D1194002

Money

MONEY

M. L. BURSTEIN
Associate Professor of Economics, Northwestern University

SCHENKMAN PUBLISHING CO.
Cambridge, Massachusetts

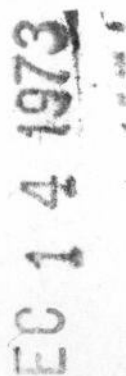

First Edition, First Printing
Designed and printed by the Nimrod Press, Boston
Composed in Linotype Baskerville with Baskerville and Futura display by Cecil H. Wrightson, Inc., Boston
Freehand illustrations by Charles Wilton
Bound by Plimpton Press, Norwood

For

Contents

Part I MONEY AND BANKING

CONTENTS

CONTENTS

Part II MONEY AND INCOME

CONTENTS

CONTENTS

Part III MONEY, INTERNATIONAL TRADE

PREFACE

I summarize my book in Chapter XVII. It attempts to apply economic theory to monetary problems. Since economic theory is of a piece, the book's reasoning is unspecialized: the arguments are like those used in studying concentration in steel or effects of protective tariffs on agriculture. Monetary institutions must be broadly understood if correct theoretical applications are to be made. And monetary history also is important. Furthermore, the book is biased towards general equilibrium and process analysis.

I have tried to keep straight my stocks and flows and my statics and dynamics. To the extent that I have succeeded, I am indebted to Robert Clower. In fact I am indebted to Clower in so many ways that sometimes I hate him. There are two other economists I should like to single out for thanks: Mitchell Harwitz and Franco Modigliani. Harwitz has helped me in innumerable ways. I met Modigliani only after the book was well along and was with him only for nine months. But a lot can be gestated in nine months. My commanding intellectual debt is to J. M. Keynes.

My major personal debts are to friends at Aspen, Colorado where I wrote the first draft of Part I, and to Ralph Andreano, Walter Tower, William Beazer, and Axel Leijonhufvud. If I were not so anti-holistic, I would express my obligation to "Aspen" itself. I wanted to dedicate the book to Had Deane, but that would have embarrassed him.

Parts I and III are to comprise a normal one-semester course in Money and Banking. Part II and part of Chapter XV are pretty stiff. Still, I hope many undergraduates will find these materials manageable. *Money* can be part of a one-year university course in macroeconomics. The book may also be used as a basis for systematic study courses sponsored by banks. Graduate students and professional readers, studying monetary economics as a whole, should read the book in order. I hope that serious readers will read the Notes, which seek to fill in the outlines drawn in the text.

Bankers and financial analysts will find many sections of the book pertinent to their everyday business. Of course, I am especially concerned to relate the financial sector to the rest of the economy. That the financial community is increasingly interested in such analysis is clear.

I have tried to respect the reader's intelligence while starting from the beginning. The book is not easy. How can it be? But never forget Silvanus Thompson's Simian Proverb:

WHAT ONE FOOL CAN DO, ANOTHER CAN.

Evanston, Illinois
May 1963

PART I

MONEY & BANKING

CHAPTER ONE

The Essential Properties of Money

A. DEFINITIONS

Money belongs to the class of things performing monetary functions. Monetary functions include service as a medium of exchange, a store of assured nominal value, and a standard of value.[1] Some goods perform all three monetary functions and no others, e.g., paper currency. Others perform one or more monetary *and* nonmonetary functions.

We define *money* as currency (including coin) and demand deposits of commercial banks. Currency is corporeal;[2] bank deposits are incorporeal. Other definitions might be appealing for various purposes. Thus, time deposits surely are stores of assured nominal value, but not means of payment. For certain purposes, the sum of the value of time and demand deposits is more relevant than is either component.[3]

---

1 However, a standard of value necessarily has assured nominal value and is by law (as I define a standard of value) eligible to be a medium of exchange.

2 Currency can be regarded as physical evidence of an incorporeal claim. True, the issuer need only cough up currency upon presentation.

3 Indeed statistical time series for the 19th century in the U. S. do not distinguish between demand and time deposits. Except for the fact that, today, interest cannot be paid on demand deposits, the text's point would be more obvious. . . . The spectrum is continuous: sometimes Treasury Bills are hard to distinguish from time deposits. . . . In this book demand deposits *always* are subject to check.

Noting that deposits are convertible into currency, a Platonist or some other Essentialist philosopher might ask, "if a demand deposit is convertible or 'realizable' into something else is not that something else *truly* money?" We justify calling certain claims "money" on the ground that scientific definitions should be *operational.* Thus, deposits do most monetary work; *prediction* of next year's Consumer Price Index or tomorrow's Treasury bill rate can be more accurate if demand deposits as well as currency are called money.

The most pervasive monetary function is service as a *medium of exchange* (or *means of payment*). A medium of exchange in a modern economy is traded in all markets; most modern transactions give rise to *debts* expressed in money of account and dischargeable by certain means of payment. Another crucial monetary function is service as a *standard of value.* A vital role of a standard of value is as a *standard for deferred payments;* most financial transactions call for settlement at a future date. Any durable good is a *store of value.* However, only a narrow class of durables have *assured nominal value.* A perfect example is hand-to-hand currency; a dollar bill always is worth a dollar.

B. MEDIA OF EXCHANGE

It has long been recognized that a *good* traded in all markets — a medium of exchange — should be durable, portable, and readily divisible. Durability, of course, is crucial for a store of value. But the medium of exchange necessarily is a revolving *stock;* pools of it must always be about. A medium of exchange should not have a "high" physical depreciation rate. (Nor should its real or nominal exchange value be volatile.) Portability refers to substantial exchange value for a given physical quantity — particularly for a given weight and volume. Helium gas is, in a sense, portable enough, but its exchange value is so low that enormous social cost would be entailed in using it as a medium of exchange. Divisibility is rather the obverse of portability. The important thing here is that conveniently large lumps of the stuff be available for low-valued exchanges. Consider precious metals. Surely, they are easy to chop into little pieces; the trouble is that the pieces, if they are not to be invisible, are too valuable for use in low-valued exchanges.

As for incorporeal media of exchange (means of payment), it is obvious that a claim against a bank is perfectly durable. It also is portable. Bank claims, in practice, are not perfectly divisible: people are not expected to write checks for two cents.

We are accustomed to the set of things used as media of exchange containing only a few objects. This was not always the case. The Spanish Conquistadores found silver and gold to be in great abundance in the Mexican and Andean civilizations, so much so that gold and silver had slight exchange value in Mexico and Peru.[4] Sir Thomas More pointed out in *Utopia* (Book II):

> "whereas they eat and drink in earthen and glass vessels . . . of gold and silver, they commonly make chamber pots and other vessels that serve for most vile uses."

The Indians (of Mexico and Peru) resorted to such commodities as pimentoes, cotton, maize, bird feathers, salt, cocoa, beans, fish, and T-shaped pieces of copper as media of exchange. In Colonial America media of exchange included tobacco, wheat, corn, cattle, beaver skins, and wampum — emphasizing that changed circumstances can result in almost anything assuming monetary functions. Witness how cigarettes were means of payment in Germany in 1945–1946.

C. STORES OF VALUE AND LIQUID ASSETS

1

To take up service of things as *stores of value* is to encounter general theories of economic choice. We find ourselves inquiring into the determinants of the composition of business and household asset portfolios and into the principles of intertemporal planning (of planning in terms of distant time horizons, making allocative choices between periods). It is impossible to treat systematically the holding of, say, demand liabilities of commercial banks without developing the lineaments of the theory of portfolio management. Once the theory of portfolio management (asset holding) has been developed, we can consider with no little rigor the consequences of monetary policies for employment and prices.

Assets of special interest to us are *liquid assets*: assets which can be converted with little expense at short notice into means of payment.

[4] The following is based on A. J. Toynbee, *A Study of History,* Vol. VII (London: Oxford University Press, 1954), pp. 307-317.

For assets to be liquid, they also must not be subject to physical deterioration and/or high storage costs. Their nominal values must be stable (or montonically increasing).[5]

An ideally monetary good would be perfectly liquid. Consider hand-to-hand currency. Common usage of "liquidity" boils down to ranking goods in terms of ease of conversion into money (as ordinarily defined) and stability of "money" prices.

If a good happened to be a medium of exchange, it would have general acceptability, even at short notice, but might be disqualified as a liquid store of value — perhaps because it was not durable enough. On the other hand, many goods not qualified as media of exchange might earn high marks as liquid stores of value. Imagine an agricultural society using some crop as a medium of exchange. It is likely that land would be the major liquid asset: if a person wishes to hoard, he would plan to increase his land holdings. While cotton and tobacco would be durable and portable enough to be media of exchange for many purposes, their modest durability and high storage costs would work against them as liquid assets. And even paper claims to land probably would not be a satisfactory medium of exchange. Thus, no one *good* in the imaginary society would perform enough monetary functions uniquely to be called *money*. Tobacco and wheat or cotton might serve some of the monetary functions, land others.

2

It begins to appear that the study of money is to an important extent a study of performance of certain functions. Thus, money's role as a liquid store of value has received much attention from theorists of income and employment. *Liquidity preference* is a key element in Keynesian income theory. It is possible that, as stocks of money increase, the "convenience yield" of money declines only grudgingly. Also note that if traders wished, *ceteris paribus,* to increase substantially their hoards of some liquid asset, this could imply that there were excess supplies of labor and commodities throughout the system;

5 An essential property of a liquid store of value or standard of deferred payment is that prices be sticky in terms of this good. If prices (in terms of it) were perfectly flexible, its real purchasing power would be subject to wild gyrations from day to day. Liquidity would be a much less desirable quality if the real value of money were very unstable over short periods. In fact, no good subject to such short-term variation in real value could be sustained as a store of value and standard for deferred payment nor, for that matter, as a means of payment. Substantial price inflexibility (using the standard as *numeraire*) is *necessary* in a monetary system.

the rate of supply might exceed the rate of demand for labor and various commodities.[6] Unemployment could, under certain conditions, persist for some time if the liquid asset either were not reproducible or could be produced only at sharply-increasing incremental cost. On the other hand, if the liquid asset were readily reproducible at constant cost, desires for increased hoards could be satisfied by a transfer of productive resources without implications for the over-all level of economic activity: factors of production would turn to producing the liquid asset instead of automobiles, sports equipment, etc. Properties of goods performing monetary functions have much to do with over-all performance of the economic system.

D. STANDARDS OF VALUE

1

A *standard of value* need not be important as a medium of exchange, nor need it be a primary liquid asset. It is true that, anciently, metals, very important as media of exchange, became standards of value. Also monetary legislation and custom generally assure that circulating media will be rigidly linked to standards of value. On the other hand, demand deposits of commercial banks — the major circulating medium in the United States and United Kingdom today — do not comprise a standard of value.

It is easy to show that a standard of value can be insignificant as a store of value. George Washington measured his wealth on the British scale. Indeed, it might have been true that his assets would exchange for more British coins than those of any contemporary. Yet Washington, to the end of his life, carried a very small balance of cash of any description; he was a perfect example of land-poorness. (*Cf.* Douglas Southall Freeman, *George Washington.*)

Perhaps the most pervasive and obvious distinction between technologically and economically advanced and primitive societies is the much greater *quantification* of the former. Surely modern trade could not be accomplished without a system of measurement of exchange value. Quantification in the realm of trade followed this course:

[6] People legally cannot plan to increase holdings of Good A without decreasing or increasing less their holdings of Goods B, C, . . . or decreasing their consumption. Paraphrasing Lord Robbins, economics largely is concerned with allocation of scarce resources among competing wants.

a) long ago values were expressed in terms of weights of precious metals that could be obtained for sundry goods and services.[7]

b) finally governments produced authenticated quantums of precious metals. Unit coins were of unit weight on relevant scales (calibrated in pounds, marks, etc.).

c) early metallic standards of value led to measures of value being measures of weight. A unit coin, although of unit weight, was not itself a measure; rather it weighed (measured) out at unity on the appropriate scale. (Measures — "ton" being an example — are purely abstractions.)

d) as time passed, coins were lightened, sometimes retaining their original symbols, sometimes being assigned new symbols. Measures of value were less likely to be identical with (although they could be transformed into) measures of weight.[8] Accounting schemes under which (physical) monetary units need not have unitary nominal value became appropriate. In any case, monetary equivalents to wealth no longer were directly expressed in true measures of weight. Coins became accepted by tale rather than by weight.

e) just *what* is measured at unit value is metaphysically immaterial.

f) basic monetary laws provide calibrated scales or rulers on which debt is measured and also the "terms of trade" between specified property — often assigned the same symbols as money of account — and debt, measured in money of account.

g) when "dollar (money of account) appears *infra.*, my tacit instruction is: "treat 'dollar' here as a measure in the sense of 'inch' or 'gram.' "[9]

---

7 The origin — zero exchange value — of a system of measurement of value is easily defined: the *ith* good has zero exchange value when a unit quantum will exchange for *none* of the standard substance.

8 Thus, "pound" measures value instead of weight in the British monetary system. *Cf.* R. G. Hawtrey, *Currency and Credit* (London: Longmans, Green & Co., 1950), Ch. II. Also his *The Gold Standard in Theory and Practice* (5th ed.; London: Longmans, Green & Co., 1947), Ch. I. Also F. A. Mann, *The Legal Aspect of Money,* 2nd ed. (London: Oxford University Press, 1953), p. 39 *ff.*

The text asserts that, anciently, the metrics for the price and weight (of gold obtainable in exchange) spaces were identical, but that, as time passed, their mapping no longer was one-for-one.

9 Hawtrey appears to offer strong support for my usage of "money of account."

> ". . . the idea of money is dependent on that of a debt, while that of a debt is not dependent on that of money. A debt, it is true, is reckoned, like money, in pounds, shillings, and pence. But that is because money, being essentially that with which debts can legally be discharged, must be reckoned in the same units as debts. These familiar units form . . . "money of account." . . . A sovereign is a coin, but a pound is not. The Coinage Acts valued a sovereign at a pound. . . . A debt of a pound could be discharged with a sovereign. The Currency . . . Act of 1914 gave the same debt-paying power to a one-pound currency note. . . . The word "shilling" is ambiguous, meaning equally a twentieth part of a pound and the coin with

American history verifies that a standard of value might be insignificant as a means of payment and/or liquid asset. European economic history in the 14th and 15th centuries shows divorce of monetary standards from "actual" money.

Recalling that a wide variety of things were means of payment in Colonial America,[10] it is conceivable that business could have been carried on using wampum as a medium of exchange under the British measure, parties voluntarily agreeing to accept the market's valuation of wampum when (promptly) tendered. Wampum prices would fluctuate from day to day. However, as the history of bimetallism makes clear, debtors like to know just how much of what stuff they are to hand over. Accordingly, Colonial practices took these forms:

a) if wampum or tobacco were the agreed-upon tender, agreements would be couched in wampum or tobacco; A would promise to pay B so much wampum or tobacco at the due date.

b) occasionally legislatures made commodities legal tender, specifying "rates of conversion" into money of account.[11]

c) more often, legislation made tobacco, for example, legal tender *for taxes,* specifying the applicable price for tobacco in the British measure. Tax obligations were expressed in the pound measure; tender of a sovereign would satisfy tax obligation measured at £ 1.

d) records ordinarily were kept in pounds, shillings, and pence. The nominal value (in pounds, shillings, and pence) of unit stocks of commodity media of exchange varied from day to day.

---

which a debt of that amount may be paid. An enactment making a coin or note money has no meaning unless the units in which it values the coin or note are already known. The money of account must exist before the money." (*The Gold Standard,* pp. 7-8.)

The statement "I, MLB, promise to pay 10 dollars to John Everyman . . ." is somewhat ambiguous, although its operational purport is not. Interpreting "dollar" as an abstract measure, I am promising to pay over unspecified property valued at 10 dollars. The legal-tender law and/or custom will specify admissible classes of property. The legal-tender law and/or custom will specify what things answer to the description "dollar." The latter is Lord Keynes's approach:

> ". . . Money-of-account is the *description* or *title* and . . . money is the *thing* which answers to the description. . . . The difference is like that between the King of England . . . and King George. . . . It is for the State to declare, when the time comes, who the King of England is." (J. M. Keynes, *A Treatise on Money,* Vol. I (London: Macmillan & Co., Ltd., 1930), pp. 3-4.)

Following Hawtrey, I favor a Nominalist as against Keynes's Essentialist or Platonist approach. Following Karl Popper (*cf.* his *The Open Society and Its Enemies*), *I* eschew Plato's Doctrine of Ideas as a scientific concept.

10 *Cf.* Chester W. Wright, *Economic History of the United States* (2nd ed.; New York: McGraw-Hill Book Co., 1949), pp. 133-145.

11 *Cf.* Arthur Nussbaum, *A History of the Dollar* (New York: Columbia University Press, 1957), p. 4.

The pound was a measure. It is today. Indeed so is the guinea. Thus, there once was a guinea coin with 1/20 more gold content than a sovereign. Today there are no guinea notes — and no active gold coins of any description — in Britain. Yet prices (especially of "snob" goods) frequently are quoted in guineas. The pound-sterling measure transforms into the guinea measure so that a 1-guinea variation is equivalent to a 21s(£ 1.05) valuation. The guinea, of course, now is exclusively an abstract accounting unit.

2

Pathological experiences such as hyperinflations sometimes reveal the bare bones of the theory of monetary standards. Thus, during the 1922–1923 German inflation, some accounts were kept in sterling and some agreements specified tender in British exchange. During their post-World War II inflation, many Germans used cigarettes as a medium of exchange, suitably altering the style of the measure of value. (Consider German bookkeepers using a dollar measure and traders using cigarettes as means of payment.)

Luigi Einaudi brilliantly discussed these issues in the context of 14th and 15th century Europe. Note, however, that "imaginary money" in the middle ages was imaginary coins; the concept of abstract measure was not quite complete.

> "The difficulty of finding a satisfactory definition for "money of account" results from its history. Money of account was not credited by decree but grew almost spontaneously out of men's habit of keeping accounts in monetary units, some of which corresponded in the time of Charlemagne to real coins. . . . Little by little — and this happened during the 14th and 15th centuries — the penny in coin lost its equivalence with the penny in money of account and was coined first in an alloy of copper and silver and then in pure copper.
>
> Sooner or later, but generally at the beginning of modern times, the different monetary systems in various European countries reached a state in which they were governed by a seemingly very odd principle, very different from our modern conception.
>
> Today each country has only one monetary unit: the lira, franc, etc. This is the system established by the French assemblies at the end of the 18th century. . . . Furthermore, if in the country in question convertibility . . . is suspended . . . the fact remains that the monetary unit is defined as a real physical quantity of gold, silver, some other metal, or perhaps another commodity.[12]
>
> There was then a monetary unit used only as a standard of deferred payments or the purpose of keeping accounts. This was the function

[12] For Einaudi a "monetary unit" is a standard quantum of a *numeraire* good.

of . . . imaginary or ideal money. The public made contracts, kept books, etc., in pounds, shillings, and pence. . . . Although it was possible to make contracts or keep accounts in imaginary money — that is in pounds, shillings, and pence — it was impossible to make actual payments in these monetary units, since they had not been coined for centuries.

The discovery of imaginary money as an instrument of monetary policy was not the work of a theorist, but the result of a long process of historical change. However, if among many contingent factors, one wanted to indicate which one came closest to being determined by individual choice, one should mention the longing of medieval men for the eternal, the immutable . . . accompanied by an abhorrence for the transitory, the mutable. . . . They stubbornly looked for an invariable standard of value and called it the pound; they pretended that it was immutable in the monetary chaos in which abraded, clipped, and adulterated foreign and domestic coins circulated side by side. . . .

From the Middle Ages down to the end of the 18th century, men saw much better than we do that *money is a negotiable commodity like any other* [emphasis supplied.] Because we exchange money at national boundaries, it appears . . . inside a country to be a super-commodity whose value is stable. . . . In former times because of the existence of money of account, men every day set a price on the florins, doubloons, etc., which they received and paid out. Every day, in every single transaction, it was made clear to their minds that the money which they paid, even bank money and paper money, was a commodity like any other, that its price was governed by the market and, like any other price, was the result of an infinite number of economic and noneconomic forces which determine the general equilibrium of all prices."[13]

---

[13] Luigi Einaudi, "The Theory of Imaginary Money," *Enterprise and Secular Change* (Homewood, Ill.: Richard D. Irwin, Inc., 1952), pp. 229-261. *Cf.* especially p. 233 *ff.*

Einaudi points out that it was possible in the 14th and 15th centuries for distributive effects of inflation or deflation to be avoided simply by changing the accounting price of, say, silver and gold. Thus, if the value of monetary metals in terms of other goods were to be cut in half, a debt contracted in "imaginary" units could be maintained at its original real value simply by crying down the price of money in terms of the imaginary unit. Similarly, increases in the value of money could be offset by crying up the price of money in terms of the imaginary unit. In the first instance, twice as much money would have to be offered to satisfy the debt, in the second instance, half as much.

Professor Toynbee's discussion of the over-all problem is distinguished. He takes up development of money of account as part of the over-all development of systems of weights and measures. (*A Study of History,* Vol. VII, pp. 293-317.) He shows how there pressed upon the most simple cultures the necessity of maintaining uniform standards of weights and measures, including measurement of the passage of time. (*Ibid.,* p. 293 *ff.*)

3

The history of attempts to secure stable *standards for deferred payments* is one of continuous failure.[14] Of course, *inflation* is a subhead under the general topic of standards for deferred payment.

The following homely example illustrates the special problems of establishing a standard for deferred payments:

> Consider a piece of paper on which is written "I, MLB, promise to pay John Everyman 100 dollars twenty years from this date, July 16, 1961." A signature — perhaps duly attested — would follow. Assume that the piece of paper is placed in John Everyman's strongbox in the vault of his bank and that physical conditions of storage are well defined.

One can be confident about the weight, length, width, chemical content, etc. of the piece of paper on July 16, 1981. Furthermore, one can be sure that, if the note's maker or his heirs are solvent and honest on July 16, 1981, the piece of paper will exchange for 100 dollars[14] on that date. But history tells us that its *real value* in 1981 cannot be predicted with precision. Our technically-advanced society has not achieved a precise measure for deferred payments.

The explanation is partly *a priori* and partly political. Consider the *a priori* reasons. John Everyman does not plan to eat or wear the hundred dollars[15] he will receive in 1981. Rather he intends to convert "them" into such things as bonds and consumption goods, although it is possible that he plans to retain some of the repaid dollars as part of his cash balance (valued in turn because it confers command over real resources).

At this point we must pause to explain a postulate of rational behavior: absence of money illusion. Standard economic theory requires that plans for holding intrinsically worthless assets be formulated in terms of command over "real" resources.[16] Thus, a *purely monetary*

---

14 This subsection treats a "dollar" as a monetary object valued at one dollar (money of account); "y dollars" as a monetary object(s) worth y dollars (money of account). Clearly, if Good X is a standard of deferred payments, a debt valued at y units of account has a fixed equivalent in physical units of X.

15 "Hundred dollars" here means "property worth $100." *Cf.* footnote 14.

16 The *jth* trader lacks money illusion if his excess demand functions for all goods, including real balances of cash and other assets, are zero-order homogeneous in prices and initial *nominal* balances. In the absence of money illusion (where money is intrinsically worthless), a change in prices of goods, services and non-money-fixed-claims in the proportion λ, together with a change in initial holdings of money-fixed claims (positive or negative) in the same proportion, is treated as a change in measure.

store of value has no economic worth except as a store of value. Arable land never could qualify; non-arable land could and, indeed, certain rocks off the island of Yap have. But, if one holds a good only because it is a way of securing command over non-monetary things (ignoring the regress involved where money is being held because of its command over bonds), proportional changes in the latters' prices and in the nominal values of monetary stocks amount to a mere change in measure.[17] Money illusion is a state in which among other things importance is attached to a purely monetary store beyond its ability to purchase non-monetary things: if all prices were reduced by $\frac{1}{2}$, one with money illusion — even in a pure-credit-money system — would not in full equilibrium reduce his cash by $\frac{1}{2}$; his utility function would respond to *nominal* values.[18]

Certain invariance theorems, one of which is a form of the *quantity theory of money,* can hold if absence of money illusion (together with a number of other restrictions) can be postulated. In any event, it is clear that (even in a society with money illusion) a promise to pay x units of A in the future arouses curiosity as to the future purchasing power of a unit of A. If A's purchasing power varies with time, a promise to pay over x units of A at time t will be of uncertain real worth.

Perhaps we almost are home free. Might not the IOU to John Everyman read:

> I promise to pay John Everyman legal tender twenty years from this date (July 16, 1961) such that its purchasing power will equal that of legal tender valued at 100 dollars on this date.

4

We have run into a mare's nest or Augean stable, depending on how you mix your metaphors. It is the *index-number* problem. We are not going to solve it, but can appreciate its broader facets. Begin by asking what is meant by the purchasing power of money (or any other good)? In order to answer this question, construct an imaginary

17 Of course, if the money stock has intrinsic value, rational behavior would *not* lead the *jth* trader to behave as in footnote 16 in response to, say, a scaling-down of all prices, debts and physical monetary quantities by the factor λ. Nor would the quantity-theory hold. (After all, if prices of Picassos were fixed, I surely would not be indifferent to holding 2λ against λ Picassos, quite aside from the prices of other goods, UNLESS I were utterly indifferent to the paintings.)

18 The context is what we shall come to call an individual experiment.

world in which the only categories of goods are food, clothing, and transportation. Food includes pork, beef, and vegetables. Clothing includes woolens and cottons. Transportation services are provided by automobiles and horses. Consider these alternative sets of prices (in dollars — money of account):

	SET I	SET II	SET III
FOOD			
1 lb. pork	0.20	5.00	15.00
1 lb. beef	2.00	0.10	10.00
1 lb. vegetables	0.50	10.00	0.20
CLOTHING			
1 yd. wool	10.00	1.00	40.00
1 yd. cotton	0.50	20.00	0.25
TRANSPORTATION			
rental: 1 auto for 1 day	3.50	30.00	30.00
rental: 1 horse for 1 day	30.00	0.50	0.80

TABLE I-I

Now consider the following three types of persons: (a) Mohammedans who love proteins, are allergic to cotton, and live in a country without highways; (b) Hindus, allergic to horses, living in a country with good roads and a warm climate; (c) Vegetarian Seventh Day Adventists who are allergic to wool. For type (a) persons, Set II offers a low cost of living (high purchasing power of money); Set I is a nightmare. But Set II would be a severe test of the faith of the most devout Hindu; for a Hindu (or Buddhist if you insist) Set I conditions are a veritable Nirvana. Type (c) persons would count their blessings under Set III prices and would rue the day they were born under Set II prices — except when they had occasion to travel. Imagine the reaction of a vegetarian Seventh Day Adventist, faced with Set II prices contemplating ebullient Mohammedans, also on horseback (at the frontier), full of praise of the golden sixties and Set II prices.

It is abundantly clear that alternative sets of prices cannot ordinarily be considered independently of the tastes and habits of the persons involved when one ranks purchasing powers of money. This can be stated more elegantly and concretely, if the price level is defined (where the price of the *numeraire* good is unity) as

$$P = w_1p_1 + w_2p_2 + \ldots + w_np_n.$$

The p's show the quantities (the number of standard units) of the *numeraire* good (here the $n+1th$) that must be surrendered in order to obtain unit quantities of the first, second, . . . and *nth* other goods. (We use *numeraire* and *numeraire good* interchangeably.) The w's are weights. $w_1 + w_2 + \ldots + w_n = 1$. We have seen, rather fantastically, that alternative sets of weights lead to different rankings of alternative sets of prices: P depends on the w's as well as the p's. In order to see this more clearly, let us suggest weights that would be appropriate for Type (a) and Type (b) persons, examining outcomes for price sets I

Good	Type (a) Weight	Type (b) Weight	I/a	I/b	II/a	II/b
pork	0.00	0.15				
beef	0.45	0.00				
vegetables	0.05	0.35				
wool	0.30	0.10				
cotton	0.00	0.25				
autos	0.00	0.15				
horses	0.20	0.00				
P Calculation			9.93	1.86	0.95	13.85

TABLE I-II

and II. Transition from Price Set I to Price Set II finds P less than 1/10 of its original value — using (a) weights. (This is to specify a corresponding rise in the purchasing power of money.) However, if one uses (b) weights, P rises more than eight-fold when we move from I to II prices.

Of course, to deny that the purchasing power of a good *must* unambiguously have increased, decreased, or stayed the same; is not to deny that there can be unambiguous statements. Thus, if we could be sure that *relative* prices 20 years from now would be the same as today, and if the number and quality of available goods were unchanged, the hypothetical IOU could be precise in its "real" meaning if it read

> I promise to pay John Everyman legal tender twenty years from this date (July 16, 1961) such that its purchasing power, using the set of weights classified as Type (a), will equal that of legal tender valued at 100 dollars on this date.

It really would not matter what were the constituent weights *if* relative prices remained the same: if all nominal prices changed by the factor k, repayment of (k) (100) dollars in 1981 would leave the parties in precisely the real position created by repayment of 100 dollars in 1981 where all nominal prices remained the same (again subject to the *caveat* of the next paragraph). On the other hand, a shift in relative prices could very substantially alter the real positions of the parties if their tastes differed. Thus, if the debtor were a Mohammedan and the creditor a Hindu, and if Set I prices prevailed in 1961 and Set II prices in 1981, the revised IOU would ruin the creditor: he would receive back less than ten dollars in circumstances in which he would have to receive more than 800 dollars in order to continue to purchase his 1961 budget in 1981.[19]

There are difficulties in longer-run comparisons of the purchasing power of money transcending differences in habits and tastes among people. These concern technological change and innovation, changes in supply conditions, and uniform changes in taste over time. They can be exemplified by problems arising from comparison of the cost of living in the United States in 1900 and in 1961. No doubt prices of whalebone corset stays, patent-leather pumps, carriages, and lard had increased very substantially. On the other hand, television sets, helicopters, radios, electric refrigerators, penicillin, Cadillacs, and water skis did not exist in 1900. How would you propose to write a constant-purchasing-power clause into a 1900 instrument promising to pay $100 to bearer in 1961 even if you knew in 1900 what 1961 would look like? Would your 1961 price-index number be based on the number of dollars required in 1961 to purchase a basket of 1900 goods (leaving aside the fact that the dollar is defined differently in 1961 than in 1900)? Obviously, you cannot sensibly ask what a basket of 1961 goods would have cost in 1900. The matter need not be pushed further: there are very substantial *a priori* difficulties preventing precise comparisons of purchasing power of money (or of any other good) over time; precise measures for real deferred payments are logically impossible in other than a completely static world. No better summary of these difficulties exists than is in J. M. Keynes's *Treatise on Money,* one of Keynes's two great books that will claim much of our attention:

> "When the composite commodity representative of expenditure is stable in its constitution for different classes and different situations, and tastes are unchanged, comparisons of purchasing power raise no

[19] This abstracts from substitution effects of price changes.

theoretical difficulty. . . . In fact, however, the composite commodities representative of the actual expenditure of money incomes are not stable in their constitution as between different places, times, or groups. They are unstable for three reasons — either (1) because the need which the object of expenditure is intended to satisfy, i.e., the purpose of the expenditure, varies, or (2) because the efficiency of the object of expenditure to attain its purpose varies, or (3) because there is a change in what distribution of expenditure between different objects is the most economical means of attaining the purpose. The first of these reasons we may classify as a change in tastes, the second as a change in environment, and the third as a change in relative prices. For these reasons, every change in the distribution of real incomes or in habits and education, every change in climate and national customs, and every change in relative prices and in character and qualities of the goods offering for purchase, will affect in some degree the character of average expenditure."[20]

5

The history of money is a history of inflation of money prices. Gibbon writes of the Emperor Julian the Apostate exhorting the merchants of Antioch to practice self-restraint in pricing their wares and inveighing against the tide of rising prices in the manner of Canute[21] as have American Presidents of our own day. Referring to services and incidents of feudal land tenures, A. W. B. Simpson writes:

> "In the course of the Middle Ages the economic importance of the services gradually declined — largely because they were fixed burdens which a lord could not vary unilaterally when a change in money values or social needs made them outdated. The incidents . . . tended to maintain their value and keep pace with inflation. . . ."[22]

Keynes, writing in 1923, gave a succinct précis of monetary history:

> ". . . There is no record of a prolonged war or a great social upheaval which has not been accompanied by a change in the legal tender, but an almost unbroken chronicle in every country which has a history, back to the earliest dawn of economic record, of a progressive deterioration in the real value of the successive legal tenders which have represented money.
>
> Moreover, this progressive deterioration in the value of money throughout history is not an accident, and has behind it two great

20 J. M. Keynes, *A Treatise on Money*, Vol. I, pp. 95-96.

21 Edward Gibbon, *The Decline and Fall of the Roman Empire*, Vol. I (New York: The Modern Library), p. 801.

22 A. W. B. Simpson, *An Introduction to the History of the Land Law* (London: Oxford University Press, 1961), p. 6.

> driving forces — the impecuniosity of governments and the superior political influence of the debtor class.
>
> The power of taxation by currency depreciation is one which has been inherent in the State since Rome discovered it [actually China did].
>
> The creation of legal tender has been and is a government's ultimate reserve; and no state or government is likely to decree its own downfall, so long as this instrument still lies at hand unused."[23]

On the surface, then, it might seem surprising that "contracts to receive fixed sums of money at future dates [made without provision for possible changes in the real value of money . . .] must have existed as long as money has been lent and borrowed."[24] Further reflection suggests that this is not as extraordinary as it seems. Interest charges are likely to reflect anticipated changes in the purchasing power of money, and the notion of constant purchasing power is so imprecise that it is difficult to give it institutional form — certainly in times and places in which collection of price statistics is haphazard or non-existent. There can be little doubt that politics has reinforced pure logic in making imprecise the "real" meaning of promises to pay stated amounts of money at future dates.

SUMMARY

It is not easy to begin to study money. This is partly because we are attempting to deal systematically and rigorously with phenomena so integral in our workaday lives as to make our reactions almost instinctual. To ask "what is money, what does it do, what can it do?" is like asking "why do two and two equal four?" Very hard questions! But it is important to ask them and eventually to answer them. Environments ultimately are controlled through analysis; societies have not secured anything like full control of their monetary environments.

So far we have asked only about *essential* monetary properties. Questions such as "what serves as money in the United States?"; "how is money created and destroyed?"; "what is the relation of the quantity of money to the level of prices and the rate of economic activity?" — all have been put aside. These remain for the future. History, anthro-

[23] J. M. Keynes, *A Tract on Monetary Reform* (London: Macmillan and Co., Ltd., 1923), p. 9.

[24] *Ibid.*, p. 6.

pology, and sociology have been touched on in order to explain key concepts. It remains to shape these concepts into an engine of analysis.

1. Money is a class of things.[25] Things called "money" perform monetary functions, including service as a medium of exchange, a standard of value, and a store of assured nominal value. Service as a standard of deferred payments is subsumed under the head "standard of value."
2. We generally define money as including hand-to-hand currency and demand deposits of commercial banks.
3. Paper money qualifies as an economic good only through performance of monetary functions, in contrast with commodity money which has intrinsic value as well.
4. A medium of exchange ideally would be traded in all markets.
5. Development of a standard of value is one of the class of problems concerned with weights and measures.
6. Study of the functioning of goods as stores of value is part and parcel of the theory of asset holding, in turn important for the theory of income and employment: plans to increase holdings of liquid assets may or may not be concomitant with plans to increase holdings of *produced* goods.
7. In Colonial America, tobacco, wampum, and wheat often were media of exchange; the English pound sterling the money of account; and land the chief liquid asset.
8. Changes in tastes and technology make the concept of "constant purchasing power of money" undefinable in any strict, but meaningful, sense. "Real world" standards of measurement for deferred payments necessarily are imprecise. Historically, politics has contributed to the imprecision and to persistent inflationary forces over the longer run.

[25] The following Venn Diagram clarifies matters. A is *the* class of things performing one or more monetary functions. B is *a* class of things, included in A, that we call "money."

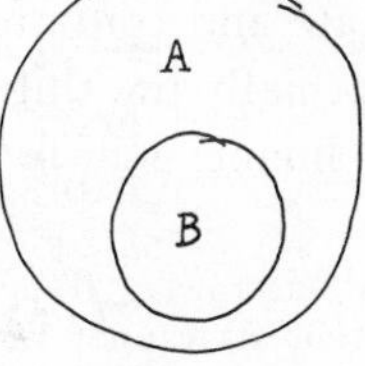

Figure I-1

CHAPTER TWO

Monetary Standards

A. THEORY AND TECHNIQUE

1. Theory of Monetary Standards

Social institutions are not necessarily dominated by government, but the role of government is pervasive and dominant in the story of monetary institutions. This becomes clear in the monetary histories of the United States and Britain which conclude this chapter.

The chapter's burden is easy to deliver. Government's role in monetary[1] matters has been threefold:

1) establishment of uniform standards of measurement of value and securing uniformity and integrity of circulating media;

2) establishment of conditions for satisfaction of debt expressed in money of account;

3) provision for "adequate" stocks of primary liquid assets sometimes leading to acquisition of resources through issue of phony warehouse receipts or fiat paper.

The first theme is easy to state and contains little drama except as it verges on the second and especially the third. The third theme is full of political excitement: the financial history of governments is com-

[1] Chapter II construes "monetary" narrowly. It largely, but not entirely, ignores banking. However, banking problems cannot be disentangled from the second theme.

posed of variations on a theme of impecuniosity; the struggles of successive governments and the effects of their insatiable desire for continued power are melodramatic. The second theme — integrated as it is with the other two — is significant for a wide variety of monetary phenomena.

This is a synopsis of Part A.

I. *The threefold role of government in monetary affairs*
  - A. The establishment of standards for measuring value, requiring, in the real world,
  - B. assertion of criteria for satisfaction of debt expressed in money of account
  - C. provision for stocks of primary liquid assets, etc.

II. *Two senses of "monetary standard"*
  - A. Selection of a standard of value (role I-A) requiring monetary legislation specifying how debt can be discharged (role I-B)
  - B. Convertibility properties of circulating media (another aspect of I-B)
    1. instruments might be convertible into gold, silver, gold or silver, gold and silver, paper, etc.
    2. metallic standards impose exogeneous restraints on governments; paper standards, endogeneous restraints

III. *Properties of real-world standards*
  - A. Monometallic standards, specifically gold standards
    1. gold coin standards
    2. gold bullion standards
    3. gold exchange standards
  - B. Bimetallic standards
    1. mint and market ratios
    2. relation to full-bodied subsidiary coinage
    3. political aspects
       a. United States, *fin de siècle:* the silver tongue from the banks of the Platte
  - C. Symmetallic standards
    1. the Marshallian concept
    2. extension to commodity-reserve money generally
  - D. Paper standards
    1. close relation to role I-C

IV. *Concluding topics; tying loose ends*
  - A. Representative paper money
  - B. Gresham's Law
    1. relation to effects of disparity of mint and market ratios

1

The first theme concerns establishment of uniform systems of measurement of values and securing uniformity of coinage. Toynbee proves to be a valuable source:

> "As soon as it has come to be recognized and accepted that honest dealing in weights and measures is a matter of social concern transcending the personal interests of the parties involved, and that, therefore, any government that aspires to be worthy of that name must make the giving of false weight and measure a prosecutable offense at law, the invention of [money of account] lies just around the corner. Yet this corner can be turned only by the taking of certain precise successive steps, and the requisite combination of moves in fact remained unachieved until the seventh century, B.C., though by that time the species of societies called civilizations has already been in existence for perhaps as long as 3,000 years."[2]

Toynbee goes on to point out that for thousands of years "the use of precious metals in bar form as measures of value had been a regular institution." But for these bars to be used as a means of payment they had to be weighed and verified like anything else. There was no coinage.

> "The decisive steps which conjured [official] money into existence were taken in the seventh century, B.C., by some Greek city-state [which] took the two revolutionary steps of making the issue of these metallic units of value a government monopoly and of stamping this exclusive governmental currency with a distinctive official image [so that] its weight and quality were to be accepted as being what they purported to be on the face of them . . . The clipping and filing of authentic coins became a political crime against the state."[3]

The only explicit references in the Constitution to the vesting of monetary powers are altogether in accordance with the first theme, containing little more than a hint of the second and third. The Constitution provides that

> ". . . the Congress shall have the power to coin money, regulate the value thereof, and of foreign coin, and fix the standard of weights and measures."[4]

Also

> ". . . to borrow money on the credit of the United States,[5] . . . to

---

[2] A. J. Toynbee, *op. cit.*, p. 307.
[3] *Ibid.*, p. 309.
[4] The Constitution of the United States, Art. I, Sec. 8, §§5.
[5] *Ibid.*, Art. I, Sec. 8, §§2.

provide for the punishment of counterfeiting the securities and current coin of the United States . . ."[6]

And then

"... no state shall . . . coin money, emit bills of credit, make anything but gold and silver coin a tender in payment of debts."[7]

The apposition of the coinage and weights-and-measures provisions of Article I, Section 8 is interesting and intellectually satisfying. Of course, Section 10, §§ 1 bears the seed of other themes. And the words "regulate the value thereof" have proved important.

2

A monetary standard as one of a number of standards of weights and measures is easily established. An accounting unit is chosen, together with the price of the chosen standard of value. If the standard of value is a metal, a coinage operation might be undertaken. The *simpliste* monetary standard would value a unit coin (e.g., the sovereign) at unity (e.g., one pound).[8]

Realization of the *simpliste* standard requires, or at least is much abetted by, a legal tender law indicating what tenders discharge obligations requiring money payment, and what are the terms of trade between legal tender and debt; the act determines nominal prices of legal tenders. Debt has been defined as "negative wealth stated in a unit of account." (*See Note A.*)*

Central bank notes might be *the* legal tender. If so, the *simpliste* standard of value would be "paper." Monetary legislation might also provide that the notes are convertible on fixed terms into some "back-

6 *Ibid.*, Art. I, Sec. 8, §§6.

7 *Ibid.*, Art. I, Sec. 10, §§1.

8 The text oversimplifies monetary legislation. In truth American legal tender laws, for example, enact "polymetallism" without "free coinage." Unity 2, 5, 10, etc. on the value scale implicitly are legislatively defined. However, official willingness to exchange one form of currency (a term technically encompassing "coin") for another, at par, assures that these always exchange at par in the market. If there are m kinds of currency, m prices are fixed by monetary legislation, but m degrees of freedom are regained: particular monetary stocks are not predetermined. What is predetermined is the *aggregate* nominal value of stocks of currency. Theory usually is concerned with this aggregate, not its components. Of course, since the law fixes prices of legal tenders, the well known (Hicksian) theorem permits one to treat the lot as one good. . . . Complications arising from "n-metallism" where inter-convertibility is not provided for also are ignored, not to be considered until bimetallism is taken up in detail.

* All lettered Notes are at the end of the chapter in which they occur.

ing," say specie. If so, there would apply another sense of "standard." In that other sense, there would be a specie standard. The second sense of standard pertains to *convertibility* of monetary claims. Once measurement and convertibility are accommodated, a complete monetary standard is established.

A vital conclusion emerges: once a bounded "ultimate" stock is established, equilibrium financial asset (liability) values become pegged to that of the "ultimate" stock. The way in which this happens is the subject of much attention later in the book. For the time being it is sufficient to see that the volume of tenders convertible into the ultimate substance (including the volume of bank credit convertible into legal tender convertible into the ultimate substance) must be governed by that of the latter.[9]

Since A's debt is B's source of liquidity, there are important implications for the theory of income: in our society demand obligations of commercal banks are vitally important in providing liquidity for the non-banking public;[10] the paper of building societies, insurance companies, and other non-banking financial institutions provides the public with interest-bearing liquid assets. Directly or indirectly (more or less directly for demand deposits), the volume of financial assets (liabilities) is pegged to that of the monetary base.[11] If the base contracts, the total of the public's liquid assets must contract, generally leading to at least temporarily depressing effects on prices, output, and employment. And what if the monetary base were gold and the government had little control over the national gold stock? The monetary standard would impose a severe discipline, one sometimes seeming to be capricious and cruel. Much more on this later.

The key word has been *convertibility*. The relation to the third theme is clear: governments can be found chafing under limitations imposed by convertibility of their debt obligations into gold or something else limited in supply. Similarly it is easy to see that govern-

9 At least the value of the base leads to an upper limit.

10 Partly because demand deposits are ready substitutes for legal tender in most circumstances.

11 Thus, if the stock of currency comprised a primitive monetary base, a reduction in that stock would, if the public have well defined preferences for mixes of currency and bank credit, lead to deterioration in the reserve position of banks.

It is shown in Chapters IV and V how the public's currency-deposit preferences affect the equilibrium distribution of sources of bank reserves. Also how changes in the monetary base led to changes in many nominal stocks in sophisticated systems.

ments would be attracted to the possibility of establishing *inconvertible* paper as the standard, since they would then be in a position to control the stock of the ultimate stuff; governments under fiat paper standards need not fear for their solvency. But, how important it is to make clear that the fact that paper standards can arise and have arisen out of fiscal irresponsibility does not detract one whit from what might be crippling disadvantages imposed by a monetary base fluctuating independently of agents of the economic system, including the government.

Metallic standards (we concentrate on gold) have been viewed by some as profound expressions of probity and economic logic and by others as lurid mixtures of ignorance, superstition, and psychosis. Keynes took the latter view, stressing as he did the importance of central authorities being able to "manage money" in the sense of manipulating interest rates and running deficits and surpluses without being subject to the mercurial discipline of an international gold standard. Advocates of non-discretionary central banking policies such as Milton Friedman also oppose "gold" on the ground that it prevents adherence to rules that they feel should govern the time profile of the money supply. On the other hand, advocates of strict gold standards are apt to be particularly conscious of the inflationist tendencies of twentieth century government and, accordingly, welcome the discipline of gold. My own predilections being Keynesian on this question, I quote additional passages from Chapter 35 of his *Treatise*:

> "The choice of gold as a standard of value is chiefly based on tradition . . . Some four or five thousand years ago the civilized world settled down to the use of gold, silver, and copper . . . but with silver in the first place of importance and copper in the second. The Mycenaeans put gold in the first place. Next, under Celtic or Dorian influences, came a brief invasion of iron in place of copper over Europe . . . With the Achaemenid Persian Empire, which maintained a bimetallic standard of gold and silver at a fixed ratio . . . the world settled down again to gold, silver, and copper, with silver once more of predominant importance; and there followed silver's long hegemony . . . chequered by imperfectly successful attempts at gold and silver bimetallism . . . and only concluded by the final victory of gold during the fifty years before the war [1914–1918].
>
> Dr. Freud relates that there are peculiar reasons deep in our subconsciousness why gold in particular should satisfy strong instincts and serve as a symbol. The magical properties, with which Egyptian priestcraft anciently imbued the yellow metal, it has never altogether lost . . . Gold is, and always has been, an extraordinarily scarce commodity.

> A modern liner could convey across the Atlantic in a single voyage all the gold which has been dredged or mined in seven thousand years . . .
>
> Of late years the *auri sacra fames* [insatiable desire for gold] has sought to envelop itself in a garment of respectability as densely respectable as was ever met with, even in the realms of sex or religion. Whether this was first put on as a necessary armour to win the hard won fight against bimetallism and is still worn, as the gold advocates allege, because gold is the sole prophylactic against the plague of fiat moneys, or whether it is a furtive Freudian cloak, we need not be curious to inquire. But before we proceed with a scientific and would-be unbiased examination of its claims, we had better remind the reader of what he well knows — namely, that gold has become part of the apparatus of conservatism and is one of the matters which we cannot expect to see handled without prejudice . . .
>
> It is claimed for gold that it has been fairly successful over longish periods in maintaining a reasonable stability of purchasing power . . . But this is certainly not to be attributed to any inherent tendency on the part of the supplies of the metal to keep step with the demand for it [without deflated money prices] . . . If any metal is to make this claim on the basis of long historical experience, it must be silver and not gold . . . Such stability of price levels — which was nothing to be proud of, far from it — which the gold standard can claim to have secured for the fifty years before the war, is certainly to be attributed in large measure to management on the part of the users of gold."[12]

3

Preparations for surveying monetary history are not yet finished; understanding of monetary standards — while broadly correct in its focus on the convertibility question — is incomplete. We must develop a more detailed appreciation of standards and of kinds of money. Once this has been achieved, the narrative can be unfolded.

We first take up monometallic standards, then bimetallism, symmetalism, and paper standards, stressing in the case of paper the chapter's third theme (impecuniosity of governments). *En passant,* the logic of subsidiary and token coinage is considered.

2. Monometallic Standards

1

We concentrate on gold; the logic of silver, copper, or, for that matter, common-brick standards is the same. It is customary to subclassify gold standards into gold coin, gold bullion, and gold exchange

[12] J. M. Keynes, *op. cit.*, pp. 289-290, 290-291, 293-294.

standards; actual standards often combine elements of all three. The gold coin standard or gold circulation system features active circulation of coined gold.[13] Its logic is that of any gold standard: "a state of affairs in which a country keeps the value of its monetary unit and the value of a defined weight of gold equal with one another."[14] The accounting price of gold is guaranteed; convertibility, at a fixed rate, of non-gold monetary assets into gold is provided for. Under a rigid (and hypothetical) gold coin standard, the state of affairs could be described as follows:

> Legal tender money shall be coined gold of specified weight and fineness. Unit gold coins (dollars) satisfy unit indebtedness, measured in dollars (money of account). Gold may be coined at the mint subject only to a small seignorage charge. Similarly, bullion will be supplied for coin. The simplistic standard of value is gold coin, not "gold."

"Free" coinage and melting privileges result in the price of gold being rigidly fixed. Such no longer would be the case if, for example, coinage were suspended at a time when bullion holders desired coin. They would have to seek out holders of coin who presumably would require a premium before surrendering legal tender for gold not intrinsically superior to that in the coins. What if melting of coin were prohibited? It would then be possible for bullion to sell at a premium if the commodity demand for gold became intense. If you were desperately anxious to have a tooth filled with gold and owned no gold bullion, but did possess gold coin, you might very well offer gold coin containing more grains of gold than the gold bullion you would be willing to accept in exchange. If the system were opened so as to include other nations, a provision for unlimited importation and exportation of gold should be added to the catalog. Its effect would be very similar to that produced by free coinage and melting privileges: maintenance of a fixed dollar price of gold. If there were a prohibition against exportation of gold (at a time when there would otherwise be exportation), the excess of claims against us could in the short run be eliminated only if dollar prices of foreign currencies rose. The dollar price of gold would rise in the free market; there would be a disparity between official and unofficial gold prices.

---

[13] *Cf.* Lester V. Chandler, *The Economics of Money and Banking* (Rev. Ed., New York: Harper & Bros., 1953), Ch. V, esp. pp. 87-103.

[14] D. H. Robertson, *Money* (London: Pitman, 1948), p. 64. Think of "monetary unit" as property.

The discussion leads to a simple and far-reaching summarization: what is interesting about a gold standard are its convertibility properties; maintenance of a fixed value of a country's money in terms of gold requires that the monetary authority stand willing to buy and sell gold in exchange for its money in unlimited quantities at a fixed ratio. (*See Note B.*)

2

Gold coin standards might classify as legal tender gold coins *and* other forms of money, all convertible into gold. But, once we have relaxed our grip to this extent, we are at the threshold of a gold bullion standard, featured by withdrawal of gold coin from circulation.[15] Keynes has described the process of transition from a gold coin to a gold bullion standard in a characteristically felicitous way:

> ". . . thus, almost throughout the world, gold has been withdrawn from circulation. It no longer passes from hand to hand, and the touch of metal has been taken away from men's greedy palms. The little household gods, who dwelt in purses and stockings and tin boxes, have been swallowed by a single golden image in each country, which lives underground and is not seen. Gold is out of sight — gone back again into the soil. But when gods are no longer seen in a yellow panoply walking the earth, we begin to rationalize them; and it is not long before there is nothing left."[16]

We should note *en passant* that it was almost universally the case that governments operating under gold bullion standards dealt only in bars of a certain minimum weight. "For example, the smallest bar that could be bought from the government under Britain's gold bullion standard of the 1920's was worth about $7,585. French peasants bitterly christened their own gold standard of this type 'the rich man's standard.' These gold bars were usually sold freely, however, whether they were used for hoarding, industry, or export."[17]

---

15 It is often said that withdrawal of gold from circulation leads to economy in the sense that less resources need be invested in gold. This view, however, is fallacious: a system can always achieve that sort of economy by having a low enough price level or through revaluation. However, transitions can be important.

The correct analysis is offered by Milton Friedman, "Commodity Reserve Currency," *Essays in Positive Economics* (Chicago: University of Chicago Press, 1953), p. 215.

16 *A Treatise on Money,* Vol. II, p. 291.

17 Lester V. Chandler, *op. cit.,* p. 93.

We have described what Chandler terms a *full* gold bullion standard, but, as we soon shall see, the United States, together with almost all of the rest of the world, is on a *limited* gold bullion standard. United States citizens are forbidden to hoard gold; gold will be sold by the United States government to American citizens only under very special circumstances; American money is convertible only externally. And it follows that free-market prices may differ from the official price of gold.

The logic of gold bullion standards is that of a convertible paper standard. Thus, in the United States today, producers of gold will find a guaranteed market at a trifle less than $35 per ounce, while foreign central banks and similar agencies are assured of being able to exchange monetary claims against the United States for gold at a price a trifle more than $35 per ounce. Of course, free-market sales of gold to persons ineligible to present dollar claims to the United States authorities might take place at higher prices.

3

A variation of the gold bullion standard is the gold exchange standard, the lineaments of which can be put with some precision: a country's money is redeemable in claims against a foreign government (or against foreign governments) which *does* maintain convertibility of these into gold at a fixed rate; monetary reserves can be held in the form of interest-bearing claims against the foreign government. Historically, gold exchange networks found the countries involved to be closely tied as a result of consanguinity, colonial relationships, etc. Thus, the Philippine Islands and India almost always are mentioned. More recently, modified gold exchange standards (under which governments hold monetary reserves in the form of dollar assets) have become prominent (*cf.* Ch. XVI).[18] It can easily be imagined that "pyramiding" of this sort can lead to severe aggravation of global liquidity crises . . . but there is little point in ringing more changes on a distressingly familiar theme.

---

[18] Chandler, *op. cit.*, pp. 95 *ff.*, has a good account of gold exchange standards. Stabilization of, say, the peso-dollar exchange ratio might not follow from an overt commitment of the peso country. That country might simply follow a practice of buying and selling peso claims (selling and buying dollar claims) whenever exchange rates violated certain upper and lower bounds.

4

We pause to consolidate some hard won ground. So far *convertibility* has been emphasized. We have seen that a change in the size of a "small," perhaps incorporeal, basic stock has multiplied effects on "large" derivative stocks of monetary and other short-term indebtedness, claims that are assets for others. It has been seen that under a gold bullion standard, for example, discipline is imposed independently of governmental authority. Under a fiat paper standard, the government is not subject to exogenous discipline; it can, at least in a closed system, impose whatever degree of discipline it wishes.

There is a more subtle, but perhaps more important, sense — not fully explained until Ch. XIV — in which control of the nominal value of the monetary base can permit one to determine the equilibrium level of prices and nominal values of *all* other stocks. Perpetuities would be just as much subject to this *diktat* as demand deposits. The controlling topic is the *neutrality* of money.

3. Bimetallic Standards

1

Bimetallism, aside from aspects taken up in the Appendix to Ch. II, is interesting in two disconnected ways: (1) as one of a set of problems under the heading "subsidiary and token coinage"; (2) as a string in the bow of "inflationists," persons advocating substantial increases in the stock of money in order to increase liquidity and reduce interest rates (even if only transitionally). An epochal moment in American political oratory was achieved during the bimetallism controversy: the Cross of Gold speech of William Jennings Bryan (D) in the presidential campaign of 1896 ("ye shall not crucify mankind on a cross of gold"). Certain of the "inflationists" were called by Keynes a "brave band of heretics."

What is bimetallism? Two metals (customarily gold and silver) are monetized. Their nominal values as legal tender are fixed. Gold and silver coins and/or "warehouse receipts" (representative paper) have unlimited legal tender powers. Coinage, or its equivalent, is free.

A strict bimetallic standard would find legislation enacted that a gold coin weighing x grains and a silver coin weighing y grains, each denoted "one dollar," could be tendered at par against debts contracted in dollars (money of account). Another pure form of bimetallism, one never put into practice,[19] would be a type of bimetallic bullion standard: the government would stand ready to provide the tenderer of x grains of gold *or* y grains of silver (each of a suitable degree of fineness) with a paper dollar *and* to provide the tenderer of a paper dollar with x grains of gold or y grains of silver as *he* wishes. Maintenance of a bimetallic bullion standard of this sort would require that the authorities possess large enough stocks of the metals to be able to impose their "view" on the market; otherwise convertibility into what we shall come to call the "under-valued" metal will have to be abandoned.[20]

Under either subsystem, there is established a *mint ratio* between gold and silver. Thus, as Chandler points out,[21] in 1834 the gold dollar contained 23.22 grains of pure gold and the silver dollar 371.25 grains of pure silver, so that the weight of the silver dollar was 16 times that of the gold dollar; the mint ratio was 16:1. Either dollar could be tendered to satisfy a one dollar (money of account) claim.

Would it be possible for the market ratio between gold and silver to be other than 16:1? Assume, for example, that a closed system, a system not in interaction with other systems, was initially in equilibrium with a market ratio of 17:1, but that the government now proceeds to work with a mint ratio of 16:1 (the legal tender act being adjusted accordingly). At the outset, silver is over-valued (and gold under-valued) at the mint. *So long as the 371.25 grain silver dollar could be tendered at par with the 23.22 grain gold dollar,* it would be foolish for traders to hold gold in coined form: simply by exchanging 23.22 grains of gold (contained in a gold dollar) for 394.74 grains of

---

19 *Cf.* Edwin W. Kemmerer, *Money* (New York: The Macmillan Co., 1937), pp. 83-84. Chapters VI, XIV, and XV of Kemmerer's book concern bimetallism. Kemmerer writes (pp. 83-84):

> ". . . although bimetallism under a gold and silver bullion standard, without the coinage of either gold or silver standard money but with the interconvertibility of paper money with gold and silver bullion at fixed rates of equivalence has never existed, such a system is possible and would be entitled to be called 'true bimetallism.' "

The text *infra.* suggests a bimetallic bullion standard with interconvertibility. Other variants are possible: there could be paper, some of which promises to pay only gold and some only silver; there could be paper promising to pay either gold or silver at the discretion of the debtor, as was true of bank notes under historical bimetallism.

20 *Cf. infra.,* Ch. XVI, for a discussion of difficulties faced by the United States Treasury in maintaining a price for silver between $0.905 and $0.91 per ounce, leading President Kennedy to propose (on November 28, 1961) that the policy be abandoned.

21 *Op. cit.,* p. 103.

silver in the open market, the holder of a gold dollar could acquire approximately 17/16 silver dollars by presenting the 394.74 grains of silver bullion at the mint.[22] *So long as the dollars circulated at par,* gold, the under-valued metal, would be withdrawn from circulation. If, even after all the coined gold were melted down and used as a commodity, there still were excess demand for gold at the 16:1 ratio, a permanent disparity of market and mint ratios could exist. Although the "ultimate" market ratio in our closed system would be less than 17:1, it would be greater than 16:1. If we were to "open" our economy, postulating that the foreign mint and/or market ratios were 16:1, we quickly find again that the under-valued metal would disappear from circulation. This is what seems to have happened in the course of American bimetallic experimentation, causing observers here and abroad to conclude that *bi*metallism is a misnomer, and that in fact *either* gold *or* silver will serve exclusively as the monetary metal.

Continuing to assume that the gold and silver dollars will circulate at par, is there a way out? Well, there is a partial escape: mint ratios could continually be adjusted to meet market conditions, admittedly a difficult trick. The trouble with this "solution" is that uncertainty would attach to the *nominal* value tomorrow of the monetary stock; an essential monetary property could not be sustained in such a system. And, then, there is an unqualified escape: if equipped with sufficiently large stocks of the metals, governments could offer to buy and sell unlimited quantities at prescribed ratios. This "solution" is quite meaningless in any but a closed economy; the possibilities for chaos would be large indeed if governments set different mint ratios and attempted to support these in the open market; the ratio would become exogenous for all but the government with the biggest stocks.

Note that we have been assuming that gold and silver dollars circulate on a 1:1 basis even if mint and market ratios are disparate, an assumption which, despite the fact that most writers on bimetallism adhere to it, seems to me to violate economic rationality. Just because gold and silver dollars can be tendered at par for taxes, why should we observe traders throughout the system insisting upon this parity? Why should we not see price quotations in the form "Finalist Golf Ball, $1.00 (Au), $1.06 (Ag)"? (*See Note C.*) A bit awkward to be sure, but seemingly consistent with agio phenomena generally. (Needless to

22 Since the mint would not deal with fractions, the above transaction would have to be scaled 16-fold. This is a completely niggling point.

say, anyone in his right mind will tender silver for taxes.) In other words, my hypothesis implies that disparity of mint and market ratios should not lead to disappearance of the under-valued metal from coinage, but, instead, to agio phenomena. Sir Ralph Hawtrey, and, so far as I can determine, nobody else, has seen the point. Permit me to quote him at length:

> "If a debtor holds some coins which are, and others which are not, worth more as metal than as money [at official rates], his creditor cannot compel him to pay the former. The debtor may stipulate that the more valuable coins be accepted at something above their nominal value. Usually the inconvenience of making payments in a medium the money value of which varies with the market prevents this, but that is not invariably the case. In England in the latter part of the seventeenth century the gold coin issued from the mint was the guinea, which was intended to be worth twenty shillings of silver. This represented an under-valuation of gold as compared with its market price in England and abroad, and according to Gresham's Law the guinea ought to have been driven from circulation. But at that period the growing volume of trade made so bulky a medium of payment as silver intolerably inconvenient. The merchants and goldsmiths or bankers found gold indispensable for large payments. Instead of the twenty shilling guinea being driven out of circulation its nominal value became a dead letter [clearly, 20s is to be taken as an accounting price], and it regularly passed for 21s. 6d. or 22s.
>
> A legal tender law can do no more than prescribe the means of discharging a debt expressed in the existing unit of account. People who choose to make bargains in terms of another medium can thereby evolve a new unit of account. When a seventeenth century merchant made a bargain in terms of guineas, the guinea became for that purpose the unit of account, and fulfilment of the contract required either delivery of guineas, or a setoff against another guinea debt. A court of law, it is true, if it awarded damages for a default on the contract, would reckon them in pounds, shillings, and pence, but the current silver money would be the compensation for the failure to deliver guineas, not a fulfilment of the obligation."[23]

As Hawtrey makes clear, the variability of the nominal prices of the under-valued metal (under no circumstances can the accounting value of the over-valued metal fall below the par established in the legal tender act) makes for awkwardness, reducing the "moneyness" of that metal. When other institutional considerations are taken into account, including, perhaps, psychological forces operating against dual price quotations, we might be able to explain the historical data, cited by Kemmerer and others, and confirmed by whatever independent investi-

[23] R. G. Hawtrey, *Currency and Credit,* pp. 48-49.

gation I have attempted, showing that disparity in mint and market ratios often leads to disappearance of the under-valued metal from the coinage.

2

Now that you know what bimetallism is, we can consider the relation between it and problems of subsidiary and token coinage. Consider a gold coin standard. In the absence of some supplementary monetary form, transactions of small value could be conducted only arduously. If a child wished to purchase an ice cream cone, he would have to clutch a gold coin so small that it would practically be invisible unless either a *subsidiary coinage* or some other subsidiary medium were developed.

A characteristic of the gold coinage under consideration is that it is *full-bodied.* That is to say, if a coin containing 25.8 grains of gold were melted down, the lump of gold remaining (assuming it also weighed 25.8 grains) would have the same exchange value, less seignorage, as did the coin; the 25.8 grain lump of gold could purchase a basket of goods valued at one dollar (always less seignorage). After all, the recipient of the lump of gold could obtain coins valued at one dollar less seignorage. Consequently, competition would guarantee our result, guaranteed to persist so long as the government stands ready to mint all gold offered to it.

This definition of full-bodiedness is at variance with that commonly offered. Full-bodiedness usually is defined as a state in which the coin "does not lose value if it deserts its monetary job and takes up other uses, if too much of it does not leave monetary uses." But how much is "too much"? Sir Dennis Robertson's animated bank note gave the definitive answer:

> ". . . And let me tell you this, too. If a great many of those haughty gold coins were to lose their money job simultaneously, they wouldn't be worth as much as they flatter themselves they would, not by a long way . . . The chief reason men run after them now is because they're *money* . . . If they all got the sack at once, goodness knows where they'd be: for this dentistry yarn has worn a bit thin — there aren't all that number of rickety teeth in this world."[24]

There is another moral: expressions like "need," "too much," etc. merely muddy the waters and certainly are misplaced in technical definitions.

---

24 D. H. Robertson, *op. cit.,* pp. 46-47.

3

Should the subsidiary coinage — that used for small-value transactions — be full-bodied? Two issues are posed at once:

1) if the metal used in subsidiary coinage is fairly common in the sense that the cost of production of the metal that could be used in a "conveniently sized" coin is small compared with that of a comparable amount of gold, the subsidiary coinage — if full-bodied — might be very cumbersome;
2) if the subsidiary coinage is to be full-bodied, a *bimetallic* or *polymetallic standard* must be established if there are not to be multiple price quotations. It is this issue that binds the problem of subsidiary coinage to bimetallism.

By way of digression, then, we take up the first issue, abstracting from the second through the assumption that the world price of copper — assumed to be the only feasible metal for subsidiary coinage — is and will remain 1/50 that of gold. It is obvious that, if the price of copper is low enough relative to the price of gold (in whatever units these are expressed), our child must flounder to the soda fountain under the oppressive weight of his (full-bodied) copper penny. The problem of convenience would not be solved. In fact the only way in which a convenient subsidiary coinage could be achieved under these circumstances would be for copper coins to be assigned values in excess of that of the copper contained in the coins. Of course, the authorities would have to avoid free coinage of copper if the economy were not to become bereft of gold coin: otherwise holders of gold coins would exchange these for copper in the world market at the lower world price (with gold as *numeraire*), have their copper minted, exchange newly minted copper for gold coins, buy copper in the world market, etc. The economy's gold stock would soon enough be exhausted; it would have to leave gold.[25] In fact, then, the government will mint a limited number of copper coins, purchasing the requisite copper in the open market. These coins will function as a medium of exchange but not as a standard of value. The government may choose to enact legal tender legislation, requiring that tender of copper coins be accepted at face value in payment of debts below a certain value. Even if it does not, the convenience of the coins will

[25] *Always abstracting from dual price possibilities.* I also abstract from a complicated case in which there would be free coinage of copper but where copper coins (which would be "over-valued") would be legal tender only for debts below a certain value. This case need not have a corner solution. Nor, for that matter, need that of the text if the legal tender powers of copper coin are restricted.

assure that their exchange value will exceed that of the copper in the coins. Of course, in the absence of legislation, ordinary considerations of supply and demand will determine the precise rate of exchange between the various copper coins and gold. (The problem has been worked out on the assumption of a gold coin standard, but the argument is readily generalized.) [26] In any case, convenience ordinarily requires that the subsidiary coinage not be full-bodied in the sense that constituent elements could command approximately the same basket of goods as does a given coin. The net result in the United States for June 1958 has been summarized by Chandler [*The Economics of Money and Banking*].

Coin	Composition	Mkt. Val. of Comm. Cont.
Dollar	90% Ag, 10% Cu	$0.672
Half-dollar	90% Ag, 10% Cu	0.319
Quarter	90% Ag, 10% Cu	0.160
Dime	90% Ag, 10% Cu	0.064
Nickel	75% Cu, 25% Ni	0.004
Penny	95% Cu, 5% Sn and Zn	0.002

TABLE II-I

Obviously, there is good reason to prohibit free coinage of these coins.

The application of bimetallism to the subsidiary coinage issues is direct. Consider the possibility of issuing full-bodied silver coinage, silver being sufficiently valuable so as not to overwhelm small children carrying coins to the market, but not so valuable as to require issue of coins of infinitesimal size. If full-bodiedness of coinage has appeal to your sense of aesthetic or moral rightness, you might be highly pleased. But, if a coin of given nominal value is to be full-bodied, its ingredients must have the selfsame nominal value in the market. This means that, if you are to employ more than one metal in the full-bodied coinage, each coin consisting of but one metal, you must attempt to fix the relative price of these metals.

[26] The text abstracts from the fact that subsidiary coinage in fact is nominally valued other than in proportion to the value of constituent materials. Convenience dictates that our imaginary economy's copper dime not be 10 times as heavy as its copper penny. However, in the absence of free coinage, this is not important.

One is reminded of stories to the effect that the purchasing power of British pennies exceeded that of British shillings (smaller coins than pennies) in parts of colonial Africa.

4

We now turn to certain of the political aspects of bimetallism, bearing on broader issues of monetary policy occupying much of our later attention: specifically, the *fin de siècle* Free Silver controversy in the United States subsequent to the Crime of 1873 which saw this country "go on gold." 1873–1896 saw a 40 per cent fall in the American wholesale price index, implying a corresponding increase in the purchasing power of gold. Casual empirical observation already has suggested the severe consequences for solvency of debtors, and perhaps income and employment, latent in such deflation. Econometric studies emphasize this point. If liquidity were to be restored, at least two proposals might have been considered.

One was an overtly Robin Hood approach: substitution of a new standard of value for gold. Legislation could make tender of y grains of the new substance discharge an obligation incurred under the gold standard to pay x dollars. Such an approach was politically infeasible.[27] An alternative plan was offered: *free silver.* Monetize silver, permitting free interconvertibility between silver bullion and coin, so that silver would become a perfect monetary substitute for gold, without demonetizing gold.

Before analyzing the Free Silver proposal, consider the factual background, based on the work of Edwin M. Kemmerer.[28] There was a world wide decrease in commodity prices in terms of gold of about 41 per cent between 1873 and 1896. American prices fell correspondingly. If they had not, the United States would have lost its gold to other countries (where it would have purchased more). Such a contraction of the monetary base would have led either to a catastrophic collapse of liquidity or a departure from gold, an eventuality striking terror in bourgeois hearts. Meanwhile the value of silver in terms of gold fell about 50 per cent from 1873 to 1896. Production of silver increased by leaps and bounds in the latter part of the 19th century — in contrast with gold production which failed to keep pace with the

[27] Outright devaluation will be considered later. Refer to Ch. XVI for discussion of devaluation in recent days.

Note that the abundance of a new standard metal is irrelevant if its price is correctly chosen. On the other hand, if there were not to be repeated devaluations under the new standard, prospects for discovery and conditions of production of the new metal would be important.

[28] Kemmerer, *Money,* pp. 359-372.

substantial increase in overall economic activity.[29] The effects of the deflation were especially marked in agriculture. Kemmerer gives a simple, but dramatic illustration. It goes far to explain political radicalism in the Midwest late in the last century:

> "A farmer giving a mortgage for $2,000 with interest of 6% in 1873 could have bought for $2,000 1,492.5 bushels of wheat in 1873 and could have bought for $120 (his annual interest charge) 89.5 bushels. If he paid off the entire principal of the mortgage in 1896, together with one year's interest then due, the payment of principal would have required the equivalent of 3,125 bushels of wheat, and that of the interest the equivalent of 187.5 bushels."[30]

The Free Silverites, including William Jennings Bryan, proposed almost to double the price of silver, implying a mint ratio completely out of line with global market prices of silver and gold.[31] Bryan's silver dollar's ingredients would exchange for little more than half a gold dollar in the free market of the time. Thus, there was a strong Robin Hood tinge to Bryan's proposal — just how strong a tinge partly would depend on how rapidly American prices (taking the price of a unit silver coin as unity) would rise, bringing the real value of silver in the United States into line with its global value. Cost curves of silver mines, foreign trade price elasticities (including capital account response), wealth effects operating on those holding silver and with equities in silver mines, etc. would come into play.[32] Needless to say, gold could be expected to be displaced as money in the United States; a *de facto* silver standard would emerge. And reasonable men could have expected prices to be more stable as a result.

Consider now a hypothetical Bryan proposal, one monetizing silver but equating the mint ratio with the "correct" market ratio. This proposal would have some immediate inflationary potential: the nominal value of silver stocks would become assured, leading *ceteris paribus* to excess supply of money.[33] (Indeed, enhanced demand for silver artifacts might delay the début of substantial amounts of coined

29 From 1861 to 1865, the average annual production of silver was 35.4 fine ounces. The figures for subsequent quinquenniums are: 1871-1875, 61.5; 1881-1885, 85.6; 1891-1895, 157.6. Comparable statistics for gold are: 1861-1865, 5.95; 1871-1875, 5.59; 1881-1885, 4.79; 1886-1890, 5.46; 1891-1895, 7.88. The last statistic reflects new discoveries finally stilling the controversy.

30 *Ibid.*, p. 368.

31 Hawtrey, *Currency and Credit*, p. 314.

32 *Cf.* Ch. VIII *infra*.

33 Keep in mind that American monetization of silver would not lead *per se* to exportation of silver to the United States. It always had been possible to convert silver into money in the market.

silver for some time.) But the real importance of the proposal would depend on future discoveries of gold and silver lodes and changes in mining technology. Thus, if silver were fated to become more abundant relative to gold, the hypothetical proposal would lead to higher prices than would have prevailed under a gold standard and, of course, to a *de facto* silver standard.[34]

Perhaps in the 1960's the tenor of the Free Silverites' proposals would be thought too orthodox, too trusting in purely monetary policy. In their own day, they were attacked and defended as only could be Heresy and Revelation. Indeed I hope, among other things, to depict the development of monetary theory since 1896, as leading to drastic changes in political atmosphere. Not drastic enough, I fear. Recall Keynes's *mot*:

> "Practical men, who believe themselves to be quite exempt from any intellectual influences, are usually the slaves of some defunct economist. Madmen in authority, who hear voices in the air, are distilling their frenzy from some academic scribbler of a few years back."[35]

4. Symmetallic Standards

These standards exist only in the febrile brains of economic theorists. Yet, even more than the bimetallism controversy, the symmetallism literature enriches understanding of economic theory — particularly relationships between money, prices, and national income. The dominant chord relating monetary standards to the theory of employment seldom is recognized.

> "Impressed with the deficiencies of gold or silver separately, a number of economists, including Marshall, proposed towards the end of the nineteenth century that the two be wedded together in what was called symmetallism. Under this proposal the currency unit would have been a specified weight of silver plus a specified weight of gold —

[34] Always remember that the value of gold was increasing globally over these years. It would have been impossible for the U. S. to keep golden money in circulation (certainly other than at a premium) *and* to maintain a steady or rising price level without increasing the coinage price of gold.

Global bimetallism might have had brighter prospects. If silver and gold were perfect monetary substitutes everywhere and at the same mint ratio — and if non-monetary applications were not important enough to permit absorption of all of one or the other metal under certain assumptions — increased silver production could drive down the value of silver *and* gold everywhere. (*Cf.* Appendix to Ch. II.)

[35] J. M. Keynes, *The General Theory of Employment, Interest, and Money* (New York: Harcourt, Brace & Co., 1936), p. 383.

> one can, if he wishes, think of a physical combination of the two in a single bar. The price of silver relative to that of gold could vary to any extent at all; the price of a particular combination of the two not at all . . . In principle, the ultimate extension of the idea of symmetallism is to include in the standard every commodity and service produced in the economy roughly in proportion to the amounts produced (presumably as measured by the 'value added' in their production)."[36]

Our comments concentrate on what Professor Friedman calls the "ultimate extension" of symmetallism. Its practical difficulties — impossibilities rather — are discussed by Friedman.

If perishability, changes in product mix over time, difficulties of specification and standardization, etc. could be averted, the purchasing power of the paper money convertible into the bundle of goods would be rigidly fixed over time; the functioning of money as a standard of deferred payments would be perfected. After all, to say that the government stands ready to exchange paper money for the bundle on a fixed basis is to say that the money value of the bundle will not fluctuate; the over-all purchasing power of money will be fixed.[37]

My interest in symmetallism, however, derives from a different source. Note that excess supplies of labor and commodities could not persist under an ideally symmetallic monetary system. The reason is easy to understand: there is a guaranteed (governmental) demand at a fixed average price level for goods and services, automatically compensating for any non-governmental short-fall. Once relative prices are adjusted, firms will be able to sell all they wish to produce at the going set of money prices. If this set of outputs finds workers involuntarily unemployed, and if money wages are at all flexible downward, lower labor costs will encourage entrepreneurs to augment labor forces in order to cash in on the profit bonanza implicit in reduced money costs of production, accompanied by fixed prices for the final product.

The argument is so simple that some would dismiss it contemptuously: "of course, if the government is ready to purchase the composite output at a fixed aggregate price, there cannot be persistent unemployment, if the money wage is low enough." But simplicity

---

36 Milton Friedman, "Commodity-Reserve Currency," *Essays in Positive Economics*, pp. 204-250, at p. 213. This has come to be the classic article on the subject.

37 The upper limit of the price level is defined by the symmetallic feature so long as positive cash holdings are desired. The price level will become "detached" only when all the cash holdings of the public are exhausted — always assuming government stocks are adequate to maintain the "mint price."

is not always a vice. It is intriguing that there is some sense in which the monetary system can be at the heart of unemployment.

The relationship between kinds of money and persistent involuntary unemployment must be handled rather crudely at this stage; there is a full-scale assault in Ch. VIII. But much ground can be gained now if one recalls Ch. I: if the community's desire to increase its money balances leads to as much demand for economic resources as does a desire to increase the stock of automobiles, persistent unemployment would be unlikely. Eventually we will have a full analytic grasp of the relationship of the essential properties of money to problems of economic stagnation.

5. Paper Standards

1

Paper monetary standards are associated emotionally (but not necessarily analytically) with an aspect of the third major theme of this section: historical impecuniosity of governments. Non-representative paper standards are *fiat* in character. Paper standards permit divorce of governments from the formal rigor of convertibility requirements. Paper standards sometimes have appealed to authorities as *entrées* into a paradise of fiscal freedom, and in fact sometimes have led to the horrors of hyperinflation.

Toynbee interestingly describes the origins of paper money, citing as authority the following lines from C. P. Fitzgerald:

> "In the imperial park at Ch'ang Ngan the Emperor had a white stag, a very rare beast, which had no fellow in the empire. On the advice of a minister, the Emperor had this animal killed and made a kind of treasury note out of its skin, which, he believed, could not be copied. These pieces of skin were a foot square [each piece being assigned the arbitrary value of 400,000 copper coins]. The princes, when they came to pay their respects to the throne, were compelled to buy one of these pieces of skin for cash and present their gifts to the Emperor upon it. This precaution ensured the circulation of the 'White Stag Notes.' The skin of the white stag was, however, a limited quantity, and the time soon came when this device ceased to supply the Treasury with much needed money."[38]

[38] A. J. Toynbee, *op. cit.*, p. 313, quoting C. P. Fitzgerald, *China, A Short Cultural History*, p. 165.

Toynbee continues:

> "In A. D. 970 the invention of printed paper money was taken up by the Sung government, and in China and its dependencies from that date onwards [until A. D. 1425] paper money was continuously and ubiquitously current [when it was withdrawn in the aftermath of hyper-inflation]. No further issues of paper money were made in China until A. D. 1851 when the Manchu dynasty, in its turn, was declining towards its fall."[39]

There can be little doubt that fiat paper money was conceived in sin, and, as often is the case with sinful things, is surrounded with an aura of excitement and legerdemain persisting into our own day. People still cannot quite believe that paper money is "right" or that it would work in the absence of mysterious metallic "backings."[40]

How does it become possible for governments to get hold of resources by issuing pieces of engraved paper that cost next to nothing in terms of other resources?[41] Partly through legal tender acts, although legal tender acts merely specify what is acceptable tender for debts expressed in money of account. If the public for any reason did not want to employ paper money, agreements *could* be drawn requiring payment in just about anything and without reference to money of account. But inconvertible paper money has generally received ready acceptance. J. S. Mill has explained this:

> "After experience had shown that pieces of paper, of no intrinsic value, by merely bearing upon them the written profession of being equivalent to a certain number of francs, dollars or pounds, could be made to circulate as such, and to produce all the benefit to the issuers which could have been produced by the coins which they purported to represent; governments began to think that it would be a happy device if they could appropriate to themselves this benefit, free from the condition to which individuals issuing such paper substitutes for money were subject, of giving, when required, for the sign the thing signified. They determined to try whether they could emancipate themselves from this unpleasant obligation, and make a piece of paper issued by them pass for a pound, by merely calling it a pound, and consenting to receive it in payment of taxes. And such is the influence of almost all established governments, that they have generally succeeded in attaining this object: I believe I might say they have always succeeded for a time, and the power has only been lost to them after they had compromised it by the most flagrant abuse.

---

39 *Loc. cit. supra,* p. 313.

40 *Cf.* p. 52 for another appraisal of paper money standards.

41 Recall the strictures of Sir Dennis Robertson's animated bank note. Practically nothing that has served as money would have the same value otherwise.

> In the case supposed, the functions of money are performed by a thing which derives its power for performing them solely from convention; but convention is quite sufficient to confer the power; since nothing more is needful to make a person accept anything as money, and even at any arbitrary value, than the persuasion that it will be taken from him on the same terms by others."[42]

There is every reason, then, to find paper money able to circulate (to have currency) in the presence of a functioning full-bodied alternative. In view of the close substitutability of paper and its (metallic) counterpart, we could expect to see an increase in the supply of one lead to a decrease in the real value of a unit of the other, at least within the context of a closed system. This is precisely what happened in China. (*See Note D.*) But "excessive" issue of fiat paper money can lead effectively to demonetization of the full-bodied alternative and to a purely fiat standard. What if people come to yearn for the old, hard money, days? Are they likely to cease using paper money? Hardly! The advantages of a system featured by official money, together with the advantages of reckoning and contracting in money of account, are so enormous that our study of hyperinflation (Ch. VI) will reveal that people are found willing to hold paper money even when it is depreciating in real value at rates in excess of 50 per cent per month.[43]

We now are in a position to set out the fundamentals of pure fiat (inconvertible) paper monetary standards. We find the government issuing certain quantities of printed paper. If it is strong enough to insure against massive counterfeit, the knowledge that the stock of this paper cannot be augmented other than by the official presses, together with the prestige conferred upon the paper through its association with the government which accepts the paper in payment of taxes, permits it to be set to work as money. The utility of official money being so great, it becomes possible for these bits of paper to purchase split-

[42] J. S. Mill, *Principles of Political Economy,* W. J. Ashley, ed. (8th ed., London: Longmans, Green and Co., 1940), p. 542.

[43] History indicates the introduction of fiat paper money often is accompanied by outlawing the use of gold and/or silver for monetary purposes and might be accompanied by legislation requiring that the public turn in their stocks of these metals in exchange for paper money. The background is usually that of the White Stag Notes: issue as a means of taxation. However, the fact that issuance of inconvertible paper money has been accompanied by outlawing of monetary use of substitutes does not mean that it would have been unable to survive otherwise. Rather the coincidence points up the theme of impecuniosity. Note that mercantilist theory stressed the advantage to the State of possessing large metallic war chests.

level houses, sports cars, cabbages, kings, and all sorts of things. Ultimately, the fact that paper of this sort has circulated so long will endow it with the sanctity of established custom and attract to it some of the reverence accorded metal.

Once we have traced the processes leading to established use of fiat paper money, we are home. All that remains is to recognize that conventional principles of the theory of value apply to the determination of the purchasing power of inconvertible paper money — implicit in the prices of other commodities. In fact the lines of fiat paper standards are cleanly etched. Since the mumbo-jumbo adhering to gold has been stripped away, the elements of a fiat paper standard can be succinctly summarized:

> The government issues a volume of paper whose real value will depend on the nominal value of that volume and the strength of demand for it. The legal tender act will rigidly determine the price of a unit of paper money.

2

For political authorities, fiat paper standards present both an opportunity to do good and a temptation to tread the primrose path of dalliance.[44] The opportunity is centered upon possibilities of scientific management largely excluded by the arbitrary discipline of the gold standard. The temptation is political in origin and concerns the use of fiat paper — or even representative paper money ("warehouse receipts") — issues as a means of commanding resources not available through conventional taxation. Governments have succumbed to the temptation from the beginning. Indeed, more generally, monetary history is replete with sweating, abrading, and clipping of coinage admixture of foreign substances into the coinage, issue of phony warehouse receipts acknowledging deposit of gold or silver that did not exist, and prolific issue of inconvertible (fiat) paper. Sometimes the temptation has arisen from the profligate propensities of sybaritic rulers, at other times from the exigencies of great wars or celebrated revolutions.

Perhaps the crucial aspect of the temptation is the relation of deliberate inflation to taxation — to be exhaustively considered in Ch. VI. Keynes put it well:

44
Do not, as some ungracious pastors do,
Show me the steep and thorny way to heaven,
Whiles, like a puff'd and reckless libertine,
Himself the primrose path of dalliance treads.
Hamlet, I, iii.

> "A government can live for a long time by printing paper money. That is to say, it can by this means secure command over real resources . . . The method is condemned, but its efficacy up to a point must be admitted. A government can live by this means when it can live by no other. It is the form of taxation which the public find hardest to evade and which even the weakest government can enforce when it can enforce nothing else . . . What is there to prevent the government from repeating this process over and over again? . . . Has the public in the last resort no remedy, no means of protecting itself against these ingeneous depredations? It has only one remedy — to change its habits in the use of money . . . The public discovers that it is the holders of notes which suffer taxation and defray the expenses of government and they begin to change their habits in economizing in notes . . . [leading to hyperinflation]."[45]

6. Loose Ends

Staggering to the finish line of a long and difficult discourse on monetary standards, only two loose ends remain to be tied: representative paper money and Gresham's Law. The latter permits discussion of abuse of coinage, and, in fact, the next paragraphs are a pot-pourri, clearing the ground for the historical surveys completing Ch. II.

1

Note the difference between paper issue merely purporting to be a warehouse receipt for gold or silver *(representative paper money)* and fiat paper money. If the warehouse receipt is convertible, the context is one of a metallic standard — whether or not "receipts" have been issued for more gold or silver than "lives underground." The ultimate stuff of the system is gold or silver; the exchange rate between specie and paper is rigidly maintained through the convertibility privilege. At the same time, issue of phony receipts will depress the value of their perfect (monetary) substitute: gold or silver.

2

Gresham's Law is widely cited and often misunderstood:

> "Where two or more forms of money of the same nominal or face value are in concurrent circulation and if one is relatively overvalued for monetary purposes, the self interest of the public . . . will lead them to discriminate between the two forms. The undervalued form

[45] Keynes, *A Tract on Monetary Reform,* pp. 41-73.

> will be retained, and the overvalued form will be passed along to others . . . In time the form of money which is undervalued for monetary purposes will disappear from circulation . . . [I]f the community is in a position to refuse to accept the bad money, . . . the good money will not disappear but will continue to circulate *at a premium*."[46]

When we argued that most writers on bimetallism have reasoned falsely, we could have said that they applied Gresham's Law without seeing that the under-valued metal will *not* be driven from circulation if it can circulate at a premium over its official nominal value. Another, and perhaps better known, application of Gresham's Law concerns metallic coin standards of other days. Public and private impecuniosity, greed and simple dishonesty led to lightening of the coinage through shaving, sweating, etc. (Milling of coins developed in order to limit shaving.) So long as there were innocents about or, for that matter, people without appropriate weighing machinery, those in the know could pass on light coins, retaining heavy coins. But too much has been made of this. Legal tender acts or their equivalents made clear enough what was to be the weight of standard coins. Only market imperfections (admittedly serious) led to disappearance of heavy coins in real-world systems. Indeed the case is on all fours with the bimetallism analysis.

3

Gresham's Law, calling forth images of debased currency, is hard to discuss outside of a context of interaction of monetary policies and fundamental fiscal disorder. Accordingly, we refer *en passant* (and not for the first time) to another mechanism through which governments have relieved their fiscal distress: redefinition of the accounting price of the standard metal so that obligations expressed in money of account could be discharged by tender of less gold or silver than had been the case. Thus, if a government owed 1,000,000 francs in the context of a gold standard system where francs were money of account and where the price of gold had been defined as 100 francs per ounce, the obligation, expressed in gold, would fall from 10,000 to 1,000 ounces if the price of gold were cried up to 1,000 francs. Assuming that the government had been farsighted enough to issue its IOU's in terms of francs without expressing their "gold content," it could wipe out 90 per cent of its gold obligation with a stroke of a pen.

[46] W. H. Steiner, Eli Shapiro, and Ezra Solomon, *Money and Banking* (4th ed., New York: Henry Holt & Co., 1958), pp. 32-33. A correct statement.

B. HISTORY

We turn to a sweeping survey of the monetary history of the United States and Britain.

1. Monetary History of the United States

1

We rely heavily upon Arthur Nussbaum, *A History of the Dollar* (New York: Columbia University Press, 1957), an excellent, readable book.

The American Colonial period saw a wide variety of media of exchange, with the British Pound serving as money of account. Legal tender acts, passed by colonial legislatures, often attempted to initiate "polymetallic" systems (specified tenders being beaver skins and corn, etc.). Needless to say, divergence of markets from "mint" ratios was the rule rather than the exception; debtors tendered the over-valued goods. Metallic money also was in circulation. Among the variety of coins were Spanish silver pieces which came to be known as dollars. There was in the colonies extreme consciousness of a "scarcity" of coin, a "scarcity" apparently encouraged by a usually unfavorable trade balance with England, prohibition against the export of specie from England, and prohibition of the colonies minting their own coins. Undoubtedly, it would be more correct to say that the colonists' demand for real cash balances was small, reflecting the high marginal productivity of capital.[47]

Nussbaum's account of introduction of paper money by colonial governments is fascinating:

> ". . . Massachusetts issued in 1690 printed bills of credit [reading 'this bill of 5 shillings shall be in value equal to money and shall accordingly be accepted by the Treasurer in all public payments'] . . . [I]n England bank notes . . . were printed . . . about 1729. As early as 1692 the Massachusetts bills were made legal tender . . . Issued in limited amounts, . . . they proved for two decades a sound substitute for coin . . ."[48]

Not surprisingly, there were "grave inflationary abuses."

---

[47] For an account of Thomas Jefferson's monetary arrangements as late as 1800, see Dumas Malone, *Jefferson and the Ordeal of Liberty* (Boston: Little, Brown & Co., 1962), pp. 179 and 218-219.

[48] Arthur Nussbaum, *op. cit., pp.* 14-15. At pp. 14-15 *et seq.*, Nussbaum details a number of fascinating episodes.

Doubtless, paper money made it possible for specie revenues (and capital) to be used for importations. It buttressed liquidity and avoided deflationary pressure and unfavorable terms of trade. Benjamin Franklin certainly thought so — and then some:

> "Pennsylvania before it made any paper money, was totally stript of its gold and silver . . . The difficulties for want of cash were accordingly very great, the chief part of the trade being carried on by the extremely inconvenient method of barter; when, in 1723, paper money was first made here [it] gave new life to business . . . whereby the province has so greatly increased . . . they have been able to obtain great quantities of gold and silver, to remit hither in return for manufactures of this country [England]."[49]

Needless to say, the fiscal problems of the Continental Congress, at the outbreak of the Revolutionary War in 1775 and during its prosecution, were immense. Congress could not conceivably finance the Revolution through specie stocks and/or tax revenues: resources had to be obtained through classical processes of inflation. The "Continentals" were born. These were bills of credit issued by the Congress under a resolution pledging the colonies' faith to their redemption — sometime. Nussbaum (pp. 35-37) reports that a typical Continental read:

THE UNITED COLONIES *THREE DOLLARS*

> This bill entitles the Bearer to receive three Spanish milled dollars according to the Resolution of the Congress . . .

> "The bills were made legal tender by the individual colonies, Congress having no power to do so." Fearful penalties were threatened to those refusing to accept the bills.
>
> Strangely enough, the main sufferers were Quakers who . . . would not accept . . . war money."

Issue of the Continentals followed the classical pattern in these matters.[50] The point is not that "not worth a Continental" became a phrase signifying utter worthlessness, but that Congress achieved as much command of resources as it did, an achievement that must be judged in the light of the fact that the Revolution was aided and abetted by a comparative few. In any event, the Funding Act of 1790,

49 Statement to the English Board of Trade, 1764, cited by Nussbaum, *op. cit.*, p. 27.
50 *Cf.* Ch. VI.

permitting Continentals to be accepted for bond subscriptions on a 1:100 basis, ended the episode.[51]

2

Interesting stories can be told of the colorful history of paper money issues by various American states. However, we turn to the development of a national currency in this sketch of the history of American monetary standards. The Coinage Act of 1792 was the key enactment, these being its main provisions:

1) bimetallism was established at the rate of 1:15;

2) the unit of account and the standard coin both were to be called "the dollar";

3) free coinage was established; the Mint would coin gold and silver free of charge. English history and practice were much attended: the 1:15 ratio dated back to Newton's 1717 report; there was free coinage in England as well.

Many foreign coins remained in circulation. Indeed, Spanish dollars were made legal tender.[52]

3

Starting in 1794, the 1:15 gold-silver ratio diverged from the market ratio, silver having begun to depreciate relative to gold. The expected occurred: gold began to disappear from coinage.[53]

The United States experienced great economic growth from 1794 to 1834. The stock of money increased correspondingly, although the important growth in monetary assets was in bank credit, especially bank notes. The resulting fractional reserve system was rendered more than usually vulnerable by irresponsible and often dishonest management of many of the state banks. This, combined with monumental political thrust and riposte, set the stage for the panic of 1837.

---

51 It seems that Alexander Hamilton, the Secretary of the Treasury, tipped off financiers or speculators (depending on one's taste in these matters) that Continentals were to be redeemed. Fast schooners left northern ports, permitting insiders to buy up Continentals before local yokels knew what had happened. However, two points are worth stressing: (1) Hamilton is not known to have profited personally; his was an action of state policy; (2) only $6 million was involved; the total issue exceeded $241 million.

52 "The dollar sign, $, is connected with the peso, contrary to popular belief which considers it . . . an abbreviation of 'U. S.' The two parallel lines represented one of the many abbreviations of 'P' and the 'S' indicated the plural." (Nussbaum, *op. cit.*, p. 56.)

53 Concededly more expected by others than by me.

It is impossible to continue the narrative without introducing Andrew Jackson, who became president in 1829 and whose epic struggle with the Second Bank of the United States and its president, Nicholas Biddle, will be discussed in Ch. V. But we must say something about Jackson and the Bank now if we are to understand 1837. We turn to Nussbaum.

> ". . . [Jackson] disliked the wealthy capitalist class of the eastern seaboard and the private banks altogether. Worst of all, in his estimation, was the Bank of the United States [a largely private institution enjoying a special relationship with the U. S. government] which he termed 'a monster,' and 'a hydra of corruption . . .'
>
> In 1833 the federal government ceased depositing its money in the Bank. Instead, its new deposits were entrusted to various state-chartered banks. . . . Inevitably, the Bank of the United States had to curtail the credits which it had given to customers, including state-chartered banks, and Biddle purposely reduced the credits more than was necessary. The result was widespread financial stringency, which aroused popular sentiment more than ever against the bank. Pressed from all sides, it had to liquidate its affairs . . . [I]t was turned into a local institution under a Pennsylvania charter . . . [and] after a few years it failed and went out of existence . . .
>
> [I]ts notes had always been fully redeemed. Their disappearance was a heavy blow to the economy of the United States."[54]

Such is the squalid tale of the battle between the prig and the demagogue.

The impending demise of the Second Bank and its note circulation intensified interest in expansion of the monetary base so that coin could be substituted for bank notes and the note issue of state banks could better be sustained.[55] Accordingly, currency legislation was passed in 1834. In accordance with the unhappy, sometimes perverse, history of bimetallism in the United States, the mint ratio was set at 1:16 "although the gold-silver ratio in the market of 1834 was 1:15.625.

---

[54] *Ibid.*, pp. 74-75.

[55] Jackson was himself a hard money man. Perhaps a moral of this incident, leading to the tragedies of 1837 and various subsequent years, is that a politician, relying on base appeal to popular prejudice, becomes particularly dangerous when convinced of the moral righteousness of his argument. He loses his perspective.

Nussbaum offers a tepid defense of Jackson at p. 79. ". . . [T]his great President, then does not lack merit even in the monetary field. However, there is a growing consensus of opinion among historians [*not* including Arthur Schlesinger Jr.] that he did not contribute to his glory by his furious fight against the Second Bank of the United States . . . His mistake led to grave consequences."

Hence, although bimetallism was legally maintained, the new regulation meant an over-valuation of gold, mainly in order to have the notes of the bank . . . replaced by gold coins."[56] The short-run effects of the over-valuation of gold were favorable from the viewpoint of the authors of the 1834 legislation. The over-valuation of gold led to "capital inflow" as holders of gold bullion abroad recognized the United States as a haven for their gold assets, a place where the monetary value of gold was exceptionally high. Although silver dollars had been out of circulation since 1806 as a result of persistent loss to South America, where they were highly esteemed for their aesthetic qualities, there was some silver coinage in the United States: silver was so convenient as a lower denomination form of coinage that *these* coins did not leave circulation, at least up to 1837. This meant that there was little enough silver circulation to lose in 1834, and what there was was, so to speak, inelastic in demand. There was little loss of monetary circulation to offset the increased coinage of gold bullion.

Thus, the monetary base did increase. However, the catastrophe of 1837 was not to be avoided. A fillip was contributed by the Jackson administration when the Specie Circular was issued in 1836. It provided that public lands must be purchased in gold or silver or notes recognized by the Treasurer of the United States as convertible into specie. This ruling primarily affected lands in the West.[57]

The appalling crisis of 1837 is a remarkably textbook-like illustration of the dread consequences of first signing articles of submission to the discipline of a metallic standard and then neglecting the most important aspect of this submission: keying the value of the paper issue to that of the metallic stock and/or providing a lender of last resort commanding confidence and a large enough specie reserve.[58] The disaster will be intensified if the monetary authorities belatedly insist upon a drastic contraction of credit in order to defend the metallic standard — to keep it afloat on a sea of bankruptcies — rather than

[56] *Ibid.*, p. 77.

[57] *Ibid.*, p. 78. Nussbaum goes on to write (pp. 78-79): "they had been purchased by settlers and speculators on credit granted by western banks through their notes, a situation which resulted in a wide overexpansion of credit. The Specie Circular was therefore based on sound considerations, but it contributed to an approaching crisis, which was caused, among other factors, by the elimination of the Second Bank of the United States, which had provided the only control over the credit structure."

[58] Of course, it always is possible for a fractional reserve system to collapse, even if buttressing arrangements are optimal.

abandon the mystique of metallic standards and support the credit structure with fiat paper. But, we shall not pursue these reflections at this time. This is but a narrative, and we have not been introduced to Walter Bagehot who understood these issues very early and wrote about them with unrivalled lucidity. Nussbaum writes:

> ". . . The Crisis of 1837 was inaugurated, so to speak, by a monetary event: in May 1837, all banks suspended payment of specie . . . More than 600 banks broke down . . . [R]egular banking service was not restored until 1843. But meanwhile the circulation of notes shrunk to $59 million [from $149 million in 1837]; the $100 million level was not reached again until 1846."[59]

As our discussion of the 1931–1933 crisis in the United States will reveal, a breakdown in liquidity of this magnitude leads to deep and widespread maladjustment of the entire economic machine. Such was the case after 1837.

4

The year 1848 ushered in a period of great expansion in the gold stock. American production of gold — less than $1 million in 1847 — exceeded $50 million in 1850. This development, together with the fact that gold was already over-valued at the Mint under the terms of 1834 legislation, led toward disappearance of silver coinage which, recall, was largely small change. (One touch is pleasing to the Hawtrey-MLB camp: railways paid premia in order to obtain change for their offices.) The upshot was introduction of subsidiary coinage through legislation in 1851 and 1853. Naturally there was not free coinage of subsidiary coins.

The trend of events from 1848 to 1860 — especially the California gold discoveries — was favorable to liquidity, but the American financial system remained unsound. Witness the crisis of 1857 and the lesser crisis at the outset of the Civil War in 1861. The causes of the *malaise* were straightforward enough: decentralization of reserves; effects of Van Buren's Independent Treasury System which diverted specie reserves from the banks to the subtreasuries. (Nussbaum — p. 95 — reports that "in 1855 the Treasury possessed half as much gold as the 1,300 banks [of the country].") Another source of strain on bank solvency was the requirement that payments to the government be in specie. The Jacksonian legacy continued to brood over the financial and monetary systems. But such is the sway of "the golden image"

[59] *Ibid.*, p. 80.

over men's minds that wholesale relief through release from the hegemony of specie did not attract the interest of responsible persons. It was not until the wrench of the tremendous fiscal pressures of the Civil War that such expedience was practiced — and then with great reluctance and with fervent protestation that "gold" would be reinstated when peace returned.[60]

5

Discussion of the monetary aspects of the Civil War (particularly the Greenbacks) will be confined to the Union side. The Confederate system is discussed at the end of Ch. VI.

An early (and predictable) development in the Civil War was the hoarding of specie — partly because of a general sense of insecurity and partly because of belief that the specie value of circulating paper would fall. By December 1861, banks had to suspend specie payments. The upshot was the Legal Tender Act of February 1862 and the advent of the Greenbacks.

Kemmerer summarizes the main provisions of the Legal Tender Act of 1862:

> "1) The Secretary of the Treasury was authorized to issue $150 millions of United States notes . . . These notes were to bear no interest and were nominally 'payable to bearer on demand.' . . .
>
> 2) The new notes were made receivable in payment of all taxes, debts, and other obligations of any kind due to the United States, except duties on imports . . . and were likewise made receivable in payment of all claims and demands against the United States, except those for interest upon bonds and notes which were to be paid in coin.
>
> 3) The new notes were declared to be 'lawful money and a legal tender in payment of all debts public and private, within the United States' [except duties on imports and interest on notes]."[61]

The initial act made the Greenbacks convertible into gold bonds, but this provision was cancelled by congressional legislation in 1863 making the Greenbacks a truly fiat currency. The legislation aroused surprisingly little controversy.

Not that the waters were altogether placid. Witness Representa-

60 The solution of deflation for "inadequate liquidity" seldom is happy: there are irksome redistributive effects; stickiness of prices and wages will keep market above natural rates of interest for some time. There will be excess supply of goods over long intervals.

61 *Op. cit.*, p. 237.

tive Roscoe Conkling (N. Y.) in a speech delivered in February 1862. Addressing himself to the moral imperfections of the bill, he said:

> "It will, of course, proclaim throughout the country a saturnalia of fraud — a carnival for rogues. Every agent, attorney, treasurer . . . and every debtor of a fiduciary character who has received for others money, hard money, worth a hundred cents in the dollar, will forever release himself from that liability by buying up for that knavish purpose, at its depreciated value, the spurious currency which we shall have put afloat . . . Think of savings banks entrusted with enormous aggregates of pittances of the poor, the hungry, and the homeless, the stranger . . ."[62]

The peak circulation of the Greenbacks was reached in 1864: $431 million. The over-all increase in the money supply — including currency, bank notes, and bank demand deposits — was more than 120 per cent. Prices (quoted with paper dollars as *numeraire*) increased, but not by as much as did the money stock. Since gold was now a commodity like any other — the linkage between gold and the unit of account being broken and replaced with a link between Greenbacks and the unit of account (the dollar) — the dollar value of gold was subject to day-to-day fluctuation in the gold market.[63]

> "During the entire period of inconvertibility, gold was bought and sold as a commodity. It was needed by the public for the payment of customs duties, for making certain settlements abroad, and for merchandise purposes. It continued during the entire period to circulate as money on the Pacific Coast. The National Government needed substantial quantities for paying interest on a large part of its national debt."[64]

By 1862 the rate of exchange of 23.22 grains of gold (a gold dollar) against a unit Greenback exceeded unity, standing at 1.13 (on the

---

[62] Cited by Kemmerer, *ibid.*, p. 242.

[63] Kemmerer points out that the bullion value of silver now became so great compared to its nominal value as money that silver coins were driven from circulation. Likewise nickel and copper coins, which now became more valuable as metal than as coin; before the war, these were subsidiary coins. "To meet the resulting need for fractional money, the government issued legal tender, fractional notes in denominations less than one dollar, which popularly were called 'shinplasters.' The smallest of these notes was for three cents." (Kemmerer, *op. cit.*, p. 246.)

This rather dramatizes what appear usually to be overwhelming institutional obstacles to coinage circulating at values different from those stamped on the coins' faces.

[64] Kemmerer, *op. cit.*, p. 247.

average) during 1862. Corresponding statistics for 1864 and 1865 were 2.03 and 1.57. The premium on gold did not altogether reflect increases in the cost of living (with Greenbacks as *numeraire*): the retail price index was 156 (1860 = 100) in 1864; the price of gold, indexed on the same base year, was 203. Various speculative considerations, often hinging on the fortunes of war, determined the gold value of the Greenbacks. And then, it certainly would have seemed logical to a trader during the Civil War that ultimate resumption of the gold standard would not be at the old price of $20.67 per ounce (the nominal price of gold). "After all," he would reason, "resumption at $20.67 requires a sharp decline in prices from levels that will have been reached at the end of the war. Otherwise, the purchasing power of gold in the United States would be substantially less than elsewhere; there would be ruinous gold outflow. Rather than accept the 'heads I win, tails you lose' alternatives of drastic deflation or drastic gold outflow, resumption will be above $20.67." This was perfectly sound reasoning, suggesting that, if resumption occurred soon after the war, rather more than 20.67 Greenbacks (each nominally valued at one dollar) would exchange for an ounce of gold. In fact, resumption was delayed until 1879 when the American price level had fallen enough and specie reserves had increased enough to allay fear of external and internal drains at the venerable $20.67 price for gold.

Discussion of gold premiums, resumption prices, etc., serves three purposes: (1) it points up that a rise in the price of gold subsequent to resort to a paper standard need not reflect "over-issue," a point emphasized in discussion of the British restriction of 1797; (2) it illuminates "resumption," an important policy problem often obscured by mumbo-jumbo; (3) it suggests consequences of sticky nominal prices and costs that make important the choice of the "gold content of the monetary unit."

Greenbacks were not the only inconvertible paper issued by the federal government, but were by far the most important.[65] The United States emerged from the Civil War with a money stock of $1.54 billion, $850 million more than the prewar stock of $0.69 billion. Since the national gold reserve had not much increased (if at all), convertibility

[65] Nussbaum, *op. cit.*, describes other federal paper.

of the vastly increased volume of paper could not be assured except by revaluation.[66] It is not hard to understand why convertibility (at $20.67) was delayed until 1879.

6

In the meanwhile, litigation reached the Supreme Court. It conjures up some of the basic metaphysics of money. And, since the legal tender cases had important bearing on litigation pursuant to the 1934 act, it might be worthwhile to study them — with the help of the ubiquitous Nussbaum.

The Constitution — while prohibiting states from making "any Thing but gold and silver Coin a Tender in Payment of Debts" and from emitting bills of credit — is silent on federal powers in these matters. Legal precedent of some vintage, together with the fact that 16 of 17 state supreme courts had ruled the Greenback legislation constitutional, suggested that the case of *Hepburn v. Griswold,* taken to the Supreme Court in 1867, would find the Greenbacks supported. "The highest court of Kentucky . . . in a divided opinion, took the view that the legal tender acts could not be applied to contracts made before their enactment."[67] This was the case of *Hepburn v. Griswold,* a case dramatized by the fact that Chief Justice Salmon P. Chase was the Secretary of the Treasury who originally issued the Greenbacks. After more than two years — and after some interesting personality conflicts — the Court handed down its judgment in February 1870. The legal tender acts were declared unconstitutional! Justice Chase wrote the *majority* opinion (the split being four-three), implying by way of *obiter dictum* that the acts did not apply to contracts made *after* their enactment. Even apart from the *dictum,* the decision would have led to a very heavy burden on debtors who had made payment since 1862 and now would have to pay over the difference between the value of Greenbacks paid and that of gold dollars at the time of payment. At the time of the decision the gold premium was 13 per cent:

[66] Chapter IV permits more precise analysis of how the gold base can affect nominal values of equilibrium stocks of paper issue, bank deposits, etc. Thus, if the public wishes to maintain a certain ratio between holdings of specie and currency and holdings of bank issue, banks will be unable to issue more than a given amount without jeopardizing their reserves. Chapter XIV shows that there can be unique equilibrium ratios of values of financial assets, including, of course, bank issue.

[67] *Ibid.,* p. 128.

current debtors would find their obligations substantially heavier. But chaos and perhaps serious conflict were averted in the nick of time: President Grant was able to appoint two justices known to favor the acts, as the Supreme Court's membership was increased to nine.

The inevitable happened: the acts were found to be constitutional in 1871, the Court splitting 5-4. By 1884, the power of the federal government to issue legal tender notes was established, although its scope was limited: ". . . the Court recognized the validity of contractual 'gold clauses,' and even the validity of the California and Oregon enactments which excluded Greenbacks from payment of state taxes."[68] . . . Gold clauses are taken up again when the legislation of 1934 is considered.

The next major event in American monetary history centers on the Resumption Act of 1875 which restored the gold standard as of January 1, 1879 when Greenbacks were to be redeemable in gold so that $20.67 in Greenbacks were convertible into one ounce of gold. The deflationary pressures abetted by this decision already have been considered. We have seen how the aftermath led to the bimetallic controversy culminating in the Cross of Gold speech of 1896. From 1873 to 1896 there was a worldwide movement towards adoption of gold standards, accompanied by demonetization of silver (production of which was greatly increasing). Since the global stock of gold did not increase in this period at the same rate as did economic activity, and since demand for gold was also increased because of growing adoption of the gold standard, deflationary pressure predominated (with gold as *numeraire*): this might have put a drag on economic progress; it certainly applied continuous pressure against debtors with nominally fixed obligations.

If silver had not been demonetized, inflationary forces would have dominated — especially if gold had been kept in the money stock through appropriate adjustment of mint ratios (*see Note E*); the global money stock would have grown at a faster rate than that of real economic activity. However, the world took the deflationist — at least the relatively deflationist — option. The result was that the United States, in the absence of revaluation, had the choice of accepting deflation or going off gold; we could not refuse to let the purchasing power of gold increase here as it was increasing throughout the world.

---

[68] *Ibid.*, p. 123.

8

1900–1914 was a golden age in more ways than one. Certainly the gold standard enjoyed salad days as Alaskan and South African discoveries relieved deflationary pressure. The stock of money and price levels both substantially increased; debtors were relieved. It was alleged that imperfections in the national banking system produced or exaggerated liquidity crises such as the panic of 1907, but certainly there was no secular shortage of liquidity. While 1900–1914 was a period of fundamental change in our banking system, it was not a period of ferment for monetary standards.

9

World War I (1914–1918) imposed relatively little strain on the American monetary system. The events of the 1914–1918 period can be capsulated, relying partly on Nussbaum.[69]

1) In August 1914 "foreign assets in this country exceeded American assets abroad by at least $3.7 billion," a fact encouraging substantial gold outflow from the U. S. if Europeans decided to cash some of their dollar chips.

2) They did to the tune of some hundreds of millions of dollars. Fears that America would abandon full convertibility led to depreciation of the dollar in terms of European currencies of more than 40 per cent during August-September 1914. These fears were abetted by "a run on currency by bank depositors in the panic following the outbreak of the war." Emergency (convertible) notes were issued, but the panic was short-lived and the emergency notes were withdrawn in 1915.

3) By October 1914, increasing war orders improved the American balance of payments and "the sterling-dollar rate returned to normal." By April 1917, when we entered the war, cumulated favorable merchandise balances of payments led to the United States having accumulated unprecedently large specie reserves, despite the fact that huge sales of European-owned dollar securities had occurred.

4) After April 1917, the Allies were no longer required to make payments in gold. We experienced gold outflow, as U. S. gold payments to neutrals increased. As a result, exportation of gold from the United States was prohibited, with certain narrow exceptions, until June 1918 when President Wilson removed the prohibitions. During this interval in which American obligations were externally inconvertible,

69 *Op. cit.*, p. 162 *ff*.

large premiums were commanded by various hard neutral currencies; the dollar price of gold abroad exceeded the internal price. However, from June 1918 onward, the American gold reserve position was "solid."

10

The 1920's were a period of calm in American *monetary* history; neither inflationary nor deflationary pressure was prominent after 1921. But, as we shall see, certain harsh facts of life were brought home with brutal force in the early 1930's.

The monetary scene abroad was much less placid than that at home. In fact American central banking policy contributed somewhat to the over-all turbulence. Globally, the nominal value of gold-convertible obligations bore unusually high proportion to the nominal value of gold reserves. The gold standards of the 1920's, bullion standards except in the United States and France, frequently were of the gold exchange type, meaning that ultimate reserves for some countries comprised holdings of foreign securities, themselves convertible into gold; Ch. XVI contains a full account of the inherent defects of international economies in which monetary reserves are held in the form of national currencies. Another element of instability was contributed by "over-valuation" upon returning to gold, by Britain and other European countries (a problem considered in some detail later in this chapter). Suffice it to say at this point that the choice in Britain in the 1920's was the same as that for the United States in 1879: establishment of prewar accounting prices for gold in the face of substantial wartime inflation (more substantial than in the United States) meant that prices of British goods had to decline if the purchasing power of the pound *vis-a-vis* the dollar was to reflect the difference in "gold content" of the pound and the dollar. The deflationary process proved to be grindingly slow and painful.

11

It is here that we can pick up the interaction of American central banking policies of the 1920's and the developing world monetary crisis. As is shown in Ch. XV, an important aspect of the functioning of an international gold standard concerns impact of gold flows on national price levels and interest rates. Thus, gold inflow "should" lead to higher prices and lower interest rates, at least transitionally. Consider Table II-II.

FRENCH, BRITISH AND AMERICAN STOCKS, 1919-1929[70]

(in millions of pounds sterling)

	France	U. K.	U.S.
End of 1919	143	120	520
End of 1929	336	146	800

TABLE II-II

Note to Table II: In view of the substantial South African production during the decade and Britain's role as banker for what became the Commonwealth, the U. K. statistic is consistent with substantial gold ouflow.

The huge increase in the American monetary base might have been expected to lead to substantial price inflation, accompanied by downward pressure on real interest rates as American banks attempted to increase their loans and investments in response to their increased liquidity. Most of the increase in the American monetary gold stock occurred before the end of 1924. If American prices had risen in relation to foreign prices, our merchandise balance of payments could have been expected to deteriorate, while lower American interest rates would encourage foreigners to sell dollar securities, convert the proceeds into gold, and invest the proceeds in sterling securities, for example, with a resulting increase in the British gold stock.

But this was not to be the case. The American authorities "sterilized" gold inflows through open market sales of securities, which reduced bank reserves, and employed other devices so that the gold inflows did not exert substantial influence on American prices and interest rates. The same story can be told of France so that, at the end of 1928, the United States and France held between them 43 per cent of the world's stock of monetary gold. Surely a highly unsound situation from the standpoint of the viability of an international gold standard.

The groundwork was laid for global collapse of the system. Keynes, writing in the late 1920's, makes some interesting comments on the degree to which blame rested with the American and French authorities for the ultimate crash, usually dated in 1931, but at least incipient in 1929:

> "It is on some such assumptions as these as to what the International Gold Standard ought to mean that accusations are sometimes made

70 *Cf.* Keynes, *A Treatise on Money*, Vol. II, pp. 296-297.

against the United States or against France that they are breaking the rules of the 'Gold Standard Game,' when in recent times they have, for purely local and domestic reasons, chosen to pursue a credit policy which attracted large quantities of gold to their vaults without allowing this influx materially to modify their policy. Yet it may be too much to expect that these countries will voluntarily sacrifice what they believe to be their own interests, in order to pursue a credit policy which would suit certain other countries better."[71]

One of these "domestic reasons" was the tremendous bull market of 1927–1929 which exercised at least some of the American authorities to no little degree.

The inevitable began to happen in 1929 when a few countries abandoned the gold standard and came to a head in May 1931 with the failure of the Credit-Anstalt, the largest Austrian bank. Chandler describes the consequent panic:

> ". . . This raised doubts as to the ability of any Austrian bank to meet its obligations, and not only foreigners but many Austrians . . . withdrew large amounts of funds . . . So great was the flood of withdrawals that it exhausted large loans from the Bank of England and the Bank of International Settlements as well as Austrian holdings of gold and foreign money; consequently, Austria was forced to terminate the convertibility of its money into gold . . .
>
> The panic was now on. Fearful creditors . . . withdrew their credits from Berlin, and frightened Germans joined the run . . . Germany suspended gold payments in July 1931 . . .
>
> Reinforced, the panic swept on to London, from where credits were rapidly withdrawn . . . England departed from gold on September 21, 1931. The retreat from gold now became a rout."[72]

The principal element in the monetary equation making possible these panics and consequent collapses of liquidity can be labelled "fractional reserves." So long as the nominal value of claims convertible into gold was in excess of the nominal value of gold — the entire monetary stock of the world was only about $10 billion in 1928 — there was the chance of the entire house of cards tumbling down. Any general scepticism about the capacity of redemption was bound to prove justified: there simply was not enough ultimate stuff to provide redemption if enough people wanted it; doubt bred doubt and panic produced panic. This was inevitable in a fractional reserve system where the ultimate backing could not be reproduced at will.

---

71 Keynes, *A Treatise on Money,* Vol. II, p. 306.

72 Chandler, *op. cit.,* pp. 143-144.

12

Domestic factors in America in 1930–1932, together with international financial panic, produced monetary and general economic crisis that for sheer horror, destructiveness, and longevity has seldom been equalled in economic history. Chapter II is confined to a single aspect of the Great Depression: the end of the gold standard in the United States. However, some of the background is provided in these paragraphs, together with the notation that the reaction of the monetary authorities to the crisis was hesitant and sometimes even perverse.[73]

These are some of the details of the American crisis:

> total individual and corporate debt fell from $72.3 billion in 1929 to $49.4 billion in 1935, a largely involuntary liquidation of almost $23 billion sending millions to the wall of bankruptcy and causing many banks to fail so that "by March 4, 1933 every state in the Union had declared bank holidays and bank deposits were no longer redeemable in cash."[74]
>
> ". . . during February and until March 4 [1933], $624 million in gold had been withdrawn, partly for export, from the Treasury and the Federal Reserve Banks, and circulation of currency had grown by about $1.8 billion."[75]
>
> the supply of money, including demand deposits and currency, fell from $54.7 billion in 1929 to $42.6 billion in 1933, demand deposits having fallen from $22.8 to $15.0 billion; the decrease in the money stock exceeded 30 per cent, reflecting in part the over-all debt liquidation statistic reported above and the data of the next paragraph;
>
> loans of commercial banks fell from $35.7 billion in 1929 to $16.3 billion in 1933, reaching a trough of $15.2 billion in 1935; over this same period commercial bank holdings of U. S. government securities rose from $4.9 billion in June 1929 to $7.5 billion in June 1933 and stood at $13.8 billion in 1935;
>
> the collapse of the stock market, usually dated at Black Friday, October 19, 1929, could be said to have led the way to collapse of nominal values of assets generally; the Standard and Poor industrial stock price index fell from a monthly average of 171.9 in 1929 to 127.0 in 1930, and 78.5 in 1931, reaching its nadir of 41.8 in 1932, rising to 59.9 in 1933; the *New York Times* index fell from 469 to 221 from Sep-

73 Although it is doubtful that the United States could indefinitely sustain a gold standard operated on fractional-reserve principles all alone, it is true that when the U. S. went off gold in 1933 the national gold reserves were not under severe pressure. The critical realized drain was that of currency from banks, not of specie. On the other hand, domestic policies were constrained by the discipline imposed by the necessity of assuring convertibility.

74 Chandler, *op. cit.*, p. 145.

75 Nussbaum, *op. cit.*, p. 173.

> tember to November, 1929; the value of securities listed on the New York Stock Exchange fell from $67,478 million on January 1, 1929 to $22,768 million on January 1, 1933.

These data reflect an incredible collapse of nominal values of assets and of liquidity in the economic system, but it should not be thought that, at the outset of 1930, ordinary criteria suggested that the liquidity position of the economy was peculiarly at risk (save for the fantastic inflation of common shares). In fact we have already learned that national gold reserves, for example, were exceptionally high and, indeed, increased until 1931. What happened could have happened at any time for many years; the catastrophe reflects possibilities inherent in any system in which the aggregate value of obligations to pay, say, currency on short notice exceeds that of available currency or at least that of the amount the authorities are willing to make available.

Viewed from retrospect, an historic task of the New Deal administration of Franklin Roosevelt was to bring to an end in America the effective dominion of specie reserve requirements. That this was in fact an effect of the New Deal is not easy to determine from the statute books. If you peruse these, you will find formal requirements that look very similar to pre-1934 stipulations. However, we shall see that these specie requirements are largely a hoax. One might aver safely that never will the liquidity position of the American economy be allowed to deteriorate drastically because of *internal* pressures threateningly legally specified relationships between nominal values of specie holdings and of debt obligations of the Treasury, Federal Reserve, and member banks. And one can at least say that the government is more likely to confess *external* insolvency than to protect its external position through measures drastic enough to induce dramatic domestic illiquidity.

We turn to the actual procedures of the F.D.R. administration in at least partially abandoning gold. On Sunday March 5, 1933 — the day after his inauguration — President Roosevelt called Congress into extraordinary session. On March 6, 1933 he proclaimed a national bank holiday which was to last until March 9:

> "During this period banks were forbidden to transact any business whatsoever, and especially prohibited from paying out coin or bullion or currency, except with the permission of the Secretary of the Treasury." [76]

[76] Nussbaum, *op. cit.*, p. 174.

Congress adopted on March 9 an emergency banking act which, among other things, authorized creation of $3 billion in inconvertible U. S. notes that would be fed into the banking system through central bank purchases of eligible paper and which would be legal tender. This presaged the main tenor of subsequent measures: draw the fangs of potential internal drains by establishing inconvertible paper as legal tender. This paper readily can be provided by governments rid of the yellow incubus. There can be greater reliance on "discretion." The external discipline of the international gold standard can be relaxed. The new policy found the public required to turn over to the government almost all gold coins, gold bullion, and gold certificates. The only exceptions were rare coins and gold required for aesthetic and industrial purposes. Domestic convertibility of dollar liabilities into gold was ended.[77]

January 1934 saw establishment of the monetary system that essentially prevails today. It is a sort of gold standard, but certainly differs profoundly from the pre-1933 standard: domestically held dollar liabilities are not convertible into gold. The following is a good statement of the main provisions of the Gold Reserve Act of January 1934, contrasting these with the pre-1933 standard:

> "Up to the beginning of 1933 the United States operated on the basis of a full gold standard . . . The price of the metal was . . . fixed by statute at $20.67 per ounce. All forms of U. S. currency were by law directly or indirectly exchangeable for gold at the rate set by the statutory price, and all gold was exchangeable for currency at the same rate. There was free coinage of gold, no limitation on private holdings or of dealings in the metal, and complete freedom of gold imports and exports. Under this system, the exchange value of the dollar in terms of other gold currencies remained stable, within narrow and defined limits, while its exchange value in terms of non-gold currencies fluctuated in accordance with the degree to which these other currencies depreciated with respect to gold . . . The abandonment of the gold standard took place not so much as a result of external strain as in pursuance of a domestic policy which was believed to require definite action in the monetary field [i.e., to increase the supply of money].
>
> The gold standard was suspended in the United States in connection with the national banking holiday proclaimed by President Roosevelt . . . Shortly after, suspension of the gold standard was converted into its virtual abandonment. All gold held within the country was

[77] More than 2,300 member banks and 2,700 non-member state banks were liquidated after the bank holiday. Thus, 24 per cent of the member banks were forced to close. This emphasizes the depth of the crisis.

> nationalized and expropriated by the government at its statutory price. The gold clause, which had been widely used in connection with debt obligations, was abrogated . . .
>
> [The authors go on to explain that the Administration's intention was to operate in foreign exchange markets, steadily increasing the dollar price of gold simply by offering dollar claims of greater and greater value in exchange for an ounce of gold, permitting a foreigner to obtain more and more U. S. paper money for an ounce of gold. We discuss the underlying theory later.]
>
> On January 30, 1934, Congress passed the Gold Reserve Act which laid the foundation for the restoration of a monetary system based upon the principles of a gold standard . . . The statutory price of gold . . . became fixed at $35 rather than $20.67 per ounce . . .
> The Gold Reserve Act didn't restore the convertibility of currency into gold nor the right of individuals to hold or deal in the metal. All gold remained the property of the federal government. However, the Secretary of the Treasury announced . . . that he was prepared to release gold for exportation to countries still on the gold standard, whenever the exchange rate of the dollar in terms of the currencies of such countries should reach the gold export point . . .
>
> As a result of the Gold Reserve Act . . . the dollar became again to all intents and purposes a gold currency. The combined effect of these . . . measures was to restore the operation of the essential features of the gold standard mechanism as it relates to the maintenance of [foreign] exchange stability."[78]

As things stood in 1934, and as they stand in 1962, the discipline of gold on the American monetary system is imposed through the convertibility of dollar claims presented by foreign governments and central banks. (*See Note F.*) Until recent years, the gold stock of the United States was so huge, and seemingly so immune to depletion, that this discipline was negligible. But recent important declines in the American gold stock remind us that the discipline of our truncated gold standard might assert itself.

13

I cannot resist discussing a controversial section of a 1933 congressional resolution abrogating gold clauses. The topic probes too deeply into the heart of monetary metaphysics to be neglected. Nussbaum points out that gold clauses have their origin in the immemorial struggle of sovereignties to reduce the real value of claims against them

78 *The Recovery Problem in the United States* (Washington: Brookings Institution, 1936), pp. 426-435.

simply by crying up the accounting price of the standard of value. Of course, the American devaluation of 1934 was quite another thing. As Nussbaum says:

> "Though devaluation had been achieved, a number of dollar creditors claimed that their rights had not been affected by it.
>
> Since the Middle Ages, when an economy based on monetary exchange developed, creditors have tried to protect themselves against harmful changes in the medium of payment by clauses which were designed to prevent the debtor from making use of such changes. The most frequent type of these protective agreements were the 'gold clauses' by which the debtor obligates himself to make payment in a specified amount of contractually defined gold coins irrespective of later changes in the law or the currency circulation. The use of such clauses spread from the latter part of the nineteenth century, particularly in this country, as a reaction to the bimetallist agitation. It became a matter of routine to insert in bonds and mortgage deeds a phrase such as this 'to pay dollars in gold coin of the United States of the standard and fineness existing on [date of contracting].' Most bonds of the federal government, especially the Liberty bonds, contained such a promise. Estimates of the total amount included in these clauses in this country vary from $75 billion to $123 billion . . ."[79]

In a 5-4 decision the United States Supreme Court generally upheld abrogation of gold clauses. However, insofar as the joint resolution of 1933 applied to the U. S. government (as debtor), it was held unconstitutional. Still:

> "the claims of the government's creditors were dismissed . . . on the ground that owing to the nationalization of gold they were no longer entitled to gold as such."[80]

A nice bit of legal flotsam.

14

New Deal monetary policy can only be understood in its factual context. The wholesale price index for the United States (1947–49 =

[79] Nussbaum, *op. cit.*, p. 188.

[80] *Ibid.*, p. 190. Gold clauses might be interpreted in this way. The traders contract out of the official value scale, adopting a differently calibrated scale: one on which a given gold dollar is valued at unity but on which the value of Greenbacks, subsequent gold dollar coins, etc. is "open." Two other scales exist, one on which the value of a "Greenback" is unity and that of a gold dollar open; one on which the value of both is unity. The last is nugatory so long as interconvertibility is not provided for.

Insofar as gold clause type agreements bypass use of money of account, they might be said strictly to be non-monetary in character, at least not in the modern sense of "monetary." Weight replaces tale . . . In any case, prices can be described only through a pure money of account.

100) fell from 61.9 in 1929 to 42.1 in 1933. (The index for farm commodities fell from 58.6 to 26.9.) The increase in the real burden of debtors was enormous. Even at this stage we can appreciate the major cause of the precipitous price decline: the effort to obtain more currency than existed, forced (attempted) liquidation which could do little more than nourish the fears of those who wanted cash.[81] A vicious cycle was initiated. If only in order to restore the real position of debtors, the New Deal wanted to raise American prices.

Professor George Warren held that increasing the nominal value of gold would promptly inflate prices. Warren became a financial adviser to F.D.R., generally considered to have been an indifferent economist. (*See Note G.*) Following policies suggested by Warren's theory, the administration strongly relied on devaluation for its internal as well as external (import-export and international capital movement) effects.

More specifically, inflationary effects of increasing the price of gold (devaluing the paper dollar) can be dichotomized: (1) effects related to changes in excess reserve positions of the treasury and central bank (recalling that member banks no longer held gold); (2) effects on demand-supply conditions in commodity markets stemming from the increased *relative* value of gold implicit in its higher nominal price; "correction" of relative price discrepancy here would require increased prices of commodities generally.

The first subset of effects has meaning only in terms of what are essentially self-denying ordinances. However, the spirit of the 1934 legislation — largely emasculating gold as an internal force — suggests that self imposed restraints would be abandoned if found to be binding.

The second subset — albeit based on fallacious reasoning in this instance — is much more interesting: it poses problems of general equilibrium of markets (*cf.* Appendix, Ch. II). If gold were to be produced and/or held (in coined or uncoined form) domestically in "meaningful" quantity ("meaningfulness" not being *strictly* necessary), an arbitrary increase in its nominal price, leading to excess supply of gold and excess demand for other goods, might — if nominally valued quantities of one or more other goods were not fixed — lead to proportionate increase in *equilibrium* accounting prices for all goods.

81 There also are income-theoretical considerations suggesting that we could expect to see a decline in prices.

Of course, adjustment processes might be painfully slow even under basically favorable circumstances. The 1934 circumstances surely were unfavorable: the New Deal legislation made it illegal (with few exceptions) for Americans to hold gold; American gold production was (and is) not substantial. Since there were no meaningful direct effects on monetary asset holdings, it would be chimerical to expect devaluation to have prompt or important inflationary effects within a *closed system* of the sort just described for the United States in 1934.

If we open the system and consider effects of devaluation of the dollar on foreign producers of gold and the balance of payments, the outlook for reflation becomes brighter: the increased dollar price of gold encourages foreigners to mine gold and ship it to the custody of the United States government. This will increase bank reserves unless the gold inflow is "sterilized."[82] If this in turn has inflationary effects — *usually* it does — the American price level will rise until the dollar price of gold is no longer attractive to foreigners.

It remains true that the forces unleashed in the second (open) variant of the "Warren hypothesis" will necessarily take time to work themselves out. An important drag will arise from sharply increasing marginal costs of production of gold: the increase in annual output is unlikely to be impressive; the accumulated stock of gold far overshadows annual outputs within the realm of our discourse.

The data contradict the Warren hypothesis: the price of gold was raised more than 40 per cent, from $20.67 to $35 per ounce in January 1934, but the wholesale price index, for example, rose only from 42.8 in December 1933 to 48.7 in December 1934, reaching 52.0 in 1935 and 52.5 in 1936. These increases in the price level are accounted for by other causes.

15

The influx of gold was considerable. The American monetary gold stock was $4 billion in January 1934, when it was revalued to more than $6.75 billion. By the end of 1937 the value of the American gold stock had risen to almost $13 billion, an immense augmentation. The causes were manifold: the deepening political crisis in Europe led to large specie shipments to the United States; the fact that only

82 Influx of gold leads to increased member bank reserves. *Cf.* Ch. VB. This process is to be contrasted with the revaluation procedure, *per se,* which has no direct effect on bank reserve positions: the banks cannot hold gold.

Belgium, France, Luxembourg, the Netherlands and Switzerland continued to purchase gold at fixed prices (in monies of account)[83] meant that outlets for gold sales had decreased, making the fixed American price more attractive; American devaluation led to European exchange having greater purchasing power in the United States than at home, encouraging foreigners to purchase American assets (including interests in physical capital); the merchandise balance of trade turned more in America's favor from 1934 to 1939; production of gold was more profitable at the higher dollar price.

One effect of the gold influx was a vast increase in the liquidity of the American banking system. But, contrary to previous experience, this did not lead so much to increased bank investments as to large excess reserves (perhaps partly a reaction by bankers to their ghastly experiences of 1932–1933). This prompted a good deal of discussion.

Another facet of the inflationary — or reflationary — policy of the New Deal was in silver. There was a welter of silver legislation, replete with the paraphernalia of mystique-laden metallic standards, but centered in its motive force in the political influence of the Silver Bloc. The practical effects were slight enough in America — being largely confined to consequences of increased purchases of silver, not a crucial commodity — but unintentionally drove such countries as China off the silver standard. The dollar price of silver increased considerably more than did the American wholesale price level.[84] Thus, the Chinese had an incentive to convert paper claims into silver, planning to convert the silver into dollar claims — unless the value of silver increased in China. But, if the value of silver were to increase in China, there would have to be either an outright devaluation of its currency — apparently impractical in a country in which metallic content means a great deal — or a substantial deflation of commodity prices, never a pleasant alternative.

---

[83] France abandoned the gold standard in 1936, a step usually associated with the accession to power of Leon Blum's Popular Front.

The operations of the British Exchange Equalization Account, established nine months after Britain left gold, steadied the price of sterling exchange in terms of the exchanges of hard currency countries. However, there was no rigid obligation for the Account; the underlying policy was one of a "floating pound."

[84] I hesitate to provide statistics. At one time there were no less than three prices paid by the United States Treasury for silver.

16

The recovery from 1933 or 1934 to the time of the 1937–1938 recession was limited: millions remained unemployed; business firms would have been delighted to produce billions of dollars worth of additional output at going prices; the enormous increase in the banking system's liquidity did not have traditional effects, as is dramatized by the fact that excess reserves of member banks exceeded $2.5 billion in 1936. If the "Keynesian revolution" inaugurated in 1936 with the publication of the *General Theory* had been better established, the authorities might have been able serenely to contemplate excess liquidity. But the Keynesian revolution was only in its infancy, and the "Chicago School" — also sophisticated about the implications of excess reserves in these circumstances — had little influence on policy. As a result, in 1936–1937 certain automatic manifestations of economic orthodoxy occurred.[85] These included restrictive fiscal policies, including curtailment of relief expenditures and public works plans, and increased reserve requirements for commercial banks, and sterilization of gold inflows so that excess reserves fell below $1 billion during 1937. Sterilization, beginning in December 1936, found the authorities making open market sales of securities offsetting gold inflows. The effects of these measures, as relentless as those preceding the Panic of 1837, and as inane to a contemporary eye, were registered in the sharp contraction of 1937–1938, which, despite its precipitousness, was not marked by a crisis of liquidity. Such a crisis was most unlikely in view of domestic inconvertibility into gold and the functioning of the Federal Deposit Insurance Corporation.

17

The onset of World War II (1939–1945) and our official entry into it in 1941 had purely *monetary* effects much milder than those experienced during either the Civil War or World War I. One reason has already been offered: the national specie reserves could not be subject to assault from citizens forbidden to hold them. Another lies in the terrific impact of the war on areas outside the United States; the United States seemed to be just about as safe a place as foreigners could find in which to hold gold (or rather warehouse receipts for gold or claims convertible into it). Our balance of payments was favorable; service as the "arsenal of democracy," prior to lend-lease and

85 *Cf.* Ch. VC *infra.*

similar arrangements, led to a strongly favorable balance; even the enormous external transfers of 1942–1945 led to no profound disturbance.

This does not mean that slight technical monetary adjustments were not undertaken: "in June, 1945 . . . , an amendment to the Federal Reserve Act reduced the minimum of gold reserves [to cover FR notes] to 25 per cent [although] actually the gold reserve for Federal Reserve Notes invariably remained above 40 per cent";[86] adjustments were made in silver legislation permitting the Treasury to "lease" silver to industrial users, but to count "leased" silver as part of the "cover" for silver certificates. The scale of the war effort and of monetary expansion meant that certain of the mystical procedures of the acolytes of the yellow gods and white demigods were altered. Nor was the cult allowed to flourish in Britain during the Napoleonic Wars[87] and other dire occasions, nor during our Civil War, nor during World War I when it became insupportable.

18

There is nothing in post-World War II experience of sufficient importance to enter this account of the purely *monetary* history of the United States other than material bearing on the interval of international "dollar shortage" from 1946 to about 1957 and the outflow of gold from the United States from 1958 to the date of writing (December 1962). These events are taken up in Ch. XVI, where we are reminded that

> No joy so great but runneth to an end,
> No hap so hard but may in time amend.
>
> R. Southwell, *Times Go by Turns*

2. Monetary History of the United Kingdom

One can understand neither American monetary history nor the history of monetary theory in the United States without learning a good deal about British history. Before World War I British monetary history was far more important than ours. And monetary theory largely has been secreted in the interstices of British history. Most advances

86 Nussbaum, *op. cit.*, p. 210.

87 Napoleon maintained a gold standard, however. As is shown *infra.*, he viewed his ability to do so as an important triumph of policy.

in monetary theory have been in response to circumstances in which monetary policy, often precipitously and unhappily, was in the political foreground.

This section heavily relies upon Sir Ralph Hawtrey's work, particularly *The Gold Standard in Theory and Practice* and *Currency and Credit.*

1

It is never easy to know where to begin in British history. We shall arbitrarily designate as Genesis an event often held to inaugurate modern British monetary history: the machinations of Sir Isaac Newton, Master of the Mint, in 1717 in establishing the gold standard in Britain. But certain background material is required, even as it is for the better known Genesis.

Gold and silver each had important monetary uses in Europe although

> "[s]o far as Western Europe is concerned, the gold standard is a modern development. In the Middle Ages the Byzantine Empire, which preserved unbroken the great tradition of Roman civilization, maintained a gold standard, and when this tradition spread during and after the Crusades to the Italian mercantile cities on the fringe of feudal barbarism, the use of gold spread with it . . . But gold became and remained only a merchants' medium. The principal standard of value continued throughout Western Europe to be silver."[88]

The numerous political entities of Europe maintained bimetallism, and the differing mint ratios led to erratic flows of gold and silver from principality to principality, gold flowing to where it was "overvalued" and silver to where *it* was "over-valued."[89] The picture drawn by Einaudi and cited in Ch. I should be recalled.

Closing in on British experience, we turn again to Hawtrey:

> "So far as Western Europe was concerned, the gold standard was practically originated in England. The valuation of gold in terms of silver had been modified several times in the seventeenth century. In 1663 Charles II issued a new gold coin called a guinea, officially valued at £1 [the precision of Hawtrey's usage is splendid to behold]. A troy pound of gold, 11/12 fine, was coined into 44½ guineas. As silver, 37/40 fine, was coined at the rate of 62s. a pound, the ratio of gold to silver . . . was 14.485 . . .

88 Hawtrey, *The Gold Standard in Theory and Practice,* p. 65.

89 The predominance of metallic flows over offer of discounts for profferment of the undervalued metal is irritating to me.

> This ratio was too low. Gold was undervalued in terms of silver, in comparison with its value in the European market . . . *Creditors were willing to accept gold in payment at a premium over its official valuation.* [Emphasis supplied.] Debtors, being entitled to pay, if they chose, in silver, could stipulate for a premium on gold. Guineas were treated as a commodity, the price being determined like that of wheat or iron in a free market. [Thus, the accounting price of the over-valued metal was the fixed peg. Law and custom assured that the over-valued metal's price would not fall below the official level.] Yet, while their price varied, they were used as a medium of exchange, and the merchants were free to make bargains expressly denominated in guineas if they chose.
>
> The premium on guineas had risen high, especially in 1695, in consequence of the defective condition of the silver coinage, but even after the restoration of the coinage there was still a premium."[90]

By 1717, however, silver had almost disappeared from the English coinage; the purchasing power of silver was greater abroad than in England. This state of affairs was more or less made permanent in 1717 when the guinea (recalling that this was a basic gold coin) was valued at 21s. This, in effect, made the mint ratio, 1:15.21, the highest in Europe. Such silver coin as remained in circulation was worn and thin: it was not profitable to melt it down or export it; silver was relegated to a subsidiary coinage despite the fact that "it remained unlimited legal tender until 1774,"[91] Gold was the dominant medium of exchange and standard of value. It appears that convenience was not strong enough to make it worthwhile for traders in Britain to offer to accept tenders of silver at a discount. (*See Note H.*)

Because silver was undervalued at the Mint, Britain from 1717 to 1795 was effectively on a gold standard. The virtual gold standard began to be undermined in 1785 when a new gold coinage was introduced in France. The French mint ratio became 1:15.5. However, the French seignorage charges were high enough to make "switching" costs more than offset the difference between the 1:15.21 and 1:15.3 ratios: for some time there was insufficient arbitrage profit for Frenchmen to be induced to melt their silver coins; there was no influx of silver into England for some years.

2

Inconvertible paper currency began to be issued in France in 1788 before the Revolution. Kemmerer writes that:

90 *Ibid.,* pp. 66-67.
91 Hawtrey, *op. cit.,* p. 68.

> "the first serious threat of paper money was an edict of the king dated August 16, 1788, creating a form of short-time, interest-bearing paper, intended to circulate as money. It met with such a storm of public protest, however, that it was revoked within a month."[92]

The exigencies of the Revolution stilled these protests, especially since its tone encouraged inflationism to some degree. The Assignats began to be issued in December 1789; the early issues were interest-bearing. At least invidious experience of the flight of the Jews and others who had much to fear from Hitler in the 1930's suggests that many would strongly desire to convert Assignat holdings into precious metal in the open market, planning to ship the specie out of the country. Indeed this is what happened, despite the revolutionary government's prohibition which, to the extent that it did dam specie outflow, encouraged widespread hoarding (still a basic feature of French monetary life).

Hawtrey states that silver tended to leave France before gold, because silver was undervalued at the mint.[93] This surely accords with traditional analysis. In any event, by the time the Assignats collapsed in 1795, French gold and silver either had fled abroad (particularly to Britain) or were hoarded at home.

France returned to a specie standard in 1796, setting the mint ratio at the pre-1789 1:15.5 ratio (the 1785 ratio). Gold was attracted back first. Why?

1) gold was over-valued at the French mint;

2) the French public had a preference for gold.

3

The flow of gold from England to France and also to other countries at a time when the two countries were at war had two basic effects, one of which deeply concerns us; the other can be quickly dismissed:[94]

1) suspension of free coinage of silver and limitation of its legal tender properties;

2) suspension of specie payments by the Bank of England.

---

92 Kemmerer, *op. cit.*, p. 175.

93 *Ibid.*, p. 68.

94 Recall that the undermining of the virtual gold standard in England began in 1785 when France over-valued gold. By 1796 transaction costs, relative price levels, etc. encouraged gold flows.

The first effect is not of great concern to us. The influx of gold into France and other Continental countries led to the English silver stock increasing, relative to the English gold stock, driving down the market price of silver until silver actually came to be over-valued at the mint. Silver came to the mint to be coined.

> "The virtual gold standard to which the English public had become accustomed was founded on nothing but the overvaluation of gold in the coinage system . . . If nothing were done, the country would revert to a silver standard. In 1798 the decisive step was taken. The coinage of silver was suspended, and it again became legal tender . . . only for payments not exceeding £25."[95]

The second effect was much more broad and powerful in its ramifications both for political-economic history and for the history of economics. As Professor Viner writes:

> "The suspension of specie payments by the Bank of England in 1797, and the currency, exchange, and price phenomena which followed it, gave rise to a controversial literature of great extent, and, on the whole, surprisingly high quality. Until the resumption of specie payments was approaching, the general trend of prices and of prosperity was upward; but resumption was followed by a long and trying period of falling prices and of economic distress."[96]

The key topic for debate among economic writers was whether the appearance of a premium on bullion should be taken as evidence of mismanagement of the currency. Those, including Ricardo, who took the affirmative were called *bullionists*; those, including Bosanquet, who took the negative, *anti-bullionists.*

We seek more of the factual background for the suspension of convertibility, the Restriction of 1797, which lasted for more than twenty years.

The outbreak of the war with France found the British government putting heavy pressure on the Bank of England for advances. This pressure proved irresistible and, as a result, the Bank's liquidity was reduced. Then, early in 1797, fears of French landings and failures of country banks "led to a general clamor for gold." (Effects of the French Resumption of 1796 on the British gold stock already have been considered.) Since the Bank's reserves were but a fraction of its

95 Hawtrey, *Gold Standard,* p. 69.

96 Jacob Viner, *Studies in the Theory of International Trade* (New York: Harper & Bros., 1937), p. 119. The classic work in the field.

liabilities, restriction became inevitable and was imposed on February 26, 1797: an Order in Council prohibited the Bank from redeeming its notes in specie. Once specie payments were suspended, there was an inward flow of specie; the Bank's solvency was now protected by law. (A paradox commonly observed in monetary history.) Indeed, there was no premium of bullion over paper until the end of 1799.[97]

At no time did the premium on bullion exceed 9 per cent from 1797 to 1808; it was at its peak — 36 per cent — in 1813. Similarly, "exchange on Hamburg" never rose above 144 (in 1811) where 100 would represent the pre-restriction norm.[98] Price levels did not rise spectacularly. Taking the 1790 price level as 100, prices of commodities did not rise above 166 from 1797 to 1808 and reached a peak over the 1797–1819 period of 198 in 1814 (always measuring in money of account). If the price index were calculated in terms of the purchasing power of silver in England, equivalent statistics would be 155 (in 1809) and 159 (in 1814). The market ratio of gold to silver at Hamburg was lower in 1814 than in 1797 (15.04:1 vs. 15.41:1) implying that the purchasing power of gold in England would have behaved so that a price index with gold as the standard of value would have stood at more than 159 in 1814 (1790 = 100). (Always remember that the higher a price index the less the purchasing power of the standard of value on which it is based.)

The statistics bring out an important point: the 1797–1808 data

---

97 Viner proceeds to outline the British monetary system as it was just prior to the restriction. We already have done this, but it might be good to make an independent check:

> "England . . . had for some time been in effect on a gold standard basis, since the mint ratio of silver to gold was such as generally to undervalue silver and thus keep it out of circulation . . . Of the silver coins, only the underweight coins remained in circulation . . . English coin could not legally be melted down unless underweight, and was not legally exportable, and gold bullion was exportable only subject to oath that it had not been obtained by melting down English coin. The metallic currency was supplemented by Bank of England notes. London bankers had, in 1793, voluntarily ceased to issue their own notes . . . Bank deposits subject to check were also in existence and constituted a part of what today would be regarded as the circulating medium." (*Op. cit.*, pp. 123-124.)

98 Data from Hawtrey, *Currency and Credit*, p. 283.

The premium is measured as follows: consider that amount of appropriately defined gold bullion assigned the accounting price of £1 in 1797. Then consider a unit of the new paper standard of value, a note bearing the inscription "£1." How many such notes will exchange for the appropriate quantity of gold? Say the answer is 1.08. Then the premium is 8 per cent.

substantially sustain J. S. Mill's view as to the ease with which paper can be instituted as the standard; after all, the American wholesale price index stood at 50.1 in 1939 and 119.6 in 1960 without there being much talk of a breakdown in the monetary system. The British Restriction can be viewed as an example of responsible management of a fiat paper standard accompanied by flexible foreign exchange rates. The fact that major intellectual concern has been with the whys and wherefores of the premium on gold reflects the interest of the bullionist controversy for the history of economics rather than any pathological behavior of the paper pound. And indeed the Restriction of 1797 *is* important to the history of economics, if for no other reason, because of the essential light it sheds on the *banking* and *currency school* conflict later in the century.

The bullionist/anti-bullionist controversy, at least before 1819, was in terms of a criterion that might seem absurd today but is easily understandable in a context of centuries of life under metallic standards:

> "The bullionists argued, or more often simply asserted, that a circulation exceeding in amount what, under otherwise like conditions, could have been maintained under a metallic standard, was in excess. There was little express objection to this criterion [prior to 1819]."[99]

Accordingly, the controversy centered on appropriate criteria for determining the existence of excess of issue. The criteria relied on by bullionists have already been reported in another connection: the premium on bullion, the rate of foreign exchange against hard currencies, and the prices of commodities.

David Ricardo, the bullionist writer of most interest to us, put special stress on the premium on bullion as a measure of the degree of excess of the quantity of paper money:

> ". . . also the degree in which prices at any time, say 1810, during the suspension of cash payments were higher, not than they would have been in 1797, but than they would have been in 1810 if the currency were in 1810 at the amount which could then have been maintained in circulation under a metallic standard."[100]

99 Jacob Viner, *op. cit.*, p. 125.

100 *Ibid.*, p. 127. Viner adds, "Ricardo, however, put much stress on the question of the extent of the depreciation, as providing an answer to the question of how great a reduction in the currency would be needed to end the depreciation."

The bullionists accepted these qualifications, among others, to their doctrine:

1) insofar as exchange rates were to be used as a measure of the existence and/or extent of depreciation, account should be taken of shipping costs which would lead to a certain degree of variation in foreign exchange that would not be arbitraged by specie flows.

2) "even before 1797, English gold coin or bullion derived therefrom" could not be exported. This meant that when England was running an unfavorable balance of payments, traders would be willing to pay a premium for stuff they could ship out; a given amount of gold in bullion form could exchange for a greater amount of gold in coined form. However, Ricardo argued that false swearing, smuggling, etc. were common before 1797 so that — even when account is taken of a minor allowance for lightness of some of the coinage, reducing its melted equivalent — no more than a 5 per cent premium (for payment of smugglers and adjustment of weight of coins) of bullion over paper and coin should be conceded. Viner writes that the data appear to support Ricardo.

3) to the extent that gold had been exported from Britain, there would tend to be an increase in prices abroad (with gold as *numeraire*): Britain could to that extent sustain a higher price level without there being a premium on bullion. This qualification to the use of price level criteria was scouted by the bullionists on the ground that the actual release of specie was small, a point that seems to have been well taken.

Viner points out that the speculative factor should have been added to the list:[101]

> ". . . under inconvertibility speculative anticipations of depreciation or appreciation of the currency would affect the willingness of individuals to hold the currency and would thus influence . . . its value in relation to gold, to foreign currencies, and to commodities, independently of the effects of variations in its quantity."[102]

The force of this point was not much appreciated on either side.

The anti-bullionists largely agreed to play the game implicit in the overissue criterion — until deflation set in after 1819. The most powerful and important of their arguments (against the proposition that a premium on gold revealed over-issue of paper) centered on balance-of-payments effects. It went something like this: when two

101 An important point, frequently appearing in one guise or another, during subsequent treatment of monetary policy in this book.

102 *Ibid.*, pp. 131-132.

countries are on gold standards, only a narrow range of fluctuation in the rate of exchange between their currencies is possible; but, when one or both abandon(s) convertibility, a much wider range of fluctuation is possible. Specifically, if there are heavy military remittances abroad and unusually large grain importations, the value of the paper pound in terms of convertible foreign currency (and gold) might fall almost without limit, quite apart from over-issue. Viner punctures this plausible argument, pointing out that there cannot be large depreciation in the exchange value of a gold standard currency because unfavorable balances of payments are met by gold shipments, *forcing contraction of the monetary base and the money supply,* until prices fall and interest rates rise enough to stem the outflow of gold.[103] If a similar contraction in the supply of money were to occur under a paper standard, the same set of effects on prices and interest rates would balance international payments with the same set of product flows as under a gold standard:

> ". . . it was primarily because under the paper standard the English currency was not contracted as it necessarily would have been contracted under a metallic standard that the foreign remittances resulted in such marked depreciation of the paper pound on the exchanges."[104]

It appears that, despite attempts of Professors Silberling and Angell to buttress the anti-bullionist case, the garlands of victory have to be handed to the bullionists — so long as they are permitted the privileged sanctuary of the over-issue criterion. If the criterion is to be that paper money is over-issued if its aggregate nominal value exceeds that which would be sustained under a metallic standard, *cet. par.*, the bullionists win. Indeed it was not until the post-resumption deflation that serious and widespread opposition to this criterion was expressed and not until our own time that what might be regarded as extreme anti-bullionism prevailed among economists. Politicians probably were converted at the dawn of history.

4

Consider the factual background of the resumption of specie payments in Britain — picking up the main thread of the narrative while preparing to examine the sequel of the debate. Preparations for resumption began in 1816 when acts were passed definitely relegating

[103] *Ibid.*, pp. 135-136 and note 15, p. 145 include an intricate qualification.
[104] *Ibid.*, p. 145.

silver to a subsidiary status: silver coins were essentially to be tokens. The Bank made tentative probes in the direction of specie resumption in 1817, but these proved premature, partly because of unfavorable balances of payments. By early 1819, even limited convertibility was barred. However, by July 1819, resumption seemed plausible. And on July 2, 1819 legislation providing for convertibility of the notes of the Bank of England was passed; even the ancient restrictions on export of coin and bullion were repealed; a gold bullion standard was enacted, the Bank being required to pay its notes in gold bars of a minimum weight of 60 ounces; the terms of redemption were by May 1821 to be £3. 17s. 10½ d. in notes for each ounce of gold. The gold bullion standard was to be permissive after May 1, 1822, when the Bank could pay in gold coin or in ingots as it chose.

Note that the price of gold — £3. 17s. 10½d. per ounce — was that of 1797. In the meanwhile, prices had risen 36 per cent (with the paper pound as *numeraire*), although the peak level of the price index (198) was reached in 1814. And prices were to fall steadily from 1819 to 1830; the Silberling index falls from 136 in 1819 to 106 in 1824 to 93 in 1830. This reveals considerable deflationary pressure. Debtors were tightly squeezed; consider the rise in the real interest rate implicit in a more than 31 per cent fall in prices in 11 years. There was substantial unemployment and idle capacity; the banking system's liquidity constantly was threatened. The story has familiar overtones when one recalls that of the United States in 1879 and, surprisingly, parallels that of the resumption of specie payments in Britain in 1924. The cruel and unyielding yellow gods continued to command allegiance more than a century later.

Ricardo had advocated resumption at the old nominal price of gold. He had predicted that, if this were done, prices would decline between five and eight per cent — reflecting the premium on bullion just prior to the resumption. His prediction was, as we have seen, completely wrong. Still he was unwilling to admit (publicly at least) that he had been in error, citing what he termed the incorrect manner in which the Bank of England managed resumption, together with independent — and more or less global — deflationary tendencies manifested in 1814–1815 and violating the *ceteris paribus* of his hypothesis. Ricardo relied on a proposition not unnoticed by later economists: a hypothesis specifying a relationship between r variables, holding constant s other variables, is going to be hard to disprove in a world where nothing remains fixed very long.

It is not conclusively proven that Ricardo should have made a different prediction on the basis of the evidence before him. Surely the Bank of England *did* exacerbate the deflationary consequences of resumption at the old price of gold. (*See Note I.*) That is the key element in the puzzle: resumption at the old price of gold. Since there had been no large increase in the world's gold stock from 1797 to 1819, it should have been quite clear that it would not be possible to back a stock of convertible obligations of much larger nominal value in 1819 than in 1797. There would have to be contraction in the stock of money. The necessary deflationary effects on the economy were bound to be heightened by secular growth in population and output requiring *expansion* in the supply of liquid assets for conventional ratios to remain intact.

Contraction was, in fact, initiated by the Bank: total advances fell from £27.2 million in 1819 to £10.6 million in 1830; note circulation fell from £25.2 million to £20.8 million over the same interval. Since the Bank's bullion reserves were valued at only £10.2 million in 1830 — standing at £10.7 million in *1817* — and since its 1830 deposit obligation (£11.2 million) still was greater than ever before, it appears that the Bank had little choice.[105] At least if the price of gold were to be £3. 17s. 10½d.

The simple and obvious alternative was devaluation (increasing the price of gold) upon resumption. Larger volumes of convertible liabilities could have been supported. But the prospect of devaluation was met with scorn and horror by the bullionists. "A stale and wretched experiment," according to Huskisson. Ricardo termed it "a shocking injustice." "The Bullion Committee held that devaluation would be a 'breach of public faith and dereliction of a primary duty of government.' "[106] Perhaps only the history of medicine can offer

---

[105] Of course, the 1830 ratio of bullion to deposits plus notes (all in £) of 31.9 per cent seems large indeed to moderns. Viner has some interesting things to say about reserve ratios:

"... It is difficult to find a basis for an estimate of what would have been a ... safe gold reserve for the Bank ... If we use the ratio of its gold holdings to its own total demand liabilities ... it would seem clear that from 1821 to 1825 the Bank maintained larger reserves than were necessary. But with reserves at their peak in 1825, the Bank barely managed to survive the crisis of 826 without suspension of cash payments ... [T]he rapidity and extent of the drain ... demonstrated that large reserves were necessary, given the quality of the Bank's management and the nervous state of public opinion [on] the solidity of the paper circulation in times of financial strain ..." (*Ibid.*, p. 178.)

[106] Jacob Viner, *op. cit.*, p. 203.

such evidence of the o'erwhelming of reason by emotion. But do not scorn Englishmen of 1819. Simply peruse the record of the 20th century.

After resumption and its deflationary aftermath, it became difficult for the bullionists and their successors to limit debate to the narrow issue of criteria for *excess of paper issue.* A metallic system hardly could be held up as an exemplar in view of bankruptcies, unemployment, and economic stagnation. The anti-bullionists took heart and enlarged the frame of the argument so that it encompassed broad questions of liquidity and interest rates, and even elementary issues of contracyclical fiscal policy. Indeed the scope of the second round of argument becomes too large for the purview of this chapter. Later we shall attempt to integrate issues of monetary standards with those of employment and economic growth.

5

The problem of secular deflation was finally modified by the enormous gold discoveries of the late 19th century. This, together with other factors, eased monetary agitation so that the supremacy of the gold standard in Britain, and the western world, from about 1870 to 1914 stood unchallenged.[107] And at the very top of this eminence stood Britain and the London money market.

> "The pre-eminence of sterling as an international currency was established and grew up with the pre-eminence of Great Britain as an international trader in the 19th century. In developing the first modern industrial economy based on raw materials and foodstuffs drawn from distant lands, British traders not only handled a larger volume of merchandise than the traders of other nations but carried their explorations and developments into more countries . . . Part of their exploration and development took the form of colonization. Where that happened . . . the local currency of the colonial territory tended to be that of the mother country or, as time went on, a local variant of it, printed or minted for the colonial territory but based on, and supported by, its connection with sterling.
>
> Elsewhere the connection between the local domestic currency and sterling was less close, but the use of sterling for international payments was equally taken for granted. New territories, whether British or foreign, received sterling in the natural course of business for the bulk of their exports. Even where the ultimate place of consumption

107 Bank rate policy as a means of countering effects of external and internal drains will be discussed in Ch. VB. During the golden age of the gold standard (*circa.* 1870-1914), British monetary policy seemed to many a mechanism of superhuman perfection.

was not in the United Kingdom the commodity market to which the produce was consigned for sale or through which it was negotiated very often was. The sterling thus acquired was readily acceptable to the sellers because it was the currency in which they or their compatriots would most naturally pay for their imports . . . from these islands or elsewhere, British agents and merchant houses being the most usual, or the broadest, channel through which such requirements were supplied.

But the payments system was not confined to bilateral interchanges between outlying British countries and the United Kingdom. The banking connections . . . which spread outwards to all parts of the world . . . provided the most widespread and convenient machinery of international payments between third countries outside the immediate British connection . . .

An incidental consequence of the system . . . was that the ultimate net inflow or outflow of gold and foreign exchange arising from the transactions of the system as a whole was centered on London; . . . [a] . . . natural consequence of sterling being used as the almost universal medium for international transactions and of London being left to take care of such foreign exchange or gold business as needed to be done."[108]

London was the world's banker! Sterling balances were held by traders of all descriptions from all over the world. These balances, convertible into gold, were a natural outgrowth of sterling's eminence as a global medium of exchange. Safety and convenience dictated in the years before 1914 that sterling balances, the most liquid of all assets, be held by persons with international commercial connections or who did not want to hold obligations of their own country. The external sterling obligation comprised a gigantic potential external drain on British gold balances. Yet, at the end of 1913, Britain held but 9.5 per cent of the world's monetary gold reserves (the U. S. held 24.8 per cent and *Argentina,* 3.1 per cent). The British central gold reserve's value aggregated but £35 million! Surely a stupendous feat, bordering on legerdemain. Yet the over-all impression conveyed to the world was one of staidness and solid conservatism. A great triumph for the British genius for self deception as well.

The relationship between interest yields on short-term paper in London and other financial centers became crucial: most foreign sterling balances were in the form of short-term securities. Working

108 "Memoranda of Evidence Submitted by the Bank of England," *Principal Memoranda of Evidence,* Committee on the Working of the Monetary System, Vol. 1 (London: HMSO, 1960), p. 16.

on so narrow a margin, it was indispensable for the Bank of England to be extremely sensitive to interest rate differentials and quickly to raise London money market rates when an external drain threatened and to lower them when influxes of gold threatened to produce inflationary pressure.[109] Here was operation of Bank rate policy in its most impressive and important phase. It was aided by extreme sensitivity throughout the world to changes in London rates: a natural byproduct of so truly international a market . . . Sometimes there were unhappy internal consequences, but analysis of these must wait.

6

The events of 1914 and their aftermath smashed the antebellum system. The pieces have been put together from time to time with varying success, but the magic no longer is there. Indeed World War I had more serious monetary consequences for Britain than did World War II.

The initial crisis in 1914 was peculiar and complicated. It stemmed directly from the enormous importance of the London money market. Remember:

> "Everywhere trade was financed by bills on London; purchasers of goods had arranged for bills to be drawn by vendors on London accepting houses or banks, and were under an obligation to provide the necessary funds in British currency to meet the bills at maturity."[110]

As we have seen, a large portion of this paper was related to goods bought and sold by residents of other countries; sterling claims provided an international medium of exchange; a great portion of international trade was financed by a revolving fund of sterling assets. The onset of World War I led to increased pressure on debtors to remit sterling. However, the normal flow of supply of sterling claims seeking foreign currency — as vendors sought to return to their own currency — was dammed; remember sterling was the most liquid of all assets. As Hawtrey eloquently puts it:

> "[T]he New York foreign exchange market, congested with demand for remittances to London, broke down, and the world felt the first dreadful thrill of panic. The exchange market between New York

[109] Critics such as Walter Bagehot thought the reserves should be larger. Only timely intervention by the Bank of France saved the solvency of the Bank of England on a number of occasions. *Cf.* Ch. V *infra.*

[110] Hawtrey, *Currency and Credit,* p. 351.

and London was an exquisitely sensitive nervous ganglion; to touch it was to inhibit vital reactions throughout the organism of world finance."[111]

With the breakdown of the foreign exchange market (the war itself paralysed the gold shipment mechanism), there was pressure on foreign sterling-debtors to find sterling cash and also on British creditors who were not receiving normal remittances. Indeed, in attempting to acquire cash, owners of sterling securities hurled these onto the market which soon panicked. The London Stock Exchange (and the New York Stock Exchange) closed on July 13, 1914. The entire system of credit was jeopardized: failure of accepting-house customers soon would cause the houses themselves to fail; the houses were major customers of the commercial banks . . . The crisis finally was met through advances from the Bank of England.

Oddly enough, Britain did not formally suspend the gold standard until 1919.[112] For some time she was gaining, not losing, gold. There were three reasons for this:

1) London, "the great international short-term lender" (*ibid.*, p. 353), on net called loans;

2) exportation of gold was prohibited;

3) for years before 1914, Britain purchased large quantities of foreign securities; this ceased during the war, making her balance of payments more favorable to this extent.

Thus, inflationary finance could be combined with domestic convertibility; there was a substantial increase in the nominal value of obligations convertible into gold.

As the war progressed, the British were forced to surrender the greater part of their gold reserve in order to pay for supplies from the United States and various neutral countries. By 1919, the British inflation had so much exceeded that of the neutrals that it became clear that the only alternative to abandonment of the international gold standard would be a substantial devaluation. Britain left gold.

7

The story of Britain's World War I monetary experiences is not profoundly interesting as an isolated tale: we are familiar with the

111 *Ibid.*, p. 351. Bank rate went to 10 per cent.

112 Various restrictions alloyed the purity of the standard; exportation of gold was prohibited (due to wartime shipping risks as much as anything).

tested proposition that the mumbo-jumbo of metallic standards will not be allowed (except perhaps by Napoleon) to interfere in any fundamental way with prosecution of wars. No, the dramatic aspect is in the implicit consequences of World War I for London's future as an international money market. Never again would it achieve its antebellum glory. Also, henceforward, there would be conflict between internal and external goals. Due either to bad luck or bad management, there would be few occasions when monetary policies promoting full employment and high rates of economic growth would not conflict with balance of payments requirements. This became the main theme of British monetary economics in the 1920's, and remains so. No episode better illustrates the interaction of these forces than the controversy over the restoration of the gold standard in Britain in 1925 until Britain finally left gold in 1931.

After studying American experience in 1879 and British experience in 1819, it is hard to believe that the 1925 episode can be true. But it is, and its telling is embellished with the names of Sir Winston Churchill and John Maynard Keynes. Indeed the best account is Keynes's: "The Economic Consequences of Mr. Churchill."[113]

It should be made clear that the dispute over the price of gold *circa* 1925 was not *directly* concerned with the relation of the nominal value of gold to that of convertible sterling claims; there was no problem of internal drain or capital outflow. Rather the issue was how much deflation Britain would have to experience if a deteriorating balance of payments on current account were not to threaten its gold reserves:

> "The policy of improving the foreign exchange value of sterling up to its pre-war value in gold from being about 10 per cent below it means that, whenever we sell anything abroad, either the foreign buyer has to pay 10 per cent *more in his money* or we have to accept 10 per cent *less in our money*. That is to say, we have to reduce our sterling prices, for coal or iron or shipping freights or whatever it might be, by 10 per cent in order to be on a competitive level, unless prices rise elsewhere. Thus the policy of improving the exchange by 10 per cent involves a reduction of 10 per cent in the sterling receipts of our export industries."[114]

Keynes proceeded to point out that the Churchillian policy (Winston Churchill was Chancellor of the Exchequer in the Baldwin government

[113] J. M. Keynes, *Essays in Persuasion* (London: Macmillan and Co., Ltd., 1931), *cf. esp.* pp. 181-296.

[114] Keynes, *op. cit.,* p. 244.

of 1925) required that wages also be reduced by 10 per cent: "He who wills the end wills the means. What now faces the Government is the ticklish task of carrying out their own dangerous and unnecessary decision."[115] In fact, the general strike of 1927 might be seen as a consequence of the Churchillian venture into finance: casual observation confirms the difficulty of persuading trade unions to accept money-wage cuts.

Another consequence of the "heavy pound" was high interest rates. It was necessary to protect gold reserves by encouraging foreigners to hold sterling securities. But high interest rates can discourage business spending on inventories and fixed investments. The dilemma becomes sharply etched.

Hawtrey, a reluctant advocate of the return to gold in 1925, juggles these balls with great dexterity:

> "Early in 1925, confronted with the approaching restoration of the gold standard and with the need to raise the value of the pound up to parity, the Bank of England put Bank rate up from 4 to 5 per cent. This is a high rate. In the 47½ years that elapsed between the beginning of 1867 . . . and the outbreak of war in 1914, Bank rate was at 5 per cent or more for 319 weeks or only one week in every eight. *Long* spells at or above 5 per cent (say 10 weeks or over) hardly ever occurred otherwise than at times of great trade activity.
>
> In fact the only exceptions were in the years 1878 . . . and 1884 and it is significant that these years were followed by the most severe unemployment recorded before 1914 . . .
>
> At a time of excessive activity, a high Bank rate is imposed to check the rise of prices. But to apply a rate suitable for such a situation to a state of *depression* is to put the brakes on when going uphill. . . ."[116]

Keynes argued that the unhappy coincidence of high interest rates and trade depression — British industry, in contrast with that of other industrial nations, slumped from 1925 onward — was a consequence of Mr. Churchill: Britain's gold reserves had to be protected by this device (particularly since world commodity prices slumped in the meanwhile). And then the task of the British authorities was not made easier by the refusal of America and France to play the game and permit their gold inflows to lead to higher prices and lower interest rates.

We need not again develop the background for Britain's depar-

115 *Ibid.*, p. 241.
116 Hawtrey, *op. cit.*, pp. 107-108.

ture from gold — bringing to an end six years of failure or at least misfortune of the noble experiment. The demise occurred September 21, 1931.[117] Keynes failed to maintain a somber face:

> "There are few Englishmen who do not rejoice at the breaking of our golden fetters. We feel that we have at least a free hand to do what is sensible. The romantic phase is over, and we can begin to discuss realistically what policy is for the best . . .
>
> The City of London considered that it was under an obligation of *honour* to make every possible effort to maintain the value of money in terms of which it had accepted large deposits from foreigners, even though the result of this was to place an intolerable strain on British industry . . ."[118]

It is hard to quarrel with Keynes: from 1925 to September 1931 the British wholesale price index fell 37.6 per cent; the price index for manufactured exports, 26.8 per cent.

8

The 1931–1939 interval featured stable prices, 2 per cent Bank rate, and foreign exchange rates for the pound that were free to vary, subject to official market operations.[119] The 1931–1939 experience was, on the whole more satisfactory than that of 1925–1931. However it

---

117 Hawtrey points out that the monetary-legislative aspects of departure from gold were somewhat different in 1931 than in 1797. In 1797, a Bank of England note was a debt redeemable in gold; the Restriction was a default. "But the Gold Standard Act of 1925 merely required the Bank to 'sell' gold bullion at the coinage [official] price." (*Ibid.*, pp. 135-136.) Indeed, the Bank was actually relieved of the obligation to convert currency notes into gold coin. [This obligation had remained on the books until 1925, although made nugatory by the prohibitions against melting gold coin (since 1916) and exporting gold (since 1919).] "The restoration of *freedom of export* was the essence of the return to the gold standard in 1925. (*Ibid.*, p. 136.)

Thus, under the 1925 act, a unit currency note was *numeraire;* its price was defined as £1. The act required *the Bank* to sell bullion at a price of £3. 17s. 10½d. per standard ounce. AN OBLIGATION TO PAY STERLING WAS NOT IN GENERAL AN OBLIGATION TO PAY GOLD. The Bank simply was required to maintain exchange between paper and gold at a certain rate. Once the Bank was relieved of that obligation, the gold price of sterling obligations was free to vary, but the legal attributes of indebtedness were left unchanged.

118 J. M. Keynes, "The End of the Gold Standard," *The Sunday Express,* Sept. 27, 1931, reprinted in *Essays in Persuasion,* pp. 288-294, at p. 288.

119 The government was under no obligation to maintain a fixed relation between sterling and gold dollars or some other currency. In fact sterling soon fell in value in terms of dollars.

was by no means spectacularly successful. The 1930's are notable as a period of *managed money,* a policy persisting to our own day.

9

1939–1961 did not produce any striking developments *for monetary standards.* After all, there was by 1939 insufficient formal "metallic" limitation on the stock of money and debt generally for any dramatic "liberalizing" change to be possible. There was, however, a rather charming change in the regulatory principle governing the currency introduced in the Currency and Bank Notes Acts of 1939 (and elaborated in Ch. V *infra.*):

> "[I]t provided that the size of the note issue should always be equal to the *market value* of the gold and other assets held by the Issue Department . . . This logically turns the basic principle of the gold standard . . . upside down."[120]

Any depreciation of sterling in terms of gold increases the market value (measured in £) of the gold reserves. The requirement does not build in any real restriction. But, then, it is not supposed to.

This does not mean that British monetary authorities are rid of a severe and sometimes ruthless discipline. Not at all. In one way or another, Britain has since 1936 been committed to maintaining a fixed dollar value for its currency, or, more correctly, for sterling assets.[121] (This commitment has been subject to change from time to time — as in 1949 when the pound was devalued.) The commitment can be sustained only through open market purchases and sales of sterling (aided in one way or another by international monetary authorities). It requires that there be a buffer stock of gold and hard currencies.

120 W. Manning Dacey, *The British Banking Mechanism* (London: Hutchinson, 1951), p. 117.

121 There was in 1936 a Tripartite Monetary Agreement between the United States, France, and Great Britain, an agreement later joined by a number of West European nations. As Crowther puts it, the agreement "was an assurance that there would be substantial day-to-day stability of the exchange rates, that large changes would be done by agreement [Geoffrey Crowther, *An Outline of Money* (London: Thomas Nelson & Sons, Ltd., 1948), pp. 324-325]. The agreement lasted until September 1939 and was not formally ended by the war, dollar rates of exchange being maintained by various controls during the war and for some time afterwards. The Bretton Woods Conference of July 1944 led to the International Monetary Fund discussed in Ch. XVI. *Cf.* also Crowther, *op. cit.,* pp. 332-335. A central theme of the IMF system is day-to-day exchange stability accompanied by infrequent changes in exchange rates, these to be accomplished only under great stress. It follows that much of the "discipline" of gold persists.

If this stock threatens to evaporate, Britain is faced with possible inability to convert sterling obligations; it would then have to rely on default, moratoria, emergency loans from abroad, or devaluation (before the fact). These are prospects most unpalatable to the international banking community, providers of much of Britain's foreign exchange earnings. Keynes's 1931 comments remain true: "the City of London consider[s] that it [is] under an obligation . . . to make every possible effort to maintain the value of money in terms of which it has accepted large deposits from foreigners." Not surprisingly, the effort to maintain a fixed price of gold imposes many of the restraints of an out and out gold standard.

The *Economist* of London for July 22, 1961, stated that:

> ". . . the immediate new short-term threat to the exchange rate was one that could and should have been largely met by a rise in Britain's bank rate several weeks ago . . . A two per cent rise in bank rate would have the double advantage of being a bait to make it more profitable for foreigners to hold sterling and a regulator to cut home demand."

Consider the complications when external considerations make it desirable to attract foreign "capital" and you want to *stimulate* home demand.

Indeed Britain retains something like "golden fetters," and must do so as long as it attempts to maintain convertibility at fixed rates of its exchange into hard currencies and gold. "And the way up is the way down; the way forward is the way back." There is remarkable continuity in British monetary history, at least from 1797 to 1961. It seems that certain basic principles persist despite overwhelming surface changes.

SUMMARY

1. The study of money as a social institution cannot be divorced from the study of governments. The role of government has been threefold: (1), establishment of uniform standards of measurement of values and securing uniformity and integrity of coinage; (2), establishment of conditions of convertibility of debt expressed in money of account; (3) provision of assured supplies of liquid assets, sometimes associated with acquisition of resources beyond yields from taxation.

2. The first role is politically neutral. It concerns selection of a *numeraire* good and of a money of account.
3. The second and third roles are pregnant with dramatic possibility which often has been manifested. These lead to monetary standards in the important (convertibility) sense and to struggles of governments and parties against self-denying ordinances.
4. We say that an economy is on a gold standard when there is a fixed rate of exchange between its money and gold. It is *convertibility* that contains the juice: starting with a stock of bullion of given nominal value, a society finds that the nominal value of the volume of financial assets that can be created is limited by that of the metallic stock.
5. Metallic systems came to be featured by inverted pyramids of convertible obligations. History shows that, from time to time, metallic standards collapsed because people wanted to hold more metal than was available. There was great excitement, since individuals were legally entitled to metal but could not have it. The ageless appeal of the glitter of gold made the problem seem moral. Today convenience and conscience both are served by limited bullion standards precluding domestic convertibility.
6. When governments have wanted to get hold of more economic resources than their taxation power permits, they have tended to break self-denying ordinances and issue *inconvertible* currency, severing the link between the nominal value of metallic reserves and that of financial assets.
7. Sometimes the accounting prices of two metals (gold and silver in our illustration) are fixed. This system is called *bimetallism.* Bimetallism is in fact an ancient system, now *passé.* Discussion of bimetallism features the counterpoint of mint and market ratios: exchange ratios fixed by the Legal Tender Act and determined in bullion markets. When mint and market ratios diverge, there is a tendency — one which we qualified — for the under-valued metal to desert monetary uses in accordance with Gresham's Law until either the ratios are brought into equality or the undervalued metal is demonetized (*de facto*). If a country has large enough metallic stocks, it conceivably could govern world market ratios. Otherwise it finds that only one metal or another continues to serve monetary uses unless its mint frequently adjusts the mint ratio, destroying the fixity in nominal value of at least one of the metals.

8. Bimetallism leads to issues of subsidiary coinage. It can be considered as part of an effort to develop a full-bodied (silver) coinage for low-valued transactions. "Full-bodiedness" often is confused with a state in which the ingredients of a coin would have the same exchange value whether or not they were monetized (eligible to be money). Instead, fullbodiedness of coinage should be associated with *free coinage.*
9. The American bimetallism controversy is associated with deflation and the desire of debtors that the money supply be increased. Key dates are 1873, 1879, and 1896.
10. The politics and economics of resumption were strikingly parallel in Britain in 1819 and 1925 and in the United States in 1879. Similarly, the underlying issues of the bimetallist controversy were little different in the United States in 1834, 1873, and 1934. As for resumption controversies, the crucial issue concerned the relation of the nominal value of the monetary base and of the stock of convertible obligations — more indirectly, financial assets generally.
11. The underlying philosophy of the free silver agitation has, to some extent, carried the day. But fixed exchanges between national currencies have led to golden fetters surprisingly like those of former days, featuring external rather than internal pressures.
12. *Symmetallism* pertains to monetary aspects of the theory of income and employment. Its (unattainable) ideal state assures stable prices. If the government stood ready to purchase unlimited quantities of appropriate commodity bundles at a fixed price, the least bit of factor-price flexibility would assure full employment.
13. Paragraph 12 suggests that strongly increasing marginal costs of production of gold work against it as an ideal money.
14. The stability of the purchasing power of gold has not been very great.
15. *Fiat paper* standards really are the simplest of all. J. S. Mill, writing more than a century ago, put it better than anyone has:

> "[paper money] derives its power for performing [monetary functions] solely from convention; but convention is quite sufficient to confer the power; since nothing more is need[ed] . . . than the persuasion that it will be taken from him on the same terms from others."

Under paper standards, appropriately engraved paper serves as the *numeraire* good, and is — in the pure case — convertible into *nothing.*

16. Fiat standards often being accompanied by rampant inflationism by governments whose fiscal process has broken down or was inadequate to the task, are associated in the public mind with glamorous sin. Oddly enough, the most celebrated instance of a paper standard replacing a gold standard — the English Restriction of 1797–1819 — reveals moderate use of fiat power. The Restriction was the occasion for a famous debate on a rather silly premise: namely that there was a certain rectitude in that stock of money which might have prevailed under a metallic standard. History suggests that governments are unlikely to adhere to self-denying ordinances about the size of the money stock if they feel their existence is at stake.
17. Modern economies feature large amounts of non-representative but convertible paper — whether convertible into a metallic substance or some other paper. The value of stocks of these convertible obligations far exceeds that of the "basic stuff" backing their issue: inverted pyramids of credit are created. The monetary history of the United States included rather frequent crises of liquidity occurring when holders of convertible currency wished to "cash their chips," almost always for currency.
18. There are more subtle relationships between the value of the monetary base and that of other stocks in equilibrium; the equilibrium value of perpetuities is affected by the value of the monetary base even though issuers of perpetuities cannot be called. There are crucial relationships between the monetary base and equilibrium values of variables of the economic system. Analysis of these relationships must be deferred to Part II, largely to Ch. XIV.
19. The monetary histories (more or less histories of the monetary standards) of the United States and Britain richly embroider the abstract argument of Chs. I and II. . . . "And the way up is the way down; the way forward is the way back."

NOTES

Note A: More precisely, "[p]roffer of legal tender by a debtor to his creditor at the maturity of the obligation stops the accumulation of interest charges and relieves the debtor of any collection costs." [Edward S. Shaw, *Money, Income, and Monetary Policy*. (Homewood, Ill.: Richard D. Irwin, Inc., 1950), p. 5.] How are prices of legal tender determined? A Federal Reserve note labelled "10" discharges debt measured at 10 dollars (money of account). A price quotation can be viewed as nothing more than an offer to acquire a debt (or credit) on stated terms; the market price today of a Federal Reserve note labelled "10" *cannot* be less than ten dollars.

These words of Sir Ralph Hawtrey explain much: "[A debt] . . . must not be thought of as arising only from the borrowing of money or the postponement of payment. Every sale of goods or service gives rise to a debt. The quotation of a price is an offer to create a debt." [Hawtrey, *The Gold Standard in Theory and Practice,* p. 3.]

I do not explicitly discuss the State theory of money, associated with Knapp and holding that, in Keynes's words, "money is peculiarly a creation of the State." [*Cf.* Ludwig von Mises, *The Theory of Money and Credit* (New Haven: Yale University Press, 1953), Ch. IV. Also F. A. Mann, *The Legal Aspect of Money* (2nd ed.; London: Oxford University Press, 1953), Chs. I and II.] Hawtrey's (and my) position favors Knapp to the extent that:

> ". . . the Age of Chartalist or State Money was reached when the State claimed the right to declare what thing should answer as money to the current money-of-account — when it claimed the right not only to enforce the dictionary but also to write the dictionary . . ." [Keynes, *A Treatise on Money,* Vol. 1, pp. 4-5.]

On the other hand, Custom often has sufficed to turn the trick.

NOTE B: If the mint produces *alloyed* coins containing x grains of gold (for example), exchanging these for (x + h) grains of gold, seignorage (including brassage) per coin is h grains of gold. (Ignoring the market value of the alloying material.) If the marginal utility of coin is high enough — presumably only coin is legal tender — gold and coin might exchange in the free market at the mint ratio. However, the proportion of coined gold to the total gold stock will fall with increasing h. If h is high enough, and if demand for gold as a commodity is elastic enough, gold will not be presented to the mint and the coinage will be melted down. Gold will sell at a premium over its official coin price.

Even if the alloying material has market value, the system should not be confused with symmetallism (*cf.* text *infra.*): coin is obtained by presentation of gold *not* of gold plus not-gold. On the other hand, the seigniorage analogy breaks down unless the market value of the alloying material is less than that of h grains of gold.

Rulers often lightened and alloyed the coinage, decreeing that the debased coins should satisfy nominally-valued claims at par. The "heavy" coins would disappear from circulation — being hoarded or reminted — unless accepted at a premium.

NOTE C: In other words, alternative price scales can develop. The *jth* element of the price set using silver as a standard of value (calibrated so that the silver dollar has unit value) is 1.10 times greater than the corresponding element of the price set using gold as a standard of value (calibrated so that the gold dollar has unit value). The text's example assumes that the price scale is calibrated with silver as the standard, silver being putatively overvalued.

The Greenback-gold-dollar case leads to the same construction. Statements about prices logically require appropriately defined scales of measurement of value.

NOTE D: The text describes a system with the logical properties of a bimetallic system in which one of the "metals" has no non-monetary use; ours is a *limiting* case. Thus, assume that we originally are on a gold standard and that the standard gold coin (the dollar) is assigned the accounting price 1 guinea, the guinea being money of account. Now assume that inconvertible paper money is introduced and is made legal tender, the accounting price of a paper dollar being set at 1 guinea. Keep the system closed. Mill and Toynbee and Fitzgerald tell us that the paper dollar can circulate at par with the gold dollar. Guinea prices of other goods will rise. There will be excess demand for non-monetary gold (its relative price having fallen); a portion of the monetary gold stock will become demonetized. If the paper issue becomes large enough, the entire monetary gold stock will become demonetized, and partly because of developing expectations of collapse of the standard, the parity of paper and gold dollars might be destroyed. There will then be a paper standard. The guinea price of gold will exceed 35 guineas per ounce (assuming that the gold dollar contained 1/35 ounce of gold) as the paper issue mounts. In other words, once the monetary stock of gold is exhausted, it no longer is possible to arbitrage differences in the guinea price of gold as a commodity and as money; the guinea price of gold becomes unstuck, even if paper and gold dollars had to exchange at par in obedience to the government's ukase; there are no gold dollars. On the other hand, if gold had no non-monetary use in a closed system, gold and paper dollars would be perfect substitutes, and could continue to circulate side by side as the paper issue mounted.

The most interesting aspect of the analysis finds partial transfer of the monetary gold stock to non-monetary uses once fiat paper money is issued. If the latter issue is modest, the equivalent of bimetallism can be sustained indefinitely if gold output is high enough to offset the steady flow of gold into commodity uses.

NOTE E: Consider a strange animal called the "limping standard." The limping standard was featured in France and other members of the Latin Union which France joined for monetary purposes from the 1870's until 1914. These countries had abolished free coinage of silver, but reserved the right to make payments in silver coins rather than gold coins despite the fact that the silver coins were token money. ". . . [T]he idea being that the standard had as it were two legs, one of gold and one of silver, but that the silver leg was crippled and deformed." (Robertson, *Money,* p. 69.) Robertson points out that, insofar as the authorities were refusing to honor monetary obligations in gold, the standard was practically fiat or arbitrary in character. The silver that was tendered by the authorities was logically the same as a paper tender. "It was not a standard at all" (*ibid.,* p. 69).

NOTE F: Compare Sir Roy Harrod, *The Dollar* (London: Macmillan and Co., Ltd., 1953), p. 69. Sir Roy writes: "The effect of this measure was nil until the outbreak of the Second World War. This was due to the operation of the free market for gold bullion in London. There any individual holder of the dollar could obtain gold at the official United States valuation via sterling, the sterling price of gold bullion being governed in that period by the dollar shipping parity. It would not be an exaggeration to say that we in Britain maintained the United States gold standard for them during this period." Thus, dollars could be exchanged for sterling and the latter sold for gold at London. These transactions conceivably could have led to excess supply of dollars. If so, British officials could, of course, have exchanged the dollars for gold at New York. "The war brought the free bullion market in London to an end. Thereafter a premium on gold against the dollar developed and has been very high in certain post-war years. For a time the International Monetary Fund frowned upon the sales of newly mined gold direct to the free markets but later relaxed its attitude. The free markets then received gold in large quantities and the premium has accordingly been reduced to a low level, but only at the price of the loss of much newly mined gold from the monetary circulation." The free market gold price of the dollar remains an important indicator of the dollar's strength.

NOTE G: Some, including Mrs. Perkins, have said that F.D.R. was especially influenced by Warren's colored charts. For discussion of *l'affaire* Warren, *cf.* James MacGregor Burns, *Roosevelt: the Lion and the Fox* (New York: Harcourt, Brace & Co., 1956), pp. 195-196 and Arthur M. Schlesinger, Jr., *The Coming of the New Deal* (Boston: Houghton Mifflin Company, 1959), pp. 234-249. Schlesinger's account is detailed and interesting. As for Roosevelt's fascination with Warren's charts, Schlesinger reports (p. 235) only that James Warburg was ". . . increasingly disturbed by Roosevelt's *apparent* (emphasis supplied) absorption in Warren's charts."

Churchill, de Gaulle, and Adenauer are notably bad economists and are notably bored by the subject. Before negatively correlating statecraft with economic wisdom, consult Schlesinger, *op. cit.*, p. 235, for Irving Fisher's 1934 judgment that F.D.R. was "informed and receptive."

The standard analytical discussions of the Warren theory are Charles O. Hardy, *The Warren-Pearson Price Theory,* Brookings Institution Pamphlet Series, No. 17 (Washington: Brookings Institution, 1935) and Seymour E. Harris, *Exchange Depreciation* (Cambridge: Harvard University Press, 1936).

NOTE H: Of course, traders accepting the under-valued metal at a premium (selling goods at a discount) had to accept the risk that the market ratio would take an adverse turn for them. Needless to say, the *real* value of gold (here the over-valued metal) was also subject to fluctuation. The point is that, under the hypothesized circumstances, the nominal value of the over-valued metal (gold) could not fall; under no circumstances would the price of a legal tender fall below its official price (in money of account). This necessarily explains *part* of what has seemed to me to be a mystery: fixed nominal value is part and parcel of moneyness. I remain dissatisfied. Transactions costs, etc. would explain the size of the premium — noting that merchants always could convert their silver receipts into gold if they wished — but not a corner solution. *Cf.* Hawtrey, *Currency and Credit,* for the only good discussion of the problem known to me.

NOTE I: It must be said in Ricardo's favor that the insistence of the Bank's management that a gold coin standard be instituted — the 1819 act was amended so that gold coin could be effected a year ahead of time — increased the deflationary potential of resumption. As Viner writes:

> ". . . [T]he chief virtue of the ingot plan lay in the fact that at a time when the general return to metallic currencies was threatening to cause a price deflation, it would enable England to make her return to the gold standard with a minimum drain on the world supply of gold." (*Ibid.*, p. 180.)

Furthermore, as Viner also points out, there will be times when firms and households wish to increase holdings of cash as against other assets, quite aside from lack of confidence in the solvency of the banking system. If the economy is on a gold bullion standard, there will be no important drain of specie from central reserves. If it is essentially on a gold coin standard — or if lower valued notes have been withdrawn as quickly as was true in Britain — there will be a gold tranche. The Bank's policies made a bad situation worse. Still it was confronted with a global deflation. The British authorities had some of the problems of the 1879 American authorities. Without a successful flexible exchange system, economies find it very hard to insulate themselves from global conditions.

NOTE J: If the demand function for money is differently characterized, namely if equation 1 is deleted and replaced by equations 1′ and 1″

$$(1') \qquad D_{2a} \equiv f_{2a}[\qquad\qquad]$$

$$(1'') \qquad D_{3a} \equiv f_{3a}[\qquad\qquad]$$

the system becomes overdetermined. The model then does not leave the authorities free to do more than passively adapt $\bar{p}_3/\bar{p}_2$ to $(p_3/p_2)^*$, a component of the system's real solution set. Any other choice for $\bar{p}_3/\bar{p}_2$ is inconsistent with general equilibrium and, presumably, with bimetallism.

The alternative formulation is inconsistent with perfect substitution of gold and silver for monetary purposes. Assume that the mint ratio is 1:16. Graph A suggests the appendix's model; Graph B, the alternative model.

Graph A tells us that there can be an infinity of Au-Ag combinations consistent with a given "monetary" plan. Each combination implies a different pair of nonmonetary gold and silver stocks. Bimetallism at 1:16 is possible if 1:16 can be achieved in the market with D_{2a} and D_{3a} both greater than zero.

If Graph B is appropriate, the unique proportion of monetary gold to monetary silver described by tan θ will be consistent with equilibrium—making certain homogeneity assumptions and noting that the indifference map must be redrawn if the mint ratio is altered. For given $S_2(t)$ and $S_3(t)$ — ignoring production and consumption components in this intuitive proof — there are specified unique monetary stocks of gold and silver. These stocks, $\bar{S}_{2a}(t)$ and $\bar{S}_{3a}(t)$, will in general be inconsistent with the solution of the system.

The text (Ch. II) is based on the model of Equations 1′ and 1″. Of course, the case of an open system is easier to handle than either of the models of the Appendix. Also, it is much more decisive.

Perfect Substitution (Indifference Curve Analysis)

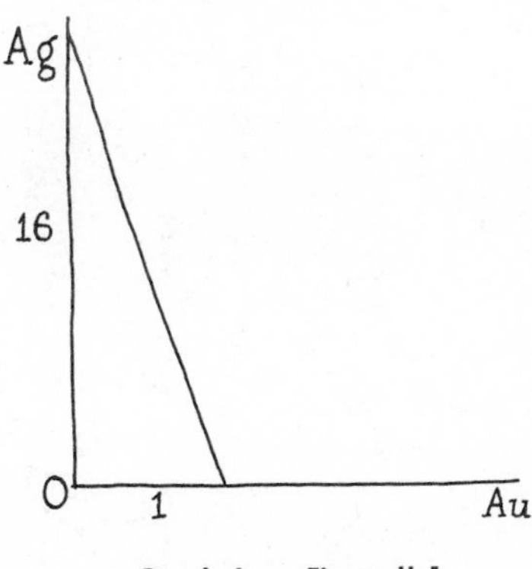

Graph A — Figure II-1

Imperfect Substitution
(Indifference Curve
Analysis)

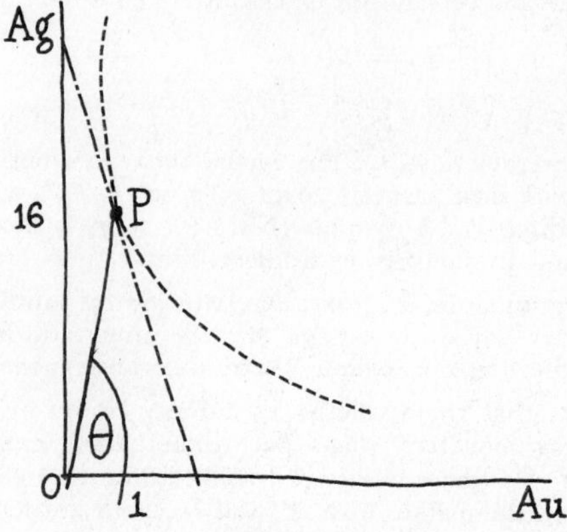

Graph B — Figure II-2

APPENDIX

Formal statement of monetary standards; gold bullion standards; bimetallism[122]

THIS APPENDIX ATTACKS THE BIMETALLISM PROBLEM, BUT the context is that of monetary standards generally: two birds can be killed with one stone.

A. A GOLD BULLION STANDARD

Consider a system with n goods: paper money, gold, silver, and $n-3$ non-durable goods. Paper money is the medium of exchange and the legal tender; there is no coined gold, and gold is never used as a medium of exchange. It is assumed that the durables do not deteriorate except as gold and silver are "devoured" in industrial uses — literally destroyed. Of course, paper money is convertible into gold. Silver is, for the time being, just another commodity. The unit of account (money of account) is the guinea. Subscripts for paper money, gold, and silver are respectively 1, 2, and 3. Set the price of paper money at unity $(p_1 = 1)$; fix the price of gold $(p_2 = \bar{p}_2)$. The following equation system applies:

(1) $f_1[\bar{p}_2, \ldots, p_n; S_{21}(t-1), S_3(t-1), S_1(t-1)] = S_1(t)$

(2) $f_2[\quad] + h_2[\quad] + S_{22}(t) = S_{21}(t-1) + S_{22}(t-1) + g_2[\quad]$

(3) $\bar{p}_2\, S_{22}(t) = kS_1(t)$

(4) $f_3[\quad] + h_3[\quad] = S_3(t-1) + g_3[\quad]$

[122] Walras has an excellent treatment of bimetallic standards. *Cf.* Léon Walras (William Jaffé, trans.), *Elements of Pure Economics* (London: George Allen & Unwin, 1954), Lessons 31 and 32, pp. 338-361. Our results and Walras' are, so far as I can see, the same. Ironically Walras chose not to use a general equilibrium framework.

(5) $F_4[\quad] = 0$

. . . .

$n+1)$ $F_n[\quad] = 0$

$S_{21}(t-1)$ are gold holdings of the public at the end of the last period; $S_3(t-1)$, its holdings of silver at the end of the last period. $S_{22}(t)$ is the government's desired gold stock. $h_2[\quad]$ and $h_3[\quad]$ show the functional determination of industrial consumption of gold and silver — consumption meaning destruction. The $f_i[\quad]$ forms are functional relations determining desired stocks for the end of the *t-th* period; it is assumed that adjustment is planned to be complete within the current period. Equation 3 implies the relationship between government bullion holdings and the nominal value of warehouse receipts issued. $F_4[\quad], \ldots, F_n[\quad]$ are excess demand functions for the $n-3$ commodities. Initial stocks are independent variables in demand and supply functions and, among other things, have wealth effects.

There are $n + 1$ equations in n unknowns ($n-2$ *prices*, $S_1(t)$, and $S_{22}(t)$). However, at most n of the equations are independent: if there is no excess demand (positive or negative) in any of $n-1$ markets, the budget constraints imbedded in the system — requiring that what is bought must be paid for — assure that the *nth* market also is cleared. Thus, a necessary condition — albeit simple-minded — for solution of the system is not violated because there are $n + 1$ equations. Indeed, it is assumed that a solution set can be obtained.

Consider the solution set $[p_3, \ldots, p_n, S_1(t), S_{22}(t)]^*$. Observe that governments, once they subject themselves to the discipline of gold — promising to convert at a fixed rate — are not free to issue any amount of paper they wish if all markets are to clear. Rather they must be guided by conditions in the gold market, the tastes and preferences of the community, etc. On the other hand, conventional assumptions suggest that, if the above is a solution set, so is

$$[\lambda\bar{p}_2, \lambda p_3^*, \ldots \lambda p_n^*, \lambda S_1^*(t), S_{22}(t)].$$

If the stock of paper money, the price of gold, and the prices of commodities rise in the same proportion, λ, no change will have occurred in any real variables of the system: the real value of money holdings will be unchanged; real values of all other asset holdings are unchanged; relative prices are the same; profitability of gold and silver production is unchanged, their nominal values having increased in the same proportion as their costs of production.[123] On the other hand, if prices are sticky, an increase in the guinea price of gold (p_2) stimulates gold production, at least transitorily. If the system's full equilibrium state (*cf. infra*) is unique, wealth effects of higher gold stocks eventually will be offset by increased "consumption" of gold through the $h_2[\quad]$ relation. If there is no way of "eating up" gold, initial price stickiness will permanently change the system's equilibrium state: there will be no way to restore the initial state because of wealth effects.

If the price of gold is increased, together with an increase in k, so that $S_1(t)=S_1(t-1)$, it cannot be expected that the real properties of the solution for the *t-th* period will be invariant against the price of gold even if prices are flexible.

What of the system's full-equilibrium properties? Since holdings of gold and of paper money are *not* treated as a single variable,

$$\frac{S_1 + p_2 S_2}{P},$$

where P is the general price level, the real solution state of the system will *not* be invariant against a change in p_2 unless S_1 is changed proportionately. This is in line with a broader theorem stating that fixity in the nominal value of a stock precludes invariance of the real solution state against parametric shifts in a second money fixed claim.

The full-equilibrium solution is obtained by treating $S_1(t-1)$, $S_{21}(t-1)$, $S_{22}(t-1)$, and $S_3(t-1)$ as unknowns — adding equations $n+2$, $n+3$, and $n+4$ to the system (noting that satisfaction of $n+2$ assures that $S_{22}(t)=S_{22}(t-1)$):

$n+2)$ $$S_1(t) = S_1(t-1)$$

$n+3)$ $$f_2[\quad] = S_{21}(t-1)$$

123 The real price of real cash balances can be *defined* as equal to unity. In order to see this, it is convenient to define the general price level, p, as a weighted average of prices of the goods of the system, excluding paper money. A unit of real cash balances is comprised of a stock of nominal monetary units capable of purchasing what 1 nominal unit could in the base year. The nominal price of a unit of real cash balances, then, is p where $p=1$ for the base period. The relative price for the jth good is defined as

$$pj/p.$$

It follows that in the case of real cash balances, real price is defined as

$$p/p \equiv 1.$$

An heuristic explanation is that a 1 per cent rise in the price level finds the quantum of cash comprising a real unit increasing by 1 per cent with each unit worth 1 per cent less.

$$f_3[\quad] = S_3(t-1). \tag{n+4}$$

If, for the sake of argument, gold had no non-monetary use, and gold and paper money could be treated as a single variable, the full-equilibrium state of the system could be invariant against a change in p_2: if p_2 were increased by a factor λ, commodity prices would increase in lesser proportion during the transition period; gold production would be stimulated until finally gold stocks would be large enough in period θ for

$$\frac{S_1(0) + [\lambda \bar{p}_2 S_2(\theta)]}{\lambda P(0)} = \frac{S_1(0) + \bar{p}_2 S_2(0)}{P(0)}$$

where P is the general price level and where there is full equilibrium in period zero. (But $S_2(\theta) - S_2(0)$ must not have become too large relative to $S_1(0)$; otherwise there would be too much real cash in the system at λP for the initial real state to be restored.) The real variables of the system are identical at $t = \theta$ and $t = 0$: if the initial equilibrium state was unique, the new full-equilibrium state must have the above properties.

B. A BIMETALLIC STANDARD

We shall here assume that the state does not issue money. Also, for now, that the authorities do not hold stocks either of gold or silver — although, when convenient, we shall assume that official stocks are infinite (and disregarded by the public in its wealth calculations). We must agree in advance that, if a predetermined relative price of gold and silver, $\bar{p}_3/\bar{p}_2$, cannot be sustained both at the mint and in global markets for the metals, bimetallism will be unworkable — *ignoring qualifications of the text.* As it happens, the important results can be ground out for a closed system in which gold and silver have non-monetary uses. We seek conditions consistent with maintenance of a uniform mint and market ratio, the ratio to be determined by the monetary authorities. Indeed, the ratios can be permanently at variance only when all gold or silver is in one use or the other so that no further arbitrage is possible. IF BOTH GOLD AND SILVER ARE IN THE MONETARY STOCK IN EQUILIBRIUM, THEN THE MINT AND MARKET RATIOS ARE THE SAME.

The essence of bimetallism is in fixing p_3 as well as p_2, thereby establishing the rate of exchange between silver and gold. If the ratio $\bar{p}_3/\bar{p}_2$ can be maintained, bimetallism can be established. Otherwise demonetization of the under-valued metal will lead to effective monometallism; the effective price of the under-valued metal will be determined in the market. We have not bothered to normalize accounting prices. This is the system:

$$
\begin{array}{ll}
(1) & \bar{p}_2 D_{2a} + \bar{p}_3 D_{3a} \equiv f_M[\bar{p}_2, \bar{p}_3, p_{10}, \ldots, p_n; S(t-1)] \\
(2) & D_{2b} \equiv f_{2b}[\qquad] \\
(3) & D_{2a} = S_{2a} \\
(4) & D_{2b} = S_{2b} \\
(5) & S_{2a} + S_{2b} \equiv S_{2a}(t-1) + S_{2b}(t-1) + g_2[\quad] - h_2[\quad] \\
(6) & D_{3b} \equiv f_{3b}[\qquad] \\
(7) & D_{3a} = S_{3a} \\
(8) & D_{3b} = S_{3b} \\
(9) & S_{3a} + S_{3b} \equiv S_{3a}(t-1) + S_{3b}(t-1) + g_3[\quad] - h_3[\quad]. \\
(10) & F_{10}[\qquad] = 0 \\
\cdot & \cdot \quad \cdot \quad \cdot \quad \cdot \quad \cdot \quad \cdot \quad \cdot \quad \cdot \\
(n) & F_n[\qquad] = 0
\end{array}
$$

Non-monetary commodities are indexed from 10 to n. Gold and silver are assumed to be perfect monetary substitutes, as is expressed in equation 1. $S(t-1)$ is a vector of initial stocks. The D's give desired monetary (indexed by a) and non-monetary (indexed by b) stocks of gold and silver. Equations 3 and 4 are market clearance conditions for the gold market, equations 7 and 8 for the silver market. Equation 5 tell us that the total stock of gold at the end of the *t-th* period — measuring in ounces — is defined by initial stocks plus new production minus consumption. Equation 9 tells the same story for silver. The equation system implies that stocks can be transferred from one use to another.

There are $n-1$ independent equations in $n-1$ unknowns: $n-9$ non-metallic commodity prices, D_{2a}, D_{2b}, D_{3a}, D_{3b}, S_{2a} S_{2b}, S_{3a}, and S_{3b}. Bimetallism (at the mint ratio $\bar{p}_2/\bar{p}_3$) can be established if solution values for monetary stocks are positive. Otherwise it cannot be imposed even in a closed system. A *range* of workable mint ratios emerges *(see Note J)*.

There is an obvious way out if the model of p. 101 reveals that bimetallism cannot be effectuated at a given mint ratio. If the authorities had a cornucopia containing gold and silver, initial stocks of one or both of the metals could be "arranged" so that selected gold and silver prices were consistent with market clearance. In fact, the officials could dip into their horn of plenty and establish stocks permitting full equilibrium. Needless to say, we have ignored agio possibilities. Agio, however practically important, is not theoretically interesting at this stage.

Some comments on the bimetallism model before closing:

a) if all prices, including those of gold and silver, are changed in the same proportion, real solution values are unchanged.

b) if gold and silver are revalued in the same proportion, maintaining an initial (solution) ratio, while commodity prices are sticky, there will be a stimulus to production of the metals and a tendency towards excess demand in the other $n-3$ markets.

c) if the system can be opened, if ours is a small country in a big world so that at least p_2 and p_3 are parametric, our authorities must maintain a mint ratio in accordance with external prices if they are not to submit to virtual monometallism; if a country is to impose its mint ratio on the world it must have very large stocks of gold and silver, permitting global open-market operations.

d) continuous adjustment of mint to market ratios is inconsistent with what should be a basic attribute of a money: stability of nominal value. Clearly the guinea price of but one of the metals could be maintained constant in that event.

The logical problems of bimetallism are interesting and important, although the subject itself surely is moot. In Ch. XVI, the argument of this Appendix is applied to some present day issues.

CHAPTER THREE

Financial Assets and Financial Institutions

In modern economies media of exchange (means of payment) are financial assets, predominantly debt instruments.[1] It is impossible intelligently to discuss money except in the context of financial assets (liabilities); the former is a subset of the latter.

A. THE MATRIX OF CLAIMS

1

Chapter III is devoted to the "matrix of claims." The role of debt and financial institutions is examined. Eventually we are concerned with interaction of financial markets with rates of output and employment. For now, we content ourselves with understanding the financial side of things, rather in isolation.

Table III-I is a schematic partial view of the matrix of claims in a modern economic system. It might better be called an asset matrix:

[1] Hart and Kenen have an excellent definition of debt:

> ". . . 'debt' is negative wealth stated in a unit of account." A. G. Hart and P. B. Kenen, *Money, Debt, and Economic Activity,* 3rd ed. (Englewood Cliffs, N.J.: Prentice-Hall, Inc., 1961), p. 6.

A rate of interest is a rate of growth of a cumulant, usually of money. It is usually expressed in per cent *per annum.*

MATRIX OF CLAIMS: INCOMPLETE

	is owed by					
	Households [1]	Unincorporated (non-farm) Business [2]	Non Fin. Corp. [3]	Non-Banking Fin. [4]	Banks [5]	Government [6]
[1]	M_{11} A_{H1} L_{11} A_{pd1} b_{11} A_{cd1} A_{L1}	E_{21} M_{21} L_{21} b_{21}	c_{31} M_{31} p_{31} b_{31} L_{31}	c_{41} R_{41} p_{41} T_{41} b_{41} S_{41}	c_{51} p_{51} D_{51} T_{51}	N_{61} F_{61} b_{61}
[2]	t_{12} b_{12} L_{12} C_{12} M_{12}	M_{22} E_{22} A_{H2} t_{22} b_{22} A_{pd2} L_{22} A_{cd2} A_{L2} A_{I2}	c_{32} L_{32} p_{32} M_{32} b_{32} t_{32}	c_{42} R_{42} p_{42} S_{42} b_{42} T_{42}	c_{52} D_{52} p_{52} T_{52}	N_{62} F_{62} b_{62} t_{62}
[3]	t_{13} b_{13} L_{13} C_{13} M_{13}	E_{23} M_{23} b_{23} t_{23} L_{23}	M_{33} c_{33} A_{cd3} t_{33} p_{33} A_{I3} L_{33} A_{H3} b_{33} A_{pd3}	c_{43} S_{43} p_{43} R_{43} b_{43} T_{43}	c_{53} D_{53} p_{53} T_{53}	N_{63} F_{63} b_{63} t_{63}
[4]	M_{14} b_{14} C_{14}	b_{24} L_{24} M_{24}	c_{34} M_{34} p_{34} L_{34}	c_{44} b_{44} p_{44} S_{44} T_{44}	D_{54} p_{54} T_{54} c_{54}	N_{64} F_{64} b_{64}
[5]	B_{15} b_{15} M_{15} C_{15}	B_{25} M_{25} b_{25} L_{25}	B_{35} L_{35} c_{35} M_{35} p_{35}	B_{45} b_{45} c_{45} S_{45} p_{45}	B_{55} c_{55} T_{55} p_{55} D_{55}	c_{65} b_{65} N_{65} F_{65} D_{65}
[6]	t_{16} M_{16} b_{16}	t_{26} M_{26} b_{26}	t_{36} M_{36} c_{36} b_{36} p_{36}	c_{46} b_{46} p_{46} T_{46}	D_{56} T_{56} b_{56}	b_{66} A_{cd6} N_{66} A_{pd6} F_{66} A_{I6} A_{L6} D_{66} A_{M6} A_{H6}

TABLE III-I

The letter symbols are as follows:

M = mortgages; L = non-bank loans; b = bonds and notes
E = equity; c = common stock; p = preferred stock
D = demand deposits; T = time deposits; R = life insurance reserves
S = retirement funds, equities in mutual funds, and other claims against Sector 4 other than time (inc. savings) deposits.
N = treasury currency; F = federal reserve notes; t = trade credit
C = consumer credit; B = bank loans.
A_H, A_{pd}, A_{cd}, A_L, A_I, and A_M are physical assets: structures, producer durables, consumer durables, land, inventories, and monetary metals.

physical as well as financial assets are included. For the time being, think of financial assets as being those things which have value because they commit others to pay over valuable consideration. Include fiat paper money among financial assets. Physical assets might be thought of as those things, capable of ownership, which have intrinsic value. The numerical subscripts indicate who owes whom. Thus E_{21} gives the equity interest of households in non-incorporated enterprises. D_{53} = demand deposits held by non-financial corporations. M_{21} = mortgages of unincorporated business held by households. M_{12} = mortgages of households held by unincorporated business. t_{33} = trade credit extended by non-financial corporations to other non-financial corporations.

Notice that physical asset holdings are obtained by tracing down the matrix's diagonal. Unlike financial assets, all of which can in some sense be considered to represent debts, physical assets are identified by a single numerical subscript. The value to the owner of a physical asset derives from rights, privileges, powers, and immunities against society generally rather than from the obligation of some particular person.

2

A few comments about treatment of a number of items in Table I are in order. "Unincorporated Businesses" are treated as legal persons, contrary to the law. The net worth of Sector 2 is attributed back to other sectors, particularly households and non-financial corporations. *"b"* and *"L"* are distinguished by different degrees of formality, *"L,"* of course, being the more informal. "C" deals with paper generated by deficit household expenditure units purchasing consumer durables. Direct obligations to banks, "B," are distinguished. At the same time, b_{36}, for example, makes clear that banks might purchase paper as well as make direct loans. The central banking sector, implicitly in the United States, is placed within the government sector, Sector 6. c_{65} reflects the fact that member banks own stock in the Federal Reserve banks. D_{66} reflects U. S. government demand deposits with the Federal Reserve. b_{66} reflects holdings of U. S. debt by the Federal Reserve and by agencies of the United States. (State and local government is ignored in Table 1, or alternatively can be viewed as combined in Sector 6.) How might t_{16}, trade credit outstanding from the government to households, arise? Remember that governments engage in much ordinary business. Consider a resident of Tennessee who has not paid his electricity bill. Once you have the numerical subscript notation straight, you might even be entertained by deriving some of the more arcane elements of the matrix, and you surely will be able to contribute new items.

A useful hint for easier reading of Table I can be offered to baseball fans. Recall the form used by the New York *Times* and New

HOUSEHOLDS BALANCE SHEET

(December 31, 1958)

Assets		Liabilities	
Equity in unincorporated bus.	78.8	Mortgages	101.0
Common stock	327.2	Consumer credit	45.6
Time dep. and shares, non-bank	74.8	Other	23.9
Life insurance reserves	99.8		
Retirement funds	86.9		
Demand deposits and currency	53.2		
Time deposits, banks	65.8		
Government securities	75.7		
Other financial assets	88.3		
Residential structures	346.8		
Consumer durables	180.0		
Other physical assets	120.4	Net Worth	1427.2
	1597.7		1597.7

NON-FINANCIAL CORPORATE BUSINESS

(December 31, 1958)

Assets		Liabilities	
Trade credit	81.6	Bank loans	24.7
Demand deposits and currency	33.4	Bonds and notes	66.9
Government securities	18.4	Preferred stock	18.2
Other financial assets	94.0	Other liabilities	142.4
Structures	202.0	Common stock	445.4
Producer durables	145.6		
Other physical assets	122.6		
	697.6		697.6

TABLE III-II

York *Herald Tribune* for exhibiting won-and-lost records. If the Yankees were Team 1, [1]-[1] would have no interpretation; the items [1]-[1] in Table I would have to be viewed as the number of intra-squad games played. The second element in the first row would give Yankee wins over Team 2. The total number of Yankee wins is obtained by summing across the first row. Similarly the square [2]-[1] gives Yankee losses to Team 2. The total number of Yankee losses — if any — is obtained by summing down the first column. Similarly, the sum of the elements of the last five squares of the first column gives household liabilities to other sectors of the economy. And, just as there is a loser for every winner in a ball game, so there is a debtor for every creditor. The aggregate algebraic value of financial assets (liabilities) in a closed system must be zero. The theme is pursued later in the chapter.

Table III gives values (in billions of dollars) for selected items of Table I for the United States as of December 31, 1958. It is based on unpublished computations of Franco Modigliani. Meanwhile, Table II gives simplified, unconsolidated balance sheets for Sectors 1 and 3,

PORTIONS OF THE CLAIMS MATRIX

	[1]	[2]	[3]	[4]	[5]	[6]
[1]	$A_{H1} = 346.8$ $A_{cd1} = 180.0$	$E_{21} = 78.8$	$c_{31} = 327.2$ $b_{31} = 13.6$	$T_{41} = 74.8$ $R_{41} = 99.8$	$D_{51} = 53.2$ $T_{51} = 65.8$	$b_{61} = 75.7$
[2]	$C_{12} = 5.1$	$A_{pd2} = 26.9$	$t_{32} = 67.2$		$D_{52} = 15.0$	$b_{62} = 5.8$
[3]	$C_{13} = 7.5$	$t_{23} = 14.4$	$A_{H3} = 202$	$T_{43} = 1.6$	$D_{53} = 33.4$	$b_{63} = 18.4$
[4]	$M_{14} = 76.3$ $C_{14} = 17.2$	$M_{24} = 13.0$	$b_{34} = 64.4$ $c_{34} = 38.1$		$D_{54} = 9.1$	$b_{64} = 36.7$
[5]	$M_{15} = 18.6$ $B_{15} = 15.8$	$B_{25} = 13.7$	$B_{35} = 24.7$	$B_{45} = 6.2$		$b_{65} = 67.0$
[6]			tax liability $= 20.0$	$T_{46} = 3.9$	$D_{56} = 4.9$	$A_{H6} = 168.2$

Note: items D_{51}, D_{52}, D_{53}, and D_{54} include currency.

TABLE III-III

household and non-financial corporate business. Balance sheets for financial sectors are provided elsewhere in Chapters III and IV.

Note the huge outstanding debt of business enterprises to other sectors of the system: items b_{31}, b_{34}, and B_{35} alone total more than 100 billion dollars. These debts reflect a history of deficit finance: shortfalls of cash receipts against cash expenditure have been accommodated by securities sales. And there is another interpretation of these data: they describe the way in which firms have become *levered.* Firms have chosen to increase their holdings of physical assets much more substantially than would be permitted by their earnings; they have induced the public (ignoring expansion of the commercial banking sector through an expanding monetary base) to devote their savings to securities; proceeds of securities sales have been diverted into accumulation of physical capital.[2] Needless to say, the scale of debt much exceeds that of currency and demand deposits: the stock of means of payment is dwarfed by that of debt instruments generally. This implies that widespread efforts to reduce financial assets to money — to liquidate debt — are doomed, and that, indeed, they harbor liquidity crises. Of course, aggregated statistics hide the process: billions of dollars worth of loans are repaid each year by firms in cash surplus, creating the wherewithal for additional loans to deficit firms.

B. FINANCIAL ASSETS

1

Consider a complete matrix of the form of Table 1 for a *closed* system (one excluding foreign lenders and borrowers). What would be your offer price for the "concern"? How would you — an outsider or the Great Engineer contemplating the scene from on high — treat such items as government bonds, cash values of life insurance policies, demand deposits, etc., in making up your offer? After all, the book value of financial assets is measured in hundreds of billions of dollars! Or should I have said, "the book value of financial *liabilities* is meas-

[2] Of course, securities might be issued to offset losses. Furthermore, some of the physical investment necessarily has proved to be worthless. Incidentally, this is easier to determine in a capitalist country than in a country in which there are no markets for physical capital.

ured in hundreds of billions of dollars!"[3] Is this to say that financial assets make no contribution to welfare? No, indeed not! All I have said thus far is that I could recreate the matrix of claims costlessly. This reasoning clearly is inapplicable to American physical assets.

The crux is in these words: it is the EXISTENCE of financial assets that permits their contribution to economic welfare; their quantity (in truth, nominal value) is, at least in a *de novo* sense, immaterial. Certainly no such statement could be made of plant and equipment.

Along these lines, consider the economics of automobiles and books. There is the pleasure and convenience of driving or contemplating an automobile, or from long evenings perusing a book. But automobiles and books might be — and in a sense are — stores of value. Thus a professor, a tweedy Silas Marner, might have put his life savings into books that neither he nor anyone else ever reads. Say that the 5,000 volume library is valued at $20,000. Now assume that there occurs a singular holocaust: books are destroyed in wholesale lots but other things are left untouched; he is left with but one book, now worth $20,000; all other prices are unchanged. From the professor's viewpoint, if his book were divisible and the market priced snippets pro-rata, his wealth would be the same as before the holocaust. Indeed he might be ahead: storage space is released.

The analogy to financial assets is obvious. Assume that the value of demand deposits — taken here to be the only medium of exchange — is cut from $x to $0.1x billion, and that nominal values of all other financial and physical assets, income streams, and prices are reduced in the same proportion. In fact, assume that debt is scaled down so that there are no redistributive effects among creditors and debtors. No meaningful change will have occurred in a society without money

[3] Coin, fiat currency, and monetary metals without value in alternative uses are best treated as financial assets in a *closed* system (fiat currency in any system). These items are useful because they confer liquid command over resources; their nominal values, not their real quantity, is what counts.

Equities in non-incorporated businesses and common stock are financial assets in that they have value because of their owners' claims against firms' assets. Since we treat all firms as legal persons, equities and common stock have the logical attributes of debt instruments; their value is directly associated with the weight of their burden on the firm.

Be sure to remember that *for the individual* financial wealth is just as important as physical wealth and surely is convertible into physical wealth. When dealing with government debt, almost all writers treat its value as a *net* plus for the non-government sectors of the economy. This is emphasized by the fact that governments use different criteria than do individuals in making economic decisions.

illusion: ratios of cash to various values are the same all around; probabilities of inability to meet tomorrow's cash demands are unchanged. *Real* values of stocks and flows would be unchanged, despite the 90 per cent deflation in *nominal* values. The real value of new indebtedness and of physical capital and that of the *stock* of cash *flowing* through the system would be unaffected by the deflation. If the transition could be managed effortlessly — *an impossible task* — the system's real performance would be unaffected. There is then a basic distinction between financial and non-financial functions of assets: the former can be performed by a miniscule stock if prices are low enough; the latter are better or more happily performed by larger physical quantities.

2

Agreeing that financial assets can perform socially useful functions without its being necessary to devote scarce resources to their manufacture, it is time to analyse these in greater detail. Broadly, as Modigliani points out, financial assets permit economic units to assume desired degrees of risk. Among other things, wealth holders without entrepreneur skills, or risk-taking propensities, can invest in residual rights. Entrepreneurs without "much" wealth can become levered. An infinite variety of combinations of expected yield and risk can be achieved if financial assets are available. It becomes immediately apparent that cash need not perform many of these functions very well. It can lead to corner solutions or be otherwise inappropriate. Indeed, many writers are moved to emphasize the role of currency and demand deposits as media of exchange (means of payment), minimizing their importance as stores of value.[4]

There has come to be a traditional trichotomization of motives for holding *liquid* assets (not all financial assets are liquid; *cf. infra.*) owing to Keynes: transactions, precautionary, and speculative motives. A task of Ch. III is briefly to compare cash with other assets as means of satisfying these traditional motives. The main effort along these lines is in Ch. VII where utility-theoretic foundations are laid.

Liquid alternatives to cash, as well as much cash itself, have been

[4] W. T. Newlyn considers five characteristics of financial assets: transactions costs of acquisition; marketability; money value certainty; income certainty; real value certainty. [*Cf.* W. T. Newlyn, *Theory of Money* (London: Oxford University Press, 1962), p. 51 *ff*. A valuable book.] I discuss these characteristics at some length in Appendix A to Ch. VA and in Ch. VII.

secreted by *financial institutions,* thus far neglected. Institutions *mediating* between debtors and creditors, some able to create means of payment, almost all affecting monetary velocity, are at the center of things. So is the word *liquidity.* Recall that liquidity is a property of an asset portfolio enabling the holder readily and cheaply to convert into other assets without fear of loss of value (measured in money of account). Financial institutions have provided liquid assets to firms and households at the expense of their own liquidity — *by ordinary standards.* Certainly they have greatly increased the marketability of debt instruments and have resulted in there being large amounts of assets readily able to substitute for currency and demand deposits (which first substituted for currency) in roles the latter might play, other than as means of payment. (*Cf. infra.* for discussion of how cash can be substituted for in transactions balances.)

Turn now to alternative means of satisfying traditional motives for holding liquid assets. Clearly there are collections of assets *almost* as liquid as a mattressful of currency or a checking deposit with a commercial bank. Consider a man whose assets consist of a life insurance policy with a cash value of $3,000, a $5,000 account with Talman Federal (a savings and loan association), and $2,000 in U. S. Government Series E savings bonds. Apparently a blameless, sober fellow, he can be just as sure as his brother who sleeps on a lumpy mattress that the nominal value of his assets will be the same tomorrow, and tomorrow, and tomorrow. Certain distinctions between our man's portfolio and one comprised of $10,000 in cash are striking: the former earns interest and is not *immediately* available as a means of payment; the latter does not earn interest and is immediately available as a means of payment.

Ready, but not instantaneous, convertibility. There is the rub. Insofar as it is ordinarily necessary to make cash payments from day to day — certainly from hour to hour — or to be prepared instantaneously to meet unexpected cash demands, the cash portfolio is the more useful. It is better able to satisfy *transactions motives* for holding financial assets. (*See Note A.*)

Keynes defines the *precautionary motive* for holding liquid assets as "the desire for security as to the future cash equivalent of a certain proportion of total resources." (*General Theory,* p. 170.) (Of course, if one wished to assure his future money income, short-term assets, let alone cash, would ill serve him. And clearly cash has done miserably as a store of assured *real* value.) In assuring the nominal value of one's portfolio, surely one need not hold his entire financial asset portfolio in cash in order to be certain of the future cash equivalent of his resources: he could obtain all the protection he wanted against fluctuation in market values by investing in interest-bearing deposits.

Speculative motives for holding assets are examined in Ch. VII. Briefly, if one expects *some* price to fall, he has reason to sell holdings of that good (perhaps a fixed income security). Suffice it to say that the decision whether to invest the proceeds in cash, time deposits, or bills depends on transactions costs, the length of time before one plans to re-enter the market, etc. It is unlikely that speculative motives for holding *cash* account for substantial cash holdings, at least when time-deposit rate is not miniscule.

3

It follows that liquidity properties of financial assets (including government securities) have caused cash to be much less important than one might suppose. The literature stresses the way in which other financial assets have substituted for cash.[5] Perhaps it has not enough stressed that so much substitution may already have taken place (especially since interest has not been paid on demand deposits) that marginal substitutability may be less substantial than is supposed. (*See Note B.*) Still, data show considerable fluctuation in monetary velocities. A crude illustration might be profitable.

Consider the sale of $100 million in 30-year debentures (unsecured bonds) by General Motors. Presumably GM raised the funds in order to finance expenditures — although firms sometimes borrow in order to increase cash balances. Once the $100 million has been spent, the public's cash will be the same as before the transaction occurred. However, GM debentures, although not of assured nominal value until close to maturity, are liquid assets; it can be assumed that their issue leads to less aggregate demand for cash, *ceteris paribus*.[6] Arbitrarily assign the value $20 million to reduced public demand for cash. Of course, there will be a partial offset because of GM's increased cash requirements for service and eventual repayment of principal. Assume that the interest service is $5 million per annum, payable on December

[5] *Cf.* R. N. McKean. "Liquidity and a National Balance Sheet," *Journal of Political Economy*, Vol. 57, p. 406 *ff*. Reprinted in Lutz and Mints (eds.), *Readings in Monetary Theory* (Homewood, Ill.: Richard D. Irwin, Inc., 1951), p. 63 *ff*.

[6] The argument is heuristic at best. Strictly, a parametric change should be specified.

31, and that GM simply accumulates cash at a steady rate throughout the year anticipating the year-end obligation, an outlandish assumption permitting an *a fortiori* argument. There will be on this account an increase in GM's average pool of cash of $2.5 million, leaving an "average excess supply of cash" for the system of $17.5 million (ignoring amortization and the liquidity of assets GM might purchase with debenture proceeds). Amortization does not ordinarily find the debtor accumulating cash until very near the due date. Instead, securities are purchased, always supposing that GM does not plan to refloat the issue on its maturity. When GM repays, it will sell securities from its portfolio to other firms building up amortization funds. Cash will flow serenely through the GM conduit to GM creditors who (crudely speaking) will reinvest in new issues. Practically no pools of cash need accumulate in the process. The over-all picture is one of substitution for cash by debt instruments accompanied by much lower increments of cash requirement for debt service.[7] It easily accommodates steady growth of *all* financial assets and explains how the growth of non-monetary assets can accommodate much of increasing demand for liquidity.

4

We almost are prepared to zero in on the peculiar role of financial institutions in the growth of the modern structure of financial assets. You may have noticed, that *in the ordinary course of events,* the more liquid is a claim, the more cash the prudent debtor will have to hold against his debt (the creditor's claim). Consider this illustration: I issue a note, payable in 30 days, for $20,000 and turn it over to the builder of my new house. I have thereby created a highly liquid claim — my note. However, an incomplete, or even a complete, house is not a liquid asset. I now must maintain a substantially higher balance of cash and short-term assets in order to be able to redeem my paper if it cannot be renewed. And then there are many aspects of the drawings from Nature's Urn comprising Life that are out of my control: I cannot take advantage of the Law of Large Numbers. The relative dispersion of my financial status about its expected value is very large compared with that of a building society.

[7] If demand deposits bore interest, the substitutional relationship between cash (*sans* currency) and other assets would be more apparent. But there is plenty of evidence that over-all demand for cash responds to changes in opportunity costs. One need not concentrate on motivations for holding cash once the over-all relationship is established. *Cf.* Ch. VII *infra.* and Note B, Ch. III.

Indeed it becomes clear that ordinary individuals cannot seriously consider acquiring substantial volumes of short-dated liability unless their assets are of similarly short maturity. Furthermore, if we had to depend on individuals to take up savings, issuing back short-dated deposit certificates and purchasing securities of long or short maturity, the financial system would be shaky. Either there would be large premiums charged by risk-avoiding financial middlemen or frequent financial crises as risk-preferring middlemen failed from time to time.

C. FINANCIAL INSTITUTIONS, BANK AND NON-BANK

1

The logical chain can be broken through the *mediation of financial institutions.* Study of financial institutions is begun by taking up the generation and function of the paper of certain non-banking financial intermediaries. Commercial banks will make an appearance soon enough.

Resorting again to the homebuilding case, instead of borrowing $20,000 from my contractor or some other individual, I could borrow $20,000 from Talman Federal who in turn acquired the funds through the "savings deposits" (savings capital) of various depositors, taken to be savers for the nonce. Talman will take from me a long-term mortgage; my liquidity will be little strained. Furthermore, as interest and principal on mortgages is repaid, Talman can relend to new homebuilders; the process generates a stock of mortgage paper, growing over time and continually turning over. Throughout, strain on the cash of mortgagors will be slight.

Meanwhile Talman depositors own claims that, aside from being unusable as means of payment, are almost ideally money-like. Potential strain on cash has been shifted to Talman. But Talman will carry reserves that are exceedingly low compared to its deposit liability. It can rely on the Law of Large Numbers to pacify the natural turbulence of Nature's Urn.

The same reasoning applies to insurance companies. Their cash holdings are tiny compared to cash values of issued policies. Mutual savings banks tell the same story all the more forcefully. We find financial institutions' liabilities convertible into legal tender (into demand deposits as a matter of practice for institutions other than commercial banks) on shorter terms than assets. Financial institutions specialize in accepting what would be dangerously illiquid portfolios for others — creating very quick liabilities of their own. These liabilities are, for others, highly liquid assets.[8]

2

We shortly shall be able to take up the mechanics of non-banking financial institutions. Commercial banks are exhaustively treated in Ch. IV. However, a few tasks must be accomplished in the meanwhile. Specifically:

a) Professors Gurley and Shaw's exposition of the logic of financial mediation;

b) a brief contrast of the logical principles of banking and non-banking financial intermediaries;

c) some statistics of the importance of financial mediation; also statistics concerning the relative growth of banking and non-banking financial institutions;

d) implications of the importance of non-banking financial institutions for the effectiveness of conventional monetary policy;

e) a digression from the non-parametric nature of money stocks and liquidity from the *micro* viewpoint.

3

Financial (inter)mediation channels some of the community's savings — to take up the simplest case — into intermediaries' *indirect securities.* Gurley and Shaw define indirect securities as "obligations of financial intermediaries, including currency, demand deposits, savings deposits and shares, policy reserves, and similar claims."[9] Savers might not wish to touch *primary securities* with a barge pole: "obligations of nonfinancial spending units including government securities, corporate bonds and stocks, mortgages, and various short-term and

8 *Cf.* R. N. McKean, *loc. cit.,* Note J, pp. 74-75.

9 John G. Gurley and Edward S. Shaw, *Money in a Theory of Finance* (Washington: Brookings Institution, 1960), p. 363.

intermediate-term debt."[10] The institutions can acquire primary securities, and are faced with a relatively less risky prospect (due to the Law of Large Numbers). The process reduces risk premiums demanded by lenders in a risk-avoiding society and would seem to encourage savings plans in any society, as well as to reduce demand for money, *ceteris paribus.*

4

Commercial banks are dramatically important in our society: they provide the larger portion of our means of payment. Needless to say, indirect exchange enormously augments liquidity of assets, along with economic efficiency. A business firm without access to media of exchange would be in sad shape: it would be stuck with its existing collection of assets unless willing to pay the huge transactions costs of indirect exchange; in its very nature, a firm must continually transform its assets from raw material to finished product to inventory to cash to raw material, etc. Accordingly, firms become willing to pay substantial sums for the right to own bank deposits, even if offset by bank claims against them.

The commercial banking *system* makes payments almost without reserve loss. Consequently, there is an important difference between expansion processes of commercial banking and other financial systems. A $1 increment in reserves of the commercial banking system permits approximately a $6 expansion in the system's equilibrium loans and investments through a process in which *systematic* leakage is quite small. However, equilibrium levels of building society deposits are attained through cumulative net receipts of savings capital, almost all of which leaves the *system* soon after it comes in. (*Cf.* footnote 21, Ch. IV.)

It follows that, historically, development of the two systems (separating out savings departments of commercial banks) was very different. One expanded multiplicatively on its reserve base; the other simply transmitted flows from surplus to deficit spending units. The one built up the means of payments, the other built up a highly liquid store of wealth. Yet in equilibrium the functioning of the two systems is little different. Neither can contribute to the stream of loanable funds unless some spending unit either is in cash surplus on current account or wishes to run down its cash balance. Indeed a "pure de-

[10] *Ibid.*, p. 364.

mand deposit" commercial banking system is stripped of all possibilities of creation of new claims if it is up against its reserve constraint and confronted with a stony faced central bank — save for cash being removed from mattresses. On the other hand, the absence of reserve requirements (at the central bank) for institutional time deposits permits non-banking institutions to create new liquid assets in the course of their mediation. Needless to say, the balance sheets of the two financial systems are strikingly similar.

5

Financial institutions are of obvious importance to the American economy. Consider these statistics for December 1959 (based on the *Economic Report of the President* (Washington: Government Printing Office, 1961) and the Federal Reserve *Bulletin*, June 1961):

1) the money supply was $144.9 billion, including $115.5 billion in demand deposits. Time deposits at member banks were $53.7 billion.

2) loans and investments of commercial banks totalled $190.3 billion, including $58.9 billion in government securities.

3) net federal debt totalled $243.2 billion, that of state and local governments, $55.5 billion — these being *primary* securities of course.

4) total assets of life insurance companies were $113.65 billion while cash assets could not have exceeded $4.9 billion (the total of "other assets"). Life insurance companies held $45.105 billion in securities of business firms and $39.197 billion in mortgages.

5) savings and loan associations held $53.194 billion in mortgages, owed approximately $54 billion to depositors and held $2.183 billion in cash. (Membership in the Federal Home Loan Bank System requires maintenance of a minimum of 6 per cent of total assets in cash and U. S. securities.)

6) Mutual savings held almost $25 billion in mortgages, had deposit liabilities of about $35 billion and held $0.829 billion in cash.

There has been a considerable and heated controversy in recent years about the trend in the importance of commercial banks among financial institutions. We prove not to be deeply concerned: commercial banks are, in any and all cases, important enough for pressures against them to have profound effects on the economy. (*Cf.* the next subsection.) In any event, Table III-IV suggests what has been going on:

ASSETS OF COMMERCIAL BANKS AND OTHER PRIVATE FINANCIAL INSTITUTIONS

Year	Commercial bank assets as per cent of assets of private financial institutions (including banks of all kinds, insurance companies, pension funds, *et. al.*)
1900	52.8
1912	53.6
1922	51.6
1929	41.4
1933	37.3
1939	39.9
1945	53.5
1949	46.3
1952	44.5

TABLE III-IV

Source: Raymond E. Goldsmith, *Financial Intermediaries in the American Economy since 1900* (Princeton: Princeton University Press, 1958) through Joseph Aschheim, *Techniques of Monetary Control* (Baltimore: The Johns Hopkins Press, 1961), p. 114.

And:

> ". . . by the end of 1959 commercial banks held 41 per cent of the deposit type savings held by financial institutions. In 1945 they held 57 per cent of such savings . . . Savings and other time deposits in commercial banks increased by 119 per cent between 1945 and 1959. But savings in savings and loan associations rose by 638 per cent . . . Because of tax and regulatory inequalities, including the ceiling upon interest rates that they may pay . . . the commercial banks found themselves under a severe handicap in competing for deposit-type savings during the post-war era."[11]

Aschheim points out that, ". . . had the growth of time deposits [in commercial banks] kept pace with that of demand deposits . . . the share of commercial bank assets [would by 1952 have increased] to 55.8 per cent of the assets of all private financial institutions, a higher share than in 1900! Thus the smallness of the over-all growth of commercial banks relative to other private financial institutions since 1929 is due to the relative decline of their time-deposit business. And it is in this type of business that commercial banks are akin to other financial institutions."[12]

As of January 1, 1962, commercial banks in the Federal Reserve

[11] Jules I. Bogen, *The Changing Composition of Bank Assets* (New York: New York University, 1961), p. 11.

[12] *Op. cit.*, pp. 115-116.

system were allowed to pay as much as 4 (instead of 3) per cent per annum on various time deposits held for one year or more.[13] As a result of this amendment to Federal Reserve Regulation Q, or so it would seem (keeping in mind that *aggregate* time deposits have increased above their trend), commercial bank time deposits increased markedly. More importantly, the *relative* share of commercial banks' time deposits increased. Consult this little table:

TIME DEPOSITS

(billions of dollars)

	Commercial Banks	Mutual Savings Banks
March 29, 1961	74.2	37.0
March 28, 1962	87.7	39.0

TABLE III-V

6

The importance of the paper of non-banking financial institutions has been so striking that some have become skeptical of prospects for effective monetary control on this ground alone. Witness this snippet from the Radcliffe *Report*:

> ". . . the factor which monetary policy should seek to influence or control is something that reaches beyond what is known as the "supply of money." It is nothing less than the state of liquidity of the whole economy . . . We have found it impossible to treat any one group of institutions as exclusively important in this connection."[14]

[13] The very fact that some institutions need not hold central bank deposits as reserves against time deposits means that the sum of demand and time deposits can increase without the sum of high-powered money increasing, quite aside from differential reserve requirements on demand and time deposits. Of course, as S and L associations increase their time-deposit liability, the stock of idle demand deposits will slightly increase on this account.

Note that, if the banking system obtains more time-deposit business, it must reduce its demand-deposit obligation if it cannot increase its reserves; commercial banks hold reserves against time deposits in the form of high-powered money. If S and L Associations and Mutual Savings Banks were eliminated and commercial bank reserves unchanged, the sum of demand and time deposits would have to fall very substantially. Individual commercial bankers see the consequences of demise of the associations in a brilliant light: they see themselves obtaining new primary deposits; the light cast by a systematic view is heavily filtered.

[14] Committee on the Working of the Monetary System, *Report* (London: HMSO, 1959), p. 357. The Committee, chaired by Lord Radcliffe, was appointed in May 1957 "to inquire into the working of the monetary and credit system." See also its three volumes of written submissions and one volume of oral evidence.

It drags a red herring across the trail: whereas the true issue concerns the speed and magnitude of potential "countervailing" *changes* in non-bank credit, the Radcliffe *Report* repeatedly stresses the magnitude of initial *stocks* of non-bank credit and its secular growth rate. Thus, consider the impact of pressure brought against commercial banks (implicitly confined to demand deposits), requiring them promptly to reduce their deposit liability by $x billion, perhaps a very large amount. Some of the public will be forced, others induced, to direct cash flows to the banks. Can non-banking financial institutions importantly mitigate the effects of official policy in a way *peculiar unto themselves?* No. Certainly, some non-banking institutions can "sell" interest-bearing deposits. Needless to say, if demand depositors can be induced to accept institutional interest-bearing deposits, the institutions will be able to purchase bank held securities. The public will hold non-bank time deposits instead of demand deposits; banks will transfer some securities to institutions.[15] The process will augment (or keep intact) the stream of loanable funds (sometimes called finance). BUT in order to buy primary securities, the institutions must sell demand deposits; they cannot sustain the stream of loanable funds unless either they acquire additional demand deposits from the public or disgorge some of their own small holdings. Demand, not time, deposits are means of payment.[16]

15 What of possible initial "excess reserves" of intermediaries? (If officials sold securities in the open market, however, intermediaries' reserves would be reduced to the extent that time deposits were cashed in order to buy Governments.) To the extent that they begin with excess reserves, intermediaries (institutions) might be able to make "barter" exchanges of new time deposits for primary securities. The new time depositors might then be able to release demand deposits to deficit spending units. This accomplishes indirectly what is in the text direct: demand deposits are exchanged for time deposits; institutionally acquired demand deposits are then exchanged for primary securities of deficit spending units. (In contrast with footnote 16, footnote 15 assumes that only demand deposits of commercial banks are means of payment.)

16 Radcliffe School men drag out another red herring when they stress possibilities of interest-bearing deposits at institutions becoming subject to check and serving as means of payment (sometimes citing exotic cases from current practice). Let us assume that this happens, that a portion of the sector issuing means of payment operates on a *laissez-faire* principle. True, there would be sinister potential for substantial increases in credit to feed booms (and for later drastic contractions to induce crises); wildcat banking is notoriously unstable. But surely Professor Sayers *et al.* do not have this wild fantasy in mind. It is more likely that the Radcliffe School confuses increases in *average* levels with *countervailing* increases in hypothetical non-bank means of payment. Surely countervailing increases in non-bank means of payment would require corresponding increases in reserves of non-banking financial institutions. We come a full circle. . . . Still I do not deny that, if time deposits were widely used as means of payment, conventional controls would be harder to enforce.

Of course, there are important potential countervailing forces—pertaining, as it happens, more to impact than equilibrium. These forces are unrelated to *essential* properties of non-banking financial intermediaries. Commercial banks and others might find it easy to exchange securities with demand depositors with slack balances by offering favorable prices (and therefore higher interest rates). Portfolio managers might be highly sensitive to asset prices. If reinforcements arrived in time, advances could be maintained to firms and households. Possibly they would not plan to reduce their borrowing despite the rise in interest rates: there can be large increases in monetary velocities of circulation with little change either in interest rates or transactions matrixes.[17]

The institutions tend to increase average velocity, but it is not at all clear that they make it harder for the authorities to affect the bond market, or that they increase the cyclical volatility of velocity.[18] Finally, it is easy to show that intermediaries (institutions) cannot prevent the central bank from affecting yields: it simply can announce its willingness to buy and sell securities in unlimited quantities at announced rates. The effects of higher interest rates can be achieved despite anything intermediaries can do. The upshot cannot be entirely clear until Ch. VA: intermediaries can impede the central bank's policy only to the extent that they facilitate the mobilization of alternatives to bank finance; they cannot affect the cost of credit if the authorities are firm.

7

So long as we have digressed to some considerations of monetary policy, let us distinguish changes in securities prices from changes in the supply of money or "liquidity" as these appear to the individual. Taking an analogous case, assume that the supply of arable land in Country Z is halved. There will be a substantial increase in land values *and* total land holdings will be halved. But, for the individual, the key thing will be that land is more expensive. If he

17 If spending units are sufficiently insensitive to interest rates, increases in monetary velocity could overwhelm monetary restraint if new credit arteries could be established in time. (*Cf.* Ch. VA.) Such arteries are not likely to be established in time unless portfolio managers are sensitive to interest rates in their cash holding policies and respond promptly.

18 Increased availability of monetary substitutes generally leads to increased elasticities of substitution, requiring larger operations for given (transitional) effects on interest rates.

wishes, he can hold more land than before the catastrophe if his wealth permits. He chooses not to do so because land has become expensive: for the individual, the price of land is a *parameter;* it rations the supply so that individuals *choose* to hold no more land than is available.

From the standpoint of policy makers, it is perfectly appropriate to take the quantity of land as a parameter; formally, it might be possible arbitrarily to fix the price of land.

The case of money and bonds is a bit harder because the assumption of market clearance — absence of a "fringe of unsatisfied borrowers" — usually is not justified. If market clearance can be assumed, a change in the supply of money would lead to price changes — including bond price changes — so that individuals finally would become satisfied to hold the new quantity of money: for the individual, only prices would be parametric. The nightmare for monetary authorities is the possibility that these price changes will have little effect on non-financial markets.

D. MECHANICS

1

We have discussed in some detail the main properties of financial paper and financial institutions, together with implications for monetary theory and policy, but we have neglected mechanics. We proceed to repair that neglect, omitting the ordinary business of commercial banking, the subject of Ch. IV.

Steiner, Shapiro, and Solomon give excellent thumbnail sketches of four prominent intermediaries: mutual savings banks, savings departments of commercial banks, savings and loan associations, and life insurance companies:

> "*Mutual savings banks* are non-profit, thrift organizations operated solely for the benefit of depositors under the supervision of state banking departments." [Many savings and loan associations and life insurance companies are mutualized. Mutualization has been abetted by tax advantages.] [19]
>
> "*Commercial banks* entered the *savings business* long after the mutual savings banks . . . Ordinarily there is no complete segregation nor are savings funds segregated from commercial funds." [20]

[19] W. H. Steiner, Eli Shapiro, and Ezra Solomon, *op. cit.*, p. 533.
[20] *Ibid.*, p. 534.

"*Savings and loan associations* (also known as building and loan associations, cooperative banks or homestead associations) . . . accept savings chiefly through the sale of "shares" and reinvest them primarily in amortized first mortgage loans on homes . . . [They] have two classes of accounts. "Savings accounts" permit investment at regular or irregular intervals. "Investment accounts" are full paid in multiples of $100 . . . These accounts are generally withdrawable in practice without notice . . ."[21]

"[*Life Insurance Companies*] . . . [T]he primary purpose of life insurance companies is not investment. However, in the course of their insurance activities they acquire substantial funds which they must invest . . . The accumulated value of the saving element in a policy is represented by the cash-surrender value of the contract . . ."[22]

Consider the mechanics of savings and loan associations in greater detail. Here is a consolidated balance sheet for U. S. savings and loan associations as of the end of 1960.[23] It is in billions of dollars.

Assets		Liabilities	
Mortgages	60.084	Savings capital	62.154
U. S. gov't obl.	4.586	Reserves and undivided profits	4.982
Cash	2.715	Borrowed money	2.191
Other	4.104	Loans in process	1.183
		Other	0.979
Total	71.489	Total	71.489

TABLE III-VI

How did they grow? Consider the genesis of a fictional but representative association, Alpha Savings and Loan, working through some simplified balance sheets. Recall that a balance sheet requires that flight be arrested and the instantaneous condition photographed: all assets and liabilities can be attributed to economic units. But being is becoming. We must show how today's balance sheet came about. And it is most important to understand how savings and loan associations can maintain so low a ratio of cash to quick liabilities and still be unable to contribute massively to *incremental* loanable funds.

Initially depositors put $2 million in Alpha; its only asset was cash. Then:

21 *Ibid.*, p. 536.
22 *Ibid.*, p. 538.
23 Federal Reserve *Bulletin, op. cit.*, p. 687.

1) Alpha acquired $1.5 million in mortgages;
2) Alpha acquired $0.3 million in U. S. securities;
3) depositors withdraw $0.05 million.

The resulting balance sheet (in millions of dollars) was:

Assets		Liabilities	
Mortgages	1.50	Savings capital	1.95
U. S. sec.	0.30		
Cash	0.15		
	1.95		1.95

TABLE III-VII

The conventionally minimum ratio of cash-plus-U. S.-securities to savings capital is 6 per cent. Since 6 per cent of Alpha's deposit liability was but $117 thousand and Alpha's cash alone $150 thousand, its management was operating more conservatively than was common. Of course, an economic crisis leading to the failure of many mortgagors could force Alpha into the arms of the government. On the other hand, the management knew from the beginning that it would sink in the event of a *general* financial collapse — *in the absence of official intervention.* Nevertheless, Alpha's shareholders (not mutualized) put in $550 thousand in cash, crediting a newly created reserve account. After Alpha was in operation long enough, it received $300 thousand in interest payments and paid out $250 thousand in interest to savers. The balance sheet (again in millions of dollars) then read:

Assets		Liabilities	
Mortgages	1.50	Savings capital	1.95
U. S. sec.	0.30	Reserves and undivided profits	0.60
Cash	0.75		
	2.55		2.55

TABLE III-VIII

Alpha would be ridiculously solvent — and highly unprofitable. Cash assets do not earn interest. Accordingly, Alpha's board would listen sympathetically when requested by a contractor to lend $1 million on the security of a first mortgage. But there is a sticking point: Alpha simply would not have $1 million in cash to lend.[24] A deal is swung by borrowing $600 thousand from a commercial bank and then writing a $1 million check against the bank in favor of a contractor (in exchange for his mortgage). Its balance sheet finally reads:

Assets		Liabilities	
Mortgages	2.50	Savings capital	1.95
U. S. obl.	0.30	Reserves and undis. profits	0.60
Cash	0.35	Borrowed money	0.60
	3.15		3.15

TABLE III-IX

Alpha might be asked why it did not sell some of its Governments instead of borrowing from the bank. It might reply — to the intense irritation of economists — that it did not wish to show a loss in its bond portfolio, that it purchased its bonds when the market was stronger. (Economists also would berate Alpha for recording its holdings at cost rather than at market value.) A more soothing reply would be that Alpha expected bond prices to increase in the near future and was willing to bear the running cost of the bank loan in the meanwhile. Furthermore, it desired to maintain "conventional" balance between mortgages and Governments in the portfolio.

Finally, note well that non-banking financial intermediaries convert most cash into non-cash assets as soon as possible, so that equilibrium balance sheets always show a very small ratio of cash to total assets.

SUMMARY

1. Chapter III dealt with a broad spectrum of financial assets, concentrating on claims issued by non-banking financial institutions.

[24] It is assumed for the sake of simplicity that the entire proceeds of lines of credit are turned over to the borrower upon negotiation of the agreement. In real life, the borrower would use up his license to borrow only as he needed cash. If transactions balances typically are held in cash, the latter arrangement permits more rapid circulation: pools of idle cash would be reduced.

2. Financial assets, being claims, *can* be netted out in social accounts for closed systems. However, for many purposes, netting out would be misleading and would not permit explanation of economic behavior; sometimes disaggregation is necessary.
3. The contribution of financial assets to economic welfare is accomplished by their *existence*: if goods and services are assigned low enough nominal values, an arbitrarily small, nominally valued quantum of financial assets could serve as well as could an arbitrarily large quantum if prices were correspondingly higher.
4. Financial institutions specialize in creating highly liquid, basically short-term claims against themselves. In turn the institutions mostly acquire less liquid, longer-term debt instruments. Being specialized, financial institutions can hold small margins of cash against their liabilities. They can rely on the Law of Large Numbers to reduce the turbulence of Nature's Urn.
5. Of course, some financial institutions such as pension trusts issue longer-term claims.
6. Financial institutions other than commercial banks mediate between individuals issuing primary debt and others wishing to commit part of their incomes to savings but preferring the greater certainty of short-term securities. Primary debt usually is issued in order to obtain means of payment, with which to conduct business, build plant and equipment, houses, etc. This is not a complete statement: non-banking intermediaries make loans on the basis of repayments and acquire "savings capital" that is the result of inventory liquidation and other acts which do not lead to saving.
7. Commercial banks up against legal reserve constraints can make new loans and investments only if repaid by surplus spending units. Oddly enough, the ordinary business of commercial banks does not give rise to new liquid assets (on net) once their historical development — featured by multiple expansion on the reserve base — is complete. This is in contrast with the ordinary business of non-banking intermediaries.
8. Securities of non-banking financial intermediaries often are close substitutes for currency and demand deposits other than service as a medium of exchange.
9. The more liquid the financial asset, the more impaired is the liquidity position of the debtor. However, intermediaries untie

the knot through their ability to exploit the Law of Large Numbers.

10. The enormous scope of non-banking financial institutions in the United States and the United Kingdom has led some to argue that attempts to affect financial markets through operations with direct impact only on commercial banks must fail. This argument is incorrect. Non-banking financial intermediaries can *peculiarly* blunt the impact of conventional monetary restraint only to the finite (albeit palpable) extent that they can increase their deposit liability at a rate above their secular growth rate by offering higher rates of interest. This process can be important if the elasticity of substitution between demand and time deposits is high enough: a given reduction in demand-deposit liability will be importantly offset by increased time-deposit liability with interest rates only slightly higher (implicitly abstracting from time-deposit business of commercial banks: *cf.* Ch. VA for a fuller analysis).
11. We discover in Ch. VA that the effects of paragraph 10 are transitional. But then monetary policy largely is concerned with diverting dynamic sequences.
12. The mechanism of monetary policy is based on official manipulation of such *parameters* as central bank holdings of securities, U. S. deposits with member banks, etc. Once a new set of parameters is plugged into the computer, lights flash, gears clang, and out pops a new set of values for such dependent (endogenous) variables as *next period's* price level, bond prices, employment, etc. The nightmare for the friend of monetary policy is the prospect that, after the machine has shivered to a halt, "financial" variables such as bond prices, rates of interest on time deposits, and monetary velocity will have changed substantially (although perhaps transitorily), but that variables such as *next period's* prices, rates of excess demand for commodities, etc. will have changed very little. Chapter III has nothing to say about *ultimate* effects of monetary policy.
13. The mechanics of the individual savings and loan association and the individual commercial bank are similar, as are some systematic aspects. But there is an important systematic difference: a $1 increase in commercial banking reserve soon leads to about a $6 increase in loans and investments. The dynamics of savings and loan association expansionary processes are very different. The latter processes are accompanied by very large leakages.

NOTES

NOTE A: We ultimately come to distinguish between transactions motives based on poor synchronization of receipts and payments and those based on *uncertainties* of payments and receipts. (*Cf.* Ch. VI.) It is clear that one can achieve at least moderate protection against irregularity of cash flows through a portfolio of non-cash liquid assets, that such a portfolio would enable one to meet reasonably deferrable cash demands within the range of his wealth. We can agree that the commercial equivalent to Job's boils can descend upon a non-liquid firm when one bad break follows another. However one need not have a *lot* of cash in order to be liquid. (*Cf. Note B infra.*)

Two further comments: (a) income and transactions velocities of circulation are subject to rather wide variation, although important empirical regularities have been found; (b) it is a matter of fairly recent law that deposits subject to check do not bear interest, nor is there a logically insuperable barrier to the use of other claims as means of payment.

"Velocity" hits upon a sensitive nerve. Sir Dennis Robertson's explanation — adapted from F. Y. Edgeworth — is pleasing:

> "On Derby Day two men, Bob and Joe, invested in a barrel of beer, and set off to Epsom with the intention of selling it retail on the race-course at 6d. a pint, the proceeds to be shared equally between them. On the way Bob, who had one threepenny-bit left in the world, began to feel at great thirst, and drank a pint of the beer, paying Joe 3d as his share of the market price. A little later, Joe yielded to the same desire, and drank a pint of beer, returning the 3d. to Bob. The day was hot, and before long Bob was thirsty again, and so, a little later, was Joe. When they arrived at Epsom, the 3d. was back in Bob's pocket, and each had discharged in full his debts to the other, but the beer was all gone. One single threepenny-bit had performed a volume of transactions which would have required many shillings if the beer had been sold to the public in accordance with the original intention." (Robertson, *Money,* p. 33.)

National income and its component flows (wages, profits, etc.) as well as national product and its component flows (consumption, investment, etc.) are measured in money of account. These data, together with that on vertical integration, the size of the subsistence sector, etc., define the work to be done by the money stock. Depending on institutional arrangements described in Ch. VI and on endogenous variables such as interest rates, varying stocks might be shunted back and forth through the system to do the necessary work, even for given price levels.

It also will be shown in Ch. VI how reduced payments periods, for example, lead to initial excess supply of cash. This excess supply can augment loanable funds, leading to absorption of additional new securities issues. Reduced liquidity preference can lead to a "permanent" increase in "equilibrium" real output through the investment multiplier. Interest rates will be "permanently" lower than before the change in monetary habits. The flow rate of savings as well as of new issues will be augmented.

Once the "vascular structure" of the payments matrix is fully taxed so that there is no excess supply of money, new issues will have to be absorbed by current savings. Asset holders collectively will want to maintain their cash balances. Savers running cash surpluses will be the only source of net demand for new issues.

NOTE B: Increases in non-monetary liquid assets probably led to more substitution against money in the 1920's when demand deposits paid interest — and were more likely to be used to satisfy Keynesian precautionary motives — than in the 1960's when money balances are more likely to concern transactions.

Once demand deposits have been driven into a transactions-balance corner, substitutability with other financial assets can be weak. If I hold money only as a lubricant for transactions, and if I do not enjoy scale economies, my possibilities for further substitution against money might be nil.

Showing proper caution about compartmentalizing motives for holding financial assets — perhaps eschewing these non-operational concepts — one might merely say that empirical work supports the hypothesis that planned holdings of money show some sensitivity to interest rates and that cash and certain other financial assets appear to be gross substitutes (as might be watermelon and roller skates). *Cf.* D. Meiselman, *op. cit.*, Ch. VA.

The text deals with a time span during which liquidity of various securities and their quantities increased. Successive temporary equilibria found portfolio managers increasing their securities holdings. It is plausible that desired cash holdings might be less than they otherwise would have been even if cash were the only means of reducing "transactions risks" and if, say, interest-bearing deposits and cash were perfect substitutes as precautionary balances. The following formulation shows this.

Assume that the typical portfolio manager maximizes, subject to constraints, a criterion function of the form

$$U \equiv U(\pi, y)$$

where π is *expected* receipts from the portfolio and "other business" of the decision maker and y an index number reflecting the portfolio's vulnerability to changes in asset prices. Unspecified constraints permit us to ignore bankruptcy risks. Wealth can be held in the form of non-interest-bearing-deposits subject to cheque and currency (M), interest-bearing deposits (D), and equities (E), all measured in dollars. The initial value of the portfolio is specified; $M + D + E = W°$. Initial prices and yields also are specified.

$$\pi \equiv \pi(D, E, M)$$

M enters because of a stochastic penalty function specifying transactions costs of liquidation of non-monetary assets in order to meet shortfalls of receipts, penalties for late payment, effects on good will, etc. It is permitted to assume that the penalties cannot be much mitigated except through initial money balances.

$$y \equiv y(D{+}M, E)$$

Note that a switch of \$1 from D to M or *vice versa* has no effect on y.

Now if there is a parametric change so that $\partial y/\partial\ (E/W)$ is less for given E/W, initial π can be achieved with y lower. However a substitution effect now operates against M: it is possible to switch from M to E without y increasing as much as before; this effect might lead to M being reduced in the new portfolio; one might choose to be more vulnerable to "shortfall" penalties in order to take advantage of less risky equity possibilities . . . It goes without saying that there will usually be substitution against D in these circumstances.

CHAPTER FOUR

Commercial Banking: Theory, Practice and History

A. ORIGINS, THEORY, TECHNIQUE

1. Some Facts of Banking Life

1

Commercial banking is characterized by demand deposits subject to check.[1] Demand deposits — claims against commercial banks immediately reducible to hand-to-hand currency — comprise the greater part of American media of exchange.

At least until the reforms of this century were enacted, commercial banking was a very risky business. There always has been danger that depositors would try to reduce their ethereal claims — invisible, and comprehensible only in terms of money-of-account[2] — to solid substance: currency or, at one time, gold. Indeed, on December 31, 1960 American commercial banks had adjusted demand deposits[3] of $115.12 billion and time-deposit liability in excess of $70 billion, but aggregate reserves consisted only of $16.72 billion in deposit liability of the Federal Reserve banks together with $3.50 billion in vault cash.

1 The individual bank thinks of itself as *receiving* deposits and thereby being able to purchase securities, including customers' IOU's. It is shown *infra.* that the systematic interpretation of this process largely is one of issue.

2 Deposit claims against banks are, of course, measured in money of account. "$x in deposit liability" means that banks are obligated to provide legal tender of nominal value $x. Commercial banks traditionally also have issued notes.

3 The adjustment finds inter-bank and U. S. government deposits deducted along with cash items in process of collection. We shun the ineffable details.

It surely is not clear to individual bankers that they are doing a juggling act. After all, bankers have bought financial assets — other airy figments — with the claims they issued against themselves. Thus, commercial banks held over $61 billion in U. S. government obligations alone on December 31, 1960. Also more than $7 billion in loans to non-banking financial institutions and over $43 billion in open-market paper . . . Talk of the Rock ot Gibraltar! . . . But wait! . . . These tens of billions of dollars worth of liquid assets would contribute not a whit to bank liquidity if depositors of *all* banks insisted on currency *now!* To whom would a banker sell his liquid assets? Not to his brother banker. His brother in fact would try to unload on him . . . and so on down the line. The sad fact is that banks have put themselves into what might be an impossible fix: they have contracted to deliver merchandise they do not have and cannot get (without help) if their bluff were called.

But we cannot afford to accept lightly the jeopardy of commercial bankers. Their solvency is utterly indispensable; if, in a monetary system, the means of payment suddenly became unacceptable and if a major component of the society's financial wealth — the liabilities of commercial banks — were to disintegrate, there surely would be economic collapse and there easily could be political revolution. It is universally agreed today that, if the banks' bluff were called, the government (including the central bank) would intervene, and replace bank liabilities with crisp currency, not allowing the banks to skirt insolvency. The government would, in the event of a crisis in liquidity, purchase huge quantities of non-monetary claims, supplying its own unexcelled paper or promises to print paper on demand.

There was a time when the government could not survey the domestic scene with the confidence it exhibits today. Before 1934, it could be forced to supply gold to Americans for its maturing liabilities; it, too, was subject to exogenous discipline, however remote. This was one reason why the Federal Reserve authorities did not respond aggressively in the early 1930's when the banking house of cards collapsed. Hindsight, of course, shows that they were wrong.

2

Commercial banking reminds a jejune lawyer of certain problems in the law of conspiracy. And the conspirators would appear to have nerves of steel at that. Yet the individual members of the conspiracy, the commercial bankers, could cry with at least a moiety of justice that their probity is unexcelled in the society (nobody ever challenged their self-righteousness). The fact is that *fallacies of composition* — unjustified reasoning from the parts to the whole — are rife in banking theory. We already have seen that the individual banker is ordinarily swimming in liquidity. Indeed, if the authorities assure the solvency of the system at all times without making any fuss, the individual banker would find our remarks pointless; our problems simply will not arise.

There are in fact two major props for *fractional-reserve banking* as it exists in the United States today: (a) J. S. Mill's *dictum* (repeatedly cited in Ch. II) on the acceptability of paper money so long as *others* will take it; (b) the willingness of the government to come to the rescue if necessary, an earnest being the Federal Deposit Insurance Corporation. Of course, if bankers are to operate under the cloak of the central government's authority in protecting their liquidity, they must accept the rigors of regulation.

Do not be deceived by what we have said, and assume that manipulation of regulatory parameters by the authorities centers on issues of bank solvency. Far from it. Bank solvency is assured by the basic structural arrangements just discussed. The important day-to-day actions of the monetary authorities are governed by judgments about effects on prices, interest rates, employment, etc. Central banking study belongs much more to income theory than it does to regulation of industry — at least in modern systems.

3

This is a statement of the condition of all commercial banks in the United States as of the end of August 1961. It is in millions of dollars.

Assets		Liabilities and Capital	
Loans	118,450	Demand deposits	128,530
U. S. govt. obl.	64,160	Time deposits	80,540
Other securities	22,510	Interbank deposits	13,800
Cash assets	42,370	Borrowings	1,880
		Capital accounts	21,870
		Statistical discrepancy	870
	247,490		247,490

TABLE IV-I

Source: Federal Reserve *Bulletin* (Board of Governors, Federal Reserve System, Washington: November 1961).

4

Finally it is impossible to convey an impression either of the importance of commercial banks or of the gigantic amount of work done by money in a modern economy without indicating rates of turnover of demand deposits: 60.0 for New York banks; 34.8 for six other leading centers; 25.7 for 337 other reporting centers in 1960.[4] Earlier, Keynes provided impressive statistics for Britain: he estimated non-financial clearings at £46.495 billion in 1929, total non-financial deposits being £1.940 billion in December 1929; his figures imply that the rate of turnover of financial deposits exceeded 100.[5] The annual work done by bank money alone in the United States today is measured in trillions of dollars.[6]

2. Banking's Origins

1

"How did Topsey grow?" A highly stylized account of banking's origins might be a good beginning. Sir Geoffrey Crowther's is good.[7] But, since Crowther's story rather concentrates on English experience, I should like first to apply broader strokes.

Banking, as we know it, essentially developed from 1200 to 1600 in Italy and Spain. It often is said that its origins are in the activities of the money changers of that time. (This assertion is challenged by modern research but admirably serves my purposes.) Money changers found considerable sums — let us say in gold — left in their care. They noted an all important fact:

> On any given day only a fraction of the gold left in them was called for by depositors.

Remember that the procedure was to give what amounted to warehouse receipts for gold deposits. The receipts read:

> I have on deposit $X in gold from Mr. A and promise to return said deposit on demand.

4 *Ibid.*, p. 673. The New York circulation includes a large "financial circulation," featured by very rapid turnover. These are annual rates.

5 J. M. Keynes, *A Treatise on Money,* Vol. II, p. 31 *ff*. Keynes provides his and other calculations for Great Britain and the United States in the 1920's.

6 Since, in full equilibrium, new bank loans are financed by repayments (the revolving fund image), commercial banks also can be viewed as mediating between surplus and deficit spending units.

7 Geoffrey Crowther, *An Outline of Money*, p. 22 *ff*.

These receipts eventually were recognized as negotiable and essentially served as representative money. The money changers, goldsmiths, etc., finding themselves with these deposits, saw a chance to make easy money:

> Why not make loans at interest, issuing certificates in excess of the amount of gold we actually have?[8] If $1,000 in gold is left with me, and if depositors are unlikely to call for their gold at once, *I can make loans*. It is true that my obligations to the public will exceed in nominal value that of the gold reserves available to meet them, but chances are that the depositors will not call for their funds all at once. (Footnote 8 admits that this paragraph is somewhat misleading.)

Thus, the birth of fractional-reserve banking, an institution providing some of the most exciting moments in economic history. The early banks, not unlike the later banks, tended to fail right and left. Laws were passed forbidding banks to make loans, this at the pain of a wretched death. All was unavailing. Banks persisted, and so did lending. One reason was that governments could not resist the temptation to borrow.

And then the taking of interest was considered to violate canon law, but the invisible hand refused to be stilled; in fact evidence exists that monasteries lent at interest. Finally, there were the Jews, permitted to lend at interest — to gentiles — and the financiers of Lombardy, the Lombards — distinguishable from the barbarians of that name to some degree — who lent at interest to all, apparently with a clear conscience.

2

Sir Geoffrey's scholarship much surpasses mine:

> "Having in the first chapter of our story, introduced the hero (or villain — the gradual unfolding of this plot tells which) and described one or two of his actions, we must now give his genealogy and a brief outline of his character.

[8] It would be more accurate to say that the smiths lent out gold that had been entrusted to them. Purposive note issue came quite late.

If we were to draw a parallel — however farfetched — to the modern system, we would specify that the gold thus lent out was redeposited, lent out again, etc. until a "satisfactory" reserve-deposit relationship were achieved. We would note that redeposit of loaned-out gold led to increasing deposit liability of the "system" of smiths. The analogy to modern day processes of cumulative expansion will become obvious: Bank A's cashier's checks (paying for investments) will be *deposited* by customers of Banks B, C, . . .

The present-day banker has three ancestors of particular note. One we have already met: the merchant, whose high and widespread reputation, or credit, enables him to issue documents that will be taken all over the known world as titles to money. To this day the title of 'merchant banker' is reserved . . . to the older, cosmopolitan and more exclusive private banking firms, nearly every one of which can trace its ancestry back to a trader in commodities more tangible (though hardly more profitable) than money.

The banker's two other ancestors are the money-lender and the goldsmith. Lending and borrowing are almost as old as money itself, and the village money-lender is found even in quite primitive communities. He is not usually regarded as a very lovely object; usury is one of the very oldest forms of abuse. But the services he performs are undoubtedly useful and necessary, even though the reward he exacts in return may usually be rapacious . . . The money-lender works, of course, with his own capital. [Voltaire was a rather rapacious usurer who made a great fortune. *Cf.* Harold Nicholson, *The Age of Reason.*] But if there are any other members of the community with money to spare, it will be quite natural for them to entrust it to the money-lender for investment . . . As soon as the money-lender reaches this stage, he is an embryonic banker. He has become a money-borrower as well as a money-lender. At first he may merely lend out his clients' money on commission. But it is obviously both more convenient for his clients and more profitable for him to borrow their money outright, paying interest on it and mingling it with his own capital, and then to lend out the whole lot [at a higher rate] . . .

The goldsmith-ancestry of the modern bank is purely an English affair. Indeed, the bank as a provider of circulating money is almost entirely an English invention, which has not yet spread to every part of the civilized world . . . In a period in which money consisted entirely of gold and silver . . . [w]hat more natural than to entrust [gold and silver money] to the goldsmiths for safekeeping and to get a receipt? . . . In the beginning this was a pure safe-deposit business [referring to the first half of the 17th century or before] and the deposit receipts were used only for the purpose of withdrawing the gold. But the stages of development into the full-blown banks were rapid and easy. First, the deposit-receipts began to be handed round as money . . . So the deposit receipt became the embryonic bank note. Second, even the deposit receipt could be dispensed with. The goldsmith could merely be instructed by letter to transfer the ownership of such-and-such an amount of gold from the original depositor to his creditor. This is the birth of the cheque (the earliest cheque on a London goldsmith-banker which has been reserved to posterity is dated 1675). And finally, the goldsmith, now fully developed into banker, makes the discovery that he can safely issue deposit-receipts in excess of his gold stock . . ."[9] (*See Note A.*)

[9] *Ibid.*, pp. 22-26.

3. Basic Concepts

1

The basic functions and analytical problems of commercial banking can be described by simple extension of the histories somewhat in the manner of Pirandello.

Three basic concepts have emerged: reserve, deposit, and loan. It is these that must be fixed more definitely. The position of a representative goldsmith upon deposit with him of $1,000 in gold would be:

Assets		Liabilities	
Gold	$1,000	Deposits	$1,000

TABLE IV-II

This proves an irresistible temptation. He issues — or so we anachronistically assume — a fake warehouse receipt, a precursor to a cashier's check, to a third person in exchange for his IOU, leading to this balance sheet:

Assets		Liabilities	
Gold	$1,000	Deposits[10]	$1,100
Loans	100		
	$1,100		$1,100

TABLE IV-III

The reserve ratio is now 10:11. And the borrower presumably intended to spend all or part of the proceeds of his loan. Inevitably, he will "redeem" part of the claim created for him by the goldsmith. Assume that he draws out $50 in gold, paying the gold to payees not doing business with our goldsmith. The goldsmith's balance sheet now reads:[11]

Assets		Liabilities	
Gold	$ 950	Deposits	$1,050
Loans	100		
	$1,050		$1,050

TABLE IV-IV

10 The value of fake as well as genuine receipts is included in Deposits. The proportion is found by comparing the Gold and Deposits items. But *cf.* footnote 8.

11 We keep the rest of the goldsmith's banking-type business on ice for convenience.

Reserves and deposits each fall by $50. But, since reserves were not initially as great as deposits, the reserve-deposit ratio falls to 19/21 from 10/11. This useful piece of arithmetic illuminates the effects of, say, open-market sales by central banks.

The last transaction poses the problem of safe reserve-deposit ratios and a number of broader issues. Thus, as an individual banker (Pirandello enters the scene) expands his portfolio, he should expect to lose reserves to other banks in the system. But when one bank loses reserves to others, there is no net contractive effect for the system: other banks are able to increase *their* liabilities. Two conclusions emerge:

1) the absolute potential for expansion of a system of banks receiving additional reserves exceeds that of an individual bank receiving the same increment;

2) while it is instructive to work through hypothetical series of transactions in order to show how banks got to be what they are, it must be stressed that day-to-day banking business is mostly concerned with selection of an optimal portfolio of assets.[12] Changes in portfolio composition can be achieved through exchanges of assets in the portfolio for "outside" assets. A bank is just as much subject to budget constraints as other economic units. The fact that commercial bank liabilities provide a medium of exchange does not affect the basic orthodoxy of the economics of bank management. (*Cf.* Appendix to Ch. IV.)

2

These conclusions — basic to modern banking — can be elucidated through T-account exercises. A surrealist tone is sustained by metamorphosing the goldsmiths into modern commercial banks and the gold into reserve accounts with a ghostly central bank.

First, assume that there is but one bank, First National, which at the outset has no assets or liabilities. It is to be subject to a legal reserve ratio of 10 per cent. $1,000 in currency is deposited by the charter customer. Anxious to do profitable business, First National begins to make loans, let us say to the extent of $2,000. Its balance sheet will read

Assets		Liabilities	
Reserves	$1,000	Deposits	$3,000
Loans	2,000		
	3,000		3,000

TABLE IV-V

12 Over the years a given bank will have acquired its reserves through net inflows of currency and claims against other banks. It will have acquired its security holdings with "that part of deposits not kept in reserve." The counterpoint of micro- and macroanalysis is striking here.

Even though the charter customer begins to draw down his balance, it might seem that First National, a banking monopolist, will experience no loss of reserves: drawers and payees of checks will be customers of First National. But it will lose some reserves. To the extent that a society tends to maintain a certain proportion of its monetary assets in currency, even a monopolist banker will experience some drain of reserves as he expands his deposit liability: there will be a currency drain.[13] We specify that, if the entire $2,000 is remitted, $100 will be lost through currency withdrawals, the rest to be "re-deposited" in the monopoly bank; the rate of this drain is specified at 0.05.

Nor have we detailed the process finding First National obtaining currency from the central bank, and it is not clear that First National has vault cash readily available. Accordingly, assume that the bank transforms part of its total reserves into vault cash.[14] The balance sheet now reads:

Assets		Liabilities	
Central bank credit	$ 600	Deposits	$2,900
Vault cash	300		
Loans	2,000		
	2,900		2,900

TABLE IV-VI

Excess reserves total $610. First National will further increase its loans, keeping in mind that a $10 expansion in loans (and deposits, *pari passu* in this case) leads to a loss of $0.50 in vault cash. Furthermore, to the extent that deposit liability is increased, additional reserves must be held; excess reserves will be absorbed.

4. Systematic Coefficients

One can develop an underlying algebraic model. Assume that there is a systematic relationship between desired holdings of currency,

13 The current proportion of currency to adjusted demand deposits in the United States is about 1:4. Sir Ralph Hawtrey has stressed that one endogenous restraint on spontaneous economic expansion is loss of currency to workers as the wage bill rises.

14 Legislation passed in July 1959 permitted member banks of the Federal Reserve system to count vault cash as part of reserve requirements effective November 24, 1960.

X, and total cash holdings of the non-banking public, $X + D$, where D is the sum of bank deposits.

(1) $$X = c(D + X),$$

where c is a positive fraction. Equation 2 follows,

(2) $$X = c'D,$$

where c' is another positive fraction $\left(\frac{c}{1-c}\right)$. The banking system (or, of course, the monopoly bank) adheres to a legal reserve/deposit ratio r (inverse r being denoted r').

(3) $$D = r'A,$$

where A represents bank reserves. The total of bank reserves is defined by potential reserves, $\bar{A}$, less currency in the hands of the public, X. Of course, currency in the hands of the public has escaped the bankers' net. Hence, Equation 4:

(4) $$A \equiv \bar{A} - X.$$

Working with Equations 2-4, there is a system of three linear equations in the unknowns D, X, and A. The really interesting problem concerns the effect of a change in reserve potential $\bar{A}$ — or in some other parameter of the system — on equilibrium values of, say, X and D, and L, the sum of loans and investments of the banking system. Solution of the problem requires that equilibrium values for X and D, X^* and D^*, be expressed in terms of $\bar{A}$. Equations 5 and 6, derived through a series of cumbersome substitutions, do just that:

(5) $$X^* \equiv \left(\frac{c'}{r + c'}\right) \bar{A}$$

(6) $$D^* \equiv \left(\frac{1}{r + c'}\right) \bar{A}$$

Equation 7 follows[15]

(7) $$\Delta D^*/\Delta\bar{A} \equiv \frac{1}{r + c'}$$

Effects of changes in reserve potential on equilibrium deposits can be traced out. What about $\Delta L^*/\Delta\bar{A}$? *This ratio is called the coefficient of expansion.* The answer is latent in the logic of the cash-drainage proc-

[15] I distinguish between definitions (≡) and "imposed" equalities (=).

esses of Equations 1 and 2. Assume, for example, that as a result of an initial increase in reserves, equilibrium deposits increase \$E and the public's equilibrium currency holdings \$B. Obviously, the \$E increase in deposits has a loan-expansion counterpart. Reflection shows that this also is true of the \$B item: the increase in the public's currency holdings derived from drawing down deposits created as part of the loan expansion. In other words, if we assume that banks create deposits up to their reserve limits, the identity

$$\Delta L^* \equiv \Delta X^* + \Delta D^*$$

holds. The coefficient of expansion is

$$\Delta L^*/\Delta \bar{A} \equiv \frac{\Delta(D^* + X^*)}{\Delta \bar{A}} \equiv \frac{l + c'}{r + c'} \tag{8}$$

and necessarily is larger than $\Delta D^*/\Delta \bar{A}$, since the currency drain leads, *pari passu, to reduced deposit obligation.*[16] ($\Delta \bar{A}$ must here be taken as initial excess reserves of banks.)

First National's *coefficient of expansion* (recalling $r' = 10$ and $c' = 0.05$) is about 7. (Remember it is a monopolist.) It can consider about a \$4,270 expansion in loans and investments on its \$610 in excess reserves.[17]

5. Multi-bank Systems

1

The major factors influencing expansion and contraction of commercial bank liabilities and the ways in which banks exchange monetary liabilities for non-monetary assets have been exhibited. It becomes clear that awesome consequences can flow from a decision by the

16 The rate of change of ΔD^* with respect to c' is $-(r + c')^{-2}$. If c' and r are 0.10, a small change in c' or r causes the expression to change 25 times as much in the opposite direction. A similar derivation exists for the coefficient of expansion. System (1)-(4) is linear. But one often can linearize a more general system in the neighborhood of, say, a solution point and approximate its comparative statics in that vicinity.

17 Consider a closed system containing the Sartoris Bank of Jefferson — after Flem Snopes took over — as the monopoly bank. Take $c = 1.0$, so that c' is indefinitely large. $dD^*/d\bar{A} = 0$. The coefficient of expansion is unity. An increment of reserves could lead to purchase of securities in the same amount. The proceeds would immediately be checked out; the change in deposits would be zero. All the excess reserves would be absorbed.

public to hold more currency or a change in the required reserve ratio. We see why reserves often are called *high-powered* money and how the central authorities can expect to obtain leverage by changing bank reserve positions.

We now strip from First National its monopoly status and introduce other banks, starting with Second Cottonpickers' Bank of Atlanta. No new principle is introduced, but the practical consequences are considerable and potential fallacies of composition are brought into play. Assume for convenience that the currency drain parameter is zero and that the distribution of business between the two banks is such that a $1 expansion in deposit liability (*ceteris paribus*) by either leads to loss of $0.50 in reserves to the other during the period. The leakage coefficient, q, has a time dimension (that of the period); $q = 0.5$. What happens when First National begins period 1 with $1,000 in excess reserves and expands its loans by, say, $2,000? First National will be in danger of passing into the crowded Valhalla of commercial banking — not because its liabilities exceed its assets, but because it has become palpably illiquid.

2

In seeking a formal *rationale*, one might reflect as follows (putting aside niceties pertaining to currency drains):

1. If First National expands its deposits by $1,[18] "first round" adverse clearings will cause $0.50 to be lost to Second Cottonpickers'.

2. "One-period" expansion possibilities are given by the formula

$$\frac{dL}{dA} = \frac{1}{q + r(1-q)} .$$

Here $dL/A = 1.8$.

On the same reasoning,

$$\frac{dD}{dA} = \frac{1-q}{q + r(1-q)}$$

Here $dD/dA = 0.91$.

3. But Second Cottonpickers' eventually will expand deposits as a result of having received incremental reserves. First National's reserves will increase during subsequent "weeks" leading to additional

[18] Say, as a result of a "gift" of reserves. We assume that First National *never* wants to borrow reserves. This assumption can affect the way in which the final result is reached.

deposit creation, etc. Furthermore, if First National (temporarily) increases its size relative to Second Cottonpickers', it will continue to have adverse clearings; q has a time dimension.

How can we get off the merry-go-round? There are a number of ways, but the most simple and penetrating procedure is to set up an equilibrium system after that of pp. 139-140. This will exhibit effects of autonomous changes in the system's reserve potential on equilibrium values of deposits of its members.

We develop an equation system for an n-bank model. Later, we shall turn to three- and two-bank systems. First, deposits for each bank must bear the "proper" relation to reserves:

$$(9) \qquad D_i = r'A_i \qquad i = 1, 2, \ldots, n$$

Equation 10 determines rates of outflow of reserves:

$$(10) \qquad x_i \equiv D_i \sum_j q_{ij} + c'\dot{D}_i. \qquad i, j = 1, 2, \ldots n, \quad i \neq j$$

x_i is the rate at which reserves are flowing out of the ith bank. It is composed of the sum of flows into the remaining $n-1$ banks and currency drain where $\dot{D}_i$ is the rate of deposit expansion for the ith bank.[19] The q_{ij}'s are coefficients of the system. $q_{12}\dot{D}_1$ gives the time rate of flow of reserves from the first to the second bank. In general, $q_{ij} \neq q_{ji}$. There can be "triangular trade" among banks much like the England-West Indies-Colonial America triad of high school history books. We shall find that the q_{ij}'s are singularly important.

If the system is to be in equilibrium, the rate of increase in deposits, $\dot{D}$ must be zero for all banks:

$$(11) \qquad \dot{D}_i = O \qquad i = 1, 2, \ldots, n \qquad i \neq j$$

Furthermore, inflow of reserves of other banks into the ith bank must equal the outflow, x_i, determined in Equations 10 and 11:

$$(12) \qquad x_i = \sum_j q_{ji} D_j \qquad i = 1, 2, \ldots, n$$

Finally, it is necessary that the sum of bank reserves conform to the total of potential reserves, $\bar{A}$, less currency in the hands of the public, $c'\Sigma D_i$:

$$(13) \qquad \Sigma A_i = \bar{A} - c'\Sigma D_i.$$

We find it convenient to use Equations 9 and formulate the alternative equation

$$(13') \qquad \Sigma D_i = \bar{D}.$$

[19] c' here has no time dimension.

In other words, the authorities might be considered to take account of the currency-drain parameter in setting the level of A, equivalent to determining $\overline{D}$.

It becomes obvious that ours is representative of a broad class of economic reasoning. You will come to draw an analogy with traditional models dichotomizing price determination: relative prices being determined in commodity markets and absolute prices through the "Cambridge" equation. Also of the Archibald-Lipsey model of Ch. XIV.[20, 21]

Above all, the relative size of the *ith* bank, $D_j^*/\overline{D}$ is dependent upon the structural coefficients (the q_{ij}'s) *and nothing else.* This can be shown for a 3-bank system, readily generalizable into an n-bank system, in the following way:

$$\begin{aligned}
&(a) \quad (q_{12}+q_{13})D_1 - q_{21}D_2 - q_{31}D_3 = 0\\
&(b) \quad -q_{12}D_1 + (q_{21}+q_{23})D_2 - q_{32}D_3 = 0\\
&(c) \quad -q_{13}D_1 - q_{23}D_2 + (q_{31}+q_{32})D_3 = 0\\
&(d) \quad -D_1 - D_2 - D_3 = -\overline{D}
\end{aligned}$$

Add $(D_1 + D_2 + D_3)$ and $\overline{D}$ to the right- and left-hand sides of (a)-(c) and then multiply through by $1/\overline{D}$, obtaining this system. *See Note B.)*

$$\begin{aligned}
&(e) \quad (1+q_{12}+q_{13})(D_1/\overline{D}) + (1-q_{21})(D_2/\overline{D}) + (1-q_{31})(D_3/\overline{D}) = 1\\
&(f) \quad (1-q_{12})(D_1/\overline{D}) + (1+q_{21}+q_{23})(D_2/\overline{D}) + (1-q_{32})(D_3/\overline{D}) = 1\\
&(g) \quad (1-q_{13})(D_1/\overline{D}) + (1-q_{23})(D_2/\overline{D}) + (1+q_{31}+q_{32})(D_3/\overline{D}) = 1
\end{aligned}$$

The solution values $(D_i^*/\overline{D})$ can be expressed as

$$(h) \quad D_i^*/\overline{D} = \frac{\Delta_i}{\Delta} \qquad i = 1, 2, \ldots, n$$

20 *Cf.* R. Dorfman, P. A. Samuelson, and R. M. Solow, *Linear Programming and Economic Analysis* (New York: McGraw-Hill Book Co., 1958), p. 245 *ff.*

21 Indeed the model is based on an ergodic Markov chain and states an "ergodic theorem." Professors Harwitz and Oi have caused me to regret that I did not formulate the model directly as a Markov process.

Note that $\partial D^*/\partial \overline{A}$ is in general determinate for savings intermediaries as well as for commercial banks. Indeed the ratio D_1^*/D_2^*, where 1 and 2 index the two systems, might be invariant against $\overline{A}$. But transitional processes find the S-L system losing reserves almost as fast as they are pumped in (via receipt of savings capital), while the commercial-banking system will not lose reserves beyond currency-efflux effects. The latter system will reach its equilibrium level more quickly in all likelihood. The text's is a "pure" demand-deposit system.

where the Δ's have the usual determinant connotation and are, of course, dependent only upon the q's.

The two-bank case is extremely simple. Since we know that $q_{12}D_1 = q_{21}D_2$ in equilibrium, $D_1^*/D_2^* = q_{21}/q_{12}$; the relative size of the two banks is determined. This result can be derived from the more general formulation immediately above.

Since Equation (d) will be satisfied, we are assured $\Sigma(D_i^*/\overline{D}) = 1$. It is convenient to denote the $D_i^*/\overline{D}$ expressions as $\lambda_1, \lambda_2, \ldots, \lambda_n$. The λ's give the relative sizes of the banks, the proportions that the respective banks have of total deposits in equilibrium. Of course $\Sigma\lambda_i = 1$. But, if the relative size of banks is determined by the q_{ij}'s, their shares of any increase in the system's deposit liability must be in the same proportion as their initial (equilibrium) shares. Thus, if $\lambda_1 = 0.8$ and $\lambda_2 = 0.2$ in a two-bank system, and if the systematic coefficient of deposit expansion is 10, a $1 increase in reserves for the system, *however initially distributed,* leads to an expansion of $8 in D_1 and $2 in D_2. So long as deposit liabilities are not in the proper ratios, some banks are gaining reserves on net from the other banks. Of course, it is clear that, in a two-bank system, q_{ij}'s of 0.0008 and 0.0002 (say per annum), while leading to the same equilibrium proportions, imply that transitory profits from "favorable distribution" will be larger than for values of 0.8 and 0.2.

We finally are prepared to relate individual coefficients of deposit expansion to the systematic coefficient. Taking the latter to be η, we can write

$$(i) \qquad dD_i^*/d\bar{A} = \lambda_i \eta \qquad i = 1, 2, \ldots, n$$

noting that $\Sigma\lambda_i = 1$, so that

$$(j) \qquad d(\Sigma D_i^*)/d\bar{A} = (\Sigma\lambda_i)\eta = \eta.$$

For the Sartoris Bank of Jefferson, λ is 0. The q_{ij}'s have the properties of demand relations: a successful advertising campaign might lead to the *ith* bank reducing its q_{ij} coefficients while increasing its q_{ij}'s: on the other hand, we saw that Flem Snopes finally caused the Sartoris Bank to become so odious that persons receiving loans from it immediately transferred the proceeds to other banks. The q_{ij} constellation was so unfavorable for the Sartoris Bank that it became nothing more than an investment company holding securities equal to its capitalization. The Albert Schweitzer Bank of Memphis is likely to be much better endowed in its q_{ij} constellation.

Two concluding observations:

1. In the event of a "diagonal" payments matrix within the economy — a state in which intraregional trade is much more important than interregional trade, the q_{ij}'s, in contrast with the q_{ii}'s, will tend to be small. So long as the former are not zero, the size dis-

tribution of banks remains determinate, but, as we have seen, the adjustment process will be slower if the system is forced out of equilibrium. Recall the two-bank case in which $D_1^*/D_2^* = q_{21}/q_{12}$: the ratio of the q_{ji}'s determines the equilibrium sizes of the bank, but, if the q_{ji}'s are small enough, adjustment might be a long, painful, process.

2. the rate of flow from the *ith* to the *jth* bank probably should depend, among other things, on the size of *both* banks. This suggests the general formulation

$$f^i(D; q) = 0 \qquad\qquad i = 1, 2, \ldots, n$$

where D is a vector of deposit levels and q a vector of parameters. There are described "excess flow functions," each set equal to zero. The system is to be solved for the D's. We refrain from specifying it more precisely.[22]

3

Return to the simple story, focusing on one commercial bank among many.

$$\frac{(1-q)}{q + r(1-q)}$$

determines potential (end of) first-round deposit-expansion equilibrium for the *ith* bank. More rigorous argument showed that equilibrium deposit levels could be ascertained only in the context of the entire banking system. Do not assume that the increase for one of many banks necessarily is small:[23]

1) small banks' customers may do business in a closed circle so that the rate of leakage to other banks might be rather small;

---

[22] A pioneering study in multiple-expansion of banking systems is C. A. Phillips, *Bank Credit* (New York: The Macmillan Co., 1921). See especially Part I, pp. 13-122. *Bank Credit* remains a useful book.

I am much indebted to Fred M. Westfield and Walter Y. Oi for useful discussion of this model.

[23] Bankers are assumed to harken to first-round losses in reserves consequent to deposit expansion; we assume that they wish never to have deficient reserves. The length of the period is chosen consistently with the time dimensionality of the q's. It has been shown that $dD_1^*/dA_4 = 0$ unless the increment to reserves is *systematic*.

2) it is customary, especially during tight money, for part of the proceeds of loans to remain unspent; this can be the result of duress.[24]

Firms might borrow in order to increase their liquidity. Also a firm is likely to build up its cash balance as it prepares to repay a loan and finds frictional costs too great to make it worthwhile to keep funds in the money market on short term.

6. Rudimentary Dynamics

1

In any event, we are equipped to avoid fallacies of composition: we understand how accretions of reserves for, say, First National might have small effects for that bank, but can work their way through the system; the system's deposits finally will settle down at a new equilibrium level reflecting the systematic coefficient of (deposit) expansion.

2

The nettle can be grasped more firmly by doing a simple set of accounts for First National, Second Cottonpickers', and Third Mercantile. And in order to be *really* sure that we know what is going on, we shall reverse gears and deal with a systematic *contraction,* introducing a more operational central bank.

We retain the system we have built up, using a marginal currency drain parameter of 0.10. Third Mercantile plays an "all other" role, being taken as much larger than the other two banks. The ad-

[24] Since loss of $1 in deposits means loss of $1 in reserves for the individual bank, it has an incentive to discourage checking out of deposits. *Cf.* George Garvy, *Deposit Velocity and Its Significance* (New York: Federal Reserve Bank of New York, 1959), pp. 31 *ff.* The model of A 5 strictly should have taken account of factors such as this by specifying vectors of outstanding loans of different maturities and dates of origin (generating cash build-up patterns). Cash outflows at "t" would, of course, be related to these vectors. Imposition of minimum-balance requirements by the *jth* bank would reduce outflow of its reserves for a specified loan vector. Note that monetary velocity will be less to the extent that minimum-balance requirements are binding.

A full model would have led to an equilibrium distribution of loans as well as deposits. The dynamics of adjustment of loan distribution might be something like this. If the *rth* bank's loans are above its equilibrium level, some customers will repay and apply to other banks. These will sell investments in order to make loans (*cf.* Appendix, Ch. IV). Some depositors of the *rth* bank will be among those buying investments. The *rth* bank will lose reserves (temporarily increased by loan repayment), etc.

justment process is to be contrasted with the final equilibrium, partly through an optional (mathematical) exercise.

We begin with a set of balance sheets for the three banks at period 0, a time when the banking system is in full equilibrium:

Assets	First National	Second Cottonpickers'	Third Mercantile
Loans	$6,600	$3,000	$ 69,000
U. S. bonds	3,300	1,950	30,000
Vault cash	100	50	1,000
Reserve account	1,000	500	10,000
Asset — Liability Total	11,000	5,500	110,000
Liabilities			
Deposits	11,000	5,500	110,000

TABLE IV-VII

Assume that at the onset of period 1 the central bank sells $1,000 in government bonds to First National customers who pay the central bank by drawing checks against First National, drawing down its reserve account by $1,000. First National's balance sheet at the end of period 1 reads

Assets		Liabilities	
Loans	$6,600	Deposits	$10,000
U. S. bonds	3,300		
Vault cash	100		
Reserve account	0		
	10,000		10,000

TABLE IV-VIII

The board takes two steps: (1) borrows $1,000 from the central bank, anticipating further strain on reserves, so that First National will have $100 in excess reserves and–$900 in *free reserves* (excess minus borrowed reserves); (2) plans to correct its position and get out of debt as soon as possible. Accordingly it is planned to reduce the government bond portfolio. It is desired not to place pressure on valued customers at this juncture. How much in bonds should be sold? It turns out that only $810 in bonds need be disgorged.[25]

3

If First National is a small enough pea in the banking pod, it is going to be hard to convince its directors that there is much mystery to banking or that contraction in bank reserve items leads to *multiplied* contraction in earnings items.

Still the banking system is out of joint. First National's bond sales absorbed reserves of other banks, say Third Mercantile. Before it returns to equilibrium, the sum total of adjustments throughout the system will find a multiple contraction of earnings assets unless depositors surrender additional currency. Unless this happens, bank borrowers will be under pressure (unless depositors are induced to surrender some of their balances for bank-held securities).

These processes soon will be unravelled, but it should be reiterated that it takes some sophistication for individual bankers to be aware of multiplicative processes of deposit expansion and contraction. At any point in time, the representative banker can correct reserve deficiencies by sales of investments about equal in value to the deficiencies.[26] Multiple contraction finds the individual banker subject to a whole series of such jogs; the calendar duration of this series of events may be as long or short as you wish.

Similarly, the representative banker finds himself with excess reserves during the expansion process. These will be worked off (at the beginning of each "day" for the "day") through expansion in investments equal in value to the excess reserves.[27] Cumulative processes of

[25] Currency reflux will add $100 to reserves. But, since this will increase deposits by $100, free reserves will increase by $90.

[26] Ignoring currency-drain considerations.

If there were a (binding) linear relationship between desired and required minimum balances and loans, First National would have to contract loans more than investments in order to correct the reserve deficiency. Thus non-renewal of a $1,000 loan might generate only $800 in favorable clearings; reserves might rise by $800 and deposits fall by $200 (freeing an additional $20 in reserves). There would remain a deficiency of $180. . . . There is no *systematic* distinction between loans and investments.

[27] At least for purchases in "distant" markets.

If loans were increased, and if we take the period to be such that only a fraction of the proceeds would be checked out at the end of one period, one-period loan expansion possibilities for the representative bank would be considerable. But presumably banks will make loan commitments in terms of an n-period horizon; they will not want to make unmaintainable commitments.

Bank notes have been ignored: perfectly proper for the United States, quite improper for France and Germany.

deposit expansion find bankers *purposively* expanding loans and investments in response to increased reserves. For the individual banker these accrue through *deposit* of checks (including cashiers' checks) against other banks. Thus an increment of systematic reserves will carom about the pinball machine (banking system) — leaving a residue of deposit liability at each contact — until finally the tilt sign flashes, and an equilibrium reserve-deposit relationship is re-established.

4

Float might have led to there being an interval in which *both* First National and Third Mercantile were in temporary equilibrium:

> "Float is a form of Federal Reserve credit which arises as a byproduct of the check clearing and collection system . . . Each check received for clearance is entered in two accounts at the Federal Reserve bank. It is entered into an asset account known as "uncollected cash items." When the check has been finally cleared and the appropriate account of the bank on which it is drawn has been debited, the item is removed from the uncollected cash items account [this might take several days] . . . When the check is first deposited at the Reserve Bank it is also entered into a liability account known as "deferred availability items" . . . In practice, the time interval set in the deferred availability schedule is generally shorter than the actual time required to collect a check. Thus, on the average, depositing banks receive a credit to their account *before* the account on which the check is drawn is debited. This difference is known as float, and it amounts to a net credit extended by Federal Reserve banks to member banks . . ."[28]

Of course, in not too many days, Third Mercantile must face up to its predicament. Third Mercantile's problems are on all fours with those of First National. Repercussions of Third Mercantile's actions are, of course, broader and perhaps more severe: Second Cottonpickers' almost certainly will be out of whack.

7. Methodological Implications of the Multibank System

1

We have reached a critical juncture: the schematic survey has broken open a number of usually obscured issues and has, in fact, counterpointed them in an interesting way. A problem in systematic

[28] Steiner, Solomon, and Shapiro, *op. cit.*, pp. 282-283.

expansion and contraction of bank deposits and investments has been posed as initiating from actions of central authorities. The contrast between individual and group perspective has been illuminated. An adjustment process — a dynamic sequence — has been developed in which the various economic units find themselves in positions that they do not wish to or cannot sustain. The way in which such institutional factors as float and outright borrowed reserves affect the adjustment path has been suggested. The properties of the new solution (*cf.* Ch. VA) generated by the shifted parameters become interesting. We note what happens to bond prices, the total of bank advances, deposit liability, etc. The mechanism underlying the system's motion concerns markets for various financial paper — markets to which the banks will resort in their response to the "shifted" environment. Finally, the question arises whether these processes are *stable,* whether equilibrium states can be achieved if initial conditions are "wrong."

It is important that you see the stuff of which economic theory is made. It is concerned with *formal* relationships between such variables as bond holdings, bond prices, reserve requirements, etc. Some of these variables are peculiarly in the control of economic policy-makers. These are the *policy variables* of the system and are included among its *parameters.* Each set of values for policy variables leads to a set of *solution values* for the variables determined within the system, the *endogenous* variables. If an endogenous variable is next period's rate of employment in the steel industry and one of the policy variables is the required reserve-deposit ratio for commercial banks, theorists — the most important of whom *must* be the men who make official decisions — might and do disagree whether manipulation of the latter has much to do with even the "temporary" solution value of the former.

The newly formulated operating procedure can be applied to other portions of the problem posed a few paragraphs ago. Dealing with a TRANSITIONAL OR TEMPORARY "equilibrium" state, we conclude our statement of effects of central bank action with presentation of a new consolidated balance sheet, the TEMPORARY solution balance sheet — it need not pertain to period $t+h+1$, where it does pertain to period $t+h$.

This balance sheet can only be specified if we know a good deal about behavioral parameters; differences between hypothetical balance sheets can be decisively important. Here is *one* set of possibilities:

1) in trying to attract reserves, banks offer more favorable rates on time deposits, drawing some currency out of circulation and into bank reserves, mitigating effects of the system's initial loss of reserves; also some demand deposits will be switched;

2) the price of short-term government paper falls, making this more attractive for depositors, hitherto accustomed to "lavish" cash balances; the banks are enabled to maintain their holdings of high-yield investments by surrendering other paper for deposits — hitherto idle — which now can be turned over to issuers of higher-yield paper (price theory suggests absolute and relative yields of this paper will increase);

3) business firms, faced with higher interest rates on financial paper, reduce their indebtedness. Since business firms are indebted to banks, there is a powerful link between firms' demand deposits and their debt positions; if willing to reduce their holdings of deposits, they can reduce their indebtedness to the bank, reflecting a general substitutional relationship between bank money and bonds. (Firms also could reduce inventories, indirectly transferring some of the public's deposits to the banks, reducing their own indebtedness.)

2

Assume that these possibilities lead to the following concrete effects:

1) vault cash rises by $250, $90 of which is associated with increased time-deposit liability (from zero). Assume that time deposits require an 8 per cent reserve;

2) $500 in demand deposits are moved into time deposits in response to the latter's more attractive yield;

3) $200 in deposits are exchanged for bank holdings of government bonds;

4) bank holdings of business paper decline, reflected in a decline in "loans" of approximately $6,400.

This is the set of balance sheets for period $t+h$:

Assets	First National	Second Cottonpickers'	Third Mercantile
Loans	$ 5,918	$2,740	$ 63,518
U. S. bonds	3,280	1,940	29,830
Vault cash	120	70	1,210
Reserve account	900	450	9,150
Asset — Liability Total	10,218	5,200	103,700
Liabilities			
Time deposits	90		500
Demand deposits	10,128	5,200	103,200

The implications of this new balance sheet for the economy's "real" variables are the subject of much of our later work. For example, lurking in the background is a new set of interest rates. What effects might these have for planned inventory holdings and investment in fixed plant and equipment? And then there has been an approximately $8,000 decrease in demand deposits, together with a $250 reduction in the public's currency holdings, partially offset by an increase of $590 in the very near money, time deposits. This decrease in liquidity is voluntary in the sense that, given the new set of prices, the public choose to hold the new set of currency, time deposits, and demand deposits. The public felt free to hold more cash — the stock of money is *not* a parameter for the individual decision maker — but choose not to. What is the new set of commodity prices? If prices have fallen relatively less than has the circulating medium, we become interested in the mechanical means through which velocity increased (if the rate of economic activity did not decline, velocity must have increased). A whole chapter (VI) is devoted to the theory of velocity of monetary circulation. Finally, the implications of liquidation of more than $6,400 in loans (of an initial total of $78,600) are intriguing. They would be slight if it merely reflected decisions by some firms to work with smaller cash balances. On the other hand, if reduced loans reflected decisions to liquidate inventory and abandon construction projects, counterpart effects in the real sector of the economy would be large indeed; severe deflationary pressures may have been induced.

Always remember that balance sheets merely capture magnitudes of a number of stock variables at a point in time. Say that you were to examine the set of balance sheets shown at p. 151 — applying to period $t+h$—and were then to examine another set for period $t+h+1$. What if every item were identical for the two periods for each of the banks? Would this imply that nothing had happened? Not at all! No more than it would be true that water had not flowed in a river measured at the same height on successive days. Take the "loans" item: $63,518 for Third Mercantile. This is consistent with the entire sum having been repaid and re-lent in successive periods. And for observations one year apart, we saw that, on the average, each dollar in deposits was transferred more than 30 times.

8. A Mathematical Model

This subsection is appended in order to give those with some mathematical training a feeling for the meaning of *stability* of economic systems and for dynamical processes describing the system's motion. It contains a dynamic bank-expansion problem. These are the basic assumptions:

1) banks adjust this period's deposit liability to their reserve position at the end of last period. There is but one type of deposit. Algebraically,

$$D(t) = 10A\,(t-1), \qquad (a)$$

where $A(t-1)$ gives reserves at the end of last period, and where the required reserve-deposit ratio is 0.10.

2) demand for currency, assumed always to be realized, is some fraction of deposits:

$$X(t) = kD(t), \qquad (b)$$

where $X(t)$ is the public's demand for currency in period t.

3) planned deposit levels always are realized, implying member-bank access to the central bank on more-permissive terms than are true in the real world.

4) reserves are defined by the relation

$$A(t-1) = A(0) + X(0) - X(t-1), \qquad (c)$$

where $A(0)$ and $X(0)$ are, respectively, initial values for reserves and for currency. $X(t-1)$ is currency held by the public at the end of period $t-1$. Take $A(0) = 100$.

These assumptions can be compressed into a single equation. Substitute Equation *(b)* into Equation *(c)*, obtaining

$$A(t-1) = 100 + X(0) - kD(t-1). \qquad (d)$$

Substitute *(d)* into *(a)*, obtaining

$$D(t) = 10[100] + X(0) - k[D(t-1)] \qquad (e)$$

or

$$D(t) + (10k)[D(t-1)] = 1000 + 10X(0), \qquad (f)$$

recalling that k and $X(0)$ are fixed numbers, their values not yet being assigned.

The level of deposits at $t=n$ can be obtained by solving the first-order difference Equation *(f)*. If $k=0.2$, the coefficient for $D(t-1)$ is 2. The general solution is obtained by finding a particular solution and then a general solution for the homogeneous form. For convenience, take $X(0)=0$, so that the equation to be solved is

$$(g) \qquad D(t) + 2D(t-1) = 1000.$$

A particular solution is $D(t) = D(t-1) = 333$. The problem is solved down to

$$(h) \qquad D(t) = 333 + R,$$

where R is the remainder term. R is obtained by solving the homogeneous difference equation

$$(i) \qquad D(t) + 2D(t-1) = 0.$$

The solution is

$$(j) \qquad D(t) = [D(0)](-2)^t.$$

where $D(0)$ is an arbitrary constant that can be determined by specifying an initial deposit level, say $D(0) = 67$. The general solution then is

$$(k) \qquad D(t) = 333 + 67(-2)^t.$$

Equation *(k)* calls for explosive oscillations, bigger and bigger swings above and below the "benchmark" level 333. Unless steps are taken to complicate the behavior rule of the central bank, the specified system will tend to "run away."

Note that the sense in which the system runs away is special: the solution specifies a perfectly well defined motion; but this motion happens to be inconsistent with a steady state unless the initial deposit level is just right.

The mathematical requirement for the remainder part to tend to zero over time — independently of initial specifications — is clarified if it is recalled that the coefficient of $D(t-1)$ in Equations *(f)* and *(j)* is vk, where v is the reciprocal of the required-reserve ratio. Thus, Equation *(k)* can be written

$$(l) \qquad D(t) = Y^* + [D(0)]\ (-vk)^t,$$

where Y^* is some particular solution. The remainder part, $[D(0)]$ $(-vk)^t$ will tend to zero as t increases only if vk is less than unity. Thus, the system's stability properties improve as the required-reserve ratio increases (its reciprocal decreasing) and as the parameter of the currency-demand function decreases. If, for example, v should be 6 and k 0.05, Equation *(l)* would read

$$D(t) = Y^* + [D(0)]\,(-0.30)^t, \tag{m}$$

obviously stable. Or, if we continued to work with $k = 0.05$, but took $v = 10$, we should have

$$D(t) = Y^{**}\,[D(0)]\,(-0.50)^t. \tag{n}$$

The solutions of Equations *(m)* and *(n)* feature *damped oscillations.*

For $X(0)$ greater than zero, the value of the particular solution increases: there is currency available other than from initial bank reserves.

If demand for currency is determined by

$$X(t) = k'[D(t) + X(t)], \tag{o}$$

it is still possible to reduce the expression to the form exhibited in Equation *(p)*:

$$X(t) = \frac{k'}{1-k'}\,D(t). \tag{p}$$

Denote $k'/(1-kp')$ as r. Referring to Equation *(l)*, we see that stability is enhanced if r is smaller rather than larger. It is clear on inspection that r declines with k'. The analysis is unaffected by more complicated assumptions about the demand for currency.

9. Rudiments of Central Banking

Why not finish this introduction to banking theory with a brief treatment of central banking, the subject of Ch. V?

The origins of central banking are various: sometimes being found in governments granting privileges to a bank which promises to provide it finance; sometimes in elaborate statutory procedure concerning protection of reserves and guarantee of prudent banking practices. There is at least one peculiarly interesting theme. Central banks perform dichotomous functions. One concerns the benefits of centralized reserves and member-bank restraint. The other function — often clad in the garments of the first — concerns manipulation of reserve requirements, rediscount rates, central bank bond holdings, etc. in order to affect the price of credit and, through this, such variables as the general price level and the rate of employment. In a closed system essentially on a fiat paper standard, the first function tends to lack interest and importance. This contrasts with its crucial role in an open system on a metallic standard (even if only externally).

To transmogrify the three commercial banks back into goldsmiths for the nonce, it is easy to understand the advantages of centralized reserves for backsliding fiduciaries. Once a central reserve were established, and arrangements were made permitting any smith in difficulty to borrow gold from his fellows until the tide receded, sources of danger would be limited to causes operating on the entire group at once. Centralization of reserves has a military analog: the principle of mass of manoeuvre.[29] A military leader should not commit his entire force so long as there is a palpable chance of stress on other portions of his front. Furthermore, if we adhere to the mass-of-manoeuvre principle, it will be hard for the enemy optimally to concentrate his forces.[30]

Needless to say, if the smiths — and now we transmogrify them back into banks again — commit themselves to a common defense, it is likely that the allies will be asked to subscribe to practices assuring that they will impose no more than a fair burden on their fellows. Thus, a bank operating on a 1 per cent reserve might do famously so long as it could rely upon being able to call out friendly volunteer firemen each time a drawing from Nature's Urn threatened its solvency. Striking relationships appear between regulatory and defensive functions of central banks and between defensive central bank functions and statistical laws. The analogy to life insurance principles is obvious.

It is easy to understand the source of bleakness and lack of cheer in the lives of bygone central banks: the value of banking system commitments to pay exceeded the value of its holdings of ultimate stuff. Ultimately the domestic scene was transformed: the internal commitment was reduced so that suitably engraved paper could be supplied. But most sovereignties continue to maintain fixed rates of exchange between their money and that of other nations: the classical problems

29 Sir Winston Churchill writes of the shock he received in 1940 upon being told by the French Staff that the French army was fully committed, hard beset, and without any mass of manoeuvre.

30 Many economic problems, ranging from duopoly to programming of firms' activities, have been handled through applications of the theory of games. In game-theoretic applications, nature frequently is treated as a particularly knowledgeable and implacable foe.

and, accordingly, some of the classical techniques of central banking persist.

Even in a closed system with a virtually fiat standard, some sort of pretense of "backing" for currency and bank paper is likely to be made. The public will feel that the thin line of "backing" is all that stands between it and monetary catastrophe — at least until the "backing" is removed by natural or unnatural causes, and nothing much happens. Still the sacredness of the metallic undergarments will be restored if the "backing" happens to be recaptured. Thus the *Bulletin* of the Board of Governors for June 1961 assures us that collateral was held against the $28.81 billion in Federal Reserve notes then outstanding. The collateral included $8.98 billion in gold certificates (essentially warehouse receipts). Also $11 *million* in certain commercial paper and $21.2 billion in U. S. government securities ("collateral" that could at best be encashed for F. R. notes). The charade is climaxed by the observation that the value of the collateral ($30.2 billion) is about $1.4 billion more than that of the notes. Crabbed obeisance to a shady past.

10. Special Banking Topics

In order to preserve the clarity of the outline, certain more specialized features have been bypassed. Accordingly, before closing the chapter with a few historical topics and some intellectual history of commercial banking (particularly the Real Bills Heresy), we shall do a backtrack.

The backtrack specifically concerns these topics: (a) correspondent relations among banks; (b) the federal funds market; (c) commercial acceptances and open-market paper, including treasury bills; (d) a more complete statement of investments of American commercial banks; (e) a word on capital-account items, stressing the small proportion of capital to total bank assets; (f) comment on the non-interest-bearing character of demand deposits. None of the additional material adds profound insights, but it is important to know a lot about the environment about which we are theorizing.[31]

a) Correspondent Relations

One aspect of *correspondent relations* is purely mechanical and need not long detain us: if I am a New York bank and you a Chicago

[31] *Cf.* Steiner, Shapiro, and Solomon, *op. cit.*, for a detailed characterization of American commercial banking. Two excellent short works on the British mechanism are W. M. Dacey, *The British Banking Mechanism* and R. S. Sayers, *Modern Banking* (London: Oxford University Press, 1951).

bank, and our customers do business in both cities, it will be convenient for us to maintain accounts with one another, permitting issue of letters of credit, etc.

A much more interesting correspondent relationship ensues when that parties are, say, the First State Bank of Oak, Eldorado (a fictitious American state) and the First National City Bank of New York. The banking laws of Eldorado might permit First State to count deposits with the New York bank as part of its legal reserve — reflecting the precursor to the Federal Reserve System, the National Banking System. One is reminded of a gold exchange international currency standard. Details are implicit in Ch. VC's discussion of the National Banking System.

b) The Federal Funds Market

Discussion of interbank relationships leads us to the *Federal funds market.* Not surprisingly, the normal give-and-take of banking finds some banks with excess reserves and others with reserve deficiencies on a given day. Clearly, claims against the Federal Reserve (high-powered money) are valuable, especially for banks with deficient reserves. The federal funds market performs the necessary mediation between buyers and sellers. Transactions in federal funds are in two major categories: unsecured overnight loans (accounting for 75 per cent of transactions); repurchase agreements. A typical loan transaction finds Bank A lending a deposit balance at the Federal Reserve to Bank B in exchange for B's check, including one day's interest. Since bank clearings are reflected in balances at the Federal Reserve, this is equivalent to B's promise to return the borrowed reserves.[32] "Under a repurchase agreement, the lender of funds buys securities, mostly short-term Government securities, and the seller agrees to repurchase them within a stated time at an agreed price and rate of interest . . . (S)ettlement is in federal funds [demand claims against the Federal Reserve]."[33]

32 ". . . Loans are reckoned in days . . . This particular segment of the market deals in loans for such brief periods that it distinguishes between funds actually available to the borrower the *same* day . . . and funds which go through normal check-clearing procedures . . . The latter are called *clearing-house funds.*" Steiner, Shapiro, and Solomon, *op. cit.,* p. 188. As SSS explain, although the borrower of federal funds might hand over his check at the time the transaction is consummated, one day's interest is borne because it will take a day for the borrower's check to clear, while the federal funds are transferred at once through bank wire.

33 *The Federal Funds Market* (Washington: Federal Reserve System, 1959), p. 5.

Bond dealers often acquired, in the course of their dealings with the New York Federal Reserve Bank (the System's "open-market operator"), more federal funds than they wanted to hold as transactions balances. This was the origin of the market in the 1920's.

The federal funds market is dominated by banks, although "Government securities dealers have become active participants in recent years . . . drawn into the market by the practice . . . of settling Government securities transactions in Federal funds."[34] Indeed the market is used only by larger banks (about 150 in all): "smaller banks, regardless of their attitude towards the market, are handicapped because of the legal limit on loans to a single borrower and because the amounts of their excesses and deficiencies of reserves are well below the unit in which Federal funds are customarily traded." As a result, country banks, hamstrung by relatively high transactions costs, normally hold the vast majority of excess reserves. Thus for the four weeks ending February 21, 1962, excess reserves of all member banks averaged $505 million; country banks neld $442 million; New York and Chicago central reserve city banks, a total of $18 million.

A number of factors determine the extent of participation in the federal funds market:

(a) the scale of a bank's operations;

(b) the interval over which the bank seeks adjustment. As *Federal Funds Market* points out (p. 8), larger banks have in recent years "in order to keep fully invested . . . followed a policy of daily or at least very short-term adjustment in their reserve position." A bank can operate in the federal funds market without risk of capital loss and "without absorbing any cost from a spread between buying and selling prices." Banks no longer can rely on call loans for this purpose, because it is no longer *de rigueur* to ask for immediate payment on these; for longer-term adjustment, bills are more attractive; thus, a bank can profit more from being invested in bills for 90 days than in federal funds over that interval;[35]

(c) attitudes towards borrowing at the Federal Reserve.

---

[34] *Ibid.*, p. 4.

[35] Banks have the same problems of synchronization of receipts and payments as do other firms. *Cf.* Ch. VI. The federal funds market serves exactly the purpose of securities substituting for cash transactions balances for non-banking firms. Just as in the non-banking case, average transactions costs are a decreasing function of scale. For a bank excess reserves are the counterpart of cash for an individual. As *Federal Funds Market* puts it: ". . . the . . . market, by facilitating use of existing reserves, tends to reduce the level of reserves which otherwise would be outstanding [because of borrowing at the Federal Reserve] under a given set of circumstances and to minimize repercussions from the temporary shifting of reserve funds among banks."

One thing becomes clear: "the fact that . . . Federal funds rate does not rise above discount rate . . . is evidence that preferences for the Federal funds market are not strong enough to induce banks to pay more than the cost of borrowing from a Reserve bank." (*Ibid.*, p. 10.)

"The Federal funds rate is inherently a sensitive indicator of bank reserve positions."[36] Clearly, I can command more for my federal funds when there is over-all excess demand for reserves. Of course, as we have seen, "in periods of credit restraint the Federal funds rate tends to move up to the discount rate and remain there for extended periods.[37] On the other hand, when there are over-all excess reserves, federal funds rate can fall well below discount rate (an administered price). The federal funds rate can be positive, even during periods of over-all excess reserves, since *some* banks even then normally will have reserve deficiencies.

c) Acceptances and Open-Market Paper

In seeking highly-marketable paper not subject to substantial market fluctuations, banks buy *commercial acceptances.* These essentially are IOU's of firms that have been accepted by houses specialized to evaluating such paper. These houses have added their names (and liability) to the paper. *Open-market paper* includes private paper—largely *bankers' acceptances* eligible for purchase in the open market by the Federal Reserve. The fact is, however, that the total of commercial and finance company paper outstanding—in and out of commercial banks—at the end of December 1960 was but $4.30 billion of which only $1.25 billion had been placed through dealers. The total of bankers' acceptances in the U. S. at that date was a little over $2.0 billion, of which $0.662 billion was held by banks. Of this $0.662 billion, $0.490 billion represented paper accepted by the same bank holding it at the end of 1960. In contrast, commercial banks alone in the United States held over $8.07 billion in treasury bills at the end of December 1960. These 90-92 day obligations of the U. S. have come to dominate the open-market paper scene.

The British scene is much the same. British Treasury bills have

---

36 *Ibid.*, p. 11.

37 *Ibid.*, p. 11.

Steiner, Shapiro, and Solomon point out that the federal fund rate *could* (it very rarely does) rise above discount rate from time to time because of the "tradition" against prolonged borrowing at the Federal Reserve by individual member banks. The desire not to borrow from the Federal Reserve *might* lead banks to be willing to pay more in the funds market than at the discount window.

become the major asset of British discount houses, although these firms developed through centuries of acceptance of *commercial* paper.[38] As a matter of fact the Treasury bill has British antecedents:

> "In 1876 a high official of the Treasury consulted Walter Bagehot on the question of devising a more satisfactory instrument of short-term Government borrowing than the old Exchequer bill. Bagehot advised that the best results would be obtained from a promissory note resembling as closely as possible the ordinary commercial bill, the ideal banking asset. The outcome was the Treasury Bill."[39]

Treasury bills were first issued in the United States in November 1929.[40] Their growth in importance is demonstrated in the table below:

TREASURY BILL DOLLAR VOLUME, U. S.
(in millions)

1933 (Dec)	1,003
1935 (Mar)	2,079
1937 (Aug)	2,653
1945 (June)	17,041
1955 (May)	19,500

TABLE IV-IX

Source: Marcus Nadler *et al., The Money Market and its Institutions* (New York: Ronald Press Co., 1955), pp. 108-109.

Commercial bank holdings of Treasury bills were over $8 billion at the end of 1960. This account is subject to substantial fluctuation, seasonal and otherwise. Consider these statistics of commercial bank bill holdings:

December 31, 1947	$2,193 million
December 31, 1958	6,294 "
December 31, 1959	6,300 "
June 15, 1960	3,593 "

This leads to the next topic. An important thing to remember is that the Treasury bill has come to overshadow commercial and bank acceptances among first-class short-term paper.

38 "Acceptance" has a broad connotation here: the traditional function of the British houses did not necessarily find them adding their signature to bills they handled.

39 W. M. Dacey, *The British Banking Mechanism* p. 66.

40 Treasury bills do not *bear* interest. Say a bill promises to pay $1,000,000 in 90 days. When sold in the market, it will yield the Treasury something less than $1,000,000. This discount implies a yield.

d. Commercial Bank Asset Position

We undertake a more complete statement of the *asset position of commercial banks.* The following is derived from the Federal Reserve *Bulletin,* June 1961.[41]

LOANS AND INVESTMENTS FOR COMMERCIAL BANKS IN THE UNITED STATES, DECEMBER 31, 1960

(in billions of dollars)

Total loans and investments	199.509
Total loans	117.642
Commercial, including open-market, paper	43.125
Agricultural loans	5.676
Loans to brokers and dealers for purchasing or carrying securities	3.284
Loans to others for purchase or carrying securities	1.833
Loans to banks	0.966
Loans to other financial institutions	7.106
Real estate loans	28.713
Other loans to individuals	26.396
Other loans	2.901
Total holdings of U. S. government obligations	61.003
Obligations of states and political subdivisions	17.570
Other securities	3.294

TABLE IV-X

41 The following charts loans as a percentage of commercial-bank earning assets, 1834-1960:

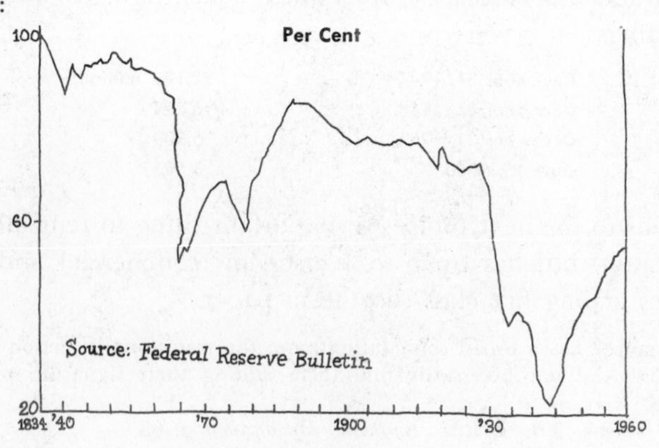

Figure IV-1

Source: Federal Reserve *Bulletin.*

[Adjusted demand deposits totalled $115.120 billion on December 31, 1960. Commercial banks had outstanding something over $71 billion in time-deposit obligations on the same date.]

Roughly one-third of bank loans have been for real-estate purposes throughout. This suggests that, as the reserve base has expanded, additional bank credit has been placed in the hands of persons who exchange it for real estate. Sellers of real estate, usually not showing gratuitous increases in liquidity preference, ultimately exchanged cash for primary securities of firms and households seeking to enter commodities markets. Ultimately the bank credit worked its way into transactions balances; *non*-financial intermediaries intervened between banks and sellers of securities.

The general interpretative comments already offered adequately explain the Table. However, two additional comments might be in order: (1) portfolio flexibility will be greater from the point of view of the single bank than from that of the system. For most items, drastic changes in systematic holdings can be achieved only by offering terms of trade so favorable that non-bank asset holders would be induced to make corresponding (and opposite) portfolio changes;[42] (2) the massive and pervasive effects of a severe credit squeeze are obvious upon perusal of the table. Assume, for example, that banks, squeezed through higher reserve requirements, lower actual reserves, etc. — are forced collectively to plan a 25 per cent reduction in their nearly 200-billion-dollar portfolio. There would be something like $50 billion in excess supply in the financial markets (not considering impact on non-banking financial institutions). Joseph Alsop would call this a *crunch.* It is hard to believe that this crunch would not quash incipient inflationary pressure, although it might be hard to endorse *all* of its consequences.

e) Capital Account Items

Loans and investments of commercial banks increased from $126.3 billion in December 1947 to $199.5 billion in December 1960, an increase of more than $73 billion. Although the GNP Deflator rose from 83.0 to 114.5 in the interim, this is very substantial growth. But the underlying source of this growth is much different from the sources of growth in the assets of the postwar steel industry, commercial aviation,

42 Within any ninety-day period, an exception would be Treasury bill and similar holdings. Substantial quantities of these come due each day.

jet fuel, etc.; *capital account items for commercial banks* rose less than $11 billion dollars from the end of 1947 to the end of 1960 (from $10.059 to $20.986 billion).

The most important factor permitting member banks to increase their asset holdings since 1939 was the increase in the Federal Reserve System's holdings of U. S. securities from $2.510 to $23.708 billion over 1939–1945; when the Federal Reserve increases its liabilities to the banks, the banks are able multiplicatively to increase their liabilities to the public, offsetting these by increases in bank loans and investments. Despite an increase of more than $5 billion in Federal Reserve holdings of U. S. securities over the 1947–1960 interval, *member bank* reserves only increased from $17.261 billion in December 1947 to $19.283 billion in December 1960. However, reserve requirements fell by about 17 per cent (from about 20 per cent to about 16.5 per cent) over the interim so that the reserve base might be said to have increased about 30 per cent (11.5 per cent more high-powered dollars each enabled to support 16.5 per cent more deposit liability) on these grounds alone. And then there is the effect of granting reserve status to vault cash, adding another $3.5 billion in reserves for all banks ($2.5 billion for member banks) over the 1947–1960 period.[43] Considering increases in reserves of non-member banks, effects of increased "Federal Reserve credit" account for about $50 billion of the $73 billion increase in the

---

43 *Cf.* Note C *infra*.

44 The way in which an expansion in capital account items permits a bank to increase its loans and investments is obvious. By inducing depositors to exchange their deposits for shares in the bank, the bank acquires excess reserves (*not pari passu* as we have seen).

The way in which we have starkly simplified bank balance sheets has distracted us from a major source of increase in bank capital: retained earnings (which can be viewed as sales of equities by the shareholders to themselves).

Two final comments: (a), in contrast with investment banks, commercial banks' profits are based on their ability to issue claims against themselves (a medium of exchange) far in excess of the value of their capital. These claims are, of course, exchanged for income-earning assets; (b), the fact that bank liabilities (demand deposits at least) come to be a revolving fund of "liquid capital" is not crucial for a microanalysis of the bank as a firm. The banker looks to his asset portfolio. Of course, the monetary theorist often is concerned with circulation of bankers' liabilities. Such turnover is a pain in the neck to the banker who must keep records of transfers of deposits.

45 As a matter of fact, if time deposits were to become a medium of exchange, it is likely that rates offered for them by financial institutions would fall: turnover rates and handling costs would much increase. And then if time deposits began to serve as a medium of exchange, reserve requirements against time deposits probably would rise.

nominal value of commercial bank asset portfolios. Such factors as the relative increase in time deposits (requiring less reserves) account for about $12 billion. Only the residual, less than $11 billion, can be associated with effects of increased bank capital accounts. We see that the main source of growth of banking assets is in the process of expansion of the monetary base. No industry in the United States is and has been more beholden to the central authorities for its growth prospects and its growth experience.[44]

f) Interest on Demand Deposits

The *non-interest-bearing character of demand deposits* is the last of the six topics chosen in our reworking of the mechanical material of Ch. IV.

It was possible to earn rather more than 4 per cent per annum on time deposit holdings in the United States during 1960. At the same time, the tens of billions of dollars held in the form of demand deposits were earning no interest. Among other things, this expresses the very great utility afforded by a medium of exchange.[45]

True enough, the very high rates of turnover of demand deposit liabilities cause banks a good deal of clerical expense.[46] But this is consistent with banks wishing to have demand deposits transferred to them: these transfers are for them transfers of *reserves.* If Bank B

---

[46] These statistics on turnover of bank deposits and of share accounts in American savings and loan associations tell an important and self-evident story:

Year	Comm. Bk. Demand Dep.	Comm. Bk. Time Dep.	Mut. Sav. Bk. Dep.	Share Accounts
1945	19.8	.50	.20	.19
1948	21.4	.51	.26	.26
1952	25.4	.46	.25	.27
1955	30.2	.47	.27	.29

TABLE IV-XI

Source: Economic Policy Commission, American Bankers Association, *Member Bank Reserve Requirements* (New York: 1957), p. 132. Reported by J. Aschheim, *op. cit.*, p. 150.

It is clear that competitive processes would lead to higher interest rates being offered on time than on demand deposits. On the other hand, it is shown in Chapter VA that yields offered by banks might be invariant (proportionately) against various cyclical factors. Monetary restraint necessarily leads to changes in money income rather than even to transitory changes in the mix of deposit liability in a system in which interest is paid on demand deposits and in which our other requirements are met.

receives a check drawn by Mr. X against Bank A and endorsed "for deposit only," Bank B will now have excess reserves; it can purchase earning assets simply by writing cashier's checks.

Which of the factors (clerical expense vs. profitability of reserves) outweighs the other? Are bankers willing to accept additional demand-deposit liability? If they answer "yes," and their advertising programs suggest they would, we can safely assume that, at present, the marginal profitability of demand deposits to commercial bankers is positive and that, if the prohibition against paying interest on demand deposits were lifted today, banks would begin to offer to pay interest tomorrow, and all would be found paying interest on demand deposits next week.

Standard economic theory suggests that it might be a good thing too, at least to the extent that any shift from time to demand deposits would be in response to prices better reflecting considerations of social cost and benefit so that appropriate marginal conditions might be fulfilled.

Relying on Friedman, these are the salient points at issue:[47]

1) the prohibition against payment of interest on demand deposits was enacted after the banking collapse of the early 1930's ". . . on the grounds that the payment of interest on deposits had led banks to follow a riskier investment policy in order to increase earnings than they otherwise would have done."[48]

2) the limitation in fact constitutes a publicly enforced cartel arrangement on the part of the bankers which, in the absence of entry, would, *cet. par.*, lead to "excessive" profits and, in the presence of entry, to overinvestment in banking without any increase in return on banking capital;

3) ". . . [i]n practice, the prohibition of the payment of interest on demand deposits has largely been ineffective. It was imposed at a time when interest rates were so low that banks were led to impose service charges and, prohibition or no prohibition, would have paid little or no interest. For most of the time since, there has been ample scope for competition in services rendered and charges for them;"[49]

4) the limitations originally were welcomed by the banks just as any group would welcome imposition of a ceiling on prices paid for an input, but, as non-banking financial institutions have become more

47 Milton Friedman, *A Program for Monetary Stability* (New York: Fordham University Press, 1960), pp. 28-29.

48 *Ibid.*, p. 28.

49 *Ibid.*, p. 29.

prominent, bankers have been frustrated in efforts to attract business to themselves by legal limitations on deposit rates, including time-deposit rates, a frustration that is more painful to individual banks than to the commercial banking *system*.

B. DOCTRINAL ISSUES

We turn to two doctrinal issues: (1) the real bills doctrine or commercial loan theory of banking; (2) proposals for 100 per cent reserve commercial banking. We append a brief history of the (British) banking school/currency school controversy to (1).

1. The Real Bills Doctrine (Commercial Loan Theory of Banking)

a) Introduction

1

Before defining terms, we might delve into dark recesses of psychological insight permitting appreciation of the origins of various fallacies comprising the theme and variations of the real bills doctrine.

A businessman, say a retail merchant carrying a stock of merchandise, sees himself as being carried, at least in part, by his bank or a commercial factor (in turn usually financed by banks). The size of his bank loan will depend on the value of his stock. If his stock turns over on the average of once a year, the businessman's vantage leads him to believe that his loan is self-liquidating: the natural course of business makes it possible for him to repay each year's loan out of the proceeds of the liquidation of the stock purchased with that loan. Accordingly, mercantile loans appear to be self-liquidating, to derive from the needs of trade, to support productive enterprise . . . It is not hard to see how men from Adam Smith to the founders of the American Federal Reserve System felt that a banking system founded on real bills would contain built-in guarantees against over-issue of bank money and perverse fluctuations in the stock of money, and would be immune to unhealthy speculation.

The logical defects of the doctrine show up as soon as we see that to limit bank advances to defined categories of loans is to say nothing about the total nominal value of these loans. In other words, if, as is the case, the total potential deposit liability is determined by forces exogenous to the lending process itself, there could be tremendous fluctuations in the stock of money and in prices without the idyllic tale changing at all. It would not matter if we specified that prices were doubled or halved. The tale is consistent with *any* price level.

Is not the source of instability precisely in the fact that the stock of money might be determined independently of "the needs of trade"? Thus, imagine a reform of the banking system requiring that bankers be prohibited from changing the scale of their loans and investments except in passive response to demand for loans in order to finance trade. The reform would eliminate reserve requirements: the *needs of trade* are to control the volume of bank money. Starting at full employment, if, for any reason, merchants wanted to increase their inventories, the rules of the game would require that the banks extend them lines of credit.[50] But they will fail to increase their holdings: prices simply will be bid up. Additional bank money would seep through the entire system as merchants made payments to factors of production: universal wage-price inflation ensues. But nothing has happened to discourage merchants from continuing to try to increase their inventories. They will continue to fail to do so. Prices will be bid up further. More bank money will be obtained in order to finance higher nominal values of constant physical stocks, raising collateral values, etc. The self-sustaining inflationary spiral will continue.

The reformed principle for bank advances similarly can induce a cumulative contraction in the money supply and in prices. Assume, for example, that firms decide to reduce their inventories. Resulting excess supply in commodities markets leads to falling prices. The needs of trade can be financed by a lower nominal value of bank credit. Under the new rule, bank liabilities necessarily will decline. The value of bills presented for discount will decline even if actual inventories do not decline. Loans must be liquidated in view of deteriorated collateral values, leading to even lower prices and to bankruptcies. Attempted liquidation of stocks will only be abetted by the banking system. Instead of deflation leading to increased real money balances, such balances either will be constant or will decline as the nominal money supply contracts. Thus, the processes prove to be unstable in both directions. A horrible example of the deflationary

50 Businessmen will be able to offer part of their equity in present stocks (inventories) as collateral or, knowing that presentation of real bills asures bank credit, gladly will sell goods for bills.

potential of the commercial loan theory of banking is that of the Great Depression (*cf.* Ch. V).

The "self-liquidating" properties of "real bank loans" (or bills) are, if anything, more chimerical than the needs-of-trade or elasticity-of-currency themes of commercial loan theorists. In fractional-reserve banking the nominal value of quick liabilities will exceed that of banking reserves. It is logically impossible for the banks to convert their asset portfolios into currency (or specie). The value of the former much exceeds that of the latter. Attempts at liquidation merely erode the nominal value of bank assets.

This is not to deny that, if banks wish to contract their portfolios *and* their liability, the contraction would be facilitated if bank assets were of 90-day term or less. However, this point is no better a guide for bank policy than the view that "Rome should be of frame construction so that, if the Emperor Nero wishes to burn the city, he can be accommodated" is for building standards.

Lauchlin Currie attacks the liquidity of real bills more narrowly:

> "Practical bankers have never regarded their local commercial loans as the liquid portion of their assets. Rather they have considered them as the least liquid and have classified their holdings of active bonds and security loans as their liquid assets . . . The conclusion is that the liquidity argument supporting the Commercial Loan Theory is untenable."[51]

2

We had better define our terms. A dubious convenience has been served by talking about a substantive doctrine without providing definitions, but a reckoning is at hand. Mints, who probably devoted more attention to the subject than anyone, says ". . . the real-bills doctrine runs to the effect that restriction of bank earning assets to real bills of exchange [or commercial loans of the type already described] will automatically limit, in the most desirable manner, the *quantity* of bank liabilities; it will cause them to *vary* in quantity in accordance with the 'needs of business'; and it will mean that the banks' assets will be of such a nature that they can be turned into cash

[51] Lauchlin Currie, *The Supply and Control of Money in the United States* (Cambridge: Harvard University Press, 1934), pp. 38-39. Chapter 4, "The Monetary Theory vs. the Commercial Loan Theory of Banking," pp. 34 *ff.* is especially valuable.

on short notice and thus place the bank in a position to meet unlooked-for calls for cash."[52]

We have already met these propositions almost point by point. In concluding our general remarks on the doctrine, two additional points are in order: (1) the fact that the real bills doctrine fell into fallacies of composition in formulating rules for behavior of the stock of bank liabilities should not blind us to the fact that almost all responsible writers have advocated that the stock of money be increased *pari passu* (or more) with real output; on the other hand, there are no logical reasons why banks should be narrowly confined in the classes of paper they purchase; (2) dramatic illustrations of the pernicious potential of the real bills doctrine can be drawn from deflations induced or accompanied by increased liquidity preference; if bank credit decreases in response to an initial decline in prices, there will develop pressures leading to forced liquidation, still greater declines in prices, etc. Where one of the sources of deflation is increased demand for money, *cet. par.*, most writers would argue that appropriate official action would be to announce willingness to purchase a wide variety of assets at a given set of prices. Such purchases could sate the desire for liquidity without ruinous deflation of asset prices. Furthermore, the fact that the offer was outstanding might go far to squelch the liquidity crisis, since confidence in future levels of asset prices would be restored. It is quite clear that a real bills (commercial loan) approach to banking theory would not provide the basis for compensatory monetary policy. Rather there is required what Currie terms a "monetary theory of banking."

b) Banking School vs. Currency School

1

We left the history of British monetary controversy with the Resumption of 1819 and its deflationary aftermath. We now turn to banking theory controversies in Britain from about 1825 to the time of our own Civil War, although the climax really occurs in 1844 with the passage of Peel's Act. This period is particularly noted for the controversial *banking* and *currency* schools. The monetary debate was not untouched by the real bills doctrine. In fact one is tempted to say that the banking school adhered to the real bills doctrine (commer-

52 Lloyd W. Mints, *A History of Banking Theory* (Chicago: University of Chicago Press, 1945), p. 29. None of the standard references specifies behavior of Bank rate. Presumably the official sector is excluded.

cial loan theory), the currency school to the monetary theory. Surely the stock of money, under banking school rules, would become an endogenous variable of the system, reacting to changes in business climate, while, under currency school prescriptions, the volume of notes would be subject to the operation of a rigid rule. However, the dichotomization is upset by the failure of currency school writers to deal with *deposits* in any precise way.

None of the parties to the dispute we now consider was in favor of inconvertible paper. Both agreed that an inconvertible paper standard might see different price behavior than would be the case under a metallic standard; things would be pretty hopeless if parties to any economic dispute could not stipulate agreement to *that* proposition. We have already pointed out that the question "who cares how prices would behave under a metallic standard?" simply was not considered in the first half of the nineteenth century. The subject narrows down to *convertible* paper and coin. "And bank deposits," *banking school* men would add. "No, deposits are not part of the universe of discourse," *currency school* men would rejoin. The currency school position, influential and persuasive as it was, is absurd on its face: how can issuance of claims to specie, whether or not these claims circulate at par, fail to influence specie's purchasing power when substitution is so close? Professor Viner describes the final outcome:

> "[t]he final outcome of the discussion was that the currency school agreed with the banking school that deposits and other forms of 'auxiliary currency' or 'economizing expedients,' as well as bank notes could be a source of difficulty, but the two groups appraised differently the relative importance of variations in the two types of means of payment as causes of currency and credit disturbances. The currency school were not prepared to support government regulation of the credit operations of the banking system [witness Peel's Act of 1844], but believed that statutory limitation of the note issues would bring a substantial measure of improvement. The banking school refused to support statutory restrictions on either bank deposits or bank notes, and maintained that the strict limitation of the amount of uncovered note issue would either have no effect or would operate to accentuate rather than to moderate the fluctuations in business conditions."[53]

The *res* then includes convertible paper and coin *and* bank deposits,

[53] Jacob Viner, *op. cit.*, p. 252.

although the treatment of the latter by the currency school was reluctant, sullen, and inconclusive.[54]

The initiative was with the currency school, the drafters and enacters of legislation. Let us then first state the currency school proposals, and then take up the banking school rebuttal, surrebuttals, etc.

The *currency principle,* governing the issue of notes by the Bank of England, was intimately related to the bullionist principle that an inconvertible currency should behave like a convertible currency. Viner states the currency principle as "the doctrine that a mixed currency should be made to operate as would a purely metallic currency . . ."[55] The currency principle would seem first to have been formulated in the 1820's when a 100 per cent reserve plan (for notes) was proposed. How might the note circulation be regulated so that the sum of coin and bank notes would fluctuate as would a metallic currency?

The first answer was the Palmer Rule or the Rule of 1832. It might be said to have had currency school backing, although there was far from complete doctrinal unity among members of the schools. The upshot of the Palmer Rule (named after the Bank's governor, J. Horsley Palmer) is easy to state: the Bank should endeavor to keep its securities holdings (including discounted paper) constant. Following Viner,

> "An influx of gold from abroad would thus act to increase the note circulation by a corresponding amount [if gold were tendered for notes]; an efflux of gold or a demand for coin for internal circulation would result in a corresponding decrease in note circulation. The internal circulation, specie plus paper, would thus remain constant unless acted upon by external gold movements."[56]

The Palmer Rule contained a fatal flaw. Exhibiting currency school perversity, the Rule ignored fluctuations in the *deposits* of the Bank of England. Thus, the governor of the Bank might be steering

---

[54] If there were a well defined "normal" proportion between deposits and notes that the public wished to maintain, it is clear that *ultimate* control of deposits could be achieved through control of the note issue. It would remain true that transitory departure from the equilibrium ratio could be substantial and that return to the equilibrium ratio could have dangerous effects on bank liquidity.

The problem recalls "analysis" in Ch. II of the way in which the stock of gold could, under a full gold standard, ultimately affect the stock of perpetuities in the system.

[55] *Ibid.,* p. 225.

[56] *Ibid.,* p. 225.

steadily according to the Rule, maintaining securities constant, but depositors could be draining off the Bank's gold by cashing their claims.[57] The Rule could be inviolate, the note circulation unchanged, but the Bank could be suffering a fatal gold hemorrhage: not from submission of notes for redemption, but through the open deposit door.

Experience under the Palmer Rule was rather horrendous:

> "[f]rom 1836 to 1839 in particular, while the Rule was presumably being followed, the Bank was in serious difficulties much of the time."[58]

Indeed, the Bank broke the Palmer Rule on a number of occasions from 1836 to 1839. At least two prominent currency schoolmen, Torrens and Overstone, proposed to correct the faults of the Palmer Rule through a drastic device: sever the banking and issue departments of the Bank of England; the issue department would be confined to exchanging notes for bullion and *vice versa*; its total note issue would be "covered" by bullion except for a fiduciary issue "covered" by securities; the banking department was to behave as just another bank. The monetary authorities were to wash their hands of the banking department.

The currency school also was concerned about the note issues of country banks (London private banks having discontinued issue during the 18th century):

> "[t]he currency school undoubtedly wanted the note issue powers of the country banks to be withdrawn, or at least drastically reduced, but they did not enlarge upon this phase . . . , as a precaution, perhaps, against providing further stimulus to the already vigorous opposition of the country's bankers to the currency school proposals."[59]

The new currency school proposals were incorporated into the Bank Act of 1844 (Peel's Act). The Act of 1844 has been called the Charter of English Banking up to World War I. Its fossil remains to this day. Under the Act, the issue department managed nicely. But the banking department had frightful experiences. By fall, 1847, the

57 Of course, an *influx* of gold might find expression through an increase in the Bank's deposits and *pari passu* its gold holdings. The Palmer Rule would not permit the Bank to increase its note circulation by buying securities.

58 Viner, *op. cit.*, p. 227. And, as Hawtrey points out *(Art of Central Banking)*, the Rule prevented the Bank from succoring the money market; it was inconsistent with the Bank's role as lender of last resort.

59 *Ibid.*, pp. 228-229.

Bank was experiencing the effects of a panic. The sources were readily visible: an initial decline in the reserves of the banking department, coupled with the knowledge of depositors that the banking department had no recourse to the gold or even notes of the issue department, caused alarm; deposits began to be checked out. The Act was suspended on October 22, 1847; the Bank was authorized to issue uncovered notes in addition to the fiduciary issue permitted by law and was requested to discount freely at a high rate of interest. Indeed these measures so much enhanced confidence that the gold tranche was reversed and the authorized note issue never had to be made. The Bank Act had to be suspended in 1857 and 1866 under similar circumstances, but the Act survived, a monument to the currency school.

Certain critical problems of the administration of the Act are discussed in Ch. VC. Let us now summarize the major facts of life under the Act:

1) the currency principle was assured without suspension of the Act. The volume of the issue department's notes outstanding would fluctuate precisely with its gold holdings;

2) the banking department was left without close guidance. No simple rule could be formulated to govern it. Grasp of central banking theory was not achieved until later and is tied up with the work of Walter Bagehot. In any case, convertibility of bank liabilities in Britain was not firmly assured;

3) the Act set a maximum limit on the note issues of country banks. It was felt that otherwise it would be possible for the country banks to expand their issues relative to the Bank of England for some time before being checked by loss of gold through local redemption and adverse clearings with London.

2

We now consider *banking school* reaction to this legislation and whatever countermeasures were generated. As Mints points out:

> ". . . they very cogently criticized the proposal to separate the departments of the Bank, because, as they held, a drain of gold might reduce deposits rather than the volume of notes outstanding."[60]

Banking school writers were much more aware of the monetary role of bank credit, or at least much more willing to express such awareness. J. S. Mill well reflects banking school skepticism of achieving

[60] Mints, *op. cit.*, p. 86.

effective control of monetary conditions through the currency principle (and currency schoolmen, although tinctured by strong *laissez-faire* bias, did desire such control):

> "It is well known that, of late years, an artificial limitation of the issue of bank notes has been regarded by many political economists, and by a large portion of the public, as an expedient of supreme efficacy for preventing, and when it cannot prevent, for moderating, the fever of speculation; and this opinion received the recognition and sanction of the legislature by the Currency Act of 1844. At the point, however, which our inquiries have reached, though we have conceded bank notes a greater power over prices than is possessed by bills or book credits [*cf.* Ch. VI *infra* for further discussion of book credit], we have not found reason to think that this superior efficacy has much share in producing the rise in prices which accompanies a period of speculation [Mill stressed book credit as fuel for speculation], nor consequently that any restraint applied to this one instrument can be efficacious to the degree which is often supposed, in moderating either that rise or the recoil which follows it. We shall be less inclined to think so, when we consider that there is a fourth form of credit transactions, by cheques on bankers, and transfers in a banker's books which is exactly parallel in every respect to bank notes, giving equal facilities to an extension of credit, and capable of acting on prices quite as powerfully."[61]

Still, banking school writers did not propose legislation limiting deposit creation by joint-stock banks. Viner suggests that this may have been "partly because they thought it impracticable, partly because, like the currency school, they objected to such control on general *laissez-faire* grounds." And then, for some at least, a reason can be gleaned from the *banking principle* itself. (There need be no regulation of a convertible note issue based on real bills; *laissez-faire* will assure that the volume of issue, based on real bills, will fluctuate with the needs of trade.) Stressing, as did Mill, the similarities of notes and deposits, some banking school writers applied the banking principle to deposits as well as notes, at least implicitly. On the other hand, John Fullarton *did* write that, if the banking principle is adhered to, "any redundance of *bank-note* issue is rendered impossible."[62] The issue is opaque.

The banking school opposed restrictions on note issue, such as those of Peel's Act, as being unnecessary and likely to be harmful, be-

---

61 J. S. Mill. *Principles of Political Economy* (Ashley Ed.) Book III, Ch. XII, §6, pp. 536-537.

62 Quoted by L. W. Mints, *op. cit.*, p. 91. Emphasis is mine.

ing in conflict with natural economic law. "Natural economic law" was its celebrated *principle of reflux*. "Reflux" refers to the process of returning notes to banks upon abatement of the needs of trade and consequent repayment of bank loans. Viner's summary is acute:

> "The essential fallacy of the banking school doctrine . . . lay in its assumption that the 'needs of business' for currency were a definite quantity independent of the state of business psychology and the activities of the banks. The banking school were right in insisting that the volume of bank credit was dependent on the willingness of businessmen to borrow as well as on the willingness of banks to lend. But the willingness of businessmen to borrow depended on their anticipations of the trend of business, on interest rate, and on their anticipations as to the willingness of the banks, in case of need, to renew loans upon their maturity. The banks, by lowering their interest rates, or . . . their credit standards, could place more loans, and the increase of loans, by increasing prices and physical volume of sales, would in turn increase the willingness of businessmen to borrow . . . [B]ankers ordinarily do not see this, because they do not see that they themselves as a group had created the conditions which make an expansion of credit possible and appear to make it 'necessary' . . ."[63]

Banking school writers were not terribly rigid about specific classes of commercial paper that qualified as proper bank assets. They preferred short-term paper, allegedly contributing to the adequacy of the reflux. They made pious invocations against "speculative" loans. But no real attempt was made at scientific definition.

The banking school were aware that "over-issue" would be found out and punished (through loss of bullion) more rapidly for individual banks than for entire systems that had expanded issue. Nevertheless, it was confident that the habits of the public with respect to the proportion it maintained between notes and specie and the effects of higher domestic prices on national bullion reserves would impose a distinct and insurmountable barrier to over-issue. (*Cf.* footnote 54 for a similar argument pertaining to currency school neglect of the volume of deposits.)

3

The surrebuttal of the currency school basically was twofold: (1) the fact remained that the note issue of the Bank assuredly was

63 The spirit of the Radcliffe *Report* cited at p. 119 *ff.* is remarkably similar to that of the banking school insofar as the *Report* stresses that control of *bank* credit may not suffice to control credit.

convertible and behaved, with rare exception, as would a metallic currency. This defense, of course, is based on a narrow construction of the Act. Its economic significance is dim to modern ears. (2) the problem of deposit creation would arise just as much under a metallic as under a mixed currency circulation. Again, under a narrow construction of the Act, a plea of confession and avoidance could be entered. There is a nightmarish lack of economic reality in this defense, but this is not the first time that the rosy hue of resolution sicklied o'er the pale cast of thought.

4

Relying on Mints,[64] the viewpoints of the two schools can be broadly summarized. First the currency school:

1) the currency should vary as would a specie circulation. The authorities should be denied discretion.

2) the currency should be convertible.

3) the real bills doctrine or commercial loan theory of banking is invalid.

As for the banking school:

1) the principle of reflux should control the volume of bank notes (to make the weaker statement) — when bank credit is confined to proper ends.

2) the currency should be convertible. (1) and (2) may appear contradictory — *cf.* Mints, p. 90. Of course, when bank credit is not confined to real bills, the principle of reflux does not apply; also convertibility permits external forces to regulate the price level and, hence, the total volume of money (Viner's point).

3) the level and variations of deposits are important components of monetary circulation and change. Failure of the Act of 1844 to regulate deposits would prove discomforting. (Again seeming contradiction with (1) is resolved by the last paragraph's argument, possibilities of speculative issue, etc. Furthermore, it is not clear that Fullerton, for example, applied the principle of reflux to deposits.)

4) internal drains of gold are more likely to concern encashment of deposits than of notes.

As a group, currency school writers were much more sanguine about effects of interest-rate manipulation on the demand for credit and on international gold flows. Banking school writers, on the other

64 *Ibid.*, pp. 75-100, esp. pp. 75, 86.

hand, much stressed the way in which currency substitutes might be created and destroyed over the business cycle.[65]

2. 100 Per Cent Reserve Banking

1

There are two reasons for discussing this topic now: (1) the theoretical position of the 100 per cent reserve advocates is beautifully antithetical to that underlying a commercial loan theory of banking; (2) analysis of 100 per cent reserve proposals shows that the fractional-reserve principle, while inherent in the functional concept of such financial institutions as savings and loan associations, is not absolutely necessary for that of commercial banking.[66]

As for (2), imagine that commercial banks simultaneously are ordered to maintain 100 per cent reserves and are presented with something more than $150 billion in reserves with the Federal Reserve, meeting the 100 per cent reserve requirement. Nothing fundamental in the nature of commercial banking would be changed — at least not from bankers' standpoints. After all, the banks cannot now substantially expand their asset portfolios unless either new reserves are made available or additional share capital is provided by the public.[67] Now imagine that a 100 per cent reserve requirement also is imposed on savings and loan associations and that a peculiarly restricted gift of $50 billion in cash is conferred upon them, somehow leaving unchanged the wealth positions of shareholders. Something fundamental *would* be altered: the associations could no longer intermediate between savers and deficit spending units; they could not afford to accept new savings, because such acceptance would impose an obligation upon them to increase their reserves *pari passu.* All that would be left for the savings and loan associations would be to manage their present portfolios; they would make loans only by liquidating assets now in their portfolios.

The analysis brings out a fundamental distinction between the

---

65 *Cf.* J. S. Mill citation, pp. 223-224.

Cf. also Lionel Robbins, *Robert Torrens and the Evolution of Classical Economics* (London: Macmillan and Co., Ltd., 1958), Esp. pp. 97-143. Chapter IV of *Torrens* (pp. 73-96) takes up the bullionist controversy.

66 Footnote 44 is based on current institutional arrangements. Leverage of bank shareholders' capital would, of course, be sustained by a gift of reserves.

67 The government would have a rigid grip on the supply of money. We soon see that this is important in the large, but not from a worm's eye point of view.

basic role of commercial banks and of non-banking financial intermediaries. Commercial banking has relevance in a stationary state; non-banking intermediaries would have to be gelded in order to fit into a stationary process. It is easy to visualize repayment of bank loans without positive saving taking place; for example, Firm A repays its loan through inventory liquidation, enabling Firm B to accumulate additional inventory when the proceeds of repayment are in turn lent to it. Theoretically, financial intermediaries other than commercial banks could be fitted into the stationary state as managers of a constant portfolio; the savings of some could be offset by the dissavings of others. And, of course, their balance sheets reveal deposit obligations important in the society's asset structure. But in fact the *raison d'être* of non-banking financial intermediaries is mediation between savers and borrowers, a mediation leaving a residue of liabilities forming highly liquid claims in the hands of the public.

2

The antithesis of the underpinnings of 100 per cent reserve banking and of commercial-loan theories is perfect. The core of the complaint of Milton Friedman[68] and other supporters of 100 per cent reserve banking is that changes in the demand for currency, changes in the distribution of deposits between demand and time liabilities, or changes in desired free reserves now generate changes in the supply of money quite independently of the authorities; fractional-reserve banking and absolutely rigid control of the stock of money are incompatible. What could more contradict the banking principle or the real bills doctrine in any of its forms? Indeed, Friedman is concerned lest banks, responding to any pressure whatever, might be able to expand or contract the money supply.[69] One hundred per cent reserve

[68] *Op. cit.*, pp. 65-76. A particularly lucid exposition. *Cf.* also A. G. Hart, "The 'Chicago Plan' of Banking Reform," *The Review of Economic Studies* (1935), pp. 104-116, reprinted in Lutz and Mints (eds.) *Readings in Monetary Theory.*

[69] The Chicago Plan — so-called because of close association with a group of economists at the University of Chicago — was promulgated *circa* 1933. Much of its motive force was generated by the bank failures of that time. The Federal Deposit Insurance Corporation, easily able to come up with whatever ultimate stuff (paper) is necessary to staunch a drain, together with more enlightened concepts of the role of the central bank during crises of liquidity, dissolves this basis for reform. Friedman recognizes this. Together with the desirability of achieving more precise control of the supply of money, he emphasizes that 100 per cent reserve banking would permit reduction of government intervention in the banking business. For me the latter argument is somewhat farfetched.

banking is suggested as a means of making the banks tractable. Let us see why.

Define the stock of money as consisting of bank deposits and currency in circulation. Assume that 100 per cent reserve banking is in effect. Obviously, bankers' deposits could not legally exceed their reserves. Bankers collectively would have no way of increasing their reserves beyond 100 per cent other than by making contributions to capital or inducing the public to buy shares.[70] It would be passing brave to find banks wishing to cut their incomes further, although speculative motivation could lead banks to increase reserves beyond 100 per cent from time to time — revealing an imperfection in the plan. What if the public wishes to hold currency instead of deposits? It simply converts the one into the other. Bank deposits and reserves fall by the same amount. The banks remain in balance; the supply of money is unchanged. The deck is clear for government control of the stock of money through creation (destruction) of currency and issuance of new reserves (positive and negative). This is to be done through deficit (surplus) finance and open-market transactions in securities.[71]

3

Practical problems of implementation of the 100 per cent reserve plan here, now, and in the U. S. have all the relevance of conversion of automobile bumpers into green cheese. Still the issues are intriguing. A few are listed below:

1) we have assumed that the banks simply would be given the reserves necessary to bring them within the 100 per cent rule; otherwise there would be real problems of transition if deflation were to be avoided. Friedman's proposal is different, to wit,

> "there is no technical problem of achieving a transition . . . Required reserves could be raised in a sequence of steps . . . culminating to a final rise to 100% in, say, two years. The Reserve System would provide the additional reserves needed to prevent the increases in required reserves from reducing the stock of money by purchasing government securities in the open market . . . Thereafter, the funds acquired by non-bank holders of government securities would be available to purchase the assets that banks would have to dispose of to meet the additional reserve requirements or to purchase the capital

70 An individual banker converts securities into reserves through favorable clearings. But this reduces the reserves (and deposits) of some other banker.

71 Changes in the stock of money would be equal to changes in bank reserves. The systematic coefficient of expansion would be unity.

stock and bonds issued by the investment trusts that banks would form to take over their lending and investment activities."[72]

2) there would be severe disruption in the banking business due to the loss of banks' earning assets (unless additional reserves simply were given to them). The fact that deposits would not be maintained by banks unless they received what might be heavy service charges might lead to *sub rosa* deals finding savings deposits substituted for demand deposits under fractional-reserve principles. These problems might be overcome by paying interest on bank reserves, a proposal Professor Friedman recommends on several other grounds as well.

3) "if savings deposits remained in their present form, but most of the present reserves were absorbed in the 100 per cent reserve against chequing deposits, the reserve proportions of the successor institutions would be so thin as to make them very vulnerable to runs. But to encourage savings bankers to carry large reserves, or to insure savings deposits, would be to revive many of the aspects of banking which the '100 per cent plan' is aimed to abolish [changes in depositors' desired currency positions leading to changes in the money stock, etc. In fact savings deposits are insured.]."[73]

Henry Simons proposed that the obligations of savings banks be converted into common stock. Friedman implicitly recommends the same solution when he writes:

"[in connection with the non-depository side of banking operations] the other institution that would be formed would be an investment trust or brokerage firm. It would acquire capital by selling shares or debentures and would use the capital to make loans or acquire investments."[74]

C. SOME HISTORY

1

As it happens, the big historical guns are not fired until Ch. VC. It is easier to talk about the history of banking in the United States and Britain after central banks are in the picture. Just as conventional political histories center on princes and presidents, so do banking his-

[72] *Ibid.*, p. 70.

[73] A. G. Hart, *op. cit.*, p. 453. *In re* (2), *cf.* J. Tobin, *Review of Economics and Statistics*, August, 1960.

[74] Friedman, *op. cit.*, p. 70.

tories concentrate on Governors of the Bank of England and Chairmen of the Federal Reserve Board. All that is done in Ch. IV is to discuss concentration in banking and the growth of deposit banking as against note issue — after this preface.

Adjusting for price-level changes, one discovers a rough correspondence in the expansion of bank credit in the U. S. from 1914 to 1960 with the expansion in industrial production, taking the latter as a measure of economic activity. This correspondence — no more than a poetic sortee ignoring important movements in velocity taken up in Ch. XIV — suggests part of the process that finds the real and financial sectors of the economy interlocked.[75] The expansion of the monetary base ("high powered" money) has permitted large increases in real activity to proceed with, as it happens, greater-than-proportional expansion of banking liabilities. All in all, deflationary pressure has been avoided. The secular growth of the money stock has been such that the supply of liquid assets *par excellence* has not lagged behind the growth of non-financial assets. When the even more rapid growth of non-banking financial institutions is accounted for, one is not surprised that the 1914–1960 interval was featured by inflation *and* growth in the real stock of liquid assets per capita.[76] The peculiar interaction of "nominal" parameters and tastes that explains movement of real as against nominal financial asset holdings cannot be explained until Part II.

2

The enormous concentration of British banking has been described: a handful of members of the London clearing association control more than 90 per cent of the country's banking business. Concentration in the United States, while substantial, is less pronounced. Recalling that total loans and investments of American commercial banks on December 31, 1960 were $199.5 billion, consider these statistics (for the same date):

a) 15 New York City banks held $27.8 billion in loans and investments;

b) 10 Chicago banks held $7.1 billion;

[75] The fact that prices have about tripled from 1914 to 1960 suggests further interaction between nominal and real values. Such interaction will occupy much of our attention in Ch. VA and in Part II of the book.

[76] Alternatively, the process saw continuous exchange by firms and households of their securities (non-monetary liabilities) for bank liabilities. Banks were able to carry out their role through the secular expansion of the monetary base.

c) 205 other member banks, classified as reserve city banks, accounted for $63.7 billion in loans and investments;

d) the remaining 5,917 members of the Federal Reserve System accounted for $68.9 billion;

e) in recent years there has been a wave of bank mergers.

3

Deposits were beginning drastically to increase in importance in the first half of the nineteenth century, a matter of considerable importance for the banking school/currency school controversy. Bank notes continued to be important in the United States rather later than in Britain, although the dollar volume of deposits at American state banks exceeded that of notes as early as 1855. However, as late as 1861 deposits ($257 million) exceeded notes ($202 million) by only $55 million. The importance of bank notes steadily declined until, with the onset of the Federal Reserve in 1914, central bank notes virtually took over the bank currency role altogether.

SUMMARY

1. A consolidated balance sheet for commercial banks shows that banks have deposit obligations far in excess of the sum of their vault cash and reserve accounts.
2. This does not disturb the individual banker who is conscious of the possibility of selling such highly liquid assets as government bonds if he becomes strapped for cash. However, such liquidation can be accomplished only at the expense of some other banker's reserves. The ultimate guarantee of the system's solvency must be that of the central authority. This is inherent in the logic of fractional-reserve banking. The guarantee has been made easy to execute by eliminating gold as the system's ultimate reserve for internal payments.
3. The annual work done by bank deposits is measured in *trillions* of dollars. Deposits typically turn over many times during the year.
4. The growth of fractional-reserve banking is bound up in the terms "reserve," "deposit," and "loans and investments." Primary deposits formed reserves which permitted banks to make loans and purchase marketable securities, in exchange for claims against

themselves. Over the centuries, steady growth in reserves, now largely accounts with central banks, have enabled banks to acquire enormous quantities of debt instruments issued by the public and by governments. Bank indebtedness to the public (deposit liability) has grown correspondingly.

5. Bank liabilities form the greater part of modern media of exchange. Demand obligations of commercial banks being the most liquid of assets, commercial banking can be interpreted as the exchange of extremely short-term, highly liquid claims for longer-term, less liquid assets. In this way the liquidity of economic units has been increased.

6. Coefficients of expansion give ratios of potential expansion in loans and investments — or deposit liability — to increments of excess reserves. The coefficient of expansion of loans and investments for a closed system is given by

$$\frac{1 + c'}{r + c'} .$$

The coefficient of expansion for the United States exceeds 6. Expansion possibilities for individual banks must be described differently. A model was set out in which $dD_i^*/dA_i = 0$, excluding structural change or increase in systematic reserves. The model led to $dD_i^*/d\bar{A} = \lambda_i\eta$ where η is the systematic coefficient of expansion, λ_i the equilibrium "relative size" of the *ith* banks, and $\bar{A}$ aggregate reserves. The analysis was one of general equilibrium.

7. Fallacies of composition prevent understanding of how changes in aggregate reserves work their way through the system. A $1 decrease in systematic reserves — leading to a $x contraction in systematic deposit liability — finds individual banks at each stage of the process reducing asset portfolios and deposit liability only about one-for-one with reductions in reserves. But Bank A's retrenchment, finding it exchanging securities for claims against other banks, leads to pressure against these banks. Unless one focuses on the entire picture, he does not see that expansion and contraction effects are multiplied. The pedestrian character of the separate stages is deceiving. The text concentrated on the dynamical process leading to a new systemic equilibrium state.

8. The dynamics of expansion of savings banks find fresh deposits quickly leaving the system as loan proceeds are checked out.

9. Economic theory is concerned with effects of changes in parameters on dependent variables of the system. Parameters governing bank decision-making include reserve requirements, rediscount rates, etc. Dependent variables include asset portfolios of banks, households, and firms, bond prices and, perhaps, rates of industrial activity and employment. Among other things, economists are concerned with predicting effects of changes in variables under official control on solution values for prices and outputs.
10. A hypothetical problem concerning contraction of bank reserves suggested substantial possibilities for households and firms to economize on cash balances. Since the stimulus for economizing on currency and demand-deposit holdings (the sum of which we define as "cash") centers on effects of higher interest rates, one senses that an important question concerns effects of higher interest rates on expenditure decisions.
11. The origins of central banking might be found in problems of mitigating dangers of fractional-reserve banking: "mass of manoeuvre" has special meaning. As time has passed, central banks have concentrated on influencing financial markets, partly in the hope that effects will be indirectly registered in labor and commodities markets.
12. The Treasury bill has come to play the premier role among short-term paper. This is ironic. The Federal Reserve System — founded on a commercial loan theory of banking — was intended to encourage banks to hold large volumes of trade bills, once a thick commercial-acceptances market was established.
13. Balance sheets of American commercial banks show how important have become government security holdings in bank portfolios. Actual portfolios are vastly different from the image of old-time commercial loan theorists. The finance of World War II had much to do with the present picture.
14. The fact that demand deposits do not bear interest reflects historical accident and political pressures. Indeed the prohibition against interest-bearing demand deposits violates standard criteria of welfare economics.
15. Contrast of the real bills doctrine (commercial loan theory of banking) with proposals for 100 per cent reserve commercial banking develops an almost perfect antithesis. The former theory

envisages expansion and contraction of bank credit as proceeding ideally from response to pressures from firms and households summarized in "needs of trade." The latter approach stresses that deposit liability, together with currency in circulation, should be subject to firm control, remaining unresponsive to endogenous pressures; indeed the supply of money, however defined, is to behave contracyclically, dropping from its secular expansion path during booms and exceeding it during depressions.

16. One hundred per cent reserve banking mostly is interesting for intellectual rather than for politically immediate reasons.
17. The real bills doctrine has been approved by some economists of great reputation. Adam Smith appears to have been one. It was gingerly embraced by John Stuart Mill and was part of the basic thinking of the founders of the Federal Reserve System.
18. The basic weakness of the doctrine is that it supposes that the monetary "requirements" of the business community are a quantum that can be defined independently of the behavior of banks and the psychology of businessmen. The doctrine appears founded on a fallacy of composition: the individual businessman goes to his bank to float a loan or refinance an existing loan faced with prices of goods and securities that for him are data. The fact that these prices, together with inventory plans, result from the *collective* behavior of businessmen is not apparent to the individual businessman. Here it is fallacious to reason from the parts to the whole.
19. The controversies in the nineteenth century between conflicting British schools are important for understanding banking theory, ancient and modern. Banking school writers, supporting the banking principle of reflux also supported convertibility of bank obligations into gold: their support of the real bills doctrine was not complete. Also they often were much concerned about consequences of "speculation."

NOTES

NOTE A: Appendix E of Alfred Marshall, *Money Credit and Commerce* (London: Macmillan & Co., 1923), p. 295 *ff*. contains an excellent short history of the development of banking, calling attention to Adam Smith, *The Wealth of Nations*. These are some of the main features of the Marshallian account:

1) Traces of "rudimentary banks" can be found in Chaldean, Egyptian, and Phoenician history.

2) "In Greece, the temples of Delphi and other safe places acted as storehouses for the precious metals before the days of coinage, and in later times they lent out money for public and private purposes at interest, though they paid none themselves. Private money changers began with the task of reducing many metallic currencies, more or less exactly, to a common unit of value; and went on to accept money on deposit, at interest, and to let it out at higher interest, permitting meanwhile drafts to be drawn on them." (Marshall, *op. cit.*, p. 295.)

3) Roman history followed the Greek pattern.

4) ". . . And when trade and industry began to revive in the Middle Ages, the lessons of finance were learnt anew from the beginning." (*Ibid.*, p. 295.) Money lending was largely a province of the Jews until about the 13th century when "it came to be taken over by Christians, whose business competition was aided by frequent outbursts of crude popular violence against the Jews . . ." (*Ibid.*, p. 296.) Marshall stresses the intimacy between the business of money changing and the growth of commercial (fractional-reserve) banking.

5) There was, however, another strand: the exigent financial requirements of political authorities. Bank privileges were granted in exchange for loans. Consider Adam Smith's account:

> "The earliest banks of Italy, where the name began, were finance companies . . . to make loans to, and float loans for, the governments of cities in which they were formed . . . After these banks had been long established, they began to do what we call banking business; but at first they never thought of it . . . The currency of a small state, such as Genoa or Hamburg . . . must be made up, in great measure, of coins of all the neighboring states, with which its inhabitants have continual intercourse [calling for money changers]." *Wealth of Nations,* Book IV, Chapter III, Part I.)

6) The Bank of Amsterdam was the great bank of the 17th century, holding "for a long time a position in international commerce as prominent as the Bank of England does now." (Marshall, *op. cit.*, p. 298.) The History of the Bank of Amsterdam is typical of the life story of many banks in the later Middle Ages: foundation in order to accumulate a stock of capital to lend without intention to make additional loans; making of additional loans, thereby becoming a fractional-reserve institution; failure when a run revealed that "fraud" had been practiced. Marshall writes that banks such as the Bank of Amsterdam acted as fiscal agents for the government and "in addition they were responsible for the counterpart of much of the work of modern stock exchanges." They facilitated conjunction of lenders and borrowers and holders of cash and of "old" securities. But the bank's main function was described by Adam Smith:

> "It received both foreign coin and the light and worn coin of the country at its intrinsic value in the good standard money of the country, deducting only so much as was necessary for defraying the expense of coinage, and the other necessary expenses of management. For the value which remained . . . it gave a credit on its books. This credit was called bank money, which, as it represented money exactly according to the standard of the mint, was always of the same real value and intrinsically worth more than current money . . . It could be paid away by a simple transfer, without the trouble of counting, or the risk of transporting it from one place to another." *(Wealth of Nations,* Book IV, Ch. III, Part I.)

The Bank of Amsterdam issued *Recipissen* for bullion deposited. Marshall calls them "transferable (and divisible) pawn tickets." But the *Recipissen* were not bearer instruments: the Bank required a series of endorsements before it would pay out bullion to the *nth* person in a chain of transfers of the original receipt. The Riksbank of Sweden originated the modern bank note in 1661.

The Bank of Amsterdam was induced by the Dutch government to "lend its deposits" to the Government. Marshall puts the matter with a touch of pure Victorianism: "the fraud committed by the Bank of Amsterdam in lending its deposits was without taint of private selfishness . . . [T]he State, which ordered the fraud, ultimately made good the loss occasioned by it to the bank's customers." (*Op. cit.*, p. 299.)

7) Marshall (p. 299) cites an author named Harris (writing in 1757) indicating the historical inevitability of the tale just told. Fractional reserve-banking stems from forces deep within man's rapacious soul. Harris wrote:

> "Should [bills of undoubted credit] increase much beyond the real stock of bullion that ought to be in their stead, they would prove mischievous in two ways: [by increasing the stock of money]; and by endangering, on a cloudy day, their own credit. But the profits to be made by lending . . . are temptations too strong to be resisted . . ."

Marshall points out that, in contrast with other commodity storehouses, a monetary storehouse "can perform its chief functions without yielding up any considerable part of its contents." It can issue warehouse receipts, passing from hand to hand This leads to the crucial role of *opinion* for the success of fractional-reserve banking. He points out that the credit of the Bank of Amsterdam was at its zenith when its "solid basis . . . had been undermined by the secret lending of its metallic stores for various public purposes."

8) Do not neglect the *Wealth of Nations.* It is fresh and stimulating. Particularly in its account of the Bank of Amsterdam. *Cf.* also A. P. Usher, "The Origins of Banking," *Economic History Review,* Vol. IV, 1934, pp. 399-428.

NOTE B: Inspection will show that Equation *(e)* can be formed by adding Equations *(f)* and *(g)* and multiplying the left- and right-hand sides of the resulting equation by *(—1)*. It follows that the determinant of the matrix Q has the value zero and that the necessary condition for existence of a solution (up to a factor of proportionality) of Equations *(e-g)* is met. These results can be generalized on inspection for an $n \times n$ matrix Q. In the case of the system *(e-g)*, eliminating Equation *(e)*, we can derive Equations *(k)* and *(l)*:

$$(k) \qquad -q_{12}(D_1/D_3) + (q_{21} + q_{23})(D_2/D_3) = q_{32}$$

$$(l) \qquad -q_{13}(D_1/D_3) - q_{23}(D_2/D_3) = -q_{31} - q_{32}$$

Equation *(h)* can be written

$$(m) \qquad D_1/D_3 + D_2/D_3 = \overline{D}/D_3 - 1.$$

Since Equations *(k)* and *(l)* have determined D_1/D_3 and D_2/D_3, Equation *(m)* can be solved for D_3. It becomes easy to solve for D_1 and D_2.

Check your understanding by doing the 2-bank case with the general technique.

$$(n) \qquad q_{12}D_1 - q_{21}D_2 = 0$$

$$(o) \qquad -q_{12}D_1 + q_{21}D_2 = 0$$

$$(p) \qquad D_1 + D_2 = \overline{D}$$

Equations *(n)* and *(o)* clearly are linearly dependent. Eliminate *(o)*, for example. Equation *(n)* can be written

$$D_1/D_2 = q_{21}/q_{12}$$

(p) is rewritten

$$(q) \qquad D_1/D_2 = \overline{D}/D_2 - 1.$$

The rest is easy.

NOTE C: Milton Friedman contributes an important *caveat* and also provides a more precise formulation of the general issue in his note "Vault Cash and Free Reserves," *Journal of Political Economy* (Vol. 69, No. 2), April 1961, pp. 181-82. He makes these points:

1) ". . . the economically relevant variable is not free reserves but the difference between actual free reserves and desired free reserves . . . Hence, a given absolute level of free reserves may be expansionary or contractionary according as it exceeds or falls short of the desired level." (p. 181).

2) ". . . The change in the status of vault cash has almost surely raised the level of free reserves that banks desire to keep for given other conditions" (p. 181).

Friedman supports points 1 and 2 by showing that, if we were to define "free cash" as the excess of deposits with the Federal Reserve plus vault cash over required reserves plus borrowings from the Federal Reserve, we should find that ". . . [b]efore the change, free reserves were less than free cash by the amount of vault cash. After the change, free reserves equaled free cash. If the altered status of vault cash had had no effect on the desired amount of free cash, it would have raised desired free reserves by the amount of the vault cash . . . In order for the altered status of vault cash to have left desired free reserves unchanged, it would have had to reduce desired free cash by the full amount of vault cash" (p. 181).

3) the most likely outcome lies between the extremes: desired free cash should decrease because vault cash now serves as a reserve item as well (it is no longer necessary to reduce reserves in order to increase vault cash) but he concedes that "[i]t is less easy to see why desired free cash should not decline by the full amount of the vault cash released to count as reserves" (p. 182). He offers two reasons: (a) vault cash probably exhibits greater variability in its behavior than do other reserve items, thus adding to the variability of reserve items as a whole and suggesting that banks might want to hold larger free reserves; (b) since the permission to use vault cash as a reserve item has the mien of a reduction in reserve requirements, the case falls under the general rule that "[i]n general, it seems unlikely that a reduction in required reserves will produce a full dollar-for-dollar reduction in desired total reserves. This is clear in the extreme case. Reduction of required reserves to zero, even at a time when excess reserves were negligible, would not reduce desired total reserves to zero" (p. 182). He concedes, however, that the fraction giving the desired reduction in total reserves over the reduction in required reserves approaches unity today in contrast with 1936-1937 when it approached zero.

APPENDIX

The Bank as a Firm

We attempt a formal statement of the commercial bank as a firm. Of course, formal theories of behavior of firms are couched in terms of maximization subject to side conditions. What might banks be maximizing? Net earnings? Not exactly: vulnerability to capital loss, portfolio flexibility, liquidity, etc., enter into bankers' calculations. Banks seek to achieve the best combination of interest earnings, liquidity, etc. open to them in the surrounding environment. Formally, think of the representative bank as maximizing

$$U \equiv f(\pi, S, u). \tag{1}$$

π is the bank's expected net income for the Hicksian day. S is an index number measuring vulnerability to capital loss during the day due to interest rate changes. u is an index number measuring the bank's vulnerability to risk factors such as business depression, liquidity crises, etc. (The latter can force the bank into liquidation at the beginning of tomorrow.) The indices can be assumed to decrease as risk increases; reciprocals of variances might be calculated.

The bank must make its portfolio plan at the beginning of the Hicksian day. All transactions are made at the beginning of the day at prices posted at the beginning of the day. There will in general be a new set of prices facing the bank at the beginning of tomorrow. There is one sticky bit of fudge: promotional expense is assumed to be associated only with today's supplies of deposits to the bank; a problem in capital theory is converted into one of analysis of current dated flows. This suggests (correctly) that intertemporal maximization would be used in a more rigorous formulation. Perhaps we should have consulted the calculus of variations. We did not. Also, bank capital and retained earnings are ignored, except as residual legatees.

Currency is ignored. All money is assumed to be bank money; vault cash is nonexistent.

Equations *(1a)*, *(1b)*, and *(1c)* define the independent variables of Equation *(1)*:

(1a) $$\pi \equiv g^1(x, y_1, y_2, V, r_1, r_2, r_3, c, p) - G(x, y) - A.$$

x is a vector of holdings of securities (including IOU's underlying advances) contracted for at the beginning of the day. c is a vector of *expected* capital gains (losses) on the securities contracted for at the beginning of the day at the vector of securities prices p (implying running yields). y_1 and y_2 (the vector y) are demand- and time-deposit liability contracted for at the beginning of the day. V is borrowings from the central bank contracted for at the beginning of the day. r_1, r_2, and r_3 (the vector r) are interest charges prevailing at the beginning of the day for demand and time deposits and central bank discounts. These rates govern transactions for this period. (Demand-deposit rates now are zero, as are rates paid by the Federal Reserve.) A is promotional expenditure. Thus $g^1(\quad)$ gives an expected gross revenue position, while $G(\quad)$ expresses the relationship between bank expenses and bank activity net of promotional expense.

(1b) $$S \equiv g^2(x, y, V, r, c, p),$$

(1c) $$u \equiv g^3(x, y, V, r, c, p, R),$$

where R gives total reserves planned for the end of the day. Introduction of legal reserve requirements leads to the constraint

(2) $$R \geqslant k_1 y_1 + k_2 y_2$$

where the k's are the reciprocals of the legal reserve ratios.

The bank is constrained by the conditions of supply of primary deposits and demand for advances facing it. Securities prices are assumed to be parametric for the representative bank — either because the bank is atomistic with respect to all n classes of securities or because of assumptions analogous to those underlying kinky oligopoly demand curves for categories $s+1, \ldots, n$, these being categories for IOU's associated with advances. It follows that systems 3 and 4, describing the relationship between maximum attainable positions for $x_{s+1}, \ldots, x_n$ and for y on the one hand and for promotional expenditure (and other variables) on the other hand, should distinguish between these and variables parametric for the representative bank. The balance, Equation (5), must be observed. (In)equalities 2-5 (together with the implicit constraint of the $G(\quad)$ function) constrain the bank and must be observed simultaneously:

$$(3) \qquad x_i \leq g^{4i}(A; r_1, r_2, p) \qquad i = s+1, \ldots, n$$

$$(4) \qquad y_i \leq g^{5i}(A; r_1, r_2, p, x) \qquad i = 1, 2$$

$$(5) \qquad \sum^{n} p_i x_i + R = y_1 + y_2 + V$$

One of the key techniques of commercial banking is exposed: obtaining deposits so that the asset portfolio can be enlarged; the bank's assets yield more than it must pay to depositors.

Equation *(1)* can be rewritten:

$$(1') \qquad U \equiv F(x, y, r, c, p, V, R, A, C)$$

where C is the cost variable determined as in Equation *(1a)*. U is to be maximized subject to (in)equalities 2-5 and Equation *(6)*:

$$(6) \qquad C \equiv G(x, y).$$

(For computational purposes c will have to be represented by a surrogate: say, a function of lagged changes in securities prices.)

In general, the solution technique will be that of non-linear programming.

Finally, formalize bank response to changes in parameters. Consider the system's reduced form, expressing solution values of the dependent variables — x, y, V, R, A, and C — as functions of the independent variables — r, p, k, and lagged changes in securities prices. Denoting the vector of dependent variables by w and that of independent variables by z, the reduced form can be expressed:

$$7) \qquad w_j^* \equiv w_j^*(z) \qquad j = 1, 2, \ldots, m$$

or, linearizing the system and denoting the matrix of coefficients as B,

$$8) \qquad w^* \equiv Bz.$$

Surely we said more than that!

This model contains a very important implication: constraints on some loan categories of the *jth* bank seldom are binding; banks advertise, inviting loan applications. Thus, when money is tight, banks seek to dispose of investments in order to accommodate customers.[77] *(Cf.*

[77] Hart and Kenen raise other important considerations:

"The borrowers are his [the banker's] 'customers.' They feel that they have a claim upon the bank's lending power . . . Refusal of an expected loan is a blow to their business and their dignity. The banker's good will is involved . . ." A. G. Hart and P. B. Kenen, *Money, Debt, and Economic Activity* (3rd ed.; Englewood Cliffs, N.J.: Prentice-Hall, Inc., 1961), p. 57.

Ch. VA, which discusses the dynamics of changes in bank portfolios when money is tight.)[78]

Our model can, by virtue of its emptiness, accommodate a large number of bank portfolio problems. (For rich probabilistic treatment see Harry M. Markowitz, *Portfolio Selection* (New York: John Wiley & Sons, Inc., 1959). Also, D. Orr and W. J. Mellon, "Stochastic Reserve Losses and Bank Credit," *American Economic Review,* Vol. 51, September, 1961, pp. 614-623.) Thus, during 1962, attention was called to increased bank activity in the mortgage market at a time when banks had substantially increased (absolutely and relatively) their interest-bearing deposit liability *and* deposit rates. At least two factors help explain lengthening out of bank portfolios in these circumstances:

1) variability of withdrawals becoming less, bank liquidity and invulnerability to forced liquidation could be assured with a longer-dated portfolio;

2) the coincidence of higher deposit rates with rather slack conditions in securities markets made it necessary for banks to accept less certainty of nominal portfolio value in order to achieve given profits. It appears that the rate of substitution between risk and profit was high at initial "equilibria"; banks were willing to accept a good deal of additional risk rather than surrender more profits.

---

78 How does this square with theories based on "unsatisfied fringes of borrowers"? The answer is that the narrow range in which loan charges are permitted to vary leads banks to prefer to invest in securities rather than extend loans (at least beyond well defined limits) to "poor credit risks." Thus, with respect to categories $1, 2 \ldots, r$, banks would like to lend more at going rates. With respect to categories $(r + 1), \ldots, n$, supply of IOU's exceeds demand by banks. When banks are permitted to expand their aggregate portfolios, they are likely to increase their loans in the $(r + 1), \ldots, n$ categories, according to the functional relation

$$Q_i^j \equiv f_i^j(\bar{r}, D_i) \qquad j = 1, 2, \ldots, n$$

Demand for the *jth* category of IOU by the *ith* bank depends upon the set of interest rates facing the bank and its attainable deposits.

Of course, when banks have excess reserves and begin to bid down money-market rates, loan rates are sure to follow.

CHAPTER FIVE A

Central Banking: Theory

CENTRAL BANKING THEORY LINKS SOME OF THE NICEST theoretical reasoning in economics with, perhaps, its most elegant terminology, all overlaid with some of its hoariest history. Pure theory, history, politics, institutions all merge together. It is next to impossible to offer a coherent treatment of the strands of analysis, one by one.

A synopsis follows. Also, in Ch. VA "effects of contraction of bank liabilities" can subsume "effects of non-expansion of bank liabilities."

A. *Mechanisms of Central Bank Policy:* measures calculated to affect bank liquidity, in turn affecting securities prices and availability of credit.

B. *Underbrush:* ultimately concern is with how changes in securities prices affect "real" markets, but first underbrush must be cleared. Specifically

1. effects of straitening or relaxing of bank liquidity on long- and short-term interest rates
2. the "bills only" controversy, including discussion of possibilities of twisting the yield curve without affecting bank reserves or required-reserve ratios
    a. theoretical discussion: "On the Invariance of Interest Rates to the Funding of Public Debt"
3. "fringe of unsatisfied borrowers"; importance, if any, of non-price rationing of credit in "equilibrium"

C. *Theory of central bank policy:*

1. correlation with mechanisms
2. open-market operations in financial markets

3. statics and dynamics
   a. preliminary distinctions
   b. central bankers mostly are concerned with disequilibrium states and short-run market clearance
   c. speed of response, as well as magnitude of adjusted response, is important
4. full employment context: price stabilization policy
   a. flexible *vs.* sticky prices
   b. responses of portfolio managers and spenders to changes in interest rates: flexible prices
   c. subsets of responses: sticky prices
5. under-employment context: income stabilization policy
   a. general case
   b. special case of cost-push inflation
      (1) *Cf.* Appendix to Ch. XIII

D. *International Aspects.*

Note: at least one usage is undeviating; *cash* in this chapter means hand-to-hand currency plus demand deposits of commercial banks.

A. MECHANISMS OF CENTRAL BANK POLICY

1

We work with a central authority merging the monetary powers of the Federal Reserve System and the United States Treasury. In keeping with the American system, the authority's key powers are to be: (1) control of required (minimum) reserve-deposit ratios; (2) establishment of (re)discount rates; (3) purchases and sales of securities in the open market; (4) transfer of government deposits to and from member banks; and (5) use of central government surpluses and deficits to reduce or increase the money supply (not a strictly monetary power).

In dealing with the British system at least four amendments should be made:

a) the reserve-deposit ratio for London clearing banks is fixed by custom at 8 per cent, although "special deposits" have the flavor of regulation of reserve-deposit ratios;

b) the British government does not keep meaningful deposits with joint-stock banks;

c) the "liquidity ratio" is important in British banking; it gives the proportion of call money, cash, and bills to deposits and is expected to be maintained at at least 30 per cent; monetary policy *might* be able to concentrate on the composition of public debt, directly affecting commercial banks;

d) Bank rate always is above Treasury bill rate; the Bank's front door is open to the money market but usually not to the banks.

In the United States the central bank's discount rate can stand below relevant market rates.[1] (*See Note A.*) However, we work for the time being on the assumption that rediscount rate is penal in the United States.

We can carry out operations with a simple para-American system with little institutional specification. Assume that all banks belong to the central banking system, maintaining deposits with the central bank, that the central authorities simply promulgate decrees as to required ratios, that all currency is issued by the central bank (not true in America), that the central bank is supplied with adequate initial stocks of government securities to carry on open-market sales and that restrictions on central bank note issue and deposit liability can be ignored. Finally, confine commercial banks to demand deposits.

The puny apparatus being in place, cogitate on its application to a closed system (ignoring international complications). Begin with an exercise in *restriction*. All five of the techniques of control of the central authorities could be concerted: (1) the required reserve ratio could be raised; (2) the rediscount rate could be raised; (3) securities could be sold in the open market; (4) government deposits could be transferred from member banks; (5) a surplus could be run by the Treasury, the proceeds being deposited at the central bank. Ignore (5) for the nonce: it is a powerful admixture of fiscal and monetary policy, but its impurity makes it unsuitable for us.

Technique (1)'s impact on the banks is immediate and obvious. Technique (4) finds the banks losing reserves and deposits one-for-one.

---

1 There have been times in the United States when rediscount rate has been below commercial bill rates but above bankers' acceptances rates. Since a bank converts a trade bill into a bank bill when it discounts, rediscount rate was technically penal (when Federal Reserve buying rates were not below bankers' acceptances rates). However, "many banks do not figure so carefully" (Randolph Burgess, *The Federal Reserve Banks and the Money Market* [Rev. Ed.; New York: Harper & Bros.], p. 227). Banks often borrowed large sums from the Federal Reserve at a (second-best) profit. In more recent years, rediscount rate and Treasury bill rate often have been so close that transactions costs, among other reasons, encouraged banks to borrow from the Federal Reserve. Except for the "open-back-door" years, British Bank rate has been effectively penal. For a discussion of Federal Reserve "buying rate" in the 1920's *cf.* Burgess, *op. cit.*, p. 171 *ff*. A theoretical analysis of this is outlined in Note A.

Technique (2) can be important in that it *announces* what the authorities are up to and can prevent "abuse" of the discount window even for short periods.

The third technique, open-market sales, requires more elaboration; it focuses attention on the broad spectrum of (securities') maturities, each with its own price (and, hence, yield). Perplexing issues are posed by compound implications for the *structure of interest rates* generated by alternative monetary policies.

2

Begin with the more obvious mechanics of open-market techniques. The immediate impact of an open-market operation (i.e., immediately after clearings are completed) is on (a) reserve positions of member banks, (b) cash balances of the public, (c) the public's currency-cash ratio, (d) the public's asset portfolio (assuming for convenience and with perfect safety that purchases are not made directly from banks), (e) stocks of securities of various maturities (both absolute and relative stocks), and (f) absolute and relative securities prices. It is most unlikely that the state of the system immediately after an open-market transaction will be sustained; just about everyone will wish to change his position in the fairly near future.[2]

Working with a 0.10 reserve ratio, assume that the initial consolidated balance sheet for the banking system reads:

Assets		Liabilities	
Loans	$100,000	Deposits	$188,800
Bonds	50,000		
Bills	20,000		
Vault cash	5,000		
Reserve account	13,800		
	188,800		188,800

TABLE VA-I

[2] Say that Treasury bills are pushed on the market by the central bank, forcing down their price. Purchasers run down their cash today, planning to dispose of private paper or government bonds tomorrow. When they place selling orders, quotations on private paper and government bonds will fall. Furthermore, there will be excess demand for cash at the beginning of tomorrow. More cash will be given up today than is intended to be done in future. Interest rates must rise still more. (And banks must contract.) If the officials stay out of the market after their initial transaction, the end result of what might be a rather prolonged sequence will find the public's cash lower (ignoring initial free reserve possibilities), a lower stock of non-government bills, perhaps some change in rates on government relative to non-government securities and in the term structure of rates, etc. Dynamics and comparative statics must in any event be carefully distinguished.

Now assume that the central bank sells $5,000 in 90-day government bills. Total central government debt is taken to be about $270,000, other debt several times as great. Although the impact on aggregate securities holdings is small, that on bank reserves is large indeed. So must be the impact on holdings of cash relative to securities. Specifically, the banking system finds its reserve account with the central bank reduced from $13,800 to $8,800. Its deposit liability has also declined $5,000 to $183,800. There is a $4,580 reserve deficiency. But we assume a once-and-for-all currency reflux of $580 that reduces the reserve deficiency to $4,000. (Currency reflux is henceforth ignored.)

The deposit liability of the banking system must decline to $143,800 (from $183,800). The banks' fate is inevitable: loans and investments must fall $40,000. That is to say, the public must be induced to substitute $40,000 in securities (including *less negative* positions *vis a vis* the banks) for $40,000 in bank-deposit balances.[3] The immediate stimulus for the public to make this substitution is provided by falling securities prices as banks are forced into the market. Perhaps liquidation will at first be concentrated at the shorter end of the market. As these securities are more attractively priced (as yields, including rates on short-term bank loans, increase) firms and households are encouraged to substitute securities for cash.

B. UNDERBRUSH

1. Term Structure of Interest Rates

1

Will prices of longer maturities be affected? "It may . . . seem illogical that the rate of interest fixed for a period of three months should have any noticeable effect on the terms asked for loans of twenty years or more."[4] Remembering that we are dealing with tran-

---

[3] One way to achieve the substitution would be for bank borrowers to turn in currency. We have agreed to ignore currency reflux from now on. "Securities" include obligations of non-banking intermediaries.

[4] Keynes, *A Treatise on Money*, Vol. II, pp. 352-353. Keynes proceeds to show that it is *not* illogical. The *Treatise* is invaluable for Ch. V. See especially Chapters 13 ("The Modus Operandi of Bank Rate") and 37 ("The Control of Investment"). Another invaluable reference for this chapter is R. G. Hawtrey's *The Art of Central Banking* (London: Longmans, Green and Co., 1932).

sitional states, not with comparisons of equilibrium positions,[5] it would seem that long rate must be affected to *some* degree. There are elasticities of substitution between long- and short-dated securities on both the supply and demand sides.

But let us first cite a limiting case working against that proposition. If *all* investors were *convinced* that short rate for *all* future periods would be 5 per cent, the fact that current short rate were 8 or 2 per cent would not influence long rate. If long rate were to rise in response to higher current short rate, there would be terrific demand for bonds; the opportunity to assure better-than-5-per-cent yield for twenty years in the face of future short yields of 5 per cent would be irresistible. Under such extreme expectational rigidity, bonds priced on a yield basis better than 5 per cent appear overwhelmingly attractive to all traders. Yield differentials would be disregarded unless short rate became astronomical. Long rate simply would not respond to momentary increases in short rate. Similarly if current short rate were to fall to 2 per cent in the face of rigid expectation of a future short rate of 5 per cent, long rate could not even momentarily fall below 5 per cent. Terrific selling pressure would be generated; there would be no reason to contract for lower yields in view of moral certainty that "5 per cent" would be restored tomorrow. *Rentiers* would expect speculators to put unbearable pressure on bond prices. Lower long rate would allow "sure" profit on positions in which traders borrowed long, planning to invest short starting tomorrow when short rate would return to 5 per cent. (*See Note B.*) . . . And then pure liquidity properties of bills and cash *might* impose a lower limit on long rate, an argument quite apart from expectations.

2

We have worked hard to conjure up circumstances in which long rate would be immune (even in the very short run) to movements in short rate, but it is time to take more plausible ground. Surely the more sensible assumption is that each trader can be assigned a subjective probability density function indicating probabilities attached to alternative prices for the spectrum of securities at future dates. Both the central tendencies and dispersions of these distributions will vary from trader to trader. For most traders the future is closely veiled. The chiaroscuro of a Rembrandt portrait is recalled: highlighted current yields against a somber background, the heavily discounted future.

[5] *Cf.* Section C *infra.*

Thus modifying communal behavior, consider the effects of 8 per cent short rate. Elasticities of substitution come into play. Take the demand side first:

> "There are a number of financial institutions — amongst which the banks themselves are the most important, but also including insurance offices, investment trusts, finance houses, etc. -- which vary from time to time the proportionate division of their assets between long-term and short-term securities respectively. Where short-term yields are high, the safety and liquidity of short-term securities appear extremely attractive. But when short-term yields are very low, not only does this attraction disappear, but another motive enters in, namely a fear lest the institution may be unable to maintain its established level of income, any serious falling off in which would be injurious to its reputation . . ."[6]

For many, short-term yields of 8 per cent would be a juicy bird in hand. Selling pressure would be induced in the long end of the market.

What of operators who are so confident of re-emergence of the "normal" 5 per cent short rate re-establishing firm conviction in 5 per cent long rate? It is going to cost them a good deal to back up their convictions. In order to take up offers of bonds they must either borrow at something like 8 per cent or sell bills and run down cash balances, foregoing an 8 per cent yield (imputed to the convenience of holding cash; *cf.* Ch. VII). And their credit is not unlimited.

Elasticity of substitution of supply also operates. An increase in short, relative to long, rate causes some corporations to plan to "fund" their debt, to replace short- with long-term debt. Similarly, an opposite rate movement would encourage shortening of the term structure of corporate debt, despite added illiquidity and heightened sensitivity to short-lived market forces.

3

We have reached a tentative conclusion: open-market sales, *irrespective of the maturities unloaded by the authorities,* put pressure on bank liquidity, leading to a tendency towards higher interest rates along the entire spectrum of maturities.[7] Open-market purchases have converse effects, although there are at least two *caveats*: (1) it might be impossible to force down long rate once a certain level is reached; (2)

[6] Keynes, *op. cit.*, pp. 357-358.

[7] We are not here concerned with comparative statics.

"real" effects of open-market purchases and sales might be asymmetrical, depending on the phase of the business cycle.

So far only positive correlation has been established. Nothing has been proved about the *degree* to which long rates may be sensitive to open-market operations, and this can be important. What if planned expenditure is much more sensitive to long than to short rate? We become exercised about *how much* long rate will be affected.[8] Indeed rigid expectations can lead to grave difficulty for contracyclical policy when it is important to move long rate *quickly*. And lagged reaction here (and elsewhere) can paralyze monetary policy, a point stressed by many writers.

2. Bills Only?

1

Turn to the *bills-only* controversy. First a précis of "bills only" (now officially in discard):

> "In the spring of 1953 . . . the Open Market Committee adopted the policy of confining its . . . operations to short-dated securities, namely Treasury Bills [except to intervene in 'disorderly markets'] . . . The decision to operate in the short-dated securities came to be known as the 'bills only' doctrine."[9]

M. W. Riefler, long with the Federal Reserve Board, expressed his position in the Federal Reserve *Bulletin* (November 1958, "Open

[8] We have argued that simultaneous purchases and sales of different maturities — if not on *massive* scales — will have little effect on the structure of rates. Professor Sayers has said that British authorities since the end of 1957 have had a good grip on long rates for at least two reasons: (1) rigid expectations of future short rate have been broken up by post-1951 experience; (2) relying on the market's knowledge of their cornucopia of ammunition, the authorities have been able to force up long rates by indicating, rather elliptically, where they think these rates ought to rest. Market operators hesitate to purchase on lower yield bases (at higher prices), since enforcement of the official point of view would cost them heavy capital losses. *Cf.* Ch. V, "The Work of the Bank of England," of the Radcliffe *Report*.

The argument is difficult to support statistically, since it maintains that authorities can importantly affect long rates without much *quantitative* intervention. It should be easier to force long rates up than down. In the former case, buyers run to cover, refusing to pay "high" prices, perhaps soon to be attacked. In the latter case, to pay "suggested" prices (above the recent market) is to be in jeopardy if the Government is unable to enforce its position or if its resolution falters.

[9] A. C. L. Day and S. T. Beza, *Money and Income* (New York: Oxford University Press, 1960), p. 220. *Cf.* pp. 220-225.

Market Operations in Long-Term Securities," pp. 1260-1274) and before the Radcliffe Committee [*Minutes of Evidence,* London: HMSO, 1960), pp. 613-627, 639-648]. His views are summarized at pages 1264-1267 of the *Bulletin*:

> "The major open money markets, particularly the markets for United State government securities, are usually characterized by a high degree of fluidity as between the various maturity sectors, in the sense that fluctuations of any magnitude in one sector are likely to be paralleled . . . in other sectors. This phenomenon is often attributed to arbitrage . . . In accounting for fluidity among the various sectors of the market, too much importance should not be attributed to the transactions of market professionals who engage in arbitrage. Much more important . . . is the high degree of substitutability . . . that exists for many lenders and many borrowers . . . Large commercial banks in particular, when their liquidity positions permit, operate actively . . . In addition . . . insurance companies and pension and trust funds . . . operate with great flexibility as between categories of investments and, when they think it will pay, between different maturity sectors.
>
> Among borrowers, also, many can adopt a variety of financial plans to meet their financing needs . . .
>
> The speed with which changes in the availability of reserves are reflected in . . . the long-term sector will depend basically . . . on the attractiveness of the yield offered in the light of the risks involved and . . . on the liquidity position of the banking system . . . [T]ime is needed before bank activity in long-term investment is likely to be affected."

The more positive argument for "bills only" — alternatives lead to disruption of securities markets — seems to me much overwrought. It is not pursued here. Furthermore, *some* disruption of securities markets is indispensable for contractionary monetary policy. *Cf.* Section C 4b *infra.*

2

Consider this objection to "bills only": operations in the long end of the market are necessary and sufficient for moving long rates; operations at the short end will tend not to affect long rates.[10] The latter portion of the statement could be true without relieving the former's incorrectness. Writers stressing that operations on the long end

---

[10] Delicate problems in timing, conceded by Riefler. might be involved. We hasten to admit that transitional effects on long rates might be achieved and might be important. Needless to say, imperfect fluidity between the long and short ends of the market would undermine "bills only."

uniquely affect long rate misunderstand open-market operations. These, on familiar scales, can have important impact on bank liquidity but NOT on the make-up of the collective securities portfolio. We suggested as much in our artificial example: more than a 25-per-cent reduction in bank reserves was achieved by a sale having little effect on aggregate bond holdings. Furthermore, as Keynes and Riefler have pointed out, it is very simple for the society substantially to adjust for whatever change has been made in the balance of long- and short-term securities. Debt issues *can* be refinanced.[11] Indeed under certain (strict) assumptions, this adjustment *can* be perfect.[12]

3

Lest you feel that the distinction between major impact on bank liquidity and on the collective securities portfolio is chimerical, consider these data:

a) at the end of December 1960, member banks of the Federal Reserve System had total reserves of $19.283 billion;

b) on that date total U. S. government debt held outside U. S. government investment accounts and Federal Reserve Banks was $208 billion;

c) total state and local government debt was $60 billion;

d) total corporate debt was $294.5 billion;

e) individual and non-corporate debt totalled $286.5 billion.

The sum of debt approaches one *trillion* dollars. An open-market operation of $4 billion within one year would be substantial. The impact on bank reserves would be of the first order of magnitude. But — within the setting of the enormous superstructure of debt in which even the national debt nestles comfortably — would it matter whether a $4 billion operation was carried on with long-, short-, or intermediate-term securities? Effects on relative holdings of various maturities would be infinitesimal. (Again, this does not deny that the immediate impact on bond prices might be substantial. It might take some time for underlying stock conditions to assert themselves.)

To repeat, normally, open-market operations do not work important direct changes in the proportions of various maturities in the hands of the public. *Their important effect is on the stock of money*

[11] *Cf.* Note C *infra.* for a fuller discussion.
[12] *Cf.* Section B 3 *infra.*

and on the proportion borne by the stock of money to securities holdings, income streams, etc.[13]

4

And yet there are times when it appears desirable for short and long rates to move in opposite directions. Witness the coincidence in 1960 of a business recession and substantial gold outflow from the United States. It seemed desirable to increase short rates, attracting hot money (funds seeking differentially higher yields) from abroad, while depressing long rates, hopefully stimulating domestic investment. Such a movement in rates would have had to rest upon very substantial "disfunding" of the national debt: *large* amounts of bonds would have to be replaced by bills. Even assuming low elasticities of substitution,[14] it would seem that any program within contemplated orders of magnitude would have little chance of success.[15] In fact the argument of Section B 3 is that such a program would have *no* chance of success.

3. On the Invariance of Interest Rates Against the Funding of Public Debt[16]

1

This note is an exercise in comparative statics purporting to demonstrate that the equilibrium structure of interest rates can be independent of the composition of public debt. It is argued that, if

13 Inelastic expectations, however, can cause open-market operations to impart torsion to the yield curve around a fixed "long end."

14 Elasticity of substitution between X and Y is defined

$$\sigma = \frac{d[log(x/y)]}{d[log(p_x/p_y)]}$$

σ gives the percentage change in the ratio of a pair of *ex ante* quantities pursuant to the percentage change in the ratio of their prices. If σ were large on both the demand and supply sides for long- and short-dated securities, a disturbance changing initial proportions would be accommodated by security holders with little change in relative prices. There would be a strong response in subsequent supplies so that the new equilibrium would look very much like the old. There would be little room for changes in relative yields without structural changes in the system. (*6* describes intended response to term-structure changes and is influenced by expectations. Thus *6* $= 0$ in Section B1, §§1.)

15 During 1961 switching operations finding about $7 billion in Federal Reserve short-term holdings converted into "long" apparently had little effect on the pattern of interest rates.

16 The reader may choose to omit this subsection. Two prominent editors already have done so.

standard axioms are maintained, the long- or short-term character of the public debt should not affect the "yield curve." These are the basic assumptions:

1) standard units of debt of any maturity can be defined operationally. Taking a unit government IOU of any given maturity as "numeraire," a unit non-government IOU of the same maturity is perfectly substitutable with the government IOU at a given ratio. It follows that we can deal with *the* yield for each maturity. We shall measure stocks in terms of standard (government) units;

2) there is a fixed distribution of liability to taxation to meet public debt obligations. Economic units have apportioned among them liabilities for debt service precisely as do share holders' claims to corporate equity;

3) tax liabilities are treated analogously with personally issued obligations. If I am liable for 1 per cent of the service of the public debt, I am assumed to treat this liability precisely as I would issuance of my own securities in the exact proportion corresponding securities occupy in the public debt structure, their aggregate value being 1 per cent of the public debt. It follows that, in general, only *net* asset positions matter;

4) the initial equilibrium is unique and stable, once parameters are specified.

Assume that the initial equilibrium state is characterized, among other things, by a vector of interest rates, r^*. By definition, the absolute value of the aggregate of public-debt holdings (ignoring holdings of government agencies) will be equal to the absolute value of the capitalized debt service obligations. Furthermore, each unit of public debt has its negative or mirror-image twin in the form of debt service obligation. Assume that there are three economic units in the system (generalization to n units being immediate and obvious) characterized by 18 Treasury bills and 12 Consols (noting the implicit convention that units of debt are defined so that at r^* a unit of each type of debt has the same market value), and that the distribution of assets, positive and negative, recalling assumptions 2 and 3, is:

ASSET MATRIX ONE

period 1

Economic Unit

	I	II	III
owns	0, 0	13TB, 5C	5TB, 7C
owes	6TB, 4C	6TB, 4C	6TB, 4C
net	—6TB, —4C	7TB, 1C	—1TB, 3C

TABLE VA-II

Now assume that a gremlin inserts himself into the economy's safes and "refinances" the public debt so that at the outset of period 2 half of the debt is in Treasury bills and half in consols. The asset matrix will now be (omitting the TB and C symbols, but maintaining the ordering of Matrix One):

ASSET MATRIX TWO

period 2

	I	II	III
owns	0, 0	10.5, 7.5	4.5, 7.5
owes	5, 5	5, 5	5, 5
net	—5, —5	5.5, 2.5	—0.5, 2.5

TABLE VA-III

Is it open to the traders (economic units) to undertake transactions that will leave them in positions identical with their original positions? If such transactions *can* be performed, they *will* be performed: assumption 4 states that the initial equilibrium state is unique and stable. Once such transactions took place, r^* would, of course, continue to be an equilibrium vector. In other words, we wish to determine whether the structure of public debt enters parametrically into the system.

We proceed to show that it does not. Before doing the mechanics, let us state the general algebraic proposition leading to the result: any refinance operation by the Treasury erases liabilities (*cf.* assumption 3) equal in amount and identical in term with the assets removed from non-government portfolios; it creates liabilities equal in amount and identical in term with the assets added to non-government portfolios. The erased liabilities can be recreated by private issue if necessary, and exchanged for some of the newly created public securities so that the net holdings of each economic unit of each maturity will be identical with the net holdings preceding the refinance operation.[17] It follows that r^* can and will be maintained.

[17] Define a_{ij} as the change in the jth trader's net position with respect to the ith asset. The text shows that $\sum_j a_{ij} = 0$ for all i (and that $\sum\sum a_{ij} = 0$) as a result of a refinance operation when $r = r^*$. The *cet. par.* assures that desired asset positions will be unchanged at r^*. Accordingly, negative a_{ij}'s give rise to market demand (restoring asset positions) while positive a_{ij}'s give rise to market supply (restoring liability or reducing asset positions). The equality

$$\sum_j a_{ij} = 0$$

assures absence of net excess supply, while implying that traders who, for example, initially lacked nominal holdings of the ith asset, assumed to be reduced

These are the mechanics associated with this proposition. Beginning with Asset Matrix Two, assume that the following transactions occur:

1) I issues a unit of debt equivalent to a Treasury bill, exchanging this with II for a consol;

2) III turns over 0.5 Treasury bill to II in exchange for 0.5 consol.

These transactions result in a final asset matrix, Matrix Three.

ASSET MATRIX THREE

period 3

	I	II	III
owns	0, 1	12, 6	4, 8
owes	6, 5	5, 5	5, 5
net	—6, —4	7, 1	—1, 3

TABLE VA-IV

The net asset positions are identical with those previous to the refinance operation. It *is* open to the traders to restore the initial position. Summoning assumption 4, the equilibrium vector continues to be r^* and is invariant against the structure of public debt. A contrary result emerges from the assumption that debt service obligation is not capitalized. Of course, once a model is constructed so that government bonds play the role of Marshallian meteor stones, it is easy to see that equilibrium r is functionally dependent upon the structure of public debt.

2

The theorem is by no means isolated. Its ancestry is readily traced to such sources as Modigliani and Miller,[18] Bushaw and Clower,[19] and Clower and Burstein.[20] The model developed here finds the economic unit maintaining a desired asset portfolio through private issue in re-

---

in supply by the Treasury, will plan to issue their own paper in order to restore liability positions.

18 Franco Modigliani and M. H. Miller, "The Cost of Capital, Corporation Finance, and the Theory of Investment," *American Economic Review*, June 1958, pp. 261-297.

19 D. W. Bushaw and R. W. Clower, *Introduction to Mathematical Economics* (Homewood, Ill.: Richard D. Irwin, 1957 [sponsored by the American Economic Association]), pp. 128-134, 160-163, 166-171.

20 R. W. Clower and M. L. Burstein, "On the Invariance of Demand for Cash and Other Assets," *Review of Economic Studies*, October 1960, pp. 32-36.

sponse to change in the structure of public debt — analogous to Modigliani and Miller's private levering process. Clower and Burstein showed that, in a system in which commodities accrued like manna from heaven, but in which there was paper money and in which bond could be issued, *individual experiments* would find equilibrium wealth independent of the manna stream and initial cash balances. But, much more important for our purposes, they showed that, where assets can be produced (or in the case of bonds, issued), equilibrium stocks and asset prices are invariant against initial stocks, which merely enter as initial conditions, not as parameters of the system: *market experiments also* produce invariance.

3

The implications for current American controversy about "bills only" and Federal Reserve open-market operations are immediate and obvious, although it should be stressed that transitional effects can be important and that the dynamics of the various markets have not been explored here. It is well known that financial markets are capable of rapid adjustment.

There also are important implications for the effects of "treasury policy by funding," an issue in British financial literature.[21] Noting that the tax obligation of the banking sector (II) is ignored, see Asset Matrix Four:

ASSET MATRIX FOUR

period 1

	I	II	III
owns	0, 0	13, 5	5, 7
owes	9, 6	0, 0	9, 6
net	—9, —6	13, 5	—4, 1

TABLE VA-V

Now assume that part of the public debt is funded, leading to Asset Matrix Five:

---

[21] *Cf.* Warren L. Smith and Raymond F. Mikesell, "The Effectiveness of Monetary Policy. Recent British Experience," *Journal of Political Economy,* Vol. 65, No. 1, February 1957, pp. 18-39.

British banks have for some years maintained liquid reserves, including cash, call money, and bills, equal to least 30 per cent of their net deposits.

ASSET MATRIX FIVE
period 2

	I	II	III
owns	0, 0	9, 9	4.5, 7.5
owes	6.75, 8.25	0, 0	6.75, 8.25
net	—6.75, —8.25	9, 9	—2.25, —0.75

TABLE VA-VI

The following transactions can lead to Asset Matrix Six:

I) II transfers 4 Consols to III, receiving back 4 Treasury bills;

2) I issues 2.25 of *equivalent* Treasury bills, exchanging these with III for 2.25 Consols. (It is *not* necessary for banks to acquire only Treasury bills in order to restore their liquidity: commercial bills also are eligible. The II-III, I-III sequence of transactions is sufficient but not necessary.)

ASSET MATRIX SIX
period 3

	I	II	III
owns	0, 2.25	13, 5	2.75, 9.25
owes	9, 8.25	0, 0	6.75, 8.25
net	—9, —6	13, 5	—4, 1

TABLE VA-VII

The net asset positions are unchanged and, due to the assumption that II has no debt-service obligation, so does the gross asset position of II.

Of course, the algebraic relation developed earlier guarantees this result. Equilibrium money (and real) prices of goods and services and the equilibrium vector of interest rates will be invariant to Treasury funding operations.

Finally, the equilibrium state of the system will be invariant against the absolute value of public debt. Our assumptions assure that the algebraic value of the public debt (a sum including capitalized debt service liability) is definitionally zero. Nor will there be liquidity effects — because of assumption 3.[22]

4

Thus, distinctions between effects of changes in the money supply generated by open-market operations and those generated by outright issue (or reflux) of paper money are invalid. For example, Professor

[22] Perhaps making assumption 3 hard to swallow.

Metzler's demonstration that equilibrium r is not invariant to changes in the money stock generated by open-market operations relies on the assumption that a proportional change in the money stock and prices with r unchanged would find the public's wealth decreased if the money stock had been increased through open-market purchases of bonds.[23] Similarly, Gurley and Shaw[24] distinguish between "inside money" generated by government purchases of debt and "outside money." They hold that the comparative statics of their system will vary according to whether all money is inside or outside or there is a mixture of the two. Enthoven's mathematical appendix shows that, if bonds held by the government (B_g) are identically zero, equilibrium r will be invariant against changes in the stock of money, apart from how the stock has been generated or changed.

In models as abstract as those of Metzler and Gurley and Shaw, it seems to me (but NOT to Franco Modigliani[25]) to be unnatural to assume that debt service liability is not fully capitalized. If it is capitalized, the "variances" obtained by these authors are inconsistent with their specific assumption that the government's own portfolio position is not allowed to affect the public's income flows; they assume that the flows are adjusted by taxes and subsidies so that the algebraic sum of government interest payments (receipts) plus taxes (subsidies) incident thereto is identically zero. This assumption makes the value of the government's bond holdings (positive or negative) *plus* capitalized tax obligation of the public (negative or positive) incident to the government's bond portfolio identically zero.

4. Fringe of Unsatisfied Borrowers

1

It is almost certain that, subsequent to central-bank contractionary measures, bank charges and interest rates will not immediately rise

23 Lloyd A. Metzler, "Wealth, Interest, and the Rate of Saving," *Journal of Political Economy,* April 1951, pp. 93-116.

The argument that the public's wealth will be decreased is as follows: if prices were to double, final money stock would equal initial money stock in real value. However, the real value of its bond holdings would be less.

24 Gurley and Shaw, *op. cit.*

25 Franco Modigliani, "Long-run Implications of Alternative Fiscal Policies and the Burden of the National Debt," *Economic Journal,* December 1961, pp. 730-755. Modigliani has convinced me that my argument probably holds only for infinitely-lived sterile adults. But that applies as much to the other contributors to the discussion.

enough to choke off demand for credit on the scale of necessary contraction in bank asset portfolios. At least transitorily, the *availability* of credit will be less: borrowers willing to borrow at current rates will be rejected, adding to "the fringe of unsatisfied borrowers." Keynes has written:

> "The relaxation or contraction of credit by the banking system does not operate, however, merely through a change in the rate charged to borrowers; it also functions through a change in the abundance of credit. If the supply of credit were distributed in an absolutely competitive market, these two conditions — quantity and price — would be uniquely correlated with one another and we should not need to consider them separately. But in practice there is the contingency to be considered that the conditions of a free competitive market for bank-loans are imperfectly fulfilled. For it is not in fact the case — at least not in Britain; I believe that the market in the United States is much more freely competitive — that anyone offering security can borrow as much as he likes from the British banking system merely by offering a rate of interest high enough to outbid other borrowers. There is, that is to say, in Great Britain an habitual system of rationing in the attitude of banks to borrowers — the amount lent to any individual being governed not solely by security and the rate of interest offered, but also by reference to the borrower's purposes and his standing with the bank as a valuable or influential client. Thus there is normally a fringe of unsatisfied borrowers who are not considered to have the first claims on a bank's favours, but to whom the bank would be quite ready to lend if it were in a position to lend more."[26]

---

[26] Keynes, Vol. II, pp. 364-365.

Keynes proceeds (at pp. 365-367) to work out implications of the "fringe" for Bank-rate policy:

> ". . . the Bank of England does not fix bank-rate and leave the quantity of bank money to find its own level; nor does it fix the quantity of money and leave bank rate to find its own level. It fixes *both* — and fixes them to a certain extent independently. It then — in effect — invites the member banks and the money-market to co-operate in keeping the bank rate, thus fixed, effective on the basis of the quantity of bank-money also thus fixed. Its weapons for securing this cooperation are terror, agreement, and convention . . ."

Terror arises from the possibility that the Bank will make Bank rate effective by altering the quantity of money "so that it is not safe to enter into transactions which are based on the assumption that [Bank rate will remain ineffective] for some little time." *Agreement* "comes in because the clearing banks have agreed to pay interest . . . at a rate bearing a defined relationship to the official bank-rate." Finally, ". . . there are a number of *customs and conventions* [emphasis supplied] by which the rate of interest charged for bank-loans bears a more or less fixed relationship to the official bank rate."

It is unlikely that the incremental availability as against cost of bank credit is important after impact effects of contractionary measures are acknowledged. (*Incremental* is to be emphasized: we do not want to bog down in a discussion of the basic perfection of the capital market, or whether Keynes paid proper heed to differential risk premiums.) It seems unlikely that ongoing borrowers long will be permitted to pay lower interest rates, allowing for risk, than are offered by others, now excluded; certainly not when the unsatisfied fringe has been increased. (If bank reserves are increased, the same forces that will induce banks to lend to less preferred customers will encourage reduction of interest charges to preferred customers.) An increased fringe of unsatisfied borrowers inevitably creates excess supply in more formal securities markets as rejected bank clients seek other sources, perhaps successfully. And unsatisfied borrowers might have liquid assets to unload. The unsatisfied fringe will come to deal directly with holders of "idle" deposits, offering securities at favorable prices; other financial institutions will be enlisted; banks will be encouraged to exchange investments for "idle" deposits. (*See Note C.*)

2

Let us summarize section B 4:

1) at impact, changes in credit availability are likely to be more important than changes in the cost of credit; there will be additional unsatisfied demand for credit (*cf.* C4b *infra.*);

2) "ultimately" — how soon is not certain — higher interest rates will become more important — how important might be debated — in rationing credit; indeed, if higher interest rates cannot restrain expenditure plans, inflationary pressures might be constrained only by mechanical limits to increasing velocity.

C. THEORY OF CENTRAL BANK POLICY

1. Correlation with Mechanisms

Things might be clarified by continuing the story line of Section A. An open-market sale of government securities of $5,000 was undertaken by the authorities, resulting in a deficiency of bank reserves of $4,000, requiring a $40,000 reduction in bank asset portfolios. A new set of prices must emerge: the public must become satisfied to hold $45,000 less in commercial-bank liabilities (ignoring hand-to-hand currency) and $45,000 more in other securities, including deposit liabilities of non-banking financial institutions. (*See Note D.*) It will be shown that it is possible that the ultimate effects of the open-market sale will be on commodity rather than securities prices. At the outset, however, the burden of adjustment will be carried by securities prices.

Six disequilibria that might exist immediately after the open-market sale have been depicted. The last three concerned the impact of the operation on the proportion of long- to short-dated maturities held by the public. Subsequent discussion showed that these disequilibria were apt to be slight at the outset and quickly eliminated by small changes in relative yields and through rather slight refunding. The third of the disequilibria concerned the proportion of currency to total cash (currency plus demand deposits) in the hands of the public. It was agreed to ignore this in Ch. VA . . . Only two of the original six sore spots remain: (a) the reserve position of the member banks; (b) the cash balances of the public.

But, once the ambit of discussion has been narrowed to these two disequilibria, stringency of member banks can be discussed without concern for the particular way in which it was brought about; this is in fact the main burden of our treatment of the "bills only" controversy. We concentrate on open-market operations.

2. Open-Market Operations in Financial Markets

There is an important distinction between such open-market operations as government purchases of agricultural commodities and official purchases and sales of securities. Our interest in government purchases of cotton, corn, wheat, etc. is largely confined to the agricultural markets themselves. Repercussions beyond the immediate markets in which purchases (or sales) are made are not of critical concern.

Such decidedly is *not* the case for open-market operations in security markets. Effects of official purchases and sales of securities on prices of credit instruments, while interesting to market operators, have little interest for outside observers *except* for portended impact on other markets. That is to say, open-market operations of central banks have their *direct* impact on highly technical, specialized markets dealing with instruments not requiring meaningful inputs. Why, then, is there widespread interest in securities transactions of central authorities on the part of participants in goods and services markets? Because these transactions can be expected to induce chain reactions throughout the economy, relying upon various relationships of economic substitution and complementarity; it is the *indirect* effects of open-market operations that are important. The same is true for alternative mechanisms of monetary policy.

3. Statics and Dynamics

1

One can imagine the monetary authorities asking "what will be the effect of the sale on the *equilibrium* path of the system?" or "how will the sale affect the transitional behavior of the system?" The first question, certainly if we could confine ourselves to stationary states, concerns *comparative statics,* the second, *dynamics.* Subordinate to the first question would be queries as to effects of the sale on interest rates, prices, employment, etc., once perturbatory effects had washed out and the system was "back on its own." Subordinate to the second question would be queries as to how long it would take the system to adjust to the new stock of cash it would be permitted to hold, how high interest rates would have to go before prices started to fall, how long it would take for changes in interest rates to have impact on expenditure plans, how drastically security prices would have to fall before spending units would be shocked, etc.

The second question poses the following problem: the authorities might judge that, without action on their part, important inflationary pressure will develop, leading to a speculatively dominated boom and subsequent steep decline; they wish to determine whether a given open-market sale of securities would soon develop counter forces powerful enough to nip the unhealthy cycle in the bud. Perhaps, if the banks can be placed in a position where their reserves are deficient, the excess supply that will be generated in securities markets as banks strive to regain equilibrium will, in conjunction with the augmented flotations of would-be deficit spending units, depress securities markets in an important way. The boom's back might be broken if the cost of credit could rise and the availability of bank loans fall rapidly and substantially enough, excess demand in commodities markets might be eliminated; whatever elements of cost inflation that might persist might find an unfavorable climate. The second question concentrates on impact effects.

2

It is the second question and its satellite queries that exercise central bankers; theirs are problems in economic dynamics (macro-dynamics if you will). The context for domestic central bank policy is that of *contracyclical* policy generally. Central bankers are not so much concerned with problems of long-run adjustment as with anticipating forces sufficiently strong to knock the system off its gently ascending track with enough violence to send it crashing downwards, leaping upwards (later to crash downwards) or into wildly gyrating motion. It is not enough to anticipate the onset of such forces. Central bankers must plan their defenses before the storm descends. Are they already too late? How large a dose is called for? Will the effects of deflationary monetary policy be delayed until the diarrheac has become constipated (recalling Keynes's bismuth-castor oil cycle)? Which markets will be promptly affected? Which markets can be influenced only after a delay? How long will the delay be? How powerfully will such markets react once the lag is overcome? Secular problems such as the long-run growth of liquid assets and its relationship to the growth of real output interest central bankers, but for them the important thing is the ability of monetary policy to interrupt the course of events.

3

A crucial dynamic theme is this. If, in the face of central bank restriction, portfolio managers can be induced to plan to change their *balance sheets* so as to hold less cash and more primary securities (including book credits), *flows* will ensue that will permit deficit spending units to replace bank with non-bank finance. Bank customers will be a conduit in a process that finds banks exchanging non-monetary assets for monetary liabilities.

4

A few more general comments on statics and dynamics. The theory of money pays what might be inordinate heed to the invariance in equilibrium of real variables of the system including the real value of cash balances, against changes in the stock of money or, more sophisticatedly, changes in monetary parameters such as the required:reserve ratio. Whatever their philosophical merit, such theorems have no interest for the student of contracyclical monetary policy: there can be no doubt that operations performed today on the liquidity of the banking system will have very definite effects on securities prices tomorrow, next week, next month, and probably next year, and that effects of some importance will develop in other markets during the interval separating equilibrium states.

4. Full Employment Context: Price Stabilization Policy

a) Flexible v. Sticky Prices

1

It is shown in Ch. VII that considerable stickiness of money prices is indispensable if money is to be a standard of deferred payments. On the other hand, if price movements are altogether independent of excess demand (supply), there is little point in studying the theory of price stabilization. Only cases of intermediate price flexibility are interesting.

Sticky prices usually are associated either with ancient user or concentration of market power leading to wage bargains with unions and administered prices. We eschew industrial organization theory, confining ourselves to this observation: if prices are fairly flexible, slighter pressure can offset inflationary or deflationary trends than if prices are sticky. If prices are fairly flexible, smaller movements of interest rates will do the trick, *cet. par.,* than if prices are very sticky in one or both directions. Of course, if prices are sticky, the authorities might have to exert enormous pressure to have any influence on events.

2

We turn to taxonomical analysis under full employment conditions. The analysis flows from the table below, a 2x2 contingency table containing dichotomous classifications of aggregate sensitivities of holders of cash (portfolio managers) and spenders to interest rate changes. Square 1 indicates a state in which portfolio managers and purchasers of durable goods (and perhaps savers) are sensitive to interest rates; square 4 a state in which both groups are insensitive; square 2 finds portfolio managers sensitive and spenders insensitive; square 3 finds the converse. (Portfolio managers' "responsiveness" is in terms of desire to substitute cash for other financial assets or *vice versa* in response to interest rate changes. Substitution of physical assets is reflected in "spenders" responses; investment behavior will reflect portfolio decisions.)

RESPONSIVENESS TO INTEREST RATES

		SPENDERS	
		Sensitive	Insensitive
PORTFOLIO MANAGERS	Sens.	1	2
	Insens.	3	4

TABLE VA-VIII

We shall argue that 1 is ideal for effectiveness of monetary policy when prices are flexible and that 3 is ideal when prices are sticky. But, before detailing the argument, it should be shown how responses to changed interest rates are generated, noting that we are in most cases dealing with different sides of the economic behavior of the same economic units. To repeat, we are concerned throughout with *temporary equilibrium* reflecting transitional effects.

b) Responses of Portfolio Managers to Changes in Interest Rates

1

Restriction of bank liquidity, wrenching banks out of portfolio balance, will have impact effects on securities prices: these will fall — yields will increase — under the pressure of excess supply as banks are forced into the market. Noting that the argument also accommodates effects of relaxed bank liquidity,[27] we ask how *hypothetically* unchanged business payments flows *might* be accommodated by firms and households planning to substitute securities for cash.[28] Consider the

[27] Impact effects necessarily are weaker for policies of monetary ease however. In the case of restraint, banks *must* reduce advances and, to a considerable extent, can execute such reductions promptly. In the case of ease, banks must *induce* the market to accept more cash. And, of course, acceptance of more cash does not imply such prompt and substantial effects on spending as does the necessity of repaying the bank, especially when this comes out of the blue sky.

You will want to note that what I call "pure Bank rate policy" does not contain the impact effect introduced later in Section C 4 b.

[28] The formalization of this analysis is to be found in Note K, Ch. VA.

following catalog, keeping in mind that the time-deposit side of commercial bank operations is being ignored:

1) cash being held for precautionary motives might be reduced in order to enjoy attractive yields on securities including institutional deposits (Note B, Ch. III lumps (1)-(4));

2) unchanged subjective probability density functions of future long rate will result in higher long rate today encouraging traders to plan to buy longs in order to realize capital gains. This incentive to reduce cash will be the stronger as it is felt that securities prices have been forced below normal levels;

3) planned transactions balances could be reduced, and it could be planned to hold a larger proportion of these balances in securities instead of cash;

4) in general the ratio of the volume of the stock of cash to nominally valued rates of economic activity could fall. Monetary velocity could substantially increase;

5) trade credit could expand. Scrip might even be issued.

2

(5) requires elaboration. First, note that substitution of trade for bank credit reduces over-all liquidity of the non-banking public: the banking sector is specialized to very short liabilities. Secondly, there are built in limitations on continued expansion of book crédit (*cf.* Appendix, Ch. VI): firms depend on confidence in their ability to *redeem* their obligations in money; there are well established and unbending criteria for financial soundness. Third, *deferral* of payment is at the heart of book credit or scrip transactions; creditors (noting that the *jth* trader will be both creditor and debtor) must *wait*. But it is stupid to wait — once one sees what is going on — unless one is rewarded: cash assets can be converted into interest-bearing assets or enjoyed for their liquidity yields; there is a clear-cut opportunity cost of waiting. Thus, a substantial increase in the stock of book credit is consistent only with higher (ex)implicit yields on such credit.[29] Fourth

[29] The stock flow model of Ch. VII nicely explains impact effects of credit restriction. There must be a net increase in the flow of funds to bank coffers. If this process is not to lead to excess supply in commodities markets, the flow of cash from "idle" to "active" balances, together with the rate of increase of non-bank credit, must increase. (This ignores possibilities of initial slack in cash transactions balances.) The central bank will be thwarted if non-banking traders offset the banking system's "favorable balance on current account" with the business community (a favorable balance brought about by central bank policies).

Once non-bank has been substituted for bank credit, there need be no net flow of cash from non-banking portfolio managers to deficit spending units. Debtors recontract with non-banks instead of banks.

expansion of book credit can have important inflationary (deflationary) effects in the short-run, in turn very important in a context of contracyclical policy. (*See Notes E, F, and H.*)

3

Both the speed and magnitude of asset holders' (or portfolio managers') responsiveness to changes in interest rates are important.

As for speed, unless portfolio managers rapidly respond to changes in interest rates, restricted bank liabilities (credit) can lead to substantial excess supply in commodities markets before alternative circuits are put into operation. Payment streams will be diverted into the bank sink. If the accelerator is important, such impact effects can be very important. Indeed, to some extent they might be inevitable. There must be some time lag of response by portfolio managers (including non-banking financial institutions). And firms forced immediately to repay banks will cancel orders, make emergency selling offers, etc., while seeking new finance.[30] Surely, if the authorities — perhaps with a Romanov tinge — think big, they hardly can be thwarted: if banks had to liquidate $10 billion in loans and investments in two weeks, there would be awesome deflationary pressure under any reasonable specifications; pressure that would crush inflationary forces for many months. The "speed of response" factor integrates the theory of central bank policy with that of "availability" doctrines. Obviously, continuous clearance of financial markets is practically impossible.

As for magnitude, the less the amount of "idle" cash that can be mobilized to replace withdrawn bank credit, once portfolio managers are "fully adjusted," for specified interest rates, the higher interest rates will have to be if specified levels of economic activity and prices are to find demand for money consistent with the stock of money.

The rate of change and the level of the stock of bank credit both have effects at time t. At time $t + h$, only the latter is in play.[31] (*See Note I.*)

---

30 Financial disorganization can lead to output cutbacks — here suppressed — which, if accelerator effects are ignored, can *be* inflationary.

31 For expositional convenience sales by banks of securities to depositors have been neglected immediately above. These can be very important and have the same effect as "alternative circuits" set up outside the banking system.

Note that the initial impact of a credit crunch will be more severe as the public's initial cash buffers are lower. Similarly, the higher are initial free reserves the less will be the impact effect of a given open-market sale. *Cf.* footnote 75, Ch. VB.

c) *Response of Spenders to Changes in Interest Rates*[32]

1

It has been shown that, for "other things equal" in the labor and commodities markets (including prices), interest rates must rise if the public is to be induced to accept an asset portfolio featuring less cash and more securities. After all, the fact that the total stock of money has been reduced is immaterial for the individual: the parameters governing his decisions are tastes, prices, wealth constraints,[33] and the like; for firms and households to be satisfied to hold less cash (money) it is necessary that the opportunity cost of holding cash increase. Securities' yields must increase *unless* the "monetary requirement is reduced as a result of decreased rates of real economic activity or lower prices of goods and services.[34] (This paragraph ignores availability effects.)

We have arrived at the heart of the uniquely interesting aspect of open-market operations in financial markets: their indirect effects. We proceed to indicate the general nature of the impact of changed interest rates on "real" markets. Once this has been done, we can take up the relationship between the degree of sensitivity of economic units as asset holders (holders of cash *et al.*) and as spenders and the effectiveness of contracyclical monetary policy, and also the prospects for monetary policy as a means of relieving unemployment.

2

Changes in interest rates affect valuations of future prospects. We shall discuss the technique of valuing future prospects in later chapters, but now can stress casual empiricism. The cost of borrowing and the return that can be earned in alternative investments (including securities) are pertinent for plans for construction of plant and equipment for example. If the appropriate discount rate is 10 per cent, it would be senseless to carry out investment in plant and equipment beyond the point where the *risk-adjusted* rate of return were 10 per cent. Thus, when, say, 9 per cent can be earned on bonds, marginal

---

32 Needless to say, we are dealing separately with portfolio management and spending behavior only for didactic convenience.

33 Wealth constraints are not parametric if the horizon is long enough. Among the things determined by my economic behavior today is tomorrow's wealth (and income) constraint. *Cf.* Ch. XIV, Sec. C §§ 6.

34 "Monetary requirements" ultimately can be reduced enough for interest rates to be restored to their initial levels. *Cf.* Note K.

projects are postponed.[35] The advantages of large inventories shrink when money is dear; inventory liquidation can yield cash that can be profitably invested in the money market or used to retire now-higher-interest-bearing short-term debt; planned housing starts would be adversely affected. The more pervasive the effects of tight money along the maturity spectrum, the more important will be its effects in the real sector, although lagged responses might disappoint the authorities.

3

This has not been to say that a given change in interest rates will have *much* impact on expenditure plans. However, at least one invalid argument often is advanced. It states that, if anything, higher interest rates are inflationary because they lead to higher costs of production; only supply prices of goods are affected. The fact is that interest expense is a trivial portion of production costs.[36] Correct formulations are concerned with effects of interest rate changes on *demand prices,* maximum amounts purchasers are willing to pay. Thus I should be willing to pay $100 for the right to receive $1 forever if the appropriate discount rate were 1 per cent and but $10 if it were 10 per cent. There could be tremendous impact on demand price even if the supply price of the source of the stream were substantially unaffected. Consider more valid grounds of scepticism about effects of interest rates on demand for goods. Thus, when entrepreneurs are sceptical about future business, they might refuse *interest-free* loans for finance of plant and equipment. Why undertake to build still more plant that cannot profitably be utilized? During booms, firms may anticipate rates of return of 20, 30 or more per cent per annum. An increase in interest charges from, say, 6 to 10 per cent is unlikely to ruffle any feathers.

35 Consider effects on "real" markets from the vantage of views stressing non-price-rationing of credit. Even if bank charges have not risen for a preferred client, the appropriate opportunity cost may have increased. It makes little sense to invest in plant and equipment with a (non-risk adjusted) expected return of 7 per cent when one can borrow at 6 per cent, but when 30-year bond rate also is 7 per cent.

The text has stressed that at impact non-price-rationing can be important. And, clearly, it is going to be harder for firms and households without access to broader capital markets to obtain substitutes for bank credit, even though they might be willing to pay high rates of interest.

36 As Hawtrey has pointed out, interest costs are important in holding inventory. But here the effect of an increase in interest rates also is on the demand side. Demand for the purpose of replenishing stocks will be cut back as a result of increased storage cost.

d) Integration of Response Patterns: Flexible Prices

It is time to relate asset management and expenditure responses to changes in interest rates to prospects for effective monetary policy, whether in a full employment context or one of involuntary unemployment.[37]

Referring to section C 4a, how can the proposition that type 1 conditions are ideal for monetary policy when prices are flexible be defended? Admittedly, our position is rooted in a subjective criterion: namely, that it is desirable, *cet. par.,* that open-market operations be small and that fluctuations of securities prices be narrowly bounded. The way home is short and direct: if portfolio managers are sensitive to interest rates, only slightly higher interest rates are necessary in order to induce the public to plan to hold less cash and more securities; but slightly higher interest rates will permit substantial deflationary pressure, or, alternatively, initial inflationary pressure can be forcefully repelled with very little effort, since the slightest excess supply of goods occasioned by higher interest rates will cause prices to fall rapidly . . . In fact, price flexibility will permit monetary policy to do a reasonably good job under almost any circumstances; higher interest rates need only exert *some* depressing influence on planned expenditure. But always keep in mind that, if prices are *too* flexible, monetary institutions will break down. (*Cf.* Ch. VII.)

e) Integration of Response Patterns: Sticky Prices

1

We now defend the assertion that type 3 conditions are ideal for price stabilization policy when prices are sticky.[38] But, first, we must anticipate criticism to the effect that price stabilization policy in a world of sticky prices is a *non sequitur.* The rebuttal is twofold:

1) prices may be flexible upwards but sticky downwards;

2) the problem is one of reversing or arresting the direction of motion of prices. The upward movement might be glacial, but it might be necessary to exert tremendous force to reverse the movement (as it would to arrest a glacier).

---

37 The remainder of the chapter's argument concerns the *magnitude, not* the *speed* of portfolio managers' responsiveness to interest rate changes.

38 Indeed type 3 conditions are ideal for monetary policy to be effective in combatting unemployment.

2

Somehow it is easier to show why type 3 conditions are favorable for monetary policy by showing why type 2 conditions are unfavorable.[39] If cash holders are sensitive to interest rates, a given official sale of securities will lead to increased interest rates, but the increases need not be great: cash is readily substituted against in asset portfolios.[40] Insensitive spenders will not be much affected by what is in any case a small change in interest rates. Interest-elastic demand for cash combined with interest insensitivity of spending units can make it next to impossible for moderate doses of monetary restraint to arrest the movement of prices. The effects of monetary policy would tend to be confined to the markets in which it is initiated — the securities markets. But we have seen that the essence of effective monetary policy is in its *indirect* effects.[41]

Adopt this type 3 specification: there is meaningful interest elasticity of demand for goods and services, together with almost complete insensitivity (almost zero elasticity) of demand for cash (money balances) to interest rate changes. Planned substitution between money and securities can be ruled out.[42] The type 3 specification implies that interest rates will rise promptly and substantially once open-market sales are accomplished, but that the money market cannot be cleared unless real output and/or prices fall. Also that prices will respond fairly quickly. The assumption that there is at least moderate responsiveness of spending units to rising interest rates provides a clue to the mechanism that will be utilized: although higher interest rates, *cet. par.*, might have practically no effect on the public's desired money (cash) balances, they do lead to reduced planned rates of expenditure, implying reduced offerings of new securities and reduced planned transaction balances.[42] These developments will relieve pressure in the securities markets: the one reduces the rate of supply of securities to the market; the other meshes with reduced bank deposits.[43] Here the

[39] Type 2 conditions also stymie monetary policy in combatting unemployment.

[40] Again, reference is to *magnitude* of response of portfolio managers. It would be natural to correlate speed with magnitude.

[41] The text carefully distinguishes between *sluggishness* of monetary policy's effects and theorems of comparative statics. Here we say *nothing* about comparative statics. *Cf.* Note K.

[42] The conventional explanation of such a state of affairs is two-pronged: (a) transactions-balance demand for cash — as against demand for speculative or precautionary purposes (in either sense of that term) — dominates; (b) possibilities of securities substituting for cash in transactions balances are very limited.

[43] *Cf.* Note K for a fuller statement of the process taking us from one state to another.

impact of monetary policy is registered in commodities markets without being blunted by forces associated with conservation of cash balances.

3

Do not neglect price stabilization in response to deflationary pressure. Counterdeflationary policy finds the authorities purchasing securities: the banks find themselves with excess reserves; they remain until their deposit liabilities increase by a multiple of the value of the securities purchases. The result is excess demand in securities markets as banks try to increase their portfolios. Securities prices will rise.

Will rising securities prices (falling yields) soon have important impact on "real" markets? We are concerned with the delay between onset of easy money and responses of spending units. And, of course, with expectations (will traders expect yields to fall still more?), and with the strength of responses once initiated. Only then can it be determined whether easy money can reverse a deflationary trend that has developed a fair amount of momentum.[44]

"Moderate" assumptions about underlying parameters lead to this process: interest rates fall, encouraging more lavish use of cash in portfolios, decreasing velocities of circulation; lower interest rates stimulate demand for goods and services; to the extent there is reflation, there is greater demand for transactions balances. In this way the increased volume of bank deposits would come to be matched by increased demand for cash: partly because of increased planned "idle" cash, partly because of augmented demand for "active" (transactions) balances.[45]

If we assumed that there were long lags in the response of spending units to changes in interest rates or that the response was weak, the effects of "easy money" would tend to be confined to financial markets; no meaningful pressure countering the deflationary trend would be exerted. On the other hand, if we assumed that desired cash holdings were independent of interest rate considerations, but that spend-

44 What of the "fringe of unsatisfied borrowers" and non-price-rationing of credit generally? To the extent that there are economic Pariahs desperately anxious to borrow, planning to buy goods with the proceeds, and unable to obtain credit, increased bank reserves will have marvelous — albeit transitional — effects. But the dynamics are less helpful during deliberate monetary ease.

45 This sentence implies a process of adjustment in which excess demand in the securities markets leads to a temporary decline in interest rates below the "natural" rate, permitting reflation until transactions demands for cash increase enough to permit the demand for cash to be equal to the new stock at the "natural" rate of interest.

ing decisions reacted promptly and forcefully, the impact of "easy money" on the markets for goods and services, including labor, would be substantial and prompt: falling interest rates would not cause demand for idle cash to increase; there would be no mitigation of excess demand in the securities markets until the "real" markets responded, increasing desired transactions balances. If there were initial slack in the labor and goods and services markets, the latter parameter specifications imply that the central bank would have it within its power to increase output and employment by performing technical operations in the "remote" money and securities markets. (*Cf.* subsection 5. *See Notes H, I, and J.*)

5. Under-Employment Context: Income Stabilization Policy

This topic is better treated after the income-theoretic preparation of Part II. But it is now possible to provide the rudiments of the impact of "easy money" on the "real" markets of the system. If responses of spending units to interest rate changes are weak in contrast with those of portfolio managers, effects of "easy money" would be confined to financial markets: interest rates would fall until firms and households came to desire to substitute cash for securities to the same extent that the banks wished to supply cash in exchange for securities — excluding the possibility that banks would want to hold free reserves, perhaps because they anticipated declines in securities prices back to "normal" levels. The central bank would not have the means at its disposal to stimulate demand for goods and services and, derivatively, labor.

If we assume that portfolio managers, in contrast with spending units, are insensitive to interest rate changes, the central bank has it within its power to increase output and employment by working in financial markets.

D. CONCLUDING TOPIC: INTERNATIONAL ASPECTS

1

We shall conclude the theoretical portion of this chapter with a discussion of the complications that external considerations can impose for planners basically concerned with internal (national) goals; we shall open the system a wee bit, having kept it sealed shut throughout this chapter. A full-scale assault on this topic is not attempted until Chapters XIV-XVI.

Walter Bagehot, writing in 1873, described the primary function of the most famous of central banks, the Bank of England, as follows:

> "In consequence all our credit system depends upon the Bank of England for its security. On the wisdom of the directors of that one joint-stock company it depends whether *England shall be solvent or insolvent.* This may seem too strong, but it is not. All banks depend on the Bank of England, and all merchants depend on some banker . . .
>
> The directors of the bank are, therefore, in fact, if not in name, trustees for the public, to keep a banking reserve on their behalf."
>
> *Lombard Street* (London: John Murray, 1915), p. 36

Keynes described the dilemma inherent in Bagehot's prescription in Ch. 36 of his *Treatise:*

> "We have seen that the Management of Money, national or international, always presents a dual aspect. There are long-period movements in the equilibrium price level . . . due to permanent changes in the quantities of the monetary factors relatively to the volume of output. And there are the short period movements round the long-period trend of the equilibrium price level due to the temporary disequilibrium of the investment factors . . .
>
> Now, so far as the first aspect is concerned, membership in an international system necessarily binds the long-period value of the local money to the long-period value of the international standard . . . But, as regards the second aspect, each country naturally wants to save itself from temporary disturbances as much as it possibly can. When investment disequilibria are being initiated within its own borders, it will endeavor to counteract them, whatever may be happening abroad; and when investment disequilibria are arising outside its own borders, it will endeavor not to share them. Since, therefore, investment disequilibria do not arise everywhere in the same degree at the same time, a given national system may be under an incentive to take measures to preserve its own investment equilibrium, which may not suit other members of the same international system."[46]

We reserve detailed comment on this dilemma for Part III, confining ourselves at this point to remarking on a few obvious facets:

a) if foreign exchange rates are to remain rigid, it becomes most

[46] Keynes, *op. cit.,* Vol. II, pp. 302-303.

difficult for individual nations to ignore global deflation unless they are possessed of huge reserves of foreign exchange or of gold;

b) if foreign exchange rates are to remain rigid and if members of the international community refuse to permit gold inflow (stemming from globally inflationary pressures for example) to influence their economies, it is likely that such nations — witness France and the United States in the 1920's — will acquire all the chips, causing other players to quit the game;

c) monetary adjustments intended to correct balance of payments difficulties almost inevitably will have impact on "real" markets; we have offered theoretical reasons suggesting that it would be difficult for the authorities to manipulate the rate pattern; more or less unselective movements in interest rates will tend to stem from official monetary reactions to balance of payments disequilibria;

d) it follows that proper treatment of the dilemma requires understanding of interaction of fiscal and monetary policy which might find adverse balances of payments attacked through monetary stringency accompanied by budget deficits and increased government spending;

e) central banks of the nineteenth century were reluctant to acknowledge even their "Bagehotian" responsibility to protect the national specie reserves (recalling the treatment of the banking department in the Act of 1844), let alone responsibility for the amplitude of the trade cycle; and, for that matter, the record of central banks in the twentieth century, including that of our own, does not reveal outstanding appreciation of the dilemma; the development of central banking in the United Kingdom and the United States can be described in terms of a process finding certain joint-stock banks invested with unusually heavy responsibilities (usually as an offshoot of profit-seeking behavior) for protection of the mass of manoeuvre, the central specie reserves; it has not always been easy to gain recognition of these responsibilities;

f) finally, full recognition of the narrow "strategic" responsibility, often leading to adoption of a general overseer role, was obtained, but, by that time, more enlightened views of the interaction of economic forces in the determination of general equilibrium of markets were at hand; new battles had to be fought to force central banking authorities to acknowledge their responsibility in this broader field, battles that have been won, although fossils of former ages remain in the form of independence of such banking authorities as the Federal Reserve System, often leading to clashes, sometimes irresponsibly played out on a political stage.

SUMMARY

1. Central bank policy traditionally has focused on manipulation of member bank reserves through open market policy, although other devices, including alteration of reserve requirements and transfers of government deposits to and from member banks, are available.
2. All agree that the Federal Reserve promptly can affect short-term rates of interest. Effects of conventional measures on long rates might not prove prompt. Yet it commonly is held that long rates are much more important for expenditure decisions.
3. Skepticism about effects of monetary policy on long rates arises from demand and supply prices of long-term securities being much influenced by expectations of *future* rates of interest. Current bill rate is part of a larger picture. These expectations might be rigid and might be revised only after sustained contradictory experience.
4. The main obstacle to reducing long rate by saturating the system with liquidity is that — given formation of expectations along lines suggested in the text — lower long rates arouse fears of capital loss dominating running-yield considerations. (*Cf.* Keynes, *General Theory,* p. 202, for an excellent illustration.)
5. We argued that bills-preferably foes often reasoned fallaciously, not recognizing that the volumes of securities involved in open-market operations are much smaller than those of aggregate holdings. The important direct effect of open-market operations is on bank liquidity rather than on the mix of securities. If open-market operations prove substantially to affect interest rates, this is because the non-banking public is reluctant to change its mix of bank deposits and securities. But thin bond markets might permit sharp impact effects.
6. Imperfections of financial markets, captured in the phrase "the fringe of unsatisfied borrowers," are especially important in connection with impact effects of open-market sales. At the outset of monetary contraction, non-price rationing is important. Unless

there are Pariahs longing but unable to borrow under ordinary conditions, availability considerations will be less important during deliberate monetary ease than during deliberate constraint.

7. Two instances of official intervention calculated to reduce long-term rates of interest will be considered: U. S. Treasury policy in 1949–1951 and British Treasury policy in 1945–1947. In neither case did the officials want bill rate to increase: this would have undermined traders' confidence in the likelihood of continued cheap money. Bank reserves had to be increased so that holders of long-term securities — stubbornly disbelieving that cheap money would be sustained — could be offered bank deposits in exchange for securities sold at support prices. These interventions were unsuccessful.
8. A crucial characteristic of central bank open-market operations is that indirect effects are much more important than direct effects.
9. If interest-rate sensitivity of demand for goods and services can be ignored, operations in securities markets might have to rely on effects of diversion of cash flows into bank sinks pending establishment of alternative conduits, or, more realistically, on inability of bank customers to obtain more credit from banks unable to expand their liabilities. Customers must await opening-up of non-bank channels. Authorities fear that effects of open-market operations will be confined to financial markets. It is easiest to establish monetary velocity if "portfolio managers" are insensitive and "spenders" sensitive to interest rate changes.
10. The student of central banking can be confused by juxtaposition of two seemingly contradictory sets of propositions. One set is comprised of invariance theorems; the other concerns transitional states. Treatises will explain at page x why the equilibrium interest rate is invariant against the stock of money, at page y that open-market operations accomplish their purposes through changed interest rates. Statics and dynamics have to be sorted out. Thus:

a) equilibrium values of interest rates and sundry real variables will in most models be invariant against the quantity of money or, better, certain monetary parameters.

b) policy makers are primarily concerned with affecting the "day to day" motion of the system. They ask whether managed money can transform an oscillatory motion around a rising trend into a steadily rising motion.

c) the equilibrium price level is not invariant against central bank policy. The process by which central bank policy can change the equilibrium price level is keyed to what might be transitional movements in interest rates. Under some conditions, once the new equilibrium price level (or path) is achieved, interest rates and other real variables can revert to their original equilibrium values (or paths).

d) equilibria and states in which all markets are cleared should be distinguished. Securities and commodities markets might be cleared over a number of periods with interest rates constant *or* with interest rates rising and falling irregularly. Only the former time path is consistent with what conventionally is called an equilibrium state; equilibrium must be identified with some steady motion. Of course, transitional states might find some or all of the markets continuously *un*cleared.

NOTES

NOTE A: A theoretical analysis of Federal Reserve buying rate policy in the '20's is suggested. It can be outlined in outline form.

A. Background

1. Federal Reserve buying rates for bank bills often were below market rates.
   a. This did not disturb real-bills-oriented authorities seeking to support the New York acceptances market.
   b. One reason was that dealers were expected to resort to the Federal Reserve (at the special buying rate) only when under pressure from banks, in turn expected properly to confine their loans to "commercial" transactions.
      i.e., recourse to the central bank was to take place only when demand for credit was increasing; a nice illustration of real bills thinking.
   c. Another reason is found in institutional arrangements described below.

B. Appearance

1. At time *t*, upward movements in market rates were likely to be constrained by buying rate.
   Limits on recourse, already described, meant that the market rate-buying rate spread could grow from time to time.
2. It might seem that cumulative inflation was a likely event.

C. Reality

1. Buying rate's dynamic laws found $d(BR)/dt > 0$ if advances to the market were increasing or, perhaps, if these were above a critical level.
   a. Hence buying rate could rise with increased demand for accommodation.

b. Here Bank rate need not be penal.

2. There could be considerable intervals over which buying rate was rising *and* below market rate.

3. If the dynamic law governing buying rates found buying rate moving sluggishly, the central bank could on this account be important as an engine of inflation.

D. Hypothetical Structure Suggested by Above

1. Assume that Bank rate is subject to the dynamic law $d(BR)/dt \gtrless 0$ as Bank advances are greater than equal to a defined critical level, perhaps the initial level. Perhaps initial Bank rate [$BR(0)$] is below market rate, and there is initial excess supply of securities (excess demand for credit).

   a. Bank rate will be increasing as the inflation proceeds. It cannot indefinitely be profitable to discount at the Bank unless market rate is rising.

   b. Admittedly it is possible for the process to go out of control if, for example, the expected rate of increase in the price level leads to "permanent" excess demand for loans.

NOTE B: Needless to say, the "arbitrage" formula implicit in the text at p. 199 and explicit in Appendix A, p. 253, requires that any unexpected change in short rate at *t* thought capable of persisting beyond tomorrow or, more correctly, enough affecting subjective probability density functions to change mathematical expectations of future short rates (so that expectations are not zero elastic) must affect bond prices. The text's illustration (p. 199) is a polar case. The "arbitrage" process pertinent to the more general case is simple: if long rate were rigid despite higher short rate, a plan calling for selling-out long positions, switching to bills, would lead to expected profit. *Arbitrage* is put between quotes for good cause: switching to bills *risks* sacrifice of capital gains on bonds ensuing from possible later revision of market opinion.

A variant of the expectations hypothesis is consistent with Bills Only: putative unit elastic expectations would induce parallel shifts in the yield curve after initial pressure on bills. Of course, what are called *error-learning models* are inconsistent with unit-elastic expectations; traders' implicit wait-and-see attitudes preclude immediate conversion of today's "surprise" into a one-for-one shift (on a log-linear scale) of expectations about subsequent short rates. *Cf.* John H. Wood, "Expectations, Errors, and . . . Interest Rates," *Journal of Political Economy,* April, 1963.

NOTE C: The text deals with two idealized cases: (a) bank reserves are changed without affecting the composition of public debt; (b) the composition of public debt is changed without affecting bank reserves. In both cases, government securities are treated as parameters of the system. In this note it is assumed that refinance of government debt is *substantial.* It must be — in the context of a trillion dollar portfolio — for the problem to be at all interesting.

It was argued that case (a) might find the yield-curve lowered and twisted: short rate will be more likely than long rate substantially to change over fairish intervals. Of course, suppliers of securities, *might* respond mightily to a slight reduction in long rate (following a reduction in reserve requirements). If not, banks, *inter alia,* would seek short-term securities or to increase free reserves: they will be unwilling, if their expectations are inelastic, to hold long-terms at more-than-slightly-reduced yields. If banks are provided with *enough* reserves, relative yields are likely to be substantially altered for at least some time.

Case (a) found bank demand functions for securities altered. Case (b) finds non-government supply and demand functions for securities (not, repeat not, *excess* supply and demand functions) unaltered, but the composition of the public debt *is* altered. Thus long-dated might be replaced with short-dated stock. If securities-portfolios' maturity compositions are to be maintained, private debt must be refinanced. Presumably asset holders would be willing to accept additional long-dated securities from private issuers — "returning" short-dated private securities now in their portfolios — at going rates: this would enable them to restore portfolio balance. *But* securities issuers presumably will not be willing to be so accommodating: they also have portfolio-balance criteria. If securities suppliers would leap at the chance of funding their debt if long rate declined slightly, private refinance largely would offset public refinance. If not, elastic expectations would make portfolio managers willing to absorb additional short-term securities — accepting reduced long-term holdings — rather than accept lower yields on longs. Since bank reserves would be unchanged, the absorption could occur at going short rates: $\Delta_B{}^1 = -\Delta_B{}^2$. It follows that high elasticities of substitution — perhaps because of low elasticities of expectation — would leave the yield curve largely unaltered. Note that in case (a) low elasticities of expectation led to a *changed* yield curve; in case (a) short rate had to fall because of over-all excess demand for securities. In case (b), bank reserves are just adequate to absorb the new short-dated securities.

Needless to say, if expectations are unit elastic and very firm, long and short rates would tend to be very close to each other at all times. (This is a naive model assuming that every element in the vector $r(t)$ is the same.)

If expectations are unit elastic but infirm, risk preferences will be important. If securities issuers are not willing to undertake substantial refunding at roughly initial interest rates, and if portfolio managers attach great importance to composition, the yield curve can be twisted: in our example, long rate must fall relative to short rate.

NOTE D: Ch. VA largely ignores non-banking financial institutions, although it *does* take up cases in which demand for currency and demand deposits is very sensitive to interest rates. In these cases, very large changes in bank reserves are associated with very small changes — even transitorily — in market-clearing interest rates. This is precisely the effect of intermediaries able greatly to increase their deposits against the grain of monetary policy — although the empirical significance of such movements does not appear to have been great.

Take up the case of non-banking financial institutions (intermediaries). Assume that commercial banks issue and most hold reserves against time deposits. IS IT POSSIBLE FOR INTERMEDIARIES TO EXPAND THEIR TIME DEPOSITS AT THE EXPENSE OF COMMERCIAL BANKS SO THAT THE NEW SOLUTION FINDS DEMAND DEPOSITS AND TOTAL TIME DEPOSITS UNCHANGED? The answer, roughly, is *yes,* provided commercial banks are limited by maximum deposit rates, and if depositors are highly sensitive to differentials between deposit rates. In that case, slight increases in money-market rates (including "free" deposit rates) would lead to substantial transfers to intermediaries. Also, substitution between demand and time deposits must be weak. Then the transfer can be accomplished without demand deposits, being meaningfully affected . . . The authorities will not know what hit them.

The answer is *no* if commercial banks can be competitive in their time-deposit rates. In this case it can be assumed that non-colluding banks will not permit their deposit rates to be noncompetitive; there will not be important substitution against commercial bank time deposits, always welcomed by individual banks. As banks try to escape the contractionary vise, interest rates — including deposit rates — will rise, encouraging substitution of all of these assets for demand deposits. The proportion of commercial-bank time deposits to total commercial bank liability — as well as their absolute quantity — will rise. The brunt of the attack must be borne by demand deposits.

The discussion emphasizes that the stock of demand deposits, of time deposits, and the sum of the two, are not directly under the authorities' control. Keynes and others have pointed out that, if banks' time deposits did not require reserves, there would be sure direct control of the volume of demand deposits. Commercial banks obviously would be in separate businesses in connection with issue of demand and time deposits.

Moving out of the contemporary scene, consider a system in which interest can be paid on demand deposits. Assume that banks do not issue time deposits or at least do not hold reserves against them. Reduced bank reserves would require that the *relative* rate of return on demand deposits increase *if* cost differentials are to be unchanged. *Absolute* rates certainly will be higher; higher money-market rates induce banks to offer more for demand deposits. In fact, competition among banks for more profitable demand deposits would assure that the system would be violently agitated until money income had declined enough for the demand schedule for demand deposits shift far enough leftward to restore the initial relative relationships between demand-deposit and other rates. An additional dimension would be added to monetary policy: competition between banks would prevent reduced demand for deposits except through the force of lower money income.

For an excellent — and empirically buttressed — discussion of demand and interest-bearing deposits, *cf.* R. G. Davis and J. M. Guttentag, "Time and Savings Deposits in the Cycle," Federal Reserve Bank of New York *Monthly Review,* Vol. 44, No. 6, June 1962, pp. 86-91.

Finally, we do *not* make the mistake of assuming that individual banks profit from intra-bank switches from demand to time deposits. Surely, it is not pleasing for a bank to contemplate paying, say, 3¢ a year in order to lend an additional 12¢ a year.

NOTE E: The Keynesian argument must be treated gingerly. It is not enough for banks to be terrorized into keeping excess reserves: idle deposits must be sopped up through bank sales of gilt-edged securities to the public. Nor is it enough for advances to be constrained: firms large enough to issue paper in securities markets will turn to these markets; banks might supply the securities markets, since they have traditionally, in response to official pressure, restricted investments more readily than advances . . . Of course, firms not large or well established enough to borrow in "formal" markets will, at least in the short run, feel the "unavailability" impact of tighter credit unless they have liquid assets to unload.

It is almost inconceivable to me that Bank rate could be reduced without the officials supplying the banks with ample reserves. (Indeed, to the extent that deposit rates fall, the public will be encouraged to hold more currency: bank reserves will fall.) Surely the officials would not want banks to be under pressure to unload long-term securities in order to satisfy customers' requests for advances. It is unusual, although not impossible, for officials to want relaxation of advances and tightening in the gilt-edged markets. (But consider a country experiencing inflation and undesired surplus in its balance of payments; the obverse of the American problem circa 1960-1961.) But to the extent that banks are unable to satisfy demand for credit at lower rates, queues will form. Credit will not be *effectively* easier. There is a snare and delusion bound up in this problem: if price is arbitrarily depressed, the amount supplied to demanders can fall even if the amount demanded increases.

NOTE F: *Exact* interpretation of Ch. VA requires the assumption that commercial banks either do not issue time or savings deposits or are not required to hold reserves against them. In the latter case, banks would be engaged in altogether separate businesses. (*Cf.* Chs. III and IV for discussion of mitigating effects of expanded time and savings deposits of non-banking institutions and effects of reserve requirements for time deposits.)

In VA, time deposits are lumped with securities generally offering the composite yield r. Open-market sales by the central bank would lead to higher yields for broad ranges of securities, causing intermediaries to offer higher deposit rates. Indeed, if a small rise in deposit rate would lead to substantial desired substitution of time for demand deposits, it would be possible for the intermediaries to take very large quantities of securities off the hands of the commercial banks as demand deposits are chequed into intermediaries' coffers. On the other hand, if the elasticity of substitution between the two classes of deposits were small, interest rates would have to become very high before substitution were attempted.

NOTE G: Transitional and "permanent" effects of changes in the equilibrium volume of bank liabilities should be distinguished. Thus, if banks are forced to contract deposit liability, initially there will be excess flow supply of securities. But, once the contraction has been accomplished, there is no *mechanical* reason for the nominal value of the flow of net issue of new securities to fall. The sources for accommodation of an increase in the stock of securities are (1) reduction in "idle" cash balances of purchasers of securities, perhaps through bank mediation finding them exchanging old securities for deposits; (2) current saving and physical disinvestment. (1) is based on a once-and-for-all effect; (2) can be available in undiminished strength if the smaller volume of money could be pumped faster through the system. Consider a physical analogy: a closed system containing x gallons of water. The flow rate past point P can be increased by increasing pressure on the water.

Banks up against a binding constraint on their deposit liability cannot collectively increase the total of their net assets except through contributions to capital. They can extend new credit only by selling securities to depositors or devoting repayments on loans to purchases of new securities. To the extent that spending units are repaying banks more dollars per period (out of current receipts, ignoring (1)), the rate of leakage from the system's expenditure circuit is greater: a corresponding increase in the rate of issue of new loans does not produce inflationary pressure, nor add to the rate of flow of payments. Of course, new loans will tend to be greater in any one period when the level of bank credit is higher; repayments will be greater also. If all loans were for one period, new loans per period would have to be enormous in order to avoid *deflation*.

Once effects of *falling* bank credit have been registered, the effects of restriction of bank advances (as a stock) arise from the necessity of higher interest rates in order to permit a smaller stock of means of payments to turn over more frequently. (The text discusses countervailing increases in non-bank credit.)

It will be shown in Ch. VII that the rate of planned demand for commodities plus bonds at time t is given by the planned rates of *gross* disinvestment in cash and that, if plans are consistent, aggregate planned *net* investment in cash will be zero.

Price-level effects of trade credit flow from its first and second time derivatives. The first time derivative affects the price level, the second the rate of increase of the price level. It is the second time derivative of trade credit that governs the engine of inflation. Of course, workers must be paid in cash. It is not enough for firms to extend the fabled finger of Midas only to each other.

NOTE H: Some have written that scrip might be issued as interest rates increase. suggesting in fact that, if yields on "Governments" become high enough, all cash tenderable for Governments will be turned in to the officials. Scrip would replace cash as a medium of exchange. These writers infer that the authorities will thereby lose touch with interest rates on non-government debt, that deflationary policies would be frustrated. (A good can serve as *numeraire* even if people choose not to hold it.)

This is nonsense. Assume that the Treasury bill rate is put up to 32 per cent per annum. What kind of scrip is meant? Scrip payable in cash on demand (instant scrip)? Putting aside legal restrictions on issue and the doubtful wisdom of ordinary firms choosing so illiquid a position, instant scrip assures that non-government securities will yield as much as government securities (adjusting for risk). (There is a *vague* resemblance to post-Civil War America when U. S. securities were payable in gold, but not all securities were.) Otherwise, holders of non-governments simply would plan to sell their securities for scrip and convert the scrip, moving into Governments. Fiat scrip? Why should I suddenly be willing to take scrip when legal tender acts entitle me to cash — and 32-per-cent Treasury bills? Nor is there any reason for traders to contract outside of the legal tender acts. The fact the bill rate is 32 per cent will not make me willing to take a piece of paper with a graven image of a Cadillac. One suspects I would be less willing on that account. (Remember that *cash balances always are endogenous for the individual.*) High interest rates, *cet. par.*, never will cause planned cash balances to be *zero*. Of course, the public's stock of cash could fall to a number of dollars equal to one millisecond's flow rate of payments if certain amazing correspondences were achieved. (*Cf.* Ch. VI.)

We have not considered the hundreds of billions of dollars of existing contractual obligation, some in the form of securities. Surely creditors are not going to surrender the right to receive stuff that can be invested in 32-per-cent bills.

Scrip was issued during various banking panics when the public's circulating media was from it untimely ripped. Certain (locally) august firms were permitted to pay for goods and services in scrip, so desperate was the desire for circulating media. (I believe it was understood the scrip ultimately was to be redeemed in cash.) No correct analogy can be drawn to the present case. Here creditors need not be in the least desperate. Cash stocks are reduced because people *wanted* less cash. Debtors have plenty of *convertible* Treasury bills which they will convert and fork over the proceeds, once it is made clear to them that no scrip nonsense will be suffered. It is *institutionally* impossible for private persons to pay rates lower than those paid by the government in a country such as the United States or the United Kingdom.

NOTE I: The text's argument takes for granted that interest rates will not ration credit while bank portfolios are contracting or securities markets are congested as banks are unable to expand portfolios during booms. (Although some might argue that interest rates will ration credit in the way the predetermined wage unit "clears" the Keynesian labor market. Thus the gap between potential supply and demand at quoted prices sometimes can be called "reservation demand." *Cf.* (2), (3), and (4) below.) These considerations buttress the argument:

1) the nexus in which bank customers seek credit finds each taking his "share," while his banker seeks to enlarge the available melon by selling-off assets. And, for most, it is no easy matter to shift from bank finance to the open market.

2) sellers' quotations are marked-down only as securities markets fail to clear day after day. Taking sellers as price quoters, they surely are not going substantially to mark-down offer prices until convinced that it was no accident that they could not move their stock yesterday at a price they are shaving only a bit today. This will be true even of households and firms with spending plans highly insensitive to *permanent* increases in interest rates.

3) traders, knowing that alternative conduits ultimately will be opened, are willing — rather than pay "outlandish" rates of interest — to run-down their cash for the nonce (bad for the authorities) and to postpone financing projects until the market becomes uncongested (good for the authorities except to the extent that there are long lags between securities placements and real expenditures).

4) there are distinct practical limits on loan rates and their rates of increase. Accordingly, banks will have "high" reservation prices on securities. Recall also that reservation prices are influenced by expectations of future short rates.

5) slack cash in the system is disproportionately in the hands of smaller traders less responsive to money-market prices. Hence, mobilization of alternative funds tends to be sluggish.

6) purchasers of bank-held securities, if they plan to replenish cash, will contribute to the market's congestion.

7) while some of these arguments evoke those of lock-in theorists, they are not in fact based on the assumption that financial institutions are peculiarly reluctant to realize capital losses; a kernel of truth in the "lock-in effect" nevertheless is uncovered.

Aside from anything else, rates of realized sales cannot exceed rates of inflow of funds into securities markets. The specific way in which the former adjust to the latter during squeezes is not critical: does it matter whether sellers sullenly recall securities from a "crazy" market or trudge home with empty pockets? Whether we characterize offerers of securities as resisting "high" yields or simply as unable to make placements at prices falling according to rather sluggishly operating dynamic laws, the fact remains that credit outstanding to spending units decreases. Furthermore, if naïve *tatonnement* assumptions are abandoned, falling prices usually reflect inability of increasingly pessimistic sellers to sell what they wish at quoted prices. Often the credit market is subject to what Professor Clower calls income constraints (*cf.* Chapters IX and X *infra*). Their reservation demand might be nil. A seller would balance risk and expected return even in offering an isotope with a half life of 10 minutes — assuming that the market imposes on the seller a once-and-for-all decision subject to later acceptance or rejection by unknown buyers. Of course, the rate of increase of inflow of funds into the market will depend partly on the rate of increase of yields. Also, if "decelerative" impact effects of credit shortage cannot be depended on, ultimately inflationary pressure must be forestalled by the level of interest rates.

TE J: See footnote 39a, Appendix A, Ch. XII.

TE K: The argument of Ch. VA, save for availability effects, can be put analytically. First employ a *CC-BB* apparatus described in Ch. X. This model can be interpreted only in terms of *tatonnement.* Its dynamics are confined to the auctioneer's quotations, in turn governed by a law such as

$$dp_i/dt \gtreqless 0 \text{ as } x_i \gtreqless 0,$$

where x_i is excess demand as ascertained by answers to questionnaires specifying the vector $p(t)$.

Assume that the entire money stock is supplied by banks in exchange for IOU's of the non-banking public. It follows that excess demand functions will be zero-order homogeneous in w and p. (Following Professor Patinkin, w and p are in lock-step in the ratio σ, the "natural wage rate," assuring continuous equilibration of labor demand and supply.) There will be a unique natural rate of interest.

Consult Diagram A, beginning at P. Now assume that there is an upward shift in the CC curve so that the new equilibrium position is Q *unless* the authorities cut back bank reserves. Indeed assume that the authorities wish to sustain Os as the equilibrium price level and correctly force the BB curve to position B_2B_2. This having been done, equilibration will occur at once.

OFFICIAL PRESCIENCE

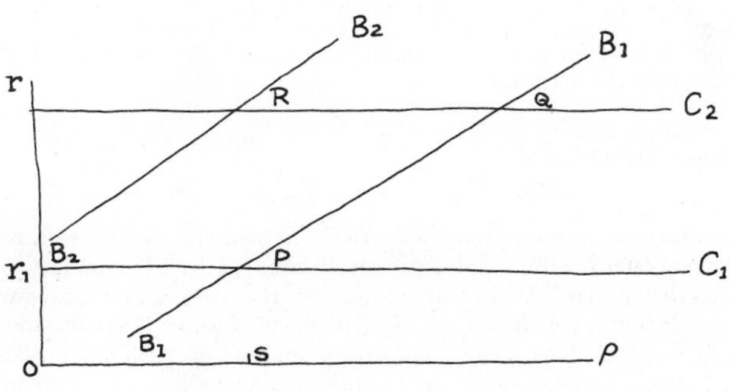

Diagram A, Figure VA-6

Now assume that the authorities underestimate the shift in CC and establish B_3B_3.

AN OFFICIAL MISTAKE LEADING TO INFLATION

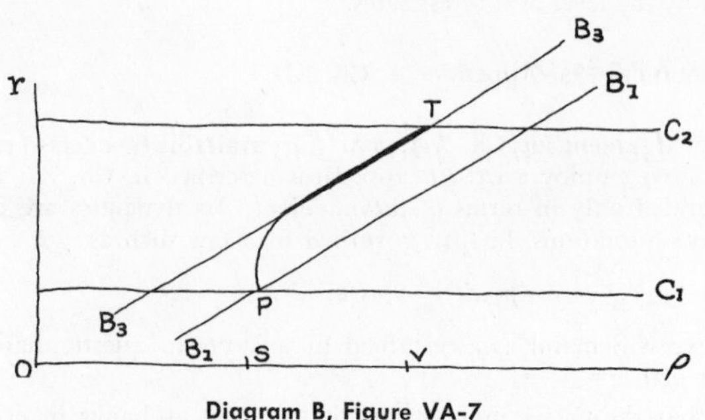

Diagram B, Figure VA-7

Prices and interest rates will rise until the position described by T is reached. The solid line PT describes one of many possible adjustment paths: the omniscient but perverse auctioneer decides that he always will call out interest rates that are consistent with clearance of the bond market (the model only has an *ex ante* interpretation) but constrains the time path of prices to conform to B_3B_3, thereby crying a series of r-p combinations at which there is excess demand in commodities markets (and excess supply of money; traders plan to use proceeds of bond sales and initial cash balances to purchase unavailable goods). At T, higher interest rates have restrained planned demand for commodities and money; there is general equilibrium.

Again consulting Diagram A, if the auctioneer insists on crying an interest rate not r_1, refusing *ever* to alter that quotation, he will go crazy; there will be cumulative (de)inflation. *Cf.* Ch. XIII *infra*.

Now resort to a *non-tatonnement* (Keynesian) system suggested to me by R. W. Clower. In this system the vector $p(t)$ can be discovered by solving mixed differential-integral equations of the form

$$(i) \qquad \dot{p} = f[x(t), \int_{t-h}^{t} x(\theta)d\theta]$$

where $x(t)$ is a vector of excess demands at $\theta = t$. Equations i are assumed to have the particular solution

$$(ii) \qquad p = p^*$$

and the general solution

$$(iii) \qquad p(\theta) = p^* + F(\theta).$$

p^*, including as it does securities prices, is assumed to be a unique steady solution consistent with steady growth if time paths of monetary parameters are correctly chosen. At t, transactions in the *ith* market are governed by supply or demand, whichever is less. (*Cf.* R. W. Clower, "Keynes and the Classics: A Dynamical Perspective," *Quarterly Journal of Economics*, Vol. 74, May 1960). If the authorities have set instrumental variables r, a subset of p, below or above r^*, there will develop inflationary or deflationary forces in commodities markets. Thus, if the system had achieved p^*, and the authorities altered Bank rate, the remainder parts of the equations' solutions would become reactivated and (in)deflationary processes would ensue. If the authorities stubbornly insisted on the new Bank rate, there might develop various cumulative processes. *Cf.* Ch. XIII *infra*.

I am indebted to Mr. Robert Coen in connection with Note K.

APPENDIX A

Long- and Short-Term Rates of Interest

PART II, COMMENCING WITH CH. VII, PERMITS A RIGOROUS basis for the theory of monetary policy. The first portion of Appendix A relies on "one period" statics techniques developed in Part II.

1. A Formal Model

1

We concentrate on developing simultaneous-equation models consistent with "full employment," somewhat in the manner of Don Patinkin.[1] The system's markets are aggregated up to four sectors: labor, commodities, bonds, and money. We work with a homogeneous commodity that can be consumed or added to capital. The problem is to determine, simultaneously, solution values for the rate of employment (N), the money-wage rate (w), the commodity price level (p), the rate of supply of commodities (Y), the rate of demand for commodities (Z), the stock of money (M), short- and long-term security prices $(R_1$ and $R_2)$, and net issue of short- and long-term securities $(B_1$ and $B_2)$ by the non-banking public to the banking sector where a short-term security is a standard promise to pay $1 in 30 days, and a long-term security is a promise to pay $1 per year forever. We impose market clearance conditions, just exhausting initial degrees of freedom, there being determined a set of values, assumed to be unique, for the endogenous variables of the system consistent with the definitions, behavioral relations, and clearance conditions of the model. We choose from an infinity of models that *could* be selected, one which explains more formally propositions advanced earlier in the book.

Planned rates of demand and supply of labor are assumed to depend on the money-wage rate and the price level:

[1] *Money, Interest, and Prices* (Evanston, Ill.: Row, Peterson and Co., 1956). Ch. X will make clear that Appendix A's models are Keynesian (as against neoclassical).

$$N = f(w, p) \tag{1}$$

$$N = g(w, p), \tag{2}$$

implicitly containing a market clearing condition. The functions are assumed to be homogeneous in degree zero in w and p — demand and supply of labor depend only on the ratio w/p — so that Equations 1 and 2 suffice to determine full-employment rate of labor utilization and the equilibrium real-wage rate, N^* and $(w/p)^*$.

The net output possibilities for the system are described in Equation 3:

$$Y^* = \Phi(N^*, K^\circ). \tag{3}$$

K° is a predetermined variable at each point in time: the stock of stored commodities devoted to production of additional commodities. (The system lacks inventories of working capital.) Equation 3 is written to make clear that full-employment production, Y^*, is determined once Equations 1 and 2 are solved: we simply plug N^* into the production function.

Equation 4 establishes a clearance condition for the commodity market and shows how commodity demand is determined:

$$Y^* = \psi(Y^*, R_1, R_2, K^\circ). \tag{4}$$

K° is a wealth variable. Money balances are not included in wealth, nor are security holdings. Applying what is known as a net money doctrine, and assuming that "money" is demand deposits of commercial banks (ignoring time deposits) acquired by sale of primary securities to the banks, bank deposits and security issues net out when taken together. There are no government bonds in the model.[2]

[2] Consider a credit money system in which the government has sold bonds to the banks, using the proceeds to purchase goods and services from the general public (as in the United States and the United Kingdom in finance of World War II). The banks will emerge with basically the same net asset position: their deposit liability to the non-banking public offsets acquisitions of government bonds. The public's net assets will have increased by the amount of the bond issue.

Consider in more detail why there can be no wealth effects from price changes in this model — if distribution effects are ignored. In the absence of money illusion, the public's desired real cash balances and desired real indebtedness will depend only on interest rates, relative prices, and physical wealth — for given tastes and preferences. If prices are halved and interest rates are unchanged, the representative man will want to retain his physical asset portfolio, cutting in half his *nominal* cash balance and *nominal* indebtedness to banks. (On *net* the public supplies primary securities to the banks.)

Compare the demonstration in the Appendix to Ch. II, showing that the relative price of real cash is *definitionally* unity. This is why desired real cash here is invariant to changes in p.

The form of $\psi(\quad)$ makes clear that the term structure of maturities is determined within the system. It would be incorrect to view the term structure as a parameter of the system.

This brings us to the model's financial markets. Equation 5 describes the determination of the money supply:

$$M^* = sV, \tag{5}$$

where s and V are officially determined constants: respectively the systematic coefficient of deposit expansion and the level of bank reserves. It is assumed that member banks are not permitted to borrow from the central bank and that free reserves always are nil.

Equation 6 describes the determination of the demand for money, $L(\quad)$ giving demand for real balances. If Equation 6 is satisfied, the quantity of money demanded will be equal to that supplied.

$$sV = p.L(Y^*, R_1, R_2, K^\circ). \tag{6}$$

Equations 7-10 apply to the securities markets:

$$\phi^1(Y^*, K^\circ, p, R_1, R_2) = R_1B_1{}^b \tag{7}$$

$$R_1B_1{}^b = F^1(R_1, R_2; s, V) \tag{8}$$

$$\phi^2(\qquad\qquad) = R_2B_2{}^b \tag{9}$$

$$B_2{}^b = sV - B_1{}^b \tag{10}$$

The content of Equations 6-10 is summarized in Equations 11 and 12:

$$\phi^1(\qquad\qquad) = F^1(\qquad) \tag{11}$$

$$\phi^2(\qquad\qquad) = p.L(\qquad) - F^1(\qquad). \tag{12}$$

Another "hint": since halved prices double both initial real cash and initial indebtedness, the *representative* trader's wealth position is unaffected, since his cash is equal to his indebtedness to banks.

The accounting framework of Equations 10-12 holds strictly only for an economy without history. Otherwise interest-rate history leads to divergence of M from $\Sigma R_jB_j{}^\Delta$ (giving bank holdings valued at market). If history is admitted you will want to write (10) as

$$R_2B_2{}^b = F^2(R_1, R_2; s, v), \tag{10}$$

delete Equations 11 and 12 and rewrite (16) as

$$\phi^2(\quad) = F^2(\qquad) \tag{16}$$

It follows from the fact that the public's monetary assets are acquired by securities sales to banks that in equilibrium the planned rate of increase of money supply must always be equal to the sum of planned rates of net issue of securities by the public (to the banks). It also is true that the planned increase in money supply minus planned bank purchases of bonds $\equiv$ planned bank purchases of bills.

The function $\phi^1(\quad)$ gives the nominal value of excess supply of short-term securities by the non-banking public, which must, in equilibrium, be equal to the nominal value of bank holdings, $R_1B^b{}_1$. The function $F^1(\quad)$ describes bank determination of desired holdings of short-term securities. Equation 9 applies to long terms. Equation 10 informs us that the nominal value of bank investments will be equal to deposit liability in equilibrium — under our peculiar accounting rules.

The system can be boiled down to Equations 13-16:

$$(13)\quad w = \eta p$$

$$(14)\quad Y^* = \psi(Y^*, K^\circ, R_1, R_2)$$

$$(15)\quad \phi^1(Y^*, K^\circ, R_1, R_2, p) = F^1(R_1, R_2; s, V)$$

$$(16)\quad \phi^2(\qquad) = [p.L(Y^*, K^\circ, R_1, R_2)] - F^1(\qquad).$$

Equations 13-16 contain the unknowns R_1, R_2, p, and w. The equations can be interpreted as giving clearance conditions for the labor, commodities, and securities markets. If they are satisfied, we know that the money market must be cleared, since budget constraints imbedded in the model assure "conservation of value." If there is no excess demand in four of the five markets, the fifth *must* be cleared.

Having fulfilled a necessary condition for determining the model's solution, we shall assume that the solution in fact exists and is unique: once parameters are specified, we can obtain a complete set of predictions for endogenous variables.

We pause to note some properties of the solution set for Equations 13-16. First, only p^* and w^* are affected by changes in the parameters s and V. This follows from absence of money illusion on the part of the non-banking public: $\phi^1(\quad)$ and $\phi^2(\quad)$ are first-order homogeneous in p: desired real net issues of *real* securities are independent of the commodity price level. Now, if we assume that F^1 is first-order homogeneous in sV, it follows that a set of values that finds the supply of money increased by the factor λ, together with w and p (now λw and λp), has excess-demand properties identical with those of the original set. Specifically, if $[p^*, w^*, R_1, R_2; \overline{M}]$ is a solution, so will be $[\lambda p^*, \lambda w^*, R_1, R_2; \lambda\overline{M}]$. This is *quantity theory of money* in somewhat exotic dress.

Secondly, and implicit in the first property, *equilibrium* bond prices (interest rates) are invariant against the quantity of money.

However, if the new set of equilibrium prices (as a result of a change in the quantity of money) is to be established, interest rates must change *transitorily,* and it is to this crucial matter that we now turn.

2

The dynamics of monetary policy become important. Taking up contractive measures, pressure is exerted against commodity prices through higher interest rates. Banks, unable to sustain initial deposits, must unload securities, creating excess supply in securities markets. Securities prices will fall. If contractionary measures are vigorous enough, interest rates might rise quickly and substantially enough to choke off excess demand before prices rise. (And then there are deflationary effects of non-availability of credit pending establishment of alternative circuits.

Responsiveness of portfolio managers and spending units to interest rate changes has much to do with the impact and transitional effects of a dose of monetary policy. The text argued that these effects determined the ability of monetary authorities to avert and reverse movements of economic variables, that they go to the heart of monetary policy.

Have we made things too easy for ourselves? Perhaps only the long rate has meaningful effect on decisions in the commodities markets. The coefficient for R_1 in Equations 4 and 14 might be zero. And then excess demand (supply) for long-dated securities might be unresponsive to changes in the short rate; excess demand contours might be inelastic. The adjustment process might be paralyzed. Monetary restraint might initially lead only to higher short rate (lower R_1) with miniscule effects on long rate. Higher short rate could lead to substitution of short-term securities issued by non-banking institutions for cash. Monetary policy having failed to more than dent excess demand for commodities, prices would continue to rise. In fact, destabilizing changes in expectations might cause natural rate to rise faster than long rate. Rising velocity could feed *growing* inflationary forces. At best, prices would not be brought under control for some time: excess demand would persist until long rate was finally dragged up to its "natural" level.

Consider the diagram below. The initial expectational structure is such that, over "n" periods, bill rate of *32 per cent* will push down the price of perpetuities only from *OC* to *OB*. (Practically zero bill rate would push up the price only from *OC* to *OA*.) Expectation of quick capital gains would, if perpetuities were lower priced, be so strong that the deterrence of so monstrous a bill rate proves to be

EXCESS DEMAND FOR PERPETUITIES

[for $t = \theta, \theta = 1, 2, \ldots n$]

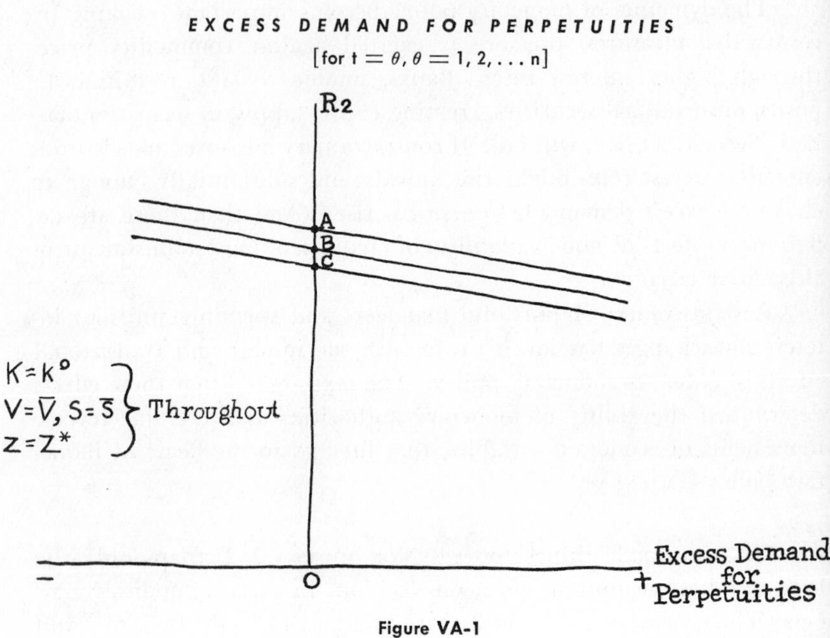

Figure VA-1

slight; potential suppliers of perpetuities would be so confident that long rate *soon* would fall from higher levels that they would be willing to accept finance at 32 per cent in the meantime . . . but a decrease of *CB* in the price of perpetuities would have practically no effect on the demand for commodities.

No doubt the case has been made too hard. But the exaggeration is not without utility:

a) it precipitates the analytical grounds for concern that sticky long rate will result in the effects of monetary policy being confined to an increase in the non-banking public's holdings of short-term securities (and/or reductions in short-term indebtedness to banks);

b) it counterpoints statics and dynamics, revealing that the size of parameters and the length of lags are important for dynamic analysis. Thus, if insensitivity of spending units to long rate is pronounced

> enough, an upward shift in real expectations might lead to a large increase in the "natural" long rate. If long rate is sticky, it might be impossible for monetary authorities to raise it (through conventional procedures) in time to prevent substantial inflation from developing. There might be a lengthy time interval featured by continuous excess demand in the commodities market accompanied by rising bill rate (reconciling the public to smaller real cash balances) and only gently rising long rate. Share prices will, of course, be booming all the while.

Post-1952 American experience utterly contradicts Figure VA-1. And mortgage rate, e.g., necessarily is tied to deposit rate.

3

Let us turn to a system featured by involuntary unemployment, a system such as that of Keynes's *General Theory*. Assume that the money wage rate, w, cannot fall short of $\overline{w}$ (*cf.* Chapters IX and X). The wage unit will not exceed $\overline{w}$ since the system will not solve out at full employment. In essence, the supply function for labor is decommissioned. We are left with Equation 17:

$$(17) \qquad N \equiv f(\overline{w}, p).$$

Equations 18-20 apply to the commodities market:

$$(18) \qquad Y \equiv \phi(N, K^\circ)$$

$$(19) \qquad Z \equiv \psi(Y, R_1, R_2, K^\circ)$$

$$(20) \qquad Y = Z$$

We want to avoid problems associated with employment effects of wage unit values. In order to do this, while extracting the essential flavor of the model, we assume that the authorities set a high enough value for the control parameter, β for R_1 to be driven high enough to imply a short rate, r_1, either almost at zero or so low that further downward movements can be ignored. Under these conditions, the banking system might choose to hold free reserves (and/or to make additional investment in long-term securities). This possibility is recognized in Equation 21:

$$(21) \qquad H(R_1, R_2, p, \beta) = p.L(Y, R_1, R_2, K^\circ),$$

where $H(\quad)$ is the supply function for (bank) money. The price level is included among the variables affecting bank behavior because the free reserve possibility gives banks room to think in real terms. However $H(\quad)$ is *not* first-order homogeneous in p, nor is $F^1(\quad)$.

The securities market equations are familiar:

$$(22) \qquad \phi^1(Y, K^\circ, p, R_1, R_2) = F^1(R_1, R_2, \beta, p),$$

$$(23) \qquad \phi^2(\qquad) = H(\qquad) - F^1(\qquad).$$

Equations 17-23 comprise a system of seven equations in the six unknowns N, p, Z, Y, R_1, and R_2. However, one of Equations 20-23 can be eliminated through Walras' Law.

Real solution values of the second model are not generally invariant to the policy parameter β: as β increases, interest rates tend to fall (perhaps towards lower bounds).

Let us assume that in fact the banks have been supplied with so much deposit-creating potential that short rate is depressed to near-zero levels as banks seek investment outlets. What will be the fate of long rate? The diagram above suggests that long rate might be little influenced, at least for some time. Open-market purchases might be carried out without driving long rate below, say, 2 per cent. Banks might prefer to hold excess reserves rather than buy long-terms on a yield basis less favorable than 2 per cent: they might fear capital losses.

A definite limit to the effectiveness of monetary policy becomes established. This might be clarified if the system is shown in a "reduced" form:

$$(24) \qquad y^* = f(\beta; \overline{w}, K^\circ).$$

where y^* is a vector of solution values for endogenous variables and $f(\quad)$ a vector of functional forms relating the endogenous variables to parameters. Increases in β and reduction of $\overline{w}$ have the same effect: creation of excess supply of money and excess demand for securities. Chapter V is concerned with one of the reduced-form equations:

$$(25) \qquad R_2{}^* = f^s(\beta; \overline{w}, K^\circ).$$

We have dealt with the possibility that a curve in R_2-β space asymptotically approaches a value for $R_2{}^*$ implying a yield of 2 per cent per annum or some such value.

Of course, these functional relationships depend upon experience of traders. It is likely that, if 0.25 per cent bill rate were to persist for economic eons, $f^s(\quad)$ would change: expectations will have changed. On the other hand, if we have correctly argued that *speed* of effect is important in monetary policy — certainly if collapse of expectation of investment profitability is to be avoided — such functional changes probably can be ignored. Relatively short time intervals are involved.

4

We conclude the pure theory of Appendix A with a discussion of possibilities for official intervention in the long-term market through direct sale and purchase. This intervention will be assumed not to affect reserve positions of banks. Thus, we are interested in the consequences of official purchase of long-term securities financed by sale of short-term paper. Similarly, we are concerned with possibilities of increasing long rate through official sales of long-term securities accompanied by purchase of short-term securities.

What are the possibilities for success in driving up R_2 through direct official purchases without affecting bank reserves? Theoretically, they are considerable: the officials need only stand ready to purchase any long-term securities offered to them on, say, a 0.5 per cent yield basis. True, if the banking and non-banking public are of the opinion that a 0.5 per cent yield is outlandish, the officials may be forced to take up all of the public's long-term securities and to finance almost all new issues. Long-terms would be considered a decidedly poor thing. Issuers of securities — including speculators in the "real world" — would jump at the chance of funding debt on a yield basis lower than anticipated future short rate. Doubtless, the non-banking public would switch to cash and short-term securities while the banks might hold free reserves and more short-terms, unloading their long-terms on the officials. But the officials could create enough short-term obligations (including reserves) to satisfy demand.

The prospects for driving down R_2 also are bright from a purely theoretical viewpoint. If the officials wish to put long-term securities on a 12 per cent per annum yield basis, they need only announce their willingness to sell to all comers on that basis. The results might be spectacular but in the domain of pure theory are easily accommodated: there might be huge reductions in desired holdings of bank deposits and short-term securities in the face of the opportunity to earn 12 per cent per annum "forever"; business firms would rush to purchase their outstanding long-term obligations and issue bills instead, anticipating that they could refund later — selling bonds for much higher prices than are now being paid.[3] Officials would have to be prepared to take up what might be huge quantities of short-term issues and cash, selling long-term issues. An extreme case would find

[3] If short rate is not so high that additional interest cost would swamp out what really are capital gains possibilities.

the officials holding the community's entire stock of short-term securities.

The banks would be subject to the officially determined β parameter. Vigorous-reduction of β undoubtedly will lead to meaningful increase in long-term yields without additional apparatus. If banks become so strapped that the resulting excess supply of bills drives bill rate to spectacular heights, capital gain considerations in the long-term market will be swamped out by the attractive bill rate, permitting long rate to rise under otherwise difficult conditions.

The formal properties of models finding the officials setting interest rates and the price level, and then accommodating themselves to the appropriate supply and demand relations, are easily stated through systems of simultaneous equations (*cf.* Ch. XIII). Assume that the short rate does not affect demand for goods and services but that there is a non-negative long rate permitting clearance in the labor and commodity markets.[4] Solve Equation 26 for this rate implicitly:

$$(26) \qquad Y^* = \psi(Y^*, K^\circ, R_2),$$

obtaining R_2^*. The task now is to make R_2^* effective in the money and securities markets: Equations 27-29 must be satisfied

$$(27) \qquad H(R_1, R_2^*, \bar{p}, \beta) = \bar{p}.L(Y^*, R_1, R_2^*, K^\circ),$$

$$(28) \qquad \phi^1(Y^*, R_1, R_2^*, p, K^\circ), = F^1(R_1, R_2^*, \bar{p}, \beta),$$

$$(29) \qquad \phi^2(\qquad) = H(\qquad) - F^1(\qquad).$$

Equations 27-29 are in the unknowns β and R_1. β is endogenous in the sense that its appropriate level is *discovered* by solving out the equation system; β is an instrumental variable. Walras' Law assures that only two of the equations are independent; the degrees-of-freedom criterion is met.

What if system 27-29 *cannot* be solved when $R_2 = R_2^*$ *and* $p = \bar{p}$? Obviously, official intervention will be necessary. Consult identities 30-32:

[4] Alternatively, we could assume that R_1 did register effects in the commodities market and could solve the equation

$$Y^* = \Psi(Y^*, K^\circ, R_1, R_2),$$

obtaining an expression in R_1 and R_2. One then chooses a *combination* of R_2 and R_1 from the resulting locus of combinations consistent with full employment and makes the combination (pair) effective in the securities and money markets. The text's method is simpler, but we *can* accommodate the "Hawtreyian models. . . . Obviously the argument of Ch. VA, B 3 is subsumed here.

$$(30) \qquad X^M \equiv \bar{p}.L(\qquad) - H(\bar{R}_1, K^\circ, R_2^*, \beta, \bar{p})$$

$$(31) \qquad X^1 \equiv \phi^1(\qquad) - F^1(\qquad)$$

$$(32) \qquad X^2 \equiv \phi^2(\qquad) - [H(\qquad) - F^1(\qquad)]$$

The X variables describe excess demand for money and excess supplies of securities with R_1 and β now "arbitrarily" specified (presumably at very high levels). The authorities need only "pick up" excess bonds by issuing money to the public through the central bank (whose issue function hitherto has been suppressed). Alternatively, so much intervention having been specified, perhaps the authorities will issue directives forcing the banks to reduce free reserves.

Chapter XIII considers the theory of official intervention contrived to establish interest rates consistent with price stability, especially the "Daltonism" discussion of Ch. VC.[5]

2. Reconsideration of Monetary History

Having theorized about determination of long- and short-term rates of interest in general-equilibrium systems with and without official intervention, we might reconsider monetary history recorded in Ch. VC, especially in the charts showing bill rate and long-term yields in the United States and Britain.

Sometimes exceptionally low short rate, even over intervals of several years, has not been able to produce *drastic* declines in long rate. It appears that, if officials are to achieve rapid and *drastic* reductions in long rate, they might have to intervene directly at the long end of the market on a scale much larger than anything yet seen. Direct purchases on the scale of the pioneering operations of 1937 are likely to have minor and extremely short-lived effects on an economy in which stocks of public and private debt aggregate many hundreds of billions of dollars. An exacerbating factor is that, the lower long rate, the more capital loss possibilities dominate running yield.

---

[5] The solutions referred to concern instantaneous market clearance. Capital stock is increasing as positive investment takes place. In general, the endogenous variables will have non-stationary time paths, perhaps *eventuating* in some regular motion, perhaps not. In any case, values imposed for R_1 and R_2 inconsistent with over-all market clearance, would tend to put the system on a different course, at least on a different adjustment path. The sequence of investment in plant and equipment, for example, might be altered. As is pointed out in Section A, §§ 6, Ch. XIII, there is nothing sacred about market clearance.

Even if skeptical about securing large and timely decreases in long rate through official purchases at conventional activity levels, this *caveat* should be attached: the *direction* of the movement of long rate can be determined by conventional policy. Another *caveat*: during a serious depression, firms unable to utilize existing capacity are unlikely to be enthralled by cheap money; its stimulatory effects likely are confined to earlier stages of downturns (and even more to upturns).

Practical difficulties of securing higher long rate through large doses of conventional policy (reducing bank liquidity) appear less formidable. As interest rates rise, running yield becomes more important. Empirical evidence suggests that elasticities of expectation are fairly large. Offers of non-banking financial institutions depend upon deposit rate. Still there are important obstacles to increased amplitude of interest rate fluctuations: concern for orderly conditions in securities markets is prominent. Such obstacles appear misplaced in a highly developed country: wider fluctuations in securities prices, reducing securities' liquidity, would give the officials firmer control.

Chapter VA showed that substantial increases in bill rate (perhaps induced by conventional open-market sales) would exert pressure against the prices of long terms: there are few persons with expectations so firmly fixed that they would be willing to hold long-term securities on a 4 per cent yield basis when bill rate stood at 12 per cent. Such persons would have to be confident that long rates soon were going to fall. But I do not know how much Treasury bill rate would have to rise to cause the long rate *quickly* to increase by 2½ points, nor can I deny that most academicians and practitioners consider variations of 5 or 6 points in Treasury bill rate to be intolerable. Some of these persons think that monetary policy can work because short rate also is important for expenditure decisions or because small changes in long rate will have important effects on credit availability (*cf.* Appendix B) or, for that matter, planned expenditure. Others would largely jettison monetary policy in favor of fiscal policy or direct controls.

It often is held that expectations are apt to be so sanguine during a boom that quite substantial increases in long rate would do little to curb the plans of euphoric businessmen, that the major effect of monetary restraint would be increased velocity of monetary circulation. Remember, however, that monetary restraint in the face of powerful and irregular upward surges of demand might be viewed in the light of what we come to call *accelerator theory*. Continuation of the expansionary process can depend upon *maintenance* of growth rates so that restraining measures which do no more than diminish the rate of growth soon can curb the boom.[6]

3. Final Topics

We have broadly conformed to the major themes of the considerable literature on the term structure of interest rates. These themes include volatile short rate *vis-a-vis* stickier long rate; better prospects for monetary policy in achieving higher than lower long rate, due to asymmetrical running yield effects; doubtful effects of lower long rate on expenditure during depressions, etc.

There remain but two tasks to be accomplished in Appendix A: discussion of the Hawtreyian position; brief discussion of whether "hedging pressure" causes long rate "normally" to be above short rate.[7]

a) Hawtreyian Position

Sir Ralph Hawtrey's *A Century of Bank Rate* (Chs. V and VI, pp. 167-207) covers much of the ground of this chapter and appendix. This excellent book also contains an extensive bibliography on the subject. Along with "accelerator" theorists, Hawtrey is concerned with effects of increased interest rates on postponement of expenditure decisions. He argues that postponement effects will be more important for inventories than for fixed capital, that, once investment

[6] The last sentence is deliberately loosely phrased. Accelerator theory is expressed in terms of *real* output. To the extent that monetary restraint is influencing prices rather than output, the connection with accelerator theory is doubtful. But, *cf.* the Appendix to Ch. XII, "Genesis and Life History of a Credit Cycle." Underlying inflationary forces might be stemmed if the rate of increase in prices is restrained at an early stage.

[7] Recall the reason for assuming that long rate is important for purchases of long-lived goods: in discounting the value of the right to receive one dollar 15 years from now, the appropriate comparison is with a 15-year security; that for an investment yielding a net income stream of $1 per year forever is a perpetual bond. If the yield stream associated with a capital expenditure is dominated by long-deferred elements, its market value will be dominated by that of long-dated IOU's. Consider the case of a durable good that yields (certain) increments to income of $100 for each of the next 20 years at the end of which it will roll over and die. The present value of the increment for the 20th year is the value in the bond market of a promise to pay one hundred dollars 20 years from now. We then move backwards, using the yield of a maturity of one year to discount the first element of the machine's income stream.

in fixed capital is under way, it is very difficult to stop. This implies a longer lag between stimulus and response for fixed capital than for inventory expenditures.

Needless to say, direct effects of inventory reduction are rather short-lived: once new levels of stock are achieved, replacement orders from manufacturers are planned as before. But this is not a drawback to breaking the pace of acceleration.

In the course of his argument that changes in short rate exert substantial impact on inventory decisions, Hawtrey writes:

> "if it were a question not of interest but of a tax varying from 4 to 8 per cent per annum on the holding of stocks of goods, no economist would be put off for a moment by the practical trader's argument that it would have no effect on his business."[8]

We have space only to note that Keynes and others have questioned whether "reasonable" increases in short rate would be able to damp inventory demand based on expected increases in prices: if I expect the price of *X* to rise 1 per cent within the next week, I would be undeterred by a short rate of 51 per cent per annum — if I were sure of myself.

Hawtrey's peroration summarizes (if broadly interpreted) much of my own argument about flexible bank rate and orderly markets and effects of conventional open-market operations on long rate. His final sentence is a great favorite of mine.

> "A high Bank rate is imposed as a deterrent upon short-term borrowing. If a rate of, say, 6 per cent were found to be negligible, the rate could be raised indefinitely. No one would regard a rate of 60 per cent as negligible. Some rate could undoubtedly be found far short of that which would affect trading operations perceptibly . . . But whatever the critical level is, as soon as the rate is high enough to call for the trader's consideration, the burden is bound to be felt in the special region of working capital long before it is felt as an item in costs as a whole . . . [M]ost traders can escape the greater part or even the whole of the extra burden by keeping their stocks of goods within narrower limits.
>
> There is nothing to prevent Bank rate from being raised to 10, 15, or 30 per cent, if business is insensitive to any lower rate. The only reason why it has stopped short at 10 per cent or less in the past is that business has in fact responded."

---

8 *Ibid.*, pp. 194-195.

b) Will Long Rate "Normally" be Above Short Rate?

Everything has pointed to long rate being less volatile than short rate. Long rate is influenced by future more than by current short rates; expectations must be elastic for long rate to be more volatile. This means that from time to time we might expect short rate to be well below or above long rate. Can anything be said of the *normal* relationship of the rates? Less than one might think. But, first, we turn to the analysis of Professor Hicks, justly celebrated for having broken open formal analysis of long and short rates in his *Value and Capital*.[9]

Hicks points out that, in a world of certainty, long rates would be arithmetic averages (using simple *vis-a-vis* compound interest) of present and forward short rates. Using compound interest, the going is stickier. Thus, if the market on loans of one year's maturity is r_1, that expected to prevail one year from date, r_2, that expected to prevail two years from date, r_3, and the rate on a three-year (long-term) maturity, ρ_3, the following relationship would have to hold in a competitive loan market:

$$(1+\rho_3)^3 = (1+r_1)(1+r_2)(1+r_3).$$

The right-hand side gives the sum that $1 would cumulate to at the end of three year's investment in the short market (compounded annually).

Turning to an uncertain world, Hicks writes that if risk aversion predominates, and

> "[i]f no extra return is offered for long lending, most people (and institutions) would prefer to lend short, at least in the sense that they would prefer to hold their money on deposit in some way or other. But this situation would leave a large excess of demands to borrow long which would not be met. Borrowers would thus tend to offer better terms in order to persuade lenders to switch over into the long market . . . A lender who did this would be in a position exactly analogous to that of a speculator in a commodity market . . . The forward short rate will thus exceed the expected short rate by a risk-premium which corresponds exactly to the "normal backwardation" of the commodity markets. [*Cf.* J. M. Keynes, *Treatise,* Vol. II, p. 135 *ff.*] If short rates are not expected to change in the future, the forward rate will exceed the current short rate by the extent of this premium; if short rates are expected to rise, the excess will be greater than this normal level . . . The same rules must apply to the

[9] Oxford: The Clarendon Press, 1938, 1946 (*cf.* especially Ch. XI, "Interest").

> long rates themselves, which . . . are effectively an average of the forward rates. If short rates are not expected to change, the long rate will exceed the short rate by a normal risk premium; if the current short rate is regarded as abnormally low, the long rate will lie decidedly above it."[10]

As H. G. Johnson (*cf.* Ch. VII *infra*) and others have pointed out, the safety of a short portfolio is very considerable for a bank, but surely not for a pension trust fund. The latter is more concerned (as a risk avoider) with being able to sustain a predetermined stream of outgoings than with fluctuations in their market value. Perhaps the pension trust is one's own: it hardly could be said that a man who invests in Consols with the intention of using the income in his old age and bequeathing the principal is a reckless gambler.

A general principle emerges: a short-dated portfolio provides safety for a firm (such as a bank) with quick liabilities; a long-dated portfolio provides safety for a firm (such as a pension trust or an insurance company) whose fixed obligation is extended in time.[11] "Normal backwardation" in securities markets is hard to justify on "hedging" grounds.[12] Nor are there *a priori* grounds for assuming that expectations dominate hedging pressure. (*Cf. Note B.*)

---

10 *Op. cit.*, pp. 146-147.

11 Consider also corporations committed to level dividend pay-outs.

Analogous arguments apply to the supply side. A firm investing in long-term investment has a better hedge when it borrows long. On the other hand, a firm buying inventory stock has a better hedge if it borrows short: if the marginal efficiency of capital later decreases, it might, if it borrows long, be unable to sustain its debt service obligations.

12 As is pointed out in Ch. VII, the theory of liquidity preference of *General Theory*, Ch. 17 was based on normal backwardation, in turn rooted in emphasis on market value certainty.

APPENDIX B

The Locked-in Effect

1

By the early 1950's economists were generally skeptical about effects of interest changes on the willingness to borrow. Furthermore, the tolerable range of fluctuation of interest rates was thought to be even smaller than was true a decade later. There was much anxiety about orderly securities markets. Massive government intervention in securities markets since at least 1941 suggested that a "free" securities market might be a thing of the past.

There was a response to this challenge, a response identified with Robert V. Roosa, then of the New York Federal Reserve Bank, appointed Undersecretary of the Treasury in January 1961.[1] It was possible, Roosa and others maintained, that small changes in interest rates would — through "locked in" effects and lags — meaningfully retard mobilization of idle deposits so that *higher* interest rates would result in a larger unsatisfied fringe of borrowers. The effect would be through the supply side of the loan market, stressing non-price rationing of credit. It was conceded that effects of any one dose of monetary restraint probably would be short-lived. But, we have seen that stemming the tide can be important.

"New School" writers heavily stressed that their approach centered on effects of *higher* interest rates, *not* on *high* interest rates. They at least implied that "conventional" writers stressed the level rather than changes in rates.[2] This was something of a canard: orthodox

[1] *Cf.* R. V. Roosa, "Interest Rates and the Central Bank," in Wright *et al., Money, Trade and Economic Growth, in honor of John Henry Williams* (New York: The Macmillan Co., 1951), pp. 270-295.

[2] The context of the early 1950's was inflation. The New School concentrated on control of inflation. So shall we.

students of bank rate policy always (correctly) dealt with effects of *higher* or *lower* bank rate in analyzing contracyclical policy. Of course the level of bank rate is *not* immaterial: its relation to natural rate can be crucial. Orthodox writers thought in terms of changes in interest rates: traditional full-employment models have "equilibrium" interest rates invariant against monetary parameters. For orthodox writers, monetary policy *necessarily* concerned transitional processes.[3]

2

Turn to more detailed presentation of New School arguments. Then to critique, relying heavily on James Tobin and Paul Samuelson.[4]

The heart of the New School's position is that *increasing* yields on government securities cause deterrence regardless of the *level* of yields: the flow of loanable funds will be slowed. Why?

> 1) If holders of government securities are to sell out, intending to use the proceeds to make loans to firms and households, they must realize capital losses. It is argued that they will be most reluctant to realize such losses.[5] (Of course, bills and maturing bonds can be less painfully liquidated. *Cf.* Hart and Kenen, *op. cit.*, pp. 271-74.)
>
> 2) Putative lags in non-government *vs.* government yields will prevent the former from showing important sympathy with the latter. Yield considerations will encourage hanging on to government securities. It might even encourage lenders — including banks — to *acquire* Governments. Banks might intend to *reduce* loans to customers.
>
> 3) Uncertainty introduced by increasing yields will encourage lenders to seek more liquid portfolio positions. They will be reluctant to acquire less liquid securities.

---

3 This paragraph ignores such writers as Gurley and Shaw. Dealing with the rate of interest, they found the equilibrium interest rate invariant against changes in the money supply brought about by airplane drops, but not when open-market operations were used. We showed that this result depended on their assumption that the government's obligation to return its interest receipts was not capitalized by the public. Very strict assumptions were necessary for the equilibrium yield curve to be invariant against the funding of public debt.

4 James Tobin, "Review of Patman Hearings (sic)," *Review of Economics and Statistics*, May 1953.
Paul A. Samuelson, testimony before the Patman Committee, cited *infra*.

5 It is assumed that depositors will be slow or unwilling to move directly into private primary securities. The New Theory is concerned to show that intermediaries (including commercial banks) will be deterred from aiding in switching idle deposits to would-be deficit spending units. Our criticism centers on the locked-in effect mechanism, *not* on the focus of the theory.

Thus, so the argument goes, small decreases in prices of Governments, whether produced by open-market operations or otherwise, will cause banks either to cease liquidation of, or to purchase government securities. Less credit will be available to private borrowers. Of course, lagged response in other markets, making Governments more attractive, and uncertainty effects are frosting on the New School cake. The upshot is longer queues of unsatisfied borrowers seeking to borrow at the old stale, flat, and unprofitable rates.[6]

3

Now for critique. Surely some sort of empirical test — however crude — should be available. After all, an admirable characteristic of the New Theory is that it yields hypotheses about what should be observed in securities markets. We attempt some crude testing by using snippets from the *Chart Book.*

CONDITION OF MEMBER BANKS

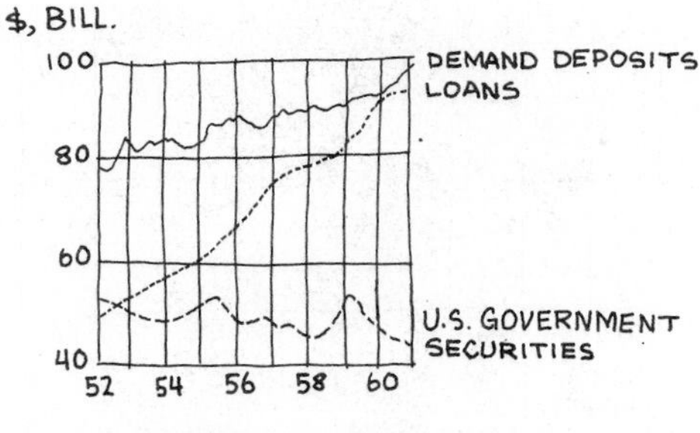

Chart A — Figure VA-2

6 New Theorists admit that higher yields probably will lead to reduced demand for cash, but do not attach much importance to this; they have their eye on the mobilization-of-the-idle-deposits ball, recognizing that the context is one of excess flow demand for cash. Nor does the New Theory stress greater incentives of lenders to *increase* their cash because of anticipated further declines in bond prices. . . . Of course, banks' bill holdings can be unloaded without important capital loss. Here New Theorists stress various liquidity constraints.

YIELDS ON U. S. GOVERNMENT SECURITIES

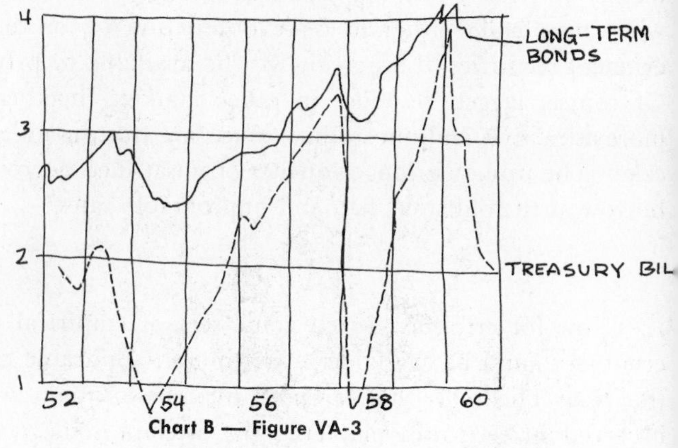

Chart B — Figure VA-3

RATES CHARGED BY BANKS ON SHORT-TERM LOANS TO BUSINESS

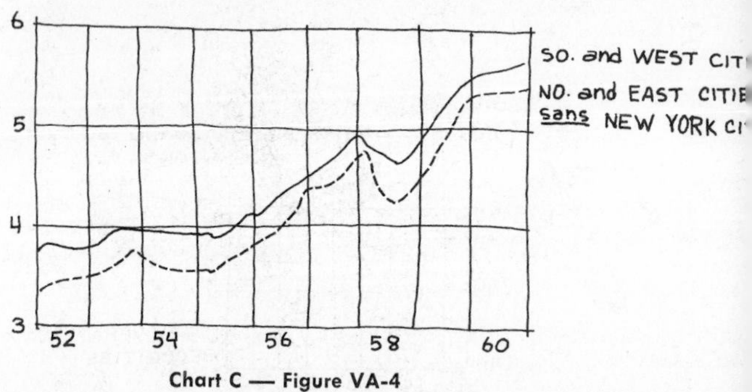

Chart C — Figure VA-4

It would be hard not to give the New Theory failing marks on the basis of these data. We observe a very large reduction in bank holdings of United States securities over the 1955–1957 period despite steady increases in their yields. Chart A shows that banks were able to make large increases in loans — despite stationary deposit liability — because of their willingness and ability to unload Governments. Chart B indicates prompt and sympathetic increases in rates charged by

LONG- AND SHORT-TERM INTEREST RATES

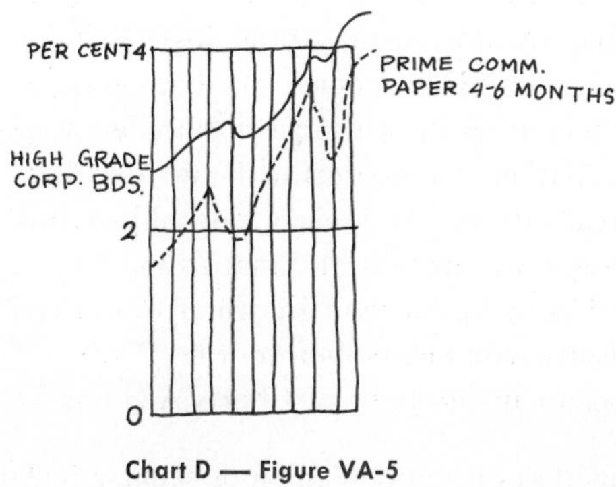

Chart D — Figure VA-5

banks on short-term loans as the yields on Governments increased. Indeed we would have been prepared for these curves to be much flatter; it is well known that statistics on rates charged by banks on loans are misleading; not taking into account changes in minimum (borrowers') balances, quality of admissable collateral, etc. Chart D is similarly disconcerting: over the boom years of 1955–1957 yields on corporate bonds *increased* relative to yields on long-term government bonds.

The data appear to tell a story of strongly linked markets of a considerable degree of perfection permitting banks to unload holdings of government securities rather rapidly. The data also suggest banks to be less subject to locked-in effects in handling their government security portfolios than has been claimed. The New Theory does not seem to survive the rigors of empirical test.

A priori reasoning and empirical observation as far back as the late 1940's and the early 1950's led such critics as Tobin and Samuelson to be skeptical about the New Theory. Tobin pointed out that there seemed no reason to believe that lending rates were particularly sticky. Uncertainty effects, allegedly encouraging lenders to stick with initial portfolios, did not and do not seem to ring true: it seems more likely that official policy leading to lower bond prices should induce expectation of still greater losses on capital account; that holders should want to *unload* Governments, shifting to private securities for the time being (if their prices *really* are sticky) or to cash or free reserves.[7] The data seem to show that hesitation to realize capital losses gives way before the importunities of borrowers (customers). Indeed, the argument that realization of capital losses will be postponed because of concern for childish fancies of shareholders definitely is fishy.[8] Elementary reasoning informs security holders when the milk has been spilt: when market values declined and decidedly not with the formality of realization. And even capital-loss-conscious bankers have available large stocks of bills and maturing bonds, subject to the caveat of footnote 6 as to formal and informal liquidity ratios.

Samuelson's comments before the Patman Committee in 1952 proved prescient in the light of Charts A-C and D:

> "The imperfect competition aspect of banking is absolutely crucial for the recently fashionable doctrine that the central bank gains its leverage not through its effects upon the cost of credit but by its effects on the availability of credit . . .
>
> The loan market is an imperfectly competitive one only in small part because of what might be called monopolistic impurities . . . The more crucial factor is tied up with the imperfections of competition inevitably associated with uncertainty. No one can read the future and therefore each lender must necessarily have a different opinion as to the credit worthiness of different borrowers. This lack of perfect knowledge and differentiation of opinion in the market place inevitably means that the infinite elasticities assumed by the theorist of perfect competition are unrealistic . . . It is quite possible therefore that, in the period immediately after open market contractionary operations by the Federal Reserve System or after an increase in legal reserve requirements, the individual banker will react to the credit stringency not by raising his posted interest rates but by rationing out the smaller supply of credit more stringently . . . but . . . the extra tightness of rationing that the central banker can induce by his ordinary operations will disappear after a few months and be replaced by a firming of interest charges and a return to normal stringency of rationing . . . [Bankers will become sensitive to opportunities to obtain higher yields on advances in view of obvious excess demand at going rates and will post higher rates so that] . . . it will be essentially up to the borrower and to the elasticity of his demand schedule to determine whether the extra one-half percent charged to him will discourage him from borrowing . . .

[7] Needless to say, this is even more ominous for "conventional" theorists.

[8] Except for legal considerations. Legal reasons may impel banks not to shift the valuation bases of their securities. Usually a cost basis can be used in the absence of realization. I have been informed that in 1960 a number of large banks would have been in legal trouble if forced to value their securities at market.

I think all monetary policy must pass through the eye of this needle of interest rates. I say this with due deference to the imperfect competition aspects of the problem, which is quite important in the first three months after you do something [subsequent experience might cause Professor Samuelson to shorten that interval]. It seems to me that the true debate between the hot adherents of this policy and of tight money and the opponents of this policy . . . would be on the question: What is the likely quantitative degree of elasticity?" [9]

[9] *Op. cit.*, pp. 696-698.

APPENDIX C

Bank Rate, Interest Arbitrage, and Forward Exchange

1

CHAPTER VA USUALLY HAS ASSUMED THAT HOT MONEY, moving from one financial center to another in response to changing interest rate differentials, is "uncovered." It sometimes has been assumed that holders of foreign balances are willing to assume exchange risks, as indeed they often are, or that such risk does not exist. Concomitant with this assumption has been the implicit dual role of Bank-rate policy: Bank rate is used in order to correct domestic *and* foreign "disequilibrium." But, an external drain may be accompanied by sluggish trade at home. Might it not be possible to confine Bank-rate policy to the domestic scene, resorting to some other device to regulate the balance of payments?

Keynes proposed a way out as far back as 1923. (See [1] *infra.*) He suggested that forward exchange rates be manipulated so that, for example, American authorities wishing to attract short-term capital would push prices of the forward dollar above interest parities.

We pause briefly to define the realm of discourse. Forward transactions in sterling, for example, find the seller promising to deliver a pound at a future date in exchange for the right to receive x dollars (francs, lira, etc.) on that date.

As for interest parities, consult Charles P. Kindelberger [4], p. 591:

> "The link between the forward and spot rates of exchange is the rate of interest in the two markets involved and what is known as interest arbitrage . . . If the three months' interest rate is 3 per cent per annum in London and 1 per cent in New York . . . three months' sterling should sell at a discount equivalent to 2 per cent per annum.

> This rate, by the way, is $2.786, given a spot rate of $2.80 and a discount of $0.014 . . .
>
> If forward sterling sold at any higher figure, it would be profitable for banks in New York to put more spot funds in London and sell these forward."

One last bit of background: *susceptible funds.* "Amidst normal conditions interest arbitrage is undertaken only by banks which possess liquid funds for that purpose."[1] Movements of "arbitrage" funds within intervals as long as a week, a month, or more, are likely to be strongly bounded; departure of forward rates from interest parities will not result in overwhelming flows.

2

The Keynesian scheme can be applied to the United States, disturbed in 1961 about gold outflow. Assume that the forward dollar is supported at prices overvaluing it in terms of interest parities. Both speculators and arbitrageurs will be attracted. Speculators will sell forward dollars for forward marks (lira, francs). (It would not matter if they could sell forward dollars for spot marks.) Arbitrageurs, heroes of the story, will plan to buy spot dollars, simultaneously exchanging forward dollars for forward marks. Hot money flows to New York, countering a deficit in the American balance of payments (excluding short-term capital movements) or leading to favorable clearings against foreign central banks.[2]

True, the remedy is highly transitory, containing its antithesis in the form of potential reverse flows. However, conventional bank-rate policy is at the same disadvantage. Moreover, the Keynesian remedy is consistent with autarchic bank-rate.

Observe that the authorities are (in the example) buying forward dollars and selling forward marks. Interest arbitrageurs and specula-

---

1 Paul Einzig, [2], p. 115.

2 Potential exchange risk on uncovered positions is bounded by gold points — excluding devaluation fears. Forward exchange manipulation can be bootless if exchange risk does not inhibit uncovered arbitrage. This was one reason why Keynes advocated wider spaced gold points.

If the forward dollar were supported above spot parities, when it came time to unwind deals, speculators could meet their commitments with fewer dollars than the United States authorities would need to satisfy their mark (lira, franc) commitment. If the scale of speculation were huge enough, the unwinding process could drive the spot dollar to its gold-export point, and gold might flow. . . . A somewhat fantastic conjury. The "unwinding discrepancy" would comprise a tiny percentage of the volume of forward dealings.

tors are selling forward dollars and buying forward marks. Each transaction consummates a marriage: there is "one for one" *ex post* correspondence between the increase in the United States short position in marks and the short position in dollars of the arbitrageurs and speculators. To the extent that the United States will need marks to fulfill its contracts, others will need dollars to fulfill *theirs*. The *scale* of the forward operations cannot be a jeopardizing factor (but *cf.* footnote 2). There is a principle of the Widow's Cruse.[3] It is impossible for official forward operations of the sort described here to exacerbate balance of payments difficulties n months hence: the worst that can happen is for forward dollar obligations to be met by sales of dollar assets by foreigners deciding at that time to convert their "hot" as well as "initial" dollar assets. But surely this is a capital outflow risk disconnected with forward operations *per se*. As Mr. Spraos puts it [3]:

> ". . . [O]perators who had sold sterling 'short' are in the nature of things compelled to reverse their initial deals. Whilst those who possessed convertible sterling but chose to cover it by a forward transaction instead of converting it via the spot market, would also be expected to reverse their initial deals if they were rational. For just as in the first place the authorities' support of the forward rate made spot conversion less desirable than forward cover, so their continuing support would make conversion more costly than reversal of the initial deal combined (if desired) with renewal of forward cover."

In other words, logic suggests that forward arrangements will be renewed. If not, the tranche, however serious, is independent of the fact that hot money had been attracted or retained through manipulation of forward exchange rates instead of through orthodox bank-rate policy.

Intervention by American authorities in the forward exchange market in the spring of 1961 has renewed interest in forward exchange policy.[4]

---

[3] Keynes, *A Treatise on Money,* Vol. I, Ch. X. Also Appendix to Ch. XII *infra.* If forward dollars are purchased with spot marks, there is a similar reckoning. Sellers of forward dollars ultimately must find spot dollars to close their commitments. This will find foreign exchange being offered for dollars or American purchases from foreigners being financed without debiting the American balance of payments.

[4] *Cf. The Economist,* February 10, 1962, pp. 541-542. Also *loc. cit.,* April 28, 1962, pp. 366-368. Needless to say, Appendix C can apply, say, to British response to initial speculative short sales of sterling, inducing interest arbitrageurs to sell spot sterling.

Partial Bibliography

[1] J. M. Keynes, *A Tract on Monetary Reform,* pp. 115-139.

[2] Paul Einzig, *A Dynamic Theory of Forward Exchange* (London: Macmillan and Co., Ltd., 1961). The standard work in the field.

[3] J. Spraos, "Speculation, Arbitrage and Sterling," *The Economic Journal,* Vol. 69, No. 273, March 1959. *Cf.* notes 2-4, p. 1, for reference.

[4] Charles P. Kindleberger, *International Economics* (Rev. Ed., Homewood, Ill.: Richard D. Irwin, Inc., 1958), pp. 340-341, 591-594.

[5] A. I. Bloomfield, *Capital Imports and the American Balance of Payments* (Chicago: University of Chicago Press, 1950). *Cf.* especially note, p. 21.

[6] J. M. Keynes, *A Treatise on Money,* Vol. II, pp. 319-327.

[7] A. E. Jasay, "Memorandum of Evidence," *Memoranda of Evidence,* Vol. III, pp. 132-136.

CHAPTER FIVE B

Central Banking: Practice

We turn to a survey of the institutional structure and certain major data of the central banking systems of the United States and Great Britain, beginning with that of the United States. The survey is concerned with the appearance of central banking systems *in esse* rather than with their historical development. The latter is the subject of Ch. VC. We swoop down on the American central banking system using as a map the excellent book published by the Federal Reserve System, *The Federal Reserve System, Purposes and Functions.*

A. CENTRAL BANKING IN THE UNITED STATES

1. Description

1

We begin with a purely descriptive account of the Federal Reserve's structure. The major administrative functions of the Federal Reserve System (or the "Fed," a portmanteau term sometimes referring to the system as a whole, sometimes to the panjandrums at its head) are performed by twelve Federal Reserve banks, organized as corporations. The stockholders are the more than 6,700 member banks, each required to subscribe 6 per cent of its capital and surplus to the capital of its Reserve bank (although only 3 per cent need be paid in). The banks are operated for public service rather than for profit. "The Federal Reserve banks differ essentially from privately managed banks in that profits are not the object of their operations, and their shareholders . . . do not have the powers and privileges that customarily belong to the stockholders of privately-managed corporations."[47] The objects of these administrative processes are, oddly enough, the stockholders: the member banks. They assume these basic obligations:

1) maintenance of reserves at required levels with Reserve banks in the form of non-interest-bearing deposits;

2) subjection to federal legal requirements concerning such technical matters as branch banking, interlocking directorates, etc.;

3) subjection to examination by the Federal Reserve — along with other agencies, depending on whether the member bank operates under national or state charter.

The principal privileges of member banks are six-fold:

1) borrowing privileges at Federal Reserve Banks;

2) use of Federal Reserve facilities for "collecting checks, settling clearing balances, and transferring funds to other cities" (*ibid.,* p. 71);

3) ability to obtain currency by requesting debiting of reserve accounts;

4) sharing in informational facilities of the system;

5) participation in the election of six of the nine directors of the appropriate Reserve Bank, the other three directors being designated by the Board of Governors of the System;

6) the right to receive a 6 per cent dividend on paid-in stock holdings.

2

While there is a good deal of statutory decentralization within the System, *de facto,* the decisions of the Board of Governors contain what is for us the critical content. Thus, individual Reserve banks establish their discount rates. But these are "subject to review and determination by the Board of Governors." (*Ibid.,* p. 77.) The official explanation of member-bank reserve requirements is more frank: ". . . the

[47] *The Federal Reserve System, Purposes and Functions* (Washington: Board of Governors, Federal Reserve System, 1954), p. 73. Hereafter denoted *System.*

Board has full authority over changes in reserve requirements." (*Ibid.*, pp. 79-80.) Similarly for open-market operations. The Reserve banks must conduct operations in the open market in accordance with the decisions of the Open Market Committee which in turn is effectively controlled by the Board.

The System's finances have been embarrassingly easy and have led to the sumptuous Board headquarters at Washington and liberal support for peripatetic research. Needless to say, *System* puts the matter more circumspectly:

> "while the Federal Reserve Banks earn an income, their operations are not carried on for this purpose, but are determined by . . . credit policies . . . For many years the System's net earnings were turned over in large part to the Government as a franchise tax [later repealed, but by 1947 the large interest income earned from heavily-augmented Federal Reserve holdings of U. S. securities led to greatly-increased Federal Reserve profits so] the Federal Reserve therefore adopted a procedure by which it pays to the Treasury nine-tenths of its earnings above expenses and dividends, as interest on Federal Reserve notes."[48]

3

The Board of Governors and the Open Market Committee are very important for our purposes. The seven members of the Board are appointed by the President of the United States "and are appointed for terms of fourteen years, with the terms arranged so that one expires every two years. This means that the political — perhaps better the ideological — complexion of the Board can be much at variance with that of the Administration (including, of course, the Treasury). Interesting conflicts have arisen. Witness that between Marriner Eccles and Harry Truman (and John Snyder). A rather severe conflict was expected between John F. Kennedy and William McChesney Martin, but it has not materialized (as of Feb. 1, 1963).

The Board's "political independence," often praised as an example of separation of powers, leads, I think, to a multiplication of confusion. It strikes me as chimerical that the Congress and the President should execute self-denying ordinances conferring vital power on their own creatures.

In any event, the Board's economic powers are of the highest importance: effective control of the Federal Open Market Committee;

---

[48] *Ibid.*, pp. 76-77.

effective control of discount rates charged by Federal Reserve banks; explicit control of member-bank reserve requirements; "responsibility for the determination of selective regulation of stock market credit;" (and, for limited periods, it has had "responsibility for regulating consumer credit and real estate credit [controlling margins for purchases of securities, appliances and other consumer durables, and housing]");[49] establishment of maximum rates that member banks may pay on time deposits. Needless to say, Ch. VA points up the importance of these powers.

The two most interesting things about the Federal Open Market Committee are that it is under the thumb of the Board and that it is rather closely tied to the Federal Reserve Bank of New York — partly because these transactions are supervised by the "Manager of the Account," an officer of the New York Federal Reserve Bank. And then there is the global importance of New York securities markets. It is hard to grasp the unique importance of the city of New York.

The subservience of the Committee to the Board, if indeed one can take for granted a certain harmony among the Board's membership, arises from the fact that

> "[t]his Committee comprises the seven members of the Board of Governors and five representatives elected by the Federal Reserve Banks.
>
> [The Committee] has the responsibility for deciding on changes to be made in the System's portfolio of Government securities . . .
>
> [P]urchases and sales of securities for the . . . Committee are effected in the name of the System Open Market Account, participations in which are allocated among the twelve Federal Reserve Banks in accordance with the ratio of each Reserve Bank's total assets to the total assets for all Reserve Banks combined."

2. The Federal Reserve and United States Currency

1

Little more need be said about the administrative and political structure of the System. The main stream of our discussion continues with development of balance sheets for Federal Reserve banks, but first there must be sandwiched in a brief commentary on United States currency, about 85 per cent of which is provided by the Federal Reserve System.

49 *Ibid.*, p. 80.

2

Federal Reserve notes are domestically inconvertible, but their issue is surrounded by hocus pocus for collateral backing. Specifically Federal Reserve notes, issued in denominations not less than $5[50] by the Reserve banks,[51] are secured by the following collateral (pledged with an authority known as a Federal Reserve Agent and representing the United States government): which must aggregate in nominal value that of the note issues:

> 1) gold certificates (interpretable as warehouse receipts for gold), including certificates "pledged as collateral with the Federal Reserve Agent and gold certificates deposited by the Reserve bank with the Treasury of the United States as a redemption fund against Federal Reserve notes,"[52] which must aggregate at least 25 per cent of the nominal value of Federal Reserve notes in active circulation;
>
> 2) remaining forms of eligible collateral include "United States Government securities and eligible short-term paper discounted or purchased by the Reserve Bank."

Exchange of deposits for currency reduces member bank reserves, *cet. par.*, but the Federal Reserve *usually* chooses to counteract contractionary effects of currency efflux.

American currency now has considerable seasonal elasticity. This is in contrast with the situation under the National Banking Act (*cf. infra*). Currency elasticity often is discussed in terms redolent with real bills heresy, but in fact is only distantly related: it concerns the mix, not the size, of the monetary stock and is closely tied to seasonal forces.

3

The remaining American currency is Treasury currency, including United States notes (greenbacks), various coins, and silver certificates. The latter are known as "representative token money," representative because the circulating medium is paper rather than silver, token because the ingredients obtainable at the Treasury for a $1 silver certificate do not sell for $1 in the market. Silver certificates were convertible into silver dollars as late as October 1962, but the President proposed in

---

50 The President proposed in 1961 to remove this limitation.

51 The Federal Reserve banks are corporate entities capable of owning and owing. The Open Market Committee or the Board are mere agencies.

52 *Ibid.*, p. 90.

December 1961 that they be abandoned in favor of additional inconvertible Federal Reserve currency.

3. Federal Reserve Balance Sheets

We turn to the consolidated balance sheet of the Federal Reserve System. Examine the "consolidated statement of condition of all Federal Reserve banks" for the end of May, 1961:

Assets		
1. Gold certificate reserves (holdings of)		$17.095 billion
2. Cash		0.374
3. Discounts and advances		0.148
4. Total U. S. government securities		26.887
5. Cash items in process of collection		3.666
6. Bank premises		0.108
7. Other assets		0.204
Total Assets		48.482
Liabilities		
1. Federal Reserve notes		27.238
2. Deposits		
Member bank reserves	16.107	16.966
Other	0.859	2.895
3. Deferred availability cash items		2.895
4. Other liabilities		0.047
Total Liabilities		47.146
Capital Accounts		
1. Capital paid in		0.423
2. Surplus		0.817
3. Other capital accounts		0.096
Total Liabilities and Capital Accounts		48.482

TABLE VB-I

The tableau of Federal Reserve notes and their collateral was as follows at the end of May, 1961:

Federal Reserve notes outstanding		$28.809 billion
Collateral against notes outstanding		30.196
Gold certificate account[53]	8.975	
Eligible paper	0.011	
U. S. government securities	21.210	
	30.196	

TABLE VB-II

a) Gold Certificates; Member-Bank Deposits

The Federal Reserve banks are not permitted to own gold but can aquire *gold certificates,* or — what is the same thing from their point of view — claims to gold certificates from the Treasury upon turning over gold or claims to gold. The fact is that "[a]ll gold that enters the monetary mechanism becomes reserve money for the Federal Reserve banks, not directly as gold but in the form of gold certificates."[54] Any direct purchases of gold by the Treasury are paid for (at the rate of $35 per ounce) by checks drawn against the Federal Reserve banks — the Treasury's bankers.[55] However, the Treasury is entitled to issue gold certificates of nominal value of $35 for each ounce of gold it acquires. Thus, upon acquiring an ounce of gold, the Treasury will draw down its account with the Federal Reserve by $35 but will pay in $35 in gold certificates (which cannot be held by institutions other than Reserve banks); its deposit account with the Federal Reserve is unchanged. Such a transaction will have the effect of increasing the Federal Reserve's asset item, *gold certificate holdings,* by $35 and, once the Treasury's check is cashed, increasing its liability item, *member bank deposits,* by the same amount. In this way, gold inflow increases the monetary base.

53 Thus, the System has gold certificate holdings well in excess of the amount required to "back" its notes, but gold certificates must also "back" its deposits.

54 *Ibid.,* pp. 98-99.

55 Under the law, the Treasury exchanges Federal Reserve credit for gold at about $35 per ounce. It pays out gold for paper — to proper parties, *not* including U. S. citizens — on about the same terms. Some prefer to say: "[i]n the American monetary system the standard dollar is defined as a weight of gold." (*System,* p. 98.)

The gold certificate account of the Federal Reserve banks fell from an amount in excess of $21.280 billion at the end of June 1953 to $17.095 billion at the end of May 1961. When the Treasury pays out gold, checks deposited with the Federal Reserve are offset by withdrawal of the same amount in gold certificates: the deposit account of the Treasury is unchanged. The Federal Reserve (Federal Reserve banks) suffers a corresponding decrease in gold certificate holdings, matched by an identical decrease in member-bank deposits. In this way, gold outflow decreases the monetary base.

b) Discounts and Advances; Analysis of Discount Rate Policy

1

Discounts and advances reflect liability (including that acquired by adding bank names to paper) of member banks who

> "borrow from the Federal Reserve banks either by discounting commercial, industrial, and agricultural paper of appropriate quality and short maturity [reflecting the commercial-loan theory orientation of the system's founders] or by offering their promissory notes secured by such eligible paper, by Government securities, or by other satisfactory collateral . . . Most member bank discounts represent advances secured by short-term Government securities. Borrowing against eligible paper or Government securities is done at the established discount rate; borrowing secured by other collateral . . . is charged a rate not less than one-half per cent higher."[56]

It matters little whether member banks borrow on their own IOU's or add their names to paper in their possession and discount it with the Federal Reserve: in either case repayment finds member-bank deposits with the Federal Reserve reduced. (*Cf.* Reg. A, rev. 1955.)

2

Federal Reserve bank discount rates (often called rediscount rates) stood at 3 per cent on May 31, 1961 and had been at that level since August-September 1960. *The Economic Report of the President* (1961) reports (on p. 178) that during December 1960 yields on Treasury bills were 2.272 per cent and those on 9-12 month U. S. issues 2.79 per cent. The average rate on short-term bank loans to businesses in selected cities was 4.99 per cent, that on prime commer-

[56] *Ibid.*, pp. 176-177.

cial paper 3.23 per cent. The discount rate was penal: commercial banks held more than $8 billion in U. S. bills at the end of December 1960; banks in debt to the Federal Reserve could *from their point of view* restore their free reserve position by selling bills yielding less than they were paying to the Federal Reserve.

3

Some readers will be quite dissatisfied with this concept of "penal" and might insist upon elaboration of a subheading of Ch. 32 of Keynes's *Treatise:* "Will Member Banks Borrow from the Central Bank at a Rate Above the Market?"

The discussion on pp. 243-250 of Vol. II of the *Treatise* is both lucid and entertaining. Keynes begins by pointing out that if we were to collapse all member banks into a single bank, the single bank's coefficient of expansion would be so large that it surely would seem in its interest to obtain additional reserves at rates well above market rates:

> "In short — so the argument runs — the profitableness of member-banking against a cash reserve of 10 per cent is so great that there is an inherent tendency, in the absence of checks, for member banks to increase the sale of their operations in a manner which is inflationary in its consequences."[57]

Keynes immediately turns his attention to "the impediments to this inherent tendency." The first impediment is the multiplicity of banks, reducing the expansion potential of individual banks. Thus, if Bank A is one of a multitude of banks, it can assume that it could initially increase its loans and investments by only $100 if it borrowed $100 from the central bank. In this case, polar to that of a single member bank, Bank rate equal to market rate would be penal; the expenses of expanding bank business would have to be considered.

The argument finally comes to grips with intermediate cases. The British instance is reminiscent of the first case: there were but five leading member banks by the late 1920's. Keynes states (rather cautiously) ". . . an individual bank may still gain some advantage from an isolated act of expansion at a cost above the market rate [in Britain]."[58] In the United States profitability for member banks to borrow

[57] Keynes, *Treatise,* Vol. II, p. 247.

[58] *Ibid.,* p. 248.

at Bank rate above the market rate depends on individual expansion possibilities in a less concentrated system. Keynes refers to a dispute, dating back to the 1920's, between Professors Lawrence and Phillips. The former estimated the representative American coefficient at 1.8, the latter, 1.25. (These concern *transitional* expansion. *Cf.* Ch. IV.) When the costs of doing bank business are considered, Phillips held that Bank rate slightly above market rate would make bank borrowing unprofitable, Lawrence that Bank rate must be rather higher.

It would seemingly be profitable for American banks to form a cartel and agree to borrow above market rate: they could share in gains achievable by a hypothetical giant member bank. Otherwise, as we have seen:

> ". . . a bank which borrows from the central bank at a cost above the market rate pays the whole cost of expanding credit, but reaps only a proportion, and perhaps only a small proportion of the benefit . . ."[59]

For the nonce, we wish to treat the British case (without collusion). Although Bank rate of 7 per cent might not seem penal for the "big" bank, when Treasury bills yield, say, 6.5 per cent,

> "there is, however, a further consideration — and one likely, perhaps, to have more influence in practice than it should have on the basis of strict calculation — namely, the fact that, so long as market rates are below the official rate, it will always appear to a bank, which is desirous of increasing its reserve-balances, that it will pay it better to steal away the reserve-balances of other member banks than to borrow itself from the Reserve Bank. Why — I think almost any practical banker would ask — should a member bank re-discount if it can increase its reserve-resources more cheaply by withdrawing funds from the call-market or by selling an acceptance or an investment?"[60]

The argument holds then so long as member banks do not act collusively or with "conscious parallelism." The fact that a meaningful subset of market rates is lower than rediscount rate encourages individual bankers to attempt to obtain reserves by selling securities in the market rather than by borrowing from the central bank. The difference between individual and systematic perspective can be relied

59 *Ibid.*, p. 248.
60 *Ibid.*, p. 249. *Cf.* footnote 61 for a modification of Keynes's dictum.

upon to insure that bankers (acting non-collusively) will not upset the monetary policy applecart.[61]

Keynes's discussion (and ours) concludes with consideration of the possibility that member banks will form a cartel, that there will be ". . . a concerted insurrection of the member banks against the deliberate policy of the central bank."[62] This insurrection would find the member banks borrowing above the market rate, recognizing that member banks might share in the profits that such action would reap for the aggregate. He considers this to be "a purely academic risk which does not materialize in practice," but proceeds nevertheless to show how the central bank could break such defiance: it might conduct huge open-market sales the proceeds of which would be governed by market rates of interest; the banks would be forced to borrow back their reserves at penal bank rate. Presumably the banks would abandon their defiance as a losing proposition. The alternative would be to sustain continuous levels of massive borrowing (at ruinously unfavorable differentials) with the central bank.[63] Let Keynes tell the story:

> ". . . Even if such concerted action were to occur, or if, for any other reason, the above deterrents were to be all of them inoperative, the Central Bank would still have weapons at its disposal in the shape of open-market policy — so long as it possesses suitable ammunition. For if the member banks start borrowing from it above the market rate, the Central Bank can make a tiresome profit at their expense by selling all its open-market assets at the market-rate, and so forcing the member banks to borrow back from it the equivalent of these at above the market rate.
> Thus the assumption that the official rate is 'effective' if it is in touch with the market-rate need not be abated."[64]

---

61 The text does not deny that banks will borrow from the central bank if rediscount rate is penal. Obviously they do. If rediscount rate is not very penal, frictional expense of going out of and into bills encourages short-run borrowing for example.

There is more in Keynes's *caveat* about "strict calculation" than may meet the eye. *Cf.* Appendix to Ch. IV. Banks *choose* to hold lower-yield assets. Indeed, formal or informal liquidity ratio constraints might, if binding, make it impossible for banks to support loan expansion by liquidating bills.

62 *Ibid.*, p. 250.

63 The punishment of the member banks could be awesome. Assume that the spread between market and bank rate leads but to a difference of $1 per $100 bundle of securities. The central bank, if it turned over its portfolio daily, could earn a running yield of 365 per cent per annum on its capital.

64 *Ibid.*, p. 250.

Of course, the Keynesian argument can be applied to deviations from a normal level of member-bank borrowing.

c) Other Assets

1

United States security holdings, almost $27 billion at the end of May, 1961, were $2.3 billion at the end of 1941, implying net open-market purchases and/or direct purchases from the Treasury of rather more than $24 billion. The contribution of these purchases to the monetary base (together with the systematic coefficient of expansion) explain much of the $150 billion increase in commercial bank loans and investments from 1941 to 1960.

2

Cash items in process of collection, together with the *deferred availability cash items,* registered on the liabilities side of the ledger, relate to the float discussion of Ch. IV: float essentially is the difference between these asset and liability accounts. There are involved highly technical problems of timing of bookkeeping entries that can produce rather substantial changes in bank reserve positions for short periods of time.

3

Taking up the *asset accounts as a whole,* one is struck by the fact that the great bulk of Reserve Bank business is with member banks and with the Treasury.[65] Of the $48.482 billion in assets held at the end of May 1961, almost $44 billion are explained by gold certificate and United States government securities holdings. The great bulk of the remaining $4 billion or so is "cash items in process of collection."

d) Federal Reserve Notes: Qualitative Analysis

The *liabilities* are dominated by "Federal Reserve Notes" and "Member Bank Reserves." *System* describes the Federal Reserve note liability item rather breathlessly:

> "Federal Reserve notes, which constitute the principal part of currency in circulation, are liabilities of the Federal Reserve Banks and also obligations of the United States government. They are a first lien on all the assets of the issuing Reserve Bank and . . . are

[65] *System,* p. 177, reveals that the Federal Reserve has outstanding certain loans and advances to non-banking agencies. These can safely be ignored.

> backed by not less than a 25 per cent reserve of gold certificates. The amount not covered by the pledge of gold certificates must be covered by eligible paper or Government securities pledged as collateral."[66]

But this (typical) description is only persiflage. A holder of a Federal Reserve note is entitled to one thing and one thing only: another Federal Reserve note of the same denomination. The gold requirements imposed on the Federal Reserve System have nothing to do with the kind of redemption obligation that is characteristic of metallic standards. Institutions outside of the Federal Reserve cannot hold gold certificates, and the Federal Reserve itself cannot hold gold. The only meaningful reserve function of Federal Reserve gold certificate holdings concerns potential foreign claims to gold.[67]

The United States securities-collateral item is complete nonsense: (a) the most ultimate thing that these securities could be converted into would be Treasury currency or Federal Reserve notes; (b) the idea of the Federal Reserve selling its security holdings other than as part of a deliberate program of monetary management is terrifying, in fact inconceivable. The standard explanation of collateral for Federal Reserve notes is a good example of how a passion for expositional symmetry sometimes can destroy understanding of substance.

e) Deposits

1

Significance of the *deposits* account arises from these Federal Reserve liabilities being the reserves of the member banks. To repeat, the Federal Reserve's deposit liability does not in any important way directly reflect the potential call on the national gold stock. Rather, this arises from dollar liabilities to foreigners, including foreigners' demand deposits with Federal Reserve (approximately $200 million) and member banks, their time deposits, currency, and other financial assets of all descriptions.[68]

66 *System,* p. 180.

67 We already have worked through the effects of a loss of gold abroad. We might find a foreign authority drawing a check on a member bank in favor of the Federal Reserve. The Federal Reserve turns in gold certificates to the Treasury which supplies the gold to the foreign authority. The net result is a reduction in member-bank reserves, Federal Reserve gold-certificate holdings, and Treasury gold holdings.

68 U. S. citizens' holdings of foreign securities are *potentially* capable of countering capital outflows. But, as is shown in Ch. XVI, the same forces that encourage foreigners to switch out of American securities discourage Americans from selling their foreign holdings.

2

At the end of May, 1961, Treasury deposits with Federal Reserve banks totalled $372 million. We have seen that movements in the level of United States deposits with member banks imply one-for-one shifts in the reserve positions of the member banks *to the extent that these movements reflect shifts of United States deposits between Federal Reserve and member banks.* Since bank reserves might be called "high power money," such shifts *might* have significant effects even if small in comparison with over-all deposit liabilities of member banks; switching of United States deposits is a potential lever of monetary policy. Have United States deposits been "exploited" in this way?

The range of variation of United States deposits with the Federal Reserve banks from 1947 to 1960 has been from $0.358 to $.563 billion: $205 million. That for United States accounts with banks is in a different order of magnitude; it is measured in billions of dollars.[69] The conclusion is easy to draw: the scale of the total of United States deposits in the last decade or so has been large enough to permit variations in their distribution between member banks and Federal Reserve banks to have important effects on bank reserve positions *if* the United States government wished to pursue such a policy, but such a policy has *not* been pursued. Rather, United States balances with the Federal Reserve have been featured by a rather small range of absolute variation (less than a quarter of a billion dollars); the important variation has been in deposits with commercial and savings banks. But such variation does not affect the reserve positions of members of the banking system.

This is not to deny that switches of deposit ownership between the government and members of the public have significant monetary effects, albeit as a side effect of fiscal policy. A transfer of $x billion from the public to the government, for example, reduces monetary assets of the public by the full amount of the transfer, reducing the public's money stock relatively more than its wealth. We should expect that there will be excess supply of securities and perhaps goods

69 In December 1960, commercial bank deposits with the Federal Reserve stood at $16,720 billion, not more than five times the range of variation of U. S. deposits with commercial and savings banks.

and services and excess demand for money as the public attempts to restore its liquidity position.[70]

f) Reserve Ratios

We have already touched on *reserve ratios* in discussing Federal Reserve notes and deposits. Specifically, "the law prescribes that gold certificate reserves must be maintained equal to at least 25 per cent of Federal Reserve deposit and note liabilities, unless the requirement is suspended by the Board of Governors subject to a graduated tax on any reserve deficiency."[71] *System* proceeds to point out that the Federal Reserve traditionally has maintained large excess reserves. The ratio stood at 43.9 per cent in December 1953 and at about 39 per cent in December 1960. "During most of the existence of the Federal Reserve System, excess or unused monetary reserves have been sufficient . . . to permit a further large expansion of Federal Reserve credit if that had been desirable in the public interest . . . That Federal Reserve Bank reserves exceed the minimum legal requirement reflects the fact that these Banks are not operated to make a profit and consequently do not extend additional credit simply because they have enough reserves to do so."[72] In other words, the central banking functions of the Federal Reserve System have not been impaired by the hodge-podge of provisos concerning gold, provisos that *could* be crippling if gold certificate requirements became binding. We receive a hint that, if these provisos did bind, they would be amended.

[70] As has been explained, liquidity positions are not parameters from the standpoint of individuals; economic decision units choose liquidity positions in the same way that they choose how much food to consume, how many ball games to attend, etc. Initial wealth, prices, and interest rates are parameters from the individual point of view. It makes no sense to say that a man decides not to buy a car because he awoke holding a $10,000 bond instead of $10,000 in cash. He can plan to convert the bond back into cash. Similarly, it makes no sense for a person to reduce his planned money balances because he woke up with a bond instead of an automobile; he always can plan to sell his "extra" bonds and buy an automobile and *will* plan to do so if the wealth constraint is unchanged and if tastes and prices are unchanged.

If adjustment reactions are slow enough, initial positions can have great importance even if endogenous. Finally, from the macro point of view, liquidity is exogenous in the sense that individual plans must conform with the supplies of liquid assets provided by the banking authorities; from the macro point of view prices of goods and services and bonds are *endogenous.*

[71] *System*, p. 183.

[72] *Ibid.*, pp. 183-184.

4. Reflections Based on Federal Reserve Balance Sheets

We are prepared to contrast central banks (including the Federal Reserve) with member banks: central banks acquire leverage for execution of economic policy through their ability to affect member-bank reserves. The *modi operandi* are reserve requirements and open-market operations, abetted by the rediscount rate. Since the Federal Reserve, for example, alters member-bank reserve positions largely for contracyclical purposes, its motives for acquiring and disposing of assets differ from those of member banks. The Federal Reserve forbears from expanding its assets in the face of profitable opportunity. It might sell securities in the open market in a deliberate effort to lower their value and accordingly the value of its own portfolio. Since prices of government securities tend to be higher during recessions than during booms, the Federal Reserve tends to sell securities when they already are "cheap" and to buy securities when they already are "dear." The Federal Reserve should be found anxious to purchase commercial paper during liquidity crises when the quality of such paper is perforce subject to doubt, and stony-faced to requests to purchase such paper or accept it as collateral during booms when the quality of the paper might be enhanced. In sum, the Federal Reserve is an agency of policy rather than a profit-maximizing firm. It is cold to its stockholders and warmly responsive to what it deems the interests of the outside public. We must not be deceived by the Federal Reserve's balance sheets, looking so much like balance sheets of other banks.

5. The Bank Reserve Equation and Member Bank Reserve Requirements

It would be convenient if we could systematically set forth the determinants of bank reserves. And, as it happens, there is a *bank reserve equation* doing just that. We shall work it out. Our survey of American central banking *in esse* concludes with some exercises manipulating the equation, hopefully leading to insight into the interaction of component parts of the financial sectors of the economy. We follow the general pattern of Ch. VIII, pp. 107-119, of *System*.

1

Sharing importance with the accounting identity, and governing factors which generate the potential supply of reserves to the banks, and those which use up this potential, are the *reserve requirements* imposed on member banks by the Board. Changes in these requirements will have immediate and direct impact on the *excess* (positive or negative) reserve positions of member banks. For one reason or another, required reserve changes have been denigrated as a major weapon of economic policy. Steiner, Shapiro, and Solomon offer the orthodox explanation:

> ". . . Changes in reserve requirements are regarded as a blunt instrument of monetary control. When reserve requirements are changed, they apply to all banks in one of the three reserve classifications . . . Even though there may be a large volume of excess reserves in the aggregate, some banks are likely to have none. An increase in reserve requirements . . . impose[s] hardships on the banks with no excess reserves no matter how much they may merit exceptions . . . Because of the disturbing effects of changes in reserve requirements, they have not been used to adapt the monetary system to day-to-day changes in the reserve position of the banking system. Rather they have been employed to adjust the banking system to large-scale changes in the factors supplying reserves."[73]

This argument is not altogether satisfactory. Open-market operations are by no means selective in their impact on banks. Furthermore, large banks at least trade excess reserves in the federal funds market. On the other hand there is a certain cumbersomeness in the reserve requirement apparatus that precludes it from being used from day to day. In this sense open-market operations *are* much more deft. Keynes is sympathetic to the "method of varying member bank reserve ratios." He proposes that a central bank should be able to "vary with due notice and by small degrees the proportion of legal reserves which the member banks are required to hold."[74]

---

[73] Steiner, Shapiro, and Solomon, *op. cit.*, pp. 320-321. Reserve requirements vary with whether a member is a central reserve city, reserve city, or country bank. These distinctions date back to the National Banking System when it was customary for country banks to keep reserves with city banks. The latter would, on Bagehotian principles, be expected to maintain larger reserves.

A consequence is that the total volume of bank credit can — transitorily — depend on disturbances in the distribution of deposits among categories of banks. But permanent effects can be wrought by changes in the q_{ij} coefficients. Mellon and Orr, *op. cit., American Economic Review*, December 1961, have an interesting and important discussion of related matters.

[74] *Op. cit.*, Vol. II, p. 260.

". . . It goes straight to the root of the matter, instead of relying on the indirect and roundabout influences which our empirical systems of monetary management have evolved for themselves . . . [T]he variation in [member bank] reserve proportions puts on them the directest possible pressure to move in the desired direction. I have proposed accordingly . . . the introduction of this feature into the British system."[75]

2

Finally, an empirical note. As of June 1, 1961, reserve requirements for demand deposits were 16.5 per cent for central reserve city banks and reserve city banks and 12 per cent for country banks. Time-deposit reserve requirements were a uniform 5 per cent. Reserve requirements for demand deposits in September 1948 were 26 per cent for central reserve city banks, 22 per cent for reserve city banks, 14 per cent for country banks, and uniformly 7 per cent for time deposits. Potential variation in the money supply though switching deposits between banks and between demand and time deposits was rather more pronounced than in 1960. (Time deposit reserve requirements were 4% by January 1963.)

3

We now turn to the bank reserve equation itself. It can be written as

$$G + F + T \equiv C + V + U + R.$$

Define the symbols:

1) *G, monetary gold stock. G* refers to gold held by the Treasury in contrast with commodity holdings of dentists, etc.

2) *F, Federal Reserve credit. F* substantially is comprised of Federal Reserve holdings of U. S. and other securities, including IOU's generated by advances to member banks. *F* does *not* include gold certificate holdings. Only the Federal Reserve can hold gold certificates, save, of course, the Treasury.

3) *T, Treasury currency.* If Treasury currency can enter bank coffers, it comprises a source of bank reserves.

---

75 *Ibid.*, p. 261. More recent discussion is found in J. Aschheim, "Open-Market Operations v. Reserve-Requirement Variation," *Economic Journal*, December 1959. See Aschheim's bibliography and also Comments by Goode and Gurley, and Aschheim's reply, *loc. cit.*, September 1960. The discussion appears to have ground to a halt, *loc. cit.*, December 1962. None of the discussants employs a non-trivial criterion function. An excellent discussion casting light on this and related questions is that of A. James Meigs, *Free Reserves and the Money Supply* (Chicago: University of Chicago Press, 1962). Meigs' work also is relevant for my Ch. VA, Section C 4 b.

4) *C, currency in circulation.* C represents a loss of potential reserves to the banking system.

5) *V, Treasury cash accounts.* V includes holdings by the Treasury of currency already listed under T and also includes gold holdings by the Treasury not represented by gold certificates issued to the Federal Reserve.

6) *U, credits at the Federal Reserve not held by member banks.* These would include non-member bank, foreign, and U. S. balances at the Federal Reserve among others.

7) *R, member-bank reserve balances.*

The left-hand items, G, F, and T account for potential supply of reserves to the banking system; these can be called *expansive items.* The right-hand items tell us just where the left-hand items went; these give the sinks accounting for the use of reserves and might be called *contractive items.*

The bank reserve equation does not claim to perform more than a housekeeping function. Any expansive factor *must* be utilized somehow. The categories are taxonomic, including as a matter of definition everything that could possibly happen to a given source of reserves and cover all such sources.

4

How might member banks at any point in time have acquired reserves? First, the Treasury might have issued gold certificates in exchange for deposits with the Federal Reserve, the deposits finding their way to member-bank credit. Secondly, Federal Reserve purchases of IOU's of all descriptions, including government securities, leads to creation of Federal Reserve liability, expressed through deposit liability and/or note issue which, if acquired by member banks, can serve as reserves. Thirdly, Treasury currency can serve as reserves for the banks, either as vault cash or through exchange at the Federal Reserve for Federal Reserve deposits. Federal Reserve notes are *not* expansive. These are but an alternative form in which Federal Reserve liability is expressed. A unit of Federal Reserve liability takes the form either of a deposit obligation or a note. The notes have to be purchased with member-bank reserves (directly or indirectly) and accordingly appear as a *contractive* item, as a means of disposal of potential reserves (although, of course, some are included in bank vault cash). The sum $G + F + T$ accounts for everything that has happened that might contribute to member-bank reserves. It gives the sum of potential Federal Reserve liability and Treasury currency, the reservoir from which member-bank reserves must be drawn.

But other events transpired, events described by items V, C, and U, subtracting from the potential reserves of member banks, the residual being R, reserves of member banks, expressed as

$$R \equiv G + F + T - C - V - U.$$

Specifically, currency went into circulation, escaping from the coffers of banks. Included in C are Federal Reserve notes, since, as has just been indicated, these notes, if "refluxed," could augment member-bank reserves through increased vault cash or exchange at the Federal Reserve for deposits. Holdings of cash in Treasury vaults also deprive banks of reserves since Treasury cash or warehouse receipts for it could comprise additional bank reserves. It is important to include V among contractive items, because G and T take no account of Treasury cash holdings (noting that the same reasoning applies with respect to other right hand items). The final source of contraction is U. We must subtract credits with the Federal Reserve held by non-member-banking sources from potential member-bank reserves.

5

Let us set out the equation for April 30, 1961, using the convenient form employed in *System* at p. 109.

FACTORS IN THE BANK RESERVE EQUATION
April 30, 1961
(in billions of dollars)

Factors accounting for supply of reserves:	
Monetary gold stock	17.4
Federal Reserve Credit	27.4
Treasury currency	5.4
Total	50.2
Factors accounting for use of reserves:	
Currency in circulation	32.0
Treasury cash accounts	0.4
Other accounts at the Federal Reserve	1.4
Total	33.8
Member bank reserve balances	16.4
Total	50.2

TABLE VB-III

Almost $27 billion in Federal Reserve credit is accounted for by Federal Reserve holdings of United States government securities. Federal Reserve holdings of United States securities were $2.22 billion in December 1941 and $23.71 billion in December 1945; this accounts for most of the increase in the supply of reserves during World War II. There is enormous inflationary potential latent in Federal Reserve powers to purchase assets in the open market, substituting its deposit liabilities; this leads to more than six-fold expansion in the nominal value of bank assets (liabilities).

Note that currency and member-bank reserve items dominate among the factors accounting for use of reserves. It is clear that there are four items — two expansive and two contractive — that will claim most of our attention: monetary gold stock and Federal Reserve credit; currency in circulation and member-bank reserve balances.

6

Now for headier wine. Let us use the equation to interpret the sweep of monetary experience in the United States from 1934 to 1961. One minor alteration: instead of working with values of various items at given dates, use differences in values from one point in time to another. Thus monetary gold stock declined from $22.5 billion in mid-1953 to $17.4 billion in April 1961. The item "change in monetary gold stock" is registered at $5.1 billion.

Run the locomotive of history backwards, tracing from 1961 to 1934, 27 years in which a great deal of history was written. The 1953–1961 interval is the only one of the four in which the reserve base declined (due to gold outflow), although you will recall that there had been a more than compensating decrease in reserve requirements. The anti-inflationary bias of the Eisenhower Administration (January 1953–January 1961) is suggested by the modest increase in Federal Reserve credit and Treasury currency, although currency plus demand deposits did increase by about $14 billion from January 1953 to January 1961. The fact that currency in circulation increased by only $1.9 billion is interesting: it reflects changes in the monetary habits of the public, here restraining absorption of reserves.

The 1951–1953 period is especially interesting when contrasted with 1941–1951. Spring 1951 saw conclusion of an accord between the Federal Reserve and the Treasury; the Federal Reserve was allowed to cease pouring reserves into the banking system (through U. S. bond

CHANGES IN FACTORS IN THE BANK RESERVE EQUATION[76]

(in billions of dollars)

Factors accounting for changes in the supply of reserves:	1961-1953	1953-1951	1951-1941	1941-1934
Change in monetary gold stock	—5.1	1.4	—1.0	14.9
Change in Federal Reserve credit	2.0	0.7	21.7	—0.1
Change in Treasury currency	0.5	0.7	2.5	
Algebraic Sum	—2.6	2.8	23.2	14.8
Factors accounting for changes in reserve absorption:				
Change in currency in circulation	1.9	2.3	16.6	5.8
Change in Treasury cash accounts	—1.0			0.4 (V+U)
Change in other acc'ts at Federal Reserve	—0.3			
Algebraic Sum	0.6	2.3	16.6	6.2
Change in bank reserve balances	—3.2	0.5	6.6	8.6
Algebraic Sum	—2.6	2.8	23.2	14.8

TABLE VB-IV

purchases). Thus the dramatic surcease in the ΔF item, 21.7 for 1941–1951, 0.7 for 1951–1953. Table VB-IV dramatically indicates the scale of Federal Reserve purchases of United States securities during World War II and its more immediate aftermath. The money supply increased from $76 billion in 1941 to $186 billion in 1951, an increase partly accounted for by the increase in the monetary base provided by Federal Reserve securities purchases. That there was not a still greater increase in the money supply is explained by the $16.6 billion increase in currency in circulation from 1941 to 1951, an increase absorbing a large part of the increase in the reserve base.

The 1934–1941 period is notable for two things, one revealed by the Table, the other not. The very substantial increase in the monetary base is explained by the massive inflow of gold, valued at $14.9 billion (recalling the 1934 devaluation). However, the impact of the $8.6 billion increase in the monetary base was muted by unprecedentedly

76 More precise dating is: April 30, 1961-midyear 1953; June 30, 1953-June 30, 1951; June 30, 1951-December 31, 1941; December 31, 1941-June 30, 1934. April 1961 data are from the *Bulletin* for June 1961. Other data are from *System*, pp. 107-119.

large free reserves (excess reserves less borrowings) of member banks. Free reserves increased by almost $1.25 billion in 1934, reaching $1.535 billion. At the end of 1940, free reserves were $6.323 billion. The enormity of this statistic is better appreciated if you recall that free reserves of member banks at the end of May 1961 were less than $0.5 billion. Some said banks were supercautious after their 1931–1933 experiences — an argument that must have lost its force by 1940. Others stressed the "liquidity trap," a state in which there is a surfeit of liquidity so that further increases in the monetary base would be bootless.

7

Let us first make sure that our reach does not exceed our grasp of the bank reserve equation. Assume that one of the following hypothetical events occurs: the United States government runs a surplus, diverting the surplus cash flow into its Federal Reserve accounts (an unlikely event, we have seen); the government experiences an adverse balance of payments; the public's preference for currency changes; desired free reserves change.

This is the bank reserve equation with April 1961 values for its components:

$$R = G + F + T - C - V - U$$

$$16.4 = 17.4 + 27.4 + 5.4 - 32.0 - 0.4 - 1.4$$

Assume that the *surplus* aggregated $3 billion (and was diverted to the government's Federal Reserve account). Take the April 1961 position as the system's initial state. The only right-hand item affected is U which will have increased by $3 billion (ignoring reflux of C for now). R must decline by $3 billion. This result will come about automatically as member bank balances at the Federal Reserve are transferred to the Treasury. Of course, part of the reserve deficiency will probably be met for a time by increased borrowing at the discount window; there will be something of a compensating increase in F. But, if the rediscount rate is penal, and/or the "tradition against borrowing" is effective, this factor will be highly transitory. There *will* be an inevitable and "permanent" partially compensating effect on R through a reduction in C. Aggregate money balances will now be less, the decline thus far being confined to the nonbanking public's deposits. This suggests that — ignoring effects of lower price levels or lower levels of economic activity on desired cash balances — the public, wishing to maintain conventional deposit-currency ratios, will exchange some of their currency holdings for bank deposits. This permits the member banks to purchase new reserves at the Federal Reserve with the refluxed currency (if they do not wish to increase vault cash).

Likely effects of an *adverse balance of payments* are familiar; it remains only to fit the familiar pieces into the equation. Assume that foreign central banks, finding themselves with an undesired increment of $1 billion in dollar claims, decide to convert the dollar claims into gold balances. The Federal Reserve System will be the foreign authority's agent in the transaction. The foreign authority will first pay over dollar claims to the Federal Reserve by liquidating the claims and checking the proceeds to the Federal Reserve. The first step finds *R* reduced by $1 billion and *U* increased by $1 billion. The second step finds the Federal Reserve paying over $1 billion to the Treasury which in turn pays out the gold. This step does not affect *U*; there simply is a transfer from the foreign authority to the Treasury. The third step finds the Treasury exchanging its deposit balance (i.e., $1 billion) for gold certificates, reflecting the decline of the monetary gold stock. *U* decreases by $1 billion (returning to its initial level of $1.4 billion) and *G* decreases by $1 billion. (We must take up effects of consequent contraction of bank deposits in a complete analysis.)

If the *public wished to hold more currency, cet. par.,* initial impact will be on *C*. Now that vault cash counts as reserves, this process is exceedingly simple to grasp. *R* decreases *pari passu*. Once again, certain second-order effects are relevant, since the consequent contraction in the total stock of money will exceed the initial loss of bank reserves: unless further action is taken, the proportion of currency to total public cash holdings will be higher than was initially planned. We need not repeat how this modifies the increase in *C*.

On the surface, an *increase in desired free reserves* would not seem to be reflected in the equation unless execution of the revised plan finds member banks repaying borrowings to the Federal Reserve (thereby reducing *F* and *R* but leaving *free* reserves unchanged) as part of their program of retraction. But the second-order effects we have stressed would, for reasons now clear, lead to a reduction in *C*, thereby increasing *R*. Finally, an *increase in float* would reflect itself in identical increases in *F* and *R*. . . . And *that* is the Federal Reserve *in esse*.[77]

[77] Chapter VC provides much additional information about practice. Thus, Federal Reserve-Dealer relationships can be made perfectly clear only within an historical context.

B. CENTRAL BANKING IN THE UNITED KINGDOM

1. Dramatis Personae

1

The *dramatis personae* of the British central banking system include the Bank of England (which is in fact nationalized), the Treasury, the joint-stock banks, and the discount market (money market). Bit players include the non-banking financial institutions and the ubiquitous general public.[78] We follow the procedure used in working through the American system, offering some political or "constitutional" background and then explaining the system's mechanics.

2

The Bank of England is on the surface a joint-stock company like any other, but in fact the Government acquired all of its capital stock under the Bank of England Act of 1946. The Bank is nationalized, but it would be wrong to assume that it is a mere functionary of the government; it is not. The Bank of England lacked formal authority to attempt to govern the affairs of commercial banks until 1946 when the Bank Act gave the Bank of England wide powers over the joint stock banks — subject to the approval of the Treasury. As Professor Sayers puts it:

> "[the Bank] can issue directions compelling bankers . . . to hold certain reserves with itself, to vary those reserves, to alter their charges for any class of business."[79]

But he goes on to say:

> "though its formal powers are thus very considerable, the position in fact remains that the Bank exercises its influence mainly by informal communication and persuasion behind the scenes."[80]

3

For the American, the strangest thing about the British system probably is the discounting procedure: British banks customarily do

---

78 Good general sources include R. S. Sayers, *Modern Banking* (3rd ed.; Oxford: The Clarendon Press, 1951) and the *Economist*, a weekly published in London.

79 R. S. Sayers, *op. cit.*, pp. 75-76. In 1960-1961 the Bank of England called for "special deposits" from the joint-stock banks, thereby reducing the availability of bank credit.

80 *Ibid.*, p. 76.

not have direct access to the central bank discount window; instead this access is given to *discount houses* who in turn are heavily indebted to the banks on an overnight and 7-day maturity basis.[81]

The fact is that by far the most important asset category for the houses is government securities. How odd that little short of $2 billion in banking assets should be devoted to loans (largely at call) to discount houses who invest the proceeds in government securities.

If the Treasury bill had always been as important as it is now, the discount houses probably would not have taken their present form. However, there was a time when the most important short-term financial assets were liabilities of commercial firms. Firms specialized in the evaluation of commercial paper performed a valuable service by more or less insuring paper they considered to be sound or by actually purchasing such paper *at a discount.* They paid for the paper by borrowing from the banks or the public, who would be saved the pains of selecting commercial paper for themselves; they could invest in the paper of the discount houses. Of course, the system was not foolproof: the fractional-reserve banking principle applied. Furthermore, discount houses borrowed on shorter term than they lent and always were in a precarious position on that account; their position could become hopeless during a liquidity crisis. In due course, the delicacy of the discount house position — together with the intimate relationship they had come to form with the banks (acting simultaneously as bank agents and debtors) — led to their being accorded discounting privileges at the bank.

Mr. Dacey explains the evolution of the London discount market.[82] This is a patch of history profoundly important to the understanding of the British finance. Dacey writes that there have been several phases in the evolution of the discount market since the early part of the nineteenth century. The first phase covers the early decades of the last century in which the function of the London bill brokers was

> "to collect the bills sent in from the industrial areas, which needed working capital to finance their expanding trade, and sell them to banks in the rich agricultural areas . . . where most of the savings of the country originated."[83]

The function of the London houses in this first phase was merely that

81 The houses obtain about half of their capital from the banks.
82 *The British Banking Mechanism,* Ch. VI.
83 Dacey, *op. cit.,* pp. 56-57.

of brokerage: while they lent their names to commercial paper, they did not issue paper; they were not financial intermediaries in the sense we have used that term.

The second phase, occupying the second half of the nineteenth century (but dated by Hawtrey from 1825), found the brokerage function of the London houses less significant: direct lending became more common; communications had improved, making it less important for lenders to discover qualities of commercial paper through jobbers. However, the London market continued to recommend bills to banks. The second phase also saw the full development of the *call loan* which is just what it says: a loan without fixed maturity that can be called at any time. Thus, a substantial portion of bank portfolios came to be devoted to loans at call to the London money market — or what now came to be called discount houses — who invested the proceeds in commercial bills. As we have seen, the upshot was to leave the discount houses in a dangerous position made more tenable by the development of a tradition permitting discount houses (but not banks) to borrow from the Bank of England on the security of eligible commercial paper. As Dacey puts it:

> "This development of the call loan was of fundamental importance in shaping the British banking system, and accounts for some of its most characteristic features. In most other countries the commercial banks are accustomed to rediscount bills or obtain accommodation direct from the central bank in some other form when they are pressed for cash. The British system developed differently. Thanks to the call-loan system, however, the banks lost nothing through the severance of direct relations with the central bank. Call money became fully as effective a second-line reserve as rediscountable bills."[84]

The third phase in the evolution of the London market is dated by Dacey in the last quarter of the nineteenth century. It marked the decline in importance of the domestic bill of exchange or inland bill and the rise of the foreign bill of exchange in the London money market. The inland bill became less popular, Dacey avers, because

> "[a], . . . many traders came to dislike seeing their names circulating in the open market as borrowers on bills [pointing up differences between Victorians and Texans]; . . .

[84] *Ibid.,* p. 57. Dacey goes on claim that the indirect British system is more sensitive than the conventional system: "in the British system the discount market acts *inter alia* as a mechanism for the clearing of day-to-day surpluses of funds between banks . . ." This neglects the federal funds market, etc.

[b] . . . they grew to prefer the greater elasticity of the bank overdraft compared with the inflexible maturity date of a bill . . ."[85]

The foreign bill differed in no substantive way from an inland bill; it was a commitment to pay in sterling but happened to be drawn by a foreigner, usually in favor of another foreigner, neither of whom may have had any direct economic relation with Britain.[86]

The fourth phase, 1918–1931, marks the predominance of government paper and leads directly to today's strange relationship between the money market and the joint-stock banks. While the discount houses found dealing in Treasury bills profitable, their function became much less clear. Dacey agrees:

". . . the discount broker in the heyday of the market was essentially an expert in the assessment and fine grading of credit risks, and no nice discrimination is required in the election of Treasury bills."[87]

Furthermore, as Dacey points out:

"the rise of the Treasury bill tended to diminish somewhat the advantages to the banks of a call loan as compared with a direct purchase of bills, since the credit even of the strongest discount house can scarcely add to that of the British Government."[88]

And then the short-dated government bonds began to make their appearance as money-market assets, although not as yet on an important scale.

The 1932–1935 period was unhappy for the discount houses. Their viability came into question. The reasons were tied to the "cheap money era" ushered in with 2 per cent bank rate in 1932. As a result of the world-wide depression, the supply of commercial paper to London declined by as much as 65 per cent. Furthermore, the government did not permit the aggregate of Treasury bill issues to exceed about

85 *Ibid.*, p. 58.

86 The broader aspects of the rise of London as *the* international money market prior to World War I were discussed in Ch. II. Dacey makes much of the sensitivity to Bank rate generated in the third phase (pp. 58-59). Thus, increased Bank rate would bring about a rather prompt improvement in the balance of payments on capital account. There were two reasons (1) London would become a more attractive place in which to hold securities; (2) the higher rates in the London market would encourage borrowers to repay — requiring that they liquidate sterling claims against them — once again improving the balance of payments.

87 *Ibid.*, p. 60.

88 *Ibid.*, pp. 60-61.

£1 billion. It is not hard to see why bill prices became very high, why yields on bills fell sharply. "Throughout the 'thirties, in consequence, the margin between money [rates charged the discount houses] and bill rates remained infinitesimal and at one time actually became negative. Such conditions threatened the very existence of the discount market."[89] In 1934–1935 measures were adopted to help the houses: the rate on call loans against bill collateral was reduced to 0.5 per cent per annum; bank competition for bills was restricted; the discount houses were allowed to form a syndicate in bidding for bills. Still the money market was forced to hold a much larger portion of its portfolio in bonds (one-third of their portfolio by 1934) in order to obtain higher differentials in yields earned and rates paid — despite risks of capital losses, due to interest-rate changes, that could be critical for firms with so narrow an equity margin.[90]

The finance of World War II found direct government dealings with banks much increased: "despite the sweeping war-time expansion in bank deposits and therefore in bank assets as a whole, the money-market assets of the banks at times actually fell below the pre-war level . . ."[91] However, the market has had some resurgence since 1951 when monetary orthodoxy returned with the Conservatives. It should be stressed, in conclusion, that the discount houses' position remains large enough for them to continue to operate as intermediaries between the joint-stock banks and the Bank of England; the order of magnitude of open-market operations of the Bank is decidedly lower than that of the aggregate portfolio of the discount houses.

4

The contrast in concentration ratios in commercial banks in the United Kingdom and the United States is startling; there are only about twenty banks in the United Kingdom and these have about 12,000 branches. The eleven members of the London Clearing House have about 80 per cent of these branches and about 85 per cent of all deposits. In turn they are dominated by a Big Five.

It is customary, but not legally required, for British banks to hold balances at the Bank of England and vault cash equal to 8 per cent of their deposit liability. (The 8 per cent figure is quite apart from

89 *Ibid.*, pp. 62-63.

90 There are 12 discount houses, 3 of which are especially important.

91 *Ibid.*, p. 65.

special deposits at the Bank which banks might have to hold from time to time under directives.) Furthermore, banks have come to be expected to maintain a *liquidity ratio* of at least 30 per cent: bank holdings of "liquid reserves" comprised of vault cash, balances at the Bank of England, money at call and short notice (usually 7 days), and commercial and Treasury bills, are expected to be equal in value to at least 30 per cent of their net deposit obligations. ". . . [T]he banks must so conduct their policies as to hold a minimum of 30 per cent of their assets in liquid form in March, when the Treasury Bill issue is at its seasonal minimum, which implies that at other times of the year their liquid assets must be a correspondingly larger proportion of the total . . ."[92] While the system's Treasury bill portfolio can be reduced to reserve money within 90 days, it would be fatuous to suggest that the liquidity ratio is a prop for bank solvency. No, it is part of the apparatus of central control of "member bank" behavior. The liquidity ratio belongs to the realm of control of the financial environment rather than to that of protection of standards of probity.

2. Balance Sheets for the Bank of England

1

The cast is assembled. The major lineaments of structure have been completed. We wish to work through the features of the British system of control. But first consider the balance sheet of the Bank of England. This reveals it to be, for all intents and purposes, a bank whose important connections are with the joint-stock banks, the money market, and the Treasury. Next, a consolidated balance sheet for the joint-stock banks is presented: a quantitative counterpart to the word picture. Only then is it appropriate to discuss the Bank's (*cum* Treasury) techniques of control: Bank rate, open-market operations, and funding. There is not space for *theoretically* less interesting direct controls.

The *Economist* for August 5, 1961 (p. 586) publishes the Return of the Bank of England for August 2, 1961. The Bank always has been loath to publish more than convention and statutory enactment requires. (And recall the separation of the issue and banking departments dating back to 1844.)

[92] H. G. Johnson, "The Revival of Monetary Policy in Britain," *Three Banks Review,* June 1956, pp. 3-20, at pp. 6-7.

BANK OF ENGLAND
Return for August 2, 1961

Issue Department

Liabilities (£ million)		Assets (£ million)	
Notes issued in circulation	2,415.4	Government debt[93]	11.0151
" " in banking dept.	35.0	Other government securities	2,437.7
		Other securities	0.8
		Coin	0.5
		Fiduciary issue	2,450.0
		Gold	0.4
	2,450.4		2,450.4

Banking Department

Liabilities (£ million)			Assets (£ million)		
Capital		15.553	Securities:		
Rest		2.7	Government	415.8	
Deposits:			Dis. and adv.	37.3	
Pub. accts.	13.2		Other	17.7	
Special dep.	163.1		Total		470.8
Bankers	243.8				
Others	68.3		Banking dept. reserve:		
			Notes	35.0	
			Coin	0.9	
Total		488.4	Total Reserves		35.9
		506.7			506.7

TABLE VB-V

There are a few entries for the banking department that might require explanation before we launch into a more general commentary on the Return. "Capital" is the amount subscribed by the Bank's stockholders over its long history and is now held by the Treasury. "Rest" is undistributed profit. Its puny size indicates that the Bank

93 Sayers gives an entertaining account of the origins of "Government Debt": ". . . a book entry that the government has borrowed so much directly from the bank. It dates from the earliest days of the bank, when the latter was allowed to issue notes to a certain amount if it lent that amount to the government." (*Op. cit.*, p. 86.)

serves public office rather than private interest (in general small undistributed profit accounts can reflect large dividend pay-outs over time). "Public Accounts"

> "shows the balance of the main normal British Government accounts . . . An increase in this item means that the Government is . . . having more money paid to it than it is paying to members of the public, and vice versa."[94]

"Special Deposits" reflects credit restraints imposed in 1960. The *Economist* for July 29, 1961 (p. 468) informs us that London clearing banks had to maintain non-reserve eligible special deposits equal to 2 per cent of their deposit liability, and that this percentage was to rise to 3 by September 1961. Because of counterpart open-market purchases by the Bank, the upshot has been to reduce bank liquidity but not to impose multiple contraction.[94a] "The sub-item *Other Accounts* shows the balances of the Bank of England's ordinary banking customers. Among these are other governments and foreign and commonwealth banks . . . There are also the balances of a few great companies and long-established houses for whom the Bank of England was acting as banker long before it was suggested that such business was not the proper field of the Bank . . . The Bank does not accept any new private customers, and the balances of its established customers are very small."[95] Of course, accounts are kept open at the Bank for the discount houses.[96] The "Discounts and Advances" item mixes together advances made to the Bank's own customers and to discount houses applying to the Bank as a last resort. The penal nature of Bank rate severely constrains money-market indebtedness to the Bank.[97]

And then there is "the Proportion." The Proportion, not explicitly reported in the Return, gives the ratio of banking department reserve holdings to deposit liability. It was 7.3 per cent for the Return of August 2, 1961.

---

94 *Ibid.*

94a Special deposit requirements were removed in 1963. For a clear exposition of special deposits, see the *Quarterly Bulletin* of the Bank of England for December 1960, p. 18. Also W. T. Newlyn, *Theory of Money,* pp. 36-37.

95 *Ibid.,* p. 88.

96 Advances to the money market are reflected in bankers' deposits with the Bank of England almost at once.

97 For more arcane usages, *cf.* Sayers, *op. cit.,* pp. 84-91. Mr. Jasay *et al.* might not agree with this sentence.

2

The balance sheet for the issue department is notable for its simplicity and its formal adherence to the currency principle, which is, of course, completely inappropriate as a substantive description of the department's work. This work is simple: the issue department "manufactures" currency which it will sell to the banking department (we avoid other channels) in exchange for suitable assets, substantially Government securities.[98] The banking department in turn will sell the currency to its own "customers." The upper limit for the fiduciary issue is subject to continual adjustment at the "whim" of the authorities. Thus it was £1,300,000,000 as recently as 1949 and £2,450,000,000 in August 1961. There really is nothing terribly *fiduciary* about the issue: the Bank is not obligated to redeem its currency in anything but its currency. Indeed the operations of the issue department, governed by the Currency and Bank Notes Act of 1939, are still farther afield from the currency principle (that the sum of paper and specie should fluctuate as would a purely metallic currency): the 1939 Act, as Dacey puts it, "introduced an entirely new principle for the regulation of the note issue."[99] It provided that the size of the note issue, taking the fiduciary issue as fixed at some level, should fluctuate with the *market value* (in sterling) of the gold backing. This means that all the government need do to increase the size of the note issue — assuming that it did not want to take the simple step of increasing the fiduciary limit — is to permit or cause the nominal price of gold to increase. Indeed there is no strong link between the British gold stock and the volume of its currency other than that forged by official reaction to balance of payment considerations.

3

Taking up the balance sheet for the banking department, note the absence of gold items: the banking department is not obligated to redeem its obligations in gold, but rather in currency and coin. And then, if worse came to worst, the banking department could sell its assets to the issue department.

This is not to deny that gold flows affect Britain's monetary base.

98 Writers on monetary theory obtain exquisite pleasure from reporting that the issue department exchanges its monetary liabilities for non-monetary assets, and that an expansion in the non-monetary asset portfolio of the issue department corresponds to an expansion in the monetary assets of the public.

99 *Op. cit.*, p. 117. Space prohibits discussion of the 1954 Act.

Recalling that, aside from the trivial Bank holdings, British gold reserves are held by the Exchange Equalization Account, consider the results of a favorable British balance of payments, say, with the United States. Surplus dollar exchange would be sold to banks who in turn would sell it to the Treasury. The banks acquire correspondingly increased balances with the Bank of England. The Treasury could exchange the dollars for gold. In the United States the next step would find the Treasury balance being restored through sale of gold certificates to the Federal Reserve. In Britain the Treasury merely sells securities to the Bank. In any case, Treasury-Account holdings of gold will have increased, Treasury balances with the Bank will be unchanged, and balances of the joint-stock banks at the Bank of England will have increased.[100] Very similar to the American case.

An unfavorable balance of payments with the United States generates a similar sequence: dollars and/or gold are purchased from the Treasury (speaking generally) leading to reduced bank balances with the Bank of England. The Treasury purchases securities from the Bank, leaving its cash position unchanged but not countering the reduction in bank reserves. Of course, the national reserve of gold and dollars is reduced.[101]

The banking department's balance sheet makes clear that the Bank is an ordinary corporation in form only: its impact on the economy derives from transactions it chooses to make with the banks (perhaps indirectly through the public). The Bank can increase the liquidity of the banking system simply by increasing its own non-monetary assets, exchanging monetary liabilities for its additional assets. (As it happens, however, large open-market sales have not characterized monetary restraint in Britain in recent years.)

3. Changes in Bank Reserves

The way in which the Bank lent its aegis to monetary expansion from 1939 to 1961 can be shown by superimposing a number of Bank returns. Examine returns for June 1939, October 1947, and August 1961, the former two being lifted from Sir Geoffrey Crowther.[102]

---

100 The complicated interrelationship of the Treasury and the Exchange Equalization Account is ignored.

101 British currency is entirely comprised of Bank notes and coin.

102 *An Outline of Money,* pp. 50-51.

COMPARATIVE RETURNS FOR THE BANK OF ENGLAND, 1939-1961
(£ million)

LIABILITIES	14 Jun 1939	15 Oct 1947	2 Aug 1961
Notes	494.9	1,368.6	2,415.4
Public deposits	22.1	11.5	13.2
Bankers' deposits	100.3	295.8	243.8
Other deposits[103]	36.4	94.6	231.4
Capital and surplus	17.9	17.7	18.3
ASSETS			
Gold and silver	227.6	2.4	1.8
Government securities	415.4	1,759.9	2,864.5
Other securities	23.0	20.1	18.5
Discounts and advances	5.6	5.8	37.3
VALUE OF ASSETS OR LIABILITIES	671.6	1,788.2	2,922.1

TABLE VB-VI

A "classical process of monetary expansion" is revealed. The central bank has vastly increased its non-monetary assets (largely government securities). These were purchased with new currency and through creation of deposit liability. Insofar as securities were purchased directly from the government, the proceeds quickly were spent and became reflected in bankers' deposits and public currency holdings. Insofar as securities were purchased in the open market, there was a *pari passu* an increase in bankers' deposits.

4. Clearing Bank Balance Sheets

1

Simply by pilfering material from the excellent Chapters 13-15 of A. C. L. Day's *Outline of Monetary Economics,*[104] we can present consolidated balance sheets for the London clearing banks from 1928 to 1954. The Radcliffe Committee's *Report* (p. 45) permits updating to 1958.[105]

103 Special deposits (2 Aug. 1961) are included in "Other Deposits."
104 Oxford: The Clarendon Press, 1957.
105 Radcliffe Committee materials comprise a vast mine of financial data. See especially Vol. 1 of the *Memoranda of Evidence.*

BALANCE SHEETS FOR LONDON CLEARING BANKS, 1928-1958

(in £ million)[106]

LIABILITIES	End 1928	End 1938	End 1950	End 1954	End 1958
Current accounts		1,249	4,159	4,314	4,227
Deposits and other accounts		1,004	2,116	2,430	2,972
Total deposits	1,807	2,253	6,275	6,744	7,199
ASSETS					
Coin, notes and bal. with Bank of England	200	237	517	546	586
Money at call or short notice	153	152	566	462	587
Bills discounted	254	264	1,422	1,303	1,320
TDR's			476		
Investments	258	641	1,516	2,360	2,102
Advances	959	966	1,617	1,860	2,126
Adjustment for interbank dep.					581
	1,824	2,260	6,114	6,531	7,302

TABLE VB-VII

Once again there are problems of nomenclature. "Current accounts" simply are demand deposits. "Deposit accounts," roughly, are time deposits. "Money at call or short notice" largely are advances to the discount houses. "Bills discounted" are, in Sayers's felicitous phrase, "post-dated checks purchased by the banks."[107] Treasury bills account for a large part of this total (after 1928). "TDR's," Treasury deposit receipts, stemmed from direct loans to the government in the wartime and early post-war periods. These had maturities of from five to seven months, were compulsory, and were non-negotiable. "Advances" are

> "loans . . . to industrialists, professional men, and others. The banks allow the business man to pay deposits to other people on the understanding that they will, at the end of three months or so, obtain deposits for repaying the bank if called upon to do so."[108]

106 Since shareholders' capital, bank premises, etc. are not shown, totals of "asset" and "liability" items need not be the same.

107 These are short-dated, generally about 90 days.

108 R. S. Sayers, *op. cit.*, p. 32.

"Investments" are "non-bills."

2

One way of determining whether any profound changes have occurred in the banking structure would be to construct a table showing the percentages borne by values of various bank assets to total deposits. (These may not sum to 100 because of the "imbalance" of balance sheets already noted.)

ASSETS OF LONDON BANKS

(per cent of deposits)

ASSET CATEGORY	1928	1938	1950	1954	1958
Coin, notes, etc.	11.1	10.5	8.2	8.1	8.1
Money at call, etc.	8.5	6.8	9.0	6.9	8.2
Bills discounted	14.1	11.7	22.7	19.3	18.3
Liquidity ratio	33.7	29.0	39.9	34.3	34.6
TDR's		–	7.6		
Investments	14.3	28.4	24.2	35.0	29.2
Advances	53.1	42.9	25.8	27.6	29.5
Interbank items					8.1[109]

TABLE VB-VIII

The decline in the "coin, notes, and bal. with bank" item from the prewar to the postwar era mostly reflects abandonment of "window-dressing." This custom found banks taking special steps to increase cash ratios on return days.

It is striking that almost 48 per cent of the asset portfolio of London banks was comprised of Government securities in 1958. (The corresponding statistic for American commercial banks is almost 36.) The corresponding statistic for 1928 would not appear to exceed 25 per cent. That for 1938 is about 33-37 per cent. Underlying these statistics are two economically important events:

a) the cheap money policy of British Governments from 1932 to 1951 when Bank rate remained at 2 per cent;

109 The deposit totals for 1958 entries are not *net,* as they are for other years reported. Accordingly, the adjustment shown in table had to be made.

b) the exigencies of war finance and the response of British wartime Governments.

Since it always is interesting to link up dreary statistics with flesh and blood events, let us touch on the background.

Before World War II, securities bore very low yields: time deposits earned 0.5 per cent; fine commercial bills about 1.5 per cent. The public found it attractive to substitute current accounts for securities (there was no important substitution against deposit accounts). In this way the banks increased their holdings of Government securities (including bills and gilt-edged stock). Deposit expansion was abetted by the Government's concern that there be no excess supply in the securities markets at the "low" yields. In this way the liquidity of the public was allowed to increase so that, as Day points out, "in 1925–1928 bank deposits averaged about 42 per cent of the national income; in 1935–1938 they averaged nearly 49 per cent."[110] The banks were kept amply supplied with reserves.

Liquidity preference effects of cheap money obtained from 1932–1951 but surely were less important for bank portfolios than was the finance of the 1939–1945 war. Bank Returns and London clearing bank balance sheets show how the Government financed that part of the financial costs of the war not covered by taxation. (Taxation accounted for something less than 50 per cent of the requirement.) Bonds were sold directly to the Bank of England, the proceeds quickly being disbursed to contractors. These purchases made possible substantial increases in bank deposits, since they led *pari passu* to increased reserves. The potential increase in bank deposits was realized by the Government which acquired bank credit through securities sales, quickly returning these deposits to the banking system through purchase of war material, payment of armed forces, etc. The parallel to the American experience is obvious.

The wartime process led, as we saw, to very substantial increases in the public's cash without corresponding issue of (non-monetary) debt by members of the public. Rather the Government increased *its* debt. Some would say the public was able to acquire highly liquid

[110] A. C. L. Day, *op. cit.*, p. 188. Another factor causing high liquidity preference was political uncertainty. Also the politically disturbed Continent increased its balances at London, causing a capital inflow and consequent eased bank liquidity.

assets without issuing debt certificates, leading to a huge increase in the public's net liquidity. (I have indicated that I should pay more heed to the citizen *qua* taxpayer responsible for service of public debt.)

The banks emerged from the war and its aftermath with bloated portfolios of Government securities and with correspondingly increased deposit liability; the public with greatly expanded deposit holdings not offset by their own debt issue; the Treasury with a greatly increased debt obligation. Banks would have to accept a more important role for Government bonds in their portfolios unless a new inflationary process would so much increase nominal values as to roll back the real value of the national debt. Increased bank holdings of non-Government securities holdings are generated by the following processes:

a) exchange of Government for non-Government securities by the banks trading with members of the public;

b) exchange of Government securities for deposit claims, followed by new loans and advances by the banks to the public, a sub-case under (a) but worth distinguishing.

3

Before taking up the last of our comments on the London clearing bank balance sheets — concerning the decline in importance of advances from 1928 to 1938[111] — consider the crude dynamics of the monetary expansions connected with finance of the 1939–1945 war. The initial impact of the wartime expansion of the money supply was felt primarily in the markets for commodities (including goods and services) and labor. The Government, while to some extent seeking to increase its average cash balance,[112] went into these markets with its newly obtained cash just about as soon as it acquired it. The newly created money quickly found its way into private and corporate pockets.

Subsequent stages of the analysis are not so easy to develop, but a rough idea can be conveyed. The combination of wartime price control and rationing of most consumer goods (together with cessation of production of many consumer durables) caused this new money to have

111 Advances remained stationary. The decline of importance in advances from 1938 to 1950 more reflects the huge increase in government securities holdings than noteworthy stagnation in the private security sector.

112 For convenience, the ordinary lag between obtaining finance and using it is ignored. This lag suffices, quite automatically, to increase the average desired cash balance of the deficit spending unit.

a checkered history. To some extent, members of the public luxuriated in higher cash balances — holding the new money idle — but a goodly portion of it was returned to the Government in exchange for securities that could, among other things, be encashed after the war for — as the public thought — consumer goods and plant and equipment foregone during the war. Each new bundle of cash created by the Government in the course of its "conspiracy" with the banking system was turned over to the public who withheld some of the cash and returned the rest to the Government in exchange for securities. The Government again returned the cash to the public who once again refluxed much of it in exchange for securities. . . . The war saw continuous production of new cash bundles, each leading to a new process contributing to the huge increase in the public's financial wealth during the war (always ignoring the public *qua* taxpayer).

The final phase concerns the later post-war period when controls were removed or much relaxed. Just prior to relaxation of controls, one visualizes the enormous potential excess demand in the commodities and labor markets, together with corresponding excess supply in the money and securities markets. A public that had refrained from consumption during a terrible war and had neglected repair and renewal of much of its producer durable stock, and which *might* be considered to be greatly enriched by its enormously augmented securities and money holdings, surely would plan to enter the "real" markets of the system, offering the proceeds of securities sales and part of their existing cash balances for goods and services. Now consider the impact of an official policy supporting securities prices at "high" levels so that the cost of refinancing floating debt could be kept low. Not only would it be possible for securities to be cashed without capital loss; additional bank reserves would be created adding further force to the inflationary pressure. These essentially were the policies of the Truman Administration (at least until spring 1951) and the British Labor Government (1945–1951). Under the new rules of the game, prices were able substantially to increase and did. Finally, once the process of money creation ceased, excess supply of money rather quickly was eliminated: higher price levels led to increased desired transactions and asset balances (a process tempered by effects of higher interest rates accompanying restoration of monetary orthodoxy). Similarly, more attractive yields, together with inflation induced decline in the real value of war-swollen holdings, helped to bring the securities markets into equilibrium. The cash created during the war and directly introduced into income streams is, at the end of the story, found to be living a staid, bourgeois existence. Its nominal value stands in "normal" relation to that of income streams, etc. A glance at major movements of financial assets reflected in the comparative balance sheets of the London clearing banks reveals much about the dynamics and comparative statics of macroeconomic systems, hinting at propositions about invariance in equilibrium of deflated values of wide classes of goods against the nominal money stock.

4

We conclude the survey of bank balance sheets with a more careful look at the "Advances" row,[113] focusing attention on the 1928–1938 interim when total advances increased by only £7 million while the aggregate of London bank assets increased by more than £400 million. Since the major increase was in gilt-edged (longer-term Government) securities holdings, we see that bank portfolio proportions changed drastically over the decade. Day[114] points out that

> "it probably would have been impossible in any case to maintain the ratio of advances to deposits of the twenties, because that would have implied a big rise in advances in relation to national income. In fact, the tendency of the time was in the reverse direction; whereas advances had averaged nearly 22.5 per cent of national income in 1925-1928, they had fallen to little over 19.5 per cent in 1935-1938."

Why? Not because banks were leery about making advances. The evidence points in the opposite direction: their higher yields made ad-

113 Rough calculations based on the Radcliffe *Report* (p. 45) and Federal Reserve *Bulletins* suggest that at the end of 1958 "Loans" comprised 53 per cent of the financial assets of commercial banks in the United States while "Advances" comprised 42 per cent of the same total for London clearing banks.

In neither calculation are government securities holdings in the numerator of course. However, advances to discount houses *are* in the London numerator, comprising something like 8 per cent of London bank assets. These funds largely are invested in Governments. Thus, British banks conduct relatively less "ordinary banking business" than do American banks.

In making a similar comparison for 1941, Professor Sayers (*op. cit.*, p. 31) noticed that "in England loans of various kinds formed a much larger proportion of the total than they do in America. . ." However, bank holdings of U. S. securities fell by almost $3 billion from 1947 to 1958. As U. S. banking reserves increased after 1949, the banks enlarged their non-Government portfolios, reducing the importance of Governments in the over-all portfolio. Thus, Sayers' calculation is reversed.

114 *Op. cit.*, pp. 189-190.

vances particularly attractive during the cheap money era.[115] In fact, as Day points out, banks became willing, in contrast with their former practice, to grant medium-term finance to business; through a technical arrangement known as *bridging* (the gap between expenditure and permanent funding), they even were willing to finance fixed investment.[116] Day suggests that the following might be reasons for the stagnation of advances between 1928 and 1938:

1) vertical integration of industry increased, reducing cash requirements. Branches need not make cash payments to one another;

2) interest rates on long-term securities fell relative to advances rates in the 1930's, encouraging firms to acquire cash by selling longer-term securities (sometimes temporarily investing the proceeds in shorter-dated stocks);

3) from 1928–1938, partly because of the public's increased liquidity, charge accounts became less important. The retail sector experienced a more even cash inflow, reducing average finance requirements below those of a "peaked" receipt pattern.

A fourth factor might be added: growth of non-banking financial intermediaries offering increasingly severe competition in the advances sector.

5. The British System of Control

We now understand enough of the environment of British banking and finance to take up the British system of control. Major concern is with interaction of funding, bank-rate, and open-market operations. Although not airtight compartments, the categories are distinct enough to permit attack under separate heads.

a) *Open-Market Policy*

1

After showing how open-market policy might work *in a system in which the money market were not obligated to "cover the tender,"* we

115 There are more-rigid price patterns in the highly concentrated British banking system than in the United States. Thus, the basic rate on advances was not competed down by the banks.

116 In a society with highly developed financial intermediaries, bank willingness to finance longer-term projects is not very important. The substance is the same if banks lend on shorter term to intermediaries — specialized to this kind of risk — who make longer-term loans to entrepreneurs.

ask why it is not taken more seriously in Britain today.[117] Keep in mind that Bank rate, the discount rate at the Bank of England, is penal; it stands above rates governing yields of most money-market assets. The money market (discount houses) is punished if it "goes into the Bank."

2

Taking up a problem in monetary contraction, assume that the Bank's operator (a firm representing the Bank in securities markets) sold £x million in securities in the open market. [b]ank balances with the Bank of England would fall by the same amount. If banks were working with an initial 8 per cent reserve, they would have to reduce their deposit liability by £(12.5)(x) million unless they somehow were able to restore their reserve position. How? (1) The rate paid on deposit accounts (time deposits) might be increased, perhaps inducing a currency inflow. We ignore this possibility. (2) Holdings of Government securities, particularly Treasury bills, might be allowed to run off, permitting banks to acquire claims against the Bank of England. The Bank would have to continue to sell assets in the open market so long as bank holdings of Governments were being run off: scheme 2 can work; officials must be aware of it and, as part of their initial plan, be ready to deliver a surrebuttal through additional sales.[118] (3) The banks might call loans outstanding to the money market, forcing discount houses into the Bank, paying off indebtedness to the banks by drawing against balances newly created for them at the Bank of England. But Bank rate is penal. Discount houses would be under severe pressure to sell securities in the market or let holdings run off in order to get out of the Bank. Insofar as discount houses sold securities and used the proceeds to repay indebtedness to the Bank of England, the joint-stock banks again would have been thwarted. On the other hand, if the discount houses repaid the Bank by permitting Government paper to run

117 Britain's post-war life has been dominated by problems of gold outflow and inflation. Naturally, bank liquidity could be increased through open-market purchases, perhaps combined with "disfunding, shortening the term structure of public debt." Appendix A to Ch. V takes up problems of open-market policy, including those concerning lower limits to long-term rates.

The discussion on weapons of monetary control in Keynes's *Treatise* is *excellent*. I should say unmatched.

118 If initial Treaury cash balances were "small," the adjustment process (the Battle of the Run-Off) might find the Bank buying tap bills and selling other securities at roughly equal rates. Treasury cash could be kept intact; clearing banks could be kept under unrelaxed discipline.

off, they would be agents for the banks' second escape mechanism, and countermeasures (described above) would be necessary. Unless the discount houses stood ready to pay penal Bank rate on what might be very large advances, the joint-stock banks could not escape the jaws of the official trap.[119] Perhaps the officials must pay a price in the form of higher interest charges on floating debt and on new issues of longer maturity, but open-market sales could work irresistibly to force contraction of the deposit liability and accordingly the asset portfolios of the joint-stock banks.

3

Up to this point we have told a story seeming to depict the operation of a cruel, remorseless, but irresistible mechanism. The joint-stock bankers have been cast as Kafka's K, subject to the absolute, albeit incomprehensible, perhaps capricious, dictates of the powers of the Castle. Where is the rub?

The answer is indirect. Imagine a system in which there were no Government debt or in which Government debt were funded in perpetual (irredeemable) bonds so that the short-term assets of the banking system — including the discount houses — consisted solely of private paper. Now assume once again that an open-market sale of £x million took place (perhaps using private securities). Equilibrium deposit liability of the banks would decline by a multiple of £x million. Banking assets would be reduced accordingly. The public must be induced, presumably through higher interest rates, to substitute securities for bank deposits. *The Treasury would be subjected to no inconvenience. It has no debt management problem.*

There is the rub! In the real world there is an enormous floating (short-term) Government debt. Government securities form a large part of banking assets and predominate among assets held by the discount houses. *The direct impact of a credit squeeze will in fact be greater for the Treasury than for any other sector.* The enormous increase in Government debt and the crucial role Government securities have come to play in the banking sector mean that it is impossible to discuss mechanisms of monetary control without inserting the Treasury into the center of the scene. (For discussion of the market's obligation to cover the tender, see Note A.)

Now it is reasonable to assume — at least in a purely monetary

119 Again compare Note A.

analysis — that the over-all supply of Government securities will be unresponsive to interest rates.[120] Among other things, a Government concerned about inflation will not print currency with which to redeem its debt. This implies that the new (temporary) equilibrium of the economy will find the non-Government sector's holdings of Government securities increased by an amount corresponding to the size of the sale and the sum of bank deposits multiplicatively contracted. Holdings of privately issued securities will be reduced, a reduction tempered to the extent that depositors are induced "permanently" to exchange deposits for securities. On net, the public must substitute securities for current and/or deposit accounts, a substitution that, at least in the case of current accounts, will be induced by higher interest rates.[121] Higher interest rates surely will lead to some contraction in the total of private issue.[122]

4

Others might say that I have painted too rosy a picture of the functioning of open-market devices in regulating the monetary system.[123] I have conceded only that the Treasury will be discomfited by a credit squeeze. Not that alternative procedures, including funding,

120 Not to deny that the distribution of Government securities among maturities can be responsive to the term structure of interest rates.

121 If bank deposit rate is not kept in line with bill rate, both classes of deposits can be expected to contract. Of course, to the extent that deposit accounts simply are shifted to institutions such as building societies, the authorities will have been thwarted.

If bank deposit rate *is* kept in line with bill rate, the new temporary equilibrium will find deposit accounts no smaller, and probably larger, because of substitution of deposit for current accounts. On the other hand, there will have been a substantial contraction in current accounts, since deposit liabilities will not have been shifted to non-banking institutions. To some extent, reduced current accounts will reflect economizing of transactions balances at unchanged rates of business activity. The authorities would hope that a considerable portion of the reduction reflected transactions requirements as inventory build-ups cease, prices cease to rise, etc.; more precisely, the process of contraction of current-account liability concerns streams of expenditure rather than economizing of cash.

122 If government and non-government securities are imperfect substitutes, yields on Governments will increase relatively as well as absolutely, the proportion of government issue to the total having increased. An exception might be Treasury bills if funding is part of the disinflationary process. *Cf. infra.*

We do not consider whether changes in interest rates will *persist*. "Equilibrium" here concerns today's market clearance.

123 E.g., Mikesell and Smith, *op. cit.;* R. S. Sayers, *op. cit.;* W. M. Dacey, *op. cit.;* the Radcliffe *Report.*

avoid this result. Smith and Mikesell offer a standard statement of the new orthodoxy:

> "the cash ratio [8 per cent] does not serve as an independent limitation on the supply of bank credit, because as long as the Bank of England continues its traditional practice of serving as a lender of last resort, the banks can translate other liquid assets into cash by calling loans to the discount houses and forcing the market into the Bank . . ."[124]

This explanation seems to be invalid. So long as the authorities do not relax their grip, equilibrium of the banking system after an official open-market sale of securities will require a multiplied reduction in bank deposits. True, the discount market's obligation to cover the Treasury bill tender and the unique environment make for intricate intermediate stages, but the upshot supports defenders of the virility of the 8-per-cent constraint. (*See Note A.*)

Concededly, there might be a sound basis for skepticism about monetary policy: one applying to all its variants, not just to open-market operations. Specifically, interest rate fluctuations might have to be so large, and perhaps so sporadic, for meaningful impact to be registered in "real" markets (where prices are determined) that monetary policy may prove to be politically intolerable and may lead to "disorganization" of securities markets, profoundly disturbing the stability of financial institutions. The picture is the more somber if indeed it is true that very large changes in short rates are necessary to move long rates and if the latter are the rates that matter in "real" markets. It is brightened if the dynamical considerations of Ch. VA are brought into play. (*See Note B.*)

b) Funding[125]

1

In British banking disinflation by funding is tied to the 30 per cent liquidity ratio.[126] Funding is conversion of short- into long-term debt. It reduces the supply of Treasury bills. At the outset, the discount market will find its allotment of bills cut back and banks will

124 *Op. cit.*, p. 25. Of course, the market can also borrow from non-banks.

125 *Cf.* W. M. Dacey, "The Floating Debt Problem," Lloyds Bank *Review*, April 1956, pp. 24-38. Also his *British Banking Mechanism*, Ch. X.

126 Recall that liquid reserves are comprised of cash, money at call and short notice and Treasury and (much less important) commercial bills. Money-at-call mostly consists of loans to the discount market. Recall also that the liquidity ratio is normally above 30 per cent. There is an analogy to desired free reserves.

not be able to satisfy their appetite for stale bills. The 30 per cent ratio will be threatened. The banks can sustain their liquidity ratios — without reducing deposit liability — only by inducing the public either to part with Treasury and commercial bills or to issue more commercial bills destined for discount market and bank portfolios.[127] How might the public be so tempted? (1) long rate might become relatively higher; (2) bill rates might fall to "the" floor imposed by basic call rate,[128] encouraging "outside" holders of bills to substitute deposit accounts (time deposits) for bills, keeping in mind that clearing banks have agreed to peg deposit rate 2 per cent below Bank rate.[129]

2

The pattern of response to a funding operation begins to clarify: the non-banking public will be encouraged to surrender part of its bill holdings and to issue more commercial bills by relatively higher yields on time deposits and on securities other than bills. Otherwise the banks will have to contract their deposit liability.[130] Effects on commodities and labor markets will depend on the operation of a scissors with monetary and "real" blades. The first set of queries that emerges includes:

> How much must yields on securities alternative to bills rise (once bill rate reaches the floor imposed by basic call rate, pegged to Bank rate) if the nonbanking public is to be induced to surrender and issue enough bills to keep bank liquidity ratios unimpaired?
>
> Will banks become significantly more reluctant to make advances?[131]

127 Of course, banks could maintain advances if they could induce some depositors to exchange deposits for securities.

128 Prices for stale bills out of line with basic call rate (let alone marginal call rate) cannot be sustained: the discount market would leap at the opportunity to dispose (to outsiders) of bills priced on a lower yield basis than their call money. Money-market rates for maturities up to 90 days are bounded by marginal call rate and the rate on 90-day fine trade bills (subject to a slight qualification imposed by elimination of discount house stocks of a maturity).

Needless to say, it is bootless for banks to purchase bills from discount houses in order to bolster their liquidity ratios: money at call is among eligible assets.

129 A binding 8 per cent cash ratio would not permit banks to increase deposits. . . We have not discussed advances by banks to discount houses leading to expansion of the latter's holdings of short-dated bonds. The Governor would not view this as an appropriate response to a funding operation.

130 But compare footnote 127.

131 Compare Note B on overdraft. It shows that use of overdraft can lead to a less than one-for-one relationship between increases in deposits and advances (without banks selling securities). On the other hand, it shows that a binding cash proportion cannot be evaded by use of overdraft except under outlandish assumptions.

The rate of interest on advances is tied to Bank rate.

How much will bank demand prices for investments decrease?

How important will be bank reluctance to turn down valued clients at the "advance window"?

After all, the opportunity cost to banks of making advances and investments will have been increased: the marginal deposit associated with the marginal advance is "backed" with relatively low-yield bills. . . . One pictures a leftward shift of a supply curve paired with a (hopefully) downward sloping demand curve.

This brings up the second set of questions:

How much would a given rise in the cost of credit affect plans of merchants and others holding inventories, firms and households planning expenditures on durables, etc.?

How fluid are the relationships between markets for loanable funds; will those turned away at banks find it easy to make contact elsewhere?

3

By way of evaluating funding as a lever of policy, some would stress that sources for replenishment of liquid banking assets are few and infertile. Thus, the Bank would frown at any trend finding banks resorting to bill finance in place of advances. The fact that basic call rate is tied to Bank rate (about 1¾% below it) severely constrains discount houses and banks in competing for bills. Others point out that the sum of public and private debt in Britain is so huge that a given funding operation might barely be noticed. They argue that operations of manageable size would easily be offset by private issue ("disfunding" of private debt),[132] that elasticities of substitution are large enough to permit banks' liquid assets to be replenished after small changes in the term structure of interest rates. They stress that markets for longer maturities are very thin, that substantial funding over short intervals might literally be impossible. I refrain from weighing the evidence; the "institutional" finesse required for a judgment is large indeed.

c) Bank Rate Policy

1

We refer to direct effects of changes in the rate of interest at which the Bank of England will accommodate the discount market.

[132] In January 1963 the Bank announced that in future its advances *could* be at rates above Bank rate. The new procedure makes it possible to open up wider differentials between deposit rate and bill rate.

"Pure" Bank rate policy is accompanied by open-market operations only to the extent that it is desired to keep the discount market in the Bank so that Bank rate is "effective."[133] The authorities are *not* necessarily thinking of effects on the cash base of the banks. Bank rate policy may indeed have little effect on the cash base. For that matter it is not essential that Bank rate be effective; Bank rate policy can be working even if Treasury bill rate is not up against Bank rate.

The direct effects of changes in Bank rate are very important in Britain, partly because of the highly concentrated, indeed benevolently cartelized, character of the British financial sector: mere announcement of a change in Bank rate produces immediate and persistent changes in a wide variety of interest rates.

2

The summer of 1961 saw a dramatic application of a policy that, at least in its early stages, featured the lineaments of our hypothetical pure Bank rate policy. The *Economist* (July 12, July 29, and August 12, 1961) tells much of the story.

First, a few words of background. British gold reserves fell by more than £600 million from the end of 1960 to the end of July 1961. While Britain's *true* reserves are unknown, its official reserves at the

133 Bank rate is effective when Bill rate is close to it.

It seems that open-market operations have had a different connotation in British than in American financial parlance, although, as Professor Kenen has pointed out, the *Treatise* has a strong American flavor in this respect. (We must avoid here debate over equivalence of official decisions on Bank rate and on the money supply.) When the Bank sells securities in the open market, banks almost certainly will increase marginal call rates (the opportunity cost of call money supply having increased) and reduce the amount of bad money offered to the market. Being obligated to guarantee the bill tender, the discount market, upon being forced into the Bank, surely will reduce its tender price and offer more for bad money. Ergo, open-market sales can keep Bank rate effective. . . . It goes for granted that the discount houses would then offer to sell stale bills at lower prices: (a) they would be anxious to get out of the Bank; (b) fresh bills would offer higher yields . . . The discount market never would tender for bills on a yield basis greater than Bank rate. It simply is not done: a dark-visaged Bank would, among other things, keep Bank rate penal. Finally, we characterize ineffective Bank rate: banks are able to accommodate demand for advances without impinging on their cash or liquidity ratios; they do not wish to extend their commitments in longer-dated securities enough to close a considerable gap between their desired commitments and the discount market's good money; ergo, they offer marginal call money on favorable terms; it becomes in the interest of the market to offer more for bills (or at least in the interest of a syndicate not expected to exert full monopsonistic power).

end of 1960 were $3.231 billion, roughly £1.15 billion. Thus, the tranche was ghastly. This gold outflow took place at a time when Britain was not experiencing particularly heavy inflationary pressure; its cost of living index rose from 120 to 121 from 1959 to 1960 and stood at 125 in June 1961.[134] The West German index, for example, rose from 112 in 1959 to 116 in June 1961. At the same time, British money-market rates were high compared to leading foreign rates. Take Treasury bill rate. In Britain it stood at 4.45 per cent per annum in April 1961. Corresponding rates in Canada, Germany, and the Netherlands were 3.30, 2.38, and 0.77 per cent per annum. Furthermore, the German and Dutch rates had *fallen* in recent months. Also, Germany and the Netherlands had revalued their currency so that German and Dutch exchange were more expensive in terms of dollars or sterling. What happened then? The *Economist* for July 22, 1961 (p. 315) puts it well:

> "In cool retrospect, the main thing that has happened in 1961 is that the previous illogical speculation against the dollar, which had dominated the international currency scene in the first two years after Europe's return to convertibility at the end of 1958, pretty well stopped in its tracks after America's new image Kennedy administration came to power in January; and the diverted tide of speculation then turned strongly against sterling instead. This unwillingness of foreigners to hold sterling at the existing level of interest rates was itself a warning that Britain's long-term weaknesses — its continuing cost inflation and adverse balance of current payments — had made sterling seem to be a sensible currency to speculate against . . ."

Britain faced an external drain challenging the convertibility of sterling claims into gold and hard currencies. At the same time, latent internal inflationary pressures suggested that drastic measures were in order (these pressures not including a demand inflation). And so Bank rate was put up to the crisis level of 7 per cent on July 26, 1961. The purpose was to encourage capital inflow from abroad and reduce demand for goods and services at home. At least at the outset, there was no apparent tincture of funding or open-market sales. The total of tender Treasury bills (bills held by the non-government sector) was £3.48 billion on July 16, 1960. On May 6, 1961 the total was £3.13 billion and had risen to £3.28 billion by July 8, 1961. The tender issue

134 However the spurt in prices in 1961 was quite alarming to many observers. There was a growing feeling that important inflationary pressure was in the offing, partly because of exogenous increases in factor prices.

was £3.28 on August 5, 1961. Thus, funding was not taking place. As for open-market sales, the total of government securities held by the departments of the Bank of England *increased* by more than £150 million from July 20, 1960 to July 19, 1961, although by August 5, 1961 there had been a slight decrease from the mid-July total. We can examine substantially unalloyed Bank rate policy in operation.

The setting being completed, we can return to the *Economist,* compiling "money rates" before and after Bank rate was put up to 7 per cent. Consult Table VB-IX:

MONEY RATES, SUMMER 1961

(in per cent per annum)

	July 21	July 28	August 11
Bank rate	5	7	7
Deposit rates paid by banks	3	5	5
Day-to-day loans	3⅜ to 4⅜	5⅜ to 5⅞	5⅜ to 6⅛
Treasury bills	4½ (approx.)		6¼ (approx.)
3 mo. bank acceptances	4¾	6½	6⅞
3 mo. fine trade accept.	5¾	7¾	8

TABLE VB-IX

Previous discussion immediately comes to mind: deposit rate is locked 2 percentage points below Bank rate; basic call rate is tied to Bank rate. These rates clearly are not the outcome of the free play of market forces. As for Treasury bill rate:

> ". . . the basic call loan rate is, while the Bill rate is not fixed relative to Bank rate. Movements of the Bill rate between the two limits set by the basic call rate and Bank rate determine current gross profit of the market from carrying Bills and the current loss from rediscounting them."[135]

We have seen that this means that the lower bound for bill rate movements is increased by an increase in Bank rate.[136] The outcome for

135 Jasay, "Memoranda of Evidence," Vol. 3, p. 131.

136 Outside tenderers are not going to upset the apple cart. They can obtain fresh Bills at the tender so long as they quote as much as does the syndicate, and, indeed are not subject to allotment. Similarly, outside tenderers will be governed in their bids for trade bills and stale Treasury Bills by the behavior of the "classic" price leader, the discount market. There is no reason for them to bid over the market.

bankers' and trade acceptances is obvious: the price that can be obtained by a seller of such a bill is remorselessly bounded by that which can be obtained by the Treasury for its bills. Keynes, writing no later than 1930, but not requiring important revision, describes additional repercussions of changes in Bank rate:

> ". . . And in addition to these matters of agreement [deposit and call-money rates], there are a number of customs and conventions by which the rate of interest charged for bank loans bears a more or less fixed relationship to official bank rate; for example loans to the Stock Exchange, and the innumerable standing arrangements for overdrafts and advances, the rate for which is agreed beforehand at a figure fixed relatively to the official bank-rate and is not lightly altered. Accordingly when, for example the official rate is raised, the rate for many bank loans goes up automatically by the same amount. If some previous borrowers no longer care to borrow at the higher rate, then more of the unsatisfied fringe gets the accommodation for which it has been asking . . ."[137]

Finally, rates paid by building societies (savings and loan associations) and the like to depositors necessarily will rise in response to increased deposit rate (reducing demand prices for mortgages).

Indeed a wide spectrum of interest rates will increase as a more or less direct result of increased Bank rate. This cannot help but affect yields in other markets, at least to the extent that changes in short rates *can* influence longer-term rates. But the reader trained in price theory is apt to ask: "if securities markets were cleared and if desired and actual cash were equal before Bank rate was put up, will not higher interest rates lead to excess demand for securities and excess supply of cash?" The answer requires that implications be drawn from the "cartelized" nature of the banking system and from the intimate relationship of the banks and the authorities. The banks must adjust their portfolios to the structure of securities prices. Their criteria for portfolio management cannot altogether be those of profit maximization. Indeed, the banks in the context of Bank rate policy almost are quasi-officials. Specifically, the banks stand ready to provide deposit accounts for current accounts. They must step aside if the public and foreign investors choose to hold more Treasury bills. If the "unsatisfied fringe of borrowers" does not absorb advances that might be turned back by regular customers (because of increased interest rates) the banks must stand prepared either to reduce deposit

[137] J. M. Keynes, *op. cit.*, Vol. II, pp. 366-367.

liability or switch to longer-dated stocks. To a considerable degree, Bank rate policy requires that the great banks perform as a safety valve: they must accept substantial modifications in their portfolio in order to accommodate the non-banking public's reaction to the new structure of rates. (The banks appear to be regaining their freedom rapidly, however.)

3

Bank rate has been taken more seriously as a means of correcting the balance of payments than as a means for dealing with domestic imbalance. The impact of changed Bank rate on the short end of the market is prompt, persistent, and decisive, and it is short rates that attract and disgorge hot money (uncovered funds sensitive to international differentials in interest rates).[138] On the other hand, if real expenditure is insensitive to short-term rates, Bank rate policy can fail on the domestic scene. Indeed to the extent that higher overdraft rates have led to reduced bank advances and banks have (directly or indirectly) been forced to disgorge bills in order to satisfy the public's heightened appetite, banks, pushed towards long-terms, might buoy up the long end of the market.

Finally, it is by no means clear that Bank rate can exert powerful influence on international movements of short-term capital these days. Traders are reluctant to take *exchange risks;* Americans, for example, do not want to be vulnerable to devaluation of sterling. Accordingly, capital movements typically are covered: Americans investing in London bills buy dollar exchange for future delivery. This means that, *cet. par.,* a movement of covered funds from New York to London strengthens the forward dollar, making higher London bill rates less attractive. "Interest parities" of forward exchange rates (*cf.* Appendix C, Ch. VA) might be restored after rather small capital movements. (Indeed, if all forward cover must be supplied by interest arbitrageurs, covered movements of hot money will lead to *no* improvement in today's capital account.)

SUMMARY

1. At the outset of discussing central banking *in esse,* the contrast with the central bank *anschaungen* of Walter Bagehot (nineteenth

138 See Appendix C to Ch. VA for an alternative to Bank rate as a means of dealing with capital (in)outflow.

century) and J. M. Keynes (twentieth century) was stressed. Bagehot thought in terms of protecting the national reserve, insuring convertibility of sterling obligations. Keynes in 1930 stressed the role of the central bank as manager of the price level and as the agency responsible for maintenance of more or less continuous equilibration of planned saving and planned investment. Conflict can arise between domestic goals and protection of the national gold reserve.

2. The American Federal Reserve System is a true central banking apparatus. Its functions include almost all of the traditional tasks of a central bank: issue; service as a banker for the government and as its agent and adviser; custodianship of cash reserves of commercial banks; service as a bank of rediscount and lender of last resort; service as a bank of central clearing, settlement, and transfer; exercise of control of credit; executor of open-market and discount-rate policy.
3. Although rather decentralized on the surface, the Federal Reserve System has come more and more to be controlled *de facto* by the Board of Governors at Washington.
4. The independence of the Federal Reserve has been a long-standing issue in the United States. The Federal Reserve has been in conflict with the Treasury from time to time, notably from 1949 to the spring of 1951 when the Federal Reserve won a great political victory expressed in the Accord of that year. It is not obvious that the resulting division of power is logical.
5. The consolidated balance sheet for Federal Reserve banks shows that their most important assets are gold certificates and United States government securities. Their most important liabilities are Federal Reserve notes and deposits of member banks.
6. Gold inflow and outflow affects the Federal Reserve's gold certificate holdings and the member bank reserve account. Gold inflow finds the Treasury acquiring gold by writing checks against its Federal Reserve deposits and replenishing its cash by issuing gold certificates to the Federal Reserve in exchange for renewed deposits. Gold outflow finds the Treasury receiving checks against member banks in exchange for gold, followed by "reflux" of gold certificates and erasure of the additional Treasury deposit. These movements can be countered by open-market policy so that member bank reserves are unaffected by the *combination* of gold flows

and open-market operations. When undertaken in response to gold inflow, this is called *sterilization* and featured Federal Reserve policy *circa* 1924.

7. The *bank reserve equation* is helpful in working through the mechanics of key central banking activity: exchange of monetary assets for non-monetary assets and *vice versa.* When the central bank increases its holdings of non-monetary assets, it provides the economy with corresponding increments of reserve money (deposit claims against itself); when it reduces its portfolio of non-monetary assets, it forces the system to reduce its holdings of reserve money. In both instances, the member banks will generally be found making adjustments in *their* portfolios much greater than the size of the open-market operation. This expansion will find the public surrendering non-monetary assets (or creating liabilities) for monetary assets (bank deposits). Insofar as there are expansionary effects through inflation and/or increased real output, part of the increased supply of bank money will be devoted to transactions balances. There will be new securities issues as the "monetary requirement" increases. There might be transitional substitution of bank deposits for securities, as securities prices temporarily rise during open-market purchases, prior to return to the equilibrium path — a comment strictly applicable only when full employment is assumed throughout.
8. The British central banking system differs from the American: British banks do not have direct access to the Bank of England (when the back door is closed); Bank rate always is penal; liquidity ratios are very important; and, partly because British banking is so concentrated, pure Bank rate policy is plausible.
9. As in the United States, the British monetary base enormously increased during World War II when the central bank purchased government debt, leading to multiple expansion of bank assets. Comparison of consolidated banking balance sheets from 1928 to 1958 shows that the relative importance of government securities has greatly increased.
10. The huge increment of government debt during World War II, together with the banks' practice of maintaining at least a 30 per cent liquidity ratio, has opened up new possibilities for monetary control. These are based on changes in the proportion of debt funded in long-term securities.

11. In postwar Britain and the United States tight money much affects the Treasury. Both countries are featured by huge stocks of floating debt. Hence, the cost to the Treasury of servicing the national debt can be substantially increased by central bank policies. Severe conflict can arise between the Treasury and the central bank, each concerned with its parochial responsibility.

NOTES

NOTE A: For example, J. R. Sargent's letter to the *Economist,* May 19, 1956, p. 681 ("Disinflation by Funding"). The *Economist* replies at p. 717 of that issue.

A more technical analysis would have considered at least these further points:

a) about 80 per cent of the discount market's borrowings are what is called "good money" on which minimum or basic call rate applies). I should think that discount houses can expect to have their good money available to them come hell or high water. Mikesell and Smith *et al.* ignore this point. Their argument hinges on bank recall of "bad" money (on which negotiated, higher, rates apply).

b) to repeat, the discount house syndicate is obligated to "cover" the Treasury bill tender. (Outside tenderers obtain bills for which they bid at least as much as does the syndicate.) Accordingly, if contractionary authorities were not to rupture the present institutional fabric subsequent to open-market sales of securities — we ignore (a) above and permit the assumption that clearing banks might even call in all of their loans to the discount market — the Bank might even be found succoring discount houses at market rates, all the while raising Bank rate (and thus basic call rate) and hence lowering the syndicate's tendering price. Finally, money-market rates would become sufficiently high to discourage supply of IOU's to the point where return of call money to the discount market and the increased outside tender eliminated any need for official help. . . Obviously, the Treasury is not going to be sent into the cold night peddling its bills; the tender will be taken up in an orderly manner throughout. If the Treasury were less sensitive, and if the discount market were not obligated to take up the tender, open-market policy could function simply through reluctance of the discount market to carry bills by borrowing at penal rates.

c) the analysis of (b) above ignores liquidity ratio (30%) considerations, which, of course, make the specified process outlandish. But this is in keeping with the economist's game. "30%" considerations here support the "old orthodoxy."

d) most process analyses ignore the discount market's holdings of short-dated bonds. This is indeed a harmless simplification: since these bonds yield more than Bank rate, for a house to carry bills by sloughing bonds is even worse for it than to carry bills by going into the Bank.

An excellent statement of the "new orthodoxy" is A. E. Jasay, "Memoranda of Evidence," *Principal Memoranda of Evidence,* Vol. III, pp. 129-132. Jasay argues that implicit in the relationship between the market and the clearing banks is an obligation of the former to relieve pressure on the latter by going into the bank from time to time. "It would be a needless sacrifice of revenue on the part of the clearing banks to maintain their generous basic call loan arrangements with the discount houses if the latter were not prepared, as the occasion arose, to keep 'Discounts and Advances' and hence the cash base at a figure satisfactory to the banks." (*Ibid.*, p. 130.) His appendix (pp. 131-132) shows, Jasay says, that the Bank's Discounts and Advances portfolio was "both positive and volatile" throughout the 148-week period from January 1955-October 1957 (during a squeeze). Over that period, the portfolio was "larger by £24.4 millions on the average . . . than it should have been in order for the traditional theory to be true. . . [T]he quantity of money appears to have been £305 millions larger on the average of the whole period, and £591 millions larger in the peak month, than it should have been under the alleged traditional mechanism of control."

I have two comments: (1) there were five occasions during Jasay's period when Discounts and Advances exceeded £50 million. On four of these occasions the account fell by 25-to-50 million within one week. On the remaining occasion, a decline from 65 to 27 million took five weeks to transpire; (2) his data suggest that the officials could, if they had wished, impose £25 million more in pressure by making incremental open-market sales in that amount.

NOTE B: The text has ignored *overdraft,* very important in British practice. Overdraft facilities permit bank customers to write checks over and above current accounts.

Overdraft facility plays the same role as the more familiar (for Americans) lines of credit. It confers to potential deficit spending units the power to incur indebtedness. This is in contrast with another source of liquidity, cash, permitting a deficit spending unit to *avoid* further indebtedness. Overdraft facility and cash clearly are imperfect substitutes.

Increased overdraft facility, while a source of increased liquidity, is not captured in the social accounts, surely not by measurements of "the stock of money." What about the *exercise* of overdraft facility? Will this affect measurements of bank deposits for example? Almost certainly, yes. There is in fact only one *conceivable* circumstance in which it would not. Namely when payers, relying on overdraft, draw checks in favor of payees, each with overdraft at the same bank in excess of the amount of his check. (A number of banks can be introduced if clearings mesh perfectly.) Overdraft of payees would fall *pari passu* with increased overdraft of payers; reserve positions of banks would be unchanged; deposits would be unaffected.

Note that use of lines of credit must lead to a change in deposits in the absence of overdraft. The borrower's deposit account is credited; the credit is transferred to his payee. In the "pure" case accounts never are overdrawn; expansion of credit, *cet. par.*, leads to expansion of deposits.

Even an hypothetical example of executed credit facility only reducing indebtedness of payees — themselves free to "restore their illiquidity" tomorrow — is intriguing. What a nightmare for monetary authorities! Payments streams could increase without limit, but even bank advances, let alone deposits, would be unchanged when measured at the end of the day! But, alas, ours is the dismal science. The house of cards collapses if there are *any* "unrequited" deposits — deposits by payees without executed overdraft or whose overdraft has been less than the value of checks paid in. If increased payments flows lead to *any* unrequited deposits, and if the 8 per cent proportion initially were binding, banks cannot increase their advances. Payments flows can increase only if "idle" deposits are surrendered.

Finally, why are current accounts maintained, since unused overdraft facility is just as liquid? Overdraft rate exceeds marginal market opportunity rate for many contemplating reliance on overdraft to meet deficits.

CHAPTER FIVE C

Central Banking: History

A. INTRODUCTION

1

We deliberately are parochial. The history concentrates on central banking in the United States and the United Kingdom. It is distorted so that we can concentrate on application of theoretical principles.

Global perspective is not altogether foregone. There are signal uniformities in central banking history: development of subtle techniques of control in haphazard ways; transformation of substantive mission behind unchanged procedural façades. Mr. Crowther puts the matter well for the oldest of true central banks, the Bank of England:

> "Central banking is almost entirely a development of the last few decades. It originated in England almost by chance, because the banks other than the Bank of England found it convenient to settle their clearing balances by cheques on the Bank of England, and came to regard their balances with the Bank as being as good as cash. The system was working in a rudimentary way, and the directors of the Bank of England were vaguely aware of the effects of raising and lowering their Bank rate . . . but the principles of the system of credit control were not discovered and enunciated until the appearance of Walter Bagehot's *Lombard Street* in 1873. Even then the criteria by which the Bank acted were almost entirely rules of thumb, and there was very little attempt at conscious control in pursuit of a consist policy before the outbreak of the war of 1914–1918."[139]

139 Crowther, *op. cit.*, p. 59.

Mr. Crowther has put his finger on another theme that crops up from time to time in central banking history, usually under the most damaging circumstances: the unwillingness of the directors of central banks to admit that theirs is *really* a central bank. However, this theme belongs to the past.

M. H. De Kock begins his book [140] with a very good statement on the evolution of central banking. Changes are rung on Crowther's theme:

> "Prior to the commencement of the twentieth century there had been no clearly defined concept of central banking. A gradual evolution had been taking place in various countries over a long period of years, but the process had not always been a conscious one, and a systematic and continuous technique had not yet been developed and formulated. The temperament and discretion of individual managements had played the principal part in the decisions and operations of the bank which had, as it were, become the centre of the monetary and banking system in each of the several countries." (p. 11.)

The origins of central banking in a given country usually are in note issue and other privileges conferred by the government in the course of intimate (often illicitly so) relationships with what is to become the central bank. Central banks often have been conceived in sin. Thus the Bank of England in 1694 received its charter granting privileges of note issue as part of a deal in which it agreed to make loans to the government.

2

We turn to a sweeping survey. The Riksbank of Sweden was the first central bank, but "the Bank of England was the first bank of issue to assume the position of a central bank and to develop what are now generally recognized as the fundamentals of the art of central banking." [141]

De Kock organizes events around a functional pattern. We take up various central bank histories as banks of issue, as bankers for the government, as custodians of cash reserves of the commercial banks,

140 *Central Banking* (London: Staples Press Ltd., 1954).

141 M. H. De Kock, *op. cit.*, p. 11. He adds, "the history of the Bank of England is thus universally accepted as illustrating the evolution of central banking principles and technique." Indeed monetary economics — at least the theory of monetary policy — cannot properly be understood unless one knows something about the history of British banking.

as custodians of the nation's reserves of international currency, as lenders of last resort, and as controllers of credit. We do not pursue each of these headings for each bank, nor do we pursue any heading in great detail.[142]

The *Riksbank of Sweden,* founded in 1656, was "reorganized as a State bank in 1668, followed in the footsteps of the Bank of England and gradually developed into a central bank." [143] The Riksbank, however, seems notable only for its antiquity. It did not cement its monopoly as a bank of issue until 1897 and did not pioneer in custodianship of cash reserves of commercial banks or in control of credit.

The *Bank of France* was founded in 1800 by Napoleon Bonaparte. It now is nationalized. Although most of its initial capital was from private sources, its initial conception was broad. As Napoleon put it, the bank was to be "national in its operations as well as in name." Evolution of central banking in France was more systematic, less colored by sheer happenstance, than was generally true elsewhere. From its inception it was the government's banker and was granted a monopoly of note issue in Paris. By 1848 it was well on its way towards securing a monopoly of note issue for the whole of France, particularly important in a country which to this day relies more heavily on bank notes than bank deposits. It became "the custodian of bank reserves and the ultimate source of credit in an emergency." [144]

The fact that the Bank of France was called upon to save the Bank of England on a number of occasions in the nineteenth century — and responded — makes its discount rate and gold holding policies especially interesting. But distinguish between the years before and after the Franco-Prussian War of 1870. France was on a "limping standard" by 1878. (*Cf.* Ch. II.) From roughly 1850 to 1870 the Bank of France maintained notably larger gold reserves than did the Bank of England. And then recall the huge gold reserves maintained by France — perhaps in contravention of the rules of the international gold standard game — in the 1920's.

The discount rate of the Bank of France was not nearly so sensitive an indicator of the economic climate as that of the Bank of England: the Bank of France's gold stocks were larger relative to its

---

142 In contrast with our treatment of the U. S. and the U. K.

143 *Ibid.*, p. 13.

144 *Ibid.*, p. 14.

obligations over much of the nineteenth century and the limping standard of *fin de siècle* permitted it freely to abandon its obligation to pay in gold: "In 1877 the Bank of France adopted the policy, which was subsequently adhered to, of charging a premium on gold when it was called upon to deliver gold in redemption of its notes."[145] The range and frequency of changes in the discount rate of the Bank of France were much smaller in the halcyon days of gold than was true of the Bank of England. Specifically, between 1844 and 1900 the French discount rate changed 111 times while the British rate changed 400 times. Between 1901 and July 1914 the French rate changed 10 times, the British rate 66 times. De Kock pointed out that in the crises of 1866 and 1907, whereas French Bank rate rose from 3 to 5 and from 3 to 4 per cent, British Bank rate rose from 3.5 to 10 and from 4.5 to 7 per cent.

French banking history does not feature important innovation or world leadership, prizes almost exclusively reserved for Britain in this field.

The *Reichsbank of Germany,* founded in 1875, was largely based on the Bank of Prussia. At least four things pop into one's mind in connection with German banking experience: (a) the adverse effects on the gold bases of gold standard countries caused by Germany's adoption of the gold standard in 1871;[146] (b) the hyperinflation of the early 1920's, fed with Reichsbank notes; (c) the fact that German commercial banks for many years lent to business firms on long-term for finance of fixed investment; and (d) the incredible events since 1949, seeing the mark become one of the hardest of world currencies.

B. NEW COUNTRIES

1

What about underdeveloped countries or simply new countries? First, observe that the United States in 1789 was in many ways an underdeveloped country. The fact that American development took

---

145 *Ibid.*, p. 150. In other words, a person delivering x ounces of gold to the Bank of France in exchange for Bank notes and later delivering back the notes would end up with x–h ounces of gold.

146 *Cf.* Ch. II. We do *not* refer to France's problems in making gold reparation payments to Germany.

the course it did and achieved the results it did should, I think, interest modern thinkers and rulers more than it does.

2

What are the peculiar problems of underdeveloped countries in the sphere of money and banking and how might central banks intervene? Casual empirical observation suggests these major categories: (1) suspicion of credit mechanisms, leading to hoarding of coins and precious metals — very high liquidity preference — and difficult soil for fractional-reserve banking; (2) absence of strong non-banking financial intermediaries taking up the savings of the public in exchange for short-term liabilities and investing the proceeds in primary securities issued by firms contemplating investment in fixed capital; facet 2 is related to facet 1 but also is rooted in the absence of a broad base of firms with widely recognized financial strength; (3) absence of highly developed markets for commercial paper; (4) a tendency — perhaps due to political instability and certainly related to facets 1-3 above — for savers to seek to invest liquid savings abroad, earning returns rather lower than the marginal efficiency of capital at home; the capital outflow being financed by favorable merchandise balances of payments; (5) certainly related to facets 1-3 while partially explaining facet 4, lack of well organized markets in long-term securities; such securities, when not well known in foreign markets, tend to be highly illiquid; (6) absence of large volumes of liquid assets, other than metallic hoards, so that manipulation of asset prices leads to slight response in the crude markets in which these are traded; (7) the importance of "subsistence" sectors featuring barter exchange so that money is *not* traded in many markets; leading, among other things, to inefficient use of economic resources, whether in terms of maximization of the value of national product or criteria of welfare economics; (8) great uncertainty about convertibility into gold or hard currencies of claims against citizens and governments of new countries; fears of expropriation or nationalization (receiving inconvertible securities) so that foreigners require huge risk premia and citizens try to convert their savings into foreign securities.

3

An impressive list of challenges. And then we have concentrated merely on monetary problems. One can appreciate the problems of governments of underdeveloped economies. Furthermore, these governments are often staffed by men untrained in theory, without practical experience and with an emotional heritage likely to make them unfriendly towards foreign capital and financial markets. These men often must deal with an economy offering no better than subsistence for many of its members, themselves illiterate. The drama of political leaders — not necessarily gifted or free from lust for power — obsessed with the desire to achieve development, but moved by forces of colonial heritage and race running deeper than the theory of economic policy, is indeed exciting.

How can central banking policy and technique deal with these eight facets of the monetary and financial problems of new countries? It would appear wise for the central bank of a new country to engage in a general banking business on its own account.[147] It is unlikely that there could be assembled private persons with resources, skills, willingness, and political power to undertake a large scale banking operation in a hostile atmosphere. Official aegis becomes especially important. It would be too much to expect that deposit banking could be brought into sudden efflorescence. Central bank liabilities largely would consist of notes. Of course, it could be disastrous if banks of questionable standing proliferated such issues.

The key policy objective concerns creation of well organized securities markets so that savings flows could be directed into investment, presumably accompanied by creation of highly liquid assets in the intermediate steps.[148] Establishment of a bank of issue might, for a time, permit some increase in investment through forced savings processes even in the absence of budgetary surpluses or increases in planned savings by households and firms, but the concomitant expansion of note issue could soon lead to hyperinflation.

4

How might the central bank improve the functioning of financial markets? *First,* it should recognize the importance of improving liquidity properties of the whole spectrum of non-government securities.

147 *Cf.* R. S. Sayers, *Central Banking After Bagehot* (Oxford: The Clarendon Press, 1957), pp. 108-133, especially pp. 115-123. This chapter, "Central Banking in Underdeveloped Countries," together with Ch. 12 of his *Modern Banking,* comprise an excellent discussion of a neglected set of problems.

148 Perhaps such aspirations are quixotic in view of illiterate masses barely achieving subsistence, etc. However, we can do no more than define goals. Others must judge their feasibility.

Once it had established its notes as being sufficiently "ultimate" to be desirable, the central bank would want to stand ready to *re-discount* paper, to purchase paper in the open market in large volumes in the face of liquidity crises, standing ready to recall its notes and reduce its holdings of financial assets when confidence was restored. In new countries the central bank cannot afford to be choosy about the paper it accepts. It has the task literally of creating financial markets, largely through the assurance its implicit imprimatur affords buyers of financial paper. *Second,* the same forces impelling the central bank to entertain a general commercial banking business impel it either to go into the savings bank business or offer guarantees to entrepreneurs that do. This strikes me as the most critical of the policy decisions: it would be too much to expect that direct relations between individual savers and suppliers of primary securities could be established in short order. Reliance would have to be placed upon attracting savings into savings accounts or, if so incorporeal an asset were suspect, into beautifully engraved, interest-bearing 30-or-60-day notes issued by the savings department or by insured savings and loan associations. *Third,* "cheap money" would have to be eschewed, particularly at the outset. Attractive yields would be necessary, both to get the ball rolling and to draw forth the savings of a suspicious public. However, the over-all result of development of financial markets increasing the liquidity of wide ranges of securities holdings, the creation of new liquid assets in the form of savings deposits, and increased confidence in mystique laden bank notes would be a reduction in cash preference. And reduced cash preference would tend to lower market-clearing rates of interest. *Fourth,* it would be hoped that the improvement in performance of financial markets could be extended to flotation of long-dated primary securities to the public. Private issue is likely to be of secondary importance in a new country, but government "stock" is another matter. We have learned enough about management of floating debt to conclude that funded indebtedness (indebtedness represented by long-term securities) offers greater opportunity for stable finance. In fact it would be doubly desirable if this debt could be placed with persons now hoarding gold and overseas securities. These could be diverted to a national stock helping to insure external convertibility of the new country's debt. And more binding ties could be created between the wealthy classes and the government. As creditors of the government, these classes would be more anxious about its survival and would exert themselves in its interest. We are reminded of Alexander Hamilton's Assumption policy (the federal government assumed state debt). We confess possible contradiction with twentieth century *Realpolitik.*

Turning to facet 7, enlargement of the exchange sector of the economy would be enormously abetted by solidification of commercial banking, perhaps through direct central bank action. Commercial banking in the best commercial loan theory tradition would provide working balances for merchants (who appear always to be overseas Chinese) mediating between producers and consumers. Also for producers who now would require money balances to meet payments for seed, transportation, etc., and in due course to meet payrolls. This would be an expansion of the money supply of a basically non-inflationary character: it accompanies a corresponding increase in the amount of work done by the money stock. New revolving funds would be created, but these would flow in newly opened channels of monetary activity.

On the whole, the suggested central banking policy probably has an inflationary bias that might discourage foreign investment. Why? There will have been a striking increase in the quantity and "liquidity" of financial assets that previously were poor substitutes for money. Liquidity (cash) preference will have decreased once the success of the program is fairly well assured. It is probable that one of the offsetting factors, an increased propensity to save, will take some time to develop. This suggests that the government might launch a program of fiscal stringency, using its budgetary surplus to purchase some of its debt from the public, thereby adding buoyancy to financial markets while restricting demand by restraining disposable income. Or the government might use its surplus, really the slack in demand created by its fiscal stringency, for construction, education, and other projects complementary with investment financed by new savings.[149]

We conclude with facets 4 and 8. In the United States' formative years crucial social-overhead capital — canals, toll roads, and later railroads — were provided mostly by English and Dutch interests. English and Dutch financiers provided the materials and paid for the labor costs of installation in exchange for bonds or equities in the projects. In the twentieth century, movements of private long-term capital (in the underdeveloped country context) are subordinated to intergovernmental transfers. We dare not explore ramifications.

149 In fact it is dangerous to separate savings and investment decisions in a system of family firms.

It is easy to see why new countries usually rely so heavily upon foreign capital: the great overhead projects — dams, hydroelectric projects, irrigation, construction of railways, canals, highways — that are *sine qua non* for other investment programs, require enormous expenditure of economic resources. Such expenditures can exceed the capability of an advanced, let alone an economically substandard, new country. Domestic securities must be exchanged for foreign material in the absence of gifts, unlikely to be more than a drop in the bucket when the full scope of development problems is understood.

What is the role of the central bank in attracting foreign capital? The answer is simple, perhaps deceptively simple: make securities more attractive to foreigners; also to nationals now "in" foreign securities. Hamilton had a firm grasp of this nettle. He wanted foreigners to have confidence in the intention of the American government that (1) they be able to collect their debts in dollars, and (2) they be able to convert dollar claims into sterling and guilders on a fixed basis. Of course, Jefferson and later Jackson were for hard money, Jackson to a ruinous degree (*cf.* Ch. II).

There are two steps in making domestic securities attractive to foreigners: (1) assuring their internal liquidity; if the relevant measure is the Y pound, the Y-pound value of Country Y's securities should be stable and readily realizable;[150] (2) assuring their exchange value in terms of gold and/or "hard" currencies.[151] We have discussed policies for achieving (1). What about (2)? The heart of the matter is *convertibility*. And convertibility, whatever form it might take, is keyed to acquisition of stocks of gold or hard currencies. We have already discussed central bank acquisition of gold hoards and foreign securities in exchange for now more palatable domestic securities. However, it is likely that credits from hard-currency countries would be necessary. Also that, if such credits were granted, there would be no need to use them.

Consider more detailed external problems.[152] Fixed exchange

150 Providing grounds for *a priori* sympathy with official efforts to prevent important fluctuations in interest rates. Reduced amplitude of interest-rate fluctuations would tend to stabilize securities prices. Of course, heed must be paid to foreign interest rates.

151 Hard currencies are currencies externally convertible into gold on fixed terms.

152 It is hard to generalize about *internal* convertibility. Intangibles are involved: history; the degree of the mystique of gold or silver. Of course, advocates of managed money would prefer an internally inconvertible standard — at least if the government were strong. The text argues that even such persons are unlikely to advocate freely fluctuating foreign exchanges.

rates appear desirable for a new country. Exchange risk reduces liquidity of a country's securities for foreigners. Furthermore, guarantees to foreigners that securities can be converted into given *dollar* sums would seem desirable, again pointing up foreign aid in the form of dollar balances for stabilization of foreign exchange values.

We have proposed a set of measures calculated, when taken in conjunction with more political actions outside of our ambit, to attract foreigners to a new country's securities, creating the wherewithal for economic expansion. Needless to say, many, if not most, governments would find our City-oriented remedies to be repulsive.[153]

C. A HISTORY OF CENTRAL BANKING IN THE UNITED STATES

1. Early Banks

We can depict the status of banking in the United States before 1790 when Hamilton detailed his proposals for the First Bank of the United States.[154]

The important examples of successful private banking in the United States available to Washington's first administration were the Bank of North America and the Bank of New York. The former was chartered by the Continental Congress in 1781, the latter by the State of New York in 1791 (although it began banking in 1784). The Bank of North America was a successor to the Bank of Pennsylvania, founded in 1780 with a capital of £300,000 presumably comprised of specie, British and French securities, promises of established persons to pay specie, etc. The Bank of Pennsylvania — led by "the financier of the American Revolution," Robert Morris — appears to be the progenitor of large scale banking in the United States and of our central banking history as well. Remembering that the Bank of England was founded in 1697 to provide funds for the English government's continental war with Louis XIV, it is interesting that the purpose of the Bank of Penn-

[153] We have stressed the contrast with early American governments. These showed great awareness of the "eight facets" and seemed sympathetic with our suggested measures.

[154] Hamilton's bank raised important Constitutional as well as economic issues. The Constitutional questions concerned the implied powers of the national government and ultimately were resolved in Hamilton's favor by John Marshall's court, later Supreme Courts, and powerful currents of history.

sylvania was "to give the Continental government financial assistance in the conduct of the war and more especially to establish the necessary contacts with France."[155] This recalls the etymology of the word *bank:* the root is Latin, concerning accumulations of capital. These early banks interested straitened governments because of their potential for intermediation between individuals who commanded ready purchasing power and the government. *Issue* of notes and deposit banking were not stressed. Nevertheless, both the Bank of North America and the Bank of New York (and, to a lesser extent, the Bank of Pennsylvania) issued notes and worked to fractional reserves. These banks, in contrast with the more typical and careless Massachusetts Bank (est. 1784) followed highly conservative policies. Nussbaum in fact waxes eloquent over the probity of these banks, referring to the "high standard of commercial punctuality" of the Bank of North America,[156] and saying of the Bank of New York:

> "the bank was very strict in its regulations and practices and became rather unpopular, but it proved to be prosperous and was able to weather all financial storms. The Bank of New York is the oldest bank still existing in the United States."[157]

2. The First Bank of the United States

1

The first Bank of the United States received its twenty-year charter in 1791. Obviously it was not conceived as a central bank in any modern sense: (a) modern views of central banking did not begin to form until well into the nineteenth century; (b) there was little banking going on in the United States in 1791; the Bank of the United States could be a general only in an Army of Oz. Rather, it was hoped that the first Bank would abet a deeper penetration of banking than had existed in the United States. It was a response to challenges included among the eight facets of Section B. While it was to be chartered by Congress and was to have a rather close relationship to the government, the first Bank definitely was not formed in order to afford direct financial aid to the government by mobilizing ready purchasing power. Broad economic statesmanship lay behind its conception.

---

[155] Nussbaum, *op. cit.*, p. 44.

[156] It received a Pennsylvania charter in 1787, more or less severing its intimacy with Congress.

[157] *Ibid.*, p. 46.

Specifically, the capitalization of the Bank was fixed at $10 million, $2 million of which was to be subscribed by the federal government, which "paid" its subscription by issuing a $2 million IOU to the bank, promising to repay (in legal tender) in ten annual installments. "Capital," as in the case of the Bank of North America, was to be comprised of specie and specie-redeemable stock (such as U. S. government IOU's). It is not surprising that foreigners became major subscribers: there was very little specie in the United States; Americans did not own large quantities of liquid assets. In fact ". . . after 1802 when the government sold its shares . . . 18,000 of the Bank's 25,000 shares were held abroad."[158] However, foreigners were not permitted to vote.

The Bank was granted issue powers and its notes were legal tender for obligations to the United States. However, "this sole legal prerogative over other bank notes was even made dependent upon the continued redemption of the notes in silver and gold coin, an obligation which was invariably carried out by the Bank."[159] The size of the Bank's note issue was limited by the amount of its capital: aside from deposit banking, it would have to operate on a 100-per-cent-reserve basis (including specie-redeemable stock among reserves). I lack detailed information on the deposit liability of the first Bank but Walter Buckingham Smith reports that the deposit and note liabilities of the Second Bank of the United States were about equal.[160] The first Bank of the United States was a fractional-reserve institution.

Steiner, Shapiro and Solomon provide a good description of other powers, privileges, liabilities, and duties of the first Bank.[161] The maximum rate of interest the Bank was allowed to charge on loans was 6 per cent. It was subject to Treasury inspection. It was permitted to establish branches, and did establish eight. In the course of its business it refused to accept notes of state banks unable to make specie redemption, a policy putting it in opposition to the inflationary forces of the rural districts. "Finally, it transacted the fiscal business of the

158 Steiner, Shapiro, Solomon, *op. cit.*, p. 215.

159 Nussbaum, *op. cit.*, p. 51. He gives details about the first bank's note issue. Denominations were $5, $10 and up. "In design and appearance they resembled very closely commercial instruments. The name of the individual endorsee appears on each note, though with the decisive addendum, 'or [payable] to bearer on demand' . . ."

160 *Economic Aspects of the Second Bank of the United States* (Cambridge, Mass.: Harvard University Press, 1953), p. 48.

161 *Op. cit.*, pp. 214-215.

Government, aiding in the collection of taxes and providing safekeeping for the funds."[162]

The Bank was a great success. As Nussbaum puts it:

> "From the beginning the outlook for the Bank was very favorable. The stock was over-subscribed and to a great extent taken by foreign, especially English, investors. In fact the Bank was a complete success commercially and paid high dividends to the stockholders."[163]

It also appears that the Bank provided highly useful commercial banking service by providing a revolving fund of credit for business enterprise.[164] No important savings-intermediary task was assigned. Only initial infusions of credit led to incremental claims against resources; subsequent credits had to be based on repayments by bank customers. And the Bank's obligation to redeem in specie limited possibilities of note issue. One hesitates to say more than that the large increase in banking service made possible by the Bank increased the liquidity of the assets of much mercantile enterprise and gave it access to aids hitherto denied American merchants.

It would be unwise to attribute more to the first Bank than its contribution of a sound note circulation and conventional banking services. It was in no position to conduct open-market operations on a meaningful scale. It could do little deliberately to regulate irresponsible state banks, beyond refusing to accept unsound notes. In other words, the first Bank of the United States was a very big, very important bank whose decisions and practices, including its interest charges, were important to the mercantile and financial communities. But it was not a Keynesian sun surrounded by satellites. Perhaps Steiner, Shapiro and Solomon are taking too narrow a view of central banking when they write:

> ". . . it is often forgotten that the first and Second Banks of the United States performed most, if not all, of the functions conducted by a modern central bank. They held the funds of the government, lent money to it, and aided in the sale of bonds and other fiscal functions. Moreover these banks attempted to provide a national currency of uniform value by issuing their own notes and presenting state bank notes for redemption in order to prevent their overissue. The Banks fought for sound government fiscal policy and attempted to stabilize domestic exchange rates and interest rates by providing mobility of

162 *Ibid.*, p. 214.

163 Nussbaum, *op. cit.*, p. 52.

164 Lacking social accounting data, the appreciation must be qualitative.

funds [elliptically referring to highly profitable arbitrage operations]."[165]

2

The first Bank of the United States, take it for all in all, seems to have been a smashing success both for its shareholders and from the standpoint of the national interest. Nevertheless its charter was not renewed in 1811. Why? The Bank of the United States was a Federalist institution, perhaps an archetype Federalist institution. It could not fail to be a bone in the throat of the Democratic-Republican politicians in power in 1811. The heavy representation of foreigners on the stockholder roll was, of course, a political natural for the Bank's enemies.

It would be unfair to counterpoint selfless friends of the Bank — together with its management — with political ogres seeking its destruction at the risk of national disaster. There were forces deep within American life, some within the authentic Jeffersonian tradition, assuring opposition to the Bank. Recall rural, later Populist and Bryan-Democratic, inflationism. Agricultural capital is notably illiquid. Furthermore, real forces guaranteed that interest rates would be high in early nineteenth century America. The state banks were cherished by the rural West, a source of the political power of the Jeffersonian Democrats. And one might suspect the Bank's motives in presenting volumes of state bank paper for redemption: the owners and managers of the bank had economic and political motivation for hamstringing state banking.[166] Oddly enough, the inflationist forces of the rural West were balanced within the dominant party by the aversion of others to paper money, including bank notes; Jefferson and Jackson were hard money men. The constitutionality of the Bank was still challenged by the Democrats in 1811: *McCullough v. Maryland* was not handed down until 1819, and John Marshall's decision would not have moderated Democratic feeling in any case. Finally, the basic social-political antagonism between Tidewater and the West was bound to be exacerbated by the bank, the very incarnation of Tidewater Politics. In all events, the Bank of the United States fell in 1811.

---

[165] *Op. cit.*, p. 226.

[166] On balance, I suspect that the verdict lies with the Bank in this connection; in interbank equilibrium, the result of the Bank's presenting others' notes for redemption upon receipt merely controlled the aggregate of note issue, not its size relative to others. (*Not* an obvious conclusion.)

3

Nussbaum and Chandler have described the aftermath of the bank's fall with particular vividness:

> "Seldom have party politics been refuted so fast by subsequent events. Shortly before the War of 1812 began, more than $7 million in cash had to be sent to the foreign stockholders in refund of their shares and $15 million had to be paid in specie to the holders of the withdrawn notes of the Bank . . . The local banks proved unable to fill the gap. The result was the 1814 suspension of specie payments and the protracted crisis that followed . . ."[167]

> "Freed from the moderating influence of the First Bank and favored by the inflationary financing of the War of 1812, state banks went on a spree . . . [T]heir note issue rose from $45 million in 1812 to $100 million in 1817. Virtually all of them ceased redeeming their notes in gold or silver, and their notes depreciated by varying amounts; the notes of many banks became virtually worthless . . . It was largely because of these gross abuses of the banking privilege by state banks and because of the extreme disorder of the monetary system that the Second Bank of the United States was established in 1816."[168]

In 1816, powerful political forces in the United States, favoring sound money, secured the charter of the Second Bank of the United States. It went into operation in January 1817.

3. The Second Bank of the United States

1

The major outlines of the Second Bank of the United States closely resemble those of the first Bank. Once again the government "contributed" 20 per cent of the capital (seven of thirty-five million dollars), this time in the form of 5 per cent government bonds. Once again, the remaining 80 per cent of the share capital was easily obtained from private, including foreign, sources.

We begin by listing major attributes of the Second Bank's constitution.

> 1) branch banking was provided for. After some uncertainty, the subordination of the branches to the home office (Philadelphia) was assured.

---

167 Nussbaum, *op. cit.*, pp. 70-71.

168 Chandler, *The Economics of Money and Banking*, pp. 252-253.

2) rather complex voting provisions resulted, for reasons not entertained here, in it being easy for insiders to gain control.

3) the Bank was forbidden "to purchase any public debt whatsoever, not [to] take more than . . . six per centum per annum for or upon its loans or discounts," the language of the Charter.

4) the Charter read in part, "the said corporation shall not, directly or indirectly, deal or trade in any thing except bills of exchange, gold, or silver bullion, or in the sale of goods really and truly pledged for money lent and not redeemed in time, or goods which shall be the proceeds of its lands."

5) the Bank was forbidden to extend loans to the federal government beyond $500,000 nor to any state beyond $50,000, and it was forbidden to make loans to "any foreign prince or state, unless previously authorized by a law of the United States," an interesting contrast with the foundation of the Bank of England and the Bank of Pennsylvania — especially in conjunction with (3). (Clause 3 shows that there was little connection between the Second Bank and a modern central bank.)

6) the notes of the Bank were to be acceptable in meeting obligations owing to the United States.

7) convertibility was to be maintained by the Bank: "the said corporation shall not at any time suspend or refuse payment in gold or silver, of any of its notes, bills, or obligations." The Charter goes on to provide that the Bank's obligation on liabilities that it failed to redeem in specie should mount at the rate of 12 per cent per annum.

8) the Bank was obligated to transfer U. S. funds from one part of the country to another and to disburse these upon request without charging commission.

9) the Bank and its branches were to be the depositories of Treasury funds "unless the Secretary of the Treasury shall at any time otherwise order and direct."

2

The pattern of actual operation of the Second Bank, after its bad start, was not much different from that of the first. The story of the bad start is told by Smith (Ch. VII). The Bank received but a small amount of specie in payment for its stock. Almost $21 million of the stock subscription was paid for with U. S. obligations. "Important blocks of stockholders in Philadelphia and Baltimore paid for their stocks by drawing on balances created at the Bank by discounting the Bank's stock as collateral security. [A report of a later date characterized this as] 'an operation of more potency in creating specie than was ever ascribed to the fabled finger of Midas.' "[169] Accordingly,

169 *Ibid.*, p. 100.

specie had to be obtained elsewhere. The Bank went to London where it obtained about $7 million in specie, not without considerable expense. Its first president, William Jones, remained sanguine, feeling that successful operations by the Bank would bring American specie out of hiding. But he was wrong.

Needless to say, the very forces leading to the Second Bank's charter created pressure for prompt resumption of specie payments despite the small specie balances available to the banking system. (Recall that the total of nominal issue was comparatively large.) As a result, by February 20, 1817, payments to the United States had to be made in gold and silver, Treasury notes, or notes of the Bank and those of state banks committed to redeem their note issues in specie and at par.

Resumption by state banks was scattered. It was effectively achieved in some of the coastal cities but not in the back country. Notes of the back country banks circulated at considerable discounts against specie. The Bank proceeded to render a delicate situation unsupportable by making large loans; the volume of nominal credit supported by a tenuous specie base was increased still further. This expansion in loans and discounts was largely concentrated in the western and southern branches of the Bank. By the middle of 1818 the precariousness of the situation was clear to its officers. They took action to reduce the Bank's liabilities, to contract the country's stock of monetary assets. The result was severe deflationary pressure as firms were forced to attempt to reduce their assets to cash. Also the Bank began to put severe pressure on the state banks. Such pressure easily applied: the Bank was a large creditor of the state banks from whom Treasury balances had been transferred to the Second Bank. The state banks owed the Second Bank more than $2.4 million in July 1818 and more than $3.6 million in December 1818. In Ohio, for example, the Bank's Cincinnati branch put indirect pressure on state banks to make specie payments. The result was widespread bank and financial failure.

The Bank's second president, Langdon Cheeves, managed to save it — with the aid of the Supreme Court's decision in *McCullough v. Maryland* supporting the Bank's constitutionality. But not without continuing highly deflationary contraction of the Bank's monetary liabilities (and loans and investments), particularly in the South and West. "Even before Cheeves took command, the Bank had established the policy of reducing loans secured by Bank stock at the rate of 5 per cent every sixty days."[170] At the same time, specie was obtained from abroad. The crisis was averted. The Bank's notes remained substantially convertible throughout, although redemption was limited to the branch location at which the notes had been issued. This meant, since exchanges ran against the South and West and transportation and communication facilities were so poor, that it was common for there to be serious difficulty in securing redemption. Probably the major lasting effect of the crisis on the Bank's political viability arose from the scandals associated with loans granted against Bank stock collateral — inside jobs.

3

The Bank increased its specie holdings to almost $8 million by April 1821. From then until about 1832 the Second Bank enjoyed a staid progress much like that of the first Bank. Circulation, which had fallen below $5 million, rose above $20 million by 1832, and was accompanied by a more modest rise in deposit liability. The proportion of specie to current demand liabilities of the Bank, built up to 61 per cent in 1821, was 17 per cent in 1832. The proportion was subject to a good deal of variation, but its decline well reflects the Bank's enhanced confidence in its position. At the same time there was a great increase in state banking. Between 1820 and 1840 the state bank issue rose from $41 to $107 million. This vast increase in financial assets accompanied great expansion in the economy's real sector: gainful employment in agriculture, commerce, and manufacturing rose from about 2.5 million in 1820 to almost 5 million in 1840; tremendous increases in fixed capital (including canal construction) took place, accompanied by large increases in real product. The period of 1820–1840 did *not* see price inflation.

4

Certain embryonic developments of modern central banking characterized the Second Bank's career, particularly under Nicholas Biddle. Interaction of the Second Bank with state banks was more pronounced than under the first Bank when the total of banking activity was so much less. The limitations of the Second Bank as a central bank — together with an interesting parallel to issues taken up by Walter Bagehot some years later — can be developed through an account of bank policy in 1828.

170 *Ibid.*, p. 120.

The Tariff Act of 1828 was passed in May, to become effective in September. Since duties were to be raised, "traders hastened to stock up on foreign goods,"[171] creating a short-term specie outflow. Biddle's policy called for contraction of bank credit, not as a facet of Bank rate policy, but as a passive response to pressure on the Bank's liquidity. However, other banks continued to discount freely, seemingly unmindful of the dangers of specie outflow. New York banks were particularly notable in providing notes for purchasers of imported goods, notes which tended to be converted into specie. These banks presumably were confident of their ability to liquidate various assets (for specie) if the need arose. An interesting fallacy of composition.

Biddle's papers include correspondence in which he reflected on bank policy in this situation:

> "[Against the ruinous consequences of these policies] it is the business of the Bank . . . to guard. It has accordingly placed itself in an attitude of security and strength, so as to interpose whenever it may be necessary to protect the community. The precise point of that interposition is the interesting question. While the state banks go on in their present career, it is hardly fair to throw on the stockholders of the Bank of the U. S. the burden of protecting them against the effects of their own improvidence . . . It seems more just that the Bank of the U. S. should reserve its strength — and let the state banks feel the pressure which their thoughtlessness occasions. Such is the present position of this Bank. It keeps within its limits — discounting cautiously — and when demands for specie come, it turns them over to the state banks."[172]

As a matter of fact, Biddle exceeded the 1832 prescription for watchful waiting as he had about two years earlier: he made open-market sales of government securities, thereby increasing indebtedness of state banks to the Second Bank and increasing his leverage for potential calls for specie redemption of state bank notes.[173] Smith interprets the sales as follows:

> "These sales were made at a time when demand for specie for export seemed possible. The disposal of government securities was no routine feature of central bank control of the money market such as has become customary under the Federal Reserve System in recent years. . . . The sales noted above were emergency measures undertaken to

171 *Ibid.*, p. 142.

172 Biddle to Ingersoll, Feb. 6, 1832. Biddle Papers cited in Smith, *op. cit.*, p. 143.

173 Recall that bank open-market purchases were forbidden by its charter. It had large holdings of U. S. securities due to the way in which it received its capital.

> strengthen the Bank rather than to restrain credit creation by the banking system . . . The Bank was severely criticized for making these sales."[174]

I believe that Smith understates the central banking attributes of these sales. After all, he wrote at the preceding page (p. 52):

> "In its relations with the state banks the Bank played a three-fold role. First, it acted as a watchdog of the bank-note circulation. The branches were discouraged from paying out state bank notes, and they were advised to send them in once a week for redemption, usually in specie or bills of exchange [referring to ordinary receipts of notes, receipts above and beyond the Bank's continuing stock held under its plan for keeping state banks in debtor positions]. Second, it occasionally made loans to solvent banks in temporary need . . . Third and most important, it acted as disciplinarian of the state banks through its collection of balances owing to it arising from the ordinary operations of banking."

I hasten to concede that the weight of evidence suggests that Smith's interpretation is on the whole correct. However, if Biddle were to conduct himself as a true central banker, and were concerned with protection of the national specie reserve, the Bagehotian formula would call for contraction of the stock of money.

It is interesting to watch the historical process of central bank regulation of bank liquidity unfold, however tentatively. Biddle's soliloquy displays contradictions inherent in a profit-making private enterprise assuming central banking functions: shareholder interest surely could be contradictory to the Bank's increasing — or not decreasing — its discounts during a liquidity crisis, risking throwing its treasure to the ground; nor is it profitable for a bank to reduce its earning assets and increase its specie holdings (or holdings of state bank notes) during booms.

5

The demise of the Second Bank resembled that of the first. It has been discussed in Ch. II. The fate of the Bank was sealed with Andrew Jackson's re-election in 1832. Withdrawal of U. S. Treasury deposits followed in 1833, but the Bank's technical soundness was not challenged even then. Its late stages featured severe contraction that appears to have been, at least in part, politically motivated (on Biddle's part). But why make these ugly events a twice-told tale?

174 *Ibid.*, p. 53.

4. The Wildcat Banking Era

1

The history has another hiatus, that between the demise of the Second Bank in 1836 and establishment of the National Banking System in 1863. Perhaps the Second Bank came closer to exercise of central bank functions than did any subsequent American institution until 1914. An outsider appreciating modern banking theory in 1830 might have anticipated that the United States would lead in development of central banking — it stood in the van. Instead this country was about to enter the dark ages of its central banking history.

1836–1863 sometimes is called the *Wildcat Banking Era*. The banking system was made up of banks operating under state charters or without charters at all. As time went on, state charters became available on a "free" basis: entrepreneurs meeting certain objective requirements could enter the banking business without seeking the particular favor of state legislatures. Requirements varied a good deal between states. As Professor Chandler puts it:

> "in some states the requirements were strict; banks could issue notes only by depositing with a state official an equivalent amount of high-quality bonds . . . But in more of the states the collateral requirements for notes were hopelessly inadequate, and capital and reserve requirements were virtually meaningless."[175]

Even in the "good" states bank note issue was not keyed to specie reserves: U. S. securities could create specie for *the system* only if gifted with "the fabled finger of Midas."

2

Doubtless the years 1836–1863 contain a number of outrageous practices. Data show almost unbelievable fluctuation in the volume of bank money accompanied by frequent and violent liquidity crises (although the United States did achieve spectacular economic growth in these years). At the same time do not assume that *laissez faire* fractional-reserve banking contains no internal checks to the volume of issue, that notes and deposits automatically will skyrocket in the absence of formal reserve requirements. Chapter IV's discussion of the fabled goldsmiths showed that simple concern for one's own solvency imposes limits on bank issue. On the other hand a few proba-

[175] Chandler, *op. cit.*, p. 257.

bilistic considerations suggest that *laissez faire* fractional-reserve banking will tend to be unstable quite apart from outright fraud:

1) Nature's Urn is apt to be turbulent. A probability distribution of specie claims for various volumes of demand liability for a given bank will feature considerable dispersion. To the extent that men without aversion to, or even preference for, risk became bankers, expected profit is likely to be preferred to certainty, leading to systematic instability;

2) during "normal" times a single bank expanding its deposits will have adverse clearings with the great bulk of bankers who are not expanding, but, during booms, expansion of deposit liability by one bank does not lead to adverse clearings with fellow banks expanding correspondingly. Adverse clearings become substantially inoperative as a check during expansionary periods except when currency drains are adverse clearings with the public;

3) inoperability of internal checks during booms does not alter the crisis-of-liquidity potential of an expansion in convertible bank liabilities without corresponding expansion of specie reserves. This is especally true in a system lacking provision for official purchase of wide ranges of paper during crises. It would require only a small disturbance in the form of heightened concern for convertibility of bank notes or loss of confidence by banks in credit worthiness of customers to set off the train of disaster always lurking in the background of a fractional-reserve banking system.

Statistics from 1836 to the Civil War show considerable expansion in the average level of bank money. First an abridgement of one of Chandler's tables:

STATE BANK NOTES AND DEPOSITS[176]

Year	No. State Banks	State Bank Notes Outstanding	Deposits at State Banks	Notes Plus Deposits
1834	506	$95 million	$76 million	$171 million
1836	704	104	83	187
1841	784	107	65	172
1846	707	106	97	203
1850	824	131	110	241
1855	1307	187	190	377
1859	1476	193	260	453
1860	1562	207	254	461
1861	1601	202	257	459

TABLE VC-I

176 Chandler, *op. cit.*, p. 258. The deflationary impact of the 1834-1836 statistics is understated. They do not indicate the contraction in the Second Bank of the United States' position.

Table I reflects the secular increase in the stock of bank money. Table II indicates the volatility of the stock of bank money from 1836 to 1860. It is taken from Chandler[177] and applies to state banks.

CHANGES IN STATE BANK NOTES AND DEPOSITS

(Percentages Expansion)
(+) or Contraction (—)

Period	Bank Notes	Bank Deposits	Notes Plus Deposits
1834-1837	+56	+67	+61
1837-1843	—60	—56	—58
1843-1848	+119	+84	+102
1848-1849	—11	—12	—11
1849-1854	+78	+107	+91
1854-1855	—9	+2	—4
1855-1857	+15	+21	+18
1857-1858	—28	—19	—24
1858-1860	+36	+37	+35

TABLE VC-II

Before attempting some interpretative comment, the operation of the Independent Treasury System should be considered. The system was established by President Martin Van Buren in 1840, abolished by the Whigs in 1841, and restored in 1846, not to cease functioning until 1920. In essence the Treasury established subtreasuries which performed the government's banking business, accepting receipts (which could only be in specie under the 1840 law) and making payments on vouchers, also in specie. The subtreasuries held huge specie working balances. In fact, "in 1855 the Treasury possessed half as much gold as the 1,300 banks in the country put together . . ."[178] In other words, this very large portion of the country's specie reserve was unavailable to support the structure of claims convertible into specie. The central banking mechanism, however primitive, was removed and a great part of the specie reserve immobilized; no important check was imposed on state bank note issue to replace that exerted, however imperfectly, by the Second Bank. We are prepared to unveil a scene of monetary chaos that builds up from Table II, no mean thing in itself.

177 *Ibid.*, p. 259.
178 Nussbaum, *op. cit.*, p. 95. *Cf.* Ch. II *supra*.

3

Keep in mind in reading what follows that the contraction of the American money supply from 1929 to 1933 was no more than 15 per cent. The decrease of 58 per cent in the stock of bank money from 1837 to 1843 defies the imagination. It largely reflects a corresponding reduction in bank advances to business firms operating in imperfect capital markets. The $161 million decline in the supply of bank money from 1837 to 1843 was an involuntary process, wrenching cash balances from households and firms. It produced many enforced liquidations as firms struggled to reduce their assets to cash. The liquidation process saw payments-expenditures streams diverted from normal commodity and bond market channels into bank coffers as banks desperately tried to pull in their horns, reducing their advances and note and deposit liability. There was, of course, concomitant excess supply in these markets: commodity prices fell precipitously; bond prices also plummeted. (Alternatively, you might say that the banks forced *ex ante* disinvestment and lower *ex ante* consumption on the system, necessarily bringing about liquidity-crisis side effects.) The fact that the system's real equilibrium state might be invariant against the reduction in the stock of money surely paled into insignificance beside the horrible transitional events.

The 102 per cent increase in the stock of bank money from 1843 to 1848 is impressive even though it is a trough-peak comparison. So rapid an expansion in the supply of bank money usually leads to briskly rising commodity prices, often encouraging further speculation and eventually leading to a catastrophic decline in values once the bubble bursts. The land-speculative factor in the expansion and contraction of bank money after 1836 (as before) was considerable, just as in the days of George Washington and in parts of the American West today. Sometimes frantic interest was expressed in development possibilities of sundry land parcels as the over-all expansion of population and economic activity produced a secularly rising land market. Banks lent large sums to customers planning to purchase land. Although a certain proportion of such loans was "refluxed" as sellers of Blackacre(s) repaid loans previously negotiated to "carry" Blackacres(s), a large portion of the proceeds found their way into channels of general circulation. Conversely, when bankers became queasy about the land market and called loans made to support land purchases, land values quickly collapsed. Fear bred fear. Of course, this meant that highly liquid traders could make large fortunes like those reaped by traders with bear positions at the end of the bull market of the late 1920's; they could offer cash for land when land owners were desperately pressed for cash in order to pay off their loans.

Finally, the narrow specie base for the stock of bank money made bank failure a routine event. The monetary system of the United States was excitingly untrammeled between 1836 and the Civil War; while boom and panic were part of the nature of things, the system *did* provide that secular increase in liquid assets that most economists think is necessary for economic development.[179]

4

We close discussion of the 1836–1863 era with passing reference to an observation of Steiner, Shapiro, and Solomon.[180] Their theme is that "even the pre-Civil War period was not without some of the characteristics commonly attributed to central banking." Specifically, centralization of reserves, special heed being paid to a plan of the Suffolk Bank of Boston which agreed to accept at par the notes of participating banks maintaining with it appropriate redemption funds.

5. The National Banking System

1

Discussion of the National Banking System (1863–1914) focuses on controversies crucial to the debate leading to establishment of the Federal Reserve System in 1914. These can be outlined.

A. Inelasticity of the money supply and its components
   1. secular unresponsiveness to the "needs of trade"; poor interconvertibility of notes and deposits
   2. seasonal inelasticity and poor interconvertibility

B. Reserve requirement provisions
   1. responsibility for volatility of American banking
   2. centralization of reserves

179 Chandler, *op. cit.*, pp. 260-262, provides some interesting background data. (a) there was wide discrepancy in specie prices of various banks' notes; some notes circulated at face value, others at a discount; (b) since about 1,600 banks issued notes by 1860, it was impossible for the ordinary person to know much about most of the notes he encountered; (c) some enterprising persons set up banks on the principle of recent Tangiers insurance companies, the "bank" being a tree stump in a swamp, the entrepreneur being ahead so long as he received valuable coneration for his notes, and staying ahead so long as he kept on the lam; (d) counterfeiting was rife; counterfeiters found it easy to copy the pedestrian workmanship of the great majority of bank notes.

180 *Op. cit.*, pp. 217-218.

C. Absence of a perfected acceptances market
   1. desirability of improving liquidity of commercial paper; real bills tincture
   2. transition from real-bills orientation to modern open-market practice (not without disastrous regression during the Panic of 1931–1933)

2

We pause to note more or less juridicial features of the National Banking System. Once this is done, mechanical features and the "transitional" controversies are studied.

Here is a partial list of features of the legislation of 1863 and 1864 (here called the National Banking Act after the 1864 legislation). There is no pretense here of either a complete catalog or a complete history.[181]

1) Note that enabling legislation for the National Banking System was passed during the Civil War. The legislative fathers wished to establish solid markets for U. S. securities, issued in volume as the war progressed. The title of the Act of 1863 was "An Act to provide a National Currency, secured by a Pledge of United States Stocks and to provide for the Circulation and Redemption thereof," implying well-warranted concern for stability of the money stock.

2) Capitalization requirements were imposed for recipients of National Bank Charters. The requirements worked against wildcatting but had no effect on the specie base of the supply of bank money. Banks were required until 1900 to deliver U. S. bonds to the Treasury in amounts tied to bank capitalization (but not less than $30,000). These could serve as collateral for national bank notes. Clearly the bond provision was a rather barefaced attempt to increase demand for U. S. bonds: the provision encouraged paying-in bonds as capital (transferring that portion of the capital to the Treasury).

3) Various restrictions were placed on loans, including a prohibition against loans on real estate collateral.

4) The note issue requirements were complex and important. These must be detailed. The notes of national banks[182] — redeemable in

[181] For a thorough and data-oriented discussion see Milton Friedman and Anna Schwartz, *The United States Money Stock* (Princeton: Princeton University Press, 1963), Ch. 2. Chandler has an excellent discussion in both the revised and third editions of his *Economics of Money and Banking*.

[182] The Act concerned banks qualifying for national charters and did not *directly* interfere with state banking. However, as Friedman and Schwartz point out, "shortly thereafter . . . a tax of 10 per cent was imposed on note issues of state banks paid out after . . . August 1, 1866, denying state banks *de facto* the privilege of note issue." (Quoted from Ch. 2 of a pre-publication manuscript.)

lawful money, including greenbacks — were to be issued against U. S. government bonds deposited with a factotum created by the Act, the Comptroller of the Currency.[183] *The nominal value of a national bank's notes was not to exceed 90 per cent of the bonds' par value or 90 per cent of their market value, whichever was smaller.*[184] No national bank could issue a volume of notes exceeding its capitalization.[185] National banks also were to maintain a redemption fund equal to 5 per cent of the nominal value of their notes. This fund — counting towards reserves to be held against deposits — was to be comprised of lawful money. (Bank notes were *not* "lawful money.") National banks were to accept the notes of other national banks at par.[186]

5) Reserve requirements for deposits were complex and important. As in the Federal Reserve System, banks were categorized as country, reserve city, and central reserve city banks. Country banks could hold 60 per cent of their reserves in deposits with reserve city or central reserve city banks; reserve city banks could hold 50 per cent of their

183 It is important to understand that reserve requirements for deposits and notes did not intersect except for the redemption fund which simultaneously satisfied both requirements.

184 The bond reserve requirement *per se* did not, of course, generate systematic specie or currency reserves. It *did* improve the marketability of Treasury securities and tended to lower their yields. It also created possibilities for Treasury policy by funding, possibilities that do not appear to have been exploited.

The bond reserve requirement led to a strange set of mechanics for the national bank note issue. The higher the price of bonds, the less profitable the issue of bank notes. Say that a bank owned $1,000 in U. S. bonds and had issued $900 in notes (for customers' IOU's). Assume that the bonds, originally selling at par, rise above par to $1,100. Assets worth $1,100 are tied up in support of a $900 note issue. Alternative investment opportunities might encourage sale of some of the bonds. The note issue might deliberately be contracted. Of course, note issue was *more* profitable when U. S. bonds sold below par.

Friedman and Schwartz, *op. cit.*, Ch. 2, discuss the profitability of note issue in some detail. They call attention to the fact that note issues (and, of course, bond holdings of banks) seem to have fallen short of optimal volumes (from the aspect of the banks). *Cf.* also a forthcoming volume of Phillip Cagan, *The Determinants of the Money Supply in the United States Since 1875* (New York: NBER, 1963). And, above all else, interconvertibility between notes and deposits was poor.

Note issue under the National Banking Act resembles a typical programming problem: multiple constraints (capitalization, U. S. securities, Comptroller balances), opportunity costs, etc. The aggregate result does not seem to meet sensible criteria for supply of bank notes.

185 The capitalization requirements concerned nominal value of assets turned in for bank stock. Reserve requirements were another matter.

186 Friedman and Schwartz, *loc. cit.*, point out that national bank notes — because of "government bond security required and the conditions of their redemption" — were "indirect liabilities of the Federal government . . . Their value did not . . . depend on the financial condition of the issuing bank. If a bank failed, the law provided for the immediate redemption of all its notes at the U. S. Treasury . . . The one respect in which national bank notes differed in usefulness from [U. S.] currency was that [they could not be used to meet] the legal reserve requirements of national banks, though most state laws did permit them to be used for this purpose by state banks."

reserves in deposits with central reserve city banks. Thus, *country banks* had to hold a reserve equal to at least 15 per cent of their deposit liability, but only 40 per cent (6 per cent of deposit liability) had to be vault cash: specie and Treasury currency. The *reserve city banks* worked to an over-all reserve requirement of 25 per cent of which at least 50 per cent (12.5 per cent of deposit liability) had to be vault cash. The central reserve city banks worked to a reserve requirement of 25 per cent, all in the form of vault cash.

6) The Comptroller of the Currency was entrusted with bank examination powers.

3

Consider the "mechanical" operation of the National Banking System. First, the *reserve system*. The burden on the central reserve city banks — most importantly those in New York City — was very great indeed. If country and reserve city banks held minimum vault cash, central reserve city banks could hold more than half of the reserves of the rest of the national banking system. Reserve requirements for country and reserve city banks were misleading: double-counting must be avoided; to the extent that country banks maintained reserves with central reserve city banks, the *system's* reserves were no larger; *aggregate* reserves were comprised of vault cash of all these categories.

The central reserve city banks (here called the New York banks) competed for deposits by the country and reserve city banks. These deposits, increasing reserves of receiving banks through favorable clearings, would permit corresponding expansion of earning assets. New York banks were encouraged all the more to pay favorable interest rates on demand deposits.[187] Also, the New York banks, like others, tended to expand their deposit liability to the legal maximum.

Continuing to fit together pieces of the puzzle of banking relations between the country and New York, there were withdrawals from New York by interior banks during, say, the Easter and Christmas seasons when demand for currency was high. Again, during periods of financial tension, featured by heightened currency preference, interior banks would tend to convert their New York balances into currency to be fed to their customers or held in their vaults. New York banks had to be in a position sharply to reduce their deposit liability from time to time. And, of course, there would be multiplied deposit contraction for the group of New York banks responding to a loss of currency. Accordingly

187 Demand deposits generally earned interest throughout the country.

New York banks wished to hold a substantial portion of their assets in very quick form: call loans to the stock market and other financial markets. Thus losses of currency to the interior led to multiplied contraction of the financial circulation — transactions balances of market operators. The stock market was made more unstable. From time to time operators had to try to sell securities in order to obtain monetary claims. *None* could succeed if *all* tried. Securities prices simply would plunge. More moderately, enforced liquidation by *some* operators, if accompanied by broad skepticism about the Market, could lead to panic. Whatever the reasons, financial panics were rather frequent from 1863 to 1914.

Mints[188] illustrates additional contraction necessitated by the country bank—central reserve—city bank relationship upon an increase in demand for hand-to-hand currency when the banking system was "loaned up." (So far the analysis has been confined to New York.) Keeping the systems closed, he first assumes that reserves are held locally and that the public withdraws $1 in currency from the country bank system.[189] This creates a reserve deficiency of $0.85 and would require a contraction of country bank deposit liability of about $(0.85) (6.66). Next, he assumes that three-fifths of country bank reserves are kept in New York, and that a $1 increase in the public's demand for currency would lead to a $0.60 withdrawal from New York by the country banks. The country bank picture is unchanged: currency withdrawn from New York already was included in their reserves. However, the New York banks, having lost $0.60 in deposits *and* reserves, have a reserve deficiency of $0.45 and will as a (closed) system be forced into a further deposit contraction of $1.80.

4

It has been assumed that increased demand for currency did not lead to issue of more bank notes. Additional notes could not be issued unless banks bought more U. S. bonds: deposit reduction would not relax the constraint on note issue. But considerable red tape and delay would be involved in acquiring bonds, having notes printed and shipped, etc. Additional bank note issue was not a feasible response to exigent demand for hand-to-hand currency. And the

188 *Op. cit.*, pp. 238-239.

189 Treasury currency. Bank note expansion is excluded from the analysis. *Cf. infra.*

country banks sometimes were reluctant to pay premiums for U. S. bonds when they simply could cash their New York deposits.[190]

Thus, the *sum* of bank liabilities depended on the public's preference for currency. To verge on critique *vis a vis* mechanics, there was not ready *interconvertibility* between notes and deposits: "if we assume fractional-reserve banking, then the major defect in the monetary system was that of a lack of a high degree of interconvertibility of hand-to-hand currency and deposits."[191]

Turn again to the mechanics of note issue, observing that, effective in 1900, banks were permitted to issue notes up to the par value of their bond holdings. Very briefly, footnote 184 showed that higher United States bond prices — certainly higher *relative* United States bond prices — led to substitution effects encouraging banks to reduce their note issues, especially if United States bonds already were at par. Similarly, lower United States bond prices led to substitution effects encouraging banks to increase their note issues, especially if the price reduction led to United States bonds falling below par. Expansion effects resulting from implicit capital gains and losses largely can be ignored: United States bonds were not a large enough component of bank portfolios to lead to "Giffen" results although United States bonds would be more likely to be inferior than superior as banking assets (noting that wealth effects here are from capital gains).

Consider effects of the business cycle on the volume of United States bonds. If government debt were retired during upswings and increased during downswings, the volume of United States bonds (measured at par) would fall during upswings and rise during downswings. Still, changes in demand for transactions balances and risk-premiums, etc., over the cycle led to contracyclical behavior of United States bond prices and hence to cyclically sympathetic movements in bank note issue.

5

Completing discussion of the mechanics of the National Banking System, consider the *absence of central banking*. Again it is difficult to avoid normative statements. In perusing the literature you will find writer after writer noting the absence of a central authority capable of feeding reserves into the banking system during liquidity

---

190 Country bank reserves would be reduced by the same amount under either method. Certainly no *individual* country bank would expect that sellers of U. S. bonds would deposit *its* cashier's check when it bought a bond.

191 Mints, *op. cit.*, pp. 236-237.

crises and extracting reserves when "speculative" expansion was feared. Of course, the Treasury could have performed this function to some extent, but Treasury officials had their own problems and genuflected to other idols.

Strengthening the pattern of inflexibility were the rigid reserve requirements. Banks could not legally make new loans when their reserves were deficient.[192] Squeezes on bank liquidity were quite irrevocable: banks could not help themselves, and the authorities were aloof. This picture can be colored white as well as black: major inflationary expansion of the money supply was precluded in the absence of specie inflow.[193] On the other hand, once reserves were lost through specie or currency outflow, a multiplied decline in the stock of bank liabilities could not be averted — perhaps at a time when substantial reduction in the community's liquidity was undesirable.

6

What of the over-all performance of the National Banking System?[194] We focus on the central controversies outlined at pp. 347-48. Chandler concludes his review of the System with a statement typical of majority opinion:

> "The inelasticity of national bank notes and the defects — or at least the inadequacy — of bank reserve requirements were dramatized by the recurring banking panics that occurred under the National Banking System before 1914. There were full-fledged panics in 1873, in 1884, in 1893, and in 1907, and serious credit stringencies threatened at other times. Unable to meet their obligations to pay cash on demand, most banks suspended payments for periods of varying lengths; some of them never reopened, a mad scramble to call loans ensued, and business activity suffered. The panic of 1907 was the last straw; popular disgust with recurrent panics made the Federal Reserve Act

192 But the practice of holding deposits in New York led to the equivalent of a federal funds market. Country and reserve city banks could earn interest on excess reserves (in the form of New York deposits). Presumably other banks, deficient in reserves, could obtain additional deposits at New York upon hypothecation of appropriate collateral.

Much the greater portion of excess reserves today are held by country banks. (Central reserve city banks hold practically none.) Transactions costs keep them out of the federal funds market.

193 Abstracting from effects of currency reflux.

194 This is a blanket citation of Friedman and Schwartz's definitive study (*op. cit.*, footnote 178 *supra*). Cf. also Milton Friedman, "An Essay in *Petitio Principii*," *American Economic Review*, May, 1962, pp. 291-301. Friedman shows that widespread suspensions prevented worse evils, in view of the poor inconvertibility of deposits and currency.

politically possible, though it had objectives beyond that of panic prevention."[195]

My slight statistical investigations are not altogether consistent with received doctrine. Consider first the chart below. While stressing the gravity of the 1907 experience, it does not reveal an erratically fluctuating money stock. As a matter of fact, the curves describe a smoother path of secular increase in the money stock than those projected for subsequent years. The year 1907, while "disgusting," pales in comparison with 1929–1933 when the sum of currency and demand deposits fell from $54.7 billion to $42.6 billion and demand deposits from $26.4 to $19.8 billion.

The gnawing suspicion that nature and art might not be in accord is further fed by data provided by W. Randolph Burgess, *The Federal Reserve Banks and the Money Market,* pp. 132-134. Burgess's data on bank failures and suspensions from 1876 to 1935 shows that from 1876 to 1878 there were on the average 2,075 national and 4,474 state banks in operation and that the average number of failures per annum of national banks was 11 and that of state banks 70. Corresponding statistics for 1898–1902 are 3,919 national banks and 10,672 state banks with annual failure rates of 7.6 and 42.0.[196] Burgess then offers the tables below on bank suspensions (inability to make cash payments).

DEPOSITS AND CURRENCY,
ALL BANKS IN THE UNITED STATES, JUNE DATES

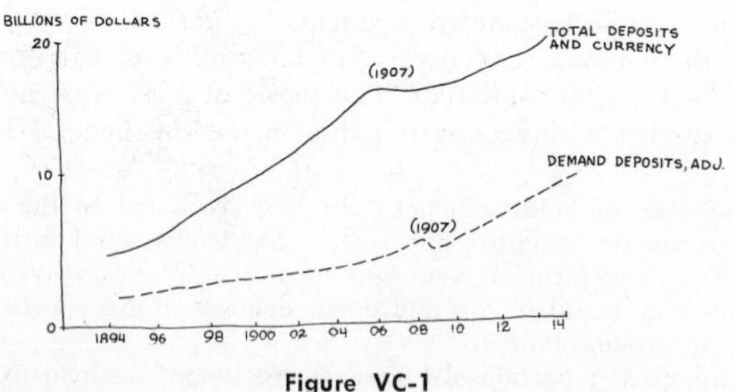

Figure VC-1

Source: Federal Reserve *Chart Book* (Washington: September 1960), p. 8.

[195] Chandler, *The Economics of Money and Banking,* p. 270.

[196] Notice the growth in state banking. This much displeased the federal government. (Recall that Congress imposed a 10 per cent turnover tax on state bank notes.) However, the decline in the importance of note issue relative to deposit banking, together with more liberal state regulation, stimulated state banking.

SUSPENSIONS, NATIONAL BANKS AND BANKS OTHER THAN NATIONAL

Average Per Cent Per Annum

	National	All Other
1863-1870	0.12	—
1871-1880	0.34	—
1881-1890	0.25	—
1891-1900	0.68	—
1892-1900	0.68	1.36
1901-1910	0.21	0.41
1911-1920	0.11	0.38
1921-1930	1.18	3.15

TABLE VC-III

The table can be continued, incorporating some of the data shown by Burgess, *op. cit.*, p. 134.

BANK FAILURES AND SUSPENSIONS

	National Bank Failures	Member Bank Suspensions
1921	0.64	0.73
1924	1.51	1.66
1927	1.17	1.34
1929	0.85	0.93
1930	2.22	2.26
1931	6.01	6.63
1932	4.49	4.74
1933	19.68	19.95
1934	0.02	0.02
1935	0.07	0.06

TABLE VC-IV

The scales fall from our eyes.

The data fail to support the hypothesis that the National Banking System tempests were succeeded by the fair breezes of the Federal Reserve.

7

At last we pick up the controversial threads of pp. 347-48.

(1) *Inelasticity of the money supply and its components*

(a) *unresponsiveness to the needs of trade, etc.*

Real bills forces were exceedingly powerful from the turn of the century right up to the formation of the Federal Reserve System. National banking controversy is heavily overlaid with this heresy: valid and invalid arguments often are hopelessly intertwined. We try to confine ourselves to the logically valid kernel of the argument, having exhaustively studied the fallacy in Ch. IV.

I suspect that valid criticisms of the "elasticity" of the money supply under the National Banking System centered on poor interconvertibility between notes and deposits. Devices for pouring currency into the system in the event of a panic did not exist. Changes in desired structures of holdings of monetary assets could undermine bank liquidity.

Professor Mints (*op. cit.*) offers a valuable discussion at pp. 201-204. Referring to the views of Wesley C. Mitchell, he writes:

> ". . . he charged that . . . just when they [banks] should be bold in using their reserves, they become timid and try to increase them. There should be more willingness to 'go below the legal reserves' when alarm is spreading."[197]

He points out that while lending without stint in the face of an internal drain is desirable, execution should be left to a central bank rather than to member banks:

> "the former can reasonably hope by a policy of liberality to reduce the severity of a panic, but the individual member-bank must assume, on the contrary, that the actions of other banks and conditions generally will not be substantially influenced by its own operations. Consequently, it is justified in assuming that a liberal policy on its part may merely mean loss of much-needed cash and a resulting impairment of its solvency. Under these conditions the need for concerted action by the banks is evident; and if this can be had, then the policy of liberality is appropriate, even for the member banks."[198]

Clearly there was no mechanism for "concerted action by the banks" built into the National Banking System. On the contrary, interior banks had every incentive to remove their deposits from New York during crises; any bank at any time had an incentive to steal away

[197] *Ibid.*, p. 203.
[198] *Ibid.*, p. 203.

the reserves of fellow banks. Either a central banking authority would have to be established or Treasury policy would have to become much more sophisticated and vigorous.

(b) *seasonal or within-year elasticity*

Officials might wish to minimize effects of seasonal movements in trade on money-market rates. This policy need not be based on a real bills approach; it is consistent with a monetary theory of banking. It is one thing for the authorities to respond to well-defined periodic "real" movements, another to be inert when irregular or fitful parametric changes occur.

The National Banking System lacked explicit mechanisms for countering seasonal forces. In the absence of excess reserves, deposits would shrink during seasonal peak demands for currency. The only countering force would be lower U. S. bond prices as the money-market became generally tighter, encouraging banks to issue more notes.[199] The Treasury simply was not sensitive or important enough to make a decisive impact.[200]

It follows that there would be seasonal fluctuations in money-market rates, reflecting movements in desired money holdings and encouraging (dis) economies in planned money holdings. And then, as Mints points out:

> ". . . a more important factor would be the building-up of cash balances by those anticipating increased needs for cash later in the year, which is merely a way of saying that velocity would be relatively low at other times than those of greatest need."[201]

Mints then shows that seasonal price movements would tend to be damped by "reducing seasonality in those industries in which interseasonal shifts in activity could be introduced without greatly affecting costs."

(2) *Structure of reserve requirements*

We saw that the practice of interior banks, of keeping deposits in

199 Recall that the national banks typically had substantially smaller U. S. bond holdings (in terms of the available supply) and, hence, note issues than were called for by profit maximization criteria. The details are in Friedman and Schwartz, *op. cit.* "Either bankers did not recognize a profitable course of action . . . or we have overlooked some costs of bank note issue that appeared large to them, which seems more likely." (*Ibid.*, Ch. 2.)

200 The share of the U. S. government in total expenditures on goods and services was but 1.5 per cent as late as 1929, and 11 per cent in 1960.

201 *Ibid.*, p. 236.

New York abetted instability of the banking sector.[202] It helped exacerbate problems of poor interconvertibility of deposits and currency. In event of panic the ultimate stress was felt by the New York banks — private firms not holding substantial excess reserves. Even conceding that the system worked pretty well, it is obvious that there were grounds for profound disquiet.

There was another "reserve" issue attracting much attention and of great importance in the transition to the Federal Reserve System: centralization vs. scattering of reserves. Arguments for centralization of reserves based on paramilitary and probabilistic considerations have already been advanced. Writers before 1913 were well aware of them:

> "Warburg likened centralized reserves to a centralized water supply for the purpose of fighting fires; and George E. Roberts compared scattered reserves with a defending array that had been broken up into small units and given no common command."[203]

But the National Banking System was without succor from its foes who also charged that the inverted pyramid of reserves — with New York City at the apex — was unsound or "wholly vicious."

There seem to me to be two really vital points. i) it was not impossible under the National Banking System for banks to borrow from each other. The crux is the adequacy of the *system's* reserves. Are there means of pouring reserves into the system if need be? Not under the National Banking System. Rediscounting and open-market purchases provide such means under the Federal Reserve System. The whole leads to the third controversy, absence of a perfected acceptances market. ii) the fractional-reserve banking house of cards can collapse if the public demands more reserves than exist.

(3) *Absence of a perfected acceptances market*

There was widespread desire, at least within financially "U" groups, for an American commercial paper market rivaling the money market of the City of London. Motivations differed widely from person to person.

It was hoped that an improved acceptances market would reduce

202 Poetic license, not without some justification, equates central reserve city banks with "New York banks." Recall that country banks could lodge reserves with reserve city as well as central reserve city banks.

203 *Ibid.*, p. 251.

the volume of call loans in New York. However, it is difficult to understand why one would want to see the vagaries of the National Banking System shifted from the call loan to the commercial acceptances market. And then, as Mints puts it, "it was also claimed that a discount market would facilitate international lending, thus steadying rates, and that it would be an aid in the promotion of foreign trade."[204] Why? If American commercial paper were to become a highly liquid asset, the American (presumably the New York) money market would attract more foreign funds, *cet. par.*; bills generated by foreign trade as well as inland bills would find a readier market with domestic and foreign investors. One wonders whether it was realized how difficult it would be to develop the subtle techniques necessary for copying the London model and subjecting the American financial system to the continuous overhang of foreign claims with its incipient, sometimes urgent, external drains.

We are led directly to the crucial arguments. Mints writes that Paul Warburg (circa 1910) showed awareness of the relationship between the acceptance market, liquidity of commercial paper, and a central bank:

> "he did not . . . contend that commercial paper is self liquidating, but rather, he argued that a discount market was necessary in order that it be liquid. He then pointed out very cogently that a central bank is essential to the satisfactory functioning of a discount market and that elasticity is dependent upon both."[205]

It is easy to see how commercial paper would become more liquid in a more perfect market, but how does the central bank enter the picture? Without occasional official intervention, heavy pressure on issuers of commercial paper and market dealers could panic the acceptance market. The liquidity of commercial paper and the supply of acceptance entrepreneurship are reduced by this prospect. Again, the London model, linking the money market to the banks, was appealing.

We are close to home. It is but a short step from Warburg's argument to central bank intervention in the acceptances market as

204 *Ibid.*, p. 252.
205 *Ibid.*, p. 252.

part of over-all banking policy. Increased liquidity of commercial paper can be a side effect of the ability of a central bank to accommodate a straitened acceptance market. Such accommodation is a necessary corollary to assurance of member bank solvency: collapse of the acceptances market is tantamount to collapse of the commercial banks, certainly in a world in which government stock comprises a small portion of aggregate bank assets.

There was also an illegitimate argument for meshing central bank policy with a perfected acceptances market, an argument that probably had the greatest influence. "Real bills" suggests that when the supply of short-term acceptances — generated by mercantile and manufacturing transactions — expands, the authorities should ensure that any excess be taken off the market, just as they should reduce the volume of available credit when the needs of trade diminish. Perfection of the acceptances market together with creation of a sympathetically reacting central bank would fulfill the fondest dreams of real bills theorists. The latent content of these dreams — never quite fulfilled — was manifested in economic psychosis in 1931.

In many ways the most virulent and influential opposition to the National Banking System had real bills sources. Real bills tainted the opposition's main theme: inelasticity of the money supply. But the successor system, the Federal Reserve, albeit partially conceived in sin, ultimately emerged as an advanced system, substantially free of real bills taint in its practice. Its story is next.[206]

---

[206] There remains another facet to the economic controversies surrounding the National Banking System: the independent treasury system, persisting until 1920 but much more important before 1914. According to Mints, "during the later years of the period . . . opinion seems to have been almost unanimously adverse to the independent treasury." (*Ibid.*, p. 250.) We know that the independent treasury system, among other things, locked up specie reserves.

As for possible Treasury intervention in the National Banking System, compare Mints:

> "the Treasury early developed the practice of using its balances in such a manner as either not to disturb the market or to come to its relief in time of trouble; but these operations of the Secretary [Leslie M. Shaw, Secretary under Theodore Roosevelt, President from 1901 to 1909] were looked upon as an evil which might be avoided, as it was believed, if the independent treasury were abolished." (*Ibid.*, p. 250.)

The slightest acquaintance with American history suggests the hopelessness of Shaw's task.

6. The Federal Reserve System

The *Federal Reserve System* came into being in 1914. This history features three lines of attack: (a) projection of the transitional themes, blending into; (b) a functional history of Federal Reserve development following De Kock's categories — custodianship of member bank reserves, service as a bank of rediscount and lender of last resort, discount rate policy, open-market operations, and certain direct credit controls; (c) integrated treatment of several major incidents, including the Federal Reserve's reaction to the gold inflow of the 1920's, its response to the earlier stages of the Great Depression, its role in U. S. bond support operations from World War II to the Treasury Accord of 1951, and the contracyclical quality of Federal Reserve policy from 1948 to 1960.

a) Projection of transitional themes

1

This section is rather a whimper. It is confined to the Federal Reserve's discount practices until about 1924. It stresses that (i), the Federal Reserve's infancy was prolonged by the coincidence of World War I with its birth, normalcy not being restored until March 1921; and (ii) open-market operations did not become a meaningful feature of Federal Reserve policy until 1923.

It is not surprising that projection of transitional themes boils down to so small a lump. Recall that discussion of elasticity of the money supply and reserve requirements under the National Banking System led to the conclusion that effective remedial action called for help for the money market from time to time and stress being (deliberately) imposed upon it at other times. And, since federal debt did not aggregate more than $1 billion in 1913 (and grew to no more than $30 billion by 1919), it is not surprising that Federal Reserve operations would be in private paper.[207]

What transitional ingredient has been omitted? The real bills doctrine (the commercial loan theory of banking). The doctrine appeared with a vengeance in Federal Reserve money-market operations

[207] The mechanics and laws of the Federal Reserve System have remained roughly the same since 1914. The basic pattern of reserve requirements and the way in which member banks purchase Federal Reserve notes and the effects such purchases have on bank reserve positions are the same throughout.

in the 1920's. Originally it was intended that paper eligible for rediscount should

> "have arisen out of transactions actually related to agricultural, industrial or commercial purposes, and the proceeds from such paper must have been used for producing, carrying, or marketing goods, and not for financing fixed investments or investments of a purely speculative character or for relending operations. Furthermore, eligible paper was not to have a maturity exceeding ninety days, except in the case of agricultural paper arising out of the activities of farmers in connection with the production, marketing and carrying of agricultural products and the breeding, raising, fattening, and marketing of livestock. For agricultural paper the maturity allowed was six months."[208]

Pure commercial-loan theory! Not surprisingly, the Federal Reserve's pattern of relationship with the acceptance (money) market caused it to lose touch with the realities of control. Real-bills adherents do not worry about the relation of rediscount rates to market rates and the amount of member bank indebtedness to the central bank, at least not if eligibility requirements are fulfilled.

Keynes gives an excellent account of the resulting policy slough, together with later attainment of higher ground.[209] The heart of the matter is easy to state: at least until 1925, the Federal Reserve often willingly took up commercial paper at less than penal rates. Witness Figure VC-2.[210]

---

[208] De Kock, *Central Banking,* p. 104. The pristine eligibility requirements were soon enough altered: "it was soon found [that] the restrictive provisions . . . did not allow of sufficient scope for the creation of central bank credit." (De Kock, *op. cit.,* p. 104.) By 1917 Federal Reserve Banks were allowed to make *advances* to member banks against government-security collateral. Indeed the rate on advances was *preferential.* In 1932 banks without eligible assets were allowed to hypothecate any collateral acceptable to the Federal Reserve, receiving *advances* from the Federal Reserve. This policy was reaffirmed in 1937.

The present-day situation is: actual rediscounting of paper (i.e., sale of paper to the Federal Reserve) is pretty much subject to the original requirements; advances to banks, the most common form of bank borrowing, can also be secured by government paper, and, of course, the 1932 policy, supported by the Banking Act of 1935 and the policy statement of 1937, would permit other collateral as well. Keep in mind the enormous increase in the importance of government paper, together with a relative, if not absolute, decrease in transactions financed by trade acceptances since 1914.

[209] *Treatise,* Vol. II, pp. 234-243.

[210] Treasury bills were not a significant item in the period covered by Figure VC-2. The chart shows that the vast majority of eligible paper held by banks offered yields above the Federal Reserve rate — certainly when the Federal Reserve's "buying rate" is considered.

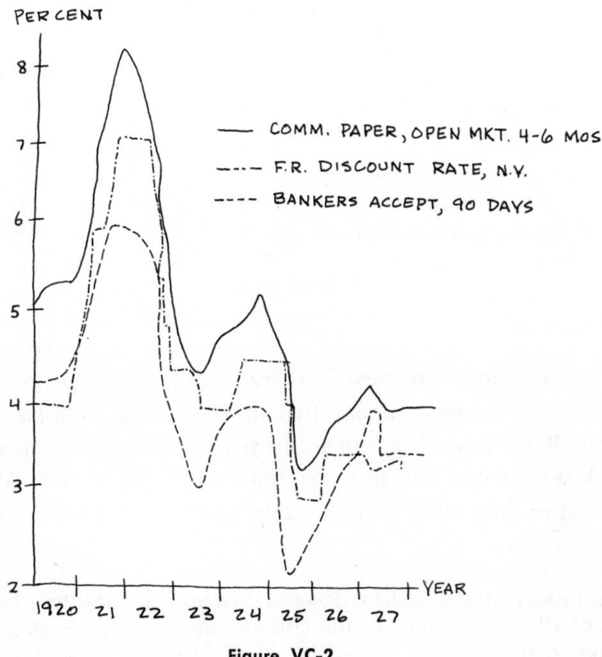

Figure VC-2

Source: Chart Book, September 1960, pp. 40-41.

The chart understates the case:

> ". . . in order to develop the New York bill market and to encourage bill-broking, which was thought to be a necessary preliminary to a functioning of the New York system like the London model, it was, more especially at first, made particularly easy and advantageous for dealers in bank acceptances to hand on their paper to the Reserve Banks."[211]

Specifically, the Federal Reserve had "buying rates" at which it was willing to take bank acceptances off the market which were below the official discount rate. These buying rates appear usually to have been beneath the market rates on bankers' acceptances. (*See Note A.*) Keynes appears to have been correct when he cited Table VC-VI,

211 Keynes, *op. cit.,* Vol. II, p. 236.

LONDON AND NEW YORK MONEY MARKET RATES
(July 1926)

	London	New York
Call money	3¾	4
Bank bills	4¼	3⅜
Central bank rediscount rate for 90-day bills	5	3¼
Central bank rediscount rate	5	3½

TABLE VC-VI

comparing London and New York rates, as being typical. The table shouts out its message: penal British Bank rate *vis-a-vis* permissive American Bank rate. Keep in mind that the "tradition against member bank borrowing" did not take hold until about 1925. Writing (as he tells us) in July 1926, Keynes summarizes the over-all results of the American system:

> "the history of the Federal Reserve System since the war has been, first of all, a great abuse of the latitude thus accorded to the Member Banks to increase the "advances" of the Reserve Banks, and subsequently a series of efforts by the Reserve authorities to invent gadgets and conventions which shall give them a power, more nearly similar to that which the Bank of England has, without any overt alteration of the law."[212]

What Keynes terms "the first phase before the above flaw in the system had been discovered," was from the latter part of 1919 to mid-1921. The price index for all commodities (1947–1949 = 100) stood at 87 in mid-1919 and at about 100 at the beginning of 1920. A peak of about 110 was reached in early fall, 1920, followed by a precipitous slide. The index was 60 in summer, 1921, when it bottomed out. Figure VC-2 above shows that money rates rose drastically during the inflationary and fell rapidly during the deflationary phase.

What was the Federal Reserve doing during this early test of its technique? It was leaning *with,* not against, the wind. This is not surprising if you recall that no onus was attached to bank borrowing or rediscounting with the Federal Reserve. Consult Figure VC-2: the relation of Federal Reserve discount rate to market rates frequently en-

212 *Ibid.*, p. 239.

couraged such borrowing. I cannot resist quoting Keynes, although it is abundantly clear that the reason Federal Reserve discounts moved sympathetically with the cycle, instead of against it, was the perverse relationship of Bank to market rate:

> ". . . For in 1920 those responsible for the management of the Federal Reserve System had not yet realized the enormous latent possibilities of inflation resulting from its failure to imitate the Bank of England system in one essential particular, and no one seems to have noticed that the main check on which the Bank of England relies was missing from the machine."[213]

Federal Reserve holdings of discounted bills stood at $2.2 billion in January 1920 and increased by 30 per cent by October 1920 when discounts were $2.8 billion. By August 1922, Federal Reserve holdings had fallen 85 per cent to $0.4 billion. These statistics are of an order of magnitude little less than total loans and investments of member banks: $25 billion in 1920. And Federal Reserve purchases and sales of securities — whether through rediscount or otherwise — have direct impact on bank reserves, leading to multiplied effects of bank loans and investments and deposit liability. The figures reflect the fallaciousness of the commercial loan theory of banking. The 1920 commodity price inflation could be said to have "increased the needs of trade." "Needs of trade" fell during the deflationary phase. Yet the Federal Reserve's actions increased and decreased these "needs." Influenced by the commercial loan theory of banking, the Federal Reserve was indeed a "wounded surgeon" — distorting Eliot's metaphor — operating on the economic system.

2

The transitional themes are concluded with something of an encroachment on the functional history. We pursue Keynes's account of the attainment of higher ground following official realization that the discount and bill buying policies of the early 1920's were inconsistent with central bank management of economic affairs. Keynes quotes the *Annual Report of the Federal Reserve Board for 1925,* stressing (p. 240) that the following passage "well expresses the twilight in which the Board still dwelt at that date as to how its system functions":

---

213 *Ibid.,* p. 239.

". . . Recent experience has shown that in general it is not necessary to maintain a discount rate above the prevailing level of call-loan rates in order to prevent member banks from borrowing at the reserve banks for the purpose of increasing their loans on securities. Member banks generally recognize that the proper occasion for borrowing at the reserve bank is for the purpose of meeting temporary and seasonal needs of their customers . . .; borrowing from the reserve bank for the purpose of enlarging their own operations is not considered a proper use of reserve bank credit . . ."

Thus, the birth of the "tradition" against member bank borrowing. From this time forward, one cannot merely consult tables and charts of yields on money-market assets and Federal Reserve bank discount and buying rates. He must keep in mind institutional constraints on member bank borrowing. "The general result is that the Federal Reserve system has approached nearer to the Bank of England system than was the case at first, and also that 'open-market policy' has come to be of fundamental importance in determining the volume of bank money." [214]

b) Functional History of the Federal Reserve System

1) Custodianship of Member Bank Reserves

The custodian function has roots in the controversies ushering out the National Banking System. "Logical" centralization of reserves concerns not their physical location, but rather their service as *systemic* reserves available — through discounts and advances and open-market purchases — more or less independently of members' initial contributions. The Federal Reserve System earned high marks on "logical centralization" from the outset. The failure of the early 1930's was due to poor execution and Nature's Urn which could be *very* capricious before 1934.

Pending detailed discussion of the early 1930's, certain purely factual matters can be disposed of:

1) it would seem that *statutory* provision for commercial banks holding minimum credits with a central bank was pioneered by the Federal Reserve Act. Manipulation of these requirements never has appealed to the authorities as much as one might expect. Still, while perhaps once associated with standards for banking probity, reserve requirements now belong more to the realm of price and employment policy.

2) under the 1914 Act member banks had to hold minimum reserves amounting to 5 per cent of their time-deposits and 12, 15, or 18 per cent of their demand-deposits, depending upon whether they were

214 *Ibid.*, p. 243.

country, reserve city, or central reserve city banks.[215] Certain portions of these reserves had to be held in vault cash, the rest in deposits with the Federal Reserve. Then, in 1917 the legal reserve requirements were altered so that legal reserves were restricted to deposits with the Federal Reserve, vault cash not counting as reserve money. The per centum reserve requirements became 3, 7, 10, and 13. The 1917 requirements remained unchanged until 1935 when discretionary power over reserve requirements was granted to the Board within well defined limits. Finally there was the amendment of July, 1959 permitting vault cash to count as part of legal reserves, effective November 24, 1960.

3) under the Federal Reserve there always have been different reserve requirements for demand and time deposits and for different kinds of banks. The supply of money can change independently of official policy. To repeat, much of the criticism of this seems to me to be pseudo-science. The authorities can respond rather soon to undesired changes in the money supply. On the other hand, critics have been virtually unanimous in damning this feature of the Federal Reserve.

2) Bank of Rediscount and Lender of Last Resort[216]

1

This topic was treated at length while projecting the transitional themes. Surely we need not re-engage the date for 1920-1925. To repeat, the long-run view is dominated by the secular increase in the importance of government as against private debt, together with the secular decline in the importance of trade acceptances — *not* including paper generated by instalment credit. Attention has shifted from Federal Reserve rediscount of commercial paper to Federal Reserve advances against U. S. securities collateral.

There are three other subthemes. *First,* the 1934 legislation, together with sundry deposit insurance programs, precludes catastrophic internal drains. Effective discard of the domestic gold standard has diluted the dramatic potential of the Federal Reserve's role as a lender of last resort. The FDIC has done the rest. *Second,* substantial abandonment of real bills (commercial loan) theories of banking has led the Federal Reserve to react to changed Discounts and Advances,

[215] I have not compared total reserve requirements (with inter-bank deposits netted out) for the national banks before and after the Federal Reserve Act. (National banks had to join the Federal Reserve System.) To the extent that reserve-eligible items simply were transferred to new repositories, the problem of transition is trivial. If additional reserves were required, it would be simple for the central bank to issue monetary liabilities for non-monetary financial assets. Differential effects on country *vis-a-vis* central reserve banks, for example, also have been ignored.

[216] *Cf.* also Ch. VB.

whether due to bank reflex (to Federal Reserve sales) or not, in accordance with Federal Reserve views of desirable bank reserve positions instead of passively to respond to demands for credit generated by the "needs of trade." Substantively, the "rediscount-and-lender-of-last-resort" function has considerably changed, but not the surface appearance. The 1925 *Annual Report,* together with Regulation A, as revised in 1955, have led the Federal Reserve to take initiative in controlling at least its secular discounts and advances; continuous member bank borrowing is not kosher. This purposiveness should not be exaggerated; Meigs, for example, has developed strong evidence that member banks' borrowing from the Federal Reserve is apt to be cyclical in character (*cf.* A. James Meigs, *Free Reserves and the Money Supply* [Chicago: University of Chicago Press, 1962]). Still, Meigs also suggests that a Board unbeguiled by free-reserve criteria for the state of monetary ease can obtain a good grip on the money supply; total-reserve (*v.* reserve-position) criteria would abet monetary control and can be achieved with present tools. (*See Note B.*) Third, the *Chart Book* (Sept. 1960, pp. 40-41) will show that Federal Reserve discount rate has more often been penal as time has passed: it has tended to be above Treasury bill rate. But the relationship has been irregular since 1952. Furthermore differences between the rates have often been very slight — especially since about 1954 — so that *this* impediment to member bank borrowing has not been very firm. (*See Note C.*)

2

It would be helpful to collect basic data for the post-1925 period, data such as member bank borrowings from the Federal Reserve, excess reserves, and free reserves. Consult Table VC-VII.

Referring to the 1930's and 1940's, De Kock writes:

> "in the United States, apart from the effects of the inflow of gold and the revaluation of gold reserves, the open-market operations of the Federal Reserve System virtually nullified the normal working of rediscounts."[217]

True enough. In due course, this phenomenon of enormous "excess" bank liquidity will be exhaustively considered. But the data speak for themselves: the banks of the later 1930's and the 1940's needed no help from the central bank as a lender of last resort.

[217] *Op. cit.,* p. 108. He refers to huge Federal Reserve purchases of U. S. securities during World War II, building up member bank reserves *pari passu.*

MEMBER BANK BORROWINGS

(discounts and advances for 1926–1928),

OTHER CREDIT TO BANKS, EXCESS AND FREE RESERVES,
1926–1960 (end of year)
(in millions of dollars)

Year	Member Bank Borrowings	All Other, Mainly Float	Excess Reserves	Free Reserves
1926	680			
1927	500			
1928	1,050			
1929	801	396	48	— 753
1930	337	292	73	— 264
1931	763	410	60	— 703
1932	281	– 57	526	245
1933	95	142	766	671
1934	10	32	1,748	1,738
1935	6	58	2,983	2,977
1936	7	57	2,046	2,039
1937	16	47	1,071	1,055
1938	7	47	3,226	3,219
1939	3	99	5,011	5,088
1940	3	114	6,646	6,643
1941	5	180	3,390	3,385
1942	4	483	2,376	2,372
1943	90	659	1,048	958
1944	265	654	1,284	1,019
1945	334	702	1,491	1,157
1946	157	821	900	743
1947	224	729	986	762
1948	134	842	797	663
1949	118	607	803	685
1950	142	1,119	1,027	885
1951	657	1,380	826	169
1952	1,593	1,306	723	— 870
1953	441	1,027	693	252
1954	246	1,154	703	457
1955	839	1,412	594	— 245
1956	688	1,703	652	— 36
1957	710	1,494	577	— 133
1958	557	1,543	516	— 41
1959	906	1,493	482	— 424
1960	94	1,723	768	674

TABLE VC-VII

Source: Economic Report of the President, January, 1961, p. 176.

Member bank borrowings in the late 1950's, while of the same order of magnitude as in the late 1920's, are relatively much smaller (also *nominally*): commercial bank loans and investments rose from $49.4 billion in June 1929 to more than $190 billion in December 1959.[218] The Federal Reserve's discipline was much stiffer in the late 1950's. What might have been pious hopes in the *Annual Report* for 1925 perhaps may come to fruition.[219]

3) *Discount Rate (Bank Rate) Policy*

1

Earlier, pure Bank rate policy was defined as being based on the effects of changes in Bank rate unaccompanied by funding or open-market operations. Practically from the beginning, people have been concerned with "announcement effects" of discount rate changes. On the other hand, it becomes obvious that — at least when banking is not concentrated — announcement effects are more likely to be psychological than tangible. In the United States, money-market rates are not tied to Bank rate with anything like the precision of British practice. Governor Strong (of the New York Federal Reserve Bank) was much impressed (in 1927) with psychological effects:

> ". . . Unfortunately, it has always seemed to me that the country has given exaggerated importance to change of the discount rate sentimentally. The danger is that an advance of rate will operate as a sort of sledge hammer blow to the feeling of confidence and security of the country as to credit . . . [T]hat reaction has been somewhat modified by these open-market operations . . . The effect is less dramatic and less alarming to the country."[220]

---

218 It is shown in Appendix A to Ch. VA and in Ch. XIV that banks in a system such as ours must show money illusion.

219 Be careful in interpreting the table. Excess reserves might decline, not because of Federal Reserve restriction, but because the banks increased their investments. Furthermore, the table does not reflect open-market operations. Thus the 1941-1945 data gaze at us with downy-cheeked innocence, but this was a period of drastic monetary expansion.

It cannot be emphasized enough that the influential Riefler-Burgess reserve-position hypotheses does not distinguish between changes in reserve positions brought about by decreased unborrowed reserves accompanied by correspondingly increased bank borrowing from those unaccompanied by such borrowing.

Finally, remember that member bank borrowings — discounts *per se* are no longer important — fluctuate over short periods somewhat exogenously to Federal Reserve planning.

220 Quoted by J. M. Keynes, *op. cit.*, Vol. II, p. 258.

What are these psychological effects supposed to be? It is held that discount rate changes announce that "we will huff and puff and blow your house down." Decision units see that official teeth are bared. They anticipate that borrowing soon is going to be more costly, that demand for goods and services is likely to be damped down. Accordingly, they plan retrenchment of expenditures and inventory commitments. They postpone physical investment programs.[221]

There is a flaw in Governor Strong's ogre. Announcement effects may be in the wrong direction. Warren L. Smith[222] runs through the analysis. He first points out that it is possible for an announcement of higher discount rate, *cet. par.* to produce pessimistic expectations. But what if this announcement had been anticipated?

> "The increase may serve to confirm and perhaps to strengthen their expectations of rising sales and prices and may well produce some acceleration of production and capital expansion plans."[223]

And then there is a point not stressed by Smith: business men (not having anticipated the announcement) will be aware of the lag between announcement and execution: they might desperately attempt to borrow before rates rise and to buy before the inflationary spiral (announced by the authorities to be impending). This will permit a renewed increase in monetary velocity. The short-run effects of the announcement again are perverse.

The upshot seems so clouded to Smith that he recommends adoption of an automatic rule that discount rate be placed about 1 per cent above Treasury bill rate (the discount rate being subject to weekly change). Hoped-for effects include:

1) control of member-bank borrowing offsetting open-market sales (my quarrel with his phrasing, if not purport, is set out in Note B);

2) discouraging the business community from reading things into announced changes in discount rate.

Under Smith's rule discount rate would respond to market forces, making open-market operations more effective; it would not be playing a regulatory role on its own account. Discount rate would be a pale

---

221 Discount rate stood at 1 per cent from 1947 to 1948. Its variance was very small during the Truman administration. During the Eisenhower administration, the Federal Reserve seems to have relied to a certain extent on announcement effects. Clearly, the doctrine's halcyon days were in the 1920's.

222 *Loc. cit.*, pp. 174-175.

223 *Ibid.*, p. 174.

reflection of substantive policies being pursued through different mechanisms.

2

It was hoped at the outset of the Federal Reserve that its discount rate would emulate British Bank rate, but it was not realized that at the heart of the British mechanism was the Bank of England's open commitment to perform as lender of last resort at penal Bank rate. As Keynes pointed out, Federal Reserve Lender of Last Resort and Rediscount Policy were muddled. In much of the 1920's, the Federal Reserve performed as lender of last resort at a permissive discount rate. Then in the crisis of 1931–1932, it made its discount rate penal but deserted its responsibility as lender of last resort. "After such knowledge what forgiveness."[224]

4) Open-Market Operations

(a) chronology

1

Open-market operations, for some time the most important arrow in the Federal Reserve quiver, were not important in early conceptions of Federal Reserve policy. I suspect that the commercial loan theory of banking explains much. Open-market operations have come to reflect direct and purposive intervention by central banks in securities markets. But, early conceptions of Federal Reserve policy stressed sympathetic response to the needs of trade. Rediscounting and allied procedures seemed to be more to the point and held the center of the stage. Furthermore, modern open-market operations have been contra-cyclical. Purchases are made by the central bank during the down-swing of the business cycle (or in response to an increase in liquidity preference) and sales during the up-swing of the cycle (or in response to decreased liquidity preference). Needless to say, countercyclicality and the commercial loan theory of banking are incompatible: the needs of trade are expanding during the up-swing and contracting during the down-swing. The fact is that the development of open-market technique by the Federal Reserve was rather haphazard.

---

[224] Still there was in the 1920's widespread euphoria about the powerful impact of the smallest measures of central bank policy. Compare Keynes's *Treatise* with his *General Theory*.

2

It might be better to tabulate some basic data first. The data that are of particular interest concern Federal Reserve security holdings and discounts and advances to member banks. We rely on the September 1960 *Chart Book* (p. 4) for the pre-1929 data. (Note that the order of magnitude of member bank reserves was $2 billion.)

RESERVE BANK CREDIT

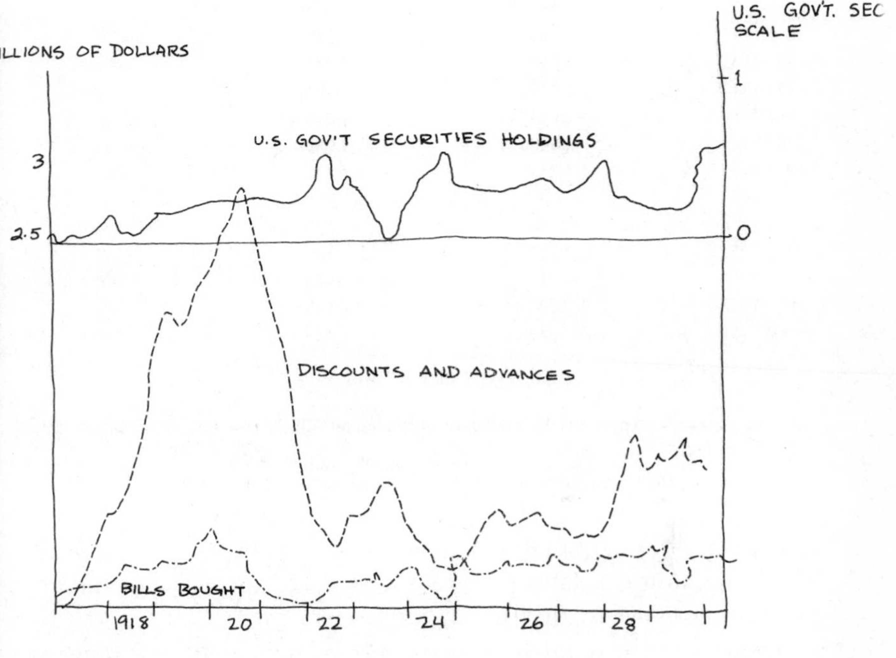

Figure VC-3

The 1929–1960 data are shown in difference form (changes) in Table VC-VIII.

What inferences can be drawn from these data? Are these inferences consistent with history?

From 1922 through 1924 movements in Federal Reserve holdings of U. S. securities and in its discounts and advances were negatively

RESERVE BANK CREDIT

(End of year in millions of dollars)

Period	U. S. Government Securities	Member Bank Borrowings	All Other, Mainly Float
1930-1929	+198	—464	—104
1931-1930	+133	+426	+118
1932-1931	+1,077	—482	—353
1933-1932	+578	—186	+85
1934-1933	—2	—85	—110
1937-1934	+135	+6	+15
1938-1937	—1	—9	0
1941-1938	—345	—2	+133
1945-1941	+21,489	+329	+522
1949-1945	—5.421	—216	—95
1950-1949	+2,058	+24	+512
1951-1950	+3,064	+515	+161
1952-1951	+991	+936	—74
1953-1952	+1,239	—1,152	—279
1954-1953	—722	—195	+127
1955-1954	—315	+593	+258
1956-1955	+163	—151	+291
1957-1956	—783	—22	—209
1958-1957	+2,330	—153	+49
1960-1958	+653	—463	+180

TABLE VC-VIII

Source: Economic Report of the President (Washington: Government Printing Office, 1961), p. 176.

Note: The post-1951 order of magnitude of reserve balances is $20 billion.

correlated.[225] Interpretation is difficult: this was the end of a transition from the absurd heights reached by discounts and advances in 1920. One thing is clear: the two policy levers were working in opposite directions; there could have been no consistent policy of constraint or expansion. Recall that rediscount policy did not begin to get straightened out until about 1925.

[225] Recall that Federal Reserve holdings of bills tended to reflect the same forces as did discounts and advances. The Federal Reserve did not appear to deal aggressively with its bill holdings until about 1928. The Federal Reserve maintained a buying rate for bills lower than its rediscount rate. These pieces of information are linked by the continuing concern of the Federal Reserve officials to perfect the New York acceptances market.

Figure VC-3 would justify the following conclusion: until 1928, the "bills bought" account should be lumped with "discounts and advances" — the sympathy of their movements was very great; open-market operations proper were performed with government securities.

The 1925–1927 record is different: holdings of United States securities and discounts-and-advances were positively correlated. However, open-market policy was not very important. Considerable expansion of discounts and advances (especially through 1926) was not meaningfully offset by open-market sales. Deliberate ease was practiced. Discount rate was particularly low in relation to market rates from 1925 to 1927. Credit was expanding with the connivance of Federal Reserve officials, perhaps hoist by their "reserve-position" petard.

The 1928–1929 story is futile and tragic. The Bull Market proceeded apace until Fall 1929. Hesitant reduction of Federal Reserve holdings of commercial and Government paper indicates that the authorities were taking mincing steps towards reducing the flow of credit into the financial circulation, but the discount window was kept open as call-money rates zoomed upwards. It still is not clear as to just what concitations of what backward devils caused the Federal Reserve to pursue such a policy, although it must be remembered that the System's coordination was much worse than it is now.

The 1922 to 1929 period permits some general comment: (1) open-market *sales* were crucial in open-market policy; the Federal Reserve's "governments" ammunition was limited in supply — sales of some $450 million of United States securities from the end of 1927 to mid-1929 left the Federal Reserve with less than $150 million in Governments — but Federal Reserve holdings were not insignificant and probably would have been adequate to do the trick in 1928–1929 if discounts and advances had been kept under control; (2) the Federal Reserve obviously was very hesitant to use its commercial-bill holdings in open-market sales; its commitment to support the liquidity of these instruments was important and was taken very seriously; (3) the scale of operations was not imaginative; it took World War II to demonstrate what could be done; (4) it seems that economic indicators in the 1920's pointed in all directions at once; hindsight should not cause too dim a view of Federal Reserve leadership.

Turn to the Table of Reserve Bank Credit. It shows the markedly timid over-all performance of the Federal Reserve from the end of 1929 to the end of 1931, a period in which unemployment rose from 1,550,000 to 8,020,000.[226] Bank failures markedly increased. The sum

[226] Gross National Product fell from $207 to $173 billion (both in 1960 prices), GNP deflator from 57.4 to 49.9 (1954 = 100), wholesale prices from 61.9 to 47.4 (1947-1949 = 100), and, on the same base, farm product prices from 58.6 to 36.2.

of demand deposits and currency fell from $26.4 billion to $21.9 billion, time deposits falling $2.2 billion. Growing concern for bank solvency led depositors to increase their currency holdings by $0.9 billion. It seems that the Federal Reserve should have sought to inject massive stocks of liquidity into the system, but it did not.

The December 1931 (really February 1932)–December 1933 story is quite different.[227] The Federal Reserve purchased more than $1.6 billion in government securities. Nevertheless, the total of demand deposits and currency declined another $2 billion as banks, badly singed by the panic, built up excess and free reserve positions. More than $660 million in borrowings were repaid by member banks over this period. By the end of 1933 Treasury bill rate had fallen to 0.515 per cent per annum (from 1.402 per cent in 1931) and prime commercial paper yielded less than 1.75 per cent. However, since discount rate stood well above money-market rates in 1932 and 1933, the banks (individually) had all the more incentive to reduce indebtedness with the Federal Reserve.[228]

The end of 1933 found free reserves of $671 million. It ushered in an era of massive excess and free reserves that was to last until we entered World War II. The state of the system was equivalent to one in which open-market purchases had been "carried to the point of saturation" (in Keynes's phrase).[229] Short-term pure interest rates were driven down to miniscule levels, long term rates to a point where traders, including banks, may have feared capital loss more than they treasured running yields. Banks became satisfied to hold unprecedentedly large excess reserves. Monetary policy had reached a dead end. Needless to say, open-market purchases would have had a muffled impact in the presence of these enormous excess reserves and in fact did not play an important role before 1942.

Such was the lull before the storm. Monetary expansion over the 1941–1946 period was accomplished through almost pure open-market policy. The implications (and mechanics) of the +$21,489 million entry for 1945–1941 in column 2 of the Reserve Bank Credit Table, have been considered. It was then that the primacy of open-market policy among central bank vehicles was secured in this country. The

227 Note the habitual indebtedness of American banks to the central bank.

228 Of course, there was a banking panic in 1932–1933, culminated by the moratorium of spring 1933. The text compares Dec. 1931 with *Dec.* 1933 when the panic was ended. The panic itself is discussed elsewhere.

229 *Cf.* Ch. II *supra.* The importance of gold inflow is stressed there.

Federal Reserve was supplied with ammunition. Member bank holdings of government paper — as well as those of the non-banking public — were enormously augmented, establishing a broad market. Commercial paper simply was swamped out. Remaining doubts about the potential of open-market operations were dispelled.

The enormous overhang of short-term U. S. debt characterizing the post-war period — together with the Korean Conflict and sundry politics — led to support programs initiated by the Treasury and executed by a blushing Federal Reserve.[230] The origin of such programs goes back at least as far as 1937. Suffice it to say for the nonce that the years 1950–1952 saw marked expansion of the reserve base through open-market purchases and member bank borrowings.

In 1953, the first year of the Eisenhower administration, open-market purchases were accompanied by approximately equal reduction in member bank indebtedness to the Federal Reserve. It can be assumed that this was a deliberate act of policy. Table VC-VIII fails to reveal vigorous use of the open-market weapon after 1954 until 1957 when open-market sales were made and float reduced without permitting meaningful increase in member bank borrowing, although rediscount rate was below Treasury bill rate. The Federal Reserve's biggest operations during the Eisenhower years were in 1958: more than $2 billion in purchases were made. The years 1959 and 1960 are not happy for discretionary monetary policy. The data offer a confused pattern. Substantial open-market purchases were made, but rediscount rate was above Treasury bill rate, encouraging reduction in member bank indebtedness. On net the money supply fell from $140.8 to $140.4 billion from December 1958 to December 1960, but free reserves increased more than $700 million, again demonstrating that the free-reserve criterion contains dangerous flaws.

3

In closing the 1920–1960 "record," we note that "discount rate" refers also to the rate at which the central bank will make advances. If discount rate has not been penal and if banks have been allowed to borrow heavily from the central bank, then an increase in discount rate to a penal level can have pronounced restrictive effects. Banks will have strong incentive to plan to sell securities in order to reduce

230 After which the Federal Reserve carried out modified support programs, but did not blush. *Cf. infra.*

their indebtedness. The more permissive the central bank has been, the more dramatic will be the effects of a penal rate. The member banks will be under all the more pressure to scurry to cover.

(b) institutional orientation

1

We turn to a more institutionally-oriented history of the Federal Reserve's open-market policy, concentrating on its origins. We have discussed effects of wartime purchases on the money supply and banking system. Sterilization policies and pegging operations are discussed later.

"Open market operations by the U. S. Federal Reserve banks date, as a fact, on an important scale, from the spring of 1922 and as a systemized policy from April 1923."[231] The birth of open-market policy was indeed humble. No sophisticated considerations of the pure theory of central bank policy were involved. Hardly! The fact is that reduction in member bank indebtedness to the Federal Reserve from the 1920 peak, abetted by effects of gold inflows increasing member bank reserves, led by spring, 1922, to so severe a decline in what was then the Federal Reserve's major earning asset that the System was strapped for income. It purchased what was for the time a large volume of United States securities. All this is made clear by Figure VC-4.

Figure VC-4 describes the American monetary gold stock time profile.[232] Consider the mechanism relating gold flows to Federal Reserve income. Recipients of bullion turned over their bullion receipts to their banks who in turn transferred the bullion to the Federal Reserve. Member-bank deposits and reserves rose by equal amounts, creating excess reserves. To the extent that member banks used excess reserves to repay indebtedness to the Federal Reserve — and the chart

231 Keynes, *op. cit.*, Vol. II, p. 255.

232 The dramatic increase in the monetary gold stock (above and beyond the revaluation "profit") after 1934 was partly due to the developing European political crisis. However the purchasing power of gold was greater in the United States than abroad as a result of revaluation. Classically, this would put into motion two forces for *decreasing* purchasing power of gold in the United States; (a) a favorable balance of trade; (b) increased bank reserves leading to rising securities prices. However, the peculiar conditions of the 1930's prevented these forces, although activated, from having important inflationary effects. Unemployment and excess capacity were so high that favorable merchandise balances were a drop in the bucket. The enormous increase in bank reserves had effects of open-market purchases beyond the point of saturation: yields were driven to lower limits, but, once this was done, monetary forces were spent.

GOLD STOCKS AND MEMBER-BANK RESERVE BALANCES

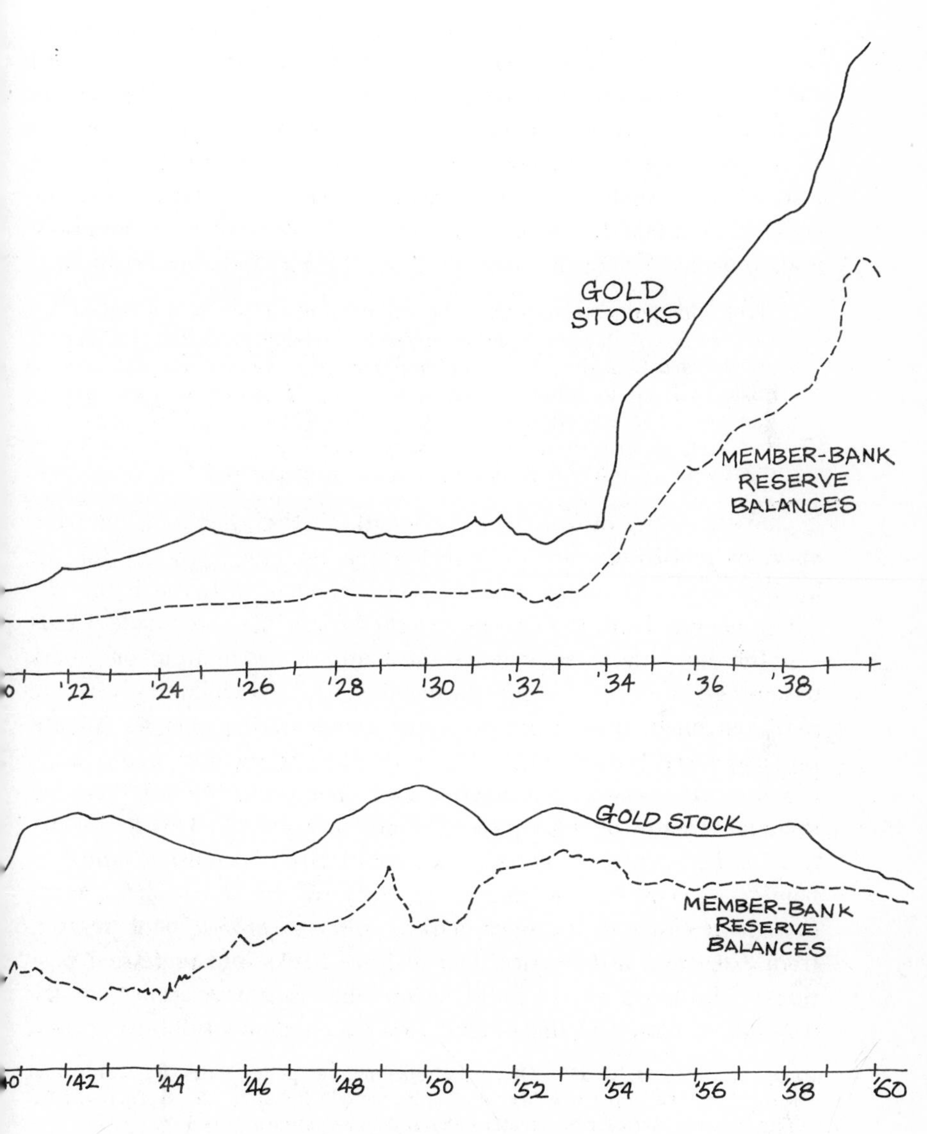

Figure VC-4

Source: *Chart Book, loc. cit.*, pp. 2-3.

implies that they did — member-bank reserves and Federal Reserve deposit liability fell off, *and so did advances to member banks.*

As Keynes puts it, "the Reserve Banks, acting each for itself and with no co-ordinated policy or far-reaching intentions, bought on the open market . . . a very large volume of U. S. Government securities."[233] However, it became apparent to the Board as early as April 1923 that the combination of gold inflow and open-market purchases could lead to a repetition of the 1920 experience. Furthermore the Board, expressing awareness of the role of open-market policy as an instrument of monetary management, "[did] . . . prescribe that securities must not be purchased merely to increase the earnings of reserve banks."[234] Keynes thought April 1923 a landmark occasion:

> "From this point we may date the empirical discovery by the Federal Reserve Board that the London method of relying on discount policy for the management of the national monetary system was not adequate by itself to control a system built on the American lines, but that open-market policy, by going straight to the root of the matter and affecting directly the volume of member bank reserves, furnished them with an instrument more adequate to their task."

At the outset of conscious open-market policy, however, the tendency for rediscount rate to be below market rate (certainly for the buying rate to be below market rate), together with the habitually heavy member bank indebtedness to the Federal Reserve, made it difficult for the authorities to move the banking system from one mark to another. Since fluctuations in member bank indebtedness were not well controlled, there were persisting compensating changes in bills purchased and rediscounted and in advances to member banks when the authorities engaged in open-market operations. Indeed there are vestigial remains of this problem in our own day.[235] This led to distinction between what Robert Roosa has termed "defensive" and "dynamic" open-market operations as early as the *Treatise*.[236] Many thought it easier to use open-market policy to *protect* bank reserves from exogenous disturbance than to force banks into undesired positions. The latter effects could be undone, so it was argued, at the discount window and the Federal Reserve operator's bill-buying desk.

---

233 *Op. cit.*, Vol. II, p. 255. Of course, open-market policy today is co-ordinated through the Federal Open Market Committee which was in fact created in 1922. The Banking Act of 1935 greatly enhanced the Committee's power.

234 *Ibid.*, p. 256.

235 But compare footnote 237, p. 381.

236 Vol. II, p. 256.

Federal Reserve open-market operations between 1923 and 1927 were defensive, partly intended to offset gold inflow. Indeed member bank reserves did not expand nearly so much as would otherwise have been the case. Still I cannot follow Keynes in deeming these operations a "triumph." Enough is known about Federal Reserve policies in 1928–1929 — suggesting that the Board did not grasp the essentials of integrated open-market and discount policy — to fear that Keynes was spinning something of a romance about the five preceding years.[237]

2

Only one task remains before concluding our history of open-market policy:[238] a 1937 incident that proved to be as the proverbial "small cloud the size of a man's hand." Chandler writes:

> ". . . in 1937 for the first time in its history, the Federal Reserve bought long-term government securities primarily because of the direct effects of its purchases upon their market prices. In this case it bought long-terms to bolster their prices and sold short-terms to prevent the operation from increasing member bank reserves."[239]

There are some interesting sidelights on the 1937 incident and several other prewar interventions. These center on variations of the theme "methinks the lady doth protest too much." Officials insisted that they were not engaged in pegging operations or, for that matter, in substantial interference with the market. Rather they were seeking to prevent "disorderly" markets and were smoothing out paths of ad-

---

237 But compare Burgess, *The Federal Reserve Banks and the Money Market,* pp. 249-254. Burgess claims that "from 1922 to 1927 the response of the economic organism to relatively small changes in Federal Reserve policy was extraordinary." He claims that Federal Reserve policy exhibited beautiful contracyclical timing.

It is important to remember that performance by the central bank of its lender-of-last-resort function almost inevitably finds its discounts and advances *temporarily* increasing when its securities are decreasing — at least when Bank rate always is penal. Contractionary effects of open-market sales largely will develop as banks (or the "market") get out of the Bank. It follows that the dynamical effects developed at p. 219 *supra* are unlikely to be generated in American or British practice.

Finally, the text perhaps has insufficiently heeded *defensive* operations offsetting undesired disturbances in bank reserves. *Cf.* Note A.

238 The 1935 legislation has been noted, as have the nullifying effects (on open-market policy) of huge prewar excess reserves. Also huge Federal Reserve purchases of U. S. securities from 1941 to 1946, the importance of open-market policy after World War II, and the relation of open-market policy to rediscount policy and rediscount rate. Pegging operations are treated in a special subsection.

239 Chandler, *The Economics of Money and Banking,* p. 417.

justment. The ground was prepared for the pegging operations of World War II.

The term-structure of interest rates is a familiar topic. We know something about effects of orthodox monetary policy on long and short rates and the extent to which authorities can affect long rates by direct intervention. Knowing the crucial importance of the general topic, it would be well to consider the factual background and whatever can be gleaned of the impact of the 1937 operation.

Page 44 of the (September 1960) *Chart Book* shows a definite trend towards increased non-government bond yields, albeit more pronounced among corporate Baa bonds than among Aaa, high-grade-municipal, or state-and-local government bonds. Page 38 (*ibid.*) shows that, during 1937, Treasury bill rate and the yield of 3-to-5-year Treasury notes increased from January levels but declined from peaks reached during the year so that by December the Treasury bill rate was lower than in January. Here is a portion of the chart concerning U. S. government bond yields:

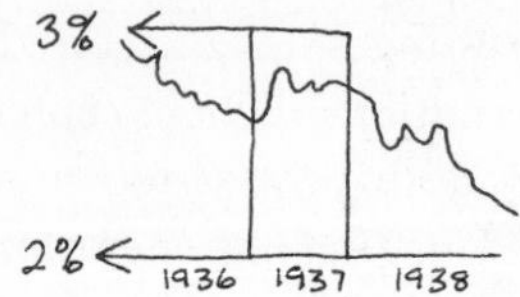

Figure VC-5

It is indeed difficult to conclude that official intervention during 1937 had much effect on long-term security prices. The curve indicates that yields did not begin to fall appreciably until the following year when forces quite beyond these open-market operations took over. Of course, official intervention may have prevented long-term rates from going higher than they did in 1937, but the general impression conveyed to me is that of Peter at the Dyke.

5) Direct Controls

1

Direct controls do not receive as much attention as they might deserve. A perhaps spurious reason is that they are difficult to work into statements of economic theory. Another, undeniably virtuous, is that direct controls are so simple that it is unnecessary to dilate on them: disequilibrium is imposed on lenders and borrowers; the role of the rate of interest as a rationing device is abrogated. Aims of orthodox measures of (restrictive) monetary policy are more or less decreed in that credit available to various spending units is officially predetermined. Little is gained by reciting the endless variations: Regulation X, Regulation W, margin requirements for purchase of this and that, etc.

Of course, rationing of credit is one of the more ancient devices of monetary control:

> "Towards the end of the 18th century, rationing of credit was found to be employed as an instrument of credit control by the Bank of England, which placed a limit upon its discounts for any one house or rejected a proportion of each discount application whenever total demands exceeded the sum which it was prepared to discount on any one day."[240]

Nor do we deny the importance direct controls can have for one convinced that changes in interest rates have little effect on decisions to purchase goods and services. For him, orthodox policy might lead to reduced stocks of money turning over at faster rates without effect on the time-path of prices. Direct controls would offer more hope: savers simply could be forbidden to turn purchasing power over to deficit spending units. It would be *verboten* for banks to sell securities to depositors with the idea of augmenting advances. It might be made impossible for me to purchase a new consumer durable unless I was prepared to offer cash or to liquidate some other assets on the spot. In other words, direct controls can forestall increases in the velocity of monetary circulation that would spell death to orthodox policy.

Objections have been raised to direct controls on the ground that decommission of the price system is in itself to be deplored. But presumably direct controls are proposed becaues it is felt that the price mechanism will not work.

2

Having filled in the background, we can turn to some history of direct controls in the United States.

---

240 De Kock, *op. cit.*, p. 222.

The Securities and Exchange Act of 1934 usually is taken as a starting point in discussion of direct controls. Steiner, Shapiro, and Solomon, among others, maintain that the late 1920's would have been an ideal time for direct controls. They point out that the general level of business activity was "relatively stable" so that severe restriction of credit generally might have had undesirable effects on real output, and yet broad quantitative controls would not permit restriction of credit to the stock market without these side effects. How convenient it would have been if more selective controls had been available. The Securities and Exchange Act provides such controls. Under this act, the Board has been delegated the power to set margin requirements on securities loans and has used this power rather vigorously: margin requirements have varied from 25 to 100 per cent. The Board has exercised its margin requirement power through Regulations T and U, the former regulating loans by brokers and dealers to their customers, the latter controlling bank loans.

Sporadic consumer credit controls, administered by the Board under its Regulation W from 1941 to 1952, came into being through an executive order of President Roosevelt in August 1941. Objects of control included down payment requirements and periods over which payments are to be made. Controls have been imposed on a wide variety of semi-durable and durable goods. Similar controls were imposed in September 1950 on credit for residential building (and were administered under Regulation X). Direct controls over consumer credit and real estate credit were allowed to lapse over May-September 1952.

3

In conclusion, the case for direct controls is double-faceted: (a) they permit the authorities to launch attacks against narrow strategic or even tactical objectives without summoning up siege guns able to attack only broad objectives and unable to achieve pinpoint accuracy; (b) if expenditure plans are very insensitive to (or much lagged in response to) interest rate changes, orthodox monetary policy will not much affect flow rates of expenditure; direct controls can slow down these flow rates through the direct fiat of the government . . . The case against direct controls also has been considered. Still another objection can be entered: direct controls might operate with particular force against narrow classes of sellers and buyers.

4

I should like to append the following excerpts from the hearings of the (Patman) Subcommittee on Credit Control and Debt Management of the Joint Committee on the Economic Report of the U. S. Congress held on March 25, 1952 and published at pp. 685-746 of *Hearings Before . . .*, March 10-31.[241] This is a valuable volume, and the March 25 hearings, including Professors Ellis, Friedman, Mikesell, Samuelson, and Whittlesley, are especially useful.

> "*Senator Flanders.* Would you have worked through specific restrictions of credit . . .? (Referring to the post-Korea inflation control problem.)
>
> *Mr. Friedman.* No; I would have worked solely through general monetary measures of selling bonds and keeping down the supply of money. I think that selective credit controls are bad, like other direct controls; that they discriminate against certain classes of borrowers for reasons that are not really relevant; and that it would be much better to do without them and to rely exclusively on general monetary controls. . . .
>
> *Mr. Samuelson.* . . . Now, the hateful and the harmful thing is that if you freeze an ancient system of relative prices, a system of allocation and quotas and priorities, gradually you are building up more and more poisonous inefficiencies in that system . . . Consider for example direct controls over housing. They seem to me to be fairly impersonal and my primary objection to them is . . . in connection with long-range inefficiencies. Nevertheless by means of regulations on housing credit, you may much more efficiently channel the construction industry into defense areas . . . *Moreover, by making specific credit controls in this area, and at the same time having gilt-edged Government bonds at 93, you might get the same deflationary impact on the system as could be achieved without Regulation X and Regulation W with Government bonds at 80. Thus judicious specific controls may greatly lighten the load on quantitative credit policy and make its use feasible* [Emphasis supplied.] . . . I use a figure like 80 in Government bonds with a certain amount of trepidation and trembling. Even a little bit as a reductio ad absurdum.
>
> *Mr. Friedman.* Professor Samuelson argues as if a fall in the price of bonds to 80, which he regards as drastic, could be prevented by a mild selective credit control. The two kinds of measures ought to be treated at the same level. If it takes drastic general credit control measures, why then, it will take really drastic selective control measures."

241 United States Congress. Washington: Government Printing Office, 1952.

c) Selected Major Incidents in Federal Reserve History

1) Reaction to Gold Inflow, Circa 1923–1928

This incident bears repetition because of the confluence of forces represented: (a) the occasion of the Federal Reserve's discovery of the rudiments of the theory of open-market operations; (b) the occasion for an increase of approximately 60 per cent in the American monetary gold stock, accompanied by only a small increase in member bank reserves and by stable, if not declining, consumer and wholesale prices, a serious departure from the way in which the international-gold-standard game is supposed to be played; (c) the occasion for the first serious and sustained effort at managed money, giving rise to enthusiastic claims until untoward incidents, beginning in 1928, came to the fore.

Factor (c) makes the incident "major" for this book. "Scientific" monetary management requires appreciation of the interaction of the various markets and particularly of the way in which open-market operations can succeed or fail to have impact on commodities and labor markets.

2) Response to the Great Depression, 1929–1933

Table VC-VIII introduced the calamitous events generally dated from October 1929 when the Bull Market utterly collapsed. Placing the 1929–1933 episode in a broader contact, two basic central banking problems emerge: (1) the appropriate conduct of a central bank during a crisis of liquidity; (2) the appropriate conduct of a central bank in the event of a collapse of investment expenditure ("a collapse in the marginal efficiency of capital"). The problems first are studied in broad generality — anticipating Bagehot and relying again on Keynes's remarkable *Treatise*. Then Federal Reserve policies are compared with theoretical norms.

(a) the appropriate conduct of a central bank during a crisis of liquidity

A "crisis of liquidity" can exist in two universes of discourse (a) circumstances in which bank depositors have come to doubt the ability of banks to provide specie and/or currency upon "presentation" of deposit liabilities and wish to change the form of their money; (b) the public's desire to hold a larger portion of its assets in money balances (best shown with a fiat paper currency in a bankless system, or one with 100-per-cent reserve banking, and in which all debt is in perpetuities).

Taking up (a), common sense suggests that the central bank take dramatic action to demonstrate to the public that it need have no fear of bank suspension or failure. The central bank might be expected to lower eligibility requirements for discount of commercial paper, to lend freely and openly on hitherto excluded collateral, and to make large open-market purchases in order to improve reserve positions of banks *and* to provide buoyancy to securities markets generally. Surely circumstances inducing depositors' fears for convertibility of bank deposits will encourage creditors to call for payment on maturing obligations and to hesitate to renew. Massive open-market purchases will provide outlets for debtors, support securities prices, and give the lie to speculators relying on declining securities prices.

We expect the central bank to rush into the arena, providing liquidity for any and all who wish to become more liquid, in that way alleviating whatever pressure is being placed on debtors and probably stemming the increase in liquidity preference. Once it becomes clear that prices are not going to fall and that debtors, including banks, are not going to fail, the main incentives for holding additional cash will have been dissipated. But a critical *caveat* must be imposed when the "ultimate stuff" of the monetary system is not paper and when there is an internal specie drain: the central bank may be drained of *its* specie reserve. However, experience of many countries over many years indicates that, once the public is convinced that it *can* have specie, "surfeiting, the appetite . . . sicken(s) and so die(s)." The public again becomes content with paper. Such was the experience of central banks with much lower gold reserves than the Federal Reserve's in 1931 (to anticipate the story a bit).

Taking up (b), a crisis of liquidity becomes important in its impact on commodity markets rather than on solvency of debtors: issuers of perpetuities never can be called. Now, if the public wishes to hold more money, *and if the central bank does not provide more money for the public to hold,* what will happen? Since the public is constrained by budget equations, the plan to hold more money is part of a plan to hold less of other assets (excluding decreased propensities to consume): excess supply will develop in markets for securities and physical capital, leading to falling prices and rising interest rates; multiplier-accelerator effects will reduce disposable income and planned consumption. Of course, as prices fall, *real* money balances are increasing. If the central bank wishes to maintain stable prices — let alone avoid the unemployment and excess capacity inevitably accompanying a deflation — it will expand the money supply through support operations. If it chooses deflation — either deliberately or, just as inevitably, through inaction — it also must assume risks of destabilizing expectations (price declines leading to the conviction that prices will fall even more, strengthening the desire to hold cash and discouraging expenditure today). In fact, these "dynamic" considerations suggest that it is important that the central bank's expansionary response be vigorous and widely published in order to combat expectations that could lead to cumulative contraction.

(b) the appropriate conduct of a central bank in the event of a collapse of investment expenditure

1

Most writers agree that the latitude of central bank action under this head is much more restricted than under the first, particularly if a collapse in investment expenditure has already occurred. Businessmen anticipating inability to sell additional output hardly can be interested in plant expansion, even if interest charges are zero; expansion of planned inventory holdings when sales are declining is most unlikely, although it is true that cheap money might modify planned inventory contraction.

Conceding all of this, central banks still should conduct open-market purchases, to the "point of saturation" if necessary, as soon as they become convinced that a collapse of investment (the marginal efficiency of capital) is in the offing. Whatever stimulus to expenditure can be offered by cheap money should be proffered. Perhaps we impose an unbearable burden of responsibility on central banks: data that they receive often are internally contradictory; there are important lags between occurrence of economic events and receipt of intelligence about these events and again between receipt of intelligence and formation of decisions, and once again between formation of policy and its execution. Usually the central bank can do no more than attach probabilities to outcomes. Open-market purchases in the light of *seemingly* adverse intelligence *might* initiate undesired inflation. Open-market sales *might* set off a dangerous down-turn if intelligence has been faulty or misinterpreted or if the train of consequence is more severe than originally had been anticipated. Here there never can be more than *moral* certainty.

2

The foundation having been laid, we can turn to what is, so far as I know, the best account of the theory of central bank policy during a down-turn in expenditure: Ch. 37, "The Control of Investment," of Keynes's *Treatise*. Permit a *précis* of Keynes's analysis.

One of the major themes of the chapter is sounded at pp. 370-371 of his *Treatise* (a note similar to that of our discussion of the role of direct controls in curbing stock market inflation):

> "The risk of bringing to bear too rapidly and severely on the industrial circulation, when it is the financial circulation which is being aimed at, is greater, I think, in the case of a contraction of credit than in the case of an expansion. But, on the other hand, it is less likely to be necessary to resort to extreme measures to check a boom than to check a slump. Booms, I suspect, are almost always due to tardy or inadequate action by the banking system such as could be avoidable; — there is much more foundation for the view that it is slumps which may sometimes get out of hand and defy all normal methods of control. It will be, therefore, on the problem of checking a slump that we shall now concentrate our attention."

This passage can be construed to mean that, while there must be interest rates high enough to check a boom (misquoting Hawtrey, "Bank rate never went above 10 per cent because it never had to"), it is not clear that positive interest rates low enough to check a slump can be achieved by conventional means.

Keynes makes clear that central bankers, when confronted with a severe slump, should carry out open-market purchases *à outrance:*

> "my remedy in the event of the obstinate persistence of a slump would consist . . . in the purchase of securities by the Central Bank until the long-term market rate of interest has been brought down to the limiting point."[242]

3

Being concerned with relationships of long and short rates and their lower limits, we pause to consider the implications of the phrase "until the long . . . rate . . . has been brought down to the limiting point." Figure VC-6, p. 391 shows that the pure short rate has been depressed practically to zero: banks and other financial institutions hardly will refuse to hold riskless short-dated paper so long as running yield exceeds marginal expense *and alternative outlets are similarly*

[242] *Ibid.,* p. 371. Sir Ralph Hawtrey would emphasize changes in short rate. *Cf.* Appendix A. Meanwhile we follow Keynes rather uncritically. If short rate is important for spending decisions, life is easy for the central bank.

unattractive.[243] How could a long rate considerably higher than the short rate be "unattractive"? Abstracting from "normal backwardation," *capital loss possibilities* might be the answer. These can limit the power of open-market policy *à outrance* to move the long rate, at least for some time.

> "if, for example, the long-term rate is 3 per cent per annum above the short-term rate, this means that the mathematical expectation for bond prices in the minds of [persons preferring to sell long-terms and hold the proceeds at lower running yields] is for a fall of 3 per cent per annum."[244]

To repeat Keynes's argument: if I can earn 3 more points by holding bonds instead of bills, why should I not do so *unless* I expect the price of bonds to fall 3 points or more during the year.

We are nearly home! Assume that the short rate is driven to 0.25 per cent per annum but that traders firmly believe that "normal" short rate is 3.25 per cent per annum. It might be impossible for authorities *quickly* to drive longs below 3.25 per cent without purchasing all the long-term debt in existence. There can be insurmountable obstacles even to open-market purchases carried to the point of saturation. Figure VC-6 on the following page suggests this:

Long-term yield fell just below 2 per cent — its nadir — during 1940. Although the decline from 3.3 to about 2.5 per cent over the period of observation is not trivial,[245] one is left with a distinct impression of the limitations of effects of open-market policy on long-term rates (especially in connection with obviously temporary contracyclical policy).

---

243 Keynes deals with crises of liquidity as well: "when prices are falling, profits low, and the future uncertain . . . lenders are most exigent and least inclined to embark their resources on long-term unless it be on the most unexceptionable security; so that the bond rate, far from falling towards nothing, may be expected — apart from the operations of the Central Bank — to be higher than normal." (*Ibid.*, p. 372.)

In the fullness of your wisdom, you will describe this as a leftward shift of the *LL* curve consequent to a leftward shift in the *CC* curve.

244 *Ibid.*, p. 371.

245 Dacey makes an interesting observation along these lines (*British Banking Mechanism*, pp. 129-130). During a general discussion of effects of interest-rate changes (effects which he feels might not be great), he cites a case of "high gearing" (leverage). He supposes "that a factory which costs £5.5 million to build

YIELDS ON U. S. GOVERNMENT SECURITIES

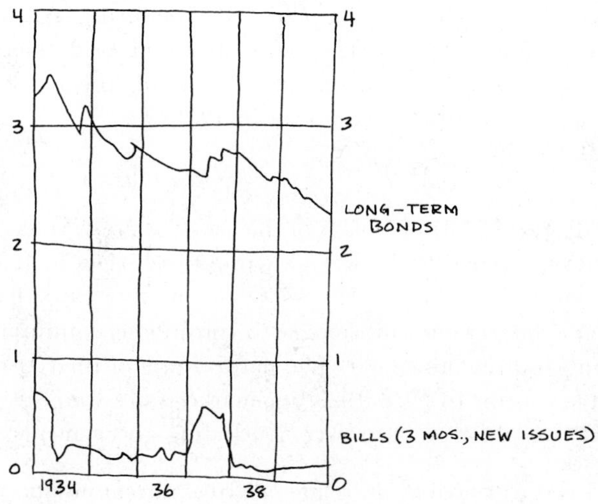

Figure VC-6

Source: *Chart Book*, September, 1960, p. 38.

4

Keynes cites two other factors limiting the degree to which open-market operations might succeed in "push[ing] such a policy home": (a) lack of ammunition; (b) international complications.

Factor (a) is easily enough overcome: eligibility requirements can be relaxed; reserve requirements for the central bank can be eased; and,

---

can be let at an annual rental of £220,000, equivalent to 4 per cent on the cost of construction. If the undertakers of the enterprise can float £5 million of debentures at 3 per cent, they will make an annual return of . . . 14 per cent on their own investment of £500,000, of which 11 per cent can be regarded as the reward for risk-bearing, etc. If the debenture rate rises to 4 per cent, the entrepreneurs will themselves obtain a return of only 4 per cent, or no more than they could earn by investing their own funds in debentures, and the enterprise will clearly not be worth while . . . In principle, of course, all of this applies equally to merchants trading on borrowed capital and thus assists Sir Ralph Hawtrey's diagnosis."

Of course, an increase in interest rates on debentures from 3 to 4 per cent is equivalent to a reduction of 33 per cent in the present value of the expected income stream. This is no small change and could be important quite apart from leverage.

finally, reserve requirements for member banks can be reduced so that the member banks can conduct open-market purchases in lieu of the central bank if they are not panicked. Factor (b), international complications, especially concerns maintenance of gold reserves when on a gold standard or when committed to rigid foreign exchanges. It influenced Federal Reserve policy in 1931.[246]

5

Pages 377-387 of Vol. II of the *Treatise* are devoted to the heading, "The Slump of 1930." (Keynes wrote these pages in 1930.) What were his specific reactions? He felt that interest rates had risen above *natural rates,* rates consistent with continuous equilbration of planned saving and investment.[247] The natural rate of interest fell, in Keynes's opinion, prior to 1928–1929 but market rates were sustained by "artificial" or "distress" borrowers (including governments)

> "not influenced by the return on actual current investment [who had] to meet their urgent liabilities, to satisfy their creditors, and to comply with their treaty obligations [these being governments] who were borrowing . . . to build up liquid reserves . . . with which to protect their newly-restored currencies. We had the extraordinary situation in 1927-1928 of the United States lending on long-term at high rates of interest, largely to Europe, amounts several times greater than her favorable balance, and being able to do so because these borrowers at once redeposited with her on short-term the major part of what they had just borrowed on long term."

The ranks of long-term borrowers were augmented by the speculative borrowers feeding the Bull Market: call money rates rose very high indeed as the financial circulation increased.[248]

For these reasons market rate stood above natural rate. Saving

246 Keynes proceeds to recommend that, if monetary measures do not do the trick, the Government increases its spending. In fact at p. 382 *ff.* one sees glimmerings of multiplier and accelerator analysis.

247 Due to peculiar circumstances such as the need to restore working capital after World War I and the growth of certain heavy industries stimulating investment demand.

248 The key thing was not new loans to securities purchasers, since these funds were quickly paid over to sellers of securities who would have the opportunity to ease the market by repaying their own loans. Rather it was in increased transactions balances flowing in a more or less closed circuit within Wall Street (after which Wall Street Panic Snopes was named). As Wall Street activity became more and more intense, these balances mounted to great heights.

tended to outrun planned investment: firms were forced into unintended accumulations of inventory and unprofitable liquidations of merchandise.[249] Keynes describes how various cumulative contractions might develop in the real sector. In view of the outcome, he was rather optimistic.

His particular prescription — radically modified in his *General Theory* (1936)[250] — is set out at pp. 383-387 of Ch. 37. Central banks in the United States and elsewhere must try to force down interest rates, particularly long-term rates, because ". . . the fall in the rate of interest is likely to be a long and tedious process, unless it is accelerated by deliberate policy."[251] He thought the stakes to be very high: "if we leave matters to cure themselves, the results may be disastrous" (p. 385), and urged that the Bank of England and the Federal Reserve Board (1) pressure member banks to reduce deposit rates to a figure as low as 0.5 per cent per annum, and (2) pursue bank-rate policy *à outrance,* making sure that steps are taken to "prevent difficulties due to international gold movements from interfering with this."[252] One wonders what the *General Theory* would have been if the Keynesian prescription of 1930 had been adopted. I do not know.

---

[249] Keynes developed a formal apparatus yielding these results in Volume I of the *Treatise.* This apparatus used certain fundamental equations (developed in the appendix to Ch. XII *infra*) described by Hicks as a "stupendous transfiguration of the Quantity Theory of Money."

[250] By 1936, he had lost confidence in the possibilities of central-bank intervention in the slump.

[251] At pp. 383-384 (Vol. II), he offers a reason for this that supports Hugh Rose in his brilliant article, "Liquidity Preference and Loanable Funds" (*Review of Economic Studies,* Vol. XXIV, February 1957). Keynes points out that "the slump itself produces a new queue of 'distress' borrowers . . ." The reference is to governments, but it is easy to extend the argument to firms with unintended inventory accumulations that must be financed either through borrowing or reducion of cash balances. Keynes himself appears to accept the generalization when he writes "the thing will never cure itself by the lack of borrowers forcing down the rate; *for it absorbs just as much savings to finance losses as to finance investment.*" (p. 384, his emphasis.)

Another reason offered by Keynes is that the post-World War I generation had become accustomed to interest rates much higher than were prewar rates: there would be a tendency for long rate to be sticky (the accepted norm being so high) — certainly unless there is dramatic central bank action.

[252] "That is say, they should combine to maintain a very low short-term rate of interest, and buy long-dated securities either against an expansion of Central Bank money or against the sale of short-dated securities until the short-term market is saturated . . ."

(c) *The Federal Reserve and the Great Depression*

1

What actually happened?[253] Much of the story is told in Note C. Discount rate averaged 3.04, 2.11, 2.82, and 2.56 per annum for the years 1930, 1931, 1932, and 1933; commercial paper rates, 3.59, 2.64, 2.73, and 1.73 per cent; Treasury bill rates (for 1931–1933) 1.40, 0.88, and 0.52 per cent. Long-term rates — even riskless rates — behaved perversely. Witness Figure VC-7.

YIELDS ON LONG-TERM U. S. GOVERNMENT SECURITIES

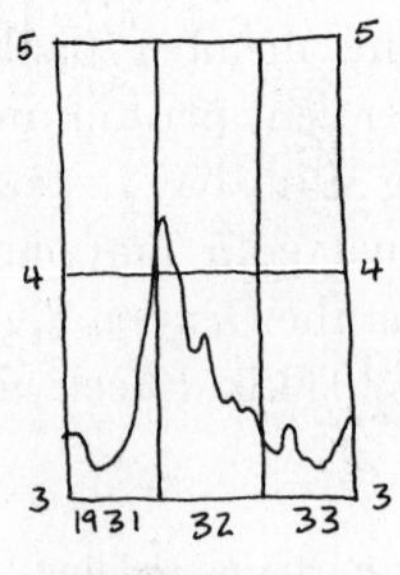

Figure VC-7

Source: Chart Book, **September 1960, page 38. Yields during 1929 averaged about 3.6 per cent per annum.**

Open-market operations *à outrance?* Purchases of U. S. securities totalled little more than $330 million from the end of 1929 to the end of 1931 (the initial portfolio being $446 million). True, the more than $1.5 billion in U. S. securities purchased from the end of 1931 to the end of 1933 was very large in relation to the time. But not in terms of the magnitude of the economic problems. The scale of open-market operations fell woefully short of what was needed either to supply desired liquidity[254] or to provide the dramatic flourish necessary to depress long rates. (*See Note D.*)

Figure VC-8 describes behavior of the bills-bought account.

[253] *Cf.* Table VC-VIII and related discussion.

[254] The real stock of money rose from 1929 to 1933 even though the nominal stock fell. Increased liquidity preference was satisfied through falling prices.

BILLS BOUGHT BY THE FEDERAL RESERVE SYSTEM

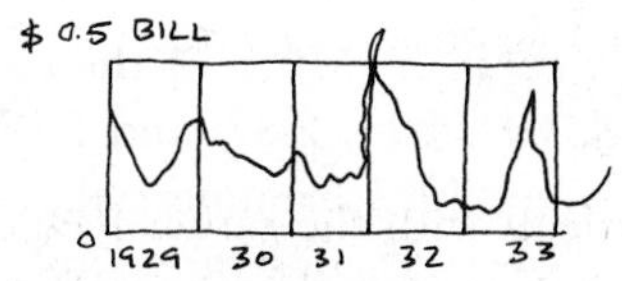

Figure VC-8

Source: Chart Book, September 1960, p. 4.

The curve reflects drying up of the supply of commercial bills as business activity slackened. Then the impact to tighter credit in the Fall, 1931: banks had to have recourse to the Federal Reserve in order to sustain their reserves. "Bills bought" played its normally passive role. Surely the Federal Reserve did not aggressively purchase commercial paper at any time from the end of 1929 to the end of 1932.

Decreased member bank borrowing from the end of 1929 to the end of 1930 and from the *end of 1931* to the *end of 1932*[255] often are cited as evidence of improved bank liquidity. It is argued that Federal Reserve open-market purchases permitted the banks to reduce their indebtedness. This ignores two important facets:

1) repayment of member bank indebtedness to the central bank involves contraction of member bank assets — hardly to be encouraged during a deflation.

2) rediscount rate had become penal, encouraging banks to reduce their indebtedness to the Federal Reserve. In fact the upshot illustrates the deflationary consequence of going from permissive to penal rediscount rate. Additional pressure for liquidation was thus placed on bank customers.

Of course, decreased member bank indebtedness was associated with declining transactions "requirements"; the real sector sagged from late 1931 to late 1932.[256] At the same time, riskless short rates deteriorated, as did credit standing of private borrowers. One need not be a commercial loan theorist to have expected commercial banks to pull in their horns. Still, if rediscount rate had been reduced well below

[255] *Cf. infra* for treatment of *September 1931 to February 1932.*

[256] In contrast with the Keynesian argument of footnote 251, Keynes's argument is specialized to undesired *increases* in inventories. Realized inventory reductions *do* reduce finance requirements.

market rates,[257] one could reasonably have expected that a greater volume of bank credit would have been sustained and more pressure could have been exerted against long rates.

2

Thus far we have dealt with the rather feeble over-all Federal Reserve response to the challenge of the Great Depression. Federal Reserve policies from roughly September 1931 to February 1932 seem to have been perverse.

The origins of this episode were external: with Britain's departure from gold, international demand for gold shifted to the United States. The external drain, together with some internal drain, reduced reserves of member banks, who had to purchase gold from the authorities. Member banks, furthermore, were forced to apply to the Federal Reserve. The Federal Reserve's response — certainly in view of the dismal condition of the commodities and labor markets — was remarkable: (1), it increased its holdings of government securities but its total earning assets fell by more than $400 million as its holdings of commercial paper and its discounts and advances declined, partly because (2), rediscount rates were raised from 1.5 per cent to 3.5 per cent late in 1931. Higher rediscount rate encouraged member banks to reduce their borrowings at the Federal Reserve and accordingly to reduce their own advances and hold out for higher yields. There was some upward pressure on interest charges to the private sector and reduced availability of credit.[258]

Needless to say, there was a *rationale* for the Federal Reserve's conduct, retrospectively so unfortunate in view of the genuine hope for recovery earlier in 1931. Figure VC-4 shows that the American gold stock fell during 1931 and early 1932 to levels lower than any since 1923, although it remained large. The traditional role of a central bank faced with an external drain called for it to impose higher money-market rates and over-all monetary restraint. It is difficult to break up ancient patterns of thought. Furthermore it is doubtful if central bankers anywhere in the world had what we would call a so-

257 Contrary to the Bagehotian formula but practicable. The stock of monetary gold was large. The tranche was in currency, not specie.

258 The initial indebtedness of the banks to the Federal Reserve — in view of the "tradition" established in 1925 — was itself a drag on bank willingness to maintain, let alone expand, advances. It might be said that both the level and the rate of change of Federal Reserve's advances had depressing effects, although for different reasons.

phisticated understanding of the intimate linkage of financial and "real" markets.

And then the Federal Reserve faced a legal conundrum not solved until passage of the Glass-Steagall Act in February 1932 permitted government securities to be collateral for Federal Reserve notes. Hitherto only gold and rediscounted commercial paper could serve as collateral:

> "As member bank borrowings declined and reduced Federal Reserve holdings of commercial paper, more gold had to be used as collateral. To the extent that Federal Reserve purchases of government securities enabled member banks to reduce their borrowings, the problem was intensified. At one time the volume of 'free gold' was only $500 million."[259]

Of course, one reason member bank borrowings declined was that rediscount rate had been increased. Be that as it may, the legal conundrum supplies the final gloss for the tale of the ill-fated Federal Reserve policies of 1931.

3

A few words on the banking panic of 1933. Friedman and Schwartz succinctly describe its onset:

> "A renewed series of bank failures began in the last quarter [of 1932] . . . The deposit-currency ratio fell; the stock of money ceased growing and began to fall precipitously after January 1933 . . . The monetary difficulties were accompanied by a relapse on the economic front as well . . ."[260]

Bank failures numbered in the thousands, culminating in the nationwide bank holiday from March 6 to March 15, 1933. "More than 5,000 banks which were still in operation when the holiday was declared did not open their doors when [it] terminated." (*Ibid.*)

What was the Federal Reserve's role? Not distinguished. Friedman and Schwartz go so far as to accuse it of the most capital of central bank crimes: ". . . It remained impassive, showing more concern for its own liquidity than about the state of the banking system." They cite this evidence:

1) The Federal Reserve "*reduced* its government security holdings by $90 million" in January. Total Federal Reserve bank credit fell by $100 million.

---

259 Chandler, *op. cit.*, p. 404.
260 *Op. cit.*, Ch. VII.

2) "It increased its security holdings by $45 million and permitted total Reserve Bank credit to rise by $70 million" from late in January until February 15, but ". . . in these three weeks alone, member bank reserve balances declined by $280 million."

3) Friedman and Schwartz concede that Federal Reserve credit rose drastically in the last two weeks before the banking holiday. "The increase was overwhelmingly in discounts and bills bought." In other words, they stress the short-run passivity of the latter accounts under long-standing Federal Reserve practice.

3) Bond Support Programs and the Accord of 1951

1

The 1942-1951 decade poses interesting problems in the mechanics of open-market operations, in the political environment in which the Federal Reserve must operate, and in the possibilities of official influence of the long rate simply by declaring willingness to support bonds at fixed prices.

Once again, we haul out the *Chart Book* and assemble records for securities yields, bank holdings of various maturities, distribution of government debt between banks and the non-banking public, and Federal Reserve holdings of United States debt.

YIELDS ON U. S. GOVERNMENT SECURITIES

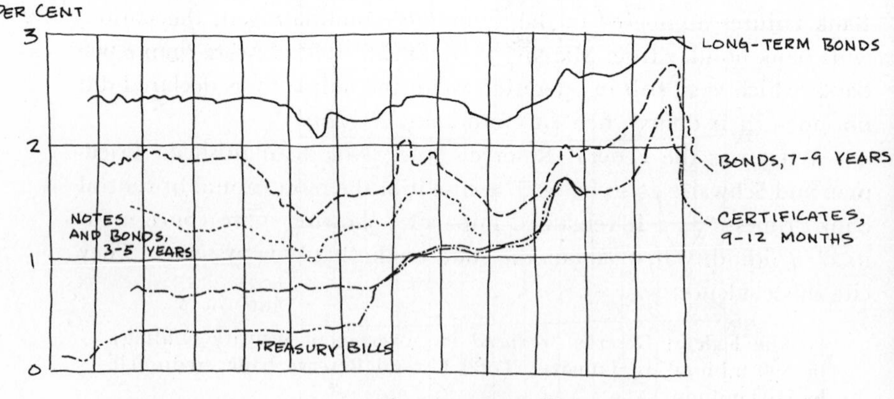

Chart A — Figure VC-9

Note: Bills and Certificates yield curves become confluent in 1947.

LONG- AND SHORT-TERM INTEREST RATES

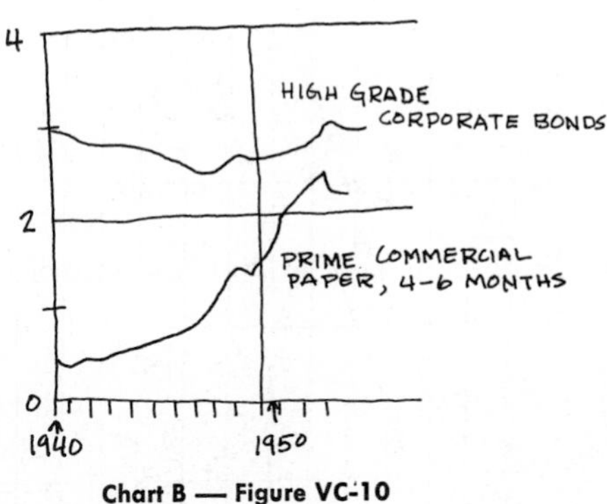

Chart B — Figure VC-10

GROSS DEBT OF THE U. S. GOVERNMENT

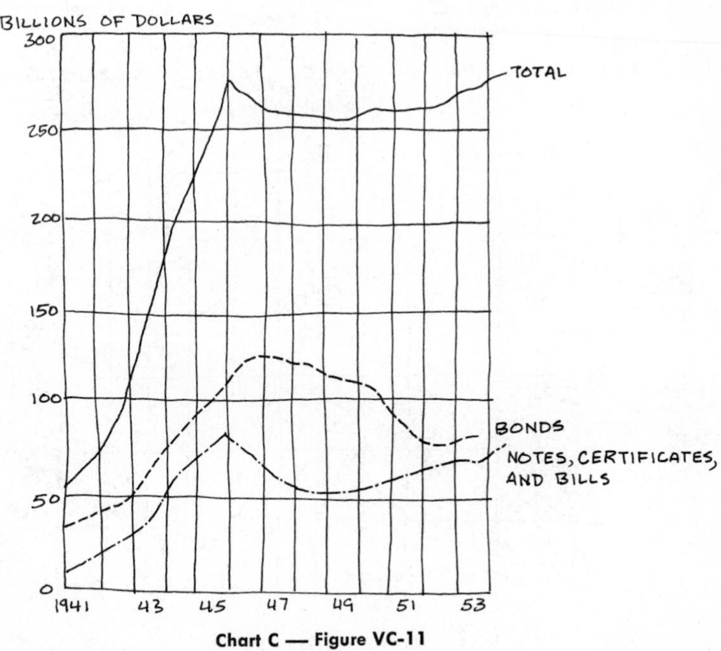

Chart C — Figure VC-11

INVESTMENT OF MEMBER BANKS IN U. S. GOVERNMENT SECURITIES

Billions of Dollars

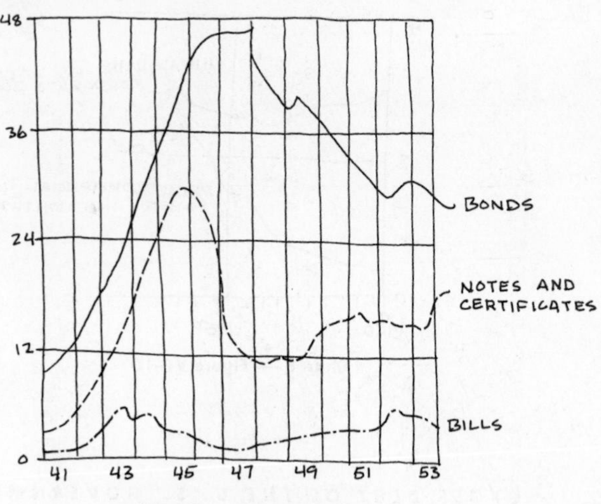

Chart D — Figure VC-12

RESERVE BANK HOLDINGS OF U. S. SECURITIES

Billions of Dollars

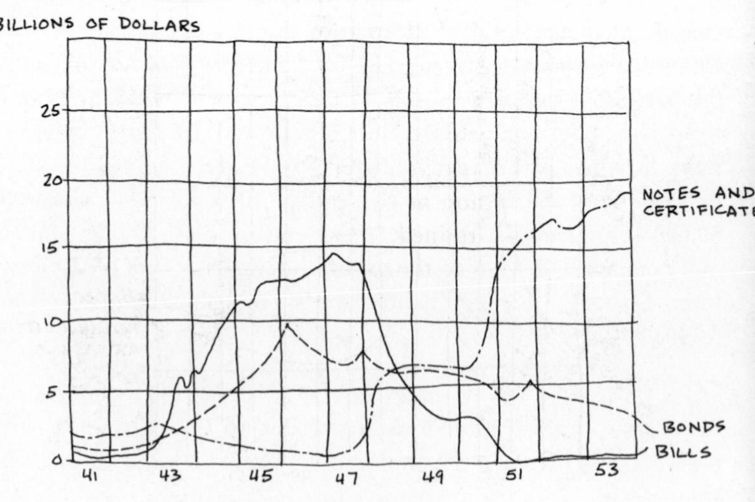

Chart E — Figure VC-13

OWNERSHIP OF U. S. GOVERNMENT SECURITIES
Billions of Dollars

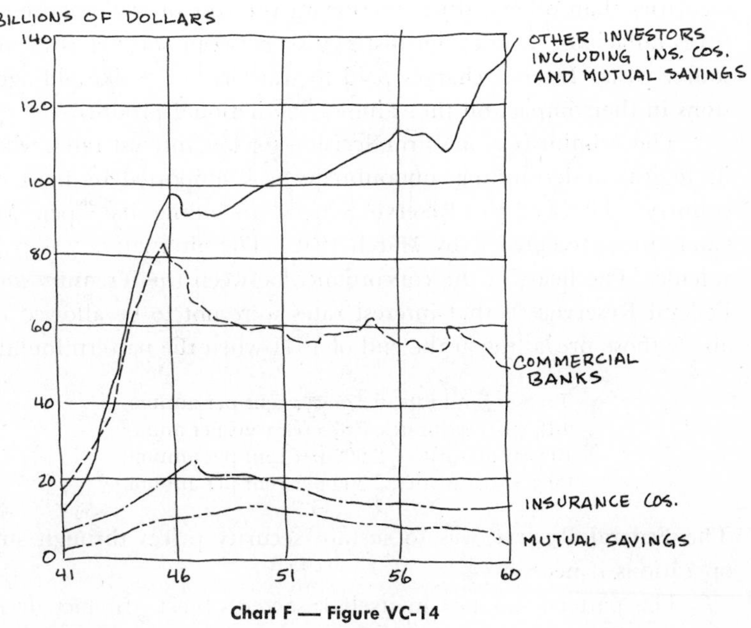

Chart F — Figure VC-14

Certain supplementary information to Chart E will be helpful. Chandler[261] shows that Federal Reserve holdings of 1-2 year maturities fell slightly from December 1941 to December 1943 and drastically from December 1944 to December 1945 and June 1946. Federal Reserve holdings of 2-5 year maturities fell from \$1.4 billion at the end of 1942 to \$0.488 billion at the end of 1943, never to rise above the \$0.620 billion mark attained at the end of 1944. These statistics are more emphatic in view of the over-all increase in Federal Reserve holdings. Federal Reserve bill holdings increased enormously from 1941 to 1946.

2

The Administration took little time to decide that (1) although taxes were to increase, the war would also be financed through borrow-

[261] *Op. cit.*, p. 425.

ing;[262] (2) interest rates should be maintained at low levels. The *rationale* underlying the second decision was two-fold: (a) minimization of distributional effects caused by some purchasing relatively more securities than others; (b) reduction in the cost of war finance. Facet (b) is fallacious. It does not distinguish between transfer costs and resource costs. Interest charges paid to Americans are like old age pensions in their impact on the value of the national product.

The Administration's firm decision for low interest rates, whatever its logical underpinning, undoubtedly was supported by most of the country. The Federal Reserve System, including its Open Market Committee, accepted it by March 1942. The alternative was political suicide. The heart of the concordance between the Treasury and the Federal Reserve was that interest rates were not to be allowed to rise above those prevailing at the end of 1941 when the pattern found

> Treasury bill rate, 0.375 per cent per annum,
> 9-12 mo. certificates, 0.875 per cent per annum,
> 10 year maturities, 2.000 per cent per annum,
> longest maturities, 2.500 per cent per annum.

The Federal Reserve was to sustain security prices through support operations if necessary.

The pattern was not in itself a sacred object. In fact declining yields of longer-dated stock are an integral part of the story.[263] The decision was for *low* interest rates. On the other hand, the pattern of rates just described is important to the story. It was characteristic of the 1930's when short rate was well below long rate and fluctuated *much* less than in the 1920's. *Rather firm expectations had come to be formed on this basis of this pattern.*

The wartime episode hinges on the interaction of a pledge and a number of expectations. The authorities, of course, were pledged to support government stock at high prices during the war. It was widely

---

[262] The desirability of increasing the public's liquid assets at the end of the war was much stressed.

[263] These declines were not spectacular. (*Cf.* Chart A.) The Treasury was placing *huge* supplies in the market. The point is that, as time passed, shorter-dated stock became unattractive at pegged rates so long as long maturities yielded 2½ per cent. Accordingly, long rate fell. It is crucially important to understand that net bill purchases by the Federal Reserve were indispensable to support long-rate at 2.5 per cent or less. If the banks had not been provided with reserves through Federal Reserve purchases of bills, the bond market would never have been buoyant enough to permit the Federal Reserve actually to dispose of some bonds (as it did).

believed that the war would be long — if we were to win. The news was desperately bad through most of 1942. There was growing conviction that cheap money was here to stay. It was anticipated that the war's end would unchain massive *de*flationary forces, that massive government intervention would be necessary to avert economic catastrophe. Finally, the American economy had been sluggish for about 12 years. There was wide belief that stagnation would return even if collapse were averted, again increasing the likelihood of cheap money after the war.

The upshot was that the prewar pattern began to look unnatural. Long-terms began to look attractive at current prices.[264] Going short rate seemed likely to persist tomorrow, and tomorrow, and tomorrow, . . .

The story of Charts A-F can be rapidly unfolded. The ½ per cent per annum differential between bills and certificates became obviously absurd. By the beginning of 1943, the Federal Reserve was forced to acquire huge quantities of bills in order to sustain their ⅜ per cent yield. These purchases added reserves to the banking system and helped to provide ammunition for subsequent assaults on an increasingly unrealistic pattern.[265] Of course, the thing that was immediately absurd was the ½ point differential in bill and certificate rates. The ⅜ bill rate looked realistic for a longer and longer future. The result is shown by Charts D and E: by the end of 1946, Treasury bills had become essentially a *Federal Reserve* asset.

There was no reason for the process to stop with maturities as short as one year. After investors took halting and tentative steps into certificates (out of bills) and found they had not been bitten, even 5-year maturities (at 1½ per cent) began to have appeal: not only because of higher yield but because more venturesome traders anticipated capital gains when broader segments of the market became convinced that cheap money was here to stay. Once again shorter-dated stock was dumped on the Federal Reserve which manfully shoveled out reserves in order to prevent short rates from rising, creating additional reserves for depredations farther out on the yield curve.[266] All the while, the long market was gaining strength. As Chandler wrote in 1949:

[264] Very liquid also. Their nominal value seemed *at least* assured over a longish horizon.

[265] Of course, American fiscal planning called for net Federal Reserve open-market purchases.

[266] *Cf.* footnote 265 *supra*.

> "An investor could rationally prefer a shorter-term government with a low yield over a longer-term government with a higher yield only to the extent (1) that the longer-term issue was selling at a premium over the support price and there was a risk that its price would decline, or (2) that the Federal Reserve would lower its support prices. In view of the fact that both official pronouncements and the problems of debt management strongly indicated that yields on longer-term governments would be prevented from rising significantly not only during the war but also for an indefinite period thereafter, it is small wonder that the Federal Reserve as residual buyer came to hold a large proportion of the shorter-term low-yield issues, thereby adding to bank reserves, while other investors bid down the yields on longer-term issues."[267]

3

A few supplemental observations on the 1942–1946 period:

1) the banks were given huge increments in reserves and non-banking financial institutions had augmented savings capital and reduced investment opportunity. Hence, the Treasury could place massive new issues. However the prices on the menu were such that short-dated securities became increasingly unattractive. The banks developed a Diamond Jim Brady appetite but found (short-term) caviar too expensive.

2) the importance of what came to be known as "playing the pattern" for continuous creation of high powered (reserve) money by the Federal Reserve can be exaggerated. The government's gigantic deficits required that new reserves be created in any case. The Korean Conflict better exemplifies side effects of support operations.

3) the 1942–1946 experience implies little about feasibility of official support of the long-term market through insertion of a peg. Long-term markets were buoyed by ⅜ per cent Treasury bill rate, or, better, by hardening conviction that low bill rate was here to stay (although the peg probably did add to the liquidity of long-dated stock). Officials were not forced *directly* to support long-term securities; Federal Reserve holdings fell.

4) Chart B shows that the buoyant long-term market was reflected in falling yields of high grade corporate bonds during World War II and

[267] Lester V. Chandler, "Federal Reserve Policy and the Federal Debt," *American Economic Review,* Vol. 39 (1949), pp. 405-429, reprinted in Lutz and Mints (eds.) *Readings in Monetary Theory,* p. 394 *ff.* The quotation is at p. 401.

See also J. S. Fforde, *The Federal Reserve System* (Oxford: The Clarendon Press, 1954), a useful book stressing problems of technique.

immediately thereafter, but there was a fairly substantial increase in the yield of prime commercial paper. Private firms had no sponge with which to mop up unsold issues.

4

The fascinating events from about the beginning of 1947 to March 1951 feature heavy political overtones and a cast of characters including such colorful personages as President Harry S. Truman, his Secretary of the Treasury, John Snyder — far from a flamboyant personality but wonderful in his Molotov-like persistence in the cause of cheap money — and Marriner Eccles, the highly articulate Chairman of the Board of Governors whose term of office — unfortunately for him — expired during the Truman administration. On the legislative sidelines were Senator Paul Douglas (D, Ill.) and Representative Wright Patman (D, Tex.), respectively anti- and pro-Treasury. The Federal Reserve finally was unleashed.

The controversy (finding the vast majority of professional opinion siding with the Federal Reserve) is easy to limn. Chart C shows that Secretary Snyder had to arrange for practically continuous refinance of tens of billions of dollars worth of short-term debt. His parochial responsibilities encouraged him to argue for low interest rates — assured by Federal Reserve open-market purchases if necessary.[268] The Federal Reserve was concerned about price inflation. The Consumer Price Index rose from 83.4 to 102.8 from 1946 to 1948, reaching 111.0 in 1951 (1947-9 = 100). Of course, bond support operations gave the banks additional reserves which could feed the inflation.

Consider the "constitutional" crux: should the Federal Reserve's open-market operations be governed by its evaluation of conditions in markets in the light of its longer-term objectives of price stability and economic growth or should Federal Reserve operations be an adjunct to Treasury convenience, the major responsibility for economic stabilization resting with fiscal problems? Doubtless, the Federal Reserve's independence was at stake.

The charts tell the more technical story. The Korean Conflict

268 The Truman administration was not fiscally irresponsible. President Truman urged higher taxes on almost all of his Congresses. Opponents dubbed him "High Tax Harry." His administration might be characterized as "biased against deflation" while the Eisenhower administration might be characterized as "biased against inflation." I think the Truman biases reached absurd heights during the bond support controversy, the Eisenhower biases during 1959 and most of 1960.

began in June 1950. It was a boom year featuring enormous investment in consumer durables and construction. The economy rapidly approached a full-employment state. Interest rates were being pushed up by "real" forces. And yet the Treasury wished the Federal Reserve to support its securities at prices above those then prevailing in the market. Until August 1950, the Federal Reserve complied without protest. Charts D, E, and F tell what happened: it absorbed huge quantities of government securities, creating new bank reserves. The banks could increase *their* portfolios by making loans financing additional demand for goods and services increasingly inelastic in supply. In Wicksellian terms, Treasury policy called for market rate to be forced below natural rate. There would be inflationary pressure so long as the banking system was able and willing to supply funds on the desired scale.[269]

Why did not the 1942–1946 magic work in 1949–1950? Primarily because, in the absence of the exigencies of a major war, it was impossible to dam-up civilian demand. Conviction grew that short rates would rise in the near future and that the long rate would be much "worse behaved" than during World War II. In fact Chart E shows that the Federal Reserve did not seriously attempt to purchase long-dated securities. Such an attempt, short of an utterly unprecedented scale, would have been futile.

Most came to believe that continuation of the 1950 policy would be disastrous, that the inflation could feed on itself as the Federal Reserve pumped reserves into the banking system. Depression of market rate below natural rate would assure rising prices of goods and services. As in one of Parkinson's Laws, nominal demand for loans could expand to take up any slack in bank reserves: "monetary requirements" would increase with rising prices, at least if expectations were not elastic. In the latter case, expectations of rising prices could become so firm that demand for cash (at least in the schedule sense) could fall, perhaps generating hyperinflationary forces.[270]

The scene was set for a Federal Reserve victory. In addition the political tide was out for President Truman in 1950. The Federal Reserve openly defied the Treasury in August 1950, announcing its intention to use its powers — including open-market operations — to combat inflationary pressure. The Treasury remained adamant and

269 Some, *not I*, would add "and the public's security holdings were too large to sustain a lower natural rate."

270 *Cf.* Note K, Ch. VA and Ch. XIII.

the controversy became hot, the Federal Reserve's rooting section becoming larger and more vocal. The first quarter of 1951 saw some remarkable political events: on different occasions Mr. Snyder and President Truman announced that the Federal Reserve had agreed to make sure that the Treasury would not have to pay more than 2½ per cent. These announcements met with heated denials, until finally, on March 4, 1951, an accord was reached. The basic independence of the Federal Reserve was assured, although it remained committed to sustain "orderly markets" and in fact continued to increase its holdings of government securities during 1951. (*Cf.* Chart E.)

The accord has not severed ties between the Federal Reserve and the Treasury. Various support operations — including removal from the market of certain unsuccessful long-dated issues — have been conducted; "maintenance of orderly markets" covers a host of evils. Rather the accord has meant that the independence of the central bank has been sustained. It is basically free to decide for itself when to become an engine of Treasury policy. This division of power may not be logical. Subsequent Federal Reserve policies have disappointed much of the professional opinion which supported it so strongly in 1951. In fact, the next time the Federal Reserve clashes with the Treasury, I believe the Treasury will win.

4) Federal Reserve Anticyclical Policy, 1948–1960

The charts below make clear that the Federal Reserve is now governed by what Currie calls a monetary as against a real bills theory of banking. It thinks in terms of affecting prices and output by controlling or at least influencing the cost and availability of credit. It does not expand credit as demand for loanable funds increases during up-swings (as the needs of trade increase). Nor does Federal Reserve credit contract with the needs of trade during downswings. The Federal Reserve tries to intensify the natural tightening of credit that occurs during upward surges of business activity — at least when the economy is operating at high levels of employment and capacity utilization. (It continued an expansionary posture during the 1961 recovery for example, when there appeared to be much slack in the economy.) (*See Note E.*) It tries to make money markets all the slacker when business activity slackens. And, when creditors become uneasy — certainly during downturns — the Federal Reserve purchases securities, seeking to allay developing fears.

Still the charts speak for themselves so far as the main point is concerned: the contracyclical quality of Federal Reserve policy is apparent. There are many articles and books containing detailed treatment. Students will especially profit from successive *Economic Report(s) of the President*. One *caveat*: consult Note E lest you attach

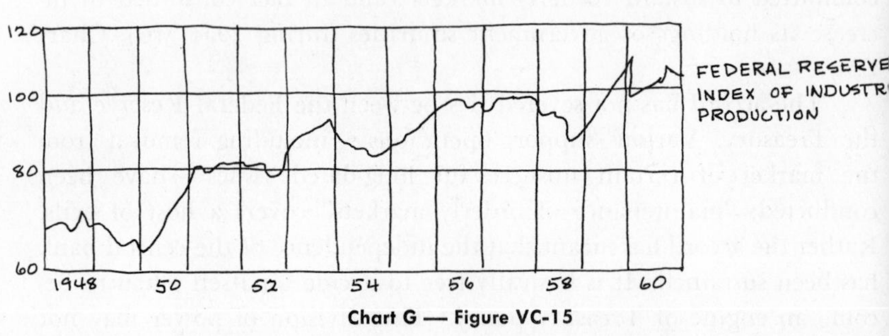

Chart G — Figure VC-15

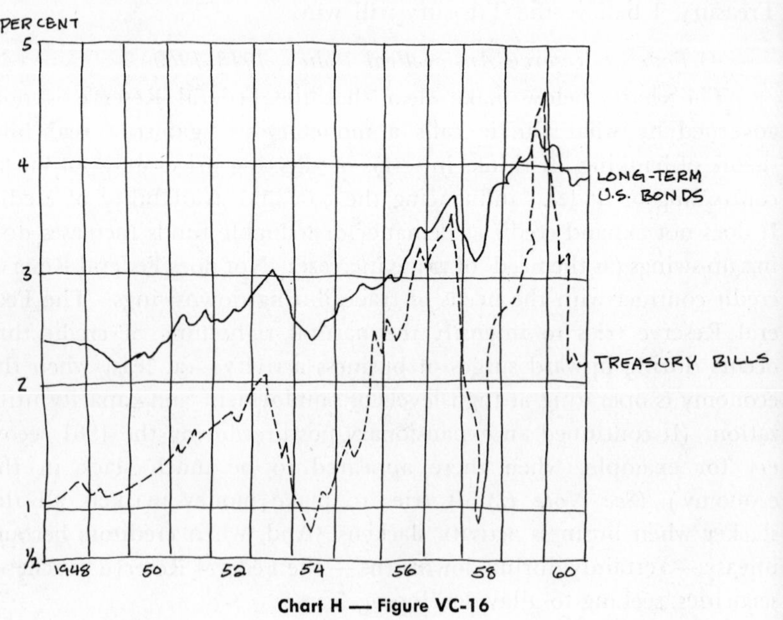

Chart H — Figure VC-16

excessive importance to Federal Reserve policy as the explanation of the strongly positive association between interest rates and industrial production; the *association* would exist quite apart from the central bank's actions.

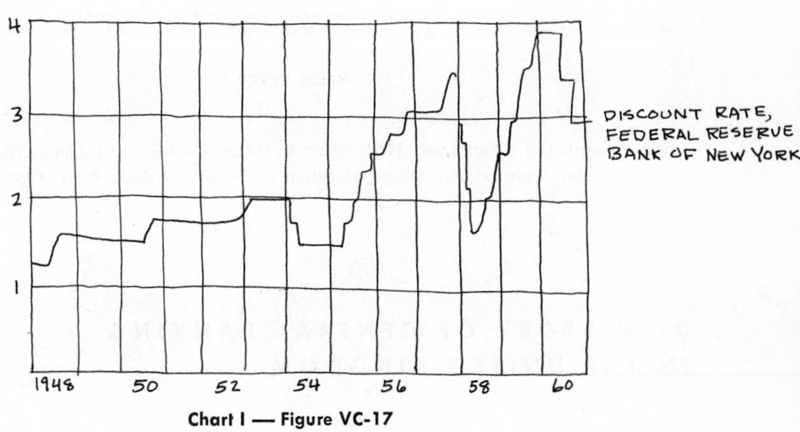

Chart I — Figure VC-17

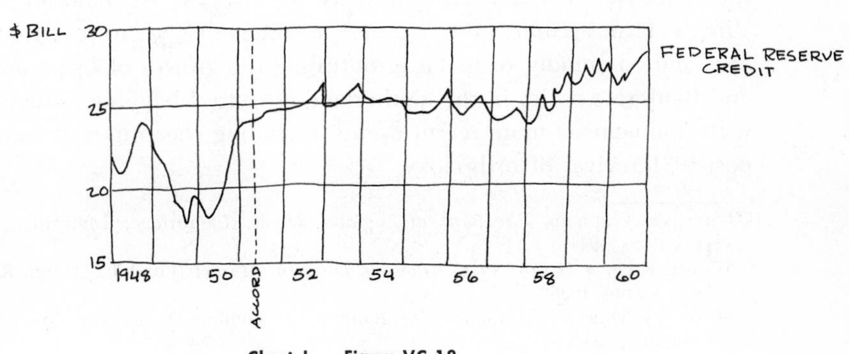

Chart J — Figure VC-18

MARGIN REQUIREMENTS, RESERVE REQUIREMENTS

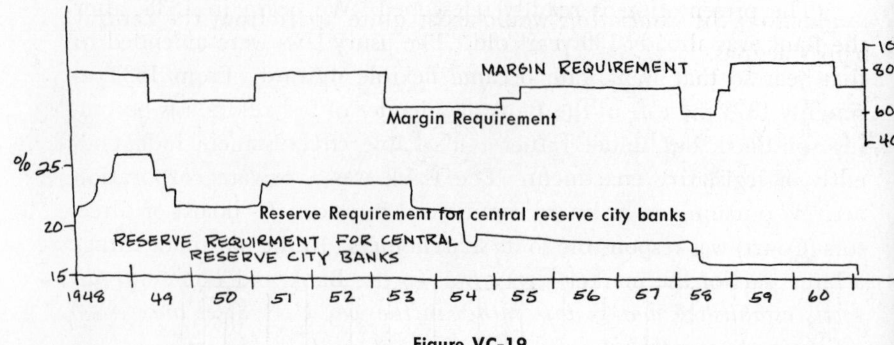

Figure VC-19

Sources: Charts G-J, *Chart Book*, 1961; Chart K, Milton Friedman and Anna J. Schwartz, *The United States Money Stock* (Princeton: Princeton University Press, 1963), Ch. XI.

D. HISTORY OF CENTRAL BANKING IN THE UNITED KINGDOM

There is an excellent literature on the Bank of England. Five authors, Clapham, King, Hawtrey, and Sayers, together with Bagehot, give a thorough, sophisticated, and elegant statement of the history of the Bank and its associated markets.[271] And we are familiar with Viner's classic account. We can, then, confine ourselves to presentation of a limited amount of material outlining the growth of open-market and Bank rate policy in the motherland of central banking — together with comment on more recent events, including cheap money and the post-1951 revival of orthodoxy.

271 Sir John Clapham, *The Bank of England,* 2 vols. (Cambridge: Cambridge University Press, 1944)
Wilfrid King, *A History of the London Discount Market* (London: George Routledge & Sons, 1936)
Sir Ralph Hawtrey, *A Century of Bank Rate* (London: Longmans, Green and Company, 1938)
Sir Ralph Hawtrey, *The Art of Central Banking*
R. S. Sayers, *Central Banking After Bagehot*
Walter Bagehot, *Lombard Street*
Needless to say, this is not meant to be a definitive list.

1. A Skeleton Account

The presentation is readily telescoped. We begin in 1833, after the Bank was already 139 years old. The usury laws were amended in that year so that Bank rate became flexible upward. From 1833 to roughly 1873 the role of the Bank as a lender of last resort was becoming solidified, but under rather remarkable circumstances independently of legislative enactment. The Bank was a private corporation actively pursuing an ordinary commercial business. Its board of directors (Court) was responsible to its shareholders. In the nature of things a large part of the market always was in the Bank and *Bank rate directly established market rate rather in the way U. S. Steel once (sic?) set the price of steel.*

Bagehot's *Lombard Street* overcame the last bastions of resistance to the concept of the Bank as the central banker responsible for the solvency of the City and protection of the national gold reserve. Still inherent contradictions within the joint-stock-central bank distorted the Bank's performance as a central bank. Also the key Bagehotian prescription — an increased gold reserve — was not warmly embraced. Rather, Bank rate policy burgeoned. At first the policy appears to have been developed in close harmony with open-market policy. Later what we have called "pure" Bank rate policy became more prominent. The success of the Bank in manoeuvering on a thin film of gold was extraordinary prior to 1914. The Bank was aided successively by sensitivity of country banks and foreign investors to money-market rates in the City of London. The latter development was abetted in turn by the certainty of foreign exchanges during the heyday of the international gold standard.

The mechanisms of British central banking were developed to a high level of subtlety and power by the turn of the century. But history was to deny the Bank continued sovereignty in the realm of money. There were at least two reasons: (a) endogenous and exogenous factors made the restored gold standard (1925–1931) unsuccessful; (b) interrelations between Bank rate and income and employment came to be stressed; adverse income and employment effects of Bank rate policy, borne with stoic indifference in the last century, became intolerable.

Of course, facets (a) and (b) are connected: the decision of 1925 to maintain so low a price of gold forced the Bank into a defensive posture and adversely affected employment — or so Keynes argued.

By the time Britain left gold in September 1931 attention was focused on the real sectors of the economy. From 1932 to October 1951 (when the Tories were returned after about 6¼ years of Labour rule) Bank rate was demobilized; the Bank was a passive agent for Treasury policy; the nationalization of the Bank more ratified than altered its status. The Tories were more "orthodox." Bank rate from 1951 to 1963 was a more flexible instrument, and one more focused on the balance of payments than on the "control of domestic investment."

2. The Rise and Decline of the Bank's Market Power

We proceed to pad the skeleton with flesh. We begin by tracing the role of the Bank of England as a profit making concern.

1

Bagehot points out (*Lombard Street,* p. 92 *ff.*) that the Bank's profitability largely derived from the politics of its origin and earlier history. The Bank was founded in 1694 in order to bolster the credit of the government of William III. In return for their charter the subscribers lent £1,200,000 at what was regarded as a very favorable (to the king) rate of 8 per cent per annum. Subsequently, the Bank made loans to the government well in excess of its capitalization. "For a long time the Bank of England was the focus of London Liberalism, and in that capacity rendered to the State inestimable services. In return for these substantial benefits the Bank of England received from the Government, either at first or afterwards three important privileges." (*Lombard Street,* p. 93.) These privileges were:

1) "exclusive possession of Government balances";

2) until 1826 a monopoly of limited liability so that the fortunes of the shareholders of only the Bank of England among banks were not subject to liability for the debts of the corporation beyond, of course, their contribution to capital;

3) "the Bank of England had the privilege of being the sole *joint stock company* permitted to issue bank notes in England."[272]

[272] Bagehot points out at pp. 96-97 that a clause in the Act of 1742, giving the Bank a monopoly of joint-stock-bank note issue, contained a clause giving the Bank the power of "exclusive banking." The clause was intended to pertain only to note issue but was broadly interpreted in subsequent years. Indeed, the clause was

> "thought to prohibit any other banking company from carrying on our present system of [deposit] banking. After joint stock banking was permitted in the country, people began to inquire why it should not exist in the Metropolis too? And then it was seen that the words I [Bagehot]

As Bagehot puts it:

> "with so many advantages over all competitors, it is quite natural that the Bank of England should have far outstripped them all. Inevitably it became *the* bank in London; all the other bankers grouped themselves round it, and lodged their reserve with it. Thus our *one*-reserve system of banking was not deliberately founded upon definite reasons; it was the gradual consequence of many singular events, and of an accumulation of legal privileges on a single bank which has now been altered, and which no one would now defend."[273]

The progress of the joint-stock banks was rapid. Compare Sayers, referring roughly to the post-1850 period:

> "though London's business, with the country's, was undergoing spectacular expansion, the staid ways of the Old Lady of Threadneedle Street were uncompetitive, and new business went rather to the rising young men of the joint-stock banks."[274]

2

In consequence, by the 1870's, the Bank of England had been "pushed out of its position as the normal source of half of the market's funds." The Bank could no longer determine money-market rates through its near monopoly of the banking business. Rather it faced market rates that were for it, *as a joint-stock company,* given (parametric). The connotation of "Bank rate" was to change from the rate charged by the Bank of England to its customers to the modern concept of a penalty rate imposed by the Bank as a lender of last resort. The transformation became quite explicit in 1878 when the Bank made it clear that it would discount for its regular customers at market rather than Bank rate. (*Cf. ibid.,* p. 16.)

Sayers's comment on the Bank's distinction between discounting for regular customers and serving as a lender of last resort dramatizes the decline of the Bank as a joint-stock company from 1826 to the 1870's:

---

have quoted only forbid the issue of negotiable instruments, and not the power of receiving money when no such instrument was given. Upon this construction, the London and Westminster Bank and all our older joint stock banks were founded. But till they began, the Bank of England had among companies not only the exclusive privilege of note issue, but that of deposit banking too. It was in every sense the only *banking* company in London."

273 *Ibid.,* p. 97.

274 R. S. Sayers, *op. cit.,* note 121, p. 11.

> "this would at first glance seem to imply a further loss of control; but the Bank's share of the ordinary business of the discount market had dwindled to such a small proportion that market rate was not now likely to be affected by what the Bank was doing for its own customers."

The Bank's directors did not surrender predominance in ordinary banking with easy grace or with chiseled comprehension of the implicit change in the Bank's function. Clapham writes that the Bank was seeking new business as late as 1894.[275] Sayers informs us:

> "although Bagehot's *Lombard Street* clearly, and to the satisfaction of almost everyone, laid the foundations of modern central banking theory, neither the [officials] nor most of the commentators were at all conscious that they were developing a theory of central banking."[276]

He cites as an illustration the protest of the Bank's governor in 1885 against government proposals to borrow from other banks: "the argument ran in terms appropriate to a private customer and private lender."

Finally, the development of open-market policy within the context of the declining affairs of a joint-stock company was halting and sporadic. Open-market sales reduce the central bank's earning assets. Open-market purchases can expand the Bank's portfolio when capital losses are expected or when the liquidity of the makers is in serious doubt.

3. An Annotated Chronicle of Bank Rate Policy

1

Certain key events can now be narrated in chronological sequence. The Bank's Charter was up for renewal in 1832. It came forward with proposals for repeal or amendment of the usury laws (limiting charges to 5 per cent) so that it might have "a free hand to charge a deterrent rate of discount."[277] Such proposals went back as far as Henry Thornton in 1797 and in his great book *Enquiry into the Nature and Effects*

275 *Op. cit.*, Vol. II, p. 255.

276 *Op. cit.*, Ch. 2, p. 18. This is from the "title" essay, "The Development of Central Banking After Bagehot."

277 Hawtrey, *op. cit.*, note 121, p. 16.

of the Paper Credit of Great Britain (1802).[278] "The recommendation of the Bank was adopted, and the usury laws were so amended by the Act of 1833 as not to apply to the rate of discount on bills of exchange maturing within three months."[279]

Recall that the period from, say, 1825 to 1844 found the Bank of England towering over its competitors (other joint-stock banks being banned until 1826). If the Bank wished to increase market rates of interest it needed only to increase charges to its own customers; the Bank could, as Sayers points out, act as a *price leader*.[280] Hawtrey writes that May 1839 witnessed "the first occasion on which Bank rate policy was seriously relied on."[281] A crisis had been precipitated by an external drain to France and Belgium, intensified by crop failures necessitating imports of grain. In truth the maiden voyage of Bank rate policy was unimpressive. Bank rate never rose above 6 per cent. The Bank even failed to exercise price leadership prerogatives: other lenders were able to obtain as much as 6½ per cent by August. Finally, bullion credits were obtained at Paris and Hamburg. However, the crisis proved to be short-lived. Bank rate fell below 2 per cent by 1844.

2

Economic history should not be done by rote. Thus, we should pause to inquire why it would be hoped in 1839 — some years before the international power of the City of London was great enough for Bank rate surely to lead to important inflow and outflow of short-term capital — that a rise in Bank rate would staunch or reverse an *external* drain of bullion. It was expected that higher money-market rates at London would produce three effects, one primary and two auxiliary. ("Primary" and "auxiliary" pertain to putative effect on the drain.) The primary effect was a decline in British price levels.

278 *Paper Credit,* among many other things, shows the most subtle comprehension of the way in which money substitutes can develop during periods of expansion.

279 Hawtrey, *A Century of Bank Rate,* pp. 17-18.

280 Pure (non-collusive) price leadership finds an important firm surrounded by very small firms for whom price is given. Demand for these firms is perfectly elastic. The large firm sets the price, taking account of supplies forthcoming from the small firms at alternative prices. In the non-collusive case, the small firms are free to produce as much as they choose. Thus, the large firm's demand curve is obtained by subtracting "supply of others" from market demand at various prices. The large firm presumably sets the price where its marginal revenue curve cuts its marginal cost curve from above.

The text makes clear that the Bank as early as 1832 was aware of its peculiar responsibilities and did not altogether act as a profit maximizer.

281 *Ibid.,* pp. 18-19.

One of the auxiliary effects (certainly related to the primary effect) was to be a reduction in the volume of bank credit; the other was concerned with high rates at London drawing cash from country banks — their reserve practices being informal.

How were these effects to be generated by Bank rate policy and why were they expected to work? The answer evokes a dilemma long associated with Bank rate policy: payment for reversal of external drains in the currency of unemployment and stunted growth.

Taking up the first auxiliary effect, it was hoped that the contraction in money-market assets (liabilities) induced by higher interest rates would permit the Bank to carry lower specie reserves: potential demand for specie would be less.[282] It is doubtful if this effect could be relied upon: a contraction large enough to produce substantial effects might lead to turmoil inducing an *internal* drain.

The second auxiliary effect pertained to an external drain only to the extent that *specie* could be attracted to London. London would enjoy favorable clearings against the country which might be forced to cough up specie. Indeed, if the Bank were to violate the Palmer Rule and sell securities to the country banks, insisting that they pay in specie, the mechanism would be crystal clear.

As for the primary effect, price deflation was to be produced by the effects of higher interest rates on demand for goods and services. We have already considered how this might come about, but contemporaries had rather unformed notions (and the same can be said about Bagehot years later: *cf. Lombard Street,* p. 47). Thus Hawtrey informs us that "[e]very one took for granted that a high Bank rate was an effective deterrent on borrowing, but it is remarkable how little consideration was given to the precise manner in which the deterrent worked."[283] (*See Note F.*) In any case Hawtrey reports testimony of Horsley Palmer (of Palmer's Rule) before a Parliamentary Committee in 1848 that is fascinating, casting light as it does on the way in which authorities in the nineteenth century weighted the importance of stability in financial as against "real" markets:

> *Question to Palmer:* "It is by producing a fall in the value of all commodities in this country that you would correct the exchange?"

---

282 Of course, the Palmer Rule, supposedly in effect in 1839 but often violated during its unhappy life, called for the Bank to keep its securities constant. In all events, operation of the first auxiliary effect would relieve pressure on other banks and, hence, on the Bank.

283 *Ibid.*, p. 33.

Palmer: "Yes; not merely in that way, but you would bring capital to this country; by the high rate of interest you stop credit." [Recent research suggests that capital flows were more important and price adjustments less important than I have indicated.]

Question to Palmer: "What would be the effect on the manufacturers and laborers in the country during such an operation?"

Palmer: "It destroys the labor of the country; at the present moment in the neighborhood of London and in the manufacturing districts you can hardly move in any direction without hearing universal complaints of the want of employment . . ."

Question to Palmer: "That you ascribe to the measures which it was necessary to adopt in order to preserve the convertibility of the note?"

Palmer: "I think that the present depressed state of labor is entirely owing to that circumstance."[284]

Hawtrey's comment shows commendable understatement:

> "from one of the most influential representatives of the Bank of England so outspoken a recognition of the price paid in the form of trade depression and unemployment for the maintenance of the gold standard is noteworthy."[285]

3

Returning to the narrative, the experience of the Crisis of 1847, the first test of the Bank Charter Act (Peel's Act) of 1844, was signally important: the Bank refused to lend in April of 1847. The disastrous consequences were repaired by suspension of the Act in October 1847, a month that also saw application of what came to be the Bagehotian recommendation of lending without stint at high rates of interest during an *internal* drain.

Recall Chapter IV: the Act of 1844 was analysed in the context of the banking and currency school controversy. The Act separated the banking and issue departments. The note issue was subject to a rigid gold cover moderated only by the statutory fiduciary issue. Short of suspension of the Act, there was unlikely to be a way for the issue department to come to the rescue of the banking department in event

284 *Ibid.*, pp. 27-28.

285 *Ibid.*, p. 28. As is suggested in the text, it is doubtful that effects of declining domestic prices on exports could be generated quickly and substantially enough to staunch a drain; it is unlikely that tremendous momentum could be achieved within a short space of time. Capital flows probably were more important than has been suggested in the text (and empirical work supports this conjecture). On the other hand, the consequences for output and employment of higher Bank rate (attracting foreign funds) could remain as described by Palmer.

of encashment of the latter's deposit liability. It is not surprising then that

> "the new Act had been placed in a sinister light. It had been interpreted to mean that if the reserve fell to zero, the Bank would refuse to lend at all. There would be *no* lender of last resort and the discount market would dry up altogether."[286]

The Bank justified this "sinister light" and restricted its discounts in April 1847, intensifying the effects of other disasters leading to the panic of that year. The panic itself increased country bank demand for notes (which held up well during the various panics) instead of money-market assets. The London market was forced to seek accommodation with the banking department; an *internal* drain developed. In the fall of 1847 the Bank did not refuse accommodation but, in Hawtrey's phrase, was "rapidly approaching the abyss." The government was moved to propose that the fiduciary issue be increased on the condition that Bank rate go to at least 8 per cent. The "proposal" was accepted by the Bank and, with abatement of the market's fear that the Bank would cease to discount, the crisis ended without an increase in the fiduciary issue in fact becoming necessary. The dramatic events of 1847 established — perhaps not as explicitly as now seems to be the case — that it simply was impossible for the banking department to behave like just another joint-stock company, but that, if the Bank clearly stood ready to discount freely, a high Bank rate would dissuade the market from resorting to the Bank; panic could be allayed without serious erosion of the central specie reserve or provision of a great volume of new notes. It became clear that, if necessary during an internal drain, the fiduciary issue would be increased — as it actually was in 1857 — rather than permit the money market to go to the wall of bankruptcy.[287] The shape of things to come was reasonably clear in 1847.

4

The stage is set for fuller introduction of Walter Bagehot and *Lombard Street,* the most readable of economic classics. *Lombard Street* issued from two basic causes: (a) Bagehot's reading of British banking experience from 1825 to 1873; (b) his altercation with a Bank director, Thomson Hankey, on the subject of the Bank's proper re-

286 *Ibid.*, p. 21.
287 *Cf.* footnote 294 *infra.*

sponsibility. Facet (a) already has been limned; Bagehot does so at p. 170 *ff.* of *Lombard Street.* There were three panics since 1844: those of 1847, 1857, and 1866.[288]

> "It is certain that in all of these panics the Bank has made very large advances indeed . . . but there is still a considerable evil; no one knows on what kind of securities the Bank of England will at such periods make the advances which it is necessary to make."[289]

More specifically, since "the *amount* of the advance is the main consideration for the Bank of England, and not the nature of the security on which the advance is made, always assuming the security to be good." Bagehot wanted the Bank to lend on a very broad base of collateral (including railway debentures) in times of internal crisis. As things stood, only fine trade bills, Consols, and India securities — basically the securities the Bank stood ready to discount — could be liquidated in a crisis. The Bank was the only source of cash. Only through the Bank's intervention could the universal quest for cash during a crisis be achieved.

Here Bagehot showed a fine appreciation of what has come to be the accepted doctrine of central bank behavior during a domestic crisis of liquidity: namely, to stand ready to purchase broad ranges of securities, damping cumulative speculative forces feeding an internal drain. Of course, Bagehot did not grasp the role that could be played by purposive open-market operations *à outrance* — a more forceful method of buoying up the market than waiting for it to come to the Bank. And he probably exaggerated the importance of extending the realm of discounting: the greater volume of trade was financed with bills and the important crunch was on short-term debtors; effects on longer-dated paper were likely merely to be sympathetic.

How was the Bagehotian policy to be executed? Through an increase in the gold reserve of the Bank. This seemed particularly im-

---

288 Bagehot feels free to ignore Peel's Act, since it had been suspended during these crises, "and that, rightly or wrongly, the world confidently expects that in all similar cases it will be suspended again." (*Ibid.*, p. 194.)

Keep in mind, throughout, that the discount houses borrowed on very short term. For the banks, call loans were a buffer stock. They were exceedingly vulnerable. To the extent that they had resold or merely guaranteed paper, they similarly were vulnerable to a liquidity crisis under ordinary principles of the law of negotiable instruments. It becomes clear how the British mechanism of central-bank control became tied to the call-loan system.

portant in 1873 when London, already very important as an international money market, had the only bullion market in Europe. The increasing vulnerability of the City to an external drain was obvious to Bagehot, and, since an external (foreign) drain called for specie and bullion — not notes — the importance of an increased gold reserve seemed all the greater.[290] Two brief excerpts from *Lombard Street* reveal the core of Bagehot's conception of the role of the Bank of England:

> ". . . all our credit system depends on the Bank of England for its security. On the wisdom of the directors of that one joint-stock company, it depends whether England shall be solvent or insolvent. This may seem too strong, but it is not. All banks depend on the Bank of England, and all merchants depend on some banker."[291]
>
> "If we remember that the liabilities of Lombard Street payable on demand are far larger than those of any like market, and that the liabilities of the country are greater still, we can conceive the magnitude of the pressure on the Bank of England when both Lombard Street and the country suddenly and at once come upon it for aid. No other bank was ever exposed to a demand so formidable, for none ever kept the banking reserve for such a nation as the English."[292]

We visualize the Bank at the apex of an inverted pyramid of credit, a fractional-reserve bank holding the reserves of fractional-reserve banks, and broadly responsible for maintaining the specie value of vast sums of debt, redeemable in specie but far exceeding the national reserves. This surely was Bagehot's vision. His remedy called for increasing gold reserves so that moderate external drains could be absorbed, while

289 *Ibid.*, p. 194.

290 Page 25 of the 1931 printing of *Lombard Street* shows that on December 30, 1869, the gold-coin-and-bullion holdings of the issue department aggregated £18.3 million and that of the banking department £0.9 million. The banking department also held £10.4 million in notes. Its deposit liability was about £27 million. Of course, this is a large reserve ratio for *ordinary* banking practice, but a large proportion of the Bank's deposits were the *reserves* of other banks. The Bank was unusually vulnerable. What is more, the total of discountable paper much exceeded the Bank's deposit obligation; the banking department's reserve — in the full extent of its function as a lender of last resort — was indeed small.

The Bagehotian call for larger reserves finally received short shrift. Witness the Bank's Return for January 1, 1914. The banking department's reserves, including £1.1 million in gold and silver coin and £22.7 million in notes, aggregated £23.8 million against a deposit liability of £71.3 million. Needless to say, the money market had enormously expanded since 1869 as had the ultimate obligations of the Bank as lender of last resort.

291 *Ibid.*, p. 36.

292 *Ibid.*, p. 61.

vigorous response (albeit at higher Bank rate) could be made to internal drains without endangering the convertibility of the note issue.

It remained unclear, or at least was not conclusively clear, that the Bank viewed itself in the same light. There was another strand of thought leading to *Lombard Street.* The overture is played at the outset of Ch. VII of *Lombard Street.* Iago, acted by Thomson Hankey, waits in the wings, ready to appear eight pages later.

> "The preceding chapters have in some degree enabled us to appreciate the importance of the duties which the Bank of England is bound to discharge as to its banking reserve . . .
>
> . . . the Bank has never by any corporate act or authorized utterance acknowledged the duty, and some of its directors deny it . . .
>
> . . . the distinct teaching of our highest authorities has often been that no public duty of any kind is imposed on the Banking Department of the Bank; that, for banking purposes, it is only a joint stock bank like any other bank; that its managers should look only to the interest of the proprietors and their dividend . . ."

Bagehot thought it imperative that this confusion be remedied:

> "In common opinion there is always great uncertainty as to the conduct of the Bank: the Bank has never laid down any clear and sound policy on the subject. As we have seen some of its directors (like Mr. Hankey) advocate an erroneous policy. The public is never sure what policy will be adopted at the most important moment: it is not sure what amount of advance will be made, or on what security it will be made. The best palliative to a panic is a confidence in the adequate amount of the bank reserve, and on the efficient use of that reserve. And until we have on this point a clear understanding with the Bank of England, both our liability to crises and our terror at crises will always be greater than they would otherwise be."[293]

We turn to the Bagehot-Hankey *contretemps.* The *Economist,* edited by Bagehot, reported a "very remarkable discussion" held at the Meeting of the Court of the Proprietors of the Bank in September 1866, the Panic of 1866 having occurred in the spring. The *Economist* interpreted remarks of the Governor to indicate that the Bank should lend without stint at a high rate of interest, thereby buttressing confidence in the solvency of the City, discouraging a test of that confidence.

293 *Ibid.,* pp. 196-197. I think Bagehot rather exaggerated the shortcomings of the Bank's *conduct* as against its *pronouncements.* His own account of Bank behavior during the post-1844 crises belies the heat of his attack.

In other words, the *Economist* interpreted the Governor to have recognized the uniqueness of the position of the banking department.[294] "This article was much disliked by many of the Bank directors, and especially by some whose opinion is of great authority."[295] These included Hankey, who proceeded to the attack:

> "The *Economist* newspaper has put forth . . . the most mischievous doctrine ever broached in the monetary or banking world in this country; viz. that it is the proper function of the Bank of England to keep money available at all times to supply the demands of bankers who have rendered their own assets unavailable. Until such a doctrine is repudiated by the banking interest, the difficulty of pursuing any sound principle of banking in London will be always very great . . . The more the conduct of the affairs of the Bank is made to assimilate to the conduct of every other well-managed bank in the United Kingdom, the better for the Bank and the better for the community at large."[296]

Hankey's fatal error lay in his failure to appreciate the high insolvency potential of fractional-reserve banking. He did not appreciate how great were prospects for recurrent panic unless reserves were subjected to a centralizing principle, nor did he see that it was the Bank of England — itself working on a fractional reserve — that was charged with this very task, one often inconsistent with its role as a profit-making concern. It was forcefully to extirpate this error that Bagehot wrote *Lombard Street.* He succeeded. But Bagehot, the central banking theorist, was not without his own fatal flaw. In proposing that Bank rate be raised during internal drains, he failed to grasp the fullness of the relationship between the securities markets

---

294 The Bagehotian prescription distinguished between internal and external drains. He called for the Bank to increase its security holdings during an internal drain but accepted the necessity of its reducing these during an external drain if its specie reserves were threatened. During an external drain, increased Bank rate was to *augment* the banking department's reserve. During an internal drain, Bank rate was also to rise, but the banking department was to *use* its reserve.

Remember that an internal drain was likely to feature increased preference for notes, only rarely for bullion. Since such a drain could be staunched with notes, notes could be provided without endangering the national specie reserve. (And, although Bagehot was silent on this, the fiduciary issue could be increased without fear.) External drains, reducing the national specie reserve, necessarily contracted the ultimate monetary base. Fundamentally contractionary measures seemed called for, perhaps because the issue department would be in no position to help (again Bagehot is silent here). And surely the underlying causes of an external drain were more likely to be substantive than psychological: foreigners were unlikely to return to their tents upon receiving Bank notes.

295 *Ibid.*, p. 161.

296 Cited by Bagehot, *op. cit.*, pp. 162-163.

and the labor and commodities markets; he exhibited rather the same blind spot as did Horsley Palmer. It was only in our own time that appreciation of the inadequacies of a monetary policy that would find money-market rates increasing under deflationary pressure became complete. Open-market purchases *à outrance* were not appreciated by Bagehot, but then neither were they by the American officials sixty years later — and it is not clear that they would be appreciated by many central banking officials ninety years later.[297]

5

We now examine the development of the technique of the Bank of England after 1873 ("central banking after Bagehot").

The period after 1855 and before the end of the century saw the Bank's open-market operations become particularly important. The Bank's share of ordinary banking business fell drastically, but Bank rate was not yet rigidly linked to various short-term rates. The Bank surely could not increase money-market rates merely by announcing higher Bank rate; it simply did not have enough customers for Bank rate to be that decisive. Rather it had to make its rate *effective* through open-market sales. Keep in mind that open-market operations at London came to be for the purpose of making effective (bringing bill rate up against) the Bank's discount rate; the Bank as lender of last resort came to recognize a duty to accommodate the market at Bank rate which came to stand above bill rate.

Open-market sales often were at the expense of the Bank's profits. The specific technique used from roughly 1850 to 1880 is itself interesting: operating through the agency of the firm of Mullens and Marshall, the Bank borrowed in the market (took up funds), leaving government securities as collateral; directly reducing reserves of the joint-stock banks but paying interest to Mullens and Marshall. As Sayers writes:

> "The costliness of these operations was a source of discomfort to a Court that felt a tightness in its own income account. When the Bank's responsibility as the central bank clearly called for such action, it did bear the expense, but it did it grudgingly."[298]

Since open-market sales were expensive for the Bank, it is not surprising that it tended to be less than energetic in pursuing contractionary

[297] Perhaps we are not fair to Bagehot. If the Bank's gold reserves were increased enough, the probability of a crisis occurring would be much reduced.

[298] Sayers, *op. cit.*, p. 12.

policies and from time to time attempted to enlarge its portfolio of income earning assets when economic indicators would tell a central bank to contract. Over much of the 1858-1878 period Bank rate chased market rate, suggesting that the Bank was behaving as a member of the ordinary profit maximizing banking community, albeit an increasingly less important member.

The formalization by the Bank in 1878 of its growing practice of discounting for its customers at market rate regardless of Bank rate distinguished its "public" role as a lender of last resort from its "private" role as a firm. Bank rate came to possess its modern connotations. The most important connotation, *penality,* became distinct. Bank rate was now definitely irrelevant in the context of Bank efforts to attract ordinary business. Then, with the growing concentration of English banking as country banks were absorbed by the great London banks, Bank rate began during the second half of the nineteenth century to become formally tied to a broad spectrum of interest charges. Pure Bank rate policy emerged. These trends gathered momentum between 1878 and 1914 so that by 1914 the Bank of England's performance as an ordinary bank was little more than an obeisance to ancient practice.

Bank rate would not have acquired its aura of legerdemain—permitting "unenforced" changes in Bank rate to affect market rates—except for its potency during the nineteenth century when Bank rate was made effective by open-market policy.[299] So potent was Bank rate in the latter part of the nineteenth century that it came to be the exclusive means by which the liquidity of the City of London was protected. The Bank of England was able to operate with gold reserves relatively thinner than in Bagehot's day. The crucial determinants of the success of Bank rate later in the nineteenth century and from 1900 to 1914 have been discussed. During the first half of the period the sensitivity of country bankers to London money-market rates made it possible for increases in Bank rate (when made effective) to draw cash to London; later in the century, when country banking became less important, the growing and in fact predominant role of London as a center for international finance meant that gold could in short order be attracted to the City through higher money-market rates. The rigid and stable foreign exchanges made these international

[299] This is *not* to say that Bank rate in the 20th century is not enforced. It has been on *many* occasions.

movements remarkably sensitive to international differentials in short-term rates. Finally, the world's gold stock increased rapidly late in the nineteenth century: there was an over-all upward push to global liquidity; the environment discouraged sustained pressure on liquidity positions.

6

In chronicling the development of the Bank of England in the nineteenth and early twentieth centuries as a true central bank, one must not forget that Bank rate was from the beginning a device to protect Britain's gold stock; use of Bank rate policy to control the price level of a closed fiat paper system would be foreign to its progenitors. If in fact Bank rate policy (including open-market operations) *can* be useful in "controlling investment," one can thank a benign Providence. (*See Note G.*)

4. Ultra-cheap Money

1

We conclude with an analysis of the ultra-cheap money drive ("Daltonism" after the late Hugh Dalton, Labour Chancellor of the Exchequer) of 1945–1947. It feeds our interest in sustained official intervention in the market for long-dated securities. I have primarily relied on three sources: W. M. Dacey, *British Banking Mechanism;* R. S. Sayers, *Modern Banking;* F. W. Paish, *The Post-War Financial Problem* (London: Macmillan and Co., Ltd., 1950) — specifically "Cheap Money Policy," p. 16 *ff.*, originally published in *Economica*, August 1947. (*See Note H.*)

The objective of the Chancellor (Dalton) was to drive down the yield of Consols from about 2.75 per cent per annum to 2.5 per cent or perhaps less than that. The chart on the following page gives the context.

How might this be accomplished? (1) it could be made clear that the government was determined to sustain cheap money for the indefinite future; (2) Treasury bill rate could be forced down, the Bank standing ready to purchase bills on a lower yield basis; purchase operations would create bank reserves, making it more likely that the lower rate could be sustained; lower Treasury bill yields might influence the price of Consols through substitutional effects and through increasing

PATTERN OF INTEREST RATES, U.K.[300]

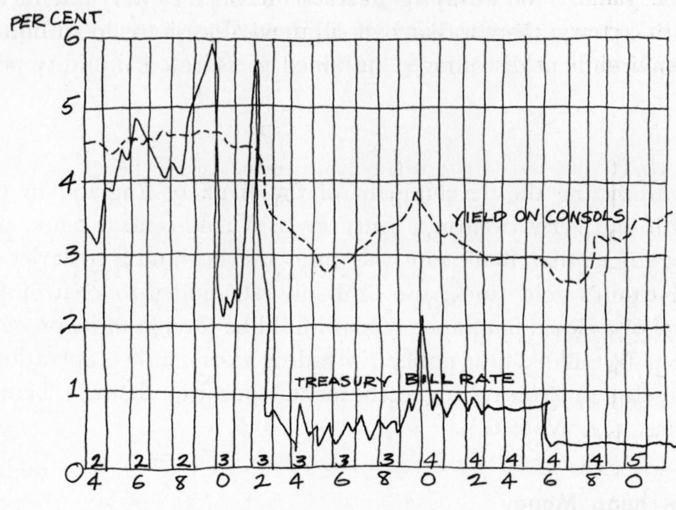

Figure VC-20

Source: W. M. Dacey, *British Banking Mechanism,* p. 144.

conviction of traders that cheap money was here to stay; (3) the officials could stand ready to support Consols through purchase operations.

Precisely these measures were taken during the 1945–1947 drive. But long rates, much dependent on market expectations about future short rate — modified by differences in current running yield — proved recalcitrant. Government departments had to step into the breach which proved to be a yawning chasm. They began to buy up large quantities of long-term securities, acquiring the means of payment by selling Treasury bills to the banks.

"Hold on! Sales of Treasury bills to the banks reduce their reserves. How can short rates be kept low if this is done?" The answer is that the Bank, through its "ever-open-back-door" system, stood ready to purchase bills in the open market at ½ per cent per annum. The picture is clarified: the government purchased long-term securities,

300 *Note:* from 1924 to 1932 the pattern of Treasury-bill yield adheres very closely to that of Bank rate which was at 2 per cent (except for a brief interval in 1939) from 1932 to 1951. The open back door breaks up this relationship later (*cf.* Note H).

simultaneously selling short terms to the banks (let us say). But the Bank of England stood ready to purchase bills at $\frac{1}{2}$ per cent. The wherewithal, created by the Bank of England, was there to sustain a low bill rate while supporting bonds.[301]

2

The chart shows that the ultra-cheap money drive failed. In due course the authorities saw that stubborn expectations would force them to purchase fantastic quantities of securities, and that prospects for success would still be dim.[302]

Consider carefully why the drive failed. The reasons were both "real" and monetary.

The 1945–1947 period in Britain was one of enormous potential excess demand in the commodities and labor markets. (It was held in check by controls.) The smallish margin of resources available beyond consumption expenditures was dwarfed by exigent demands of households and firms seeking to accomplish capital formation: "in the prevailing economic circumstances, even 3 per cent was an unnaturally low rate, defended only by the stringent physical controls of capital investment."[303] If controls were abolished, there would have been substantial excess supply in securities markets: because of massive new issues and firms' attempts to transform liquid assets into fixed assets. It was impossible for the market to believe that *lower* interest rates could be sustained, especially as physical controls became harder to impose with the passage of time. By the same token, recognition of

[301] The text's process has the public reducing Consol holdings, taking cash instead. The banks buy bills from the Government and are able to supply cash for the public by exchanging bills for deposits at the Bank of England. In fact the fractional-reserve principle permits the banks to achieve multiple expansion of asset portfolios. The Bank will provide the reserve basis for the public's initial cash increment *and* for secondary expansion of bank portfolios and deposits. Sayers, *op. cit.*, pp. 210-212, works through the process with T-accounts.

Other variants are possible: the public might wish to exchange Consols for bills instead of cash, in which case the clearing banks would not have to rescue the Government; the banks might unload Consols; etc. In all variants stubborn expectations force the Government to absorb long-term securities.

[302] Of course, the aggregate stock of securities is of a larger order of magnitude than department-held public debt.

[303] R. S. Sayers, *Modern Banking*, p. 217. He goes on to comment on expectational factors that wrecked Daltonism: ". . . But 3 per cent had after all been held for years, and it was the attempt, the patently juggling attempt, to press it down yet farther, flying in the face of basic conditions, that the market found so difficult to swallow. The distrust . . . was perhaps heightened by the tone of the propaganda speeches of the then Chancellor . . ."

powerful inflationary potential made for reluctance to hold long terms at yield that could become *negative* in real terms with inflation. In fact the chart above shows this is exactly what would have happened on a 2.5 per cent yield basis and that, all in all, those holding Consols postwar have been losers for this reason alone. The real factors worked against Daltonism.[304]

3

It remains true that securities prices are determined in securities markets. Dacey and Paish have summarized proximate "financial" causes of the collapse of ultra-cheap money. Their analyses readily apply to U. S. Treasury policy during the Korean Conflict.

1) Since the long rate is influenced by expectations of future short rates, and it is impossible for the government of a country with free elections to bind future governments, the impact of official pronouncements and of a near-zero bill rate is bounded.

2) As latent inflationary forces build up, consequences of the pot boiling over become more and more severe. Fixed-income securities become less and less attractive. Excess supply in the gilt-edged market increases, as does the difficulty of the officials' self-assigned task.

3) Speculative factors, which can work in favor of the policy at its onset (increased prices of long-term securities might spur hopes of further capital gains) are likely to work against the policy once it runs into trouble. Expectations of even a small increase in yields tomorrow or next week induce strong selling pressure: the running-yield sacrifice is miniscule over so short a period. "When interest rates are low, it takes several years even of gross income to make up for the capital loss due to a small rise in interest rates . . ."[305]

---

304 What would be the result of Daltonism *à outrance* without controls? Since planned bond sales would exceed planned buying at 2.5 per cent, the authorities would have to take up securities. Surely bank depositors would not want to switch to long-terms. Bond markets simply could not be cleared without official purchases. It follows that: (1) in due course the public would have surrendered its long-term Governments to the departments; (2) inflation would persist throughout. The officials indirectly would provide funds for firms planning physical expansion, at least until complete departmental absorption of long-term Governments led to detachment of private and public yields. Initial windfall profits might permit these plans partially to be realized, but soon would be offset by increased factory prices and diversion of resources to the consumer goods sector. (*Cf.* Appendix A, Ch. XII.)

This has been an exercise in central banking pathology. Up until now we have dealt (except for the counterpart American illustration) with open-market purchases during stagnant trade and sales during booms. Here we have purchases during booms. (*Cf.* also Ch. XIII.)

305 Paish, *op. cit.*, p. 20. *Cf.* also Dacey, *op. cit.*, p. 165 *ff.*

4) Pursuance of ultra-cheap money in a world in which interest rates have more or less been set free can require exchange controls and lead to bureaucratically regimented foreign trade. Of course, there was no pretence of convertibility of the pound between 1945 and 1947.

SUMMARY

1. *A priori* discussion of central banking problems of under-developed or new countries leads to these conclusions:

   a) the analogy to the United States of 1789, which adopted monetary policies appealing to foreign investors, is perhaps too much neglected.

   b) a primary function of a central bank in a new country is to create financial markets so that debt instruments can become more liquid. The central bank is likely to engage in regular banking business.

   c) convertibility is critically tied to attraction of physical capital from abroad. The central bank should go to some lengths to inspire confidence in the convertibility of debt obligations into gold and hard currency. Convertibility also can be advanced by foreign aid and by surrender of foreign-held securities for now-more-liquid domestic securities. Fixed exchange rates seem appealing.

   d) development of financial markets is important both for lowering the equilibrium rate of interest and for stimulating planned savings.

2. The central banking concept got off to a fast start in this country with the chartering of the first Bank of the United States in 1791. The Bank's history actually tells little about early central banking: the satellite system was rather trivial. An exception: the Bank supplied a sound note issue.

3. The history of the Second Bank of the United States, however fascinating in its political ramifications (explored in Ch. II), adds relatively little to the story of the functional evolution of central banking. However, note that

   a) economic growth was accompanied by great expansion in banking enterprise; the central banking function of the Second Bank is more relevant;

   b) Nicholas Biddle showed consciousness of the Second Bank's central banking function.

4. 1836 to 1863 was in the United States an essentially *laissez faire* interval marked by massive dishonesty and shady banking prac-

tice. The State's police functions were not performed. Honest banks often failed. The stock of money fluctuated violently. Cumulative monetary expansion and contraction was encouraged by the absence of either constitutional or discretionary checks. We suggested that probabilistic considerations exacerbated things.

5. Analysis of the National Banking System (1863–1914) centered on the prolonged debate prior to establishment of the Federal Reserve System rather than on its actual functioning. We did observe that the system performed rather better than its critics allowed and contemporary writers imply.

6. The debate centered on three basic issues: (a) inelasticity of the supply of money; (b) the structure of the reserve system; (c) absence of a perfected commercial-acceptances market.

7. There was a strong real bills tinge to most of the criticisms of the inelasticity of the money supply under the National Banking System. On the other hand, criticisms of *seasonal* inelasticity would have to be accorded higher marks.

8. The National Banking System's "constitution" led to heightened fluctuation in the stock of bank money when country banks were faced with drains and to poor interconvertibility of notes and deposits. However, the record of bank failures under the National Banking Act seems superior to that under the Federal Reserve System through the 1920's and, of course, during the early 1930's.

9. Some discussants of the acceptances-market issue showed profound insight into the nature of central banking. Others espoused sheer real bills doctrine. Thus some recognized that commercial paper's liquidity would increase if there were a central bank ready to accommodate a distressed market, albeit at penal discount rate. (Remember also that significant open-market operations would have to be in commercial paper: the aggregate of national debt was small.) These writers (*circa* 1910) understood that development of open-market policy and of a Bagehotian mechanism depended upon linkage of central banking institutions with the (improved) commercial-paper market. But there were others, concerned that the money market be supplied with new cash during periods of expansion and that cash be withdrawn from it when the needs of trade subsided. Commercial-loan theorists envisaged a passive role for the new central bank. And in fact the Federal Reserve did play a passive role in 1920–1921.

10. Open-market policy was not important for the Federal Reserve's founders: it suggests purposive intervention in contrast with the passive role suggested by real bills. Open-market policy was somewhat impeded by countervailing movements in "bills purchased," but, before the end of the 1920's, it became the Big Bertha of the Federal Reserve armory. Open-market policy from 1928 to 1933 was not distinguished.
11. The economic crisis of the early 1930's failed to elicit massive response from the Federal Reserve — or from the Congress or Treasury. The liquidity crisis was not countered by massive security purchases. There was no attempt to avert a collapse of investment expenditure through a timely and vigorous cheap-money policy. In fact concern for national gold reserves led the Federal Reserve in 1931 to raise its discount rate and generally tighten credit.
12. Open-market policy — voided in the later 1930's by enormous excess and free member bank reserves — was massively reactivated during World War II.
13. The chapter concluded with a synoptic and selective account of British central banking history. The major themes were evolution of a joint stock company as a central bank against the will of influential members of the company, and the evolution of Bank rate policy. In the nineteenth century, income and employment effects of central bank actions in defense of specie reserves received little attention, but they are extremely important in the twentieth century.

NOTES

NOTE A: But *cf.* Randolph Burgess, *op. cit.*, for limitations imposed by the Federal Reserve on its bill buying (and Ch. VA, Note A, for a theoretical analysis). Burgess described Federal Reserve — bill market relations:

". . . the bill market provides a medium by means of which additional Federal Reserve credit is obtained in times of temporary money strain and returned when the strain is passed. If the money market incurs a loss of funds so that bank reserves are impaired, the banks promptly sell bills to the market or to the Reserve Banks. If the dealers find funds difficult to obtain at reasonable rates, they sell bills to the Reserve Banks either outright or under repurchase agreement." (*Ibid.*, p. 175.)

Thus dealers in bank acceptances might be asked to take up additional bills when their own bank credit was under restraint. The Federal Reserve stood ready to intervene. The upshot was a caricature of the London system: accommodation was offered below market rates.

The present-day bill market, including Federal Reserve-dealer relationships, is authoritatively and lucidly described in Robert V. Roosa, *Federal Reserve Operations in the Money and Government Securities Markets* (New York: Federal Reserve Board, 1956), *must reading.* These are some of Roosa's important points:

1) dealers play an important role in the New York market. They "make markets" (performing crucial brokerage in thin markets) and are buffers between the public, the banks, and the Federal Reserve.

2) dealer accommodation by the Federal Reserve today usually is at Federal Reserve (New York) discount rate, subject to a Treasury bill rate floor.

3) dealer accommodation, often under 15-day repurchase agreements (obligating the dealer to repurchase securities sold to the Federal Reserve), is offered as a smoothing device, as part of what Roosa calls *defensive* central bank operations.

4) the bank-dealer-Federal Reserve nexus could build up an engine of inflation. After all, "one part of the dealer's 'buffer' role is his readiness to take short-term government securities in some volume at a reasonable price whenever banks or others are trying to obtain funds on balance by selling them. At the same time, banks . . . [will] . . . perhaps call back their loans." (*Ibid.*, p. 16.) But today recourse to the Federal Reserve is not automatic. If it suits official purposes, dealers will be forced to sell-off holdings in order to repay dunning banks. Or perhaps the dealer will have to accept the cold comfort that "at a price some New York bank will usually find a way to lend him the last bit he needs." (*Ibid.*, p. 17.)

5) dealers are not permitted adventitiously to exploit spreads between discount and market rates; repurchase agreements can be used to assure that dealers are ". . . kept on a short leash."

NOTE B: Compare W. L. Smith, "The Discount Rate as a Control Weapon," *Journal of Political Economy*, April 1958, pp. 171-177. Referring to the 1954–1956 restriction, he writes:

> "if the discount rate had been kept high enough relative to interest rates on shorter-term government securities to have induced the banking system to have liquidated additional securities [pointing out that banks reduced governments holdings by $10.2 billion from the end of 1954 to the end of 1956] rather than increasing their borrowings from the Federal Reserve to this extent, I believe that the restrictive policy might have been developed somewhat more effectively than it was." (*Ibid.*, p. 173.)

Caution is indicated:

1) the Federal Reserve no longer looks at member bank borrowing during booms as natural events to be accommodated willy-nilly. As Keynes put it, "no member has an absolute *right* to borrow." Recourses looking like continuous borrowing have been *permitted* by the Federal Reserve.

2) if member bank borrowing were to exceed expectations, the Federal Reserve can make additional sales. The all-important question concerns the Federal Reserve's choice of target: concern for free as against total reserves can lead to fatuity. Criticisms of monetary policy dating back to the early 1920's have stressed that open-market sales can be countered by easy access to the discount window. To repeat, since 1925 the Federal Reserve has assumed responsibility for continuous borrowing quite apart from penality of discount rate; the rub is in its *criteria.* For an excellent discussion, *cf.* W. G. Dewald, "Free Reserves, etc.," *Journal of Political Economy*, April, 1963.

On the other hand, Smith's proposal that rediscount rate be put a full point above Treasury bill rate is appealing and would add precision and simplicity, as well as improving the timing of open-market operations. (*Cf. ibid.*, pp. 176-177.)

There is a passage at p. 172 (*loc. cit.*) that goes far to clarify matters: "there has been a tendency to look upon increased member-bank borrowing as a force intensifying credit restraint. The reasoning behind this attitude is that member banks, being reluctant to borrow, are likely to tighten their credit standards and turn away more borrowers, when they are forced to turn to the Federal Reserve for accommodation."

The view *described* by Smith is illogical. Banks come to the Federal Reserve because the demand curve for loans has shifted rightwards. Accommodation gives the banks high powered money, perhaps leading to increased supply prices. Market clearance might very well find the cost of borrowing higher. But so what! Equilibrium supply price after an increase in demand (in the schedule sense) almost always is higher. *But*, if the Federal Reserve nabobs should adopt this fallacy, they will stand by unconcernedly despite unexpectedly large member bank borrowing. To the extent that this has happened, I should be quick to share Smith's misgivings. *Cf.* p. 368 *supra*.

We have neglected to point out that, even if banks wished to sell bills in order to accommodate customers seeking additional loans, failure to accomplish these plans in a congested market (responding sluggishly) may lead to their borrowing from the central bank at rates above prime-bill rates, although below loan rate . . . There are a number of features of our monetary institutions augmenting cyclical instability.

NOTE C: The table gives yields on 3-month Treasury bills, 4-6 month prime commercial paper, and also Federal Reserve discount rate for 1929–1960. Yields are per cent per annum and are averaged annually.

Year	T. B.	Commercial Paper	Dis. R.	Year	T. B.	Commercial Paper	Dis. R.
1929		5.85	5.16	1945	0.375	0.75	1.00
1930		3.59	3.04	1946	0.375	0.81	1.00
1931	1.40	2.64	2.11	1947	0.56	1.03	1.00
1932	0.88	2.73	2.82	1948	1.04	1.44	1.34
1933	0.52	1.73	2.56	1949	1.10	1.49	1.50
1934	0.26	1.02	1.54	1950	1.22	1.45	1.59
1935	0.14	0.75	1.50	1951	1.55	2.16	1.75
1936	0.14	0.75	1.50	1952	1.77	2.33	1.75
1937	0.45	0.94	1.33	1953	1.93	2.52	1.99
1938	0.05	0.81	1.00	1954	0.95	1.58	1.60
1939	0.02	0.59	1.00	1955	1.75	2.18	1.89
1940	0.014	0.56	1.00	1956	2.66	3.31	2.77
1941	0.10	0.53	1.00	1957	3.27	3.81	3.12
1942	0.33	0.66	1.00	1958	1.84	2.46	2.16
1943	0.37	0.69	1.00	1959	3.41	3.97	3.36
1944	0.375	0.73	1.00	1960	2.93	3.85	4.53

Source: Economic Report of the President.

From October 1942 to April 1946 a preferential rate of 0.50 per cent applied to advances secured by Government securities maturing or callable in one year or less.

Commercial paper rates above discount rate have no significance for member-bank borrowings if discount rate is above Treasury bill rate, perhaps subject to this *caveat*: when the margin is as close as it often has been, costs of disposing of bills *vis-a-vis* borrowing from the Federal Reserve can be decisive; slight "locked-in" effects might be generated by a rise in bill rate.

Finally, when the Federal Reserve's discount rate became penal in 1960, member-bank indebtedness fell more than $800 million. It had risen almost $350 million in 1959 when the discount rate fell below Bill rate. When the authorities *sometimes* are permissive, they can gain all the more leverage by making discount rate penal. 1960 does not seem to have been an ideal year for the experiment.

NOTE D:

EARNING ASSETS OF THE FEDERAL RESERVE BANKS, PRICES, AND INDUSTRIAL PRODUCTION

Date	Earning Assets (in millions of dollars)	Wholesale Price Index (1926=100)	Index of Industrial Production (1923–1925=100)
Jul 1829	1,380	96.5	120
Oct 1929	1,450	95.1	121
Dec 1929	1.643	93.3	96
Mar 1930	1,095	90.2	106
Jul 1931	954	72.0	80
Oct 1931	2,088	70.3	75
Mar 1932	1,652	66.0	68
Jul 1932	2,422	64.5	56
Feb 1933	2,224	59.8	64
Dec 1933	2,669	70.8	69

Sources: Annual Report of the Federal Reserve Board (1933), pp. 74-75, 240-241, 251. Set out in Lloyd W. Mints, *Monetary Policy in a Competitive Society* (New York: McGraw-Hill Book Co., 1950), p. 45. Used by permission.

NOTE E: Keynes refers to "the well-established and easily-explained tendency of prices and interest to rise together on the upward phase of the credit cycle, and to fall together on the downward phase . . ." (*Treatise,* Vol. II, p. 198.) Chapter VA and Part II of this book make it clear that there will be a tendency for interest rates to rise during the upswing as the demand for loanable funds increases, the supply of loanable funds being augmentable only by the flow of idle cash into active circulation if the system is near full employment. Similarly, on the downswing, there will be a tendency for desired transactions balances to fall as business activity slackens, leading to excess supply of cash. In neither case, does Keynes accept as an explanation of changing interest rates over the cycle discrepancies of *ex ante* savings and investment; these are, he argues, offset by equal and opposite changes in finance requirements.

What Keynes called the "Gibson Paradox" is yet another thing: "For some years past Mr. A. H. Gibson has published a series of articles . . . emphasizing the extraordinarily close [positive] correlation over a period of more than a hundred years between the rate of interest, as measured by the yield of Consols, and the level of prices, as measured by the Wholesale Index-Number." (Keynes, *Treatise,* Vol. II, p. 198.)

As Keynes writes, ". . . the correlation is a long-period, or intermediate, rather than a strictly short-period phenomenon, and is not less striking if the sharp oscillations . . . associated with credit cycles are smoothed out . . ." (*Op. cit.*, p. 201.) His explanation (p. 201 *ff.*) of the *secular* phenomenon of the Gibson Paradox essentially is that there will be a tendency for market rates of interest to be sticky: when natural rate falls, market rate will tend to fall at a much slower rate; there will be a lengthy deflationary period, a natural outgrowth of market being above natural rate.

NOTE F: Hawtrey deals with "deterrence" at pp. 32-36.

He reminds us of the domination of the Currency Principle, that "[Bank rate] was raised in order to prevent an over-issue of notes." Perhaps the text attributes too much sophistication to the Court of the Bank in discussing the first auxiliary effect.

He points out that after April, 1847, for reasons the text explores, "the Bank definitely abandoned the expedient of refusing to lend. The use of Bank rate as a deterrent on borrowers was then the only policy available."

He points out that trade in those days was financed by bills. If I were to purchase $100 worth of cloth from you and lacked cash, I would issue an IOU which you or another could present for cash payment 90 days from now. If you had sold the bill and if I went bankrupt, *you* would be on the spot: your name would appear on my "rubber bill." Today such a transaction would find me borrowing $100 from my bank (giving it my IOU for something more than $100), writing a check in your favor. If I went broke (after the check was cashed), you would *not* be on the spot. "Under the bill system traders were terribly dependent on one another's solvency. A 'shock to credit' would result in a general reluctance to purchase goods by the acceptance of bills. A decline of orders to manufacturers would follow, and so general depression and unemployment and a fall of prices." (*Ibid.*, pp. 35-36.) Today banking and non-banking financial intermediaries — backed by agencies of the federal government — absorb much of this risk.

NOTE G: Hawtrey writes of the traditional purposes of Bank rate policy: "the broad conclusion to which an examination of the facts leads us is that the policy followed in the use of Bank rate from 1858 to 1914 continued on the whole to be guided by the principles enunciated in the earlier period. Since the aim of the Bank of England was to keep its banking operations within the limits appropriate to its reserve, *the reserve is always the governing factor* [emphasis supplied]. Any change in Bank rate is usually associated in an obvious manner with the state of the reserve, and, even where this is not so, that is because causes were believed to be at work to affect the reserve in the near future, such as the existence of gold in transit." (*Op. cit.*, p. 40.)

The text underplays the historical relationship between the Bank and the discount houses. But we hasten to admit that Bank-rate policy long has been conditioned by the Bank's responsibility as lender of last resort. Hawtrey gives an authoritative account at pp. 36-37 of *A Century of Bank Rate*. These are his essential points:

1) "the London bankers from 1825 onwards made a point of never offering bills for rediscount."

2) the discount houses fell into their present relationship with the London banks by 1825, although the banks also were substantial holders of trade bills. "The banks . . . could strengthen their cash by ceasing to buy; if that was too tardy an expedient, they called up the money they lent to the discount houses."

3) *Circa* 1858 it was not uncommon, when the banks were strengthening their cash, for market rate to rise above Bank rate, nor was it uncommon for traders to bring bills directly to the Bank of England, although it was also a regular practice for discount houses to rediscount when the market was under stress.

4) in 1858 the Bank announced that it would no longer discount bills for the discount houses and would make advances to the houses only by special arrangements. "This course was not ultimately compatible with the call money system, which for the banks was a substitute for rediscounting." Of course, so long as traders were permitted to go to the Bank, the banks could gain some succor by permitting bills to run off (implicitly), sending payers of such bills to the Bank. In any event, it was not until 1890 that the Bank definitely accepted the discount houses as the principal channel through which bills came for rediscount.

Hawtrey's *The Art of Central Banking* is invaluable for Chapters VA and VC, especially Ch. IV, "The Art of Central Banking." *Art* makes these points, among others:

1) The Bank's position as lender of last resort made it crucial that Bank rate be raised promptly and "enough" in event of an external drain; unless foreigners could be induced to hold London assets, the banking department soon would be stripped of its reserves. As the Governor said of the 1866 crisis, ". . . before the Chancellor . . . was perhaps out of his bed, we had advanced one-half of our reserves . . ."

2) It seems that the Bank sometimes expanded its discounts in response to increasing supplies of trade bills rather than merely to relieve the money market from *contractionary* pressure.

NOTE H: Spaced throughout the book, there is an account of British monetary policy from 1932 to 1961. Bank rate was immobilized from 1932 to 1951. Treasury bill rate averaged about 0.5 per cent per annum from 1932 to 1939, the yield on Consols falling rather steadily from about 4.5 per cent in 1931 to a low of 2.75 per cent in 1934, rising to a peak of 4 per cent during 1939, never falling below 2.5 per cent, and rising from the 1946 nadir to about 3.75 per cent in 1951. Treasury bill rate never meaningfully exceeded 1 per cent from 1940 through 1950. (The Bank maintained an open back door for Treasury bills during most of the Atlee premiership. It stood ready to purchase Bills on a 0.5 per cent yield basis under the open-back-door policy.) Bank rate essentially was invariant at 2 per cent. Thus, the government, aided by the Bank, assured that short rate would be sustained at low levels and succeeded in bringing down long-term rates although these remained well above short-term rates, reflecting the market's persistent disbelief in the future of cheap money. The 1932–1951 period saw the authorities willing to provide the banking system with whatever reserves were necessary to maintain short-term money rates at low levels.

The interval — fall 1951 through summer 1961 — saw a return to monetary orthodoxy. Bank rate reached 7 per cent on two occasions and was subject to substantial fluctuation. Monetary policy largely was keyed to external drains, although it was mobilized from time to time against the secular inflationary pressure (from the side of demand and/or costs) featuring the postwar British economy.

There follows a chart, "Yield on Treasury Bills, Consols, and Changes in Bank Rate, 1951–1959," copied from p. 146 of the *Report* of the Radcliffe Committee. Yields are monthly averages except for Bank rate.

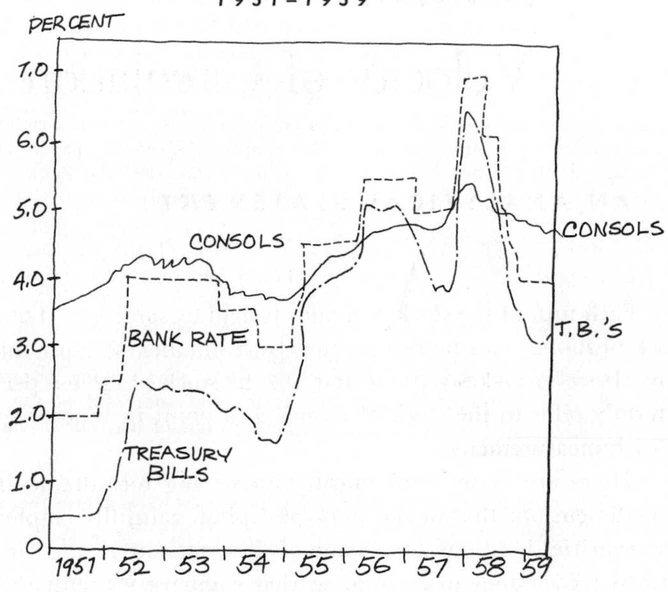

Figure VC-21

We are again struck by the way in which Consols resist short-rate changes. Finally, this is the curve for retail prices in Great Britain (1953 = 100) for 1948-1958 (*ibid.*, p. 10):

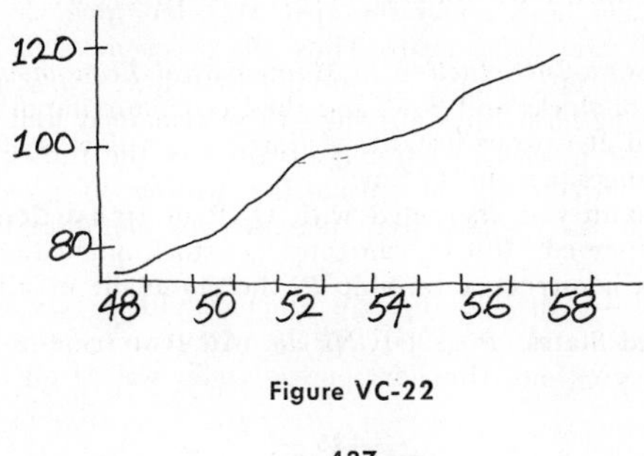

Figure VC-22

CHAPTER SIX

Velocity of Circulation

A. AN ANALYTICAL STATEMENT

1

Each unit of the stock of money is held by someone. The aggregate stock of money can be represented by a number without time dimension. It never makes sense to refer to the stock of money per day. We can only refer to the stock of money *at* a point in time or to averages of such measurements.

There are many economically interesting measurements without time dimension: that of the stock of capital, gainfully employed workers, securities holdings, etc. Some of these measurements can be transformed into money of account so that comparisons with the nominal value of the stock of money are easy. But, as it happens, the value of the stock of money more often is compared with numbers making no sense unless associated with a time dimension. Relationships between monetary *stocks* and various *flows* have special importance in monetary theory and are in the special province of the theory of velocity.[1]

Consider two *flows* of special economic interest: rates of transac-

---

[1] *Cf.* Bushaw and Clower, *Introduction to Mathematical Economics,* Ch. 2, esp. pp. 9-10, for definition of stocks and flows and their economic importance: "a stock is a quantity measured at various instants of time . . ."; a flow is "the rate at which a stock quantity changes per unit of time."

What stock quantity is associated with GNP or transaction activity? None that is ordinarily observed. But we can construct stock quantities that will clarify the concept. Thus, construct a variable *P,* the cumulant of all GNP ever produced in the United States. $P \equiv \int_{-\infty}^{t} (GNP)d\theta$. All that remains is to specify the time dimension.

tions activity and gross national product. Just as it would be inane to refer to the stock of money *per day,* it would be inane to say that gross national product was being generated at the rate of $100,000,000. $100,000,000 per what? If the referant were the United States and the time unit one year, the statistic would imply that, if its present rate were sustained for one year, gross output during the year would be valued at $100 million! On the other hand, if the appropriate time unit were one hour, the statistic would imply an annual rate of GNP of $854.4 billion!

2

Having expressed numerically the stock variable (money supply) and the flow variable (transaction activity or GNP), it is a simple and natural step to construct mathematical relationships between them. The first step is to construct accounting identities. These permit us to describe relationships among variables without claiming anything about the structure of the economic system, without claiming to have discovered imposing regularities of economic behavior.

Proceed to do just that, defining X as the annual rate of nominally valued transactions. *NNP* is the familiar (nominally-valued) net national product, hereafter denoted Y'. The lower case symbols are explained anon.

$$Mv_X \equiv X \tag{1}$$

$$M \equiv k_X X \tag{2}$$

$$Mv_{NNP} \equiv NNP \tag{3}$$

$$M \equiv k_{NNP} NNP \tag{4}$$

There is an indefinitely large number of such accounting relationships: the transactions and national product or income variables are subject to many nuances of definition, just as is M. Spheres of activity might be isolated so that accounting identities could be constructed for mercantile, financial, and industrial circulations, etc. However, the heart of the matter is in identities 1-4.

It is the lower case symbols, the v's and k's, that contain the juice. These are assigned values so that the right- and left-hand sides of the equations are certain to be equal; Equations 1-4 are *identities.* This permits us to issue instructions to computational assistants, informing them how to "quantify" Equations 1-4:

1) measure the stock of money according to our instructions which might tell you to include currency and adjusted demand deposits or again might include non-governmental time deposits, or — when prices of some securities are rigidly supported by the authorities — even some securities;

2) measure values of instantaneous transactions rates or of Y or, perhaps, take an average of such rates over a considerable period;

3) calculate a value for k_i or v_j that will satisfy the equation.

3

We have progressed as bookkeepers but not as economists. Why should economists be concerned about the measurements associated with Equations 1-4? Is it the fact that one side of these equations poses a stock variable and the other a flow variable of damaging significance? The answer to the first query is double tined; that to the second is negative.

The two tines have been produced, (a), by forces embedded in the history of economic doctrine (especially that of the quantity theory of money), and (b), by practical concerns of twentieth century monetary policy, more and more centered on influencing Y' through manipulation of parameters controlling M.[2] The first tine arises from long standing dispute about the *predictability* of Y' from M.

Pursuing our explanation of why identities 1-4 are interesting to economists, imagine that we frequently have taken measurements suitable for the identity

$$(5) \qquad M_t \equiv (k_{Yt}')(Y_t'),$$

where the t subscript indexes time and Y' gives net national product or national income in undeflated money of account.[3] Assume that values recorded for k_{Yt}, for the last 50 years ranged from $(1.5)^{-1}$ to $(1.7)^{-1}$. We might be willing to work with an equation of the form

$$(6) \qquad M_t = 0.6Y_t' + u_t$$

where u is a *disturbance term* and usually is assumed to have an expected value of zero and the "scatter" characteristics of a normally distributed random variable. We would assume that there is an *exact*

---

[2] Interest may be in the components of Y': Y and p. *Cf.* Ch. VA, Appendix A.

[3] For simplicity, M, however defined, is taken as a parameter of the system. In the models of Appendix A, Ch. VA, s and V were the parameters. The banks *chose* how much deposit liability to supply. The flavor of the argument would be unchanged if we pursued the more intricate line of attack. But *cf.* Ch. XIII.

relationship between Y' and M, continuously disturbed by drawings from Nature's Urn. These drawings take on values scattered in a familiar bell-shaped pattern about zero.

Real significance attaches to a decision to use Equation 6 as a basis for prediction. It contains a testable hypothesis about the economic world. If subsequent values for u are much larger than over the interval for which the equation was estimated, statistical criteria might no longer permit us to assume that the "true" relation beween the parameter M and Y' is given by $M = 0.6Y'_t$. The fit might become so poor that it becomes ridiculous to pretend that discrepancies arise merely because of rumblings in the bowels of Nature's Urn. Indeed subsequent data might not be consistent with *any* estimator such as that of Equation 6. The issue might not be whether *0.6* is the "right" value for the *parameter* $k_{Y'_t}$ but whether the model is "right."

Parameter was not italicized for trivial reasons. In Equation 4, k_{NNP} is *not* a parameter: it serves as a slack variable guaranteeing satisfaction of the equation, assuring that Equation 4 is an identity. On the other hand, *0.6* in Equation 6 *is* a parameter. It is assumed to be determined outside the system but to govern the system's behavior. It is changed only by alteration of basic specifications embedded in the system. The slack variable in Equation 6 is u_t, but the operational procedure underlying the use of Equation 6 calls for feeding calculated values of u_t into a computational apparatus providing continuous information on the consistency of the exact equation — $M_t = 0.6Y'_t$ — with observed errors of prediction. If these errors become large enough, the computational apparatus will sound an alarum, informing us that it no longer can honestly state that the data could be generated by the exact relationship, at least not at a 5 per cent level of significance. Or, worse, the apparatus might refuse to concede that there is any exact relationship of this form. Equation 6, then, has predictive content and offers a refutable hypothesis about the world. The testing process finds us repeatedly solving for $k_{Y'_t}$ in Equation 5 and feeding the results into the apparatus. Equations of the form of Equation 6 state that there are important uniformities between variables such as Y' or X and parameters of monetary policy — permitting officials to presume that, if $Y = Y'$, there will be a strong tendency for prices to change proportionately with the money supply . . . We largely avoid the quantity theory of money until Ch. XIV.

Even if equations such as Equation 6 fail to fit the data, adjustments might permit their kind to work very well indeed. Assume, for example, that originally you claimed that an equation of the form $M_t = kY'_t + u_t$ could be fitted with great accuracy over long intervals of time but that, somehow, the data proved intractable and the resulting fits were very poor. Perhaps you will spot what looks like a systematic tendency for the value of k to increase with time. You beat a strategic retreat, suggesting a new equation:

(7) $$M_t = kY_t' + \beta T_t + u_t,$$

where T is a trend variable exhibiting some sort of regular progression.[4] Another way of framing your suggestion would be a concession that k was not a true parameter of the system, *but* that it could be explained by a relationship no more complicated than

(8) $$k_t = f(T_t).$$

If correct, you will have surrendered very little of the substance of your initial position; the officials can achieve complete control of the price level by making well-defined adjustments in the quantity of money.

What if the data continue to be intractable? What if Equation 7 yields a poor fit, particularly, let us say, when quarterly data are used? (Your hypothesis is singularly ineffective when the fuller impact of the business cycle is brought to bear on it for example.) You might conduct extensive empirical investigations, finally concluding that velocity was functionally dependent upon interest rates; perhaps also on changes in the purchasing power of money. Indeed you might emerge with a formulation like

(9) $$M = f[r_b, r_e, (1/p)(dp/dt), w, P/Y', u].Y',$$

omitting the subscript t, and where r_b is the yield of perpetual bonds, r_e the market rate yield of equities, p the price level of goods and services, and w the ratio of non-human to human wealth.[5] Let us

[4] A statistician probably would estimate equations of the form

$$Y_t' = f(M_t, T_t, u_t)$$

since presumably M_t is measured with much greater accuracy than is Y'. However, the proportion borne by the stock of money to, say, national income is more illuminating at this stage than would be a turnover rate.

[5] Equation 9 is taken from Milton Friedman, "The Quantity Theory of Money—A Restatement," at p. 11 (in Milton Friedman [ed.], *Studies in the Quantity Theory of Money* [Chicago: University of Chicago Press, 1956]) with minor notational changes. Friedman's researches suggest that the relationship of k with various interest rates is weak. Others, including Modigliani and Latanne, have reported contrary results.

assume that you do and that the fit is good. Might you support conventional monetary policy?[6] For some the answer depends on whether manipulation of monetary parameters leads to perverse movements in k so that effects on the price level might be slight.

Before continuing this line of attack, rewrite identity 5:

$$M(t) \equiv [k_{Y'}(t)]\; pY^{\circ}, \tag{10}$$

where Y° is full-employment *real* income. Next write the *stochastic* reduced form Equations 11-14.[7] These relate $k_Y'(t)$, $r_b(t)$, $r_e(t)$, and $p(t)$ — values observed at time t — to parameters (perhaps including trends and lagged endogenous and exogenous variables) of the system, subject to a disturbance term. The time unit is chosen so that short-run responses are described: the data are monthly, quarterly, or annual for example.

$$k_Y'(t) = f^1[z_1(t), \ldots, z_m(t), M(t), u_1(t)] \tag{11}$$

$$r_b(t) = f^2[\qquad\qquad\qquad\qquad, u_2(t)] \tag{12}$$

$$r_e(t) = f^3[\qquad\qquad\qquad\qquad, u_3(t)] \tag{13}$$

$$p(t) = f^4[\qquad\qquad\qquad\qquad, u_4(t)] \tag{14}$$

The z's are predetermined and otherwise exogenous variables as is $M(t)$, taken here to be policy determined. The u's are disturbance terms. Confine parametric variation to M.[8] What might happen to k?[8] Equation 9 indicates that k is linked to the r's.[9] Specifically, it is as-

---

[6] You would want to allege that stable demand for money *implies* a steady relationship with Y', that manipulation of M would lead to desired changes in Y'.

[7] Recall that a reduced form of a *statical* simultaneous-equation system contains as many equations as there are dependent (endogenous) variables. Each equation contains one endogenous variable and expresses its functional relationship with the parameters of the system.

In System 11-14, the vector z generally includes lagged endogenous and exogenous variables. If the exact model underlying the system has an equilibrium solution, the value of the *rth* endogenous variable y_r, at time t can be expressed

$$y_r(t) = y^*_r + g^r\,[z(t), M(t), u_r(t)].$$

The text argues that, if the dynamical properties of the system are unfavorable for monetary policy, System 11-14 will generate vectors $y(t)$ widely different from the solution vector y^* long after, say, M is changed. (y^* of course is appropriate for the "new" M.)

[8] w, the proportion of non-human to human wealth, and Y'/p (defined as Y^*) are fixed in our analysis. We neglect $(1/p)(dp/dt)$, the relative rate of change of prices. Of course, the purpose of monetary policy in the simplest case is to make this term nil. But *cf.* Ch. XIV.

[9] The r's are endogenous. They do not appear on the right-hand sides of Equations 11-14.

sumed that k is negatively correlated with the r's ($\rho_{k.rj}<0$ or $\rho_{v.rj}>0$).[9a] It was shown in Ch. VA that changes in monetary parameters could affect the price level only through transitional changes in interest rates: short-run changes in the stock of money would be closely associated with opposite changes in interest rates if the *cet. par.* always held. If portfolio managers were sensitive and spending units insensitive to interest rates, changes in M would be associated with large short-run shifts of k in the same direction (shifts of v in the opposite direction). Thus reduced M might be transitorily associated with higher interest rates and much higher velocity. Effects of monetary measures on commodity prices might be slight — at least over considerable periods of observation. In the short run k and M might be very strongly and positively correlated (v and M negatively correlated). Huge doses of monetary policy might be necessary in order to damp down or reverse economic events.

But this is consistent with the partial variation of p with M being well defined and subject to a small standard error of estimate (and, for the sake of your sanity, in the right direction — $\rho_{p.m}>0$).[10] If in fact these are the statistical properties, you can be left with an impregnable position *if* you are willing to go into the limit: if unconcerned with the size of the dosage, you can affect indifference about the size of M's regression coefficient (if it is large relative to its standard error). Presumably, monetary policy can do the job.[11] Of course, all of this is consistent with long-run (comparative statical) proportionate variation of M and p and invariance of interest rates. Equations 11-14 describe short-run variation.[12] The setting is contracyclical policy. We are concerned with the possibility of monetary policy achieving prompt and massive effects in the labor and commodities markets. We have not in Ch. VI been directly concerned with long-run equilibrium states. Still it is obvious that if desired holdings of money balances are sensitive to interest rates in contrast with insensitive real expenditure,

[9a] Otherwise the long-run equilibrium relationship between M and p is likely to change. The quantity theory of money properly is concerned with dp^*/dM, *cet. par.*

[10] In this exercise the only parametric variation is in M—. Remember that $z(t)$ includes lagged values of M. This means that, if the long-run relationship is one of proportionate variation between p and M, equation 14 might predict θ periods after a once-and-for-all increase in M that prices will rise: there can be positive correlation between $[M(t) - M(t-1)]$ and $[p(t+h) - p(t+1)]$.

[11] We have ignored identification problems. (*Cf.* "Rainfall in Siam," Ch. XIV.) On the other hand, the underlying system easily can be made recursive.

[12] *Cf.* Note K, Ch. VA.

even stable adjustment processes might be featured by prolonged failure of prices to conform to "equilibrium" relationships with money stock.[13]

4

We have gone to great pains to answer the first of the questions: "why should economists be concerned . . . with Equations 1-4?" The answer forced us to delve into distinctions between identities and statements with predictive (and hence refutable) content and into processes of adjustment of economic systems resulting from changes in the supply of money. The answer to the second question, "is the fact that one side of Equations 1-4 poses a stock variable and the other a flow variable of damaging significance?" is "No." The explanation probes into the very nature of theorizing in economics and suggests something about the nature of positive economics.

Equations 1-15 can be interpreted as merely describing putative correlations between variables. If one were confident of the persistence of these relationships in magnitude and sign, he presumably would not hesitate to make the suggested change in, say, the money supply when he desired to change prices. He need not be concerned with philosophical questions of cause and effect nor with the "structure" of underlying models; he would be unconcerned with identification of structural parameters. He might not even have an underlying model in mind.

Witness the spirit of *positivism:* data are collected and regularities sought among variables; upon discovery of such regularities tentative hypotheses are advanced, subject to being accepted or rejected as more data are collected; the whole takes on a mathematical shape in order that predictions and testing can be quantitatively precise; the overriding concern is with association of series of numbers, each series being collected according to precise instructions. In the context of algebraic relationships between quantitative series it hardly matters whether some numbers measured stocks and others flows. Surely, regularities can link stocks and flows.

13 *Cf.* Note I, Ch. VA.

B. A MECHANICAL STATEMENT

1

Mechanics as well as mathematics have to be brought into play. We shall work through Irving Fisher's classification of the determinants of velocity, developing practical relationships between cash balances and various flow rates, noting that a given instantaneous rate of nominally valued economic activity is consistent with a wide range of values for money balances. It is easy to show how transition matrixes relating cash holdings at t to those at $t + h$ can change so that given aggregate cash stocks sustain different "nominal" activity matrixes.[14] Thus, if workers were paid every micro-second, spending their incomes at precisely the rates they were being paid, transactions balances could approach zero in the limit.

2

We turn to Fisher's elegant classification of the factors *directly* affecting monetary velocity.[15] These direct agents exclude interest rates, the "general state of expectations" and price expectations, necessarily affecting velocity indirectly. The latter factors must work through one or more of the Fisherine agents. In other words, Fisher has listed immediate mechanical agencies, but not the levers activating them.

1. Habits of the individual
    a) As to thrift and hoarding
    b) As to book credit
    c) As to the use of checks
2. Systems of payments in the community
    a) As to frequency of receipts and disbursements
    b) As to regularity of receipts and disbursements
    c) As to correspondence between times and amounts of receipts and disbursements
3. General causes
    a) Density of population
    b) Rapidity of transportation[16]

---

[14] *Cf.* Kemeny and Snell, *op. cit.*, Ch. IV, for discussion of transitions matrixes and Markov Processes.

[15] Repeated in Hart and Kenen, *Money, Debt, and Economic Activity*, p. 161.

[16] Irving Fisher, *Purchasing Power of Money* (New York: The Macmillan Co., 1926), p. 79.

Hoarding, 1-a, already has been discussed. As for 3-a and 3-b, the denser is the population the more rapid will be transit of a given economic distance, *cet. par.*[17]

Taking up 3-a and 3-b, work with a simple fiat-currency economy composed of two sectors — North and South — in which cash is sent with orders. $1 million per day is transmitted by each sector to the other. Orders are sent in at 9 a.m. The mail is delivered at 5 p.m. Assume further that it takes 56 hours for mail to travel between North and South. A letter dispatched from N at 9 a.m. Monday does not reach the correspondent at S until 5 p.m. Wednesday. It follows that the economy's affairs cannot be conducted with a money stock less than $6 million, all of which is in the transportation pipe lines at 9:01 a.m. each day. Furthermore, the $6 million figure assumes that traders are willing to go without cash for all but an instant of each day and ignores transactions within sectors.

How was the $6 million figure arrived at? North and South each must be able to transmit $1 million at 9 a.m. each day; their respective remittances for the two preceding days will be in transit. It is easy to see how more rapid transportation reduces the amount of cash necessary for transaction of a given volume of business. Simply work through the effects of a reduction in the time required to transmit mail from N to S, say a reduction of 24 hours so that the transmittal time becomes 32 hours. The minimum monetary requirement becomes $4 million: only $2 million need be in transit at all times under the new assumption. If the initial stock of money were $6 million, there would develop excess supply of money balances: at current prices, firms would find themselves with undesired idle balances of $2 million.

Effects of differing levels of book credit (1-b) are two-fold: reduction in desired contingency balances; more efficient utilization of aggregate cash balances in satisfying individual demands. The omnibus credit-card services are a fine example of book credit. Within 30-day intervals, card-holders need have no concern about the *timing* of receipts and expenditures for the broad class of purchases that can be made with credit cards.

Effects of book credit, including credit cards, on more efficient

[17] Of course, in Fisher's day bank deposits sometimes were not included in measures of the money stock; "checking" *per se* would then have important effects on velocity measurements.

utilization of aggregate cash holdings are less easy to explain.[18] (Book credit refers to purchases financed by creation of debit entries on sellers' books.) Briefly, book credit finds firms and households with surplus liquidity permitting others, short of cash, to defer making cash payment until the tables are turned, until the debtors' ships come in, at which time the creditors will experience cash outflow and will want to encash their claims and perhaps acquire credits on their own hook. The economy's cash is mobilized, ready to respond to requirements at the sundry fronts.

One role played by credit card systems concerns mobilization of cash, offsetting "poor synchronization." Persons making important use of credit cards find themselves turning over cash receipts to the credit card companies very soon after these "lumps" of cash are received; these persons seldom are found to hold pools of idle cash. Almost as soon as the credit card companies receive cash from their "members," they "ship it off" to affiliated firms; "members'" cash receipts become massively and readily available to the business community, the credit card system overcoming otherwise dominant frictions that would prevent "members" from holding balances in non-cash forms.

We have worked with specified payments impulses; the equivalents of dyne-seconds and number of impulses per time unit have been predetermined in the analysis. Always keep in mind that, if frequency of payments impulses were high enough, if transmittal times were short enough, and other "frictions" were minimal, so that "capacitors" for example could virtually be empty, there could be enormous velocities of circulation.

Factors 2-a-b-c are perhaps the best known in the standard literature on the theory of velocity, but they cannot be analyzed unless we understand what is meant by "frequency" and "correspondence" of receipts and expenditures.

Frequency of payments or expenditures is in the sense of "thus many times a year."[19] We assume *in the discrete case* that payments

---

[18] We neglect offsetting book entries which, of course, reduce monetary requirements, as does vertical integration which takes whole sectors of activity outside of monetary exchange. Vertically integrated enterprises can, except to the extent they must deal with outsiders, confine themselves to bookkeeping entries. Here we consider only the *level* of book credit.

[19] The time units could be in weeks, months, bienniums, etc.

and expenditures are made periodically.[20] Each "lump" is the same size. Thus frequency can be defined as the number of "lumps" of payments (and/or expenditures) for an economic unit per year (for example). If payments were made daily, frequency would be 365, and the payments period would be one day.[21]

Correspondence essentially is concerned with the coincidence of receipts and disbursements. If factors of production, for example, go to market once a month and are paid daily, lack of coincidence would lead to the piling up of money balances within the household sector if balances were kept in cash.[22, 23]

Consult these crude diagrams:

CORRESPONDENCE, ILLUSTRATED

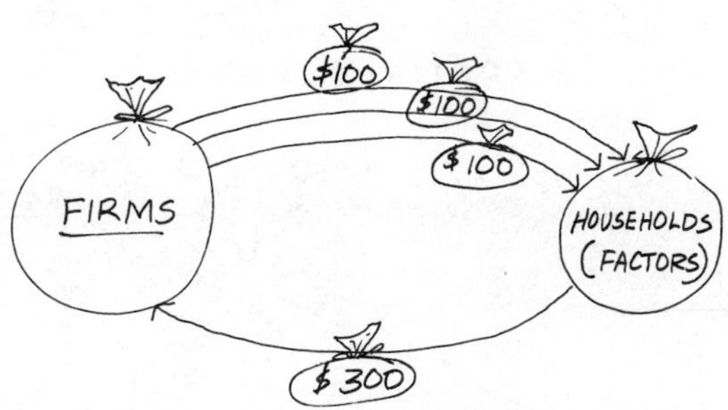

Diagram A — Figure VI-1

The first diagram indicates an income payments period of one day and an income expenditure period of three days. Each day firms pay factors $100. Their receipts are zero on the first and second days of each three-day week; $300 on the third day. In other words, if all firms and households are on the same time schedule, a system gener-

20 If continuous time is used, frequency must be redefined.

21 In continuous time, the physical analogy to shorter income payments and expenditure periods is more frequent, but "smaller," impulses capable of accomplishing the same amount of work (nominally valued activity) over a given time interval.

22 If households had different marketing days, firms could have the same receipts each day. Nevertheless pools of cash would be found in the household sector.

23 In discussing frequency and correspondence, it is assumed that payments, once attempted, are accomplished instantaneously, that transportation, etc. can be ignored. . . . When synchronization is perfect, all cash above that required for asset balances is in the hands of those preparing to spend it *now*. In general, velocity measurements concern clearings over $t+h$ as against monetary stocks at t.

CORRESPONDENCE, ILLUSTRATED

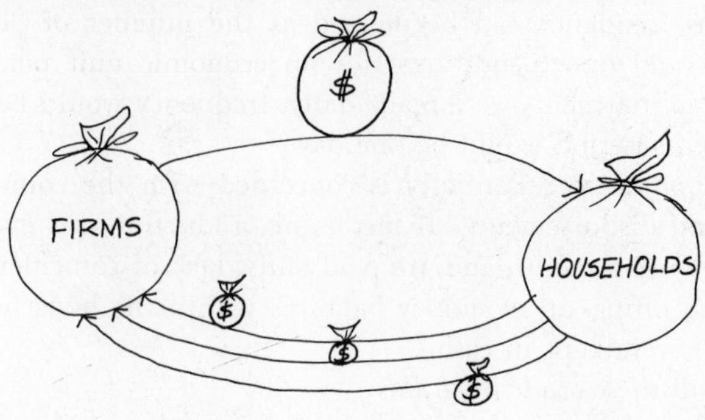

Diagram B — Figure VI-2

A CONTINUOUS CASE

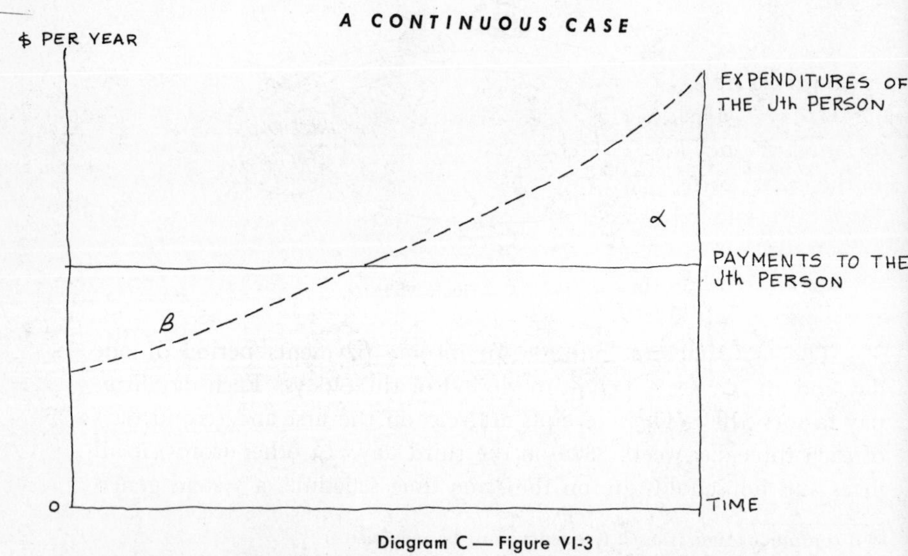

Diagram C — Figure VI-3

ating net national product at a rate of $100 per day requires a money stock of at least $300. Aggregate cash balances of the two sectors (separately) will range from $0 to $300 over the three-day week.

What if phasing varied among households?[24] Thus, assume there are three households, each receiving $33 ⅓ per day, and that (work-

24 Split billing produces this effect.

A CONTINUOUS CASE; PERFECT CORRESPONDENCE

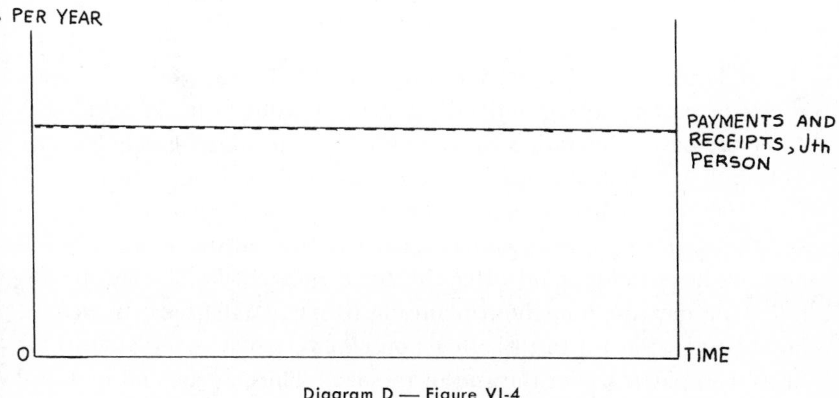

Diagram D — Figure VI-4

ing with a three-day week) Household I spends $100 on Day 1, Household II on Day 2, and Household III on Day 3. Even if household balances are not kept in securities there will be excess supply of cash at the initial prices. (Supply = $300.) If households invest all accumulated cash balances in securities (ignoring frictional expense and time lags), results of perfect correspondence can be achieved. The *shorter* of the two periods can dominate: in our example of a one-week payment period, only $100 in cash is required.

Let us elaborate, first ignoring household securities balances and then incorporating them.

(1) *household balances kept in cash*

The modified phasing assumption reduces required average cash balances of firms: the range is now from $0 to $100 instead of from $0 to $300. As for households — recalling the implicit assumption that payments are made at the end of each day and expenditures during the day — Household I will hold $33 ⅓ in cash at the end of Day I; Household II, $100; Household III, $66 ⅔. The total monetary requirement is reduced to $200. (Firms hold no cash after meeting their payrolls at the end of the day.) Correspondence between aggregate streams will have been improved as a result of "differential phasing" among households, reducing the aggregate sum of cash necessary to conduct business at going valuations.

(2) *household balances kept in securities ("bonds")*

> "The failure of receipts and expenditures to be perfectly synchronized certainly creates the need for transactions balances, but it is not obvious that these balances must be cash." [25]

If households plan to keep all balances in the form of bonds, effects of perfect correspondence (synchronization) can be achieved.[26] Alter the basic illustration in these ways: (1) assume households wish to keep balances in bonds; (2) assume that the total stock of money is but $100, although income payments and weekly expenditures persist at original rates. At the end of each day, the entire money stock is held by households (paid after the bond market closes). During the following day, the household planning to spend $100 sells its accumulated bonds ($66 ⅔) to the other households, paying over $100 to the firms who pay it out at the end of the day. Thus, at the end of Day 1 the asset positions of the households are as follows:

Households	Cash Holdings	Bond Holdings
I	$33⅓	0
II	$33⅓	$66⅔
III	$33⅓	$33⅓

During Day 2, II will sell his bonds to I and III, acquiring the wherewithal to make $100 in purchases during that day. And around and around we go.[27]

Needless to say, if households do not hold transactions balances in bonds, only perfect correspondence can reduce the cash requirement to the largest quantity disbursed by firms or households at any single

---

25 James Tobin, "The Interest Elasticity of Transactions Demand for Cash," *Review of Economics and Statistics,* Vol. 38, No. 3, August 1956, pp. 241-247 at p. 241.

26 For a good (non-mathematical) discussion, *cf.* William J. Baumol, *Economic Theory and Operations Analysis* (Englewood Cliffs, N. J.: Prentice-Hall, Inc., 1961), pp. 241-245.

27 Firms continue to hold cash during the day and individuals overnight. The model must be defined so that cash is desired (or accepted) by some people at all times. Otherwise money prices could become indefinitely large. Our model does the trick: only cash is acceptable as a means of payment; the securities markets close before households are paid. If securities markets remained open "too long," households would wish to convert their wages into securities to be held overnight (in the extreme case) or longer.

Frictional expense and scale economies are very important in the real world which finds only large transactors holding even weekly transactions balances in securities.

time. Further reductions in cash requirements — insofar as frequency and correspondence control — can be achieved only by reducing payments and disbursements periods.[28] Thus, in our illustration, perfect correspondence requires the households' disbursements period to be reduced to one day, permitting an aggregate cash requirement of $100. Now work with Diagram B, showing a three-day income payments period and a one-day disbursement (by households) period. The analysis is symmetrical with that for Diagram A.

Diagrams C and D are in *continuous time.* They can be used to illustrate the role of correspondence in the "real world" where all balances are *not* in bonds. Correspondence is perfect in Diagram D. If taken literally, the diagram implies a very small cash requirement indeed! Payments to and expenditures by households are *continuously* in phase. The effect is that of infinitesimal payments and expenditures periods in discrete time. Diagram C describes behavior rather like that of Diagrams A and B: phasing is imperfect. Of course, households *can* (directly or through intermediaries) make loans to firms earlier in the year, permitting the firms to meet cash deficits. Planning to spend in excess of their collective receipts later in the year, the households must either stockpile cash or redeem bonds that have been issued by firms. Needless to say, the wherewithal for redemption is there: the households' cash deficit is matched by the firms' cash surplus.

There is no need to belabor the fact that real-world frictions and scale effects make the "pure securities" case impossible. Nor is it worthwhile to collect the model's orts. ("Let him have time a beggar's orts to crave.")

Two further comments on correspondence, one on differential phasing, the other a generalization of Diagram D:

---

28 Assume, for example, that both periods are reduced to one hour. Firms and households need never hold more than one hour's worth of receipts and payments in cash. Working with a 10-hour day, the monetary requirement falls to $10. For simplicity, it is assumed that all firms pay at the same instant in calendar time. If not, further economies are available through differential phasing.

Tobin, *op. cit.,* uses a convenient illustration. He considers an individual who receives $100 in income on the first of each month, spreading his expenditures evenly through the month in all events. His average cash holdings would be $50. If he were to be paid once a week, his average cash balance would be $12.50 or 12.5/1200 of his annual income in contrast with 50/1200 — 1/24.

1) we could construct a set of diagrams for the *m* households so that, while each household exhibited curves similar to those of Diagram C, the aggregate curves (applying to the *sector*) would be those of Diagram D. Always assuming — very realistically — that a large portion of transactions balances are held in cash, this would reduce cash requirements. But there would not be perfect correspondence. Individuals would be found stockpiling cash, although, under our assumptions, firms would be able to work with average cash balances no greater than $50 (in the case of discrete daily payments).[29]

2) Diagram C is drawn on the assumption of seasonal merchandise sales but constant rates of manufacturing activity and payments to all factors of production (including retail clerks spending off-months preparing for the season). Correspondence is imperfect. But if expenditures *and* receipts of all persons were identical with the disbursements (expenditures) curve of Diagram C, there would be perfect correspondence; and a set of problems like those discussed in connection with seasonal elasticity of currency under the National Banking Act would emerge. These problems are rather afield from velocity theory, save for the following: assuming that seasonal movements in prices were not nearly so violent as changes in the degree of economic activity over the year, there would be a tendency for cash to pile up in the earlier portions of the year conventional velocity measurements would be lower earlier in the year. (*See Note A.*)

We conclude discussion of the Fisherine direct determinants of velocity with *regularity* of receipts and disbursements. This determinant poses a nice set of problems considered at some length in Ch. VII: stochastic elements in demand for cash balances. Still they can be understood in a general way at this time. Consult Diagrams E and F, applying to a typical trader in the system.

Diagram E is drawn on the assumption that streams of expenditures and receipts are known with certainty. The *irregularity* of the streams makes it necessary for firms, in the real world, to hold buffer stocks of cash. Difficulties and expense of cashing other assets to meet cash demands — let alone the time involved and the possibility of being forced into sales at inopportune times make it desirable to hold cash somewhat in advance of intervals of net cash outflow. (Not to deny that such instruments as tax-anticipation certificates play an important role.)

It is obvious that non-stochastic "irregularity of receipts and payments" is related to the correspondence problem. The more interesting subset under 2-b) concerns stochastic properties.

[29] "Piled-up cash" at t is cash not meant to be spent at $t+h$, where h can approach zero in the limit.

A CYCLE

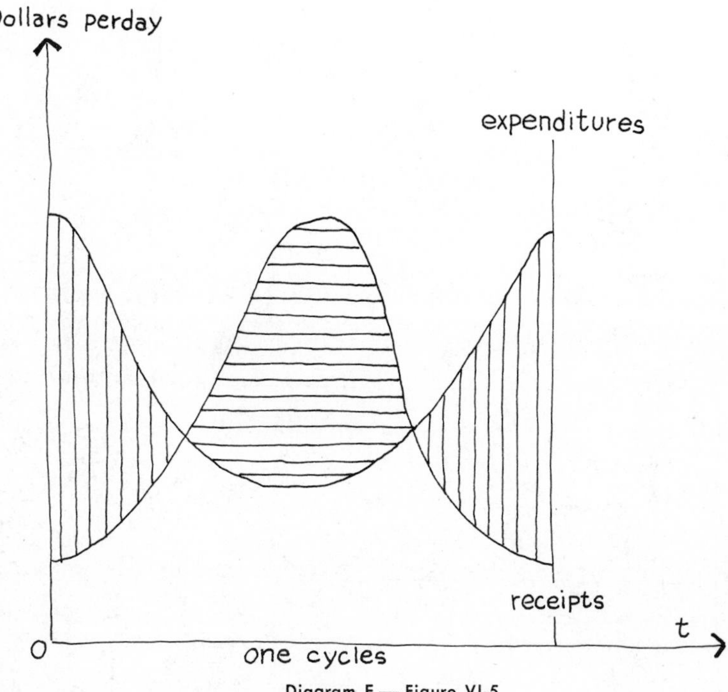

Diagram E — Figure VI-5

The role of drawings from Nature's Urn is best developed by assuming that the *expected* phasing of receipts and expenditures is perfect. This assumption is reflected in the horizontal line, identical with the abscissa of Diagram F. Next assume that these streams always are subject to disturbances generated by random drawings from Nature's Urn. At each moment in time, the mathematical expectation of the disturbance term is zero, and there are approximately 19 chances in 20 that actually realized receipts minus expenditures will fall between the horizontal dotted lines. There remains one chance in twenty that actual experience will be even more extreme, that receipts minus expenditures will fall outside the dotted lines. More rigorously we can expect to be correct 95 per cent of the time as we repeatedly assert that the range of experience will be within the dotted lines, drawn so as to be about two standard deviations (2σ) from the base line. The larger a standard deviation (σ), the greater is the range of experience consistent with the (now-wider) confidence belt.

A STOCHASTIC MODEL

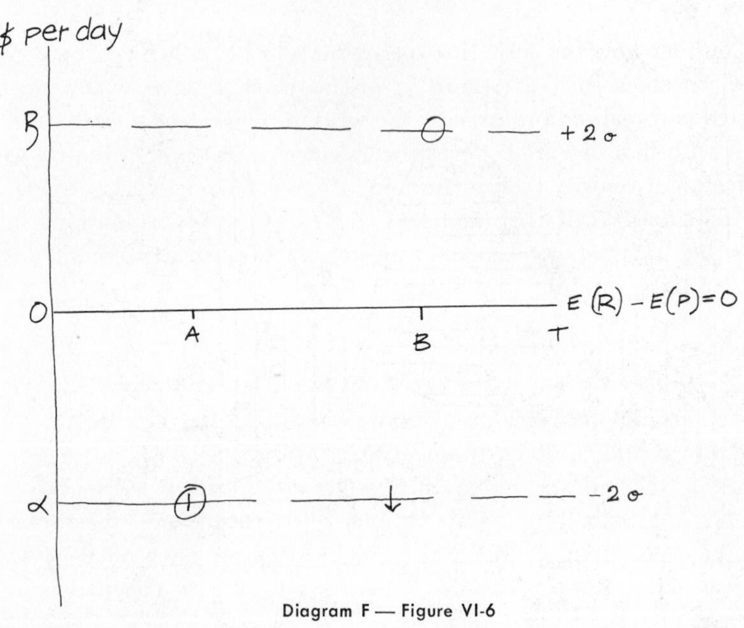

Diagram F — Figure VI-6

"Regularity of receipts and disbursements" can refer to the width of the confidence limits of Diagram F. The wider the limits, the more important it becomes to hold cash in order to avoid embarrassment or, worse, insolvency. If the intervals are wide enough, a trader without substantial cash balances would be skating on very thin ice even if he held large stocks of liquid, but less than perfectly liquid, assets. Of course, overdraft facility reduces demand for cash buffer stocks.

Diagram F illustrates the argument. Consider instant A: there is a short-fall of cash receipts at the rate of 0α dollars per day. A state of affairs just within the assigned probability limits, although there is a palpable chance that things could become worse. At B there is a surplus at the rate of 0β dollars per day.

Finally, when holding cash as a buffer against drawings from Nature's Urn, one must consider *persistence* as well as *incidence* of drains.[30] One must calculate conceivable *accumulated* drains. An integral rather than an instantaneous rate of change is appropriate. Still the structure of the argument is intact.[31]

3

Consider how the Fisherine mechanics can be influenced by economic variables such as securities prices, price change experience, expected and realized profits, etc. We wish to integrate the analysis of Part A with that of Part B, revealing the mechanical underpinning of the algebra of velocity theory. In doing this we encounter what economists felicitously call the "monetary dynamics of hyperinflation," a fascinating exercise in economic pathology. We turn, then, to the levers bringing into play the Fisherine forces.

Changes in Interest Rates

Changes in interest rates exert obvious pressure on speculative holdings of cash balances or on those simply having a strong taste for highly liquid asset portfolios. More attractive yields encourage ventures farther out on the liquidity spectrum.[32] Cash could be made available to economic units intent upon purchasing goods, sustaining larger payrolls, etc. In other words, higher interest rates can lead to idle cash being pumped through the system instead of congealing in mattresses.

As has been pointed out, cash intended to guard against deficits in balances of payments is not of a different color than are speculative balances or Silas Marner's holdings. Higher interest rates will discourage emergency transactions balances: the cost of insurance against insolvency has increased; it becomes worthwhile to take a larger risk of insolvency rather than forgo the opportunity to earn generous yields. Furthermore, if interest rates are increasing during a surge of economic expansion, Nature's Urn is apt to seem more serene. Of course, if demand for money at given levels of economic activity de-

30 Abstract from bankruptcy possibilities. That is to say, assume that stocks of non-monetary assets are "large" compared to possible drains. Of course, during liquidity crises, frantic efforts to liquidate might enough depress asset prices to precipitate many ordinarily unthinkable bankruptcies.

31 A trader deeply concerned about insolvency possibilities will maintain a cash reserve against the possibility of over-all crisis *vis a vis* personal bad luck.

32 Effects of interest rates on asset portfolio selection are considered more deeply in Ch. VII when James Tobin's seminal paper is studied. Franco Modigliani stresses the role played by bonds in reducing the variance of expected income streams.

clines, money national income must increase before demand and supply of money balances can be equated.

Finally, interest rates affect desired ordinary transactions balances. At higher interest rates, firms have greater incentive to invest funds that have piled up under the aegis of favorable cash flows; funds awaiting dispersal later in the receipts-disbursements cycle. Inconvenience and frictional expense seem less important with increased opportunity cost of holding cash. Similarly, even if payments periods were unaffected by changed interest rates, households (*et al.*) would be spurred by higher interest rates to place idle funds in securities while awaiting the active phase of their expenditure cycle. (There are converse effects of lower interest rates.) Thus firms might be able to command larger cash balances than appears true on the surface.

You might say that it is absurd to imagine workers investing in Treasury bills prior to Saturday when they (hypothetically) spend most of their weekly receipts. So it is, but surely 22 per cent bill rate would revolutionize norms of transactions-balance behavior.[33] And then consider Christmas clubs. . . . In all these ways higher interest rates can accelerate the flow of cash through the system, or, alternatively, can lower the desired ratio between the stock of cash and that representing such flow rates as national product per annum. *(See Note B.)*

Changes in Expectations of Profitability of Investment

This factor's impact is like that of changing interest rates. However its sphere of influence is apt to be narrower. In any event, rising entrepreneurial spirits are almost certain to be accompanied by reduced desired cash *stocks. (See Note C.)*

[33] "By virtually common consent . . . transactions demand for cash has been taken to be independent of the rate of interest." James Tobin, *op. cit.*, p. 572. Of course, Tobin shows that standard economic theory suggests the opposite. He states that priority for rigorous demonstration of this proposition belongs to W. J. Baumol, "The Transactions Demand for Cash: An Inventory Theoretic Approach," *Quarterly Journal of Economics*, November 1952, pp. 545-556.

Tobin deals with the interaction of the cost of transactions in going to and from (cash and) interest-bearing assets and the opportunity costs (expressed through interest yields) of holding cash. He ingeniously shows how optimal holdings can be expected to vary with interest rates, transactions levels, etc. There is a threshold level of interest below which transactions balances always would be kept in cash.

C. EXPERIENCE OF CHANGING PRICES: HYPERINFLATION

1

To expect prices to increase is to expect to be subject to a continuing tax on cash balances. Once these expectations become firm, pressures for higher velocity become exigent. However, study of hyperinflation shows that the pressures are more bounded than would seem true at first glance. We begin by working through the logical chain from increasing prices to increasing velocity.

As inflationary forces mount, money becomes more and more of a hot potato. If rapid inflation is expected, it becomes lunatic to hold money for precautionary or speculative purposes: real capital losses on cash become prohibitive. Planned transactions balances are similarly affected by the general desire to reduce proportions of wealth held in cash. An upshot is that workers will come to be paid more frequently and will more rapidly rid themselves of the proceeds. So will firms.[34] In a polar case, the whole money stock could be paid out to factors each hour. They might return the lot to the firms within the hour — buying precisely 1/8960 of the annual product as it is relentlessly ground out. All concede that the stability of monetary velocity ultimately can collapse under inflationary pressure: once the public decides to reduce the proportion of their wealth held in cash, acceleration of the time rate of change of prices can set off a train of events destroying money's capacity to perform its traditional functions.

[34] Keynes writes of Moscow grocers who, upon selling cheese, ran to the central market in order to replenish their stocks rather than hold steadily depreciating money. Also of a Viennese witticism that "a prudent man at a café ordering a bock of beer should order a second bock at the same time, even at the expense of drinking it tepid, lest the price should rise in the meanwhile." (*Tract,* p. 46.) Mr. James Hicks reports that it became customary for patrons of Chilean sporting houses also to place double orders, even at the expense of fatigue. Chile long has experienced inflationary pressure.

Competition for labor will lead to a shorter income payment period: the value of a worker's contract will be greater if he is paid more frequently (and therefore better able to synchronize his expenditures and receipts).

Of course, holders of cash will try to switch to physical assets or augment (temporarily) their consumption; we have seen that workers will want to do as much of their purchasing as they can on their pay day, meanwhile trying to reduce transactions balances previously accumulated. Firms will have an incentive to reduce income payments periods in order to reduce the proportion of their assets that must be held in liquid balances. (Firms will especially be pressed in this direction if most income payments occur on, say, Monday: otherwise they will have to hold Monday's receipts — equal to the whole payroll if the workers can help it — for a week.)

The economics of liquidity crises and collapses of expected profitability of investment, like many economically pathological experiences, expose the subject's bare bones, but hyperinflation is a truly pyrotechnic display. There is no better way to study the theory of velocity.[35]

2

Generally speaking, a state of affairs in which prices are increasing at the rate of at least 50 per cent per month is described as hyperinflation. The table below shows some aspects of the German inflation of August 1922–November 1923 and the Greek inflation of November 1943–November 1944:

GERMAN AND GREEK INFLATIONS

No. of months	16	13
Ratio of prices*	10^{10}	4.7×10^8
Ratio of hand-to-hand currency*	7.3×10^9	$10^6 \times 3.6$
Average monthly rate of price increase (per cent)	322	365

TABLE VI-I

Source: P. Cagan, *op. cit.*, p. 26.

* Ratio of value at end to that at beginning of interval.

How could *this* have happened? Turn first to Keynes's description of the German inflation of 1922–1923 (*Tract,* Ch. II).

Some of the background has been provided in Ch. II *supra.* Governments can print paper money as a means of taxation, securing command over real resources, but the public has a means of protecting itself if it is willing to change its monetary habits. It is not likely to do so at the outset. On the other hand, once the public does change its habits (with a vengeance), the purchasing power of additional paper issues might fall short of their real cost of production.

35 Sources include Keynes's *Tract*; Phillip Cagan, "The Monetary Dynamics of Hyperinflation," and Eugene Lerner, "Inflation in the Confederacy, 1861-1865," in Milton Friedman (ed.), *Studies in the Quantity Theory of Money,* pp. 25-117, 163-175; C. Bresciana-Turroni, *The Economics of Inflation* (New York: Barnes & Noble, 1937); C. D. Campbell and G. C. Tullock, "Hyperinflation in China, 1937–1949," *Journal of Political Economy,* June 1954, pp. 236-245. *Cf.* also Kessel and Alchain, *Journal of Political Economy,* December 1962.

Keynes gets to the heart of the matter:

> "The collapse of the currency in Germany was due not so much to taxing by inflation — for that had been going on for years — as to an increase in the *rate* of inflation to a level almost prohibitive . . . We have seen that what concerns the use of money in the retail transactions of daily life is the rate of depreciation, rather than the absolute amount of depreciation as compared with some earlier date."[36]

Keynes estimated that in the middle of 1922 the German government had for some time past been obtaining £75 to £100 million (in mid-1920's pounds sterling) per annum in goods and services through resort to the printing press. The value of the German note issue was about £100 million in the middle of 1922. By the end of 1922 prices had increased so much that, despite lavish issues of new paper, the value of the note issue had fallen to £60 million. By the middle of 1923 it had fallen to £20 million. Underlying these statistics was an increasingly firm determination by the public to reduce cash holdings. Cash was a rotten investment. Excess supply of money was generated by planned disinvestment by holders of "old" cash as well as through new issues. The intense desire to reduce cash balances and assets fixed in nominal value led to drastic increases in monetary velocity (*cf.* Note H, Ch. VII). Everything led to accelerated excess supply of money. A familiar note is sounded: universal efforts to reduce cash holdings led to none succeeding and to all experiencing further deterioration in the value of their balances.

Do not assume, however, the the public became alarmed at the very outset of what was to be a hyperinflationary process. Not at all. In the tradition of hyperinflations, velocity actually *fell* during the early stages of the German inflation of 1922–1923. Originally there were strong notions of "normal" prices expected to persist despite temporary interruption. Initial "elasticities of expectation" were less than unity. The fact that prices rose more than usual gave rise to the expectation that prices later might even fall: it would then be profitable to hold cash. Of course, declining velocity or — what is the same thing — an increasing ratio of cash holdings to nominal income, is grist for the mill of governments operating printing presses in order

[36] *Op. cit.*, p. 58. The impetus to the German inflation was provided by the government's fiscal exigencies. It attempted to raise £3 million per week through the printing press instead of its "customary" £1 million per week. As inflation took over, tax revenues, not easily re-rated, fell off enormously in real value.

to levy on resources. Keynes describes these early stages of hyperinflations before the public awakes and all hell breaks loose:

> "... Experience shows that the public are generally very slow to grasp the situation and embrace the remedy [change in habits in the use of money]. Indeed, at first there may be a change of habit in the wrong direction which actually facilitates the Government's operations. The public are so much accustomed to thinking of money as the ultimate standard, that, when prices begin to rise, believing the rise must be temporary, they tend to hoard their money and to postpone purchases ... But sooner or later the second phase sets in ..."

We have described the second phase. Accelerating velocity leads to declining real cash balances, but the authorities still can increase their command over resources by printing money. In the second phase, money still has meaningful, albeit declining value. It remains to describe the tragic *dénouement* of the third phase.[37]

The stage is set for the third phase by the implications of the declining real cash balances of the second phase: the faster the rate of increase of prices, the greater must be acceleration of the printing presses for the government to continue to levy resources at the same rate; the greater the acceleration of the money supply, the faster prices rise.[38] A vicious circle takes over. By November 1923 the immense sea of paper was worth only £4 million. In order to raise £4 million (in real purchasing power) the government would have to double the money supply *if* velocity did not increase. The end had come. In the last throes of the hyperinflation, German currency and bank notes (important in Germany) lost much of their standing as media of exchange and standards of value. Mark exchange became unacceptable as a trading medium and reckoning was done in pounds sterling for many transactions. Hyperinflation laid bare elemental monetary properties described in Ch. II.

But the persistence of the use of money during hyperinflation, even in almost its last throes, is truly remarkable. It shows how crucial are the basic monetary functions and emphasizes the staying power of established social practices. As Keynes wrote:

---

[37] Nominal interest rates can rise to fantastic heights during hyperinflations. Thus if prices are likely to rise 500 per cent over the next year, and if a lender and borrower can agree upon a real rate of 5 per cent per annum, a nominal rate of 505 per cent per annum will express their intention.

". . . The convenience of using money in daily life is so great that the public are prepared [rather than forego it, to pay the inflationary tax] . . . Suppose that the rate of inflation is such that the value of money falls by half every year, and suppose that the cash used by the public turns over 100 times a year; this is only equivalent to a turnover tax of ½ per cent on each transaction. The public will gladly pay such a tax rather than suffer the trouble and inconvenience of barter . . . For certain other purposes . . . the inflationary tax becomes prohibitive at a much earlier stage. As a store of value, for example, money is rapidly discarded as soon as further depreciation is confidently anticipated. As a unit of account for contracts and balance sheets [a standard of value and for deferred payments] it quickly becomes worse than useless . . . In the last phase, when the use of legal-tender money has been discarded for all purposes except trifling out-of-pocket expenditure, inflationary taxation has at last defeated itself."

3

Pursue "the monetary dynamics of hyperinflation" through Eugene Lerner's account (*op. cit. supra*) of inflation in the Confederacy from 1861 to 1865. He ably sets the stage:

". . . for 31 consecutive months, from October 1861 to March 1864, the Confederate commodity price index rose at the average rate of 10 per cent per month [making this a quasi hyperinflation] . . . In April 1865 the index was 92 times the prewar base. Like all people living through rapid inflation, southerners directed their invective against the instrumentality through which the increase in prices occurred. They exhorted, threatened, villified, and enacted legislation to regulate and control businessmen and farmers who sold goods at more than 'fair' prices . . . But prices continued to rise . . . The rapid and continuous rise of the commodity-price level was caused by an ever expanding stock of money, a sharp rise in velocity, and a drop in real income [fewer goods becoming available in the contracting area in which Southern money could circulate]."

The Confederacy was never able to obtain much through taxation; less than five per cent of its receipts up to October 1864 came

38 Compare Note C. Abstract from interest rate changes. If, in a statical model, people are planning to reduce real cash balances, prices must rise until real balances fall to desired levels. In a dynamical model, where desired cash holdings depend on price experience, lagged adjustment assumptions usually are appropriate. Bresciana-Turroni (Ch. V) treats "real" aspects of the German inflation.

Note that excess demand for goods flows from two sources: dM/dt, expressed as government demand for goods; the public's desire to reduce real cash balances.

from taxes.[39] The inevitable printing press came to the fore, this time so spectacularly that even the physical circumstances are notable: the note-signing bureau was expanded from 72 employees in July 1962 to 262 in July 1863, but its efforts proved inadequate; even bogus notes were called in (in exchange for Confederate interest-bearing paper) to be stamped "valid" and put into circulation. Lerner supplies statistics on the money supply.

TOTAL STOCK OF MONEY IN THE SOUTH

(in millions of dollars)

	Bank Notes and Dep.[40]	Confed. Gov't. Notes	Index of Total
1861:			
January	94.6	....	100
October	146.3	24.5	180
1862:			
January	165.2	74.6	250
October	181.5	287.3	500
1863:			
January	239.1	410.5	690
October	274.7	792.4	1130
1864:			
January	268.1	826.8	1160

TABLE VI-II

39 The system of tax collection is worth noting. Its makeshiftness reflects early Southern confidence in victory over — at least appeasement by — the shopkeeping North. The states were offered the equivalent of a commission for collecting taxes for the Confederate Government. This agency could be performed by turning over bank notes or deposits. The states earned their commission neatly and simply: they borrowed from the banks. The fiscal procedure thus led to an increased money supply. Bond sales were paralysed by the insistence of the Confederate Secretary of the Treasury that bonds not be sold to yield more than 4 per cent per annum. A 4 per cent nominal yield could be negative in real terms under a moderate inflation. Surely the 4 per cent yield did not reflect the risk involved in investing in a rebel authority's securities. The incident goes far to confirm generalizations about Treasury biases.

40 Southern banks carried increasingly large reserves as the Rebellion proceeded. The expansion in bank deposits was not in line with pre-1861 reserve practices. (Banks acquired much of the enormous note issues through customer's deposits.) The explanation appears to be that Southern bankers, anticipating mass withdrawals of funds with the approach of Union troops (an event that became more common in 1864) chose to carry exceptionally large reserves.

As the inflation proceeded, the standard landmarks appeared:

> 1) lenders required that standards of deferred payment be gold, leather, or some other commodity, not Confederate paper;
>
> 2) the index number for the price level, taking January 1861 as 100, rose to 9211 in April 1865;
>
> 3) prices rose more rapidly than did the stock of money. Thus, from the first quarter of 1861 to the beginning of 1864, the money stock increased 11 fold and the price level 28 fold. Real cash balances fell 42 per cent;
>
> 4) Confederate notes continued to have currency until the very end. Recall Keynes's remarks on the persistence of the use of money as a medium of exchange under the most adverse circumstances.

As Lerner concludes:

> "What is remarkable is that so large a fraction of the Southern war effort could, in fact, be financed by currency issue. It betokens the enormous importance that people attach to having a currency, even a depreciating one, and the great amount of real resources they are willing to pay for it."

The Chinese story — related by Campbell and Tullock[41] — confirms the pattern. Witness again the amazing tenacity of money as a medium of exchange despite raging inflation. Government issue never was altogether abandoned — even when the government collapsed. Instead, enormous nominal interest rates prevailed, standards of deferred payment were altered, etc. (*See Note D.*)

SUMMARY

1. Velocity theory keys to stock-flow analysis. The interesting relationships concern monetary stocks and income or transaction flows.
2. There is no mathematical principle precluding meaningful regularities between numbers representing stocks and numbers representing flows. However, careful heed should be paid to dimensions.
3. If important empirical regularities can be discovered between changes in money stocks and such flows as net national product,

[41] *Op. cit.*, footnote 35.

the case for monetary policy as a means of controlling the price level is helped.

4. Identities can link monetary stocks and various flow variables. Examples are $M \equiv kY'$ and $Mv \equiv Y'$.
5. k and v obviously are related algebraically. The "k" form makes it easier to focus on the integration of monetary and general equilibrium theory, the task of Part II.
6. Predictive content can be injected to putative relationships between monetary stocks and income flows through testable hypotheses about the variation of observed k's or v's.
7. Ornate hypotheses might "explain" short- and long-run behavior of velocity with great precision but might imply short-run ineffectiveness of monetary policy in controlling the price level or stimulating trade. Thus, interest rate changes might substantially affect planned cash holdings while having small effect on expenditure decisions. If price adjustment is sluggish, this can lead to a highly-erratic short-run relationship between M and Y'.
8. The roles of frequency and correspondence in determining desired transactions balances were considered. Also the ways in which bond transactions, with or without financial intermediation, could offset poor correspondence (synchronization).
9. Interest rates and price experience (leading to expectations) might influence desired cash balances. The impact of interest rate changes on speculative and precautionary balances is widely recognized, but that on transactions balances has been neglected. The whole is subsumed under *opportunity cost.*
10. Persistent inflation is a tax on cash balances, or, alternatively, a turnover tax. History shows that, once firm expectations of rising money prices have been formed, monetary habits drastically change. However, inflated currencies have exhibited remarkable persistence as media of exchange in the midst of prolonged and drastic inflation.

NOTES

NOTE A: Chapter VII develops a stock-flow model uniquely suited to exposition of velocity theory. Its message can be developed heuristically as follows.

Imagine that half of the money stock is red; the other half, green. Assume that initially the red money is held by firms, the green money by households.

Then assume that the real product of the system is sausage, ground out at an inexorable pace by the firms for the households.

Mathematically, there is no limit to the value that might be taken by velocity. The two money stocks could change hands each minute — or millisecond — if income payments and expenditures periods are short enough. The table explicates the model.

SIMPLE MATHEMATICS OF VELOCITY

Period	Firms	Households
0	R	G
1	G	R
2	R	G

TABLE VI-III

NOTE B: I have not considered the circuit velocity approach. The interested reader should compare W. T. Newlyn, *Theory of Money,* Ch. IV, pp. 38-50.

The circuit velocity approach risks Böhm-Bawerkian chaos. I consider an activity matrix for each (very short) period until a complete cycle is accomplished. Then I check planned holdings of cash for each economic unit at each "point in time." *Cf.* Ch. VII for further discussion of how changes in planned time paths for cash holdings affect velocity.

I have neglected detailed treatment of effects of the number of stages in transforming of raw materials into finished goods. The crude diagrammatics of Diagrams G and H partially repair this neglect. Diagram H suggests the effects of an additional stage: planned cash holdings increase; Stage II producers must accumulate cash over the week in order to meet Saturday's payments to Stage I producers. Obviously, the crude model neglects possibilities for holding balances in bonds.

ONE STAGE PRODUCTION

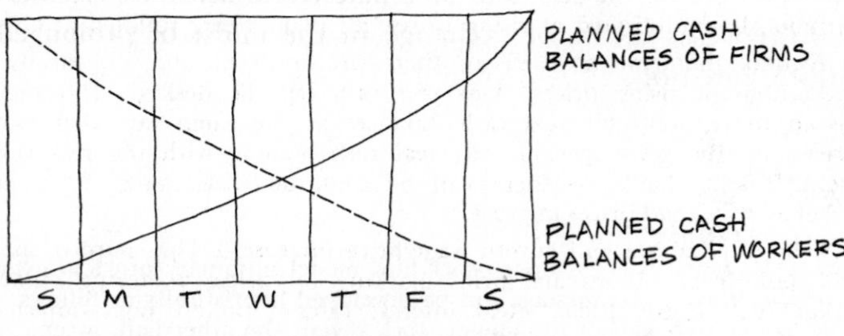

Diagram G — Figure VI-7

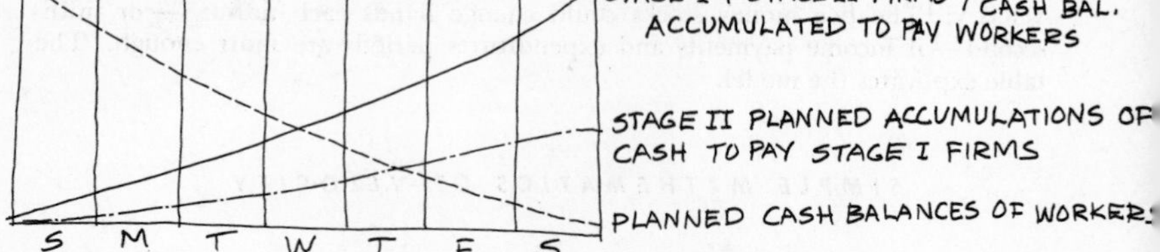

Diagram H — Figure VI-8

Note C: It is shown in Ch. VII that, for the micro-unit, money is like a stock-flow good. Ch. VI has concentrated on demand for money *stocks.*

The approaches are reconcilable. In the notation of Ch. VII, equilibrium of the money market requires that

a) $x'_{rj}(t)_{ex\ ante} = z_{rj}(t) - x_{rj}(t) \qquad j = 1, 2, \ldots, m$

b) $\sum_j x'_{rj}(t)_{ex\ ante} = 0 \qquad \text{for } dM/dt = 0$

Recalling that

c) $x'_{rj}(t) \equiv k_{rj}\ [D_{rj}(t) - S_{rj}(t)],$

it is necessary that

d) $\sum_j k_{rj}([D_{rj}(t) - S_{rj}(t)] = 0$

holds for Equation *b* to hold. If monetary habits are changed, reducing many of the $D_{rj}(t)$ elements, there will be excess supply of cash stocks. The representative $z_{rj}(t)$ will exceed the representative $x_{rj}(t) + x'_{rj}(t)_{ex\ ante}$. Price levels will increase until Equation *b* again holds at time *t if* the system is stable.

(*Ex ante* is in the sense of desired; this usage of a term rooted in discrete analysis probably is unfortunate. Furthermore "desired" investment in cash stocks at *t* might be conditioned by inability to fulfill other plans.)

Note D: A variant of Chapter VI's analysis explains sequences in which inflation is accompanied by unchanged unemployment (either "Keynesian" or "structural" in the sense that capital, but not labor, constraints are binding). Indeed it is possible in this model, based on a pure credit money, for markets to be continuously equilibrated at rising prices, all plans being fulfilled at all times.

Assume that, for any reason, there are uniform and universally held expectations of rising prices. Less *real* cash will be desired. If traders are satisfied to reduce their real cash balances at the same rate that expected increases in the price level devour real cash — along with the real value of indebtedness to banks — there will be continuous clearance of the money market as wages and prices increase.

What mechanism will govern wage-price increases? The simplest specification would have unions and firms marking up prices "knowing" that "the market" will justify them. Real interest rates — interest rates adjusted for expected price increases — will be unchanged, as will be excess demand functions for assets, services, etc. Effective demand will be unchanged.

To the extent that it is desired to reduce real cash balances at a rate faster than it is expected prices will rise (while planning, for example, to increase holdings of equities), real equity yields will tend to fall, encouraging increased real investment expenditures, etc. Here rising prices would be accompanied by increasing real income and employment, starting from a Keynesian state.

The first specifications appear to have special application to a country like Argentina . . . Mark-up phenomena have largely been neglected by theorists.

Consider also inflation in the Congo and other places where unsettled conditions lead to "more diagonal" input-output *tableaux* and to loss of confidence in the ability of the currency to be a means of payment tomorrow.

NOTE: E: Thornton wrote, ". . . if bank paper were abolished, a substitute for it would be likely to be found, to a certain degree in bills of exchange . . ." (*loc. cit.*, pp. 100-101). These words must be treated gingerly. In the face of severe official restrictions, imposing the need for liquidation on many firms and households, there is more likely to be strong resistance against extending credit. On the other hand, at high enough rates of interest, extant trade bills — certainly those of faceless colossi like General Motors — would be used much more as means of payment: traders planning to hold transactions balances in securities would be pleased to receive securities of the sort they otherwise were planning to buy. Such securities can acquire currency. The upshot falls under "interest elasticity of demand for money"; the analysis' flavor is much affected by laws concerning payment of interest on demand deposits.

We have been careful to distinguish between expansion of book credit and increased use of existing (or for that matter a smaller volume of) trade bills as a means of payment. The latter, already conceded as a possibility, is likely in any case to be much inhibited today: there are enormous economies present in a system of checking against demand deposits as against cumbersome multiple endorsements of bills; clearly, GM could not profitably or legally convert itself into a commercial bank issuing interest-bearing deposits.

A. B. Cramp enriches the discussion in his article "Two Views on Money," *Lloyds Bank Review,* July 1962, pp. 1-15. His major purpose is to relate the Banking School — Currency School controversy to the environment of the Radcliffe Committee. As for trade or book credit, Cramp notes, ". . . an important part of Mill's argument against the Currency School was that in the earlier stages of the trade cycle boom increased purchases were largely financed by trade credit. It followed that the strain on the cash base . . . appeared too late to moderate the boom either automatically or with the conscious assistance of the monetary authorities." (*Ibid.*, p. 10.) As for trade bills serving as means of payment before bank deposits became the predominant transactions balance, Cramp, referring to early-19th-century Lancashire where bank notes were suspected, writes, ". . . bills of exchange for extremely small amounts virtually monopolized the payments function over a very wide range of transactions . . ." (*Ibid.*, p. 10.)

A nagging problem for some in economic theory is the possibility that the *jth* trader will, so to speak, plan to die (or simply declare bankruptcy) as a net debtor, violating his intertemporal budget constraint.

It might be said that credit managers' main function is to ferret out such persons so that their firms do not hold the bag(s). A more or less inductive proof shows how eagle-eyed credit managers would avert loss. Say that n periods are involved. Obviously, the *nth* potential creditor will refuse to lend. Knowing this, the *(n—1)th* will not be willing to lend . . . The process proceeds all the way to the second and hence the first potential creditor.

APPENDIX

Financial Markets, Trade Credit, and Facets of a Monetary Economy

1

PART I HAVING BEEN COMPLETED, IT IS POSSIBLE TO penetrate some of its issues with deeper insight. We can peer into dark recesses. And informal reflection sometimes destroys stately mathematical processions.

The term structure of interest rates is determined through interaction of technology, settlement practices, expectations, time preference, and liquidity preference. It is dangerous to stress any one factor. Thus, consider a system in which there is very strong demand for short-term paper: short rate might fall far below the marginal efficiency of capital. Still there readily can be substantial issues of long-term securities at higher yields (in turn permitted by normal backwardation or expectations of securities-market traders); advantages of secured finance over long periods offset those of cheaper short-term rates at the margin. (Default risks are ignored in this paragraph.)

We devote much space to determinants of demand for securities of various forms and duration. Effects of concern for income and/or principal security and of the degree to which firms prefer to be paid in cash and invest in bills of their own choosing are considered. Less attention is paid to the supply side, especially to *technology*. Consider alternative brewing operations. Assume that A beer is aged, beginning each November 1, for 120 days, while B beer is continuously produced under a chemical aging process. Only 2 days' output of B beer need be in process. A is incented each year to acquire its borrowed capital by issuing paper of long enough maturity to tide it over its gestation period. Indeed, one visualizes a farmer in an A world using harvest proceeds to repay his bank, enabling it to lend to A. When A's ship comes in, it repays the bank, enabling the bank to make a loan to the farmer . . . Brewery B need not look askance at floating 7-day paper . . . The preference for long-term finance by a firm building an aluminum plant is obvious.

Of course, issue partly adapts to demand considerations. We have seen that a firm's debt service requirements and cash flow can have very different time shapes: a firm *might* largely be financed by 30-day paper even if its lumps of receipts are annual.

Settlement practices also affect the structure of rates and *vice versa*: if *all* settlements were made on December 31, there would neither be demand nor supply of loans from, say, June 10 to July 10. But in a monetary economy it is in fact true that it always is possible to buy goods, including productive capital, for cash (at least for suitable legal tender) and that incremental cash leads to incremental opportunities or assurance.

A fundamental determinant of settlement patterns is the reluctance of ordinary persons to be dependent upon consistency of would-be purchasers' plans with solvency on economic Judgment Day(s). Acceptance of primary securities is a dangerous business. The simple solution is for payments to be made in cash (within customary intervals rarely more than 90 days). Credit is arranged through specialists: debtors and customers of the *jth* trader are intersecting but not congruent sets . . . And then there is bookkeeping expense.[42] Unless there are frequent settlements using conventional means of payment, there would tend to be a chaos.

An important aspect of the settlements pattern finds workers paid weekly in cash. This partly is founded in custom, partly in the desire of tradesmen to minimize indebtedness of clients without well established credit standing, partly in the diseconomies of management of small scale liquid balances. Indeed most people are incapable of keeping accounts. And most of those who can have better things to do. Cash payments make life much simpler.

2

At the bottom of a monetary economy is a concept of *redemption*.[43] Modern practice finds bank credit ordinarily suitable as a

42 Imagine a Wyoming tourist buying soda pop on credit at a New York lunch counter!

43 Compare R. G. Hawtrey, *Currency and Credit*, 4th ed., Ch. I, "Credit Without Money." "Monetary" here is *not* contrasted with "barter."

reduced substance. However, the convertibility of bank credit into lawful money is assured by a massive apparatus of law and custom; a commercial bank balance sheet reveals a special asset-liability structure, unsuited to an ordinary enterprise.

This leads directly to the metaphysics of trade (book) credit.[44] Continuing powers of issue of irredeemable legal tender are restricted to the state. The alternative is farcical. Nor are there historical or sociological bases for private fiat issue. Firms, households, and local authorities can sustain their credit only as long as they are believed able to redeem maturing claims in official money or bank credit.

Nobody, then, in our economy, is free of the ultimate duty of *redeeming* his debts, cast in money of account, in legal tender.[45] The onus can be postponed through refinance, but is inexorable. It follows as a practical matter that no financial claim against another has value unless it can directly or indirectly be reduced to ultimate substances; no paper can have currency unless it can be reduced to official money. The linkage between money of account and official money is ineluctable; its origins can be found only in the bottomless well of history.

Once this is understood the role of tested notions of financial soundness in limiting expansion of trade credit (or punishing its excess) becomes clear. Balance sheet norms emerge. Given these norms and re-emphasizing that the value of accounts receivable depends on the market's assessment of their redeemability, it is easy to see how the system develops endogenous restraints on trade credit expansion. As A's accounts payable increase relative to his cash assets, red lights flash down the line: finally A might be thought extended beyond prudent limits; he will have to apply for fresh cash if he is not to be forced to direct normal cash inflows to creditors instead of suppliers . . . Of course, as J. S. Mill and others have stressed, if built in limitations (comptrollers' yardsticks, etc.) on expansion of credit are suppressed, the stage is set for financial panic. Once a few large and respected firms are found insolvent, panic buttons might be pressed everywhere.

---

44 For a discussion of trade credit and monetary policy see the Radcliffe *Report*, pp. 102-106. The classic and undimmed reference is Henry Thornton, *An Enquiry into the Nature and Effects of the Paper Credit of Great Britain* (New York: Rinehart & Co., 1939). *Paper Credit* was first published in 1802. J. S. Mill's *Principles* contain rich discussions of the pertinent issues.

45 And, for that matter, remedies at common law ordinarily call for money compositions.

There is a strong analogy to the instability of *laissez faire* (wildcat) banking. (*See Note E.*)

Thus, technology and tastes require that there be means of payment reducible to legal tender. Part I has shown that commercial banks have generated almost perfectly liquid liabilities (assets), *and* that non-financial firms cannot produce such claims consistently with their organic functions. Absurd fantasies in which 18th century American payments practices based on repeatedly-endorsed trade bills would be restored without catastrophic deflation despite a drastically reduced monetary base should be put aside. This subsection, together with elementary statistical inference, suggests what can happen when quick liabilities o'erreach cash assets. Traders know this also.

3

Finally, we have not directly considered whether there are theorems peculiar to a monetary economy (noting that a barter economy can have money of account). That is part of the task of Part II, but this much can be said now. Since, as shall be made more explicit in Ch. VII, an essential property of a monetary economy is sticky money prices, and since money-fixed claims are bound to be important in such an economy, price adjustments, together with new issue and retirement of debt, will not be instantaneous or complete. *Nominal quantities matter in a monetary economy;* even the most rigid adherence to preconditions for monetary neutrality cannot prevent there being long intervals in which the performance of a monetary economy importantly depends on various nominally-defined parameters.

PART II

MONEY & INCOME

PART II

*Money and Income**

INTRODUCTION

The theme of Part I, Money and Banking, was that the impact of monetary policy on an economic system cannot be understood if the student concentrates on financial markets rather than on the interaction of financial with "real" sectors (markets for goods, services, and labor). We have not yet attempted a careful, formal statement of the formation of prices and outputs either instantaneously or in terms of time sequences. Part II seeks to correct this deficiency. Once this has been done, we shall return to monetary problems proper, devoting no little space to the pure theory of central bank policy and the quantity theory of money.

In the meanwhile we shall try to fit the theory of demand for money into wider realms of the theory of choice. It is hoped to consolidate the argument of Part I on the reasons for holding money and why money holdings might contribute to utility. After contemplating necessary conditions for optimization of asset portfolios, we consider how what Keynes called "essential properties of money and interest" might establish lower bounds to asset yields throughout the system, possibly exerting depressive effects on demand prices for newly-produced assets. Then we launch into a fairly formidable statement of the modern theory of income and employment. Most of this theory is contained in Keynes's *General Theory of Employment, Interest, and Money;* the remainder in literature more or less stemming from this masterful but turbulent book. Next we attempt to extend Keynes's theory of instantaneous equilibrium to cover theories of growth and fluctuation.

* I am particularly indebted to Don Patinkin (for his book) and to Robert Clower and Mitchell Harwitz (my colleagues) in connection with Part II.

Part II, especially Chapters VII and VIII, stresses certain peculiar features of paper money. An increase in the demand for paper money generally involves a diversion of demand from goods and services requiring labor and other inputs to a good that can be produced without meaningful factor input. Sufficient price flexibility to achieve prompt and massive changes in the real value of paper money — in the absence of official intervention — contradicts what proves to be another of the essential properties of money; prices must be somewhat sticky if money is to function as a standard of value. We find that income and employment theory can be much simplified when implication of alternative monetary standards are understood.

It will seem at times during Chapter IX-XII that the subject matter of money and monetary theory has been swallowed up in the great seascape of the modern economy. But the last chapters of Part II, Chapters XIII and XIV, on the pure theory of central bank policy and the quantity theory of money, seek completely to integrate theories of money, prices, and income.

CHAPTER SEVEN

The Demand for Money and the Theory of Choice

A. THE HICKSIAN CHARGE

Dr. Hicks posed a challenge (in 1935) to which most of modern monetary theory can be considered a response. In his celebrated article, "A Suggestion for Simplifying the Theory of Money," *Economica,* New Series, Vol. 2 (1935), pp. 1-19,[1] he pointed out that monetary theory had diverged from the course set by the more highly developed theory of value and was unlikely to be fruitful unless brought within the pale. Since this chapter will be organized around the facets of the Hicksian challenge and whatever response has developed, we would be well advised to detail the Hicksian argument. These were his main points:

1) In their concentration on various equations of exchange ($M = kY'$, $vM = Y'$, etc.), monetary theorists overlooked that the demand for money should be analysable in terms of marginal utility theory.[2] As Hicks put it, "people do choose to have money rather than other things, and therefore, in the relevant sense, money must have a marginal utility." (*Ibid.,* p. 15.)

2) Since money is a stock (and an asset for the non-banking public), we might ask just what determines the decision to hold money

[1] Reprinted in Lutz and Mints, eds., *Readings in Monetary Theory,* p. 13 *ff*.
[2] "It was marginal utility that really made sense of the theory of value." ("A Suggestion . . .", p. 14.)

at a point in time. The answer to this query should be expected to range well beyond the confines of equations of exchange relating money holdings to income flows, but should bring us into the realm of the theory of portfolio management:

"what has to be explained is the decision to hold assets in the form of barren money, rather than of interest- or profit-yielding securities . . . So long as rates of interest are positive, the decision to hold money rather than lend it, or use it to pay off old debts is apparently an unprofitable one . . . This, as I see it, is really the central issue in the pure theory of money. Either we have to give an explanation of the fact that people do hold money when rates of interest are positive, or we have to evade the difficulty somehow. It is the great traditional evasions which have led to Velocities of Circulation, Natural Rates of Interest, *et id genus omne*." (*Ibid.*, p. 18.)

3) Explanations of the holding of money should rely on reasoning applied to houses, automobiles, etc. Riskiness of alternative portfolios is important. And, of course, money is a stock; capital accounts or balance sheets are the appropriate tools. "We have to concentrate on the forces which make assets and liabilities what they are." (*Ibid.*, p. 25.)

B. CHOICE THEORY

1

We now proceed to carry out the Hicksian charge. Begin with a very simple model, one in which stocks actually are precluded.[3] Assume that the typical economic unit has the opportunity of acquiring either or both of goods X_1 and X_2, both completely perishable. These goods are assigned accounting values (with, say, the dollar as the unit or money of account). The economic unit does not hold money. Money in fact does not exist. Rather each unit is assigned a budget at each point in time defining the maximum accounting value of his purchases — a time rate. Temporal interdependence is precluded.

It is further assumed that the economic unit is capable of ranking "bundles" of X_1 and X_2 and that his tastes and preferences can be ex-

[3] In this subsection, the text deals with two-good cases amenable to elementary geometry. Footnotes and Notes carry the burden of n-commodity cases, presented algebraically.

pressed mathematically through a *utility function* associating index numbers (which increase as more-preferred bundles are plugged into the function) with combinations of X_1 and X_2. A number of axioms are maintained, those important for us being axioms of comparison, transitivity, and nonsatiety.[4] The axioms assure that alternative bundles can be compared in the sense that the subject can announce that he prefers one or the other or is indifferent between them; that if Bundle A is preferred to Bundle B and Bundle B to Bundle C, then A is preferred to C;[5] and that, if Bundle D contains more of everything than does Bundle E, D will be preferred to E. We also assume diminishing rates of substitution (sometimes called diminishing rates of marginal substitution or marginal significance), implying that the rate at which X_1 must be substituted for X_2 in order for me to sustain the same level of utility increases as it is supposed that my initial rate of consumption of X_1 was larger compared to that of X_2.

The set of assumptions, axiomatic and otherwise, is diagrammatically represented in the diagram below. Rates of consumption of X_1 and X_2, x_1 and x_2, are measured along the respective axes. Curves I-IV link combinations of x_1 and x_2 towards which the economic unit (consumer) is indifferent. These curves will be downward sloping,

INDIFFERENCE-CURVE ANALYSIS

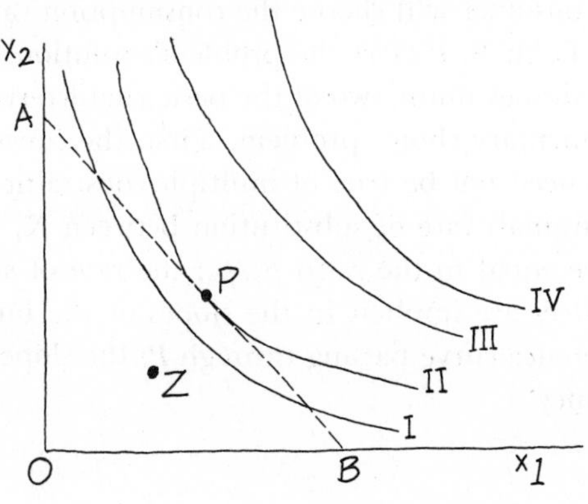

Figure VII-1

[4] *Cf.* D. W. Bushaw and R. W. Clower, *Introduction to Mathematical Economics*, Ch. V, p. 102 *ff*.

[5] The transitivity axiom, when combined with the nonsatiety axiom, can be used to show that indifference curves do not intersect.

convex to the origin, and nonintersecting. (*See Note A.*) They are crosscuts of a utility surface constructed in a third dimension: each curve represents the same height (measuring the utility index number); the indifference map is a contour map. *AB* is the budget line. Its slope infers the ratio of accounting prices facing the consumer. (If the budget and the prices are increased in the same proportion, *AB* will be unchanged.) All points lying on *AB* or below it are attainable; all points above it are unattainable.

2

All that has been done thus far is to erect a framework for analysing a problem; no problem has been stated. In fact the problem is to select the most preferred position compatible with the budget constraint; the classic problems of the theory of economic choice hinge upon maximization or minimization subject to side conditions.

The solution will find the consumer on his budget line *AB*; the nonsatiety axiom assures that any point such as *Z* lying below *AB* is inferior to some point on *AB*. The same axiom assures that Curve I is less preferred than Curve II which is less preferred than Curve III, etc.: more-preferred curves always lie to the right of less-preferred curves. The consumer will wish to attain the most-rightward curve consistent with *AB*. Clearly, no attainable curve could be more rightward than one barely touching *AB*, than the curve tangent to *AB*.[6] Accordingly the consumer will choose the consumption rates given by the coordinates of Point *P*; *P* gives the problem's solution.

We proceed to examine two of the basic characteristics of the solution to the elementary choice problem. First, the constraint is exactly satisfied. This need not be true of multiple-constraint problems. Secondly, the (marginal) rate of substitution between X_1 and X_2 will, in the solution, be equal to the ratio p_1/p_2: the rate of substitution and the ratio of prices are implicit in the slopes of the budget constraint and the indifference curve passing through *P*; the slopes are equal at a point of tangency.

3

The next step is to examine the comparative statics of the model. Compare the diagram below. *P* is an initial solution. Assume that p_1

[6] The assumption of uniformly-diminishing marginal significance, together with nonsatiety and transitivity axioms, assure that there can be only one indifference curve tangent to *AB*. This is intuitively obvious from the above diagram.

is reduced, *cet. par.*; the new budget line is AC. What are the general characteristics of movements such as from P to Q where Q is the new solution point?

COMPARATIVE STATICS

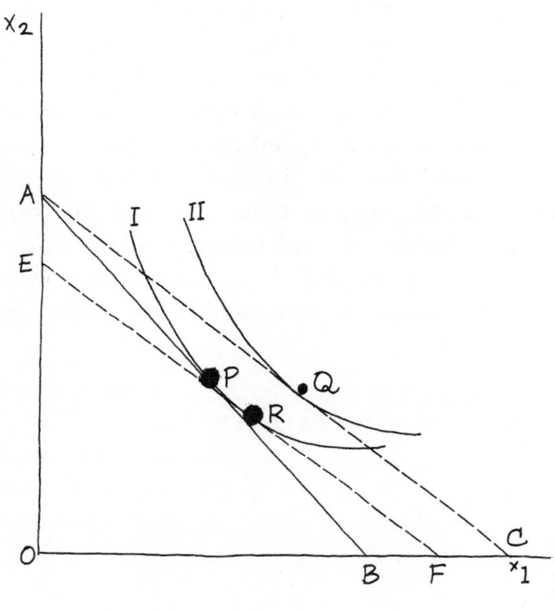

Figure VII-2

"Comparative statics" involves comparisons of solution points. The analysis here emphasizes substitution and income effects of price changes, together comprising the price effect. These "effects" are changes in planned rates of purchases (consumption in a model without durables) consequent to a change in price. An important concomitant is the concept of the *income-compensated* price change which leads to the price effect being solely comprised of a substitution effect.

A decrease in p_1, *cet. par.* has two impacts: (a) encouragement of substitution of X_1 for X_2; X_1 is now cheaper relative to X_2; (b) effects based on the consumer's real income having increased, since he would have purchasing power left over if he continued to purchase the old collection. The diagram above separates out these effects by conceiving of a price effect as generated through a two-stage process. The first stage finds p_1 reduced so that the slope of lines AC and EF reflect the new price ratio, in contrast with the original budget-line, AB. The first stage finds the consumer's income reduced so that he will be unable to achieve a more preferred state than is described by Indifference Curve I: the appropriate budget line is EF. The movement from P to R reflects a *pure-substitution effect* accompanying an *income-compensated* price change. The second stage involves a parallel movement of the budget line from EF to AC. This "takes" the consumer to the ultimate solution point, Q. The movement from R to Q reflects a pure *income effect;* relative prices are unchanged. In this way price effects are decomposed into substitution and income effects.

The axioms assure that the direction of substitution effects will be unambiguous in the two-good case: if p_1 falls, the consumer *certainly* will plan to increase x_1 and reduce x_2 if the price change is accompanied by a compensating change in nominal income. This follows from the assumption that indifference curves are convex

INFERIORITY

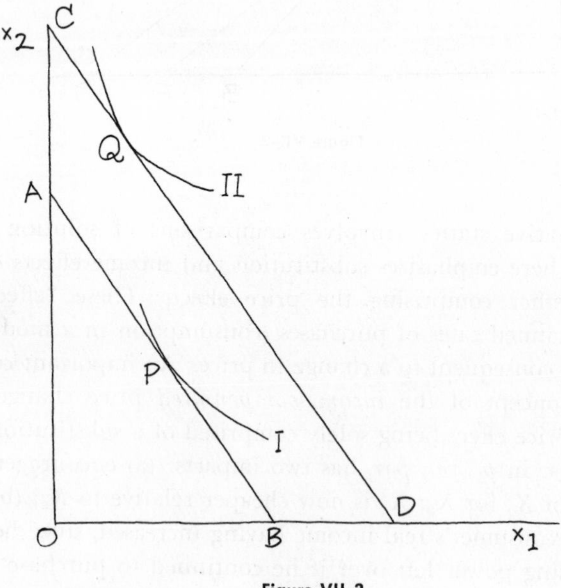

Figure VII-3

throughout.[7] If p_1 falls, p_2 unchanged, the budget line becomes flatter. If income is to be compensated so that tangency continues to occur on Curve *I*, the point of tangency must be to the right of *P*: Curve *I* becomes flatter as we move along it to the right.

There is no assurance that the income effect of a price reduction will lead to increased purchase of any one good. The axioms are consistent with goods being superior or inferior. (Income effects are positive for superior goods.) On the other hand, the axioms require at least one superior good: nonsatiety dictates that the budget always be exhausted. The diagram below demonstrates inferiority. A movement of the budget line from *AB* to *CD* leads to a shift from point *P* to *Q*. x_1 is lower at *Q* than at *P* although Indifference Curve *II* is preferred to Indifference Curve *I*. X_1 might be hamburger, sowbelly, or bus rides. X_2 might be filet mignon or racquets equipment.

C. STOCK-FLOW MODELS

1

Unfortunately the simple two-good model does not permit us to say as much about substitution and complementarity as we should like: the axioms require that at least one pair be substitutional, and there is only one pair. In general, the *ith* and *jth* goods are substitutional if the rate of purchase of the *jth* good falls when there is an income-compensated reduction in p_i (and *vice versa*). The *ith* and *jth* goods are complementary when such a reduction in p_i leads to an increase in the rate of purchase (consumption) of the *jth* good.[8] Substitution and complementarity are important in monetary theory. Indeed Part I put great stress on effects of prices of long- and short-dated securities on desired securities and cash holdings. Clearly, pursuit of the Hicksian golden fleece cannot begin in earnest without a model that permits holding of durable goods. Then we can handle balance-sheet problems

7 Otherwise the assertion would necessarily hold only for small changes in price. It can be shown that a necessary condition for a point to be a solution point is that the indifference curve passing through that point be convex in its neighborhood.

8 *Cf.* J. R. Hicks, *Value and Capital,* 2nd ed. Chapters I-III of this celebrated book are verbal and geometrical. The mathematical appendix also is a primary source.

Hicks defines substitution and complementarity in terms of effects of income-compensated changes in the price of one good on the maximum price the subject is willing to pay for the other. (P. 44.)

— effects of changes in asset prices on desired portfolios.[9] (*See Note B.*)

2

Bushaw and Clower provide such a model (p. 128 *ff.* and p. 160 *ff.*). Taking up a model of consumer choice, we discover at once that the criterion function must contain twice as many variables as before if we assume that *all* goods can either be held or otherwise used. Specifically,

$$(1) \qquad U \equiv U(x_1, \ldots, x_n; D_1, \ldots, D_n),$$

> "where the flow demand (or supply) variables [x] represent quantities of various commodities purchased for current consumption (or sold as current "output"), and the stock demand variables [D] represent corresponding quantities of the same commodities which the consumer wishes to hold for future disposal (through use or by sale). The D_i's may assume any real values, negative values indicating that D_i is a quantity of individual *debt* rather than assets." (*Op. cit.*, p. 128.)

Now consider definition of the budget equation for a consumer in what Bushaw and Clower call a "stock-flow" economy, one in which goods are produced, held, and consumed. The budget equation should be formulated in terms of flow rates, but account must be taken of stocks: we now are concerned with *investment* behavior, with rates of change of stock holdings. (Inventory and investment theory have obvious relevance to the theory of demand for money.) The consumer's actual holdings of the *ith* commodity, S_i, must be distinguished from the quantity of the *ith* commodity he wishes to hold, D_i. *Desired excess stock demand* for the *ith* commodity is defined as

$$(2) \qquad X_i \equiv D_i - S_i.$$[10]

However, as is common in investment behavior, the rate of market demand, while directly variant with X_i, will fall short of instantaneous correction of the short-fall. A simple assumption about the relation of

9 The transition from the theory of consumer choice and the theory of the firm to theories of market demand is part of the transition to general-equilibrium theory. [Consumer choice and firm behavior can be handled simultaneously. *Cf.* J. deGraaf, *Theoretical Welfare Economics* (Cambridge: Cambridge University Press. 1958)]. If all markets are to clear, prices and outputs must validate plans. When all markets are cleared, what Patinkin calls individual and market experiments lead to consistent results.

10 My exposition of the stock-flow model simply follows Bushaw-Clower as best I can. I also adopt their notation.

investment demand (x'_i) to desired excess stock demand is contained in Equation 3

$$(3) \qquad x_i' \equiv k_i X_i,$$

where k_i is "a positive fixed number."[11]

We now are prepared to state the budget equation proper, observing that the consumer, lacking privileges accorded Al Capone, will have to use his (positive or negative) money income, M (acquired from sources other than purchase or disposal of goods and including such items as interest on bonds) to pay for net purchases of commodities for consumption and for net investment in stocks. Specifically, the budget equation can be written as

$$(4) \qquad \sum_{1}^{n} p_i (x_i + k_i [D_i - S_i]) = M$$

or as

$$(5) \qquad \Sigma p_i (x_i + x_i') = M.$$

3

The groundwork has been laid for construction of a problem of constrained maximization analogous to that of the pure-flow model. Taking the S_i's, p_i's, and M as fixed, the problem can be reduced to selection of D_i's and x_i's consistent with the budget equation — establishing linkage between the D_i's and the x_i's. (*See Note C.*)

The next step distinguishes between what Bushaw and Clower call "plan equilibrium" and "consumer equilibrium": sets of solution values inconsistent and consistent with asset positions remaining fixed over time. This distinction becomes very important in later work dealing with motions of variables. A state of consumer equilibrium is defined as one in which $\overline{D}_i = S_i$ ($\overline{D}_i$ being a solution value), so that $x_i' = 0$ for all i. Of course, in plan equilibrium investment plans ($x_i' \neq 0$ for some i) are fulfilled, along with consumption plans.

The distinction between plan and consumer equilibrium suggests that between full equilibrium and market clearance. When the latter distinction is understood, one gains fruitful insight into the properties of motions of economic systems, motions including the still point of

[11] Bushaw and Clower point out in note 16, p. 129, that in a continuous-time analysis k_i must have a time dimension so that the right- and left-hand sides of the equation can become commensurable as flows. X_i has no time dimension; it is a stock quantity. The time dimension for k_i will be the same as that for x_i'.

the turning world: full equilibrium. (*Cf.* Ch. VA for a piece of analysis turning on this point.)

Implicit in solving the maximization problem is construction of demand and supply functions for stocks and flows (including investment). These functions can comprise a peg on which to hang results obtained from the comparative-statics properties of the system. The demand and supply equations can be written

$$(6) \qquad \bar{x}_i = f^i(p_1, \ldots, p_n; S_1, \ldots, S_n; M) \quad (i = 1, \ldots, n)$$

$$(7) \qquad \bar{D}_i = F^i(\qquad\qquad\qquad\qquad) \quad (i = 1, \ldots, n)$$

$$(8) \qquad \bar{x}_i' = k_i(\bar{D}_i - S_i) \quad (i = 1, \ldots, n)$$

where the barred quantities are solution values for the respective variables, and where Equations 8 can be rewritten

$$(9) \qquad \bar{x}_i' = g^i(p; S; M; k_i).$$

p and S are vectors. Equations 6, 7, and 9 comprise a reduced-form system.

4

What are the comparative-statics properties of the stock-flow system? Since these properties are to be derived mathematically, we can only state some of the results in the text, providing somewhat more background in footnote discussion. The following concrete results can be reported:

1) the empirically-observable variables are x and x', variables having special importance in income theory;

2) it remains true that the signs of price effects on demand for the *ith* commodity in responses to changes in the *jth* price are ambiguous;

3) the effects of a change in the *ith* price on demand for the *ith* good are interesting:

a) the total substitution effect, concerning the sum of consumption and investment demand, behaves as before; a reduction in the price of the *ith* good leads to a positive over-all substitution effect, but
b) one or the other of the solution values for consumption and investment demand for the *ith* commodity might *decrease* in response to a decrease in the *ith* price: "purchases of a commodity for current consumption may be either a substitute for or a complement to purchases of the same commodity to add to stocks (and similarly for

sales)." (*Ibid.*, p. 135.) Thus, if the price of peanuts falls, I might plan to eat some of my current stock;

4) results 1-3 were obtained for given S_i's. Abandonment of that assumption leads to the conclusion that, as between states of consumer equilibrium (X_i and $x_i' = 0$ for all i), the substitution terms $\partial \bar{x}_i / \partial p_i$ are ambiguous in sign;[12] "moreover, the income term in the expression [for price effect], which indicates among other things the effect on $\bar{x}_i$ [the bars denoting solution values] of changes in various asset holdings, and which is probably of more empirical significance than the substitution term, is always ambiguous in sign." (*Ibid.*, p. 133.) (*See Note D.*)

5

We have two more tasks to perform: (a) apply flow-stock models to the theory of the firm; (b) show how cash balances are entered into the model.

a) The Firm

There are no budget constraints in the formal theory of the firm (faced with perfect capital markets). The problem is to maximize a linear objective function subject to a production function — describing the terms under which inputs can be transformed into outputs — and functions linking maximum prices that can be obtained for outputs and minimum prices that must be paid for inputs with output-input combinations. The first- and second-order conditions for extreme values are of the same form as in the consumer-choice problem. These conditions imply that the contribution to the maximand of the "last" penny held in cash balance should be equal to that of the "last" penny's worth of any and all other assets in the firm's portfolio; it should be impossible to increase the present value of the firm, for example, by transferring from one asset to another. (*See Note E.*)

b) Entry of Cash Balances Into the Model

Cash balances at the micro level look like a stock-flow good. At each point in time there is an equivalent of consumption utilization, the gross rate of cash outflow. Define the rate at which the *jth*

[12] There can be no change in investment demand between full-equilibrium states since $x' = 0$ in both states.

trader is supplying cash to the market as x_{rj} and the rate at which the market is supplying cash to the trader (the rate at which he is buying cash) as z_{rj}. His planned investment demand for cash x'_{rj}, is

$$(i) \qquad x'_{rj}(t) \equiv [k_{rj}(t)]\,[D_{rj}(t) - S_{rj}(t)].$$

The *jth* trader's temporary equilibrium requires that

$$(ii) \qquad x'_{rj}(t) = z_{rj}(t) - x_{rj}(t).$$

Of course, for a fixed stock of aggregate cash balances, market equilibrium requires that $\sum_j x'_{rj}(t) = 0$. *(See Notes F and G.)*

It is important to keep in mind that a trader can be satisfied with his cash position even if his over-all plans are not being fulfilled: a firm accumulating undesired inventory might increase its bank loan, although it surely is unlikely that $D_{rj}(t)$ is independent of the *jth* trader's ability to fulfill other plans. At the macro level, $D_{rj}(t) = S_{rj}(t)$ might hold for all traders although output is running ahead of effective demand; firms can restore depletions of their cash (as, say, inventories accumulate undesirably so that $x_{rj} > z_{rj}$) by selling securities. *(Cf. Notes F and G.)*

It is desirable to use continuous time in order to handle periodicity: D_{rj} varies over the week, or the day for that matter. The k's are functions of time. Consider a businessman walking to the bond mart with surplus cash: at the *moment* we observe him his k_{rj} is zero. *(See Note H.)*

We assume that, unlike candy, no utility or disutility attaches to the act of "consuming" (spending) cash. Silas Marner is outside our purview. "Equilibrium" cash flows express the outcome of a set of decisions concerned with determining optimal values for arguments entering into the expression being maximized or minimized. On the other hand, cash can be entered into utility functions and surely can affect productive efficiency, marginal demand prices of purchasers of the firm's securities, etc. Cash stocks can be seen to yield streams of liquidity services, streams which should be entered in utility and other transformation functions. These streams are NOT measured by the x_{rj} terms. Entry of D_{rj} into the *jth* criterion function is surrogate for the stream of liquidity services mapping into D_{rj}. Since contribution to utility or present value is associated with *holding* a perfectly-durable good, cash is a stock commodity in the sense that the stock of cash (but no explicit flow variable for cash) is entered into criterion functions. *(See Note I infra and Note B, Ch. III.)*

Bushaw and Clower suggest at pp. 134-135 that "[one can] make theoretical provision for the fact that assets are normally held in part as a store of value as well as for their own sake [by] the introduction of price variables [as parameters] into the utility index." It is impossible rationally to consider contributions of cash holdings, for example, without taking account of the prices of other goods. Thus Patinkin works with a composite price variable, p, introducing money (cash) balances into individual criterion functions in the form M/p.[13]

Durable goods performing services in addition to those tied to their nominal value require different treatment, although prices must be introduced into a criterion function whenever liquidity services are rendered (at the least in order to define its arguments). "True" stock-flow goods such as automobiles have a place in the consumption plan.[14] Furthermore, assets such as bonds yield interest income as well as liquidity services. Account must be taken of the marginal utility of income in balancing off the contribution of the "last" penny's worth of cash and of bonds. *(See Note I.)* Similar adjustment must be made in a model for the firm. All of these considerations can be fitted into the generalized stock-flow model.

D. MOTIVES FOR HOLDING CASH

1

The Hicksian injunction has been diligently and painfully fulfilled. Let us extract the essence of comments made at least as early as

---

13 In Ch. VA, Appendix A, money balances did not enter into aggregate *demand* functions. We assumed that all money balances had an indebtedness offset, that all money was "inside" money. Whether it is appropriate to include a variable in a given function depends on the problem at stake. In Ch. VII we are dealing with micro problems.

Needless to say, $D_{rj}(t)$ can be linked by stochastic penalty functions and similar constructions to time profiles of cash flows. *(See Note J infra and Note B, Ch. III.)*

14 The formal model requires that the consumer have control of the consumption decision to a greater extent than is likely to be true in the "real world." In the model a decision to increase holdings of the *ith* stock-flow good is independent of the decision about consumption of the services of the *ith* good. Perfect markets make this possible: even if automobiles remorselessly eroded at a given rate whether or not used, it would be possible for me to maintain a stock without consuming automobile services; I could rent out my automobile stock and use the proceeds continuously to replace "dying" stock. Similarly, I could consume automobile services without holding stocks of autos simply by renting from others.

Ch. III. Why do households and firms hold money? Why hold assets in the form of barren money? Or, as Hart has put it:

> "Why do individuals and business firms hold cash? Cash cannot be eaten, worn, slept in, or used to keep off the weather. In itself it is useless; it is valued only because it can be used to buy other things. There is always something you can buy with cash on hand. Why keep cash unspent?"[15]

One almost would expect money prices to become infinite as traders try to rid themselves of the barren stuff — and none can succeed.

At least since the *General Theory,* it has become conventional to classify motives for holding cash under three heads:[16]

> "The three divisions of liquidity preference which we have distinguished . . . may be defined as depending on (i) the *transactions-motive,* i.e., the need of cash for the current transactions of personal and business exchanges; (ii) the *precautionary-motive,* i.e., the desire for security as to the future cash equivalent of a certain proportion of total resources; and (iii) the *speculative-motive,* i.e., the object of securing profit from knowing better than the market what the future will bring forth." (J. M. Keynes, *General Theory,* p. 170. All emphasis supplied.)

Before canvassing the Keynesian categories, we capsulate the argument at pp. 170-174 of the *General Theory:*

> ". . . the question of the desirability of having a highly organized market for dealing with debts presents us with a dilemma. For, in the absence of an organized market, liquidity-preference due to the precautionary-motive would be greatly increased; whereas the existence of an organized market gives an opportunity for wide fluctuations in liquidity-preference due to the speculative motive.
>
> . . . if the liquidity preferences due to the transactions-motive and the precautionary-motive are assumed to absorb a quantity of cash which is not very sensitive to changes in the rate of interest as such and apart from its reactions on the level of income . . . each increase in the quantity of money must raise the price of bonds sufficiently to exceed the expectations of some 'bull' and so influence him to sell his bond for cash and join the 'bear' brigade. If, however, there is a negligible demand for cash from the speculative motive . . . an increase in the quantity of money will have to lower the rate of interest.

[15] A. G. Hart, *Money, Debt; and Economic Activity,* p. 199.

[16] The tripartite classification was informally treated in Ch. III in connection with the liquidity services of savings deposits, insurance policies, cash values, etc. *Cf.* also Ch. VI.

> . . . in whatever degree is necessary to raise employment . . . sufficiently to cause the additional cash to be absorbed by the transactions-motive and the precautionary-motive." (*Ibid.*, pp. 170-171.)

Keynes then suggests (somewhat repetitiously) why "the schedule . . . relating the [desired] quantity of money to the rate of interest" is given by a smooth curve which shows the rate of interest falling as the quantity of money is increased:

> 1) assuming initial unemployment, the larger quantity of money might lead to lower interest rates, stimulating economic activity and requiring larger transactions balances;
>
> 2) desired transactions balances should increase, since the interest cost of the convenience of ready cash is less;
>
> 3) implicitly assuming open-market purchases, the public will be induced by lower interest rates to substitute money for securities.

After pointing out that *hoarding,* or rather the *propensity to hoard,* "may be regarded as a first approximation to . . . *liquidity-preference,*" Keynes concludes (Ch. 13, *General Theory*) with an admonishment to the reader, stressing the distinction between demand in the schedule and the quantity sense:

> ". . . [I]t is impossible for the actual amount of hoarding to change as a result of decisions on the part of the public, so long as we mean by "hoarding" the actual holding of cash. For the amount of hoarding must be equal to the quantity of money . . .; and the quantity of money is not determined by the public. All that the propensity of the public towards hoarding can achieve is to determine the rate of interest at which the aggregate desire to hoard becomes equal to the available cash. [In fact, the equilibrium rate of interest *might* be independent of the propensity to hoard.]" (*Ibid.*, p. 174.)

2

We shall take up the three motives, consolidating and reviewing material of earlier chapters. But first pay careful heed to the next two paragraphs. Otherwise dire confusion probably will engulf you.

The *speculative motive* of Ch. 13 (*General Theory*) is, as Tobin and others have shown (*cf. Note J*), a dubious foundation for a theory of holding *cash* beyond transactions "requirements." I detail it but confess I think it a thin reed. Some argue that Keynes's *precautionary motive* can be molded into a much more convincing explanation of "investment cash balances"; Keynes does this in Ch. 17 (*General The-*

ory). Note B, Ch. III, shows speculative, precautionary, and transactions motives to be inextricable, but gets Ch. 13's results. Acknowledging dissatisfaction with arguments compartmentalizing motivations for holding cash, Ch. 17 also can be used to get Ch. 13's results on the assumption that subjective probability distributions center on *expected* future interest rates equal to current rates — *but not for sure.*

The argument of Ch. 17, difficult in any case, is almost incomprehensible except in terms of general portfolio management. Accordingly, instead of a subheading "Precautionary Motive," the argument is integrated into Section E of this chapter, "Liquidity Preference, Financial Assets as Stores of Wealth, Income Theory." It is crucially important to understand that the theoretical foundations of liquidity preference do *not* lead to unique theorems about cash; only to theorems about assets of various degrees of liquidity.[17]

3

As for the *transactions* motive, Chapters III and VI need only be recalled. Deal first with a world of certainty. The costs of going in and out of securities being considerable, and interest yields over spans as short as a day or week being miniscule, traders planning to pay out cash rather shortly plan to hold cash balances today: balances will be cumulated for pay-day, market-day, etc. Clearly, the problem is one of synchronization[18] . . . Turning to uncertainty, seated in the darkly-rumbling bowels of Nature's Urn, recall Ch. III's discussion of displacement of cash by "near-monies" in providing a buffer against insolvency; interest-bearing deposits, credit cards, overdraft facilities,

---

17 Professor Harry G. Johnson focused my attention on the *General Theory's* two theories of liquidity preference as behavior towards risk. *Cf.* his "Monetary Theory and Policy," *American Economic Review,* Vol. 52, June 1962, pp. 335-384. Of course, the theory of Ch. 13 *(General Theory)* does not purport to explain "normal backwardation," only *rigidity* of long rate.

18 This note is digressive, but gives a feeling for stock-flow analysis of cash. Consider firms building new plant and equipment whose other payments and receipts can be ignored. They acquire cash by selling securities. Such firms (or "aspects of firms") form a sector with persistent net cash outflow; the sector's membership always is changing. Acquired cash leaves its possession as quickly as it arrives — subject to some pools being accumulated because of ill-synchronized securities sales and factor payments. It continuously sells bonds, acquiring fresh cash — partly from members of the sector paying-up and leaving. Chapter IV's revolving-fund interpretation of the banking sector becomes animated.

One visualizes a reservoir, the cash stock of the firms in the deficit-spending sector. The reservoir's water level is constant. It is being replenished by some of the very cash that flowed out shortly before, returning under the aegis of financial institutions.

etc. permit firms and households to obtain cash easily and cheaply when emergencies arise.[19]

Of course, there often are sound reasons for holding at least some cash against the fickle finger of fate: if shortfalls occur frequently, frictional expense — including that associated with removing and redepositing interest-bearing deposits — might overcome interest earnings; sometimes time can be of the essence.[20]

4

The *speculative motive* for holding cash is rooted in a "bear" attitude towards one or more goods. For a trader to hold *cash* speculatively, his bear view must extend to short-term securities and/or transactions costs must be relatively important for him. Also it is more than likely that the trader holding cash for speculative purposes wants to be able to jump back into the market at a moment's notice.

Let us unwind the verbal tangle. Once one decides that some price is likely soon to fall, perhaps tomorrow, he first must reflect on the strength of his conviction. Is his expectation firm enough to justify risk taking? Say the answer is affirmative. If the good is now in his possession, bearish expectations call for its sale today. If not, or if it is a pure-flow good, bearish expectations might call for a short sale — to contract to deliver the good to a customer or broker at a future date, anticipating that its price will fall by the delivery date.[21,22] However,

19 In fact, Americans do not hold much cash. United States cash balances amount to less than the value of two weeks' transactions. Annual rates of turnover of bank deposits are as high as 63 in New York City and exceed 26 in less important American reporting centers.

20 Where securities markets are imperfect, the danger of unexpectedly having to cough-up cash is more sinister: prices facing one as a seller might be much less than if I were a buyer; enforced liquidation, even in a generally-tranquil atmosphere, can impose serious financial sacrifice. Demand for what Ch. VI called "precautionary transactions balances" tends to be greater in less-developed countries: non-monetary assets do a poorer job of substitution for cash.

21 "*Might* call for a short sale" because, after all, one is guessing about the future. Risk avoiders require that the game be unfair before they will play; some require that it be more unfair than do others.

22 Say that I have sold short a share in Chrysler Corporation. This means that my broker borrowed a share (selling it spot) and that I deposited cash with the broker equal to at least 50 per cent of the share's value. The short sale is unwound when I replace the share. The short sale itself does not realize cash for me. On the other hand, the broker's handling of the sale's proceeds and the cash I deposited with him will be governed by transactions and precautionary considerations.

Short sales of commodities and foreign exchange almost never lead to current cash realizations for the seller. There remains, however, the decision when to cover the short position. If I announce I want to cover, my broker might build up cash today in order to purchase the stock tomorrow. The fact is that analysis of short sales does not permit more penetrating light to be shed.

the juice is extracted by concentrating on a good now in the portfolio, thought likely soon to fall in price, and accordingly sold today.

The first step is completed: an asset is exchanged for cash. Should the cash be exchanged for some other asset today? The answer hinges on at least four considerations:

1) transactions costs, the core concept keyed to 2-4;
2) running yields on alternative assets;
3) probabilities attached to various asset prices falling tomorrow as against next week, month, or year;
4) view as to when will be the nadir of the price of the asset sold today.

Thus, if one were certain that an asset's price would fall tomorrow and rise the day after tomorrow, he would sell today, hold cash overnight, and buy tomorrow.[23] Transactions costs would o'erwhelm any but astronomical running yields of assets alternative to cash. If one felt that the price, starting tomorrow, were likely to fall for some months when it would reach its nadir, and if the relevant short rate were very high, he almost certainly would plan to invest the sale's proceeds in a non-cash asset. Now consider an intermediate case: the relevant short rate (it might be that for interest-bearing deposits) is $2\frac{1}{2}$ or 3 per cent; the price's nadir is expected *some* time within the next 60 days. The decision whether to hold proceeds in cash will hinge on all four of the above factors. All that can be said is that lower transactions costs, higher yields on alternative investments, lower probabilities attached to price declines *tomorrow,* and anticipation that the nadir will occur in the rather distant future all encourage plans to hold non-cash balances.[24]

Put aside distinctions between motives for holding cash. Deal with observables: cash balances, period. Everything suggests negative asso-

[23] For simplicity it is assumed that all is expected to be the same the day after tomorrow as it is today.

[24] Potential capital losses on short-term securities have been ignored. For any set of expectations about tomorrow's bill rate, the lower is today's rate, the larger the number of traders who are "convinced" it will rise tomorrow. The less is running yield, the less is the offset to potential bear profit.

Cautiously distinguish between the arguments of Chapters VA and VII on speculative factors in securities markets. Chapter VA was concerned with the fact that Treasury bill rate in the United States ranged from 0.014 to 0.103 per cent from 1938–1941 when long-term United States bonds yielded more than 2.25 per cent. Chapter VII explains criteria that would be used in deciding what to do with cash obtained from the sale of, say, a long-term security priced "too high."

ciation between desired cash balances and interest rates. And do not neglect the Keynesian *caveat:* ultimately interest rates must reconcile the public's plans and the actual stock of cash.

E. LIQUIDITY PREFERENCE, FINANCIAL ASSETS AS STORES OF WEALTH, INCOME THEORY

1

We attempt to integrate the Keynesian Precautionary Motive (security of nominal value of wealth) into a theory of portfolio balance. It suggests why, at least from time to time, long rate can be sticky at "high" levels. It explains how demand prices for physical assets can be held down because of strong preferences for financial assets. It attempts the transition from the theory of demand for cash and other assets to the theory of income and employment.

We are in trouble unless the chapter's message can be condensed into a simple relationship such as

$$M^{d} = p.f(r, Y) \text{ or } M^{d}/p = f(r, Y)$$

where M^{d} is the desired stock of cash, p a general price level, r a vector of interest rates, and Y real income. The functional relationship accounts for such institutional factors as quality of transportation, synchronization properties not influenced by interest rates, attitudes towards securities as liquid assets, etc. The luxury of compartmentalized motivations for holding cash becomes too expensive. Instead the goal becomes to relate *observables* such as money balances (although M^{d} is *not* observable), income wealth and interest rates.

Assume that cash balances contribute to consumers' utility indexes and to the profitability of firms so that cash is among the stocks of the formal model. It is expected that desired cash balances will vary inversely with yields of alternative assets. (*See Note I.*)

It is convenient to couch the equivalent of the stock-flow model's first-order conditions in nominal yields. Assume that the marginal liquidity yield from money holdings can be expressed as a per annum rate, l_n. If l_n were 0.10 (10 per cent per annum), the "last dollar" of cash would yield services for which the economic unit were willing to pay 10 cents a year. In fact additional symbols are required, loosely following Keynes (*General Theory,* p. 225 *ff.*): q_i, c_i, and a_i.[25] q_i re-

[25] *This* Keynesian model is close to Tobin's: inelastic expectations are not needed here. (*Cf.* footnote 30 *infra.*) It pursues the Keynesian precautionary motive.

flects the fact that "some assets produce a yield or output . . . by assisting some process of production or supplying services to a consumer." (*General Theory*, p. 225.) Let q_i be the proportion borne by the net value of the (non-monetary) services generated by a unit asset — if cumulated at that rate for, say, one year — to that of the initial price of the asset. (We do not follow Keynes strictly.) If $q_{machinery}$ were 0.10, the services rendered over one year by the asset are valued at 10 per cent of the asset's initial price. And then

> "most assets, except money, suffer some wastage or involve some cost through the mere passage of time (apart from any change in their relative value), irrespective of their being used to produce a yield; i.e., they involve a carrying cost c_i . . ." (*General Theory*, pp. 225-226.)

If c_i were 0.05, 5 per cent of the initial value of the *ith* asset would be wasted on this account. l_i is the liquidity yield (including the "precautionary" premium) for the *ith* asset, again using the beginning-of-the-period price as the base.[26] Finally, a_i measures the rate of expected capital gain or loss for the *ith* asset (measuring in money). *All yields are marginal.*

Be sure you understand the symbols. How would we obtain a yield statistic for automobiles comparable with that for money? Assume, for example, that q_3 (where 3 indexes autos) $= 0.30$,[27] $l_3 = 0$, $c_3 = 0.25$, and that $a_3 = -0.01$. The net yield is 0.0425 (the capital loss being calculated on what is left of the car). Indexing money as n, assume that $l_n = 0.0425$, with q_n and $c_n = 0$, a_n being definitionally zero (a dollar always exchanges for a dollar). Net yields realizable through holding a dollar's worth of automobile and one dollar are equal.[28] The form of the first-order conditions becomes obvious:

$$q_i - c_i + l_i + a_i(1-c_i) = q_j - c_j + l_j + a_j(1-c_j)^{29}$$

For paper money and the *ith* good, the condition is written

$$q_i - c_i + l_i + a_i(1-c_i) = l_n$$

(You might not want to ignore carrying costs for money.)

26 Keynes considers only precaution against variability of nominal wealth. *Cf.* footnote 30 and Appendix A, Ch. VA, and p. 110 *ff. supra.*

27 Consumer-durable yields are assumed to be derived from objective market prices.

28 As is so often true, a period analysis facilitates exposition at the expense of logic. In continuous time, the asset portfolio would be continuously scrutinized. We would not be plagued by problems of whether prices changed at the beginning or the end of the period, etc. This ugly and unproductive difficulty permeates period analysis; one's choice of usage generally affects present values of outcomes.

29 Appreciation is realized at the *end* of the period. Recall the more formal first-order conditions of Note H.

The form of the equations belies the elements of uncertainty that have been introduced into the problem through the l terms. (Conventional solutions of problems of choice often do not hold-up under uncertainty.) Still in some crude sense an "optimal" asset portfolio can be characterized by equality of marginal net yields of a dollar's worth of each of its components.[29a]

[29a] The text ignores frictional costs; the model applies to a micro-interval. An explicitly multiperiod horizon (together with the calculus of variations) must be introduced in order to accommodate frictional costs.

Assume Asset A has a coupon yield of 6 per cent per annum; Asset B, 5 per cent. Assume further that the *jth* trader expects Asset B to increase in price at the rate of 20 per cent per annum over the next day, only to return to its current price the day after tomorrow. Moderate assumptions about frictional expense make it likely that the trader will not take action even if his expectation is held with well-nigh absolute confidence.

Frictional expense sometimes explains what is meant by "buying for long-run appreciation." Consult this expected time path for the price of Asset B.

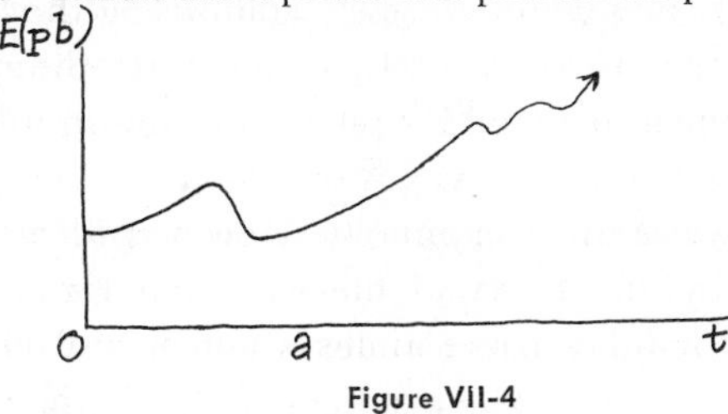

Figure VII-4

I might choose to buy at $t = a$: transitional possibilities are not worth the buying and selling expense.

The following chart illustrates another aspect of buying for long-run appreciation.

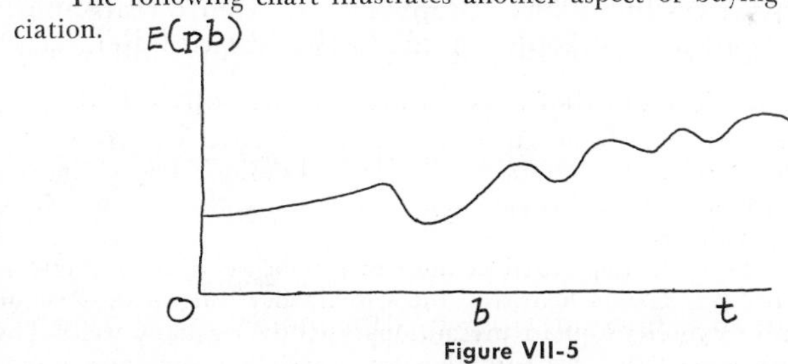

Figure VII-5

I might buy now instead of at b because I am not *sure* that p^b will be lower at $t = c$. The vicissitudes of price might mean nothing to me. Selling and buying expenses might be high enough to keep me on the B bandwagon throughout.

It becomes clear that realistic theories of portfolio management must deal with choices among *time paths* of asset holdings, among *sequences* of sales and purchases for given initial portfolios. Nor can target dates (end points) be neglected. *Quite apart from risk-and-uncertainty influences,* a rational real-world portfolio manager will be found to violate the text's instantaneous marginal conditions.

2

The end of the tortuous path leading from the theory of asset holding to that of income and employment is in sight. But there is another preliminary step: relation of equilibrium conditions for asset portfolios to *investment* behavior. Begin with a three-asset model: paper money, perpetual bonds and homogeneous physical capital. Assume that the liquidity yield from money holdings, l_n, is and remains at 5 per cent throughout. Next assume that the liquidity yield of a dollar's worth of perpetual bonds is 1 per cent and that $a_{bonds} = 0$. Long rate cannot fall below nor exceed 4 per cent: at a lower yield cash would be preferred; at a higher yield excess supply of cash (excess demand for bonds) would drive up bond prices.[30] This means in turn that physical capital must offer a marginal net yield of 5 per cent in equilibrium. (It presumably has no liquidity yield.) If the marginal yield of the existing stock of physical capital were 5 per cent, there would be no incentive to increase that stock: investment demand would be nil. Investment demand for physical capital can be restricted by the floor imposed by liquidity yields of cash and other financial assets. The vistas of Keynesian economics have been approached through a route dominated by the theory of money, although it has become customary to follow another route along which monetary factors are ignored.

3

Terminological and analytical underbrush having been cleared, we can plunge into a series of topics going to the heart of Part II of

[30] Ignoring convenience yields supporting transactions and speculative motives for holding cash, the ℓ terms become negatively surrogate for Tobin's σ. The ℓ become slack variables in the equilibrium conditions explaining away willingness to accept lower marginal expected yields from some assets than from others. Higher ℓ's associate with lower σ's.

However, transactions (and speculative) motives cannot be ignored: the correspondence of l_n and σ is merely heuristic: the sets are not congruent. Assume that demand and time deposits support precautionary motives equally well. The ℓ term for cash must exceed that for any other asset; cash can serve as a means of payment. When deposit rate is, say, 4 per cent, the marginal convenience yield for non-precautionary purposes of demand deposits exceeds that of time deposits by 4 per cent in equilibrium. When deposit rates are, say, 1 per cent, equilibrium marginal convenience yields for demand deposits are substantially driven down. *N. B.*, in the text the *l*'s, encompass all benefits from liquidity not otherwise explicitly entered; transactions motives are encompassed. David Meiselman (*cf.* Appendix A, Ch. VA) points out, however, that if expectations (as against hedging pressure) determine the yield curve, nominal-value certainty has nothing to do with market yields.

this book and treated by Keynes, Lerner, and Kaldor.[31] Specifically, it remains (a) briefly to restate the relationship of the theory of asset holding to the theory of investment; (b) to examine the essential properties of money in order to determine whether monetary phenomena can impose persistent barriers to full employment and growth — not neglecting historical experience.

a) restatement of theoretical results through a homely example

The following statement might be illuminating. It ignores the a_i factor:

At a given point in time, men can be observed to hold money, bonds, producers' durables and consumers' durables — and, indeed, many other goods not ordinarily labeled "durable" but not *instantaneously* consumed upon manufacture. Yields can be expressed nominally: one deals with dollar's worth(s) of assets and values of service yields, ultimately reduced to percentages. Optimality requires that marginal yields be equal. Furthermore, the typical individual "owns" negative assets, namely, bonds that he has issued. At the margin negative yields associated with borrowings (comprised of interest cost and illiquidity disservice) are equal to the common positive net yield of his assets. The constituent elements of the yield streams are q_i, c_i, and l_i.

Begin with this postulate: purchase of any asset can be made equivalent to purchase of a perpetual bond promising to pay $r per year forever. Assume that a machine can be purchased for $100 and that it will yield a certainty-equivalent *net* stream of $10 per year forever. One would be indifferent between it and a perpetuity promising to pay $10 a year and costing $100. Now take the case of a very compact automobile costing $100. At τ, the auto's service yield, adjusted for depreciation, must permit indifference between it and alternative investments. In equilibrium, portfolios must be distributed so that the last dollar's worth of each asset is earning the same yield.[32] What

31 Ch. 17 ("The Essential Properties of Interest and Money") of the *General Theory*. A. P. Lerner, "The Essential Properties of Interest and Money," *Quarterly Journal of Economics,* May 1952, reprinted in his *Essays in Economic Analysis* (London: Macmillan & Co., Ltd., 1953), pp. 354-383. Nicholas Kaldor, *Essays on Economic Stability and Growth* (London: Duckworth, 1960), pp. 59-74.

32 Here continuous "instantaneous efficiency" assures inter-temporal efficiency in portfolio management. Future transformation possibilities here depend only on values of portfolios. One can neglect the consumption plan, focusing solely on *some* of the necessary conditions for optimization. For a general discussion, see R. Dorfman, P. A. Samuelson, and R. M. Solow, *Linear Programming and Economic Analysis,* pp. 309-318 (especially pp. 317-318). But *cf.* footnote 29a.

if it were inconceivable that $1 held in cash balances would produce a convenience yield of less than 2 per cent per annum? Then 2 per cent would be the minimum rate of interest that could be borne by non-liquid assets, although assets as liquid as Treasury bills might carry very low interest rates, but be attractive because of their liquidity.[33] And surely this applies to time deposits. (Recall the 1930's and 1940's when short rates were very low compared to short rates of the 1920's and to long rates in the 1930's and 1940's. *See Note J.*)

High liquidity preference, such as that often attributed to India, can cramp demand for new machines (and consumption goods as well), investment demand hinging as it does on plans to increase initial stocks. Investment will not be contemplated unless expected rates of net return are at least equal to the liquidity yield from cash holdings. (*See Note I.*)

b) role of essential properties of money

The theory of asset holding has taken us to a point where it is evident that "if there is any asset whose marginal efficiency of holding stays high, all the other marginal efficiencies and all the rates of interest must be equally high because they must be equal in equilibrium — all being measured on the same commodity yardstick." (A. P. Lerner, *op. cit.*, p. 371.) The effects of high interest rates already have

33 *Certainly for banks.* The added safety of a short-dated portfolio pertains only to day-to-day certainty of its expected value. The extended time-profile of the *yield stream* is more uncertain for the holder of bills than of consols. Risk considerations are a two-way street. As H. G. Johnson writes in his 1962 article "Monetary Theory and Policy" (*American Economic Review*): "In the first place there is a tendency to follow too closely Hicks' original sketch of the approach in identifying the typical asset-holder with a bank, borrowing for shorter term than it lends and therefore preferring the shorter term assets." Thus, if one is in very short-dated stock, the net worth of his portfolio is never in jeopardy: this can be important for banks; long-terms can vary substantially in market value from day to day; one must hold on to the bitter end to be sure of his capital. But the yield stream (excluding capital gain and loss) from long-terms is certain. The holder of long-terms can be sure of being able to spend at a certain rate without increasing his investment. A pension-fund manager who did not want to have to chance eating into his capital in order to meet his fixed annuity obligation would have greater safety in long-terms; for him these would be a perfect hedge against his annuity obligation.

Cf. Joan Robinson, "The Rate of Interest," *Econometrica,* Vol. 19, April 1951, pp. 92-111. Also Joseph W. Conard, *Introduction to the Theory of Interest* (Berkeley: University of California Press, 1959), Part III, and Ch. III *supra.*

received much attention.[34] Are money and other highly-liquid assets the culprits?

Try an indirect approach. Might not a non-monetary asset such as land be culpable? Keynes thought so:

> "It may be that in certain historical environments the possession of land has been characterized by a high liquidity-premium in the minds of owners of wealth; and since land resembles money in that its elasticities of production and substitution may be very low, it is conceivable that there have been occasions in history in which the desire to hold land has played the same role in keeping up the rate of interest at too high a level which money has played in recent times . . . The high rates of interest from mortgages on land, often exceeding the probable net yield from cultivating the land [reflecting landowners' high liquidity premiums . . .] have been a familiar feature of many agricultural economies. Usury laws have been directed primarily against encumbrances of this character. And rightly so. For in earlier social organizations where long-term bonds in the modern sense were non-existent, the competition of a high interest-rate on mortgages may well have had the same effect in retarding the growth of wealth from current investment in newly produced capital-assets, as high interest rates on long-term debts have had in more recent times.
>
> That the world after several millennia of steady individual saving is so poor as it is in accumulated capital-assets is to be explained, in my opinion, neither by the improvident propensities of mankind, nor even by destruction of war, but by the high liquidity-premiums formerly attaching to the ownership of land and now attaching to money . . ." (*General Theory,* pp. 241-242.)

Lerner's comment on what he terms "this intriguing speculation" — he is supported by Kaldor — is both negative and enlightening. He writes that Keynes's argument "falls to the ground" because "there is nothing to stop the value of land from rising rapidly in the way in which money-wage stickiness stops the value of money from rising rapidly." (*Op. cit.,* p. 377.) In other words, excess demand for land could be expected to lead to an increase in its price, thereby increasing the stock of land *as a liquid asset* — as a means of storing purchasing power. As Lerner puts it, "any conceivable desire for holding wealth in the form of land can therefore be filled until it overflows into the demand for other forms of wealth that *can* be produced." (*Ibid.,* p.

[34] The context is unemployment. Of course transitional effects on interest rates of monetary expansion (contraction) can be important. *Cf.* Ch. VA.

377.) Presumably there would be some real value of land high enough to depress its marginal liquidity yield to any desired level.[35] Of course, if liquid balances were not subject to diminishing marginal utility, any non-reproducible liquid asset could impose a floor on interest rates in the way described by Keynes. Such an assumption, however, while consistent with long-lasting involuntary unemployment, is inconsistent with economic theory. We prefer to seek out another monetary property — consistent with economic theory — imposing a floor on long-term interest rates. We wish to avoid speculative forces (although we discover that the essential property activates speculative forces working against falling long rate).

Money wages and hence money costs and prices of produced goods (unlike unreproducible goods such as land) tend to be sticky, certainly downwards. Considerable stickiness in the general purchasing power of money proves essential to its (and money-fixed claims) usefulness as a liquid asset and a standard for deferred payments. But this means that the system is unlikely soon to generate important (spontaneous) increases in *real* liquid balances. And then a very large cumulative fall in the general price level might be necessary for there to be a meaningful reduction in liquidity yields: very low carrying costs and the very generality of the uses of money, for example, might cause l_n to bottom-out at a fairly high level. Finally the fact that excess supply in labor and commodities markets leads to gradually falling wages and prices, instead of to drastic once-and-for-all declines, can encourage speculative holding of money-fixed claims: a terms for real commodities might be negative. Thus, it is possible that large cumulative

[35] Or, alternatively, a price high enough for the marginal yield, expressed in dollars, to bear a low-enough ratio to that price. Be careful to understand that higher land prices do not *per se* increase the cost of storing value through holding land: the quantum of liquidity associated with a unit of land increases *pari passu* with the price of land. The same applies to money or any other store of value. The Appendix to Ch. II shows that the relative price of real cash balances is definitionally equal to unity. Of course, higher land prices reduce q for land.

The Lerner-Kaldor argument pertains more to a statical than to a dynamical framework. One should distinguish between the possibility of land being a barrier to ultimate achievement of a positive natural interest rate and the possibility of its liquidity paralysing or severely hampering adjustment processes requiring rapid decline in interest rates. Thus deficient aggregate demand can ensue from a collapse of expectations rather than from fundamental structural maladjustment. Of course, if the price of land is highly flexible, land is much less likely to be a drag on the system.

decreases in the general price level will be necessary to reduce liquidity yields, but that sticky money costs and prices will make the rate of decline small. This can generate perverse speculative forces reducing the likelihood of lower long-term interest rates. On the other hand, if the more important liquid asset were land, Lerner argues that excess demand for liquidity would lead to rapidly-increasing land prices. The aggregate real value of land soon would satisfy demands for liquidity, eliminating excess supply in the "real" markets.[36]

Why are sticky money prices essential for money to perform its functions? "The central proposition that emerges from Keynes's Ch. 17 is that stickiness of wages, and therefore also of costs and of prices, is an essential property of money." (A. P. Lerner, *op. cit.*, p. 378.) Why? If money wages could be "unstuck" so that excess supply in the labor market would lead to rapid and large price declines, any conceivable demand for liquidity could be satisfied at an arbitrarily low (positive) rate of interest. Lerner responds that highly-flexible money wages and prices would cause the baby to be thrown out with the bath water. If there were all-out price flexibility, money could not serve its primary functions:

> "If . . . we assume a thoroughgoing wage and price flexibility so that there could be a rapid movement to the position where adequate liquidity has been produced by the wage and price declines, we find ourselves in a strange world in which we can no longer make use of money for its normal purposes." (*Ibid.*, p. 382.)

Why? Hyperdeflation would damage the functioning of money as a

---

If the stock of money is fixed, and if nominal wages and commodity prices are sticky while land prices are flexible, increased land preference, unaccompanied by increased money preference, results in higher land prices but either in lower or unchanged interest rates. Land and money here would be substitutional; marginal yields of initial stocks of real cash balances would be lower at initial wages, commodity prices, interest rates, and employment. (*Cf.* Kaldor, *op. cit.*, pp. 73-74; Patinkin, *Money, Interest and Prices,* pp. 168, 342-351.)

36 Of course, if land prices were highly flexible in both directions, it would be unlikely to qualify as a liquid asset unless there were a strong upward secular trend in land prices. Indeed, if there were no asset with stable purchasing power, the importance of secure nominal value would seem much less. If money were unique in immunity to drastic declines in value over short periods, it could serve uniquely as a liquid asset. This property would permit it to be an obstacle to lower interest rates.

standard of deferred payment just as would hyperinflation.[37] And thoroughgoing price flexibility makes the holding of monetary assets a highly-speculative venture even in the short run, a means of conducting a speculative operation rather than holding buffer stocks against transactions requirements and sacrificing yield for security. "Assured nominal value" would be a chimerical property. Even sundry constant-purchasing-power clauses will not much help: "some prices will . . . fall much more than others and some incomes will fall much more than others . . . Everything will be in disorder and nothing predictable . . . [The monetary unit] will have been rendered quite unfit to do its main job." (*Ibid.*, p. 384.) I cannot improve on Lerner's peroration:

> "This is the essential lesson of the chapter. The usefulness of money depends intimately on a certain degree of stability in its purchasing power. This stability in turn encourages the making of contracts and the development of other institutions that help to establish a rigidity of the general price level. The rigidity in turn gives further stability to the purchasing power of money so that its positions in the economy reinforces itself in the mould of custom.
>
> One effect of the rigidity is that the automatic adjustment to a change in the demand for liquidity is not socially satisfactory . . . [Changes requiring] a larger supply of liquidity to maintain a satisfactory level of employment [are not automatically accommodated] . . . [P]rice rigidity is not an appendage that can be removed without harm. Wage and price rigidity is an essential property of money and the most successful of operations to remove it would mean the death of the patient so transformed. Any money which was completely cured of wage and price rigidity would not be able to survive as money." (*Ibid.*, pp. 384-385.)

3

The Hicksian call has been answered. The theory of demand for

[37] Employment effects of inflation and deflation are not symmetrical: one wipes out widows and orphans; the other, entrepreneurs. As severe deflation proceeds, entrepreneurs, hoisted by their own leverage, offer their equities at a song but inevitably are packed off to debtors' gaol. Plunging equity values terrify potential securities purchasers and make prohibitive the cost of equity finance. Investors with revealed preference for leverage must turn over their interests to creditors' representatives; management of the financial ruins is turned over to insipid receivers (points made to me by Mr. Axel Leijonhufvud). Corporate bankruptcy proceedings are prolonged and paralyzing. Finally, debtors are forced to divert receipts into clogged creditor sinks. Inevitably there is a collapse of investment in plant and equipment; the outcome is decided even if final-product markets initially are buoyant. The presence of money-fixed claims in the system leads to crucial asymmetry.

money has been integrated into a theory of portfolio management. The transition from the theory of money to the theory of income, employment, prices, interest rates, *and* money has been made. One dividend already is at hand: we see that monetary properties can be important in explaining persistence of "high" long rate during slack times. (But *cf.* footnote 33.) The full-scale assault on the theory of income is about to be mounted. (*See Note K.*)

SUMMARY

1. The theory of demand for money must be part of a theory of portfolio determination.
2. Money is a thing(s). The demand for it is to be explained by choice theory. But the standard model of consumer choice is a pure-flow model.
3. A general stock-flow model was presented. The first-order conditions were reworked to deal with yields measured on a common yardstick.
4. Material from Part I, together with some new material, was collected to describe sundry motives for holding cash. Of course, empirically all there is to be seen is *cash* (indeed demand deposits, incorporeal herididaments, cannot be seen).
5. Transactions motives for holding cash have non-stochastic sources — based on poor synchronization of payments and receipts — and stochastic sources — based on uncertainties of payments and receipts. Again, following Baumol and Tobin, balances and *cash* balances were distinguished. Transactions costs, interest rates, etc., influence the choice.
6. The speculative motive for holding cash relates to bear views on one or more assets. (Long-term securities often are mentioned.) Should sales proceeds be held in *cash*? The answer depends on transactions costs, interest rates, when the "nadir" is expected, etc.
7. Following Tobin, Note J seeks broader grounds for an inverse relationship between planned holdings of "idle" cash balances and interest rates, assuming unit-elastic expectations.
8. The own-rates analysis of Ch. 17 of the *General Theory* was explained. What if l_n, encompassing the spectrum of liquidity yield,

including satisfaction of transaction motives, were sticky at a "high" level? Interest rates would be correspondingly sticky at "high" levels: in equilibrium marginal yields must be equal for all assets.

9. Various other assets feature liquidity yields. Thus, Treasury bill rate lower than ½ per cent is consistent with quite-substantial *total* yield. Of course, Treasury bills' liquidity is affected by policies of monetary authorities who can, for example, cause bill rate to fluctuate widely from day to day. (*But see Note J.*)

10. Non-monetary, non-reproducible assets held as liquid assets are not likely to be persistent encumbrances to full employment and growth: excess demand for these assets quickly can lead to substantial price increases until their real values have increased enough to satisfy demand.

11. On the other hand, our society is characterized by sticky money wages, at least on the down side. Excess demand for liquidity is unlikely to be corrected by spontaneous generation of additional real cash balances through price deflation of goods. Furthermore, secular deflation can set-up destabilizing expectations. Finally, the functioning of money as a liquid asset and a standard of deferred payments would be seriously impaired by thoroughgoing wage-price flexibility.

12. Paragraphs 8-11 indicate that interaction of sticky prices with high liquidity preference can sustain "high" long rate despite persistent unemployment. But, needless to say, the officials could saturate the banking system with liquidity so that short-dated claims could be exchanged for money on a miniscule yield basis.

13. Despite easy money, there can be at least two barriers to lower long rate: (a) stability of "precautionary" liquidity yield over a *wide* range of money-fixed holdings; (b) rigid views of "normal" short rates. And of course, gloomy prognoses of the profitability of investment in physical capital could prevent "very low" long rates from stimulating expenditure.

14. The transition from the pure theory of money to the theory of income and employment is complete.

NOTES

NOTE A: The negative slopes of the curves reflect the assumption (implicit in the text) that both goods provide utility. Convexity follows from the assumption of diminishing rate of substitution. Non-intersection also follows from the axioms. Examine this simple diagram.

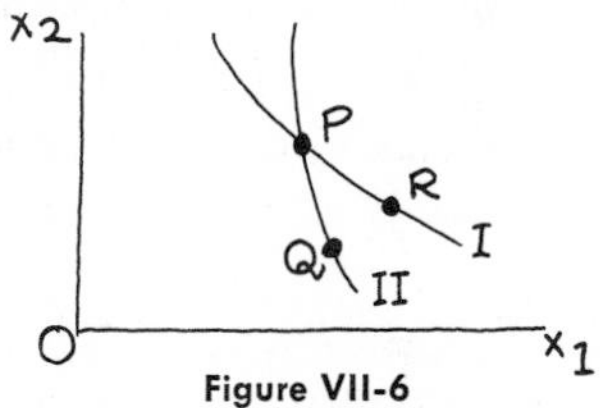

Figure VII-6

Points P and Q are indifferent for the consumer: both are on Indifference Curve II. The consumer also is indifferent between P and R: both are on I. The transitivity axiom states that, since $Q = P$ and $R = P$, $Q = R$. However, the nonsatiety axiom requires that R be preferred to Q: rates of consumption x_1 and x_2 both are greater at R than at Q. *Q. E. D.*, intersecting indifference curves are inconsistent with the model's axiomatic underpinning.

NOTE B: There follows an algebraic statement of the argument of Section B. It obviously is more general. It also is highly compressed, and is not intended to deal with its topics *de novo*.

The problem is to maximize the utility function

$$U \equiv U(x_1, x_2, \ldots, x_n) \tag{1}$$

subject to the constraint

$$\Sigma p_i x_i = Y^\circ. \tag{2}$$

Equation 2 is the budget equation.

A standard method for solution of this basic problem in constrained maximization is that of Lagrange multipliers. Form the Lagrangian function

$$U(\quad) + \lambda(\Sigma p_i x_i - Y^\circ) \equiv F(\quad) \tag{3}$$

where λ is an arbitrary constant to be determined in the solution. The next step is to maximize the Lagrangian function. The first order conditions require that its partials with respect to the x's and λ be set equal to zero. The p's are parametric in individual experiments. Equations 4 result:

$$\partial U/\partial x_i + \lambda p_i = 0 \qquad (i = 1, 2, \ldots, n) \tag{4}$$

Also Equation 5

$$\Sigma p_i x_i - Y^\circ = 0. \tag{5}$$

Equations 4 and 5 comprise $n+1$ equations in the unknowns $x_1, \ldots, x_n$ and λ. Equation 5's satisfaction assures satisfaction of the budget constraint.

As between any two goods,

$$U_r/U_s = p_r/p_s, \tag{6}$$

where $U_r \equiv \partial U/\partial x_r$. The marginal utilities are proportional to the prices.

Moreover, U_r/U_s can be interpreted as the marginal rate of substitution between X_r and X_s . . . We have, thus, examined the properties of a solution which takes as given the consumer's tastes and preferences and the prices facing him.

Now for comparative statistics. You might want to consult such sources as the Mathematical Appendix to *Value and Capital;* Bushaw and Clower; R. G. D. Allen, *Mathematical Analysis for Economists* (London: Macmillan and Co., Ltd., 1938) and *Mathematical Economics* (London: Macmillan and Co., Ltd., 1956); James M. Henderson and Richard E. Quandt, *Microeconomic Theory* (New York: McGraw-Hill Book Co., 1958). Substitution and income effects are calculated by differentiating equilibrium conditions 4 and 5. We are concerned with equilibrium values for the x's. First express the effects of an increase in nominal income, *cet. par.*:

$$
\begin{aligned}
& p_1(\partial x_1/\partial Y) + U_{12}(\partial x_2/\partial Y) + \cdots + p_1(\partial\lambda/\partial Y) = 0 \\
(7)\quad & \cdot \quad \cdot \quad \cdot \quad \cdot \quad \cdot \quad \cdot \quad \cdot \quad \cdot \quad \cdot \\
& p_1(\partial x_1/\partial Y) + \cdots\cdots + p_n(\partial x_n/\partial Y) \qquad = 1
\end{aligned}
$$

The upper left-hand corner term gives the rate of change of U_1 as x_1 changes with Y; the first of Equations 7 requires that the first of the equilibrium conditions of Equations 4 continue to be observed.

We can follow Bushaw and Clower (p. 125) in stating in determinantial notation the solution of the preceding system of equations:

$$\partial\bar{x}_i/\partial Y \, \frac{\Delta_{n+1,\ i}}{\Delta}.$$

$\bar{x}_i$ indicates that we are dealing with an equilibrium value for x_i. Δ is the bordered determinant

$$
\begin{vmatrix}
U_{11} & U_{12} \cdots & U_{1n} & p_1 \\
\cdot & \cdot & \cdot & \cdot \\
U_{n1} & U_{n2} \cdots & U_{nn} & p_n \\
p_1 & p_2 \cdots & p_n & 0
\end{vmatrix}
$$

$\Delta_{n+1,i}$ is the determinant obtained by substituting the right-hand column of (7) for the *ith* column in Δ.

Now proceed to obtain expressions for the effects of a change in the *jth* price (with nominal income constant), maintaining equilibrium conditions 4 and 5

$$
\begin{aligned}
& U_{11}(\partial x_1/\partial p_j) + \cdots + U_{1n}(\partial x_n/\partial p_j) + p_1(\partial\lambda/\partial p_j) = 0 \\
& \cdot \quad \cdot \quad \cdot \quad \cdot \quad \cdot \quad \cdot \quad \cdot \quad \cdot \quad \cdot \quad \cdot \\
(8)\quad & U_{n1}(\partial x_n/\partial p_j) + \cdots + U_{nn}(\partial x/\partial p_j) + p_n(\partial\lambda/\partial p_j) = 0 \\
& p_1(\partial x)/\partial p_j) + \cdots p_n(\partial x_n/\partial p_j) = -x_j
\end{aligned}
$$

System (8) can be solved with determinants:

$$(9)\qquad \frac{\partial x_i}{\partial p_j} = -x_j \frac{\partial x_i}{\partial Y} - \lambda \frac{\Delta_{ji}}{\Delta}.$$

Δ_{ji} is the cofactor of the *ijth* element of Δ. Always recall that the initial set of x's is a solution set (so that the U_{ij} terms are fixed values) and that the equilibrium conditions are imbedded in the problem so that the rates of change are consistent with maintenance of equilibrium and are in fact the *only* rates of change that are consistent with equilibrium.

Consider a change in nominal income just compensating a change in price in the sense that the consumer could continue barely to purchase his original budget (a compensation accurate only in the limit). Such a change in response to an increase in p_j, *cet. par.*, would have to be equal to initial purchases of X_j, x_j, times the change in the price of X_j: ·ᶠdpᶠx Thus, $dY = x_j dp_j$ *or* $dY/dp_j = x_j$; income must increase by $x_j dp_j$ if the consumer is to be compensated.

Now multiply both sides of Equation 9 by dp_j and proceed to compensate the consumer so that $dY = x_j dp_j$. The price effect, dx_i, now is equal to

$$-x_j(\partial x_i/\partial Y)dp_j - \lambda(\Delta_{ij}/\Delta)dp_j + x_j(\partial x_i/\partial Y)dp_j = \lambda(\Delta_{ji}/\Delta dp_j.$$

This is the pure substitution effect. Or perhaps you will wish to express it as

$$dx_i/dp_j \text{ (real-income and other prices constant)} = -\lambda(\Delta_{ji}/\Delta).$$

The second-order conditions do not impose any limitation on the sign of the $\partial x/\partial Y$ terms, but do require that $-\lambda(\Delta_{ii}/\Delta) < 0$: the pure substitution effect of an increase in own-price must be negative. The second order conditions require that not *all the* $-\lambda(\Delta_{ji}/\Delta)$ terms for $j \neq i$ be negative: there must be *some* substitution in the system. This follows from the requirement that pure-substitution effects of own-price changes cannot be positive.

NOTE C: Thus, the problem also can be viewed as one of selection of the vectors x and x', a selection accomplished by maximizing the criterion function (1) subject to (4).

It can be useful to think of maximization of utility subject to constraints imposed by initial holdings (and their income yields) together with what *can* be regarded as physical k-constraints. [If these "constraints" are assumed to be psychical *vis a vis* physical — and Bushaw and Clower do not require that they be physical — should not the *psychics* be in the utility function?] Recalling that there are $2n$ variables, $x_1, \ldots, x_n$ being flow rates of consumption — and $2n$ k's, the first n of which are unity (the x variables are indexed from 1 to n), we can follow Bushaw and Clower in listing the first-order conditions as

$$\text{(i)} \qquad U_i + \lambda k_i p_i = 0 \qquad (i = 1, 2, \ldots, 2n)$$

$$\text{(ii)} \qquad \sum^{n} p_i(x_i + k_{i+n}\,[D_i - S_i]) - M = 0,$$

where $p_i = pi{+}n$ for all i. A good's price is independent of the purpose for which it is being bought. Note that x_1 is the consumption rate for the first commodity and that D_1, the $(n+1)$st variable, is "potential" stock demand for the first commodity. The indexing is continuous: the D's are indexed from $1+n$ to $2n$.

If k_{1+n} and k_{2+n} are equated, the first-order conditions take on the familiar form

$$\frac{U_{1+n}}{U_{2+n}} = \frac{p_1}{p_2}.$$

If the only source of utility for certain stocks were their income yields — so that no utility could be gained by using up these stocks for consumption purposes (imagine one chewing his bond certificates) and the equivalent x's would be zero — the first-order conditions call for equation of yields at the margin: income could not be increased by switching a penny's worth of one asset into a penny's worth of another. Unfortunately, uncertainty is very hard to introduce, even heuristically, into this formulation.

NOTE D: This is a sketchy mathematical derivation of the comparative-statics results. The basic determinant, Δ, is

$$\begin{matrix} U_{11} & U_{12} & \cdots & U_{1n} & U_{1,n+1} & \cdots & U_{1,2n} & p_1 \\ \cdot & \cdot & \cdot & \cdot & \cdot & \cdot & \cdot & \cdot \\ U_{n+1,1} & & \cdot & & \cdot & & U_{n+1,2n} & k_1 p_1 \\ \cdot & \cdot & \cdot & \cdot & \cdot & \cdot & \cdot & \cdot \\ U_{2n,1} & & \cdot & & \cdot & & U_{2n,2n} & k_n p_n \\ p_1 & \cdot & \cdot & \cdot & k_1 p_1 & & k_n p_n & 0 \end{matrix}$$

$U_{i\ n+1}, \ldots, U_{i,2n}$ give the cross partials for consumption and asset holdings. The index from $n+1$ to $2n$ is for commodities held in stock. Recall that the k's for consumption decisions are taken as unity. Of course, the elements of Δ are derived from differentiation of first-order conditions 1 and ii (*cf.* Note C).

Δ_{ij} has the same connotations as in Note B: it is a cofactor. We now define a new term:

$$K_{ji} = \frac{-\lambda \, \Delta ji}{\Delta} .$$

We dismiss income effects, noting their ambiguity, and state the substitution effects for the stock flow model. It is implicit that we are dealing with "temporary equilibria" in which stocks can be changing.

(*iii*) $\partial D_i / \partial p_j \,_{[\text{real income constant}]} = K_{ij} + k_j K_{i,n+j}$

(*iv*) $\partial x_i / \partial p_j \,_{[\text{real income constant}]} = K_{n+i,j} + k_j K_{n+i,n+j}$

(*v*) $\partial x'_i / \partial p_j = k_i \, (\partial D_i / \partial p_j)$

We cannot further consider the *rationale* for conclusion 4, Section C, but Bushaw and Clower develop the argument at p. 133 *ff.*

NOTE E: The text works on the assumption that the decision unit makes choices over time so that "while each step, being determined by a conscious act of choice satisfies certain maximizing conditions, this sequence as a whole does not." (Wassily Leontief, "Time Preference and Economic Growth: Reply [to F. M. Westfield]," *American Economic Review,* Vol. 49 [No. 5], December 1959, pp. 1041-1043, at p. 1041.) It was pointed out by F. M. Westfield, *loc. cit.,* pp. 1037-1041, that plans formulated so that the solution values are determined over the entire time span "in one piece by a grand act of one single choice" [Leontief, *loc. cit.,* p. 1042] can lead to different sequences than those generated by a series of "instantaneous horizon" choices.

The cruder model suffices for our purposes. These are a few references on n-period horizon problems: (a) Frank Ramsey, "A Mathematical Theory of Saving," *Economic Journal,* 1928, discussed in R. G. D. Allen, *Mathematical Analysis for Economists,* p. 537 *ff.*; (b) R. H. Strotz, "Myopia and Inconsistency in Dynamic Utility Maximization," *Review of Economic Studies,* Vol. XXIII (No. 3), 1955-6, pp. 165-180; (c) R. Dorfman, P. A. Samuelson, R. M. Solow, *Linear Programming and Economic Analysis,* Chapters 11 and 12; (d) "Prices and the Turnpike," a symposium featuring J. R. Hicks, M. Morishima, and R.

Radner, *Review of Economic Studies,* Vol. XXVIII (No. 2), Feb. 1961, pp. 77-104; (e) P. A. Samuelson, "An Exact Consumption Loan Model of Interest with or without the Social Contrivance of Money," *Journal of Political Economy,* Vol. 66 (No. 6), Dec. 1958, pp. 467-482; (f) F. M. Westfield, *loc. cit., supra.*

NOTE F: $\sum_j D_{rj}(t) = \sum_j S_{rj}(t)$, where $S_r(t) = S°_{rj}$ is neither necessary nor sufficient for $\Sigma x'_{rj}(t) = 0$ unless the $k_{rj}(t)$ terms are the same for all j. In that case $D_r(t) = S_r(t)$ is necessary and sufficient: since $\sum_j [z_{rj}(t)] \equiv 0$, undesired increments to cash holdings surely will offset undesired decrements if $\Sigma D_{rj}(t) = \Sigma S_{rj}(t)$.

Throughout the text, we take $k_{ri}(t) = k_{r2}(t) = \ldots = k_{rm}(t)$ where $j = 1, 2, \ldots m$. Thus $D_r(t) = S_r(t)$ assures that investment demands for cash are compatible.

If $n—2$ of the other $n—1$ markets of the systems are cleared, *ex ante,* and $D_r(t) = S_r(t)$ — making our special assumption about the k's — clearance of the $(n—1)th$ market is assured: there remains no source of imbalance in this market. On the other hand, if plans in one of the other markets are known to be inconsistent, so must be plans in at least one more market.

Continuing to take $D_r(t) = S°_r$, assume that there is excess supply in a commodity market and excess demand in a bond market, the remaining $(n—3)$ markets being cleared. Blithely departing from *tatonnement* dynamics and assuming that inventories pile up in the commodity market, we see that — if all producers miraculously decide to maintain their cash-balance plans in the face of failure of various of their other plans — they will supply bonds, satisfying the *ex ante* excess demand in the bond market ("coincidentally" issuing the "right" bonds), thereby permitting *all* cash balance plans to be fulfilled — making unplanned new issues to finance unplanned inventory investment.

It cannot be enough stressed that Walras' Law (Principle) refers to *ex ante* flow rates. Any time it is alleged that satisfaction of an equation of the form $D_i = S°_i$ confers market clearance, at least these things must be assumed:

(1) $k_{i1}(t) = \ldots = k_{im}(t) \qquad j = 1, 2, \ldots, m$

(2) $dS_i/dt = 0$

Consider an analysis using discontinuous time and in which $D_i(t)$ and $S_i(t)$ refer to stocks planned for the end of the period. Choose the length of the period so that a number giving initial stock disequilibrium minus a number giving the flow rate of planned net output equals the number giving disparity of flow rates of demand and supply. Of course, the dimension of the latter numbers differs from that of the first.

Patinkin conducts such an analysis in MIP and elsewhere. Most of the models of this book are most easily interpreted in terms of it.

NOTE G: Since money is a medium of exchange, all market transactions have a monetary counterpart. It follows that an ongoing state of excess demand in the *ith* market finds money tenders exceeding in value offers of X_i. It should *not* be deduced from this that there is excess supply of money.

Milk, the *sth* good, is analogous to money. D_{sj} is a stock of milk, z_{sj} a rate of purchase of milk and x_{sj} a rate of consumption. It is absurd to say that a man drinking milk is *definitionally* out of equilibrium. He can be in *stock-flow equilibrium.* In the same way a man spending money can be satisfied with his money stock: $x'_{rj}(t) = z_{rj}(t) — x_{rj}(t)$ might hold.

In a similar vein, the fact that the value of money being offered for goods exceeds the value of the goods being offered is perfectly consistent with *ex ante* clearance of the money market; it could imply *ex ante* excess supply of bonds. This is not to deny that *ex ante* clearance of the money market, when associated with *ex ante* disequilibrium in other markets, usually leads to *ex post* disequilibrium in the money market. (Note that we implicitly deal with non-auction markets.)

An alternative formulation is

$$x'_{rj}(t)_{ex\ ante} \equiv z_{rj}(t)_{ex\ ante} - x_{rj}(t)_{ex\ ante}.$$

This formulation makes clear the association between purchase, consumption, and stock for a stock-flow good. When your intuition becomes unstuck (as sometimes does mine) return to the Milk Case. Of course, my consumption of milk does not *automatically* provide milk for another, while my use of money *does* automatically provide money for another.

NOTE H: The model easily interprets changes in velocity: the z_{rj} and x_{rj} elements increase with ΣS_{rj} constant (for example). Chapter VI shows that, for specified parameters, increases in planned transactions rates are associated with increases in planned cash holdings. Thus, if correspondence is imperfect, increased transactions rates require that the representative $S_{rj}(t)$ increase: if the transactions matrix is scaled by $\lambda(>1)$, pools of cash must increase unless some structural improvement is made or higher interest rates induce firms and households to dispatch favorable cash balances to the bond market. Improved synchronization can be expressed this way: representative planned receipts and disbursements of cash,

$$x_{rj}(t) \equiv f^1_{rj}(t); \qquad z_{rj}(t) \equiv f^2_{rj}(t),$$

change so that the elements of the time path for monetary stocks are excessive at original prices and real transactions flows. (Bond transactions are included among cash receipts and disbursements.)

There is another way to express a change in velocity. The vector of parameters, η, describing the time profile of monetary stocks maps into the set of parameters, β. A shift in β changes the *ex-ante* time path for S_{rj} for given prices, outputs, etc.

The diagram below shows how an oversimplified representative firm's $S_{rj}(t)$ profile changes when it pays factors, say, daily, instead of weekly. We assume that transactions balances are held in cash.

CHANGE IN PAYMENTS PERIOD:

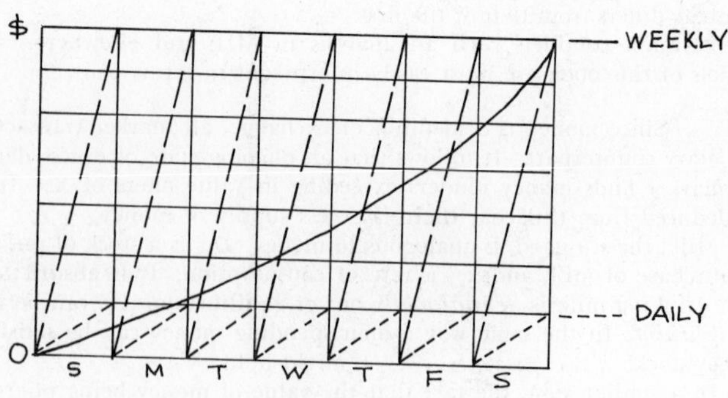

Figure VII-7

Cash is to be run down to zero at the end of each day (when payments are made to factors). *But,* if the receipt pattern of the representative firm is unchanged, firms will have excess cash balances most of the week unless they are able to dispose of these in the bond market. (It is assumed that households always have purchased in an even stream throughout the week. Say that the reform goes into effect after the end of Saturday's business and before Sunday's.) There will be excess demand for securities, interest rate will fall below natural rate, there will be excess demand for goods, prices will rise, etc. Finally, prices and wages will be so high that the entire stock of cash must — in our simple world — be paid out at the end of each day.

The model's plasticity (emptiness) seems boundless. It nicely interprets a situation in which planned saving equals planned investment but in which there is excess supply of securities (excess demand for money). Firms will be unable to produce at planned rates without letting their cash run down. Of course, usually firms collectively pay out more in factor incomes than factors buy back from them through purchases of goods. The excess of planned output over planned purchases by factors of production is balanced by investment-expenditure plans of firms. This is what is meant by planned saving being equal to planned investment. However, firms must float securities to households if they (firms) are not to run down their cash. (Retained earnings are treated in the same way as dividends in this model.) Firms must sell securities as well as goods to households in order to maintain their cash. ("Firms" are to be interpreted as disembodied entrepreneurs who are the sole owners of physical capital. They also issue securities, hold cash, contract for factors, and sell output.)

A dynamical interpretation is suggested: firms (acting independently) unable to place securities (in an ongoing situation) will cut back investment expenditures in order to protect their cash. Excess supply in the goods markets results from initial excess supply of bonds, despite the fact that *ex ante* saving and investment are equal.

NOTE I: The model of Note C is best interpreted on the assumption that none of the goods has an income yield. Here is how bonds would be treated if that model were to be adjusted. The text *infra* will assume that these adjustments have been made.

a) The marginal contribution to the utility index of the *ith* stock-flow good could not be calculated unless heed were paid to the marginal utility of income, λ, so that we would write $U_i + \lambda(\partial M/\partial D_i)$ instead of U_i. Denote $\partial M/\partial D_i$ as v_i.

b) ignore the k's — already set equal to 1 for $k_1, \ldots k_n$ — taking these as unity or, at least, as having the same value. This step is not necessary for our adjustment but greatly simplifies its exposition.

c) continue to maintain the assumptions about independence of consumption and stock-holding plans described in footnote 14. The first *n* first-order conditions are unaltered.

d) the "equilibrium" conditions for the stocks, conditions $n+1, \ldots, 2n$, will have to reflect the budget equation

$$\Sigma p_i(x_i + x'_i) - M - v_i S_i = 0,$$

where $v_i = 0$ for $i = 1, 2, \ldots, n$. M flows from exogenous causes and is not related to the portfolio. The first-order conditions take the form (for all stocks)

$$\frac{U_r + \lambda v_r}{U_s + \lambda v_s} = p_r/p_s \qquad r, s > n$$

Here we take account of income yield. If $U_r = U_s = 0$, the condition merely requires that the same income yield be obtained by a penny's worth of investment in any direction. (The yields take account of depreciation.)

Don Patinkin, *op. cit.*, discusses bonds as liquid assets in Ch. VI, Section 4 and pp. 324-326 of the mathematical appendix.

Inclusion of assets in criterion functions is controversial. Thus, under certainty, only the aggregate value of terminal stocks need appear in a micro criterion function. Nor would it be strictly necessary to insert financial assets under uncertainty: the criteria could concern parameters of time profiles of E's and σ's; financial assets can be viewed as means of transforming one such time profile into another, and appear (implicitly) only in the constraints.

Admittedly a jejune utility theorist, I am more comfortable with financial assets in criterion functions . . . I have much profited from conversations with Franco Modigliani on these matters but emphatically exonerate him from responsibility for these remarks.

NOTE J: Professor Tobin shows how to obtain an inverse relationship between interest rates and "investment balances" independently of interest-rate *expectations.* ["Liquidity Preference as Behavior towards Risk," *Review of Economic Studies,* No. 67, February, 1958, pp. 65-86, reprinted as *Cowles Foundation Paper No. 118* (New Haven, Conn.: 1958).] Investment balances are ". . . balances of an economic unit . . . that will survive all the expected seasonal excesses of cumulative expenditures over cumulative receipts during the year ahead." Investment balances are over and above transactions "requirements" flowing from stochastic and non-stochastic considerations.

He points out that the Keynesian speculative motive (narrowly interpreted) derives from sticky expectations about future interest rates. Damaging criticisms were delivered by Leontief and Fellner *et al.* who pointed out that *in equilibrium* there would be no speculative motive. Also there seemed no reason to confine inelasticity of expectations to interest rates. As Tobin paraphrases Fellner, "why don't wealth owners and others regard predepression price levels as 'normal' levels to which prices will return? If they did, consumption and investment demand would respond to reductions in money wages and prices, no matter how strong and how elastic the liquidity preference of investors." (*Op. cit.*, p. 70.)

Tobin assumes that interest rates are expected to remain at present levels. This is his argument:

1) any asset portfolio can be described by expected return and risk, the latter being measured by the dispersion of possible returns around the mean value.

2) "The investor is assumed to have preferences between expected return . . . and risk . . . that can be represented by a field of indifference curves." (*Op. cit.*, p. 72.)

3) It is easy to show how increased interest rates *could* lead to lower planned cash balances, although this need not be the case. Consider a simple case in which the alternatives are cash and consols. Recall that the rate of interest is *expected* to remain at whatever level it is at but is known to be subject to a symmetrical disturbance term. Assume risk aversion (preference for certainty). Consult this diagram:

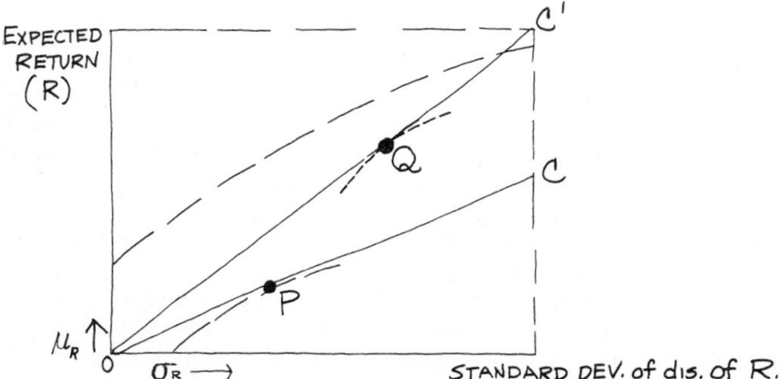

Figure VII-8

The (dashed) indifference loci show that the representative trader must expect to receive a greater return on his portfolio if he is to assume greater risk. The rays OC and OC' are opportunity loci, subject to the trader's initial wealth constraint (shown by the dotted perpendiculars to the axes — the trader cannot obtain more income than is permitted by his initial bond-buying capacity). As one moves out from the origin along a ray such as OC, he is switching from cash to consols. Increased interest rates shift the opportunity locus from OC to OC'. The solution point moves from P to Q. "This relationship is, of course, in the direction liquidity preference theory has taught us to expect, but it is not the only possible direction of relationship. It is quite possible to draw indifference curves so that the point of tangency moves left as the opportunity locus is rotated counterclockwise. The ambiguity is a familiar one in the theory of choice, and reflects the ubiquitous conflict between income and substitution effects." (*Ibid.*, p. 79.) Substitution effects of higher interest rates encourage risk bearing but make it possible to enjoy greater safety without sacrificing income. If "safety" is strongly superior, higher interest rates might lead traders to plan to hold more cash, actually reducing the number of promises to pay one dollar a year forever that they hold. The text concentrates on substitution effects.

W. T. Newlyn in Ch. VI of *Theory of Money* proposes an "encashment function," relating desired cash holdings at $t = 0$ to expected deficits over the next n periods. The model's usefulness pretty much is confined to cases in which an initial stock of cash might be invested in sundry securities maturing in phase with sundry disbursement obligations.

The following construction might be more helpful.

Define complex variables describing expected cash inflows and outflows "on current account," together with their dispersions, on the variable t. Thus

$$(E_t, \sigma_t)^1{}_j = f^1{}_j(t)$$

describes the time profile of expected receipts and their variability for the *jth* trader. Now inject financial assets, including money, into the model, defining time profiles of expected prices (and price dispersion) of these. Each time profile of financial assets holdings yields a different path of expected outcomes; the trader chooses the set of planned holdings of financial assets over time "recommended" by his criterion function. And, of course, we can take note of the M-co-ordinate of the optimal time path at $t = 0$. We doubtlessly will find that, if expected deficits on current account increase for $t = 30$ (years), traders will want to hold less cash at $t = 0$ than if these deficits were for 1 hour from now.

In general, money can serve as a buffer stock over the planning period guarding against shocks on current account, as a means of reducing transactions costs and illiquidity penalties (*cf. Note B, Ch. III*), as a buffer against calls or capital-account shocks. And, if short rates are not high enough to outweigh frictional expense, one would plan to hold money to meet net deficits (after bond redemptions) of short duration over *any* interval included in the plan.

Do *not* think that just because my cash deficit is to be $A between $t = \lambda$ and $t = \tau$, I will purchase $A of a security of maturity λ. Aside from interest-rate expectations, I must take account of the shape and "certainty" of receipt-expenditure patterns. Thus, if I *knew* that I would be balanced on current account until $t = \lambda - \eta$ and that I would be in surplus to a tune of $A from $\lambda - \eta$ to λ, I would have no incentive on "encashment" grounds to buy a λ-maturity security now.

NOTE K: We have not seriously analyzed *equities*. The formal neoclassical model excludes equities, and, indeed, eschews the concept of the *firm*. However, it contains markets for physical capital which in turn earns rent. In full equilibrium, included activities earn barely enough gross profit to pay rent on capital; excluded activities would be unable to "pay their rent."

Meaningful models dealing with accumulation posit firms, here legal entities (corporations). Equities confer residual rights on shareholders. Such a model stipulates that employment of physical assets occurs within firms, implying that physical assets could not profitably (considering rents) be deployed by households. Organization and other technologies demand *indirect* ownership of the means of production. As a result, producers' goods will be acquired through collective decisions. Analogously to "King in Parliament," such decisions will be made by "Management in the Board."

The revised model oversimplifies the financial-asset nexus. It already is implied that households manage purely financial portfolios, consumer durables having been put aside. Similarly, firms, as Management-Board decision units, largely are dealt with as deciding whether, if at all, to acquire physical assets with bonds or equities — retained earnings being imputed to equity account. In the simplest case, management, perhaps coerced by takeover-bid threats, tried to maximize net worth. Thus, lower interest rates can encourage demand for physical capital in at least two ways: effects of cheaper borrowing; effects of lower costs of equity finance to the extent that the common-share market is buoyed.

The text's money-bonds-physical assets trichotomy, while an heroic simplification, gets the right results: it generates higher or lower demand prices for physical assets under the same circumstances as does the more sophisticated model.

CHAPTER EIGHT

Monetary Standards and Involuntary Unemployment

WE BEGIN INVESTIGATION OF MODERN INCOME THEORY for which J. M. Keynes' *General Theory of Employment, Interest, and Money* comes near to being the Book of Genesis. The connection between the monetary standard (gold, paper, etc.) and involuntary unemployment, although intimate, seems to have received little attention since 1947–1948.[1]

Keynes was acutely aware of the link between monetary standards and persistent unemployment:

> ". . . Thus the characteristic that money cannot be readily produced by labor gives at once some *prima facie* presumption for the view that its own-rate of interest will be relatively reluctant to fall; whereas if money could be grown like a crop or manufactured like a motor-car, depressions would be avoided or mitigated because, if the price of other assets was tending to fall in terms of money, more labor would be diverted into the production of money; — as we see to be the case in gold-mining countries, though for the world as a whole the maximum diversion in this way is almost negligible."[2]

[1] *Cf.* Jacques Rueff, "The Fallacies of Lord Keynes's General Theory," *Quarterly Journal of Economics,* Vol. 61, No. 3, May 1947, pp. 343-367. Also Comment by James Tobin and Reply by Jacques Rueff, *ibid.,* Vol. 62, No. 5, November 1948, pp. 763-782.

Tobin's reasoning is correct, but he would seem to underplay the significance of the argument for the validity of Keynes's attacks on classical writers who were, of course, working with commodity-money standards.

[2] Keynes, *General Theory,* Ch. 17, pp. 230-231. Chapter 17 is crucially important.

The argument can be elucidated through a set of simple models in which common-brick, gold, and paper monetary standards are successively taken up. We discover that Keynesian income theory is developed from the paper-standard model, and that the classical writers worked in terms of metallic standards. Furthermore, it appears that the gulf between such classical writers as Nassau Senior and Keynes is narrower than Keynes was apt to own. (*Cf. General Theory,* p. 18.)

A. A BRICK STANDARD

1

The first model concerns an economy in which common brick is money. In fact this brick is so common that a standard brick can be produced by application of one hour's labor of a standard laborer to free raw materials. Storage costs and depreciation are nil. The economy is assumed to feature a composite shmoo-like commodity that can be consumed or put into capital-stock (invested) where it can contribute to the production of additional shmoos. Non-monetary financial assets are ignored. (*Cf.* footnote 3.)

Soon the model will be put formally, but the above assumptions, together with elementary economic reasoning, permit us to limn its salient features without further ado:

1) Using brick (money) as the standard of value, we see that the wage rate can never fall below one brick per hour, since a worker could turn to the production of bricks if the shmoo industry offered less. But there is nothing to prevent the wage rate from rising above one brick per hour; in that case money-producing activity ceases.

2) So long as there is investment demand for money balances, the money industry is activated, the stock of money is increasing.

3) Since the assumptions assure that the supply of money (bricks) is perfectly elastic within the relevant range, involuntary unemployment is impossible. If the shmoo industry does not absorb available laborers, they will turn to producing money; the money-producing activity can absorb an indefinitely large number of laborers at a wage rate (objective or shadow) of one brick per hour. This means that, if the money industry is in operation and if the labor market is perfectly competitive, the universal wage rate will be one brick per hour. The brick (money) industry can have no problem of selling output at going prices: the product itself is a perfectly general store of purchasing power. Of course, rising commodity prices would im-

ply excess supply of money, indicating in turn that forces promoting involuntary unemployment had been eliminated.

4) It would matter little if positive investment demand for money persisted over time, even if the total stock of money became indefinitely large. *Persistence of high convenience yields from money balances or weakness of any wealth effects of increasing money balances is immaterial.* Demand for money contributes to demand for labor in the same way as does demand for shmoos. If people want money instead of shmoos and if this lust proves insatiable, the money industry merely will continue to operate for the indefinite future.

2

The verbal argument suggests an algebraic model. Assume that the labor market is competitive. This is not a critical assumption; it merely facilitates neater formulation. Then assume that the system cannot sustain a wage rate above one brick per hour if the labor market is to be cleared: unless some labor is diverted to production of money, there will be excess supply of labor; full-employment planned saving exceeds planned investment if investment in money is excluded. Also assume that workers and employers lack money illusion: they react to the real wage rate and the real value of money balances; planned rates of demand for and supply of labor would be unaffected by proportional changes in commodity price levels and wage rates. (Brick, of course, is *numeraire* and is a commodity.)

Equations 1-3, governing the labor market, fit this bill:

$$N^s \equiv f(1/p) \tag{1}$$

$$N^d_c \equiv g(1/p) \tag{2}$$

$$N_M \equiv N^s - N^d_c. \tag{3}$$

N^s is the rate of supply of labor measured in standard labor hours and depends on the real wage rate, w/p, where p is the money (brick) price of shmoos, $w = 1$ by assumption. N^d_c, the rate of demand for labor by shmoo producers, depends on the real wage rate; this is the message of Equation 2. N_M, the equilibrium rate of utilization of labor in the money industry, is introduced in Equation 3. N_M takes up the slack developed by shortfall of shmoo-industry demand for labor and total supply of labor. Equations 1-3 must be simultaneously satisfied if the labor market is to clear. (The solution vector must be semi-positive definite; negative values are inadmissible.)

Turn to the demand and supply relationships in the money market, ignoring non-monetary uses of brick. Non-monetary services are rendered only by the benevolent shmoo.

$$(4)\qquad dM/dt \equiv h[N_M(t)] \qquad \text{where } h[\quad] \equiv N_M(t)$$

$$(5)\qquad M \equiv \int_{-\infty}^{t} h[N_M(\theta)d\theta]$$

$$(6)\qquad m^d \equiv k_1[\psi(Y, M, p, dM/dt, K_o) - M]$$

$$(7)\qquad m^d = dM/dt$$

Equation 4 states that the rate of increase of the money stock depends on the rate of employment in the money industry. The $N_M(t)$ notation indicates that reference is to time t. Since one hour of labor yields one brick, $N_M(t)$ can be substituted for $h[\quad]$, implicitly adopting a time dimension of one hour. Equation 5 states that the stock of money at $\theta = t$ is the cumulant of all money produced since before Economics' Adam and Eve. At each point in time, the rate of production of money is defined by $h[\quad]$. Equation 5 instructs us to sum all of these "productions," obtaining their cumulant. Equation 6 is nothing more than a standard equation for investment demand. $\psi(Y, M, p, dM/dt, K_o)$ gives desired holdings of money stocks as a function of real income and wealth. Thus nominally-valued wealth at a point in time can be calculated by taking the sum $M + pK_o$, recalling that K_o is the stock of stored shmoos and that all money is "outside money" in the sense that production of money does not lead to offsetting bookkeeping entries. From the community's point of view, money holdings are wealth in the same sense as are capitalized shmoos. Of course, wealth can be measured in shmoos by dividing $M + pK_o$ by p, *obtaining* $M/p + K_o$. Money income is given by $pY + dM/dt$, where Y is the rate of output of shmoos. Income, measured in shmoos, is

$$\frac{dM/dt}{p} + Y.$$

3

We have explored rather exhaustively the ways in which real income affects demand for money. Once desired money holdings, $\psi(\quad)$, are known, demand for newly-produced money, m^d, can be calculated by applying the positive scalar k_1 to $[\psi(\quad)]$. Assume $k_1 = 1$. Equation 7 requires that the flow demand for additional money balances be equal to the rate of output of money. If $\psi(\quad) = M$, investment demand would be nil; the money market could not be in equilibrium unless $dM/dt = 0$. If $\psi(\quad) < M$, there would, of course, be no production of money, and the shmoo value of the money stock would have to decline through price inflation. Finally, both M and $\psi(\ \ ) - M^d$ for convenience — could be growing over time; the money market might be in continuous balance (in the sense that production would be continuously equated with investment demand) with positive investment in money balances continuously occurring.

Turning to the shmoo market, we have Equations 8-11:

$$(8) \qquad Y \equiv \phi(N^d{}_c, K_o),$$

$$(9) \qquad Z \equiv C + \bar{I}$$

$$(10) \qquad C \equiv F(Y, dM/dt, M, p, K_o)$$

$$(11) \qquad Y = Z$$

Y, the rate of output of shmoos, is determined through the production function $\phi(N^d{}_c, K_o)$, where K_o is the stock of capital (shmoos used in the production of shmoos) and $N^d{}_c$ the number of hours of labor desired by shmoo producers. It is assumed that they can obtain all the labor they want at $w = 1$; it is known that there would be excess supply of labor at $w > 1$. Z, aggregate demand for shmoos, has two components: an exogenous investment component $(\bar{I})$; and a consumption component (C) determined through Equation 10. dM/dt is in (10) because the money industry generates income just as does the shmoo industry. Equation 11 is the clearance condition for the shmoo market.

The first model, then, is completed. There are 11 equations in the 10 unknowns: $N^s, N_c{}^d, N_M, p, dM/dt, M, m^d, Y, Z,$ and C. However, one of the clearance conditions is otiose; if, for example, the commodity and labor markets are cleared, the budget constraints imbedded in the model imply clearance in the money market. If various mathematical requirements are met, the equation system can be solved for a unique set of solution values. Of course, its most interesting property is the obvious assurance of full employment, assurance provided by the fundamental properties of a commodity money perfectly elastic in supply.[3]

[3] Introducing securities into the model, there might be excess supply in both the money and shmoo markets and excess demand in the securities market. There are at least two reasons why this should not affect the flavor of the model:

a) As securities prices rise, securities become less attractive compared to cash (bricks). Surely *some* liquidity premium will be demanded by securities holders. In other words, price changes seem capable of working off excess demand for securities, transferring this to cash.

b) even if I wished to exchange part of my present money (brick) balances for securities, I would continue to produce bricks so long as the marginal disutility of labor did not exceed the marginal utility of income (crudely speaking). The complication imposed by securities markets is not even transitorily important.

B. A GOLD STANDARD

1

In the second model, gold is the commodity money. The second differs from the first model in its assumption that money (gold) is produced at increasing marginal cost through the cooperation of labor and a predetermined quantity of specialized capital. This capital is assumed to be perfectly durable: no user cost is incurred in production. The new specifications about the way in which money is produced lead to terribly important changes in the model's properties. Specifically, it might be necessary for the money-wage rate to fall to very "low" levels if sufficient labor is to be diverted to the money industry to clear the labor market. (The price of currently-produced shmoos will adjust so as to content entrepreneurs with producing what proves to be the "equilibrium" output.) If money wages are rigid or sticky, there might be prolonged unemployment. Still, the assumption that money is a produced commodity assures existence of a stable full-employment solution.

2

We proceed to set out the "gold" model, once again justifying our ommission of securities markets by the argument of footnote 3 (showing that excess supply in the labor and/or commodities markets must, in any case, lead to increased employment in the money industry if wages and/or prices are flexible downward). Similarly, the investment relation is left uncomplicated: the essential results can be obtained with the simple-minded assumption that investment expenditure (expenditure on new shmoos not for consumption) is predetermined; $I = \bar{I}$. The price of gold is defined as unity.

$$N^s \equiv f(w/p) \tag{12}$$

$$N^d{}_c \equiv g(w/p) \tag{13}$$

$$N^d{}_M \equiv j(w, p) \tag{14}$$

$$N^s = N^d{}_c + N^d{}_M \tag{15}$$

$$Y \equiv \phi(N^d{}_c, K^o{}_1) \tag{16}$$

$$Z \equiv C + \bar{I} \tag{17}$$

$$C \equiv \psi(Y, dM/dt, p, M^s, K^o{}_1, K^o{}_2) \tag{18}$$

(19) $Y = Z$

(20) $dM/dt \equiv F(N^{d}_{M}, K^{o}_{2})$

(21) $M^{s} \equiv \int_{-\infty}^{t} H(\theta)d\theta$

(22) $m^{d} \equiv k_{1}[\psi(Y, dM/dt, p, K^{o}_{1}, K^{o}_{2}) - M^{s}]$

(23) $m^{d} = dM/dt$

(24) $dw/dt \equiv - k_{2}(N^{s} - N^{d}_{c} - N^{d}_{M})$

(25) $dp/dt \equiv k_{3}(Z - Y)$

Interpreting the 14 equations in 13 unknowns (N^{s}, N^{d}_{c}, N^{d}_{M}, w, p, Y, Z, C, dM/dt, M^{s}, m^{d}, dw/dt, and dp/dt), we first note that the system being solved is the statical system 12-23 in 11 unknowns (excluding dw/dt and dp/dt); Equations 24 and 25 serve only didactic purposes. Equations 12 and 13 are familiar from the brick model. Equation 14 is new. If you were a producer of gold (money), you would plan to produce at a greater rate if the purchasing power of gold should increase (if p were to fall) and/or if the cost of production of gold were to fall as a result of a decline in w. Equation 14 should reflect this. Equations 12-15, taken together, describe the labor market. Equation 15 is the labor-market clearance condition. Note that the newly-specified conditions of production of money lead to fulfillment of Equation 15 less "automatically" than was the case with Equation 3: wage-price stickiness might prevent w and p from assuming values as low as are necessary to absorb enough workers into the money industry — in accordance with Equations 14 and 20 — to clear the labor market.

Equations 16-19 are concerned with the commodity (shmoo) market and are precisely analogous to their counterparts, Equations 8-11. However, in the gold model, shmoos, once imbedded in capital stock, are not transferrable and cannot be consumed either. The price level, p, applies to currently-produced shmoos in whatever use they are put.

3

As it happens, prices of capital goods have not been introduced into the model, nor, of course, have been equations determining demands for capital goods as functions of these prices. The system could have been elaborated with the addition of equations of the form

$$K^{d}_{j} \equiv F^{j}(p_{j}, u^{j}) \qquad j = 1, 2$$

where K^{d}_{j} is the desired stock of the jth capital good, P_{j} its price, and

u^j a vector of other variables. Aggregate investment demand could be formulated

$$I^d_j(t) \equiv k_j\,(K^d_j\,(t+h) - K^s_j(t)) \qquad j = 1,2$$

It is assumed here and throughout the rest of the book — with a few carefully indicated exceptions — that aggregate production functions in the continuous case really are of the form

$$x(t) \equiv \psi[N(t), \int_{-\infty}^{t-h} Id\theta]$$

The rate of output at t depends on current labor input and the capital stock accumulated as of $t—h$. An interval of duration h must elapse before a newly-produced shmoo can "qualify" (be initiated as) a production good. This establishes a market distinction between newly-produced capital goods and capital goods already in stock.[4] Positive I^d_j implies, since user cost and depreciation are nil, that P_j exceeds p: newly-produced capital is unavailable for immediate use in production.

If these equations were introduced into the system, the $\bar{I}$ notation would be dropped. Also equations would be added requiring balance in the capital-goods markets:

$$K^d_j(t) = K^s_j(t), \qquad j = 1,2$$

adding a total of six equations, together with six unknowns: K_1, K_2, p_1, p_2, I_1, and I_2. In this way asset markets could be introduced into the model. It becomes clear that prices (and, roughly speaking, the strength of demand) in asset markets affect investment flows. Possibilities for adverse effects on investment demand of shifts in demand functions for assets become apparent.

4

However, these insights are not immediately required; treatment of the shmoo market is left in the rustic state depicted in Equations 16-19. Finally, simultaneous fulfillment of market-clearance conditions

[4] Rigorously, there is an indefinitely large number of capital-goods markets. The birthdays of all capital younger than t must be accounted for.

In the discrete case, it is assumed in §§ 3 that contracts are made at the beginning of each market day, and that transactions in assets existing at the beginning of the day are instantaneously fulfilled. On the other hand, new output is delivered at the end of the day. If asset contracts call for delivery at the end of the day, there no longer is any reason to distinguish between "old" and "new" capital.

In all cases it is assumed that unspecialized capital can instantaneously be transferred from one production application to another without cost.

15 and 19 assures harmony of plans of workers and entrepreneurs and of production plans of entrepreneurs and the demand for their output at going prices: the labor and commodity (shmoo) markets will both be cleared.

Equations 20-23 deal with the money (gold) market. Equation 20 gives the production function of the money industry. The planned labor input is N^{d}_{M}. The planned rate of output of money is determined by the planned rate of employment in the money industry, conditioned by the transformation possibilities shown in Equation 20. The remaining equations (21-23) can be disposed of quickly enough: Equation 21 describes the historical experience leading to the existing money supply; Equation 23 is a market-clearance condition; Equation 22 describes the demand for cash balances as a function of practically everything and describes the determination of the rate of demand for new cash. The model's logic is that of the brick model.

Nor is it hard to count equations and unknowns. One of the clearance conditions is otiose: there are no more than 13 independent equations to determine the 13 unknowns.

5

Equations 24 and 25, while not integrally part of the model, encourage casual dynamics. Thus, the system might solve out at wage-price levels substantially lower than those now prevailing: perhaps the money industry must absorb a great deal of labor and has sharply increasing marginal costs of production (measured in shmoos). For a sufficiently large initial discrepancy and sufficiently small k's, excess supply in the labor market might persist for a long time.

6

I wish to avoid doctrinal dispute. These seldom are rewarding. Still I cannot resist defending such classical writers as Ricardo and Senior — dealing with commodity-money systems and concerned (excessively perhaps) with full-equilibrium states — as income theorists.[5] Surely in their context wage-price flexibility would preclude "underemployment equilibrium." Excess demand for money in a commodity-money system portends no more danger for the buoyancy of the labor market than would excess demand for corn, woollens, etc. Such excess

[5] That gold was not produced in England is beside the point: *ultimately* falling prices in countries without a money industry and suffering unemployment would lead to favorable export balances for such countries — or so the theory would run.

demand might require a permanent shift of resources to the money industry in what would be for a classical writer a crazy case or, more plausibly, a temporary shift of resources to the money industry until the real value of the money stock increased enough to alleviate excess demand for money.[6] Indubitably, wage-price flexibility would assure full adjustment. *(See Note A.)*

C. A PAPER STANDARD

1. The Lange Model

The chapter concludes by taking up the effects of money being a good such as fiat paper, a good not produced with meaningful expenditure of labor and other inputs. We operate within the context of general equilibrium, following Oscar Lange, *Price Flexibility and Full Employment* (Bloomington, Indiana: Principia Press, 1944). After a crude précis of part of Lange's book, we can show that Keynes's results flow from certain characteristics of paper *vis a vis* commodity money, a point fully recognized by Keynes: "if money could be grown like a crop . . ."

Lange works with a huge set of equations of the form

$$x_i \equiv f^i(p_1, p_2, \ldots, p_n) = 0 \qquad i = 1, 2, \ldots, n, n+1$$

where the $(n+1)th$ good is paper money, p_{n+1} being unity. The x_i's are excess demands (differences between rates of market demand and supply). He interprets "the goods $1, 2, \ldots, m$ as commodities and stocks and the goods $m+1, m+2, \ldots, n$ as fixed-income-bearing securities." (Lange, *op. cit.*, p. 102.) The excess demand functions are assumed to have these attributes: (a) ". . . the excess-demand functions of commodities and stocks are homogeneous in zero degree in the prices of commodities and stocks, interest rates (or the prices of fixed-income-bearing securities) being constant" (*ibid.*, p. 102) — excess demand for these goods is assumed unaffected by proportionate changes in all prices, including those received by factors of production, classified among the commodities; this assumption ignores "real balance effects," effects on demand generated by changes in the value of the

[6] This implies that wage-price flexibility could do the trick for a paper-money system. *Cf. infra.*

money stock and can be justified by assuming that all money is non-interest-bearing debt; (b) "under these circumstances the demand and supply functions, and consequently, also the excess demand functions, of fixed-income-bearing securities are homogeneous of first degree in commodity prices (p. 102)," meaning that proportional changes in all commodity prices lead, *cet. par.,* to changes in the same proportion in excess demand for securities so that, if all prices are doubled, $10 in excess demand for securities becomes $20: "because if all commodity and stock prices increase *k*-fold the real earning power of the securities . . . decreases in inverse proportion and it takes *k* times as many securities to represent the same earning power as before." (*Ibid.,* p. 102.)

Lange then analyses the properties of a system in which the *n-m* securities prices are perfectly rigid so that the appropriate statical system becomes a set of *m* excess-demand equations in the *m* commodity prices. The *m* commodity functions are of zero-order homogeneity (that for money is first-degree homogeneous). This system can be solved for *m—1* relative of commodity prices: "the equilibrium value of one of the *m* prices . . . is arbitrary." This means that the equilibrium point about which the system is to perturbate lies on a ray defined by *m—1* commodity-price relatives.

The rank of stability of the homogeneous system is *m—1.* (*See Note B.*) Stability requires that at least one of the *m* "commodity" prices — perhaps the money-wage rate — be rigid.

2. Aspects of the Lange Model

We proceed to an heuristic proof of why a system such as that just developed would tend to experience indefinite deflation once excess supply developed in one or more markets *if* all non-securities prices were flexible. The proof is based on Oscar Lange, *op. cit.* (p. 10 *ff.*), J. R. Hicks, *Value and Capital* (pp. 254-255), and Jacob L. Mosak, *General Equilibrium Theory in International Trade* (Bloomington, Ind.: Principia Press, 1944), pp. 162-164. Chapter VIII concludes with four operations:

a) an heuristic proof

b) consideration of implications of flexible securities prices;

c) consideration of real-balance effects, albeit cursorily;

d) formal indication of how commodity monies force the system to take a different turn

a) An Heuristic Proof

Assume that all elasticities of expectation are unity so that changes in current prices do not affect expectations so as to generate intertemporal substitutions. Elastic expectations would reduce prospects for internally generated price declines to correct excess supply: traders would be all the more anxious to sell and reluctant to buy now. Conversely, inelastic expectations would contribute to stability: intertemporal substitutions might reduce excess supply in markets for current-dated commodities. The *m* commodity prices are to be flexible, the *n-m* securities prices rigid. Finally, blithely ignore distinctions between instability and neutral equilibrium: we characterize a system as being unstable or imperfectly stable if initial displacement leads to cumulatively-falling money prices.

Now the system must be started up. Assume, after Lange, that "one factor of production is in excess supply and that its price is flexible; the markets of all other factors and of all products are supposed to be in equilibrium." Corresponding excess demand is registered only in the money and/or securities markets. At the outset, the lower price for the factor, *e.g.* the *rth,* in excess supply could lead to its being substituted for other factors; the *rth* market might clear. If so, this must be at the "expense" of other markets: there would be excess supply in other commodity markets. Continuous clearance of the remaining *m—1* commodity markets requires maintenance of the initial set of price ratios. But then excess supply in the *rth* market will be unchanged. At least if we adhere to the peculiar Hicks-Lange adjustment path along which equilibrium continuously is maintained in the other *m—1* commodity markets, price flexibility leads to continuous decline in nominal prices with relative prices and initial excess supply in the *rth* market unchanged. Price flexibility simply cannot do the trick in this model: substitution effects are precluded by the "necessity" of keeping the other *m—1* commodity markets in balance; "income" effects are precluded by absence of real balance effects, the money stock being comprised of debt instruments.

Under these circumstances, additional price *in*flexibility would be welcome. It would bound the possibilities of cumulative deflation. Thus, take the *rth* market to be the labor market. If the money wage rate were rigid, it would be possible to live with excess supply in the labor market without experiencing cumulative deflation. Taking *m—1* commodity and factor prices as flexible and the *n-m* securities prices, together with p_r, the money-wage rate, as given, we can work with an equation system of the form

$$X_i = f^i(p_1, p_2, \ldots, p_{r-1}, p_{r+1}, \ldots, p_m; p_r, p_{m+1}, \ldots, p_n),$$
$$(i = 1, 2, \ldots, r-1, r+1, \ldots, m.)$$

The factor and commodities markets, other than the labor market, comprise a stable, generally "soluble" system *not* homogeneous in the $m-1$ commodity prices. The rigidity of the money-wage rate will prevent any excess supply of labor from finding expression. Finally, it is clear that similar results flow from taking a "commodity" price other than p_r, say, p_s as fixed and excluding the *sth* market from the equations, but including the labor market (the *rth*) in the truncated system.

b) What if securities prices were flexible?

The analytic results for commodities and factor markets would be considerably different if the assumption of rigid securities prices were abandoned. Consider a system with m "commodities," 2 securities, and paper money. (*See Note C.*) The rank of stability of this system could be no greater than, but could be as great as, $m+1$. Thus, if one of the two securities prices is held rigid, it is possible that flexible commodities prices, together with price flexibility in the other securities market, would be consistent with stability. Falling prices lead to excess supply of money — if the supply of money does not fall *pari passu* with the price level — which in turn leads to rising security prices, perhaps exerting expansionary effects on the real markets.[7] But we have seen that initial interest rates might be close to lower bounds dictated by institutional considerations or liquidity preference; it might be impossible for interest-rate fluctuation to play a meaningful role in the adjustment process. As Hicks puts it:

> ". . . If the rate of interest was reasonably high to begin with, it seems possible that this reaction may take place without difficulty. But if the rate of interest is very low to begin with, it may be impossible for

[7] Lange recognizes, of course, that, if securities prices are not rigid, positive monetary effects can find expression in falling interest rates (rising securities prices). He points out (p. 17 *ff.*) that "[reduction of excess supplies in commodities markets] is much less certain to follow when the increase in demand or decrease in supply, caused by the positive monetary effect, is confined to stocks and bonds. In this case the substitution effect and expansion effect are induced only indirectly . . ."

> it to fall further — since, as we have seen, securities are inferior substitutes for money, and can never command a higher price than money." (*Op. cit.*, p. 259.)

We cannot "mop up" this topic until we discuss the "liquidity trap" in Ch. X.

c) What if real-balance effects were not ignored or precluded from the model?

Concededly, then, price flexibility must lead to *expansion* effects if it is to be capable of restoring equilibrium. (*See Note D.*) And expansion effects cannot be achieved in a system in which the money stock is comprised of non-interest-bearing securities where debtor-creditor effects are netted out. The paper money must be comprised of a stock of counters, not the direct or indirect debt obligations of any traders. Lange, and later Hicks, conceded that price flexibility would induce expansionary monetary effects in this case.[8] Pigou propounded this proposition, later elaborated by Patinkin.[8] The expansionary effect of increased value of real money balances under these specifications is easy to explain: as prices fall, increased real money balances comprise an (apparent) increase in wealth leading to increased demand for all non-inferior goods. If commodities as a whole are taken to be superior, demand for commodities will increase. If prices fall enough, each person with some money will feel as rich as Croesus and surely will plan to increase his rate of spending.

Qualifications to the *real-balance effect* will be detailed in Ch. XIV, but can cryptically be catalogued now:

> 1) Credit money features modern systems. Real-balance effects can operate in these systems only through asymmetric income effects.
>
> 2) In modern systems enormous price level changes would be necessary to generate enough change in the real value of currency to produce meaningful wealth effects. Price changes of this order of magnitude would imperil the ability of money to perform its basic roles and might — if there is wage-price stickiness — take economic eons to be consummated.

---

[8] *Cf.* Oscar Lange, *op. cit.*, pp. 14-19; J. R. Hicks, *op. cit.*, 2nd ed., pp. 333-335; A. C. Pigou, "The Classical Stationary State," *Economic Journal*, Vol. 53, Dec., 1943, p. 349 *ff.*; A. C. Pigou, "Economic Progress in a Stable Environment," *Economica*, New Series, Vol. 14, 1947, pp. 180-188, reprinted at p. 241 *ff.* in *Readings in Monetary Theory;* Don Patinkin, "Price Flexibility and Full Employment," *American Economic Review*, Vol. 38, 1948, pp. 543-564, reprinted in *Readings in Monetary Theory*, p. 252 *ff.*; Don Patinkin, *Money, Interest, and Prices.* The literature has become voluminous.

3) High elasticities of expectation could result in pointless hyperdeflation.

4) Political repercussions of large and sustained deflations are dreadful. (Of course, no writer has seriously proposed spontaneous deflation as a technique of economic policy. Real-balance effects have policy interest only when produced by increased fiat issue.)

d) What if a commodity were money?

If one of the m commodities served as money, the Hicks-Lange model could have a different complexion. Excess demand for real money balances would no longer be invariant against proportional changes in money prices of factors and commodities. Lower prices of factors and other commodities (normalized on the price of the monetized commodity) would lead to increased demand for factors by the money industry; expansionary effects would materialize even if wealth effects of increases in the value of stocks of the monetized commodity were ignored. If factor and commodity prices could fall enough, any net excess supply of non-monetary commodities and factors could be accommodated by increased production of money. In sum, the new *non-homogeneous* system has excellent stability properties — surely if the monetized commodity is produced under near-constant-cost conditions.[9]

SUMMARY

1. Chapter VIII studied links between monetary standards — a commodity elastic in supply, a commodity inelastic in supply, or paper — and persistent involuntary unemployment.
2. If the monetized commodity were produced at constant cost ("bricks"), even transitory involuntary unemployment would be impossible: incipient excess supply of commodities and factors would lead to transfer of resources to the production of money (bricks) until excess demand for liquidity were satisfied. Indeed, if necessary, the transfer of resources to the money industry could be permanent.

[9] Initial excess supply of money would be partially offset by reduced — finally nil — production of the monetized commodity. But, once production fell to zero, other forces would have to come into play: for example, the inflationary process might run upon shoals of higher interest rates.

3. If the monetized commodity were produced under increasing cost ("gold"), meaningful wage-price flexibility might be necessary to avoid involuntary unemployment. Elasticities of expectation become important: elastic expectations might throw a monkey wrench into the adjustment machinery. Still price flexibility assures *existence* of a full-employment solution, and in general the solution is stable: certainly if elasticity of expectations does not exceed unity and if income effects were symmetrical.
4. The "gold model" treated asset markets and asset prices. Relationships between desired stocks and investment demand developed in Ch. VII were exemplified.
5. Chapter IX, "The First Approximation to Income Theory," is the first of a number of chapters dealing with unemployment possibilities in paper-money systems. In the meantime attention was focused on the Hicks-Lange model, primarily concerned with price flexibility as an *adjustment mechanism.*
6. The crucial issue for paragraph 5 is whether price flexibility generates corrective expansionary effects. Two possible expansionary effects were considered: effects on and of interest rates; real-balance effects. It was pointed out that elastic price expectations would work against stability and inelastic price expectations in its favor. Ch. VIII usually assumed unitary elasticities of expectation: current prices were expected to continue.
7. Chapter VIII usually assumed that securities prices were fixed. This assumption is realistic when open-market purchases have been conducted *à outrance*: short rate being driven down to an extremely low level; various factors causing long rate to stick at a higher level. Such factors are immaterial for Secs. A & B.
8. When paper money consists of debt, real-balance effects can be produced only by asymmetric income effects: any increase in the real value of cash balances is offset by increased real value of underlying debt. And then, if the assumptions of this paragraph were applied to a Hicks-Lange system, the supply of money would fall in the same proportion as prices.
9. When counters comprise the paper-money supply — counters not directly or indirectly debts of traders — real-balance effects will be generated. However, nobody seriously has suggested that spontaneous deflation would be a sensible restorative. Furthermore perverse expectations could jeopardize the process.

10. If money is a produced commodity, the Hicks-Lange excess-demand functions are non-homogeneous in the commodity-factor prices. Lower prices of non-monetary commodities and factors lead to an increased planned rate of output of money: the value of the final product will have increased; the cost of production will have decreased. Since it never can be difficult to dispose of the means of payment, price flexibility assures successful adjustment — unless very high elasticities of expectation intervene. The mathematics (the breaking up of the homogeneity of the Hicks-Lange system) lead directly to the economic argument.
11. Thus, characteristics of monetary standards — essential properties of monetary institutions — much affect systems' inflationary and deflationary potential, prospects for full employment and growth, etc.

NOTES

NOTE A: *Cf.* Nassau W. Senior, *The Cost of Obtaining Money* (London: 1830), reprinted as No. 5 in the Scarce Tract Series of the London School of Economics, Lecture I. The classical writers were very sensitive to the relation of the cost of production of money to the rate of growth of the money stock, the part played by money wages, etc. Joan Robinson cites Marx to the same effect in her *Essay in Marxian Economics* (London: Macmillan and Co., Ltd., 1947), p. 47. *Cf. Das Kapital,* Vol. II, § 12, "The Reproduction of the Money Supply."

I have avoided that reddest of herrings, Say's Law (after J. B. Say, a 19th century French economist). W. J. Baumol states Say's Law (or Identity) as do most modern theorists. He is careful to refer to it as being *attributed* to Say. "Say's law is the . . . assertion that people do not want money except to buy goods at once, so that the total supply of commodities alone (excluding money) is necessarily identical with the total demand for commodities alone." [W. J. Baumol, *Economic Theory and Operations Analysis,* pp. 237-238.]

Despite Keynes's out-of-context quotation of J. S. Mill, I do not think that this form of Say's Law can be attributed to the classical writers. (*Cf. General Theory,* p. 18 and J. S. Mill, *Principles of Political Economy,* Book III, Chapter xiv, §§ 2.) Certainly not to Mill, the author of the brilliant "Of the Influence of Consumption Upon Production." (London Scarce Tract, No. 7.)

Keynes actually quotes Mill's rendition of how Say's Law *might* be interpreted. In fact Mill proceeded to offer "much the more plausible form of the doctrine":

> ". . . It is evident enough that produce makes a market for produce, and that there is wealth in the country to purchase all the wealth in the country, but those who have the means may not have the wants, and those who have the wants may be without the means. A portion, therefore, of the commodities produced may be unable to find a market from the absence of means in those who have the desire to consume,

> and the want of desire in those who have the means." [Ashley Edition, 1909, p. 558.]

True, the quality and clarity of Ch. xiv fluctuates widely. At pp. 561-562 he recognizes that a secular fall in the marginal efficiency of capital works towards planned saving exceeding planned investment at full-employment income. But he feels free to disregard this prospect.

> "Rather [a 'glut' is not] the effect of a general excess of production. It is simply the consequence of an excess of speculative purchases. It is not a gradual advent of low prices, but a sudden recoil from prices extravagantly high: its immediate cause is a contraction in credit and the remedy is . . . a restoration of confidence." (*Ibid.*, p. 561.)

In fact he sometimes illogically equates acts of saving with acts of investment. (*Ibid.*, p. 560.)

Thus Mill recognized the possibility of "glut" in the short run but was confident that planned saving can be equated to planned investment at full-employment income in the longer run: either planned saving will fall with planned investment or interest rates will fall. Indeed, in the stationary state there would be neither net saving nor investment.

I concede that Keynes captures much of this despite his doubtful tactics at p. 18 of the *General Theory*. Still it is better to keep the record straight.

NOTE B: Stability is a property of an equilibrium state or what Hicks calls a "temporary equilibrium of the whole system," what we have been prone to call a set of solution values. Lange is dealing with the propensity of the system to regain equilibrium when displaced from it rather than with problems of *existence* of equilibrium states.

Systems are *partially* stable if price displacements about equilibria in some markets, featured by flexible prices, tend to be corrected by movement of the flexible prices of the system if, and only if, certain other prices remain rigid.

There is an alternative statement of the mathematical properties of the underlying model. We might say that, if the $n+1$ equation system of Section C has a rank of stability equal to $n-1$, it is *imperfectly* stable. ("Partial stability of order m is said to be *perfect* when the system shows partial stability of *all* lower orders with respect to *any* prices being held constant. Otherwise the partial stability is said to be imperfect."—Oscar Lange, *op. cit.*, p. 93.) Specifically, when n-m securities prices are held rigid, the system does *not* show partial stability of order m. Finally, the Hicks-Lange system is one of *tatonnement*.

NOTE C: The first degree homogeneous (in commodities prices) properties of excess demand functions for securities (and money) are lost if banks, as we know them, are introduced. Thus, if all money is supplied by banks and if we can assume that reserves remain constant and banks lend up to their limit, the supply of money will be invariant to prices of commodities and securities. On the other hand, the demand for money, in the absence of real-balance effects, would be halved if commodity prices were to be halved, neglecting redistribution effects. Hence, excess demand functions for money and securities would not be homogeneous.

Needless to say, substantial excess supply of money would develop as commodity prices fall, taking interest rates to be constant. Non-banking traders can be assumed to plan to hold the same physical stocks and to consume these at the same rates as before. However, they will be attempting to exchange claims against banks for bank claims against them. Banks can be ignored as demanders of factors and commodities and surely, then, are found attempting to increase their *real* holdings of nonmonetary securities by offering unchanged nominal quantities of banking assets. Excess demand for securities must develop so long as banks do not wish to hold idle reserves. Whether real markets and bond prices will be affected are questions we have asked earlier. Hicks (*loc. cit.*, p. 259 *ff.*) points out that banks might well reach a point where they *do* abandon the quest for securities. Furthermore, response to lower interest rates in the labor and factor markets might be inadequate (*cf.* footnote 7).

NOTE D: These results flow from properties of homogeneous equation systems. (*Cf.* Lange, *op. cit.*, pp. 99-103.) Recall that the underlying system consists of m excess-demand functions which are zero-order homogeneous in the commodity prices, n-m excess-demand functions for securities which are first-order homogeneous in the same m prices, and, finally, an excess demand function for the $(n+1)th$ good, taken to be money. Lange proves the following three proporties for the system:

1) the excess-demand function for money is first-order homogeneous in the m commodity prices. This is to say that the excess-demand function for *real* money balances is zero-order homogeneous in these prices and implies that initial excess demand for real money balances cannot be corrected by proportional reductions in commodity prices;

2) "the system is neutral of rank not less than one and the rank of stability of the system does not exceed $n-1$," (*op. cit.*, p. 100) meaning that either

a) a decline in the rth price on the assumption that other prices are adjusted so as to maintain equilibrium in the remaining markets will lead neither to excess demand nor excess supply in the rth market — the case of neutrality of degree one, or

b), a decline in the rth price on the assumption that other prices are adjusted so as to maintain equilibrium in as many as $n-1$ other markets will lead to excess supply increasing in the rth market;

3) the accounting price of one of the m commodities and factors can be chosen arbitrarily, since the conditions for market clearance can be expressed in terms of $m - 1$ ratios (*e.g.*, $p_2/p_1, \ldots p_m/p_1$) — given $p_{m+1}, \ldots p_n$ — meaning that if the vector of prices, p^*, were a market-clearing vector so would be kp^* where k, a scalar, is an arbitrary positive constant.

CHAPTER NINE

The First Approximation to Income Theory

A. BACKGROUND

Chapters IX-XI show how paper-money systems might fail to attain full-employment solutions or at least suffer prolonged departure from them. Once again the way will be round-about: we turn away from monetary theory, going so far as to develop a model largely ignoring the money and securities markets. But money-and-banking phenomena reappear in due course when we develop the pure theory of central-bank policy (Ch. XIII) and the quantity theory of money (Ch. XIV). These subjects prove easy once the main properties of highly-aggregated general-equilibrium systems are grasped.

Until Ch. XII, when we turn to models of economic growth, we are concerned with determination of such dependent variables as the rate of employment and output *at a point in time;* what has gone before is given data; the model is applied repeatedly as time passes; the generation of systematic sequences is held in abeyance.

We must run a bit ahead of the story. It turns out that the "equilibrium" level of income at each point in time is related to investment expenditure through an investment multiplier. But an important determinant of investment at each point in time is growth experience — taken to govern expectations of future sales. The level of investment is intimately related to the rate of growth of income. Sluggish growth of national product in 1963 can lead to a *downturn* in production in 1964; full employment depends on continuing *growth* in effective demand as well as on *high* effective demand.

This important facet of income theory will not appear explicitly until Ch. XII. In the meanwhile, we often treat planned investment as *exogenous* $(I_t \equiv \bar{I})$, not pointing out that a functional relation such as $I_t = f(Y_{t-1} - Y_{t-2})$ might govern the way in which "given data" determines $I_t \equiv \bar{I}_t$. In Ch. X we will write $I_t = F(Y_t, r_t)$ without stressing that Y_t implies the value of $(Y_t - Y_{t-1})$ or that the partial relationship between I_t and r_t might depend on growth experience. In other words we could have written

$$I_t = F(Y_t, r_t; Y_{t-1}, Y_{t-2}, \ldots, Y_{t-n}, K_{ot})$$

B. "THE PROPENSITY TO CONSUME AND THE RATE OF NEW INVESTMENT"

All the income theory presented in this book is broadly *Keynesian,* after Lord Keynes's *General Theory.* This chapter might have been labelled "The First Approximation to Keynesian Income Theory" if we did not wish to be free occasionally to introduce elements absent from the *General Theory.* Not surprisingly, then, our first approximation to income theory — a version largely ignoring money and securities markets — is keyed rather exegetically to these passages from the *General Theory:*

> "Thus, given the propensity to consume and the rate of new investment, there will be only one level of employment consistent with equilibrium; since any other level will lead to inequality between the aggregate supply price of output as a whole and its aggregate demand price."[1]
>
> "Thus the volume of employment is not determined by the marginal disutility of labor measured in terms of real wages, except in so far

[2] P. 30.

The essence of the "one period" Keynesian model can be retained even if the wage units falls according to a well-defined dynamic law when there is excess supply in the labor market. The value of $w(t)$ still would be fixed. The analysis would stress less the question of "existence" of equilibrium and more the kinds of experience a capitalist system might have and the properties of disequilibrium states.

Chapter IX shows that in the basic Keynesian system the differential equation for the wage unit is consistent with persistent excess supply in the labor market, while that for the price level is constrained so that the shmoo market always is cleared.

as the supply of labor available at a given wage sets a *maximum* level to employment. The propensity to consume and the rate of new investment determine between them the volume of employment, and the volume of employment is uniquely related to a given level of real wages — not the other way round. If the propensity to consume and the rate of new investment result in a deficient effective demand, the actual level of employment will fall short of the supply of labor potentially available at the existing real wage, and the equilibrium real wage will be *greater* than the marginal disutility of the equilibrium level of employment."[2]

1. The First Form of the First Approximation

1

The first approximation to income theory, attempting to put flesh on the bones of the skeletal explanation of these quotes, can be presented in two forms; one developing aggregate demand and supply functions expressed in money of account; the other relying on demand-for and supply-of goods (shmoos) functions measured in goods (shmoos). The second form is more in keeping with contemporary literature, but the first is somewhat closer to the Keynesian original. (In neither case do we measure in Keynesian "wage units".)

The first model is built on the assumption that the money-wage rate (applying to an hour of standard labor) is predetermined. $w = \overline{w}$. The price level of shmoos, which play the same role as they did in Ch. VIII, is flexible: clearance of the shmoo market requires that the rate of demand for shmoos be equal to the rate of supply; this is necessary for $dp/dt = 0$. The equilibrium condition for the labor market is that the value of the marginal product of labor be equal to the wage rate. (Industry is assumed to be competitive.) The supply side of the labor market can be ignored: the system is assumed to be incapable of generating full employment, defined as a state in which additional labor cannot be obtained except at a higher real-wage rate; the predetermined money-wage rate prevents any excess supply of labor from exerting downward pressure on money wages.[3] Finally, all income is imputed to "households," all expenditures on producers' goods to "firms."

2

The first step in the analysis requires construction of an *aggregate supply function* relating rates of output and the proceeds entrepre-

---

[2] P. 30.

[3] In Ch. X it is shown that rigor requires that $N^d \equiv N^s$ in a Keynesian system, although N^s is defined *most* peculiarly.

neurs must expect to receive in order to be induced to produce at that rate. Production possibilities must be described, but this is easy to do in view of our assumption that the universal good, the shmoo, can be produced by applying labor to the stock of stored shmoos, K_o — given data at any point in time. There results an aggregate production function of the form

$$Y \equiv f(N, K_o). \tag{1}$$

Since labor is applied to a fixed stock of capital, it can be assumed that the rate of net output, Y, increases at a decreasing rate as in Figure IX-1. (Regions of increasing returns would never be pertinent.) The slope of the production function (the slope of the diagram's curve) gives the marginal physical product of labor — the rate at which output is increasing with the rate of utilization of labor. Algebraically,

$$MPP_N \equiv \partial Y/\partial N \equiv F_N(N, K_o). \tag{2}$$

As the diagram implies, the marginal physical product of labor decreases as more labor is applied to the fixed amount of capital. Algebraically,

$$\partial^2 Y/\partial N^2 < 0. \tag{3}$$

Clearly, firms want to employ labor up to the point where the rate of increment to cost, w, is equal to the rate of increment of value product, $p.MPP_N$ or $p.F_N(N, K_o)$. This gives rise to the equilibrium condition

$$\overline{w} = p.F_N(N, K_o). \tag{4}$$

PRODUCTION FUNCTION

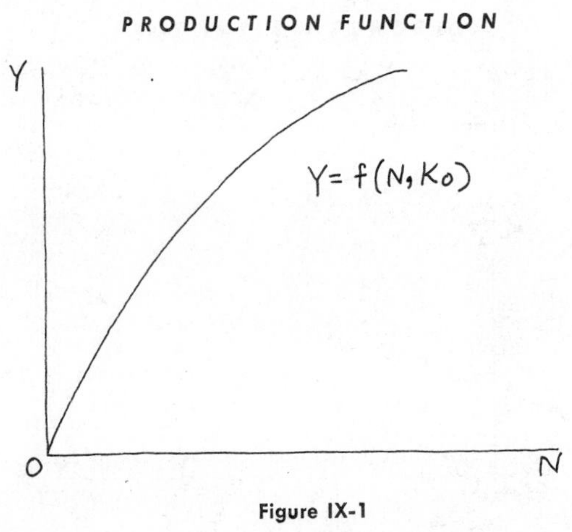

Figure IX-1

3

Now, we are prepared to develop the aggregate-supply function, at least on the assumption that current prices are expected to prevail in the future (unitary elasticity of expectations). If the rate of output is to be Y^a, plug that value into the production function (Equation 1). Out pops a value, for N, N^a. This is the rate of labor utilization necessary to sustain shmoo production at Y^a. Plug N^a into Equation 2, obtaining the marginal physical product of labor for the employment rate N^a:$F_N(N^a, K_0)$. Plug that value into Equation 4 which will then read

$$\overline{w} = p.(MPP)^a.$$

Solve for p: p^a. This is the price level necessary to induce firms to produce at the rate Y^a. Ignore *user cost* — the measure of capital burned up as a result of producing new shmoos. The product $(p^a)Y^a$ gives the proceeds that must be expected by entrepreneurs if they are to be induced to produce at the rate Y^a. A similar calculation can be made for all conceivable rates of output. The graphics are shown in Figure IX-2. The aggregate-supply curve increases at an increasing rate as Y increases. This follows from the curvature of the production function graphed in the diagram, based in turn on equation 3: higher rates of output (employment) require that the price level rise if the real wage is to continue to be equated with the marginal physical product of labor. In turn, this implies that the share of national income going to labor must decline as output increases, an implication

AGGREGATE SUPPLY

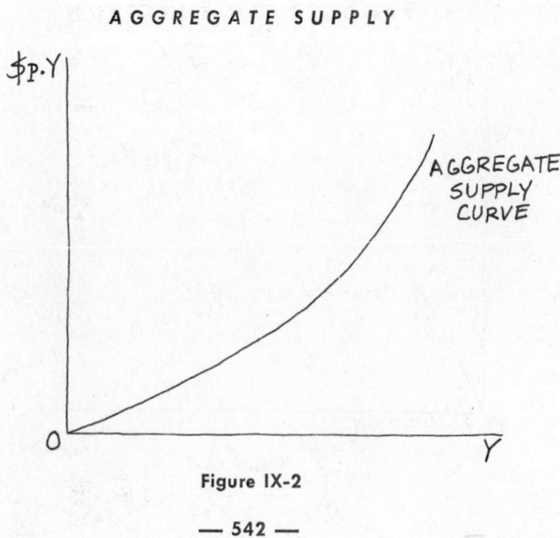

Figure IX-2

without empirical support. However, this part of the structure can be discarded once we abandon the assumption of flexible commodity prices. But we do not wish to do this before extracting the peculiarly-Keynesian flavor of the model.

4

Turn now to the *aggregate demand function*. It shows the relationship between rates of output and proceeds entrepreneurs *will* receive if they produce at that rate. Recalling that ours is a statical problem, we are not disturbed about a procedure generating the aggregate demand function by associating with a given level of output (say, Y^a) a price (say, p^a) obtained from the aggregate-supply function. After all, we are concerned with discovery of a market clearing solution: obviously the "final" price level must accord with the aggregate-supply function. The planned rate of expenditure on shmoos to be added to capital stock (I) is assumed to be predetermined or exogenous. Real investment expenditure is a given datum determined by past (perhaps very recently past) events. Thus, the nominal value of investment expenditure when $Y = Y^a$ is $p^a \bar{I}$. (Y, of course, takes on a whole range of values.) On the other hand, the planned real rate of consumption expenditure is taken to depend on the rate of shmoo output (identical with the net rate, user cost being excluded). This dependence, shown in Equation 5,

$$C \equiv \phi(Y; K_0), \tag{5}$$

is such that, as real income increases (measuring in shmoos), planned consumption increases at a lesser rate. Thus, if the rate of output increases by 1 shmoo per year, planned consumption can be expected to increase by something like 0.9 shmoos per year. Implicit in Equation 5 are distributional effects and the like, important in some contexts, but not in this.

5

What do income recipients[4] plan to do with that portion of their income not to be devoted to shmoo consumption? Alas, financial assets must be introduced into the system, however crudely. Uses of income

[4] "Capitalists" receive the residual $pY\text{-}\bar{w}N$. Markets for capital goods, equivalent here to equities markets, also have been ignored. Exogenous investment expenditure implies that prices in the equities markets will not affect this period's real investment expenditures.

Equities markets are neglected throughout the book. In general they are subsumed by markets explicitly determining prices of physical capital.

alternative to consumption include purchase of money, bonds, and equities.[5] Implicit in Equation 5 is a rate of diversion ($\equiv Y\text{-}C$) *of* income into financial markets (in this case, the "money market" activity finds workers stuffing cash into their jeans).[6] Clearly, the system cannot solve if the shmoo market is imbalanced. Indeed, in order to be sure that feed-back from financial sectors does not impinge upon the shmoo market, why not assume that "the" rate of interest is at an institutionally-bounded nadir, and that bank reserves always are large enough to permit the banks to supply additional cash balances in exchange for securities priced on a "nadir" yield basis. Real-balance effects can be excluded by postulation (in this chapter) of a pure-credit money.

6

Savings and investment decisions have been separated out.[7] This surely is a major contribution by Keynes: the identity or lack of identity of savings and investment decisions was a major source of confusion for pre-Keynesian writers. (*Cf.* citations of J. S. Mill in Ch. VIII.) Thus, in our first model, planned investment, measured in shmoos, is given by the predetermined variable, $\bar{I}$. Planned savings, defined as the difference between planned output and planned consumption of shmoos, is determined through separate function relations, and, in fact, different decision units generally plan investment expenditure and savings.[8] Once again — and this really is important — Keynesian theory makes crystal clear the distinction between planning not to consume and planning to invest in physical capital.

---

[5] Entrepreneurs placing shmoos in capital stock are considered to buy equities from themselves. Consumer durable expenditures *here* are included in consumption.

[6] In Ch. IX's models, households never *directly* acquire investment goods.

[7] To repeat, *investment* here has a rather specialized meaning: expenditure on shmoos intended to be added to capital stock. In a world with depreciation and/or user cost, *net* and *gross* investment would have to be distinguished.

[8] These are some of the points to be made in Chapters IX-XII:

i) Fulfillment of plans of all decision units requires that planned investment be equal to planned savings.

ii) Actual (realized) savings are definitionally equal to actual investment.

iii) Comparative statics are of limited usefulness in income theory. Theories of disequilibrium states are necessary for full comprehension.

iv) There is no reason to confine one's self to systems featured by stationarity or steady growth, once motions of systems are introduced into the analysis. This is the counterpart to (iii). Thus, a general growth model should be able to accommodate a state in which it never is true that all plans are fulfilled.

It is hard to keep all the balls in the air at once. Points i-iv are very close to the surface of the text at this stage, but must be dropped to footnotes for the time being.

Noting again that the appropriate price level is that pertaining to the aggregate supply function for corresponding rates of output, the aggregate demand function can be graphed.

AGGREGATE DEMAND

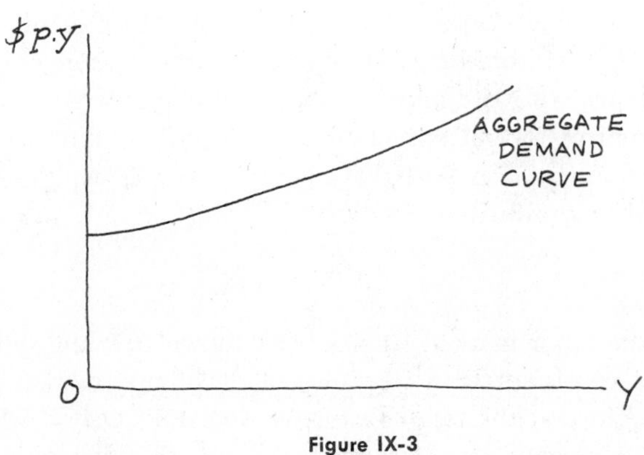

Figure IX-3

One is cautious about specifying its curvature: the price level is assumed to be rising with higher rates of output (increasing the curve's convexity); the real rate of demand is increasing *less* rapidly than output (decreasing the curve's convexity). We simply specify that the curve is less steep than the aggregate-supply curve. This is enough in the way of stability properties for present purposes.

Now draw the aggregate supply and demand curves on the same graph:

SOLUTION OF SYSTEM

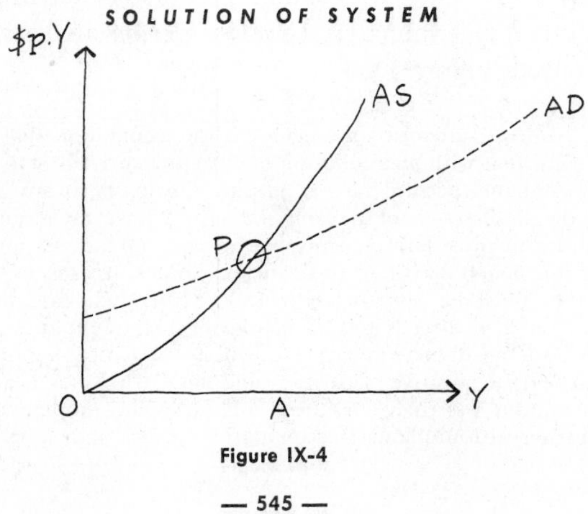

Figure IX-4

OA is called *effective demand.* Only if the rate of output is OA will the receipts that must be expected by entrepreneurs be equal to those actually received by them.[9] If the rate of output exceeded OA, entrepreneurs would find that their receipts (at the price level appropriate to that rate of output) fell short of receipts necessary to induce them to sustain that rate of output. Correspondingly, at rates of output less than OA, receipts would exceed "required levels": there would be a tendency for prices to rise and for output to expand. At $Y = OA$, there is no incentive for entrepreneurs to change their rate of output in either direction.[10] Point P of the diagram above is assumed to be a point of stable "equilibrium." Adjustment processes are unspecified.

7

Turn to the labor market. It has been shown that the only rate of employment consistent with clearance of the shmoo market is that required to produce at the rate of effective demand: $OA = Y^*$. Call this N^*. The aggregate supply function assures that the rate of demand for labor at p^* (appurtenant to Y^*) is N^*. In general, at the real wage rate $\overline{w}/p^*$ there is involuntary unemployment, measured by the additional number of hours of labor available at going wages and prices, here CD. Workers passively accept offers of employment at $\overline{w}(t)$ over the range FD on Figure IX-5. The simple-minded characterization is that there is money illusion on the supply side of the labor market. The preferred characterization is that the Keynesian labor market, in contrast with the elementary Keynesian commodity market, is a non-auction market: the labor market need not be cleared at t; $w(t)$ is "historically" determined, and of course is not in general equal to $w(t+1)$, but this is immaterial for *one-period* analysis.

Now consult Figure IX-5.

9 This and subsequent statements are made on the assumption that the price level, given $\overline{w}$, is consistent with maximization of entrepreneurial profits (from the micro point of view) at the specified rate of output. Obviously, if any other price level were used, the intersection of AS and AD would have no meaning. Of course, there is a different price level appropriate for each rate of output.

10 Integrating the shmoo market with financial markets, if firms expand output beyond OA, they must be prepared either to reduce their cash balances or issue securities (to banks or directly to factors). Firms, if they produce in excess of OA, must make unplanned inventory investment accompanied by unplanned reduction in cash and/or (positive) securities holdings. (*Cf.* Notes F and G, Ch. VII.) For rates of output less than OA, firms will experience unplanned inventory reduction, together with unplanned accumulation of cash and/or (positive) securities holdings.

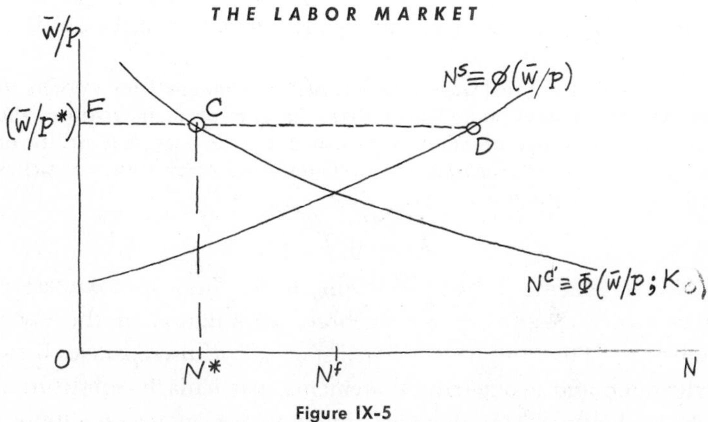

Figure IX-5

The planned rate of use of labor, N^d, is a decreasing function of the real-wage rate, reflecting the aggregate supply function. These entrepreneurial plans are independent of aggregate demand; prices are parametric for atomistically-competitive producers. However, clearance of markets featured by flexible prices require that entrepreneurial plans be consistent with demand conditions. p must induce entrepreneurs to plan to use labor at the rate N^* (producing Y^*). The potential offer of labor is an increasing function of the real-wage rate. The system solves with $p = p^*$, a price level low enough (engendering a real-wage high enough) for firms to plan to use labor only at the rate N^*.

8

The graphics are complete: the shmoo market is in balance; firms are hiring labor at their planned rate; the predetermined wage unit decommissions the supply side of the labor markets. The causal chain is much like that implied in the Keynesian extracts:

1. A (unique) rate of output consistent with clearance of the shmoo market — the rate of effective demand — is determined. Key determinants include the relationship of planned consumption to income (shmoo output) and the (predetermined) level of real investment expenditure.

2. Implicit in the determination of effective demand is determination of the equilibrium price level. Each rate of output is associated with a price level satisfying the aggregate-supply relation. The solution price level leads entrepreneurs to plan to hire labor at a rate consistent with effective demand.

3. The real-wage rate becomes $\overline{w}/p^*$ and is determined by the "effective volume of employment," not by the intersection of the curves of the diagram above.

4. In general the real-wage rate will be high enough[11] for workers to be willing to work more hours than the entrepreneurs require: the marginal disutility of labor is exceeded by the marginal utility of wages. A *deus ex machina,* the predetermined wage unit, reconciles all. (But *cf.* footnote 1.)

9

The statement of the first form of the first approximation to income theory closes with an algebraic formulation of the essential argument.[12] (The careful reader will spot minor discrepancies between the algebraic and geometrical statements, particularly substitution of supply- and demand-for-all-goods functions for aggregate supply and demand functions.) These are the equations:

$$(6) \qquad Y \equiv h(\overline{w}/p;\, K_o)$$

$$(7) \qquad Z \equiv f(N, \overline{w}/p\,;\, K_o, \overline{I})$$

$$(8) \qquad Y = Z$$

$$(9) \qquad \overline{w} = p.F_N(N, K_o) \quad \text{or } \overline{w} = p.MPP_N \text{ where the latter is given by the production function.}$$

All the variables have already been defined: Y is the rate of output of shmoos; p the money price of a shmoo; $\overline{w}$ the given wage unit (money-wage rate); K_o the predetermined stock of capital; Z the rate of demand for shmoos; N the rate of employment, $\overline{I}$ the predetermined rate of investment demand for shmoos; $F_N(\quad)$ or MPP_N the marginal physical product of labor.

Equations 6-9 are easily explained. Equation 6 defines the supply-of-all-goods function (to be honest, the supply of shmoos: the only good). $\partial Y/\partial p$ is positive: the higher the price level — given the wage unit — the higher will be the planned rate of output. Equation 7 is the demand-for-all-goods (shmoos) function. It permits distribution effects and, in fact, accounts for just about everything. Thus, if the marginal propensity to consume is less for entrepreneurs than for workers, $\partial Z/\partial p$ will be negative: at higher price levels for given wage

11 In order to content entrepreneurs with the production rate dictated by effective demand. This is made necessary by the assumption of flexible commodity prices.

12 Wage-flexibility effects are taken up at the end of the statement of the second form of the first approximation.

units, entrepreneurs receive a larger share of total income. Equation 8 is a familiar balance condition for the shmoo market. Equation 9 simply requires that the value of the marginal product of labor (here identical with the marginal value product) be equal to the wage unit; the condition automatically is fulfilled by profit-maximizing producers.

There emerges a system of four simultaneous equations in the four unknowns Y, Z, N, and p. The equations are independent.[13] Perhaps tiresomely, we assume that the system can be solved for a unique constellation of values for the unknowns, $[Y, Z, N, p]^*$, consistent with simultaneous satisfaction of Equations 6-9.

System 6-9 prompts at least two observations:

1) No supply-of-labor conditions are specified. It is assumed that the system's solution finds excess "potential supply" of labor. Once again the gruesome metaphysik of §§ 7 must be summoned.

2) Solution values for the system's "real" unknowns are independent of the wage unit (w). Thus rewrite Equation 9 as

$$\overline{w}/p = F_N(N, K_o).$$

$\overline{w}$ enters only as the numerator of the ratio $\overline{w}/p$. If the wage unit is reduced to $\lambda\overline{w}$, the system solves at $[Y^*, Z^*, N^*, \lambda p^*]$. The solution value for p falls proportionately with the wage unit; w/p's solution value is unchanged. In fact, not only are solution values for output and employment invariant against the wage unit in the first approximation, but even wage rigidity is desirable — on standard dynamical assumptions — in order to prevent endless and bootless deflation.[14]

2. The Second Form of the First Approximation

1

The first approximation's second form shares the essential properties of its mate. It simply is less-explicitly Keynesian, although more in accord with present-day convention. Begin with the algebra.

---

13 Walras' Law does not appear. There is but one explicit clearance condition: obviously *it* is not otoise.

14 System 6-9 can be reduced to a single excess-demand function for shmoos zero-order homogeneous in p and w (and set equal to zero). If the labor market were cleansed of money illusion, there would be two such equations, together with an excess demand function for securities (set equal to zero) first-order homogeneous in w and p (following Lange and explicitly assuming a pure-credit money). Chapter VIII showed that this system's rank of stability cannot exceed 1. Either prices or wages must be rigid ("the" interest rate has been assumed so all along) if equilibrium is to be restorable after the system is displaced . . . Note well that this stability analysis assumes that there *does* exist a "real" solution.

$$(10) \qquad C \equiv \phi(Y)$$

$$(11) \qquad I \equiv \bar{I}$$

$$(12) \qquad Y = C + I$$

$$(13) \qquad Y \equiv F(N, K_o)$$

$$(14) \qquad \bar{w}/p = F_N(N, K_o)$$

The symbols surely are familiar. The system is comprised of five independent equations in the five unknowns C, I, Y, N, and p. Equations 10-12 comprise a self-contained subset determining I, C, and Y; aggregate demand for shmoos $(C+I)$ will equal the rate of output (Y). It is easier to handle this model on the assumption that the consumption function (Equation 10) is unaffected by the distribution of income, and, in fact, it is obvious from Equations 10 and 11 that the path of least resistance is chosen: p and w — the determinants of distribution do not appear in the functions determining aggregate demand.[15]

Equations 10-12 can be labelled the "aggregate demand subset," determining effective demand, the rate of shmoo output consistent with aggregate demand. Lower rates of output lead to excess demand; higher rates, excess supply.

---

[15] The consumption function can accommodate distributional effects without affecting the analysis. Write Equation 10 as

$$C \equiv \phi(Y, p; \bar{w}).$$

Reduce Equations 13 and 14 to one equation in two unknowns (the wage unit being parametric):

$$\psi(Y, p; \bar{w}, K) = 0,$$

or use the related explicit form

$$p = \psi(Y).$$

Thus each Y has associated with it a p consistent with Equations 13 and 14. In determining the aggregate demand associated with rate of output Y', use the associated price (solved-for as above), p'. In this way the solution of subset 10-12 is assuredly consistent with Equations 13 and 14.

It is obvious that the only influence of the price level on aggregate demand is through distributional effects (in this model). Aggregate real income, measured in shmoos, is given by output (Y). The price level (indirectly) describes the way in which claims to output are shared-out among workers and entrepreneurs. Thus, a lower price level, given $w = \bar{w}$, implies an increased relative share for workers. Aggregate income being defined by Y, if there were no distributional effects, $\partial C/\partial p$ and $\partial C/\partial w$ would be zero: planned consumption would be independent of wage-price constellations.

Finally, remember that system 10-14 does *not* permit p (given $w = \bar{w}$) to be chosen arbitrarily: Equations 13 and 14 impose important restrictions on p that must be observed if the system as a whole is to solve out.

While we have done no more than establish properties of a temporary equilibrium, it is hard to resist some informal dynamics. Thus excess supply of shmoos leads to unintended inventory accumulation and to downward pressure on the price level, both forces encouraging contraction of output; excess demand to unintended inventory reduction and rising price levels, encouraging expansion of output.[16] A crude, highly preliminary, survey of stability properties of the model suggests a favorable verdict.

Once effective demand is determined, it is easy to solve for the price level. Plug the solution value for $Y(Y^*)$ obtained from Equations 10-12 into Equation 13 (the production function). Out pops N^*. Plug N^* into equation 14 (recalling that the supply side of the labor market can be neglected). Out pops p^*. We are home!

2

Now do the model with geometry. These are the diagrams.

THE AGGREGATE-DEMAND SUBSET

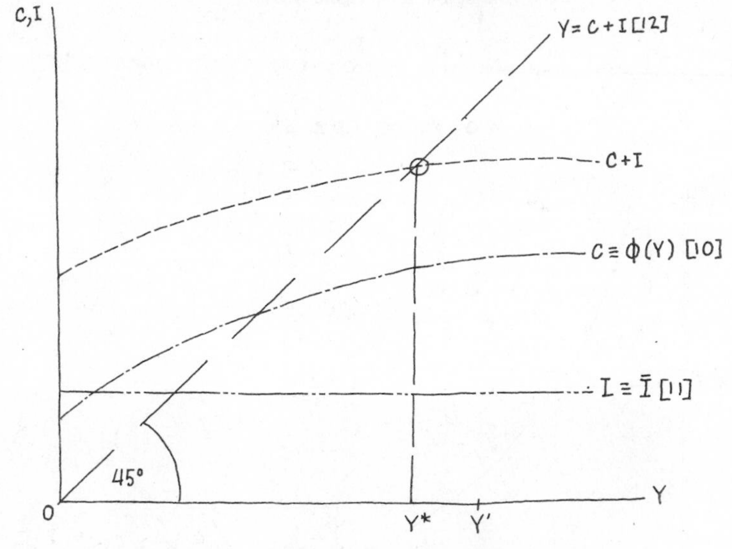

Diagram A — Figure IX-6

[16] We shall see that, if *ex ante* investment exceeds *ex ante* saving in the *t-th* period, firms are likely to plan to increase output in succeeding periods. Cash will to some extent be built up in anticipation of larger outflows "liquidity" of firms will temporarily increase. Observers might be led to find causal association between liquidity and investment behavior.

SOLVING FOR N*

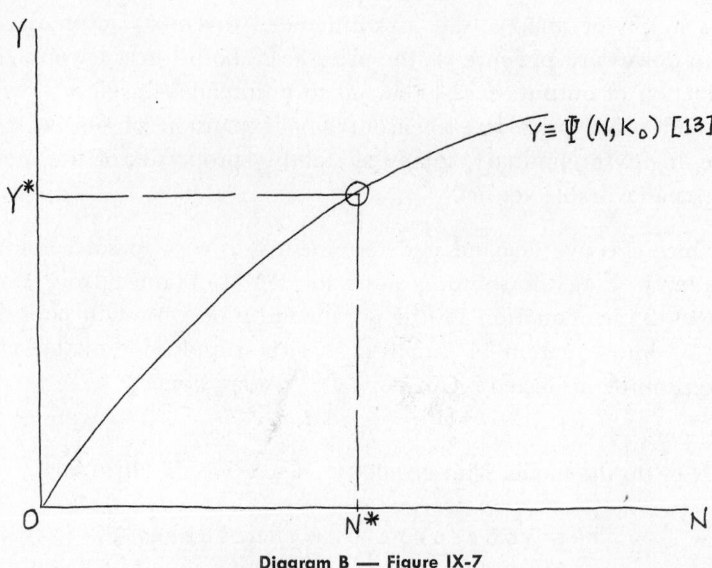

Diagram B — Figure IX-7

SOLVING FOR p*

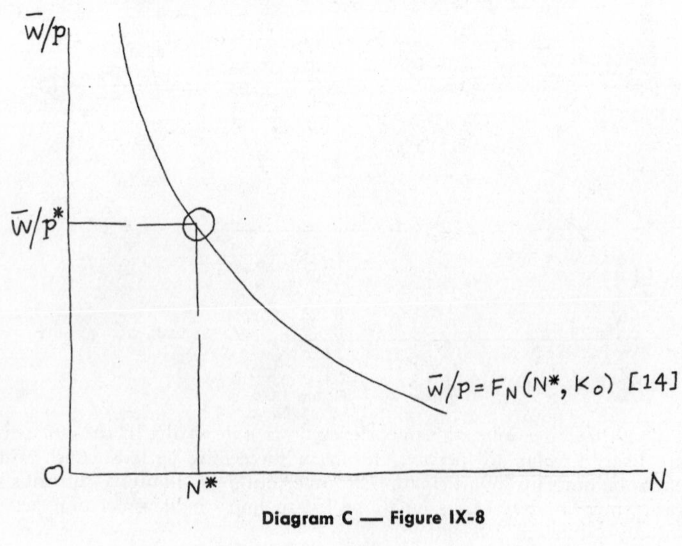

Diagram C — Figure IX-8

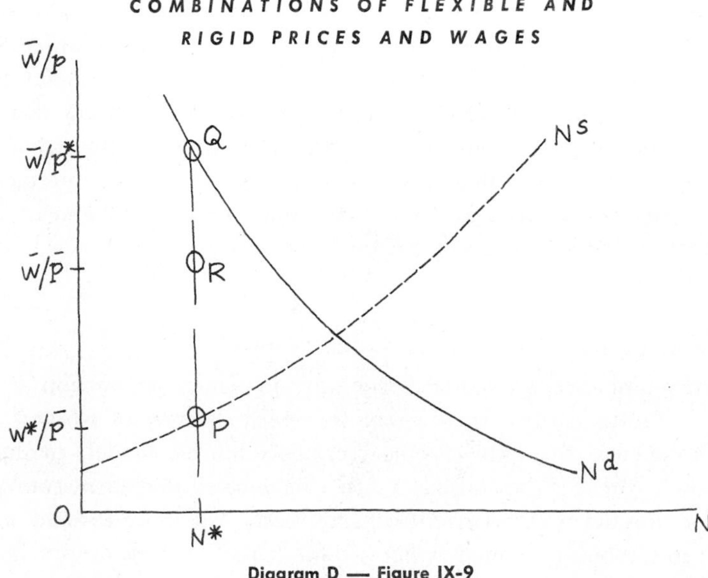

Diagram D — Figure IX-9

Diagrams A and B are easy to explain. Diagram A is simply a visual aid; nothing is contributed to the discussion. What about the dotted 45° line? It is a matter of Euclidian fact that, if perpendiculars are dropped to the ordinate and the abscissa from any point along a 45° line, the lengths cut off along the axes will be equal. It follows that, if we are on the 45° line, aggregate demand, measured along the ordinate ($\equiv C + I$) must be equal to the rate of output, Y, measured along the abscissa; indeed the $C + I = Y$ condition cannot be met unless the state of the system can be described by the coordinates of a point on the 45° line. Diagram B surely speaks for itself.

3

Diagram C suggests another important issue: clarification, even at the expense of some repititiveness, of the distinction between planned and realized (*ex ante* and *ex post*) saving and investment. The statical models of this chapter always refer to *planned* saving and investment. These models are concerned with discovery of solution values for equation systems, *not* with generation of time sequences. References to stability properties and adjustment processes either are informal or based on very special dynamical assumptions.

On the other hand, if the problem is approached from an accountant's point of view, saving and investment are defined differently. Saving (*realized, ex post*) becomes definitionally equal to investment (*realized, ex post*). More specifically, the accountant would describe the fate of all current output, Y. There are only two things that can happen to this output in a closed system (a system without interaction with other economies): it can be consumed or not consumed. The accountant recognizes this by writing the identity

$$Y \equiv C + I$$

where the category "not-consumption" is defined as "investment." He has taxonomically categorized the ways in which production is disposed. He then turns to the ways in which incomes of workers and entrepreneurs (the only income recipients in this model) might be disposed. Clearly, these also can either be devoted to current consumption or not devoted to current consumption. And since income, measured in shmoos, is defined as net income (equal to gross output in our model), the appropriate identity is

$$Y \equiv C + S,$$

where S is the value of the category not-consumption. Obviously, the identities lead to a residual identity

$$S \equiv I.$$

The symbols refer to realized, not planned, magnitudes; the concern is with what is happening, not with what planners would like to have happen.

Now test your sophistication by analyzing the consequences of the rate of output exceeding effective demand, Y^*. Try output Y^b. Observe that the planned rate of demand for goods (shmoos) will fall short of Y^b: planned investment $(\bar{I})$ will fall short of planned saving $[Y - \phi(Y)]$. Aggregate demand will be "below the 45° line." This means that — assuming the savings plan always is realized — actual (realized, *ex post*) investment will exceed $\bar{I}$.

What if output should fall short of Y^*? $\bar{I}$ will exceed $Y - \phi(Y)$. Unintended decumulation of stocks will have to take place or some planned investment expenditure will have to be unrealized. Of course, the accounting identities always hold, but the way in which they are satisfied is all important: unintended accumulation or decumulation of stocks implies decreasing or increasing output next period.

4

Once the aggregate-demand subset has been solved — a process described in Diagram A — the rest is easy. We need only move up the ordinate in Diagram B to Y^* and project a perpendicular. Its intersection with the curve of the production function describes a point whose abscissa value is the "effective" employment rate, N^*.

We proceed at once to Diagram C which can be used to obtain the price level consistent with entrepreneurs planning to employ labor at the rate N^*. The downward-sloping curve reflects the assumption that the marginal physical product of labor will decline as more labor is used with the fixed stock of capital. . . . Thus our primitive theory "determines" output, consumption, investment, employment, and the price level.

C. CONCLUDING TOPICS

Diagram D calls attention to two issues: wage-price flexibility and full employment; the stability of the solution of the first approximation to income theory.[16a]

1. Wage-price Flexibility

Diagrams A and B, together with Diagram A (*supra*), show that the only role of the price level in the model is to adjust entrepreneurial plans to the overriding reality of effective demand. Diagram D shows that this adjustment generally requires that there be excess "potential supply" in the labor market. Analysis of the model has shown that release of the wage unit (w) from the thralldom implied by the $\overline{w}$ notation would leave p undetermined in the sense that the

[16a] Diagram D and our analysis of it relies heavily on Don Patinkin's *Money, Interest, and Prices*. *Cf.* especially p. 211 *ff.* I am heavily indebted to Patinkin on many counts. There also is heavy, albeit more indirect, reliance in Ch. IX on Jacob Marschak, *Income, Employment, and the Price Level* (New York: Augustus M. Kelley, 1951).

model only can determine the ratio w/p. In fact the analytic statement of the model flooded light on the wage-price flexibility issue. Thus, use a reduced-form notation (expressing dependent variables as functions of parameters). Among the parameters is nestled the wage unit, $\overline{w}$, the "bar" stressing that it is determined by union authority or something of that ilk.

$$(15) \qquad p^* \equiv g^1(\overline{w}, z),$$

$$(16) \qquad y_i^* \equiv g^i(\overline{w}, z). \qquad i = 2, 3, \ldots, n$$

The asterisks indicate solution values. The y's are endogenous variables of the system other than the price level. z is a vector of exogenous variables and other parameters of the system. The analysis has shown that Equation 15 is first-order homogeneous in $\overline{w}$: if $\overline{w}$ is doubled, the solution value for p will double. It also has shown that $\partial y_i^*/\partial\overline{w} = 0$ for all i, that no other solution value depends on the wage unit.

It is intuitively clear that, if $w(t)$ were not predetermined, if wages, along with prices, were flexible, prices and wages would chase each other in an endless downward spiral. Excess supply of labor would persist, albeit transitorily alleviated if prices initially declined less than wages so that entrepreneurs would expand output. But entrepreneurs quickly would discover that the additional output could not be disposed of: prices would fall and employment would return to its initial level. The process could be repeated indefinitely.

Rigid wages and flexible prices lead to a position like point Q, Diagram D.[17] At Q, entrepreneurs are hiring at their planned rate: they are on their demand curves for labor. On the other hand, more than ON^* units of labor can be hired at $\overline{w}/p^*$. Point P, Diagram D, describes a point consistent with rigid prices and flexible wages. Entrepreneurs are off their demand curves for labor. They would like to hire more labor at the going real-wage rate, but they could not sell the additional output. Still there is no pressure against prices. On the other hand, the wage unit has been adjusted so that exactly ON^* units of labor can be obtained, ON^* being the rate of employment consistent with effective demand, Y^*. Point R describes a position most like what is observed during "slack times." Workers are willing to work more hours than they are being hired to work. Employers would like to hire more workers, but their sales possibilities do not

[17] *Cf.* Don Patinkin, *op. cit.*, p. 211 *ff.*

permit additional output. (Point R easily can be adapted to describe a state in which prices and wages merely were sticky.) [18]

If prices and wages were both rigid, Equation 14 could be ignored. Equations 10-13 simply would determine solution values for Y, C, I, and N.

2. Stability

The theory of "static stability" suggests that the solution of the first approximation is stable. The rate of excess demand for commodities, X, defined as $Z - Y$, can be expressed as a function of p, given $\overline{w}$. If p is specified, one can work back from Equation 14, determining Z and hence $Z - Y$. Equation 17 emerges:

$$X \equiv \phi(p; z) \tag{17}$$

where z is a vector of the system's parameters, including exogenous and predetermined variables. Following Marschak, Equation 17 can be graphed by breaking-down X into its Y and Z components as in Figure IX-10. Excess demand, $Z - Y$, decreases with p. Accordingly, if p is above its solution value ($X = 0$ at the encircled point), there will be excess supply of shmoos; excess demand if p is below its solution value. Assuming that dp/dt will be positive if there is excess demand, negative if there is excess supply, and 0 if $X = 0$, dp/dt will be negative for $p > p^*$, zero for $p = p^*$, and positive for $p < p^*$. The solution is stable.[19]

---

18 Point R suggests an "income constraint" model, recently developed by R. W. Clower. In this model — in contrast with neoclassical *tatonnement* formulations — traders' spending and output decisions are governed by experience in non-auction markets. Sellers of commodities adjust output to sales possibilities with prices following what might be a sluggishly-operating dynamic law. Workers' consumption plans are geared to employment they actually can obtain.

Of course, "income-constraint" processes convert Wicksellian Deflation (*cf.* Ch. VA, Note K, and Ch. XIII) into Keynesian states.

19 Chapter IX has not considered price-cost performance during imbalance of aggregate demand and supply; equilibrium relationships have been stressed. What happens during "overproduction?" Inventories begin to pile up of course. Relative prices change to the extent that perishables are marked-down more rapidly and drastically. Still, the hideous paradox of spoiling food and starving workers often has appeared during depressions. Inelastic expectations can lead to absorption of output through price cuts reducing propensities to save, although the upshot would find entrepreneurial receipts falling short of their aggregate supply price.

This note emphasizes the advantages of the schemata of Section B 1 over that of B 2.

EXCESS DEMAND AND PRICE

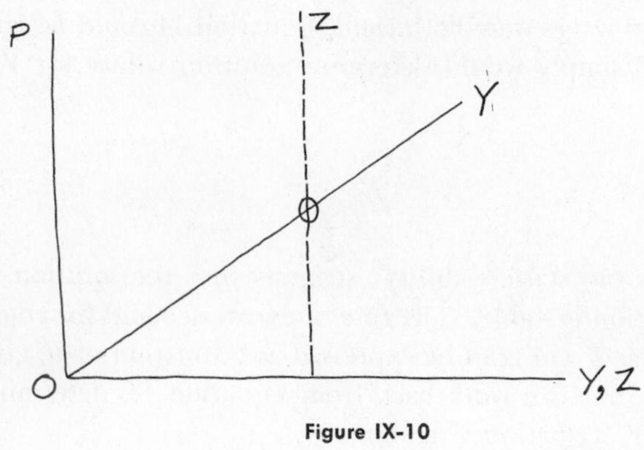

Figure IX-10

SUMMARY

1. Chapter IX developed the first approximation to Keynesian income theory. The first approximation concentrates on the commodities (shmoo) and labor markets. It substantially ignores the money and bond markets. Interest rates are fixed at an institutional minimum and bank reserves always are large enough to accommodate increased demand for cash. Banks will be able to exchange cash for securities at the fixed rate of interest.
2. The analysis uses an all-purpose good, the shmoo.
3. The first form of the first approximation uses aggregate demand and supply functions consistent with each other only at the point of effective demand. Once effective demand is determined, the solution value for employment easily is learned. N^* implies the price level inducing entrepreneurs to plan to employ labor at a rate consistent with effective demand. N^* might be called the rate of effective employment.
4. The second form of the first approximation is much like the first. It is less explicitly Keynesian but perhaps a more common formulation.
5. Saving and investment are identical *ex post* but unequal *ex ante* except at the point of effective demand. This is a crucial distinction.

6. The systems of Ch. IX can determine no more than the ratio w/p. Unless w or p is given, p or w cannot be determined through these models.
7. Furthermore, if both w and p were flexible, the models of Ch. IX would call for hyperdeflation.
8. The stability properties of the first approximation were healthy.
9. If one phrase summarized Ch. IX, it would be Keynes's: ". . . the volume of employment is uniquely related to [gives rise to] a given level of real wages — not the other way around." Dunlop and others have found evidence contradicting its *empirical* content, but its importance for us is *didactical*.[20]

[20] Workers in the vineyards of Keynesian economics easily become detached from basic neoclassical theorems of product and factor substitution. When liaison with price theory is restored, the problem of unemployment becomes more pertinent for dynamics than for statics. If, at t, factors are in excess supply, planned savings "must" be directed towards physical instead of financial assets (for a *given* propensity to save and noting that consumption and holding decisions are separable; durability is variable). This can be done if prices of sources fall relative to rents, expected rents, and to financial-asset prices; in an uncertain world, increased relative holdings of physical assets require increased premia. Thus, wages must fall relative to rents so that, as it were, Rolls Royces come to be preferred to Fords, Rolls Royces having higher labor-input coefficients and machine-hour requirements not nearly so much greater.

In a longer run, "unemployment equilibrium" surely is a chimera. If the capital stock is low enough, and, implicitly, if discount factors are high enough, an arbitrarily low level of "National Income" can be accompanied by a labor force fully engaged in rubbing one another's backs and dragging building stones into place with ropes.

Even as a statical system, the model is not Pollyanna in spirit. It implies that an economy unable to accumulate capital at a reasonably high rate must, if it is to absorb its labor force (perhaps growing exogenously), become backward.

APPENDIX

Structural Unemployment

INVOLUNTARY UNEMPLOYMENT NEED NOT BE KEYNESIAN. See for example R. Dorfman, P. Samuelson, and R. Solow, *Linear Programming and Economic Analysis,* pp. 364-366, and Joan Robinson, *The Accumulation of Capital* (London: Macmillan & Co., Ltd., 1956). (I also benefited from conversations with Mrs. Robinson in Spring 1961.)

Consider a system in which production techniques are frozen: the labor-capital ratio is 3:1. If there were more than 300 labor units, accompanying 100 capital units, there would be unemployment quite apart from any deficiency in aggregate demand. Or consider a situation in which initially there were 100 units of capital and 300 units of labor, but that innovation occurs; the ratio becomes 2:1; 100 units of labor become unemployed.[1] If all labor is to be employed, there must be a spurt in the accumulation of capital (accompanied by an increase in the rate of growth of output, of course). Once the system has caught up, it can enjoy a "golden age" if the rate of growth of population (roughly equivalent to that of the labor force) and the rate of accumulation of capital are equal. Full employment will be sustained. If growth of output and capital lag behind the rate of growth of population, as has more or less been true of the United States in recent years, a problem arises which is not unlike that of underdeveloped countries requiring capital accumulation in order to utilize their labor force.

These lines are at a very simple level of analysis: possibilities of factor substitution through alternative techniques and changed mixes of final products, absorption of labor in uses involving non-limitational inputs, etc. have been omitted.[2] But some basic insight is provided. One perceives some of the effects either of drastic changes in growth rates of factor supplies or in technique.

1 "Full employment" means exhaustion of at least one of the constraints. Here the capital constraint.

2 *Cf.* Dorfman, Samuelson, and Solow, *loc. cit.*

CHAPTER TEN

The Second Approximation to Income Theory

CHAPTER X EXPLICITLY TREATS FINANCIAL MARKETS AND takes belated notice of the banking system. It does not consider the role of the government. Nor is investment behavior formally treated as a problem in capital theory. On the other hand, there is rumination on the relation of interest rates to planned investment expenditure. Finally, the second approximation provides some rudimentary theory of asset markets; there is less dependence on a shmoo economy.

A. INTEREST RATES AND DEMAND FOR ASSETS

1

Preparation for the models of the second approximation begins with reflection on interest rates and investment plans. First consider the relationship between interest rates and demand prices (maximum offers) for capital goods ("machinery"). Take a machine with a life of two years. Assume that purchase of this machine will increase a firm's profits by $300 in period 1 and $200 in period 2 — purchase being in period 0 and "profit" defined so as *not* to account for depreciation. Exclude uncertainty.

(If profits here were calculated net of depreciation, the machine's cost would be counted twice: it would be deducted from the revenue stream and included in purchase price. Consider this simple example. Assume that a machine would augment profit [not including depreciation] by $1,000 for one period at the end of which it would "die," and that the initial cost of the machine were $500. If depreciation were deducted from "profit," the opportunity would appear to consist of paying $500 now in order to get back $500 at the end of the period. In fact the purchaser would get $1,000 at the end of the period.)

What opportunities are most like those described by the specifications? Purchase of some other machine? Assume that there is no machine purchase that could yield higher returns in both years.[1] Purchase of bonds? Yes, but what sort of bonds? Obviously, a bond with a maturity of one year, promising to pay $300 and another with a maturity of two years, promising to pay $200. These would offer a stream identical with that of the machine. How much must be paid for the equivalent collection of bonds? The answer depends on the one- and two-year interest rates, $100r_1$ and $100r_2$ per cent per annum. Once these are known, the cost of the securities (if one compounds annually) would be given by the formula

$$(1) \qquad P = \$300/(1+r_1) + \$200/(1+r_2)^2.$$

Thus, if I paid $\$300\,(1+r_1)$ now for a one-year security, I would have $300 one year from now [$\$300(1+r)^{-1}(1+r) = \$300$]: the market value of a promise to pay $300 one year from date is $\$300/(1+r_1)$. Similarly, $\$200/(1+r_2)^2$ is the market value of a promise to pay $200 two years from date.[2] The revenue stream of the right-hand side of Equation 1 is exactly that offered by the machine. *P* is the present value of the machine and gives the demand price for it.

The *r*'s might be called discount rates. If the discount rates were to decrease, the present value of the machine would increase. Increased discount rates reduce the present value of the machine. Once the elements of the revenue stream, the R_i's, are specified, definite relationship can be established between demand for investment

1 Effects of interest rates on durability of new machinery are not considered here.

2 Appendix A, Ch. VA showed, following Hicks, that $(1+r_2)^2$ should be equal to the product $(1+r_1)\,(1+\rho_2)$, where ρ_2 is the one-year rate expected to prevail at the end of the first (beginning of the second) year. Ch. X is confined to manifest rates. Also for convenience, "year" and "period" are used interchangeably. Finally, the expressions $1/(1+r_1)$ often are called discount factors.

goods and interest rates. Several relationships between demand prices for machinery and interest rates (discount rates) should be noted:

1) Demand for capital goods of very short life would be little affected by discount-rate changes. Thus the price of a right to receive $100 tomorrow would almost be invariant against a wide sweep of interest-rate changes.

2) The longer the life of the equipment, the more important should be longer-term interest rates for demand prices. The appropriate alternative to a machine expected to yield a steady *net* stream forever would be a perpetual bond.

3) Interest rates should affect the shape of desired income streams and, hence, the kind of machinery demanded. Higher interest rates encourage demand for machines yielding high returns over short intervals; lower rates, machines yielding lower returns for longer intervals.

4) In any case, ordinary opportunity-cost considerations dictate that interest-rate (discount-factor) changes affect demand prices for machinery.

2

Up to now the relationship between increment to profit in period t and machinery purchase in period *0* has been assumed certain. Clearly this is unrealistic. Furthermore this assumption obscures the central issues. In the real world purchase of producers' capital involves surrender of certain sums for lottery tickets. Think of the representative lottery tickets as bearing coupons, one for each period. Each coupon can be characterized by two parameters, although an indefinitely-large number of attributes might be specified. The parameters are expected value (E) and variance (V). If for example, a lottery ticket offered one chance in two of collecting $10, one chance in four of $20, and one chance in four of $0, the expected value of the ticket would be $10: ½($10) + ¼($20) + ¼($0). Now consider a ticket with 20 coupons, each featured by the same assortment of outcomes as the simple ticket. The analogy is to a machine with a life of 20 years.

Next consider the dispersion of outcomes, a factor we have rakishly called variance. In our particular case, the *range* of outcomes is from $0 to +$20. We might have considered a ticket offering a 90 per cent chance of collecting $1,000 and a 10 per cent chance of losing $8,900. The mathematical expectation of this ticket also is $10: (0.90)($1,000) + (0.10)($8,900). But the range is much greater: —$8,900 to +$1,000. Indeed, just about any measure of dispersion — including the second moment about the mean — will be greater.

3

Enough technique has been accumulated to deal analytically with elements of receipt streams associated with producers' capital. However, a link is needed if certain and uncertain outcomes are to be mixed together while solving problems of maximization and minimization. The concept of the *certainty equivalent* proves to be a link, however crude. Thus consider the pair of single-coupon lottery tickets. One offers the alternatives \$10, \$20, and \$0 with probabilities 0.50, 0.25, 0.25; the other \$1,000 and —\$8,900 with probabilities 0.90, 0.10. Recall that their mathematical expectations are the same. What would you be willing to pay for the first ticket? For the second? Less than \$10 in each case? Then you would be described as having an aversion to risk; you would be a risk avoider. More than \$10 in each case? You would have risk preference.[3] If you were willing to pay \$9.50 for the first ticket, the *certainty equivalent* to that probability distribution of pay-offs is \$9.50. If you were willing to pay \$11 for the ticket, the certainty equivalent would, of course, be \$11. We operate on the general assumption that investors are risk avoiders, that certainty equivalents are less than the coupons' mathematical expectations. This suggests that the certainty equivalent to the second ticket — featured by much greater dispersion around the same expected value — would be less than that to the first ticket for the representative trader.

When we refer to the contributions to profit of a machine of three-years' life — R_1, R_2, and R_3 — these are to be interpreted as certainty equivalents to subjective probability distributions of contributions to net profits that might be accomplished by the machine.[4]

It becomes clear why changes in interest rates (discount rates) might have little influence on the plans of entrepreneurs over the course of the business cycle. During a collapse of confidence, the elements of the yield stream might become zero or negative: regardless of the vector of non-negative interest rates, *r*, it does not seem worthwhile to purchase capital equipment. An access of confidence accompanying a strong upsurge of business activity might raise the *R*'s so

[3] I ignore the case in which one is willing to pay more than \$10 for one of the tickets and less than \$10 for the other. *Cf.* Milton Friedman and L. J. Savage, "The Utility Analysis of Choices Involving Risk," *Journal of Political Economy,* Vol. 56 (1948), pp. 279-304, reprinted in Boulding and Stigler (eds.), *Readings in Price Theory* (Philadelphia: Blakiston, 1951), pp. 57-96.

[4] Subjective because the probability distributions ensue from opinion rather than from the characteristics of an objectively defined experimental set-up.

much that even a substantial increase in all or most of the elements of r will not prevent a substantial increase in demand prices for machinery. Indeed, if the timing of changes in r finds r declining during downsurges and increasing during upsurges — as it does — it would be easy to form the impression that interest rates never much influenced demand for producers' durables. (*See Note K.*)

B. THE MACHINERY MARKET

1

The ingredients are at hand for a partial-equilibrium analysis of what we might call the machinery market. We deal with demand and supply of new machinery as functions of the price of machinery for various specifications of the level of interest rates. The latter are represented by a "representative" quotation, r. The analysis can be geometrical. The relationship between price and quantity — for a given value of r — is represented by a downward-sloping demand and upward-sloping supply curve.

The downward-sloping demand curve can reflect the following *ex ante* considerations:

a) entrepreneurs whose demand prices were below market price will enter the market when the price of machinery falls.

b) firms will expect the marginal profitability of machinery to decline as more is acquired, *cet. par.* This result is obvious for a monopoloid model. Limitational factors do the trick for a pure-competition model.

c) substantial costs — partly in disruption of normal production — must be incurred during installation of producers' durables. These costs might increase at an increasing rate as more investment is attempted. In all events, they can be offset by lower machinery prices.

d) lower machinery prices encourage capital-intensive production.

The upward-sloping supply curve reflects these *ex-ante* considerations:

a) as a greater proportion of the economy's resources is devoted to production of producers' goods, their cost in terms of consumer goods will rise: greater pressure is placed on resources specialized to the production of producers' goods; there are transitional costs associated with transferring resources from one to another sector of the economy.

b) more simply, it can be assumed that in the short run the machinery industry produces at increasing marginal cost.

Of course partial-equilibrium analysis is limited. The demand and supply curves are mere didactic devices: numerous specifications of values for other dependent variables of the system are required. The *relative* price of wage goods is assumed to fall as machinery output increases. Similarly, elements of the expected future income stream depend on the profile of future outputs. And then the position of the supply curve for the machinery market will depend on the total of available resources, assuming that the proportion of resources devoted to machinery production is "important." We ignore the impact of interest rates on the supply price of machinery (the minimum price that producers will accept — a price varying with the rate of output). (*See Note A.*)

Thus, we are brought to Figure X-1.

CLEARANCE OF THE (NEW) MACHINERY MARKET

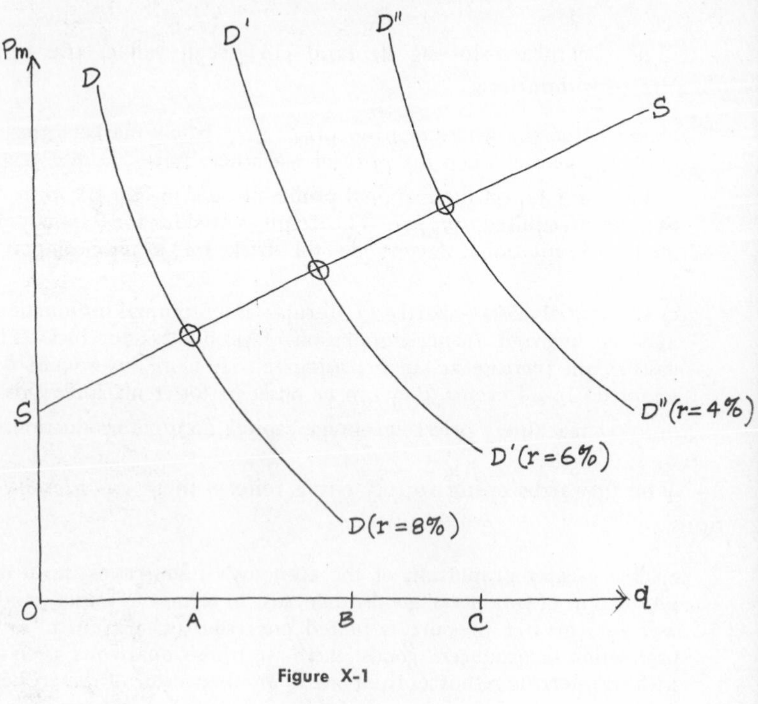

Figure X-1

The interest-rate variable, r, is a shift parameter: the position of the demand curve changes with r. Clearance of the machinery market occurs at greater rates of output as r is reduced. (The shifts might be slight.) The marginal return on machinery purchases in equilibrium decreases with security yields (opportunity costs).

Consider the response of the machinery market to interest-rate changes when the price of machinery has been rigid so that "deficient demand" has been reflected in "excess capacity" (or "availability"—*cf.* Ch. IX) rather than in falling machinery prices. The relevant portion of *SS* would be a flat line at the height $\bar{p}_m$. The curve relating the representative interest rate and the rate of output clearing the machinery market would be drawn with $p_m{}^*$ invariant against r, remaining at $\bar{p}_m$ throughout.

The general results can be summarized through a reduced-form equation

$$(ii) \qquad q_m{}^* \equiv f(r^*, u),$$

where u reflects the myriad conditions underlying the *ceteris paribus*: the production function for machinery, parameters of income streams expected to ensue from machinery purchase, etc.

The association between rates of output consistent with clearance of the machinery market and the vector of interest rates can be demonstrated with tables and graphs. Thus, Figure X-1 above leads to Table I and to Figure X-2 below.

INTEREST RATES AND RATES OF OUTPUT CLEARING THE MACHINERY MARKET

r	$q_m{}^*$ or I (planned investment)
.08	OA
.06	OB
.04	OC

TABLE X-I

INTEREST RATES AND RATES OF OUTPUT CLEARING THE MACHINERY MARKET

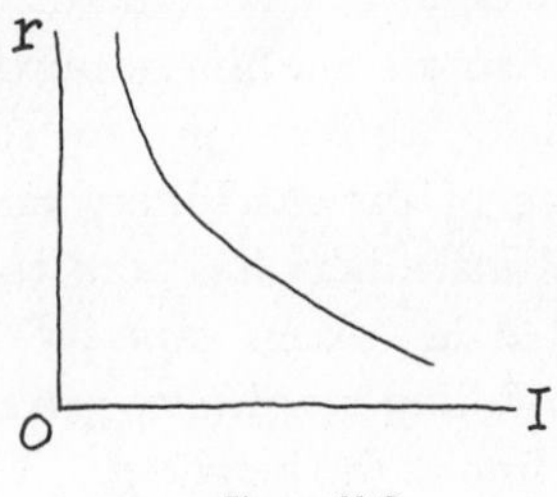

Figure X-2

Be careful *not* to interpret the diagram as a demand curve for (new) machinery. It is not. Rather it is a locus of rates of output clearing the machinery market for various interest-rate levels, *cet. par.*[5] If the supply curve for new machinery were perfectly elastic within the relevant range, however, the diagram's curve could be obtained by projecting a perpendicular to the ordinate of the diagram (Figure X-2), "collecting" the points discovered on the intercepted demand curves, and then exhibiting these points as interest rate–investment combination on the diagram above.

2

There is but one bit of dead wood to be cleared away before launching into the second approximation proper. It concerns the *marginal efficiency of capital,* a concept almost impossible to define in a fairly rigorous and complete model, but widely used and admittedly evocative. MEC is in fact defined in terms of a single discount rate (say, ρ). Assume that the market price of a given machine is p^s_m and that the certainty-equivalent yield stream is $(R_1\ R_2\ \ldots,\ R_n)$ where the machine has a life of n years. Write Equation iii:

$$(iii) \qquad p^s_m = R_1(1+\rho)^{-1} + R_2(1+\rho)^{-2} + \ldots + R_n(1+\rho)^{-n}.$$

Solve Equation iii for the discount rate ρ. The *certainty-equivalent* rate of return on the projected investment is equal to the solution value for ρ. Referring to the marginal purchase, this is the marginal efficiency of capital.

5 Or of rates of interest that must prevail if the machinery market is to clear at this or that rate of output.

The solution value for ρ is, of course, essentially a rate of return over cost. It implies the (single) discount rate which, if it were the market rate, would equate demand and supply prices of machinery. If indeed one could work with a single discount rate, a first-order condition emerges: stocks of machinery should be augmented until the rate of return over cost from the last dollar's worth of investment in machinery — the marginal efficiency of capital — is equal to the objective discount factor. Diagrammatically:

EQUILIBRIUM CONDITION
SUGGESTED BY DEFINITION OF ρ

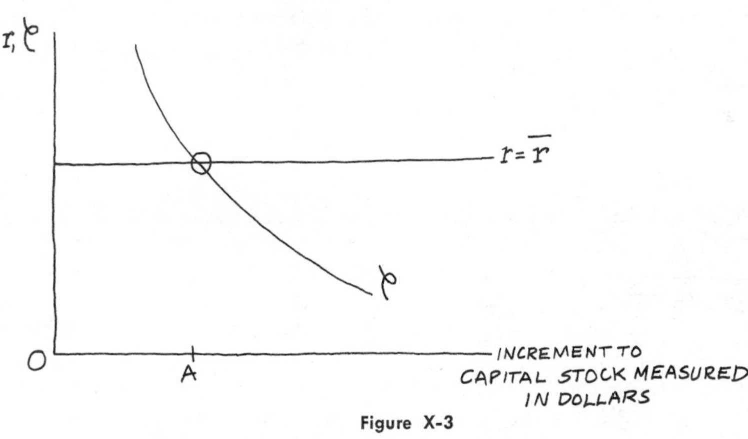

Figure X-3

This diagram above applies to a representative firm calculating rates of return over cost for increments to its stock of machinery. The downward-sloping curve — being based on certainty-equivalence — allows for reduced liquidity and increased riskiness of operations as the firm grows. The flat line segment indicates market opportunities open to the firm. It also is supposed to represent the rate at which the firm can borrow in the market, perhaps a silly assumption. It pays the firm to add to its capital stock so long as the rate of return over cost exceeds the external discount factor . . . Where it is appropriate to distinguish between the firm's opportunities to lend in the market and the cost to it of borrowing, the equilibrium condition must be put more subtly, but the flavor is unchanged: broadly speaking, lower external discount rates increase the appeal of adding to capital stock.[6]

3

In one sense the MEC concept leads to the same pass as did the multi-discount-factor approach: there is an inverse relationship between "the" interest rate and planned investment expenditure (consistent with clearance of the machinery market). Still it is disturbing to find one's self dealing with a single discount factor rather than with a family of such factors. Surely the better procedure is to calculate the demand price for a machine and compare it with the supply price. The structure — and changes in the structure — of interest rates can be accounted for. On the other hand, the imprecision of the MEC concept is the dull side of a panel: the gleaming side is the way in which expressions such as "a collapse in MEC" forcefully communicate broad movements.

C. A MACROMODEL WITH FINANCIAL ASSETS

1. Foundations

1

The building blocks are in place. There is enough apparatus to do "Keynesian economics."[7] Liquidity preference, the propensity to consume, the propensity to invest, the wage unit, production functions, long- and short-term interest rates, etc. have become bywords. What remains is to build a structure transforming this miscellany into a compact general-equilibrium theory.

[6] Regrettably, problems associated with the cost of raising capital, debt *vis-a-vis* equity finance, more precise statement of first-order conditions pertaining to portfolio decisions, etc. are suppressed in this book. *Cf.* James S. Duesenberry, *Business Cycles and Economic Growth* (New York: McGraw-Hill, 1958), especially pp. 49-170. (*See Note B.*)

[7] Following Professor Clower — *cf.* footnote 32 *infra* and the text of Section C 1 — my models are Keynesian in the sense that traders in implicitly non-auction markets obey non-price constraints. Thus, Keynesian workers are constrained by the volume of employment they can obtain at $w(t)$.

True, we, along with Keynes, are interested in circumstances in which potential supplies of labor or goods at going prices exceed actual employment and output for extended stretches of time.

As Note C makes clear, in neoclassic general-equilibrium theory, an auctioneer confronts traders with prices that, for the latter, are — together with initial asset holdings — the *only* "givens." The traders announce their plans to the auctioneer who feeds the data to a computer. *Transactions never take place unless the plans are consistent with universal market clearance.* If plans are inconsistent, the auctioneer — following well defined rules — cries new prices. To say that the system is unstable is to say the *auctioneer* will go crazy; transactions cannot occur except in cleared (clearing) markets.

In this section, however, market participants — strictly speaking, only workers in our easily generalizable models — make their plans contingent on realizations as well as on prices. The markets implicitly are not auction markets. Transactions can take place in uncleared markets, although our statical formulation permits description only of characteristics of market-clearing states at t.

We first examine "solutions" in which "contingencies" would not arise, in which a vector p^* could reconcile all plans made for $p = p^*$. Then we examine states in which $p(t) \neq p^*(t)$ and $p^*(t)$ might not exist. Recalling that the model encompasses non-auction markets, we "solve" for states in which the contingency plans of workers are invoked but in which, as it happens, firms remain "on their supply curves." More complicated Keynesian possibilities are taken up only informally.

Finally, the models are framed with a certain low cunning so that the accounting relationships underlying Walras' Law are sustained.

2

We begin with an outpouring of algebra, although geometrical interpretations will be provided. The system is broken up into five sectors: labor; consumption and investment goods comprising the current-output sector; the physical assets sector (comprised of goods already produced); money; fixed income securities. Equities are reflected in prices of physical capital. Consumption goods are assumed to be completely perishable. There are three classes of physical assets: unspecialized reproducible physical capital; non-reproducible physical capital completely specialized to production of consumption goods; non-reproducible physical capital completely specialized to production of (unespecialized) capital goods. All depreciation rates are zero. Labor is completely unspecialized. The money stock — at the outset — is comprised of fiat paper. Securities consist of bills and consols.

The government is no more than a wraith-like object adjusting the stock of fiat paper or bank reserves. (Fiscal policy is introduced in Ch. XI, the role of government debt in Ch. XIII.)

The model is less frightfully aggregated than most Keynesian models. Another thing: symbols must be conserved. Accordingly, when we wish to say that the *ith* endogenous variable, y_i, is a function of a vector of other variables, x, we write $y_i = y_i(x)$. This is *not* to be read "y_i equals y_i times x," but rather "y_i is a function of the variables x." There remain occasions when symbols such as f, F, g, and ϕ indicate functional relationships.[8]

On to the models!

2. Full-Employment Solution

1

The Labor Sector (or Market)

(1) $$N^s \equiv N^s(w, p_1),$$

where p_1 is the price of the homogeneous consumer good — a shmoo gelded so as to be unserviceable as an investment good — and where the function $N^s(w, p_1)$ is zero-order homogeneous in w and p_1: proportional changes in w and p_1 leave N^s unaffected.[9]

(2) $$N^d_1 \equiv N^d_1(w, p_1, p', p_2, p_3, p_4),$$

informing us that the planned rate of demand[10] for labor in the consumer-goods industry depends on the wage unit (w), the price of consumer goods (p_1), the price of investment goods (p'), the price of unspecialized capital (p_2), and the prices of specialized capital (p_3 and p_4). Naturally, the form of the function will depend upon various parameters, including those of the physical-transformation functions.

(3) $$N^d_2 \equiv N^d_2(w, p_1, p', p_2, p_3, p_4),$$

where N^d_2 is, of course, the rate of demand for labor in the investment-goods sector.

8 The model can be interpreted as a period model. In that event, when the term *rate* is used, the time dimensionality is that of the period. If one period is a month, and consumption is expressed as a rate per month, the cumulant of consumption for the month is represented by the same number as the time rate.

9 The "labor" functions are oversimplified. For an apology, see Don Patinkin, *op. cit.*, pp. 129-130. *The firms are assumed to be in pure competition.*

$$(4) \qquad N^s = N^d_1 + N^d_2,$$

a market-clearance condition, recalling again that we begin with a general formulation, determining values for a vector of dependent variables consistent with clearance in *all* markets.

$$(5) \qquad N \equiv N^s \quad \text{or} \quad N \equiv N^d_1 + N^d_2,$$

merely definitional, but notationally convenient. If Equation 4 is satisfied, it is obvious that it does not matter which alternative for Equation 5 is chosen.

The Current Output Sector (or Market)

$$(6) \qquad C = C^d(w, p, C, I, N, K, R, \overline{M}),$$

telling us that the desired rate of consumption[10] depends on just about everything, including the wage unit *(w)*, the vector of prices *(p)*, rates of output of consumption and investment goods (*C* and *I*), the vector of initial capital stocks *(K)*, the vector of securities prices *(R)*, the predetermined money stock *(M)*, and the rates of employment *(N)*. (*See Note C.*) Of course, the notational scheme is consistent with proportional changes in all prices and the money stock not affecting demand for consumer goods.

$$(7) \qquad C = C^s(N^d_1, K^d_{21}\ K^d_3),$$

requiring that the planned rate of supply of consumption goods [$C^s(\quad)$] be equal to *C*, the rate supplied and demanded.[11] Equation 7 provides a production function for consumption goods: output is associated with inputs. If Equations 6 and 7 are simultaneously satisfied, the consumption-goods market will be in balance.

$$(8) \qquad I = I^d(w, p, C, I, N, K, R, \overline{M}),$$

$I^d(\quad)$, the demand-for-investment-goods function, reflects the influence of just about everything on desired holdings of capital stock, which in conjunction with initial holdings and adjustment coefficients (here parameters of the system), infer desired purchases of new capital goods.

$$(9) \qquad I = I^s(N^d_2, K^d_{22}, K^d_4),$$

10 *Cf.* footnote 8 *supra.*

11 $K^d_{2,1}$ gives the planned use of unspecialized capital in the consumer-good industry. K^d_3, the planned rate of utilization of the fixed stock of capital specialized to the consumer-good industry. Later equations deal with satisfaction of community restraints on the capital stocks.

the counterpart to Equation 7. Simultaneous satisfaction of Equations 8 and 9 assures clearance of the investment-goods market.[12]

The Physical Assets Sector (or Markets)

$$(10) \qquad K^{d}_{21} \equiv K^{d}_{21}(w, p, u),$$

$$(11) \qquad K^{d}_{22} \equiv K^{d}_{22}(w, p, u),$$

$$(12) \qquad K^{d}_{21} + K^{d}_{22} = \overline{K}_2$$

Equations 10 and 11 define demand for unspecialized capital in the consumption- and investment-good industries. Equation 12 requires that the sum of planned utilization of unspecialized capital be equal to that available, always recalling that currently produced capital goods do not contribute to *current* production capability.[13] Again, p is a vector of prices, and u a vector of other variables of the system.

$$(13) \qquad K^{d}_{3} \equiv K^{d}_{3}(w, p, u)$$

$$(14) \qquad K^{d}_{3} = \overline{K}_3$$

$$(15) \qquad K^{d}_{4} \equiv K^{d}_{4}(w, p, u)$$

$$(16) \qquad K^{d}_{4} = \overline{K}_4$$

Equations 13 and 15 define demand for specialized capital. Equations 14 and 16 require that these demands be consistent with the fixed stocks.

[12] The disaggregated or, rather, incompletely aggregated, character of the current-output sector has led to disappearance of counterparts to the aggregate supply and demand variables (Y and Z) of the first approximation. It is easy to restore these variables. Define aggregate supply in nominal terms as

$$y \equiv p_1 C^s + p' I^s$$

and aggregate demand as

$$z \equiv p_1 C^d + p' I^d$$

It is necessary but not sufficient for satisfaction of the equation system that $y = z$: y could equal z with component markets uncleared . . . A highly aggregated model is used in the geometrical supplement. (*See Note E.*)

Some would here prefer to exclude C, N, and I from $I^d(\quad)$. But surely there is no harm in indicating the *association* between output in t and planned output for $t+1$. Furthermore, more general Keynesian systems would find entrepreneurs subject to "income constraint."

[13] *Cf.* Ch. VIII *supra.* Even if there were uniform and certain expectations about future prices, $p'(t)$ and $p_2(t)$ need not be rigidly linked. For example, a carrying cost can be attributed to "underaged" capital; the average carrying cost might vary with the size of stocks being carried over. . . . As for the vector u, *cf.* footnote 12.

Keep in mind that fixed *aggregate* capital stocks are perfectly consistent with individual firms taking these stocks as variables (as was shown for money stocks). An appropriate constellation of prices of consumer and investment goods and money-wage rate is necessary for individual plans to be consistent with the constraints.[14]

The Money Sector (or Market)

$$\overline{M} = M^d(w, p, C, I, N, K, R, \overline{M}). \tag{17}$$

Equation 17's right-hand side is nothing more than demand for nominal money balances. Satisfaction of Equation 17 means that demand for money balances is equal to the predetermined supply. We have shown that, if traders lack money illusion, the demand for nominal balances will be homogeneous in degree one in prices and the money stock (ignoring distribution effects). In other words, if all prices *and* nominal money balances were doubled, demand for nominal balances would double; the demand for real money balances would remain unchanged. In due course, we shall discover that this elementary proposition floods light on the quantity-theory-of-money controversy, properly a facet of general-equilibrium theory.

The Securities Sector (or Markets)

$$B^d_1(w, p, C, I, N, K, R, \overline{M}) = B^s_1(\qquad), \tag{18}$$

$$B^d_2(\qquad) = B^s_2(\qquad). \tag{19}$$

[14] It is assumed that the constraints are exactly observed in the solution of the equation system. As is indicated in the Appendix to Ch. IX, this frequently is not the case in programming problems. *Cf.* Dorfman, Samuelson, and Solow, *Linear Programming and Economic Analysis*, pp. 357-366. Recall the distinction between "structural" and "Keynesian" unemployment.

There is no K_1 in our system. It was decided to use the same index for capital goods and their prices.

Recall that the depreciation is *nil* in the model. To introduce user-cost and related considerations would be to complicate horribly an analysis that is already intricate, and would not change the flavor of the results.

It is explained in Ch. VIII that the price of unspecialized capital and that of investment goods need not be the same. The latter are not available for use in current production processes. When user cost and complicated expectational phenomena are introduced into the model — let alone technological change — any disparity between p' and p_2 hardly needs justification.

There is implicit in the model a rigid relationship between stocks of capital and derivative flows of capital-goods services. But see footnote 14, Ch. VII. The individual household or firm can plan to dispose of any surplus services or acquire additional services in the rental market. Machinery remains a stock-flow good.

Equation 18 deals with nominally-valued bills, defined as promises to pay \$1 in 30 days, and Equation 19 with nominally-valued Consols, defined as promises to pay \$1 per year forever. As Note D shows, the functions of Equations 18 and 19 can be viewed as determining flow variables. Satisfaction of Equations 18 and 19 results in planned rates of offer of securities (including planned rates of issue of new securities) being equated with planned rates of purchase of securities. The vector $R = (R_1, R_2)$ where R_1 is the price of a unit bill and R_2 the price of a unit Consol. R_2 implies the long-term interest rate, $100r_2$ per cent per annum $(R_2 = 1/r_2)$. However, it is easier to work with securities prices than with interest rates.

Be careful not to be trapped into equation of planned issue of new securities with planned demand for investment goods. There are myriads of other reasons for planned issue of securities: desire to increase cash balances, to spend on consumption goods beyond current income, etc. Similarly, it is possible that capital expenditures are planned to be financed through reduction of cash balances or reduction in the rate of purchase of consumer goods.

2

Consider the perhaps fatuous equations-unknowns criterion. The 19-equation system contains 18 explicit unknowns: $N^s, N^d_1, N^d_2, w, p_1, p' \ldots, p_4, N, C, I, R_1, R_2, K^d_{21}, K^d_{22}, K^d_3$, and K^d_4. However, one of the equations follows from the others: if, for example, the first 18 equations were satisfied, satisfaction of Equation 19 would be assured; satisfaction of Equations 4, 6-9, 12, 14, 16-18 assures that all markets other than the consol market are cleared, but it is logically impossible for there to be excess demand (supply) in that market, since that would imply excess supply (demand) for at least one other good in a system governed by imbedded budget constraints.[15] The number of *independent* equations does not exceed that of the unknowns of the system.

---

[15] Walras' Law pertains to *ex-ante* values. Interpreting $B^d(\quad)$ and $B^s(\quad)$ as determining flow demand and supply, all excess flow demands of the system will be zero if Equations 4, 6-9, 12-16 are satisfied.

The dependence of Equation 17 on Equations 4, 6-9, 12, 14, 16-18 is clear if we write 19 as

$$w(N^s - \Sigma N^d) + p_1[C^s(\quad) - C^d(\quad)] + p'[I^s(\quad) - I^d(\quad)]$$
$$+ p_2[\overline{K}_2 - \overline{K}^d_{21} - K^d_{22}] + p_3(\overline{K}_3 - K^d_3) + p_4(\overline{K}_4 - K^d_4) + [\overline{M} - M^d(\quad)]$$
$$+ R_1[B^s_1(\quad) - B^d_1(\quad) = 0.$$

We have learned to be chary of equation-counting. This criterion is shaky even when applied to linear systems.[16]

3

There is an alternative model whose discrete-time interpretation should be that all contracts are made at the beginning of the period, delivery of capital to be made at the end of the period.[17] It is assumed that all of period *t*'s output of producers' goods are "fully matured" at the beginning of period $t+1$. The specialized capitals (indexed by subscripts 3 and 4) are eliminated. In this model, capital cannot be transferred from one application to another until the end of the period. The supply functions are written so that the initial capital stocks, $\overline{K}_{21}$ and $\overline{K}_{22}$, appear as arguments . . . It is obvious that, in this model, p' and p_2 must be identical. The p' notation is dropped.

The revised system basically has the same income-theoretic properties as the original system. System *i-xiv* probably is more orthodox than System 1-19. I happen to prefer the latter.

The system is set out below. There are 13 unknowns in the 14-equation system: N^s, $N^d{}_1$, $N^d{}_2$, N, w, p_1, p_2, C, I, R_1, R_2, $K^d{}_{21}$, and $K^d{}_{22}$. Walras' Law does its usual work. Note that demand for investment goods flows out of functions determining desired holdings of capital stock. It is assumed that adjustment of capital stock to desired levels always is planned to be completed within a single period.

i) $$N^s \equiv N^s(w, p_1)$$

ii) $$N^d{}_1 \equiv N^d{}_1(w, p_1, p_2)$$

iii) $$N^d{}_2 \equiv N^d{}_2(w, p_1, p_2)$$

iv) $$N^s = N^d{}_1 + N^d{}_2$$

v) $$N \equiv N^s \quad \text{or} \quad N \equiv N^d{}_1 + N^d{}_2$$

vi) $$C = C^d(w, p, C, I, N, K, R, \overline{M})$$

[16] For example, an economically-meaningful solution generally requires that prices be non-negative.

[17] In continuous time, the alternative model states that, at the micro level, instantaneous supply decisions are constrained by initial holdings of capital. The interval *h* of System 1-19 can approach zero. In System 1-19 the supply decision of the *kth* producer was not constrained by *his* initial holdings of capital: he was free to plan to acquire initial holdings of other producers. Once the producer is denied this option, it no longer is logically necessary to separate out markets for currently produced capital and capital in place at time *t*.

$$(vii) \qquad C = C^s(N_1{}^d, K_{21})$$

$$(viii) \qquad I = I^s(N^d{}_2, \overline{K}_{22})$$

$$(ix) \qquad K^d{}_{21} + K^d{}_{22} - (\overline{K}_{21} + \overline{K}_{22}) = I$$

$$(x) \qquad K^d{}_{21} \equiv K^d{}_{21}(\qquad)$$

$$(xi) \qquad K^d{}_{22} \equiv K^d{}_{22}(\qquad)$$

$$(xii) \qquad \overline{M} = M^d(\qquad)$$

$$(xiii) \qquad B^d{}_1(\qquad) = B^s{}_1(\qquad)$$

$$(xiv) \qquad B^d{}_2(\qquad) = B^s{}_2(\qquad)$$

3. Involuntary Unemployment Solution

1

We inquire about the likelihood of some obstacle preventing the systems from solving out at full employment.[18] Chapter VIII contains an important clue. A real-balance effect is imbedded in System 1-19. There must exist a set of prices low enough to make the real value of money balances high enough for wealth effects to counteract, say, institutional requirements that interest rates be positive . . . But let us not repeat Ch. VIII.

How might we make a transition from the 19-equation model to models that do not solve out at full employment? One approach is to impose restrictions on wage-price movements. After all, real-balance effects will have little empirical significance in systems dominated by credit money unless price movements are so drastic as to destroy money's ability to perform essential functions. Thus, we might assume that initial values for w and p are rather higher than the solution vector (w^*, p^*) and that dynamic laws governing wage-price movements,

$$dp_i/dt \equiv f^i(X_i),$$

where X_i is positive or negative excess demand, permit us to assume that wage-price levels will be rigid over short intervals without much loss of accuracy. We then concentrate on properties of the system dur-

[18] In the future the text deals with System 1-19 and its variants. By "solving out, at full employment," I mean "permitting market clearance with offers of labor, commodities, physical and financial assets conditioned only by prices and initial wealth." At full employment the non-price constraints are at most exactly fulfilled.

ng what might be periods of transition. The assumptions about wage-price behavior would be empirically justifiable, and we would be free of tedious metaphysical arguments about existence of solutions. (*See Note E.*)

2

However, tradition requires more vigorous exercise. We must develop more conventional variations of the basic model of Ch. X.

Assume that the wage unit is fixed at $\overline{w} > w^*$ but that prices are flexible. (But *cf.* Ch. IX, footnote 1.) This is how the model would have to be redone:

wherever w appears, impose a bar so that the symbol reads $\overline{w}$;

drop the supply equation for the labor market, Equation 1. The tacit assumption is that the demand side of the labor market will dominate.[19] Clearance of the labor market at $w = \overline{w}$ is assured, since workers passively accept offers of employment — within the relevant range — at $\overline{w}$. (*Cf.* footnote 19.) We assume that the system's new "solution" will find a rate of employment low enough and a price level for wage goods high enough to assure that additional labor can be obtained at $\overline{w}$; the fact that more labor can be obtained at the going real-wage rate assures that w will not exceed $\overline{w}$. In sum, the assumptions that money wages cannot fall below $\overline{w}$ and that prices must be low enough for clearance of the commodity markets (*cf.* Ch. IX) permit us to decommission the labor market to impose a fixed wage unit;

Equation 4 can be written as an identity:

the $N \equiv N^d_1 + N^d_2$ formulation of Equation 5 is chosen.

[19] Examine the diagram below, describing the text's supply-of-labor curve. Under no circumstances is labor offered at $w < \overline{w}$. Unions or some other frictional force have spavined the labor market. For successively lower prices ($p^1_1 > p^2_1 > p^3_1$) for wage goods, the perfectly elastic segment becomes longer. The text assumes that the demand-for-labor curve cuts the flat part of the supply curve.

SUPPLY OF LABOR

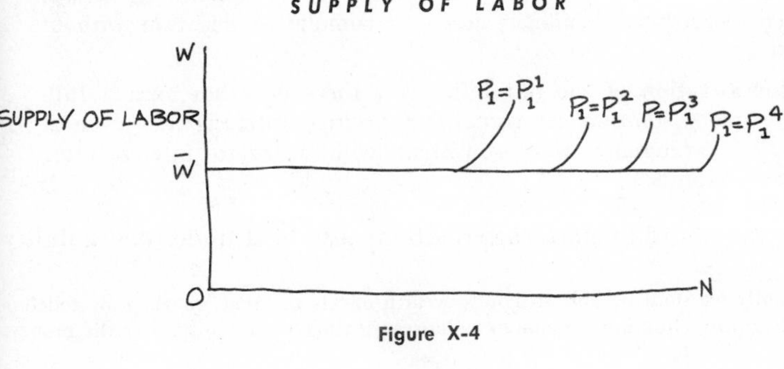

Figure X-4

There remains an 18-equation model in 17 unknowns: w is dropped as an unknown. We have guaranteed that the labor market will "clear"; Equation 4 could be written as an identity. Thus, the remaining market-clearance conditions must be dependent in the sense that satisfaction of all but one of them assures satisfaction of the last.

3

The modified model is not completely satisfying intellectually, partly because we suspect that solution values for securities prices depend on the value of the wage unit. If the wage unit is reduced with output remaining the same, prices will have to fall if entrepreneurs are to be satisfied to produce at initial rates of output. Lower prices will reduce desired transactions balances, leading to excess supply of money. (If wealth effects [in non-financial markets] of increased real money balances can be ignored,[20] *direct* effects of higher real money balances will be registered only in the securities markets, not in markets for current output and for assets.) Excess demand for securities will drive up securities prices, ordinarily leading to increased planned expenditure . . . The modified model's reduced form, expressing solution values for dependent variables as functions of the system's parameters (including $\overline{w}$), finds $\partial R_i/\partial \overline{w} < 0$, $\partial N^d{}_i/\partial \overline{w} < 0$, etc.

Since the choice of a wage unit is not neutral for the system's solution values — at least not in general — we must consider further modifications. These might include:

a) treatment of the problem as one of transition in the face of sticky wages and/or prices, perhaps elaborating the analysis by dealing with stability properties of the model;

b) consideration of how inelastic expectations (*re* interest rates) and/or liquidity preference might impose ceilings on securities prices, leading to an empty full-employment solution set. Wage-price flexibility is paralysed as an adjustment mechanism in the absence of wealth effects; wage-price flexibility leads to cumulative deflation without limit.

c) consideration of the possibility that there does not exist a full-employment solution set containing positive interest rates even if liquidity preference were consistent with near-zero interest rates. (*But see Note K.*)

We can afford to ignore approach (a): Ch. VIII undertook stability

20 Eventually we shall be able to ignore wealth effects in "real" markets by redefining the supply equation for money balances, dealing with a purely credit money.

analysis, and, furthermore, stability analysis is not crucial at this juncture.

Approach (c) is explored for a more simple model in Note E. Initial states can be imagined that would find expectations so pessimistic that near-zero long-term interest rates would not stimulate planned purchases. But approach (c) is so bound up in expectations phenomena that it had better be deferred until the dynamic models of Ch. XII.[21] *(Again see Note K.)*

4

Approach (b), then, is selected by a process of elimination. Also, it permits a scheme of argument parading under the title "liquidity trap."

We have considered *ad nauseam* how a ceiling can come to be established for the price of long-term securities. We have explored the question from at least two points of view: inelastic expectations and imposition of a lower limit on acceptable long-term yields through the liquidity yield of cash and short-term securities.

Assume that the authorities "defend" the price of bills at $\overline{R}_1$, which experience shows might imply yields of as little as one-tenth of one per cent per annum. Then assume that R_2, the price of Consols, gets hung-up in the neighborhood of $R_2°$: the yield on Consols must not fall below the marginal liquidity yield from money balances, equal in equilibrium to the marginal liquidity yield from bill holdings plus their nominal yield.[22] Otherwise holders of Consols would plan to move into bills or cash.[23, 24]

5

We again are prepared to modify Ch. X's basic model and, in so doing, enter into a highly Keynesian world featured by flexible prices, a fixed wage unit, and fixed short rate. Our attack is parallel to that

21 Keynes stressed decline in the marginal efficiency of capital, presumably relying upon the working of an increasing stock of non-human capital against a more-or-less fixed availability of other resources with the state of the arts fixed. The post-war world has seen a revolution in technology, vast expansion in investment in human capital, and evidence of insignificance of land limitation in the western world. Chapter XII will expand on this, but casual empirical observation makes it clear that the euthenasia of the *rentier* is far, far off in the absence of political intervention.

22 Analytical considerations prohibit rigidly specifying R_2 at $\overline{R}_2$.

23 How unfortunate that most models contain only one security and therefore must obscure their *Keynesian* content.

of the first modification of the 19-equation model: the text will provide an algebraic treatment; the Notes, a simpler geometrical treatment. But perhaps a preliminary verbal statement will be helpful. The stock of money must become large enough — given the wage unit — for yields on securities to be forced down to "institutional" limits.[24] The complex of securities and money markets is in a sort of "neutral equilibrium" afloat on a sea of liquidity. Under these circumstances, absolute holdings of bills and Consols are determined by supplies forthcoming at yields implicit in $\overline{R}_1$ and R_2°.[25] If the stock of money became larger — wealth effects, other than in financial markets, being cavalierly ignored prior to surgical removal[26] — asset holders would accede without a murmur to holding more money; indifference between money and securities at $\overline{R}_1$, R_2° extends over a wide range of holdings. However, supplies of securities would be practically unchanged, since no element in the vector of variables determining security supply would be meaningfully affected by further increase in the supply of money. It is the interaction of *indifference* and *surfeit* that gives the "b" modification its peculiar flavor. Surfeit suggests that monetary policy and monetary effects of changes in the wage unit will have run their course. If the yields implicit in $\overline{R}_1$ and R_2° are too high to permit "full employment," monetary policy will have reached a dead end. The system proves to have a solution featuring involuntary unemployment of labor in the sense that, if the wage unit were reduced, *cet. par.*, firms would plan to use more labor and produce more goods, and the labor would be forthcoming.[27] But the plans would prove unfulfillable because of inadequate effective demand. Since further increases in the stock of money would not lead to meaningful changes in key solution values of the system — asset holders being unwilling to hold non-monetary assets at lower-than-prevailing yields and security-issuers having been able to place all desired issues at prevailing yields — the system might be said to be in a *liquidity trap*. The only way for authorities to increase employment and output through monetary policy would be for

[24] We ignore inelastic expectations as an explanation of rigid long-term yields. Keynes's Ch. 17 rather than his speculative-motive approach is used. *Cf.* Ch. VII, footnotes 25 and 30.

[25] Equations 1″-18″ make clear that the only substitution relationships considered are between money and securities.

[26] The functions of Equations 1″-15″ are zero-order homogeneous in w and p.

[27] This somewhat distorted definition of Keynesian involuntary unemployment assumes that $w(t) = \overline{w}(t)$ is the result of dynamic forces in non-auction markets, *not* the result of workers' money illusion.

them to take up gigantic stocks of Consols at prices above R_2°. (*Cf.* Ch. VA, Appendix A and Ch. XI.)

6

The "(b) model" can be expressed algebraically through the following 18-equation system:

(1″)[28] $N^d_1 \equiv N^d_1(\overline{w}, p)$

(2″) $N^d_2 \equiv N^d_2(\overline{w}, p)$

(3″) $N \equiv N^d_1 + N^d_2$

(4″) $N^s \equiv N$

(5″) $C = C^d(\overline{w}, p, C, I, N, K, \overline{R}_1, R_2)$

(6″) $C = C^s(N^d_1, K^d_{21}, K^d_3)$

(7″) $I = I^d(\overline{w}, p, C, I, N, , \overline{R}_1, R_2)$

(8″) $I = I^s(N^d_2, K^d_{22}, K^d_4)$

(9″) $K^d_{21} \equiv K^d_{21}(\overline{w}, p, C, I, N, K, \overline{R}_1, R_2)$

(10″) $K^d_{22} \equiv K^d_{22}(\qquad\qquad\qquad\qquad)$

(11″) $K^d_{21} + K^d_{22} = \overline{K}_2$

(12″) $K^d_3 \equiv K^d_3(\overline{w}, p, C, I, N, K, \overline{R}_1, R_2)$

(13″) $K^d_3 = \overline{K}_3$

(14″) $K^d_4 \equiv K^d_4(\overline{w}, p, C, I, N, K, \overline{R}_1, R_2)$

(15″) $K^d_4 = \overline{K}_4$

(16″) $M = M^d(\overline{w}, p, C, I, N, K, \overline{R}_1, R_2, M)$

(17″) $B^d_1(\overline{w}, p, C, I, N, K, \overline{R}_1, R_2, M) = B^s_1(\overline{w}, p, C, I, N, K, \overline{R}_1, R_2, M)$

(18″) $B^d_2(\qquad\qquad\qquad\qquad) = B^s_2(\qquad\qquad\qquad\qquad)$

There are 17 unknowns: p_1, p', p_2, p_3, p_4, N^d_1, N^d_2, N, N^s, C, I, M, R_2, K^d_{21}, K^d_{22}, K^d_3, *and* K^d_4. For the usual reasons, there are no more than 17 independent restrictions. (*See Note C.*)

The ease with which the simple-minded algebraic criterion was satisfied should not lull one into believing that the analysis is particularly simple. It is not. In making the transition from system 1-19 to

[28] *Cf.* footnote 26.

1″-18″, w and R_1 were declassified as unknowns, while M was added to the list of unknowns. Why? Once w and R_1 are "fixed," M cannot be chosen arbitrarily if the system is to solve. For a given value of w, M must be large enough to "ratify" $\overline{R}_1$ (while we implicitly assume that as $\overline{r}_1 \rightarrow 0$, $r^*_2 \rightarrow r^\circ_2$, a fixed value). In a way that cannot become entirely clear until Ch. XIII, M becomes a variable (not even an instrumental variable) of the system: to repeat, the "solver" of the system cannot select M arbitrarily if $\overline{w}$ and $\overline{R}_1$ are to be ratified; rather M must be at least as large as the critical value determined above.

7

This leads to another reason why system 1″-18″ is not really so simple and why, in fact, it is somewhat deceitful. You will recall we treated verbally the possibility that the stock of money, M, might exceed the critical value M^* without affecting "real" solution values such as N^*, C^*, and I^*; system 1″-18″ determines M^* but does not handle the additional complication of the verbal account. To do so would require the paraphernalia of Note I. Equation 16″ would be rewritten

$$M \geqslant M^d(\qquad\qquad),$$

Equations 17″ and 18″ would become equalities

$$B^d{}_j(\qquad) \geqslant B^s{}_j(\qquad) \qquad j = 1, 2.$$

A *deus ex machina* from Note I in the form of $\overline{r}$ less than, say, ⅛ point above $\hat{r}$ (where movements must be in ⅛'s) might be resorted to. Or multiple solutions could be admitted so that a large number of money-securities combinations would be acceptable.

8

Why not eradicate the real-balance spectre? Relying on Appendix A to Ch. V, assume that all cash is provided by banks in exchange for securities. Unless there are distribution effects, the system will not experience real-balance effects: net financial wealth will be unaffected by changes in the quantity of money (and indeed here is zero).

The first 15 equations of the new model repeat Equations 1″-15″.[29] Of course, one need no longer apologize for excluding M. Note that M no longer is directly set by official action: manipu-

29 Compare footnote 26 *supra*.

late money-supply parameters in a naive (and unstated) banking model. The revised Equation 16″ reads

$$(16^{\Delta}) \qquad M^d(\overline{w}, p, C, I, N, K, \overline{R}_1, R_2) = M^s(\overline{R}_1, R_2; \propto)$$

Roughly following Appendix A, Ch. VA, Equations 17″ and 18″ are rewritten

$$(17^{\Delta}) \qquad \phi^1(\overline{w}, p, C, I, N, K, \overline{R}_1, R_2) = F^1(\overline{R}_1, R_2, \propto)$$

$$(18^{\Delta}) \qquad \phi^2(\qquad\qquad) = F^2(\quad)$$

The functions determine nominal quantities. $\phi^1(\quad)$ and $\phi^2(\quad)$ presumably are first-order homogeneous in w and p while demand and supply functions of Equations 1″-15″ are zero-order homogeneous in w and p in the absence of distribution effects. The parameter, $\propto$, encompassing such things as bank reserves and required reserve ratios is treated as an unknown.

D. THE HICKSIAN IS-LM MODEL

1

We almost have reached the end of the road of Ch. X. All that remains is to develop J. R. Hicks's famous *IS-LM* construction.[30] It is convenient to work with rigid prices as well as wages, although Note H shows that the results can be obtained in a model with flexible prices. Finally, since we wish to stress graphics, it is convenient to use the more highly aggregated concepts of the model of the first approximation to income theory and of the models of Notes E and F, Ch. X. The rigid wage-price assumption is developed in the diagram below. An expansion path is available such that wages and prices remain unchanged as employment and income increase; both demanders and suppliers have been forced from their respective "real" demand and supply curves as follows:

---

[30] J. R. Hicks, "Mr. Keynes and the 'Classics'; A Suggested Interpretation," *Econometrica,* Vol. 5, 1937, pp. 147-159, reprinted in Fellner and Haley (eds.), *Readings in the Theory of Income Distribution* (Philadelphia: Blakiston & Co., 1946), pp. 461-476. Rigorously, the *IS-LM* model can be interpreted only through modified *tatonnement*: there is "income constraint," but the "dynamic law for output" must deal with *planned* output, consumption, and investment; transactions take place in the Hicksian shmoo market only when that market can be cleared. (*See Note J.*)

POTENTIAL EXPANSION PATH FOR EMPLOYMENT WITH RIGID WAGES AND PRICES

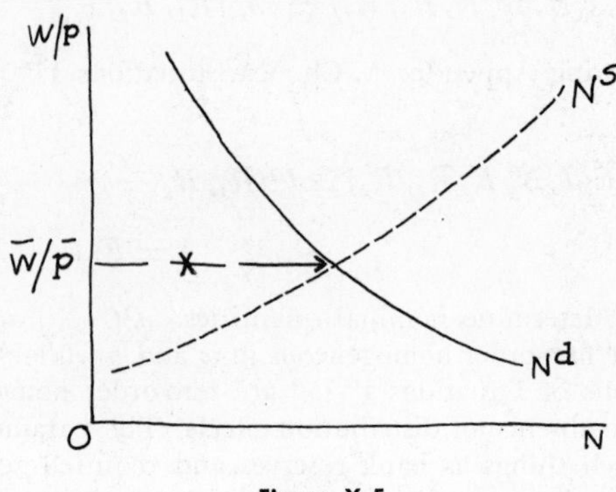

Figure X-5

Clearance conditions for the labor market can be ignored altogether, provided that the range of variation of output is consistent with dashed-line expansion path of the diagram above. Incidentally, this means that the dynamic law for output in the new model is

$$dY/dt = f[Y-(C+I)]$$

where C and I are, of course, *ex ante,* and where $dY/dt = 0$ when $Y = C + I$.

The system can be reduced to six equations in six unknowns (resuming unprimed arabic numerals):

(1) $$C \equiv C(Y, r)$$

(2) $$I \equiv I(Y, r)$$

(3) $$Y = C + I$$

(4) $$M^d \equiv \bar{p}.L(Y, r)$$

(5) $$M^s \equiv \overline{M}$$

(6) $$M^d = M^s$$

The securities-market subset is eliminated: its clearance is assured if Equations 1-6 are satisfied.[31]

[31] The securities subsector neither adds degrees of freedom to nor subtracts degrees of freedom from the system. Of course, when demand and supply functions for securities are introduced, the information obtained from solving Equations 1-6 suffices to determine the absolute value of new issues.

Dealing with Equations 1-3 and 4-6 separately, satisfaction of 1-3 assures *ex ante* balance in the commodities (shmoo) market, while satisfaction of 4-6 assures balance in the money market. Equations 1-3, containing the four unknowns C, I, Y, and r, can be reduced to one equation in two unknowns, say Y and r.

(i) $$f(Y, r) = 0 \text{ or } Y = F(r).$$

This is a locus of values of r and Y consistent with *ex ante* clearance of the commodities market. We assume, quite naturally, that $\partial Y/\partial r < 0$: lower interest rates lead to higher rates of effective demand. Lower interest rates stimulate investment expenditure and, perhaps, reduce the propensity to save. Output and employment can be tied together through a production function.

Equations 4-6 also are in four unknowns: M^d, M^s, Y, and r. They can be reduced to a single equation in Y and r,

(ii) $$g(Y, r) = 0 \text{ or } Y = G(r),$$

providing a locus of r-Y combinations consistent with *ex ante* clearance of the money market. We assume that $\partial Y/dr > 0$ (*i.e.*, $d[G(r)]/dr > 0$). Demand for money balances is inversely related to the interest rate, *cet. par.* Ch. VII shows this *ad nauseam.*

Possibilities for geometrical exploitation are rich.

THE BASIC IS-LM CONSTRUCTION

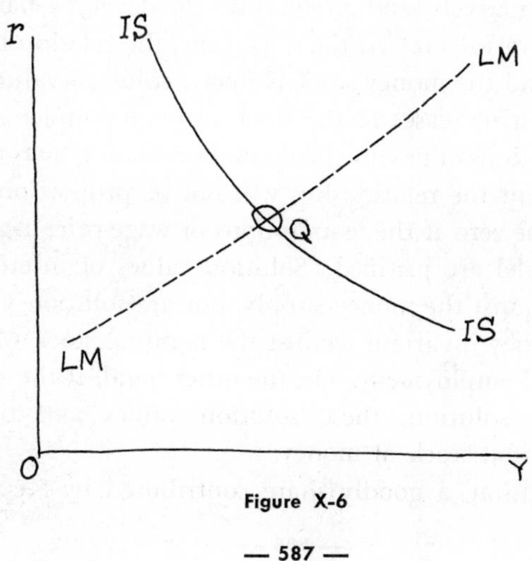

Figure X-6

The downward-sloping curve (the locus of r-Y combinations consistent with clearance of the commodities market) is labelled *IS* in view of the fact that planned savings will be equal to planned investment along this curve. "LM" follows from the fact that the stock of money is consistent with liquidity preference along the upward-sloping curve. (*See Note G.*)

Point Q reveals the unique combination of Y and r consistent with clearance of both the money and commodities markets (and, implicitly, the securities market). In other words, the abscissa value for Q gives effective demand, the ordinate, the solution value for r. (*See Note H.*)

2

The *IS-LM* construction is peculiarly well suited for comparative-statics demonstrations: the impact on the system of changes in the stock of money, the rate of government spending, etc., can be demonstrated in eye-filling ways, and such is the task of Ch. XI which is concerned with meshing fiscal and monetary policy into primary Keynesian models. At this point, we content ourselves with two comments, one concerning the "monetary" character of the Keynesian theory of interest, the other anticipating the formulation of Ch. XI in revealing the graphics of the *IS-LM* approach to "liquidity traps."

3

It has become clear that solution values for security prices in Keynesian systems are in general dependent upon the size of the money stock — or, alternatively and preferably, the level of bank reserves, required-reserve ratios, etc. At the same time, the relationship between the price level and the money stock is shaky: solution values for prices will increase with increases in the stock of money under the *General Theory's* assumptions of flexible prices and decreasing marginal productivity of labor, but the relationship will not be proportional. Indeed, $\partial p^*/\partial \overline{M}$ might be zero if the assumptions of wage-price rigidity of the basic *IS-LM* model are justified. Solution values of interest rates are not invariant against the money supply, nor are solution values of the *real* stock of money invariant against the nominal stock when the system is not at full employment. On the other hand, if the system has a full-employment solution, these solution values *will* be invariant against the nominal stock of money.

Much confusion, a goodly share contributed by Keynes, has attended discussion of Keynesian interest theory. We content ourselves with these observations:

a) the essential Keynesian results are consistent with the first-order conditions of Ch. VII; in solution yields earned at the margin will be equal for all assets (under certainty);

b) the general-equilibrium properties of interest-rate determination hold; there is no special sense in which interest rates are determined by liquidity preference or by the system's transformation possibilities — save for highly-particular specifications.

In sum, Keynesian solutions can be built up from standard micro-economic theory. Attempts to distinguish between "Keynesian" and "classical" theories have been unfortunate, usually leading to crude and misleading distinctions.[32]

4

The diagram below introduces the *IS-LM* construction as a means of tracing comparative statics.

IS-LM CURVES AND THE LIQUIDITY TRAP

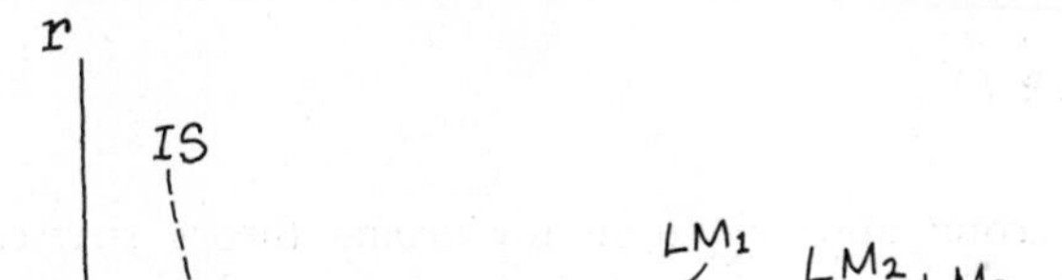

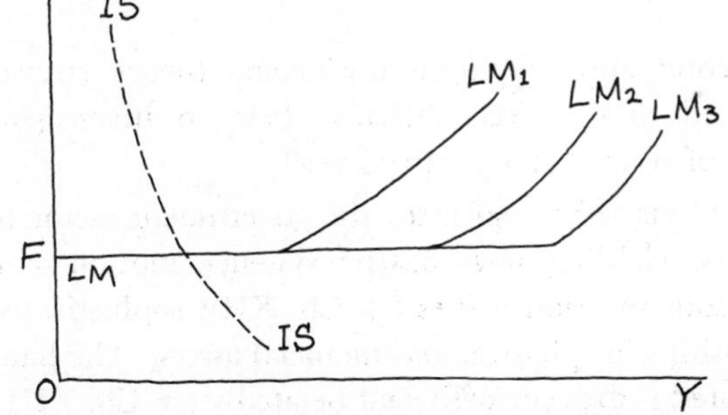

Figure X-7

[32] A signal exception is Robert Clower, "The Keynesian Counterrevolution: A Theoretical Appraisal," a paper, unpublished at the date of this publication, read to the Conference of the International Economic Association at Paris in April 1962. Clower points out that the implicit dynamics of Keynesian systems are more general than in neoclassical systems: quantities (such as *Y*) must be entered in excess-demand functions as well as prices for given initial asset positions.

The curves make clear that rates of interest below $\bar{r}$ are unattainable. (Long rates that is; short rates are ignored.) As one moves rightward from LM_1 to LM_2 to LM_3, the stock of money is increasing so that higher and higher real incomes become consistent with $\bar{r}$. By the time LM_3 is reached, the money stock is consistent with an "undreamed of" rate of income generation: for the plotted *IS* curve, there would be a huge pool of liquidity. Since economic units are indifferent between holding money and securities at the rate $\bar{r}$, the pool easily could be diverted to active balances through bond issues or otherwise. *(See Note* G.) Excluding real-balance effects in non-financial markets, further increases in the stock of money will not stimulate output and employment. Rather "excess liquidity" will increase without affecting interest rates or effective demand. The economy is in a *liquidity trap.* In order to increase effective demand, the *IS* curve must be shifted to the right, a shift that can be accomplished through fiscal policy which must now be relied upon in the absence of a change in expectations — held fixed throughout the analysis of Ch. X. Obviously, we are prepared to introduce a government sector into our models. That is the purpose of Ch. XI. (*See Note J.*)

SUMMARY

1. The second approximation to income theory stressed financial assets and their prices, relating these to investment behavior. Money, of course, is a financial asset.
2. Several facets were neglected: the government sector (*cf.* Ch. XI); dynamics, yielding laws of the system's motion — not just instantaneous solution values (*cf.* Ch. XII); sophisticated stock-flow relationships for physical and financial assets. The banking system was treated rather cursorily and belatedly (*cf.* Ch. XIII).
3. Associations between interest rates and planned expenditure on durables must allow for stochastic elements. Such concepts as "variance" and "certainty equivalent" become relevant. Investment in plant and equipment involves laying out a certain sum for a lottery ticket. The value of the ticket is affected by drawings from Nature's Urn.
4. Once expectations are defined, demand prices can be defined. In

general higher interest rates are associated with lower demand prices.

5. Section C's first model could solve at full employment. (Following Keynes, involuntary unemployment was defined as a state in which more labor could be obtained at the going money-wage rate even if prices increased.) The model demonstrated the interaction of the markets of the system: the solution of a simultaneous-equation system requires a set of values for dependent variables satisfying all of the relationships at once.

6. The basic model was modified to accommodate less-than-full-employment "equilibrium." A rigid wage unit, $\overline{w}$, was introduced, but it was seen that, unless further modifications were made, the model would have little (statical) theoretical interest. Hence, the Keynes effect was considered: the effect of the wage unit on interest rates; a lower wage unit generally leads to lower interest rates.

7. The second approach to financial markets assumed that the price of consols, R_2, was subject to a ceiling determined by limitational factors on liquidity yields from money and bills and/or speculative motives. The liquidity trap was analysed, perhaps *ad nauseum.*

8. Unyielding liquidity preference can prevent even open-market purchases *á outrance* from achieving full employment.[33]

NOTES

NOTE A: The problem can be dealt with more rigorously if the techniques of the stock-flow analysis of Ch. VII are used. (The notation of footnote 5 corresponds to that of Ch. VII.)

(1) $$s_t \equiv f(p_t)$$

(2) $$d_t \equiv x_t + x_t'$$

(3) $$s_t = d_t$$

33 Keynes summarized the *General Theory* at least twice: the *Quarterly Journal of Economics,* 1937, reprinted in Seymour Harris, ed., *The New Economics* (New York: Alfred A. Knopf, Inc., 1947), pp. 181 *ff.*; "The Theory of the Rate of Interest," *The Lessons of Monetary Experience; Essays in Honor of Irving Fisher* (New York: Farrar & Rinehart, 1937), pp. 145-152, reprinted in Fellner and Haley (eds.), *Readings in the Theory of Income Distribution.* These essays are particularly lucid.

The planned rate of output of new machinery depends on its price. The flow rate of demand for new machinery has a user-cost and an investment component. Depreciation is incorporated in x_t. If the planned rate of net investment (x_t) is zero, the rate of demand for new machinery will be equal to the rate at which machinery is being "burned up."

Investment demand is determined by Equation 4

$$x_t' \equiv k(D_t - S_t), \tag{4}$$

where D_t is determined by Equation 5:

$$D_t \equiv g(\bar{r}_t, \bar{w}_t, R_t, u_t). \tag{5}$$

r is "the" rate of interest. R is the rent that can be commanded by machinery, including its shadow rent where appropriate. u is a vector of other variables, including expectational variables. R_t is a function of S_t, *cet. par.* x_t is determined according to Equation 6:

$$x_t \equiv \phi(\bar{w}_t, R_t, \bar{y}_t). \tag{6}$$

This is a very simple formulation stating that user cost is determined by the wage rate, the rent of machinery, and the rate of output. Depreciation is subsumed within user cost.

The statical system is:

$$s_t \equiv f(p_t) \tag{7}$$

$$x_t \equiv s_t \tag{8}$$

$$x_t = \phi(\bar{w}_t, \bar{r}_t, R_t, \bar{y}_t) \tag{9}$$

$$R_t \equiv \psi(S_t) \tag{10}$$

$$D_t = g(\bar{r}_t, R_t, \bar{w}_t, u_t) \tag{11}$$

$$D_t = S_t \tag{12}$$

Six equations in the six unknowns: $s_t, x_t, p_t, D_t, S_t, R_t$. In this partial-equilibrium model, the external rate of return and the rate of aggregate output are exogenous, as is the wage rate. (p_t is the price of machinery; the general price level also is exogenous.)

In the solution, the stock becomes large enough for the rent to fall low enough for there to be no incentive to add to the stock, at the supply price of new machinery. Needless to say, if this model were transformed into a model of the economy, it would be disastrous if the stationary state were being approached *and* if the propensity to save remained positive. Consider also how a lower bound, certainly zero, may be imposed on r . . . The heart of the Keynesian insight can be extracted through this model. The relation of R and S contains the problem of diminishing marginal productivity of capital, if any. We return to this problem in Ch. XII.

The demand curve of the text pertains to the d's (flow-rates) of course.

NOTE B: Planned adjustment of consumer-durable portfolios to interest-rate changes can be analysed in similar terms.

The theoretical analysis is facilitated by assuming that there is a perfect market in rentals so that "convenience yields" become objective market prices. A rise in interest rates has no direct impact on rents in the short run except to the extent that savings decisions are affected: rents will be governed by the fixed supply of sources in the short run. On the other hand, holders of consumer goods (sources of services) can be expected to plan to reduce their holdings in the short run — assuming as we are that consumption and asset-holding decisions are divorced. The demand price for consumer durables will fall until the marginal efficiency of holding these is brought into line with the new structure of interest rates. Alternatively, taking the supply price to be fixed in the short run (including that for newly-produced sources), planned rates of purchase of new sources will decline; net investment will decline and might even become negative.

Assuming that a higher set of interest rates becomes permanently established, in the long run the ratio of rentals to asset prices must increase. Own rates must be higher, *cet. par.* Since this means that rentals, using a standard consumer durable as *numeraire,* must be higher and must in fact increase relative to non-durable prices (it being assumed that costs of production of non-durables, "measured in durables," remain unchanged), substitution effects will work against consumption of services of durables and in favor of nondurables; "equilibrium" stocks of consumer durables will be lower at each point in time; a limitation is imposed on accumulation.

The deflationary effects of the higher interest rates are twofold: (a) the transitional stages find investment decreasing; (b) net investment will be lower in absolute terms at each point in time.

NOTE C: The argument of Section C was based on work by R. W. Clower not yet published (*cf.* footnote 32). He points out that a linear neoclassical model would be of the form

$$(i) \qquad Ap = 0$$

where

$$(ii) \qquad x \equiv Ap,$$

x being a vector of excess demands. An internally consistent neoclassical model must posit auction markets; it cannot rigorously deal with transactions in markets where there is "realized" excess demand (supply).

On the other hand, what Clower calls "Keynesian" models permit traders to be out of plan equilibrium. (However, models in which simultaneous transactions can occur at different prices have not been analysed. Such models would comprise a fuller generalization of Keynesian systems.) In Keynesian models, the jth trader's excess demand function for the ith good at time t is of the form

$$(iii) \qquad x_{ij} \equiv f^{ij}(p; y_j),$$

where y_j is a vector of "income constraints" giving achievable realizations at time t. Thus the worker cannot formulate his consumption plan unless he knows how much employment he will receive at $w(t)$; the analytical basis of consumption-function theory becomes clearer. (Needless to say, imperfect competition or oligopoly constructions easily are accommodated, but the dynamics of competitive markets are such that $p_j(t)$ usually is not a market-clearing price.) "Full employment" is a special state in which the income constraints are not binding or are exactly fulfilled. The models of Ch. X, Section C are formulated in the manner of Equation *iii.*

As for Walras' Law, recall that in the models of Ch. X, Section C, "income constraints" applied only to workers; commodities markets always were cleared. However, we carefully defined planned expenditures of workers as functions of N as well as of w, R, and p (initial assets would enter into neoclassical as well as Keynesian excess demand functions). In a thought experiment in which workers were informed of their constraints, constraints reflecting entrepreneurial plans at the quoted prices, one of the clearance conditions would be otiose in the models of Ch. X, Section C.

Note D: It is important to check our model against the criteria offered by Bushaw and Clower, *op. cit.* *Cf.* also William J. Baumol, "Stocks, Flows, and Monetary Theory," *Quarterly Journal of Economics,* Vol. 76, No. 1 (February 1962), pp. 46-56 for a useful application of the Bushaw-Clower system to monetary theory.

The labor, consumption-good, and investment-good markets are pure flow markets. Recall that in stock-flow models the rate of market demand, $d_i(t)$, can be expressed

$$(i) \qquad d_i(t) \equiv c_i(t) + k_i[D_i(t) - S_i(t)],$$

where $c_i(t)$ gives the time rate of consumption demand for *ith* good, and k_i is a positive fraction relating excess stock demand to a flow rate of investment demand. Denoting the rate of new output as $s_i(t)$, market clearance requires

$$(ii) \qquad d_i(t) = s_i(t).$$

The text's model defines $c_M = s_M = 0$. Clearance of the money market requires that $D_M(t) = S_M(t) = \overline{M}$. Investment demand for money is uniquely zero when excess stock demand is zero (at least if $k_1 = k_2 = \ldots = k_m$).

Of course, $c_B = 0$: bonds are not consumed. We confine ourselves to *a* bond market and follow the text's convention of setting *k*'s equal to unity. Market clearance at a point in time requires that

$$(iii) \qquad s_B(t) = 1[D_B(t) - S_B(t)].$$

The rate of new issue must equal the rate of demand for new securities. Of course, in a growing system investment demand for bonds might continuously be positive.

If $S_B(t)$ is interpreted as the stock in existence at the beginning of the period, the general requirement for market clearance becomes

$$(iv) \qquad s_B(t) = k_B\,[D_B(t) - S_B(t)].$$

The functions of Equations 18 and 19 — $B^d(\quad)$ and $B^s(\quad)$ — should then be interpreted as flows: $s_B \equiv B^s(\quad)$; $k_B[D_B(t) - S_B(t)] \equiv d_B \equiv B^d(\quad)$.

The model can be interpreted in period terms. $D_B(t)$, of course, is *ex ante.* In period terms, it is the sum of *positive* bond holdings planned for the end of the period. $S_B(t)$ *can* be taken as the sum of issues (negative bond holdings) planned for the end of the period. (*Cf.* Baumol, *op. cit.*, pp. 55-56, for a related argument.) Satisfaction of the equality, $S_B(t) = D_B(t)$ can — certainly under our assumption that all *k*'s are unity — be assumed to assure that new issue planned for the period will equal investment demand.

Note E: There is a simpler, easily-graphed, full-employment model. It restores the shmoo as an all-purpose commodity — eliminating complications of multiple manufacturing sectors, albeit at the expense of contradicting earlier analysis of the machinery market. Also some of the richness of texture of a less-aggregated model is lost.

All shmoos must sell at the same price in this formulation. Shmoos now in capital stock can be eaten. In period terms, contracts always are made at the beginning of the period for delivery at its end.

$$K_0(t) = \sum_{-\infty}^{t-1}[Y(t) - C(t)].$$

1

The algebra of the simplified model solving at full employment follows:

LABOR SECTOR (MARKET)

(1′)	$N^s \equiv N^s(w/p)$	
(2′)	$N^d \equiv N^d(w/p)$	
(3′)	$N^s = N^d$	
(4′)	$N^s \equiv N$	or $N^d \equiv N$

COMMODITY (shmoo) SECTOR MARKET

(5′)	$Y \equiv Y(N, K_o)$
(6′)	$C \equiv C(Y, r)$
(7′)	$I \equiv I(Y, r)$
(8′)	$Y = C + I$

MONEY SECTOR (MARKET)

(9′)	$M^d \equiv p.L(Y, r)$
(10′)	$M^s \equiv \overline{M}$
(11′)	$M^d = M^s$

BOND SECTOR (MARKET)

(12′)	$B^d \equiv rp.\Phi^d(Y, r)$
(13′)	$B^s \equiv p.\Phi^s(Y, r)$
(14′)	$B^d = B^s$

No comment is needed for the first four equations. Asset effects are ignored in Equations 6′ and 9′, for example. This is consistent with most Keynesian commentaries and helps graphical treatment. We indicate how asset effects can be introduced at the end of this note. Equation 8′ is the clearance condition for the shmoo market. $L(Y, r)$ gives demand for real cash balances. You will see that this is the case if you divide both sides of Equation 9′ by p. Equation 9′ indicates that demand for nominal balances varies proportionately with the price level. It leads to an internally-contradictory system and will be modified at the end of the Note. Equations 12′ and 13′ imply that the only security in the system is the consol. A unit consol is defined as a promise to pay $1 per year forever. Hence, the nominal value of the stock of consols — the nominal value in absolute terms; the net value is definitionally zero — is B, the number of unit consols, divided by r where the rate of interest is $100r$ per cent per annum. The absolute real value of the consol stock is B/rp so that $\Phi^d(Y, r)$ and $\Phi^s(Y, r)$ are functional relationships determining demand and supply for *real* bond stocks (at the end of the period). In the text we defined $B^d(\quad)$ and $B^s(\quad)$ in flow terms. *Cf.* Baumol reference, Note D. (Note that some households may plan to direct savings directly into purchase of equity in machinery rather than in bonds.)

The 14 equations of the system are used to determine solution values for the 13 unknowns: N^s, N^d, N, w, p, Y, C, I^r, M^d, M^s, B^d, and B^s. It is easy to show, of course, that one of the market-clearance conditions is otiose. It remains to show what factors might intervene to prevent realization of full-employment potential.

The graphics of the system of Note E are marvelously simple: the system is recursive; it can be solved piece by piece, plugging solution values of the first piece into the second, etc.

THE LABOR MARKET

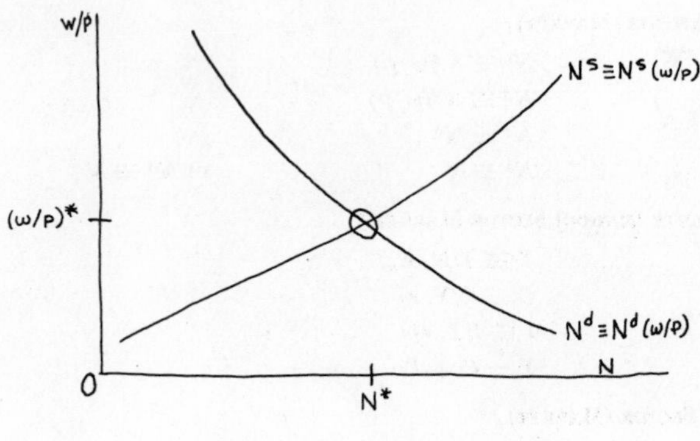

Diagram A — Figure X-8

Diagram A provides enough information to determine solution values for the rate of employment and the real-wage rate.

DETERMINATION OF Y* THROUGH THE PRODUCTION FUNCTION

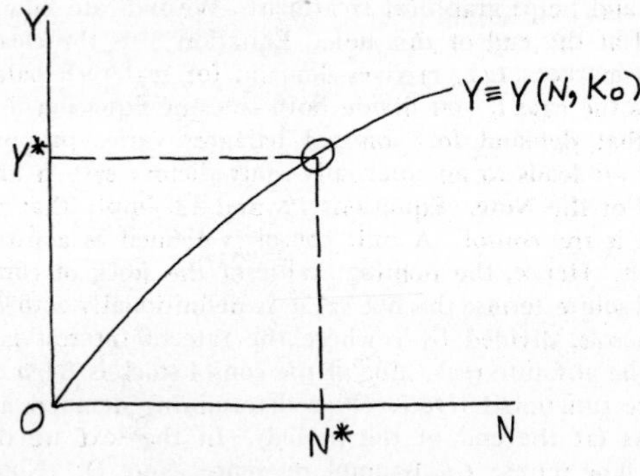

Diagram B — Figure X-9

Y^* (equal to gross income: we ignore user cost and depreciation) is determined. It is convenient to define $S = S(Y^*, r)$, where S is the planned rate of saving, definitionally equal to $Y^* - C$, where C is the planned rate of consumption. Of course, if $S = I$ (the planned rate of investment), the commodity market will be in balance. Savings are like leakage of water from a tub and investment like inflow into the tub; the level of water in the tub will remain constant when the two flows are equal.

DETERMINATION OF SOLUTION VALUE FOR r

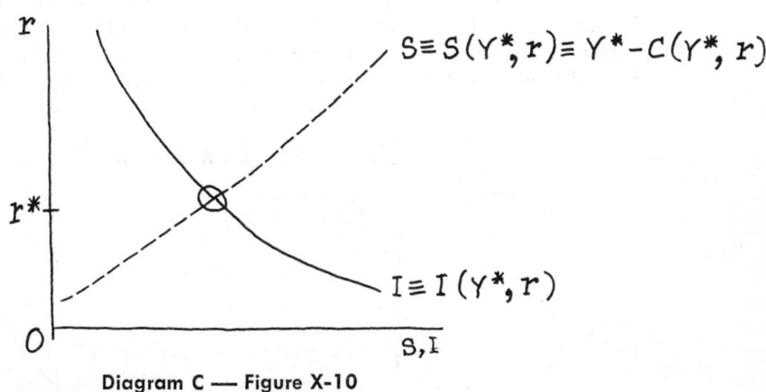

Diagram C — Figure X-10

As is indicated in Diagram C, $S = Y^* - C$, so that, if $S = I$, $Y^* - C = I$ and $C + I = Y^*$. *Q. E. D.* . . . Savings and investment variables are *ex ante*. It is commonly stated that, at $r = r^*$, full-employment income generates planned saving equal to planned investment. The rub might be in Diagram C, but more of that anon.

DETERMINATION OF THE PRICE LEVEL THROUGH THE MONETARY EQUATIONS

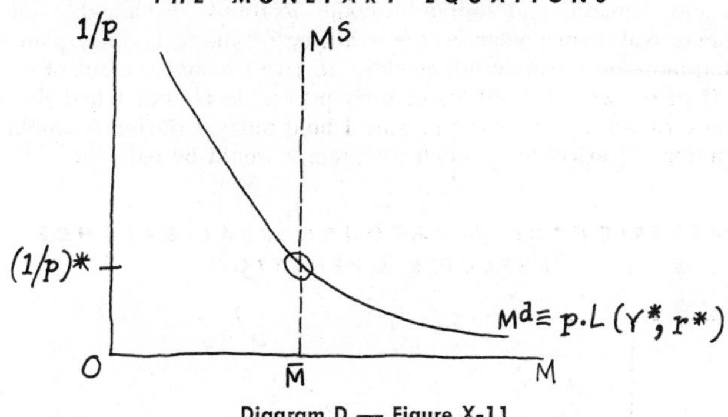

Diagram D — Figure X-11

Diagram D reveals that (M^d) $(1/p)$ is constant for $Y = Y^*$ *and* $r = r^*$: desired real money balances are invariant against the price level. $(M)(1/p) = k$ describes a rectangular hyperbola.

We solve the equation $\overline{M} = p.L(Y^*, r^*)$. The recursiveness of the system has permitted us to solve for the variables *seriatim,* save for B^d and B^s.

Values for B^d and B^s immediately emerge upon plugging r^*, p^*, and Y^* into Equations 12′ and 13′. The equality of B^d and B^s is assured by Walras' Law. The solution is completed.

2

Less-than-full-employment "solutions" of the system can be traced out and the real-balance effect introduced through a diagrammatic scheme based on

Don Patinkin, "Price Flexibility and Full Employment," *American Economic Review,* Vol. 38 (1948), pp. 543-564, reprinted in Lutz and Mints (eds.), *Readings in Monetary Theory,* pp. 252-283 and *Money, Interest, and Prices,* pp. 166-169. Consider Diagram C. Assume that the intersection of the *S* and *I* curves does not take place in the positive quadrant. Compare Diagram E. (*Also see Note K.*)

REVISED DIAGRAM D

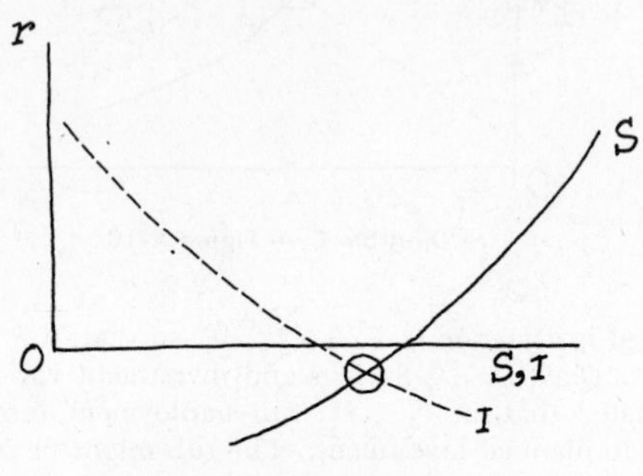

Diagram E — Figure X-12

We are brought down in a heap: admissible solution values must be positive. Now introduce wealth variables into the consumption, investment, demand-for-money, and demand- and supply-for-bonds relations. Presumably the greater the value of real money balances, the wealthier people feel. They plan to spend more and more on consumption goods — to save less and less out of current income. If prices were 1/1,000,000 of their present level, and I had the nominal cash (more rigorously, currency) balance I hold today, I obviously would step up my spending. If prices fell enough, Diagram E would be redrawn:

REVISION OF D THROUGH REAL-BALANCE EFFECT'S OPERATION

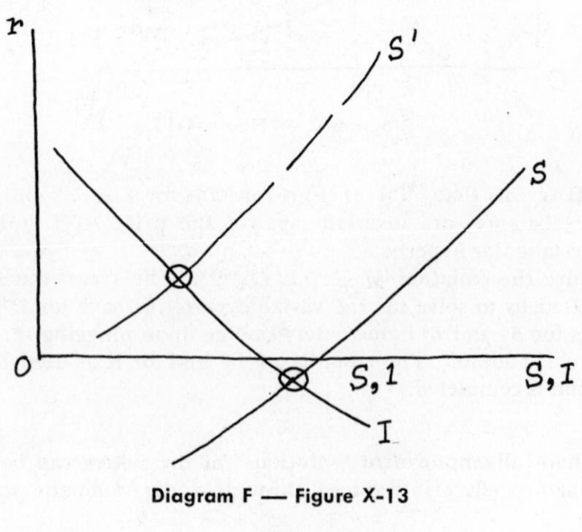

Diagram F — Figure X-13

Diagram G shows another way to get this result. Z is aggregate demand; Y, aggregate supply. The commodity (shmoo) market cannot be cleared unless $Z = Y$. Effective demand will be that rate of output consistent with intersection of the Z-function with the 45° line. For arbitrary values of r and p, the intersection can occur short of Y^*, full-employment output. Hold r fixed at $\bar{r}$. Still, if p is low enough, say, equal to p^2, the demand-for-all-goods function can be shoved upwards so that intersection with the 45° line is at $Y = Y^*$.

The special form of the curve of Diagram D disappears under the new assumption (the assumption that there are asset effects operating on the demand for goods, money, and securities). As a matter of fact, since M/p is an additional argument in the function $L(\quad)$, the geometry in two dimensions becomes unmanageable.

OPERATION OF THE REAL-BALANCE EFFECT

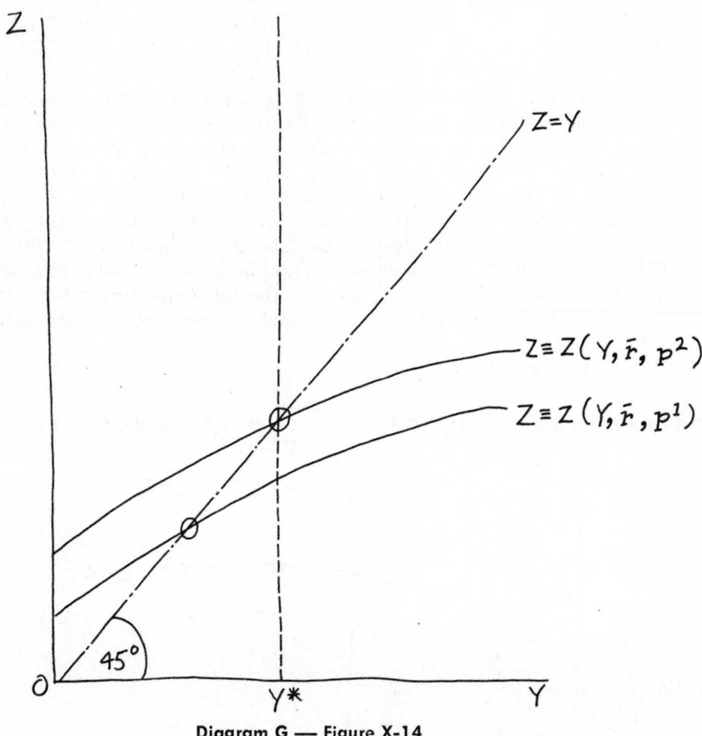

Diagram G — Figure X-14

Consider the reduced form of a system without money illusion. (Economic units are indifferent between alternatives in which factor and product prices and nominal money balances and nominal bond holdings — positive or negative — are proportionately changed.) Thus,

$$y^*_i \equiv f^i(z) \qquad i = 1, 2, \ldots, n$$

where the n y's are endogenous variables and z is a vector of the m predetermined or exogenous variables. One of the endogenous variables is p, the price of shmoos. Consider the rth equation

$$p^* \equiv f^r(\overline{M}; z')$$

where z' is a vector of exogenous variables other than the stock of fiat paper money. Ch. X has shown that

$$\partial p^* / \partial M \equiv k.$$

Solution values for p are proportional with the money stock, M. (*Cf.* Appendix A, Ch. VA.) This result does not depend on peculiar properties of demand for money: only on the absence of money illusion; a form of the quantity theory of money.

NOTE F: The model of p. 583 can be again restated, conforming to approach (b), but permitting nicely recursive treatment, easily exhibited graphically. Very little comment beyond that of the text is required.

I.	$r = \bar{r}$	VI.	$N \equiv N^d$
II.	$C \equiv C(Y, r)$	VII.	$N^d \equiv N^d(\overline{w}/p)$
III.	$I \equiv I(Y, r)^{\dagger}$	VIII.	$N^s \equiv N^s(\overline{w}/p)$
IV.	$Y = C + I$	IX.	$N^s - N^d \equiv U$
V.	$Y \equiv Y(N, K)$		

The method of solution of system I-IX is rather neat. Plug $\bar{r}$ into Equations II, III, and IV. These became a set of three equations in the unknowns Y, C, and I, recalling that IV is a market-clearance condition. This determines effective demand, Y^* as well as C^* and I^*. Plug Y^* into the production function, Equation V, recalling that the capital stock is predetermined. Out pops N^*. Substitute N^* for N^d in VII and solve for p. The solution value, p^*, is the price level consistent with demand for labor being equal to N^*. Plug p^* into VIII, solving for N^*, the maximum amount of labor obtainable at $\overline{w}/p^*$. There is enough information to determine U, the difference between the maximum amount of labor obtainable at $\overline{w}/p^*$ and the amount of labor actually demanded.

These are the graphics:

DETERMINATION OF C*, I*, AND Y*, ONCE r IS KNOWN

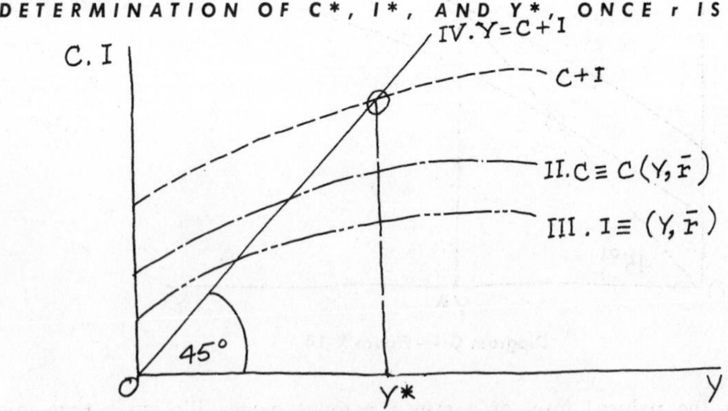

Diagram A — Figure X-15

† Rigor would require that the capital stock be included in this function. Then accelerator effects are encompassed. Also incentives for deepening provided by lower interest rates. Of course, capital stock at time t is a parameter of the system.

DETERMINATION OF N* THROUGH THE PRODUCTION FUNCTION

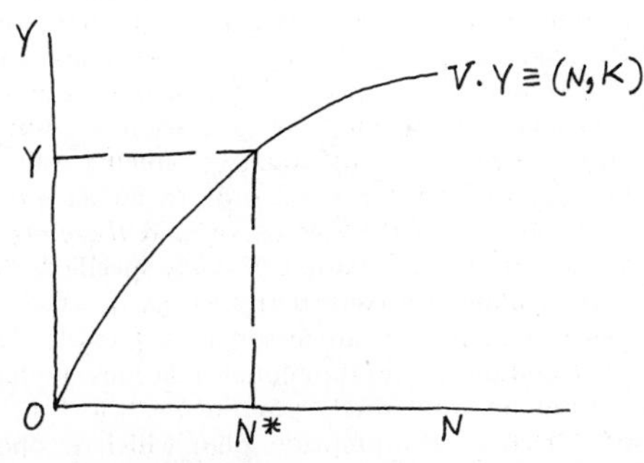

Diagram B — Figure X-16

DETERMINATION OF p*, N*, AND U

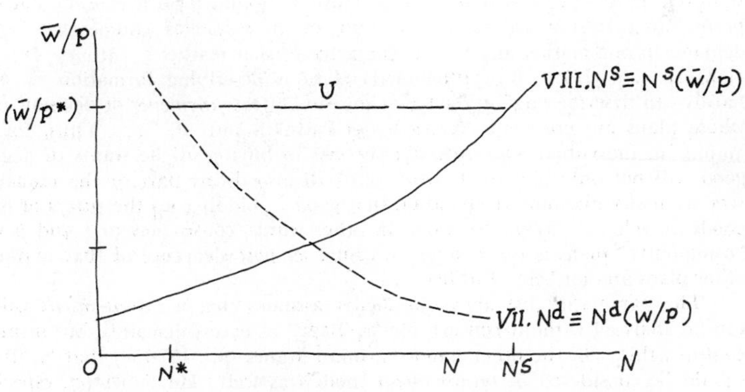

Diagram C — Figure X-17

This model has the authentic Keynesian flavor. It jibes almost perfectly with Keynes's summary of his theory. (*Cf. General Theory,* pp. 245-254.) There is an underlying assumption that the money stock is set at a high enough level to permit *the* interest rate to fall to $\bar{r}$. (The long rate presumably is meant.)

The real-bills doctrine, in the sense of treating the money stock as an endogenous variable, has valid application under liquidity-trap conditions. The quantity of currency and demand deposits in the hands of the public will respond passively to their demand.

The stability of the model of Note F seems safe. As in the case of the first approximation, there is a downward-sloping demand-for-all-goods function (of p) and an upward-sloping supply-of-all-goods function (of p). Money wages and interest rates are held rigid throughout, the context being "underemployment equilibrium."

Note G: More formally, in the *IS-LM* analysis we are concerned with three subsets in the *Y-r* space: *(Y-r)* points consistent with fulfillment of plans for production, sale, and purchase of commodities; points consistent with plans for holding money balances; points consistent with plans for purchase and sale of new securities and holding and disposal of old securities. These subsets are nothing other than the *IS, LM,* and *ZZ* curves. (It happens that *ZZ* never is drawn.) Any pair of these curves has one and only one intersection — point *Q*.

The curves are based on *m* individual experiments where there are *m* decision units. They are to be interpreted only in an *ex ante* (planned) sense. Thus, a point on the *IS* but off the *LM* curve (and *therefore* the *ZZ* curve) reflects that, if the particular combination Y_o-r_o is specified, "commodities" but not "money-securities" plans are consistent with each other. This specification is not to be thought of as part of an historical sequence. The analysis is emphatically statical. Similarly, the functional relations underlying the *IS-LM* construction are based on individual experiments: the function $C = C(Y, r)$ tells us about a "collective" consumption plan which is one of a number of plans that would be made if individuals were faced with various *Y-r* combinations. It has no interpretation other than in an *ex ante* sense; being one of a number of plans, the consumption plan can describe consumption behavior only if *all* plans are fulfilled.

Whatever rigorous dynamical content can be supplied to *IS-LM* and *CC-LL* systems probably requires assumption of a *tatonnement* process. However, stability analysis such as that of Note J usually glides by this *caveat.* Patinkin points out that standard stability analysis of these systems assume that "excess demand in one market affects only the price of that market." [*Money, Interest, and Prices,* p. 157.] But, functional relations describing formation of plans hardly can describe ongoing behavior (outside of *tatonnement*) of decision units whose plans are not being realized. As Patinkin puts it, ". . . Thus, for example, an individual who does not succeed in buying all he wants of a given good will not only bid up its price but will also divert part of the money he was originally planning to spend on that good to bidding up the prices of other goods as well . . ." (*Ibid.,* p. 157). In other words, consistency of *r* and *p* with "commodity" plans is not enough to assure *ex post* clearance of that market if other plans are not being fulfilled.

The paragraph just above implicitly assumes that a *tatonnement* process can be analysed without concern for "spillage" of excess demand. My intuition confirms this. On the other hand, Patinkin argues (pp. 157-158) that "spillage" should be considered in *tatonnement* models as well. He shows (*cf.* especially pp. 342-344) that the basic *CC-BB* model is stable on the "no-spillage" assumption, but states that "it follows [from 'spillage'] that the *tatonnement* will not necessarily succeed in reaching the equilibrium values of the economy; that . . . the system is not necessarily stable . . . In what follows we shall disregard this possibility . . . [b]ut this stability is now a matter of assumption — not a matter of proof." (*Ibid.,* p. 158.) I think Patinkin here is wrong.

Note H: The *IS-LM* formulation is consistent with price flexibility:

(1)	$N^d \equiv N^d(\overline{w}/p)$	*(5)*	$Y = C + I$
(2)	$Y \equiv Y(N^d, K)$	*(6)*	$M^d \equiv p.L(Y, r)$
(3)	$C \equiv C(Y, r)$	*(7)*	$M^s \equiv \overline{M}$
(4)	$I \equiv I(Y, r)$	*(8)*	$M^d = M^s$

The first subset contains Equations 1-5 in the six unknowns *Y, C, I, r, p,* and N^d. It can, of course, yield the reduced equation

$$(i') \qquad f(r, Y) = 0.$$

transformable into an *IS* curve. It also yields the reduced equation

$$(i'') \qquad F(p, Y) = 0.$$

Indeed, i'' can be inferred trom Equations 1 and 2 alone.

The second subset, comprised of Equations 6-8, deals with the money market. Its three equations in five unknowns can be reduced to one equation in three unknowns, say r, Y, and p:

$$(i) \qquad h(r, Y, p) = 0.$$

This is the *LM* function. Rewrite it in explicit form

$$(ii) \qquad r = H(Y, p).$$

Draw-up the *LM* curve by choosing values for Y at will and substituting values for p consistent with Equations 1 and 2 — equations governing entrepreneurial demand for labor and production possibilities. The values for p in Y-p pairs cannot be chosen arbitrarily. Equation *ii* can be rewritten

$$(iii) \qquad r = H[Y, F(Y)],$$

or simply

$$(iv) \qquad r = J(Y).$$

It shows combinations of r and Y consistent with clearance of the money market.

Fortunately we can make do with the rigid-price assumptions of the text without serious substantive loss.

NOTE I: There are a number of ways in which the liquidity trap might be treated formally. 1) A set-theoretic statement can be made of the "indifference" model of the text. Mitchell Harwitz does this below. 2) A *deus ex machina* can be summoned, permitting excess supply in the money market and excess demand in the securities markets with rigid prices in these markets and without effect in the "real" markets. 3) An "asymptotic" approach can be substituted for the "sheer" liquidity trap.

1) *Indifference, a set-theoretic approach* [*by Mitchell Harwitz*]

To define an equilibrium situation in which the money demand function and bond demand and supply functions are multiple-valued in a relevant way, one may construct these functions, denoted by Φ_M, Φ^D_{Bj}, and Φ^S_{Bj}. Φ is in general a function that maps a vector of prices and interest rates (p, r) into a set of money demand values (bond demand values, bond supply values). Treating money first

$$\Phi_M:(p, r) \rightarrow \subset M^d \;\; R \qquad (p \geqslant, o, r >, \bar{r})$$

with the property that for any p,

$$\Phi_M(p, r) = \{M^d\} \qquad r > \bar{r}$$

$$\Phi_M(p, \bar{r}) = \{M^d \mid M^d/M^d = M^d_o(t),\ t \in [1, \infty] \quad M^d_o = \lim_{h \to o} \phi_M(p, \bar{r}+h)\}$$

Equilibrium requires

$$M \in \Phi_M(p, r).$$

Φ^D_{Bj}, Φ^S_{Bj} can be similarly defined functions for the *jth* security market, and equilibrium requires that the equilibrium

$$B^*_j \in \Phi^{D\prime}_{Bj} \cap \Phi^S_{Bj}.$$

D S

2) *Deus ex Machina*

Assume there is excess supply of securities (and physical assets) regardless of the value of M at a yield as low as $\hat{r}$. It is immediately established that $\hat{r}$ is unattainable unless the authorities purchase "everything." But effective demand might fall short of full-employment income for $r > \hat{r}$ but not for $r = r' < \hat{r}$; liquidity preference might prevent attainment of full employment.

Clearly, we must work with $r > \hat{r}$, say, $r = \bar{r}$. Since we wish to deal with a dead end of monetary policy, $\bar{r}$ should be very close to $\hat{r}$. How can we be sure that $\bar{r}$ will be maintained even if bank reserves, for example, are vastly increased? Introduce a *deus ex machina.* Assume that "the" interest rate can only move in 1/8's and that $\bar{r}$ is less than 1/8 point above $\hat{r}$. Then increases in the stock of money or — more sophisticatedly — bank reserves, lead to excess supply of money and excess demand for bonds. However, it is assumed that there is no spillover into the commodity markets, a perfectly "obvious" assumption if we work with a pure-credit money. Hence, excess supply of money, accompanied by excess demand for bonds is, in these circumstances, "harmless."

3) *An asymptotic approach*

Work with a liquidity-preference function (in ρ-M space) asymptotically approaching $\bar{r}$. Omit $\hat{r}$ from the discussion. Here, increases in the money supply always lead to *some* decrease in r^*, but the decrease approaches zero in the limit. This approach has a didactic disadvantage: we must speak of "slight" or "meaningless" effects instead of *nil* effects from changes in the money supply. Of course, if $\bar{r}$ exceeds the "natural" rate, this didactic disadvantage hardly is decisive.

The "asymptotic" approach has the important advantage of being more amenable to classical mathematical analysis.

NOTE J: The text does not consider the stability properties of the *IS-LM* model. *Cf.* Don Patinkin, *Money, Interest, and Prices,* p. 228 and p. 366. "Standard" assumptions find the solution to be stable.

There are two approaches, one substantially verbal and geometrical, the other analytic. Taking up the first approach, let us assume that the appropriate dynamical laws are

(i) $dr/dt = f(X^B)$, *(ii)* $dY/dt = g(X^C)$,

namely that the time rate of change of the rate of interest is a function of excess demand in the bond market and that the time rate of change of output is a function of excess demand in the commodity market (recalling that prices are held fixed). If you wish to study the intricacies of these equations see G. L. S. Shackle, "Recent Theories Concerning the Nature and Role of Interest," *Economic Journal,* Vol. 71, June 1961, pp. 209-254, references 11-16, and 24, pp. 252-253.

Following Hugh Rose ("Liquidity Preference and Loanable Funds," *Review of Economic Studies,* Vol. 24, Feb. 1957), we can equate excess supply of money with excess demand for bonds (measured in dollars). A state of excess supply in the commodity market implies piling up of unplanned inventories or windfall losses requiring finance in a dollar amount exactly equal to the initial discrepancy in planned saving and planned investment. Hence, excess supply in the commodity market implies "finance" bond issues on the part of firms just equal to the excess of savings over *ex ante* investment that can be taken as a first approximation to excess of demand over initially-planned supply of securities. (If firms plan to reduce cash balances in order to carry inventory, there will be direct impact on the "money market.") A state of excess demand in the commodity market implies unplanned decumulation of inventories, reducing finance requirements *pari passu* with the dollar value of the excess of *ex ante* investment over planned saving . . . Thus, we can resort to the diagram below, implicitly rewriting Equation *i*

$$(i'')\ dr/dt = h(X^M).$$

The sign of ongoing excess demand in the securities market *can* be determined exclusively by *ex ante* excess demand in the money market.

STABILITY OF THE IS-LM SYSTEM

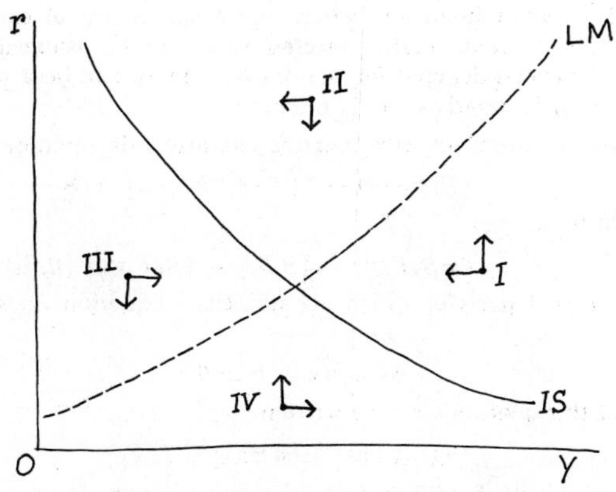

Figure X-18

The space has been divided into four sectors. Sector I features excess supply of commodities and excess demand for money (excess supply of securities). Sector II, excess supply of commodities and excess supply of money (excess demand for securities). Sector III, excess demand for commodities and excess supply of money (excess demand for securities). Sector IV, excess demand for commodities and excess demand for money (excess supply of securities). The arrows indicate the movements of output and interest rates in accordance with the dynamical laws of the system:

". . . [T]here always exist automatic market forces to drive at least one of the variables in the direction of its equilibrium value. Hence the system is stable and converges to the equilibrium point." (Patinkin, *op. cit.*, p. 228.)

The mathematical approach is suggested by Patinkin, *op. cit.*, p. 366. Represent aggregate demand for goods as

(iii) $$Z \equiv F(Y, r)$$

so that clearance of the commodity market requires that

(iv) $$F(Y, r) - Y = 0.$$

Since the planned *net* value of bond holdings must be zero in equilibrium (as is *always* the case *ex post*), Equation *v* gives the condition for clearance of the bond market. If *iv* and *v* hold, clearance of the money market is assured.

(v) $$B(Y, r) = 0.$$

By assumption, $\partial F/\partial Y$, denoted F_1 is a positive fraction. It is assumed that a dollar's worth of extra output generates less than a dollar's worth of extra spending. Also by assumption, $\partial B/\partial Y = 0$, $(B_1 = 0)$, an assumption that might be based on Rose. The system is assumed to operate according to the dynamical laws

(vi) $$dY/dt = \beta_1[F(\quad) - Y]$$

(vii) $$dr/dt = \beta_2[B(\quad)]$$

where β_1 and β_2 are positive constants. Form the expression

$$|A| = \begin{vmatrix} F_1 - 1 & F_2 \\ 0 & B_2 \end{vmatrix}$$

where $|A|$ is a determinant and where the elements are, of course, partial derivatives. B_2 is positive: higher interest rates can be assumed to lead to an increase in the excess demand for bonds. F_1 is known to be a positive fraction. Hence $(F_1-1)(B_2)$ is negative; $|A|$ is negative.

The stability condition requires that the characteristic equation

(viii) $$[\beta_1(F_1-1) - \lambda] - [\beta_2 B_2 - \lambda] = 0$$

which might be written

(ix) $$\lambda^2 + \lambda[-\beta_1(F_1-1) + [\beta_2 B_2] - [\beta_1(F_1-1)]\,[\beta_2 B_2] = 0,$$

has roots the real parts of which are negative. Equation *ix* is of the general form

(x) $$\lambda^2 + a\lambda + b = 0.$$

The roots of this quadratic can be written

(xi) $$\lambda_1, \lambda_2 = \tfrac{1}{2}(-a \pm \sqrt{a^2 - 4b}).$$

Inspection of *ix* will show that *a* necessarily is positive. If the expression under the radical is negative, the real part of the roots, —*a* must, of course, be negative. If the expression under the radical is positive, the absolute value of the negative root will exceed that of the positive root (taking the most unfavorable case, $\sqrt{}$exceeding *a*) ; the negative root will dominate. Local stability is assured.

Needless to say, rigorous interpretation of this "stability analysis" requires *tatonnement*. This is more an exercise than a serious attempt at dynamical theory.

NOTE K: The reader can profitably consult Martin J. Bailey, *National Income and the Price Level* (New York: McGraw-Hill Book Co., Inc., 1962), especially pp. 100-116.

At pp. 112-114, Bailey takes up assets that cannot be produced. For these assets, production costs cannot set upper bounds on asset prices. Thus, if ratios of expected site rents to land prices become low enough (as could happen if bond yields become low enough and the supply of money large enough), owners of land could afford to plan to sell off bits of land, planning to live in baronial splendor on the proceeds for centuries. (For produced assets, and measuring in wage units, a "very low" yield, say 0.001, requires that expected future rentals be "very low"; but shadow rents on idle equipment already are zero; effects on demand for produced assets can be negligible during bad trade. Site rents, however, will be little affected by interest rates; prices of sites will soar.)

Bailey points out that, at *very low* long-term rates of interest, investment opportunities such as coast-line fill-ins almost certainly could become highly attractive, and would absorb unemployment. (*Cf.* p. 103 *ff.*) Of course, it might take a long while for such response to become operational. Nevertheless, Bailey correctly focuses attention on dynamical phenomena rather than "existence" questions through this intriguing argument.

CHAPTER ELEVEN

The Third Approximation to Income Theory

A. INTRODUCTION

Chapter XI does not contribute new analytical devices. It contains no wholly new concepts. Rather it accounts for the impact of the *fiscal* authorities; it introduces the government sector. And it introduces *automatic stabilization,* very important since World War II. At the end of the chapter, synthetic policies — combinations of monetary and fiscal measures — are discussed.

The chapter's argument is an extension of the theory of instantaneous equilibrium pursued in Chs. IX and X. Thus, the relationship of fiscal policy[1] to time paths of national income and employment is neglected in Ch. XI, although taken up, at least inferentially, in Ch. XII.

B. MULTIPLIER THEORY AND ALPHABET SOUP

1

The *multiplier* intrigues economists. Keynes writes that the investment multiplier ". . . tells us that, when there is an increment of

1 Think of fiscal policy as being concerned with actions registered in the government's budget, in contrast with monetary policy measures — ideally not reflected in the budget.

aggregate investment, income will rise by an amount which is k times the increment of investment."[2] The origin of multiplier theory, at least in explicit form, is R. F. Kahn's celebrated article, "The Relation of Home Investment to Unemployment."[3] The multiplier's intrigue might stem from the *leverage* factor implicit in the Keynesian definition: it is striking that a firm's decision to spend $1 less on plant and equipment *might* lead to a reduction in annual national product of $4 or $5; that a government might spend $1 for otherwise idle labor, employing it to dig holes and fill them in again, with a consequent increase in national product of $4 or $5.

2

I am concerned with the "logical" as against the period multiplier. Multiplier theory is treated as a problem in comparative statics, at least until Ch. XII. Ch. XI introduces the multiplier as a problem in analysis of reduced forms of economic models. (*See Note A.*)

The kind of question asked in Ch. XI is: what will be the effect on the solution value for output if autonomous expenditure increased by $x? The answer requires that we consult the system's reduced form. Recall what is a reduced form. Consider a system of the general structure

$$(i) \qquad f^i(y_1\, y_2, \ldots, y_n; z_1, \ldots, z_m) = 0 \qquad i = 1, 2, \ldots, n$$

The system contains n independent restrictions upon the endogenous variables, the y's. The z's are autonomous or predetermined. In general, each set of z's leads to a different solution vector, y^*. Solution values of the endogenous variables can be expressed as functions of the exogenous variables,

$$(ii) \qquad y_i^* \equiv g^i(z_1, z_2, \ldots, z_m). \qquad i = 1, 2, \ldots, n$$

If linearized, the relationship can be written

$$(iii) \qquad y^* \equiv Bz.$$

Systems *ii* and *iii* are *reduced forms.* Their equations are not to be interpreted as assertions about economic behavior; these are not demand and supply relations, or anything of the kind. But Systems *ii* and *iii* do imply all that is important to know about logical multipliers.

2 *General Theory,* p. 115.

3 *Economic Journal,* June 1931.

3

Consider a model that is little more than a primitive version of the models of the first approximation to income theory. Assume that the stock of money is large enough to permit interest rates to fall to the limiting vector $\bar{r}$ and that wages and prices are rigid. Assume further that expansion of output and employment can be accomplished without interest rates rising, due either to the nature of monetary policy or the size of the initial money stock. The model can be written

$$C \equiv C(Y, \bar{r}) \tag{1}$$

$$I \equiv \bar{I} \tag{2}$$

$$Y = C + I \tag{3}$$

Equations 1 and 2 are behavioral relations: consumption and investment expenditures are distinguished according to the mathematical law they obey; Equation 1 is the consumption function. Equation 3 is the clearance condition for the commodity market; $dY/dt = f(X^c)$. The reduced-form equations of the system are

$$C^* \equiv g^1(\bar{I}, \bar{r}) \tag{4}$$

$$Y^* \equiv g^1(\bar{I}, \bar{r}) + \bar{I} \tag{5}$$

Linearizing the consumption function so that Equation 1′ applies,

$$C \equiv \beta_0 + \beta_1 Y, \tag{1'}$$

where β_1 is a positive fraction, Y^* can be obtained by solving the reduced-form Equation 6,

$$Y^* \equiv \beta_0 + \bar{I} + \beta_1 Y^*, \tag{6}$$

or

$$Y^*(1 - \beta_1) \equiv \beta_0 + \bar{I}, \tag{6'}$$

so that

$$Y^* \equiv \frac{\beta_0 + \bar{I}}{(1 - \beta_1)} \,. \tag{6''}$$

(Of course, in general β_0 and/or β_1 might be functions of r.)

A multiplier can be calculated from, say, Equation 6″. The autonomous expenditure elements of the system are β_0 and $\bar{I}$. Write $A \equiv \beta_0$. Equation 6″ now reads

$$Y^* \equiv A/(1-\beta_1). \tag{6''}$$

$dY^*/dA \equiv 1/(1-\beta_1)$. The system's investment multiplier is $1/(1-\beta_1)$, where β_1 is the marginal propensity to consume: a dollar's worth of increase in autonomous spending leads to $1/(1-\beta_1)$ dollars increase in "equilibrium" output.[3a]

4

What a strange business it is to differentiate solution values with respect to autonomous variables which, in some sense, are to be *fixed* in the analysis. But the sense in which I is fixed at $t = \tau$ is that nothing happening within the system affects $I(\tau)$; forces determining I operate independently of forces specified in the model. (Resort to a time-honored exogenous variable: rainfall in a wheat economy, *sans* cloud-seeding or belief in God.) Surely there is no difficulty in conceiving of the dependence of equilibrium price on rainfall. Rainfall is a parameter of the system: it is fixed in any one specification; it varies from specification to specification.

> ". . . an economic system consists of a designated set of unknowns which are constrained as a condition of equilibrium to satisfy an equal number of consistent and independent equations . . . These are implicitly assumed to hold within a certain environment and as of certain data. Some parts of these data are introduced as explicit parameters; and, as a result of our equilibrium conditions, our unknown variables may be expressed in function of these parameters . . .
>
> The method of *comparative statics* consists of the study of the responses of our equilibrium unknowns to designated changes in parameters . . ."[4]

5

Empirical work on the consumption function (discussed in this chapter's Appendix) suggests that values for β_1 between 0.75 and 0.90 could appropriately be assumed, implying investment multipliers between 4 and 10 for the simple model. Yet empirical estimates of the American investment multiplier for postwar years zero-in within a 1.5 to 1.8 range. What accounts for the discrepancy? The answer is tied to the "bath-tub motif" of multiplier models. Recall what it is (its

---

[3a] Of course, β_o is a parameter of the system. Equation 5 might read

$$Y^* \equiv g'(\bar{I}, \beta_o, \bar{\tau}) + \bar{I}. \tag{5}$$

$$\partial Y^*/\partial \beta_o \equiv \partial Y^*/\partial \bar{I}.$$

[4] Paul A. Samuelson, *Foundations of Economic Analysis* (Cambridge: Harvard University Press, 1947), pp. 10-20, at pp. 19-20.

origins are due to Professor Boulding). View the rate of income generation as the level of water in the tub. Assume that autonomous expenditure is pouring into the tub at a given rate, and that leakage — determined by the level of water in the tub and contributed by saving and like factors — passes through the drain. If the level, Y, is multiplied by some positive fraction, $s \equiv (1-\beta_1)$, the rate of leakage, sY, is obtained. The system's equilibrium finds the level of water in the tub constant, implying that the rate of flow of autonomous expenditure is balanced by the rate of leakage. If the rate of flow of autonomous expenditure is stepped up, the level of water in the tub can increase by $[1/(1-\beta_1)][d\bar{I}]$ units; only then will additional leakage offset the added inflow. On the other hand, if the marginal rate of leakage is increased, two things follow: (a) a given rate of inflow of autonomous expenditure will sustain a lower level of water in the tub; (b) a given increase or decrease in the rate of inflow of autonomous expenditure will lead to less response in the equilibrium level of water than had been the case; the rate of change of the multiplier as a function of the marginal propensity to save $(1-\beta_1)$ is $(-s^{-2})$.

6

The transition is completed. Clearly, changes in the rate of government spending can change the solution value for output (income). Changes in leakage factors can induce changes in the value of the multiplier. The first result need not be elaborated now: if the government wishes to increase enough its rate of expenditure — taken as a component of $\bar{I}$ — it can achieve a full-employment rate of income in this model. Assume that all expenditures are financed by borrowing, and that the stock of money is large enough to satisfy liquidity preference at the "fixed" interest rate, although the initial increment of government expenditure is financed by "idle" cash.[5] Once income increases to the equilibrium level consistent with the permanent increase in government expenditure, ΔG, sufficient additional savings will exactly offset the increase in expenditure. The permanent increase in the rate of issue of securities (to finance the deficit) is just offset by increased demand for securities.[6] *(See Note D.)*

5 Neither money balances nor Government securities enter into the consumption function.

6 For simplicity, increased demand for money balances is abstracted from. The banking system is assumed willing and able to accommodate increased demand for cash at $\bar{r}$; it will supply cash for securities.

The simplicity of the relationship of Y^* and G is disturbed by "more realistic" assumptions. What if we were to retain the simple model, add a government-expenditure variable, and require that the government always balance its budget by collecting taxes at the same rate, T, as its expenditures on goods and services?[7] The answer — containing the elementary balanced-budget-multiplier theorem due to Salant — can be developed through a linearized model:[8]

$$(7)^9 \qquad C = \beta_1 Y^d$$

$$(8) \qquad Y^d = Y - T$$

$$(9) \qquad T = \overline{G}$$

$$(10) \qquad Y = C + \overline{G} + \overline{I}$$

Y^d is *disposable income*, defined by Equation 8; disposable income is obtained by subtracting T from Y. Equation 9 imposes the balanced-budget requirement. Equation 10's satisfaction assures clearance of the commodity market. The system can be reduced to a single equation expressing Y^* as a function of the system's parameters and of T:

$$(11) \qquad Y^* \equiv \frac{\overline{G} + \overline{I} - \beta_1 T}{(1-\beta_1)}.$$

It follows that

$$(12) \qquad dY^* \equiv (1-\beta_1)^{-1} d(\overline{G} + \overline{I}) - \beta_1 (1-\beta_1)^{-1} dT.$$

For $d\overline{I} = 0$ and $d\overline{G} = dT$ — in accordance with Equation 9 — we obtain

$$(13) \qquad dY^* \equiv [(1-\beta_1)^{-1} + \beta_1 (1-\beta_1)^{-1}] d\overline{G}$$
$$\equiv [(1-\beta_1)/(1-\beta_1)] d\overline{G} \equiv d\overline{G}.$$

The "equilibrium" value for output increases by an amount equal to the increase in expenditure: the balanced-budget principle reduces the multiplier to unity . . . Do not fail to see that this result is part of a particular, and a particularly simple, model: alternative formulations lead to different expressions for $dY^*/d\overline{G}$, constrained so that $dT = d\overline{G}$.

An heuristic explanation might be in order. The period multiplier becomes a useful tool. Each dollar increment in G gives rise to a series of the form

[7] G, of course, is to be autonomous.

[8] The equation-identity distinction is dropped in Equations 7-10.

[9] Eliminating the autonomous component of consumption expenditure.

(14) $$1 + \beta_1 + \beta^2_1 + \cdots + \beta^r_1 + \cdots$$

There corresponds to each of the increments in G an identical increase in T (always keeping in mind that neither T nor G is keyed to Y), giving rise initially to a decrease in expenditure of $\$\beta_1$ and to a series of the form

(15) $$\beta_1 + \beta^2_1 + \cdots + \beta^r_1 + \cdots,$$

the elements being absolute values (their signs being negative). Assume that these processes have been in progress for an indefinitely long interval. This means that each of the slots of Equations 14 and 15 can be filled: when 15 is subtracted from 14, the positive element, *1*, remains.

The balanced-budget-multiplier theme permits transition to discussion of the impact of stabilizers on the size of the multiplier. The way in which Equation 9 constrained G and T implied stabilizing technique: it assured that increases in government spending would be offset by increased tax-take. Our general technique for handling stabilizers will be algebraic. Specifically, a series of linear models will be constructed comprising an alphabet soup. But not before some literary discussion.

7

There are forces at work within a modern economic system increasing "leakage rates." These forces are *stabilizers.* To the extent that their operation is not governed by authoritative discretion, they are called "automatic stabilizers." "Stabilization" pertains to muted responsiveness of the system to parametric changes, whether these be marginal propensities to consume, expectational factors underlying investment decisions, changes in autonomous military spending, or "Acts of God." To reduce the responsiveness of solution values of the system to parametric shifts is to reduce its multipliers.

Consider mechanisms that increase marginal leakage rates. If stockholders' spending depends more on dividends than on earnings and if dividend rates tend to be more stable than earnings, forces increasing the rate of income generation automatically lead to an increase in planned corporate saving; opposite forces automatically lead to a decrease in planned corporate saving and corresponding buttressing of stockholders' disposable income. If the government's tax take is keyed to national income, forces working to increase national income automatically tend to reduce disposable income (to that extent) as tax revenues increase; recessionary forces tend to reduce the rate at which income is being drained off by taxation. If government spending on goods and services is anti-cyclical, booms lead to diminished government spending, depressions to expansion of government spending. Similarly, anti-cyclical transfer-payment mechanisms reduce the multiplier.[10] Well known transfer-payment mechanisms include unemployment compensation, social security, etc. Finally, introduction of a foreign trade sector can be stabilizing: forces towards higher rates of income lead to increased leakage due to planned purchases of foreign goods; lower income discourages imports.[11]

8

Two tasks remain before the subsection can be closed: (a) development of an algebraic argument; (b) reference to postwar data illuminating the way in which the stabilizers actually have performed. Taking up (a), continue to use linear models patterned after the first approximation to income theory. Money is neglected: the system has a plethora of liquidity or potential liquidity; expansion of economic activity within contemplated ranges can take place with $r = \bar{r}$. Prices and wages are rigid.

First, deal with a model without automatic stabilization, say a linearized form of Equations 1-3. Assume that the marginal propensity to consume, β_1, is 0.9. The multiplier is 10: a \$1 change in autonomous expenditure leads to a \$10 change in "equilibrium" income in the same direction. Then assume that the model is modified by the assumption that the government's tax revenue varies proportionately with income, except for an autonomous portion. Algebraically,[12]

$$C = 0.9Y^d \tag{16}$$

$$Y^d = Y - T \tag{17}$$

$$T = \alpha_0 + 0.3Y \tag{18}$$

$$Y = C + \bar{I} + \bar{G} = C + A. \tag{19}$$

10 Positive transfers include expenditures not directly reflected in the labor and commodities markets; negative transfers include tax receipts and other items not directly consequent to governmental sale of goods and services to the public.

11 Imports detract from demand for *domestic* goods in the same way as does saving.

12 Ignoring the identity-equation distinction.

The special assumptions about government revenue are collected in Equations 17 and 18. The system can be reduced to Equation 20:

$$(20) \qquad Y^* - 0.9Y^* + (0.9)(0.3)Y^* \equiv A - 0.9\alpha_o$$

$$(21) \qquad Y^* \equiv (0.37)^{-1}(A - 0.9\alpha_o) \equiv 2.7(A - 0.9\alpha_o).$$

$\partial Y^*/\partial A \equiv 2.7$. The multiplier has fallen from 10 to 2.7 as a result of the introduction of a stabilizer. The system's volatility has been much reduced.

Innumerable variations could be contrived through specification of alternative sets of stabilizers. However, we are content with a single, fairly large caldron of alphabet soup (again ignoring the equation-identity distinction):

$$(22) \qquad C = 0.8Y^d$$

$$(23) \qquad J = 0.1Y^d$$

$$(24) \qquad Y^d = Y - T + V$$

$$(25) \qquad T = \alpha_o + 0.3Y$$

$$(26) \qquad V = \alpha_1 - 0.1Y$$

$$(27) \qquad G = \alpha_2 + 0.1Y$$

$$(28) \qquad Y = C + \bar{I} + G + \bar{X}$$

J is the rate of demand for imports; T the rate of tax receipts (negative transfers); V the rate of positive transfer payments; $\bar{X}$ the rate of export demand. All are measured in dollars or shmoos as you wish — the price level is fixed. The fact that X is exogenous implies that our country is a pebble in the international pond.[13]

Explicit stabilization policy, in contrast with the "unconscious" stabilization resulting from introduction of a foreign sector, is described in Equations 25-27. In this model, it is obviously confined to the government sector; more complete models would take account of dividend policy, perhaps guaranteed annual wages, and other non-government stabilizers . . . Of course, save for the Christian Businessman, these stabilizers would be accidental: "stabilization properties" of business policy are external to considerations of Board meetings, except perhaps for unconscionably large firms . . . Equation 27 shows

[13] X-J, net foreign balance, does not appear in Equation 28: C is defined in terms of demand for domestic goods only, as are all other expenditure items.

that government expenditure on goods and services has an autonomous component (α_2), governed by, say, hard-core defense requirements, but also a segment responsive to the cycle, cutting across its grain. Roughly speaking, the model contained in Equations 22-28 typifies the present-day American economy.[14]

Equation system 22-28 can be reduced to a single equation determining Y^* as a function of the parameters of the linear system:

$$(29) \quad Y^*(1.0+0.8+0.24-0.08+0.10) \equiv A' \text{ or } Y^* \equiv 2.2A'$$

where A' is the sum of the autonomous elements of expenditure. The modified system's investment multiplier is 2.2. What about its balanced-budget multiplier? If the balanced-budget multiplier is interpreted so that $G + V$ is constrained always to be equal to T, elaborate analysis of reduced forms is necessary. On the other hand, if one simply asks what would be the effect of simultaneous and equal increases in the exogenous components of T and G(α_0 and α_2), the answer is easy. Equation 29 can be rewritten:

$$(30) \quad Y^* \equiv 2.2\,[-0.8\alpha_0 + \alpha_2 + A''],$$

where A'' gives other autonomous components. Holding these constant and increasing α_0 and α_2 each by \$1, Y^* increases by \$2.20 — \$1.76 = \$0.44, emphasizing *caveats* about feckless use of balanced-budget multipliers.

9

In finishing the alphabet soup, note that, as more sophisticated models are considered *exogeneity* becomes vaguer: none of the basic national-income-accounting concepts such as net foreign balance, gross

14 Consider the effects of a reduction in the marginal rate of taxation, c, in a less-than-full-employment context. Can lower c lead to increased tax revenues? If it is to do so inequality i must hold for systems such as 16-19:

$$(i) \quad \frac{\beta c}{1-\beta+\beta c} > 1.$$

Obviously, i does not hold for System 16-19. Interpreting β as a marginal propensity to *spend* (introducing a marginal propensity to invest), it would seem that i cannot hold for a stable system. However, introducing a monetary sector, it is possible for higher interest rates to damp down upward movements (and *vice versa* for downward movements), so that even systems with marginal propensities to spend in excess of unity can be stable.

It would seem that hopes for reduced tax rates to lead to higher tax takes must be based on accelerator effects. . . . Note that the formal analysis of Ch. XI can only apply to an instant in time. Interpretation of effects on "sequences" must be heuristic.

private domestic investment, government expenditure on goods and services, etc. could survive as autonomous variables in a full system; these categories are too broad to escape subjection to the straitjacket of behavioral equations. It becomes evident that eligibility requirements for classification as a parameter of the system are stringent. Commonly classified "autonomous variables" are likely to disintegrate as such when put under pressure. There is a clear implication that very elaborate aggregate models — models pursuing sophistication into the limit — become transmogrified into naïveté; weather and other Acts of God prove to drive the system. It seems strange that unsophisticated model builders would make predictions based on planned expenditures on plant and equipment, while sophisticated model builders would rely on doubtful predictions of next year's rainfall in selected states, together with expected mean temperature. In fact, *very* sophisticated model builders would associate solution values with the putative will of God.

The resolution of the paradox is in the capacious bosom of scientific positivism: it is undesirable to refine models to a point where observation of parametric variables must be imprecise or where putative relationships are subject to large standard errors of estimate. It is better to leave the model more naïve if measurement can be more precise or if postulated relationships are subject to a minimum of disturbance. Problems of estimation cannot be dissociated from those of pure theory.

10

We turn to some postwar time series for a number of variables pertaining to automatic stabilizers: gross national product, gross private domestic investment, disposable personal income, and government receipts and expenditures.[15] The time series are in first differences: the data are *changes* from year to year. See Table XI-I.

The last three columns of the table (government transfer payments, government receipts, and surplus — all in first differences) are in current dollars in contrast with the first four columns (Gross National Product, Gross Private Domestic Investment, Disposable Personal Income, and government purchases of goods and services) which are in constant (1960) dollars — again in first differences.

[15] In what follows, the accelerator (*cf.* Ch. XII) is ignored. Of course, we are concerned with determination of solution values at points in time. In this context, the message of the accelerator can be delivered through a model in which previous incomes are given data, along with initial stocks of capital.

FIRST DIFFERENCES OF CERTAIN ECONOMIC MAGNITUDES

(in billions of dollars at 1960 prices)

					—Current Dollars—		
Year(s)	Gross Nat. Prod.	GPDI	DPI	Gov't Pur.	Transfer Pay (Gov.)	Receipts	Surplus or Def. (cash)
1948-1947	+12.5	+ 8.3	+11.3	+ 4.9	+ 1.1	+ 2.1	— 5.1
1949-1948	+ 0.6	—11.3	+ 2.9	+ 5.1	+ 2.9	— 2.8	—11.3
1950-1949	+28.1	+17.4	+18.5	— 2.1	+ 2.7	+12.9	+11.3
1951-1950	+29.7	+ 1.8	+ 7.0	+18.2	— 3.2	+16.2	— 2.1
1952-1951	+14.8	— 7.3	+ 7.0	+14.4	— 0.5	+ 5.1	—10.0
1953-1952	+18.7	+ 0.2	+13.0	+ 6.6	+ 0.8	+ 4.3	— 3.2
1954-1953	— 8.7	— 1.7	+ 2.0	— 9.0	+ 2.3	— 4.9	+ 0.4
1955-1954	+12.9	+ 4.2	+18.0	— 2.1	+ 1.5	+11.4	+ 9.6
1956-1955	+ 9.5	— 1.6	+14.8	— 0.9	+ 2.3	+ 8.1	+ 2.3
1957-1956	+ 8.6	— 1.5	+ 7.7	+ 3.2	+ 3.4	+ 6.8	— 4.2
1958-1957	— 8.1	— 9.8	+ 3.4	+ 3.8	+ 4.4	— 1.1	—12.4
1959-1958	+30.4	+ 3.4	+16.0	+ 0.9	+ 1.4	+13.9	+ 8.9
1960-1959	+12.6	— 0.8	+11.1	+ 0.1	+ 1.9	+ 8.2	+ 2.8

TABLE XI-I

Source: *Economic Report of the President*, 1961.

Table XI-I reveals rather dramatically the way in which stabilization has broken up and muffled the multiplier relationship. Compare Column 1 with the sum of Columns 2 and 4, as illustrated in Figure XI-1.

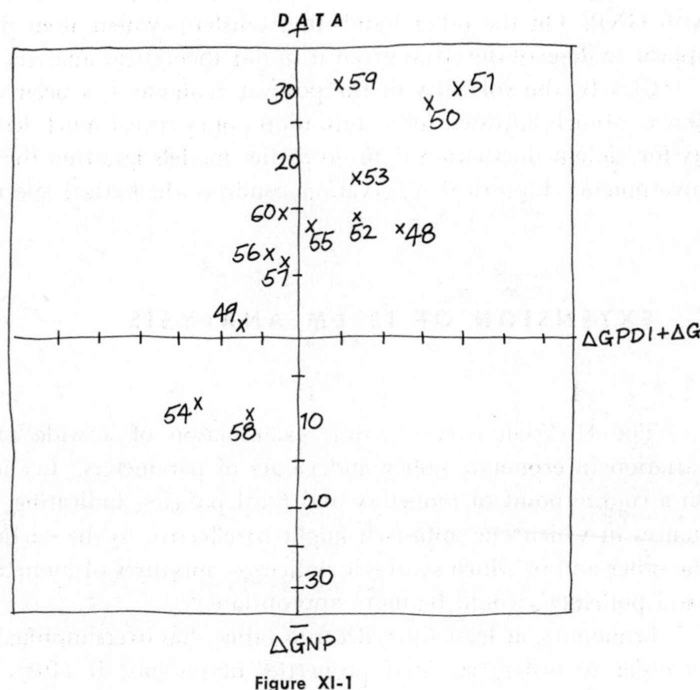

Figure XI-1

As for breaking up the multiplier relation, observe that four of the thirteen observations lie in the Northwest quadrant. These are inconsistent with a multiplier relation: positive and negative first-differences are (perversely) associated. In the recession year 1954 the decline in Gross National Product was exceeded by the decline in the sum of gross private domestic investment and government spending. In 1958 the latter sum declined by $5 billion and was associated with a decline in GNP of $8 billion. On the other hand, increases in GNP of $28.1, 29.7, and 14.8 billion in 1950, 1951, and 1952 were associated with increases in GPDI + G of $15.3, 20, and 7.1 billion. This does not suggest a very powerful multiplier relation. Stabilizing effects are suggested by other data. Disposable personal income rose in the face of lower GNP in 1954 and 1958. The over-all behavior of DPI suggests that shifts in more volatile components of expenditure are pretty much confined to the sectors in which these operate; multiplier effects are precluded by the stabilizers. Consumption data — particularly for soft goods — stress this. Column 6 shows how tax receipts rise and decline with GNP. On the other hand, the transfer-payment item does not appear to deserve the stress given it in our theoretical analysis.

Clearly, the volatility of the postwar economy has been damped down. Models adjusted for stabilization policy reveal much less capacity for violent fluctuation than do earlier models ignoring the role of government. Empirical observation confirms theoretical speculation.

C. EXTENSION OF IS-LM ANALYSIS

1

The Hicksian curves permit examination of a wide range of variation in economic policy and values of parameters. Let us focus on a counterpoint of monetary and fiscal policies, indicating circumstances in which one approach might be effective to the exclusion of the other and in which synthetic policies — mixtures of monetary and fiscal policies — would be more appropriate.[16]

Economics, at least since Ricardo's time, has oversimplified things in order to isolate essential properties of systems; it often has exhibited the Ricardian Vice. Thus, I present the *IS-LM* version of the theory of economic policy through two characters: Chrysippus, a proponent of purely monetary policy; Epicurus, an advocate of fiscal to the exclusion of monetary policy. Under what circumstances would a Chrysippus policy be appropriate? When would an Epicurus policy be appropriate?

The diagram below offers an *IS-LM* construction consistent with Chrysippus' prescription: "the important policy device for 'control'

[16] Of course, synthetic policies have been employed by Administrations facing recessions. Compare the narrative parts of Economic Reports of the President for 1950, 1955, 1959, and 1961. You should in any case. Perhaps the Truman Administration relied more on fiscal than monetary devices whilst the Eisenhower Administration was more friendly to monetary policy. Surely this would tend to be true of the respective "Court economists."

of national income is the stock of money; fiscal policy cannot be expected to exert important influence on the system."[17] Chrysippus could use a geometrical argument: measures of fiscal policy shifting the *IS* curve cannot affect the *Y* coordinate of the "equilibrium" position; the vertical *LM* curve dominates. The only way in which effective demand, *Y**, can be shifted rightwards is through a lateral displacement of the *LM* curve.[18]

GEOMETRY UNDERLYING A CHRYSIPPUS POLICY

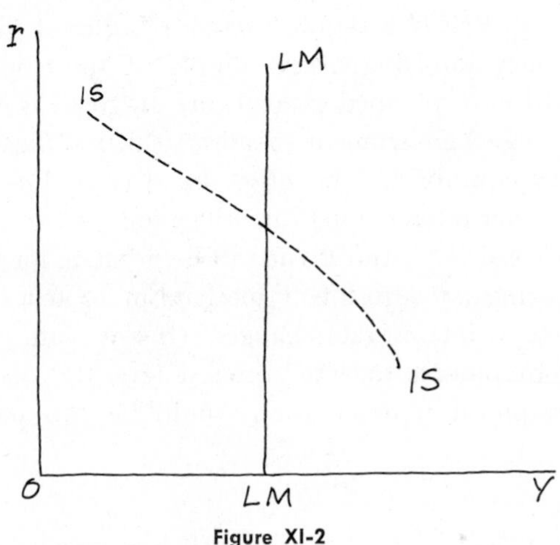

Figure XI-2

2

What can be the economic content of assumptions underlying a vertical *LM* curve? The fact that the *LM* curve is vertical implies that clearance of the money market is unaffected by "the" rate of interest but is uniquely associated with a single value of *Y*. This state of affairs

17 But compare footnote 18. In order to deal with full-employment situations, one must work with the analogous *CC-LL* construction of Note B.

18 I employ the *IS-LM* construction only for ranges of effective demand short of full-employment income. Although Hicks has extended the construction to full-employment cases (*cf.* his review of Patinkin's *Money, Interest, and Prices,* "A Rehabilitation of 'Classical' Economics?", *Economic Journal,* Vol. 67, June 1957, pp. 278-289), I think it loses its heuristic appeal in such cases. And surely there is no important non-heuristic motive for such diagrammatics.

could be generated by the following demand-supply subset for the money market:

$$(1) \qquad M^d \equiv \bar{p}.L(Y)$$

$$(2) \qquad M^s \equiv \overline{M}$$

$$(3) \qquad M^d = M^s.$$

The quantity of money demanded depends only on income, at least once certain parameters, not otherwise pertinent to the model, are specified. The supply of money is exogenous. Equation 3 imposes a clearance condition on the money market. The system of three equations in the unknowns M^d, M^s, and Y (for $p = \bar{p}$) determines the solution value for Y, Y^*. If Y should exceed Y^*, there will be excess demand for money implying excess supply of securities.[19] Securities prices must fall until planned expenditure on goods is consistent with Y^*. Thus increased government spending, shifting the *IS* curve rightward, will, in equilibrium, be offset by decreased non-government spending as higher interest rates take their toll. dr/dt will be positive so long as Y exceeds Y^*. And dr/dt will be negative for Y less than Y^* — again implying an adjustment mechanism rooted in response of spending plans to interest-rate changes. (If aggregate demand also is completely unresponsive to "the" interest rate, the system cannot be solved: its graphical representation would be two parallel vertical lines.)

3

There is at least one other approach leading to the substance of the Chrysippus position. It flows from assumptions about behavior of money, wages, prices, and the marginal physical product of labor examined in greater detail at the end of the chapter. Thus, consider

19 Effects of excess demand (supply) of money in the commodity market are ignored. Of course, the planned rate of saving should be governed by income and the *aggregate* value of the initial portfolio. If there is an undesired shift in the portfolio, traders would plan to correct the distortion by shifting asset holdings. Similarly, liquidity variables should not be introduced into micro demand functions: one can, in theory, make his portfolio as liquid as he wishes. On the other hand, excess demand for money — wealth unchanged — *might* be reflected in capital-goods markets even if the propensity to save is unchanged. If asset holders plan on net to increase money holdings at the expense of securities *and* physical capital, there will be excess supply in the market for new durables. In other words, neutral increases in liquidity preference shift both the *IS* and *LM* curves. For convenience, the text works with non-neutral shifts in liquidity preference, shifts confined to a money-bonds nexus, and eschews equities (as does fn. 19).

consequences for desired transactions balances (*cet. par.*) under one or more of these specifications:

a) a tendency for the wage unit to increase as unemployment decreases

b) sharply-decreasing marginal physical product of labor as the rate of employment increases so that satisfaction of the condition,

$$\overline{w} = p.MPP_N$$

requires substantial price increase.

c) administered prices following a dynamic law like that of (a), a law keyed to the degree of "excess capacity," the analog to involuntary unemployment.

In all of these cases prices increase with output, imposing additional pressure on the money supply. But the rate of interest *must* have *some* effect on the demand for money. Chrysippus will stoically accept the diagram below. Clearly, a small increase in output (M constant) will require a very-large increase in the interest rate if the money market is to clear. The steep (but not perfectly vertical) LM curve of the diagram suffices to paralyse fiscal policy. Huge doses of fiscal policy will be necessary for meaningful effect.

ALTERNATIVE GEOMETRY FOR A CHRYSIPPUS POLICY

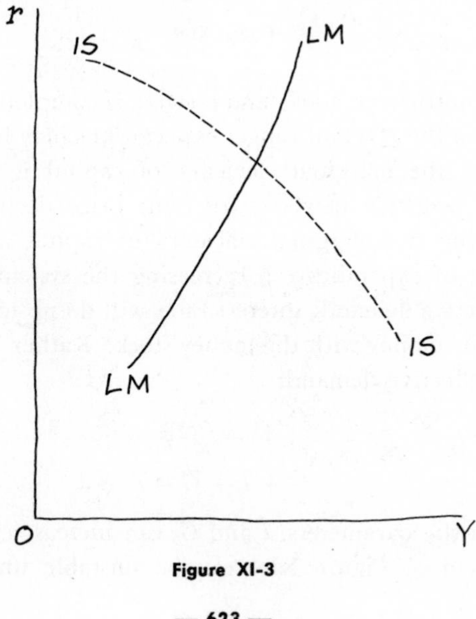

Figure XI-3

4

Before limning an environment favorable to Epicurus policy, note that — save for the liquidity trap — increased government expenditure in less-than-full-employment systems leads to higher interest rates: higher income levels lead to greater demand for transactions balances and for asset balances (if money is not inferior), *cet. par.* Interest rates must rise if nominal income is to increase and the stock of money to be unchanged.

This diagram applies to a "pure Epicurus" world:

EPICURUS GEOMETRY

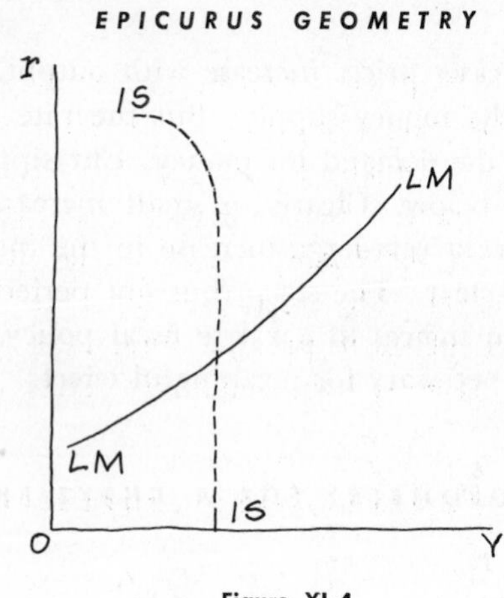

Figure XI-4

Planned expenditure on goods and services is completely insensitive to interest rates in the revelant range: expectations may have collapsed to a point where the marginal efficiency of capital is negative; excess capacity may preclude new construction; price declines may be expected, affecting the marginal efficiency of capital and encouraging postponement of expenditures. Increasing the system's liquidity will not affect effective demand: interest rates will do no more than equate the demand for money with the money stock. Rather Equations 4 and 5 determine effective demand:

(4) $$C \equiv C(Y)$$

(5) $$C + \bar{I} + \bar{G} = Y$$

Only shifts in the parameters, *I* and *G*, can increase effective demand.

The system of Figure XI-4 can be unstable under inflationary pressure if the officials confined themselves to monetary policy. Thus, assume that, beginning at full employment, aggregate demand exceeds full-employment income and that the parameters governing aggregate demand are locked into place. Rising commodity prices lead to increased demand for transactions cash balances.[20] Excess demand for cash reflects itself in excess supply of securities. But interest rates have no impact on the commodity market: they merely reconcile demand for cash with the predetermined stock of money. The inflation could proceed apace, interest rates becoming high indeed, but merely adding a fillip to increasing monetary velocity. (*See Note B.*)

Of course, the liquidity trap alone could seal the doom of monetary policy: there is little point in adding to the system's liquidity if meaningful reductions in interest rates cannot be achieved and if bank reserves are more than adequate to accommodate existing demand for cash. All that would remain for a government determined upon monetary policy would be for it to offer to purchase securities at a yield less than r°: the officials would have to hold the entire stock of securities. Epicurean forces could cry "socialism!"

5

The duel between Chrysippus and Epicurus concludes with the diagram below, the analog to Figure XI-3, depicting elastic liquidity

ALTERNATIVE GEOMETRY FOR AN EPICURUS POLICY

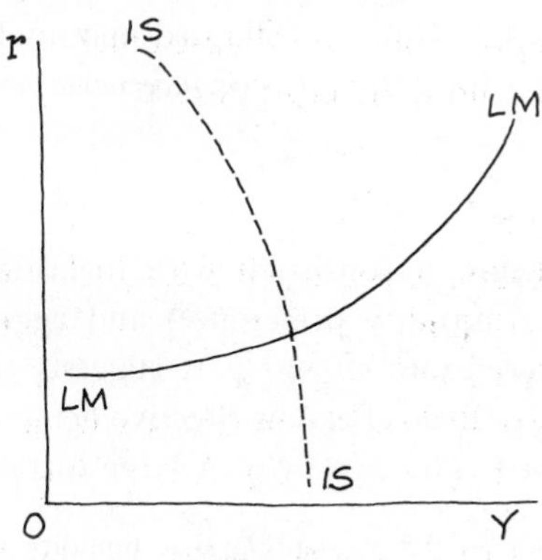

Figure XI-5

[20] Certainly if the elasticity of expectations does not exceed unity. Otherwise the case for monetary policy further deteriorates.

preference confronted by inelastic response of planned real expenditures to changes in interest rates. The range of response of effective demand to monetary changes is indeed limited: e. g., as the money stock increases, there is rightward displacement of *LM,* leading to initial excess supply of money. Excess demand in securities markets increases securities prices (reduces interest rates), but this has little effect on planned expenditure: almost all of any increase in the money stock is absorbed in asset rather than transaction balances. Lower interest rates, of course, abet this process. On the other hand, the range of response of effective demand to fiscal policy is considerable. An increase in the rate of autonomous government spending, for example, leads to a rightward shift in the *IS* curve: aggregate demand is greater for a given set of interest rates. There is initial excess demand in the commodity market leading to increased production and employment, resulting, in turn, in increased demand for transactions balances. However, elastic liquidity preference permits a slight rise in r to choke off demand for cash; inelastic response of demand for commodities to interest-rate changes means that higher interest rates have little effect on demand for commodities.[21]

6

The case of *Chrysippus v. Epicurus* has ended indecisively. There remain scheduled but two further applications of the *IS-LM* construction: (a) a pair of curves demanding synthetic policy if "practicable" doses of monetary and fiscal policy are meaningfully to ameliorate unemployment;[22] (b) application to collapsed marginal efficiency of capital, accompanied by a liquidity crisis or *vice versa,* evoking recollection of Ch. VC.

a) The "synthetic case"

The diagram below is consistent with inelastic response of both demand for money (liquidity preference) and aggregate demand for commodities to interest-rate changes. It suggests that huge doses of either policy will have little effect on effective demand if the other policy lever is untouched. (*See Note C.*) A large increase in autonomous

21 Rework these passages on the assumption that liquidity preference is inelastic and expenditure plans elastic to interest-rate changes. The conclusion will, of course, be reversed.

22 Or, in the alternative *CC-LL* construction, to control of the price level consistently with "acceptable" changes in interest rates. (*See Note B.*)

expenditure might lead initially to excess demand for commodities, but, as output increases, leading in turn to increased demand for transactions balances, huge increases in interest rates become necessary to avert excess demand for money (excess supply of securities). Even the inelastically responding aggregate-demand function succumbs. Similarly, a large increase in the stock of money results in initial excess supply in the money market (excess demand in securities markets). Interest rates are forced down. But the weak response of aggregate demand to lower interest rates means that there will be little change in effective demand.[23] The only way in which the economy can be moved

THE CASE FOR SYNTHETIC POLICY

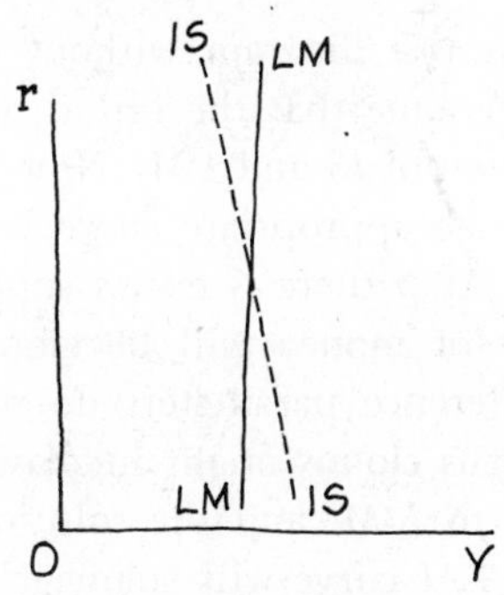

Figure XI-6

off a dime is through simultaneous doses of monetary *and* fiscal policy, reflected in shifts of both the *IS* and *LM* curves.

b) Collapse in marginal efficiency of capital accompanied by a liquidity crisis

First consult Figure XI-7.

23 It might be disturbing to deal with changes in "M" without specification of how these come about. The approach I prefer is that of Chapters V and XIII, centering on shifts of parameters governing the banking sector. Otherwise changes in *M* cannot be divorced from fiscal policy: additional money must come into the hands of the public through governmental purchases or direct transfers. For the time being, you might want to use this model: there is a banking sector always creating deposits up to the limit of legal reserves. Any change in the money-creating potential of banks is reflected in excess demand (supply) for securities. In this model, pure-credit money forecloses real-balance effects in commodities markets . . . Ignore time-deposit creation by commercial banks.

SHIFTS IN IS AND LM

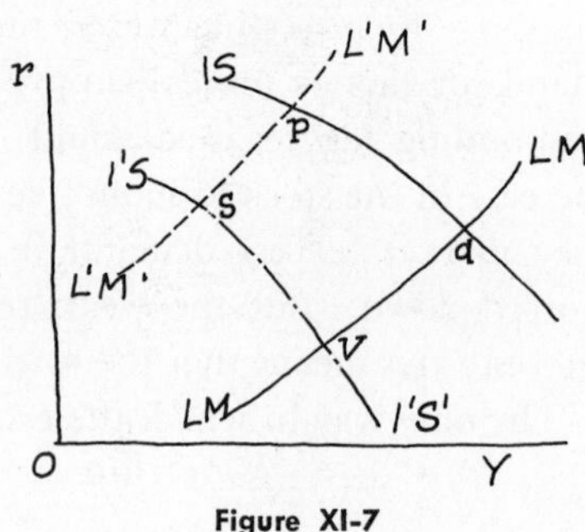

Figure XI-7

It is difficult to discuss this diagram without dubiously mixing up statics and dynamics. Assume that the initial solution for the system is point *q*, the intersection of *IS* and *LM*. Now assume that there is a downward shift in *IS*: the appropriate curve becomes *I'S'*. The new solution is at point *v*. At *p* there is excess supply in the commodity market. Excess supply of money will develop once income begins to fall, *if* liquidity-preference parameters do not change. But business failures and ominous clouds might increase liquidity preference, shifting the *LM* curve to *L'M'* and the solution point from *v* to *s*. A leftward shift of the *LM* curve will "damage" the commodity market: pressures for higher interest rates[24] will damp down whatever investment expenditure was planned under the *I'S'* specification; pressure for conversion of IOU's into cash might induce bankruptcies that otherwise might not have occurred and surely will lead to diversion of receipts from demand for commodities into retirement of securities (into the hands of persons obviously reluctant to lend). There might be an utter collapse of expectations. Quite clearly, the occasion would be ripe for open-market policy *á outrance*: infusion of liquidity into the system so as to sustain securities prices despite increased liquidity preference. Such a policy might feature official purchase of securities previously not eligible. If vigorous monetary policy is not undertaken, the induced shift of the *LM* curve can, as we have seen, reduce the economic scene to shambles.

Discussion of financial panics in Chapters II and VC made clear

[24] The standard security is issued by firms and *the* interest rate referred to is NOT riskless.

how increased liquidity preference (in the "schedule sense") might induce a leftward shift in the *IS* curve — if indeed analysis of disequilibrium can be conducted within so statical a framework. Thus, starting at *q*, assume that *LM* is replaced by *L'M'*: the new solution point is *p* if the *ceteris paribus* for the *IS* curve can be sustained. But the dynamics associated with excess demand for cash will not leave the commodity market untouched. To repeat, expenditure units pressed to make cash payment or anxious to increase their liquidity, but faced with stony-faced lenders, will plan to divert cash receipts into their own coffers instead of making normal inventory replacement; plant-and-equipment expenditures will be postponed; to the extent that expenditure units divert cash from their coffers to those of their exigent creditors, excess supply of goods will be accompanied by increased finance requirements, but cash-surplus units will find time deposits more attractive than primary securities. Of course, an epidemic of bankruptcies could disorganize the commodities markets.

The counterpart to open-market purchases *á outrance* as an antidote to secondary consequences of a collapse of the marginal efficiency of capital would be massive government expenditures. It would be advisable for such expenditures to be accompanied by infusions of liquidity in order to maintain the buoyancy of the securities markets.

D. THE KEYNESIAN ELASTICITIES

We have become inured to a reduced-form psychology. We are accustomed to thinking in terms of the impact on solution values of dependent variables of changes in parametric policy variables. The method of comparative statics is second nature. One regrets that the method is not useful in generating sequences from arbitrary initial states, but nothing more can be done about that until Ch. XII.

Obvious comparative-statics applications include effects on "equilibrium" output, prices, employment, interest rates, etc., of changes in the rate of autonomous spending, the supply of money, and other parameters. Keynes states various relationships of this sort in Ch. 20 of the *General Theory*.[25] He writes of the "elasticity of employ-

[25] *Cf.* Alvin H. Hansen, *A Guide to Keynes* (New York: McGraw-Hill Book Co., 1953), pp. 183-204. The *Guide,* together with Hansen's *Monetary Theory and Fiscal Policy* (New York: McGraw-Hill Book Co., 1949) are models of exposition.

ment," the "elasticity of effective demand with respect to changes in the quantity of money," etc. While taking leave of the *General Theory,* we might indicate conditions under which some of these elasticities would be large or small. The treatment is informal: "elasticity" will mean nothing more than "sensitivity."

1. Elasticity of the Price Levels with Respect to the Money Supply $[(dp^*/d\overline{M})(\overline{M}/p^*)]$

We must infringe upon Ch. XIV, "The Quantity Theory of Money." Keynes, of course, saw the connection (*cf. General Theory,* p. 296). Some of the factors having immediate bearing on the value of this elasticity include:

1) the dynamic law governing money-wage behavior;

2) the slope of the marginal-productivity-of-labor function, in turn affecting the elasticity of supply of all goods;

3) the extent to which prices originally were administered or were flexible;

4) the responsiveness of demand for money to changes in interest rates;

5) the sensitivity of demand for goods to changes in interest rates;

6) the strength of the real-balance effect if the change in the stock of money was accomplished in a way that increased the public's appraisal of its wealth.

Briefly analysing the six factors, the state of the labor market at the outset of monetary expansion has much to do with the final result. If there is initial excess supply of labor, effects of monetary expansion on aggregate demand might be accommodated without a higher wage-unit — say a simplistic dynamic law finds $w = \overline{w}$ so long as there is excess supply of labor.[26] If there is full employment initially, Ch. XIV shows that conventional assumptions lead to the conclusion that equilibrium output will not change and that wages and prices will rise proportionately with the increase in the money supply. On the other hand, the dynamic law governing the wage unit might be

$$dw/dt = \quad (N^d - N^s),$$

[26] As in Ch. X, the sense of "excess supply" is that additional labor can be obtained at going money-wage rates even if the price level should rise.

where dw/dt can be positive for some negative values of $(N^d - N^s)$. Perhaps the function is discontinuous, so that dw/dt never is negative. There are many variants. In any case, expansion of output could lead to higher money-wage rates under a wide range of specifications. Prices would tend to rise as a result — at least under most specifications.

Especially if commodity prices are flexible, the slope of the MPP_N function comes into play. The steeper is the rate of decline of MPP_N as N increases, the more must p rise if employers are to be induced to plan to increase production (and employment) even if the wage unit is unchanged. On the other hand, if employers were initially off their demand-for-labor curves — if they would have liked to have hired more labor if only they could have anticipated being able to sell more goods at the rigid price level — the slope of the MPP_N curve might be neglected: it hardly matters how much labor *above and beyond the rate of employment consistent with effective demand* entrepreneurs wish they could employ. In other words it is possible that the "desired" supply-of-all-goods function permits output to extend indefinitely at a particular wage-price combination $(\bar{w}, \bar{p})$. Compare Figure XI-8.

SUPPLY-OF-ALL-GOODS FUNCTION

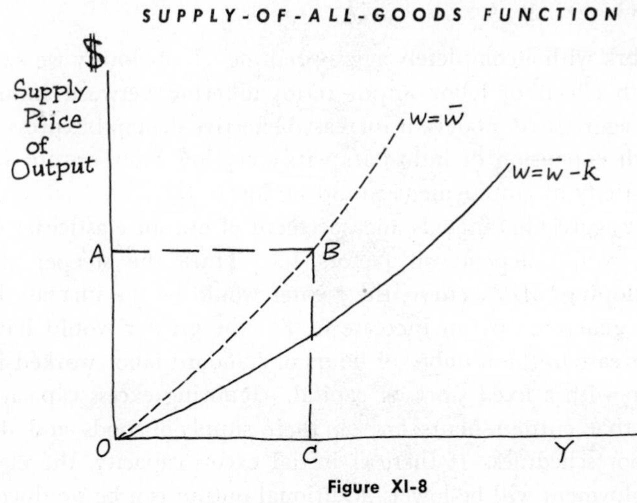

Figure XI-8

Supply price is the minimum price at which sellers are willing to supply goods for a given rate of output (sales). If the price level becomes stuck at OA, supply-of-all-goods is perfectly elastic over the output range OC and can be represented by the line segment AB.

Factors 1-3 take for granted that changes in the stock of money will influence effective demand. Factors 4-6 inquire into *how* this might come about. If demand for money balances is highly responsive to interest-rate changes, while demand for all goods is highly unresponsive, we should expect that an increase in the money stock would exert little influence on effective demand (always dealing with less-than-full-employment situations). Under this specification, a changed money stock would affect only r^* (ignoring liquidity-trap possibilities), *unless* the sixth factor, real-balance effects could rescue the situation. But, if an "increase in the money supply" resulted from a lower required reserve-deposit ratio, for example, it is clear that real-balance effects should be ignored: expansion of bank deposits is accompanied by creation of liability items *pari passu* with creation of monetary assets.[27] On the other hand, if the expansion of the money supply is achieved through airplane drops or budget deficits financed by the printing press, real-balance effects cannot be ignored, certainly not at the level of pure theory.

2. Elasticity of Employment with Respect to Effective Demand $[(dN^*/dY^*)(Y^*/N^*)]$

If we work with a completely aggregated model, obviously we cannot deal with effects of labor-output ratios differing between industries. In less aggregated models, if increased effective demand expressed itself through expansion of industries with very low labor-output ratios, the elasticity of employment would be low.

For fully-aggregated models, measurement of output elasticities of employment would depend on factors 1-3. Thus, the steeper the (negatively sloping) MPP_N curve, the greater would be the increase in employment generated by an increase in Y^*; the greater would have to be the increase in the number of hours of standard labor worked in collaboration with a fixed stock of capital. (Ignoring excess capacity. We assume that entrepreneurs are on their supply-of-goods and demand-for-labor schedules. If there *is* initial excess capacity, the elasticity of employment will be lower: additional output can be produced in part by utilizing idle equipment.)

[27] Needless to say, rigor rarely permits one to treat the stock of money as a parameter of the system. However, Ch. VA, especially its Appendix A, laid the foundation for the convenient — but not substantively important — assumption that M can be treated as parametric in income models.

3. Elasticity of Effective Demand (Equilibrium Output) with Respect to An Increase in Autonomous Expenditure $[(dY^*/dA)(A/Y^*)]$

When there is unemployment it is easy to catalog some of the factors determining the value of this elasticity: the six factors of Section D1; the "stabilizers"; the propensity to consume; etc. The *IS-LM* construction permits one to work up sets of specifications consistent with one or another value for dY^*/dA.

SUMMARY

1. Behavior of the government sector is not based on profit and utility maximization, but instead is directed towards full employment, stable prices, etc.
2. The comparative statics of economic policy concerns reduced forms of equation systems. Solution values of such endogenous variables as employment and output are related to changes in policy variables (parameters of the system) such as tax rates, official autonomous spending, money supply, etc.
3. When Ch. X models are modified by equations describing behavior of present-day governments, multipliers fall drastically. Volatility is much reduced.
4. Postwar American experience is consistent with multiplier values suggested by Ch. XI. Government behavior, especially that of the federal government, tends to be anti-cyclical.
5. The *IS-LM* construction shows how alternative parameter specifications favor monetary or fiscal policy, neither or both. In general fiscal policy, *cet. par.* is effective if demand for goods is unresponsive while demand for money is responsive to interest-rate changes. Opposite sensitivities favor monetary policy. If demand for both goods and money is interest inelastic, monetary and fiscal policy have to be used simultaneously if worthwhile results are to be achieved.
6. Chapter XI did not take up the argument that it is the stability, not the expected values of the parameters, of reduced-form relationships that is important. (*Cf.* Ch. VI.) The predictor basically is concerned with goodness of fit; estimates subject to large stand-

ard errors are not useful. Still political considerations, for example, often impose limitations on permissible variation of autonomous variables: elasticities can be important for practical purposes.

7. Chapter XI neglected another theme: *lags* in response to changes in autonomous variables. *Cf.* Milton Friedman, "A Monetary and Fiscal Framework for Economic Stability," *American Economic Review,* Vol. 38, June 1948, pp. 245-264. Friedman divides the total lag pertaining to reaction to disturbance into three parts:

> (1) the lag between the need for action and the recognition of this need; (2) the lag between recognition of the need for action and the taking of action; and (3) the lag between the action and its effects.

Comparative statics encourages neglect of lagged adjustment. But lags can be decisive. Thus, the first and second lags discourage reliance on discretionary official action and encourage built-in stabilization. The third lag reminds us that Bank-rate policy would be impaired if capital-expenditure commitments are made well in advance. So would be tax-adjustment policies. And then long delays between the letting of contracts and expenditure on labor and materials by contractors can paralyse stabilization policy.

8. Conventional analysis, rather faithfully produced in Part II, centers on properties of solutions, sometimes permitting crude stability analysis. Policy characteristically concerns motions in phase spaces. To paraphrase Clower, points rather than crosses are important. Concentration on solution points can be misleading. It has become time to learn something about the motions of economic systems.

NOTES

NOTE A: *Cf.* Paul A. Samuelson, "The Simple Mathematics of Income Determination," Metzler *et al.* (eds.), *Income, Employment and Public Policy; Essays in Honor of Alvin H. Hansen,* pp. 133-155. For explanations of the period multiplier see Joan Robinson, *Introduction to the Theory of Employment* (London: Macmillan & Co., Ltd., 1939); Lloyd A. Metzler, "Three Lags in the Circular Flow of Income," *Income, Employment and Public Policy*; *Essays in Honor of Alvin H. Hansen,* pp. 11-32.

Calculation of the period multiplier is in response to the query: when the total effects of an increase in autonomous expenditure are considered, what is the quantitative relationship between these and the initial increment to expenditure? Some sort of period analysis must be used. Thus, consider this model:

a) investment expenditure in each period is determined independently of events of previous periods;

b) consumption in the *t-th* period is determined by the relation

$$C_t = 0.9Y_{t-1}.$$

This period's consumption is equal to nine-tenths of last period's income; the consumption decision is a lagged response to last period's income;

c) there is no lag between changes in sales and changes in output nor between the earning and distribution of income; the only lag is the expenditures lag of (b).

If there were a one-shot increase in autonomous expenditure of $1 in period 0, income — defined as the sum of *ex post* consumption and *ex post* investment — increased by $1 in the initial period. In period 1, consumption will increase by $0.90 as a result of period 0's higher income. Income in period 1 will be $0.90 higher than in period (—1), leading to an increase of $0.81 in consumption expenditure over that of period (—1). We are dealing with an infinite series of the form

$$x_0 + 0.9x_0 + (0.9)^2x_0 + \cdots + (0.9)^r x_0 + \cdots$$

This series can be shown to converge to $10x_0$. The period multiplier here is 10: the total increment to expenditure resulting from an initial dose of autonomous expenditure of $1 approaches $10: it can be brought as close to $10 as one wishes; all that need be done is to take enough terms of the series.

Verbally — following Professor Metzler's classroom example — consider a football team at the enemy 10-yard line, offered an indefinitely large number of downs to cross the enemy goal line but able to traverse only 9/10 of any remaining distance. Its first play will net 9 yards, the second 0.9 yards, the third, 0.0 yards, etc. The sum of yardage gained will never *quite* equal 10, but, if enough scrimmages are allowed, the offensive team can come as close as you wish to scoring, although it never actually scores.

NOTE B: Chapter XII scouts possibilities of limitless inflation. If real output becomes jammed at full-employment output, expansionary dreams of entrepreneurs will go unfulfilled. Planned investment expenditures will be dampened. And then Ch. VA (as well as Ch. XII) discussed the Keynesian credit cycle in which the system turns down from its peak as cost-price and wage good — capital good relationships change. Finally, it is hard to imagine that a set of interest rates in which bill rate was, say, 82 per cent would not smother the most sanguine expectations.

There are no stability problems under even the most extreme Chrysippus assumptions about the demand for money, namely that only income or transaction rates — not securities prices — affect demand for money. If M can be brought under control, the money value of national product is determined by the equation

$$\overline{M} = kpY^{**}, \qquad (i)$$

imposing a specialized demand function for money. k is a rigid parameter and Y^{**} is full-employment income. On the other hand, Equation i makes clear that the price level cannot be controlled except by controlling M, just as a pure Epicurus formulation makes clear that the price level cannot be controlled except through manipulation of government expenditures and receipts and/or physical controls on non-governmental demand for goods and services.

Chapter XI has not shown how a neoclassical (*tatonnement*) system might be graphed analogously to the *IS-LM* construction for a Keynesian system. Assuming, of course, that the system has a solution, recall (from Note K, Ch. VA) the Metzler-Patinkin *CC-LL* formulation. The curves plot combinations of interest rates and prices consistent with *ex ante* clearance of commodities and money markets. Simultaneous clearance of these markets (subsuming, as it happens, clearance of the labor market) assure, through Walras' Law, that the bond market will be cleared.

Now construct *CC* and *LL* curves for Chrysippian, Epicurean and "mixed" specifications. The results pertain to effectiveness of monetary and fiscal policy in the control of inflation. Diagrams A, B, and C are generalized, Chrysippus, and Epicurus versions respectively. In Diagram A higher price levels must be associated with higher interest rates if the money market is to clear: velocity must be stimulated. The downward-sloping *CC* curve reflects a real-balance effect. Lower interest rates are assumed to stimulate planned expenditure; higher price levels are assumed to exercise a restraining influence. Balance can be sustained in the commodity market if lower interest rates are accompanied by higher price levels.

Diagram B depicts a Chrysippus world. The vertical *LL* curve implies that demand for money is governed by the price level but not by the interest rate. The pertinent equation is

(ii) $$M^d \equiv kpY^{**}.$$

GENERALIZED VERSION

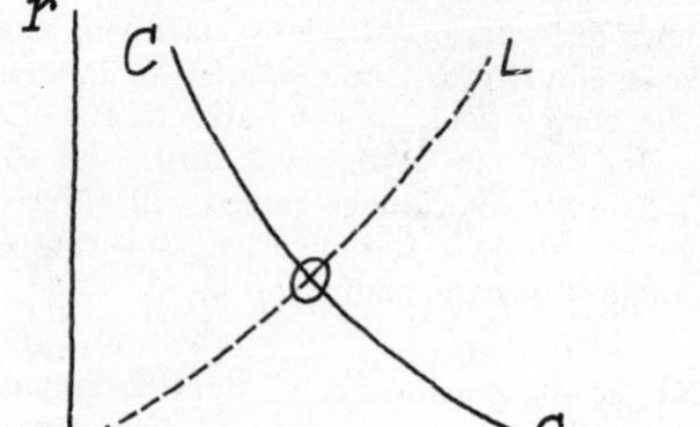

Diagram A — Figure XI-9

CHRYSIPPUS VERSION

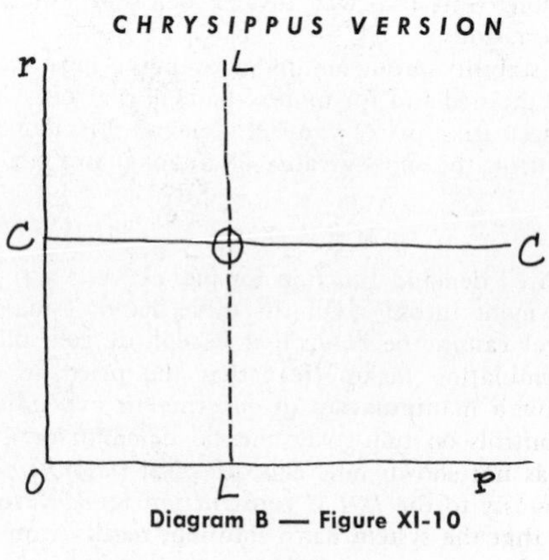

Diagram B — Figure XI-10

EPICURUS VERSION

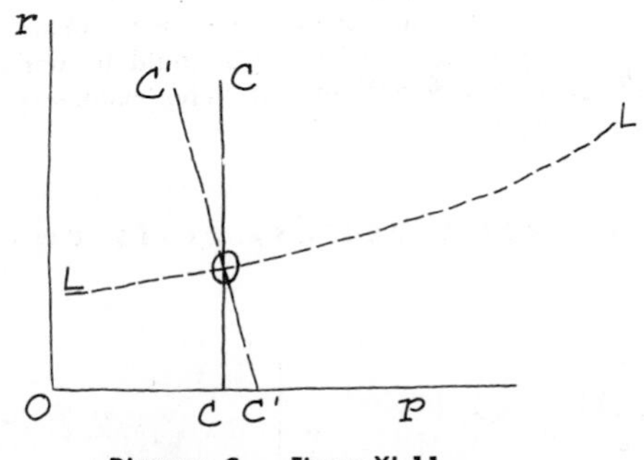

Diagram C — Figure XI-11

The only way in which the price level can be controlled is by laterally shifting the *LL* curve, implying that the stock of money is altered. The *CC* curve as drawn in Diagram B, ignores the real-balance effect. Once autonomous elements of expenditure are given, there is a unique interest rate — or set of rates — clearing the commodity market. The vertical *LL* curve means that fiscal policies will have no impact on p^*. An increase in autonomous government spending, *cet. par.*, is reflected in an upward horizontal displacement of the *CC* curve so that r^* increases: higher interest rate(s) become(s) necessary to reduce planned spending so that demand for cash remains consistent with Equation ii.

Diagram C depicts an Epicurean world. The flattish *LL* curve arises from elastic liquidity preference: a small increase in r leads to a large decrease in demand for money balances, *cet. par.* The price level must rise substantially for demand for money for transactions purposes to increase enough to offset effects of lower interest rates on portfolio-balance plans. The *CC* curve is hard to define in an Epicurean world; Epicureans are inclined to hold that planned expenditure on goods and services is insensitive to interest rates, and also to denigrate real-balance effects. One can "punt" by assuming the price level is arbitrarily determined at any point in time, partly governed by union demands; hence the vertical *CC* curve of Diagram C. Shifts in *LL* would — in that construction — have no impact on p^*: r^* adjusts so as to accommodate demand for money to the new available stock. It is hard to work fiscal policy into the essentially-disequilibrium system posed by the vertical *CC* curve, illustrating a variant of the cost-push inflation hypothesis discussed in the appendix to Ch. XIII; cost-push is expressed through lateral displacement of *CC* . . . The dashed-line, *C'C'*, is a milder version of an Epicurean approach, although, paradoxically, a real-balance effect is implicitly introduced. It is clear that large changes in the money stock, expressed through correspondingly large shifts in *LL,* have little effect on p^*: r^* adjusts to the new monetary conditions, an adjustment with very little backwash in the commodity market.

NOTE C : The diagram below gives background for the corresponding neoclassical ("full-employment") problem. If the price level is to be shoved back from p_1 to p_2, exclusive application of monetary policy, expressed in a leftward shift of *LL,* leads to a very large increase in the rate of interest, an increase that may be politically unsupportable or lead to "disruption" of the securities markets, and certainly to huge capital losses for some traders. Similarly, leftward shifts of the *CC* curve, induced, let us say, by reduced autonomous government expenditure, require very large reductions in interest rates if p^* is to be moved from p_1 to p_2. Indeed, the intercepts of the curves of the diagram might be such that some shifts in "equilibrium" price levels would be impossible without simultaneous shifts of the curves. (Note that, here, "monetary policy" cannot merely find "M" increasing.)

SYNTHETIC POLICY, CC-LL CONTEXT

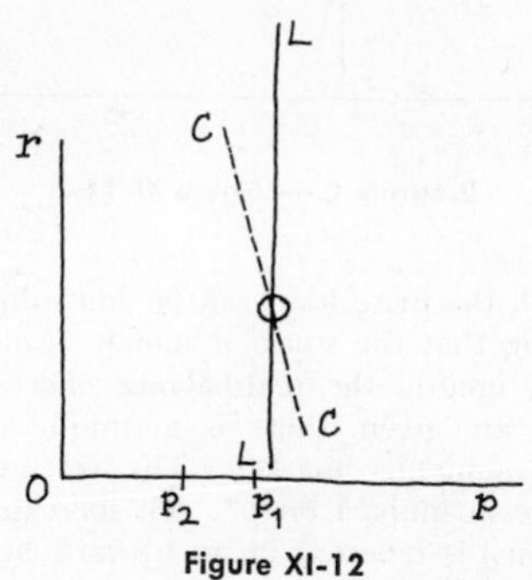

Figure XI-12

Note D: At p. 611 we consider problems of financing government deficits during transitional stages after a tax-cut or boost in exogenous expenditure. It is easy to show that the analytical framework is that of Ch. XV's *transfer problem*: an arbitrarily small "lump of money" can theoretically finance an arbitrarily large annual deficit. So long as the public does not want to add to its cash holdings — preferring to hold incremental financial wealth in bonds or wishing to acquire new bonds in order to offset imputed incremental indebtedness *qua* taxpayers — the "lump of money" repeatedly will be transferred back to the Government as it repeatedly pays out the proceeds of bond sales to its suppliers and transferees.

Postulation of the propensity to save as unity advances the argument. Incremental flow demand for bonds would then increase *pari passu* with the incremental deficit if the income elasticity of demand for cash were zero. Of course, in general, interest rates must somewhat increase if Note D's processes are to unfold. But, once interest rates have risen enough for incremental demand for cash to be arbitrarily small, the argument holds regardless of multiplier effects. A deficit of \$525,600 per annum, spread evenly over the year, could be financed by \$1 in cash in a frictionless payments process finding k in $X^s_{Mj} \equiv k(M^s_j - M^d_j)$ equal to unity for all j where the transformation converts excess stock supply into per-minute flow rates. There would, of course, be monetary-stock disequilibrium throughout the process; excess flow supplies of money would be married to fresh issues of Government bonds at t for all values of t.

APPENDIX

More on the Consumption Function

1

THE CONSUMPTION FUNCTIONS (RELATIONS SUCH AS $C = C(Y, r)$) of Part II have been outmoded. This has not damaged us: more recent work would not basically change our results. Still, the lineaments of modern consumption-function theory should be indicated, together with a *very* sketchy bibliography.

The main result of more recent work on the consumption function is easy to state: the functional relationship between current consumption and current income is not as strong as early "Keynesians" thought; a goodly part of current consumption should be regarded as exogenous to current measured income; independent variables alternative to current disposable income better explain the data.

What the alternative formulations essentially do is to introduce weighted combinations of past incomes as explanatory variables. These are to capture lagged response to economic stimuli. There is a hard core of economic theory underlying revision of the consumption function:[27] one chooses between consumption at different points in time just as he does between alternative forms of consumption today; the appropriate constraint on expenditures is a wealth variable reflecting past receipt and expenditure streams, current receipts, and receipts that can be obtained in the future. Consumption function theory is peculiarly Keynesian (as against neoclassical): it is concerned either with principles guiding households in estimating future "income restraints" and their responses to these estimates or, more naïvely, with households' current reactions to current income constraints.

Current receipts can be extremely misleading as a guide to expected receipts and accumulated wealth. It would be plausible for a

[27] Compare Note C, Ch. X, however.

married medical student to buy a cooperative apartment in a fashionable neighborhood even if his current income were nil: his expectations might justify his "extravagance." In fact, young families typically run cash deficits, repaying debt in their middle years when they accumulate additional savings to tide them over their declining years, pay for the funeral meats, etc.[28] A nonogenarian, who in his prime was a celebrated concert violinist and chose, as did Pope's father, undeviatingly to hold his savings in hard cash, might be living in some style although his receipts are nil. On the other hand, a ball player might live in virtual squalor, accumulating capital to tide him over years of retirement (from baseball) when he might otherwise be reduced to penury.

The formal micro model is complex. It must recognize this much:

1) the choice variable is a time path of consumption. A curve, not a point, is being chosen;

2) terminal stocks are important. The length of the time horizon is important;

3) the equivalent of the budget constraint must be carefully formulated. Terms of trade between consumptions at different dates are derivable from interest rates. The present value of consumption (the discounted value of consumption expenditures) of the plan — unless you are Al Capone — cannot exceed the value of current human and non-human capital less the value of terminal asset holdings. Of course, this capital valuation implicitly accounts for future receipts that can be generated by optimally utilized present equipment.

It would be impossible to formulate such a theory without touching upon the work of Frank Ramsey (*op. cit.*). But it is not enough to understand the calculus of variations. Formation of consumption plans finds one peering into a dimly lit future: the decision process necessarily is stochastic.

Irving Fisher's *The Theory of Interest*[29] — the early editions are more than 50 years old — probably is the parent of modern consumption theory. It is a great book and is touched on in Ch. XII.

In view of the considerable analytical apparatus underlying recently formulated consumption functions, their applications might be difficult. Not at all! Friedman's formulation, for example, can be

[28] Note that a good part of the expenditure of young families is on long-lived durables. Such expenditure largely should be classified as investment in a sophisticated model.

[29] Irving Fisher, *The Theory of Interest* (New York: Kelley and Millman, Inc., 1959).

expressed so that it is formally indistinguishable from Ch. X's formulations:

$$C_t \equiv \beta_{ot} + \beta_1 Y^d{}_t$$

where C_t is real consumption per capita at t and Y^d disposable personal income per capita. However β_1 in this formulation is about 0.297 (=0.9(0.33)). Consumption plans — much influenced by past experience — are relatively unresponsive to changes in current income. Even lower multipliers are implied than were suggested by the Ch. XI models β_{ot} — consumption expenditures exogenous in the *t-th period* — are obtained by solving an equation of the form

$$\beta_{ot} = 0.9\Sigma w_i Y^d{}_i$$

where i runs to $t{-}1$. The sum of the weights, the w's, is unity. The approximate sum of the weights to $t{-}1$ is 0.67; w_t is approximately 0.33.

Other formulations become similarly manageable in their empirical forms. There result distributed lagged functions consistent with extremely naïve underlying theories. But this is not surprising. If the future is to be predicted through statistical procedures, events that have already happened must serve as predictors.

2

Revised consumption functions have allowed reinterpretation of a good deal of data. Consider this Table.

DATA

(1) Period Covered	(2) Average DPI Per Cap. in 1929 Prices	(3) Sum of Consumption Divided by Sum of Real DPI Per Cap. $\Sigma C/\Sigma Y^d$	(4) MPC
1897-1906	420	0.89	0.72
1907-1916	495	0.89	0.65
1919-1929	591	0.88	0.60
1929-1941	607	0.94	0.45
1930-1949	691	0.87	0.46
1897-1949	578	0.88	0.70

TABLE XI-II

Source: Milton Friedman, *A Theory of the Consumption Function* (Princeton: Princeton University Press, 1957), p. 126.

Column 2 shows average disposable income per capita over each interval; Column 3, the ratio of the total of consumption to the total of average DPI per capita. Thus, assume that we are dealing with the interval $(t-1)-(t+1)$ and that Column 2 values are 100, 150, 200. $\Sigma Y^d = 450$. Assume that consumption values are 75, 100, 110. $\Sigma C = 285$. The corresponding entry in Column 3 would be 285/450. MPC (marginal propensity to consume) values were obtained by fitting regression lines to the annual observations contained within each of the six intervals. The statistics of Column 4 are the slopes of corresponding regression lines.

Each of the fitted regression lines has a positive intercept: average propensities to consume exceed marginal propensities. Consult the diagram below. Ignore the dashed lines comprising triangle EDO for the nonce. The *x*'s are observations. The solid line (including the segment *AP*) is fitted by least-squares. The Table indicates that the regression line is likely to have a positive intercept (*AO* in the diagram): the average propensity to consume is expected to exceed the marginal propensity to consume. Thus in a consumption function of the form

$$C = a + bY$$

(*cf.* the diagram below), the average propensity to consume for $Y = Y^*$ is

$$(a+bY^*)/Y^* = a/Y^* + b.$$

FITTED CONSUMPTION FUNCTION

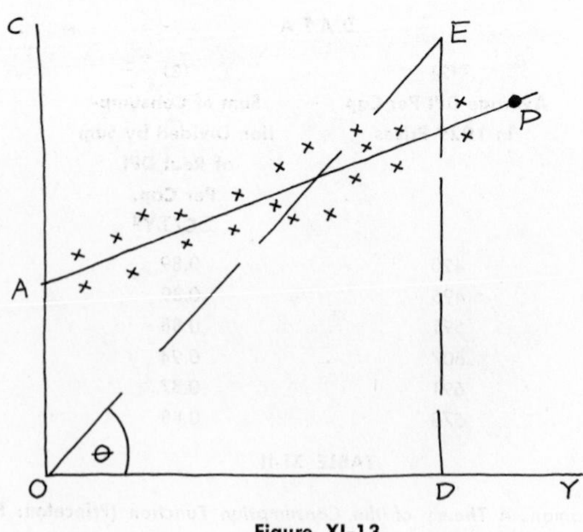

Figure XI-13

The marginal propensity to consume is b, necessarily less than $a/Y^* + b$. If the marginal and average propensities are to be equal, a must equal zero: the regression line must pass through the origin. Witness the dashed line OE. For any point on OE or its projection, $APC = MPC = \tan \theta$.

A positive intercept implies that the ratio C/Y—indefinitely large for $Y = 0$—declines towards the limiting value b as Y increases. Accordingly, consumption-income lines fitted to annual data suggest that average propensities to consume should secularly decrease as income increases. But Column 3 (in the Table) makes clear that average propensities to consume did *not* decrease from decade to decade. In fact if the data are expressed in *decade averages,* only a line of the form of OE can fit the data.

How might the paradox be resolved? Friedman suggests the "permanent income hypothesis." Roughly, he divides measured income in any period into permanent and transitory components. The permanent component is given by the rate of expenditure that could be sustained while keeping capital intact. Capital is defined to include human and non-human elements. The transitory component is the difference between measured and permanent income. As Friedman puts it:

> "The permanent component is to be interpreted as reflecting the effect of those factors that the unit regards as determining its capital value or wealth . . . It is analogous to the 'expected' value of a probability distribution. The transitory component is to be interpreted as reflecting all 'other' factors, factors that are likely to be treated by the united affected as 'accidental' or 'chance' occurrences . . ."[30]

The empirical approximation of permanent income is *expected income*: a weighted sum of current disposable income and disposable income for a number of past years.[31] Indeed we have seen that the Friedman and other models are distributed-lag characterizations.

Friedman's basic hypothesis is that

$$C_p \equiv bY_p$$

where C_p is the permanent component of consumption, defined analogously to Y_p, permanent income. If the permanent-income hypothesis

[30] *Op. cit.*, pp. 21-22.

[31] Of course, future asset positions are being determined simultaneously with the consumption decision: wealth is not a parameter in a rigorous model; only certain initial constraints are parameters. It has always seemed to me that the theoretical underpinning of consumption-function models was puny.

is correct, persons whose measured incomes far exceed their permanent incomes (persons with large positive transitory components) will be consuming smaller fractions of measured incomes than persons with large negative transitory components. Thus, if at a point in time a number of persons with "large" measured incomes were "over their heads" while a number of others with "small" measured incomes were experiencing a run of bad luck, the fitted regression line would tend to flatten out and to have a large positive intercept in contrast with some "true" relationship, a ray through the origin. If, for the sake of simplicity, we assumed that all persons were governed by the $C_p = bY_p$ relationship and that b was the same for all (transitory components for C being zero throughout), the diagram below would apply. The "true relationship" between consumption and permanent income gives rise to the measured relationship described by the line $C_m = a + b_1Y_m$, where the subscript "m" is for "measured." Thus, point Q describes the status of Mr. I whose measured income OE is well short of his permanent income OA. Mr. I is having a bad year, but his permanent income governs his consumption. Point P describes the behavior of Mr. II, aware that his permanent expectation, so to speak, is OB; he adjusts his consumption accordingly. A "flattened" line is generated.

Ours was a cross-sectional analysis, but the reasoning readily applies to the time-series problem of Table II and Figure 13. We should anticipate that decade-average data would be less influenced by transitory components than would annual data, and then Friedman shows at p. 125 *ff.* of his book that ". . . the observed income elasticity can

EFFECTS OF TRANSITORY COMPONENTS

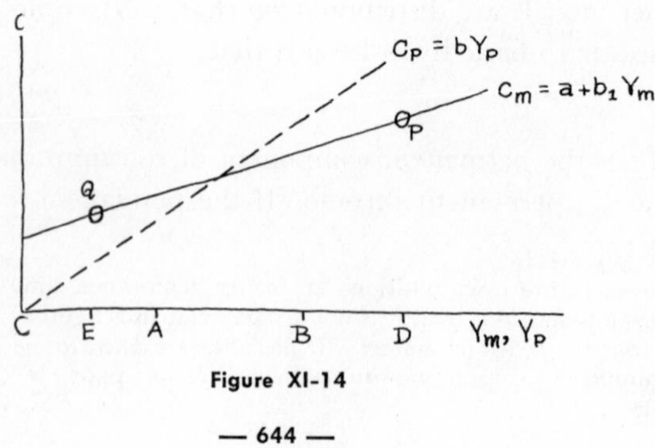

Figure XI-14

be expected to be higher the longer the period covered, provided that the society in question is undergoing a systematic secular change in income."

3

That is all I wish to say about consumption-function theory.[32] For us the key point is that multipliers will be reduced as more of consumption expenditure is predetermined at time t and $\partial Y_t/\partial G_t$ is reduced. *Some* of the major contributions to the literature are:

1) James S. Duesenberry, *Income, Saving, and the Theory of Consumer Behavior* (Cambridge: Harvard University Press, 1949). Duesenberry stresses the role played by the highest level of income previously experienced in relation to current income in the formation of consumption plans.

2) Franco Modigliani, "Fluctuations in the Saving-Income Ratio: A Problem in Economic Forecasting," *Studies in Income and Wealth*, XI (New York: National Bureau of Economic Research, 1949).

3) Franco Modigliani and Richard Brumberg, "Utility Analysis and the Consumption Function: An Interpretation of Cross-Section Data," K. Kurihara (ed.), *Post Keynesian Economics* (New Brunswick: Rutgers University Press, 1954), pp. 388-436. This is perhaps the most rigorous and elegant treatment of derivation of consumption functions in the broad context of choice and asset theory and statistical aggregation. Life cycle theories of saving are emphasized.

4) Milton Friedman, *A Theory of the Consumption Function.*

5) J. M. Keynes, *The General Theory of Employment, Interest, and Money*, pp. 89-131. Keynes's own formulation of the consumption function is in fact much more subtle than we are apt to remember — its celebration has in part resulted from its startling basic simplicity.

[32] Again remember that fuller theoretical analysis shows that *neither* the independent nor dependent variables of consumption-function theories are truly autonomous in an n-period horizon model.

CHAPTER TWELVE

The Fourth Approximation to Income Theory: Dynamics

A. INTRODUCTION

This chapter is not a comprehensive survey of dynamized versions of Keynesian income theory. Otherwise we could not justify exclusion of such writers as Kaldor,[1] Robinson,[1] Phillips, Kalecki, Domar, *et al.*[2] It merely is intended as a glimpse of the way in which theories of motions of economic systems are formulated. Certain regular motions, including stationarity, become special cases. The *General Theory* recedes as we pass to explicitly dynamical theorizing.

The heart of the matter of Ch. XII is suggested by the fact that the models of Chapters IX–XI imply ongoing processes of capital accumulation. Positive savings and investment are implied. The vector of solution values, y^*, for period $t+1$ will differ from $y^*(t)$: initial capital stocks will differ. Cannot what has thus far been a jumble of successive instantaneous solutions be organized into a systematic attack?

And then it has not been emphasized enough that net investment is a response to disequilibrium, reflecting disparity of actual and desired capital, consistent with moving but not stationary equilibrium.[3]

Observation of ongoing economic systems suggests continuous dis-

---

1 But *cf.* Appendix C, Ch. XII.

2 For analysis of work of Harrod, Kalecki, Phillips, *et al.*, *cf.* R. G. D. Allen, *Mathematical Economics,* esp. pp. 60-90, 209-313.

3 Again emphasizing the importance of imbedding investment behavior in portfolio-selection functions.

parity of actual and desired holdings of capital goods. Stationary states are empirically uninteresting. It is aesthetically and mathematically right to inquire whether economic growth will be regular or irregular, featured by explosiveness or damping, etc. And in any event we must improve our treatment of investment behavior, thus far pretty much divorced from formal capital theory; investment must be placed in the context of its intimate relationship with the theory of demand for capital.

Although income theory has been further generalized in the "macrodynamic" literature, it has not effectively been coupled with standard theory of consumer and business behavior. It is fairly clear that theories of capital accumulation positing pure competition among firms must rely on price-expectation concepts: prices, not outputs, are parametric for purely competitive producers. Monopoloid markets also are troublesome: neither output nor price, but rather parameters of demand and cost functions are exogenous for the monopolist.

Our concern will be with aggregate relationships associating the rate of change of the stock of capital $(dK/dt \equiv I)$ with that of effective demand (dY^*/dt). We sometimes associate $I(t)$ and $Y(dY/dt)$ without attempting reconciliation with such considerations as initial excess capacity, effects of relative factor prices on desired labor-capital ratios, etc. At other times, we are more careful to specify that unfolding results are based on characteristically unit-elastic price expectations, that rigidity of the capital-output ratio — seemingly inconsistent with output departing from a fixed relationship with capital stock —is offset by buffer stocks, etc.

B. LEONTIEF'S SYNTHESIS OF KEYNES AND FISHER

1

The full title of Wassily Leontief's note emphasizes its pertinence for us: "theoretical note on time-preference, productivity of capital, stagnation, and economic growth."[4] It is an ideal jumping-off point for study of *post*-Keynesian economics.

Borrowing some of Irving Fisher's expository devices, Leontief focuses on the savings decision as a choice to give up a quantum of

[4] *American Economic Review*, Vol. 48, No. 1, March 1958, pp. 105-111.

present consumption in favor of a capital asset which generates "a perpetual series of equal annual interest payments." The Leontief man (and society) at each point in time is in an intertemporal tussle. He decides how he should allocate his income between consumption and investment in standardized annuities.[5] Resolution of the tussle is explained graphically in the diagram below. The horizontal axis measures current income and consumption; the vertical axis measures annuity streams. These annuity streams are produced by capital. The 45° line has special importance: at a point on the 45° line, current consumption is equal to the perpetual annuity which can be purchased with initial capital; capital is neither increasing nor decreasing; there neither is accumulation nor decumulation. A decision to stay on the 45° line is a decision precisely to undertake current consumption expenditures equal to current income. On the other hand, a decision to

"EQUILIBRIUM" AND TIME PREFERENCE

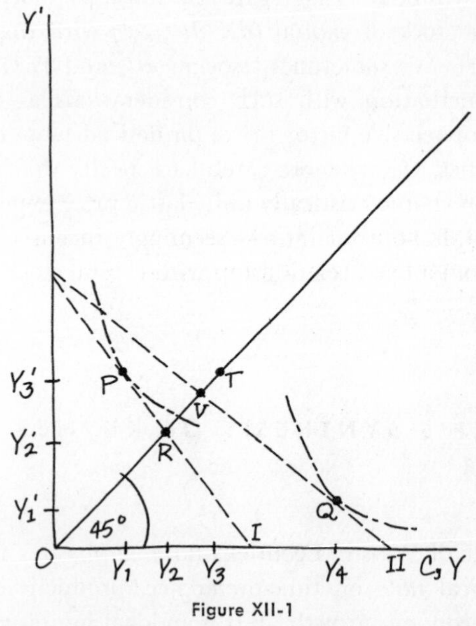

Figure XII-1

[5] F. M. Westfield points out that Leontief men, since their horizons are shorter than the time-span of the appropriate dynamical processes, may embark upon inefficient programs of capital accumulation. ("Comment," *American Economic Review,* Vol. 49, No. 5, Dec. 1959, pp. 1037-1041.) Leontief's reply (*loc. cit.,* pp. 1041-1043) makes clear that (1) he concedes Westfield's point; (2) he is concerned with stability rather than with efficiency.

move to P — given that initial capital yields the perpetual stream $Y'_2 = Y_2$ — is a decision to accumulate capital. It leads to a new level of income — defined as the rate of consumption leaving capital just intact — $Y'_3 = Y_3$. The next decision is to be made "starting from" T. A decision to move to point Q (starting at V) is a decision to decumulate capital, to eat up part of one's substance. It leads to the next decision being made "lower down" on the 45° line, at a point below V.

The terms of trade between current consumption and accretion to capital are given by the slopes of such lines as I and II. The flatter are these lines, the more current consumption must be sacrificed in order to acquire a given increment to the annuity stream, the more expensive are annuities in terms of current consumption. The slopes of lines I and II are equal to $-(1+r)$ where the rate of interest appropriate for annuity valuation is $100r$ per cent per period.

The family of curves is an indifference map. Each curve plots a locus of Y'-C combinations registering the same score on the preference-recording machine. For reasons explained in Ch. VII, we assume that these curves do not intersect and that more-rightward are preferred to less rightward curves. Again relying on Ch. VII, certain properties of solution states can be asserted. Noting that the appropriate budget line passes through that point on the 45° line given by initial income (capital), the solution occurs where the budget line is tangent to an indifference curve. A necessary condition for temporary equilibrium is that the rate of time preference be equal to *the* rate of interest. The *rate of time preference* here is defined as a rate at which annuity income can be substituted for current consumption — multiplied by 100 per cent — so that the subject remains on the same indifference curve. Thus, if I am willing to exchange \$1's worth of current consumption for a perpetual annuity of \$0.10, my time preference *here* is defined as 10 per cent per annum. Time preference will, in general, vary from point to point in C-Y' space. We assert that a man has systematic time preference when his intertemporal rate of substitution always exceeds unity on iso-consumption rays. *Die Wesenheit* is that an individual will choose a point where the rate at which he is *willing* to exchange current consumption for an increment to his annuity stream is equal to the rate at which he *can* do so.

2

We still have not forged enough tools to use Leontief's model. Recalling Ch. VII, we know that a necessary condition for the system to be in balance is that the marginal efficiency of capital (conceived as a rate of return over cost) be equal to *the* rate of interest. Following Lerner,[6] the next step is to distinguish between the *marginal efficiency of capital* and the *marginal productivity of capital.* The latter is defined as the marginal efficiency of capital when the rate of investment is arbitrarily close to zero. We should expect that, as more of the system's resources are devoted to investment as against consumption activity, the rate of return over cost will decline. Consult Diagrams A and B.

Curve *i,* Diagram A, describes a state in which the marginal productivity of capital is constant: capital might be "all inclusive" in the Knightian sense. (We return to this possibility in the next subsection; it is an organic part of the position of the "Chicago School."[7]) Curve *ii,* Diagram A, describes decreasing marginal productivity of capital: the rate of return on the first dollar's worth of investment is lower for higher values of initial capital stock.

The important thing about Diagram B is that the appropriate *MEC* curve is downward-sloping regardless of whether curve *i* or curve *ii* of Diagram A describes the corresponding *MPC* relation. Thus, if curve *i* applies, *MPC* will always be equal to, say, *(MPC)′*: curve *(1)*

MARGINAL PRODUCTIVITY OF CAPITAL

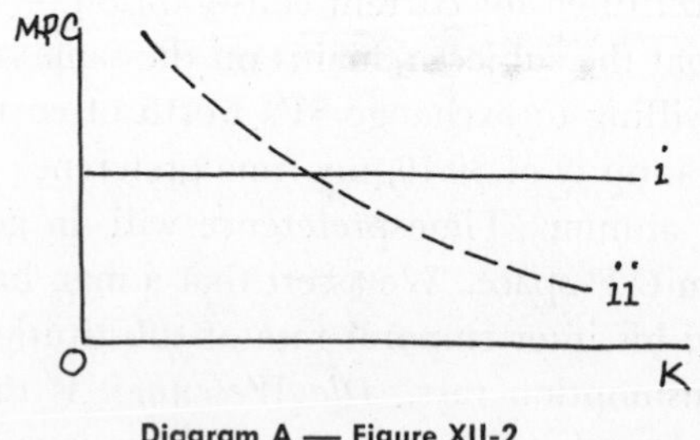

Diagram A — Figure XII-2

[6] A. P. Lerner, *Essays in Economic Analysis* (London: Macmillan & Co., 1953), pp. 347-353.

[7] *Cf.* Milton Friedman's unpublished *Lecture Notes.* It provides the basis for synthesizing the Leontief and the Knight-Friedman formulation. Indeed, Lerner and Friedman, *loc. cit.,* have (indirectly) led me somewhat to alter the Leontief model.

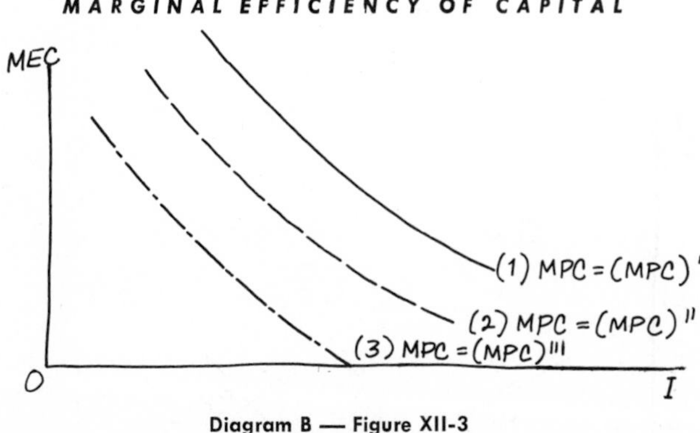

Diagram B — Figure XII-3

pertains throughout. On the other hand, if *ii* applies, the appropriate *MEC* curve shifts downward as the initial capital stock increases.

Diagram C is very useful in presenting the full Leontief system, but two preliminary points should be made. Assuming, after Fisher, that there are perfect markets for consumer and producer loans, the system cannot be in temporary equilibrium unless the marginal efficiency of capital is equal to time preference. In equilibrium these rates will be the same for all. Finally, following Leontief, we draw *social* preference maps, a step requiring much elaboration if logical consistency is to be assured, but one we take utterly blithely.

Each of the transformation loci of Diagram C is defined in terms of the initial capital stock associated with P_1 (leading to TT), P_2 (leading to $T'T'$), and P_4 (leading to $T''T''$). Starting at P_1 (the initial income is given by P_1's abscissa value), the marginal productivity of capital exceeds the rate of time preference. Accordingly, there will be excess demand for capital goods if the initial rate of investment is zero.[8] Equality of time preference and the marginal efficiency of capital *is* achieved at P'_1, leading to P_2 as the initial position for the second period. Starting at P_2, we move to P_4 through P_3. The dynamic process is under way.

In Leontief's phrase, there are "two sets of basic structural relationships," those dealing with time preference and those dealing with the marginal efficiency of capital. Their interplay is the subject of his model. One seeks a simple way of viewing these relationships at a

[8] Leontief works with a one-good system, while I am (heuristically) working with two basic goods. The modification is consistent with Professor Leontief's over-all purpose.

LEONTIEF'S SYSTEM

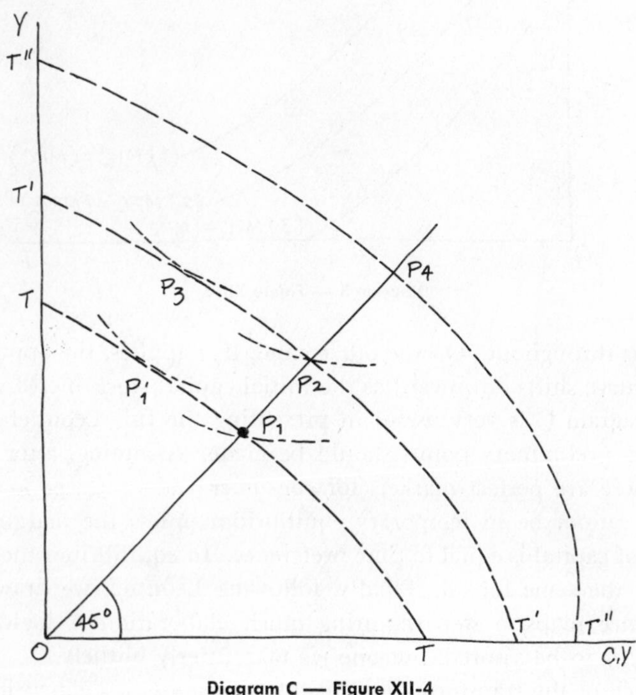

Diagram C — Figure XII-4

glance illuminating problems of stability, stagnation, etc. Leontief provides the device, reproduced as Diagram D. (*Cf.* Leontief, *loc. cit.*, p. 109.) The *TP* curve shows the slope of the indifference curve cutting the 45° line for points with abscissa values recorded on the horizontal axis of Diagram D. The *TP* curve implies rates of time preference at various incomes (capital stocks) when the rate of investment is zero. The *MP* curve — similarly derived — shows the marginal efficiency of capital at various incomes (capital stocks) when the rate of investment is zero. The *D* curve at the bottom of the diagram registers the difference between the absolute values of the slopes of the *TP* and *MP* curves *(TP-MP)*. So long as *MP* exceeds *TP* the system will be featured by accumulation of capital; income will be growing. If *TP* exceeds *MP*, capital will be eaten up; income will be decreasing over time. If *TP* = *MP*, the system will be stationary; income will neither be increasing nor decreasing.

Points *a, b,* and *c* on the *D* curve are equilibrium points in the sense that corresponding values of income give rise neither to growth nor decay; these points represent stationary states. Point *a* represents a locally-stable equilibrium: *MP* exceeds *TP* to the left of *a*; *TP* ex-

SUMMARY OF LEONTIEF'S DYNAMICS

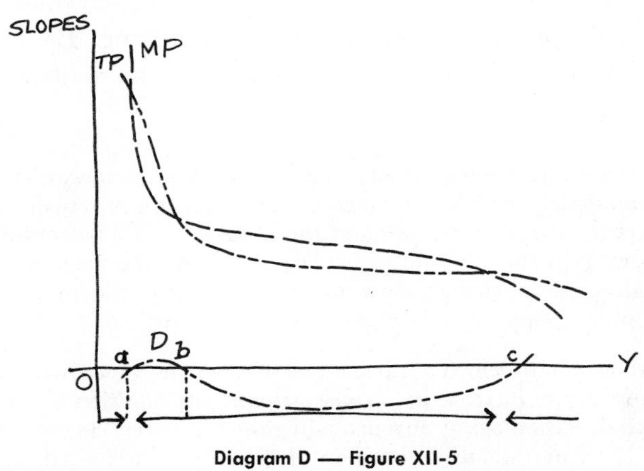

Diagram D — Figure XII-5

ceeds *MP* to the immediate right of *a*. Growth will occur if income is less than *0a* and there will be decay if income is between *0a* and *0b*. Initial values for income between *0* and *0b* start up processes moving towards *0a*. *b* is a point of unstable equilibrium. Initial incomes to the left of *b* start up processes moving income towards *0a*; initial values to the right of *b* start up processes moving income towards *0c*, another locally stable equilibrium point.

3

It is easy to apply the now completed structure to problems of development and to "Keynesian economics." If the initial rate of effective demand, *Y**, is in the *0-0b* range, it cannot escape from the low-income trap unless some outside force intervenes. Such intervention might be foreign aid, an exceptional harvest. etc. Once income is shifted into the *0b-0c* range, the system is able spontaneously to generate growth; it will have taken off. The Keynesian application is easier if we begin with *Y** in the *0b-0c* range, say, just to the right of

0b. At the outset, the system can sustain high levels of investment consistently with over-all market clearance. However, as time passes, *MEC* curves shift downward, more rapidly in fact than do *TP* curves (which might roughly stand proxy for liquidity-preference), slowing down growth. The system grinds towards the stationary state of point *c*. Insofar as accelerator relationships apply, slowing down in the system's rate of growth might lead to disastrous collapse of capital formation; the system might be subjected to a devastating downward spiral.

Leontief's concluding observations are interesting. He shows how his structure might be used to trace the effects of technological advance:

> "For instance technological advance, described as an upward shift of the capital-output curve . . . might — and most likely actually would — affect the shape of the *MP* and the *D* curve . . . The equilibrium positions *a, b,* and *c* would shift. Depending on the magnitude and the nature of the change, some of these positions of stationary state might even disappear or new ones might be created.
>
> To the extent to which a rise in the productivity of capital enables the economy to increase its income without any addition to its stock of capital, technological advance will shift the system at once to the right . . . from whatever position it had previously occupied. In fact, however, new technology as a rule requires a new type of equipment and different kinds of skills. That means that its introduction will depend itself on the current rate of saving and accumulation."[9]

C. CHICAGO SCHOOL MODIFICATION OF THE LEONTIEF MODEL

Just as the Leontief model can show how an economy might stagnate, it can show how an economy can experience indefinite expansion. Frank Knight is associated with hypotheses about marginal productivity of capital and time preference suggesting indefinite log-linear expansion to be the characteristic solution path for systems of the sort thus far described. If certain of the implications of Milton Friedman's

[9] *Op. cit.*, pp. 110-111.

permanent-income hypothesis are also considered, a "Chicago modification" of the Leontief model emerges.[10]

If capital is defined in an all-inclusive sense so that human as well as non-human capital is encompassed, and if limitational factors such as arable land can be neglected, or if technological advance can be assumed to offset pressures against fixed factors, it need not be assumed that the *MP* curve is downward sloping; curve *i* becomes the appropriate construction. *MEC* simply becomes a function of the ratio I/Y. Why should scale matter so long as *MPC* itself is independent of scale? On the other hand, as the ratio of investment to consumption increases, it is reasonable to assume that the terms of transformation of consumption into investment goods become more onerous. The analogy is to the Principle of Variable Proportions. These are a few of the strands of Knightian capital theory.

If time preference is independent of scale within the relevant range, but depends instead on the ratio of posited present and future consumption, the propensity to consume should not be affected by the level of income (size of the capital stock). Indeed, *a priori* reasoning suggests that there is at least no reason to reject this view: while a poor man may have to surrender "necessities" in order to save, he will have to go without "necessities" in the future if he does not save now.[11]

Another way of saying that the marginal productivity of capital and the rate of time preference should be independent of K (uniquely associated with income) is to say that the functions of Equations 1 and 2 are zero-degree homogeneous in C and Y':

$$\rho \equiv f(C, Y') \equiv F(C/Y'), \tag{1}$$

$$\gamma \equiv g(C, Y') \equiv G(C/Y'). \tag{2}$$

Scaling up C and Y' has no effect on the rate of time preference (ρ) and the marginal productivity of capital (γ): these values are independent of K and depend only on the ratio of current consumption to the annuity available after the consumption decision.

Diagrams A and B summarize the argument:

[10] *Cf.* Milton Friedman, *A Theory of the Consumption Function,* pp. 233-239.

[11] In the Leontief model decreasing time preference is an anti-stagnationist factor. On the other hand, the assumption that the *average* propensity to consume decreases with income (that S/Y increases with Y) implies that the proportion of investment expenditure to total income must increase with time in a growing economy, *cet. par.* (At least if the model is put in *per capita* terms.)

TP AND MPC AS FUNCTIONS OF Y (OR K)

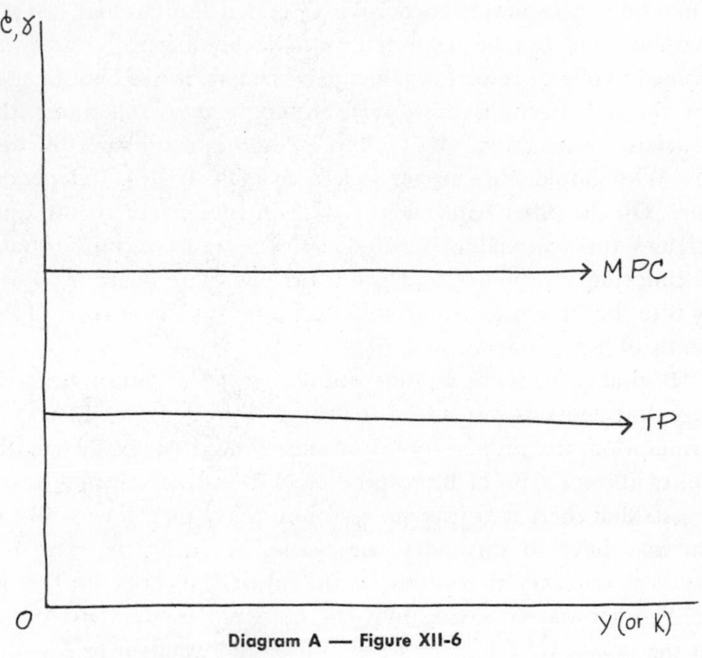

Diagram A — Figure XII-6

Since the slopes of the transformation and indifference curves depend only on the ratio C/Y', and we assume that the curvature properties are uniform, all tangencies will occur along a single ray such as OA. Starting at P_1, we move to P_2 through P_{11}. The process continues on. We move from P_r to P_{r+1} through P_{rr}, etc. The homogeneity assumptions assure that $Y_2/Y_1 = Y_3/Y_2 = \ldots = Y_{r+1}/Y_r = \ldots$ The system is capable of indefinite expansion at a constant rate. As Diagram A shows, the proportion γ/ρ is invariant against Y (and K) . . . The homogeneity of the underlying functions assures that tangencies always will occur along the ray OA, assuring in turn that the system will enjoy steady progress for the indefinite future. This result should not be used to pin a Panglossian tag on the Chicago School. It simply points out that "stagnationist" theories derive from rather special assumptions. Once this has been done, fruitful work is in the domain of empirical testing.

A "CHICAGO-ORIENTED" LEONTIEF DIAGRAM

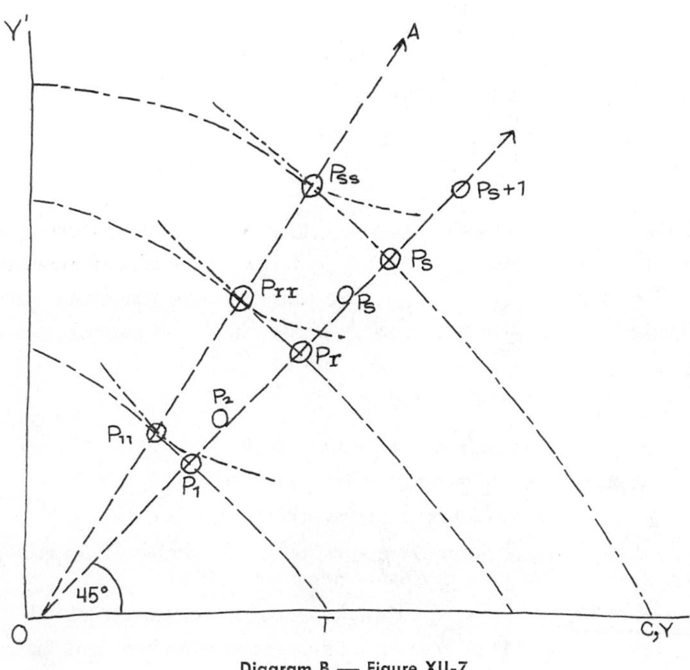

Diagram B — Figure XII-7

D. DUESENBERRY'S SYSTEM

James Duesenberry has worked out a number of rich income-generation models in his book *Business Cycles and Economic Growth.*[12] We render a sketchy account of one of the simplest of these (p. 179 *ff.*). Our purpose is to limn his procedures, move farther along the path of process analysis, and, finally, to present Duesenberry's graphical apparatus, revealing much of the message of Ch. XII.

Breaking in upon *Business Cycles* at p. 195, we find the following seven-equation system depicting a cut-down version of Duesenberry's model:

$$(1) \qquad I_t = f(Y_{t-1}, K_{t-1}, \pi_{t-1}, R_t)$$

[12] James Duesenberry, *Business Cycles and Economic Growth* (New York: McGraw-Hill Book Co., 1958).

$$(2) \qquad C_t = \phi(Y_{t-1} - \pi_{t-1} - R_{t-1} + d_t)$$

$$(3) \qquad d_t = \chi(\pi_{t-1})$$

$$(4) \qquad \pi_t = \theta(Y_t, K_t)$$

$$(5) \qquad R_t = kK_{t-1}$$

$$(6) \qquad K_t = K_{t-1} + I_t - R_t$$

$$(7) \qquad Y_t = I_t + C_t$$

Before defining the variables of System 1-7, note that it features *lagged response* to stimuli; reactions at t are in response to stimuli received at $t-1$. The more complicated the lag patterns and the more periods that elapse between stimulus and response the more complicated can be the motion of the system.

This is Duesenberry's notation:

I_t — investment expenditure in the *tth* period

C_t — consumption expenditure in the *tth* period

Y_t — gross national product in the *tth* period

R_t — capital consumption allowances in the *tth* period (in Equation 5, k, a positive fraction, is a parameter of the system)

K_t — capital stock net of depreciation at the end of the *tth* period

π_t — profits, including those of unincorporated business and farms, earned during the *tth* period

d_t — dividends and entrepreneurial withdrawals during the *tth* period

Equation 1 relates investment expenditure this period to capital stock brought into the period (when adjusted for capital-consumption allowances), last period's earnings, and last period's gross output. Technological conditions suggest desirable proportions between capital and output; last period's output influences expected future outputs. Equation 2 essentially describes a consumption — disposable income relationship built around a Robertsonian lag. The remaining equations are self-explanatory.

Next the model is linearized and reduced through substitution to Equations 8 and 9:

$$(8) \qquad r_y = \frac{Y_t - Y_{t-1}}{Y_{t-1}} = a_{11} + a_{12}(K_{t-1}/\,Y_{t-1})$$

$$(9) \qquad r_k = \frac{K_t - K_{t-1}}{K_{t-1}} = a_{21} + a_{22}(K_{t-1}/Y_{t-1})^{-1}$$

The a's are constant terms. r_y and r_k respectively are rates of growth for income and capital. r_y obviously is a linear function of the lagged capital-output ratio. r_k is less obviously an hyperbolic function of the same ratio.[13]

Duesenberry writes:

> "It must be kept in mind here that the ratio of capital to income is not technically determined. It is simply the result of the cumulative effects of investment on the capital stock and of investment and consumption on income. As we pass from low to high ratios of capital to income the rate of growth of capital tends to fall (a) because the returns on investment are reduced by an increase in the capital-output ratio (with a given state of technique), (b) because profits per unit of capital tend to fall, (c) because a given ratio of investment to income produces a smaller percentage increase in capital stock. At the same time as we pass from low to high capital-income ratios, the rate of growth of income tends to fall. For the reasons just given, the ratio of investment to income tends to fall as the capital income ratio rises. However, the ratio of saving to (lagged) income also tends to fall because of the decline in the ratio of profits to income. [Duesenberry assumes that the proportion of planned saving to income derived from profits exceeds that for non-profit income.] In general, the first effect tends to outweigh the second."[14]

One is led to the diagram below:[15]

DUESENBERRY'S BASIC SYSTEM

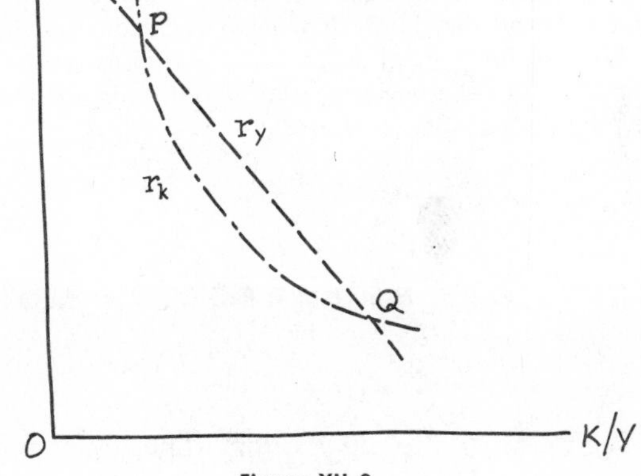

Figure XII-8

[13] Equation 9 is of the general form

(i) $\quad y = ax^{-1} + b \quad$ or $\quad (ii) \quad xy = a + bx,$

a rectangular-hyperbolic form.

[14] *Ibid.*, pp. 204-205.

[15] *Ibid.*, p. 205, Fig. 9.

Points P and Q represent "equilibria" in the sense that, if corresponding capital-output ratios are once achieved, these will be sustained indefinitely: income and capital are growing at the same rate. These capital-output ratios are consistent with sustained growth at their corresponding growth rates. Point Q represents an unstable equilibrium: a displacement of the capital-output ratio to the left of Q finds income growing more rapidly than capital; K/Y becomes still smaller; a displacement to the right of Q finds capital growing more rapidly than output, K/Y is becoming still larger. But P represents a locally stable equilibrium. A displacement of the capital-output ratio to the right of P and the left of Q finds output growing more rapidly than capital; K/Y is falling. A displacement of K/Y to the left of P finds capital growing more rapidly than output; K/Y is rising. Once again a basically Keynesian model is transformed into a dynamical system, describing motions of economic variables over time — beginning from an arbitrary initial position.

Duesenberry offers interesting variations on the theme of the diagram above.[16] Space permits only two further observations:

1) The results of the Duesenberry model sharply differ from the knife-edge equilibria characterizing many of the basic growth models; instability is not inherent in his system.

2) The diagram can be used to exhibit some business-cycle theory.[17] Thus a shock might occur when the ratio of capital to income is between that at P and that at Q, driving down income so that the ratio shifts to the right of Q, leading to a long period of capital decumulation. Recovery can begin only after "floor" phenomena discussed *infra* are brought into play.

E. ELEMENTS OF THE HARRODIAN MODEL[18]

1

In the beginning is the *accelerator.* The accelerator relates investment to *changes* in output. It is concerned with *widening* of

[16] *Op. cit.*, pp. 205-239.

[17] James S. Duesenberry, *op. cit.*, p. 206 *ff.*

[18] *Cf.* especially Sir Roy Harrod, "An Essay in Dynamic Theory, *Economic Journal,* March 1939; Sir Roy Harrod, *Towards A Dynamic Economics* (London: Mac-

capital. *Deepening* of capital — introduction of more capital-intensive techniques in response to technological change or change in the wage rate relatively to the rent of capital — is ancillary in accelerator theory. Multiplier relationships are concerned with the impact of changes in autonomous expenditure on Y^* (and lead to damped fluctuation). Accelerator relationships are concerned with the impact of changes in output on planned investment (and introduce explosive tendencies, making the system unstable unless checked).

One way in which an accelerator can be derived is to assume that, for whatever reason, there is a fixed relationship between desired capital and output,

$$(1) \qquad K_t \equiv vY_t,$$

where K_t and Y_t have the usual interpretation and where v is a fixed coefficient. It follows that (ignoring lags)

$$(2) \qquad \dot{K} \equiv I_t = v\dot{Y},$$

where the "dots" indicate time rates of change. Investment is a function of the rate of change of output. Thus, if $v = 4$, an increase in output of one unit per period leads to a 4-unit planned increase in capital stock. The *level* of income is not important for investment plans except for its connection with the size of the desired capital stock. If the capital stock is in the proportion v to output, it does not matter how large is output: there simply is no incentive to increase the capital stock.[19]

The accelerator lends drama to staid old income theory: if investment expenditure is to be sustained, income must be growing; once GNP begins to "top out," investment expenditures will fall and a

---

millan & Co., 1948). There have been many interpretations of Harrod's theory and that of Evsey D. Domar (E. D. Domar, *Essays in the Theary of Economic Growth* [New York: Oxford University Press, 1957]). W. J. Baumol's might be the clearest: (William J. Baumol, *Economic Dynamics* [New York: The Macmillan Co., 1951], pp. 36-54.)

19 An illustration I somehow associate with Alvin Hansen's *Fiscal Policy and Business Cycles* (New York: W. W. Norton and Co., 1941) might be helpful. Consider the steel rail business. If replacement can be ignored, the key determinant of sales will be the rate of new construction. The number of miles of track already laid would be immaterial. All that would matter would be the rate at which total trackage was changing.

The text continues to ignore distinctions between gross and net output. Employment would be greater for identical net output if capital is subject to depreciation than if it is not: labor must be used to produce replacement parts.

downward movement in income can be initiated. That the accelerator is destabilizing is at least intuitively clear.

2

Is there a fairly plausible basis on which we could posit that entrepreneurs wish to maintain a fixed relationship between capital and output?[20] R. C. O. Matthews suggests an answer in *The Business Cycle*.[21] (The next few sentences are keyed to his analysis, but not completely bound up in it.) As a first approximation one relies, as we have, on a quasi-technological relationship imposing a fixed desired capital-output ratio. But what if the desired ratio were variable? Changes in the relative cost of capital *vis-a-vis* labor would encourage entrepreneurs to use capital and labor in different proportions (to make their production processes deeper or more shallow). The structure of demand might change so that the output mix would be altered in favor of (labor) capital-intensive goods. Innovation might be predominantly labor or capital saving so that there will be changed desired capital-labor ratios for given relative factor prices.

On the other hand, at a point in time, production techniques are pretty much given. Firms might use more or fewer "shifts" of workers, but even here, if capital inputs are measured in machine hours, technical coefficients might remain fixed. If the setting is less-than-full-employment, it is reasonable to assume that open-market purchases *á outrance* have been made, that discount factors remain roughly fixed over the period of analysis. This implies that machine rent and/or user cost can be assumed to be constant. So can the wage unit. Furthermore, one doubts the importance of moderate changes in interest rates for the desired labor-capital ratio. Even in models less highly aggregated, as these; changing product mixes are here unlikely to be decisive. We do not consider innovation. (*Cf.* Nicholas Kaldor, "A Model of Economic Growth," *Economic Journal,* December 1957). On the other hand, the Harrodian model *can* handle changes in production coefficients and their effects on the model's solution. And surely, we

20 Obviously, if additional capital is purchased — either by manufacturers or by entrepreneurs in the machine-rental business — a view must have been formed about *future* output. We subsequently consider more sophisticated formations of output expectations. The text above blithely associates planned rates of acquisition of capital with *current* output. Needless to say, I_t does not produce C_t.

21 R. C. O. Matthews, *The Business Cycle* (Chicago: University of Chicago Press, 1959), p. 33 *ff*.

have committed more heinous crimes against "reality" than to assume neutrality of innovation.

The fixed-coefficient (v) assumption seems, then, to be less stark than it may have at first. *A priori* objections do not appear compelling enough to force us to abandon a simple model suggesting that sustained increases in output are necessary to generate increasing demand for capital, and tying investment to disequilibrium in capital-stock holdings. Still, we must concede that macro accelerator models do not achieve sure linkage with micro theory.[22]

3

Take up a simple Harrodian formulation in discrete (difference equation) form. Equation 1,

$$S_t \equiv sY_t, \tag{1}$$

defines the savings plan (working at a completely aggregated level), assumed always to be fulfilled: Equation 1 applies *ex ante* and *ex post*. s is a positive fraction. The investment *plan* is defined by Equation 2,

$$I_t \equiv v(Y_t - Y_{t-1}) \equiv v(\Delta Y). \tag{2}$$

It follows directly from simple accelerator theory (shifting the idiom

[22] Observed constancy of capital-output ratios is consistent with a wide range of production functions: the reduced-form relationship might be consistent with *many* structures.

Matthews makes greater claims for the consistency of acceleration theory with the neoclassical theory of the firm:

> "the concept of normal capital-output ratio must therefore be restated in terms of profitability. Looked at in this way, the attainment of the desired or appropriate stock of capital in an industry may be seen as substantially identical to the attainment of the state of long period equilibrium which figures so prominently in Marshallian economics." (*Op. cit.*, p. 34.)

In other words, for given specifications of factor prices and the state of the arts, profit maximization leads to optimal capital-output ratios.

Space limitations permit only these additional observations:

a) if the accelerator is to be integrated into the theory of competition, profit rates and capital-output ratios must be associated so that the equilibrium capital-output ratio follows from the equilibrium profit rate. Although they emphatically do not try to link growth theory to that of competitive industry, Joan Robinson and Nicholas Kaldor cast much light on this problem. *Cf.* Joan Robinson, *The Accumulation of Capital,* N. Kaldor, *op. cit.*, and H. Rose, *Quarterly Journal of Economics,* February, 1963.

b) for more explicit linkage of growth theory to the theory of competitive industry, see J. E. Meade, *A Neo-Classical Theory of Economic Growth* (London: Allen and Unwin, 1961).

to continuous time) that dK/dt must grow at the rate vY if the capital-output rtio is to remain at v. Equality of planned (*ex ante*) saving and investment requires that

$$sY_t = v\Delta Y \tag{3}$$

or

$$\Delta Y/Y_t = s/v. \tag{3'}$$

Equation 3′ defines the *warranted rate of growth*: the growth rate consistent with continuous equality of planned saving and investment so that entrepreneurial plans always are precisely justified. If s were 0.10 and v, 4.0, the warranted rate would be 2.5 per cent. A track is defined which in some sense is an "equilibrium" track in that its log-linear motion can be sustained indefinitely — once attained. As Baumol puts it:

> "When income is growing at the rate [s/v] required to make the entrepreneurs desire to invest just that amount that is being invested, we say income is growing at the warranted rate, i.e., we call that rate the warranted rate of growth."[23]

Of course, growth at a steady percentage rate implies ever larger increments of output from period to period: growth at 10 per cent per period, for example, develops the sequence 100, 110, 121, . . ., 1000, 1100, . . . Maintenance of "equilibrium" (in this special sense) requires that planned investment increase at an increasing rate from period to period.

4

Next consider Harrod's *natural-rate-of-growth* concept, a bridge between Harrod's theory and that of Hicks's *Trade Cycle*. First note that Harrod's formulation — as thus far presented — is invariant against the possibility that more labor and capital could be utilized at going factor and final-product prices.[24] On the other hand, for given initial stocks of capital, a maximum permissible rate of balanced growth, a natural rate of growth (r_n), can be defined at each point in

23 *Op. cit.*, p. 41.

24 As for expansion of plant equipment in spite of excess capacity, Baumol (*op. cit.*, p. 49) points out that it should reduce v, taken to be a "reduced-form" parameter rather than a technical coefficient. (And increasing the warranted rate of growth, a result with important implication for stability.) We come to rely on a not very well defined empirical relationship when dealing with excess-capacity states.

time. If the natural rate of growth should exceed the warranted rate, there need be no fear of cumulative contraction resulting from output bumping against a ceiling. Rather the problem is to adjust the parameters of the system in order to raise r_w to r_n.[25] On the other hand, if r_w exceeds r_n, and if parametric adjustments cannot be made, cumulative contraction can result from output bumping against its ceiling.[26] *(See Note C.)*

5

The *stability properties of the elementary Harrodian model* do not flow directly from equations thus far written. They can only be generated by additional specifications.

In the simple model, savings plans always are realized. Satisfaction of the *ex post* identity relating output (income) to the sum of consumption and investment expenditure is achieved by permitting *ex post* to differ from *ex ante* investment. The system's perturbance arises out of divergence of planned and realized investment expenditure.

What is the consequence of departure of the actual from the warranted rate of growth? As R. G. D. Allen (*Mathematical Economics,* pp. 68-69) points out, the elementary model can do no more than define a track along which continual equilibration of the commodity market is possible. It is not truly dynamical: sequences cannot be generated from arbitrary initial positions. But to stop here would be grossly unfair to Harrod. The basic model, rephrased in continuous time, can be written

(1′) $$S_t \equiv sY_t$$

(2′) $$I_t \equiv v\dot{Y}_t \qquad \text{(defining } ex\ ante \text{ investment)}$$

(3″) $$s/v \equiv \dot{Y}/Y \equiv r_w.$$

If the rate of output finds $\dot{Y}/Y = r_w$, entrepreneurial plans will be

[25] Factors affecting r_w ($\equiv s/v$) include those governing the aggregate propensity to save distribution of income, tax structure, etc. v might be affected by interest rates, depreciation allowances, technological change (dis)encouraging capital deepening, etc.

It is easy to intuit why decreasing s or increasing v reduces the warranted rate of growth. If v is increased, a given ΔY leads to more planned investment. If s is decreased, a given ΔY generates less saving and therefore requires less investment in order to be sustained.

[26] Needless to say, the simple Harrodian model neglects monetary factors and is not concerned with price formation.

fulfilled. Aggregate demand will be growing at the same rate as aggregate supply.

At each point in time the rate of output is immediately determined by entrepreneurial decisions; there is a supply function in Harrod just as there is in Keynes.[27] As for aggregate demand, planned investment is — we assume — inextricably linked with the supply decision through the relation

$$(4) \qquad I(t)_{ex\ ante} \equiv v\dot{Y}.$$

Consumption demand is defined as

$$(5) \qquad C(t)^{ex\ ante}_{ex\ post} \equiv (1-s)Y(t).$$

Thus, if $\dot{Y}/Y = s/v \equiv r_w$, aggregate demand and supply will be in *ex ante* balance. Entrepreneurs will adhere to the plan $\dot{Y} = r_w$. Equation 6 will hold

$$(6) \qquad \ddot{y} = 0 \text{ (for } r = r_w, \text{ where } \dot{y} \equiv r).$$

r is the rate of growth and $\ddot{y}$ $(=d^2y/dt^2)$ the time rate of change of the time rate of the logarithm of output. If $\dot{y} < r_w$, sales will grow less rapidly than output; there will be involuntary accumulation of in-

[27] The log of the *jth* firm's output at t is one of the elements of the vector $y_j = f(\theta)$ for $\theta = t$. y_j is a complex variable defined upon θ. The range of θ is from t to $t+n$. $f(\theta)$ will depend, among other things, on parameters expected to govern product demand, and factor supply over the range giving the planning horizon. Output's log at t might be denoted $y_{rj}(t)$, price $y_{sj}(t)$ and rate of purchase of machines of type *aleph*, $y_{vj}(t)$. The firms revise their plans in the light of experience; the text has shown that realized sales at $t+h$ will depend in an interesting way on sales planned for $t+h$, $t+h-1$, $t+h-2$, etc.

Peculiar features of the elementary Harrod model include: (a) linkage of the firm's investment and output plans through a linear relation; (b) neglect of such possibilities as "excessive" planned markups, leading to distributional effects forbidding sales to grow at r_w although firms are expanding output at that rate; (c) the "degeneration" of $y_r = f(\theta)$ into $\dot{y}_r = r_w$ if this value "initially" is achieved; (d), and related to *(c)*, the mysterious way in which the other elements of $f(\theta)$ fall into place to sustain $\dot{y}_r$ at r_w if r_w initially is achieved *and* are helpless to rescue matters if it is not; (e) the completeness of aggregation, masking possibilities for stability taken up in Appendixes B and C.

Finally, this footnote makes *each* firm a price quoter for goods it customarily supplies; there might be as many prices as there are transactions at t. Aside from superior accommodation to data, this formulation has the advantage of emphasizing non-price constraints on potential realizations (what Clower calls income constraints); prices are inherently *non*-parametric in this model. Kinky-oligopoly-demand formulations can be introduced suggesting sticky price behavior . . . The firms most crucial for macrodynamics are the least suited to pure-competition characterization; firms such as GM, GE, ICI, Shell, *et al.* are tremendously important as investors in plant and equipment.

ventory. If $\dot{y} > r_w$, sales will grow more rapidly than output; there will be involuntary inventory decumulation. Of course, actual investment will deviate from $v\dot{Y}$ insofar as there is involuntary (de)accumulation of inventory. If the initial output plan is "wrong," sales (including investment-demand) experience will be "wrong" in the same direction: optimistic entrepreneurial views will be more than justified; pessimism too will be self-justifying; the upshot is in the fact that sales experience depends on output decisions.

Let us state the general dynamic relationship from which Equation 6 is derived:

$$\text{(7)} \qquad \ddot{y} \gtreqless 0 \qquad \text{as} \qquad \gtreqless (r\text{-}r_w)\, 0.$$

$\ddot{y}$ is greater than, equal to, or less than zero as the discrepancy between the actual and warranted rate of growth is greater than, equal to, or less than zero. This means that the rate of change of the actual rate of growth will be negative if r is less than r_w. Thus, if r initially is less than r_w, r will begin to turn down; the rate of growth of output will decline. Eventually $\dot{y}$ will become negative; output actually will decline. Similarly, if r initially exceeds r_w, r will increase at an increasing rate; $\dot{y}$ will explode upward. The "equilibrium" path defined by r_w is unstable: initial departure from it leads to ever-increasing departure.[28] *(See Note A.)*

F. ROSE'S FORMULATION OF THE HARRODIAN PROBLEM

This section is based on Hugh Rose, "The Possibility of Warranted Growth," *Economic Journal,* Vol. 69, June 1959, pp. 313-332. Indeed it apes Rose. We work on the assumption that the desired

[28] Baumol writes:

> ". . . at this point [Harrod] goes on to argue that when entrepreneurs have been unable to sell all they have produced they will become pessimistic to such an extent that they will keep the rate of increase of output below the warranted rate. This will then again bring about a situation involving overproduction which in turn will add further fuel to their pessimism making them keep their rate of increase of output still further below the warranted rate, and so on." (*Op. cit.*, p. 47.)

Thus aggregate demand at t might be predetermined but aggregate supply still leads a life of its own.

capital stock is given by vY, where v is the desired capital-output ratio. It follows that the shortage of capital, σ, can be defined — where x is the actual stock of capital,

$$(1) \qquad \sigma \equiv vY - x.$$

Using the operator notations $D \equiv d/dt$ and $G \equiv d \log/dt$, we can derive Equation 2,

$$(2) \qquad D\sigma \equiv vDY - Dx.$$

We also assume that savings plans are continuously realized where desired saving is sY and $s \equiv 1-\beta$, where β is the marginal propensity to consume $\equiv$ average propensity to consume. Thus, actual investment and saving are identical so that

$$(3) \qquad Dx \equiv sY \quad \text{or} \quad Dx/x \equiv Gx \equiv sY/x.$$

Equations 1-3 assure that Equation 4 will hold:

$$(4) \qquad \sigma/x \equiv \frac{[Gx-(s/v)]}{s/v}$$

Also that

$$(5) \qquad \frac{D\sigma}{Y} \equiv vGY - s.$$

If $Gx = s/v$, $\sigma = 0$; there will be no shortage or surplus of capital. If $Gy = s/v$, $D\sigma = 0$. (The first derivative of capital shortage will also be zero.) It becomes established that a growth rate of s/v is consistent with continuous realization of saving plans and leaves firms satisfied with their capital positions at all times.

We must now consider the effects of initial discrepancy in $D\sigma$, assuming $\sigma(0) = 0$. Assume that, denoting investment as i,

$$(6) \qquad DGi \gtreqless 0 \quad \text{as} \quad D\sigma \gtreqless 0.$$

It is more convenient to associate DGi with $D(\sigma/Y)$ than with $D\sigma$.

Accordingly, we assume

$$(7) \qquad DGi \equiv kD(\sigma/Y).$$

By substitution from Equation 5,

$$(8) \qquad DGY \equiv k(vGY - s),$$

The assumption of continuous fulfillment of savings plans means that

$sY \equiv i$ and that, accordingly, $dY/di \equiv 1/s$: the ratio of Y to i is constant. It follows that $DGY = DGi$. Equation 8 can be rewritten,

$$DGY \equiv k(vGY - s), \tag{9}$$

a first-order differential equation, linear in GY. The solution is

$$GY \equiv s/v + [GY(0) - s/v]e^{kvt} \tag{10}$$

where the bracketed expression gives the initial discrepancy, determining the arbitrary constant — assuming that $\sigma(0) = 0$. Obviously, as t increases, the remainder part grows larger. The system is explosive. Note that, if the bracketed expression is negative, the system's growth rate GY, ultimately becomes negative, corresponding with the previous section's result.

However, the system's explosiveness is very much a matter of choice of the investment-behavior equation. For example, substitute Equation 11 for Equation 7:

$$i \equiv vDY + k\sigma, \tag{11}$$

a statement about *actual* investment. Investment is viewed as reacting to the rate of change of income and to cumulated capital deficiency.[29] Since it is assumed that the savings plans always are realized, we know that $sY = i$ will always hold, so that

$$vDY + k\sigma \equiv sY \tag{12}$$

or

$$vDY + k\sigma - sY \equiv 0. \tag{12'}$$

But Equation 2 states that $D\sigma \equiv vDY - Dx$ and Equation 3 that $Dx \equiv sY$, so that

$$D\sigma \equiv vDY - sY. \tag{13}$$

Equation 12 can now be rewritten:

$$D\sigma \equiv k\sigma,\ (D + k)\sigma \equiv 0,\ d\sigma/dt \equiv -k\sigma. \tag{14}$$

Thus, if σ is negative, $D\sigma$ is positive; if σ is positive, $D\sigma$ is negative. The system is stable: σ always tends towards zero. And, when $\sigma = 0$, 12 reads

29 Note that the analysis based on 11 does *not* proceed on the assumption that $\sigma = 0$. Analysis based on investment relation 7 ignored the role of σ; it was concerned only with $D\sigma$. Hence, σ was *there* taken as zero.

$$(15) \qquad DY \equiv \frac{sY}{v}$$

or

$$(15') \qquad DY/Y \equiv GY \equiv s/v.$$

Even if initially off the track, the system has built into it stabilization properties that keep it on the $GY = r_w$ track. It is forcefully called to our attention that economic theory is concerned with properties of models, and that models can be made to do almost anything. Selection among theories requires some sort of empirical test.

G. HICKS'S "REAL" TRADE CYCLE THEORY

1. Hicksian Building Blocks

We turn to a line of analysis based on J. R. Hicks, *A Contribution to the Theory of the Trade Cycle* (Oxford: The Clarendon Press, 1950). (Of course, multiplier-accelerator models' origins are associated with Samuelson, Metzler, *et al.*, and predate Hicks's book.) We attempt but to limn models explaining the primary pattern of time series of Gross National Product and/or National Income: cyclical fluctuations around a rising trend. While others (including Duesenberry) have simultaneously treated trends and cycles, Hicks's model has the advantage for us of being expressed in now-familiar terms.

We begin by developing the basic concepts of the Hicksian model after noting at least one important contrast with the Harrodian model: in the latter model, entrepreneurs form output plans subject to adjustment according to sales experience; in the Hicksian model, entrepreneurs respond passively to demand. Hicksian entrepreneurs increase their capital in anticipation of future demand, not as part of a "positive" output plan. (Keep in mind that prices are not defined in a Hicksian model. *See Note B.*)

a) autonomous investment

Investment expenditure has two components. One is autonomous; the other is induced. The autonomous component, $\bar{I}$, is assumed to increase from year to year at a constant percentage rate, adhering to a Parkinson's Law (and indeed $\bar{I}$ includes autonomous government spending). Equation 1 follows:

$$(1) \qquad \bar{I}_t = (1+g)\bar{I}_{t-1},$$

where g is the autonomous growth rate. The plot of autonomous investment will be a straight line on a semi-log scale.

b) induced investment

The induced component of investment expenditure is described by a distributed-lag relationship: response to stimuli is delayed one or more periods. Equation 2 describes induced investment in the *t-th* period:

$$(2) \qquad I_t = v_1(Y_{t-1} - Y_{t-2}) + v_2\,(Y_{t-2} - Y_{t-3}) + \ldots$$

Investment and consumption plans always are realized. Recalling Note B, output responds perfectly elastically to changes in aggregate demand until the *ceiling* is reached.

c) consumption

Neglecting autonomous consumption expenditures ($\bar{I}_t$ can carry the burden of all autonomous expenditures), consumption is a linear function of past income

$$(3) \qquad C_t = c_1 Y_{t-1} + c_2 Y_{t-2} + \ldots$$

There is no savings plan in this system. Consumer units simply plan consumption expenditures as in Equation 3 and save the remainder of their incomes: saving is a residual item. In the basic model, monetary factors are neglected after the fashion of the first approximation to income theory. Prices and wages are not considered. Supply simply passively accommodates itself to demand which, in turn, is predetermined at each point in time.

d) "equilibrium path" of output

The phrase "equilibrium path" is especially misleading for the Hicksian model. It means nothing more than a particular regular motion: log-linear growth. Pausing to tie up the model, we recall that supply — at least when unconstrained by upper and lower bounds soon to be introduced — adjusts to aggregate demand which in turn is generated through interaction of a multiplier and an accelerator. Induced investment is determined by an accelerator principle: it depends on *changes* in output. To the extent that investment expenditure increases, consumption expenditure will be stimulated (income having increased), generating further increases in income, etc. A multiplier-accelerator principle operates.

It can be shown (*cf.* Hicks, *op. cit.,* pp. 183-184) that a Hicksian system has an equilibrium path in the special sense just defined, namely steady growth of output in accordance with the law

$$(4) \qquad Y_t = (1+g)Y_{t-1}$$

or

$$(5) \qquad Y_t = Y_0(1+g)^t,$$

where Y_0 is an initial value for output (income). Similarly, standard assumptions about orders of magnitude of parameters of the system suggest that departure from the equilibrium path, sometimes termed the *benchmark* path, leads to explosive oscillation or to explosive divergence without oscillation. If the motion of output departs from the equilibrium path, the subsequent path of output will show increasing divergence.

e) the ceiling

Up to this point, we have not developed a model characterized by a free cycle around a secularly-increasing trend, although proper constellations of parameters *could* permit an unconstrained cycle. The peculiar flavor of the Hicksian model derives from its "non-linear" accelerator: the system is constrained by upper and lower limits to output at each point in time: its ceiling and its floor. The characteristically constrained Hicksian cycle features accelerated departure from the equilibrium path, say, in an upward direction until output bumps against the ceiling. As Hicks writes:

> "I shall follow Keynes in assuming that there is some point at which output becomes 'inelastic in response to an increase in effective demand' — and just leave it at that. I do not myself believe that the ceiling (and the behavior of the economy as it reaches the ceiling) can be at all adequately analysed in these terms; but the assumption of a rigid barrier is a convenient simplification which will serve out turn until we are ready to replace it with something better."[30]

There is a strong possibility that the economy will not be able to "crawl along the ceiling," and will plunge down to the floor, ultimately to soar to the ceiling once again.

f) the floor

We must anticipate the story somewhat in order to introduce its final element, the floor. Recall that induced investment is related to

30 *Op. cit.,* p. 96. We settle for this simple statement. If you are interested, turn to Ch. X of the *Trade Cycle* for further analysis.

the rate of increase of income in past periods. It follows that, if dY/dt should become negative, induced investment will be negative if the downward movement of income persists long enough. However, the rate of *disinvestment* cannot exceed kK, where k is the rate of depreciation. Thus, once induced disinvestment attains $-kK$, the accelerator will have to recede into the background, just as it did when the ceiling was reached. But autonomous investment is proceeding all the while: net investment equal to autonomous investment minus a constant term will be established. The floor will tilt upwards, the incline being given by the equilibrium growth rate of income. The accelerator will be reactivated . . . We are ready to begin discussion of the Hicksian cycle itself. (*See Note C.*)

2. The Cycle

The argument can be summarized through the semi-log scale chart below, essentially Figure 12, p. 97 of the *Trade Cycle*:

THE CYCLE IN OUTLINE

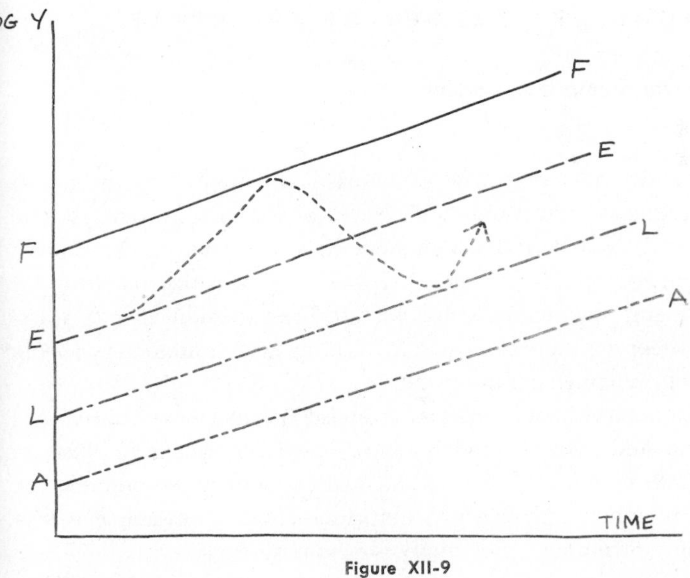

Figure XII-9

AA is the autonomous-investment time-path, *LL* the floor, *EE* the equilibrium path, and *FF* the full-employment ceiling.

We begin in moving equilibrium along *EE*. Now assume that the desired rate of investment temporarily increases so that dy/dt increases above the equilibrium rate. The accelerator swings into action, leading to intensified induced investment, leading to a still greater growth rate, etc. Income (output) blasts upward, but in due course hits the ceiling. Once we hit the ceiling, we crawl along it for some time as unaccomplished investment is fulfilled and might, for that matter, crawl along it indefinitely (*cf. Note C*). But it is also possible that the curtailed rate of growth simply cannot sustain ceiling outputs. Output might begin to turn down, leading to reversal of the system's gears as the relentless accelerator again does its dirty work — subject to limitations we have imposed on disinvestment possibilities. We plummet downward, "through" the *EE* curve, until we hit *LL*. We cannot crawl along the *EE* curve because the system was decelerating when it hit *EE*. On the other hand, we might crawl along the floor for some time. As is shown at the end of Note C, once induced investment is accomplished through depreciation, the accelerator rakes over, carrying us back to the ceiling.

H. A MONETARY THEORY OF THE CYCLE

1. A Non-Mathematical Version

1

The model has been at least heuristically appealing in that it generates sequences consistent with cycles of national income around a rising trend. Furthermore, dynamics have a certain enchantment: one can deal with points as well as crosses. Still it is disconcerting *for us* that monetary factors have thus far not been introduced into Hicksian cycle theory; chapters 11 and 12, dealing with a monetary theory of the trade cycle, become important.

The monetary theory, really an exercise, has its roots in the *IS-LM* construction and cobweb models. It is based on lagged response of plans for holding money balances and real expenditure to interest-rate changes — together with other assumptions about short-run elasticity of the supply of money. The analysis is non-rigorous.

Assume that *Y* is measured in real terms. It probably is easiest to work with a free real cycle with the level of income always below that of the ceiling. Consult the diagram below. We begin at *P*. Income and the rate of interest are such that, while existing money balances are consistent with desired money balances, planned investment exceeds actual investment. There is excess demand for goods. It is assumed that the short run elasticity of the money stock is large: banks accommodate themselves in the short run to the demand for credit, running-down their free reserves, borrowing from the central bank, etc. Also — in the short run — if money balances for transactions purposes fall short of desired levels, economic units accommodate themselves to the inconvenience, planning to remedy the situation in subsequent periods. If the "monetary lag" is long enough, we emerge at *Q*.

At *Q*, the rate of interest and income are consistent with equality of *ex ante* saving and investment, but the money market will not be in balance. Desired money balances exceed the aggregate stock of money. The banks, responding to longer-run inelasticity of money supply,

A DAMPED CYCLE

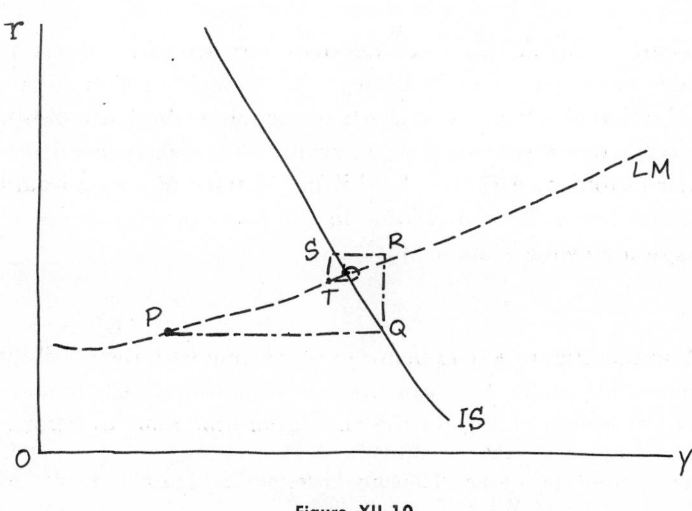

Figure XII-10

must begin retrenchment of deposit liability at a time when firms are anxious to increase their cash holdings. These forces cause excess demand for money, driving up the rate of interest. At the outset, reactions of households and firms to higher interest rates are nil: response is *lagged.* We emerge at point *R,* consistent with monetary equilibrium but inconsistent with continued equality of *ex ante* saving and investment.

Investment expenditures now are cut back and the rate of saving tends to increase. Transactions-balance requirements — especially when multiplier effects are considered — are reduced. However, there is no immediate impact on "the" rate of interest. Moving along the line segment *RS,* firms, involuntarily accumulating inventory, require finance if their cash is not to be depleted: the nominal rate of inventory accumulation corresponds to that of cash deficit.[31] If firms are willing to run down their cash so that households involuntarily accumulate cash (instead of securities as they had planned), we assume that households will not react to portfolio imbalance until next period. Hence, we emerge at *S,* a point at which savings and investment plans are consistent, but in which there is excess supply of money and excess demand for bonds. Also, finance requirements now are lower; inventories no longer are accumulating; the rate at which bonds are being offered in the market declines. There is downward pressure on the interest rate. The falling interest rate has no *immediate* impact on the savings-investment situation: we move along the line segment *ST* to point *T.*

Point *T* has all the essential characteristics of *P.* Accordingly, another, more gentle, cycle begins. But finally we zero in on the blessed union of *LM-IS.* The effects of the initial shock are dissipated. However, a new shock starts us off again in the same general pattern. (Secular factors are expressed by shifting *IS* and *LM* curves leading to a rightward movement over time in the point of intersection of the curves in a growing economy.)

2

Consider Figure XII-11 below in connection with the possibility of an undamped cycle. You can provide your own commentary. The theoretical underpinnings of the analysis are the same as before. All

---

31 Again compare Hugh Rose, "Liquidity Preference and Loanable Funds," *Review of Economic Studies,* Vol. 24, February 1957.

that has happened is that slope coefficients have been altered, leading to instability.[32]

AN UNDAMPED CYCLE

(explosive oscillations)

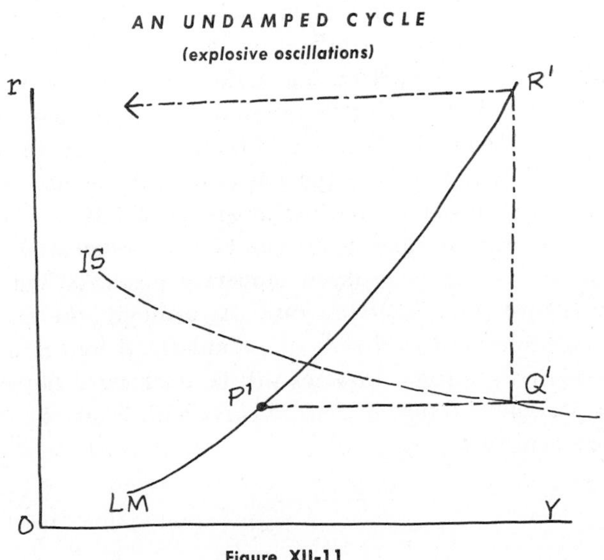

Figure XII-11

2. A Mathematical Version of the Monetary Theory

1

Begin by expressing the *LM* and *IS* curves in explicit form:

(1) $$r = f(Y) \qquad LM$$

(2) $$Y = g(r) \qquad IS$$

Linearize the model:

(3) $$r = a + bY$$

(4) $$Y = c - er,$$

where a, b, c, and d are positive constants.

Now introduce the specific dynamical assumptions of the preceding subsection. We assumed that the money supply was perfectly

[32] In the course of Chapters 11 and 12 of the *Trade Cycle,* Hicks informally discusses interaction of real and monetary factors rather as we worked through implications of changing values of s and v for the Harrodian model.

elastic in the short run, the longer run possibilities being embodied in the *LM* curve itself. We assumed that response in the money market to disparity between demand for and supply of money was lagged one period, and that adjustment, when made, would be in terms of last period's income. In other words, if on the *LM* curve in period $t-1$, it would not be attempted during period t to respond to monetary disequilibrium arising during that period. Hence the movement from *P* to *Q*. Similarly for the *IS* curve. If on the *IS* but off the *LM* curve in t, $Y_{t+1} = Y_t$, $r_{t+1} \neq r_t$; and the *LM* curve will be attained in $t+1$.

The formal model assures attainment of *IS(LM)* at the end of t if *LM(IS)* has been attained at the end of $t-1$. Beginning at *P*, there is passive acceptance of changed monetary positions and hence no pressure against $(t-1)$'s interest rate. Accordingly, the IS curve can be reached in period t with $r_t = r_{t-1}$. Similarly, if we begin on the *IS* curve in period t, output decisions will be unchanged during $t+1$: it becomes possible to return to the *LM* curve with $Y_{t+1} = Y_t$, etc.

More generally,

$$Y_t = g(r_{t-1}), \tag{5}$$

$$r_{t-1} = f(Y_{t-2}), \tag{6}$$

$$Y_t = g[f(Y_{t-2})]. \tag{7}$$

Linearizing,

$$Y_t = (c\text{-}ea) - ebY_{t-2}, \tag{8}$$

a second-order difference equation. A particular solution is

$$\overline{Y} = \frac{(c\text{-}ea)}{1+eb}. \tag{9}$$

The full solution is

$$Y_t = \overline{Y} + A(\sqrt{eb})^t \cos\left(\frac{\pi}{2} - \varepsilon\right), \tag{10}$$

where A and ε are arbitrary constants determined by initial conditions.

The solution's homogeneous *(r. h.)* part is a trigonometric function. The *amplitude* of the oscillation is given by $(\sqrt{eb})^t$. This is the key term: if the amplitude diminishes with time, the system will be stable in the sense that cycles will be damped. If $(eb)^{½}$ exceeds unity, amplitude will increase with time; the oscillations will be explosive.

If the *LM* curve should be perfectly flat, there cannot be a cycle.

Low values for e and b contribute to damping the oscillations. (A low value for b means a "flat" LM curve.) Since the slope of the IS curve gives the rate of change of r with respect to Y, rewrite Equation 4 as

$$r = -(c/e) - (1/e)Y. \tag{11}$$

The lower is e, the steeper is the IS curve. *Flat LM curves and steep IS curves contribute to damped cycles; steep LM curves and flat IS curves contribute to explosive cycles.* This result is in exact correspondence with the geometrical analysis of the preceding section.[33]

2

Regrettably, we must leave dynamical models. A fuller context has been provided for economic theory. Motions in phase spaces are encompassed. *Some* of these motions are regular. Witness log-linearity or stationarity. But "equilibrium" motions are special cases.

SUMMARY

1. In dynamical analysis, regular motions — including steady states — are special cases.
2. The models of Chapters IX-XI implied ongoing accumulation of capital, that solution values for endogenous variables will change over time. From the outset, attention is focused on stock disequilibrium.
3. Chapter XII suggests a theory of investment intimately tied to capital-stock disequilibrium. This is done through the *accelerator,* relating planned rates of capital accumulation to planned expansion of output.
4. The accelerator contributes volatility to the system in contrast with the stabilizing multiplier. Temporary displacements from "equilibrium" paths do not lead to explosion in simple multiplier systems.
5. Variants of Harrodian and Hicks-Samuelson multiplier-accelerator systems forcefully show that the rate of growth can be critical for the ability to achieve full employment. The exigency introduced

[33] *Cf.* R. G. D. Allen, *Mathematical Economics,* Ch. 6, for the technique used in this subsection.

by the accelerator is heightened when one sees how economic stagnation can lead to collapse.

6. Properties of multiplier-accelerator models can depend on rather special assumptions about parametric values. Nevertheless simple models can be "rigged" to generate a wide variety of motions. It remains true that difference or differential equations of a higher order generate more complex motions.
7. Models of Professors Leontief and Duesenberry were taken up. These models, especially Leontief's, do not flow as directly from the first three approximations to income theory as do the models of Harrod and Hicks. On the other hand, the Leontief and Duesenberry models touch upon broader reaches of economic theory.
8. Leontief synthesizes Keynes and Fisher. His basic concepts are marginal efficiency of capital, marginal productivity of capital (MEC when $dK/dt = 0$) and the rate of time preference. A Leontief system will grow so long as MPP exceeds TP (defined at an initial position on a 45° line). Stagnation and depression easily are encompassed if one assumes that MPP diminishes with K. On the other hand, the Knightian (Chicago) view can be exhibited in a Leontief model: log-linearity *can* be achieved. The Leontief model also raises interesting problems of appropriate time horizons for choice theory. It does not solve them.
9. Duesenberry's system avoid rigidities in capital-output rations, determinants of desired capital stocks, and the consumption function. He disaggregates more than do others. His system is capable of secular growth and damped cycles, and can, in fact, adapt to a large class of motions. In Duesenberry's system steady growth is likely to be accompanied by highly stable capital-output ratios, but this is a reduced-form result: it is not built into the system's technology.

NOTES

NOTE A: R. G. D. Allen (*Mathematical Economics,* pp. 76-79) offers yet another formulation of stability properties of a Harrod-like system. In order to reduce the system's rigidity, he lags the savings function, obtaining as his market-clearance condition

$$(i) \qquad sY_{t-1} = v(Y_t - Y_{t-1})$$

$$(ii) \qquad Y_t = \frac{(1+s)}{v} Y_{t-1}.$$

The equilibrium path is defined as

(iii) $$Y_t = Y^o(1+r_w)^t$$

where Y^o is the initial income. Along the equilibrium path,

(iv) $$Y_t/Y_{t-1} = 1 + r_w.$$

Y expands progressively at the warranted rate, r_w.

Define the excess of planned over realized investment in the *t-th* period as

(v) $$\overline{U}_t = I'_t - I_t = v(Y_t - Y_{t-1}) - sY_{t-1} = vY_t - (v+s)Y_{t-1}.$$

I' denotes planned investment. If planned exceeds realized investment, planned (identical with realized) savings are inadequate to sustain the investment plans. If realized exceeds planned investment, savings exceed planned investment; entrepreneurs are forced into involuntary inventory accumulation.

We must specify entrepreneurial behavior in the event of departure of actual from desired investment. We assume that investment plans in period $t+1$ are in accordance with Equation *vi*:

(vi) $$I'_{t+1} = v(Y_{t+1} - Y_t)+\overline{U}_t$$

Investment plans are in accordance with what Harrod calls "the relation," but are adjusted so as to make up for last period's discrepancy. It is seen on inspection of *vi* that the adjustment procedure is on the order of Equation 5 of the text: optimistic expectations always are more than justified; if the rate of growth of output ever is pushed beyond the warranted rate (in either direction) self-sustaining forces are generated. More formally,

(vii) $$Y_t = (1+r_w)Y_{t-1}+\overline{U}_{t-1}.$$

Output in period t will be adjusted for departure of actual from planned *investment in period t—1,* Equation *vii* is more or less derived from Equation *vi*. The appropriate difference equation is

(viii) $$Y_t = \left[1 + \frac{1+s}{v}\right] Y_{t-1} - (v+s)Y_{t-2}.$$

Equation *viii* can generate an infinite sequence once values for two Y's — usually taken as the initial Y's — are specified. It turns out that for cases in which v exceeds $(1-s)$, departure from the "equilibrium" path $[Y_t = (1+r_w) Y_{t-1}]$, leads to "an explosion."

NOTE B: J. R. Sargent points out that in the Hicksian model short-run supply freely adjusts itself to demand. ("The Supply Factor in Professor Hicks' Theory of the Cycle," *Economic Journal,* Vol. 66, Dec. 1956), pp. 635-661.

> ". . . It is curious to find . . . [freely-adjusting short-run supply] . . . in the same bed as the acceleration principle. For the acceleration principle has supply implications of the opposite kind. It tells us that entrepreneurs make their investment decisions [so] as to preserve a constant ratio between capital and output. Why should they be so concerned about this ratio? Presumably because their capital equipment has a certain closely defined capacity, and to operate it at any other ratio (if indeed it is technically possible) seriously inflates their costs . . . Increases in the output of their existing plant are costly, and only if disequilibrium between supply and demand involves a substantial increase in price will they be worth while . . ." (*Loc. cit.,* pp. 637-638.)

At p. 639 *ff.,* Sargent proposes that the contradiction be resolved by assuming that buffer stocks are held and/or that

> ". . . entrepreneurs keep a constant ratio, not between output and capi-

tal *in use,* but between output and total capital; and that these two differ because they like to keep some reserve capacity."

The reserve capacity assumption allows supply to "accommodate itself to demand in the short run by using up reserve capacity." Still, the acceleration principle is intact: capital is expanded to maintain a fixed total capital — total output relationship. Sargent weaves alternative supply assumptions into an elegant design.

NOTE C: This is the algebra of a simple Hicksian model exhibiting most of the features of the *Trade Cycle's* fuller model. Assume that the consumption function is

(i) $C_t = 0.5Y_{t-1} + 0.4Y_{t-2}.$

Difference equations need not be carried beyond second-order terms in order to generate a cycle. The induced-investment relation is

(ii) $I_t = 4(Y_{t-1} - Y_{t-2}),$

while autonomous investment is assumed to behave according to the law

(iii) $A_t = A_0(1.02)^t.$

Assuming that initial autonomous expenditure was 100,

(iv) $A_t = 100(1.02)^t.$

The fundamental equation to be solved is then

(v) $$Y_t = 100(1.02)^t + 0.5Y_{t-1} + 0.4Y_{t-2} + 4(Yt_{t-1} - Y_{t-2}) \equiv 100(1.02)^t + 4.5Y_{t-1} - 3.6Y_{t-2}.$$

We seek a *particular solution* yielding Equation *v.* Try

(vi) $Y_t = Y_0(1.02)^t,$

a solution that finds output growing at the same rate as autonomous expenditure. We anticipate that Y_0 cannot be chosen arbitrarily but is restricted by the value chosen for A_0. The solution can be started up by specifying $Y_1 = 1.02Y_0$. Then, if $Y = (1.02)^t$, Y is a solution; we are home; we will have found a path of moving equilibrium capable of being a benchmark.

We seek to determine the required value for Y_0 (and will find that, if $Y_0 \neq \overline{Y}_0$, the path of output will veer off from the equilibrium path). If *vi* is a solution, *vii* must hold:

(vii) $$(1.02)^tY_0 = (1.02)^tA_0 + (0.5)(1.02)^{t-1}\,Y_0 + (0.4)(1.02)^{t-2}Y_0 = 4Y_0\,[(1.02)^{t-1} - (1.02)^{t-2}]$$

Dividing through by $(1.02)^{t-2}$,

(viii) $$(1.02)^2Y_0 = A_0(1.02)^2 + (0.5)\,(1.02)Y_0 + (0.4)Y_0 + 0.8Y_0$$

or

(ix) $Y_0 = 2{,}066.1 \quad for\ A_0 = 100.$

Equation *vii* holds for $Y_0 = 2{,}066.1$; *vi* is *a* solution for $Y_0 = 2{,}066.1$. We have found a particular solution. The general solution of the system is:

(x) $$Y_t = (1.02)^t(2{,}066.1) + A_1(1.08)^t + A_2(3.46)^t,$$

where A_1 and A_2 are arbitrary constants to be determined by initial conditions. If initial values for Y_0 and Y_1 are not just right so that A_1 and A_2 are zero (the "right" initial values are 2,066.1 and 2,107.4), the time-path of income veers off drastically from the log-linear motion described by the particular solution.

Now we can discuss the inevitability of the downturn and upturn in the Hicksian model, relying on Sidney Alexander's review of the *Trade Cycle*

(*American Economic Review,* December 1951) and on J. R. Sargent, *op. cit.* Taking up the downturn, assume that an explosive movement has carried us to the ceiling and that the rate of growth, once the ceiling is hit, is less than the rate of growth experienced just before it was hit. We find that the downturn is *not* inevitable. Alexander demonstrates this through Equation *xi,* derived from the simple model of this note

(*xi*) $$Y_t = 0.95Y_{t-1} + 2.1(Y_{t-1} - Y_{t-2}) + (1+g)^t A_0.$$

If the rate of growth just before the ceiling was hit were 15 per cent, the solution calls for a 22 per cent increase in output. But, if the rate of growth of the ceiling is 6 per cent, output will, of course, rise only by 6 per cent. The rate of growth called for the next period will be 7 per cent, but output will increase only by 6 per cent. Similarly for the following period, and the next, and the next, *ad infinitum.* We can crawl along the ceiling so long as the ceiling rate of growth lies between the roots of the auxillary equation which here calls for growth rates of 5 and 100 per cent. The accelerator is trying to push output through the ceiling, but is thwarted. Output crawls along the ceiling.

Is the upturn inevitable in Hicks's model? Yes. Recall that, as we move along the floor, the accelerator is decommissioned. Recalling that disinvestment is continuing, and using a single-lagged consumption function, the movement of output (when induced investment is negative and including the case in which unaccomplished disinvestment for past periods is being made up) is described by Equation *xii*:

(*xii*) $$Y_t = 100(1.02)^t - k' + 0.9Y_{t-1},$$

where $A_0 = 100$ and where k' is the amount of depreciation that takes place. The solution of this first order difference equation is of the form

(*xiii*) $$Y_t = \overline{Y}(t) + A_1(0.9)^t.$$

There is a particular solution of the form

(*xiv*) $$Y_t = C(1.02)Y_{t-1}$$

where C is an arbitrary constant. The remainder part goes to zero with increasing t; the path of output is steady so long as induced disinvestment is negative. But, once unaccomplished disinvestment is worked off, the steady rise of output as it moves along the upward-sloping floor brings the accelerator back into play. In essence, the problem of "getting off the floor" can be developed through a pair of initial conditions finding income below the $2{,}066.1(1.02)^t$ track but in which $Y_1 = 1.02Y_0$ and in which unaccomplished disinvestment is nil. It necessarily follows that income will rise above the specified value for Y_1 and that output will zoom towards the ceiling under the specifications of the note's first model. Sargent is able to modify the model so that output can crawl along the floor indefinitely.

APPENDIX A

The Pure Theory of Keynes's Treatise: Rudimentary Dynamics

THIS APPENDIX HAS TWO PARTS. THE FIRST CONCERNS THE theory of the *Treatise.* Since the theory is dynamical and is more a theory of prices than income, it has attracted renewed interest in post-war economics featured by inflation and low levels of unemployment. The second part concerns geneses and life histories of credit cycles.

The sources for this appendix include:

J. M. Keynes, *Treatise,* Vol. I, Book III;

Lawrence R. Klein, *The Keynesian Revolution* (New York: The Macmillan Co., 1947), Ch. I and pp. 189-192;

W. H. Steiner, E. Shapiro and E. Solomon, *Money and Banking,* pp. 462-467.

A. W. Marget, *The Theory of Prices* (New York: Prentice-Hall, Inc., 1938), Vol. I, especially pp. 101-140.

R. G. Hawtrey, *The Art of Central Banking,* Ch. IV.

And then there is the work of Knut Wicksell. Wicksell was one of the first to appreciate appropriate distinctions between dynamical and comparative-statics analysis. His concept of the natural rate of interest and of the way in which departure of market from natural rates could lead to changing prices directly or indirectly underlies much of modern theory. Compare his "The Influence of the Rate of Interest on Commodity Prices," in *Selected Papers on Economic Theory* (London: Allen & Unwin, 1958), pp. 67-89, and *Lectures on Political Economy* (London: Geo. Routledge & Sons, 1935), Vol. 2, especially pp. 127-228. Wicksell's penetration is astounding. (*Cf.* Steiner, Shapiro, and Solomon, *op. cit.,* pp. 450-453, for a brief account of Wicksell's views). Also appropriate parts of Joseph A. Schumpeter, *History of Economic Analysis* (New York: Oxford University Press, 1954).

1. The Elements of the Pure Theory of Keynes's Treatise

Book III of the *Treatise,* "The Fundamental Equations," is heavily convoluted. Even 33 years later it is not easy to present its argument within a brief compass. Indeed our treatment is schematic, stressing the *Treatise's* implications for dynamical theory. I have adhered to Keynes's notation in order to facilitate cross reference.

It sometimes is said that Book III merely leads to a collection of identities. This is not true. Although the *fundamental equations* are identities, they are for "separating out those factors through which, in a modern economic system, the causal process actually operates during a period of change." (*Treatise,* Vol. I, p. 133.) It also is said that the *Treatise* fails to offer a theory of effective demand, that its formal structure is based on full employment. (*Cf.* L. R. Klein, *op. cit.,* Ch. I and *loc. cit. supra.*) This comment also is incorrect, although the aggregate-demand theory of Book III surely is vague. And then Book III leads easily to treatment of inflations induced by expansion of bank credit or by cost-push.

a) The Basic Identities of the System; The Fundamental Equations

Five basic infinitesimal relationships, two of them fundamental equations, require these definitions:

- R, physical volume of consumption output
- C, physical volume of investment (production of capital goods)
- O, physical volume of output, definable as $C + R$, since physical units of consumption and investment goods are defined so that their costs of production are the same. C and R are dimensionally commensurate if measured in terms of an (unchanging) real-cost of production standard[34]
- P, price level of consumption goods
- P', price level of investment goods
- π, general price level
- E, incomes paid out to (earnings of) factors of production, including user cost. When firms' receipts are equal to income pay-

[34] It was pointed out by Alvin H. Hansen, "A Fundamental Error in Keynes's "Treatise on Money," *American Economic Review,* Vol. 22 (1932), p. 462 *ff.,* and others that Keynes's definition of O breaks down if relative costs are permitted to shift during the analysis — as happens in Keynes's credit cycle. *Cf.* A. W. Marget, *The Theory of Prices* (New York: Prentice-Hall, 1938), Vol. 1, pp. 101-140, esp. p. 115 *ff.*

Marget analyses the *Treatise* in great detail. He discovers, and reports how others discovered many logical flaws, mostly at a definitional level. Still I think it worthwhile to study the Baroque model of Book III. *De gustibus non disputandum.*

ments, firms are in equilibrium, producing at just the rate appropriate to parameters facing them; E includes "normal" profits

I', cost of production of investment goods

I, nominal value of investment goods

S, nominal value of saving out of factor incomes

Q_1, windfall profits in the consumption-goods industry; excess of receipts over outlay to factors. Can be positive or negative

Q_2, ditto for the investment-goods industry

Q, defined as $Q_1 + Q_2$

The first of the fundamental equations is

$$(1) \qquad P \equiv \frac{E}{O} + \frac{I'-S}{R}.$$

It is derived as follows (*ibid.*, p. 135): $PR \equiv E - S$, assuming that windfalls are not devoted to consumption. Since $O = R + C$, we can write $PR = (E/O)(R+C) - S \equiv (E/O)R + I' - S$, since E/O is the average cost of production.

The second fundamental equation is

$$(2) \qquad \pi \equiv \frac{E}{O} + \frac{I-S}{O}.$$

It is derived as follows (*ibid.*, p. 137): define π as $\frac{PR + P'C}{O}$, definitionally equal to $\frac{(E-S)+I}{O}$.

The profit characteristics (*ibid.*, p. 137 *ff.*) are shown in Equations 3, 4, and 5:

$$(3) \qquad Q_1 \equiv I' - S$$

$$(4) \qquad Q_2 \equiv I - I'$$

$$(5) \qquad Q_1 + Q_2 \equiv I - S.$$

Equation 3 is derived from the definitional relationships, 3′, recalling that $E(O)$ gives average cost of production for either consumption or investment goods as a matter of definition.

$$(3') \qquad Q_1 \equiv PR - (E/O)R.$$

Again assuming that no part of windfalls is devoted to consumption expenditure — an absolutely harmless restriction[35] — $PR \equiv E - S$

[35] *Cf. ibid.*, p. 139. The lovely parable of the Widow's Cruse and the Danaid Jar shows that *ex post* windfalls (positive or negative) are independent of consumption out of windfalls.

while $(E/O)R$, the total of factor income generated in the consumption-good industry, is identical with E, the total of factor incomes, less I', factor income generated in the investment-goods industry. Thus,

$$Q_1 \equiv E - S - (E - I') \equiv I' - S. \quad (3'')$$

Equations 4 and 5 follow in an obvious manner.

One conclusion can be reached at once: departure of I from I' or of receipts of the consumption-good industry from outlay on consumption goods is inconsistent with equilibrium. In the competitive model underlying the aggregate-supply curve of the *Treatise on Money,* such disparity finds firms dissatisfied with current output levels; they have a longer-run incentive to expand or contract output in response to departure of profits from normal levels. It is this aspect of the model of Book III that yields its dynamical qualities. In any event, it is clear that "equilibrium" requires equality of investment expenditure and saving out of factor income so that windfalls to entrepreneurs will be zero. This is about as much juice as can be extracted from a set of definitional relationships.

b) The Underlying System

The underlying system of Book III is not so easily at hand as are the identities, perhaps explaining why the *Treatise* has been so misunderstood. However, it can be unveiled. First, attention is called to the *natural rate of interest,* the rate of interest at which investment expenditure will be equal to saving out of earnings of factors of production so that windfalls will be zero. The natural rate is in contrast with the *market rate of interest* which, together with M_3, the quantity of savings deposits, is set by the authorities (a not unnatural assumption in British practice). Reconciliation is achieved through P', the price of investment goods. The heart of the theory concerns effects of disparity of "the" rate of interest, $\bar{r}$, from the natural rate, r^*. (Note that r^* is determined within the system and varies over time.) The theory attempts to develop a long-run norm around which the purchasing power of money "oscillates below or above . . . according as the cost of current investment is running ahead of, or falling behind, savings." (*Ibid.,* p. 153, referring explicitly to the price of consumer goods.)

The basic model — capable of generating a sequence of prices for consumption and investment goods and permitting continuous disequilibrium — is dynamical. Supplies of consumption and investment goods in period t are predetermined according to the relations

$$(1) \qquad R^s \equiv \overline{R}$$

$$(2) \qquad C^s \equiv \overline{C}$$

supply functions being of the form

$$f^i(P_{t-1}, p'_{t-1}, \overline{w}),$$

where $\overline{w}$ is a predetermined wage unit. The price of investment goods, P' is determined through the seemingly innocent Equation 3,

$$(3) \qquad \overline{M}_3 = g(\overline{r}, P'),$$

where $\overline{M}_3$ is the officially determined volume of savings deposits and $\overline{r}$ is bank rate (also predetermined). The demand for savings deposits is given by $g(\quad)$. Excerpts from pp. 141-146, *ibid.*, tell the story very well:

> ". . . when an individual is more disposed than before to hold his wealth in the form of savings deposits and less disposed to hold it in other forms . . . he favours savings deposits (for whatever reason) more than before at the existing price level for other securities. But his distaste for other securities is not absolute and depends on his expectations of the future return to be obtained from savings deposits and from other securities respectively, which is obviously affected by the price of the latter — and also by the rate of interest allowed on the former[36] . . . It follows that the actual price level of investments is the resultant of the sentiment of the public and the behavior of the banking system . . . The amount by which the creation of a given quantity of deposits will raise the price of other securities above what their price would otherwise have been depends on the shape of the public's demand curve for savings deposits at different price levels of other securities . . . The price level of investments as a whole, and hence of new investments is that price level at which the desire of the public to hold savings deposits is equal to the amount of savings deposits which the banking system is willing and able to create."[37]

---

36 The portfolio choice is between securities — equity interests in capital goods — and savings deposits. These markets are taken to be mirror images of each other: clearance of one implies clearance of the other. But, since C is predetermined, determination of P' implies determination of I, the nominal value of production of investment goods — always assuming that new and old capital are perfect substitutes.

37 At pp. 141-146, Keynes shows that securities prices cannot be disrupted (in his model) by disparity of S and I: windfalls account for the difference; these, if entrepreneurial cash is not to be disturbed, will either be used to repay debt (for $I>S$) or will be reflected in demand for finance ($S>I$). (This is a crude statement, ignoring the Widow's Cruse aspect.) These passages of the *Treatise* put Hugh Rose on the right track in his "Liquidity Preference and Loanable Funds," *loc. cit.*

We can proceed to Equation 4,

$$(4) \qquad \overline{R} = \frac{E\text{-}S}{P},$$

where $R^d \equiv \frac{E\text{-}S}{P}$. Equation 5 governs planned ($\equiv$ actual) savings,

$$(5) \qquad S \equiv h(P, P', E, \overline{r}).$$

And then,

$$(6) \qquad I \equiv P'\overline{C}.$$

The system's seventh equation can be written in number of forms. We might write

$$(7) \qquad E \equiv PR + P'C - (I\text{–}S).$$

This results in a system ignoring relationship of income deposits, M_1, and/or the wage unit, $\overline{w}$, with prices — an acceptable result if one prefers to work with a system in which the monetary authorities passively adapt the stock of current (demand) deposits to the "needs of trade."

How would such a system be capable of determining prices? Of course, P_{t-1} *and* P'_{t-1} are predetermined in the *t-th* period. If Equation 7 were used, determinancy of prices in a model in which lagged values of the P's were "released" in order to determine a steady solution would arise from control of M_3, savings deposits. In general, a sequence of prices can be generated once initial conditions are established. Indeed the resulting functional's parameters can be differentiated with respect to $\overline{w}$ as well as $\overline{M}_3$.

Equations 7′, 7″, and 7‴ are alternatives to Equation 7:

$$(7') \qquad E = \overline{v}_1\overline{M}_1,$$

$$(7'') \qquad E = [\phi(\overline{r}, P')]\ [M_1],$$

$$(7''') \qquad E = \overline{k\overline{w}}.$$

Equation 7′ contains the heart of the crude quantity theory of money (*cf.* Ch. XIV): it imposes a strict relationship between factor incomes and income deposits, abstracting from transfers between current and savings (demand and time) deposits. It permits the second of the fundamental equations to be written

$$\pi \equiv \frac{\overline{v}_1\overline{M}_1}{O} + \frac{(I\text{-}S)}{O}$$

so that in equilibrium an $M\overline{v}_1 = p\overline{Y}$ relationship will hold. Equation

7″ implies that income velocity of circulation is a function of yields available from holding assets other than demand deposits [$v_1 = \phi(\bar{r}, P')$]. It accords with more sophisticated theory (except that the stock of capital is not explicitly introduced), but, as Ch. XIV shows, is consistent with equilibrium *loci* for M_1 and π describing rectangular hyperbolae. Equation 7‴ accords with what Hicks has called a "labor standard of value." (*Cf.* Appendix to Ch. XIII.) It indicates that the price level will be determined by, say, labor unions, while the monetary authorities passively adapt the volume of demand deposits to transactions requirements implied by the wage unit. $\bar{k}$ simply implies that there is a proportional relationship between the wage unit and total factor income. The *Treatise* is much in advance of its (and perhaps our) day in analysis of cost-push inflation.

Equations 1-3, then, determine outputs of consumption and investment goods and the latter's price level in period t. Plugging these values into Equations 4-7, we are able to determine the remaining unknowns of the system: E, S, I, and P.

The identities permit a neat summary of the results. Perhaps the most striking result is that — if Equation 7′ applies — the value of factor incomes at any point in time can be considered to have a "particular solution": the value for E when there are no windfall profits (losses).[38] This value is determined by Equation 7′. The particular solution is subject to disturbance induced by disproportion in streams of expenditure on and output of consumer and investment goods, creating windfall profits (losses). On the other hand, at each point in time there is an interest rate, r^* (the natural rate), consistent with factor income adhering to the particular or equilibrium solution. Since the appendix's second part — the genesis and life history of a credit cycle — concerns stability properties of systems in which market rate initially differs from natural rate, the dynamical character of the argument of Book III becomes apparent.

c) Temporary Equilibrium and the Natural Rate of Interest

Perform these adjustments to the basic model: release the restriction on r;[39] impose the equilibrium condition

[38] The value for P for unchanged O.

[39] Ch. XIII takes note of the fact that the authorities are able to control both M_3 and r so long as they are willing to permit windfall profits (losses) and "unsteady" price behavior. Empirically useful models must be able to account for disequilibrium states.

(8) $$I = S,$$

so that the system has an additional unknown (r_t) and an additional equation. The model now determines r_t at r^*_t: factor incomes will accord with the basic quantity-theory relationship if Equation 7′ applies. However, we are not assured that $r^*_{t+1} = r^*_t$: solutions for P_t and P_{t-1} may not be equal to their lagged values; π will change from period to period along with the mix of output of consumption and investment goods, the scale of the economy as capital stock changes.

We do not attempt to consider conditions, if any, under which the system could experience steady balanced growth at a constant rate of interest and constant prices and wages (along with steady and equal rates of growth of factor supplies). Nor are less restrictive long-run variants considered. These are left as exercises for the student (if he is young and strong). Suffice it to say the authorities will not be able arbitrarily to choose time profiles for M_1 and M_2 if they wish to have $r^*_t = r^*_{t+1} = \ldots = r^*_{n-1} = r^*_n$. The chapter's second appendix uses models better adapted for long-period analysis.

2. Application of the Pure Theory

a) Sketch of the Genesis and Life History of a Credit Cycle, Treatise, Ch. 18

Outline form is convenient. Correspondence with the formal model is only approximate, but the flavor lingers. Surely it is a fuller model of a monetary theory of business cycles than that appended to Hicks's *Trade Cycle.*

I. The Primary Phase
   A. Entrepreneurs come to believe that certain new investments will be profitable
      1. so they switch factors of production previously producing consumer goods to production of investment goods
         a. leading to rising consumer-good prices, since demand for consumer goods is undiminished; factors' expenditure plans are not affected by the nature of their employment
      2. consumer prices will rise more if the investment-good industry bids away factors from the consumer sector, since there will then have been an income inflation,
      3. but the commodity inflation carries on in any event.

4. the supply of money is assumed elastic in this phase, although we have seen that a commodity inflation could occur with M_1, v_1, and E (money income of factors) unchanged, implying reduced real factor income.

II. The Secondary Phase

A. Windfall gains induce efforts to increase all output (R and C), causing factor prices to be bid up (starting, let us say, at full employment); there is an income inflation; the price rise can be accounted for by the E/O terms of the fundamental equations

1. the income inflation requires that the stock of money continue to expand if demands of firms for credit at the market rate of interest are to be met

a. increased demand for cash as a result of higher factor incomes is very explicit in Equation 7′, although similar results can be obtained with less rigid alternative formulations

b. but the elasticity of supply of money can be expected to lessen

As Keynes puts it, "with the progress of the income inflation the surplus bank-resources fade away, but so long as any element of commodity inflation is still present, the stimulus continues."

III. The Collapse

A. "Now whether or not the primary phase contains within it the seeds of a reaction, the secondary phase necessarily does."

1. The secondary phase finds output of consumption goods increasing as producers of consumer goods, responding to the commodity inflation, bid away resources

a. leading to "better" proportioning of expenditure flows to output flows (*in re* consumer and investment goods), leading in turn to a decline in prices (in accordance with the r.h. terms of the fundamental equations), save for effects of further income inflation. (Certainly windfall profits will fall.)

1. This possibility leads to entrepreneurial pessimism. Entrepreneurs might cut back output. Also households might wish to save more, generating more windfall losses.

a. Another consequence of the change in "proportioning of expenditure" and its effects shown immediately above can be increased liquidity preference. This can push up market rate above (now lower) natural rate, intensifying the downturn.

IV. The Upturn

(Not specified by Keynes but presumably generated by restoration of confidence associated with "floor" phenomena.)

V. Epilogue

"All this presumes of course that the Banking System has been behaving according to the principles which have in fact governed it hitherto, and that it lies either outside its purpose or outside its power so as to fix and maintain the effective bank-rate as to keep Saving and Investment at an approximate equality throughout. For if it were to manage the Currency successfully according to the latter criterion, the Credit Cycle would not occur at all." (*Loc. cit.*, p. 291.) [*Cf.* Ch. VA, *supra,* especially Note K.]

b) The Hawtreyian Model

Sir Ralph Hawtrey's *The Art of Central Banking* (Ch. IV) develops an interesting model, not unlike that of Keynes's credit cycle. The analysis centers on *release* and *absorption* of cash. (*Cf.* Note G, Ch. VA, *supra.*)

The Hawtreyian model has an electric circuit theory counterpart. The upside of the cycle finds cash being transferred from units with very low output of current (x_{rj}) per unit of cash in capacitors to firms with much higher "output." Thus, over interval h cash acquired by firms in exchange for IOU's turned over, say, to households, flows into their capacitors. At $t+h$, the new critical stock level having been achieved, incremental expenditures (resistors' incremental output of current) match continuing flows from households. Multiplier-accelerator effects (or "full employment" analogues) enter the scene. For example, if capacity constraints are binding, and if there is a wage lag, part of the incremental increase in autonomous expenditure can be sustained out of windfall profits. Indeed, if the "circuit velocity" of expenditure is high enough, windfall profits can sustain more than the initial increase.

But, as wages and wage goods' prices rise, the more appropriate issue concerns the value of "money" national product that might be sustained if the dishoarders do not renege. (Of course $\dot{p}$ at $t+h$ might be enormous; once the process "levels off," we cannot think of $p(t+h)$ being sustained.) The central theme concerns effects of shifts of cash to more efficient circuits on prices and outputs at $t+n$. A simple model might lead to $\Delta y = v\Delta M_s$, where v is a transactions velocity of "active cash and M_s the amount of cash in active circulation.[39a]

To change the metaphor, the original transition matrixes must change considerably for these results to be accomplished: a greater proportion of cash at t must be transferred by $t+h$ $(h \rightarrow 0)$. Hawtrey suspects that, as the process develops, much of the "released" cash will be absorbed in workers' hoards, that income elasticity of demand for cash is high; this will put pressure on the securities markets. The downside of the cycle, featuring absorption of cash, can be initiated by such factors as (1) creditors refusing to renew loans as firms' liquidity ratios fall or (2), as R. Coen has pointed out to me, as Modigliani-Miller shareholders wish to increase liquid-asset holdings because of falling liquidity ratios of firms.

Finally, remember that the electrical or hydraulic analogies to cash-flow processes are no more than heuristic: in truth, increased payments-expenditures flows in bank-dominated models essentially imply nothing more than bank clerks' nibs scratching faster; in essence the stocks are always at the stations, never in the circuits (pipes); there is no inherent physical limit to velocity in such a *model.*

(I am indebted to D. Morrison in connection with these remarks.)

[39a] A "release of cash" model might find exogenous expenditure increasing by, say, \$1 million per week. If it is financed through hire purchase, if the marginal propensity to save is unity (a simplifying assumption), and the desired "industrial circulation" exactly one-half the annual rate of nominal GNP, a total of \$26 million in cash would have to be released before the \$1 million per week "transfer" could be self-sustaining. Once the "industrial circulation" was built up—ignoring other cash balances—there would develop a cash flow from income recipients precisely equal to the increment to exogenous expenditure. From this point forward, non-monetary financial assets would be increasing by \$1 million more per week whilst cash flows could replicate themselves *ad infinitum*; the new transition matrix could become locked-in.

At the outset dM_i^d/dt might be increasing more rapidly than dY/dt, although the context is expansionary. Indeed, the desired rate of accumulation of "industrial" cash at $t=0$ will be greater if expectations are more elastic. It follows that the Federal Reserve during early stages of reflations might be called upon to open up the gates especially wide in order to be sure that money did not become tight at just the wrong time.

APPENDIX B

Financial Assets and Growth Models

1

PROFESSOR TOBIN HAS BUILT AN INTERESTING MODEL whose "growth mechanism . . . is not radically different from the accelerator mechanism . . . [b]ut . . . there is not just one tenable rate of growth." [40] This is the model:

$$(1) \qquad K = S(Y),$$

where K is the rate of growth of the capital stock and $S(Y)$ the savings function. Equation 1 is a clearance condition.

$$(2) \qquad Y \equiv \Phi(K, N),$$

a linear homogeneous production function.

$$(3) \qquad w = \Phi_N(K, N),$$

$$(4) \qquad r = \Phi_K(K, N).$$

The marginal physical products are measured in shmoos. r is a rental for physical capital. Equations 3 and 4 are balance conditions for factors of production.

$$(5) \qquad W \equiv K + M/p.$$

Wealth (W) has a real and a fiat-money component. The stock of money is determined by the officials: it is a parameter.

$$(6) \qquad M/p = L(K, r, Y),$$

where $L(\quad)$ defines demand for real cash balances $L_K \gtreqless 0$, $L_r < 0$,

Vol. 63, April 1955, pp. 103-115, at p. 103.

[40] James Tobin, "A Dynamic Aggregative Model," *Journal of Political Economy*,

$L_Y > 0$. "It is possible that there are levels of r (e.g. negative rates) so low that portfolio balance requires all wealth to be in the form of currency and that there is some level of r above which wealth owners would wish to hold no currency."[41] The crucial Equation 6, the portfolio-balance equation, implies an accelerator relation, as is apparent when the equation is written in implicit form; but the accelerator is modified by variable production coefficients and portfolio-balance criteria. The Tobin model accommodates effects of decreased liquidity preference (increased willingness to accept risk) on desired capital stocks, for example.[42] Alternative portfolio-balance criteria are available — depending on specifications of risk preference and expectations.[43]

Taking $K(t)$ and $M(t)$ as given, there are six equations in the unknowns K, Y, p, r, w, and W.

2

The system can be solved for stationary equilibrium — if indeed it exists — by dropping Equation 1, replacing it by

$$S(Y) = 0, \tag{1'}$$

and adding Equation 7

$$\phi(Y, W, r, w, p) = 0, \tag{7}$$

where $\phi(\quad)$ determines the rate of growth of the labor force. N and $\dot{K}$ are endogenous in the modified model while K disappears as a variable.

3

Since the production function is first-order homogeneous, balanced growth will find r^*/w^* constant. Also, for a fixed stock of money, prices must fall steadily in order to maintain portfolio bal-

41 Presumably he refers to investment balances. *Cf.* Note J, Ch. VII.

42 The *Treatise's* model also finds the portfolio-balance equation providing the link with investment behavior.

43 Franco Modigliani has developed formal models in which the basic role of financial assets is to modify uncertainty of income streams if one exchanges a supershmoo (an *MM*) for a bond, he can reduce the variance of his income stream — at the expense of expectation in a risk-averting world. If risk aversion diminishes, equilibrium requires that physical capital be more important in portfolios and/or that yields from physical capital and bonds come closer together. The upshot suggests transitional excess demand in commodity markets. And, of course, the equilibrium balanced (and steady) growth rate can be affected by the changed configuration of asset yields, factor prices, and preferences.

ance: transactions "requirements" are increasing; increasing wealth leads to increasing demand for real investment (cash) balances. Consider the solution vector (for $t = 0$)

$$[K, Y, p, r, w; M_0, K_0, N_0]^*.$$

Tobin's specifications together with the assumption that $L(\quad)$ and $S(Y)$ are first-order homogeneous in K and Y and in Y respectively, permit balanced growth at the rate $i \equiv \dot{K}(t=0)/K_p$. In other words,

$$[(1+i)^t K^*, (1+i)^t Y^*, p^*, r^*, w^*, (1+i)^t M_0, (1+i)^t K_0, (1+i)^t N_0]$$

is a solution vector for the *t-th* period (permitting M to increase without transfer payments, contrary to Tobin's assumptions).

Tobin considers a number of other possibilities: growth with capital deepening, technological progress, wage inflexibility, cyclical fluctuations, etc.

4

Professor Solow also has made a fundamental contribution to "the analysis of the process of economic growth in an economy in which the factors of production are substitutable, subject to diminishing marginal returns and in which decision-making units have asset preferences."[44] *Cf.* Robert Solow, "A Contribution to the Theory of Economic Growth," *Quarterly Journal of Economics,* Vol. 70, Feb. 1956, pp. 65-94.

Consider the Leontief-Knight model — featured by steady growth of capital and consumption. Introduce securities, including money, into the system. Tie the money stock to a policy-determined reserve parameter. It is intuitively obvious that, if the real money stock and other financial assets (liabilities) grow at the equilibrium rate (determined in Ch. XII), the solution path for capital and consumption can be maintained.

As is shown in Ch. XIV, if the money stock does not increase at the rate i, the real solution path of the system might be altered as price expectations change. On the other hand, if only the nominal stock of cash were controlled by official discretion — all other financial stocks being "free" — it would seem that expansion of the money stock at i would assure balanced growth in a Leontief-Knight model.

44 Alain C. Enthoven, "A Neo-classical Model of Money, Debt, and Economic Growth," appendix to Gurley and Shaw, *Money in a Theory of Finance,* pp. 303-359, at p. 304. Enthoven makes a masterful presentation.

What if financial assets are relatively superior for nonbanking sectors? If monetary reserves increased at the rate *i,* deflation would be necessary for real financial assets to increase at a rate satisfactory to portfolio managers. But unit-elastic price expectations during steady deflation seem chimerical. At the same time, Tobin, Solow, and Enthoven, *inter alia,* stress that razor's-edge solutions are very special and analytically trivial: inability to achieve steady growth, for this or other reasons, need not have dramatic effects.

APPENDIX C

The Robinson and Kaldor Models

THIS APPENDIX SKETCHILY ATTEMPTS TO INCORPORATE THE work of Joan Robinson and Nicholas Kaldor into our analysis of growth theory. I have penetrated these models only gradually, having become aware of them for the first time through Mr. Kaldor's "Alternative Theories of Distribution" (*Review of Economic Studies,* Vol. XXIII (2), No. 61, 1955-1956).[45] Perhaps the most significant theme of the Kaldor-Robinson models centers on the interaction of the rate of growth, the rate of profit, and the distribution of income, a theme that I for one find to be rooted in Keynes's *Treatise.* And Keynes's intriguing phrase, "animal spirits" of entrepreneurs, is another hallmark. These factors, together with population growth, technological change, etc. are woven together in models capable of generating a wide variety of motions, including moving "equilibria."

The following diagram conveys the flavor of Mrs. Robinson's

A ROBINSON MODEL

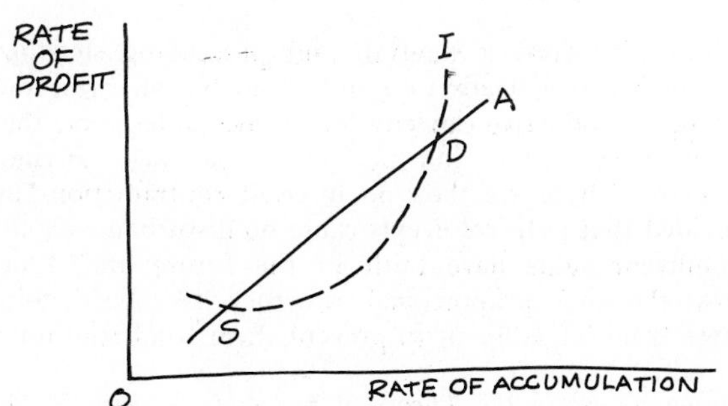

Figure XII-12

[45] Mr. Kaldor and Mrs. Robinson both excoriate marginal-productivity theories of distribution.

simplest model.[46] It shows the determination of short-period equilibrium in the context of different propensities to consume of workers and capitalists; indeed one can assume that workers consume all of their incomes and capitalists none. Aggregation is to the level of "bread," "labor," and "machines."

"The *A* curve represents the expected rate of profit on investment as a function of the rate of accumulation that generates it. The *I* curve represents the rate of accumulation as a function of the rate of profit that induces it."[47] Investment (as a fraction of real output) and the proportion borne by profits to income — and hence the rate of accumulation of capital and the rate of profit on investment — are associated through the respective propensities to consume. The higher is I/Y, the less is the share of output available to the workers; the capitalists always can acquire a larger share through an access of zeal. Lower bounds on real-wage rates are imposed through subsistence requirements, union action, the degree of competition among capitalists, etc. The *I* curve reflects the operation of animal spirits, the appetite growing upon what it feeds.

At *S* and at *D* the rate of profit generated by the rate of accumulation is exactly equal to the rate of profit necessary for generation of that rate of accumulation. Furthermore, the temporary equilibrium described by *D* is stable: a larger rate of accumulation generates animal spirits inadequate to sustain that rate; a smaller rate of accumulation generates animal spirits in excess of those required to sustain such a rate.

The pith of Mrs. Robinson's model might be in these lines:

> "When technical progress is neutral, and proceeding steadily . . . population growing at a steady rate and accumulation going on fast enough to supply productive capacity for all available labor, the rate of profit tends to be constant and the level of real wages to rise with output per man. There are then no internal contradictions in the system. Provided that political events cause no disturbances, and provided that entrepreneurs have faith in the future and desire to accumulate at the same proportional rate they have been doing in the past, there is no impediment to prevent them from continuing to

[46] *Cf.* Joan Robinson, *Essays in the Theory of Economic Growth* (London: Macmillan and Co., Ltd., 1962), p. 48. *Essays* contains a most lucid presentation of Mrs. Robinson's analysis. *Cf.* also H. Rose, *Quarterly Journal of Economics,* February, 1963.

[47] *Ibid.,* p. 48.

do so . . . Total annual output and the stock of capital . . . then grow together at a constant proportionate rate compounded of the rate of increase of the labor force and the rate of increase of output per man . . . [This is] . . . a *golden age* (thus indicating that it represents a mythical state of affairs not likely to obtain in any actual economy.)"[48]

---

[48] Joan Robinson, *The Accumulation of Capital* (London: Macmillan and Co., Ltd., 1956), p. 99. *Accumulation of Capital* is Mrs. Robinson's basic work in the area. *Essays in the Theory of Economic Growth* augments and clarifies it.

Mr. Kaldor's most important works in this area include "Alternative Theories of Distribution" (*loc. cit.*), "A Model of Economic Growth," *Economic Journal*, December 1957, and "A New Model of Economic Growth" (with J. Mirrlees), *Review of Economic Studies*, Vol. XXIX (3), No. 80, June 1962, p. 174 *ff*. A brilliant critique and extension of Kaldor's system was presented by Luigi Pasinetti in *Review of Economic Studies*, November, 1962.

CHAPTER THIRTEEN

The Pure Theory of Central Bank Policy

Chapter XIII manipulates models of earlier chapters, developing a formal statement of the theory of policy. Among other things, it is concerned about circumstances in which it might be possible for monetary authorities to control market-clearing prices *and* interest rates. The technique is quite straightforward. Underdetermined simultaneous equation systems are developed. Authorities use up the excess degrees of freedom by "arbitrarily" choosing values for some of the system's unknowns. These become instrumental variables.

We stress that economic theory deals with models. If one asserts "the authorities can, consistently with general equilibrium, control either *the* interest rate or the quantity of money, but not both," he necessarily is asserting a property of a model. Indeed the subset of models for which this assertion is correct proves to be surprisingly small.[1]

Chapter XIII concentrates on comparative statics, but does take

[1] Where we deal with a spectrum of maturities, only extreme Bills Only proponents would believe that control of the stock of money confers sensitive control over interest rates. Opponents of Bills Only would stress that the term composition of the debt as well as the stock of money would have much to do with the *i-th* interest rate.

up an essentially Wicksellian inflation model. It becomes clear that time paths of prices can be determinate even if one or more — or all — markets always are uncleared; following Note K, Ch. VA and Chapters IX and X, dynamic laws of price behavior can be formulated. In Ch. XIII, we decisively break through barriers imposed by auction-market concepts.

Chapter XIII has, then, three major purposes: to apply the analysis of Chapters VII-XII to some of the informal argument of Ch. VA; to treat more sophisticatedly the supply of money; to indicate with some rigor how "non-equilibrium" data sets are generated.

A. ADAPTATION OF MODELS FROM CHAPTERS IX-XII

1

Consider this reduction of a model from Ch. X ("The Second Approximation to Income Theory"). The model has a full-employment solution, determining Y^* at full-employment output. If $Y = Y^*$, it is assured that the labor market will clear: the wage unit will adjust to the price level (determined in Equation 2) so that the equilibrium real-wage rate is attained.

$$f(K_o, Y^*, r) = Y^*, \tag{1}$$

$$g(K_o, Y^*, r, p) = M. \tag{2}$$

It is assumed that there is a pure credit money, that the public's stock of money is offset by debt owed by the public to the banks so that changes in the general price level do not affect (apparent) net wealth. Of course, since price changes do not affect real wealth, there will be no real-balance effects in commodity markets. (The government sector is ignored in this model.) The form of the demand function for money, $g(\quad)$, makes clear that traditional motives for holding money are recognized. Barring money illusion, the demand function for money will be first-degree homogeneous in p, so that Equation 2 can be written

$$h(K_o, Y^*, r) = M/p. \tag{3}$$

Finally, Walras' Law assures clearance of the bond market.[2]

The system is recursive. The "natural rate of interest" is determined in Equation 1. Plugging r^* into Equation 3, the value of real-cash balances that will clear the money market becomes determined. The authorities are constrained by identity 4,

$$p^* \equiv kM, \tag{4}$$

the market-clearing value of the price level is proportional to the money supply. (k, a constant in the reduced form of the system, is not a behavioral constant.) The authorities must choose from a modest menu. They cannot affect the natural rate of interest — the rate of interest clearing the commodities market so that there will be neither inflation nor deflation. If they do not insist that the money supply be confined to a certain range of values, they can control the "equilibrium" price level. Alternatively, if, for some reason, they wish a certain money supply, they can sustain it consistently with general-equilibrium if they abandon control of the equilibrium price level.

What have writers meant when they asserted that monetary authorities can, in models of this sort, control the rate of interest if they are willing to buy and sell securities (selling and buying cash) in sufficient quantities? If correct, they were referring to market rates of interest (in contrast with natural rates). Indeed we shall see that, if the authorities are willing to pay a price in the form of continuous inflation or deflation (or unemployment), they can have almost any interest rate they want. Our immediate concern happens to be with

---

[2] More formally, equations defining the demand and supply functions for labor, together with the production function, can — for given initial capital stocks — be solved for the market-clearing rate of employment and full-employment output. $Y = Y^*$ assures clearance of the labor market if the real-wage rate, w/p, is "right." Thus, System 1-2 can be rewritten

$$w/p = \eta \qquad \text{where } \eta \text{ is a constant} \tag{1'}$$

$$f(K_o, Y^*, r) = Y^* \tag{1}$$

$$g(K_o, Y^*, r, p, w) = M. \tag{2}$$

This system exhibits an extra equation and an extra unknown, w. There is no change in net degrees of freedom. Substitute ηp for w in Equation 2, and we are back where we started.

Obviously, satisfaction of Equations 1′, 1, and 2 assures clearance of the securities market. The equilibrium real-wage rate and interest rate are invariant against monetary policy. To choose a specific value for w is to choose a value for p in the equilibrium system.

The dynamics of this system are clouded: excess supply in the commodity market leads to falling prices but *not* to lower planned output. w and p are locked-in so that firms always plan to produce at the full-employment rate.

equilibrium models. On the other hand, we saw in Ch. VA, while discussing contracyclical policy, that departure of market from natural rates of interest can be an important weapon for a central bank trying to move a system from one mark to another.

2

Results thus far achieved undoubtedly are related to the simplicity of the model: it is not always possible to make silk purses from sows' ears. Consult Equations 5 and 6:

$$f(K_0, Y^*, r, \beta_1) = Y^* \tag{5}$$

$$g(K_0, Y^*, r, \beta_2) = M/p \tag{6}$$

β_1 and β_2 are *shift parameters,* an arcane term for a rather simple concept. It appears as early as p. 10 of Samuelson's *Foundations.* Let us define the concept indirectly. Consider a simple demand function of the form

$$q^d \equiv \beta_3 - 0.6p. \tag{7}$$

β_3 can be viewed as a shift parameter: the demand curve shifts upward as β_3, a positive constant, is assigned higher values. It is a short step to treat β_3 as a parameter indexing "tastes," taking on higher values as preference for the good increases. In general, shift parameters are indexes for values of pertinent factors not determined within the system — including *policy-determined* variables.

Let us proceed slowly — tasting the forbidden fruit of fiscal policy — setting β_2 equal to zero and assuming that β_1 reflects a fiscal-policy variable such as autonomous government spending or tax collections.[3] The policy-determined variable, β_1, adds a degree of freedom to the system. There are but two restrictions on the three arguments: β_1, r, and M/p. For simplicity, take M to be predetermined. The authorities can choose solution values for β_1, r, or p. Of course, once one of these values is chosen, no degrees of freedom remain *if the authorities are intent upon achieving an equilibrium state.* Now unchain M. Clearly, the authorities can choose r^* and M^* if they are willing "to take what they get" for p and β_1. Similarly, it is open to the authorities to choose M^* and p^*, abandoning discretionary control of r and β_1.

[3] Of course, Walras' Law must be obeyed in the course of the parameter shifts. Think of the bond market as "absorbing" the effects of a shift in β_1, β_2 being held constant.

Check your understanding by consulting Figure XIII-1, a *CC-LL* construction, plotting loci of prices and interest rates consistent with temporary equilibrium in the commodity and money markets and, implicitly, the bond market.

CC-LL CONSTRUCTION ILLUSTRATING PERFORMANCE OF SHIFT PARAMETER β_1

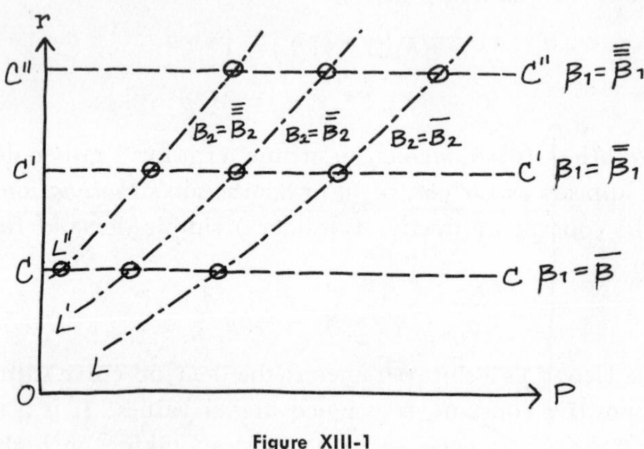

Figure XIII-1

An increase in autonomous government spending or a decrease in the autonomous tax base shifts the *CC* curve upward. The authorities can choose an equilibrium price level (the stock of money being held constant), but in order to attain it must accept the appropriate equilibrium interest rate. Similarly, if the officials are to choose an equilibrium interest rate, they must accept the appropriate equilibrium price level.

We are well on the way home. Let us now unchain β_2, the shift parameter of the demand function for money. A determinant of this parameter might be the degree of certainty attached by the representative trader to the future course of bond prices. If uncertainty is increased, liquidity properties of bonds deteriorate; liquidity preference increases. This can be indicated by an increased value for β_2. We further assume that the effects of increased liquidity preference are registered only in the securities market: capital goods and/or equities are assumed never to have been assigned liquidity properties. We now have an additional degree of freedom, bringing the net sum to two.

There are four holes to be filled and only two pegs. The two-equation system now has four unknowns: β_2 is added to a roster already including β_1, r, and M/p. Selecting a value for M, we now can choose values for r and p, accepting resultant values for β_1 and β_2: the shift parameters are established in accordance with equilibrium requirements.[4] The *LL* as well as the *CC* curve can be controlled. It is possible to attain any point in the p-r space of the diagram below even if nominal money balances are held rigid.

CC-LL CONSTRUCTION WITH β_1 AND β_2 CONTROLLED

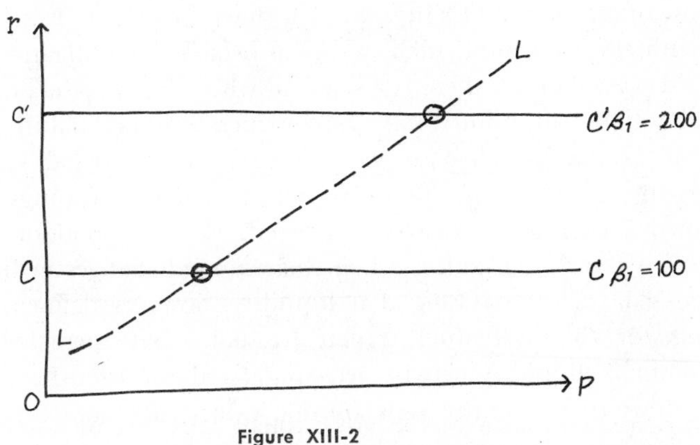

Figure XIII-2

3

We argued in Ch. V that, on some assumptions, the scale and/or composition of public debt need not affect solution values of the system. Still it is interesting to consider implications of other assumptions under which the scale and composition of public debt *do* matter. We explicitly introduce government debt in the equation system 8-9, implicitly rewriting the suppressed clearance condition of the securities market to require that the non-government sector plan aggregate net holdings of securities equal to the nominal value of the public debt.

$$f(K_o, Y^*, r, X, p, \beta_1) = Y^* \quad (8)$$

[4] It is assumed that the officials are able to affect expectations about stability of securities prices through various kinds of market behavior. Each can name his own poison in playing the game of Ch. XIII (where *securities* $\equiv$ *bonds*).

$$(9) \qquad g(K_o, Y^*, r, X, p, \beta_2) = M/p$$

Some would claim that the real value of government debt, X/rp (it is assumed to be funded in perpetuities) affects demand for commodities through conventional wealth effects.[5] Hence, the introduction of p into Equation 8 where X is the number of government promises to pay $1 per year forever and r applies uniformly to government and non-government bonds, also assumed to be funded in perpetuities. And, of course, injection of net bond holdings into the system would then directly affect the money and bond markets: interest rates must be higher, *cet. par.*

Of course, to the considerable extent that bonds can be money substitutes, the public's liquidity will have increased. Even apart from wealth effects of public debt where associated tax obligations comprise but a partial offset, there is a sense in which its introduction increased real wealth: illiquidity imposed by increased tax liability is not as great as the liquidity of the bonds; at the original set of prices and interest rates, last period's preference-meter readings can be attained even if some cash is destroyed. This "second order" wealth effect is shortly recognized when *compensated* changes in liquidity are analysed. While stressing that liquidity, however defined, is endogenous for the individual trader, we note that increased aggregate "nominal" liquidity can be accommodated consistently with general equilibrium only at different solution values for commodity prices and interest rates: among other things the proportion of liquidity provided by cash *vis-a-vis* bonds is changed.[6]

---

[5] There is another complication implicit in introducing government bonds. Insofar as the government sold bonds to banks and used the proceeds for purchases of goods from the public, the public's cash is not offset by private indebtedness to banks. If the public did not capitalize tax obligations, real-balance effects could be expected to be generated by changes in the general price level — even in a system in which all money consisted of bank obligations.

I have tried carefully to construct all models in this book so as to avoid this complication. It is easy enough to handle, but it blurs the lines of analysis of a pure-credit money.

[6] Two kinds of changes in liquidity have been discussed: (a) changes in character of instruments; (b) changes in quantities of liquid assets.

In the former case, there can be substitution effects leading to equities being substituted for cash in planned portfolios, equities for bonds, both for cash, etc. As it happens, the text has concentrated on changes in planned holdings of bonds *vis a vis* cash. In no event, *if wealth is unchanged,* should changes in initial liquidity affect consumption plans at the initial set of prices for commodities and securities. On the other hand, type (a) changes can affect desired portfolios and

4

Let us use the new technique to solve a problem calling for lower interest rates and unchanged prices in equilibrium. Perhaps the purpose is to increase the growth rate without inflation. Of course, appropriate combinations of monetary and fiscal policy can achieve a plethora of equilibrium r-p combinations. (*Cf.* Figure XIII-2.) But let us attempt the sterner task of achieving the result through monetary policy alone, using fiscal measures only in order to maintain the parameter, β_1, at its initial level (any effects of monetary policy on demand for commodities is subsumed in β_1).[7] Also, enter government securities (still ignoring possibilities for spectra of maturities) as X/rp: money illusion is forbidden. Equations 10 and 11 apply:

$$(10) \qquad f(K_0, Y^*, r, X/rp, \beta_1) = Y^*,$$

$$(11) \qquad g(K_0, Y^*, r, X/rp, \beta_2) = M/p.$$

Target values are chosen for r and p. β_1 cannot be touched according to the rules of the game. Ignoring β_2 for the time being, X and M are to be determined within the system. X and M must be consistent with values selected for p and r if a *solution* is to be achieved. The lineaments of the *solution* are fairly obvious. M will have to be increased in order to accommodate the public's desire to hold more cash at lower interest rates. Bank reserves can be increased or required-reserves reduced (bringing β_2 into the picture). (Ordinary open-market operations are neglected because these would lead to cash entering into the system that was not offset by private debt to banks.) X/rp will have to

---

lead to transitional output effects; consider effects of increased preference for equities because of improved marketability.

Taking up case (b), if bills were substituted for long-terms in the Government debt structure, the total of highly liquid assets available without (private) indebtedness offset to the private sector will have been increased: "net-bills will have increased"; "net-Consols" will have declined. There will be excess supply of money at initial prices and interest rates will fall.

Note that, while liquidity is not a "proper" exogenous variable, various measures of liquidity can be good predictors; if the public are observed not to hold "equilibrium" constellations of assets, one can predict that they will be attempting to revise their portfolios. Consider 1946, when the proportion of government securities and cash was outlandishly high: one could predict that there would be strong demand for equities and durables.

7 Tax collections are adjusted to changes in interest receipts (on government debt holdings) so that shifts in X have no effect on disposable income. In our usage, β_1 is unaffected by changes in X.

be reduced in order to damp down demand.[8] Here we must cheat a bit. The restriction on β_1 has to be temporarily relaxed. Our instructions to the authorities are to run a temporary surplus, using the proceeds to buy back bonds. Then the previous fiscal policy is to be restored except for reduced taxes in line with the reduced interest-transfer obligation. For purposes of comparative statics, β_1 is unchanged. (*Cf.* Section C, §§ 3 *infra* for a happier treatment.)

5

A number of gaps remain in the analysis. Some of these are not within the province of this chapter: dynamics; will it be possible for long rate to be moved quickly and forcibly enough to reverse the thrust of boom or bust (*cf.* Note K, Ch. VA); supply-of-loan factors (*cf.* Appendix B, Ch. VA). Two others are to be repaired in this chapter: Section C's attempt to be more sophisticated about the way in which demand liabilities of banks become determined; §§ 6's attempt to deal with essentially Wicksellian disequilibrium systems. Physical controls (especially important for disequilibrium systems of these types) continue to be ignored.

6

Chapter VC discussed attempts in the United States and the United Kingdom after World War II to establish market rates of interest well below natural rate. Indeed the authorities might choose persistently to pump reserves into the banking system so that securities markets always are cleared at "low" rates of interest.[9] The fact that these rates of interest, in conjunction with other official actions, lead to excess demand in commodities markets means that prices will continuously be rising: the commodities markets will be in continuous disequilibrium. This does not mean that the time path of prices is not determinate: once

[8] There will be negative wealth effects because of the implicit uncompensated change in the quantity of liquid assets provided by the government. Two points should be made: (a) the wealth effect does *not* arise from reduced net transfers from the government; these are unchanged; (b) as is pointed out in the text *infra.*, these "second order" wealth effects are unlikely to be very powerful.

[9] Thus, assume that finance is arranged before spending units enter commodities markets. Decision makers always are able to fulfill their finance plans, but never their real expenditure plans. As prices rise, finance requirements increase. The authorities must continue to pour reserves into the banks in order to prevent interest rates from rising.

the system's lag structure and the degree to which prices are sticky upward are known, the laws of motion of prices can be stated; the fact that market-clearance is not established does not prevent one from predicting (accurately) future prices. (*Cf.* Note K, Ch. VA.)

Official policies should not be damned merely because these are inconsistent with "equilibrium." There is nothing ethically wrong about states of affairs in which all plans are not fulfilled. On the other hand, most of us would decry a stationary equilibrium state in the United States. Once the officials choose to ignore solution states (and they almost certainly will), they can "arbitrarily" fix more variables than they have degrees of freedom in the *equilibrium* system. Keep in mind that disequilibrium is not chaos. Perhaps economists have been reluctant to consider disequilibrium states as normal because conventional welfare criteria are inapplicable, and, at least on the surface, concepts of economic freedom become vitiated: the freedom to plan for unrealizable outcomes is unlikely to be treasured. (*See Notes A, B, C.*)

B. APPLICATIONS TO THE MODEL OF THE TREATISE[10]

Consult Ch. XII, Appendix A, *supra.* Keynes's authorities normally fix savings deposits, income deposits, and the rate of interest on savings deposits, accepting emergent values for the price levels of consumption and investment goods, expenditure on investment goods, savings out of factor income, and resultant values — as given by the fundamental equations and other identities — for windfall profits, ΔP, $\Delta P'$, $(R_{t+1} - R_t)$, and $(C_{t+1} - C_t)$. If the authorities seek steady prices, planning to keep the market rate of interest at natural rate (somewhat oversimplifying the analysis), they must accept the bank rate which emerges from solving the enlarged system of equations.

The spirit of Ch. XIII is that of Volume I of the *Treatise*: "The Pure Theory of Money." Chapter VA was governed by Volume II of the *Treatise*: "The Applied Theory of Money."

---

10 *Cf.* Appendix, Ch. XII.

C. MORE SOPHISTICATED TREATMENT OF THE SUPPLY OF MONEY

1

This section relies heavily on two major sources: John G. Gurley and Edward S. Shaw, *Money in a Theory of Finance,* and Don Patinkin, "Financial Intermediaries and the Logical Structure of Monetary Theory, a review article," *American Economic Review,* Vol. 51, March 1961, pp. 95-116, esp. pp. 113-116. As Patinkin puts it:

> ". . . in most discussions of monetary theory the nominal quantity of money supplied is taken as an exogenous variable. But though we continuously shy away from this fact in our theoretical work, we do nevertheless know that in the real world this is not the case: for money is largely the creature of a banking system which responds to such endogenous variables as the rate of interest, the wages of clerks, etc. How then can we take account of these responses? And, in particular, is there a limit to the extent to which such endogenous influences can be assumed to operate? Conversely, must a determinate monetary system necessarily retain some exogenous element?"[11]

2

It proves easy to fit the more sophisticated treatment of the supply of money into the framework of Section A.[12] Assuming at the outset that banks lack money illusion, the supply-of-money function of the banking system is framed in terms of real balances:

$$(M/p)^s \equiv \Phi(r, d). \tag{12}$$

Reserve requirements (real or nominal) are ignored for the time being. d is the rate paid by banks on deposits, r the rate of interest paid on the system's only bond instrument. The rustic simplicity of the argument is maintained through a model reducing to Equations 13 and 14. These are like Equations 5 and 6, Section A, except that arguments for shift parameters and capital stock are dropped:

$$f(Y^*, r, d) = Y^* \tag{13}$$

$$g(Y^*, r, d) = \Phi(r, d), \tag{14}$$

sufficing to determine r and d. Prices do not appear in the system; only

[11] Don Patinkin, *loc. cit.,* pp. 111-112. He proceeds to give Gurley and Shaw deserved credit for breaking-open these issues.

[12] The following passages closely follow Patinkin, *loc. cit.,* pp. 113-116. Basic priority, of course, belongs to Gurley and Shaw. The system is defined *de novo. Cf.* footnote 2, Ch. VA, Appendix A. *Cf.* J. Tobin, *Review of Economics and Statistics,* Aug. 1960.

the value of the real stock of money is determined. Needless to say, there is no real-balance effect: changes in the money stock are offset by changes in nominal indebtedness to the banks. There is no fixed nominal quantity in the system: determination of real quantities implies nothing about any nominal value.

A richer model can be created by introducing a central bank with money illusion. The central bank thinks in nominal terms.[13] In fact, Gurley and Shaw posit a central bank that provides reserves by purchasing primary securities.[14] They assume that the central bank offers a rate of return, d', on its deposit liabilities, and that there are no reserve requirements. In order to obtain the important results all that need be assumed is that the banks have a convertibility onus (*cf.* footnote 13). It follows that Equation 12, dealing with the supply of money, should be revamped:

$$(M/p)^s \equiv \Phi(r, d, d'). \tag{12'}$$

Also that an equation should be added showing how demand for real reserves is determined:

$$(R/p)^d \equiv \psi(r, d, d'). \tag{15}$$

The quantity of reserves offered by the central bank is subject to its discretion.

The amount of money the banking system plans to supply no longer is equal to its *net* demand for bonds. Net bank demand for bonds is equal to the supply of money *less bank demand for reserves* (which must be purchased with bonds). Equation 16 must hold:

$$U(\quad) \equiv \Phi(\quad) - \psi(\quad). \tag{16}$$

$U(\quad)$ defines bank demand for bonds. All functions determine real values.

There emerges a system comprised of Equations 13, 17, 18, and 19:

---

13 Another approach would be to develop a system in which some good, fixed in supply, was the monetary standard. Once the unit of account (money of account) were defined, there would be a stock in the system whose nominal value was fixed. Banks, liable to convert their deposits into the good comprising the monetary standard (legal tender as well as *numeraire*), would have to take account of the nominal value of their liability. Prices would be determined. Indeed prices can be determined by fixing the nominal value of any such stock, whether or not legal tender, and whether or not there are banks in the system.

14 Recall from Ch. III that primary securities are issued by "non-financial spending units."

$$f(Y^*, r, d) = Y^* \quad \text{commodities} \tag{13}$$

$$B(Y^*, r, d) = U(r, d, d') + R/p \quad \text{bonds} \tag{17}$$

$$g(Y^*, r, d) = \Phi(r, d, d') \quad \text{money} \tag{18}$$

$$\psi(r, d, d') = R/p \quad \text{reserves} \tag{19}$$

Equation 17 requires a bit of explaining, but the scales fall from one's eyes when one recalls that Gurley and Shaw assume that the central bank creates reserves by purchasing primary securities from banks. Take $B(\quad)$ as the real value of bonds that the non-banking public (a net debtor) wishes to issue. The right-hand side of Equation 17 gives the total demand for bonds. R/p can be interpreted as central-bank demand for bonds.

The system contains the unknowns r, d, d', and R/p. It has three independent equations. Walras' Law knocks out one of the four clearance conditions (that for the labor market being subsumed by Equation 13). There is an extra degree of freedom in the system when it is expressed in r, d, d', and R/p and in a sense two extra degrees of freedom when R/p is decomposed: the numerator *or* the denominator of R/p can be fixed without losing the extra degree of freedom. The similarity to the argument of Section A of Ch. XIII becomes striking. Although we now are accustomed to thinking of the authorities as determining such variables as bank reserves in order to achieve target price levels (arrived at through free play of market forces), it might be more comfortable to follow Patinkin:

> "The decision on R is *not* analogous to the decision on d or d'. Indeed, unless the central bank makes a decision on R . . . it cannot achieve a determinate price level." (*Ibid.*, p. 115.)

I should prefer to say that, once a target level for p is decided upon, the authorities have enough freedom to permit them to fix d' and "accept" the level for R that emerges (if the selected values for d' and p are to be solution values), although R, of course, will be announced by ukase.

3

A pleasing feature of the *G-S* model, as modified by Patinkin, is that it permits the monetary authorities to determine the rate of return on primary securities and the commodity-price level without resorting to fiscal *deus ex machina*. It is true that this is done in a model lacking government bonds and in which the central bank accordingly holds only private securities, but, indeed, this was essentially the state of affairs at the foundation of the Federal Reserve System. My system (Equations 10 and 11) would — if transformed in accordance with the more sophisticated assumptions about money supply made in Section C — look like this:

$$(20) \qquad f(K_o, Y^*, r, X, p, \beta_1) = Y^*$$

$$(21)^{15} \qquad G(\qquad\qquad ,\beta_2) = p.\Phi(r, d, d')$$

$$(22) \qquad p.\psi(r, d, d') = R.$$

The system now contains an additional equation and three additional unknowns *(R, d, d')*, but *M* has disappeared. On net one degree of freedom is gained. It now is possible, for example, to choose values for *p, X,* and *r* (holding β_1 and β_2 fixed), taking what you get for *d, d',* and *R* — at least within the mathematical happy hunting grounds of this chapter.[16] And, finally, Gurley and Shaw surely deserve thanks for putting banking into the theory of money and banking. *(See Note D.)*

SUMMARY

1. Neutrality of money, employment effects of monetary changes, etc. are properties of *models.*
2. Similarly, the scope for determining *solution* values for economic variables depends on the model one uses. Introduction of shift parameters or additional variables such as government securities might permit selection of equilibrium values for the stock of money, the price level *and* interest rates without changing parameters of fiscal policy.
3. In Ch. XIII's equilibrium models (temporary equilibrium or otherwise) authorities selected target values for some unknowns — not necessarily under their direct control. Then the system was solved

15 *G(* *)* defines demand for nominal money balances. *f(* *)* is zero-degree homogeneous in *X* and *p*.

16 Keep in mind that *d'* and *R* are "mechanically" determined by the authorities. Values selected for *d'* and *R* emerge from solving an equation system (in which "arbitrary" values for *p, X,* and *r* are inserted). The authorities pull switches on instructions from their computing machine. *d* is market-determined.

for values of the remaining variables consistent with the target values for the selected variables. The officials needed only to take action with respect to variables under their "physical" control in order for the desired solution (market-clearing) set to emerge.

4. Equilibrium (always in the sense of market clearance in Ch. XIII) might not be consistent with the officials selecting as many targets as they wish. However, degrees of freedom can be regained if they are willing to abandon market clearance as an objective. Witness the Wicksellian-inflation model.
5. Following Gurley and Shaw (as modified by Patinkin), Section C treated the supply of money as "largely the creature of a banking system which responds to such endogenous variables as the rate of interest, the wages of clerks, etc." The model featured a central bank that created reserves by purchasing primary securities. Despite its simplicity, it yielded solutions of rather rich texture.
6. The basic model of Book III of the *Treatise* is highly amenable to the methods of Ch. XIII. The Keynesian authorities would lose a degree of freedom if they constrained market rate to natural rate.
7. Chapter XIII should be compared at this point with Ch. VA which treated the dynamics of central-bank policy. Chapter XIII concentrated on comparative statics, perhaps at the cost of understressing the crucialness of timing in execution of contracyclical policy.

NOTES

NOTE A: There is an important distinction between the effects of a policy forcing "the" interest rate below "the" natural rate through continuous open-market purchases and those of a once-and-for-all increase in the stock of money or, better, bank reserves. The former policy leads to continuous disequilibrium, the latter to a new *level* of prices and to unchanged equilibrium interest rates (under some assumptions) despite transitionally-changed rates. Inflation, of course, refers to rising, not to high prices.

Consider Wicksellian *deflation,* recalling "The Economic Consequences of Mr. Churchill." Following Note K, Ch. VA, there will be persistent excess supply in commodity and labor markets and concomitant deflation at $r > r^*$. "Income constraints" will come into operation; consumption and output will become conditioned to expected realizations. Depending on the laws governing wage-price velocities, the economy might experience "stagnation" of output and prices; or stagnation of output accompanied by drastic inflation; etc. The *General Theory* looms.

For a good discussion of the material of Section A, *cf.* Don Patinkin, *Money, Interest, and Prices,* Appendix E ("Wicksell's Monetary Theory"), pp. 420-433, especially p. 431.

NOTE B: The Wicksellian inflation model can be accommodated by the stock-flow model of Ch. VII. Thus, assume that expenditure units plan to discount paper at Bank rate (below natural rate), using the proceeds to purchase goods. By assumption the securities market always is cleared at the official rate of discount. At the outset of the process $x'_{rj} = 0$ for the *j-th* expenditure unit while $x_{rj}(t) > x_{rj}(t-1)$, the variables being defined *ex ante*. $x_{rj}(1) - x_{rj}(0) = \Delta z_{rj}$, where Δz_{rj} is nothing other than the proceeds of bond sales.

Excess supply of money is being generated: traders are not planning to increase stocks of cash, but the aggregate stock of cash *is* increasing. At the outset, as has been noted, the rate of increase in the stock of cash might measure the rate of excess demand in commodities markets. As the inflationary process develops, analysis becomes more complex. Some *ex ante* demand for goods is accompanied by planned reduction in cash holdings. As inflation develops, x'_{rj} may become negative. Of course, it is more than likely that rising prices will account for enough increase in *nominal* planned cash balances to guarantee that negative $x'_{rj}(1)$ will not offset increasing $x_{rj}(t)$ in the typical case. There will be continued applications for additional credit.

Note that an application for $100 from the central bank at time *t* does *not* reflect a plan to increase cash holdings by $100. The applicant may be planning to increase his cash balance by $10 and to increase his rate of expenditure so that an adverse balance of payments of $90 will have cumulated by $t+h$.

The relationship to the model of the *Treatise* is quite intimate. Thus, if the period is appropriately defined, $z_r(1) - z_r(0)$ becomes nothing other than windfall profits if factor prices are lagged.

(The model of Note B can be exhibited by an alternative mechanism. Open lines of credit at bank rate permit firms to bid for goods. They anticipate borrowing after contracts are closed. They will fail to obtain the goods. Prices will rise. They will borrow, after all, in order to maintain their real cash balances — at least during the inflation's early stages — continuing to bid up prices.)

NOTE C: These technical notes should be appended to an analysis of Wicksellian (de)inflationary processes:

1) It does not follow from the fact that a market is continuously cleared that plans are being fulfilled in that market. Thus, if the authorities are maintaining market rate above natural rate, firms might be floating unplanned securities issues in order to maintain their cash. Furthermore, if commodities prices have fallen in period *t—1*, firms might reduce indebtedness to banks at the beginning of the *t-th* period. Banks would proceed to purchase securities from the authorities. But firms will discover that they repaid "too much": they will lose cash in the course of period *t*'s business (assuming, of course, that outputs have not yet been adjusted).

2) It is better to avoid entanglement with Walras' Law, an *ex ante* concept, in this connection. Thus, the *ex ante* state of the securities markets (excluding the official operator) is not important in this context. There will be no realized excess demand (supply) of securities, due to the official operator's actions. On the other hand, there will be realized excess supply of goods so long as output exceeds effective demand at "the" pegged market rate of interest. In the realized state, firms, while continuing to fail to achieve desired cash flows from the sale of goods, might be sustaining desired cash positions by reluctantly floating securities. To repeat, there might be excess supply in commodities markets while "ex-post" selling and buying offers are in balance in all other markets; firms are found holding the amount of cash they wish to hold because they are successfully marketing securities they wish they did not have to market.

3) Remember that there is no money *agora.* The objective phenomena during "Wicksellian deflation" are falling commodities prices with unchanged interest rates.

4) During Wicksellian deflation, firms' balance sheets show deteriorating liquidity. Output must turn down towards effective demand or there will be widespread insolvency. Indeed there will be insolvencies in any case: fixed commitments to purchase inputs and effects of falling prices on net debtors with money-fixed obligations will cause some to go under.

Note D: Recalling Note K, Ch. VII, consider Ch. XIII's failure to take up equities. Recall that in our models (see especially Ch. IX) households hold producers' capital only indirectly through their equity ownership. Surely under uncertainty, the incorporeal hereditament, common stock, and the physical asset, Machine Aleph, would be very different objects in the market. However, so long as management is kept in line by arbitrageurs able to outbid those planning non-optimal utilization of company assets, the management will manipulate Machine Aleph as part of a plan maximizing net worth.

It follows that, in the real world, effects of shifting equity prices on demand prices for producers' goods (excluding here possibilities for debt finance) are generated through changes in the cost of raising capital. But again compare Note K, Ch. VII, justifying Ch. XIII's procedure.

APPENDIX

Cost inflation (Cost-Push) and Monetary Policy

1

THIS APPENDIX WORKS ALTERNATIVELY AT THE LEVEL OF simple theory and casual empiricism. It does not attempt to evaluate the *importance* of cost inflation in the United States and other countries.[17] There has been heated dispute on that issue. Considerable empirical work has had inconclusive results: both sides have been fully substantiated by their scientific investigations.

The issue of cost-push inflation, anticipated and treated with considerable flair by Keynes in Book III of the *Treatise* (*cf.* the Appendix to Ch. XII *supra*) flows out of an institutional structure in which wage rates are determined through autonomous forces. It is easily pursued along the lines of the *General Theory*. The wage unit might obey the law

$$dw'/dt = k,$$

where w' is the log of the wage unit. Intuition suggests that, if the wage unit were subject to such a law, economies could be faced with continuous inflationary pressure of an unorthodox sort: inflationary pressure originating on the supply side and leading a life of its own reasonably independently of the state of demand. J. R. Hicks, reflecting what might be greater sympathy with cost-push theories on the other side of the water, has said:

> "In the new world which began after 1931 the problem of wages is bound to have a distinctly different character from that which it had

17 Profit inflation based on administered prices is neglected here but is subject to equivalent analysis.

> in an older time. Since 1931, wages questions have been closely connected with monetary questions; it was even true that the general level of wages has become a monetary question. So long as wages were determined within a *given* monetary framework, there was some sense in saying that there was an 'equilibrium wage,' a wage that was in line with the monetary conditions that were laid down from outside. But the world we now live in is one in which the monetary system has become relatively elastic so that it can accommodate itself to changes in wages, rather than the other way about."[18]

The theme is laid down: accommodation to changes in wages rather than the other way about. To whom might we be accommodating ourselves? The leaders of organized labor. The *Economist* (May 4, 1957, p. 376) put it nicely:

> "The automatic annual process by which the unions decide on a claim in the early summer, submit it in the autumn and get perhaps half of what they asked in the following spring, has this week suffered a small variation which has reduced it to the absurd. The Amalgamated Engineering Union at its annual conference, while still involved in its old wage claim, is discussing a new one — based presumably, . . . on the rise in the cost of living since the increase they have not yet had."[19]

---

[18] J. R. Hicks, "Economic Foundations of Wage Policy," *Economic Journal,* Vol. 65, September 1955, pp. 389-404, at p. 391. Of course, the main source of this elasticity is political. Since 1955, U. S. and British authorities have not necessarily been willing to accommodate monetary policy to a "labor standard." This Appendix considers likely consequences of non-accommodation.

[19] Comments like the following are common in cost-push literature:

> "the general wage rate for 1957 [in Britain] has now been fixed at at least five percent [higher than in 1956] after a year in which there has been no general increase in productivity." (*Economist,* March 30, 1917, p. 1069.)

The phrase "increase in productivity" yields a mare's nest of troubles. If it is *marginal* productivity that is meant, standard theory suggests that, if money wages rise five per cent, so will marginal value products. If *average* productivity is meant, it is easy to be in trouble: adoption of strongly-labor-saving machinery might lead to an industry drastically reducing its employment rate so that the ratio of output to labor much increased; this has no meaning for wage policy. Clearly, the only useful sense in which "increase in productivity" might be used relates to a schedule shift. Even here, tilting effects can lead to ambiguity.

The May 4, 1957, *Economist* proceeded to point out that restriction of the money supply can, under conditions of cost inflation, lead to restriction of output without prices being much affected:

> "the immediate increase in labor costs per unit of output has therefore been greater after this year of restricted internal demand [the result of a credit squeeze] than after any of the years of less restricted demand that preceded it. It can be argued that the squeeze should have been carried much farther in order to achieve the desired effect on wage bargaining. But this is to ignore the fact that, industrially, restriction has already led to an expensive 18-month check on the growth of production . . ."

2

A new engine of inflation is suggested: an engine that operates perversely in terms of conventional criteria. Let us analyse it. Use a generalized *IS-LM* construction. Ignore real-balance effects in commodities markets. Begin at full employment (the *IS* curve has no interpretation beyond that point). If the wage unit increases while monetary parameters are unchanged — and certainly if industry is competitively organized — the *LM* curve must shift leftward: desired transactions balances will now be greater for a given rate of output and interest rate, since prices will be higher. All of this is summarized in Figure XIII-3.

***IS-LM* AND COST INFLATION**

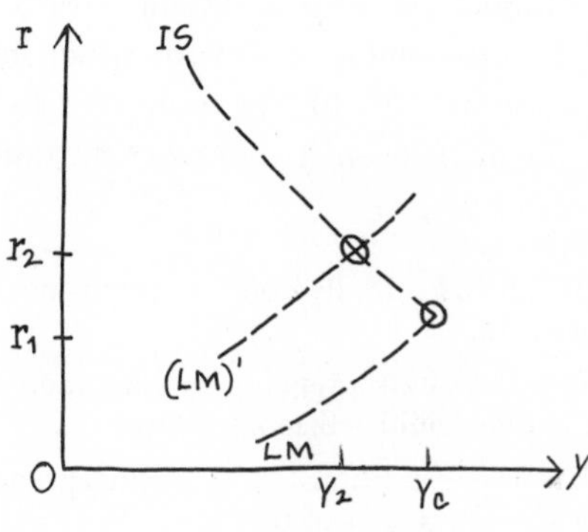

Figure XIII-3

The broad outline of the problem becomes clear: monetary restraint when prices are rising because of supply side pressures will be able to check prices only by damping demand. If there is no initial fat to cut in profit margins (*cf.* text *infra in re* Baumol), prices will not fall except to the extent that windfall profits are negative, recalling the second term of the right-hand sides of the Fundamental Equations. The cost of monetary restraint in terms of reduced output can become severe.

I am much indebted to Sir Roy Harrod for pointing out to me in 1959 the crucial relevance of the *Treatise* to the cost inflation problem. The Hicksian model just elaborated is obtained by using Equation 7''' in the basic model for Book III of the *Treatise*. The model appropriate for the *Economist's* passages just quoted includes Equation 7''' and finds the market rate of interest raised through official action. The price level would rise to the extent that factor costs increased and fall to the extent that higher interest rates made *I-S* more negative (less positive). *Cf.* Appendix A, Ch. XII.

Full-employment output no longer can be sustained, since r_1 no longer is achievable. If the monetary authorities insist on a climate consistent with full employment, they must relax monetary parameters so that the *LM* curve returns to its initial position; the wage increase must be *validated.* If the time rate of change of the wage unit is a decreasing function of involuntary unemployment (defining that term in the sophistic manner of Chs. IX and X), the authorities can gain a phyrric victory by keeping shut the monetary valves in the face of exogenous increase in the wage unit.[20] And, of course, corresponding analysis applies to exogenous movements in prices where dp/dt is a decreasing function of excess capacity.

If firms operate under a "Baumol principle" (maximization of sales revenue subject to a minimum profit restraint), our conclusions lose definition if firms initially are enjoying rates of profit greater than constraining rates.[21] But surely it is safe to assume that higher wage units lead to higher prices if a system with a given technology is to continue at full employment.[22] On the other hand, there is a set of specifications consistent with higher money wage rates not leading to increased unemployment even if monetary authorities do not react sympathetically:

a) perhaps entrepreneurs initially able to obtain more workers at the going money-wage rate;

b) initial willingness of entrepreneurs to hire more workers at the going wage rate if they could sell more output;

c) initial liquidity-trap conditions so that entrepreneurs can obtain additional finance at going rates of interest.

Under these conditions prices might not rise at all or higher prices will not lead to higher interest rates and, hence, to lower effective demand. Compare Figure XIII-4.

20 The fiscal authorities face a similar dilemma. If full employment is maintained, dw/dt increases. Furthermore, if monetary valves remain shut, deficit spending will lead to higher interest rates, discouraging private investment. On the other hand, the fiscal authorities must keep in mind that sluggish trade might cause investment expenditures to fall even more through operation of the (de)accelerator principle. The conflict between growth and price stability simply cannot be resolved.

21 *Cf.* William J. Baumol, *Business Behavior, Value, and Growth* (New York: The Macmillan Co., 1959), Ch. 6, pp. 45-53.

22 If the state of the arts is improving, you might want to impose a rate of change of money-wage rates more than enough to offset whatever deflationary effects might be generated by technological change.

Begin at point *P*. If the wage unit is increased to w_1 (from w_0), the real-wage rate is that at *Q*: w_1/p_0.[23] The price level is unchanged, but part of entrepreneurial receipt streams have been diverted to labor receipt streams. Of course, if Keynesian income balances vary (*ex ante*) with distribution of income or if Keynesian business balances (transactions requirements of firms) increases with higher payments to non-entrepreneurial factors, the liquidity-trap assumption might be summoned . . . It also is possible that prices and wages may increase in the same proportion so that, if we begin in the liquidity trap, effective demand will be unchanged: point *P* in the (w/p)-*N* space of this diagram will continue to describe the solution-state of the labor market.

LABOR MARKET WITH WAGE-PRICE RIGIDITY

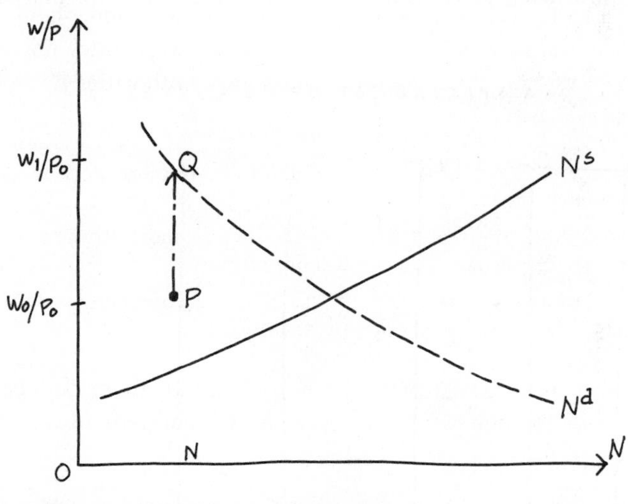

Figure XIII-4

3

Two other theoretical problems are of interest in this connection:

23 We can assume that the price level is unchanged at the outset. Ignoring distributional effects, there will have been no increase in demand for goods. We might assume that price increases will occur only if excess capacity is reduced.

1) cost inflation where expenditure plans are insensitive to interest rates over the relevant range;

2) income-and-employment effects of union-compelled increases in *real* wages where industry is competitively organized.

Taking up problem 1, how can a system be depicted in which firms and households are totally insensitive to interest rates in their expenditure decisions, in which no real-balance effects exist in commodities markets, but in which demand for money balances is conventionally affected by prices and interest rates? The *LL* curve for such a system — the locus of price-and-interest-rate combinations consistent with clearance of the money market at full employment — would be upward sloping. The *CC* curve — the locus of price-and-interest-rate combinations consistent with the commodities markets clearing at full employment — is a bird of another feather: only the strange representation of the diagram below suffices. Since the (temporary) equilibrium price level is determined in the labor market, the

A SPECIAL SET OF CC CURVES

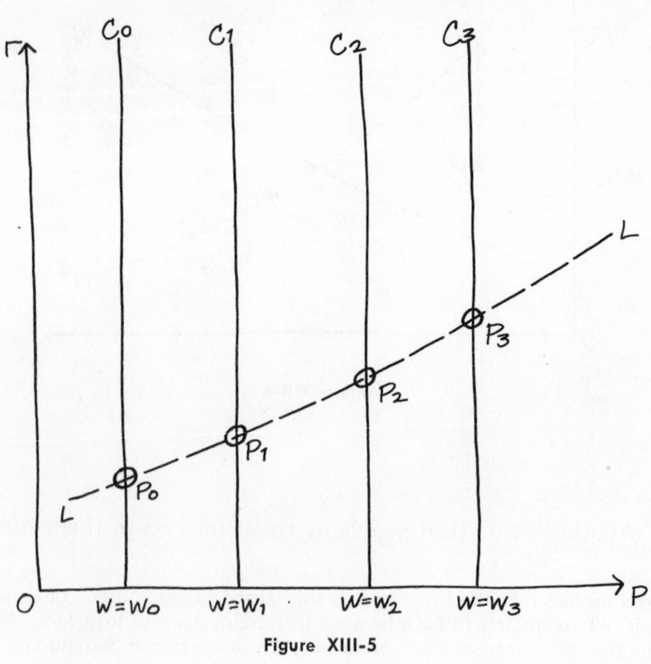

Figure XIII-5

appropriate CC curve is discovered by checking off the wage unit underlying its abscissa intercept. Each of the CC curves is vertical: interest rates have no effect on aggregate demand. If we superimpose the LL curve on the diagram, wage units (and hence price levels) can be related to solution values for interest rates; interest rates merely adjust the money market to the price level. As the wage unit is increased from w_0 to w_1 . . . to w_3, interest rates rise (transitorily and in equilibrium), inducing the money stock to turn over faster and faster. The system can move from P_0 to P_1 . . . to P_n as the wage unit is increased. Unemployment does not develop. Still the monetary authorities are quite helpless. Manipulation of the money supply permits control only of the interest rate(s). But "the" rate of interest has no effect on prices and production. If the diagram conditions prevail, the Administration might address appeals to, or bring down threats upon, labor leaders; the monetary authorities can do no more than scurry about their palace, twirling disconnected faucets.

Taking up the second problem, observe that union leaders thus far have "suffered" from money illusion: their decisions have been couched in nominal terms. What if union leaders — standing proxy for the whole set of exogenous forces operating directly on price levels — formulate policies in *real* terms? (Hold constant the state of the arts.) There are at least two immediate implications:

a) in a world operating as in the diagram above, the inflationary process might explode into hyperinflation as union leaders — anticipating sympathetic price movements — make more and more stringent demands. Prices will rise all the faster. Elastic expectations will be more than justified. An hyperinflationary spiral can develop that is undampable even by monetary stringency.

b) firms, faced with deterioration in cost price relationships (here assuming that prices lag behind wages), cut back output and employment. However, effective demand is not affected (always abstracting from distributional effects) except to the extent that accelerator effects and consequences of reduced profit margins impinge specifically upon investment plans: excess demand develops in commodities markets, driving up prices, inducing further wage increases, etc. Assuming now that interest rates affect expenditure plans, a lag structure can be specified that finds output oscillating within limits short of Y^f. If the authorities practice monetary restraint, interest rates will be forced higher and higher while the upper limit of the range in which output is oscillating moves farther away from Y^f. If the authorities adhere to cheap money in order to maintain demand at high enough levels to be sure that prices keep pace with wages, the inflationary process might go out of control in rather short order if indeed the union leadership is free of money illusion and persists in aiming at a real-wage target.[24]

4

Transition to some causal empirical observation is simple. First recall the case of cost inflation, if, indeed, it is important. Conventional monetary restraint in response to inflationary pressure unrelated to excess demand for goods proves either to be quite hopeless, as in the extreme case of the model of Figure XIII-5, or subject to a cruel dilemma forcing the authorities to buy price stability with lower rates of growth: there is concomitant adverse pressure on capital formation and persistent unemployment. The more vigorously conventional measures are applied, the greater the pressure of the nether stone. The less the resistance of the monetary authorities to powerful political pressure inevitably brought to bear against persistent unemployment and sluggish growth of output, the greater the danger that inflationary processes will be accelerated, perhaps leading in their turn to politically intolerable consequences. The lot of a monetary nabob would not be a happy one.

It remains to consider whether we live in such a world. The following much-edited excerpt from the *Economist* of June 1, 1957 (p. 785 *ff.*), interpreting the American scene, typifies an important view:

> "The persistence of inflation has plunged the government's economic managers into deep pessimism. Despite 18 months of monetary restraint and a budget surplus during the last two years, prices paid by consumers are rising steadily. . . .
>
> Two equally important elements contribute to the despondency of the moderate conservatives who run Republican economic policy. The first is the distress that always accompanies the frustration of an ideal. [The Republican advisers] came to Washington in 1953 with

[24] For useful discussions of wage-unit movements and the theory of employment, see J. R. Hicks, "A Rehabilitation of 'Classical' Economics?", and T. F. Dernburg and D. M. McDougall, *Macroeconomics* (New York: McGraw-Hill Book Co., 1960), pp. 200-211.

Keep in mind that the *IS-LM* construction applies only at a particular point in time; a single set of curves in general cannot precisely describe an ongoing process. More sophisticated treatment would concern deviation from a secularly rising level of full-employment income. "Neutral" monetary policy would perhaps find the money supply expanding at a steady rate; maintenance of a constant money supply would be a contractive policy. The more sophisticated approach would not, in this instance, contribute to over-all understanding of the theoretical issues.

great hopes of proving that a modern capitalist society could have full employment without inflation. They used all of the classic weapons with great courage and considerable vigor . . . [but prices since 1956 have been] rising month after month with depressing regularity . . .

The second cause of gloom is the almost unanimous conviction [of the authorities] that creeping inflation is bound to gather speed . . . [The late] Professor Sumner Slichter has become the most articulate spokesman of a school whose argument, in brief, is that under modern conditions creeping inflation is inevitable, that it is an acceptable price to pay for many of the benefits of modern economic organization, and that it can be lived with indefinitely . . . [The top Eisenhower advisers and the Federal Reserve] are passionately convinced that a creeping inflation cannot help but turn into a galloping one . . .

The two parties to the debate . . . are strikingly agreed on one crucial point, the responsibility of wage settlements negotiated in modern conditions of collective bargaining for the rise in prices . . . A recent study by the Bureau of Labor Statistics . . . tells the story. Payments to wage earners as a whole have risen 61 per cent in the last decade while their productivity [God only knows how this was computed! . . . MLB] rose only 26 per cent . . . Nobody wants a recession, but it seems probable that only a substantial dose of unemployment could halt the month-by-month rise in prices . . ."

I hesitate to play numbers games. Suffice it to say that it cannot be denied (nor can it be confirmed) that American data since the latter part of 1957 are consistent with hypotheses that rising prices have been due to cost inflation and that stiff doses of monetary policy in response to this kind of inflation are likely to purchase a modicum of price stability at the expense of growth and full employment.[25]

The CPI (not including food) rose about 24 per cent over the interval, wages (as defined in column 5), 33 per cent, the money stock 11 per cent.

A mere tyro, I refuse to play at this pot-limit table of statistical analysation. Suffice it to say that wage rates seem to lead a life of their own and that fundamentally restrictive monetary policy (real GNP rose 23.5 per cent from 1952 to 1960; nominal GNP 45 per cent) has not succeeded in preventing persistent inflationary pressure — this statement being subject to the *caveats* suggested by the Price Statistics Review Committee. Surely, the data do not establish the efficacy

25 It has been argued that much of the measured inflation in the postwar United States is spurious, that official measures — particularly of quality changes — have been inaccurate. *Cf.* U. S. Congress, Joint Economic Committee, *Government Price Statistics, Hearings* (Washington: Government Printing Office, 1961). For a more uncertain opinion, see M. L. Burstein, "The Measurement of Quality Changes in Consumer Durables," *Manchester School,* Vol. 29, September 1961, pp. 267-279.

of monetary policy, at least in dosages administered by the Eisenhower Administration. On the other hand, we must ask the question: what would these series look like if monetary policy had been more expansive? I do not suggest an answer.

These are some data from the *Economic Report of the President* for January 1961.

PRICES, OUTPUT, EMPLOYMENT, AND MONEY SUPPLY 1952–1960

(1) Year	(2) CPI, all items	(3) CPI, less food	(4) Unemploy. as % lab. force	(5) Av. hrly. earn. in Mfg.	(6) GNP, 1960 prices	(7) Money Supply (Dec.)
	1947-1949 = 100			$	Billions of Dollars	
1952	113.5	113.5	3.1	1.67	407	126.5
1953	114.4	115.7	2.9	1.77	426	128.1
1954	114.8	116.4	5.6	1.81	417	131.8
1955	114.5	116.7	4.4	1.88	450	134.6
1956	116.2	118.8	4.2	1.98	459	136.5
1957	120.2	122.8	4.3	2.07	468	135.5
1958	123.5	125.5	6.8	2.13	460	140.8
1959	124.6	127.9	5.5	2.22	491	141.5
1960	126.4	130.0	5.6	2.29	503	140.4

TABLE XIII-I

Finally, demand induced inflationary processes often can appear to the careless observer to be cost induced. Thus, starting at "full employment," if there is a surge in planned investment, steel prices, for example, and wages will be pushed up. Costs of production of many manufactured consumer goods might rise substantially. The Consumer Price Index will begin to rise as consumer-goods manufacturers, not necessarily experiencing any surge in demand for their products, announce price increases, pleading increased costs of doing business. Needless to say, even if initial inflationary pressure stems from attempts of consumers to purchase more durables on credit, indirect effects, including those under the "accelerator" rubric, will make it appear that the CPI is subject to cost-push.

CHAPTER FOURTEEN

The Quantity Theory of Money

DISCUSSION OF THE QUANTITY THEORY HAS BEEN POSTponed to the end of Part II because the quantity-theory literature makes sense only in a context of general equilibrium. The quantity theory of money can be viewed as a set of predictions of how *observed* prices and incomes will react over varying lengths of time to changes in monetary variables; or as a theorem on the comparative statics of certain models. Unqualified earlier formulations of the quantity theory as an empirical law have not held up. Neo-quantity theorists have made more qualified predictions. Sections B, C, and E take up the quantity theory as an exercise in pseudo (one-period) statics pertaining to variables Y^* at t. Here too the verdict is negative: quantity theorists offer a trivial theorem in the context of simple models; it is incorrect in more complex models. Thus money cannot be neutral if there is even one other financial asset whose total quantity is fixed in nominal value.

A. EMPIRICAL RELATIONS

1

"There is perhaps no other empirical relation in economics that has been observed to recur so uniformly under so wide a variety of circumstances as the relation between substantial changes over short periods in the stock of money and in prices; the one is invariably linked with the other and is in the same direction; this uniformity

> is, I suspect, of the same order as many of the uniformities that form the basis of the physical sciences. And the uniformity is more than direction. There is an extraordinary empirical stability and regularity to such magnitudes as income velocity that cannot but impress anyone who works extensively with monetary data. This very stability and regularity contributed to the downfall of the quantity theory, for it was overstated and expressed in unduly simple form; the numerical value of velocity itself, whether income or transactions, was treated as a natural constant. Now this it is not; and its failure to be so, first during and after World War I and then, to a lesser extent, after the crash of 1929, helped greatly to foster the reaction against the quantity theory."[1]

Since Professor Friedman is probably the most famous contemporary "quantity theorist," this excerpt should be a good start. However, a small cloud the size of a man's hand appears early in the game: nowhere in this essay does Friedman define the quantity theory. "The quantity theory of money is a term evocative of a general approach rather than a label for a well-defined theory."[2]

Let us pursue the method of science: observation made precise through quantification, formation of hypotheses intended to explain the data, test of hypotheses on additional data, reformulation, retesting, etc. Then a simple and natural transition can be made to discussion of whether quantity-theory statics concern *structures* or *reduced forms* of economic models, and whether comparative-statics properties are pertinent for purposes of prediction.

Friedman refers to awesome regularities demanding that close attention be given to monetary phenomena. We proceed to do just that — relying upon the *Chart Book* — but first must make a tentative statement of the *quantity theory of money*: the chapter's themes cannot be developed without using the term.

The statement should be operational and empirically oriented.[3] I consider the quantity theory to predict that changes in the quantity of money — defined as including currency and demand deposits and sometimes time deposits — in period t should be strongly and quite precisely associated with changes in the nominal value of transactions and income streams in period $t+1$, surely in period $t+6$, where the unit period is, say, a month or bimonthly. Furthermore, at full employment there should be proportional variation in the money stock

1 Milton Friedman, "The Quantity Theory of Money: A Restatement," *Studies in the Quantity Theory of Money,* pp. 20-21.

2 *Ibid.*, p. 3.

3 *Cf.* footnote 21.

and prices.[4] It holds that the single most important policy variable is the money stock or, more precisely, parameters controlling the size of the money stock. A quantity theorist puts great stress on the importance of the authorities having a firm grip on the money supply (even if this is but to facilitate execution of a non-discretionary rule). He might advocate 100 per cent reserve banking and similar reforms. He might or might not stress structural as against reduced-form relations. Still he is likely to claim that the determinants of demand for money balances are relatively few in number and sure in operation.

GROSS NATIONAL PRODUCT AND MONEY SUPPLY

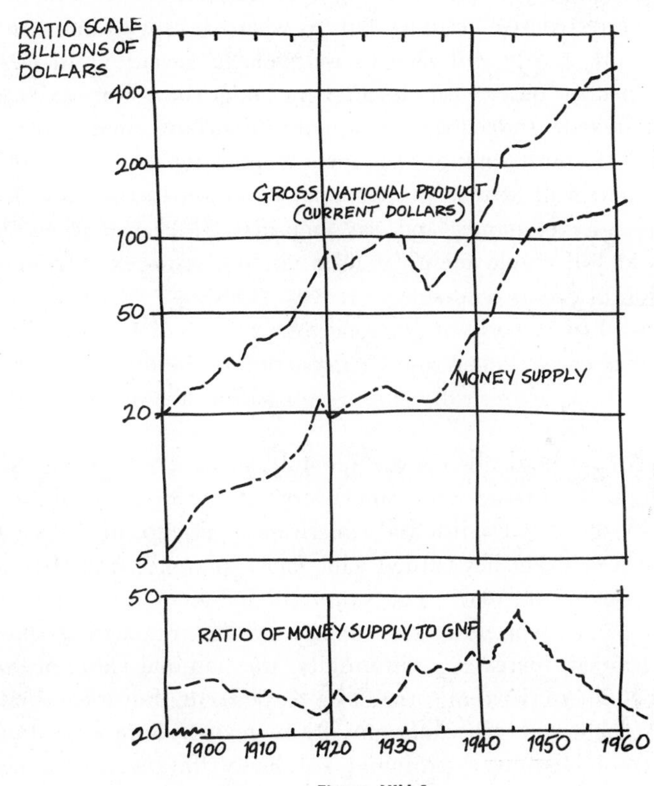

Figure XIV-1

Source: Chart Book (Washington: 1961), p. 68. (See Note A.)

[4] An exception would be made where price experience generates non-unitary elasticities of expectation. For the case of hyperinflation, *cf.* Ch. VI. For the general argument, *cf.* Section D, Ch. XIV.

We now turn to some data. The chart above shows strong positive correlation between the money stock and nominal GNP, but — as its lower part shows — this correspondence is far from those comprising the "basis of the physical sciences." Obviously the relationship between the stock of money and flows highly correlated with GNP is subject to substantial variation in both the short and long run. "Unduly simple" characterizations of the association of monetary and price (and/or income) series are apt to be crashing failures.

As Ch. VI showed, more elaborate formulations can permit better statistical fits — perhaps at the expense of introducing a large number of variables as parameters that are not controllable or even forecastable. These estimating equations might be empirically useless; they might achieve retroactive accuracy, but of what use is it to know that variations in *M* shortly will lead to well-defined variations in GNP only if innumerable other variables are kept under control or can accurately be predicted? Indeed there is a more important consequence of "complicated" formulations, at least for our immediate purposes: they imply that there will NOT be proportional variation in the short run between the stock of money and, say, nominal GNP even when the economy is at full employment; at least not unless an extraordinary concatenation of events occurs.

There is, then, a world of difference between the definition of the quantity theory of Sections A and C: in Section C the quantity theory is diminished to an empirically empty proposition about comparative statics.

Figure XIV-1 does not convey the full flavor of short-run fluctuation in ratios linking the money stock with national income, transactions rates, etc. English and American experience in the 1950's does. Table XIV-I sketches United Kingdom experience from December 1954 through Fall 1957. The supply of money — including currency and bank deposits — fell slightly while transactions flows (nominally valued) increased substantially: the nominal value of output rose by about 16 per cent, prices by 14.5 per cent, and wages by 23 per cent. Monetary velocity substantially increased. Surely the table cannot be explained by a profound regularity linking the money-supply series to any of the others.

U. K. VARIABLES 1954-1957[a]

Year	Wage Rate[b]	Prices[c]	Money Supply[d]	Output[e]
1954	236	244	5.72	130
1955	252	256	5.70	137
1956	272	263	5.76	136
1957 (Apr.)	279	278	5.39	
1957 (Oct.)	290	278	5.58 (Sept.)	143

TABLE XIV-I

[a] Based on the *Economist*, June 1, 1957, p. 824, and International Monetary Fund statistics.
[b] Money wages per hour, 1939 = 100.
[c] Consumer price index (all retail goods), 1938 = 100.
[d] Billions of pounds sterling.
[e] 1948 = 100.

The 1955-1957 episode in the U. S. is another example:

> The wholesale price index rose from an average of 110.7 during 1955 to 118.4 in August 1957. The retail price index from 114.5 to 121. Nominally valued Gross National Product increased from $397.5 billion in 1955 to $442.5 billion in 1957; its implicit price deflator from 100.7 to 107.3. The daily average of free reserves of member banks was —$21 million in 1955 and —$320 million in 1957 (—$471 million in August 1957).

Money was tight, but, once again, countervailing forces were interposed. At least the authorities could not rely on automatic linkage between money stocks and income flows and price levels. (*See Note B.*) Many other illustrations are available. It is hard to work annual, let alone quarterly, data of this kind to reveal overwhelming regularities. And then the outlandishly large free reserves of the 1930–1941 period have mercifully been repressed.

But at least two points should be noted: (1) the theoretical underpinnings of the quantity-theory literature are interesting and informative; (2) enough regularity has been turned up to suggest that impressive "simple" uniformities would appear if only the parameters of the system (other than the money stock) would stay put and that, if we account for the influence of relatively few other variables (*cf.* Ch. VI), a neo-quantity theory can be formulated, supporting monetary control if not the classical formulation. (*See Note B.*)[4] After all, Professors Friedman, Cagan, Selden, *et al.* have obtained high correlations between series of money stocks and of income and output variables when various secular, expectational, and cyclical phenomena are accounted for.[5]

2

There is another topic under the general heading of *empirical relations.* R. S. Sayers has written:

> ". . . To label something as 'money,' the supply of which is to behave according to rules laid down by legal authority, is to build on shifting sand . . . [T]here is no hard and fast line between what is money and what is not money . . . When we worry ourselves about changes in the supply of money, our concern is in fact with the shifting liquidity position of the economy . . . [T]here is not even finality in the list of financial institutions whose behavior is relevant. New financial institutions arise to exploit new opportunities . . . It is idle to say that one can somewhere find an ultimate form of money and rule that off as the grand regulator of the economic situation, a regulator that can be made to behave properly by legislator's orders . . ."[6]

As a proposition about comparative statics, the quantity theory would be undamaged *a priori* by Professor Sayers' strictures. Even if the relative importance of instruments classified as money were declining over time,[7] no dent would be made in its argument. Consider a system in which (non-banking) traders lacked money illusion. Control of the nominal stock of demand deposits (or of any other nominal stock) suffices to determine the equilibrium price level — and, *if nomi-*

4 An irregular simple empirical relationship between the stock of money and nominal GNP, for example, is not necessarily adverse for monetary policy if various exogenous and predetermined variables can be controlled or predicted. (*Cf.* Ch. VI.) But a quantity theory of money does *not* emerge. Thus, I might assert with strong confidence that a 31 per cent reduction in the money supply will cause prices to fall 2 per cent over the next six months. To me, this is not a quantity-theory assertion.

5 *Cf. Studies in the Quantity Theory of Money, loc. cit., supra.* Also Milton Friedman, "The Demand for Money: Some Theoretical and Empirical Results," *Journal of Political Economy,* Vol. 67, August 1959, pp. 327-351.

6 R. S. Sayers, *Central Banking After Bagehot,* pp. 5-6. Sayers goes on to say (footnote 1, pp. 6-7) that proposals such as 100 per cent reserve banking designed to "eliminate private creation or destruction of money and discretionary control by central-bank authority" — the words are Friedman's — are based on "the supposed possibility of identifying once and for all something called 'money' . . . I find all such proposals tempting, but they are based on a complete misconception of the origin of money."

7 Our charts do not encourage this conclusion.

nal quantities of all other stocks are free to vary, the equilibrium price level will vary proportionately with the nominal value of the "controlled" stock. (*Cf.* Clower and Burstein, Section C, §§ 6, *infra.*)[8]

The Sayers argument does imply that, at the least, transitional interest-rate changes can break up the proportionality of changes in the money supply and the price level (or nominal national income) in the short-run. (*Cf. Note B.* It is convenient to assume full employment in these arguments.) But this need not undermine the neo-quantity theorists. Surely one will want to know about mutual savings banks, building and loan associations, insurance companies, trade-credit expansion possibilities, etc.: these can determine how much pressure must be put on the commercial banks for a given end result. But the crucial concern of the neo-quantity theorists is with Equation 1:

$$(1) \qquad y_{i(t+1)} = f^i(M_t, z_t, u_{t+1}),$$

where $y_{i(t+1)}$ is the observed value of the *ith* endogenous variable (say the price level) next period and where u_{t+1} is a disturbance term. M could even be defined as the supply of currency. The question is whether $y_i(t+1)$ can accurately be predicted from M_t or whether enough evidence has accumulated to justify the assumption that manipulation of this period's stock of currency *somehow* leads to well-defined changes in y_i? The structure through which such changes occur might be unspecified. Still, if the monetary authorities know z_t, and if the expectation of u_{t+1} is small, all will be well for the neo-quantity theorist.

Perhaps this is a roundabout way of putting the following proposition: the importance of growth of non-banking financial institutions and other sources of liquid debt instruments for effectiveness of conventional monetary policy (if manipulation of the currency supply can be conventional) is not in effects of such institutions on the level of velocity or its secular trend or cyclical movement but rather on its *predictability.* If new sources of instability are not unearthed, creation and destruction of money substitutes is not a cause for concern for

8 This conclusion can be intuited: equilibrium values will always be in real (as against nominal) terms. Beginning with a set of equilibrium values change the policy-determined numerator. If the other numerators and the price level change in the same proportion, the initial real state can be restored. "The other numerators" are readily enough adjusted: more bonds are issued, etc. The italicized words in the text are crucial.

neo-quantity theorists. And one suspects that the professional managers of the institutions are more likely to add to than detract from predictability of financial variables.

3

We have done no more than explain why the inability of what had been known as the quantity theory of money to explain data does not *per se* undermine the neo-quantity theorists. We do not intend to concede them the field. Not at all. Indeed they are on uncertain ground. Since the neo-quantity theorists do not specify a model or even an elaborated mechanism of adjustment, it is impossible to grant them identification clearance (*cf.* Section F *infra*). Furthermore, their prediction has been retroactive. Their regression analysis suggests that lags are important and that the *z* vector contains variables not easily ascertained, let alone controlled, by the officials. They themselves believe that discretionary monetary control is *destabilizing.* They call for automatic rules, but are not altogether clear as to why the rules should overcome the lags. They are unclear whether interest-rates are the engine of monetary policy but do not rely on real-balance effects (and in fact cannot in a credit-money world). Thus they have not offered a precise alternative *modus operandi.* (*Cf.* Note C *infra* for the nearest thing to a precise specification.) In many ways the neo-quantity theory is more a mystique than a theory — at least when it ventures outside the stout bastion of logical positivism.

4

In past ages the sense of quantitative relationships was much less developed.

> "It will not surprise the reader to learn that the *effects* of the violent price revolutions of the fifteenth, sixteenth, and seventeenth centuries should have been zealously discussed. But it might surprise him to learn that there was any question about its causes . . . Nevertheless, though it is probably possible to find early arguments that more or less distinctly imply this obvious diagnosis [relation to the stock of money] it seems to be a fact that no explicit, full and — so far as it went — theoretically satisfactory explanation of it appeared before 1568 . . . On the strength of this, [Bodin] is universally voted the discoverer of the Quantity Theory of Money."[9]

It was common in other ages, and is not rare today, for changes in the

[9] Joseph A. Schumpeter, *History of Economic Analysis,* p. 311.

value of money to be ascribed to changes in its "quality," where "quality" applies to a broader context than that provided by mere clipping and sweating of coins.

B. THE QUANTITY THEORY AS A BEHAVIOR RELATION

1

We have thus far carried on as positivists. The discussion has been in terms of observed regularities and conclusions that might be drawn from data as to the ability of monetary authorities to affect endogenous variables. Causal mechanisms have been avoided. Demand and supply functions have been unspecified. In fact the traditional quantity theory was fundamentally a theory of the demand for money. The neo-quantity theory also appears somehow to be rooted in the demand for money:

> "the quantity theory is in the first instance a theory of the *demand* for money. It is not a theory of output, or of money income, or of the price level. Any statement about these variables requires combining the quantity theory with some specifications about the conditions of supply of money and perhaps other variables as well." [10]

Not that the demand function for money for the neo-quantity theorist is of no more importance than that for the *ith* good:

> "the quantity theorist not only regards the demand function for money as stable; he also regards it as playing a vital role in determining variables that he regards as of great importance . . . such as the level of money income or of prices . . ." [11]

2

Traditionally, interest in the quantity theory as a behavior relation flows from concern about certain propositions in comparative statics.[12]

---

[10] Milton Friedman, *op. cit.*, p. 4.

[11] *Ibid.*, p. 16.

[12] *Cf.* Don Patinkin, *Money, Interest and Prices.*
J. M. Keynes, *A Treatise on Money*, Vol. 1, pp. 221-240.
A. W. Marget, *The Theory of Prices.* This deserves more attention than it has received.

Following Patinkin (to whom I am especially indebted), it might be said that quantity-theory comparative statics can be obtained in two ways:

a) through peculiar characteristics of the demand function for money;

b) through properties of economic models not particularly focused on the money market.

The first possibility is the subject matter of Section B, the second of Section C. Finally, it is important to remember that we deal only with *once-and-for-all* changes in the money stock until Section D, "Growth."

3

Alternative (a) was stressed by the early Keynes and, at one time, by A. C. Pigou. Also by Irving Fisher, although he attached severe *caveats* (*cf.* Ch. VI.) Keynes wrote:

> "The Quantity Theory of Money states that the amount of cash which the community requires, *assuming certain habits of business and of banking to be established,* and assuming also a given level and distribution of wealth, depends on the level of prices. If the consumption and production of actual goods are unaltered but prices and wages are doubled, then twice as much cash as before is required to do the business. The truth of this, properly explained and qualified, it is foolish to deny. The Theory infers from this that the *aggregate real value* of all the paper money in circulation remains more or less the same, irrespective of the *number of units* of it in circulation, provided the habits and prosperity of the people are not changed."[13]

Pigou has been more unqualified:

> "an increase in the supply of legal tender ought always, since the elasticity of demand for legal tender is equal to unity, to raise prices in the proportion in which the supply has increased."[14]

I avoid elaboration of alternative forms of the demand-for-money function used by primal quantity theorists. Exegetes can fairly wallow in the *Treatise* and especially Marget. I confine myself to the basic Cantabrigian and Fisherine approaches, heavily relying on the *Treatise* (Vol. I, p. 229 *ff.*). Conceding (along with Keynes) that the

[13] J. M. Keynes, *A Tract on Monetary Reform,* pp. 41-42.

[14] A. C. Pigou, *Essays in Applied Economics* (London: Macmillan & Co., Ltd., 1923), pp. 41-42.

Cambridge Quantity Equation has "a much longer descent, being derived from Petty, Locke, Cantillon, and Adam Smith," it can be expressed:

$$M^{d} \equiv kpY, \tag{2}$$

where k is an institutionally determined constant (*cf.* Ch. VI), p the general price level, and Y real income so that pY is money (nominal) income; Y is highly correlated with transactions activity. The desired stock of money is linked to the flow of payments roughly proxied by "income." Keynes later made clear that there is a misleading simplicity in Equation 2:

> "The prominence given to k, namely the proportion of the bank-deposits [for simplicity taken to comprise the stock of money] to the community's *income* is misleading when it is extended beyond the income deposits . . . The equation entirely obscures disturbances which in practice are one of the most important types of disturbances — arising out of a change in the proportions in which deposits are held for different purposes . . ."[15]

4

There is a long way to travel from the *Tract* to the *Treatise.* In the *Treatise* Keynes became concerned with money as a liquid store of value as well as a means of payment. *Once this is done Y becomes important not only as a proxy for "payments requirements" but as an index of wealth.* More recently, Professor Friedman has emphasized the relationship between monetary stocks and aggregate wealth. Still Friedman has not found interest rates empirically significant as a determinant of demand for money.[16] If we posit unit-elastic price expectations,[17] Friedman's formulation can be reduced to Equation 3:

$$M^{d} \equiv p.L(w, Y). \tag{3}$$

w is the proportion borne by non-human to human wealth: since non-human wealth is more liquid, $\partial M^{d}/\partial w < 0$. But w should be fairly constant over short periods. For purposes of a "thought experiment" in which Y were held fixed, Equation 4 roughly holds:

---

15 *Treatise,* Vol. I, pp. 232-233.

16 He concedes that in his model interest rates theoretically should have influence. *Cf.* Ch. VI.

17 The neo-quantity theorists put great stress on the importance of response to price experience. Phillip Cagan has made especially important contributions on this matter. *Cf.* Ch. VI.

(4) $$M^d \equiv k'p.$$

Of course, Professor Friedman's fuller formulation avoids a simple predictive rule: lagged adjustments, cyclical phenomena, etc., are interposed. Neo-quantity theorists cannot be found pinned and wriggling on the wall as could Keynes and Pigou in 1923. (*See Note C.*)

5

The traditional (and therefore "transactions-oriented") Fisherine formula is

(5) $$Mv = pT$$

where the expected value of v, interpretable as a velocity of circulation, is specified quite narrowly and where T is the total volume of cash transactions or expenditure. As Keynes wrote:

> "The great advantage of this formula is the fact that one side of it, namely Mv, fits in better than most with the actually available banking statistics . . . Mv corresponds, more or less, to the volume of bank clearings . . . Its weakness, on the other hand, is to be found on the other side of it . . . [f]or neither p nor T corresponds to the quantities in which we are likely to be interested for their own sakes. p is not the purchasing power of money and T is not the volume of output. Professor Fisher has not, indeed, been oblivious to these defects, but he has not, I think, rated them as high as he should. Nor do the approximations which he has employed for their evaluation command confidence. For example, he has tried to arrive at p by combining the Wholesale Standard [price index], the Wages Standard [CPI], and an index of 40 stocks . . . This, of course, represented pioneer work."[18]

6

Agreed then that at least the traditional quantity theory of money can roughly be associated with a demand function for money of the form

(6) $M^d \equiv kpY$ or (6′) $M^d \equiv ky$

where y is nominal income. For a predetermined stock of money, equilibrium in the money market requires that

(7) $$\overline{M} = k'p$$

at full employment: if the money stock is increased to $2\overline{M}$ from $\overline{M}$, the equilibrium price level must double; real balances are invariant in

[18] J. M. Keynes, *op. cit.*, Vol. I, pp. 235-236.

equilibrium against nominal balances. (Of course, *sans* price flexibility, the analysis breaks down.) Abandoning the full-employment assumption and assuming that the supply-of-all-goods is perfectly elastic at $\bar{p}$, we have

$$Y^* = (k\bar{p})^{-1}M = k''M. \tag{8}$$

The seemingly innocent transformation of k from a slack variable in an identity to an institutionally-determined constant has had rather shocking consequence: it implies that manipulation of the money stock has absolutely decisive bearing on equilibrium prices and/or output.

7

Let us probe into mechanisms of adjustment capable of producing these startling comparative-statics effects. The probe has three subheads: (1) adjustment mechanism in a system of credit money; (2) adjustment mechanism in a system of fiat paper money; (3) relation to what Patinkin has called "invalid dichotomies."

8

1. Adjustment Mechanism in a System of Credit Money

Be unsophisticated. Take the quantity of potential bank-deposit liability as officially determined at each point in time. If the banks are to create more money or destroy existing money, the public must be induced to hold a correspondingly different amount of money in accordance with Keynes's dictum:

> "The volume of cash-balances depends on the decision of the bankers and is 'created' by them. [Keynes is more sophisticated than we have to be.] The volume of real-balances depends on the decisions of the depositors and is 'created' by them. The price level is the resultant of the two sets of decisions and is measured by the ratio of the volume of the cash-balances created to that of the real-balance created."[19]

But Equation 2 requires that "persuasion" be exerted by changing price and/or real-income (as proxy for transaction) levels. Interest rates are relevant in traditional Cantabrigian demand for money only to the extent that they influence planned production and consumption activities, and hence transactions. But the fact that suppliers plan to supply different amounts than demanders plan to take off markets

[19] *Ibid.*, p. 224.

need have little to do with planned demand for cash. (In models with non-price constraints on market realizations — *cf.* Chapters IX and X — it is clear that there should be included proxies for potential realizations; the traditional Cambridge equation easily is built into modern models in which money is in a transactions-balance corner.) Interest rates can enter Cantabrigian demand for money only through the back door. Let us slam it shut. The clearance condition for the money market becomes

$$\phi(p) = 0, \tag{9}$$

where $\phi(p)$ is excess demand for money balances.

The absolute price level need have no effect on plans made in the commodity market: distribution effects can be ignored; wages and prices can be assumed to march in lock-step at the "natural real wage rate"; the model need not contain non-monetary money-fixed claims; cash balances can be offset by bank-held IOU's. Clearance of the commodity market (not permitting interposition of non-price restraints on realization potential) requires that the interest rate be "right":

$$\psi(r) = 0, \tag{10}$$

where $\psi(r)$ is excess demand for commodities.[20]

There is, in Modigliani's phrase, a curious criss-cross: excess demand for money, certainly when income constraint can be ignored, depends on the price level which is determined in the commodity market; excess demand for commodities depends on the rate of interest which is determined outside of the commodity market. Creation of excess bank reserves leads to a sequence of events like this:

a) securities prices rise as banks attempt to place more funds with firms and households;

b) higher securities prices encourage firms and households to borrow from the banks, planning to increase real rates of expenditure, but succeeding only in bidding up prices of goods and services;

c) higher commodity prices lead firms and households to plan to place securities with banks in order to restore their real cash balances; the supply curve for securities issues shifts to the right as prices increase;

d) finally the money and commodity markets are cleared at the initial (natural) rate of interest with prices higher in the same proportion as the increase in the money supply; the stock of money and prices vary proportionately in equilibrium.[20]

---

[20] This argument probably can be justified rigorously only through a *tatonnement* process. An heuristic proof seems adequate for present purposes.

Bear in mind that the onset of the adjustment process does *not* find the public trying to dispose of suddenly increased money balances. At the outset, it seeks to increase the rate at which cash is flowing to it from the banks (net of repayments to banks), not mainly with the intention of increasing cash balances, but rather with the intention of exchanging most of the borrowed cash for goods and services as soon as possible. These plans lead to rising prices. As prices rise, the public in fact wishes substantially to increase its cash balances, planning to issue additional securities to banks and divert the net cash inflow from the banking sector into their reservoirs of cash. Transitorily lower interest rates encouraged the first set of plans. The second set led to interest rates being restored at initial levels. Surely it is misleading to refer to the quantity of money, an endogenous variable, as the driving force in this process of adjustment. Initial imbalance was confined to the banking sector and quickly was transferred to the securities markets. In an ongoing process *(vis-a-vis à tatonnement),*[20] money balances increase only when proceeds from sales of securities to banks start to flow through the system. Only then do traders find that, being unable to fulfill plans to purchase more goods at initial prices, they must hold their bank loans in cash instead of converting them into goods. It is at this point that rising prices take over: finally, traders *want to hold* the extra cash . . . When put this way, the quantity theory becomes a (as it happens, trivial) proposition about comparative statics derived from a well-defined set of assumptions about the demand for cash. It implies a distinct adjustment mechanism and is invulnerable to criticisms that the form of the demand function for money is inconsistent with the adjustment mechanism.[21] *Remember this: what has come to be known as the "Patinkin Business" pertains only, repeat only, to a fiat-paper-money model.*

21 On the other hand, it is shown in Section C that the same comparative statics results can be obtained from a model in which no special assumption is made about the demand function for money. Professor Friedman could have derived his conclusions (Note C) even if he assumed that demand for cash was sensitive to interest rates. The quantity theory, neo or otherwise, is trivial as a theorem of comparative statics. That is why I have insisted upon defining it as an empirically testable assertion about short-period phenomena. I have associated a statement about proportional movements of prices and the money supply over reasonably short periods with traditional quantity theorists, a weaker statement —stressing stability but not size of regression coefficients — with neo-quantity theorists. Quantity theorists must accept this cup or be dismissed as trivial. Indeed if neo-quantity theorists brew their tea weak enough, this will be their fate anyhow.

A useful bit of graphics can be performed. Now, Cantabrigians assume that Equation 9 is of the form

$$(9') \qquad k'p - M = 0,$$

$k'p$ being defined as the demand for cash. The demand curve for money is a rectangular hyperbola $[M^d(1/p) \equiv k')]$. If the parameter k' stays fixed, the demand curve of the diagram below will stay fixed:[22] the public will continue to demand the same quantity of *real* cash balances. If the supply of cash — always being indicated by a vertical line at a point in time — shifts, observed points will trace-out the demand curve for money IF the money market continually is in equilibrium. The locus of market-clearance points and the demand curve for money are then the same thing.[22] *We shall take great pains to point out that this need not be the case.*

9

This might be a good time to collect our wits, to summarize the difficult material that has been thus far developed. It is now possible to take up the argument in a different order:

a) we shall show that the locus of equilibrium points of the diagram below can be obtained from an infinity of specifications of the de-

A CANTABRIGIAN EXCESS-DEMAND-FOR-MONEY DETERMINATION

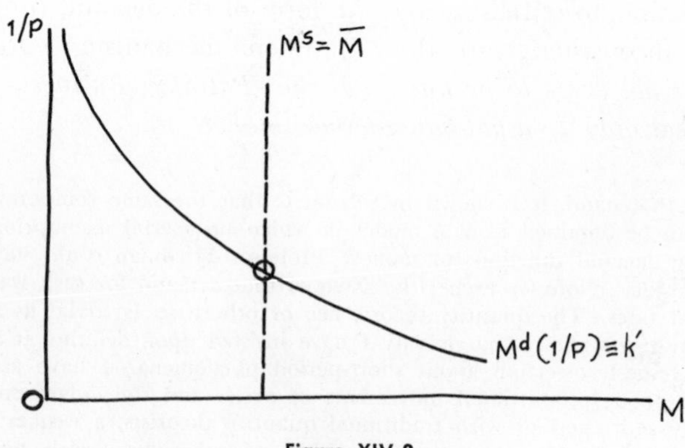

Figure XIV-2

22 Growth can be accommodated. Draw a family of rectangular hyperbolae, each corresponding to a different level of real income.

mand function for money, including, of course, traditional and neo-quantity theory specifications;

b) it follows that both quantity theories are trivial as theorems about comparative statics; *cf.* Section C;

c) lag specifications alone could make either the traditional- or the neo-quantity theory — as an hypothesis about short-run behavior — consistent with almost anything that might happen;

d) it follows that *l'affaire* quantity-theory has to be fought out in a narrowly defined empirical arena if it is not to be meaningless. It happens that traditional quantity theorists — perhaps not recognizing that their theorem applies only to comparative statics — made very strong statements about short-run correlations between money stocks and prices. They have been knocked cold. The neo-quantity theorists have recognized that the issues to be resolved by data concern monetary dynamics, not statics. They have made much weaker statements about real-world correlation between money stocks and other things but have come up with some solid results — not in conformity with "strong" quantity-theory predictions. The neo-quantity theorists' empirical results encourage belief that monetary policy affects important variables of the economic system in predictable ways over varying lengths of time.

10

2. Adjustment Mechanisms in a Fiat-Paper System

Banish the banking system from the model (as does Patinkin in *Money, Interest, and Prices*). Airplane drops and *auto da fé* will be acceptable theoretical means of altering the money supply. However, squeamish readers usually prefer once-and-for-all budgetary surpluses (deficits) accompanied by burning (printing) of paper money . . . This subsection is mercifully brief. Two observations suffice:

a) If my stock of fiat paper money were increased, *cet. par.*, my wealth would be greater, but nobody else's would be less. [Unfortunately, in a fiat-paper model changes in the quantity of money and in wealth are (transitorily) inextricably linked.] Furthermore, the balance of my asset portfolio would be disturbed. At least transitorily, I would plan to increase my rate of purchase of goods in general (on standard utility-theoretic grounds) and to rearrange my portfolio.

b) It follows that, if micro and macro excess demand functions are to have an interpretation outside of equilibrium, they should include initial money stocks and the price level as variables. On the other hand, "real" variables in micro and macro full-equilibrium states for most models are invariant against the nominal stock of cash; so are macro temporary equilibrium states if the model's dynamics are based on *tatonnement*. (*See Note D.*)

Cruder Cambridge equations find demands for money balances unaffected by initial endowments except insofar as these affect what is measured as "income"; so long as income is unchanged, demand for real cash balances is unaffected.[23] The implicit adjustment mechanism in a fiat-money model with a Cambridge equation is not much different from that of §§ 8. A new gimmick is added: wealth effects in the securities and/or goods markets. The individual trader's options are broader immediately after than before increased fiat-money balances. Thus define Y as a shmoo stream descending from the heavens as did manna upon the ancient Israelites. Assume that this manna is perfectly perishable (albeit exchangeable) in contrast with perfectly-durable fiat-paper money which — along with privately issued securities — comprise the system's stocks. There is no government sector. Since an economic unit's range of choice is determined by his initial assets and manna stream, an increment of cash (*cet. par.*) will cause him to revise his plans. There is no reason to suppose that he will choose to hold his new wealth (as it seems to him) entirely in cash. He might plan to purchase bonds, higher interest income permitting a permanent increase in consumption. Perhaps he will plan to increase his consumption for some time, ultimately running down his assets to their initial level. In any event there will be immediate effects in other markets if fiat-paper cash balances are arbitrarily augmented.

If the manna streams are predetermined, clearance of *today's* markets will require that prices rise proportionately with the increase in the nominal stock of money so that plans will be consistent with actuality. (Section C shows equilibrium interest rates to be invariant.) It becomes clear that invariance of the real stock of money balances in equilibrium is consistent with a number of behavioral assumptions other than those of the Cambridge equation.

11

3. Invalid Dichotomies

Working throughout with fiat paper money, we deal here with Say's Law as a theory of the demand for money, showing that such a theory is inconsistent with determinacy of money prices. Then we

[23] Y is crudely defined so as to exclude the real value of liquidity services yielded by money. In fact, traditional treatments exclude money from the utility function — at least under certainty.

treat certain logical inconsistencies in combining what is known as the "homogeneity postulate" with a Cambridge monetary-demand function.

a) Say's Identity (Law)

Interpret Say's Law as asserting that aggregate excess demand for commodities is identically zero; in a system comprising *n-1* goods and money there never can be net excess supply in the commodities markets.

Normalize the price vector $[p'_1, \ldots, p'_n]$ on p'_n, the accounting price of money. Assume that excess demands for commodities are zero-order homogeneous functions of the prices $p_1, \ldots, p_{n-1}$, so that $x^i \equiv f^i(\lambda p_1, \ldots, \lambda p_{n-1})$. (This is the traditional approach.) If a homogeneous system of the form $Ap = 0$ is to have a solution (p^*), it is necessary that the determinant of A be zero, in which case the solution can be obtained up to a factor of proportionality. Equations (11)

$$f^i(p_1, \ldots, p_{n-1}) = 0 \qquad i = 1, 2, \ldots, n-1 \tag{11}$$

can be solved for the solution set

$$[p_2/p_1, \ldots, p_{n-1}/p_1]^*$$

If Say's Law is added to the system,

$$\Sigma p_i x_i \equiv 0, \qquad i = 1, 2, \ldots, n-1 \tag{12}$$

"money" prices remain indeterminate (determined only to a factor of proportionality); multiplication of $[p_2/p_1, \ldots, p_{n-1}/p_1]^*$ by λ/λ will not disturb satisfaction of Equations 11, and Equation 12 is an identity in the p's. Among other things, Say's Identity is inconsistent with quantity-theory results.

b) The Cambridge Equation

Conservation of value (Walras' Law) requires here that the excess (market) demand function for money be homogeneous in degree 1 if commodity excess demand functions are homogeneous in degree zero. Scaling of prices by the factor λ does not affect excess demand in any commodity market and therefore must increase aggregate excess demand (supply) for money by the same factor, λ. But postulation of excess demand functions for commodities of zero-order homogeneity in commodity prices *and* of first order homogeneity (in commodity prices) of excess demand for money is inconsistent with *uniqueness* of equilibrium "money" prices in a model with bonds, or in a model like that of p. 747. If the prices $[p/p_1]^*$ satisfy Equations 11, so will the prices $[\lambda p/\lambda p_1]^*$. In either case the money market will be cleared: clearance of $n-1$ markets implies clearance of the *nth.*

What light is shed on the well-known dichotomization finding a "Cambridge Equation" tacked on to a set of excess demand functions homogeneous in zero degree in the $n-1$ commodity prices?

$$(11) \qquad f^i(p_1, \ldots, p_{n-1}) = 0 \qquad i = 1, 2, \ldots, n-1$$

$$(13) \qquad k\, \Sigma p_i S_i = M$$

or

$$(13') \qquad (k)(p_1)\, \Sigma(p_i/p_1)\,(S_i) = M$$

where the S_i are *equilibrium* quantities supplied and demanded of the $n-1$ commodities. In the simplest case, the S_i are predetermined as in the "manna model." Since solution values for the p_i/p_1 — as well as the S_i — are determined in Equations 11, p_1^* can be determined (for given M) through Equation 13 or Equation 13′. $[p_2 \ldots, p_{n-1}]^*$ quickly follow. This is the traditionally dichotomous process through which relative prices are determined in the real markets and money prices in the money market.[24] It cannot be gainsaid that the set of prices $[p_1, \ldots, p_{n-1}]^*$, determined by Equations 11 and 13′ is a solution of the system. "For I do not find it difficult to believe that anyone involved in the controversy was unaware that a formally consistent model was possible, despite the postulates of homogeneity and the Cambridge equation, provided that Walras' law did not hold."[25]

As Baumol makes clear, the fact that the Cambridge equation makes possible a solution does not end the story. Not being homogeneous in money prices, it is inconsistent with Walras' Law.[26] If demand functions are to be defined outside of market-clearing states, the

24 "Money" prices here are nominal (accounting) prices normalized on the accounting price of money. Money prices are a subclass of the class of nominal prices. For $p_n' = 1$ (as in text) "money" and nominal prices are indistinguishable.

25 William J. Baumol, "Monetary and Value Theory: Comments," *Review of Economic Studies,* Vol. 28, No. 1, October 1960, pp. 29-31 at p. 29.

26 The function, $k\Sigma p_i S_i - M$, obviously is not homogeneous in the p's. Assume that $M = 1{,}000$ and that at some initial set of prices, demand for money is 2,000 so that there is excess demand for money of 1,000. Double the p's. Demand for money becomes 4,000. Excess demand for money trebles, becoming 3,000. The Cambridge Equation is non-homogeneous in the p's, while Equations 11 imply that the excess demand function for money should be homogeneous in degree 1 in the p's.

axiomatic underpinning of Equations 11 is inconsistent with Equation 13 or Equation 13′.[27]

Should we not be able to observe certain regularities in movements of money stock, and of prices without specifying strange and unnatural characteristics for the demand function for money?

C. THE QUANTITY THEORY AS AN INVARIANCE PROPOSITION

1

In systems without money illusion — in systems in which scale changes in *all* nominal values do not, *cet. par.*, lead to changes in planned "real" actions — the solution value for the real quantity of money balances should be invariant against the nominal quantity. (Dealing with alternatives at a point in time in a system in which *all* markets are cleared.) Consider one of the fiat paper systems taken up at the end of Section B, adjusted to account for the influence of real money balances on planned outcomes:

$$(1)\qquad f^i(p_1/p, \ldots, p_{n-1}/p, \overline{M}/p; Z) = Z_i \qquad i = 1, 2, \ldots, n\text{-}1$$

$$(2)\qquad g(\qquad\qquad) = \overline{M}/p$$

$$(3)\qquad p = \Sigma w_i p_i, \text{ where } \Sigma w_i = 1.$$

This is a system taken from Patinkin. The Z's are exogenously determined flows of exchangeable but perishable manna. The nominal stock of money also is exogenously determined. p gives the general price level and is obtained by applying a set of fixed weights summing

27 Don Patinkin writes: ". . . [t]hus, contrary to the accepted opinion, Say's Identity and the 'homogeneity postulate' are logically equivalent properties: both are necessarily present in a barter economy; both are necessarily absent from a money economy . . ." (*Op. cit.*, p. 121.) Consider system *i*:

$$(i)\qquad f^i(p_1, \ldots, p_n) = 0 \qquad i = 1, 2, \ldots, n$$

The functions are zero-order homogeneous in the p's. Interpret Equations *i* as describing a barter system. (At least assume that no nominal quantity is fixed.) Following the text, this system can be solved for $n—1$ relative prices. The absolute price level is utterly immaterial; it can be arbitrarily specified.

System *i* also shows that the homogeneity postulate, requiring that excess demand for money be first-order homogeneous in the p's, requires that excess demand for *real* cash balances be zero-order homogeneous in the p's. *Cf.* also R. W. Clower, "Classical Monetary Theory Revisited," *Economica*, May, 1963.

to unity. The unknowns of the system are the *n-1* relative prices and p and are to be determined by *n independent* equations.

Assume that the system is solved for the solution set $p_1^*, \ldots, p_{n-1}^*, p^*$ and assume further that the solution is unique in relative prices *and* real balances. It follows that if the supply of money, together with all prices, were doubled $[2p_1^*, \ldots, 2p_{n-1}^*, 2\overline{M}]$ would also be a solution, indeed the only solution, of the system. If a series of *market experiments* were undertaken in which the quantity of fiat paper money were varied, solution values for p would vary in precise proportion with M so that

$$(4) \qquad \partial p^*/\partial M \equiv k \qquad \text{or } p^* \equiv kM.$$

Alternatively:

$$(5) \qquad p^* \equiv kM + f(\eta)$$

where η is a vector of parameters of the system other than M. When M is varied, *cet. par.*,

$$(6) \qquad \partial p^*/\partial M \equiv k.$$

Equation 4 is a reduced form, graphed as a rectangular hyperbola in M-$(1/p)$ space. It implies little about the demand function for money, and, in models of this kind, can be derived from little more than absence of money illusion.[28] There emerges an *invariance proposition* (or, alternatively, a proposition about the neutrality of money) quite divorced from special assumptions about the demand for money.

At a more heuristic level, the key is in this paradox: although the society is limited in its endowments of the *n-1* commodities, there

---

28 The models of Sections B-E are highly artificial. The reason "invariance" follows so readily in "models of this kind" is that a number of strong restraints are built into the model. The upshot of Sections B-E, of course, is that in the real world one should not find money to be neutral. This emphasizes anew the critical distinction between the quantity theory as an empirical assertion and as a proposition about comparative statics. Its latter role is vapid.

In his NBER paper, "The Monetary Mechanism and Its Interaction with Real Phenomena," (NBER Conference: April 1962), Franco Modigliani succinctly summarizes necessary conditions for the neutrality of money: (a) absence of money illusion ("a postulate of rational behavior"); (b) unit elastic price expectations "and independence of interest rate expectations from current prices"; (c) all prices flexible; (d) invariance of market demand under redistribution of wealth (a requirement not necessary in full equilibrium in some formulations — *cf. infra.*); (e) "no government bonded debt," an assumption that is necessary for neutrality under most specifications.

is a sense in which it can have any "value" of real money balances it wishes — quite apart from the nominal stock of money. Hence, the nominal stock of money should be immaterial. This can be clarified by a hypothetical and simple-minded experiment. Invoke a random process distributing a collection of *n-1* goods and paper money among a group of people. Work with a pure-exchange stock model, abstracting from production. Some find themselves with golf balls and tennis racquets, others with tennis balls and golf clubs. Some will have properly-matched equipment but will be unsuited for play. And then some may have a good deal of paper money and practically nothing else, others a goodly collection of commodities and no money. . . . This unsatisfactory state of affairs can be resolved by trade (price quotations being attached to the goods). We impose one limitation: trade cannot take place until a set of prices has been hit upon equating aggregate demand for each good with its aggregate endowment: transactions are not permitted unless each market is cleared. What are the conditions for determinate relative and nominal prices?

Alternatives open to the *jth* individual including holding any combination of goods consistent with his budget constraint

$$\sum_i p_i S_{ij} + M_j = \sum_i p_i S_{ij}(0) + M_j(0), \tag{6a}$$

where the S_{ij}'s are stocks planned for the end of the period and where the $S_{ij}(0)$'s, together with $M_j(0)$, are initial endowments. Why should he plan to hold money in a world in which future prices and endowments are known with certainty *and in which there are alternative forms of storing wealth?* Roughly speaking, Patinkin's response was to insert a random payment device into the model so that the individual could not be sure of the timing of his receipts and payments over the interval before the next market day: he has an incentive to hold money in order to protect himself against insolvency. Obviously, the representative trader's choice of a particular combination of goods will be influenced by relative prices and by his budget constraint — his wealth. Planned holdings of money similarly are influenced by prices and wealth.

And, of course, *excess demands* will also depend on the mix of the particular collection of goods with which the trader was endowed. Thus assume that an individual in an equilibrium state suddenly were presented with a mansion. Presumably his greater wealth encourages him to plan to increase his holdings of all superior goods, including housing. But it would be extraordinary if he were to plan to devote *all* of his newly-found lucre to housing. Substitute "money" (dropped from airplanes) for "mansion" and the *real balance effect* becomes clear: it creates excess supply in the money market and excess demand in the commodities markets.

Waiving aggregation problems, the community's excess demand function for the *rth* good can be written

$$(6b)\qquad X_r \equiv F^r\left[p_1/p, \ldots, p_{n-1}/p, \frac{\Sigma p_i S_i(0)}{p}, \frac{M(0)}{p}\right] - S_r(0).$$

The demand function $F^r[\quad]$ is *not* zero order homogeneous in $p_1, \ldots, p_{n-1}$, nor is the excess demand function. If an experiment were performed in which *all* prices were doubled but $M(0)$ unchanged, excess demand (X_r) would become more negative: members of the community would feel "worse off." On the other hand, the demand and excess demand functions *are* zero-order homogeneous in $p_1, \ldots, p_{n-1}$ and M (nominal money balances).[29] This is another way of postulating absence of money illusion.

It again is painfully evident that, if the set of prices

$$p_1^*, \ldots, p_{n-1}^*$$

is a solution set for the system — given $M(0) = \overline{M}$ — so is the set of prices $\lambda p_1^*, \ldots, \lambda p_{n-1}^*$, *given* $M(0) = \lambda\overline{M}$. But it also is true that the equilibrium value for real cash balances $(M/p)^*$, is invariant against $M(0)$, depending only on initial endowments and tastes (in this model).[30] Furthermore, changes in tastes can have no effect on equilibrium *aggregate* demands for the stocks, since these supplies are exogenously determined. This is in startling contrast with the possibilities for expansion of real cash balances. If there is increased liquidity preference, there will be excess supply of goods (excess demand for money) at the set of prices, p^*, forcing down prices until the value of real cash balances is "adequate."[31]

The implicit dynamical mechanism in this fiat-paper model is based on the real-balance effect. So long as real balances exceed

29 Recall that a zero-order homogeneous function's dependent variable is unaffected by proportional increases in its independent variables.

30 *Cf.* the Archibald-Lipsey and Clower-Burstein models discussed later in this section.

31 Patinkin shows that a shift in liquidity preference, neutral between bonds and commodities (and among commodities) can be treated as a change in the quantity of money. *Cf. Money, Interest and Prices,* pp. 346-350.

$(M/p)^*$, there will be *some* excess demand in commodities markets. The *strength* of the real-balance effect is immaterial: all that matters is that there be positive excess demand for commodities so long as actual real balances exceed desired real balances.

2

The quantity theory can be expressed as an invariance proposition — independently of special properties of the demand function for money — in a system of credit money.[32] Assume that all money balances result from issue of perpetual bonds to banks, the sole creators of money. These perpetual bonds, the system's only security, promise to pay $1 per year forever. There can be no wealth effects *on net*[33] as a result of changes in the general price level or of expansion in the money stock (perhaps through manipulation of the "banking parameters" as in Appendix A, Ch. VA).

The real net excess supply function for bonds issued by the non-banking public will be zero-order homogeneous in commodity prices, as will be the demand functions for commodities. On the other hand, bank demand for bonds will exhibit money illusion: desired aggregate net holdings are deemed to depend rigidly on bank reserves; aggregate demand for bonds by the banking system is defined as $\overline{M}$.[34] Eliminating the clearance condition for the money market through Walras' Law, the resulting system is:

$$f^i(p_1/p, \ldots p_{n-2}/p, r) = \overline{S}_i \qquad i = 1, 2, \ldots, n\text{-}2 \tag{7}$$

$$\phi(p_1/p, \ldots, p_{n-2}/p, r, p) = \overline{M} \tag{8}$$

$$\Sigma w_i p_i = p \tag{9}$$

Equations 7-9 comprise a set of n equations in n-2 "real" prices, r, and p. The function $\phi(\quad)$ determines nominally-valued excess supply of bonds (always planned for the end of the period) by the non-banking public. This function is taken to be homogeneous in degree

32 We take up mixed systems — what Gurley and Shaw call systems with "inside" and "outside" money — later in this section.

33 We abstract from distribution effects. *Cf.* the *A-L* and *C-B* models (footnote 30) *inter alia.*

34 The model of §§2 is based on nothing more than Patinkin's "fourth dichotomy — the Keynesian Case." *Cf. MIP,* pp. 109-110, 163-164, 335-336. There has to be *some market* influenced by "money" prices if the price level is to be uniquely determined in equilibrium.

1 in the commodity prices. Alternatively, real excess supply is homogeneous in degree zero.

The price level, p, is determinate, since the nominal value of excess supply of bonds by the non-banking public is constrained by $\overline{M}$. (You might prefer to say that the aggregate excess demand function for bonds is not homogeneous in the commodity prices.) Consider the solution set

$$[p_1^*, \ldots, p_{n-2}^*, r^*; \overline{M}].$$

Will the set

$$[\lambda p_1^*, \ldots, \lambda p_{n-2}^*, r^*; \lambda\overline{M}]$$

also be a solution for the system? Yes. Relative prices and the interest rate are unchanged. Nominally valued excess supply of bonds by the non-banking public will be scaled by λ, as will bank demand for bonds.

The dynamical mechanism is essentially that described above. Once again solution values for $(1/p)$ and designated values for M trace out a path in $(1/p)$-M space plotted by a rectangular hyperbola. But the quantity theory here has the status of an invariance relation.

3

It is but a short step to develop invariance properties of macromodels of Chapters IX-XI solving at full employment. In a credit-money system,[35] we obtain market-clearance conditions of the following form:

(10)	$N^d(w/p) = N^s(w/p) = N$	labor
(11)	$\Phi(K_o, Y, r) = \psi(K_o, N) = Y$	commodities
(12)	$\phi(Y, r, p) = \overline{M}$	bonds[36]

comprising a system of five equations (10 and 11 each contain two equations) in five unknowns: w, p, N, Y, and r. The demand-for-all goods and production-possibilities functions are respectively $\Phi(\quad)$

[35] The public's money balances will be offset by public indebtedness to the banks. Bank holdings of bonds will be offset by deposit liability to the public.

Net wealth is comprised of physical capital, K_o, which can include human capital.

[36] Equation 12 refers to planned issue and holding of bonds for the end of the period. The system nicely reveals the importance of somebody thinking in nominal terms if money prices are to be determinate. The text's system is defined *de novo*. *Cf.* footnote 2, Ch. VA, Appendix A.

and $\psi(\quad)$. The clearance condition for the money market is excluded via Walras' Law. Consider a set of solution values

$$[w^*, p^*, Y^*, r^*, N^*; \overline{M}].$$

Is the set

$$[\lambda w^*, \lambda p^*, \; Y^*, r^*, N^*; \lambda\overline{M}]$$

also a solution for the system 10-12? Yes. Real wages and the rate of interest are unchanged. Since $\phi(\quad)$ is homogeneous in degree one in p, Equation 12 continues to be satisfied. If the real solution values are unique, hypothetical changes in M will be associated with proportional changes in solution values for prices. Once again a rectangular hyperbola will be generated by the locus of solution values. Quantity-theory results are obtained without strong assumptions about the demand function for money.

4

It has been argued by Metzler and by Gurley and Shaw—I think incorrectly (*cf.* Ch. VA) —that invariance of the real value of the money stock to its nominal value in solution states of the system can be lost (in the models of this chapter) if the money stock is comprised of a mixture of outside and inside money: say, fiat paper money and money offset by issue of private domestic securities. Thus, if the money stock is doubled as a result of open-market purchases by the central bank, *and* if central-bank holdings of securities are not ingested by the public, a doubled price level with interest rates unchanged no longer is consistent with a solution state. (*Cf.* Ch. VA.) Real money balances would be unchanged, but the public's bond holdings would be less. "Wealth" is reduced. There would be excess supply of goods at doubled prices. Prices must rise less than 100 per cent, and interest rates must fall if a solution is to be achieved.[37]

[37] It was shown in Ch. VA that the assumption that the authorities return interest receipts to the public through transfers means that increased central-bank holdings increase payments streams to the public. (This assumption is necessary to establish a problem in *monetary* theory.) Indeed, these transfer streams, if capitalized, always exactly offset central-bank bond holdings. Of course, reduced central-bank bond holdings lead to similarly offsetting effects. Hence, no wealth effects could be generated by open-market operations, and the invariance properties of the model would be unaffected.

Cf. A. C. Enthoven's appendix to Gurley and Shaw, *Money in a Theory of Finance,* pp. 303-359 at pp. 330-335. Invariance of real quantities to changes in the nominal stock of money depend there upon the argument B_g (bond holdings of the government) being zero. *My* assumptions make B_g definitionally zero.

5

An important contribution to understanding the quantity theory of money as a proposition about invariance of real solution values against nominal values of cash (and, for the matter, other assets) has been made by G. C. Archibald and R. G. Lipsey.[38] Archibald and Lipsey (hereafter A-L) were able to show that individual experiments in models where money is the only asset would find full *equilibrium* cash balances invariant against initial cash balances, and that market experiments would — for an economy in which cash is the only durable — find temporary and equilibrium relative prices invariant against changes in the aggregate quantity of money. The outcome of market experiments always would be independent of the way in which a change in the quantity of money *initially* affected distribution of money stocks among traders.

These conclusions — their proofs soon will be sketched — might seem to be terribly specialized. But, as R. W. Clower and I attempted to show, rather straightforward extension of A-L's analysis leads to much more general invariance propositions.

1. Invariance of the Individual Trader's Equilibrium Demand for Cash Where Cash is the Only Asset, Proof

These proofs and those of Clower and Burstein (hereafter C-B) are for a model in which a trader's plans for the *t-th* period can be formulated in terms of his tastes and preferences, techniques (where relevant), and initial endowments. The endowments include carry-over from period *t-1* and manna-stream entitlement (a nonessential convenience). The model is not necessarily inconsistent with n-period planning horizons — leading to planned streams of expenditure and time profiles of asset holdings — but relationship to such models is not rigorously established. Finally it is assumed that there are unique full equilibrium states: once "correct" constellations are achieved, these will be repeated *ad infinitum*.

Consider a trader receiving "the same bundle of goods at the beginning of each week . . . no goods [being] carried forward from week to week," (*Ibid.*, p. 2) whose money stock is his only (possible) asset. If he were initially in full equilibrium, his nominally-valued

38 "Monetary and Value Theory: A Critique of Lange and Patinkin," *Review of Economic Studies*, Vol. 26, October 1958, pp. 1-22.

consumption would be exactly equal to his nominal income stream. His cash balance would be constant from period to period.[39] Real-balance effects of windfall increments to his money holdings would have to be transitory: so long as he were consuming above his income, he would be running down his money balances; he will approach and reattain the initial unique (and stable) full equilibrium state. Similarly, if he suffered a windfall loss of cash, his consumption would fall below his income stream until he replenished his cash.

Thus full equilibrium cash balances and equilibrium rates of consumption are, in individual experiments, independent of initial cash balances. The real-balance effect is "a transitory phenomenon, which is operative only in some disequilibrium situation," or "since in full equilibrium consumption is equal to income, a change in real balances can only change real consumption during a process of adjustment." (*Ibid.*, p. 9.) *Full equilibrium* demand for cash balances can be defined as

$$M^* \equiv kp. \tag{14}$$

While it is possible to enter into a heated methodological affray about the "invalid dichotomies" of Section B, we release a Dove of Peace: *we have not previously dealt with stationary states;* invariances thus far exhibited have been for aggregated models in which market-clearing sets of values for real variables were, *at each point in time,* invariant to the nominal stock of money; only now do we treat invariances of a higher order. These concern full equilibrium states: equilibrium so full that the term is not in inverted quotes; nor is a phrase such as "solution set" used in its stead.

2. Invariance of Relative Prices and Distribution of Cash in Equilibrium to Initial Volume and Distribution of Cash Where Cash is the Only Asset, Proof

A-L offer a clear, if informal, proof. §§ 6 concerns C-B's attempt to do something a bit more formidable: higher orders of invariance are suggested.

> ". . . consider the consequences of an increase in the stock of money which is not distributed [so that there are] equiproportionate in-

39 This is an individual experiment: we deal with an individual facing a set of parameters unaffected by his decisions.

> crease[s] in the money balances of all individuals. Since each individual's final equilibrium is fully defined by his expansion path and his real income, any given increase in the stock of money has the same effect on the position of final equilibrium as that of any other equal increase however it may be initially distributed . . . The path of adjustment, but not, of course, the final equilibrium, depends on the actual distribution of the increase of the money stock. We must notice that the conclusions obtained [in an analysis of a non-full-equilibrium state] above, that a doubling of the money stock causes the price level at which trade next takes place to be double what it otherwise would have been, depends on the absence of distribution effects. The conclusion that doubling the stock of money doubles the full equilibrium price level does not depend on this assumption."[40]

6[41]

It is not clear that A-L's first result is valid in a model in which money balances may be used to purchase and hold income-earning assets. If an individual can buy and sell bonds, for example, he can presumably effect a permanent change in his real income by substituting bonds for cash in his asset portfolio. In the A-L model real income is a parameter, even for the individual. In a model including bonds individual real income becomes a variable. The mechanical process by which operation of real-balance effects forces money balances to be run down in the A-L model can be obviated through introduction of income-earning assets. And, since the validity of A-L's second result (invariance of real full equilibrium values against initial distributions), also is derived through the same trick, making it mechanically impossible for an individual to increase his consumption without running down his money balance, the validity of this result seems to be questionable in an economy in which windfall variations in money stocks are capable of leading to permanent changes in the distribution of real income.

On closer analysis, provided we adhere to the standard assumption of the uniqueness of equilibrium states, it turns out that neither of these doubts is justified. Subject to the same proviso, invariance propositions similar to those of A-L continue to hold, not only for a bond-and-money economy but also for more general systems.

Suppose that in any given market period (say period t) the typical trader (call him trader "j") receives "like manna from heaven" quanti-

[40] *Ibid.*, pp. 8-9.

[41] §§ 6 largely reproduces R. W. Clower and M. L. Burstein, "On the Invariance of Demand for Cash and Other Assets," *Review of Economic Studies*, Oct., 1960.

ties $s_j \equiv (s_{1j}, \ldots, s_{nj})$ of n non-durable commodities which may either be consumed directly or traded during the period at market prices $p(t) \equiv [p_1(t), \ldots, p_n(t)]$ so as to achieve at the close of the period a desired consumption pattern represented by $d_j(t) \equiv [d_{1j}(t), \ldots, d_{nj}(t)]$. Suppose further that the trader holds a quantity $S_{Mj}(t)$ of money and a quantity $(S_{Bj}(t)$ of bonds at the outset of period t, but assume that these quantities may be increased or decreased through market trading so as to achieve at the end of the period a desired asset portfolio represented by the variables $D_{Mj}(t)$ and $D_{Bj}(t)$. By hypothesis, bonds are perfectly standardized perpetuities which in each market period pay one unit of money to their holder and entail payment of one unit of money by their issuer. The market rate of interest, $r(t)$, is then equal to the reciprocal of the price of bonds, and the money value of the trader's bond income in period t is numerically equal to his bond holdings, $S_{Bj}(t)$.

Turning now to behavior postulates, we follow Patinkin and suppose that the demand for each commodity and the real demand for bonds (equivalently bond income) and for cash balances is in every case a function of real income, relative commodity prices, the rate of interest, real bond income, and real money balances. The behavior of the *jth* trader is thus described in part by the relations

$$(15)\quad d_{ij}(t) \equiv d_{ij}\,[s_j;\ p(t)/P(t);\ r(t);\ S_{Bj}(t)/P(t);\ S_{Mj}(t)/P(t)],\ i = 1, 2, \ldots, n$$

$$(16)\qquad D_{Bj}(t)/P(t) \equiv D_{Bj}[\qquad\qquad\qquad\qquad]$$

$$(17)\qquad D_{Mj}(t)/P(t) \equiv D_{Mj}[\qquad\qquad\qquad\qquad]$$

where $P(t) \equiv \Sigma w_i p_i(t)$ represents "the general price level" in market period t and $j = 1, 2, \ldots, m$.

Following *A-L*, we suppose that the behavior of the stock quantities $S_{Bj}(t)$ and $S_{Mj}(t)$, respectively, are described by the relations

$$(18)\qquad S_{Bj}(t) \equiv S_{Bj}(t_o) + \sum_{\theta = t_o}^{\theta = t-1} [D_{Bj}(\theta) - S_{Bj}(\theta)]$$

and

$$(19)\qquad S_{Mj}(t) \equiv S_{Mj}(t_o) + \sum_{\theta = t_o}^{\theta = t-1} [D_{Mj}(\theta) - S_{Mj}(\theta)].$$

Then for any given set of values of the parameters s_j, $p(t)/P(t)$ and $r(t)$ and for arbitrary values of the "initial asset" quantities $S_{Bj}(t_o)$ and

$S_{Mj}(t_o)$, the recursive system (15)-(19) provides a total of $n+4$ equations for any fixed value of j to determine the value of the $n+4$ unknowns $d_j(t)$, $D_{Bj}(t)$, $D_{Mj}(t)$, $S_{Bj}(t)$, and $S_{Mj}(t)$ for all values of $t \leqq t_o$. In particular, requiring that $\Delta S_{Bj}(t) = \Delta S_{Mj}(t) = 0$ and recalling the uniqueness assumption introduced earlier, (15)-(19) yields a determinate statical model comprising $n+4$ equations to determine the *equilibrium values* d^*_j, D^*_{Bj}, D^*_{Mj}, S^*_{Bj}, S^*_{Mj} of the $n+4$ variables over which the individual trader exercises direct control. The reduced form of the system reads

$$(S1) \qquad \begin{aligned} d_{ij}^* &\equiv f_{ij}\,[s_j;\ p(t)/P(t);\ r(t)] & i &= 1, 2, \ldots, n \\ S_{kj}^*/P(t) &\equiv f_{kj}[\qquad\qquad\qquad\qquad] & k &= M, B \\ D_{kj}^*/P(t) &\equiv f_{kj}[\qquad\qquad\qquad\qquad] & k &= M, B \end{aligned}$$

The equilibrium values defined by S1 are obviously independent of "initial assets."[42] More precisely, since the quantities $S_{kj}(t_o)$ enter the dynamical system (15)-(19) as arbitrary constants (initial conditions) rather than structural parameters, they do not appear in the equations defining a stationary solution of the system. Moreover, since the system (S1) is homogeneous of order zero in the quantities $p_i(t)$, D^*_{kj} and S^*_{kj}, the uniqueness assumption implies that the real demand for money and for bond income is independent of the general price level.

The same conclusions may be reached by an alternative route, arguing directly from the properties of system (15)-(19). Starting from any initial equilibrium state, a once-over change in nominal asset balances or in the general price level involves a momentary relaxation of the dynamical assumptions underlying the system. If the initial "real" equilibrium state is stable, however, the system must ultimately tend to return to its initial "real" position. In this sense, equilibrium real balances are invariant against changes in initial asset stocks.

---

42 As Mr. Hahn has pointed out to us (Clower and Burstein), "rational behavior" on the part of an individual trader would seem to require that manna income and real income from bonds be treated as perfect substitutes. If this suggestion is carried through (i.e., if the typical trader is assumed not to discriminate among different values of S_{Bj}/P and $\sum_i p_i s_{ij}/P$ so long as the numerical sum of the two items is the same), it can be shown that the modified version of *S1* — i.e., a system of equilibrium equations in which bond variables are replaced by the "composite" income variables $S_{yj} \equiv S_{Bj} + \Sigma p_i s_{ij}$ and $D_{yi} \equiv D_{Bj} + \Sigma p_i s_{ij}$ — is independent of the manna variables s_{ij} as well as the initial asset variables. The explicit appearances of the variables s_{ij} in system S1 appear to entail "manna illusion," but this is merely a possible but not necessary consequence of our model. (Of course, the nominal value of s_{ij} is not fixed from period to period nor is the real value of any particular collection.)

Notice, however, that it is meaningless to talk about the comparative statics effects of a change in initial asset balances in any *statical* system obtained from (15)-(19): for the only asset quantities appearing in such a system are D^*_{kj} and S^*_{kj}, and these are dependent variables rather than (arbitrary) parameters. Moreover, the preceding results can be broadened to apply to a more general "individual experiment" in which individual traders buy and sell physical assets as well as securities and money and in which the "manna" quantities, s_j, are themselves functions of relative prices and other "real" variables. A striking result of these or, for that matter, more elementary models is that wealth and income become dependent variables whose equilibrium values are independent of initial conditions; consumption-function literature becomes difficult to reconcile with broader reaches of economic theory. On the other hand, it remains true that if, roughly speaking, individual traders had homogeneous utility functions leading to the possibility of indefinite accumulation, initial conditions could determine the "base" of log-linear expansion (reminiscently of the Hicksian trade-cycle model). A-L's results then could not hold: meaningful interpretation of effects of initial real balances on long-run values emerges; it becomes clear that the "uniqueness of equilibrium" assumption is crucial for A-L and for C-B, but not for Patinkin who is working with instantaneous market-clearance and need not even consider the existence of full equilibrium. And, of course, these considerations apply with equal decisiveness to distribution effects. Again, the existence and uniqueness of full equilibrium states is decisive for the arguments of A-L and C-B, while for Patinkin it is enough to point out that once-and-for-all increments of money balances, equiproportionately distributed, will not affect "real" solution values.

Extending the preceding analysis to deal with determination of commodity prices and the rate of interest, we begin by assuming that the values of the variables $p_i(t)$ and $r(t)$ are chosen via some kind of *tatonnement* process, ensuring simultaneous satisfaction of the set of $n+1$ market clearance conditions

$$(20) \qquad \sum^{m}[d_{ij}(t) - s_{ij}(t)] = 0 \qquad i = 1, 2, \ldots, n$$

$$(21) \qquad \sum^{m}[D_{Bj}(t) - S_{Bj}(t)] = 0,$$

and simply add to these requirements the relations (15)-(19). The resulting system, S2, contains a total of $m(n+4)$ relations describing *in-*

dividual behavior of which only $m(n+4) - 2$ can be specified independently from a *market* point of view. More particularly, since the total quantity of bonds held by creditors at the beginning of any period is necessarily equal to the total quantity of bonds issued by debtors up to the beginning of the same period, the set of equations (18) must satisfy the linear relation

$$(22) \qquad \sum^{m} S_{Bj} \equiv 0.$$

Similarly, since the aggregate of individual holdings of money balances in any period must equal the total stock of money in the economy, the set of equations (19) must satisfy the linear relation

$$(23) \qquad \sum^{m} S_{Mj} \equiv S_M,$$

a constant.[43]

Taking (22) and (23) into account along with (15)-(21), the recursive system (S2) is determinate in the usual sense; i.e., it contains a total of $m(n+4) + n + 1$ independent equations to determine the values of the $m(n+4) + n + 1$ variables $d_1, \ldots, d_m; D_{B1}, \ldots, D_{Bm}; D_{M1}, \ldots, D_{Mm}; S_{B1}, \ldots, S_{Bm}; S_{M1}, \ldots, S_{Mm}; p$; and r.

Now suppose that the system (S2) has a stable "steady state" solution, $p_i^*, r^*, d_{ij}, D_{Bj}^*, D_{Mj}^*, S_{Bj}^*, S_{Mj},^*$ corresponding to any given set of values $s^o{}_j, S^o{}_M$ of the parameters s_j and S_M. Then by direct inspection it can be seen that the set of values $\lambda p_i^*, r^*, d_{ij}^*, \lambda D_{Bj}^*, \lambda D_{Mj}^*, \lambda S_{Bj}^*, \lambda S_{Mj}^*$ is the unique "steady state" solution of the system when s_j retains the value $s^o{}_j$, but S_M is assigned the new value $\lambda S^o{}_M$ (λ being any positive constant). From this it follows immediately that, in equilibrium, relative commodity prices, the rate of interest, and real asset balances are all invariant with respect to changes in the aggregate stock of money. Alternatively, it may be noted that the statical system obtained from (S2) by setting $\Delta S_{kj} = 0$ $(k = B, M)$ can be solved uniquely to yield reduced-form equations from which the aggregate-money-stock parameter, S_M, is altogether absent. The "representative" equation of the statical system (S3) will be of the form

$$(24) \qquad v^* \equiv h(s_1, \ldots, s_m)$$

[43] It should be remarked that, by virtue of the constraint (23), the aggregate stock of money, S_M, may be regarded as a structural parameter in the dynamical system S2. The constraint (22), on the other hand, does not fix the value of the aggregate stock of outstanding bonds, $S_B = (\frac{1}{2}) \Sigma_j \mid S_{Bj} \mid$ where $\mid S_{Bj} \mid$ is the *absolute* value of bond holdings of the *jth* trader.

where v^* is the equilibrium value of one of the endogenous variables p_i/P, r, d_{ij}, D_{kj}/P, S_{kj}/P. The *real* stock of money is determined within the system; the parametric aspect of S_M becomes important only for the determination of the vector p, and, of course, P. The equilibrium relation between P and S_M can be plotted by a rectangular hyperbola. Finally, if account is taken of footnote 42, the parameters of the system can be reduced to tastes and "social" techniques only. Individual techniques can eventually be altered through accumulation of human capital. Fascinating variants emerge: doweries can be treated as stud fees. Or, as C-B put it (for fixed socially available techniques): "more generally, if we consider an economy in which all commodities except money are produced, consumed, and held in the form of assets, and if the relevant supply and demand functions of the system depend only on relative prices and other real variables, then it can be shown that the equilibrium demand for commodities, for real bond income, for physical assets, and for real money balances are all invariant against a change in the nominal stock of money. To put the matter another way, *the equilibrium distribution of real wealth and real income in such an economy is determined by 'tastes and technique' and is otherwise independent of historical accidents.* This, it appears, is the most general statement of the Archibald-Lipsey 'invariance principle.'" (*See Note E.*)

D. GROWTH

Sections B and C dealt *once and for all* with changes in the quantity of money, considering their impact on today's market-clearing prices and real quantities and on full equilibrium. Implicitly assuming unit-elastic price expectations, a wide range of invariance propositions (including that of the quantity theory of money) was developed. A standardized set of (strong) assumptions yielded the conclusion that once-and-for-all changes in the quantity of money or, alternatively, sporadic changes not changing expectations of future "official" behavior, should not affect "real" market-clearing or full-equilibrium states. Gurley and Shaw and Enthoven show that these conclusions need not be modified for systems experiencing (or perhaps we should say capable of experiencing) steady and balanced growth in all real dimensions but in which the nominal money stock is a parameter —

subject to sporadic shift — and in which price expectations are unit elastic.

On the other hand, and here we rely on Alvin L. Marty,[44] the law obeyed by the time-rate of change of the money supply, dM/dt, will govern that obeyed by the time-rate of change of the general price level, dP/dt.[45] It happens that our theoretical analysis has been confined to time profiles of growth of the money stock of the form $dM/dt = 0$ [alternatively, $M(t) = \overline{M}$ for all t]. We have varied M by a factor of proportionality (λ) for analytical purposes but have not relaxed the "stationarity" law except momentarily, even then retreating behind "unitary elasticity of expectations" assumptions.

It is obvious that $\dot{p}$ is related to $\dot{M}$ at all times, but it is not obvious that the time-path of *real* variables of the system, including real money balances, should be affected by the law governing the time-path of the stock of nominal money balances.[46] Gurley and Shaw would appear to assert that, as Marty puts it, "different rates of growth of the money stock are neutral in their effects on the real variables." As it happens, we can, following Marty, quickly perceive that market-clearing values for the real variables of the system at any point in time can be dependent on the time path of the nominal money stock to the extent that they are dependent on the expected time-rate of change of prices which might be related to the law governing growth of the money stock.

Thus far in Ch. XIV we have ignored the role played by $\dot{p}$ at t, implicitly justifying this by the fact that all time paths for the money stock we have considered have found $dM/dt = 0$, subject only to "once and for all" shifts in M. At each point in time $\dot{p}$ has been independent of the *level* of the stock of money. But we cannot continue to ignore $\dot{p}$ unless we maintain an assumption of unitary elasticities of expectations formed independently of price history, recalling that the rate of change of the price level at t is dependent on dM/dt. The expected time-rate of change of the general price level is an important factor in the measurement of the real return that can

---

44 *Review* of Gurley and Shaw, *Money in a Theory of Finance, Journal of Political Economy*, Vol. 69, Feb. 1961, pp. 56-62, esp. pp. 56-58.

45 Certainly if we adopt assumptions leading to the strict invariance of Section C.

46 We do not consider the role played by expansion of money substitutes, say, through growth of non-banking financial institutions, except to note that this is obviously an important factor in determining the relationship at each point in time between dM/dt and dP/dt. The theoretical underpinning is found in Note E.

be obtained from holding cash balances. To the extent that prices are rising and are going to rise, holders of cash balances are suffering, and will continue to suffer, capital loss. There are *a priori* grounds for including price-expectation variables in demand functions for money.

The argument (which I take to be Marty's) is easy to complete:

1) performance of real variables — *sans* money illusion — is determined by the real as against nominal rate of interest. The real rate of interest is obtained by adjusting the nominal rate by a factor reflecting expectations of the time-path of prices;

2) it is reasonable to assume that price experience will govern price expectations;

3) the time profile of the money stock will bear on that of the price level;

4) thus, alternative log-linear rates of growth of M will lead to differing expectations of the future time-path of prices;

5) but expectations of (4) influence desired real money balances: capital gain or loss from these holdings depends on price performance.[47] Alternatively, expected opportunity costs of holding money are influenced;

6) the dynamic law governing the growth of the money stock, then, can influence the "real" state of the system at each point in time: it can influence expected real yields of cash assets; this yield is an opportunity cost for holding any other asset in the system.[48]

The highly specialized character of the quantity theory of money, seen as a specification of a rigid relationship between the equilibrium *level* of prices and the *stock* of money, is accented. We have seen that the dynamic law governing the money stock $(M = f(t))$, affecting that observed by the price level $(p = g(t))$ must influence the real performance of the systems of Ch. XIV unless unitary elasticity of expectation of prices prevails, come hell or high water. The effects of once-and-for-

47 The capital loss arises from unchanged nominal value while prices are rising, *not* from loss of nominal value.

48 There is an alternative proof. If prices increase, nominal yields, including (nominal) capital gains, must increase if real yields of non-monetary assets are to be unchanged. Invariance of the $n-1$ real yields of non-monetary assets depends on change in their "undeflated" nominal yields. *But* this means that the real rate of return on money balances *cannot* be invariant against the rate of steady growth of the money stock *if* the real rates of return on non-monetary assets are to be invariant. Accordingly, all-round invariance of rates of return is impossible: investment and asset-portfolio behavior generally must be affected; the real state of the system at each point in time must be affected unless price expectations always are unit elastic.

all changes in the money supply and of changes in the (steady) rate of growth of the money supply prove to be asymmetrical: the former are consistent with invariance of real equilibrium values; the latter generally inconsistent with invariance even when the real variables are transformed into rates of growth.[49]

E. INTERNATIONAL TRADE

It is impossible to deal with the history of the quantity theory of money without being impressed by its close relationship to balance-of-payments questions: one need only consult Hume and Ricardo to verify the organic relationship of quantity-theory analysis with the specie-flow mechanism. Section E, however, is confined to a few theoretical themes: (1) continued invariance in full equilibrium of real variables against once-and-for-all changes in the monetary base under an international metallic standard with fixed exchange rates; (2) analogous invariance of full-equilibrium properties of flexible-exchange systems against once-and-for-all changes in the quantity of money in one or more member countries; (3) "money-illusion" effects in models featured by buffer stocks.

1. Comparative Statics for Fixed-Exchange Rate Systems

Consider a generalized model of the type used in Section C, §§ 6. Let j index m countries instead of m individual traders. Continue to ignore transportation costs: price levels in terms of a common *numeraire* and measure must be the same in all countries. Obviously tariffs and other distortions of international pricing are immaterial to the model. Introduce a globally-fixed stock of (non-reproducible) gold,

[49] In the case of once-and-for-all changes in the money stock, we dealt with invariance of solution values for such variables as output, real money balances, etc., at each point in time against the level of the stock of money. In the case of alternative steady growth rates for the money stock, we were concerned with possibilities for invariance of the rate of growth of output, real balances, etc. The latter set of relationships was beyond the (formal) ken of earlier quantity theorists.

Figure XIV-1 probably makes a lot more sense when we recognize the role that can be played by reactions to price *experience* on demand for money balances.

Price expectations were considered in the study of hyperinflation of Ch. VI.

the global standard of value, serving only monetary purposes. Assume that any paper money that might be issued is convertible into gold so that units of paper money always are perfect substitutes for gold: gold and paper money can be treated as a single good, their prices being rigidly linked. Finally, assume that specie-reserve ratios are rigidly determined.

The exact counterpart to C-B's statical system (S3) has been created. Among other things, initial distribution of real money balances is immaterial to equilibrium distribution. Once the ratios of gold to total money stocks in the various countries are known, one can predict with perfect accuracy the global distribution of gold stocks in full equilibrium. Similarly, an increase of 10 per cent in the global gold stock will lead to an increase of 10 per cent in the global price level if rigid linkage of paper issue to gold is maintained. The global distribution of real cash balances in full equilibrium depends only on tastes and globally-available techniques.

We quickly concede that the model of this subsection is highly artificial and fails to deal with shifts in real parameters of macro systems. However, this gap will be partially filled in Ch. XV, "Some Theory of the Balance of Payments." Nor have we specified adjustment mechanisms. These become clear in E 3 when we take up the determinants of market clearance at each point in time, revealing, among other things, that the nominal price level can vary from country to country at each point in time, exerting influence in real markets in each country, even under specifications precluding such influence in closed systems. (*See Note F.*)

2. Comparative Statics for Flexible-Exchange Systems

C-B type models do not easily apply to international systems featured by fiat paper money issued by each of the countries ("traders") and exchanged in international markets. But invariance in equilibrium of "real" international equilibrium against nominal monetary stocks in each of the member countries can nonetheless be shown through an aggregated model proving to be useful in Ch. XV.[50]

We proceed to construct an 11-equation model for a two-country world lacking possibilities for international movement of factors of

50 Which is not to deny that a disaggregated model could be constructed.

production and in which the shmoo reappears — with a difference. Country A's (America's) shmoos are stamped with the Stars-and-Stripes, Country B's (Britain's) with the Union Jack. The shmoos otherwise are identical. Still the perhaps chauvenistic denizens of the two countries have commodity illusion and do not treat Type A and Type B shmoos as identical: price levels — expressed in a common standard — could vary between the two countries. It is assumed that, once shmoos are put into capital stock, they cannot be converted into consumer and/or export goods.

$$(1) \quad Y^a{}_o = f(Y^a{}_o, Y^b{}_o, r_1, r_2, p_1, p_2, \sigma, B_{t-1}, B'_{t-1})$$

$$(2) \quad Y^b{}_o = F(\qquad)$$

$$(3) \quad \overline{M}^a = g(\qquad)$$

$$(4) \quad \overline{M}^b = G(\qquad)$$

$$(5) \quad B \equiv \psi(\qquad)$$

$$(6) \quad B' \equiv \Psi(\qquad)$$

$$(7) \quad B' = h(\qquad)$$

$$(8) \quad B = H(\qquad)$$

(9)[51] $$\phi(\qquad) = \Delta[\sigma(B'/r_2)] - \Delta[B/r_1]$$

or

(9′)[51] $$\phi(\qquad = [\sigma/r_2]\Delta B' - [1/r_1]\Delta B$$

$$(10) \quad \Delta B \equiv B - B_{t-1}$$

$$(11) \quad \Delta B' \equiv B' - B'_{t-1}$$

Equations 1 and 2 are clearance conditions for the commodities markets in the two countries. Subscripts 1 and 2 index countries A and B. σ is the rate of exchange between the two currencies: $\sigma = 2$ means that 2 units of A's money will exchange for 1 of B's. B_{t-1} and B'_{t-1} are the number of promises to pay 1 unit of Country A's money per period forever held by citizens of Country B at the end of the last period, and the number of promises to pay 1 unit of Country B's money per period forever held by A citizens at the end of the last period. Since internally held securities are netted out, B and B' are net domestic excess supplies of securities; these excess supplies must be offset by external demand.[52] General price levels enter into the market-clear-

51 The left-hand side is nominally valued in dollars.
52 All variables are current-dated unless otherwise specified.

ance conditions for commodities quite apart from any real-balance effects: the p_1, p_2 constellation influences exports and imports. Furthermore, since Country A(B) can be a net creditor for Country B(A), international distributional effects can be induced by price-level changes. r_1 and r_2 are rates of interest in Countries A and B on perpetual bonds issued by their citizens. They can differ for roughly the same reasons that p_1 and p_2 can differ.

Equations 3 and 4 prescribe clearance conditions for the money markets in the two countries. (Demands and supplies 3-8 are for the end of the period.) Later specifications make clear that foreign-exchange balances are held in bonds and not in cash: this greatly simplifies the algebra without affecting the argument. The nominal values of money stocks are determined by official action. Although the subsequent argument specifies fiat-paper money for simplicity (while ruling out real-balance effects in commodities markets) you might be more comfortable with the assumption that there is a pure-credit money in both countries. However, you will have to exercise exquisite care in defining excess demand functions for bonds if you choose the latter course. The right-hand sides of Equations 1-4 define demand functions.

In a sense, supply functions are defined in Equations 5 and 6. Equation 5 is concerned with the excess of supply of securities in Country A over domestic demand for its securities. The excess is defined as B. Similarly, Equation 6 concerns the excess of supply of Country B securities over domestic demand. Equations 7 and 8 establish clearance conditions for securities markets. Equation 7 requires that the excess domestic supply of Country B securities (as determined in Equation 6) be equal to Country A's demand for Country B securities; Equation 8, that the excess domestic supply of Country A securities be equal to Country B demand for A securities.

Equation 9′ (or 9) concerns clearance of the foreign exchange market. Country A's favorable balance on current account — valued in dollars — is determined by the function $\phi(\ \ )$. If positive it generates excess demand for dollars. It must be offset by an unfavorable balance on capital account. (Sales of bonds abroad are viewed as debtor country exports.) Net purchases of foreign securities create a supply of dollars capable of "picking up" excess demand for dollars generated by surplus on current account. Note again that buffer stocks of foreign cash are excluded.

Equations 10 and 11 simply define changes in Country B's holdings of A bonds and Country A's holdings of B bonds. In defining full equilibrium for the two-country system, Equations 9-11 are replaced by Equations 12-14:

$$(12) \qquad \phi(\qquad) = 0$$

$$(13) \qquad B = B_{t-1}$$

$$(14) \qquad B' = B'_{t-1}$$

The lagged values for bond holdings, B_{t-1} and B'_{t-1}, become variables; ΔB and $\Delta B'$ disappear from the system.

Equations 1-11 contain 9 unknowns: $r_1, r_2, p_1, p_2, \sigma, B, B', \Delta B, \Delta B'$. However, Walras' Law knocks out two clearance conditions: clearance of the commodities, money, and foreign exchange markets in the two countries assures clearance of their securities markets.[53] Thus, net new issue of bonds by the deficit country is assured equal to net new acquisitions by the country with a favorable merchandise account.

The functions of Equations 1 and 2 are zero-order homogeneous in p_1, p_2, B_{t-1}, and B'_{t-1} or alternatively in p_1, σ, and B_{t-1}.[54] If the American price level were doubled, along with the dollar price of sterling and initial English holdings of United States securities, all real variables affecting demand for commodities are unchanged; Americans and Englishmen continue to be able to purchase the same quantities of each other's goods for given sacrifices of domestic goods as before; initial international distribution of wealth is unchanged.[55] (Of course, the British price level is assumed unchanged.) However, the functions of Equations 1 and 2 are *not* zero-order homogeneous in p_1 and p_2 or in p_1 and σ: international distribution creeps into the analysis, unless specifically excluded.[56]

---

53 Thus eliminate ΔB and $\Delta B'$ with Equations 10 and 11. Eliminate B and B' in Equations 1, 2, and 9′ with Equations 7 and 8. Eliminate the identities 5 and 6. You emerge with five equations (1-4, 9′) in the unknowns p_1, p_2, r_1, r_2, and σ.

54 Similarly, commodities markets continue to clear if p_2 is doubled, σ halved, and B'_{t-1} doubled.

55 The fact that B_{t-1} is doubled along with p_1 and σ precludes distribution effects: the real burden of initial external debt is unchanged for American issuers of securities; the real value of initial foreign bond holdings of Englishmen is unaffected. B'_{t-1} need not be altered: Americans' sterling securities balances have unchanged sterling purchasing power and are worth twice as much in dollars, each dollar being worth half as much as before.

Recall that Equations 1-11 do not comprise a full-equilibrium system.

56 Otherwise an increase in the American price level, for example, could generate positive wealth effects (for Americans): American external debtors will be relieved. Of course there will be negative effects on Englishmen.

Turning to Equations 3-8, the demand and supply functions are first-order homogeneous in p_1, p_2, B_{t-1}, and B'_{t-1} — barring money illusion. The equalities 3-8 continue to be satisfied if these variables — together with nominal money stocks — changed in the same proportion. Of course, if B_{t-1} and B'_{t-1} are fixed (as they will be at the outset), equalities 3-8 no longer can be satisfied if p_1, p_2, M^a and M^b are altered in the same proportion: international distributional effects preclude monetary neutrality in the short run.

Turning to the full-equilibrium system, if Equations 1-8, 12-14 are satisfied by

$$[r_1^*, r_2^*, p_1^*, p_2^*, \sigma^*, B_t^* \ (=B_{t-1}^*), B'_t{}^* \ (=B'_{t-1}); \overline{M}^a, \overline{M}^b],$$

it will be satisfied either by

$$[r_1^*, r_2^*, \lambda p_1^*, \lambda p_2^*, \sigma^*, \lambda B_t^*(=\lambda B_{t-1}^*), \lambda B'_{t-1}(=\lambda B'_{t-1}); \lambda\overline{M}^a, \lambda\overline{M}^b]$$

or

$$[r_1^*, r_2^*, \lambda p_1^*, p_2^*, \lambda\sigma^*, \lambda B_t^*(=\lambda B_{t-1}^*), B'_t{}^* \ (=B'_{t-1})].^{57}$$

Invariance of "real" solution values against nominal stocks of money persists when the model is opened. It does not matter whether we work with fixed- or flexible-exchange. And, of course, we deal with once-and-for-all changes in the money stock.

3. Short Run Effects When Buffer Stocks of Gold or Foreign Cash are Inserted

Focusing on diverse movements of p_1 and p_2 and their effects on exports and imports of both countries when σ is rigid or sticky, we can ferret out interesting possibilities of non-neutrality of money even for the macro models of Ch. XIV, let alone those for Ch. XIII. Clearly, if Country A inflates, keeping rigid its exchange rate (the context is one of fiat paper), its officials must be equipped with a buffer stock of foreign bonds or cash in order to prevent σ from exceeding $\bar{\sigma}$ and maintain control of its financial markets. If they have enough ammunition, they have considerable leeway in formulating autarchic domestic price-level and interest-rate policy. The same reasoning applies to a group of countries on an international gold standard. If officials hold adequate buffer stocks, they can accommodate substantial "disequilibrium" by using their buffers. And, of course, this *deus ex machina* —

[57] Obviously, distribution effects are nil in the full-equilibrium system: distribution of wealth is *endogenous* in such a system.

discussed at length in Chapters XV and XVI — topples the structure of invariant relationships.

One final point: even if wealth effects can be neglected, absolute price levels play an important role in *processes of adjustment* to monetary changes: supplies and demands of goods from abroad and for sale abroad are affected. At each point in time, excess demand functions for commodities cannot be formulated without specifying absolute price levels. This is true even in systems which *in isolation* could be described by equations of the form

(15) $f(r) = 0$ *commodity market*

(16) $g(p) = 0$ *money market*

However, this has no bearing on properties of full-equilibrium states of multi-national systems.

F. ECONOMETRICS: RAINFALL IN SIAM

1

This brief section tries to convey a feeling for econometrics and one of its key problems, *identification*. It happens that certain of Ch. XIV's implications can better be appreciated by a reader with a slight knowledge of econometrics.

> "An econometrician's job is to express economic theories in mathematical terms in order to verify them by statistical methods, and to measure the impact of one economic variable on another so as to be able to predict future events or advise what economic policy should be followed when such and such a result is desired."[58]

Thus, an econometrician might want to formulate a simple supply-and-demand model for an isolated market as

(1) $$q^d \equiv f(p) \equiv a_{10} + a_{11}p$$

(2) $$q^s \equiv g(p) \equiv a_{20} + a_{21}p$$

(3) $$q^d = q^s.$$

Say that he is satisfied to work on the assumptions that the market always is cleared and that the functions are linear. He is particularly interested, let us assume, in the demand function and would like to

58 Stefan Valvanis, *Econometrics* (New York: McGraw-Hill Book Company, 1959, p. 1.).

know what value for the slope parameter, a_{11}, best fits data that have been generated over some years.[59] Assume that in fact the data are described by this diagram.

HYPOTHETICAL DATA FOR AN ISOLATED MARKET

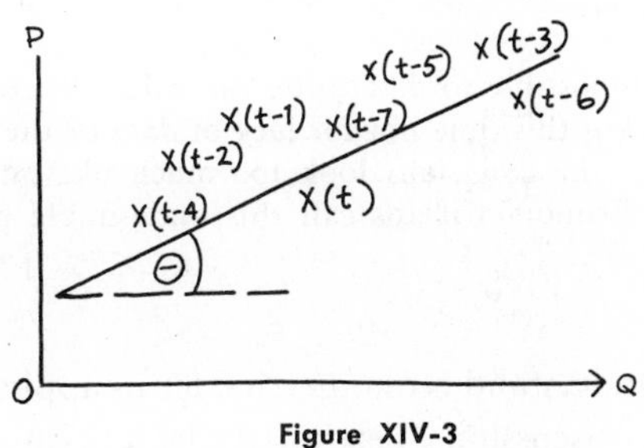

Figure XIV-3

Let us say that the best linear fit to these data is that of the line with the slope tan θ, say 1.5.

Should our estimate of $a_{11}(\hat{a}_{11})$ be 1.5? Consider this diagram.

A HYPOTHETICAL PROSPECT

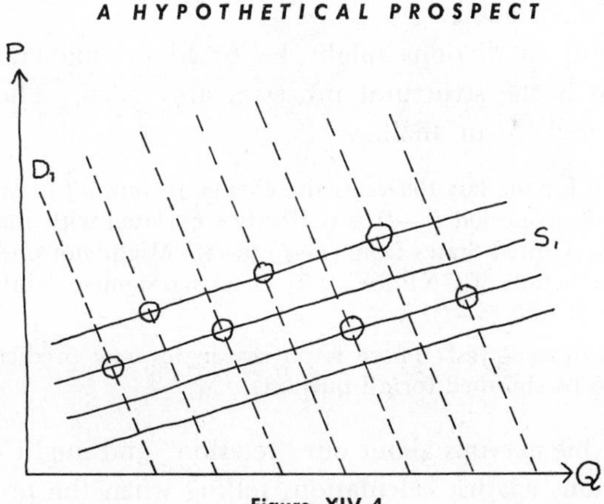

Figure XIV-4

59 The non-mathematical reader will be especially interested in E. J. Working's excellent introduction to the problems of subsection F: "What Do Statistical 'Demand Curves' Show?" *Quarterly Journal of Economics* (1927), reprinted in K. E. Boulding and G. J. Stigler (eds.), *Readings in Price Theory*, pp. 97-115. The text borrows heavily from Working's classic article.

The data could have been generated by shifting supply and demand curves, the demand curve here shifting much more than did the supply relation. Then $\hat{a}_{11}$ would suggest nothing about the slope of the demand curve; rather it would suggest the slope of the supply curve. Furthermore, it can be shown that, unless we specify the way in which the demand and supply curves shift over time, it is impossible to estimate parameters such as a_{11} and a_{21}. *There is an infinite set of structural parameters consistent with the observed outcomes.* This is the *identification problem.*

> "It is sometimes impossible to determine the value of each parameter in each equation, but this time not for lack of *data* or their monotony, but rather because the *equations* look too much like one another to be disentangled. Econometricians call this undesirable property lack of *identifiability.*"[60]

2

Now that you understand econometrics, let us apply it to the quantity-theory-of-money discussion. Section A dealt with empirical relations. Assume that when proxies for price expectations and cyclical movements are introduced, superb statistical fits are obtained. The message of Ch. XIV has been that the data might be consistent with a myriad of demand functions for money. Section F adds an arrow to our quiver: the parameters of a putative demand function for money might not be identifiable.

Still, useful predictions might be based on monetary decision variables even if the structural processes are veiled. The argument can be facilitated by an analogy:

> Assume that for the last 100 years the change in *rainfall in Siam* from period *(t—2)* to period *(t—1)* is perfectly correlated with that of real GNP in the United States from *(t—1)* to *(t)*. Might not one sensibly base his prediction of GNP for *(t)* by checking Siamese rainfall statistics for *(t—2)* and *(t—1)*?
>
> Certainly! Indeed, yes! There is no reason for raw predictive relationships to be shunned for all purposes.

We are a bit nervous about our "relation" and might continually check predictions against calculations telling when the process is out of control (when there has been a basic parametric shift in the reduced-form relation). But we continue to use the strange and unnatural predictor as long as it works.

60 Valvanis, *op. cit.*, pp. 3-4.

How would you react to a cloud-seeding experiment in Thai skies? Probably negatively. Certainly if the experiment were expensive. You would fear that there is no structural relationship between Siamese rainfall and United States GNP that could be established through controlled experiment. If the observed correlation indeed arose from coincidental association with other variables, it might be ruptured by cloud-seeding experiments.

SUMMARY

1. There has been strong positive correlation between movements of the money stock and nominally-valued national product.
2. On the other hand, the regularity of this relationship is not overwhelming in the manner of certain physical constants. Monetary velocities appear to be functions of interest rates, expected rates of price change, and other non-institutional factors.
3. Sections B-E were concerned with the (in)variance of *equilibrium* real cash balances and other real variables against the nominal stock of money.
4. Section B concerned effects of alternative postulations of demand functions for money. Concentrating on a simple form of the Cambridge equation, $M^d = ky$, we were able to show that there would be invariant $(M/p)^*$ at full employment either in a fiat- or credit-money system — provided that a number of rather strong assumptions necessary for neutral money were made.
5. In the context of a fiat-money system, the Cambridge equation has implications for effects of changes in the price level on excess demand for money that are inconsistent with excess demand functions for commodities zero-order homogeneous in nominal prices.
6. The neutrality of money is consistent with a large class of assumptions about particular characteristics of the demand function for money. Roughly speaking, absence of money illusion ("a postulate of rational behavior") is sufficient for neutral money in a *Patinkin Model.*
7. Results similar to those of (6) were obtained for pure-credit money and aggregated systems — always assuming that nominal stocks of other assets could vary so that a given real solution set could be

reproduced subsequent to variation in the stock of money. This would be done simply by scaling nominal bond stocks, income, prices, etc. If the "nominal" vector y^* were a solution vector, so would be λy^*.

8. Archibald and Lipsey emphasized differences between full- and temporary-equilibrium states. They were able to show that in a manna-and-money world, full-equilibrium values of individual real cash holdings and other real variables of the system were independent of the nominal value of the stock of money and of its initial distribution among traders.
9. Clower and Burstein were able to show that the A-L invariance propositions could be extended to systems with bonds and other assets on A-L assumptions about existence and uniqueness of equilibrium: "the equilibrium distribution of real wealth and real income . . . is determined by tastes and technique and is otherwise independent of historical accidents."
10. Real solution values at time t are not independent of the law of motion obeyed by the price level — unless price expectations are unit elastic. Rising prices imply real capital loss on nominally-fixed obligations (including cash). If nominal interest rates are adjusted so that real yields on bonds are unchanged, the real opportunity costs of holding cash are increased: the real solution path is not invariant against the time-path of prices, a function of the time-path of the money supply.
11. Once-and-for-all changes in the money stock generally must be distinguished from "steady" changes. *Cf.* par. 10.
12. Invariance propositions can be developed for open as well as closed systems.
13. The case of an international gold standard with fixed exchange rates is reducible to a C-B model.
14. Flexible-exchange-rate systems are easier to handle through a highly-aggregated model such as that of Section E, §§ 2. The logical chain of Section E, §§ 2 is highly analogous to that of Section C, §§ 3. It is useful for Ch. XV, "Some Theory of the Balance of Payments," of Part III, "Money and International Trade."
15. As for adjustment mechanisms, in open systems absolute price levels (p_1 and p_2) are directly important in commodity-market *adjustment,* although they might not be in isolation. The key is in demand and supply for imports and exports.

16. Section F — partly a truncated introduction to econometrics — showed that there are statistical as well as *a priori* grounds for distinguishing empirical relationships (such as those relating to the nominal stock of money and money income) which are "reduced forms" from those which are structural relations.

NOTES

NOTE A: *Cf. Chart Book* (1961), p. 118 for details. Pp. 68-69 offer details of relationship of total debt to GNP, of private to federal debt, and of the components of private debt issues. As Ch. XIV unfolds, relationships between various debt issues (including "money") and such variables as GNP become more important. Among other things, we become interested in the degree to which other financial assets may have come to be substituted for cash.

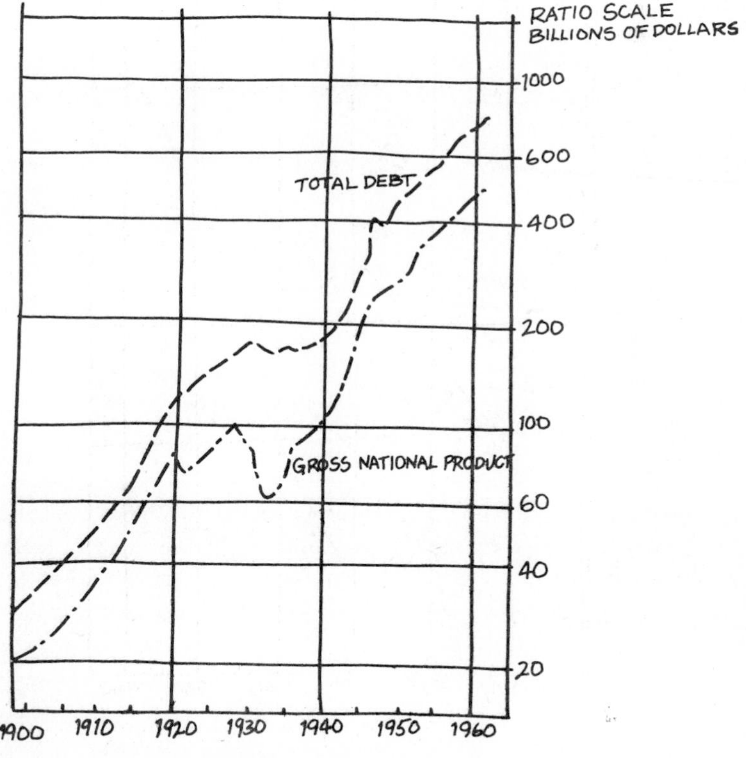

Figure XIV-5

Recalling that on a semi-log scale (as above) a given vertical distance measures a ratio so that parallel lines imply a constant ratio, we see that the value of claims and Gross National Product moved in close correspondence from 1908 to 1920, that a new long-term relationship began to be established in the 1920's and has roughly prevailed since World War II. During the Great Depression the proportion borne by GNP to total debt fell substantially; not surprising when one considers the importance of longer-term debt instruments and the finance problems of firms during periods of declining demand. There was a sharp rise in total debt during World War II, whilst GNP was understated by price controls. As is stressed in the text *infra,* Figure XIV-5 suggests that close correspondences — "invariances" at the theoretical level — are consistent with a wide range of theories of demand for money and other assets. . . . Certainly the data are consistent with the Modigliani-Brumberg consumption function. *Cf.* Appendix, Ch. XI.

FEDERAL AND NON-FEDERAL

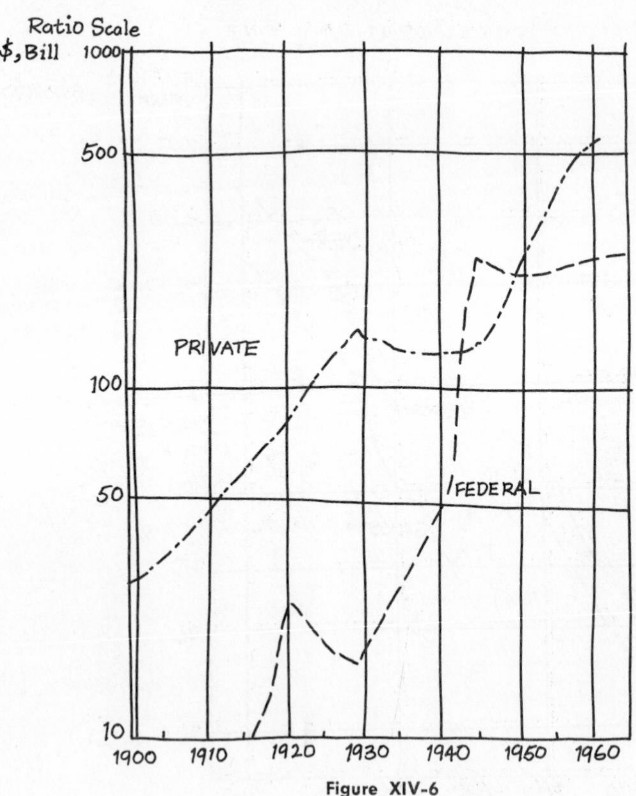

Figure XIV-6

COMPONENTS OF NON-FEDERAL DEBT

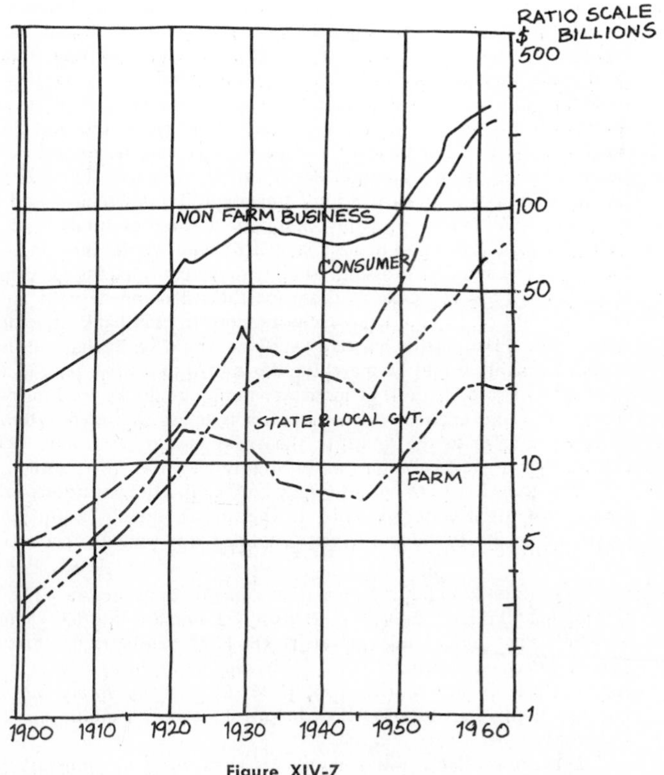

Figure XIV-7

NOTE B: These are end of year statistics over the 1955-1957 period, all in billions of dollars.

(1) Year	(2) Total of Demand and Time Deposits (exc. Govt.) and Currency	(3) Time Deposits	(4) Col. 2 minus Col. 3
1955	216.6	78.4	138.2
1956	222.0	82.2	139.8
1957 (Aug)	220.0	87.1	132.9
1957 (Dec)	222.7	89.1	133.6

TABLE XIV-II

Source: *Economic Report of the President* (Washington: 1959, 1960).

If the sum of currency and demand deposits is taken to comprise the money stock, the predictive power of a quantity-theory relation is dim indeed for this episode. If time deposits are included in *M*, things are somewhat better for ex-post prediction but not for the quantity theory: (a) insofar as time deposits increase in response to higher deposit rates, giving banks and financial institutions room to make loans to deficit spending units, it is implied that interest rates influence nominal flow rates, *cet. par.* — contrary to traditional quantity theorizing; (b) the obviously-endogenous character of the sum of demand and time deposits in the American system is revealed; the quantity of money becomes a resultant of individual decisions, not a cause. Thus, if bill rate were put up to 15 per cent, institutions' time-deposit rates soon would increase, say, to 13 per cent. There probably would be a surge of funds to the institutions (essentially on a demand-deposit standard) who would then increase their bill holdings. For simplicity, assume that reserve requirements for commercial-bank time deposits are the same as those for their demand deposits and that official measures limit demand-deposit contraction to non-bank time-deposit expansion.) The $TD + DD +$ currency statistic would be unchanged, but prices and output probably would be marching downward at a brisk pace in the face of 15 per cent bill rate. Note that monetary policy might be working with powerful effect, while the quantity-theory relation is being shattered. One logically can refuse to adhere to the quantity theory of money (as I have defined it) and believe that monetary policy can be highly effective. (*Cf.* footnote 4.)

Over the 1955-1957 period banks and financial institutions sold billions of dollars in United States securities to the public, thereby acquiring room to increase advances. Idle deposits were mopped up; velocity increased.

NOTE C: Professor Friedman's position is lucidly expressed in "The Lag in Effect of Monetary Policy," *Journal of Polititcal Economy,* Vol. 69, October 1961, pp. 447-466. The context for this article is J. M. Culbertson, "Friedman on the Lag in Effect of Monetary Policy," *Journal of Political Economy,* Vol. 68, December 1960, p. 617 *ff.* See also, J. M. Culbertson, *Reply, loc. cit.,* Vol. 69, October 1961, pp. 467-477. Friedman's footnotes contain an excellent bibliography.

The *cause celebre* was rules *versus* authorities in monetary policy. Friedman's support of rules partly was based on the argument that effects of monetary policy were so lagged that, if the authorities did not properly anticipate events, the Keynesian bismuth-castor oil cycle would be precipitated: the authorities might prescribe bismuth for last week's diarrhea, diagnosed as such only today, after it had ceased. The patient would become constipated. The tortoise-like authorities would prescribe castor oil next week, days after the patient had been cured, leading to diarrhea, etc. Friedman had argued elsewhere that the authorities have to be right at least 75 per cent of the time if their policies are not to be destabilizing. Of course, long lags tend to make *any* contracyclical monetary policy less effective. But Friedman argues that non-discretionary policies can have built into them reaction processes so that reversal can be accomplished more readily when the initial policy proves wrong. (*Cf.* A. P. Lerner's *Review, Journal of the American Statistical Association,* Vol. 57, March 1962, pp. 211-220, for an interesting discussion of these and other problems of monetary policy.)

At pp. 462-463 of "The Lag," Professor Friedman offers a schematic account of the way in which the effects of an open-market purchase work through the system. The initial effects are on balance sheets. Those who sold securities to the government for cash do not plan to retain cash: "indeed the prime function of money is to permit a barter transaction to be separated . . . into a purchase and a sale." Rather they plan to purchase other government securities, commercial paper, etc.: their sales were induced by the favorable price that day of the asset sold. Heightened demand for other securities will drive up securities prices, leading to sympathetic movements in equities' prices and making durables more attractive: "the key feature of this process is that it tends to raise the prices of the sources of both producer and consumer services relative to the prices of the services themselves . . . encourag[ing] the production of such sources." Furthermore, the increased price of sources relative to services encourages "direct acquisition of services rather than of the source": consumption is stimulated (but, I should think, only to the extent that lower interest rates discourage saving). He concludes by showing that — once these effects have seeped through the system — the system might settle down with interest rates and other real variables unchanged and prices higher. This result can be obtained only if government bonds are treated as I suggest in Ch. VA.

Notice that the effects of monetary measures depend upon those of "deranged" asset prices: the real effects of monetary policy depend on reaction to portfolio imbalance. The crucial role of response lags becomes obvious. Notice also that effects of interest rates on desired cash balances are not considered. If these were considerable, correlations between monetary and real variables would be even worse: the adjustment process would be much slower. (*Cf.* Ch. VA and Ch. VI.) Finally, the comparative statics analysis is unaffected by these "transitional" issues.

NOTE D: The adjustment process for Patinkin models and others of that ilk is quite artificial. It is a process of *tatonnement* finding the "crier" adhering to the following decision rules: announce higher prices for goods for which there is excess demand and lower prices for goods for which there is excess supply, this in some proportion to the degree of excess demand and supply; do not allow actual dealings to take place until all plans are consistent, until a set of prices is discovered at which all markets will clear.

It follows that we expect interest rates *not* to be invariant during the *tatonnement* process, although, on the assumption that there is no stock, other than money, the net nominal value of which is fixed, interest rates will be invariant in "equilibrium." Thus, we are permitted to describe adjustment processes although transactions never take place except in cleared markets.

Finally, a Patinkin model would be said to be unstable when the crier's rules lead him into a sequence of announcements taking the system farther and farther from a displaced equilibrium state. (*Cf.* Note K, Ch. VA and Ch. X.)

NOTE E: *Cf.* Bushaw and Clower, *Introduction to Mathematical Economics,* esp. pp. 36, 76, 128-134, 160-163, 166-171.) Also R. W. Clower, "An Investigation into the Dynamics of Investment," *American Economic Review,* March 1954, pp. 69-71 and pp. 73-77.

The *C-B* conclusions have to be modified for a model in which the total nominal stock of bonds also is fixed in advance. It can be shown that the ratio between the aggregate stock of bonds and the aggregate stock of money (S_B/S_M) appears as an explicit parameter in the reduced-form equations corresponding to *(S3)*. Even in this instance, however, all "real" quantities are invariant against equiproportionate changes in the aggregate stock of money *and* bonds. This emphasizes what is perhaps the most interesting feature of the system (S2): the stock of bonds is "geared" to the stock of money via a market adjustment mechanism; changes in the aggregate stock of bonds are, *ceteris paribus,* directly proportional to changes in the stock of money. (This paragraph is crucially important for understanding many of the Gurley-Shaw results.)

The *C-B* conclusions need not be modified if fixed supplies of physical assets yielding income in "kind" are inserted into the system. Provided no trader suffers from money illusion, and provided individual traders are permitted to issue new securities and to retire outstanding debts in the light of changing market conditions, the effects of a change in the aggregate stock of money can and will be entirely offset by an equiproportionate rise in money prices and in nominal asset balances.

NOTE F: Adhering to convention, the text assumes that the *jth* country's "money" is strictly national. But consider this international system. Each country has different official money of account and legal-tender currency. However, it is conventional in each country to cast up agreements in sundry monies of account, adhering to the convention that terms of discharge of debt should conform to the appropriate legal-tender laws and settlement conventions. Thus, an agreement cast in British pounds requires payment in British exchange in accord with British law and/or convention.

Assume that all countries are on fiat-paper standards with freely-floating exchange rates. The "quantity of money" in the *jth* country becomes difficult to define. The aggregate value of monies in the *jth* country varies from day to day with exchange rates and quantities; index-number problems crop up. If issue of Country A currency is increased, *cet. par.,* its value will diminish everywhere, of course.

In general, traders will not be indifferent towards composition of monetary balances. For fixed global means-of-payment preferences (admittedly easily unstuck by effects of monetary experience), there will emerge unique equilibrium real balances of dollars, lira, marks, . . . in each country.

The recent development of Eurodollars makes these musings more pertinent: a small but palpable portion of international, but intra-European, payments is accomplished with dollar exchange, contracts being in dollars (money of account).

Consider the system's adjustment process. Say that there is excess demand for dollar exchange (e.g., United States bank credit) and excess supply of lira exchange in Italy and that all American markets are cleared. Then, using a lira (money of account) measure, the price of dollar exchange will increase in Italy; dollar exchange will buy more in Italy. Americans will be incented to acquire lira balances. Italy will be likely to run a temporary favorable balance of payments. A "final" result of a positive shift in Italian demand for dollar balances is substitution of lira for dollars in the United States. Equilibrium requires that prices in the lira measure rise everywhere and that prices of dollar exchange rise. Also that American prices (in the dollar measure) fall. In the new equilibrium, Americans will "require" less dollar and more lira exchange.

PART III

MONEY & INTERNATIONAL TRADE

PART III

Money and International Trade

INTRODUCTION

The framework for Part III is already built. The major purpose of Chapters XV and XVI (comprising Part III) is to demonstrate that monetary theory can be applied to open as well as closed models, a task begun in Section E of Ch. XIV. Chapter XV's title, "Some Theory of the Balance of Payments," is self-explanatory. Chapter XVI, "Some Problems of International Monetary Policy," is confined to the International Monetary Fund and topics under the general heading of international central banking and post-war convertibility issues, including dollar shortages (surpluses). Chapter XV impinges upon a number of policy issues in the course of analysing the transfer problem and "disciplinary" implications of alternative international monetary standards. After all, theories are propounded to explain data.

International trade has a massive literature of high quality and surely does not require my ministration. Part III merely tidies up loose ends and projects some of our major themes into new areas; it does not offer training in trade theory. But, just as we do not claim to make contributions to the theory of international trade, we do not restate elementary mechanics.

A vital theme of Part III concerns impingement of international considerations on the autonomy of national authorities.* Under an international gold standard featured by fixed exchange rates and full internal and external convertibility, national authorities have very little room for maneuver. Their primary concern becomes protection of specie reserves, often requiring obedient response to changes in ex-

* This might be said to have been the central *res* of Keynes's work of the 1920's—culminating in the *Treatise*. Indeed the theme made an appearance in Part I of this book when Keynes was cited in some detail.

ternal conditions. This was dramatized in nineteenth-century Britain during the genesis of Bank rate policy. On the other hand, while "golden fetters" surely bind national authorities faced with loss of specie reserves, it is rather easy for nations gaining gold to undertake sterlization and other policies offsetting pressures towards higher commodity and securities prices in *their* countries. Even greater onus is placed on authorities of deficit countries. The urgency of their taking deflationary measures increases.

It is this onus, so disturbing to Keynes *et al.* before 1931, which plagues British and American authorities to this day. How might national authorities achieve autonomy permitting them to undertake policies suitable for domestic needs without courting insolvency resulting from collapse of the balance of payments? Proposals calculated to provide some insulation from international forces come under two heads:

1), provision for national and/or international buffer stocks of liquidity within a context of basically fixed exchange rates and international gold convertibility;

2), establishment of largely fiat-paper monetary standards, mostly relying on flexible exchange rates to maintain clearance in foreign exchange markets.**

It was pointed out in Ch. XIV that flexible exchange systems (at least if stable) are consistent with authorities "choosing" their own equilibrium price levels. But flexible-exchange does cost a degree of freedom in the sense that officials for whom the equilibrium price level *and* "the" interest rate would be choice variables (in the special sense of Ch. XIII) must, *cet. par.,* surrender "arbitrary" control of the equilibrium value of another real variable if the system is opened to international trade. Thus, if we were to raise our price level 10 per cent and reduce our interest rates, a 10 per cent devaluation of our currency would *not* correct the balance of payments: even if the real surplus on current account were maintained through the devaluation, there still would be capital outflow. Something would have to give. There might have to be a shift in a parameter of fiscal policy, or, perhaps, physical controls. If a devaluation of more than 10 per cent were acceptable to the officials, the new policy for prices and interest rates might be sustainable: but net exports would have to increase to offset increased

** *Cf.* Appendix C to Ch. VA (on forward-exchange manipulation) for a more technical, but substantively less important, device.

"capital outflow," implying changes in the production mix and necessary fiscal adjustments. There cannot be *complete* insulation of an economy from international forces.

In Part III invariance propositions largely are put aside: we are concerned with transient phenomena. Concern is in the forces causing period-to-period changes in balances of payments (sometimes, indeed, these periods are as long as decades or generations), not in properties of full-equilibrium states.

> Once more into the breach dear friends, once more
> . . .
> Stiffen the sinews, summon up the blood,
> Disguise fair nature with hard-favoured rage;
> Then lend the eye a terrible aspect.
>
> *Henry V,* III, i

CHAPTER FIFTEEN

Some Theory of the Balance of Payments

A. COMPOSITION OF THE BALANCE OF PAYMENTS

All transactions with foreigners can be classified in terms of whether these have occasioned dollar receipts or dollar payments. To the extent that the dollar value of goods sold abroad exceeded the dollar value of American purchases of goods from abroad, we must either have received IOU's or metallic stuff. Alternatively, to the extent that the dollar value of American purchases of foreign securities exceeded that of foreign purchases of American securities, foreigners either must have received gold from us or purchased goods from us of greater dollar value than our purchases from them. One can work within the confines of an accounting identity based on double-entry bookkeeping.

Briefly, all things involved in international trade, whether these be corporeal or incorporeal, can be classified as goods and services, securities, or gold. Goods and services enter into calculation of the current-account position, securities into the capital account (machinery, note well, is a good). Gifts are treated as imports of an incorporeal good — goodwill, let us say. Each transaction leads to an entry within one of the three categories and to a debit or credit of "surplus on balance of payments." If one delays posting gold flow to the very last, he knows that, aside from statistical discrepancy, it will be equal in value and opposite in sign to the net debit or credit accumulated at that point in his calculations. The reason already has been suggested: if our transactions, excluding gold transactions, gave rise to a net deficit, this can be only because foreigners have refused to make a gift; there is only one thing left to be done, ship gold. If our transactions, excluding gold transactions, gave rise to a net surplus, that can be only because we have refused to make additional gifts to them; there is but one thing for them to do, ship gold to us. *The categories are all-inclusive.*

Tables I–III, showing German, British, and American experience in recent years, are informative about balance-of-payments analysis. The data are in marks, pounds, and dollars respectively. The official exchange rate of dollars for pounds was 2.80 over 1958–1960 (and still is the mid-point). The official exchange rate of marks for dollars was 4.20 over 1958–1960, but was set at 4.00 during 1961 — this as part of a revaluation that led to speculative pressure against the pound described in Ch. VB and further discussed in Ch. XVI.

GERMAN BALANCE OF PAYMENTS

GOODS AND SERVICES	1958		1959		1960	
1) Goods and Services Proper		7,880		7,177		7,704
2) Merchandise Balance	4,880		5,104		5,385	
3) Other	3,000		2,073		2,319	
4) Private Donations		— 195		— 247		— 313
5) Official Donations		—1,454		—2,389		—2,363
6) Net Bal. on Current Acct.		6,231		4,541		5,028
CAPITAL ACCOUNT						
7) Private Capital		—519		—1,274		1,623
8) Long Term	—516		—1,105		986	
9) Short Term	— 3		— 169		637	
10) Official and Bank Cap.		—4,022		—2,682		—6,376
11) Net Bal. on Capital Acct.		—4,541		—3,956		—4,753
12) Line 6 + Line 11		1,690		585		275
GOLD AND RELATED ITEMS						
13) Monetary Gold		— 411		8		—1,402
14) IMF Balance		— 271		— 509		— 169
15) EPU Balance		— 355		411		
16) Line 13 + Line 14 + Line 15		—1,037		— 90		—1,571
17) Net Errors and Omissions		— 653		— 495		1,296

TABLE XV-I

Source: International Monetary Fund.

UNITED KINGDOM BALANCE OF PAYMENTS

GOODS AND SERVICES	**1958**		**1959**		**1960**	
1) Goods and Services Proper		515		285		— 57
2) Merchandise Balance	—430		—522		—902	
3) Other	945		807		845	
4) Official Donations		—222		—234		—287
5) Private Donations		— 2		— 1		
6) Net Bal. on Current Acct.		291		51		—344
CAPITAL ACCOUNT						
7) Private Capital		—128		—134		18
8) Long Term	—130		—142		—101	
9) Short Term	2		8		119	
10) Official and Bank Cap.		37		28		277
11) Net Bal. on Capital Acct.		— 91		—106		295
12) Line 6 + Line 11		200		— 55		— 49
GOLD AND RELATED ITEMS						
13) Monetary Gold and Convert Curr		—284		119		—177
14) IMF Balance		— 5		—137		—151
15) EPU Balance		— 10		9		
16) Line 13 + Line 14 + Line 15		—299		— 9		—328
17) Net Errors and Omissions		99		64		377

TABLE XV-II

Source: International Monetary Fund.

Possibilities for confusion over signs are boundless. Thus, consider the American data (Table III). Plus items (items without minus signs) concern transactions leading to demand for dollars (for payments purposes). Minus signs characterize transactions supplying dollars to foreigners (including the International Monetary Fund) or reducing the value of Americans' dollar claims against foreigners. Thus, the \$3,260 million increase in the private capital account in 1958 is a minus item in the American balance of payments: it led to supply of dollars; securities can be viewed as an import. Similarly, the \$2,275 million reduction in American monetary gold in 1958 is a plus item in our balance of payments: the gold was paid for with foreigners' claims against Americans, reducing excess supply of dollar exchange; gold loss can be viewed as an export item. Similarly, increases in American IMF holdings are minus items in our balance of payments: dollars are being supplied for IMF credit; from the balance-of-pay-

UNITED STATES BALANCE OF PAYMENTS

GOODS AND SERVICES		1958		1959		1960
1) Goods and Services Proper		2,272		172		3,973
2) Merchandise Balance	3,219		965		4,698	
3) Other	— 947		— 793		— 725	
4) Official Donations		—1,798		—1,849		—1,856
5) Private Donations		— 540		— 575		— 633
6) Net Bal. on Current Acct.		— 66		—2,253		1,484
CAPITAL ACCOUNT						
7) Nonmonetary Sectors		—3,260		—1,909		—3,548
8) Short Term Assets	— 339		— 356		— 527	
9) Other	—2,961		—1,553		—3,021	
10) Monetary Sectors		664		2,596		569
11) Net Bal. on Capital Acct.		—2,596		687		—2,979
12) Line 6 + Line 11		—2,662		—1,564		—1,495
GOLD AND RELATED ITEMS						
13) Monetary Gold		2,275		1,075		1,702
14) IMF Balance		17		— 39		441
16) Line 13 + Line 14		2,282		1,036		2,143
17) Net Errors and Omissions		380		528		— 648
Military Aid*		[2,281]		[1,944]		[1,765]

TABLE XV-III

Source: International Monetary Fund.

* Military Aid is not included in goods and services, nor is it included in Official Donations.

ments viewpoint such a transaction is just like American importation of Volkswagens.

The European Payments Union is a now defunct international settlement arrangement, transactions with which should be treated analogously with those with the International Monetary Fund . . . And perhaps you are disturbed by the huge "Net Errors and Omissions" items on lines 17. One reason for the size of these items is inaccurate measurement of service flows and capital-outflow.

Tables I–III tell some rather dramatic tales. Newspaper readers know about the highly favorable West German current-account balances in the late 1950's and in 1960, but line 6 (Table I) remains stunning. You might recall that Secretaries Anderson and Dillon allegedly were sent to Germany in 1960 to urge the Germans to make larger foreign aid contributions. The Secretaries were reported to have been given short shrift, and lines 4 and 5, Table I might suggest why: German contributions — including reparations to Israel — have been large. Lines 13 and 14 of Table I reveal the large expansion of German gold reserves; lines 7-9 that German purchases of foreign securities have been modest. The accounting identity provides the link. We have seen in Ch. VB that this led to the mark being revalued upward in 1961. The upshot was especially disappointing for Britain: speculation developed against the pound leading to the crisis of summer 1961 and to 7 per cent Bank rate. (High Bank rate was successful: hot money flowed to London and Bank rate was put down to 6 per cent by the end of October 1961.)

Table II makes clear that British balance-of-payments difficulties had deeper roots than mere speculation; Britain's current account deteriorated steadily from 1958 to 1960.[1] You might be surprised at the magnitude of the items of line 4, Table II: official donations, valued in dollars, were 621.6, 655.2, and 803.6 million for 1958, 1959, and 1960. Corresponding American non-military aid was 1,798, 1,849, 1,856 million dollars. British GNP is only about 1/10 that of the United States. Nevertheless Britain gained gold and convertible currencies over the 1958–1960 interval: capital account items were but slightly negative in 1958 and 1959 and substantially positive in 1960 when Britain exported £295 millions in securities. The crisis of 1961 was sudden.

The American balance of payments, described in Table III, deteriorated dramatically from 1958 to 1960: losses of monetary gold exceeded $5 billion; IMF credits fell more than $400 million. There was tremendous expansion in American holdings of foreign IOU's. In the topsy-turvy mercantilistic world of balance-of-payments, exchange of yellow dross for income-earning assets is a bad thing; unrequited export of IOU's is good. (Some call *B/P* surplus: net increase in monetary gold plus *short-term* claims against foreigners.)

B. FIXED EXCHANGE RATES

1

Sections B, C, and D are closely linked. Section B is concerned with economies whose money is externally convertible into gold (al-

---

[1] Dividend and interest payments from abroad are included in the "Other" item of line 3. Despite substantial sell-offs during the world wars, these are important positive items in the British balance of payments.

though perhaps featuring a limited gold-bullion standard of the American sort). Transitional stages and the way in which these are influenced by buffer stocks are not stressed in Section B, which primarily deals with comparative statics. It is concerned with constellations of variables consistent with *cessation* of gold flows, at least if there is no further disturbance. In theoretical analysis of international gold standards, exchange-rate adjustments revaluations ideally are eschewed: adjustment is accomplished through reaction to specie flow, perhaps including Ch. XIV E 3 effects on the level of output. However, we live in an impure world and must acknowledge hybrid institutional arrangements: external convertibility accompanied by exchange-rate manipulation. We try, however, to defer analysis of these bastard systems until Ch. XVI.

Section C 1 concerns a hypothetical community of economies none of which maintains convertibility in any form (although there is no *a priori* obstacle to some economies maintaining convertibility and others not). Here the central mechanism of adjustment is in foreign-exchange quotations, although in Section C 2 the real world intrudes: support operations based on official ammunition in the form of foreign-exchange holdings must be recognized. These buffers might be large enough for national officials to offset "parametric" changes in global asset functions by altering the size of their own holdings in response to changed market conditions. They might be able to sustain initial exchange rates as equilibrium rates. In other instances, official buffers prove to be hopelessly inadequate.

Section D is concerned with stability properties of the adjustment mechanisms of Sections B and C, although it sometimes is hard to separate out problems of existence and stability of exchange equilibrium. As it happens, problems concerned with reattainment of equilibrium positions after disturbance have been especially important in the flexible-exchange literature.

2

Surely the classical specie-flow mechanism of international gold standards with fixed exchange rates can fall into the "what every schoolboy knows" category. Again and again something like the following is asserted:

1) Begin without considering effects of real-income changes on the balance of payments.[2] What are called Keynesian adjustments

[2] Reference is to ultimate balance without further specie flows.

(after the Keynes of the *General Theory*) are ignored. Deal with a set of economies, each characterized by convertible money, specified liquidity preference, tastes (including preferences for foreign *vis-a-vis* domestic goods), techniques, tariff laws, etc.

2) Once parameters have been specified the system can be solved for a global set of prices, interest rates, real cash balances, gold stocks, etc., consistent with clearance of markets everywhere (including foreign-exchange markets) *without gold flows.* Generally speaking, the analysis is not at the level of *full* equilibrium; "equilibrium" is accompanied by capital flows; solution values change from period to period.

3) The general properties of solution states having been discovered, or, rather, posited, it is now assumed that the system initially is in imbalance. Perhaps prices are too high in Country A and interest rates too low to be consistent with payments balancing without gold flows. Stability questions can be ignored until Section D. (Section D is concerned with characteristics leading to instability; prior to that it is taken for granted that adjustment mechanisms will work save for certain Section C passages.)

4) The monetary systems are such that specie outflow is identified with monetary contraction and specie inflow with monetary expansion.

5) It is said that contraction in the stock of money in Country A, following specie outflow associated with an unfavorable balance of payments, will result in falling prices and rising interest rates in A, while expansion in the stock of money in other parts of the world, following specie inflow associated with favorable balances of payments with A, will result in rising prices and falling interest rates in not-A. These assertions necessarily are based on the assumption that variations in monetary parameters will lead to movements in the price level and in interest rates. (One or the other, if not both, would be called for by almost any doctrine, certainly if there were to be continuous full employment.) While movements in interest rates might be important in the adjustment process, the new equilibrium might find interest rates unchanged.

6) Similar reasoning applies where initially Country A — due to gold discoveries or the like — starts with real cash balances in excess of those desired. Effects will be registered throughout the world, the end results recalling C-B in Ch. XIV: invariance of solution values for real variables against initial distribution of cash and other assets.

7) Freedom of action of authorities of the individual economies

is very limited: deflation (inflation) abroad leads to deflation (inflation) at home; when Europe sneezes, America catches cold — unless the rules of the game are violated.

8) At least since 1930, there has been greater awareness of the impact of changes in real output and income on the balance of payments. The mechanisms of paragraphs 1-7 are impinged upon (intellectually and economically) by income and output effects.[3] (*Cf.* Sections E and F.) A country whose prices are "high" is caught up in a train of events leading to lower real output.[3] This discourages its imports. Not-A countries enjoy higher real incomes. This encourages demand for A exports. Some claim that paragraph-8 mechanisms are the more important in the real world. What sometimes is called the Keynesian adjustment mechanism permits (at least partial) adjustment of balance-of-payments difficulties through income changes even if the price-adjustment mechanism does not work. In any case, it relieves the burden on the latter mechanism.

9) The *transfer problem* (Section F) is especially interesting because it contains strands of almost all the analysis of these paragraphs.

Metzler has described the classical mechanism succinctly:

> ". . . For more than a century and a half, English economists and others in the English tradition had believed that [monetary forces cause] a country's balance of payments [to tend] automatically toward a state of equilibrium. If one country had a deficit in its balance of payments with another . . . it was recognized that part of its payments abroad would have to be made in gold, and it was believed that the gold movement would bring about certain price changes which eventually would restore an even balance of payments. As a result of the increased supply of money in the surplus country, and the reduced supply in the deficit country, prices and costs would rise in the former and fall in the latter . . . The classical explanation of the balancing process was eventually modified to consider the influence of interest rates on capital movements, to allow for a fractional reserve banking system, to recognize the similarity of gold movements and changes in foreign balances, and in other respects as well, but in substance the theory remained essentially as it was originally developed by the early English economists."[4]

---

3 Some of these effects flow from monetary contraction, others directly from reduced exports and/or increased imports.

4 Lloyd A. Metzler, "The Theory of International Trade," H. S. Ellis (ed.), *A Survey of Contemporary Economics* (Homewood, Ill.: Richard D. Irwin, 1948, pp. 210-254 at pp. 211-212).

Finally recall the mechanisms associating monetary events in various countries with foreign-exchange markets under international gold and other fixed exchange standards.

Taking up gold standards, if the United States government stands ready to provide a unit of its "currency" (including bank credit) for x grains of gold and to provide x grains of gold for a unit of its currency, while the British government makes a similar pair of offers, offering to buy or sell unlimited quantities of gold at an exchange rate of λx grains per unit of its currency, it follows — ignoring transportation and like costs — that a unit of British currency *must* exchange in world markets for λ units of American currency. And the same story can be told about *any* pair of countries in the international system. Nobody would be willing to pay more than λ dollars for a pound: one could acquire enough gold by selling λ dollars to the United States Treasury to buy a pound from the British Treasury. Nobody would be willing to take less than λ dollars for a pound as one could acquire λ dollars at the United States Treasury with the gold proceeds from the sale of a pound to the British Treasury.

It follows that, when the sum of items under the headings GOODS AND SERVICES and CAPITAL ACCOUNT in the American balance of payments is negative, gold will be shipped abroad, the physical quantity being [*(x).($ deficiency)*] grains. Of course, the phrase "shipped abroad" should not be taken literally: perhaps mere bookkeeping entries will be made in New York.

The mechanisms would be little different for a country not recognizing an *obligation* to exchange gold for monetary claims against it, but which chose to keep the value of its currency stable in terms of gold and hard currencies. Witness Britain in the 1930's. Reliance had to be placed on buffer stocks of gold and hard currencies when sterling was to be supported. What if the British buffer stock of dollars were so large that it could ignore consequences of gold outflow? Then Britain could pursue domestic ends without concern for its external solvency. A Bagehotian Nirvana would be achieved. Of course, precisely the same thing applies to a country legally obligated to convert its money into gold at a fixed ratio if its gold stocks were large enough. Operation of the classical mechanisms requires that would-be inflators ultimately bump against binding constraints. An example of utter futility from the point of view of the international gold standard would find Country A — possessed of an infinitely large gold stock but controlling its banks' reserves — inflating, losing gold to Country B which practices sterilization.

3

Before taking up Professor Metzler's elegant apparatus for summarizing the forces determining foreign-exchange-market clearance under fixed exchanges and in the context of Part II models, consider a theme sounded as far back as Ch. II: a tendency for the classical adjustment process to be crimped because of refusal of countries experiencing gold inflow to take the inflationary consequences.[5]

The theme is stated by Robert Triffin:

> ". . . But Keynes [in formulating a plan for an International Clearing Union in the early 1940's] was acutely concerned about the so-called 'deflationary bias' which had attended the functioning of the gold standard in the last decade before the Second World War. International balance of payments disequilibria manifest themselves in excessive or persistent deficits in some countries, but also in parallel surpluses for others. Under a managed gold standard, the full burden of readjustment tends to fall on the former countries, as a consequence of the depletion of their monetary reserves. The surplus countries, on the other hand, are always able to follow compensatory, or 'sterilization,' policies which block expansionary adjustments. Balance of payments disequilibria then tend to find their correction exclusively through the deflationary policies of the debtors, unrelieved by monetary expansion on the part of the creditors."[6]

There is no need to confine ourselves to the 1930's. The United States and France were unwilling to react "properly" to gold inflows in the 1920's. Indeed the euphoric applause in the late 1920's for central-banking as a mechanism of control was based in large part on effects of the Federal Reserve's sterilization policies circa 1923–1925. And surely post-1945 experience does not contradict Triffin.

It is not hard to resolve the chords of this subsection: so long as national authorities submit passively to the discipline of gold, adhering to automatic procedures adjusting the monetary base to gold flows,

[5] More formal and complete discussion of sources of failure of the classical adjustment mechanism is in Section D, concerned with exchange stability. If we deal with economies with involuntary unemployment so that monetary phenomena are unlikely to exert much influence on price levels and interest rates (assumed to be at institutional minima), the adjustment mechanism has to be based on effects of output changes in the various countries. This topic is detailed in Section E.

[6] *Europe and the Money Muddle* (New Haven: Yale University Press, 1957), p. 94.

and so long as none of the players accumulates so many chips that he can afford to lose interest in the game, classical adjustment processes have a chance to work; only inherent instability can thwart them.

4

This subsection consists of an analysis based on 1955 classroom presentations of Professor Metzler that have not, so far as I know, been published. I have attempted to fill in some of the gaps inevitable in an informal presentation.

We perform comparative-statics analysis of systems always at full employment and featured by fixed exchange rates (reflected in the model's use of a common unit of account). The two-country system is on an international gold standard. We work with simple shmoo economies. The model was, I believe, suggested by Section 4 of Ch. 13 (Vol. 1) of the *Treatise* and indeed points up the *Treatise's* chaotic richness.

Begin by defining the functions

$$(1) \qquad (S\text{-}I)^a \equiv f(r_a, r_b, p_a, p_b),$$

$$(2) \qquad (S\text{-}I)^b \equiv F(r_a, r_b, p_a, p_b).$$

The positive or negative excesses of planned saving over planned investment, measured in shmoos, in Countries A and B are functions of r_a and r_b, the interest rates in Countries A and B, and their price levels. The functions are zero-order homogeneous in the prices: only the ratio p_a/p_b can be determined by Equations 1-4. A and B shmoos are identical except that the former are stamped with Stars and Stripes, and the latter with Union Jacks. I^a and I^b give planned rates of demand for domestic goods for investment purposes; S^a and S^b are planned differences between receipts from production and the sum of planned expenditures on domestic consumption goods and all foreign goods, always measuring in shmoos. (There is patriotic shmoo illusion of course.)

Turn to Equations 3 and 4:

$$(3) \qquad (E\text{-}J)^a \equiv g(r_a, r_b, p_a, p_b),$$

$$(4) \qquad (E\text{-}J)^a \equiv -(E\text{-}J)^b.$$

Of course, $E^a \equiv J^b$ and $E^b \equiv J^a$. E^a and J^a are real exports and imports of A; $(E\text{-}J)^a$ measures the real export surplus, positive or negative, of A. (Transfers are not included.) Recall that $g(\quad)$ is zero-order homogeneous in p_a and p_b.

Consider Equation 5:

$$(5) \qquad E^a - J^a = S^a - I^a \qquad \text{or} \qquad E^a + I^a = S^a + J^a.$$

This is nothing more than a clearance condition for A's commodities market. The rate of leakage from the system is given by the sum of savings and imports. The rate at which consumption expenditure is being augmented is given by the sum of investment expenditures and exports — always measuring in shmoos.

Now assign an arbitrary value to $(E\text{-}J)^a$, assigning the same value to $(S\text{-}I)^a$. Equation 4 tells us that a value equal in amount but opposite in sign to that chosen for $(E\text{-}J)^a$ is definitionally appropriate for $(E\text{-}J)^b$. Equate $(S\text{-}I)^b$ with $(E\text{-}J)^b$. We are then assured that the commodities markets of the two countries will clear simultaneously, implying that the excess of saving over investment in A is equal to the excess of investment over saving in B.

Having done this, Equations 1-4 can be solved for interest rates and for the ratio p_a/p_b. The *jth* value chosen for $(E\text{-}J)^a$ becomes associated with the pair $(r_a, r_b)^{aj}$ and, of course, with a relative price ratio. (Put aside the latter for the nonce.) Indeed the *jth* pair can be expressed

$$(r_b - r_a)^j.$$

THE BB CURVE

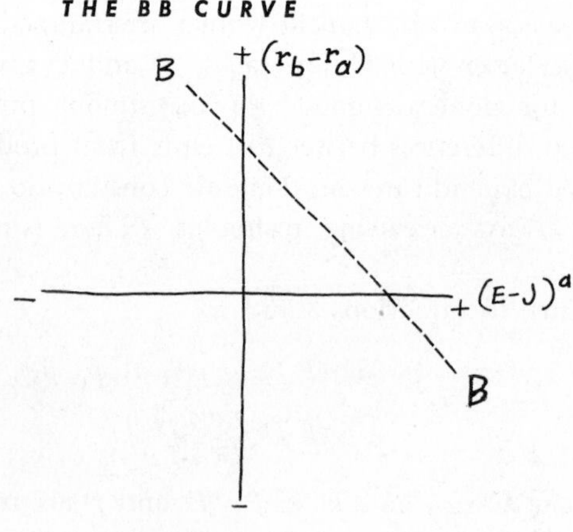

Figure XV-1

Assume for convenience that $(r_b - r_a)^*$ is positive for $(E - J)^a = 0$, that, in some sense, the "natural rate of interest" is higher in B than in A. It can be anticipated that the difference between interest rates will become smaller in solution as $(E\text{-}J)^a$ is taken to be larger: for larger values of $(S\text{-}I)^a$, r_a^* becomes larger and r_b^* less: savings must exceed investment by a larger amount in A; investment must exceed savings by a larger amount in B. Assume that domestic interest rates dominate in the two countries in the determination of savings and investment plans. We are led to Figure XV-1.

The *BB* curve is a locus of combinations of export surpluses for Country A (import surpluses for B) and interest-rate differentials consistent with commodities markets being in balance in both countries. (We have seen that the interest-rate differentials are associated with definite solution values for interest rates in both countries.)

We turn to capital outflow and Equation 6:

$$C \equiv h(r_b - r_a). \tag{6}$$

C is the rate of excess of purchase of B securities by citizens of A over purchase of A securities by citizens of B. Income transfers, including interest and dividend payments, are incorporated into "capital outflow" and are treated as a constant of the system at any point in time. It is assumed that, on net, transfers are in favor of B. *C*, of course, is assumed to be an increasing function of the interest-rate differential. We are led to Figure XV-2.

The *CC* curve simply relates planned capital outflow to interest-rate differentials. Capital flows — measured in shmoos — are from A to B (net capital outflow from B to A is registered as a negative number). Consider the properties of point *P*, the intersection of the *BB* and *CC* curves. At *P*, Equation 7 holds:

$$C = (E\text{-}J)^a. \tag{7}$$

Capital outflow is equal to the export surplus; the foreign-exchange market is in balance. In fact, simultaneous clearance of the foreign-exchange and commodities markets in the two countries is impossible except at *P*: interest-rate differentials and the export surplus are determined through satisfaction of the clearance conditions; the equilibrium state, displacement from which is to give rise to adjustment processes, is partially defined.

Absolute price levels in the two countries (taken to comprise

BB-CC CONSTRUCTION

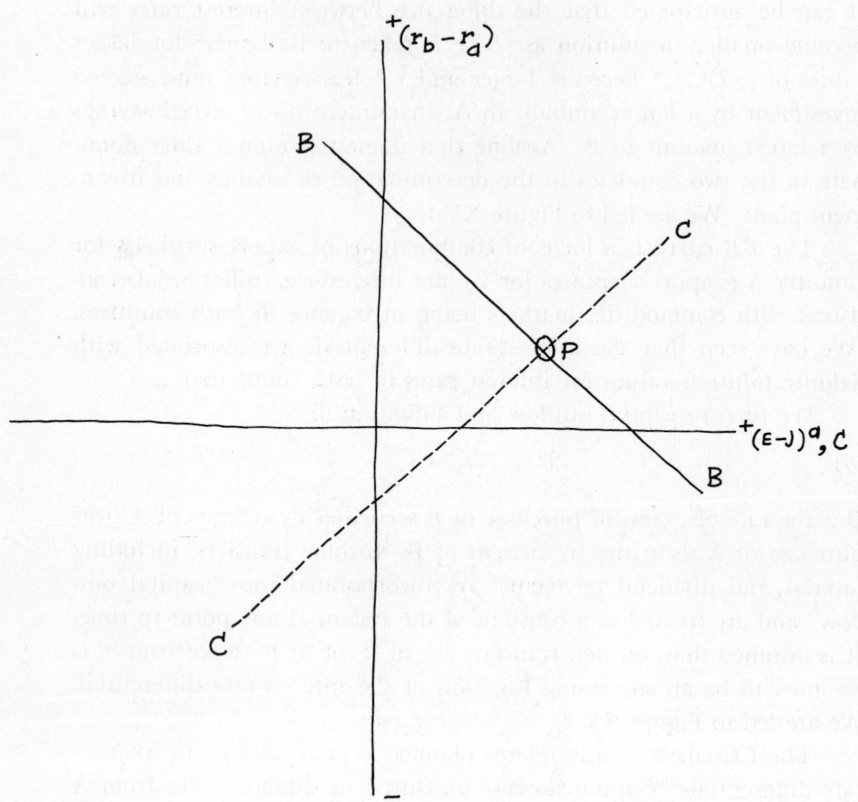

Figure XV-2

the world) have not yet been determined. However, k_1 in identity 8 already has been determined through the first four equations:

$$(8) \qquad (p_a/p_b)^* \equiv k_1.$$

Money markets must be introduced into the system. Consider Equations 9, 10, 8′, and 11:

$$(9) \qquad \phi(G_a) = \psi(p_a, p_b, r_a^*, r_b^*)$$

$$(10) \qquad \phi(G_b) = L(\qquad)$$

$$(8') \qquad P_a = k_1 p_b$$

$$(11) \qquad G_a + G_b = \overline{G}.$$

Functions $\phi(G_a)$ *and* $\phi(G_b)$ indicate that supplies of money in the two countries depend on their gold holdings, G_a and G_b. Functions $\psi(\quad)$ and $L(\quad)$ are liquidity-preference functions defining demand for money. Price levels are expressed in a common unit of account, a convenient simplification; the accounting price of money is unity in each country. In neither country is the public permitted to hold gold. Equation 11 states that aggregate gold holdings cannot exceed the globally-available stock, measured in grains of gold.

There are four equations in the four unknowns, p_a, p_b, G_a, and G_b. "Equilibrium" distribution of gold stocks and price levels are determined. The formal system is, of course, statical, although solution values generally change from period to period. All of this within the context of an international-gold-standard framework.

Finally, we turn to two problems in comparative statics: effects of an increase in the supply of gold; effects of a shift in one or both of the S-I functions. The conclusions prove to be strikingly close to those offered by Keynes in Section 4, Ch. 13 of the *Treatise.*

a) Increase in the supply of gold

The position of point P of the diagram above must be unaffected by an increase in the stock of monetary gold. There are no real-balance effects. Nor does the distribution of the gold stock enter into the diagram. In the new solution relative price levels must be unchanged. Since liquidity preference is assumed to be unchanged, prices will rise by the same proportion in both countries; *in solution,* the proportionate distribution of the gold stock will be unchanged. (*See Note A.*) Of course, the adjustment process is another matter. The monetary supply functions of Equations 9 and 10 imply that officials in both countries submit meekly to the dictates of gold; the monetary systems are not managed. We expect interest rates to fall transitorily in B — if the influx of gold initially is in that country — and B price levels to rise. Values in A will momentarily be unchanged. Then the adjustment process takes over. Eventually interest rates settle back to old levels as "monetary requirements" increase with higher price levels.

b) Shift in an S-I function

Consider a shift in the S-I function for Country A so that $(S\text{-}I)^a$ is greater for any given pair $(\bar{r}_a, \bar{r}_b)$: the *BB* curve has shifted rightward; A's export surplus must be greater for any pair $(\bar{r}_a, \bar{r}_b)$ if its greater excess of saving over investment is to be offset by a more favorable merchandise balance. Prices must fall in A relative to prices in B. On the other hand, balance in the foreign-exchange market requires that real capital outflow from A to B increase: the interest rate differential must increase, as is graphically obvious. However, since B must now sustain a more unfavorable balance on current account — since its "import drain" must increase — its excess of investment over saving will also have to increase: interest rates will fall in both countries. In the new solution, the proportion of the global gold stock in Country B might be higher, since the "monetary requirement" has fallen in A. (This might be offset by differential effects on demand for cash in the two countries resulting from lower interest rates.) However, the key thing is that parametric shifts in one country require what might be substantial adjustment in the other; the world becomes a big (un)happy family.

Remember that the model determines only temporary equilibria: solution states differ from period to period. We are not now concerned with full-equilibrium states. Accordingly, stability analysis must be phrased in terms of barren *tatonnement* concepts.

C. FLEXIBLE EXCHANGE RATES

1. Inconvertible Paper Model

Section E of Ch. XIV did a good deal of the work of this section. It was shown that autonomy over price levels can be achieved, but that autonomy over price levels *and* interest rates could not be achieved, unless control of some other variable is surrendered. Let us show how the Metzler model leads to the same results.

Graphical analysis is eschewed in favor of algebra. The new model is based on inconvertible paper currencies and flexible exchange rates.

$$(1) \qquad (S\text{-}I)^a \equiv f(r_a, r_b, p_a, p_b, \rho)$$

$$(2) \qquad (S\text{-}I)^b \equiv F(\qquad\qquad)$$

$$(3) \qquad (J^b\text{-}J^a) \equiv g(\qquad\qquad)$$

$$(4) \qquad (S\text{-}I)^a = (J^b - J^a)$$

(5) $(S\text{-}I)^{b} = -(J^{b}-J^{a})$

(6) $M_a = \Psi\ (r_a, r_b, p_a, p_b, \rho)$

(7) $M_b = L(\qquad\qquad)$

(8) $h(r_a, r_b) = (J^{b} - J^{a})$.

This comprises a system of eight equations in the 10 unknowns r_a, r_b, p_a, p_b, ρ, $(S\text{-}I)^{a}$, $(S\text{-}I)^{b}$, $(J^{b}\text{-}J^{a})$, M_a, and M_b. ρ is the price of a unit of B money in terms of A money and transforms prices stated in B's money of account into prices stated in A's money of account. Walras' Law cannot knock out any equations, since securities markets are not explicitly in the model. Accordingly, there are two extra degrees of freedom. Use these to set arbitrary price levels p_a and p_b. A solution value for the exchange rate will emerge: a ratio $(p_a/p_b)^*$ becomes established. Given $p_a = \bar{p}_a$ and $p_b = \bar{p}_b$, the price of B commodities in terms of A money is: $\rho \cdot p_b$; the price of B commodities in terms of A commodities is

$$\frac{\rho p_b}{p_a}.$$

A suitable value for ρ permits establishment of the equilibrium *relative* price for arbitrary specification of nominal prices. It becomes clear that the *BB-CC* construction is unaffected by replacement of a fixed-exchange system by a flexible-exchange system; functions zero-order homogeneous in p_a and p_b can be expressed in terms of the exchange rate, given arbitrary values of p_a and p_b. Money stocks are established in the respective countries consistently with chosen price levels and without concern for "golden fetters." The clearance conditions, explicitly set out in Equations 4-8, are satisfied in the solution.

2. Flexible Exchange

1

The remainder of Section C contains an informal discussion of essential properties of *flexible-exchange systems* (including systems subject to occasional exchange-rate changes) and a statement of Robert A. Mundell's basic statical model, our base of operations for study of stability questions.[7]

Chapters XIV and XV have paved the way for study of flexible-

[7] Probably the best treatment of flexible-exchange systems is in Milton Friedman, "The Case for Flexible Exchange Rates," p. 157 *ff.*, in Milton Friedman, *Essays in Positive Economics.*

exchange systems. We have seen that authorities can choose "equilibrium" domestic price levels without fear of international complication — if they are willing to accept corresponding values of rates at which their currencies exchange for other currencies. The setting is that of the introduction to Part III: the problem of national autonomy in international economic systems. We need only state some of the objections that have been made to flexible exchange and distinguish pure flexible-exchange systems from those featured by rigid exchange rates sporadically changed by official action. *En passant,* we do a simple graphical analysis of the excess demand function for foreign exchange that has important implication for Section D.

The most frequently voiced criticism of flexible exchange as a means of international monetary adjustment concerns stability, the subject of Section D. The argument is largely *a priori* since there is so little data on actual performance of flexible-exchange systems. It also is suggested that exchange-rate fluctuation is likely to be so violent that there may be disruption of international trade, especially if forward-exchange markets are imperfect. A related criticism, one with special importance for such centers of international banking as London, stresses the difficulty of dealing in money-fixed claims with foreigners when conversion rates are subject to drastic change.

Diagrams A, B, and C (the latter two impinging on Section D) pertain to all of these objections. Diagram A concerns "well-behaved" situations in which there are unique market-clearing foreign-exchange rates at all times, and where the solutions obviously are stable. We do not trouble to define conditions underlying these curves except to note that the steep curves of the left-hand side of Diagram A suggest that elasticities of demand for imports in Countries A and B are lower than is the case for the flatter curves of the right-hand side of Diagram A. Also that we assume the dollar prices of American goods to be parametric for Englishmen and the sterling prices of English goods to be parametric for Americans; price elasticities (in own-currency) of supply of exports are infinite in both cases. The market is assumed to be initially cleared at the exchange rate *OC.* There is a shift in the demand-for-dollars curve: more dollars are demanded at given exchange rates. The shifts are the same on both sides of the diagram: the increase in the number of dollars demanded at a given exchange rate is the same under either slope specification.

The outcome is easy to grasp: foreign-exchange market clearance

(IN)ELASTIC DEMAND AND SUPPLY FOR DOLLARS

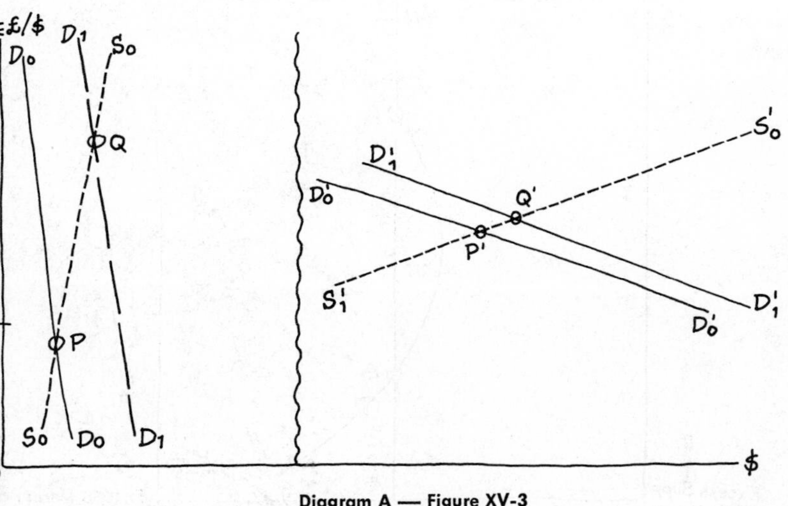

Diagram A — Figure XV-3

EFFECTS OF INELASTIC DEMAND FOR GOODS IN FOREIGN TRADE

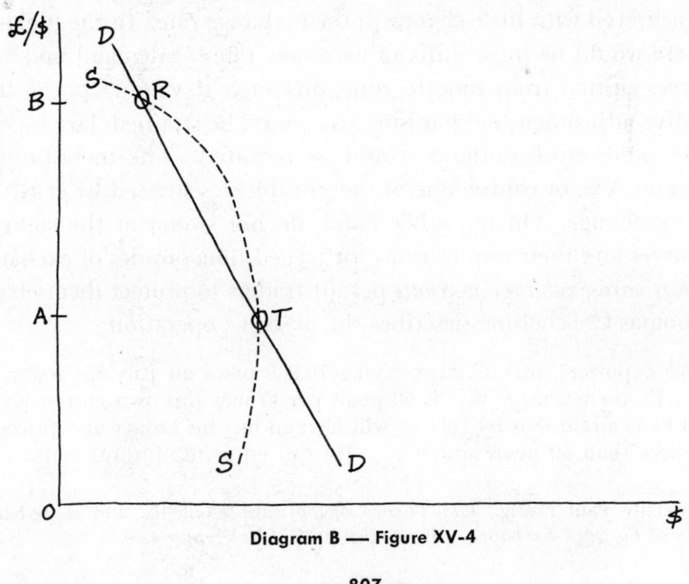

Diagram B — Figure XV-4

EXCESS DEMAND FOR DOLLARS AS A FUNCTION OF $1/\rho$

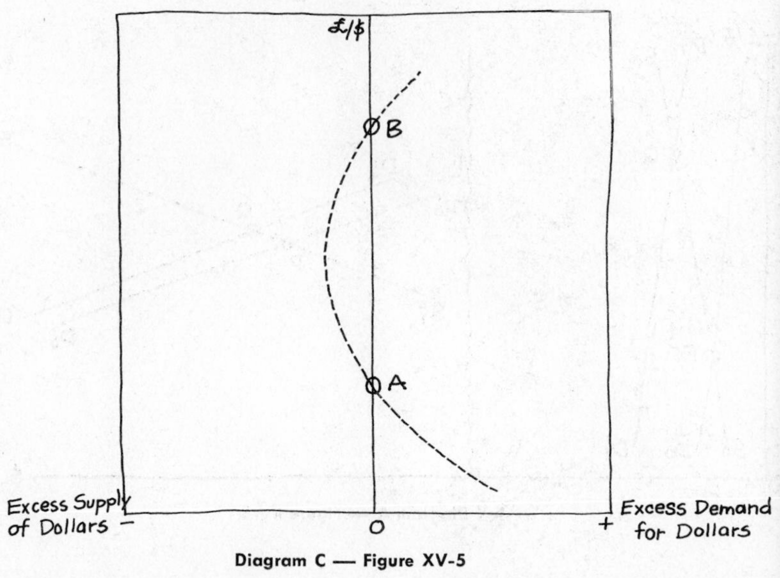

Diagram C — Figure XV-5

in the "inelastic case" requires a "large" increase in the "number of pounds sterling" commanded by a dollar; in the "elastic case" clearance can be achieved with little change in the exchange rate. In the inelastic case there would be huge shifts in exchange rates as demand and supply curves shifted from time to time, although it would appear that alternative adjustment mechanisms also would be strained; large specie or other buffer-stock outflows would be required. The inelastic case of Diagram A is, of course, one of the possibilities stressed by critics of flexible exchange. On the other hand, do not swoon at the sight of steep curves and their implications for jagged time-profiles of exchange rates. *Forward-exchange markets* permit traders to protect themselves.[8]

Thomas C. Schelling describes the market's operation:

> "[An exporter] anticipates receiving 10,000 pesos on July 15; today, May 15, the exchange rate is 50 pesos per kroner (his own currency), and he is afraid that by July he will have to buy his kroner at a price of more than 50 pesos apiece . . . He can enter the futures market,

[8] *Cf.* especially Paul Einzig, *The Theory of Forward Exchange* and *A Dynamic Theory of Forward Exchange.* Also Appendix C, Ch. VA *supra.*

> and contract at today's *futures* rate to sell 10,000 pesos on July 15 [for a stipulated number of kroner] . . .
>
> This serves the exporter's purpose; but who is on the other side of the arrangement? The answer: somebody in the exact opposite position. An importer in the kroner country has to pay 10,000 pesos in the second half of July . . . He is prepared to 'freeze' today's rate in his calculations, to forego the chance of a lower price, if he can be sure the price will not rise. So he sells kroner for July 15 delivery, against pesos at approximately today's rate . . . Thus anybody who wants to insure himself today's rate for a future transaction can use the futures market to do so."[9]

Professor Schelling proceeds to write that

> "if one can buy . . . 200 kroner for 10,000 pesos today, but could get 210 for 10,000 pesos in a July 15 futures contract, there is a sure profit for anyone who buys and sells simultaneously. He buys the 10,000 pesos for 200 kroner, enters a futures contract to sell 10,000 pesos for 210 kroner thirty or sixty days hence . . . and [nets] . . . a 5 per cent profit in 30 days . . . It should not be surprising that the two rates come into line."[10]

Appendix C, Ch. VA, shows that the analysis also should take account of interest rates in the kroner and peso countries; *interest parities* must be considered. However, departures from interest parities can occur in the face of strong speculative forces; interest arbitrage can be too little and too late:

> "Doubtless in an ideal world enveloped under a static theory forward rates would always adjust themselves promptly to their Interest Parities . . . In our real world, however, things do not work nearly so smoothly. For a variety of reasons there can be, and often are, substantial and lasting discrepancies of great practical importance . . . Even allowing for the possibility that the public may be inclined once more to take a hand in interest arbitrage . . . the volume of balances available for that purpose is by no means unlimited. . . . It is only when intrinsic premiums or discounts are abnormally wide that [private arbitrageurs] can operate. Moreover, only those private firms or individuals who know it for certain that they would not want their funds during the period concerned could afford to engage in interest arbitrage . . . [T]he main reason why abnormal intrinsic premiums or discounts ever exist over long periods is that while there are limits to the volume of direct or indirect interest arbitrage, there are virtually no limits to the speculative pressure it is supposed to counteract."[11]

9 Thomas C. Schelling, *International Economics* (Boston: Allyn & Bacon, Inc., 1958), p. 93.

10 *Ibid.*, p. 94.

11 Paul Einzig, *A Dynamic Theory of Forward Exchange*, pp. 176-185.

But assume for the sake of argument that spot and futures exchange rates will stay in line with each other. That does not mean that *both* cannot fluctuate violently and that an initial decline in, say, the rate at which dollars exchange for marks cannot lead to speculators (as against hedgers) bidding for *marks* in anticipation of further deterioration of the dollar's trading position, being confirmed by the resulting continued decline in the mark price of the dollar, increasing selling pressure, etc., *ad nauseum.*[12] Of course, destabilizing speculative pressures are apt to be abetted by "steep" curves.

2

Diagrams B and C deal with possibilities for outright perversity in the sense that excess supply of dollars (or what have you) might lead to *increased* excess supply quite apart from speculation. It is not difficult to derive the *DD* curve of Diagram B. Consult Diagrams D and E. Diagram D implies that the supply of American exports to Britain is at a fixed price, that British demand is a small enough pea in the

COUNTRY B'S DEMAND FOR THE EXPORTS OF COUNTRY A

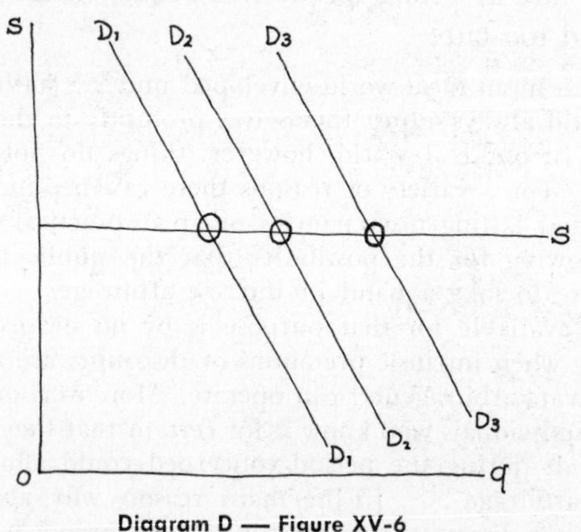

Diagram D — Figure XV-6

[12] Milton Friedman minimizes the likelihood of destabilizing speculation, stressing the role of profit taking. *Cf. op. cit.,* note 5, pp. 174-177. *Cf.* also Lester G. Telser, "A Theory of Speculation Relating Profitability and Stability," *Review of Economics and Statistics,* Vol. 41, August 1959, pp. 295 *ff.* Also William J. Baumol, "Speculation, Profitability, and Stability," *loc. cit.,* August 1957, pp. 263 *ff.* Baumol's article evoked Telser's.

TOTAL REVENUE FROM EXPORTS

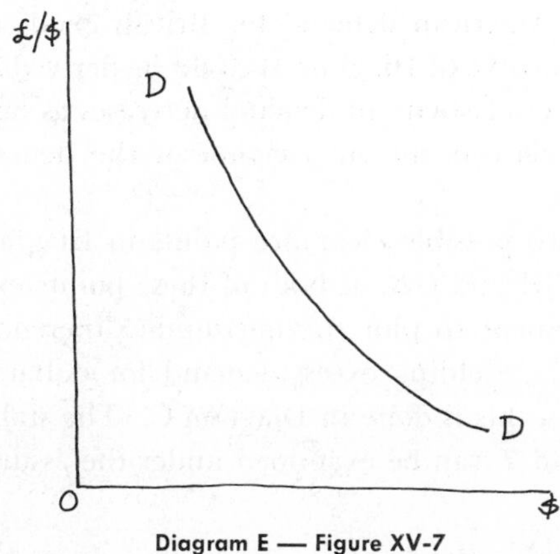

Diagram E — Figure XV-7

American pod for the supply price to be parametric for Britain. The successive demand curves are for exchange rates finding the pound worth more and more in terms of the dollar; the sterling price of American goods becomes lower as we move from D_1D_1 to D_2D_2 to D_3D_3. Just how much American revenue from exports will increase depends upon the elasticity of British demand. The results are summarized in Diagram E (drawn to a different scale). If British demand for American goods were perfectly inelastic, *DD* would be a vertical line at a value given by the product of supply price and the fixed quantum of British demand.

The *SS* curve of Diagram B is harder to derive. It is important to remember these principles:

> marginal revenue is positive when demand is elastic, zero when demand is unit elastic, and negative when demand is inelastic. Total revenue increases with an increase in price when demand is inelastic, is unchanged when demand is unit elastic, and decreases with an increase in price when demand is elastic.

A decrease in the value of the dollar in terms of the pound means that a given quotation in pounds sterling has a higher dollar equivalent; an effect of a lower value for dollars in the foreign-exchange market is for the dollar prices of British goods to increase (assuming that sterling prices of British goods are parametric for American importers). It follows that the nominal value of dollars seeking British exchange increases with a decrease in the value of the dollar in terms of sterling when American demand for British goods is inelastic, etc. The particular *SS* curve of Diagram B could be derived from a straight-line demand curve: elasticity of demand decreases as one moves to the right, becoming zero at the intersection of the demand curve with the quantity axis.

There are two possible clearance points in Diagram B: points *R* and *T* for rates *OA* and *OB*; at both of these points excess demand is zero. It is convenient to plot the horizontal differences between the *DD* and *SS* curves, yielding excess demand for dollars (a positive or negative number); this is done in Diagram C. The stability properties of solutions *R* and *T* can be examined under the assumption that the dynamic law

$$dp/dt = f(X) \tag{1}$$

applies — where p is the price of pounds sterling in terms of dollars and where X measures excess demand for dollars in the foreign-exchange market. dp/dt is assumed to be negative when X is positive, positive when X is negative, and zero when X is zero. Clearly, *T* is a stable solution point: upward displacements from *OA* lead to excess supply, downward displacements to excess demand. By the same token, *R* is unstable: downward displacements in the neighborhood of *OB* lead to excess supply and upward displacements to excess demand for dollars in the foreign-exchange market. If we begin at *OB* and experience a downward displacement, the rate will fall all the way to *OA*; initial excess supply will lead to decreasing sterling values for the dollar. This might be a painful process and might find the bottom of the foreign-exchange market seeming to drop out if *OA* is enough below *OB*. But an upward displacement from *OB* is even worse: excess demand for dollars will grow upon what it doth feed; complete disorganization might ensue — unless there were official intervention, filling the dollar gap and shoving back the sterling price of dollars through main force. Diagrams B and C pose nightmarish prospects for flexible exchange and call attention to the role of demand and supply elasticities in the theory of exchange stability.[13]

[13] For a very good discussion of the topics of this subsection and the monetary aspects of international trade generally see A. G. Hart and P. B. Kenen, *Money, Debt, and Economic Activity*, pp. 313-370, especially pp. 313-323.

3

Systems featuring exchange rates held rigid by national authorities *subject to occasional change through official action* really do not belong in Section C. On the other hand, it is evident that more or less once-and-for-all changes in exchange rates "have the same kind of effect on commodity trade and the like as those produced automatically under a system of flexible exchange rates."[14] Professor Friedman, however, proceeds to argue that official changes in exchange rates "have very different effects on speculative transactions." He argues that it is likely the authorities will not take action until "disequilibrium has grown to crisis dimensions; action, when it does occur, will be drastic." Furthermore,

> "there is seldom any doubt about the direction in which an exchange rate will be changed, if it is changed. In the interim between the suspicion of a possible change in the rate and the actual change, there is every incentive to sell the country's currency if devaluation is expected . . . This is in sharp contrast with the situation under flexible exchange rates when the decline in the exchange rate takes place along with, and as a consequence of, the sales of a currency and so discourages or penalizes sales, and conversely for purchases. With rigid rates, if the exchange rate is not changed, the only cost to the speculators is a possible loss of interest earnings from an interest-rate differential . . . In short, the system of occasional changes in temporarily rigid exchange rates seems to me the worst of two worlds: it provides neither the stability of expectations that a genuinely rigid and stable exchange rate could provide in a world of unrestricted trade and willingness and ability to adjust the internal price structure to external conditions nor the continuous sensitivity of a flexible exchange rate."[15]

4

Robert A. Mundell has provided a nice mechanism for analysis of stability properties of international-adjustment mechanisms.[16] Section D concentrates on the Mundell model. Consider now his statical system, noting that it can be used either for fixed or flexible exchange rates.

The assumptions underlying Mundell's system appear to be somewhat informal. But we are content with heuristically-appealing matter

14 Milton Friedman, *op. cit.*, p. 163.

15 *Ibid.*, p. 164.

16 Robert A. Mundell, "The Monetary Dynamics of International Adjustment under Fixed and Flexible Exchange Rates," *Quarterly Journal of Economics*, Vol. 74, May 1960, pp. 227-257.

ultimately suggesting how alternative exchange-rate systems might have very different stability properties even if their solution states are identical. These are Mundell's underlying assumptions:

1) The system is dominated by conditions of clearance in two markets: "the market for domestic goods and services, and the market for foreign exchange."

2) "When the excess of domestic saving over domestic investment is greater than the trade balance surplus there is deflationary potential, and when it falls short of the trade balance surplus there is inflationary potential."

3) Clearance in the foreign-exchange market "requires equality of foreign exchange payments and receipts (excluding central-bank transactions), or, equivalently, equality of the rate of lending (net capital exports) and the trade balance surplus."

4) The two markets are "subject to two main influences": domestic interest rates and the terms of trade.

5) "The" rate of interest in each country is determined by its central bank which stands ready to enforce the rate through unlimited open-market operations.[17]

6) ". . . all foreign prices, incomes, and interest rates are constant during the period under consideration: this means that changes in the terms of trade can result only from changes in the exchange rate or variations in the domestic price level."

These assumptions lead to the diagram below, producing the kind of structure featured in the Metzler-Patinkin CC-LL or the Metzler BB-CC constructions: the curves are to be interpreted as loci of solution values for the respective markets.

Under a system of fixed-exchange, measurements along the abscissa give Country A's price level (all analysis being in terms of a single country). Under flexible exchange, p should be interpreted as the price of A's currency in terms of B's. In either case, we measure a terms-of-trade variable along the horizontal axis. Clearance in the foreign-exchange market will require higher interest rates in A as the terms of trade move in its favor, certainly when we assume that A's balance on current account decreases with improvement in its terms of trade, *cet. par.* Accordingly, the *FF* curve, associating values for p and r

[17] It was shown in Ch. XIII that standard systems frequently do not contain enough degrees of freedom to permit the central bank to "select" an interest rate and be able to sustain market clearance even if the Bank does not insist upon an arbitrary value for the nominal stock of money. We assume that Mundell's system has left him with this degree of freedom. Indeed we showed that it is not difficult to construct a plausible system that does this trick.

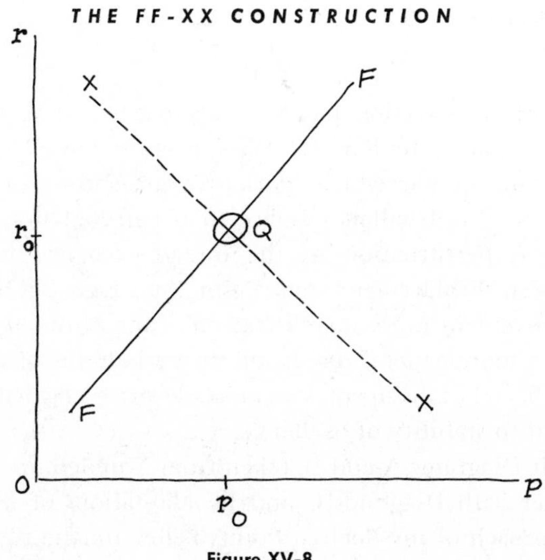

Figure XV-8

consistent with clearance in the foreign-exchange market, is upward-sloping. On the other hand, it can be assumed that the excess of planned saving over planned investment algebraically decreases with the rate of interest: the *algebraic* value of A's surplus on current account must decrease with r if there is not to be excess demand in the commodities markets. The terms of trade must move in favor of A so that A's export surplus can be reduced. It follows that the *XX* curve, associating values for r and $\dot{p}$ consistent with clearance of markets for goods and services, is downward-sloping. And, of course, A's "entire economic system" cannot be in balance except at the particular r-$\dot{p}$ combination given by $(r_o, \dot{p}_o)$, point *Q*.

One is perhaps a bit queasy about the failure to check back to Country B, more or less in order to study interaction of *A* combinations with clearance in *B* markets — there might be trouble back at the ranch. Still Mundell assures us that his structure is consistent with models specifically introducing global clearances (as did the Metzler model of Section B). If you remain nervous, assume that Country B is very large relative to Country A so that the rate of interest and the price level in *B* — the rest of the world — are parametric for *A*. In any case, the diagram permits integration of the concepts of Parts II and III. However, the real purport of the Mundell model is for stability problems, and it is to these that we turn.

D. STABILITY OF EXCHANGE

1

Obviously this section has been encroached upon by Section C, and, for that matter, by Part II. We can settle down at once to study the circumstances under which alternative mechanisms of international adjustment will and will not suffice to restore balances of payments once there is perturbation in the foreign-exchange market — once there has been displacement from Point *Q* in Figure XV-8.

It is convenient to resume discussion of the Mundell model before turning to a more general discussion of mechanisms of adjustment — including the relationship of foreign-trade price elasticities of supply and demand to stability of exchange.

Consult Diagrams A and B, taken from Mundell, *loc. cit.*, pp. 234-235, together with Diagrams C and D, adaptations of Mundell's to a cobweb approach of my device. Points below (to the right of) the *FF* curve find deficit in the foreign balance; points above (to the left of) the *FF* curve, surplus. Points above (to the right of) the *XX* curve describe excess supply in markets for goods and services; points below (to the left of) the *XX* curve, excess demand. Accordingly, Point *A*, Diagram A, finds deficit in the foreign balance together with excess supply in goods-and-services markets. Point *B* describes surplus in the foreign balance and excess supply of goods and services. Point *C*:

SIMPLE DYNAMICS WITH RIGID EXCHANGE

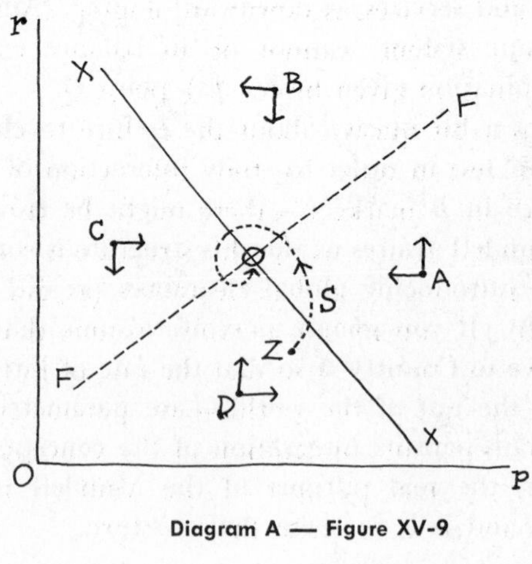

Diagram A — Figure XV-9

SIMPLE DYNAMICS WITH FLEXIBLE EXCHANGE

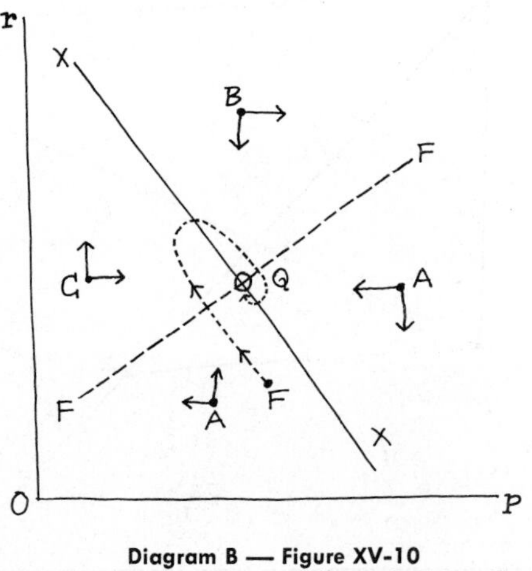

Diagram B — Figure XV-10

COBWEB MOTION WITH RIGID EXCHANGE

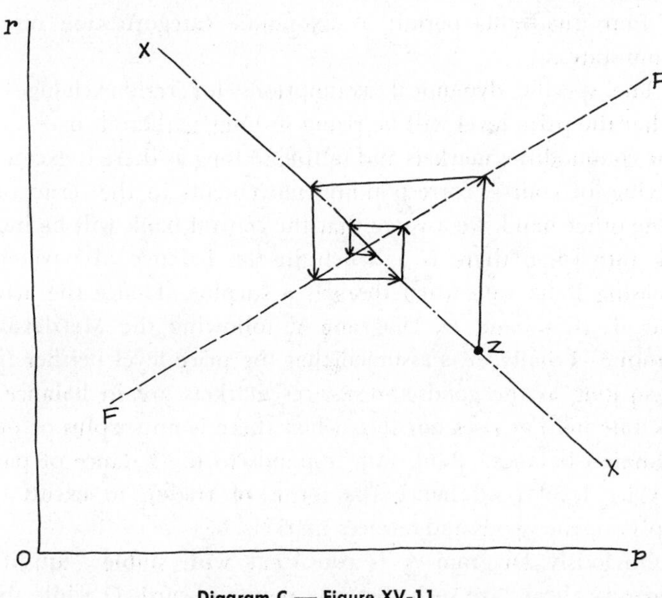

Diagram C — Figure XV-11

COBWEB MOTION WITH FLEXIBLE EXCHANGE

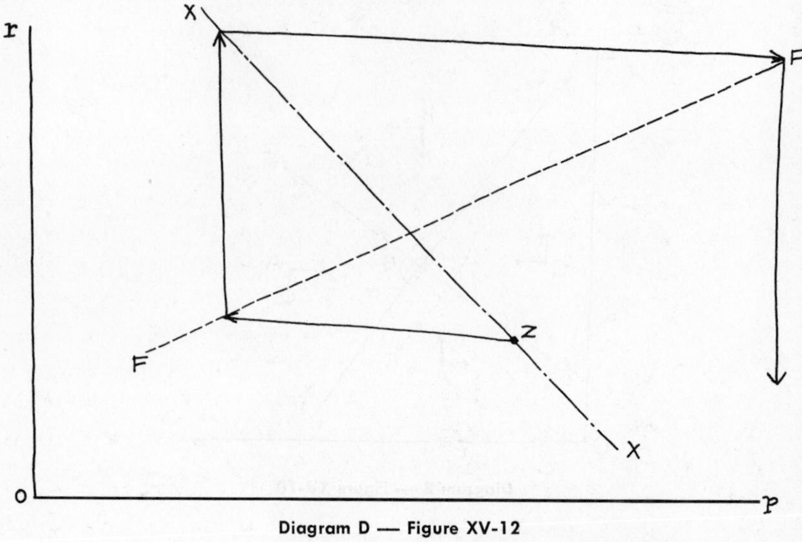

Diagram D — Figure XV-12

surplus in the foreign balance; excess demand for goods and services. Point *D*: deficit in the former, excess demand in the latter market. The four quadrants permit a taxonomic categorization of disequilibrium states.

The specific dynamical assumptions for rigid-exchange systems are that the price level will be rising so long as there is excess demand in the commodities markets and falling so long as there is excess supply, implying, of course, corresponding movements in the terms of trade. On the other hand, we assume that the central bank will be increasing Bank rate when there is a deficit in the balance of payments and decreasing Bank rate when there is a surplus. Hence the arrows for points *A, B, C,* and *D,* Diagram A, following the Metzler-Patinkin technique. Finally, it is assumed that the price level neither rises nor falls so long as the goods-and-services markets are in balance, whilst Bank rate neither rises nor falls when there is no surplus or deficit in the foreign balance. Bank rate responds to the balance of payments, the price level (and hence the terms of trade), to excess demand (supply) in the goods-and-services markets.

Obviously Diagram A is consistent with stable "equilibrium": the arrows always are such that one points towards *Q* while the other suggests a circular motion around it. Consider the initial point *Z*, lying in Quadrant *D*. The price level and Bank rate will both be increasing, leading to a resultant force taking the system to the *XX* curve. Once the *XX* curve is reached, the price level will cease to rise, but interest rates will continue to increase. There will be deflationary pressure in goods-and-services markets; we quickly pass into Quadrant *A*. Interest rates continue to rise, but prices fall. The resultant vector leads us towards *FF*. Once we reach *FF*, interest rates will cease to rise, but prices continue to fall, leading to surplus in the balance of payments, declining interest rates, etc. The process is described by the dashed lines of Diagram A.

Turn now to the flexible-exchange system described in Diagram B. The dynamical assumptions are different: the central bank manipulates Bank rate with an eye towards internal rather than external balance, while terms-of-trade movements are dominated by the state of the foreign balance. The central bank achieves autonomy by virtue of being able to rely upon the foreign-exchange market to correct external imbalance.[18] Accordingly, the terms of trade improve when there is a surplus on foreign account and deteriorate when there is a deficit. Bank rate rises when there is excess demand in goods-and-services markets and falls when there is excess supply. Bank rate is steady when we are on the *XX* curve; the time-rate of change of the terms of trade is zero when we are on the *FF* curve. Hence the arrows of Diagram B.

Diagram B also is consistent with stable equilibrium: one of the arrows always is pointing towards *Q*, while the other describes a cyclical course. On the other hand, the dashed line of Diagram B shows that the adjustment path will be very different. Starting again at *Z*, interest rates rise as before: there is excess demand for goods and services. But the trade deficit leads to deterioration of the terms of trade. The system heads in a clockwise fashion towards the *FF* curve. Interest rates will continue to rise once the *FF* curve is attained, forcing the system to the *XX* curve but producing a surplus in the foreign balance. . . . Mundell carries out a number of interesting analyses,

18 External imbalance here is defined as a state in which there is excess demand, positive or negative, in the foreign-exchange market. Existence of external imbalance over any finite interval in a flexible-exchange system will lead to unintended change in short-term foreign assets held by us and/or short-term American assets held by foreigners. (Needless to say, "liabilities" can be substituted for "assets" as the word appears.)

all showing that the dynamics of alternative mechanisms of international adjustment can be very different, although stability properties *might* be the same.

Diagrams C and D are designed to show that identical sets of *FF-XX* curves might be consistent with the stability of, say, a fixed-exchange system but inconsistent with that of a flexible-exchange system and *vice versa*. Implicit in these diagrams are the crude "dynamics" of earlier analysis of Hicks's monetary theory of the trade cycle: lagged adjustment is postulated, permitting us to be on one or the other of the curves. Taking up Diagram C (rigid exchange), if we begin in period *0* at point *Z*, Bank rate will be increased in period *0* so that reaction during period *1* puts the system on the *FF* curve. However, higher Bank rate leads to deflationary developments in markets for goods and services. Prices will fall during period *1*, putting the goods-and-services markets back into balance in period *2*, but producing a surplus in the balance of payments. Bank rate falls in period *2*, balancing the foreign account in period *3* but inducing inflationary pressure in domestic markets, etc. Bank rate responds to current imbalance in the balance of payments but has its impact only after a lag of one period. The domestic price level similarly responds to excess demand (supply) in goods-and-services markets; it also is lagged one period in its impact. Recalling that the system has been rigged in the interests of diagrammatic simplicity so that we stay on one or the other of the curves, we find that the system of Diagram C is stable.

FF and *XX* have precisely the same slopes in Diagram D as in Diagram C, but the dynamical process differs: Bank rate responds to domestic phenomena whilst the terms of trade respond to the foreign balance. Again starting at point *Z*, the terms of trade deteriorate enough in period *0* to correct the deficit in the balance of payments, but the resulting increase in exports leads to inflation in domestic markets and higher interest rates in period *1*. In period *2*, Bank rate increases *and* there is deterioration in the balance of payments, etc.[19] Diagram D shows that the system is unstable when operated under (our admittedly odd) flexible-exchange rules. It is not hard to see what Mundell means when he writes:

[19] The cobweb models might more comfortably deal with administered prices in the rigid-exchange case and officially-determined but "flexible" exchange rates in the other case.

> ". . . The dynamical differences between the two systems are based on an inversion of the roles, in the dynamic adjustment process, of the terms of trade and the rate of interest. In the fixed exchange system money income (the price level) moves to equilibrate the market for domestic goods and services, and monetary policy is directed at the requirements of the foreign balance; but in the flexible exchange system the rate of exchange moves to correct external disequilibrium, and monetary policy aims at the goal of internal stabilization. These dynamical dissimilarities have important implications for economic policy . . . [O]ne system may work well (dynamically) under one set of static parameters and speeds of adjustment, but badly under another . . ."[20]

2

We turn to a broad informal discussion of forces affecting stability of exchange (noting that Section C stole some of Section D's thunder). It is generally agreed that there are three basic mechanisms that might operate to correct adverse balances of payments, whether the context be fixed- or flexible-exchange: 1) changes in the terms of trade; 2) changes in interest rates; 3) changes in real income leading to income effects on demand for imported goods.

The last mechanism will be taken up in Sections E and F and can be dismissed in Section D with a brief comment: if official response to adverse balances of payments either does not dampen deflationary effects of specie outflow or positively abets them, it can be expected that, in addition to adjustments already considered, lower real income in deficit countries, together with higher real income in surplus countries accepting inflationary pressure, will lead to reduced demand for imports, *cet. par.*, in the former countries and to increased demand for imports, *cet. par.*, in the latter. This mechanism might stabilize otherwise volatile systems.[21]

We are familiar with Bank rate as a means of correcting imbalance of payments. Recall the crisis in Britain in summer 1961: the authorities imposed 7 per cent Bank rate; there was dramatic improvement in capital-account items in the British balance of payments; Bank rate was reduced to 6 per cent by the middle of November 1961. If there is a good deal of uncovered "hot money" sensitive to differentials in money-market rates between international centers, rising interest rates in countries experiencing specie outflow and falling rates in countries

20 Robert A. Mundell, *loc. cit.*, p. 228. Bear in mind that only two of a large number of Mundell's cases have been treated.

21 Obviously, the assumption of full employment is relaxed.

experiencing specie inflow can comprise an important short-term adjustment mechanism. The short run can be crucial for problems of destabilizing speculation and the like: British experience repeatedly has shown that timely and drastic increases in Bank rate, making it dramatically clear that the authorities intend to "defend the pound," can stamp out speculation based on anticipated devaluation; once devaluation can be ignored differential interest rates can lead to larger movements of hot money, since foreign investors cease to worry about capital losses on reconversion.[22]

Price elasticities of demand and supply can apply to the functioning either of the specie-flow or flexible-exchange mechanisms. There follows a verbal treatment of effects of various combinations of demand and supply elasticities on prospects for exchange depreciation or specie loss for correction of deficits in balances of payments. Ultimately a few algebraic formulas are provided to help explain the "verbal" results.

We use the symbols η_x and η_j for price elasticities of demand for our exports and imports; σ_x and σ_j for price elasticities of supply. Now consider some elasticity combinations.

a) High η_x and η_j, Alternative σ's

If we devalue, and if price elasticity of demand for our exports exceeds unity in absolute value, improvement in our balance of payments is facilitated if the elasticity of supply of our exports is high. Given $|\eta_x|>1$, $\sigma_x = \infty$ would be ideal. Increasing supply prices would lead to less revenues than could be earned if supply prices were constant. Total revenue increases with lower prices so long as $|\eta_x|>1$.

If we devalue, and if price elasticity of demand for our imports exceeds unity in absolute value, improvement in our balance of payments is facilitated if elasticity of supply of imported goods is high. Remember that an effect of our devaluation is to reduce a foreign exporter's proceeds (in terms of his own currency) from a given dollar yield. Thus, if foreigners were to insist upon their established yield per unit in terms of their own currency, the price of our imports would increase by the proportion of currency depreciation; foreign exporters would earn fewer dollars. On the other hand, if foreign supply were perfectly inelastic, there would be no reduction in the

[22] Implying imperfection or thinness in the forward-exchange market. Alternatively, fear of devaluation can lead to a currency selling forward far below its interest parity. *Cf.* Appendix C to Ch. VA.

foreign dollar take, at least not under crude partial-equilibrium assumptions.

b) Low η's, Alternative σ's

If $|\eta_x| < 1$, it is desirable from a balance-of-payments point of view that σ_x be as low as possible. Thus, if $\sigma_x = 0$, we will continue to offer the same quantity of exports as before, "maximizing" foreign demand for dollars:[23] demand prices (in dollars) for our exports will increase as a result of devaluation unless $\eta_x = 0$, but, still, marginal revenue will be negative for the American export-goods industry.

If $|\eta_j| < 1$, σ_j should be as low as possible: when our demand for foreign goods is inelastic, balance-of-payments considerations make us hope that foreigners will try to sell as much as possible: the more they put on the American market, the less will be their total revenue; marginal revenue is negative when demand is inelastic. Since devaluation of our currency in terms of foreign currency leads to foreign exporters realizing less in terms of their own currency from sales at given dollar prices, inelastic foreign supply (low σ_j's) means that foreign supply will be little reduced in the new equilibration of the market for American importables. If foreign supply were highly elastic, there might be large reduction in the quantity offered in the United States as a result of a moderate devaluation of the dollar: devaluation would cause foreign exporters to cut-back supply just as a foreign cartel would *choose* to do.

3

Words, words, words! If you thirst for headier wine, try this (referring to a two-country model):

> "If the discrepancy between exports and imports is small, relative to the total value of foreign trade, it can easily be shown that a devaluation of the currency of either country in the proportion K will bring about a change, positive or negative, in that country's balance of payments on current account, which has the following value, relative to the value of exports
>
> $$K\left[\frac{\eta_1\eta_2(1+e_1+e_2)+e_1e_2(\eta_1+\eta_2-1)}{(\eta_1+e_2)(\eta_2+e_1)}\right]$$

23 We assume that the various industries are competitively organized and do not exploit potential monopolistic or monopsonistic power. To penetrate this subject is to enter the forbidden realm of scientific tariffs, beggar-my-neighbor policies, reciprocal demand curves, etc.

> . . . [The η's are demand elasticities and the e's supply elasticities] . . . The foreign exchange market is obviously unstable unless the expression in the brackets is positive, for exchange stability requires that depreciation must increase a country's net supply of foreign exchange." (Lloyd A. Metzler, *loc. cit.,* footnote 4.)

The algebra for the case, $e_1 = e_2 = \infty$ is easier. Assuming that prices for imports are parametric for both countries — that supply elasticities are indefinitely large — the condition for exchange stability in Metzler's special case is the Marshall-Lerner condition: the sum of the absolute values of the demand elasticities, $\eta_x + \eta_j$, should exceed unity. This result, worked out in Note B, is heuristically appealing: if foreign demand for our exports were "zero elastic," it would follow that a 1 per cent devaluation would reduce our take of foreign currency by 1 per cent: foreign demand for dollar goods would be unchanged. Unless our demand for foreign goods — now 1 per cent more expensive — falls 1 per cent (reducing our demand for foreign currency by 1 per cent), the deficit in our balance of payments will increase. If $\eta_j = -1$, our demand for imports will fall 1 per cent. $|\eta_j| + |\eta_x|$ must exceed unity for stability. Alternatively, assume that foreign demand for our goods is of elasticity —0.5, implying that a one-per cent devaluation will result in a 0.5 per cent decrease in supply of foreign currency seeking dollars (dollar prices remaining the same throughout). If our foreign balance on current account is not to deteriorate further, Americans must reduce their demand for foreign goods by at least 0.5 per cent. (*See Note B.*)

E. FOREIGN-TRADE MULTIPLIERS

1

Sections E and F, dealing with foreign-trade multipliers and with the transfer problem, are modest in purpose. It is wished merely to outline the functioning of yet another engine of international adjustment: effects of changes in national income. It is indicated *en passant* that multipliers calculated for open and closed systems are not the same. The "matrix multipliers" of Section E indeed have many applications. Recall our analysis of member-bank coefficients of expansion. One application of Section E's technique is found in analysis of the transfer problem, in turn concerned with such matters as reparations payments, amortization and interest charges on debts owed abroad, etc.

The literature on the topics of Sections E and F is voluminous, much of it being of very high quality. Note C gives a few references and is intended to expiate sins of omission and commission.

The central theme of Section E is simple: mechanisms of adjustment of the balance of payments thus far considered (price-level, exchange-rate, and Bank-rate changes) have not accounted for possible impact of changes in national income induced by reaction to the balance of payments. Of course, changes in income lead to changes in demand for imports in the general case.

"Income effects" are isolated in that changes in price levels and interest rates are ignored. We manipulate a model much akin to those of Ch. IX. The adequacy of this "Keynesian" adjustment mechanism, if it bears the whole burden, is the topic of Section F.

Do not denigrate the theme of Section E because of its simplicity. It was shown as early as Ch. II that balance-of-payments deficits lead to restrictive monetary effects in international-gold-standard systems. Economies on flexible exchange also would tighten money if there were persistent excess supply of their currencies. (*Cf.* footnote 18.) Thus, it is likely that balance-of-payments difficulties will lead to national policies inducing unemployment and/or slackened rates of economic growth. Indeed, this was the main burden of Keynes's work in the 1920's. By the same token, countries with surpluses in their balances of payments can afford to adopt laxer monetary policies. And to the extent that its surplus is generated by strengthened autonomous demand for its exports, there is a direct real force pushing a country's output nearer to full employment levels and encouraging higher growth rates through acceleration effects. After all, there is *some* slack in almost any economy at a point in time.

2

A number of "corollaries" should be appended to the "central theme" of Section E:

1) If marginal propensities to import ($\partial J/\partial Y$ terms) are small, the mechanism of Section E will be of little importance, and *vice versa* if marginal propensities to import are large.

2) If multipliers are small in isolation, adjustment through income effects will be less powerful than if isolated multipliers are large.

This implies that the "new" mechanism is aided by there being a potential for what usually is considered undesirable volatility of national incomes.

3) Participation in an international community can either increase or decrease volatility of individual economies. Thus "a country which would be unstable when left to itself may be perfectly stable in a two-economy world because of the dampening influence of low propensities in the other country."[24]

4) In countries such as Norway and, to a lesser extent, Britain, where a large portion of costs of production is accounted for by imported goods, marginal propensities to import can be large even if consumers have small marginal propensities to import out of disposable income. This suggests a qualification to balance-of-payments adjustment through exchange-rate or price-level movements: if imports bulk large as inputs, exchange depreciation tends, on this account, to increase costs of production (and prices) in the deficit country, reducing costs of production (and prices) in the surplus country.

5) Adjustment through income effects definitely was known before Keynesian economics.

6) Results of empirical work on the efficacy of various mechanisms of international adjustment have been mixed. It does appear, however, that recent work on foreign-trade price elasticities of demand and supply has yielded higher estimates than had earlier work.

3

We turn to models of international systems patterned after the models of Ch. IX. The subsection is devoted to mechanics, but its results have important implications for the transfer problem. We confine ourselves to two-country systems, basing our analysis on Jaroslav Vanek's Appendix (E) to C. P. Kindleberger, *International Economics* (pp. 613-616). Vanek writes the basic income relations as

$$Y_a = C_a + G_a + I_a + J_b + \beta, \tag{1}$$

$$Y_b = C_b + G_b + I_b + J_a - \lambda\beta. \tag{2}$$

The symbols have their customary connotations, G_a and G_b referring to government expenditures on goods and services. A's exports are B's imports and *vice versa.* β is a shift parameter, "a parameter expressing a parallel shift in any one of the expenditure schedules." (*Ibid.*, p. 613.) λ is "an arbitrary constant relating a shift in spending in B to a shift in A." (*Ibid.*, p. 613.) Thus, if $\lambda = 1$, a $100 increase in

[24] L. A. Metzler, "Underemployment Equilibrium in International Trade," *loc. cit.*, p. 103.

exogenous expenditure in A will lead to a \$100 decrease in B. (Prices are assumed constant throughout the analysis.)

The multiplier relation of interest relates Y_j^* and β. β is assumed to be zero in some "initial equilibrium." The analysis is that of comparative statics, relating the change in the solution value for national income in the *jth* country with a shift in β from its initial zero value. Ignoring Country B's solution in what is a symmetrical analysis, we become concerned with $\partial Y_a^*/\partial \beta$. The general derivation (*cf.* Note D) is awesomely complex, but a simpler expression can be derived if one makes the following assumptions:

1) $\lambda = 0$; exogenous shifts in the two countries are unrelated;

2) investment and government spending are autonomous in both countries; $\partial I_j/\partial Y_j = \partial G_j/\partial Y_j = 0$;

3) both countries are stable in isolation. This means that aggregate marginal propensities to spend are less than unity in both countries.

Having made these assumptions, we can derive Equation 3. (*See Note D.*)

$$(3) \qquad \partial Y_a/\partial \beta = \frac{1 + m_b/s_b}{m_a + s_a + m_b\ (s_a/s_b)}\ .$$

Still a bit cumbersome, but interesting things can be learned by plugging in various combinations of parameters.

Assume first that the propensity to save is 0.1 in both countries, the propensity to consume domestic goods 0.8, and the propensity to import 0.1. In isolation these countries would have multipliers of 10 (shoving *m* into *c*). The foreign trade multipliers — the investment multipliers in the open system — are 6.7. This accords with Ch. XI. When foreign trade was introduced (imports being endogenous, exports exogenous), multipliers fell: the propensity to import was dampening.

It is one thing to say that opening of economic systems might reduce investment multipliers, and another to deny that expansionary and depressive impulses are carried from one economy to another. The latter assertion would be false. Thus Western Europe shivered in its collective boots during the 1950's lest the United States suffer a severe and prolonged depression. Europe feared that America would be an economic Typhoid Mary — despite the fact that multipliers in each country undoubtedly were lower because of the impact of international trade. Open systems have that many more sources of disturbance than do closed systems.

Now assume that $s_a = 0.4$, $s_b = 0.1$, $m_a = 0.1$, $m_b = 0.3$. The investment multiplier for A in isolation is 2.5. If we introduce foreign trade but ignore the impact of A on B (so that A's exports are exogenous), A's multiplier falls to 2.0. On the other hand, when B's large propensity to import is considered, A's multiplier becomes 2.4: opening the system decreases the multiplier by very little.

Finally assume that $s_a = 0.6$, $s_b = 0.1$, $m_a = 0.1$, $m_b = 0.8$. In isolation A's multiplier is 1.67, but, when trade is introduced and B's huge propensity to import accounted for, A's multiplier increases to about 1.8. Effects on B's imports of changes in autonomous spending in A (effects brought about by a changed solution value for Y_b) overcome the additional leakage factor (m_a). A not only becomes subject to consequences of autonomous changes in B but now is more sensitive to *its own* autonomous shifts.

F. THE TRANSFER PROBLEM

1

Consider the plight of Country A. It might have acquired a large foreign debt during its development, or it might be a country such as France in 1871 or Germany in 1919: a war loser forced to issue IOU's on which amortization and interest charges are incurred. Country A must acquire substantial sums of foreign currency each period in order to meet these charges (payable only in foreign currency). Country A's problems would not interest us if it had large stocks of gold that could be sent abroad without difficulty. We do not deign to soil our hands with so unworthy a challenge. We concentrate on countries that *must* sustain transfers of foreign currency each period through development of a favorable balance of payments. Germany *circa* the 1920's fits the bill. Much of the transfer-problem literature was stimulated by German reparations issues. (*Cf.* the Keynes and Ohlin citations of Note C.)

Why should there be a transfer *problem*? Recall Sections C and D. Acceptable changes in the terms of trade may not be able to achieve the necessary favorable balance of payments. Of course, Country A might be able to attract sufficient capital inflow through high interest rates to meet reparations payments (interpretable as capital outflow — reduction in claims against A held by foreigners). In fact there were large Allied loans to Germany during the 1920's. But to meet debt-service problems by acquiring more debts is to risk the Wrath of God, who often is held to believe in balanced budgets. Not only does such a "solution" merely postpone the way of reckoning; it is intellectually uninteresting. Somehow, some day, the means have to be found to transfer foreign currency to foreign creditors.

Perhaps only one avenue will remain: development of a favorable foreign balance through "income effects." If Country A were to contract its growth rate or incur actual decreases in output while Country B stepped up its rate of growth or at least continued to realize absolute increases in output, and if marginal propensities to import were high enough and foreign trade important enough, this addition to A's crown of thorns (B's laurels) might make possible a sufficiently favorable balance on current account for A to meet its transfer requirements. It is as simple as that.

2

One not-so-simple task remains: what relationships must there be between such parameters as marginal propensities to consume domestic goods, to import, to save, etc. for an initial transfer of $X from A to B (a dollar country) to set off a train of events improving A's balance of payments by $X or more, permitting A to transfer $X to B next period, recouping the dollars for the period after next, etc.?[25]

Notice that we have posed a rather artificial problem. Income effects have been restricted. We could simply have required A to adopt a set of domestic policies leading to contraction of its national product and have inquired whether a given set could create enough improvement in A's balance of payments to meet transfer obligations. If not, we could try still more drastic contraction in A and/or expansion in B. It is intuitively clear that, if A turns itself into a Wasteland while B becomes a nation of Sybarites fond of the delicacies concocted by A's groaning masses, A should be able to achieve a highly "favorable" balance of payments. . . . The transfer problem belongs to the realm of theoretical speculation. Still it permits exercise of matrix multipliers and other esoterica of Ch. XV.

25 Alternatively, the flow rate given by A's surplus in its balance of payments would exactly offset that specified for dollar transfer to B (Transfers are excluded from the balance of payments in this calculation.)

3

Our exposition is based on Harry G. Johnson, "The Transfer Problem and Exchange Stability," acknowledging the importance of Metzler's classic article and the work of Machlup and Meade cited in Note C.[26] Johnson makes the standard assumptions for analysis of a purely-Keynesian transfer problem: perfectly elastic domestic supplies of goods at fixed price levels "so that output, income, and employment are determined by the aggregate demand for output"; "it is also assumed that each country fixes its exchange rate and level of interest rates by appropriate monetary action, . . . and that, apart from accommodating financial transactions between monetary authorities, international capital movements are independent of the levels of national income." These assumptions permit derivation of what Johnson calls "multiplier equations."

$$y_a = i_a + c_a y_a + j_b + m_b y_b \tag{1}$$

$$y_b = i_b + c_b y_b + j_a + m_a y_a \tag{2}$$

$$b_a = j_b + m_b y_b - j_a - m_a y_a - T. \tag{3}$$

All of the arguments are *changes* in variables. i_a is the change in autonomous investment in A; j_b, the change in autonomous imports of B; b_a, the change in A's balance of payments; T, "an autonomous change in capital movements from A to B." The parameters c_a, c_b, m_a, and m_b are fixed throughout. Stability of this system is assured by positive propensities to save in both countries.

The linear system can be solved for its unknowns y_a, y_b, and b_a through determinants, but it is convenient to adjust it:

> "substitute for the various autonomous changes in demands [the *i*'s and *j*'s] . . . the proportions of the transfer [T] by which the [autonomous] demands for domestic and foreign goods are reduced in the transferor and increased in the transferee."[27]

Take account, in other words, of the way in which the initial transfer is to be effected: perhaps A will raise taxes so that its government can run a balanced budget; perhaps it will impose import restrictions; the government of B might lower taxes, remove import restrictions,

---

[26] Harry G. Johnson, *International Trade and Economic Growth* (London: Allen and Unwin, Ltd., 1958), pp. 169-195, esp. pp. 177-181.

[27] *Ibid.*, p. 179.

etc. Hence, substitute m'_aT and m'_bT for the j terms and s'_aT and s'_bT for the i terms. s'_aT — where s'_a is a positive fraction — can be interpreted as the change in the financial assets of citizens of A directly attributable to the transfer. The s'_aT term accounts for the possibility that the transfer is accompanied by forced disgorgement of securities holdings of A citizens. Disgorgement (a capital levy) is interpreted as a negative income item. Following this approach, changes in autonomous investment (i) are ignored. Finally $(1-c_a)$ and $(1-c_b)$ are defined as s_a and s_b.

Johnson reports that the solution value for b_a is

$$(4) \quad b_a = [m'_a + m'_b - (m_a/s_a)\, s'_a - (m_b/s_b)\, s'_b - 1]\ [s_a s_b/\Delta]\, T,$$

where $\Delta = s_a s_b + s_a m_b + s_b m_a$. Since s_a, s_b, m_a, and m_b all are positive, the denominator of the expression $s_a s_b/\Delta$ must exceed the numerator. If an initial transfer is to generate enough of an improvement in the balance of payments to permit a transfer next period of the same amount without dipping into foreign-exchange reserves, it is necessary (but not sufficient) that inequality 5 hold.

$$(5) \qquad m'_a + m'_b \geqslant (m_a/s_a)s'_a + (m_b/s_b)\, s'_b + 1$$

If the inequality holds, the transfer can be overeffected. If the equality holds, it can be just effected. Otherwise, it will be undereffected.

Before continuing, be sure you understand that if, say, the transfer is just effected, and the total sum to be transferred is $10T$, the *entire* procedure, including the reduction in autonomous imports, the capital levy, etc., is to be repeated 10 times in a period analysis. Differences always are measured from values at $t = 0$, the outset of the transfer process.

The m' and s' parameters are crucial. We must know how the demand for importables is affected by what Johnson calls "the financing and disposal of the transfer." If m'_a, m'_b, s'_a, and s'_b all are zero — if autonomous changes in imports and financial assets of the public are independent of the transfer process — the (in)equality cannot hold; the transfer will be undereffected. If m'_a and m'_b are zero and $s'_a = s'_b = 1$ (implying that tax receipts are increased in A and reduced in B by the amount of the transfer), neither the inequality nor the equality can hold; the requirement would now become

$$(6) \qquad 0 \geqslant m_a/s_a + m_b/s_b + 1.$$

Since marginal savings and import propensities are positive, it is obvious that (6) cannot hold.

4

Johnson's formulation offers a richer variety of outcomes than do narrower formulations; release of s'_a and s'_b from the one-or-zero bind is the lever. It reminds us that it always might be possible to make A poor enough and B rich enough to effect a transfer from A to B.

None of the contributors to the transfer-problem literature seems to have given much thought to capitalization by citizens of their share of government assets and liabilities. In that event the s' terms are definitionally zero. The consumption functions employed have been primitive as, for that matter, have the other structural specifications.

Metzler and Machlup took the s' terms to be either *0 or 1* and the m' terms to be *0*. Thus, they found that transfer would be undereffected whenever the global system was stable.

Finally, Johnson suggests that we take $m' = m$ and $s' = s$ for both countries. This is to assume that autonomous imports will be affected in the same way as induced imports when transfer payments are financed by levies on accumulated savings. Assuming positive marginal propensities to save, the transfer must be undereffected, since Equation 4 becomes

$$b_a = -\frac{s_a s_b}{\Delta} T. \tag{7}$$

b_a must be negative. (*See Note E.*)

SUMMARY

1. Chapter XV stressed impingement of international considerations on the autonomy of national authorities. *Roughly,* exchange-rate rigidity requires that authorities accept price levels and interest rates consistent with external considerations while autonomy over prices and/or interest rates requires acceptance of foreign exchange rates consistent with external considerations. (*Cf.* Introduction to Part III for important qualifications.)
2. The traditional mechanism of adjustment of international gold standards — a class of fixed-exchange-rate systems — is based on

specie flows leading to monetary expansions in "surplus" countries and monetary contraction in "deficit" countries. Of course, in equilibrium, specie flows are nil.

3. Often, countries with favorable balances of payments have been unwilling to accept inflationary consequences, placing the entire strain of adjustment on "deficit" countries.

4. Under international gold standards, Country A is affected by monetary and output phenomena in Countries B, C, . . . This point is emphasized in Sections E and F dealing with foreign-trade (matrix) multipliers and the transfer problem.

5. It was possible in Chapters XIV and XV to mould international systems into Walrasian models with real solution states invariant against initial distribution of assets, nominal quantities of money, etc.

6. Putting aside effects of specie flows on national income, stable but sluggish response of merchandise balances of payments to domestic-price-level changes places a heavier burden on generation of surpluses on capital account through high interest rates. Chapters II, VB, and VC showed that traditional Bank-rate policy has been employed in Britain for rather more than a century in correcting short-term external imbalance. Also that "hot money" movements create possibilities for new, and perhaps more serious, crises upon withdrawal of these sensitive funds. This is a major topic for discussion in Ch. XVI.

7. In the 1920's, Keynes stressed the deflationary potential of Britain's choice to "return to gold" at the *ante bellum* price. One consequence was enforcement of high interest rates during sluggish trade. Horsley Palmer frankly accepted such policies during the 19th century.

8. Sections E and F concerned "income effects" as mechanisms for adjusting the balance of payments. Although the analytics of foreign-trade (matrix) multipliers are somewhat formidable, their essence is found in the problems of the wasted vanquished nation toiling as did the ancient Israelites in Egyptian bondage, producing delicacies pleasing to the Sybaritic victors.

9. In general, opening of hitherto closed economies reduced investment multipliers but exposes these economies to more sources of perturbation. The quantitative importance of exposure to ex-

ternal disturbance depends in part on the importance of foreign trade items in national income accounts, marginal propensities to import, the importance of foreign inputs in production processes, propensities to save, etc.

10. Somewhat paradoxically, success of national-income-stabilization policies decommission foreign-trade-multiplier processes as means for rectifying disequilibria in balances of payments.
11. Economies wishing to maintain autarchical control of price levels, interest rates, levels and rates of growth of national product, etc. must rely on flexible exchange for correction of "long run" disequilibrium in the foreign-exchange market. Shorter-run disturbances might be accommodated through buffer stocks of internationally-liquid assets. More on this in Ch. XVI.
12. The theory of stability of exchange is substantially the same for fixed and flexible exchange. However, as Mundell showed, paths of adjustment might be very different even if static solutions are identical. Indeed identical "statical" parameters might be consistent with stability in one case and not in the other.
13. Under flexible exchange the terms of trade are dominated by conditions in the foreign-exchange market and interest rates (at least in the short run) by the state of the domestic markets for goods and services. Under fixed exchange terms of trade are dominated by domestic markets and interest rates (at least in the short run) by the state of the balance of payments.
14. There are important differences between systems of truly flexible exchange and systems in which exchange rates are fixed subject to sporadic official intervention. Friedman argues that, since maladjustment is apt to be pronounced before official action is taken, systems featured by sporadic revaluation tend to have poorer stability properties.
15. Ch. XV barely touched on the important and difficult problem of destabilizing speculation under flexible exchange.
16. The transfer problem — the problem of effecting systematic transfers of foreign exchange without relying on buffer stocks — was treated as a problem of adjustment of foreign balances through Keynesian (income) mechanisms. "Classical" adjustment mechanisms were abstracted from. Prospects for self-sustaining transfer processes depend not only on propensities to import and

to save but on responses by paying and receiving governments to transfers. In special cases analysed by Metzler and Machlup transfers were shown to be undereffected in two-country models in which each country was stable in isolation.

17. No attempt was made to deal formally with a model in which all of the mechanisms of adjustment of balances of payments operated at once.

NOTES

NOTE A: Consider effects of a neutral increase in liquidity preference in Country B. Price levels must fall in both countries with p_a^*/p_b^* unchanged. This can be accomplished by reducing the money stock and price level in Country A in the same proportion, while increasing the money stock of Country B until its citizens are satisfied with the new level of real balances — recalling that p_b must fall with p_a. This table might apply:

CHANGE IN LIQUIDITY PREFERENCE

	p_a	p_b	G_a	G_b
$t = 0$	100	1000	1000	1000
$t = 1$	50	500	500	1500

TABLE XV-IV

It always is possible to find values for gold stocks and prices satisfying the aggregate-gold and relative-price constraints and consistent with any values for real balances the model calls for. Thus,

(i) $$p_a = k_1 p_b$$

(ii) $$G_b/p_b = k_2$$

(iii) $$G_a/p_a = k_3$$

(iv) $$G_a + G_b = \overline{G}$$

The system *i-iv* can be solved for G_a, G_b, p_a, and p_b.

NOTE B: You might prefer to say that, since foreigners will demand 0.5 per cent more in American goods, foreign demand for dollars increases by 0.5 per cent, although foreigners reduce their total offer of their own currency by 0.5 per cent. (Each dollar is 1 per cent cheaper in terms of foreign currency.) If elasticity of American demand for foreign goods is at least as negative as —0.5, the supply of dollars seeking foreign currency will not increase by more than 0.5 per cent — again keeping in mind that each unit of foreign currency commands 1 per cent more dollars.

For a good derivation of the Marshall-Lerner condition, *cf.* Egon Sohmen's Appendix D to Charles P. Kindelberger, *International Economics,* pp. 610-612. Following Sohmen:

a) Define the balance of payments in terms of foreign currency,

$$B \equiv f(\bar{P}_x/r) \cdot (\bar{P}_x/r) - g(r\bar{p}_m) \cdot \bar{p}_m, \tag{1}$$

where $\bar{P}_x$ is the given United States price for exported goods, r the exchange rate, expressed as the number of units of domestic currency paid per unit of foreign currency, and $\bar{p}_m$, the price of our imports, expressed in the foreign measure. Thus, the price of our goods in terms of foreign currency (and indirectly the foreign measure) is given by $\bar{P}_x/r$, so that American receipts of foreign currency are given by the product

$$(X)(\bar{P}_x/r)$$

where

$$X \equiv f(\bar{P}_x/r).$$

American payments in foreign currency are expressed by the product

$$(J)(\bar{p}_m)$$

where

$$J \equiv g(r\bar{p}_m).$$

b) Differentiate the balance of payments, B, with respect to r (working, of course, with small changes in r):

$$dB/dr \equiv f'(\quad)\left[(-\bar{P}_x/r^2)(\bar{P}_x/r)\right] + X(-\bar{P}_x/r^2) - g'(\quad)[\bar{p}_m{}^2] \tag{2}$$

c) Hack through some algebraic manipulation (described by Sohmen at p. 611), so that Equation 3 applies if Giffen goods can be excluded

$$dB/dr \equiv X(\bar{P}_x/r^2)[\eta_x - 1] + \frac{J\bar{p}_m\eta_m}{r} \tag{3}$$

where η_x and η_m are absolute values for elasticities of demand for our exports and imports.

d) After some additional machete work, we are able to obtain the condition for exchange depreciation (increasing r) improving the balance of payment, namely that $dB/dr > 0$,

$$(V_x/V_j)\eta_x + \eta_m > 1 \tag{4}$$

where V_x and V_j are initial values for our exports and imports expressed in the foreign measure.

If trade were balanced to begin with, the familiar Marshall-Lerner condition

$$\Sigma\eta_i > 1$$

emerges. But if there is an initial deficit in the balance of payments, "a [small] devaluation [can] still result in an improvement even if the sum of the demand elasticities falls below unity. The permissible deficiency depends on the size of the trade deficit . . ." (*Ibid.*, p. 612.)

NOTE C: Charles P. Kindelberger, *International Economics,* is a good general reference.

On the foreign-trade multiplier, see Lloyd A. Metzler, "Underemployment Equilibrium in International Trade," *Econometrica,* Vol. 10, April 1942, pp. 97-112; Fritz Machlup, *International Trade and the National Income Multiplier* (Philadelphia: Blakiston, 1950); J. E. Meade, *The Balance of Payments* (London: Oxford University Press, 1952), pp. 99-148, esp. pp. 125-148; R. Robinson, "A Graphical Analysis of the Foreign Trade Multiplier," *Economic Journal,*

September 1952; A. G. Hart and P. G. Kenen, *Money, Debt, and Economic Activity*, pp. 323-342.

A few important references on the transfer problem are J. M. Keynes, "The German Transfer Problem," reprinted in Ellis and Metzler (eds.), *Readings in the Theory of International Trade* (Philadelphia: Blakiston, 1949), pp. 161-169; Bertil Ohlin, "The Reparation Problem: A Discussion," *loc. cit.*, pp. 170-178; Lloyd A. Metzler, "The Transfer Problem Reconsidered," *loc. cit.*, pp. 179-197; Fritz Machlup, *op. cit.*, Ch. IX; Gottfried von Haberler, *The Theory of International Trade* (London: William Hodge and Co., 1936), pp. 63-117; Paul A. Samuelson, "The Transfer Problem and Transfer Costs," *Economic Journal*, Vol. 62, June 1952, pp. 278-304 and Vol. 64, June 1954, pp. 264-289; Harry G. Johnson, *International Trade and Economic Growth*, pp. 169-195.

Harry G. Johnson, *loc. cit.*, pp. 196-199, offers an excellent synoptic statement under the title, "A Simplification of Multi-Country Multiplier Theory." The title is misleading.

NOTE D: This note deals with derivation of more general foreign-trade multiplier relations, and with propositions about stability owing to Metzler. Professor Metzler's contributions in this area obviously are profound.

1

Following Vanek, differentiate Equations 1 and 2 totally with respect to β. Detailing the operations on Equation 1 (p. 826),

(i) $dY_a = c_a(\partial Y_a/\partial\beta)d\beta + g_a(\partial Y_a/\partial\beta)\,d\beta + i_a(\partial Y_a/\partial\beta)d\beta + m_b(\partial Y_b/\partial\beta)d\beta + d\beta$

or

(ii) $$dY_a(1-c_a-g_a-i_a) = m_b dY_b + d\beta,$$

noting that $dY = (\partial Y/\partial\beta)d\beta$, or

(iii) $$(dY_a/d\beta)(1-c_a-g_a-i_a) = m_b(dY_b/d\beta) + 1$$

(iv) $$(dY_a/d\beta)(\qquad) - m_b\,(dY_b/d\beta) = 1.$$

Similarly, Equation 2 can be differentiated with respect to βm assuring that the second of the income relations will hold in the new "equilibrium." We obtain

(v) $$(dY_a/d\beta)(-m_a) + (1-c_b-g_b-i_b)(dY_b/d\beta) = -\lambda.$$

Equations *iv* and *v* are a pair of simultaneous equations linear in $dY_a/d\beta$ and dY_b/dB, where Y_a and Y_b are solution values for Y_a and Y_b. Vanek's procedure emphasizes calculation of multipliers as part of the process of differentiating equilibrium conditions with respect to parameters, an important process in *On Money*. The solution for $dY_a/d\beta$ is given by

(vi) $$dY_a/d\beta = (1/\Delta[(1-c_b-g_b-i_b)-\lambda m_b]$$

where Δ is the determinant of the coefficient matrix,"

$$\Delta = (1-c_a-g_a-i_a)(1-c_b-g_b\,i_b)-m_a m_b.$$

It is useful to know the special result for $\lambda = 1,\ i = g = 0$ with $1-c = s + m$:

(vii) $$dY_a/d\beta = \frac{1}{[m_a + s_a + m_b\,(s_a/s_b)]}\,.$$

Equation *vii* suggests a possibility that Johnson points out is of great importance in the transfer problem. (*Cf. infra.*)

2

Turn now to certain stability problems, relying on L. A. Metzler, "Underemployment Equilibrium in International Trade," *loc. cit.*, Note 15, p. 100 ff. Metzler's results are based on the dynamic system.

(viii) $C_t = f_1(Y_{t-1}) + {}_2(Y_{t-1})$

(ix) $I_t = f_3(Y_{t-1}) + g_2(Y'_{t-1}) - f_2(Y_{t-1})$

(x) $C_t' = g_1(Y'_{t-1}) + g_2(Y'_{t-1})$

(xi) $I_t' = g_3\,(Y'_{t-1}) + f_2(Y_{t-1}) - g_2(Y'_{t-1})$

Y_t is definitionally equal to $C_t + I_t$, as is Y'_{t-1}, income of the second country, to $C'_t + I'_t$. Consumption in either country is obtained by taking the sum of consumption of domestic goods and of imports. Both elements are functionally dependent upon income, lagged one period. Investment is "divided between net increases in producers' goods and stocks by domestic manufacturers and increases in foreign claims arising out of favorable trade balances." (*Ibid.*, p. 99.) Capital-account transactions are ignored. Domestic investment also is a lagged function of income.

Taking advantage of accounting identities linking the sum of consumption and investment to income, Metzler can rewrite system *viii-xi* as

(xii) $Y_t = f_1(Y_{t-1}) + f_3(Y_{t-1}) + g_3(Y'_{t-1})$

(xiii) $Y'_t = g_1(Y'_{t-1}) + g_3(Y'_{t-1}) + f_2(Y_t)$

Assume that there is a particular solution for system *xii-xiii*, $Y = Y^*$, $Y' = Y'^*$, noting that the system is non-linear. Now consider values for Y and Y' in the neighborhood of (Y^*, Y'^*), defining $Y\text{-}Y^*$ and $Y'\text{-}Y'^*$ as y_t and y'_t. Expand the functions of *xii* and *xiii* by Taylor's Series, neglecting other than first-order terms, the displacements being small. Define $/f_1/\partial Y$ as c;$/g_1/\partial Y'$ as c'. The partials for importation become m and m'; those for investment, v and v'. We obtain Equations *xiv* and *xv*:

(xiv) $y_t = (c+v)y_{t-1} + m'y'_{t-1},$

(xv) $y'_t = (c'+v')y'_{t-1} + my_{t-1}.$

Before considering the very important Equations xiv and xv, Metzler wishes "to consider two other cases with stability conditions somewhat more simple . . ." (p. 101.) The stability condition for a country in isolation, as we saw in discussion of the Hicks cycle model, is

(xvi) $c + v < 1. \qquad (m = 0)$

If trade is opened up, but the second country is so large compared to the first that the first can exert no influence upon it, the stability condition for the small country is given by *xvi*:

> "The size of the marginal propensity to consume foreign goods and hence of the marginal aggregate propensity to consume is immaterial. *Ceteris paribus*, changes in the consumption of foreign-made goods will not affect income in Y [$g_2Y'_{t-1}$, our country's exports, become given data]. Consequently, a very large marginal aggregate propensity to consume is compatible with perfect stability provided only that the marginal propensity to consume domestic goods and the marginal propensity to invest domestically be sufficiently small." (pp. 101-102.)

Returning to the general case, Metzler gives the general solution for the linearized system:

(xvii) $Y_t = Y^* + Ap^t_1 + Bp^t_2$

(xviii) $Y'_t = Y'^* + Cp^t_1 + Dp^t_2$

where p_1 and p_2 are roots of the quadratic equation

$$\begin{vmatrix} (c+v) - p & m' \\ m & (c'+v') - p \end{vmatrix} = 0$$

and where A, B, C, and D are constants determined by initial conditions. Stability of the system requires that the "remainder parts" of Equations *xvii* and *xviii* approach zero as t becomes large, a condition that is fulfilled if p_1 and p_2 are less than unity in absolute value. The "necessary and sufficient conditions for this to be true" are

$$(xx) \qquad c + v + c' + v' < 1 + (c+v)(c'+v') - mm' < 2.$$

Inequalities *xx* permit at least these inferences:

a), as is shown by the $c+v+c'+v' < 2$ condition, at least one of the countries must satisfy Equation *xvi*.

b) supposing this stable economy to be Y', and taking $c' + v = \sigma < 1$, write the first inequality of *xx* as:

$$(xxi) \qquad c + v + \sigma < 1 + \sigma(c+v) - mm'$$

or

$$(xxii) \qquad c + v < (1-\sigma) + \sigma(c+v) - mm'$$

$$(xxiii) \qquad (c+v)(1-\sigma) < (1-\sigma) - mm'$$

$$(xxiv) \qquad c + v < 1 - mm'/(1-\sigma)$$

$$(xxv) \qquad (c + v) + mm'/(1-\sigma) < 1$$

Since $1-\sigma$ must be positive if Country Y' is stable, and since the m's are positive, $c + v$ must be less than unity if the stability condition is to be met. ". . . Stability of the world economy with all reactions considered implies stability of each economy with the reactions of the other ignored," which is to say that each country must be stable on the assumption that the other is very large.

c) "if both countries are stable when isolated the world economy will likewise be stable." (p. 102.)

d) "if both countries are unstable when isolated the world economy will likewise be unstable." (p. 103.)

e) ". . . a country which would be unstable when left to itself may be perfectly stable in a two-economy world because of the dampening influence of low propensities in the other country." (p. 103.)

Opening of the system to trade does not, roughly speaking, increase instability in the *technical* sense of that word (distinguishing between stability and volatility; the system may become more volatile but be stable before and after it is opened to trade).

NOTE E: These are the rudiments of Professor Metzler's appendix to "The Transfer Problem Reconsidered," *loc. cit.*, Note 15, pp. 196-197.

His static system is

$$(i) \qquad Y = C_1(Y) + I(Y) + C'_2(Y') - \beta - \sigma$$

$$(ii) \qquad Y' = C'_1(Y') + I'(Y') + C_2(Y) + \beta' + \sigma$$

$$(iii) \qquad B = C'_2(Y') - C_2(Y)$$

$C_1(Y)$ is to be read "function C_1 of Y." It gives consumption of domestic goods in the first country. The income variables are disposable incomes: β_1 and β_2 are "transfers which affect income directly in the paying [receiving] country only"; σ is a transfer affecting income in both countries in the sense that it is assumed that taxes are adjusted in amounts equal to σ but oppositely in sign.

He then differentiates the static system partially with respect to the parameters β, β', and σ, obtaining, among others, the relation

(iv) $$\partial B/\partial \sigma = 1 - \frac{(1-I_y-C_{1y}-C_{2y})(1-I'_{y}-C'_{1y}-C'_{2y})}{\Delta},$$

I_y is the marginal propensity to invest at the initial equilibrium point.

(v) $$\Delta = (C_{1y} + I_y - 1)(C'_{1y} + I'_y - 1) - C_{2y}C'_{2y}.$$

Assuming that the systems are stable in isolation we know that

$$\frac{(\quad)(\quad)}{\Delta},$$

the right-hand side of *iv,* is positive and that the denominator exceeds the numerator:

(vi) $$0 < \partial B/\partial \sigma < 1.$$

Thus, as Metzler points out in his Table 4, p. 195, *ibid.,* "trade balance moves in favor of [the] paying country by less than the amount of the transfer." His Table 4 also points out that transfers accompanied by tax increases in paying countries equal to the size of the transfer with no tax reduction in receiving countries or tax reductions equal to the size of the transfer in receiving countries with no tax increases in paying countries improve the balance of payments (Metzler's trade balance) of the paying country but not by enough to effect the transfer. (*Cf.* text *supra.*)

CHAPTER SIXTEEN

Some Problems of International Monetary Policy

A. INTERNATIONAL LIQUIDITY

1. The Structure of the System

1

The international economy is composed of units demanding considerable autonomy over internal monetary policies, characterized by sticky or secularly rising wages and prices and unwilling to submit to flexible exchange rates. Referring to measures taken by Britain and other European countries in 1958 to increase the scope of convertibility of their currencies into gold and dollars, Robert Triffin wrote:

> "The reservations and qualifications surrounding the new convertibility decisions make it abundantly clear that no country is prepared to subordinate fully and unilaterally its domestic policy aims and techniques to the maintenance of international balance, and to renounce all recourse to exchange rate adaptations and trade and exchange controls as alternative techniques of balance of payments adjustment."[1]

---

[1] Robert Triffin, *Gold and the Dollar Crisis, Rev. Ed.* (New Haven: Yale University Press, 1961), pp. 18-19. *Cf.* also Robert Triffin, *Europe and the Money Muddle*; W. M. Scammell, *International Economic Policy*; Hart and Kenen, *op. cit.*, p. 343 *ff.*; F. A. Lutz, *International Liquidity* (Princeton: Princeton University Press, 1963).

Obviously, widespread unwillingness to accept the discipline either of the "classical" international gold standard or of flexible exchange can lead to persistent disequilibria in balances of payments. In the absence of physical controls discussed in Section B, large buffer stocks of foreign exchange are required if even short-lived storms are to be ridden out. On the other hand, it is accepted, even today, that *longer range* disturbances must be countered by changes in exchange rates and adjustment of internal policies.

Chapter XVI concentrates on the way in which buffer stocks and more or less direct controls might offset short-run disturbances. Buffer stocks are discussed in Section A, direct controls in Section B. Chapter XVI largely avoids long-term adjustment problems.

2

Let us put into place the backdrop for Section A:

1) changes in exchange rates are frowned upon and, hopefully, avoided;

2) physical controls — especially over merchandise as against "capital" movements — ideally should be avoided;

3) there should be fundamental national autonomy over monetary policies; prices and interest rates should not be sensitive to balances of payments.

Quite an order! It would seem that at least this much must be done:

> Exceptionally large reserves of gold and other internationally liquid assets should be available. These reserves should be easily mobilized and concentrated at trouble spots.

Consult Tables I and II. Table I shows that there has been a steady decrease in "international liquidity": nominal values of gold and foreign-exchange reserves have been falling relative to the volume of international business on current account. Table II suggests what might be a more ominous development: sterling and dollar liabilities have become crucially important as reserve components outside of the United States and the United Kingdom; the postwar international economy is to a large extent on a *gold-exchange* standard. As was explained in Ch. II, a gold-exchange standard finds Country B holding its reserves in the form of A liabilities which in turn are convertible into gold. The effect is to increase pressure on the gold reserves of Country A: disturbance in B affects ultimate re-

RATIO OF MONETARY RESERVES TO ANNUAL IMPORTS, 1913-1957

(in per cent)

	ALL COUNTRIES			ALL COUNTRIES EXCEPT U.S. AND U.K.				
	Total	Gold	For. Exch.	Tot.	Gold	Dollar	Sterling	Other
Including gold in circulation								
1913	39	36	2	35	32			
1928	46	35	11	44	28			
Excluding gold in circulation								
1913	22	19	2	20	17			
1928	43	32	11	42	26			
1932	97	89	8	85	74			
1938	118	110	8	62	51	3	8	
1947	87	61	26	54	19	5	31	
1949	73	55	18	40	16	6	17	
1951	58	42	16	37	15	7	13	1
1953	64	45	19	44	18	11	12	3
1955	58	40	18	42	18	12	10	2
1957	50	35	15	35	16	9	7	2

TABLE XVI-I

Source: Robert Triffin: *Gold and the Dollar Crisis,* Table 3, p. 40.

serves of A. The National Banking System is recalled. Country banks held part of their reserves in the form of deposits with reserve-city and central-reserve-city banks. The big New York banks were in a dangerously vulnerable position. Also, we recall the fallacy of composition implicit in the view that "liquid" bank portfolios aided resistance to internal drains. Pyramided and secondary reserves do not increase *systematic* reserves. Tremendous pressure simply is concentrated on a few spots. If there is a cave-in at a pressure point, the entire system can disintegrate. Triffin puts it well:

> "The basic absurdity of the gold exchange standard is that it makes the *international* monetary system highly dependent on individual countries' decisions about the continued use of one or a few *national* currencies as monetary reserves. In the absence of any widespread doubts about exchange stability, the choice of such currencies as reserves normally falls on the currencies of the countries which play a major role in world trade and finance . . . When doubts about the future stability of exchange rates begin to develop, however, the weaker currencies quickly tend to be eliminated from this competition . . .

SOURCES OF INCREASE IN MONETARY RESERVES OUTSIDE U.S., 1950-1959

TOTAL INCREASE, from	Millions of U. S. Dollars		Percent of Total		1958-1959 Percent of Total	
1. Decrease in U. S. Net Res:		6,851		63		92
a) dec. in Au assets	1,706		16		67	
b) inc. in dollar lia.	5,145		47		24	
2. Inc. in World Gold Res:		3,915		36		26
a) New prod. out. USSR	7,342		67		17	
b) USSR sales	635		6		9	
c) non-mon. absorp.	—4,062		—37			
3. Other		170		1		—18
a) sterling bal.	—1,578		—14		—2	
b) other & errors	1,748		15		—16	
4. Sum		10,396		100		100

TABLE XVI-II

Source: Ibid., Table 11, p. 54 and Table 24, p. 166.

The gold exchange standard *may*, but *does not necessarily*, help in relieving a shortage of world monetary reserves. It does so only to the extent that the key currency countries are willing to let their net reserve position decline through increases in their short-term monetary liabilities unmatched by corresponding increases in their own gross reserves [if the United States acquires gold, it is draining gold from the rest of the world.] If they allow this to happen, however, and to continue indefinitely, they tend to bring about a collapse of the system itself through the gradual weakening of foreigners' confidence in the key currencies."[2]

Table II supports Triffin. It shows that the main source of increase in foreign monetary reserves has been United States gold and United States liabilities. (*See Note A.*) The fact that Americans have purchased even larger quantities of foreign securities over the interval considered is beside the point: American holders of foreign securities

[2] Robert Triffin, *Gold and the Dollar Crisis,* Rev. Ed., p. 67.

can be expected to respond to economic stimuli as do their counterparts abroad; they will not want to switch to dollar securities when the "world" wants to get out of them. If the United States government instigates countervailing sales of foreign securities whenever the dollar is under pressure, world liquidity will be reduced, since foreign authorities will no longer be able to treat dollar holdings as equivalent to gold balances. This line of speculation forces us to recognize that, under an international gold exchange standard, growth of international liquidity can require continuing deficit in the U.S. balance of payments.

3

Time series giving "world monetary reserves" can be highly misleading: the ultimate source of reserves is, as matters stand, gold; the proportion borne by the nominal value of holdings of gold to nominally-valued international transactions has been falling, and in fact has fallen below ratios maintained in the late 1920's, ratios proved to be inadequate in 1930–1931. What are the prospects for growth of the (non-Russian) world's gold stock over the next 10 years? Assuming that gold continues to be valued on the current nominal basis ($35 per ounce), what is likely to be the relationship between the nominal value of gold stocks and that of international transactions? What might be the consequences of continued reduction in what might be termed the international liquidity ratio?

Triffin answers the first two of these questions in Ch. V (p. 47 *ff.*) of *Gold and the Dollar Crisis.* He concludes that, if a physical growth rate of 3 per cent per annum is sustained for trade and if inflation is avoided (always abstracting from revaluation in terms of gold), the likely increase in the monetary gold stock will be only 70 per cent of what is required to maintain the 1957 ratio of gold reserves to annual imports. If the physical growth rate should be as high as 6 per cent, only 27 per cent of the "requirement" will be covered. The answer to the third question would run something like this:

> simple statistical considerations suggest that considerable foreign-exchange pressures can be generated by drawings from Nature's Urn. If buffers are inadequate, and if other mechanisms of adjustment are dispensed with, the international economy, especially "key currency" countries, risks insolvency. The international financial network is apt to be ruptured. There is likely to be resort to various physical controls; barter may replace indirect exchange, a typical consequence of monetary breakdown.

These ghastly prospects are being conjured up rather artificially: the primary adjustment mechanisms of both fixed- and flexible-exchange systems are dispensed with; *we have not considered the role of the International Monetary Fund.* The IMF is an international agency intended to bring about *efficient use of existing monetary reserves.* Perhaps practical disregard of the first portion of §§ 2's prescription is not important; existing reserves may have been and perhaps might be utilized with peculiar efficiency.

4

It might be helpful, having penetrated the heartland of Section A, to integrate discussion of the IMF with what is to follow. The IMF's main features are noted: especially its potential for undoing evils of gold-exchange standards. It receives no better than a Scotch verdict. Then proposals for reform are considered, proposals within the ground rules of Ch. XVI: basically fixed exchange rates and basic national monetary autonomy. Emphasis is on the Triffin and Bernstein plans. The Triffin proposal proves similar to one of J. M. Keynes at the time of the IMF's founding: our story of IMF genesis flows from discussion of the Triffin plan. We also consider Sir Roy Harrod's proposal that the nominal value of gold be increased, a proposal so direct and simple that economists avoid it as a pariah. We then are ready to move to Section B. Section B concentrates on non-price-rationing reactions to foreign-exchange "surpluses" and "shortages." It enquires *en passant* whether or not secular dollar shortages (surpluses) are theoretically plausible.

5

Chandler[3] and Triffin[4] give very clear accounts of the IMF. Triffin[5] and Scammell[6] discuss the genesis of the IMF (Savannah, Bretton Woods, etc.). And you will want to read Sir Roy Harrod's fascinating account of the Keynes-White struggle.[7]

---

3 L. V. Chandler, *The Economics of Money and Banking,* p. 507 *ff.*

4 Robert Triffin, *Europe and the Money Muddle,* p. 88 *ff.*

5 *Ibid.*

6 *Op. cit.,* Note 1.

7 R. F. Harrod, *The Life of John Maynard Keynes* (London: Macmillan & Co., Ltd., 1952), pp. 582-585. White is Harry Dexter White, who was Assistant Secretary of the Treasury from 1945 to 1947. Subsequently he became caught up in a famous internal security investigation.

These are the IMF's major features:

1) Article I of the Agreement signed at Bretton Woods, N. H., in 1944 makes clear that the objective of the Fund should be to secure truly multilateral trade accompanied by "the elimination of foreign-exchange restrictions which hamper the growth of world trade." At the same time, it is desired "to promote exchange stability, to maintain orderly exchange arrangements among members, and to avoid competitive exchange depreciation." Also, citing purposes 5 and 6 in full

> 5) "To give confidence to members by making the Fund's resources available to them under adequate safeguards, thus providing them with opportunity to correct maladjustments in their balance of payments without resorting to measures destructive of national or international prosperity [e.g. deflationary measures that might spread depression through matrix multipliers]."
>
> 6) "In accordance with the above, to shorten the duration and lessen the degree of disequilibrium in the international balances of payments of members."

The ground rules are now familiar: a lending apparatus is to be used to correct short-term disequilibrium; secular flaws are to be corrected by revaluations and by monetary and fiscal probity of debtors.

2) Exchange rates are fixed in terms of U. S. (13.71 grain gold) dollars. Member countries are committed to maintain definite dollar prices for their currencies, subject to qualifications listed below. Naturally this provision establishes gold prices, since the American buying price is fixed. These are the exceptions to fixity of exchange rates:

> a) countries can depreciate or appreciate their currencies unilaterally up to 10 per cent regardless of their position in the Fund. Triffin makes the important point that "the Board [cannot] recommend an exchange readjustment or impose it as a condition for further drawings . . ."[8]
>
> b) larger alterations in exchange rates are permitted if there is "fundamental disequilibrium." Such alterations are to be made only with the approval of the Board of the Fund. The Board is to be guided by these criteria, among others:
>
> > i) persistence of imbalance in the balance of payments;
> >
> > ii) "a nation is not to adjust its exchange rate to offset . . . capital flight. Such a disturbance is to be met by direct control of capital movements or by other means."[9] Capital flight can summon forth direct controls;

[8] *Op. cit.*, pp. 109-110.

[9] L. V. Chandler, *op. cit.*, p. 513.

iii) it is to be permitted to revalue when balance-of-payments disequilibrium threatens to induce chronic unemployment;

iv) on the other hand, revaluations which are part of "competitive" sequences are to be frowned upon. Indeed, emphatically disapproved.

3) "Essentially each country is left free to regulate international capital movements, but cannot impose, without the approval of the Fund, any restrictions on current payments and transfers. Such restrictions are automatically authorized, however, against a currency declared scarce by the Fund."[10] In fact, multilateralism under the Fund has been qualified, and for these "structural" reasons:

a) trade, as against currency, restrictions are *not* prohibited. It hardly matters whether Country X prohibits its citizens from purchasing American currency except under license or from purchasing American goods except under license;

b) "the second major loophole is the sweeping latitude granted to members, for an ill-defined postwar transitional period, to 'maintain and adapt to changing circumstances . . . notwithstanding any other Articles of this agreement . . . restrictions on payments and transfers for current international transactions.' (Art. XIV, Sec. 2). Twelve years after the end of the war, all but 10 Fund members were still availing themselves of these post-war transitional arrangements."[11]

Triffin points out[12] that restrictions imposed under loopholes a and b largely were on imports payable in dollars and "approximated . . . a declaration of dollar scarcity under Article VII . . ." However, the Fund never declared dollar scarcity. Despite the fact that potential excess demand for dollars exceeded the Fund's supply, the Fund never had to. Early on, the Fund discouraged member borrowing. Knowing that it would be hard to pry dollars from the Fund, member countries imposed restrictions on dollar trade: ". . . dollars were never scarce in the Fund. Its dollar holdings never fell substantially below $1.3 billion, and could at all times be replenished by gold holdings ranging from $1.3 billion to $1.8 billion."[13]

4) Technically, the Fund does not engage in lending operations: it sells foreign currency to member nations at officially determined rates of exchange. The Fund's role as a central bank — as an institution ready

10 Triffin, *op. cit.*, p. 110.
11 *Ibid.*, p. 124.
12 *Ibid.*, pp. 127-128.
13 *Ibid.*, p. 127.

to provide internationally monetary claims for internationally non-monetary claims — is circumscribed by its gold stock.[14]

6

Table III gives Fund holdings of gold, United States dollars, German marks, Canadian dollars, and pounds sterling, all valued in United States dollars. Table IV tells something about the Fund's "lending" activities. Obviously, sundry restrictions on Fund purchases of national securities (including demand deposits) must be built into the Fund's structure. Disequilibrium possibilities are almost boundless in an international economy in which fundamental adjustment mechanisms are decommissioned. In the absence of restraint, perfectly enormous quantities of various currencies might be "sold" to the Fund in exchange for gold or for currencies in excess demand. Following Chandler, these are the basic restrictions imposed upon the Fund's lending operations:

a) the Fund cannot sell a nation's currency without that nation's permission;

IMF HOLDINGS OF VARIOUS CURRENCIES AND GOLD

(in millions of U. S. dollars)

Category	(1) Dec. 31, 1958	(2) July 31, 1961
U. S. Dollars	792	2,585.4
German Marks	183	329.7
Canadian Dollars	210	387.9
Pounds Sterling	1,618	1,419.0
All Currencies	6,740	10,941.7
Gold	1,532	2,507.5
Gold + All Currencies	8,272	13,449.2

TABLE XVI-III

Sources: Robert Triffin, *Europe and the Money Muddle*, Table 16, pp. 96-97 and Table 17, p. 99, *International Financial Statistics* (Washington: IMF, Sept., 1961), Vol. XIV, No. 9, p. 5.

Note: Column 1 definitely excludes unpaid subscriptions. This may not be true of Column 2.

14 If one is willing to ignore consequent pressure on key currency nations, he can include Fund holdings of "hard" currencies in the total of Fund capability for provision of "gold assets."

DRAWINGS, REPAYMENTS, AND NET FUND SALES FOR SELECTED CURRENCIES THROUGH JULY 1961

(in millions of U. S. dollars)

	DRAWINGS				
Member	1947-1950	1960	1961	Gross Drawings*	Net Drawings or, if Minus, Net Fund Sales of Currency
Brazil	37.5	47.7	60.0	368.4	200.0
Canada					— 24.6
France	125.0			518.8	— 44.6
Germany					—260.9
Netherlands	75.4			144.1	— 42.5
United Kingdom	300.0			861.5	— 43.5
United States					—483.6

TABLE XVI-IV

Source: International Financial Statistics, Vol. XIV, No. 9, pp. 6-7.
* Drawings are to be interpreted as sales of one's own currency to the fund.

b) "the Fund's resources are to be used only for temporary assistance . . . Nations are expected to repay within 3 to 5 years."[15]

c) the Fund's resources are to be used only to meet deficiencies on current account. Article VI, Section 1(a) of the Agreement states:

> "a member may not make net use of the Fund's resources to meet a large or sustained outflow of capital, and the Fund may request a member to exercise controls to prevent such use of the resources of the Fund. If, after receiving a request, a member fails to exercise appropriate controls, the Fund may declare the member ineligible to use the resources of the Fund."

Obviously, there is concern over consequences of massive security transactions (capital outflows); here, the Fund's fathers are willing to accept physical controls;

d) in the absence of waiver by Fund officials:

> "the Fund may not increase its holdings of a nation's money during any 12-month period by an amount exceeding 25 per cent of that nation's quota [*cf. infra.*], and its total holdings of a nation's money may not at any time exceed 200 per cent of that nation's quota. The Fund has often waived the first limitation in recent years but never the second."[16]

[15] Chandler, *op. cit.*, p. 515.
[16] *Ibid.*, pp. 515-517.

e) charges are imposed by the Fund on member drawings. The charges vary directly with the size and duration of the drawings.

Finally, the Fund sometimes enters into stand-by arrangements with members, as it did for the United Kingdom in summer 1961. The 1961 British experience is especially interesting: speculative pressure against sterling substantially eased when it became clear that the British Treasury *could* rely on the aid of the Fund well beyond the extent to which it *had* done so. (*See Note B.*)

7

Now for a broad summary of the Fund's essential features. The Fund must collect its resources from its members. It cannot create its own liabilities, pumping these into the stream of international payments (subject to a January 1962 modification). (*See Note C.*) The greater part of the Fund's resources are in the form of monetary obligations — not gold — of member countries, contributed in fulfillment of quota obligations. Thus, the bulk of the Fund's resources are not available to meet a global increase in "gold preference," and, of course, Fund holdings of "deficit" currencies are quite meaningless as correctives for disequilibrated balances of payments. Insofar as the Fund hands over currencies that are in excess demand to governments whose currencies are in excess supply, the Fund does indirectly what could have been done directly through extension of loans by surplus to deficit countries — if standard adjustment mechanisms were eschewed.

Review of Fund operations and perusal of its "constitution" make clear that it is specialized to short-run (transitory) disequilibrium: the Fund's major function is to provide ammunition for national monetary authorities shoring up exchange rates for their currencies. It appears to have been founded on an overriding fear that flexible exchange — if chanced — would be overwhelmed by destabilizing speculation; that basically fixed exchange rates without an international control mechanism would be cursed by competitive devaluation; rigidly fixed exchange rates (surely if there are no international controls) would find short-run imbalance metamorphosized into disastrous specie drains and globally transmitted deflationary spirals. The Fund's fathers did not hope for a great deal. Essentially they sought but to damp down effects of short-run disequilibrium. This, it was hoped, would make possible basically rigid exchange rates — trusting that the

Fund's ability to cope with destabilizing speculation and competitive devaluation would permit sporadic exchange-rate changes to correct disequilibrium. (*See Note D.*)

What can be concluded about the Fund's "capability for undoing evil consequences of gold-exchange standards?" Can the Fund somehow be expected to achieve such effective utilization of international monetary reserves that conceded inadequacy of their aggregate amount becomes unimportant? Triffin answers these questions in Ch. 3 (pp. 94-101) of *Gold and the Dollar Crisis* (Rev. Ed.). Crucial background is provided by Table III above (*cf. ibid.*, Table 16, pp. 96-97) concerning Fund holdings of gold and of most of the currencies ever lent by it.[16a] Since Fund holdings of sterling and dollars hardly can be of use in combatting a run on themselves, we cannot but agree with Triffin's conclusion:

> "the most fundamental deficiency of the present system, and the main danger to its future stability lies in the fact that it leaves the satisfactory development of world monetary liquidity primarily dependent upon an admittedly insufficient supply of new gold and an admittedly dangerous and haphazard expansion in the short-term indebtedness of key-currency countries."[17]

Assuming that nominal values of gold remain unchanged, Triffin's diagnosis would seem to be understated when account is taken of the probable course of global price inflation in coming years.

2. Proposals for Reform

We turn, then, to proposals for reform, taking up gold revaluation (particularly associated with Sir Roy Harrod), the Keynes-Triffin plan, and finally E. M. Bernstein's plan, always remembering that we operate within limitations imposed by basically rigid exchange rates *and* substantial national monetary autonomy.

16a Dutch guilders and Belgian francs are omitted. Triffin's Table 16 gives IMF holdings of these currencies on December 31, 1958 as 206 and 169 million U. S. dollars (worth). Comparable figures for July 31, 1961 are $267 million and $253 million.

17 Triffin, *op. cit.*, pp. 100-101.

a) Revaluation of Gold

1

It certainly seems plausible that, if the price of gold in terms of all currencies were increased by a factor λ, a new reservoir of international liquidity would be created. American and British gold reserves, for example, could overnight become so large — when valued in dollars or sterling — that existing American and British external obligations would fade into insignificance. True, the procedure might be accompanied by piercing cries of votaries of the little yellow gods. But this would be a small price to pay for international monetary tranquillity. Could not Professor Triffin's calculations be knocked into a cocked hat; if revaluation were drastic enough, balance-of-payments deficits in the order of hundreds of billions of dollars could be flicked aside by transfer of a few grains of the yellow elixir. The fact that foreign countries hold dollar securities well in excess of $15 billion could be contemptuously dismissed as a danger to American solvency. There hardly could be a liquidity ailment that would not yield to a few grains of gold.[18]

2

I suspect that the most ardent advocate of revaluation would attach at least these *caveats* to his proposal:

a) irresponsible governments could, as a result of devaluation, persist in inflationary policies, paying the piper in now-enhanced gold. The road to perdition would crookedly traverse more miles, but the end would be the same. On the other hand this *caveat* attaches to almost any plan to increase international liquidity;

b) (closely related to (a)) substantial release from the discipline even of *external* convertibility might encourage totally irresponsible public finance. This danger seems inherent in increased international liquidity;

c) revaluation of gold merely makes disequilibrium less painful. It does not affect root causes of balance-of-payments disequilibrium. But we have seen that the IMF system is much more keyed to correction of short-run than of secular disequilibrium. The Harrod proposal is not of a different gender.

18 Of course it might cost huge sums in domestic currency to acquire even a few grains of gold from the IMF, but it is easy enough to print currency.

d) the more the price of gold is increased (in terms of dollars, sterling, etc.), the greater will be the stimulus to production of gold, a "wasteful" enterprise. Theory suggests that the stimulus will be stronger and more persistent in systems in which the money stock is not keyed (upward at least) to gold inflow. *(See Note E.)* This *caveat* may be unimportant if gold is sufficiently inelastic in supply. It is considered *infra.*

3

It is not as if depreciation of currencies is an unheard-of thing. Compare the chart below (partly reproducing Chart III, p. 80 of *Gold and the Dollar Crisis*). Chapter II paid much heed to secular inflationary forces underlying the dramatic sweep of the curve of the chart. And yet, Triffin considers devaluation to be "basically absurd." He offers a comprehensive criticism:

GOLD PRICE IN LONDON OVER SEVEN CENTURIES

(in shillings per fine ounce)

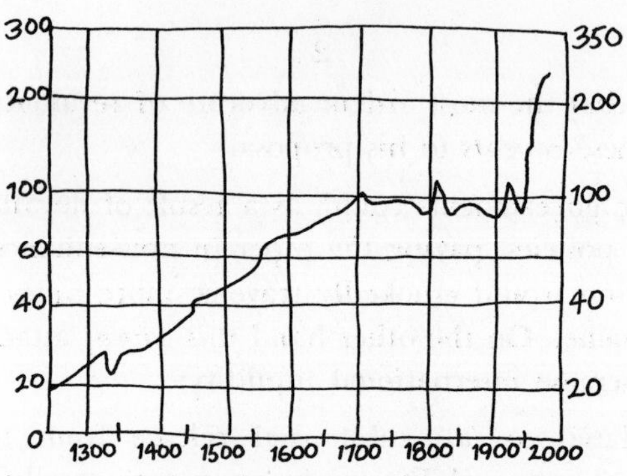

Figure XVI-1

1) Gold prices would have to be increased drastically unless there were to be repeated devaluations. The latter might induce destabilizing speculation, but huge once-and-for-all revaluation would produce an excess of liquidity that might, along the lines of our caveats, start up inflationary processes;

2) Benefits of revaluation "would be distributed very haphazardly, and indeed in just about the least desirable fashion imaginable":

countries with initially high reserves would benefit the most, together with the major gold producers, Russia and South Africa.

3) If global price levels are not permitted to rise with the price of gold — and they must not if revaluation is to increase international liquidity — more resources will be devoted to "earth-digging" throughout the world. We already have noted this point. In truth, it seems to me rather niggling: in 1960 world production of gold — excluding iron curtain countries — was between 33.6 and 33.7 million ounces, valued at $1,175 million; 1960 production exceeded that in any of the last 10 years; American production in 1960 was less than 1.7 million ounces. Obviously, no substantial diversion of resources will result from drastic changes in gold valuation; the orders of magnitude involved are petty.

4

Perhaps the objections to revaluation are not as overwhelming as some have been led to believe. Nevertheless, I should judge that there are three decisively negative considerations:

1) programs leading to meaningful enrichment of Soviet bloc countries are political poison;

2) it is likely that the inflationary potential created by dramatic revaluation of gold will dominate the thoughts of policy makers, encouraging "adamant objection";

3) reduction in "gold contents" of currency units fills right-thinking people with horror and guilt. For debtors to be able to discharge liabilities through transfer of smaller quantities of gold than they had, however implicitly, contracted to offer, seems to many to be immoral, the more so if the debtor is able painlessly to avail himself of the remedy.

b) The Keynes-Triffin Plan

1

Consider an analogy between the interbank payments matrix within an economy and the international payments matrix. A primary function of a central banking system is to create a form of liability that can constitute the reserves of member banks. In exercising its clearing function, the central bank makes offsetting debit and credit entries to the accounts of the member banks. As a lender of last resort, it stands ready to add to the total of its outstanding liability in exchange for various bank assets, and, surely, it is not rare for the central bank to be granted the power to create claims against itself that can be redeemed in suitably-engraved paper that *it* can produce.

This last is the crux. Consider a banking system in which the central bank is empowered to issue fiat paper to satisfy its obligations; the international counterpart is the Keynes-Triffin plan. Then consider a banking system in which the central bank is empowered to issue claims against itself in exchange for member-bank assets, but in which these claims are redeemable in gold or some other substance limited in supply; the international counterpart is the Bernstein plan.

The Keynes proposals *circa* 1943 were a direct attack on the problem of international liquidity in a world in which major adjustment mechanisms (price-level and interest-rate changes, exchange flexibility, and income variation) were to be put out of commission in at least the short run. The Keynesian solution was drastic: creation of an essentially fiat supplementary medium of international payments. It aroused justifiable fear that "structural imbalance" could be prolonged and perhaps aggravated as large doses of *bancor* soothing syrup were administered to countries running adverse balances of payments.

2

More specifically, the international medium of exchange to be used in transactions between central banks and like institutions was to be called *bancor*.[19] It would be issued by a Clearing Union, essentially the Keynesian counterpart to the IMF. The gold value of bancor was to be fixed; gold could satisfy bancor obligations on fixed terms. (But a bancor creditor could not demand gold.) Bancor values of national currencies would be subject to *roughly* the procedures now characterizing the IMF.

> "The practical outcome of these arrangements, therefore, would be to create bancor accounts endowed with international purchasing power in terms of any and all currencies whatsoever, equivalent to gold itself and as freely usable in international settlements among central banks."[20]

---

19 Presentation of bancor credit could offset obligations to pay over stated amounts of member exchanges. It also was intended that bancor money of account be used. But this was not important: reckoning could just as well have been in dollars, lira, francs, etc. (monies of account).

The abstractness of bancor claims brings to mind feudal tenures: seizen of Blackacre or of a right of appointment of a cleric were conceptually identical.

20 Triffin, *Europe and the Money Muddle*, p. 96.

Bancor could be provided to members of the Clearing Union through overdraft facilities. Since bancor was to be inconvertible into gold or anything else, there would be no inherent limitation on its total issue:

> "Yet the Union could not extend unlimited credits to the deficit countries without encouraging total irresponsibility on their part, and without risking stimulation of a boundless spirit of international inflation."[21]

Various restrictions were to be imposed: limitation of overdraft facility in terms of trade turnover; taxes on both debtor and creditor balances in order to encourage creditors, for example, to run unfavorable balances so as to develop adverse clearings, reducing their bancor balances with the Union.

There were various objections to the Keynes plan, and, of course, these carried the day:

> 1) Keynes's formula linking overdraft facility to trade turnover would have led to potential advances to countries other than the United States of about $95 billion by 1955 (plus $20 billion becoming available to the United States); there was inherent in the formula a real bills fallacy, since expansion in the nominal value of trade would lead to further advances, leading to further expansion in the nominal value of trade, etc.;
>
> 2) Keynes's proposed distribution of voting power would have tended to place creditor nations at the mercy of debtors, making it possible that creditors would be forced indefinitely to accumulate credits "in a bank which is itself committed in advance to lend large sums to any Tom, Dick, or Harry on the mere condition that they need the money to finance their deficits";[22]
>
> 3) while it is true that creditors could convert bancor balances into merchandise or foreign balances simply by running adverse balances of payments and that untouched bancor balances would, *cet. par.*, have all of the international liquidity of gold, the taxation scheme would put creditors under pressure as to the timing of disposition of bancor balances that might be resented: why should the United States pay a penalty to the Union simply because it does not choose to "waste its substance" at a given juncture in time?

Whatever the merit of various objections, the Keynes plan clearly was imaginative as well as elegant and simple. It envisaged genuine internationalization of political control of the Union's activities. Its

---

21 *Ibid.*, p. 97.
22 *Ibid.*, p. 106.

close family resemblance to the Triffin plan of roughly 15-16 years later is of special interest.[23]

3

Triffin's plan is outlined at pp. 102-120 of his *Gold and the Dollar Crisis* (Rev. Ed.):

> "[Needless to say] the keystone of [my] proposals would be the substitution of IMF balances for balances in national currencies — i.e., mostly dollars and sterling — in all member countries' monetary reserves. Such balances should be made equivalent in all respects to gold itself and as widely usable and acceptable in world payments."

Eventually, *national* currencies would be barred as *international* reserves: non-gold monetary reserves would be in the form of bancor accounts with the IMF:

> "Initially it might be right to say that every member of the IMF should keep at least 20 per cent of its reserve in the form of these deposits, but as they would be deposits guaranteed against any possibility of devaluation and bearing some interest most countries would be likely to choose in time to keep a far larger proportion there."[24]

Of course, the crucial issue concerns the "sources and limits of the Fund's overall lending capacity"; how would an "adequate" level of international liquidity be squared with the intention that the Fund not be endowed "with an unlimited — and potentially inflationary — lending capacity, nor that each member country commit itself in advance to accumulate unlimited amounts of bancor in settlement of its surpluses?"[25] Recall that the Keynes plan fell short in these respects.

Triffin proposes a first approximation that the Fund's net lend-

---

[23] Review the mechanics of the Clearing Union apparatus. Insofar as Country A is running a favorable balance of payments, it is building up credits at the Union in just the manner that a member bank can increase its reserve position if it has favorable clearings at the Federal Reserve. If Country B is running an unfavorable balance of payments, it will run down its bancor balance. Clearing Union overdrafts would be analogous to Federal Reserve rediscount facility; the paper exchanged for bancor balances would be B's currency. There would be no more reason for a member country to wish to switch from bancor to gold than for a member bank to switch from its balance at the Federal Reserve to Bank-of-Mishawaka notes. Finally, repayment of overdrafts at the Clearing Union is accomplished by turning over foreign "currency" to the Union. The bancor value of the paper presented to the Union is predetermined.

[24] *The Economist*, May 6, 1961, "Bernstein, Triffin, Stamp, . . .," pp. 528-530 at p. 529.

[25] Triffin, *op cit.*, p. 103.

ing over any year be limited so that, considering increases in monetary gold stocks, total world reserves would only increase from 3 to 5 per cent a year. Creditor nations would be "induced" at first to hold increased bancor reserves as a result of the 20 per cent requirement already discussed (where it was hoped that in time no special inducement would be needed). Since Triffin would limit bancor drawing privileges of countries not making efforts to correct structural causes of balance-of-payments disequilibrium, potential creditors hopefully would not be forced to extend credit indefinitely to profligate borrowers. Still the Triffin plan's structure finds pressure on debtors being exerted through an international agency rather than directly by creditor governments or potential private lenders in creditor countries. Those skeptical or disapproving of international executive power might not welcome such dsicipline.[26]

There are two other features of the Triffin plan that should be noted: (a) the Fund, it granted permission by the appropriate member country, could engage in open-market operations, using exchange obtained during the course of its business; (b) initially the Fund would acquire large holdings of "bank deposits, acceptances, and Treasury bills previously held by the central banks themselves in London and New York"; Triffin envisages progressive liquidation of these assets, albeit "at a maximum pace of, let us say, 5 per cent annually." The proceeds are to be "re-employed in other markets whose need for international capital is greater than that in the United States and the United Kingdom."[27] Feature (b) comes under particular attack from Dr. Bernstein. We defer criticism of the Triffin plan until limning the Bernstein plan: the most cogent criticisms have been voiced by Bernstein while defending his own plan.

c) The Bernstein Plan; Criticism of the Triffin Plan

The Bernstein Plan finds the IMF issuing its own liabilities — long-term debt — in exchange for gold or some scarce currency, lend-

[26] Needless to say, overtly Soviet bloc countries are not expected to be in the new plan any more than they are in the old.

[27] Open-market operations could be used by the Fund to create and destroy international monetary reserves. Thus, purchases by the Fund of United States securities at New York would create bancor credits for the United States. Sales of German securities at Hamburg would reduce German bancor balances. It seems to me that, while open-market powers would confer elasticity on Fund operations even beyond that under the Keynes plan, unavoidable conflict with national ethos would lead to the Fund's discomfort.

ing the proceeds to a member country experiencing balance-of-payments difficulty.[28] Hart and Kenen write:

> "It would not enlarge the total of reserves but would make more effective use of the existing supply. The Bernstein proposal would be especially helpful were the Fund obliged to mobilize cash to support the dollar or the pound against speculative pressure."[29]

The *Economist* wrote:

> "Mr. Bernstein's idea is that the IMF should be enabled to borrow funds under standby arrangements from countries that are increasing their international reserves (e.g., at present Germany) and lend out the D-marks thus borrowed to countries in deficit."[30]

The *Economist* stated that ". . . the Bernstein plan . . . would not increase total world liquidity," presumably meaning that the plan would not lead to creation of additional international reserves. Dr. Bernstein responded in a letter published in the *Economist,* May 20, 1961 at p. 769. Among other things, he asserted that his plan would allow the United States and United Kingdom to treat their balances with the IMF as reserves. He then pointed out that the United States and United Kingdom would become debtors of the IMF under the Triffin plan as a result of conversion dollar and sterling balances into bancor:

> "These enormous debts would be funded, but they would have to be repaid over a period of 20 years. Furthermore, any dollars or sterling acquired by other countries hereafter would be converted by them or the IMF into gold . . . With a balanced pattern of world payments, these operations, even if they could avoid disrupting the money markets, would impose on the United States and the United Kingdom a far greater burden of providing reserves for the rest of the world than they have now under the gold exchange standard."[31]

These objections to the Triffin plan seem overstated: amortization and service charges on American and British indebtedness to the IMF would not exceed $150 and $100 million per annum. And amortiza-

28 *Cf.* E. M. Bernstein, *International Effects of U. S. Monetary Policy,* Joint Economic Committee of Congress (Washington: Government Printing Office, 1960), p. 84 *ff.*

29 *Op. cit.,* p. 369.

30 *Loc cit.,* p. 529.

31 He also voices concern that "the Triffin institution could avoid being the ultimate judge of the fiscal and credit policies of all of its members, including the United States and the United Kingdom."

tion and interest charges could be offset by Fund open-market operations. It would seem that a basic function of the Triffin institution would be to provide bancor for countries subsequently accumulating dollars and sterling during transitory imbalance. If it wished it could acquire claims payable in gold *against* such countries through open-market sales of securities — forcing them to tender dollar and sterling accretions to the Fund. Of course, such intervention confirms Bernstein's concern that the Triffin institution would have to intervene forcefully in national affairs. In fact, I suspect this is the real rub: Triffin's proposals require that the IMF acquire many of the features of a central bank, and we have seen that central banks must acquire no little suzerainty in order to do their work.[32]

B. DOLLAR SHORTAGES (SURPLUSES)

1. This Night, Methinks, is but the Daylight Sick

1

In its most naïve form, the problem of dollar scarcity (surplus) can be analysed through the following examination problem, taken from a first quiz in Economics A.

> There is alleged to be a shortage of parking space in Evanston. This is best explained by the fact that
>
> (1) more parking space is needed than is available; (2) more parking space is available than is needed; (3) the price of parking space is too high to clear the market; (4) the price of parking space is too low to clear the market; (5) in university communities cars are more often parked than driven when in use.

The student's instincts usually direct him towards choice 1, but further reflection erodes this choice. Thus, if Evanston's fathers imposed

---

[32] *Cf.* J. W. Angell, "The Reorganization of the International Monetary System: An Alternative Proposal," *Economic Journal,* Vol. 71, December 1961, pp. 691-708. Professor Angell criticises the Triffin plan, proposing instead to eliminate the use of gold in international settlements. Gold is to be replaced by IMF deposit balances. Professor Triffin replies at pp. 244-249, *Economic Journal,* Vol. 72, March 1962.

The literature grows and grows. For an interesting collection of essays — including contributions by Harrod, Triffin, and Bernstein — see Seymour E. Harris, *The Dollar in Crisis* (New York: Harcourt, Brace & World, Inc., 1961).

a meter charge of $82 per hour on all of the city's streets, motorists probably would check their petrol upon approaching Evanston, making sure they would not have to stop there. It probably would be possible to shoot a cannon down an Evanston street without inflicting harm, except perhaps to an agent of Northwestern University's Traffic Office vainly seeking a parked car that might be tagged. On the other hand, if Evanston meters were reworked so that they operated on a one-armed bandit principle — if they became nickel slot machines — cars would be logjammed before the gates of the Wesleyan Paradise for miles, waiting for an opportunity to park. As a general rule, there always is a price that will clear a market.

We have stressed literally from the onset of this book that money is a class comprised of *things* bought and sold in markets and held like other stocks. It makes no more sense to talk about a need for more dollars than are available or of more dollars being available than are needed than it does to state that more platinum rings are needed than are available or more wheat is available than is needed. (If wheat were priced at $0.02 per bushel, it would be kneaded into clothing, houses, and tinker toys *if* it could be obtained at such a price.)

2

We do not want to belabor the obvious. There is little or no disagreement that if, for example, dollar prices (values in dollars) of of all foreign exchange were increased threefold — and if the devaluation were viewed as once-and-for-all — there would be no excess supply of dollar exchange in international markets.[33] Similarly, it is hard to conceive how there could *not* have been excess demand for dollars in the first decade or so after World War II. Rigid dollar prices (subject to sporadic revaluation) of foreign exchange failed to reflect profound, albeit transitory, changes brought by devastation of most of the world's great economic centers, but not, of course, the United States. Global demand for capital goods for reconstruction was enormous. There was great disruption in food supply. Instability of continental governments encouraged European investors to try to shift into dollar securities. Not only was much manufacturing equipment and transportation facility actually destroyed in Europe and Asia: cost-price relationships, determined by fiat, led to hopeless economic bottlenecks. In sum, the peculiar circumstances of the postwar economic world much increased

[33] Competitive devaluations are excluded.

the equilibrium external value of the American dollar, but foreign authorities were unwilling to accept such terms of trade. At the same time, the proverbial small black cloud was developing: the stock of dollar liabilities held abroad as monetary reserves was rising; one of the preconditions for a capricious gold-exchange standard was being established.

3

Observers during the "dollar-shortage" era, say, prior to 1958, were denied a view of the future. They were inclined to hold that the problem of dollar-gap would persist long into the future.[34] Many reasons were offered, most of them obviously chimerical. On the other hand, economists such as John H. Williams offered a hypothesis that was subtle and not *a priori* invalid.[35] Williams recognized that at each point in time there would in general exist a set of market-clearing exchange rates (although he was, of course, aware of threats to stability posed by destabilizing speculation). Nevertheless, he suspected that there might be secular forces leading to persistent excess demand for dollars unless dollar prices of foreign currencies persistently fell — a motion that could in itself lead to dangerous speculation. And, of course, to the extent that adjustment of exchange rates was lagged, there would in fact be a secular dollar shortage. In other words, Williams had in mind a schemata such as that of the diagram below. The demand curve is shifting more rapidly than the supply curve, leading to a secular increase in the good's price. Interpret the diagram as showing demand and supply for dollars in foreign-exchange markets where the price axis measures the sterling price of dollars. The higher the sterling price of dollars — where sterling is the currency of the rest of the world — the more expensive are dollars for foreigners. If the variety and quality of American goods and American productivity should be increasing more rapidly than in the rest of the world, American prices (at least when properly measured) will increase less than foreign prices, *cet. par.* The terms of trade would have to turn more

34 Triffin was a signal exception. ". . . difficulties . . . [of] foreign countries in balancing their over-all transactions with the United States were largely the result of military and political developments rather than of a fundamental and intractable balance originating in economic factors . . ." (*Europe and the Money Muddle,* p. 16.)

35 *Cf.* John H. Williams, *Economic Stability in the Modern World,* Lord Stamp Memorial Lecture (Oxford: Basil Blackwell, 1952). Also Charles P. Kindleberger, *The Dollar Shortage* (New York: John Wiley and Sons, 1950). Triffin's discussion in Ch. I of *The Money Muddle* is excellent.

SCHEMATA, SECULAR DOLLAR SHORTAGE (SURPLUS)

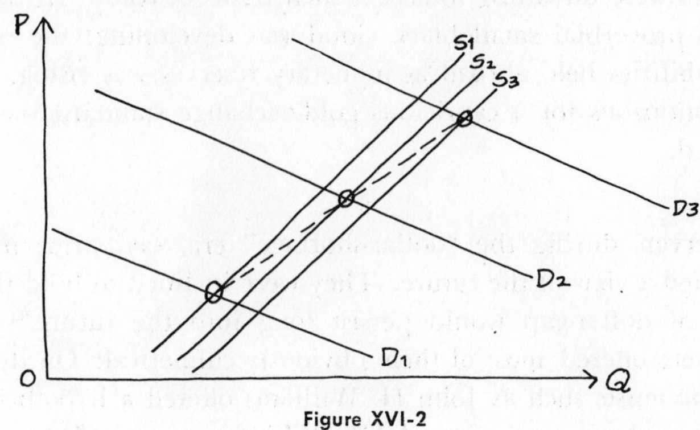

Figure XVI-2

and more in favor of the United States for the foreign-exchange market(s) to be in continuous balance. And then, if sundry inflationary biases abroad caused foreign prices to rise faster than American prices, dollar-gap pressures would be augmented. (Of course, the argument can be turned around to explain persistent dollar surpluses.)

4

We need not further pursue the Williams hypothesis.[36] Events soon mooted speculation about dollar gaps, greater inflationary biases in Europe, faster rates of technological advance in the United States, etc. By the end of 1961 serious fears were expressed about the long-run ability of the United States to maintain convertibility of the dollar into gold at $35 per ounce. Consult Table V and Figure 3.

CURRENCY SALES BY THE IMF

(percentage of total sales together with absolute amounts)

Currency	1947-1957	1958-1960	Jan-Sep 1961
U. S. Dollars	92%	68%	34%
Sterling	7	13	5
Continental Europe		19	54
Other	1		7
Total Sales in $ mill	2,886	798	2,405

TABLE XVI-V

[36] Triffin (*loc. cit.*) did. So did Professor Leontief in a different context. They both came to negative conclusions.

EXCESS OF PAYMENTS OVER RECEIPTS, U.S.

(quarterly at seasonally adjusted rates in billions of dollars)

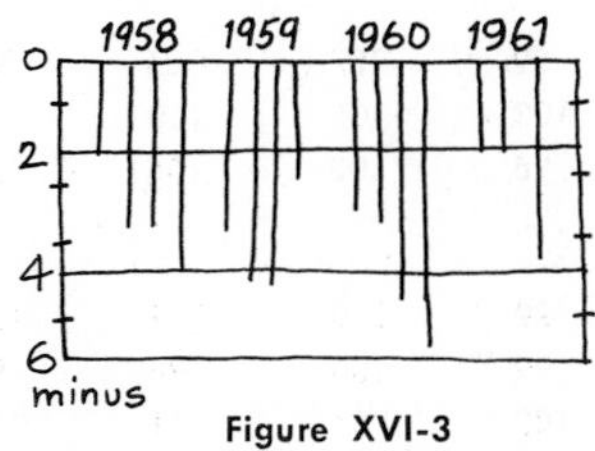

Figure XVI-3

Sources: Table, The *Economist,* November 25, 1961, p. 799; Graph, *Ibid.,* p. 762.

Note: the second-quarter 1961 bar excludes receipts from special debt repayments amounting to $2.6 billion at annual rates.

Productivity, admittedly a very crude concept, has been increasing rapidly in Europe and in Japan, and, in any event, prices of American exports have risen, both in comparison with prices of most foreign exports and with prices of American imports. Consult Table VI. Of course, to say that terms of trade have turned in favor of the United States — keeping in mind that we deal with fixed exchange rates — is to say that American exports have increased in price compared to our imports.

However, recall from Section A that the deficit in the American balance of payments has not arisen from collapse of the balance on current account. Rather the villain of the piece has been substantial capital outflow (net movements into foreign securities), a process featured by the dreaded overhang of huge foreign holdings of dollar securities, despite large American holdings of foreign securities: it cannot be expected that Americans holding foreign securities will unload these as a patriotic gesture, certainly not if they anticipate devaluation of the dollar. And, of course, such measures as prohibition of purchase of foreign securities, forced divestiture of such securities in order to provide the American Government with ammunition to support the dollar, etc., fall into the category of disequilibrium techniques. These are to be taken up at once.

SELECTED PRICE INDEXES FOR PRICES EXPRESSED IN U. S. DOLLARS
(1953 = 100)

Country	1951	1954	1957	1958	1959	1960	1961
United States							
Export Prices	101	99	107	106	106	108	111
Import Prices	111	103	105	100	98	100	98
Terms of Trade	91	96	102	106	109	108	113
United Kingdom							
Export Prices	99	99	110	109	108	110	111
Import Prices	112	99	106	98	97	98	97
Terms of Trade	88	100	104	111	111	112	114
Continental Europe							
Export Prices	113	99	103	100	96	98	
Import Prices	109	97	104	97	93	93	
Terms of Trade	104	102	100	104	105	105	
Germany							
Export Prices	98	98	103	103	100	101	107*
Import Prices	123	98	103	95	91	91	92
Terms of Trade	80	100	100	108	110	111	116
Japan							
Export Prices	129	96	98	89	92	94	94
Import Prices	124	96	97	86	83	82	84
Terms of Trade	104	100	101	103	111	115	112

TABLE XVI-VI

* Recall revaluation of the D-Mark.

Note: for this section's purposes United States export prices and export prices of other countries are the key statistics. Import prices in all cases importantly reflect exports of countries not shown in the Table. Raw materials are especially important for excluded countries. Note that United States and United Kingdom exports have become more expensive relative to those of other countries shown.

Source: International Financial Statistics (Washington: IMF, Sept. 1961), pp. 36-37.

2. Disequilibrium Techniques

1

Our final topic flows easily from treatment of genesis of excess demand and supply of dollars in foreign-exchange markets. It concerns controls imposed in order to freeze a disequilibrium situation.

We have repeatedly stressed that there is nothing fundamentally "right" about market clearance, and, correspondingly, nothing fundamentally "wrong" about non-clearance. It is worth while to explore these remarks a bit farther.

IMF members easily can run out of degrees of freedom. If they wish to maintain control over their prices, rates of output, money-market yields, terms of trade, etc. — maintaining fixed exchange rates — it is more than likely that something will have to give. An "arbitrarily" selected set of values will not sustain clearance in all markets.

Must we — as authorities — faint dead away or scurry about seeking a solution set? No. We might instead resort to non-price rationing of foreign exchange, impose restrictions on bank borrowing, require priority certifications for purchases of certain goods, etc. Indeed, great portions of global economic activity — and not just in Iron Curtain countries, far from it — are conducted under disequilibrium systems.

Concentrate on foreign exchange. Assume that Country A's authorities recognize that their currency, the peso, will exchange for the currency of Country B, the lira, on a 1:1 basis in a free market. For simplicity's sake assume further that both countries are on inconvertible paper standards. The A authorities might take the following steps:

a) require that A citizens turn in all holding of lira assets in exchange for its own securities;

b) make it illegal for A citizens to hold lira assets in the future — except with its special permission. Require that all lira receipts be turned over to it on an exchange basis of 2 lira for 1 peso;

c) the government of A is now in a position to be the sole supplier of lira to citizens wishing to purchase lira goods. It supplies 2 lira for each peso offered to it by citizens holding certificates of entitlement — or the government might nationalize importation;

d) the A government may or may not stand ready to provide lira to all foreigners currently earning pesos. It almost certainly will not finance sales of peso securities by foreigners (noting that foreign sellers have nowhere else to turn other than to non-A peso holders);

e) no other controls are imposed. B does not retaliate.

Any A importer now can obtain B goods half as cheaply as before (in terms of pesos). On the other hand, A exporters now find that peso equivalents to lira earnings are only half as great as before. Supply prices of A exports (expressed in lira) will tend to increase. B importers, buying in A markets, will have to pay 2 lira in order to obtain

1 peso if foreign earners of pesos are able to exchange them for lira at the 1:2 rate: they will be discouraged from buying A goods.[37] (And peso prices of B exports will fall.) If B demand for A goods is inelastic, A's lira earnings will increase. But assume that B's demand for A goods is elastic, that A's lira earnings fall. In that case, A's sales to B decline and A's earnings of lira exchange must be rationed to A citizens. On the other hand, the *terms of trade* have been turned in A's favor. To put it crudely, the shrinkage of the bundle of A goods going to B has been greater than that of the bundle of B goods going to A (valuing goods at initial prices).

It is quite easy to show, at least in a statical context, that unimpeded trade can (if the externalities are right) lead to a position in which both A and B in some sense are better off than is the case after A's interference with the market system. Recalling that B is assumed not to retaliate, it remains true that one or another criterion function can find A better off (albeit B might be worse off) than before its government imposed exchange control. The fact that a lot of marginal conditions no longer are observed should not obscure the possibility that, in some sense (not considering in just what sense) A is better off than in the old days when the marginal conditions may have been fulfilled: all that Pareto optimality would do is to make it possible for A to be still better off without B becoming still worse off.

Try a more concrete illustration. Perhaps A imports a class of consumer goods from B, and A's government wants A on a better war-preparedness footing without totally removing B goods from the A menu. The A Government's procedures lead to some reduction in the quantity of B goods imported, but also release A resources from production of goods exported to B. The government finds that the saving in resource cost of exporting to B (a saving partly achieved through improved terms of trade) more than makes up for any deterioration in its citizens' morale. Fortunately B elasticity of demand for A goods was not so high that it was impossible to achieve a meaningful change in the terms of trade without the bundle of B goods that could be purchased becomingly hopelessly shrunk . . . Admittedly, an authoritarian aura has been imposed: all has been subordinated to the

[37] If peso earnings are blocked, B importers would have to get pesos either from the A government or in the black market. Milton Friedman suggests that Hjahmer Schacht, Hitler's finance minister, invented inconvertibility, *defined as prohibition of trading in foreign money*. *Cf.* Friedman, *Capitalism and Freedom* (Chicago: University of Chicago Press, 1962), pp. 57-58.

tastes and preferences of A's rulers. But we seek a rationale, not an apology.

2

We have seen that Country A might find it in "its" interest (*l'état c'est moi*) to set peso prices for lira, francs, etc. that lead to foreign-exchange "shortage," excess demands for foreign currencies being controlled through non-price rationing. There is a refinement of the procedures just described — easily demonstrated once we beat a hasty retreat to the shelter of a two-country model. The A authorities might institute *multiple exchange rates*:

> "In the early 1950's, many countries practicing exchange controls maintained more than one 'price' for foreign currencies, the applicable price depending usually on what kind of payment was to be made, or what kind of commodity imported. At the beginning of 1956, 23 countries were reported by the International Monetary Fund to have multiple exchange rates."[38]

The theory underlying multiple exchange rates is that of *price discrimination*. Thus, the A authorities might be disturbed that a straightforward increase in the lira price of pesos (more lira per peso) applies to A exports that are elastic as well as those inelastic in demand. It also observes that the "overvalued" peso encourages B firms exporting goods assigned high priorities by the A government no more than B exporters of "frivolous" items.

Taking up effects on A exports, consider two of A's exports: ceramic tile and long-staple cotton. Assume that the former is much more differentiated than the latter: roughly, elasticity of demand facing A for its tile exports is substantially less than that facing it for its cotton exports. A might establish a 1:3 exchange rate for lira proceeds from tile sales (1 peso for 3 lira); a 2:1 rate for cotton. Assuming for simplicity that A's tile industry is purely competitively organized and produces at constant cost, lira prices of A ceramic tile will now be trebled. Inelastic demand will result in greater lira receipts despite reduction in the quantity of tile exported. The 1 lira-2 peso rate for proceeds of cotton sales encourages transfer of resources into exportation of cotton; high elasticity of demand for Country A cotton assures

38 Thomas C. Schelling, *International Economics* (Boston: Allyn and Bacon, Inc., 1958), pp. 106-107.

substantial increase in lira proceeds. (I abstract from the implicit two-price system for cotton, pleading mutual fatigue.)

The same sort of game can be played with A's imports. Importers of B goods highly inelastic in supply to A might be forced to pay a higher price in pesos in order to get lira. Importers of B goods elastic in supply to A will be permitted to obtain lira at lower peso prices. And then, quite apart from the terms-of-trade game, multiple exchange rates might be used to discourage demand for "frivolous" imports and encourage that for officially-favored imports without the officials imposing direct prohibitions upon importation of the former. It might be easier to control foreign-exchange transactions than to patrol long coast lines.

There are many fascinating ramifications of multiple-exchange rates. But we content ourselves with the observation that multiple exchange rates are a feature of disequilibrium systems: in general supplies of pesos seeking lira will not equal officially valued (in pesos) supplies of lira seeking pesos; non-price rationing will be practiced.

3

We are about to reach conclusion. We take up restrictions on exportation of *physical capital.*

It often is argued that exportation of physical capital involves net loss of national product because of net complementarity of capital goods with other factors of production. Putting aside external (dis)-economies, this argument is invalid under conventional specifications. On the other hand, it is easy to show that exportation of physical capital can lead to redistribution of income; straightforward assumptions suggest that the brunt will be on laborers. What follows attempts to show that exportation of capital does not lead to diminution of the Pigovian National Dividend and cannot be restricted without departure from Pareto optimality. The demonstration is for small movements, but appropriate convexity assumptions permit application to larger movements.

Assume that exported capital is leased to foreigners for one period. The rent of capital is assumed to be parametric for our country; it will be the same at home as abroad.

Begin in equilibrium "before trade." Ask yourself what will be the loss of product resulting from exportation of a unit of capital in our two-factor, one-final-product world. Assume that there are n firms $(i = 1, 2, \ldots, n)$, each with a production function

(1) $$x_i \equiv f^i(K_i, N_i).$$

Once a unit of capital is exported, there will be a realignment of factor utilization. The change in over-all labor utilization is assumed to be nil. There will be one less unit of capital employed. The over-all change in output, neglecting terms of the third order and above, is shown by Equation 2:

(2) $$\Delta(\Sigma x_i) = \Sigma f^i_K dK_i + \Sigma f^i_N dN_i + 2\Sigma f^i_{NK} dK_i\, dN_i + \Sigma f^i_{KK} dK_i^2 + \Sigma f^i_{NN} dN_i^2.$$

Neglecting second-order terms — footnote 39 shows that consideration of these second-order-of-small terms strengthens the argument — and denoting the common value for the marginal productivity of labor as A and that for capital as B (the initial state was one of equilibrium), we have

(3) $$A\Sigma dN_i + B\Sigma dK_i = d(\Sigma x_i).$$

Since $\Sigma dN_i = 0$ and $\Sigma dK_i = -1$, we have

(4) $$d(\Sigma x_i) = -B.$$

This is a very elaborate way of saying that, when an economy loses a unit of physical capital, it loses (approximately) its marginal product. Clearly, if the global rent of capital exceeds B, the National Dividend can be increased by exporting capital. In fact, there will be exportation unless B equals the global rental. Maximization of the National Dividend here requires that resources be permitted to seek out the highest returns available to them.[40]

SUMMARY

1. Present-day governments hopefully avoid price, foreign-exchange, interest-rate, and output adjustments in correcting transitory bal-

---

[39] Satisfaction of second-order conditions at the initial equilibrium requires

$$d^2(\Sigma x_i) < 0.$$

The first differential slightly *overstates* the product lost to the economy by removal of a unit of capital. Indeed this alone should resolve the argument.

[40] If exportation of capital reduced rents that could be earned in world markets, restrictions on exportation might be profitable in accord with the standard theory of monopoly pricing.

ance-of-payments disequilibria. Liquidity requirements are correspondingly high.

2. The sum of international monetary reserves — even including foreign holdings of dollars and sterling — has not grown as much as has the volume of international trade, measured nominally, since World War II.
3. The global liquidity problem is much exacerbated by the postwar gold-exchange standards. Dollars and sterling — national currencies — have become international reserves. British and, it would appear, American convertibility have been threatened.
4. The International Monetary Fund is the key institution in today's system of international payments. The IMF makes available foreign currency to members — technically as part of a transaction in which the "borrowing" member makes a sale of his own currency to the Fund.
5. The Fund's holdings of gold are in the neighborhood of $2.5 billion, a small sum in terms of global liquidity requirements. There is little that the *Fund,* as presently constituted, can do to counteract pressure against the dollar. On the other hand, as long as the dollar's convertibility is assured, the Fund's dollar holdings are useful in aiding members other than the United States. This points up the tremendous potential pressure on the dollar: the United States gold stock is — under a gold-exchange standard — subject to levy by the rest of the world.
6. Global gold production cannot be expected to increase enough in coming years to close the gap between international liquidity requirements and monetary reserves *at present valuations of gold.*
7. Three proposals for reform were considered: revaluation of gold, the Keynes-Triffin plan, and the Bernstein plan.
8. Revaluation, a very simple proposal, is unlikely to attract official favor for at least three reasons:

a) central bankers fear that increases in gold prices large enough to make an important difference and to avoid destablizing speculation (anticipating further revaluation) will be a siren lure for weak-willed governments to inflate.

b) benefits of revaluation would be substantial for Russia and for the Union of South Africa. It would increase the liquidity of large more than of small gold holders.

c) for many it carries with it emotionally displeasing connotations.

9. The Keynes-Triffin plan calls into being an international medium of exchange (bancor) that could be created by the IMF and would supplement gold. Ideally, bancor would be inconvertible but would substitute for gold in international clearances at a fixed rate. Bancor balances would be provided for members with adverse clearances through overdraft facilities.

10. The Triffin Plan's success might depend on considerable intervention by the IMF in national money markets.

11. The Bernstein Plan would permit the IMF to issue long-term debentures: it could act as a financial intermediary, purchasing scarce exchange by issuing debentures, lending the exchange to member clients.

12. None of these proposals for reform is intended to strike at fundamental causes of disequilibrium. The IMF system might permit structural disequilibrium to become extremely serious before corrective action is taken. IMF placebos, however effective, *might* induce the patient to delay his operation too long.

13. From about 1942 to 1957 many thought that structural changes had occurred requiring either secular dollar scarcity or persistent reduction in dollar prices of non-dollar currencies. Experience since 1958 moots this prophecy.

14. Economic systems typically function with excess demands (supplies), sometimes for years on end. Authorities also ration resources by non-price techniques. This bears on foreign-exchange markets, especially during and after World War II.

15. Exchange rates might be fixed in full knowledge that excess demand will develop for various foreign currencies — that one's own currency will be in excess supply. The idea might be to impose more favorable terms of trade. Such a choice is apt to be accompanied by a wide range of selective controls.

16. Among the more interesting forms of official manipulation are multiple-exchange-rate systems, permitting price discrimination and virtual prohibition or restriction of importation of some items without having to worry about smuggling.

17. There has been a steady increase in convertibility of currencies throughout the West since about 1958. Non-price rationing has become less important. This reflects at least two things: (a) the

growing economic power of the continental European powers; (b) retaliation possibilities, "all they that take the sword shall perish by the sword."

NOTES

NOTE A: Table VII shows how the overhang of foreign claims has developed more recently.

U. S. GOLD RESERVES AND SHORT-TERM LIABILITIES TO FOREIGNERS IN MILLIONS OF DOLLARS

		Short-Term Liabilities to Foreigners			
Period (End of)	U. S. Gold Stock	Grand Total	International Institutions	Foreign Countries, Official	Foreign Countries, Private
1956	22,058	14,939	1,452	8,045	5,442
1957	22,857	15,158	1,517	7,917	5,724
1958	20,582	16,159	1,544	8,665	5,950
1959	19,507	19,389	3,158	9,154	7,076
1960	17,804	21,326	3,955	10,326	7,045
March, 1961	17,433	21,090	3,877	10,309	6,904
July, 1961	17,590	21,756	3,983	10,096	7,677
September, 1961	17,331	21,943	3,434	10,929	7,580

TABLE XVI-VII

Source: Federal Reserve *Bulletin* (Board of Governors, Federal Reserve Board), November 1961, p. 1362 *ff.*

In June 1959 the United States paid $1,031 million to the IMF by way of an increase in the American subscription to the Fund.

Table VII makes clear that the American gold drain has not been caused by foreign withdrawals of funds, that in fact foreign holdings of short-term United States securities increased substantially over the interval of the gold outflow. Not nearly as much as did United States holdings of foreign securities, however.

The substantial increase in *official* foreign holdings of short term United States obligations is, of course, ominous, implying that tremendous pressure might be exerted against United States gold reserves if foreign governments choose to convert these holdings, comprising as they do a substantial portion of *their* monetary reserves. Column 5 is very much in accordance with Triffin's point.

Table VIII shows net purchases of United States government and United States corporate long-term securities by foreigners. It reveals that these items do not account for the gold drain either.

NET PURCHASES BY FOREIGNERS OF LONG-TERM AMERICAN SECURITIES

Period	U. S. Government Securities	U. S. Corporate Securities
1957	—52	194
1958	36	— 39
1959	689	435
1960	127	252
Jan.-Sept. 1961	315	155 (Jan.-Aug.)

TABLE XVI-VIII

Source: Ibid.

From January to July 1961, total private American purchases of foreign securities was in excess of $1,800 million.

NOTE B: Britain drew £535 million in August 1961 from the IMF. This is to say that she deposited that much sterling with the Fund, drawing out equivalent amounts of desired assets. She repaid £100 million in Octoer 1961 (i.e., repurchased £100 million in sterling). IMF proffered a stand-by facility for Britain of $2 billion.

The *Economist,* November 25, 1961, offers data under the heading "Financing the Deficit." There were three stages: 1960, Jan. to July 1961, and July-Oct. 1961. The data are summarized in Table IX. Remember that "gold gain" is an *outgoing* item: gold is purchased with sterling. "Ford payment" refers to purchase of British interests by American Ford. "Basle credits" refer to accommodation to Britain by European central banks. These are some of the notable events described by the table:

i) decided weakness on current account in 1960 was offset by very large investment in sterling securities by non-sterling economic units. "Private capital . . . financed the yawning basic deficit of 1960." (*Ibid.*)

ii) there was massive withdrawal of this capital in 1961, which together with continued substantial British purchases of non-sterling securities and continued deficit in the balance on current account led to a very large gold drain from Jan.-July 1961. The pressure was somewhat relieved by the Basle credits;

iii) the crisis came to a head at the end of July 1961. Drastic internal measures, featuring 7 per cent Bank rate, have been described. These were accompanied in August by aid from the IMF. Speculative attack on sterling was halted and in fact there was considerable reflux of funds into sterling securities.

FINANCING THE U. K. DEFICIT: FUNDING IN THREE STAGES

(in £ million)

	1960	Jan.-Jul. 1961	Jul.-Oct. 1961
OUTGOINGS			
Current Deficit	339	83	
Long-term Capital	196	124	
Sterling Area Drawings	224		
Official Withdrawal of £ Bal.		76	
Private Withdrawal of £ Bal.		296	
Other Capital		190	
Repayments to IMF	156		100
Repayments of Basle Credits			300
Gold Gain	175		385
TOTAL	1090	769	785
FINANCED BY			
£ bal of non-£ countries	473		
Ford Payment	131		
Basle Credits		320	
Drawing on IMF			535
Sterling Area Balances		124	
Reflux of Funds			250
Other Capital	122	47	
Gold Loss		278	
Unidentified Receipts	364		
TOTAL	1090	769	785

TABLE XVI-IX

Source: London *Economist,* Nov. 25, 1961, p. 795.

NOTE C: The *Economist,* January 13, 1962, p. 146, reports adoption of a scheme for supplementing the resources of the IMF. A new lenders' club has been formed. "Ten industrial countries [United States, United Kingdom, Germany, France, Italy, Japan, Canada, Netherlands, Belgium, and Sweden] are the club's founder members, but any country can join. All it need do is put itself down for a minimum of $100 million in freely usable money." The *Economist* continues, "the club will lend only to its own members — other members of the IMF will continue to draw on its ordinary resources, more of which will now be available to them." The club is established within the machinery of the IMF. When one of its members wishes to obtain credit, it issues debentures to the Fund. The Fund in turn issues interest-bearing non-negotiable certificates of debt for currency from one or more members of the club whose currency is in demand by debtor member(s). ["These credits are a highly-attractive central banking asset. They are gold guaranteed; they bear interest in gold at 1½ per cent a year . . ."] Accelerated payment can be had by creditors if the Fund approves. (It is likely that it will.) The Fund in turn is expected to call on the debtor. "Repayment here will be in a currency which is convertible in fact" . . . or in gold; and, if necessary, the other club members may be asked to put up more money to finance the repayment. Repayment in the ordinary case will, where possible, be in the creditor's own currency.

The *Economist* comments: "hitherto the Fund has had a fixed stock of currencies, paid in . . . on the basis of trading size. The new arrangements for contingent, returnable contributions conform to the principle of . . . a true international clearing system." The Club's schemata clearly is that of the Bernstein Plan (cf. p. 859 *ff*.) . The IMF comes very close to playing the role of a true non-banking financial intermediary. All that remains is for the debt certificates to become negotiable.

The new lending commitments are: United States, $2 billion; United Kingdom, $1 billion; continental common-market club members, a total of $2.45 billion; others, $0.550 billion. The increase in United States, United Kingdom lending commitments is rather beside the point just now (June 1962). The total increase in the commitment of Germany, France, Italy, Netherlands, and Belgium ($2.45 billion) may not be impressive, but "at the crucial point, the specific lending commitments need not be the last word either. The worth of any scheme depends on the enthusiasm . . . of the creditors. Perhaps even they may in time recognize the appeal of interest-bearing gold."

NOTE D: The table below indicates the extent to which there have been currency revaluations from December 1946 to August 15, 1961.

PAR VALUES OF SELECTED CURRENCIES IN U. S. DOLLARS

Country	Currency Unit	Initial Par (Dec 1946)	Par as of August 15, 1961
Belgium	Franc	0.023	0.020
Canada	Dollar	1.000	1.031*
Chile	Peso	0.032	0.000941**
France	Franc	0.008	0.002026***
India	Rupee	0.302	0.210
Netherlands	Guilder	0.378	0.276
United Kingdom	Pound	4.030	2.800
United States	Dollar	1.000	1.000

TABLE XVI-X

Source: International Financial Statistics, Vol. XIV, No. 9.

* Market value during July 1961.

** Market value during July 1961. On January 1, 1960, Chile's currency unit became the Escudo, valued at 1,000 Chilean pesos.

*** Quotation in old Francs. On January 1, 1960, the French monetary unit became the new Franc valued at 100 old Francs. As in the case of Chile, this was merely a change in measure. The dollar value of the French money stock of December 31, 1959, was unaffected by the changeover; the prices of all goods, *including money*, changed proportionately. Contrast this with the British devaluation of 1949: the dollar value of the British money stock was reduced.

NOTE E: The following summarizes conclusions reached on revaluation, assuming full employment throughout. *Cf.* Appendix, Ch. II and Chapters XIV and XV.

1) Assume monetary gold stocks cannot be held by the public. Ignore non-monetary gold stocks. Assume that the authorities cause the money stock to vary proportionately with the nominal value of the gold stock. Always work with a closed system. If prices are perfectly flexible, revaluation of gold will have no effect on the real variables of the system: all prices will rise in the same proportion as the price of gold. If prices are sticky, there will be transitory increases in gold production.

2) Adhere to the assumptions of (1) except that the money stock is to be held fixed by the authorities or at least not varied proportionately with official gold holdings. An increase in the price of gold *will* affect the real solution state of the system; among other things, resources devoted to gold production will be increased.

3) Work with a gold-bullion standard in which the public is permitted to hold bullion and in which gold is valued only for monetary purposes. The full-equilibrium state of the system will be invariant against the price of gold (assuming that a dollar's worth of gold bullion is treated as a perfect substitute for a dollar's worth of representative paper money — otherwise not). Prices will vary proportionately with the price of gold in full equilibrium. However, transition to the new equilibrium state finds gold production increasing from hypothesized zero levels in order that the real state of the system finally be restored.

4) Work with a gold-coin standard without bank money. An increase in the nominal price of gold leads to instantaneous proportional increase in all prices if there is perfect price flexibility.

5) Amend paragraph (4): assume sticky prices. There will be transitory increase in the production of gold. If gold cannot be "consumed" and is perfectly durable, the new solution state will find the real value of gold balances unchanged, but the price level will increase relatively more than the accounting price of gold. Otherwise, the real value of the gold stock would exceed that in the initial equilibrium. (Reminiscent of "inside-money" cases.)

6) If nominal prices of gold and silver are both increased, and if prices are sticky, the new full-equilibrium state is *not* invariant (when deflated) against the increased nominal prices. The reasoning is that of paragraph (5): prices of the monetary metals relative to other prices must change.

7) Invariance is obtainable if prices are flexible. In certain instances the government must also be willing and able to supply monetary stocks out of its own inventories.

Turning to less-than-full employment states, price levels cannot be expected to vary with changes in "the gold and/or silver content of the dollar." Hence, Professor Warren's predictions could not be fulfilled. There were other reasons detailed in Ch. II.

President Kennedy's proposals of November 28, 1961 to repeal the Silver Purchase Act of 1934, together with his executive action of that date, are interesting in this connection. He has also asked that silver certificates be replaced by Federal Reserve Notes, thereby releasing 1.2 billion oz. of silver for coinage purposes.

The President ordered the Treasury to stop selling silver at 91 cents per ounce, and said he would ask Congress to repeal legislation requiring it to buy silver at 90.5 cents per ounce, "breaking the Democratic Party's tie to silver." Increased industrial demand for silver, related to exotic uses in missilery and to other things, led to the Treasury's silver stock being seriously depleted: at the end of November all but 22 million ounces of the Government's 1.7 billion ounce stock was committed as a reserve for silver certificates.

This illuminates problems incident to authorities standing ready to buy and sell unlimited quantities of a good at stated prices. They lose a degree of freedom that can be regained only by accommodating to the stock position that must be accepted if the stated price is to clear the market. If the authorities do not have enough ammunition, they must abandon the quest.

It is hard to understand Note E unless it is seen that in a full gold standard the price of gold becomes *defined* by the buy-and-sell provisions of the coinage act; invoking Minkowski spaces, the world-line of the price of gold becomes *definitionally* horizontal. The world-line of the price of anything other than the standard of value might, indeed, be flat, but only because of purposive official action, technology, tastes, etc., *not* by definition.

CHAPTER SEVENTEEN

Summary of the Work

1. MONEY BELONGS TO THE CLASS OF THINGS PERFORMING MONETARY FUNCTIONS.

2. There is a tendency to confuse money of account, an abstract measure, with that class of things called money, a confusion largely induced by the habit of using the same symbol for both.

3. Monetary standards have come to be important not in terms of choice of the *numeraire* good, but rather in terms of establishment of convertibility requirements. Thus, metallic standards find the monetary base, on which rests a much larger stock of debt convertible into metal(s), not in control of the authorities. This is in sharp contrast with fiat paper standards.

4. Paper money, as Mill said, "derives its power for performing [the functions of money] solely from convention; but convention is quite sufficient to confer that power . . ."

5. Financial institutions acquire primary debt obligations, issuing their own liabilities in exchange. The latter are usually of much shorter duration than the former. Demand obligations of commercial banks are classified as money by just about everyone. Liabilities of non-banking financial institutions, however, have very considerable liquidity properties and are of crucial importance in modern economies.

6. Commercial banks are of special importance, since their liabilities — in the form of demand deposits — serve as a means of

payment. Commercial banking is an especially dramatic illustration of borrowing on short term and lending on larger term. A consolidated balance sheet for commercial banks shows that their deposit obligation is far in excess of the sum of their vault cash and reserve accounts. Ours is a *fractional-reserve* system of commercial banking with a systematic coefficient of expansion (contraction) in the neighborhood of 7.

7. The work done each year by bank deposits is in the *trillions* of dollars. Demand deposits typically turn over many times during the year.

8. The real-bills doctrine (commercial-loan theory of banking) and 100-per-cent-reserve banking are perfectly anithetical. The former theory envisages expansion and contraction of bank credit as response to pressures from households and firms motivated by the "needs of trade." The basic weakness of the real-bills doctrine — crucial for American banking history, the Federal Reserve System having been conceived in sin — is that it supposes the monetary "requirements" of the business community to be a quantity definable independently of the behavior of banks and the psychology of business men.

9. The traditional focus of concentration on central-bank policy concerns central-bank manipulation of member-bank reserves, affecting the cost and availability of credit, in turn expected to have at least transitory impact on labor and commodity markets.

10. Impact of central-bank policy on long- and short-term rates might be very different because of expectations, hedging pressure, and liquidity preference.

11. The appropriate theory to apply to month-by-month central bank policy is dynamical and should concentrate on transitional states of economic systems. One is not so much concerned with lingering effects of central-bank actions on, say, interest rates, as with the contribution of changes in *prevailing* interest rates to adjustment processes, including those of prices and outputs.

12. The American Federal Reserve System is a true central-banking apparatus. Its functions include almost all of the classical tasks of a central bank: issue, service as the government's banker, agent, and adviser, custodianship of cash reserves of commercial banks, service as a bank of rediscount and lender of last resort, service as a bank of central clearing, settlement and transfer, exercise of control of credit, and execution of open-market and discount-rate policy.

13. A drastic change in the environment of central banking was occasioned in the United States and Britain by the huge increase in government debt in this century. It is possible for central banks largely to confine their operations to government debt and still have broad and penetrating impact on all markets of the American and British systems.

14. Modern central banking did not spring fully grown from the brow of an economic Zeus. Central banking history in fact tells a chequered tale of woe. The haphazard nature of central-banking development is illustrated by the origins of open-market policy in the United States in the early 1920's: the Federal Reserve needed more income, and, accordingly, bought securities.

15. The concept of velocity of monetary circulation immediately suggests interest in the regularity (or lack thereof) of empirical relationships between monetary stocks and income or transactions flows.

16. Once the mechanical determinants of velocity are understood, one asks whether interest rates have important and prompt impact on velocity. If they do, execution of monetary policy can become very difficult if not impossible (for political reasons if not because of dynamical instability): huge doses of monetary policy might be required to achieve given ends. And, of course, if expenditure decisions are insensitive to interest rates, there may have to be large fluctuations in interest rates in order to budge the system.

17. The demand for money is demand for a stock. The theory of demand for money must be part of a theory of asset-portfolio determination.

18. In order for a thing to perform monetary functions, prices measured in terms of it must be sticky: otherwise money could not perform a role as a standard for deferred payments or a liquid asset.

19. Of course, if the convenience yield associated with liquidity properties of money has a lower limit — approached asymptomatically as the stock of money increases — a floor to yields throughout the system becomes established.

20. There are links between the monetary standard and the possibility of persistent involuntary unemployment of factors of production and/or excess supply of goods. If the monetized commodity were produced at constant cost, there could be no involuntary unemployment even briefly; if the monetized commodity were produced at increasing cost, meaningful wage-price flexibility might be necessary to

avoid persistent excess supply of factors and commodities; in the case of a paper standard, wage-price flexibility might not only fail to relieve unemployment — an endless spiral of deflation could ensue.

21. The first approximation to income theory (Ch. IX) concentrates on explicating the Keynesian dictum:

> "the volume of employment is uniquely related to [generates] a given level of real wages — not the other way around."

22. The second approximation to income theory (Ch. X) takes account of financial and other assets and their prices. The relationships between asset prices and investment behavior were explored.

23. The third approximation to income theory (Ch. XI) introduces a government sector whose policy (monetary and fiscal) cannot be described through conventional utility or profit-maximization criteria.

24. The fourth approximation to income theory (Ch. XII) concerns motions of economic systems over time. In dynamical analysis certain regular motions — including stationary states — are but special cases. One generally is able to deal with points anywhere within hyperspaces with time dimensions.

25. The models of Chapters IX-XI implied ongoing processes of accumulation of capital: solution values for the system's endogenous variables can be expected to change over time. Focus on investment behavior becomes imperative.

26. One must beware of paying excessive heed to models, such as those of Harrod and Hicks, capable of generating only simple motions.

27. The theory of policy boils down to analysis of reduced forms of equation systems, at least if we confine ourselves to comparative statics. One examines the behavior of solution values of endogenous variables such as employment and output in response to changes in policy variables (parameters of the system) such as taxation rates, autonomous official spending, central-banking holdings of securities, transfer-payment parameters, etc.

28. The pure theory of central-bank policy is based on models with excess degrees of freedom. The authorities select target values for some unknowns (which need not be under their direct control). They solve the system for solution values of remaining variables consistent with these targets. Once this has been done, the officials need only take appropriate action with respect to variables under their

"physical" control. Wicksellian (de)inflation models also were considered.

29. More sophisticated models of central-bank policy do not take monetary stocks as given. Rather such parameters as required-reserve ratios and rates of interest paid by central banks on deposits are considered.

30. The quantity theory of money — as a theorem of comparative statics — is concerned with the "neutrality of money." Among other things, will the equilibrium real value of the money stock be invariant against the nominal stock? Under certain strict assumptions, the answer is "yes," and is consistent with a broad range of specifications for the demand function for money.

31. From the standpoint of economic theory, the "quantity theory of money" is but one of a wide class of propositions about invariance of real variables (in equilibrium) against exogenous changes in nominal values of stocks. It evokes contrast of full- with temporary-equilibrium states.

32. The central theme of Part III — largely dealing with the theory of the balance of payments — concerns impingement of international considerations on autonomy of national authorities. Roughly speaking, exchange-rate rigidity requires that authorities accept price levels and interest rates consistent with external forces, while autonomy over prices and/or interest rates requires acceptance of externally-determined foreign-exchange rates.

33. Today's international liquidity problems are within a special setting: price, foreign-exchange, interest-rate, and output adjustments ideally are to be eschewed in correcting transitory balance-of-payments disequilibria.

34. Accordingly, liquid requirements are high. However, the existing institutional framework — centering on the International Monetary Fund — might not be capable of generating needed liquidity. The main source of international liquidity has been reserves (held by foreign countries) of national currencies, particularly United States dollars and British pounds sterling; the non-communist world is on a gold-exchange standard. There has been serious pressure on the dollar. Indeed some hold that, unless international monetary institutions are basically reformed, United States gold reserves will prove inadequate.

35. Money belongs to the class of things performing monetary functions.

BIBLIOGRAPHY

ALEXANDER, SIDNEY. Review of Hicks' *A Contribution to the Theory of the Trade Cycle*. *American Economic Review*, December, 1951.

ALLEN, R. G. D. *Mathematical Analysis for Economists*. London: Macmillan and Co., Ltd., 1938.

______. *Mathematical Economics*. London: Macmillan and Co., Ltd., 1956.

ANGELL, J. W. "The Reorganization of the International Monetary System: An Alternative Proposal," *Economic Journal*, Vol. 71, December, 1961.

ARCHIBALD, G. C., and LIPSEY, R. G. "Monetary and Value Theory: A Critique of Lange and Patinkin," *Review of Economic Studies*, Vol. 26, October, 1958.

ASCHHEIM, JOSEPH. *Techniques of Money Control*. Baltimore: The Johns Hopkins Press, 1961.

BAGEHOT, WALTER. *Lombard Street*. London: John Murray, 1915.

BAUMOL, WILLIAM J. *Business Behavior, Value, and Growth*. New York: The Macmillan Co., 1959.

______. *Economic Dynamics*. New York: The Macmillan Co., 1951.

______. *Economic Theory and Operations Analysis*. Englewood Cliffs, N. J.: Prentice-Hall, Inc., 1961.

______. "Monetary and Value Theory: Comments," *Review of Economic Studies*, Vol. 28, No. 1, October, 1960.

______. "Speculation, Profitability, and Stability," *Review of Economics and Statistics*, Vol. 41, August, 1959.

______. "Stocks, Flows, and Monetary Theory," *Quarterly Journal of Economics*, Vol. 76, No. 1, February, 1962.

______. "The Transactions Demand for Cash: An Inventory Theoretic Approach," *Quarterly Journal of Economics*, November, 1952.

BERNSTEIN, E. M. *International Effects of U. S. Monetary Policy*, Joint Economic Committee of Congress. Washington: Government Printing Office, 1960.

______. Letter to The *Economist*. May 20, 1961.

BLOOMFIELD, A. D. *Capital Imports and the American Balance of Payments*. Chicago: University of Chicago Press, 1950.

BOGEN, JULES D. *The Changing Composition of Bank Assets*. New York: New York University Press, 1961.

BOULDING and STIGLER (eds.). *Readings in Price Theory*. Philadelphia: Blakiston & Co., 1951.

BRESCIANA-TURRONI, C. *The Economics of Inflation*. New York: Barnes and Noble, Inc., 1937.

BURGESS, RANDOLPH. *The Federal Reserve Banks and the Money Market* (Rev. Ed.). New York: Harper & Bros., 1946.

BURNS, JAMES MACGREGOR. *Roosevelt: the Lion and the Fox*. New York: Harcourt, Brace & Co., 1956.

BURSTEIN, M. L. "The Measurement of Quality Changes in Consumer Durables," *Manchester School*, Vol. 29, September, 1961.

BUSHAW, D. W., and CLOWER, R. W. *Introduction to Mathematical Economics*. Homewood, Ill.: Richard D. Irwin, Inc., 1957. (Sponsored by the American Economic Association.)

CAGAN, PHILLIP. *The Determinants of the Money Supply in the United States Since 1875*. New York: National Bureau for Economic Research (forthcoming).

______. "The Monetary Dynamics of Hyperinflation," in *Studies in the Quantity Theory of Money,* ed. Milton Friedman. Chicago: University of Chicago Press, 1956.

CAMPBELL, C. D., and TULLOCK, G. C. "Hyperinflation in China, 1937-1949," *Journal of Political Economy,* June, 1954.

CHANDLER, LESTER V. *The Economics of Money and Banking* (Rev. Ed.). New York: Harper & Bros., 1953, 1959.

______. "Federal Reserve Policy and the Federal Debt," *American Economic Review,* Vol. 39, 1949. (Reprinted in Lutz and Mints (eds.), *Readings in Monetary Theory.*)

CLAPHAM, SIR JOHN. *The Bank of England* (2 Vols.). Cambridge: Cambridge University Press, 1944.

CLOWER, R. W. "An Investigation into the Dynamics of Investment," *American Economic Review,* March, 1954.

______. "The Keynesian Counterrevolution: A Theoretical Appraisal" (unpublished). Read to the Conference of the International Economic Association, Paris, April, 1962.

CLOWER, R. W., and BURSTEIN, M. L. "On the Invariance of Demand for Cash and Other Assets," *Review of Economic Studies,* Vol. 28, October, 1960.

Committee on the Working of the Monetary System. "Memoranda of Evidence submitted by the Bank of England," (A. E. Jasay), in *Principal Memoranda of Evidence.* London: Her Majesty's Stationary Office, 1960.

______. *Report.* London: Her Majesty's Stationary Office, 1959.

CONARD, JOSEPH W. *Introduction to the Theory of Interest.* Berkeley: University of California Press, 1959.

The Constitution of the United States. Article 1, Section 8, §§ 2, 5, 6. Article 1, Section 10, §§ 1.

CRAMP, A. B. "Two Views on Money," *Lloyds Bank Review,* July, 1962.

CROWTHER, GEOFFREY. *An Outline of Money.* London: Thomas Nelson & Sons, Ltd., 1948.

CULBERTSON, J. M. "Friedman on the Lag in Effect of Monetary Policy," *Journal of Political Economy,* Vol. 68, December, 1960.

______. "Reply," *Journal of Political Economy,* Vol. 69, October, 1961.

CURRIE, LAUCHLIN. *The Supply and Control of Money in the United States.* Cambridge: Harvard University Press, 1934.

DACEY, W. MANNING. *The British Banking Mechanism.* London: Hutchinson, 1951.

______. "The Floating Debt Problem," *Lloyds Bank Review,* April, 1956.

DAVIS, R. G., and GUTTENBERG, J. M. "Time and Savings Deposits in the Cycle." Federal Reserve Bank of New York *Monthly Review,* Vol. 44, No. 6, June, 1962.

DAY, A. C. L. *Outline of Monetary Economics.* Oxford: The Clarendon Press, 1957.

DAY, A. C. L., and BEZA, S. T. *Money and Income.* New York: Oxford University Press, 1960.

DE GRAAF, J. *Theoretical Welfare Economics.* Cambridge: Cambridge University Press, 1958.

DEKOCK, M. H. *Central Banking.* London: Staples Press, Ltd., 1954.

DERNBURG, T. F., and MCDOUGALL, D. M. *Macroeconomics.* New York: McGraw-Hill Book Co., 1960.

DOMAR, EVSEY D. *Essays in the Theory of Economic Growth.* New York: Oxford University Press, 1957.

DORFMAN, R., SAMUELSON, P. A., and SOLOW, R. M. *Linear Programming and Economic Analysis.* New York: McGraw-Hill Book Co., 1958.

DUESENBERRY, JAMES S. *Business Cycles and Economic Growth.* New York: McGraw-Hill Book Co., 1958.

______. *Income, Saving and the Theory of Consumer Behavior.* Cambridge: Harvard University Press, 1949.

Economic Policy Commission, American Bankers Association. *Member Bank Reserve Requirements.* New York: 1957.

Economic Report of the President. Washington: Government Printing Office, 1961.

Economic Report of the President. Washington: Government Printing Office, 1959.

The *Economist,* April 28, 1962, pp. 366-68.

The *Economist,* February 10, 1962, pp. 541-542.

The *Economist,* January 13, 1962.

The *Economist,* November 25, 1961.

The *Economist,* August 5, 1961.

The *Economist,* July 22, 1961.

The *Economist,* May 6, 1961.

The *Economist,* June 1, 1957.

The *Economist,* May 4, 1957.

The *Economist,* March 30, 1957.

EINAUDI, LUIGI. *Enterprise and Secular Change.* Homewood, Ill.: Richard D. Irwin, Inc., 1952. (Sponsored by the American Economic Association.)

EINZIG, PAUL. *A Dynamic Theory of Forward Exchange.* London: Macmillan and Co., Ltd., 1961.

ELLIS, H. S. (ed.). *A Survey of Contemporary Economics.* Homewood, Ill.: Richard D. Irwin, Inc., 1948. (Sponsored by the American Economic Association.)

ELLIS, H. S., and METZLER, LLOYD A. (eds.). *Readings in the Theory of International Trade.* Homewood, Ill.: Richard D. Irwin, Inc., 1949. (Sponsored by the American Economic Association.)

ENTHOVEN, ALAIN C. "A Neo-classical Model of Money, Debt, and Economic Growth," Appendix to Gurley and Shaw (eds.), *Money in a Theory of Finance.*

The Federal Funds Market. Washington: Board of Governors, Federal Reserve System, 1959.

Federal Reserve *Bulletin.* Washington: Board of Governors, Federal Reserve System, November, 1961.

Federal Reserve *Bulletin.* Washington: Board of Governors, Federal Reserve System, June, 1961.

Federal Reserve *Chart Book.* Washington: Board of Governors, Federal Reserve System, September, 1961; September, 1960.

The Federal Reserve System, Purposes and Functions. Washington: Board of Governors, Federal Reserve System, 1954.

FELLNER, WILLIAM, and HALEY, BERNARD (eds.). *Readings in the Theory of Income Distribution.* Philadelphia: Blakiston & Co., 1946.

FFORDE, J. S. *The Federal Reserve System.* London: Oxford University Press, 1954.

FISHER, IRVING. *Purchasing Power of Money.* New York: The Macmillan Co., 1926.

——. *The Theory of Interest.* New York: Kelley and Millman, Inc., 1954.

FRIEDMAN, MILTON. "A Monetary and Fiscal Framework for Economic Stability," *American Economic Review,* Vol. 38, June, 1948.

——. *A Program for Monetary Stability.* New York: Fordham University Press, 1960.

_____. *A Theory of the Consumption Function.* Princeton: Princeton University Press, 1957.

_____. "Commodity-Reserve Currency," in *Essays in Positive Economics.*

_____. *Essays in Positive Economics.* Chicago: University of Chicago Press, 1953.

_____ (ed). *Studies in the Quantity Theory of Money.* Chicago: University of Chicago Press, 1956.

_____. "The Case for Flexible Exchange Rates," in *Essays in Positive Economics.*

_____. "The Demand for Money: Some Theoretical and Empirical Results," *Journal of Political Economy,* Vol. 67, August, 1959.

_____. "The Lag in Effect of Monetary Policy," *Journal of Political Economy,* Vol. 69, October, 1961.

_____. "Vault Cash and Free Reserves," *Journal of Political Economy,* Vol. 69, No. 2, April 1961.

FRIEDMAN, MILTON, and SAVAGE, A. L. "The Utility Analysis of Choices Involving Risk," *Journal of Political Economy,* Vol. 56, 1948.

FRIEDMAN, MILTON, and SCHWARTZ, ANNA. *The United States Money Stock.* Princeton: Princeton University Press, 1963.

GARVEY, GEORGE. *Deposit Velocity and Its Significance.* New York: Federal Reserve Bank of New York, 1959.

GAYER, A. D. *The Lessons of Monetary Experience; Essays in the Honor of Irving Fisher.* Philadelphia: Blakiston & Co., 1949.

GIBBON, EDWARD. *The Decline and Fall of the Roman Empire* (Vol. I). New York: The Modern Library.

GOLDSMITH, RAYMOND E. *Financial Intermediaries in the American Economy Since 1900.* Princeton: Princeton University Press, 1958.

GURLEY, JOHN G., and SHAW, EDWARD S. *Money in a Theory of Finance.* Washington: Brookings Institution, 1960.

HANSEN, ALVIN H. "A Fundamental Error in Keynes' *Treatise on Money,*" *American Economic Review,* Vol. 22, 1932.

______. *A Guide to Keynes.* New York: McGraw-Hill Book Co., Inc., 1953.

______. *Fiscal Policy and Business Cycles.* New York: W. W. Norton and Co., 1941.

______. *Monetary Theory and Fiscal Policy.* New York: McGraw-Hill Book Co., Inc., 1949.

HARDY, CHARLES O. *The Warren-Pearson Price Theory.* Washington: Brookings Institution Pamphlet Series, 1935.

HARRIS, SEYMOUR E. *Exchange Depreciation.* Cambridge: Harvard University Press, 1936.

______ (ed.). *The New Economics.* New York: Alfred A. Knopf, Inc., 1947.

HARROD, R. F. *The Life of John Maynard Keynes.* London: Macmillan and Co., Ltd., 1952.

HARROD, SIR ROY. "An Essay in Dynamic Theory," *Economic Journal,* March, 1939.

______. *The Dollar.* London: Macmillan and Co., Ltd., 1933.

______. *Towards a Dynamic Economics.* London: Macmillan and Co., Ltd., 1948.

HART, A. G. "The 'Chicago Plan' of Banking Reform," *The Review of Economic Studies,* 1935. (Reprinted in Lutz and Mints (eds.), *Readings in Monetary Theory.*)

HART, A. G., and KENEN, P. B. *Money, Debt, and Economic Activity.* Englewood Cliffs, N.J.: Prentice-Hall, Inc., 1961.

HAWTREY, SIR RALPH. *A Century of Bank Rate.* London: Longmans, Green & Co., Ltd., 1938.

______. *Currency and Credit* (4th ed.). London: Longmans, Green & Co., Ltd., 1950.

______. *The Art of Central Banking.* London: Longmans, Green & Co., Ltd., 1932.

______. *The Gold Standard in Theory and Practice* (5th ed.). London: Longmans, Green & Co., Ltd., 1947.

HENDERSON, JAMES M., and QUANDT, RICHARD E. *Microeconomic Theory.* New York: McGraw-Hill Book Co., Inc., 1958.

HICKS, J. R. *A Contribution to the Theory of the Trade Cycle.* Oxford: The Clarendon Press, 1950.

______. "A Rehabilitation of 'Classical' Economics?", *Economic Journal,* Vol. 67, June, 1957.

______. "A Suggestion for Simplifying the Theory of Money," *Economica,* New Series, Vol. 2 (1935). (Reprinted in Lutz and Mints (eds.), *Readings in Monetary Theory.*)

______. "Economic Foundations of Wage Policy," *Economic Journal,* Vol. 65, September, 1955.

______. "Mr. Keynes and the 'Classics'; A Suggested Interpretation," *Econometrica,* Vol. 5, 1937. (Reprinted in Fellner and Haley (eds.), *Readings in the Theory of Income Distribution.*)

______. *Value and Capital.* Oxford: The Clarendon Press, 1938, 1946.

International Financial Statistics, Vol. XIV, No. 9. Washington: International Monetary Fund, September, 1961.

JOHNSON, HARRY G. *International Trade and Economic Growth.* London: George Allen & Unwin, Ltd., 1958.

______. "Monetary Theory and Policy," *American Economic Review,* Vol. 52, June, 1962.

______. "The Revival of Monetary Policy in Britain," *Three Banks Review,* June, 1956.

KAHN, R. F. "The Relation of Home Investment to Unemployment," *Economic Journal,* June, 1931.

KALDOR, NICHOLAS. "A Model of Economic Growth," *Economic Journal,* December, 1957.

______. *Essays on Economic Stability and Growth.* London: Duckworth, 1960.

KEMMERER, EDWIN W. *Money.* New York: The Macmillan Co., 1937.

KEYNES, J. M. *A Tract on Monetary Reform.* London: Macmillan and Co., Ltd., 1923.

______. *A Treatise on Money* (Vols. I &

II). London: Macmillan and Co., Ltd., 1930.

______. *Essays in Persuasion.* London: Macmillan and Co., Ltd., 1931.

______. *The General Theory of Employment, Interest, and Money.* New York: Harcourt, Brace & Co., 1936.

______. "The German Transfer Problem," in Ellis and Metzler (eds.), *Readings in the Theory of International Trade.*

KINDLEBERGER, CHARLES P. *International Economics* (Rev. Ed.). Homewood, Ill.: Richard D. Irwin, Inc., 1958. (Sponsored by the American Economic Association.)

______. *The Dollar Shortage.* New York: John Wiley and Sons, 1950.

KING, WILFRED. *A History of the London Discount Market.* London: George Routledge & Sons, 1936.

KLEIN, LAWRENCE R. *The Keynesian Revolution.* New York: The Macmillan Co., 1947.

KURIHARA, K. (ed.). *Post Keynesian Economics.* New Brunswick, N. J.: Rutgers University Press, 1954.

LANGE, OSCAR. *Price Flexibility and Full Employment.* Bloomington, Ind.: Principia Press, 1944.

LEONTIEF, WASSILY. "Theoretical Note on Time-Preference, Productivity of Capital, Stagnation, and Economic Growth," *American Economic Review,* Vol. 48, No. 1, March, 1958.

______. "Time Preference and Economic Growth," *American Economic Review,* Vol. 49, No. 5, December, 1959.

LERNER, A. P. *Essays in Economic Analysis.* London: Macmillan and Co., Ltd., 1953.

______. "The Essential Properties of Interest and Money," *Quarterly Journal of Economics,* May, 1952. (Reprinted in *Essays in Economic Analysis.*)

______. "Review," *Journal of the American Statistical Association,* Vol. 57, March, 1962.

LERNER, EUGENE. "Inflation in the Confederacy, 1861-1865," in Friedman (ed.), *Studies in the Quantity Theory of Money.*

LUTZ, FRIEDRICH A. *International Liquidity.* Princeton: Princeton University Press, 1963.

LUTZ, FREIDRICH A., and MINTS, LLOYD W. (eds.). *Readings in Monetary Theory.* Homewood, Ill.: Richard D. Irwin, Inc., 1951. (Sponsored by the American Economic Association.)

MACHLUP, FRITZ. *International Trade and the National Income Multiplier.* Philadelphia: Blakiston & Co., 1950.

MALONE, DUMAS. *Jefferson and the Ordeal of Liberty.* Boston: Little, Brown & Co., 1962.

MANN, F. A. *The Legal Aspect of Money* (2nd ed.). London: Oxford University Press, 1953.

MARGET, A. W. *The Theory of Prices* (2 Vols.). Englewood Cliffs, N. J.: Prentice-Hall, Inc., 1938.

MARKOWITZ, HARRY U. *Portfolio Selection.* New York: John Wiley and Sons, 1959.

MARSCHAK, JACOB. *Income, Employment, and the Price Level.* New York: Augustus M. Kelley, 1951.

MARSHALL, ALFRED. *Money Credit and Commerce.* London: Macmillan and Co., Ltd., 1923.

MARTY, ALVIN L. "Review of Gurley and Shaw, Money in a Theory of Finance," *Journal of Political Economy,* Vol. 69, February, 1961.

MARX, KARL. *Das Capital.* New York: The Modern Library.

MATTHEWS, R. C. O. *The Business Cycle.* Chicago: University of Chicago Press, 1959.

MCKEAN, R. N. "Liquidity and a National Balance Sheet," in *Journal of Political Economy,* Vol. 57. (Reprinted in Lutz and Mints (eds.), *Readings in Monetary Theory.*)

MEADE, J. E. *A Neo-Classical Theory of Economic Growth.* London: George Allen and Unwin, Ltd., 1961.

______. *The Balance of Payments.* London: Oxford University Press, 1952.

MEIGS, A. JAMES. *Free Reserves and The Money Supply.* Chicago: University of Chicago Press, 1962.

METZLER, LLOYD A. "The Theory of International Trade," in H. S. Ellis (ed.), *A Survey of Contemporary Economics.*

______. "The Transfer Problem Reconsidered," in Ellis and Metzler (eds.), *Readings in the Theory of International Trade.*

______. "Three Lags in the Circulation Flow of Income," in Metzler *et al, Income, Employment and Public Policy; Essays in Honor of Alvin H. Hansen.*

______. "Underemployment Equilibrium in International Trade," *Econometrica,* Vol. 10, April, 1942.

______. "Wealth, Interest, and the Rate of Saving," *Journal of Political Economy,* April, 1951.

METZLER, LLOYD A., *et al. Income, Employment and Public Policy; Essays in Honor of Alvin H. Hansen.* New York: W. W. Norton & Co., 1948.

MILL, J. S. *Principles of Political Economy.* J. W. Ashley, ed. (8th ed.), London: Longmans, Green & Co., Ltd., 1940.

MINTS, LLOYD W. *A History of Banking Theory.* Chicago: University of Chicago Press, 1945.

______. *Monetary Policy in a Competitive Society.* New York: McGraw-Hill Book Co., 1950.

MODIGLIANI, FRANCO. "Fluctuations in the Saving-Income Ratio: A Problem in Economic Forecasting," *Studies in Income and Wealth,* XI. New York: National Bureau of Economic Research, 1949.

______. "Liquidity Preference and the Theory of Interest and Money," in Lutz and Mints (eds.), *Readings in Monetary Theory.*

______. "Long-run Implications of Alternative Fiscal Policies and the Burden of the National Debt," *Economic Journal,* December, 1961.

______. "The Monetary Mechanism and Its Interaction with Real Phenomena," paper read at the National Bureau of Economic Research Conference, Pittsburgh, April, 1962.

MODIGLIANI, FRANCO, and BURMBERG, RICHARD. "Utility Analysis and the Consumption Function: An Interpretation of Cross-Section Data," in K. Kurihara (ed.), *Post Keynesian Economics.*

MODIGLIANI, FRANCO, and MILLER, M. H. "The Cost of Capital, Corporation Finance, and the Theory of Investment," *American Economic Review,* June, 1958.

MOSAK, JACOB L. *General Equilibrium Theory in International Trade.* Bloomington, Ind.: Principia Press, 1944.

MOULTON, HAROLD G., *et al. The Recovery Problem in the United States.* Washington: Brookings Institution, 1936.

MUNDELL, ROBERT A. "The Monetary Dynamics of International Adjustment under Fixed and Flexible Exchange Rates," *Quarterly Journal of Economics,* Vol. 74, May, 1960.

NADLER, MARCUS, *et al. The Money Market and its Institutions.* New York: The Ronald Press Co., 1955.

NEWLYN, W. T. *Theory of Money.* London: Oxford University Press, 1962.

NICHOLSON, HAROLD. *The Age of Reason.* New York: Doubleday & Co., Inc., 1960.

NUSSBAUM, ARTHUR. *A History of the Dollar.* New York: Columbia University Press, 1957.

OHLIN, BERTIL. "The Reparation Problem: A Discussion," in Ellis and Metzler (eds.), *Readings in the Theory of International Trade.*

ORR, D., and MELLON, W. J. "Stochastic Reserve Losses and Bank Credit." *American Economic Review,* Vol. 51, September, 1961.

PAISH, F. W. *The Post-War Financial Problem.* London: Macmillan and Co., Ltd., 1950.

PATINKIN, DON. "Financial Intermediaries and the Logical Structure of Monetary Theory, a review article," *American Economic Review,* Vol. 51, March, 1961.

______. *Money, Interest, and Prices.* Evanston, Ill.: Row, Peterson & Co., 1956.

______. "Price Flexibility and Full Employment," *American Economic Review,* Vol. 38, 1948. (Reprinted in Lutz and Mints (eds.), *Readings in Monetary Theory.*)

PHILLIPS, C. A. *Bank Credit.* New York: The Macmillan Co., 1921.

PIGOU, A. C. "Economic Progress in a Stable Environment," *Economica,* New Series, Vol. 14, 1947. (Reprinted in Lutz and Mints (eds.), *Readings in Monetary Theory.*)

______. *Essays in Applied Economics.* London: Macmillan and Co., Ltd., 1923.

______. "The Classical Stationary State," *Economic Journal,* Vol. 53, December, 1943.

"Prices and the Turnpike," a symposium

featuring J. R. Hicks, M. Morishima, and R. Radner, *Review of Economic Studies,* Vol. XXVIII, No. 2, February, 1961.

RAMSEY, FRANK. "A Mathematical Theory of Saving," *Economic Journal,* 1928.

RIEFLER, W. "Open Market Operations in Long-Term Securities," Federal Reserve *Bulletin*. Washington: Board of Governors, Federal Reserve System, November, 1958.

ROBBINS, LIONEL. *Robert Torrens and the Evolution of Classical Economics.* London: Macmillan and Co., Ltd., 1958.

ROBERTSON, D. H. *Money.* London: Pitman, 1948.

ROBINSON, JOAN. *The Accumulation of Capital.* London: Macmillan and Co., Ltd., 1956.

______. *Essays in Marxian Economics.* London: Macmillan and Co., Ltd., 1949.

______. *Introduction to the Theory of Employment.* London: Macmillan and Co., Ltd., 1939.

______. "The Rate of Interest," *Econometrica,* Vol. 19, April, 1951.

ROBINSON, R. "A Graphical Analysis of the Foreign Trade Multiplier," *Economic Journal,* September, 1952.

ROSA (ROOSA), ROBERT V. *Federal Reserve Operations in the Money and Government Securities Markets.* New York: Board of Governors, Federal Reserve System, 1956.

______. "Interest Rates and the Central Market," in Wright *et al.* (eds.), *"Money, Trade and Economic Growth, in honor of John Henry Williams.*

ROSE, HUGH. "Liquidity Preference and Loanable Funds," *Review of Economic Studies,* Vol. 24, February, 1957.

______. "The Possibility of Warranted Growth," *Economic Journal,* Vol. 69, June, 1959.

RUEFF, JACQUES. "The Fallacies of Lord Keynes's *General Theory," Quarterly Journal of Economics,* Vol. 61, No. 3, May, 1947.

SAMUELSON, PAUL A. "An Exact Consumption Loan Model of Interest with or without the Social Contrivance of Money," *Journal of Political Economy,* Vol. 66, No. 6, December, 1958.

______. *Foundations of Economic Analysis.* Cambridge: Harvard University Press, 1947.

______. "The Simple Mathematics of Income Determination," Metzler *et al.* (eds.), *Income, Employment and Public Policy; Essays in Honor of Alvin H. Hansen.*

______. "The Transfer Problem and Transfer Costs," *Economic Journal,* Vol. 62, June, 1952, and Vol. 64, June, 1954.

SARGENT, J. R. "Disinflation by Funding," The *Economist,* May 19, 1956.

______. "The Supply Factor in Professor Hicks' Theory of the Cycle," *Economic Journal,* Vol. 66, December, 1956.

SAYERS, R. S. *Central Banking After Bagehot.* Oxford: The Clarendon Press, 1957.

______. *Modern Banking.* Oxford: The Clarendon Press, 1951.

SCAMMELL, W. M. *International Economic Policy.* London: Macmillan and Co., Ltd., 1957.

SCHELLING, THOMAS C. *International Economics.* Boston: Allyn & Bacon, Inc., 1958.

SCHLESINGER, ARTHUR M., JR. *The Coming of the New Deal.* Boston: Houghton Mifflin Co., 1959.

SCHUMPETER, JOSEPH. *History of Economic Analysis.* New York: Oxford University Press, 1954.

SENIOR, NASSAU W. *The Cost of Obtaining Money.* London: 1830. (Reprinted as No. 5 in the Scarce Tract Series of the London School of Economics, Lecture I.)

SHACKLE, G. L. S. "Recent Theories Concerning the Nature and Role of Interest," *Economic Journal,* Vol. 71, June, 1961.

SHAW, EDWARD S. *Money, Income, and Monetary Policy.* Homewood, Ill.: Richard D. Irwin, Inc., 1950.

SIMPSON, A. W. B. *An Introduction to the History of the Land Law.* London: Oxford University Press, 1961.

SMITH, ADAM. *The Wealth of Nations.* New York: The Modern Library.

SMITH, WALTER BUCKINGHAM. *Economic Aspects of the Second Bank of the United States.* Cambridge: Harvard University Press, 1953.

SMITH, WARREN L. "The Discount Rate as a Control Weapon." *Journal of Political Economy,* April, 1958.

SMITH, WARREN L., and MICKESELL, RAYMOND F. "The Effectiveness of Monetary Policy: Recent British Experience," *Journal of Political Economy,* Vol. 65, No. 1, February, 1957.

SOLOW, ROBERT. "A Contribution to the Theory of Economic Growth," *Quarterly Journal of Economics,* Vol. 70, February, 1956.

SPRAOS, J. "Speculation, Arbitrage and Sterling," *The Economic Journal,* Vol. 69, No. 273, March, 1959.

STEINER, W. H., SHAPIRO, ELI, and SOLOMON, EZRA. *Money and Banking* (4th ed.). New York: Henry Holt & Co., 1958.

STROTZ, R. H. "Myopia and Inconsistency in Dynamic Utility Maximization," *Review of Economic Studies,* Vol. XXIII, No. 3, 1955-1956.

TELSER, LESTER G. "A Theory of Speculation Relating Profitability and Stability," *Review of Economics and Statistics,* Vol. 41, August, 1959.

THORNTON, HENRY. *An Enquiry into the Nature and Effects of the Paper Credit of Great Britain.* London: 1802. (New York: Rinehart & Co., 1939.)

TOBIN, JAMES. "A Dynamic Aggregative Model," *Journal of Political Economy,* Vol. 63, April, 1955.

———. "Liquidity Preference as Behavior towards Risk." *Review of Economic Studies,* Vol. 25, No. 67, February, 1958. (Reprinted as *Cowles Foundation Paper No. 118.* New Haven: 1958.)

———. "Review of Patman Hearings (sic)", *Review of Economics and Statistics,* May, 1953.

———. "The Interest Elasticity of Transactions Demand for Cash," *Review of Economics and Statistics,* Vol. 38, No. 3, August, 1956.

TOYNBEE, A. J. *A Study of History* (Vol. VII). London: Oxford University Press (Royal Institute of International Affairs), 1954.

TRIFFIN, ROBERT. *Europe and the Money Muddle.* New Haven: Yale University Press, 1957.

———. *Gold and the Dollar Crisis* (Rev. Ed.). New Haven: Yale University Press, 1961.

———. Reply to J. W. Angell, *Economic Journal,* Vol. 72, March, 1962.

U. S. Congress. *Hearings Before the Sub-Committee on Credit Control and Debt Management of the Joint Committee on the Economic Report of the U. S. Congress.* Washington: Government Printing Office, 1952.

———. Joint Economic Committee, *Government Price Statistics, Hearings.* Washington: Government Printing Office, 1961.

USHER, A. P. "The Origins of Banking," *Economic History Review,* Vol. IV, 1934.

VALVANIS, STEFAN. *Econometrics.* New York: McGraw-Hill Book Co., 1959.

VANEK, JAROSLAV. "Appendix" (E) to Kindleberger, *International Economics.*

VINER, JACOB. *Studies in the Theory of International Trade.* New York: Harper & Bros., 1937.

VON HABERLER, GOTTFRIED. *The Theory of International Trade.* London: William Hodge and Co., 1936.

VON MISES, LUDWIG. *The Theory of Money and Credit.* New Haven: Yale University Press, 1953.

WALRAS, LÉON. *Elements of Pure Economics* (Translated by William Jaffé). London: George Allen & Unwin, 1954.

WESTFIELD, F. M. "Comment," *American Economic Review,* Vol. 49, No. 5, December, 1959.

WICKSELL, KNUT. *Lectures on Political Economy* (Vol. 2). London: George Routledge & Sons, Ltd., 1935.

———. *Selected Papers on Economic Theory.* London: George Allen & Unwin, 1958.

WILLIAMS, JOHN H. *Economic Stability in the Modern World* (Lord Stamp Memorial Lecture). Oxford: Basil Blackwell, 1952.

WORKING, E. J. "What Do Statistical 'Demand Curves' Show?" *Quarterly Journal of Economics,* 1927.

WRIGHT, CHESTER W. *Economic History of the United States* (2nd Ed.). New York: McGraw-Hill Book Co., 1949.

WRIGHT, DAVID MCCORD, *et al. Money, Trade and Economic Growth, in honor of John Henry Williams.* New York: The Macmillan Co., 1951.

Index of Names

Index of Subjects

INDEX OF SUBJECTS

INDEX OF SUBJECTS

Supplementary Notes and Errata

Page 1, par 2. More precisely, we define money as currency held by the nonbanking public plus adjusted demand deposits of commercial banks.

Page 8, line 5. *pound* for *pound-sterling.*

Page 11, line 13. "spond to changes in measure.[18]"

Page 26, lines 7-8. Certificates representing and convertible into specie (representative full bodied money) might circulate in a pure gold coin standard. *Cf.* item for p. 43.

Page 37, line 14. Of course, bimetallism could assure "appropriate" growth of the global monetary stock even if one or the other metal typically did not circulate.

Pages 39 *ff.* In Sec. A.5, *paper standard* always means *inconvertible paper standard;* paper always is inconvertible into bullion or specie. Perhaps unorthodoxly, I equate *fiat* with *inconvertible.*

Page 39, line 14. *Inconvertible* for *non-representative.*

Page 42, lines 22-23. "use for fiat-paper — or even convertible paper — issues as a means . . ." See item for p. 39.

Page 43, Sec. A.6, § § 1. Representative money is defined as (not necessarily but ordinarily convertible) certificates "backed" by 100% specie or bullion reserves. It can be token, as were U. S. silver certificates. The crux is convertibility v. inconvertibility. "Representativeness" is tangential.

Pages 47 *ff.* (also pages 337 *ff.*). Hammond and other scholars would play down the importance of rural opposition to the Banks of the U. S., stressing mercantile rivalries, etc.

Chapter III. time deposits here include non-demand-deposit liability of commercial banks *and* of nonbanking financial institutions. In Ch. III, "S & L shares" belong to the class "time deposits."

Page 116, lines 30-31. At the *micro* level, receipt and leakage processes are alike for the two kinds of institutions. Probably the only valid distinctions are drawn in § § 4, par. 2. *Cf.* fn. 21, p. 143.

Page 140, lines 13-14. Indeed initial reserve increments are "gifts" throughout Secs. A.4 and A.5.

Page 169, line 11. *assets* for *portfolios.* Page 169, line 12. *liabilities* for *liability.* The individual bank loses and gains deposits and reserves one-for-one. Deposit contraction is a byproduct of frustrated efforts to increase reserves.

Page 193. Legal restraints relating mortgage investments of banks to non-demand deposits should have been cited. Restraints on non-mortgage investments of S & L firms, on the other hand, are even more severe.

Page 195, line 18. *I.e.,* currency in the hands of the nonbanking public.

Page 196, fn 1. A bank bill is drawn by a bank on a bank.

Pages 197 *ff*. As it happens, I work only with official open market sales to and purchases from the nonbanking public.

Page 198. See item for page 169, line 12.

Page 200, line 30. See Note B, p. 231, par. 3, at this point.

Page 201, § § 1, line 8. W. W. Riefler.

Pages 216 *ff*. Since "spending" decisions concern (dis)investing in consumer-durable and/or producer-capital portfolios, I should instead have counter-pointed "elasticity of substitution of cash against other assets" with "interest elasticity of the MEC function." In any case, p. 217, lines 2 and 3, should read: ". . . responses which, indeed, reflect but another aspect of portfolio management."

Page 218, line 8. *bonds* for *longs*.

Page 222, lines 6 *ff*. I tacitly assume that at the outset the real sector's response will be lagged so that very elastic liquidity preference minimizes transitional changes in interest rates.

Page 224, line 6. *these* for *they*.

Page 231, Note B. The following paragraphs, paragraphs 2-4, were accidentally omitted.

The text argues that, if expectations varied among traders and were held with imperfect confidence, a change in short rate at *t* would affect long rate for two reasons: (a) expectations of future short rates would be affected; some debtors who have been tempted to fund would be "convinced" by higher short rate; (b) for given expectations, higher short rates, for example, would encourage assumption of more risk by those portfolio managers (say of pension trusts) who find greater security in bonds and encourage debtors such as grocers to fund despite queasiness about financing inventories with bond issues. Thus "hedgers" are tempted to take a little risk as interest-rate differentials open up, even if elasticities of expectation are zero; expected return and uncertainty are traded-off.

I emphasize that Ch. VA is, on the whole, concerned with possibilities for changing long rate at *t*. Considerations pertinent to the secular term structure of interest rates are explored in Appen. A to Ch. VA and in Ch. VII.

Compare David Meiselman, *The Term Structure of Interest Rates* (Englewood Cliffs, N. J.: Prentice-Hall, Inc., 1962). Meiselman shows that the term structure at *t* necessarily reflects opinion about the rate that will prevail at, say, $t+9$ for a loan maturing at, say $t+11$. Traders at *t* can buy (sell) 9-period maturities, selling (buying) 11 period maturities. If $r_{9.11}$ proves to be out of line with the yield $i_{9.11}$ implicit at *t*, capital gains can be realized by such traders at t+9. Meiselman forms an expectations hypothesis, the empirical counterpart of which measures the metaphysically meaningless concept, "the market's expectation." He concludes that normal backwardation is not present in securities markets; his hypothesis is supported. An implication is that the liquidity trap cannot persist; traders will come to expect short rate to be very low in the distant future if short rate has been very low for a long enough time.

Page 231, Note B, par. 3. *I.e.*, hedgers are induced to take small flyers.

Page 241, eq. 10. $R_2B_2{}^b = sV - R_1B_1{}^b$

Page 241, eq. 10; page 246, eq. 23; page 248, eq. 29; page 585; pp. 753-4. Commercial and central banks (suppliers of reserves) are consolidated in obtaining "bank" demand for securities. *Cf.* p. 712 *ff*. Of course, one can assume alternatively that banks receive reserves through gift. Primary deposits are ignored in any case.

Page 241, eq. 12; page 242, eq. 16. Read sV for p.L(   ). This fortunately harmless slip may recur.

Page 270, § § 3. Compare item for page 43.

Pages 274-5. Page 141 *ff*. show that the j-th bank can expand its equilibrium deposits by $\$\lambda_j\eta$ for a \$1 increase in the system's reserves.

Page 310, line 8. "ings by banks of privately issued securities will be reduced, the effects being tempered."

Page 310, lines 9-12. Increased holdings of securities by the nonbanking public encompasses reduction in its indebtedness to banks.

Page 314, fn. 133, lines 14-15. Footnote 133 was written before Jan. 1963. *Cf.* fn. 132, p. 313.

Page 403, line 23. *in* for *by*. Page 403, line 34. *purchases* for *depredations*. Page 403, line 35. *bond* for *long*. Sales were by authorities who quickly spent the proceeds.

Page 405, line 30. *policies* for *problems*.

Page 440, line 11. delete *it*.

Pages 446 *ff*. In the real world the monetary authorities might make seasonal adjustments in M so that peak requirements would be less significant than in the text.

Page 452, note 27, line 9. *requirements* for *balances*.

Page 508. It should be stressed that inelastic expectations, leading to planned disinvestment in bonds, need not be accompanied by increased demand for *money*. One can plan to invest in bills. I wish to shout that Sec. E is more concerned with properties of liquid assets generally than with money proper.

Chapter X, Sec. B, pp. 565 *f*. Aggregate demand for new machinery of Type Aleph means *investment* demand and, when depreciation is nil, is represented by $k(X_a - X_{ao})$ where X_{ao} is the initial stock. See note A, pp. 591-2.

Page 576, fn. 15, line 3. "Equations 4, 6-9, 12-14, 16-18."

Page 576, fn. 15, line 4. Equation 19 instead of equation 17.

Pages 661 *ff*. Note carefully that some K's and Y's are dotted. The dots are inconspicuous.

Page 688, line 4. lower case "p′" should be upper case "P′".

Page 702, lines 8-9. "for . . . unknowns. These policy-determined variables are attained through manipulation of instrumental variables."

Page 716, Note A, line 14. *deflation* for *inflation*.

Page 742, indented pars. C and D. *prices* refer to *commodity prices*.

Page 755, § § 3. This model avoids Patinkin's second invalid dichotomy. The excess demand function for bonds *plus* money is first-order homogeneous in w and p but the component excess demand functions are nonhomogeneous, sharing the constant term M^s, bank demand for securities. (See item for p. 241, eq. 10.)

Page 763, Sec. D, line 1. "once and for all with" should read "with once and for all."

Page 797, last line. *constraining* for *controlling*.

Page 793, last line. "externally freely convertible into gold within narrow exchange-rate bounds."

Page 847, lines 21-25. Par values are defined in terms of gold (or 13.71 grain gold dollars). Members are committed to maintain exchange rates within one percent of pars, subject to qualification, or, alternatively to buy and sell gold in unlimited quantities within IMF approved limits. Only the U. S. employs the second approach, until recently to the exclusion of the first. These are the qualifications:

Pages 861 *ff*. It is crucial to separate out the international-liquidity from the U. S.-gold-outflow problem. Thus, a more favorable U. S. balance of payments implies a lower rate of accumulation of liquid balances, *cet. par*.